COMMANDER IN CHIEF

Other books by Eric Larrabee

Knoll Design, with Massimo Vignelli, 1982
The Benevolent and Necessary Institution, 1971
The Self-Conscious Society, 1960

Commander in Chief

FRANKLIN DELANO ROOSEVELT,
HIS LIEUTENANTS, AND THEIR WAR

ERIC LARRABEE

A Cornelia and Michael Bessie Book

HARPER & ROW, PUBLISHERS, New York
Cambridge, Philadelphia, San Francisco, Washington
London, Mexico City, São Paulo, Singapore, Sydney

FIRST EDITION

Designer: Sidney Feinberg

Maps by George Colbert

Copyeditor: Marjorie Horvitz

Index by Olive Holmes for Edindex

Library of Congress Cataloging-in-Publication Data

Larrabee, Eric.
  Commander in chief.

  "A Cornelia and Michael Bessie book."
  Bibliography: p.
  Includes index.
  1. Roosevelt, Franklin D. (Franklin Delano),
1882–1945—Military leadership. 2. World War,
1939–1945—United States. I. Title.
E807.L26   1987   973.917'092'4   85-42609
ISBN 0-06-039050-6

---

87 88 89 90 91 HC 10 9 8 7 6 5 4 3 2 1

CONTENTS

MAPS

COMMANDER IN CHIEF

PROLOGUE

THIS BOOK IS CONCERNED WITH FRANKLIN ROOSEVELT as war leader and with the subordinates through whom he exercised command. It assumes that the dominant part the President played in World War II has been neglected, if only because his prominence was so visible as to be taken for granted, comfortable and familiar. He had been around for so long that he was almost a part of the landscape; we have a sense even when unwarranted of knowing who he was and what he did. Moreover, he loomed so large on the domestic and political scene as to dim his outline on any other. Support can thus be found for the misapprehension that he left the conduct of the war largely to the military, and accordingly the centennial of his birth tended to emphasize his accomplishments as architect of the New Deal rather than as architect of victory. The wartime Roosevelt is a stilted and less substantial figure by comparison.

Yet this would not have been his perception of himself. Roosevelt took his position as head of the armed services more seriously than did any other President but Lincoln, and in practice he intervened more often and to better effect in military affairs than did even his battle-worn contemporaries like Churchill or Stalin. "It must be borne in mind," wrote Mark S. Watson in the official U.S. Army history of the prewar period, "that President Franklin D. Roosevelt was the real and not merely a nominal Commander in Chief. Every President has possessed the Constitutional authority which that title indicates, but few Presidents have shared Mr. Roosevelt's readiness to exercise it in fact and in detail and with such determination."[1] Roosevelt as war lord has been there all along, needing only to be recognized.

On the face of it, any effort to have a closer look at him in his warmaking capacities would seem to be hampered by the fact that he left no memoirs and was accustomed to keep his own counsel. Sometimes, for his

own reasons, he would give the impression that he thought military matters belonged in military hands. His style of administration required him
on more than one occasion to haze over his purposes, and in peacetime
he invigorated men and events as notably by shrewd manipulation as by
the overt employment of his powers. Responsibilities were vague and
overlapping, and channels of authority repeatedly ignored; he was able to
manage circumstance merely by his own presence. In the Roosevelt administrations his control of a situation was now and then evidenced only
by the inability of anyone else to control it.

He could exasperate equally by a refusal to disclose all his actions and
by insouciance in covering his tracks, nor was he always candid; an element of the devious could be found in his methods even when it was
unnecessary. He enjoyed the atmosphere of intrigue and frequently relied
on personal agents, accountable only to him. All of which seems calculated
to frustrate examination of what he was about as war loomed and then
came, and therefore of what stature he should be accorded in the history
of that now-distant conflict.

But this is not the whole story. In matters pertaining to the military,
Roosevelt behaved rather differently than he did as a civilian leader. Since
he was dealing here with men who operated under the constraints of duty
and military security, his relationships with them could be less roundabout
and less conspicuous. He gave an attention to the war more concentrated
and full of intent than he had any reason to make known except to the
commanders who carried out his directives. He found the men who suited
his needs and he kept them in his service. His wartime choices for military
posts were rarely—with one disastrous exception—supplanted or neutralized, as so often his civilian appointees had been and continued to be. His
military instructions, issued at numerous and critical points, were in the
main concise and final, contrary to his practice when the ebb and flow of
politics was the determining factor.

He arranged matters so that the Grand Alliance was directed from
Washington and its center of information was in the White House; his own
records contained the only complete and up-to-date accounting of the
war's conduct at its highest level. He kept in close contact with the progress of events, receiving daily and often hour-by-hour reports about the
course of the campaigns, and hence was in position to premeditate the
questions of strategy on which future campaigns would hinge. A large part
of this was necessarily documented. Despite the President's innate preference for doing business orally and informally, much of his military thought
and action was expressed in writing or is reflected clearly in the written
record. Roosevelt as war leader is much more observable than he has been
given credit for being.

By principle and conscious choice he was an activist commander.
While willing to leave the bulk of detail to the armed service chiefs, he

had been taught by experience as the political administrator of a military department that generals and admirals, left to their own devices, do not always manifest the initiative and drive that civilian leadership can and should demand of them. He was often far ahead of the conventional wisdom and never unwilling to set goals far beyond what competent professionals believed to be achievable. He sought and respected their advice, but he would never permit them to shape strategies contrary to his own, which were framed in a political format on a grand and world-girdling scale. If he seems a confident Commander in Chief, it must be conceded that he had always intended to be President, in the full meaning of the franchise. Virtually alone among occupants of that office, as Richard Neustadt remarks, he had no preconceptions of it to live up to, since his image of the presidency was quite simply that of himself occupying it.

"The White House was for him almost a family seat," writes Neustadt, "and like the other Roosevelt he regarded the whole country almost as a family property."[2] He could conceive of the interests of the United States being at issue in terms that were no less global for being personally felt. National strategic thinking came naturally to him; at age fifteen he had been given a copy of Mahan's *The Influence of Seapower upon History* for Christmas, and was repeatedly to make clear how fully he had absorbed its message. To take charge of the Navy in preparation for the presidency, as his cousin Theodore had done and he did in turn, seemed to him thoroughly appropriate. He had observed World War I at first hand and had not hesitated to propose ideas about its conduct. While not needing to represent himself before the public as a strategist in the Churchill mold, he was one nonetheless and, if concentration on essentials is the hallmark of good strategy, the better of the two.

For all that, the Roosevelt who presided over the internal economic reformation of the country and the Roosevelt who prosecuted a victorious global war were the same man. Among his most skillful maneuvers was to make the second seem like a logical extension of the first. "If war does come," he would say in the prewar years, "we will make it a New Deal war,"[3] and to a remarkable extent he did exactly that. The armed forces that he led partook of qualities from his peacetime administrations. The war was a crucible in which aspects of America that had been hidebound or authoritarian were fused and dissolved in the intensity of a common enterprise depending for its power on the people as a whole and bearing the mark of the President's personal political style—open, breezy, direct. Opposition to entrenched financial power on behalf of the under-privileged and opposition to Fascist tyrannies on behalf of their victims were made to appear as but two articles of the same democratic, humanitarian faith.

In this he was aided by the tendency of his domestic foes to be isolationist as well, and to oppose his foreign policies with the same vigor as they did his social reforms. His dexterity in uniting the two was naturally resented by those who failed to perceive a causal connection and sympathized with neither, and they drew the not unnatural conclusion that he was courting foreign adventures (as Hitler also accused him of doing) to distract attention from failures at home. To some it seemed inconceivable that he had not "caused" the disaster at Pearl Harbor, since it rescued him from the vise of immobility in which they were seeking to grip him. Their feelings were intense, and their bitterness still reverberates in the pages of revisionist historians of American entry into the war, which the latter considered unnecessary. For those who share this perspective, the successful transition of his government from peace to war is still a disgrace. But what is indisputable is that he brought it off.

◆

From the very beginning, Roosevelt defined American involvement in World War II as an all-out endeavor in pursuit of high principle. "We are all in it together," he said in a radio speech to the nation two days after Pearl Harbor, "—all the way. Every single man, woman, and child is a partner in the most tremendous undertaking of our American history." It was not only going to be "a long war, it will be a hard war," demanding sacrifices of everyone. These must be made because "powerful and resourceful gangsters have banded together" against "the whole human race." They must be totally defeated in order that "this Nation, and all that this Nation represents, will be safe for our children." Therefore the "true goal that we seek is far above and beyond the ugly field of battle": a world in which the threat to liberty represented by the Axis powers will have been totally eliminated. "I repeat," he said, "that the United States can accept no result save victory, final and complete."[4]

Thus the war lent itself to being seen as a crusade, an invocation of the flaming avenging sword pictured on the unit insignia of supreme Allied headquarters in Europe. Of all wars, it seemed most plausibly to be animated on the Allied side by trust in decency and responsive government, as opposed to lack of trust on the other side in anything but brutality and arbitrary power. It was a liberal's war as its predecessor, and its successors, never were. The anti-Fascist cause readily attracted and absorbed unto itself a whole panoply of other causes—against intolerance, against racial prejudice, against physical suppression of dissent, against police power based on torture and terror, against the very hosts of evil incarnate.

Generalizations that glib do not easily adapt themselves to an epic that so combined the noble and humane with the sordid, barbaric, and grotesque as did World War II. It will not escape notice that many who fought it on the winning side were either indifferent to the causes above or viewed them with skepticism, and at present remove, the postwar consequences are self-evidently not in perfect harmony with the Four Freedoms or the language of the Atlantic Charter, for which the war was presumably being waged.

To say as much is not to imply that Roosevelt and those who echoed his words were cynical, or that all who responded to them were dupes, but rather to affirm the truism that wars do not end as they begin. Why die for Danzig, indeed? The demands of war impose their own momentum on those who enter it. By all accounts, Roosevelt was a person of rudimentary and uncomplicated trust in Providence; he was, he would say when asked, a Christian and a Democrat.[5] He tried to make the war idealistic, and his conduct in directing it is not internally inconsistent with the idealist Harry Hopkins and others of his immediate circle saw in him, and attempted to encourage.

He was a gifted artist at governance, and the virtuoso hand for good or ill is just as plainly at work in his dealing with military dilemmas as it was with those of a nation needing recovery from a loss of economic self-confidence. The war was similar to the Depression in being a challenge that required a concerted national effort to meet it; we began the fighting with defeats no less devastating than the hunger and impoverishment of the early 1930s. Indeed one could argue that Roosevelt was more successful in coping with the vicissitudes of the battlefield than with those of the economy. All too sadly, it was the war that brought about the ultimate recovery, and certainly in the war he was better served.

American high military leadership in the 1940s is still impressive for its matching of individual to task, for its sloughing off of militaristic vainglory, for its coordinating of one and all with the purposes to which the President gave voice. Lincoln's long agony (and that of the Union) in searching for the overall commander he finally discovered in Grant was not repeated. Somehow the right men were found, and it is asking too much of coincidence to suppose that care had not gone into their selection.

They and their President came out of past histories surprisingly held in common, they in their turn picked other men out of the same reservoir of shared tradition, and what they did in the war years is illuminated by what had happened to them in the previous three decades of their maturity. Robert E. Lee observed to a friend as the Civil War commenced that the problem of the Confederacy lay not in its soldiers, who were unsurpassable, but in finding officers to lead them, which worried him.[6] In Roosevelt's America this problem was solved, and not by inadvertence.

To speak of Roosevelt's lieutenants is to speak of the continuum that links high strategy to the low, bloody business of carrying it out. The making of strategy, as a senior historian of World War II put it, "remains a fascinating subject if only because it represents a supreme effort of human will and intelligence to dominate the roaring flux of forces that are aroused by war."[7] Strategy includes the working out of its consequences. The ranks of martial authority from multiple stars to modest chevron correspond to an ordering of reality in which plans produce orders, orders produce actions, and actions produce isolated episodes of swirling fury where the issue hangs or falls on the skill and fortitude of individual human beings, under conditions of indescribable repulsiveness and stress.

Roosevelt knew this not because he was Commander in Chief but because he was a politician in a democratic (with a small d) society. Putting together a powerful concentration of military force is not wholly unlike assembling a successful political coalition; individual capabilities have to be combined. Woodrow Wilson spoke in his 1912 campaign about the duty of an American President to "liberate the generous energies of our people," as Roosevelt most surely did, and he did it, among other ways, by particularizing the involvement of his constituency in the panoramic drama of the war.

He was alone among the leaders of World War II in making this kind of connection. In his second wartime radio "fireside chat," on April 28, 1942, he reinforced his case for the abstract issue of economic stabilization by recounting the exploits of a naval physician named Corydon M. Wassell and a B-17 pilot named Hewitt T. Wheless. "He comes from a place called Menard, Texas," said the President of Wheless, "with a population of 2,375." Wheless had been awarded the Distinguished Service Cross for completing a mission over the Philippines and downing seven Japanese fighter planes despite the loss of two engines, radio and oxygen systems out, two crew members wounded, and one dead.

At noon on May 7 at Boeing Plant Two in Seattle, eighteen thousand workers came out on the concrete apron in front of the vast building, a recording of this passage from the President's speech was played over loudspeakers, and Captain Wheless stepped to the microphone. "The men operating the planes don't want all the credit," he said to them. "I want to thank you for myself and a lot of other pilots who more or less owe their lives to your design and workmanship. Continue the good work and together we can't lose."[8]

By such simple means are the generous energies liberated.

◆

One of the actualities most difficult to recapture about World War II is the very real possibility that the Allies could have lost it—or, what is almost equally forbidding, could have failed to win. The series of blows that reduced the Axis powers to ruin had about them at the time a rhythm and crescendo bordering on the apparently inevitable, an impression the President, as duty required, did everything to encourage. Time was on his side only in appearance. Once the industrial and manpower resources of the United States were brought to bear, it was predictable that they would overpower in matériel the output of Germany, Russia, Great Britain, and Japan combined; but this could not come about immediately, and in fact did not until 1944.[9]

Until then it was thoroughly reasonable of our enemies to reckon a total of gains they could consolidate to a point where depriving them of their acquired strength would be an arduous and costly prospect. The President's blithe assumption of eventual triumph, in which the entire nation seems to have vied in joining him, was far from rooted in military realities. The Allied cause drew its strength from convictions that were not altogether rational; Hitler was not the only one who couldn't understand why the British went on resisting him. This was in major respects a quixotic venture.

Germany in Europe by mid-1940, and Japan in Southeast Asia by mid-1942, had each achieved possession or effective control of a self-sufficient economic base surrounded by a strategically defensible perimeter. They had already won major national objectives, and had done so by the feats of military forces with a well-earned reputation for professional competence. They had options before them for further advances which, if realized, would have brought us very close to the nadir of our hopes. That all their efforts would come to naught was by no means obvious, and the progress of their undoing was frequently—in Wellington's famous phrase after Waterloo—"a damned nice thing—the closest run thing you ever saw in your life."

As more and more of the history of the war has been told, the more evident it has become that what then seemed historically foreordained was nothing of the kind. Time and again the issue was at risk, and the Allies turned out to have assets that in no way could have been counted on in advance. Many battles balanced on the knife edge where the final increment of courage or professionalism made the difference. Many foolhardy decisions on our part led only to the brink of disaster, and many wise ones would not have saved the sum of things if they had been made otherwise. Not least, the role of British (and American) military intelligence was far more vital than anyone knew but the dedicated men and women who generated it, and had it not been there the cast of the dice that all war involves would have been many times more hazardous.

War as a narrative of risk and hazard is not universally admired by historians (the "drum and trumpet" school has long been out of fashion), no more than is emphasis on personalities (the "great man" school). But strategy divorced from its consequences is singularly desiccated and—to use a necessary if unpleasant word—bloodless. The effectiveness of a strategy is a function of its execution. Bad strategies produce bad battles; men die to no good effect and causes just and unjust are consigned to the dustheap.

History is not unfair when it judges Hitler a bad strategist because he lost, especially because he came so often within an ace of winning or at worst forcing a stalemate. The events he set in train were inherent in his ideas and the kind of man he was. Military history exerts an enduring fascination not only because narrative and personality cannot be detached from it but because therein the shadow T. S. Eliot saw fall between the will and the act is absent. The conversion of intention into action—the domination of the "roaring flux"—is what the narrative of wars is all about.

And it will be done by persons. The personality of military leaders will have been shaped by their understanding of this seamless web that weaves together their deliberations, as Roosevelt did conceptually, with the fate of a single soldier or sailor. They must internalize an awareness that the efficacy of their thoughts will cause particular men and women to live or die, as well as cause nations to stand or fall. In the history of wars, the steps that lead from cause to effect are more than usually exposed, which is why the for-want-of-a-nail phenomenon is so frequently observed. For strategists and students of strategy alike, the continuity must be seen as uninterrupted between the high brass in lofty conference and the prototypes of cartoonist Bill Mauldin's Willie and Joe in the filth and horror of combat, if only because it is on the latter that defeat or victory depends.

◆

Strategy can be simply defined as The Reason Why, in that it will explain why a given number of individuals with a given mission to accomplish will find themselves at a given place at a given time. If the strategy is well conceived, they will be concentrated in greater strength than the enemy and will have caught him off balance; to contrive such circumstances is the strategist's never-ending preoccupation. But there is another Reason Why, in that men do not go to the cannon's mouth without motivation, especially in those nations that are clumsily and not always accurately known as the freedom-loving democracies. Fighting to no purpose, for a citizenry in arms, does not have the look of a productive enterprise, and to offer a sense of political purpose that could be readily understood and at least tacitly accepted was not the least of Roosevelt's achievements as war leader.

Some historians of warfare (conspicuously J. F. C. Fuller) have disparaged its entanglement with politics and deplored the process by which war as a relatively harmless game of aristocratic professionals was displaced, somewhere in the Napoleonic era, by a massive concentration of wills and peoples inflamed by ideological slogans—warfare à l'outrance on the populist rather than the elitist model.[10] Whether or not one accepts such an interpretation, the axiom has remained in effect that heads of government in wartime must concern themselves with that complex of emotions aroused when the flags are flying, and the drums and trumpets sound, lest they have no followers. "We failed to see," General George Marshall said after the war, about the Army's opposition to the President on action in North Africa in 1942, "that the leader in a democracy has to keep the people entertained." He added: "That may sound like the wrong word, but it conveys the thought."[11]

One of the ironies of World War II is that the Allies and not the Axis were the more politicized and fought from the start in the extravagant fashion subsumed by the phrase "total war" and called for by the President in his speech of December 9, 1941. Neither the Germans nor the Japanese opened hostilities with any understanding of what "total war" meant in practical terms, much as they professed to. They were seriously underprepared for it and their populations seem to have greeted the arrival of the long-expected conflicts with little more than stoic resignation.

The Japanese had no administrative machinery for centralized military or economic planning; they had failed to stockpile rubber or aluminum; they lacked adequate shipping, especially oil tankers, and had made no plans to build more (they tried to catch up, but too late). They went to war with limited goals and expected us to react, as for a time we did, with a limited defense.

Those of them who had thought the problem through, like Admiral Yamamoto, had no expectation of "ultimate" victory but, instead, hoped to attain such predominance in Southeast Asia and the central Pacific that we would see the futility of trying to dislodge them and would accept a negotiated peace, perhaps at the initiative of a third party (this was the way their most recent experience of major war, against the Russians in 1904–1905, had ended—with the United States as the third party).[12] Note that had it not been for the Battle of Midway, this line of thinking would not look so senseless as it now does.

Hitler's scheme of things, and hence the structure of his military machine, was predicated on a series of short, inexpensive wars. Before 1939, Germany lacked self-sufficiency in iron ore, oil, copper, and aluminum; efforts to control their use had been ineffective and stockpiles were low. An essentially civilian economy was being left largely untouched by a government politically unwilling to ask its people to give up material gains of which both were so proud. The labor force was not adequately mobilized and women, on doctrinal grounds, were at first excluded from it except for domestic service.

Armament manufacturing goals in Germany were set consistently too low, even after it became evident that the Allies were not going to back down and that shortages of ammunition were going to be endemic. In September 1940, at the height of the Battle of Britain, Hitler ordered a *cutback* in aircraft and other arms production. Two months after undertaking the invasion of Russia, he ordered still another reduction in output

of weapons, ammunition, and aircraft and had plans drawn up for demo-
bilizing a large number of divisions and reconverting industry to civilian
use. It was not until 1942 that Albert Speer persuaded him to stop building
the *Autobahnen* and at a meeting with his advisers on January 25, 1943
—with von Paulus and Sixth Army only a week away from surrender at
Stalingrad—Hitler discoursed at length on the importance of constructing
a new stadium at Nuremberg, large enough for celebrating the conquest
of Russia.[13]

It was the democracies, Britain above all, that organized themselves
totally for war. Their citizens were as thoroughly committed to it as only
an aroused, united, and self-reliant populace can be. "What sort of people
do they think we are?" Churchill asked a joint session of Congress, and a
roar of energy surged up at him, the chamber rising as one to cheer and
cheer. It seems unlikely now that "they" had the slightest idea. Though
both the Germans and the Japanese made much of a code of fanatical
commitment to brute force, and indulged it to excess, they showed no
premonition whatever of the rage beyond measure about to be unleashed
against their very existence. For all the atrocities the Axis perpetrated
against civilians, and they were many, it was the peace-loving Anglo-
Americans—once their blood lust was up—who proved to be utterly im-
placable in dealing destruction and death to the homes, wives, and children of the men they faced in battle.

◆

This was the route to which the President gave his powerful assent.
The choice of it led a long way, longer perhaps than any other choice the
Allies made. Their political objectives were implicit in the way they chose
to fight, and could not be readjusted retroactively as the fighting drew to
a close. That is, the total defeat of their enemies came first, and determined the strategies employed to that end. The announcement at Casablanca of "unconditional surrender" as the Allied war aim was a formality
by comparison; the underlying decision to crush incontrovertibly had
been made long before, and at some deeper level in many, many minds.[14]
Inevitably other objectives—including a postwar world that took a reborn
Germany or Japan into account—were underplayed or lost from sight, and
this was just as true of the politically astute British as it was of the supposedly naive Americans.

Much currency has been given to the theory that in contrast to the
British, the American military paid insufficient attention to "politics," with
untoward and ill-considered effects on the postwar world.[15] This will not
stand up to examination. The Americans were highly alert to political
considerations but with different aims and within a different conception
of duty to their civilian leader. "We probably devoted more time in our

discussions to such matters as any one subject . . . ," said General Marshall in 1956 about the Joint Chiefs of Staff, "we discussed political things more than anything else. . . . I repeat again that I doubt if there was any one thing . . . that came to our minds more frequently than the political factors. But we were careful, exceedingly careful, never to discuss them with the British, and from that they took the count that we didn't observe these things at all. . . . We didn't discuss it with them because we were not in any way putting our necks out as to political factors which were the business of the head of the state—the President—who happened also to be the Commander in Chief."[16]

It must be understood that the American military is attuned to politics and to civilian authority in a special way. The professionals of the World War II generation had in good part begun their careers by securing appointment to one of the service academies from a congressman. In the lean between-wars years they had struggled to persuade politicians of their needs for increased manpower and matériel. If they arrived at flag or general officer rank, they did so with congressional approval, and they continued to be dependent on it for their budgets and promotions. If they became the chiefs of their services, they did so by exercising, and being recognized by their fellow officers for their ability in exercising, political skills. Their orders would be issued in the name of civilian service secretaries who were political appointees.

The end product of such an education tended to be wary of politicians and bipartisan whenever possible, but he may nonetheless have been an intensely political animal—as Marshall, MacArthur, Arnold, and Eisenhower in their several ways all were—and they all had to deal with a Commander in Chief who was a politically elected official. The presidency is the focus where the threads from two alien but related universes gather, and neither the President nor his military advisers can afford to forget or ignore this.

Politics includes the art of leaving things alone. Roosevelt's awareness of the broad scope of his powers—while involving a willingness to intervene at any level, down to the location of buoys in the channels of naval bases—also encompassed a perception of what it was *not* necessary for him to do. Where he refrained from intervening, he did so in some knowledge of what those initiatives were that he was allowing to pursue their wayward course. No one understood better than he the inner dynamics of American strength: how to mobilize it, how to draw on it, how to gauge its limits. Once mobilized, it did not need to be driven; it needed only to be steered.

If the energy was already there to do something not too far apart from his intentions, then he was loath to restrain it—as he was, for example, to hold back the Navy in the Pacific despite an accepted and necessary strategy of Atlantic-first. The energy was the important thing. Fortunately, as he told Harry Hopkins not long after war began, in Marshall, King, and Arnold he knew that he had three men "who really like to fight."[17] As long as that was true there would be a wide range of matters with which as politico-military leader he need not concern himself.

By the same token, it was surely clear to him that political energies in open or covert conflict with his aims had to be given an outlet, one that satisfied their yearnings but could be carefully kept under control. After our entry into the war, the domestic forces that had passionately opposed it were still in being, momentarily stunned into joining the consensus for victory but still vocal and alert, still amply represented in the Congress. To keep them in the consensus there should ideally be a conservative, neo-isolationist military hero, preferably a figure who was large enough to rally around but naive enough to be no real threat, who was possessed of *bona fide* anti–New Deal credentials yet was located at a safe distance in the Far East, where isolationism paradoxically did not apply.

This goes a long way, I think, to explain the President's otherwise enigmatic handling of Douglas MacArthur, who fitted these conditions to perfection and was therefore—up to a delicately chosen point—nurtured and indulged. He drew MacArthur into his orbit. He did not *have* to recall him to active duty in the Philippines, he did not *have* to rescue him from certain capture to command in Australia, he did not *have* to overrule the Joint Chiefs and authorize his cherished return to the Philippines, he did not *have* to make him supreme ground commander for the invasion of Japan. The MacArthur of legend is in no small measure one of Roosevelt's most ingenious inventions.

Of Roosevelt's cultivation of bureaucratic disorder too much has probably been said. The observation was once made[18] that it undeniably had a negative impact, in that succeeding generations of Washington power-managers were so shaken by exposure to it that they studiously tried to inculcate the opposite as soon as they had the chance, tried to eliminate the very possibility of a President with such a debonair disregard for the organizational niceties. A standard of tidiness was later set against which Roosevelt is measured and found wanting. But we are permitted to inquire whether in terms of national policy-making the replacements for Roosevelt's "poor" administration have been all that satisfactory. The years since have witnessed catastrophic failures of coordination between politics and the military that his years in office did not. Perhaps there was more method to his maneuverings than appeared.

Yet a price was paid. His determination to go his own way, his insistence on informing himself through his own idiosyncratic avenues of communication, his deliberate short-circuiting of the proper channels of responsibility—all these had defects of their virtues that now and then led him and the country astray. His two great failures were France and China. These historic civilizations of depth and pungent flavor, to which he was instinctively and without reluctance attracted, defeated his best efforts to incorporate them in an all-embracing view of the postwar world. In each instance he was badly advised, and there is no great artfulness needed to see where the bad advice came from and why he listened to it. But evidence was also available to him that de Gaulle was a far more powerful personage than he had imagined and Chiang Kai-shek a far weaker one: he chose not to act on it. He wanted a revived but malleable France that would be willing to give up its empire and a united but nationalist China that would be a "great nation," able to fill the vacuum left by Japanese defeat. He got neither.

Nor should it be assumed that from the military's point of view Roosevelt was a parfit gentil knight beyond reproach. He eluded everyone who tried to net the butterfly of his consent. "I frankly was fearful," George Marshall said, "of Mr. Roosevelt's introducing political methods of which he was a genius into a military thing which had to be on a fixed basis. . . . You can't treat military factors in the way you do political factors." As early as spring of 1941, Marshall wrote a memo to tell his planning staff that they must "begin the education of the President as to the true strategic situation—this coming after a period of being influenced by the State Department," and even later, when he had come to respect Roosevelt with less reserve, Marshall continued to be made uneasy by what he called the President's "cigarette-holder gestures."

Marshall always worried about his boss's "tendency to shift and handle things loosely and be influenced, particularly by the British."[19] Whenever Roosevelt and Churchill met alone together, their staffs were in despair at the thought of what harebrained schemes the two might concoct, and have to be talked out of. But that is the way of staffs. It is on the issues that Roosevelt has to be watched at work and subsequently judged in the light of the outcome.

Above all else there is no doubt that he relished the role, which he wore with the same ease as he did the naval cape in which he was so memorably photographed, the wind in his hair, on the deck of the cruiser *Houston* in San Francisco Bay, reviewing the fleet he had many years before served as assistant secretary. He liked to "play soldier," Secretary of War Henry Stimson's biographer quoted one observer as saying. "The President continued not to invite me to his military meetings," Secretary of State Cordell Hull complained in his memoirs. "He loved the military side of events, and liked to hold them in his own hand."[20] When the secretary was to propose a toast to him, at a cabinet dinner in January 1942, Roosevelt told Hull beforehand that he preferred to be addressed not as President but as Commander in Chief.

II

Ample authority can be summoned up for the contrary opinion that Roosevelt did not actually take a vigorous, personal part in the war's direction. "So far as the major decisions in policy and strategy were concerned," wrote Samuel P. Huntington in *The Soldier and the State* in 1957, "the military ran the war." An equally firm statement of a common assumption is that of Alfred Vagts in his *Militarism,* to the effect that Roosevelt "usually accepted the views of the military." The President, wrote Churchill of the conference with Stalin at Teheran, "was oppressed by the prejudices of his military advisers, and drifted to and fro in the argument." Both Field Marshal Sir Alan Brooke and Secretary Stimson thought, as others have concluded since, that he relied heavily on Marshall and was governed by Marshall's advice. Robert Sherwood, in his *Roosevelt and Hopkins,* seems to have set this unanimity in motion in 1948 by maintaining, of the President and the Joint Chiefs of Staff, that "there were not more than two occasions in the entire war when he overruled them."[21]

Sherwood did admit the possibility, pointed out to him by Navy Captain Tracy B. Kittredge of the Joint Chiefs' historical section, that this might only have been because "informal discussions of the President with Leahy, Marshall, King and Arnold led them usually to know in advance the President's views," and Admiral Leahy, who said that he saw Roosevelt nearly every day (during 1942–43 this was true), reinforces that surmise. "Planning of major operations," according to Leahy, "was always done in close cooperation with the President. Frequently we had sessions in his study. . . . Churchill and Roosevelt really ran the war . . . we were just artisans, building patterns of strategy from the rough blueprints handed us by our respective Commanders-in-Chief."[22]

But one could go a great deal further and insist that Huntington, Vagts, and especially Sherwood were entirely wrong, and that Roosevelt —in contrast to Churchill, who was incidentally in neither title nor authority a "commander in chief"—not twice but repeatedly exerted his constitutional powers and disregarded his professional military colleagues on important questions.

Winston Churchill was prime minister, minister of defence, and chairman of the two defence committees concerned with operations and supply; if anyone was supreme commander of Britain's armed forces, it was he. Yet he could not issue a military "order" in his own person, as Roosevelt could, and he was at all times answerable to the War Cabinet and his legislature, the House of Commons, as Roosevelt was not. It may well be that as prime minister he so bestrode the narrow world that he could have demanded or usurped the powers of a Lord Protector Cromwell had he wished to, but he wished otherwise. He harried and browbeat his military chiefs to the margin of their endurance, but it remained his boast to the end that he never overruled them, "never wielded autocratic powers," as he put it more or less truthfully.[23]

Roosevelt's position was quite different. Since he possessed the authority, he had no need to make an issue of working his will; he needed only to express it, and the American war effort would remain very firmly under his control, as he did regularly and it did throughout. Roosevelt was in no way the creature of the Joint Chiefs of Staff; he and they were a unit of which he was the undisputed leader and they the analytical minds and operational executants. But there was no question who was Commander in Chief; the President's interventions were the rule rather than the exception. Kent Roberts Greenfield, former chief historian of the U.S. Army, listed in his *American Strategy in World War II* some twenty-two major decisions made by Roosevelt "against the advice, or over the protests, of his military advisers," and thirteen more of them made at the President's instigation, from the order of November 1938 for increased aircraft production and of June 1940 for keeping the fleet at Pearl Harbor, to the cancellation of the invasion of southern Burma in December 1943 and the recall of General Stilwell in October 1944.

"It is enough to list some of these decisions," wrote Greenfield of only the period before war began, "to feel their weight": for copious military assistance to Britain, for placing an oil embargo on Japan and reinforcing the Philippines, for establishing garrisons and convoys in the western Atlantic. But those made by the President in wartime were equally weighty: insistence on full delivery of Lend-Lease to Russia, encouragement of the Doolittle raid on Tokyo, selection of North Africa for the first Allied offensive, resolution of the British import crisis, choice of Eisenhower to command the invasion of Europe, acceptance of Chennault's proposals for air war in China, permission for MacArthur to recapture the Philippines, and pressure to speed up the bombing of Japan by the B-29s.[24]

To leave it at that would be of course to oversimplify. Scorekeeping on who made what decisions is a deceptive exercise, as closer inspection reveals most of them to have had a tangled history. The President, the Joint Chiefs, and their British counterparts worked together in a rich and complex partnership that had room in it for considerable give-and-take, and that changed over time. No one party to it had his own way exclusively (though it might be conceded that at first the British won many points, that toward the end General Marshall's austere integrity prevailed, and that throughout Admiral King saw more clearly and got more of what he wanted than did the others).

The success of the total endeavor came from compromises that can now be seen to have absorbed the correct features, and discarded the incorrect, of otherwise contradictory ways of thinking. This was most clearly true of the many vigorous confrontations with Churchill and his cohorts. "No other allies could have done it," said Rommel's chief of staff, General Hans Speidel, to *New York Times* correspondent Drew Middleton many years after the war, about the Normandy invasion. "... [Y]ou Americans and the British. You learn from each other. There is a special chemistry there."[25]

As could be expected, Roosevelt's direct involvement diminished as the war progressed, and as plans he had approved at their inception moved to the stage of execution. As his confidence in the military leaders grew, he saw less of them; he had less reason to see them. But his possession of the final word is always in evidence, and even where the evidence thins out its underlying mark is visible. "No war was better recorded than World War II . . . ," writes Maurice Matloff, one of the closest students of those records. "But all too often the historian who has struggled through mountains of paper finds the trail disappearing, at the crucial point of decision-making, somewhere in the direction of the White House."[26]

The basic outline was the President's, and for all the delight he took in playing it by ear, what is remarkable about his strategies is their consistency. While the service chiefs and the theater commanders were not always certain what a specific application might be, they were never in doubt that Roosevelt would reject any proposal in conflict with the animating principles of the American effort as he understood them.

His fellow countrymen in positions of command were quite literally his lieutenants.

◆

On July 5, 1939, by a military order that attracted little attention, the President transferred the Joint Army-Navy Board and the Joint Army-Navy Munitions Board out of the armed services departments where they had been located, into his newly created Executive Office. Those who think that Roosevelt lacked skill or interest in administration would do well to reflect on this simple and seemingly innocuous move. It was typical of his administrative arrangements—"inherently disorderly," as Stimson called them—but it was the keystone in the structure of authority that made the President Commander in Chief in fact as well as name.

The Joint Board, which in 1942 was to be superseded by the Joint Chiefs of Staff, was by this order transformed from an interdepartmental consulting group into a potential source and instrument of national strategy, lifted above the departmental level and joined in a special link to the President alone. (Questioned by Admiral Leahy as to whether this was his intention, Roosevelt protested at the time that it was not, but the Joint Board's subsequent history belies him.)[27]

The proliferating "emergency" agencies that came along in due course with the nation's economic mobilization joined the Munitions

Board in a similar place under the President's personal direction. The service secretaries—after 1940, Stimson and Secretary of the Navy Frank Knox—were put in an anomalous position and kept there. They continued in principle to be in charge of their departments—and ritualistic reverence was paid to their prerogatives—but their senior military subordinates now reported directly to the President, over their heads. During the war they were not routinely consulted about strategy, they were not on the distribution list for Joint Chiefs of Staff papers, and with few exceptions they were not invited to the major conferences with the British where joint strategies were deliberated.[28] That this system functioned at all is a tribute to their patient acceptance of the President's determination to give legitimacy and force to his own command.

When they finally drifted into being—and "drifted" is the only word —the Joint Chiefs of Staff wore an equally Rooseveltian aspect. They were never formally established; no executive order creating them was issued. They first appear as the American component of the Combined Chiefs of Staff, the supreme committee of Allied command set up in January 1942 at "Arcadia," Roosevelt's and Churchill's first wartime conference in Washington, and their inexperience and lack of orderly procedure appalled the British. "There are no regular meetings . . . ," an incredulous Sir John Dill wrote home to Alan Brooke in London, "and if they do meet there is no secretariat to record their meetings. They have no joint planners and executive planning staff. . . . Then there is the great difficulty of getting the stuff over to the President. He just sees the Chiefs of Staff at odd times, and again no record. . . . The whole organization belongs to the days of George Washington."[29]

Roosevelt was determined that ultimate direction of Allied strategy should be located physically in the capital bearing Washington's name, and his wish was heeded. The British, from Churchill and Dill on down, seem to have come there with a notion of showing the Americans how things were going to be managed. "It has not worked out quite like that," reads the diary of Sir Charles Wilson, Churchill's physician (later Lord Moran), who accompanied him. "The discussion was heated," wrote Moran of the Combined Chiefs' first meeting, "until they at last decided that there should be two committees, one in London, the other in Washington. . . . But this did not suit the President. He wanted one committee in Washington, and after what Hopkins calls 'a hell of a row' he got what he wanted."[30]

Moran's account condenses and conflates a series of somewhat complicated events. What had happened was this: The Americans came to Arcadia with a hastily prepared plan that Marshall put forward for a Supreme Allied War Council on the model of World War I, with numerous participants. British experience of working with allies was more recent, and even if Roosevelt's overtures to Stalin and Chiang Kai-shek had not already shown unpromising results, Churchill would have been the first to point out to him the disadvantages of allowing too many cooks in the kitchen.

At an early meeting, on Christmas Day 1941, Marshall made a strong and eventually successful plea for unity of command in the theater of action they were most concerned about, the South Pacific or ABDA (American-British-Dutch-Australian) area. This led inevitably to the question of whom the ABDA commander (he was to be General Wavell) would report to. The President had taken in hand several proposals already made and recomposed them into one of his own, for a special "appropriate joint body" to be set up in Washington for the purpose.

It was this idea of his, for a new entity superimposed on top of the existing chiefs of staff, that occasioned Hopkins's "hell of a row." The American and British military leaders wanted nothing of it. They were united in their rejection of the President's draft, and they returned to him with their approval the original, prepared by the British, in which decision about the ABDA theater would rest with the American chiefs meeting together in Washington with representatives of the British chiefs, leaving the authority of both intact.

Here was the critical step: It was approved by the President and the Prime Minister at a general gathering of the principals at the White House on New Year's Day 1942. In other words, the British chiefs from the start were reconciled, if reluctantly, to Washington as the main Allied headquarters. It was they who contributed the structure for ABDA command and then followed on with the sensible proposal that it be continued for post-Arcadia Anglo-American strategy in general, just as it was they who made the useful suggestion that the word "joint" refer to inter-service collaboration within one nation, and "combined" to collaboration between two or more of what henceforward were to be called the United Nations. The Combined Chiefs of Staff as they were eventually constituted came from British initiatives.

The subject did come up again toward the end of Arcadia, when Marshall discovered that Roosevelt and Churchill had agreed on machinery for munitions allocation that provided for two coequal bodies, in Washington and London. This General Marshall opposed with "unusual vehemence" in a brief consultation with Roosevelt and Hopkins just before the final White House session began, on January 14. Strategy and logistics could not be separated: There could be only *one* Combined Chiefs! Hopkins saw immediately that Marshall was right, and between them they convinced the President, much to the embarrassment of the Prime Minister when in open meeting he discovered that the American position had changed. He tactfully agreed to a one-month trial of munitions boards as subcommittees of the Combined Chiefs. "We will call it a preliminary agreement," said Roosevelt, "and try it out that way."[31] *C'est le provisoire qui dure.* Of course, the "temporary" arrangement soon became permanent.

It seems improbable that Churchill attached any great importance to all this; he makes no mention of it in his many-volume war history, where he expresses the conviction that "future historians" will view the creation of the Combined Chiefs as "the most valuable and lasting result" of his journey across the Atlantic. Moran thought that Churchill's mind was concentrated to the exclusion of all other concerns on bringing Roosevelt fully committed into the war: "If that can be done, nothing else matters." After all, the levers of Allied military force in being were still very much under the Prime Minister's hand; it was only later, when the locus of mobilized power shifted, that he made the painful discovery of what the implications were. But Moran saw at the time a consequential decision being made, and sensed its importance. "The Americans have got their way," he wrote, "and the war will be run from Washington."[32]

◆

The chartering instrument of the Combined Chiefs came to be written almost by accident. The British in a separate session on January 8 had adopted a paper intended to set forth the kind of organization they proposed to leave behind them on their return to London. It was presented to the Americans on the thirteenth, was discussed, revised, rewritten, and lo and behold was introduced the next day as a mutually-agreed-on statement in which the Combined Chiefs of Staff asserted their existence, defined themselves, and described their powers and responsibilities. Copies were sent to the President and the Prime Minister, in dutiful anticipation of a need for their approval.

But the White House copy at the outset produced no response whatever, and only after some prodding was returned three months later, with what a historian of the Joint Chiefs describes as the "airy" notation "OK FDR." That was all the authorization they ever got. Either Churchill's copy was regarded as requiring no action or else Roosevelt's casual habits were contagious: It was never formally approved.[33]

One of the happy by-products of the post-Arcadia collaborative agreement was the British choice to head their resident Washington mission, Field Marshal Sir John Dill, worn in long and honorable service, who earned himself a place of his own in the affection and trust of his American co-workers. Soon a familiar sight on Washington spring mornings was Dill and his aide, Major Reggie Macdonald-Buchanan, striding along the banks of the Potomac on their way to the office in their faultless gabardines, their Sam Browne belts, and their *chota lakris*—"small woods" in Urdu, the swagger sticks beloved of British army officers—tucked under their arms.

Dill and Marshall became particularly close; one time the two of them took the day off and went in civilian clothes to Gettysburg, where the guide was much annoyed at their evident lack of interest in all he had to tell them about a battlefield they knew better than he did. During Dill's final illness, Admiral King came to visit him in Walter Reed Hospital nearly every evening. When Dill died, Congress passed a joint resolution of appreciation and Marshall arranged, contrary to regulations barring foreign soldiers, for him to be buried, as he had wished, in the American Valhalla of Arlington National Cemetery.

As for the American Joint Chiefs, for a time it was not even quite clear who they were. At Arcadia, representation from the U.S. side had consisted for the Army of Marshall (Chief of Staff) and Arnold (his air deputy), and for the Navy of Stark (Chief of Naval Operations) and King (Commander in Chief, U.S. Fleet). Though relatively junior, and subordinate to Marshall, Arnold was there to serve as an "opposite number" to Air Chief Marshal Sir Charles Portal of the RAF. But before long it became apparent that the division of labor between CNO (Stark) and Cominch (King) was not going to work out, and Stark himself urged Roosevelt that King be given both titles.[34] This was done (Stark going to London to command U.S. naval forces in Europe) and thus the Navy was left underrepresented on the Joint Chiefs, since King refused to let his air deputy serve, and thus also grave doubts were left among the Congress, the press, and the public as to exactly who was in charge here.

Given the series of military reverses during the first half of 1942, there was understandable concern about the organization of the American armed forces at the top, especially insofar as it involved the principle of unity of command (Pearl Harbor was generally believed to have provided an object lesson in the absence of such unity). In February, the idea of a supreme Allied commander was endorsed during a speech in Boston by Wendell Willkie, the 1940 Republican presidential nominee (his candidate for the military top job was Douglas MacArthur), and in the month of March there were at least seven bills before Congress designed to establish a unified Department of National Defense under a single secretary. Marshall came out for a single head of the Army and Navy at one of the last meetings of the Joint Board. But the Navy was opposed (Rear Admiral Richmond Kelly Turner, chief of the naval plans division, was "violently opposed") and the President was unenthusiastic. At his press conference on March 17, Roosevelt ridiculed an editorial in the *New York Times* that had said, "it is time to create a joint general staff," as typical amateur advice.[35]

Realizing that avenue was closed, George Marshall tried another. He had been thinking for some time about a "chief of the joint general staff," who would be not a supreme commander but rather a source of informed knowledge on which the President could base decisions, someone above the level of involvement in one service only (with Stark gone, Marshall was uncomfortable presiding over disputes to which he was a party). Stimson supported him, and Admiral Horne (vice-chief of naval operations) was of a similar disposition. They could all feel the hot breath of Congress on their necks; if they did not resolve this, someone else would. Marshall tried his proposition on the President at a date, not precisely known, in February or March, but Roosevelt was cool to it. Who would such a paragon be?

That objection was suddenly removed by the news that Admiral William D. Leahy would be returning from his tour of duty as ambassador to Vichy France, and Marshall seized the moment to put his name forward. Leahy solved all the problems: impeccable credentials as former CNO, many years' friendship with the President, and acceptability (unique!) to Ernie King. In July, Roosevelt appointed Leahy his personal chief of staff, whatever that might mean. (His press conference of July 21, 1942, fending off questions about Leahy's position, is a vintage example of Roosevelt at his most cheerfully crafty and confusing; the exchange ends with one reporter's *sotto voce* comment: "getting nowhere fast."[36]) Leahy proved to be an ideal choice: methodical, tactful at patching up differences, and able to provide the clear and prompt passage of business to and from the President that had previously not obtained. Even his limitations became strengths, since a team that included Marshall and King had no need of another formidable personality.

So the Joint Chiefs would consist of Leahy (who chaired their meetings, as the most senior), Marshall, King, and Arnold: two Army, two Navy —a balanced ticket. The Joint Army-Navy Board was never officially abolished; it simply "lapsed into a sort of shadow existence," as JCS historian Vernon Davis puts it. King kept agitating for a piece of paper that would make them legal, but the President, fully in character, replied to a request from Leahy on this score by saying it "would provide no benefits and might in some way impair flexibility of operations."[37] By "flexibility" he meant his, not theirs; *he* was all the authorization they needed.

◆

When Churchill came to Washington for Arcadia, he brought with him a portable version of the Map Room from his underground headquarters in Storey's Gate, the nerve center of the British Empire. It was installed in the Monroe Room, across from Churchill's suite in the White House, and immediately attracted the President's attention. "He liked to come," Churchill wrote, "and study attentively the large maps of all the theatres of war which soon covered the walls, and on which the movement of fleets and armies was so swiftly and accurately recorded."[38] After Churchill had departed, nothing would do but Roosevelt must have a map room of his own, and this was speedily accomplished, under the direction of the President's naval aide, Captain John L. McCrea, and with the assistance of Lieutenant (jg) Robert Montgomery, USNR, the actor who had been naval attaché in London and was familiar with British procedures.

McCrea found an unused room with its own washroom on the ground floor of the White House (later the Curator's Office) which was admirably suited to the purpose. It was located across from the elevator and next to the offices of Rear Admiral Ross T. McIntire, surgeon general of the Navy and Roosevelt's physician, where the President was accustomed to come regularly.

This was not the first time the White House had a map room, nor was it the first to be used as a command post by the Commander in Chief. During the Spanish-American War, McKinley had a map room convenient to his study on the second floor, complete with twenty-five private telephone lines to the War and Navy departments. (Next to Washington, McKinley was militarily the best prepared of the Presidents; he had been commissioned at nineteen, served throughout the Civil War with the Ohio Volunteers, and was twice cited for gallantry in action.) Wilson had World War I maps set up in the Cabinet Room but seems never to have consulted them; Lincoln ran his war out of the telegraph office of the War Department building across Lafayette Square.[39]

But Roosevelt's Map Room was peculiarly his own, a characteristic expression of his working habits. The door said "No Admittance" and indeed no one was allowed inside but the President, Harry Hopkins, the Joint Chiefs, Captain McCrea, presidential secretary Grace Tully, rare visitors like Admiral Stark or Secretary Stimson, and the round-the-clock Army and Navy duty officers who posted current information on the maps: the progress of ground offensives and the location at sea of convoys, task forces, and capital ships. Grace Tully was thoroughly bored by the Map Room, with "its hodgepodge of varicolored pins, arrowheaded lines and generally confusing symbols," but she could see that her boss "took to that sort of thing like a duck to water."[40]

Here, too, was what the President called "the Magic Book," containing the latest reports from Magic, the cryptanalysts who had broken the enemy codes. Here also were kept action reports, future plans, records of decisions, and the President's communications with the other wartime leaders, making this the most extensive collection of secret documents in Washington. Information is control, as Roosevelt well knew. He had it in mind that no one else should monitor his dealings with Churchill, Stalin, and Chiang Kai-shek, and he cannily arranged this by sending outgoing messages through the Army and receiving incoming ones through the Navy, so that only his own set of files in the Map Room was complete.[41]

At least one or more often two daily visits to the Map Room became part of the President's routine, in which the "doctor's office" had always had a place. Toward the end of the afternoon every day or so, it had been his custom to emerge from the elevator and cross over to McIntire's rooms, where, sitting in an old dentist's chair, he would have his sinuses packed by McIntire and his legs massaged by Lieutenant Commander

George A. Fox, his physical therapist. He would read (with comment) the afternoon newspapers, feed his "anxiously awaiting" Scottie dog, Fala, and generally relax. (Fala's bowl was brought by Prettyman, Roosevelt's valet, but the idea of the occasion was that he receive it direct from the master's hand.) Sometimes McCrea would read to him out of dispatches with a security classification low enough so that the others could listen, and then Roosevelt and McCrea would go to the Map Room for any further briefing on the most recent reports from the battlefronts.

When he was not in Washington, the President was kept abreast of events by Captain McCrea on the phone or, when that was insufficiently secure, by McCrea in person. Mrs. Roosevelt has left an account of a weekend in August 1942 at the Catoctin Mountain retreat in the Maryland Blue Ridge that her husband called Shangri-La (now Camp David) when, on Sunday morning, McCrea arrived and conferred with the President in hushed tones for a half hour over a large map he unfolded. "Things are not going well in the Pacific," was all that Roosevelt said at dinner.[42] Later she realized that McCrea had brought reports hard on the event of the disastrous battle of Savo Island near Guadalcanal, where the Allies had suffered a heavy defeat that for many months the Navy tried to keep secret, in the hope the Japanese would not know the extent of their victory.

Rear Admiral Turner of the plans division told McCrea when he was appointed naval aide that his chief qualifications for the job were being over six feet tall and having a strong back. Admiral King warned him not to be surprised at "the number of people your senior, who heretofore have never given you a tumble, who will now address you as 'John, old boy.'" McCrea had been specially picked by King, over his own objections; he wanted sea duty, and had been slated to command a cruiser.

He pointed out to King and Secretary Knox that, while he had never voted, he had been raised a Republican and was no New Dealer. "Well, what do you think I am?" said Knox. "I'm a thorough-going Republican serving a Democratic President." King liked and trusted McCrea and wanted him there as a reliable channel of communication between the Navy and the White House: McCrea would attend the secretary's morning briefing, see all top-secret documents, and have access to King whenever he wished. He understood the difficulty of serving more than one superior. "If there are things going on you don't want the President to know about," he told King and Knox, "just don't tell me." They smiled at him.[43]

When McCrea had his first appointment with the President, he was startled by Roosevelt's recalling McCrea's service as an aide to Admiral Hugh Rodman with the American battle squadron that joined the British Grand Fleet in the North Sea during World War I.[44] Not to be outdone, McCrea reminded the President of the day in April 1920 when Rodman and he had been waiting for a cab at the Navy Department and the assistant secretary had not only offered them a lift but invited them home to lunch, on the grounds that the Roosevelt children had never seen an admiral (for McCrea it had been a memorably warm family affair). Roosevelt replied, "Of course I remember the incident but I didn't associate you with it."[45]

McCrea soon discovered that the President liked to talk about "when I was in the Navy" and to observe that he had known officers like King, Nimitz, and Halsey when they were "on their way up." McCrea cultivated the privilege of meeting with him in his bedroom on Sunday mornings, "an excellent time to see him," and became very much a member of the working White House family, a close-knit group. (Roosevelt's secretary Bill Hassett, who was not lavish with praise, called McCrea "skipper" and said he was "an able man.") Eventually McCrea's wish was granted: He left to command the new battleship *Iowa,* which fought in both oceans and carried the President to the Allied conferences at Cairo and Teheran in 1943.

McCrea thought "the President's knowledge of world geography was amazing," and expressed surprise "that he knew so much about an insignificant lake in a small foreign country." Roosevelt responded that this was what happened "if a stamp collector really studies his stamps." Like others who spent much time with Roosevelt, McCrea remarked on his thoughtfulness, his cheerful demeanor, and "the patience with which he bore his affliction . . . with never a reference to it." ("It's hard sometimes to tell just how he feels," Bill Hassett wrote in his diary, "because he never betrays it in ill temper."[46])

Once McCrea went with the President to church and loaned him two dollars for the collection, a debt that was duly settled a week later. "Now John," said Roosevelt, "you are a gentleman. I'll keep you in mind when in the future I want to make a small touch. You know if I had borrowed two dollars from Hopkins he would have hounded me daily until I repaid him—and you never said a word about it."

◆

Roosevelt's means of personal contact with his commanders varied with their preferences and their choice of intermediary. His notorious partiality to the Navy did not make life any easier for Admiral King. The President reserved to himself final approval of flag officer assignments. He kept at hand a well-thumbed copy of the Naval Register and could readily pronounce opinions on the merits and demerits of many of the senior officers. "Some were remembered favorably," wrote Robert G. Albion, "a few unfavorably, and some, who had not happened to be around the Department in his time, were . . . not remembered at all."[47] King had never belonged to the inner circle of the President's naval acquaintances and had been passed over by Roosevelt for appointment as Chief of Naval

Operations, to his deep and agonized disappointment, at the one time in his life when he would normally have been eligible.

The war changed all that and King became, if not a Roosevelt intimate, a trusted counselor. On the record he was in the White House forty-three times during 1942, perhaps at other meetings unofficially. (Grace Tully said that the "gold braid" came and went "by the dozens," and that a closed car speeding through the normally unused South Gate of the White House enabled them to escape the attention of reporters.) James Roosevelt thought that his father had a higher opinion of King than of any other American leader, and John Gunther heard in Washington that King was held in such esteem that he could "raise hell with FDR."[48]

Yet King was still uncertain enough of how he stood that he became uneasy when his sixty-fourth birthday, the age of mandatory retirement, approached in the fall of 1942. He wrote the President a short, formal note calling attention to the date and ending, "I am, as always, at your service." When McCrea showed him the letter, Roosevelt said, "He didn't have to remind me of that," and scrawled across the bottom of it:

> E.J.K.
> So what, old top?
> I may send you a birthday present!
> F.D.R.

and he did: an autographed photograph. The usually dour King was so elated he showed the letter to his aide.[49]

With Marshall and the Army the President was more distant. Marshall told Brooke that sometimes he did not see Roosevelt for a month or six weeks at a time. ("I was fortunate if I did not see Winston for six hours," Brooke dryly noted.[50]) In searching to fill his own needs for an emissary, Marshall had discovered the uses of Harry Hopkins, who had been among his backers when he was being considered for Chief of Staff. "I didn't see Hopkins very often," Marshall told Forrest Pogue after the war, "because I made it a business not to go to the White House [often]. . . . But whenever I hit a tough knot I couldn't handle . . . I would call him up and he would either arrange a meeting with the President for me or he and I together would see the President. He was always the strongest advocate, it seemed to me, of almost everything I proposed. . . . And there had to be a firm position taken in these matters. So he was quite invaluable to me and he was very courageous."[51]

Even at a distance it is difficult to withhold astonishment at this remarkable figure, this reformist midwestern social worker with a liking for racetracks and nightclubs, who had come up through the world of settlement houses, health associations, and welfare agencies to be Governor Roosevelt's deputy director of emergency relief in Albany and then President Roosevelt's head of the WPA (Works Progress Administration) in

Washington. In 1940, while secretary of commerce, Hopkins had gone to Chicago and taken muscular command of the convention that renominated Roosevelt for an unprecedented third term, and by 1941 he had already worked his way into the niche of presidential alter ego and right-hand man that in wartime was to be of prime importance.

His frail grasp on good health and his profound ignorance of foreign affairs (and much else) in no way diminished Hopkins's dedication to the President's cause, to which he unswervingly devoted himself. Indefatigable, and shrewdly protective of his position, he possessed to an unusual degree the ability to separate the important from the unimportant and to act accordingly. Where he had not been apprised of Roosevelt's wish, a sixth sense of it guided him. He spoke in the President's name, and action followed.

When his own judgments obtruded, the effects were sometimes less fortunate, and toward the end his influence waned, but in the early years of the war he was induplicable. Probing, questioning, demanding to be satisfied, he rode herd on the full range of the President's interests and responsibilities. Sherwood, in a biography based on Hopkins's papers—while cautioning that his subject's preferred instrument of self-expression was the telephone, which he employed with abandon—tried to convey the extent and variety of his activities through a sampling of the letters and memoranda that crossed his desk in the spring of 1941. A listing of their subject matter fills over four printed pages.

A sampling would include: the needs of Greece for aircraft, a shortage of alloy steel, a new thermal process for making aluminum, delivery of propellers for Navy fighter planes, the amount of small-arms ammunition going to private purposes, the capacity of B-24s for carrying spare engines across the North Atlantic, shipments of tin plate to England, Russian needs for raw copper, bauxite transfers in the Virgin Islands, the amount of magnesium being put to civilian use, American requirements for raw materials from Australia and Australian requirements for American machine tools, coordination of American and British tank design, airports on the ferry-service route from Takoradi to Cairo, financial assistance to Ibn Saud of Arabia, denial of U.S. gasoline and kerosene to Tahiti, and arrangements for a copy of Orson Welles's film *Citizen Kane* to be screened for the President's delectation. "The more I think of it," Secretary Stimson wrote of Hopkins in his diary in March 1941, "the more I think it is a godsend that he should be in the White House."[52]

Nor should mention be omitted of the President's military aide Major General Edwin W. Watson, known to all as "Pa," in Stimson's view another "godsend." Watson had served as President Wilson's aide at Versailles. He was a big, bluff, good-natured Virginian who had been assigned to White House duty in the first New Deal administration and had stayed on beyond the normal tour in the all-important post of President's appointments secretary. "Many people in Washington," wrote Judge Samuel Rosenman, "considered him merely a jovial companion to the President. He was much more."[53] If nothing else, Watson was sympathetic and knowledgeable (in "old army" terms) about the Army. True, he was regarded in some quarters as not very bright, an impression he did not discourage, but the fact that he decided who saw the President and who did not, thus had to say no to many important and importunate people, and still was universally described as "lovable" suggests a considerable astuteness behind his amiable exterior.

Captain McCrea tried to set down in his memoir a sketch of Watson in action on the phone, which might have gone somewhat as follows: "Now ———, I can't tell you how good it is to hear your voice. . . . So you want to see the President. I must be frank with you,———, and tell you that he is up to his neck in work. He is so darned busy that I who must see him many times in a day often stand outside his door and say to myself isn't there some way I can spare him this interruption. I always feel better about it when I can say, 'Yes Pa, there is: don't go in.' And I can't tell you how good it makes me feel to keep from going in. . . . I know the Boss well enough to know that there isn't anyone in Washington whom the President would rather see than you—but he just can't make it today or any day soon. I'll tell you, why don't you ring me up in a week or ten days from now and maybe we can work something out. It's been good to talk to you and fine to know that you are so understanding. I'll tell the President of your call at the risk of catching hell for not letting you in. It's been so good to talk to you, but you can see how it is." Then, after hanging up: "Jee*sus*, John! If I let that guy in to see the President I'd be fired from here and find myself on duty with troops in about forty-eight hours."

Watson used a particularly redolent brand of aftershave lotion, and at their first meeting of the day Roosevelt would ask McCrea, "What do you think of Pa this morning, John? Doesn't he smell pretty? Do you suppose all army officers smell pretty like this early in the morning?" while Watson "laughed uproariously." Watson told McCrea: "I've been around here a long time, and I've picked up a few things." His advice was brief: Be available but stay out of sight. "I would much rather have them say, 'Where's Pa?' than have the thought flash through their minds, 'Here he is again.' "

Watson, said Rosenman, had "an uncanny instinct for distinguishing between the fake and the genuine in human beings and human conduct," and he had become as indispensable to Roosevelt as anyone could be to that supremely self-contained man. Often the President literally relied on Watson's physical strength to help him walk and stand. Watson's death of a cerebral hemorrhage, aboard the cruiser *Quincy* on the return from Yalta, affected Roosevelt so deeply and visibly that those who knew him well were alarmed at this reflection of his own declining powers.

Behind the formal record of traffic between the President and the military—the situation reports, the plans of operations in prospect, the summaries of agreement at Allied conferences—there is much documentation of their relationships on a less elevated level. Memoranda from Marshall, King, and Arnold individually indicate that Roosevelt was always asking questions to which their memos are the answers: about weapons systems, the defenses of some outpost, possible targets for bombing, the claims of Colonel McCormick of the *Chicago Tribune* to military wisdom, the duty assignments of sons of notable personages. There is no particular pattern; they lack the ferocious concentration on every detail that Churchill's "minutes" for "action this day" have. Rather they represent the spot checking of a prudent executive who wants to keep his people on their toes, and not too much should be made of them, though they doubtless took their toll in effort by staff to answer.

But from time to time his heads of service would send the President statements of their own strategic thinking, as King significantly did on March 5, 1942, and equally he would now and then put together a thoughtful résumé of what was on his own mind, as he did for Marshall about Stilwell and the situation in China on March 8, 1943. Then again, they would send him copies of vivid combat reports or letters from commanders in the field they thought might interest him, and always there were the greetings and acknowledgments of greetings on Christmas or birthdays, an opportunity for an exposure of sentiment in what were otherwise fairly impersonal exchanges. And Roosevelt being as he was, you could never be sure you would not receive something like the following, addressed in late August 1942 to Captain McCrea:

> Will you tell the Navy Band
> that I don't like the way they
> play The Star Spangled Banner—
> it should not have a lot of
> frills in it?
>
> F.D.R.[54]

III

On March 17, 1913, at the age of thirty-one, Franklin D. Roosevelt had been sworn in as assistant secretary of the Navy. He was the youngest to hold that office and went on to serve in it the longest, seven years and five months. Twice elected to the New York State Senate as an anti-Tammany Democrat from normally Republican Dutchess County (where his family's country home at Hyde Park was located), he had hitched his wagon to the rising star of Governor Woodrow Wilson of New Jersey, and worked to gain backing in New York—despite Tammany's firm hold on the state's convention delegates—for Wilson's presidential candidacy. When Wilson won the nomination without Tammany's help, and went on to win the election as well, Roosevelt's name, his independent means, his "progressive liberalism," and his prominence as a Wilson supporter all made him a logical contender for a post in the new administration.

Wilson's choice for secretary of the Navy was Josephus Daniels, editor and publisher of the Raleigh, North Carolina, *News and Observer.* (An ardent supporter of William Jennings Bryan, Daniels had been instrumental in swinging Bryan delegates to Wilson; a position in the cabinet was his reward.) Daniels had taken note of Roosevelt at the nominating convention in Baltimore. "I thought he was as handsome a figure of an attractive young man as I had ever seen," Daniels later wrote. Two less alike it would be hard to imagine. Daniels, twenty years senior, was a pacifist and prohibitionist who believed that whatever an admiral told him was probably wrong and that any business enterprise of more than $100,000 net worth was probably up to no good (not a bad attitude to bring to bear on the U.S. Navy of 1913).

In style as in belief, Daniels was old-fashioned, with his black string tie, his pleated linen shirts, his heavy watch case, and his fervent trust in the wisdom of the people, but his affable, small-town southern manners were coupled with political and administrative shrewdness and skill. He wanted a northerner for his assistant secretary, best of all an energetic one: "I had no fear of a strong man . . . ," he wrote. Also, as Daniels was able to assure President Wilson, Roosevelt had been a naval enthusiast from boyhood and was "our kind of liberal."[55] Meeting Roosevelt at the door of the Willard Hotel on Inauguration Day, Daniels offered him the job, and Roosevelt accepted on the spot.

The parallel with Cousin Theodore, who had sat at the same desk, was on everyone's mind. "I was very much pleased that you were appointed . . . ," the older Roosevelt wrote the younger. "I am sure you will enjoy yourself to the full . . . and that you will do capital work." The Roosevelts were elaborately interrelated; Theodore was Franklin's cousin but Eleanor's uncle. When Uncle Ted was inaugurated, Franklin and Eleanor had lunched at the White House and sat with the family at the ceremony. At their marriage two weeks later in New York, it was President Theodore who gave away the bride, and on several occasions subsequently they visited him in Washington or at Oyster Bay. "Dinner at White House & have talk with President," read Franklin Roosevelt's diary for New Year's Day in 1903.

When Daniels as a matter of courtesy cleared Roosevelt's appointment with Senator Elihu Root of New York, a "queer look" came over Root's face. "You know the Roosevelts, don't you?" Root asked. "Whenever a Roosevelt rides, he wishes to ride in front . . . they like to have their own way." Daniels and Roosevelt had their picture taken standing by the pillars on the eastern portico of what was then the State, War, and Navy Building (now the Executive Offices), and when the prints came back Daniels asked Roosevelt why he was "grinning from ear to ear" in the photograph; Roosevelt said he didn't know. "I will tell you," Daniels said. "We are both looking down on the White House and you are saying to yourself . . . , 'Some day I will be living in that house.' "[56]

Roosevelt did nothing to dispel this image by bringing with him as assistant an Albany newspaperman named Louis McHenry Howe, recently director of his campaign for reelection to the state senate. Howe was an acerb personality who managed to alienate everyone in sight while relieving the assistant secretary of unpleasant features of his office, but he had a natural gift for handling publicity and the all-consuming passion of his life was to install Roosevelt in the presidency. Nor did it go unnoticed, when the Roosevelt family came to Washington from Campobello Island in the fall, that they moved into a building, at 1733 N Street, rented from Mrs. Roosevelt's aunt "Cousin Bammie" and known as the "Little White House" from the days when Theodore Roosevelt had lived there in 1901.

All things considered, it is remarkable enough that Daniels and Roosevelt managed not only to get along but to become, in afteryears, devoted to one another. Roosevelt was a brash young man on the make, not above showing a streak of insubordination. As a convinced Mahan disciple, he believed in a big navy, in a foreign policy that bordered on imperialism, and in preparedness for a coming war which Daniels and Wilson dreaded (they both believed it would fasten the hold of big-business monopolies on the United States). Before long Roosevelt was trying to commit an administration of which he was a very junior member to policies of naval expansionism in conflict with those of his President.

Roosevelt could give correspondents the impression that he was having to run the Navy Department all by himself, and he regaled his clubmates in New York with derisory imitations of his chief. Rexford Tugwell, a "brain trust" associate of Roosevelt as governor and president, and afterward his biographer, thought this was "one of the least admirable phases of his career." The man was young. Daniels understood this and for the most part put up with it; he liked Roosevelt's "spontaneity and gaiety." Years later, on the train carrying Roosevelt to his own inauguration in 1932, he introduced Tugwell to Daniels, saying, "Rex, this is a man who taught me a lot that I needed to know."[57]

Cousin Theodore had made the job conspicuous (left as acting secretary one day, he had ordered Admiral Dewey to attack Manila if war broke out with Spain), but it was a substantive one anyway and Cousin Franklin lit into it with zest. The assistant secretary traditionally had many powers: He was in charge of all civilian personnel, he negotiated most contracts, and he took a large role in preparing annual estimates for the budget. The

Navy then was clumsily organized and half obsolete—nearly all of its captains and admirals had learned their profession on sailing ships—but Roosevelt loved every aspect of it.

The company of high rank and successful business barons did not displease him, and he loved not least the perquisites of his position: As he came aboard a naval ship he got four drum ruffles, a seventeen-gun salute (four more than a rear admiral), and an honor guard of sixteen men at attention on the quarterdeck. Still he seems to have had time to play golf nearly every day and to go the rounds of Washington social life, as exhausting and compulsory for the ambitious to keep up with then as it is today. (When she arrived, Mrs. Roosevelt, by nature shy, had to make ten to thirty courtesy calls an afternoon to introduce herself to the wives of Supreme Court justices, members of Congress, and diplomats.)

Down the long perspective, the most telling aspect of these years is that during them just about everything one would want to have happen to a future Commander in Chief happened. He learned the uses (political not excepted) of inspection trips. He learned that no matter how well he understood the Navy, Secretary Daniels understood Congress. He was willy-nilly made aware that well-bred executives, like those in the corporate clients of the law firm he had briefly worked for in Wall Street, did not always behave like gentlemen. (There was something called collusive bidding: For armor plate on the battleship *Arizona*, three major steel companies turned in identical bids.) He began to learn that graduates of Annapolis were not necessarily competent to run navy yards and, most useful of all, he began to discover that there was something called labor, and that it mattered. Laboring men had votes, as Howe could have told him; admirals did not.

Much was accomplished. He took on personally the task of dealing with labor leaders and made himself the key figure in wage negotiations; it was to be his proud claim that "the Navy has not had a single strike or a single serious disagreement" during his incumbency. He cut costs: on coal by encouraging competitive bidding, on steel by persuading Carnegie to reduce its prices by seven or eight dollars a ton. (In his own household, even with as many as ten servants, he practiced small economies: ate at home because it was cheaper, rode streetcars, drove a secondhand car, wore the same suits for many years.)

He saw to it that Pearl Harbor had a drydock, which the experts had said was impossible; he built the "temporary" buildings along Constitution Avenue that were still in use long after World War II (until President Nixon tore them down); he started a program to encourage sailors to know how to swim. During World War I, he suggested the appointment of a labor administrator, promoted the use of submarine chasers, pushed on behalf of naval aviation, drew up (in 1919, unsuccessfully) a proposal for a joint army-navy "Plan Making Body," and successfully urged that a mine barrage be laid across the North Sea—his "most notable achievement during the war," according to Frank Freidel in his *Franklin D. Roosevelt: The Apprenticeship,* which treats this period in detail.[58]

He identified so completely with his work that references abound in his letters to "my cruise," or "my destroyer," or "my navy men," or "my Marines." But he also developed a healthy disenchantment with the immobility of "the Na-a-vy's" entrenched institutions. "The Admirals are really something to cope with—and I should know," he told Marriner Eccles in 1940. "To change anything in the Na-a-vy is like punching a feather bed. You punch it with your right hand and you punch it with your left until you are finally exhausted, and then you find the damn bed just as it was before you started punching."[59] During the same years, too, he got to know many in the cast of characters that would surround him as wartime President.

It is easy to forget that members of proximate generations going through the same sequences tend to encounter one another. Roosevelt sailed often on the dispatch ship *Dolphin,* whose captain was William D. Leahy. When he went with Vice-President Marshall to the Panama Pacific Exposition in San Francisco, his personal aide was Husband E. Kimmel. While recovering from an appendicitis operation, he was sent best wishes for recovery by the Japanese naval attaché, Commander Kichisaburo Nomura. When in France during World War I, he visited a naval air base where the officer in charge was Robert A. Lovett ("the son of Judge Lovett . . . ," Roosevelt wrote in his letter-diary, "he seems like an awfully nice boy"), and in Turin he found an acquaintance of his, Army Air Corps Captain Fiorello La Guardia.

He cruised on a destroyer commanded by Lieutenant Harold R. Stark, and while inspecting naval installations in Maine he offered to guide destroyer *Flusser* through the strait between Campobello and the mainland, to the dismay of *its* commander, Lieutenant William F. Halsey, Jr. "The fact that a white-flanneled yachtsman can sail a catboat out to a buoy and back is no guarantee that he can handle a high-speed destroyer in narrow waters . . . ," Halsey later wrote. "As Mr. Roosevelt made his first turn, I saw him look aft and check the swing of our stern. My worries were over; he knew his business."[60]

When Roosevelt went to France in 1918, he insisted on being given a more-than-cursory introduction to the realities of warfare. He visited Belleau Wood, recent scene of heavy fighting by U.S. Marines. At Mareuil-en-Dole, which had just been captured, he witnessed an artillery barrage and aircraft dogfighting overhead. He reviewed marines who had taken heavy losses and, with no rest period, were going back into action. At Verdun, as he climbed the slope of Fort Douamont, German shells burst on the path he had just traversed. He saw the shattered villages, the unburied dead, and the effects of combat on men in whose place he felt he should be (his efforts to get into uniform had been blocked by President Wilson).

This exposure made an intense imprint on him and was the basis for the celebrated passage in his Chautauqua speech of August 1936:

> I have seen war. I have seen war on land and sea. I have seen blood running from the wounded. I have seen men coughing out their gassed lungs. I have seen the dead in the mud. I have seen cities destroyed. I have seen two hundred limping, exhausted men come out of the line— the survivors of a regiment of one thousand that went forward forty-eight hours before. I have seen children starving. I have seen the agony of mothers and wives. I hate war.[61]

It must be admitted that at the time, he expressed no such sentiments. There is nothing in the accounts he sent home to suggest anything but exultation and pride in the prowess of Allied arms—one more among the many indications that the Roosevelt who had survived his crippling illness, mastered the national political scene, and uneasily observed the advancing worldwide clash of conflict was not the same Roosevelt as the assistant secretary. Even after Pearl Harbor, he remembered to refer to the field of battle as "ugly." What the younger man looked at with an appetite for experience in its fullness, the older man looked back on with revulsion, nor should the possibility be entirely discounted that abomination for war's evil is not inconsistent with a sense of its awesomeness.

◆

On September 11, 1939, the President of the United States addressed a letter to the First Lord of the Admiralty. Great Britain had gone to war with Germany the week before, and a warrior had been brought into the government to head the Royal Navy. Since so much came of this single piece of paper, it deserves to be quoted at least in part:

> Dear Churchill:
> It is because you and I occupied similar positions in the world war that I want you to know how glad I am that you are back in the Admiralty. Your problems are, I realize, complicated by new factors but the essential is not different. What I want you and the Prime Minister to know is that I shall at all times welcome it if you will keep me in touch personally with anything you want me to know about.[62]

The President exaggerated. By no stretch of the imagination could his position in World War I be described as "similar" to Churchill's. An adequate history of the time could be written without even mentioning Roosevelt's name, where without Churchill's it would have huge and unbridgeable gaps. But no matter: A hand had been extended and it was grasped. This was the beginning of a correspondence that lasted until the

President's death and eventually numbered more than 1,700 items. It was of monumental significance; on the relationship between these two everything else depended.

Both of them (Churchill the more) made so much of their "friendship" that curiosity is alerted as to how deep it went, especially in view of their self-evident differences in temperament and in belief about the geopolitics of Europe, the future of colonialism, and the shape of the postwar world. Lord Moran thought they had nothing in common but the war, and the suspicion does intrude that this was less a marriage of true minds than of convenience.

These were two consummate actors always on stage, two larger-than-lifesize human beings engaged in a serious task which required of them that they get along. This they did. They measured up to what history asked, and they took justified pleasure and satisfaction in doing so together. "Partnership" is a better word than "friendship," and Joseph P. Lash did not greatly exaggerate when he called it "the partnership that saved the West."[63] Certainly the principal reason for the effectiveness of the Anglo-American collaboration was the spirit of it established at the summit, and never fundamentally flawed thereafter.

To see how the thing worked in practice, one has only to dip into their collected correspondence at a crucial moment and watch the differences being ironed out—for example, the half dozen or so cables they exchanged between August 27 and September 5, 1942, on the vexed question of where and when the Allied landings in North Africa were going to take place. The British, concerned to reach Tunisia before the Germans, wanted to land inside the Mediterranean as far east as possible, certainly not short of Algiers. The Americans, mistrustful of supply lanes from the United States that could be nipped at the Strait of Gibraltar, wanted to land on the Atlantic seacoast in the west at Rabat and Casablanca. One's first impression is of total impasse, but bit by bit the compromises are effected until, eventually, Roosevelt to Churchill on September 4: "we are getting very close together," and last, Churchill's reply the next day: "We agree to the military lay-out as you propose it."[64]

Churchill, eight years older, was the senior in every respect save rank (he was not, like Roosevelt, a head of state), and yet rank and the disparity of power were enough to activate his invariable deference to the younger man; it was "Winston" for the one but always "Mr. President" for the other. Churchill had been a member of a British cabinet before Roosevelt had been elected to anything but the editorship of the Harvard *Crimson*. His philosophy of statecraft was the product of a far richer and more developed experience; he had been in the thick of great events for four decades and had known war in close proximity as both organizer and participant. "Now think of it," Moran's son John said to his wife after a visit to the aging Churchill in 1958, "that hand you shook today held a saber at Omdurman"—which was in 1898 in the Sudan, where Lieutenant Churchill of the 21st Lancers took part in one of the last cavalry charges in British history (actually his hand held not a saber but a Mauser pistol, and it saved his life).[65]

Churchill would have been less than human not to have judged some of his own gifts the greater, and if nothing else, his command of language touched a nerve of envy in Roosevelt. "Who writes Winston's speeches?" was the first question he asked Hopkins on the latter's return from London in early 1941, and Hopkins hated to have to tell him that Winston did.[66] It is impossible to imagine Roosevelt producing spontaneously the comprehensive *tours d'horizon* that were Churchill's specialty, like the three state papers on world strategy he dictated aboard the *Duke of York* in the storm-tossed Atlantic on his way to the Arcadia meetings, which read today with a force and freshness more than borne out by subsequent events that unrolled very much as he had wished and forecast.

Given Churchill's careful choice of words, when we first meet Roosevelt in his war history the introduction is more remarkable for what it does not say than for what it says. "I formed a very strong affection, which grew over our years of comradeship," he writes, "for this formidable politician who had imposed his will for nearly ten years upon the American scene, and whose heart seemed to respond to many of the impulses that stirred my own."[67] Not a word here about the champion of the downtrodden, the sage statesman, the gallant invalid who had restored a nation's vitality, the symbol of democracy triumphant in a sea of dictatorships—only "this formidable politician." It should be granted that Churchill handsomely made up for this in the encomium he inserted at the time of Roosevelt's death, but nonetheless the earlier omissions are striking.

Churchill was not overly interested in what other people thought, as to a high degree was Roosevelt, who weighed each phrase in a speech for its probable impact; Moran thought Churchill's rolling tidal waves of rhetoric were meant not for their impression on anyone else but mainly for his own amusement. Churchill's willpower animated his countrymen in their time of danger, where Roosevelt drew upon the American will in its moment of dawning strength. Churchill invented things, like tanks and the floating harbors of Normandy, that Roosevelt might never have dreamed of. But Roosevelt invented combinations of people and ideas that had not been thought of before by anybody. Facts, phrases, personalities —"a terrific variety of matters that didn't seem to have any relationship to each other," as Frances Perkins put it—would lie dormant in his memory until suddenly they coalesced in a pattern without precedent, which could break deadlocks, galvanize action, and transform dilemmas into opportunities.

Madame Perkins (his secretary of labor) described "this aptitude for knowing all kinds of diverse things at once in a flash" as almost "clairvoyant," but she saw that it came and went, so that the illumination of one day might be unavailable to him the next; sometimes he caused people to feel deceived, she thought, because he literally could not remember a combination his mind had previously put together and since forgotten.[68] Fortunately, one idea of his generated by a letter from Churchill did not suffer that fate.

The whims of fortune contrived it that Churchill again and again should be asking impossible things of Roosevelt; in the pre–Pearl Harbor dialogue, he sometimes seems to be doing little else, often with what verges on incomprehension of the limitations that the Constitution and public opinion imposed on the President. Churchill wanted the United States in the war, and this Roosevelt could not grant him. Later, too, there were moments when the Prime Minister's impatience with subordination burst forth. "I hope I have given satisfaction," reads an ironic but stinging sentence in one of his cables in 1943. At the second Quebec conference in 1944, he interrupted Roosevelt's stream of anecdotal digressions with a heartfelt "What do you want me to do? Get on my hind legs and beg like Fala?" But in his letter of December 8, 1940, at a moment when fortune held its breath, he was on the top of his form. "It was," he said, "one of the most important I ever wrote."[69]

Britain was broke.

Bound by the mandate of Congress, the British had thus far drawn on American industry only insofar as they had dollars in gold, in credit, or in investments convertible as dollars to put on the drumhead. Now all this had come to an end. "The moment approaches," Churchill wrote, "when we shall no longer be able to pay cash for shipping and other supplies." His letter reached Roosevelt by courier in the Caribbean, where the President was vacationing aboard the cruiser *Tuscaloosa,* and Hopkins has described how he sat alone in his deck chair, reading and rereading Churchill's message. "I began to get the idea that he was refueling," Hopkins wrote, "the way he so often does when he seems to be resting and carefree. . . . Then, one evening, he suddenly came out with it—the whole program."[70]

This crystallization of disparate elements was the Lend-Lease Act, which relieved Britain of the need to go on exhausting resources it no longer had for necessities it continued to require. The idea of leasing or lending, together with the metaphor of the garden hose your neighbor borrows to extinguish a fire, removed the economic obstacle to putting the American industrial powerhouse behind the Allied cause (the homely image of the garden hose was no small factor in the bill's passage). It made possible what otherwise could not have been: Britain's continuation in the war. In a decade so full of turning points that they dizzy the mind, this one still stands out. De Gaulle, who was spending the weekend with the Prime Minister, said that Churchill came to him at dawn, "literally dancing with joy," to tell him that Lend-Lease had passed. To the House of Commons, Churchill called it "the most unsordid act in the history of any nation."[71]

◆

After the Casablanca Conference ended in January 1943, Churchill persuaded Roosevelt to come with him to the oasis of Marrakech, to wind up their tasks and to watch the sun go down on the Atlas Mountains, a favorite sight of Churchill's. They were put up in a showpiece of Morocco, La Saadia, a light-red stucco villa with courtyards and black marble fountains, interiors of Oriental splendor, and a six-story tower. It had been loaned by the widow of its American millionaire owner to Kenneth Pendar, one of our advance agents brought into North Africa before the invasion thinly disguised as vice-consuls. (Pendar, a well-to-do young archaeologist and art historian, had come to this exotic assignment direct from the Harvard College Library.)

Roosevelt and Churchill, followed by their entourage, were driven from Casablanca in a Daimler limousine painted olive drab, stopping on the roadside for a picnic lunch. Thousands of American soldiers had been posted at hundred-yard intervals along the route, fighter planes circled overhead, and the Daimler's progress was reported to La Saadia every half hour by telephone.

Once arrived, Churchill prevailed on Roosevelt to allow himself to be carried bodily up the staircase of the villa's tower, the Prime Minister bringing up the rear and singing a little tune of his own composition to the words "Oh, there ain't no war, there ain't no war." Snowstorms had recently covered the mountains, which were white almost to their base; in the setting sun they turned varying shades of pink.

Pendar thought he had never seen the Atlas range, wild and rugged, with twelve-thousand-foot peaks, look more magnificent; in the clear air it seemed close enough to reach out and touch. They sat there silent for nearly a quarter hour. As the sun descended, electric lights went on, summoning the faithful to prayer, in the top of every mosque minaret in Marrakech, "like a gong announcing the end of day," wrote Pendar. The evening turned chilly and the Prime Minister sent downstairs for the President's coat, which he draped over Roosevelt's shoulders. "It's the most lovely spot in the whole world," said Churchill.[72]

Dinner—laid on by Pendar's major-domo, Louis, like his employer a graduate of the Sorbonne—was elegant and convivial. As host, Pendar seated himself between the two great men and could not resist comparing them. He was struck by the sense that though Churchill was the better conversationalist, it was Roosevelt who dominated any room they were in. To his surprise, the President proved to have "an extraordinary and profound grasp" of Arab problems and the Arab character as Pendar saw it, with its combination of materialism and intuition. "He even had all the

facts of our unique diplomatic position in Morocco at his fingertips," said
Pendar, "down to the names of the treaties and the dates."

It seems that Roosevelt held forth at some length with his views about
the future independence of Morocco, the importance of compulsory education, of fighting disease and introducing birth control. "He recognized
the rise of nationalism among the colonial peoples," wrote Averell Harriman, who was there. "He also recognized that Churchill was pretty much
a nineteenth-century colonialist. So he said some of these things partly to
jar Churchill but also from a fundamental belief that the old order could
not last." Apparently the talk was not all one-sided. Harriman later told
Pendar that he had much enjoyed hearing Pendar explain to the President, "in no uncertain terms," why in Morocco the New Deal would not
work.

Harriman thought that Churchill would have preferred an opportunity for conversation with Roosevelt alone. At Casablanca, though British
strategies had been adopted, the presence of the American power
Churchill had so devoutly sought—symbolized by those soldiers on the
road and the fighter planes above (the British had provided the picnic
lunch)—was beginning to show its other side to him; from now on it would
grow, Britain's would not, and the President's elusiveness and self-determination would reveal themselves. As for a tête-à-tête with Churchill at
La Saadia, Harriman wrote, "Roosevelt rather liked the idea that he did
not have to go through with this. . . . He always enjoyed other people's
discomfort. I think it is fair to say that it never bothered him very much
when other people were unhappy."[73]

After dinner (which ended around midnight in a certain amount of
song), to work. Space was cleared and lights arranged, a table with sandwiches and drinks provided, and together with Harriman and Hopkins,
the Big Two set about composing a summary of their recent meeting and
messages about it to Stalin and Chiang Kai-shek. This took them till about
two o'clock in the morning. Pendar thought they were well pleased with
what they had accomplished and that both had the "catching quality" of
optimism. "The Prime Minister seemed much more in the present and
more of an extrovert," Pendar wrote. "The President, on the other hand,
often sat gazing into space as he worked. That night he had a look that was
not exactly sad, yet it was the look of someone who comprehended sad-
ness."[74]

Next day, after seeing Roosevelt off, Churchill was in a vile mood until
finally he shouted to his valet, "Sawyers, my painting things. Please put
them out in the tower." A sigh of relief went up from the staff officers, who
recognized this as a sign of improving humor (it is a daunting thought that
Churchill could simply assume his "painting things" to be instantly available). At eleven o'clock he emerged in a smock and an enormous wide-brim
hat, ascended the tower, gazed for a long time at the mountains, and made

a painting of the view they had admired the day before, the only picture he painted during the entire war. (His silhouette was visible all over Marrakech, and confirmed the rumors that had been racing through town.) "He seemed reluctant to break the illusion of a holiday," Moran wrote, "which for a few hours has given him a chance to get his breath." Churchill later presented the painting to Roosevelt as a memento of the occasion and for a time it was kept in the library at Hyde Park, though it is now in a private collection.[75]

When the moment had come at seven-thirty for Roosevelt to leave Churchill was in bed and, "as usual," according to Lord Moran, not eager to get out of it, but he was determined to bid the President a proper farewell. So he came to the airfield wearing his black velvet slippers with the embroidered initials, his blue flannel coverall, which he called his "zip," and his dressing gown with the velvet collar and the red dragons, topped off by the cap of a field marshal of the Royal Air Force. When the photographers at the plane saw him coming, they jumped at the chance of a lifetime, but waving his cigar, he told them, "You simply can not do this to me," and laughing, they lowered their cameras.

Churchill said goodby to Roosevelt and then, to Pendar, at the foot of the ramp, "Come, Pendar, let's go home. I don't like to see them take off." The sun was breaking through the ground mist and the outline of the mountains was beginning to appear; the aircraft, though large by the standards of the time, seemed tiny in all that vastness. In the car, Churchill said, "Don't tell me when they take off. It makes me far too nervous."

He put his hand on Pendar's arm. "If anything happened to that man," he said, "I couldn't stand it. He is the truest friend; he has the farthest vision; he is the greatest man I have ever known."[76]

I

ROOSEVELT

IN WASHINGTON, D.C., which has never lacked for warm summers, the spring of 1941 ushered in one of the hottest on record. Its mood was restive. "The situation," wrote the secretary of war in his diary, "has been very trying for the past few days . . . everybody asking what is going to be done and no way of finding out whether anything will be done."[1] For nearly five months, in the face of events daily more threatening, the President had made no statement of how he proposed to deal with them. The war was going badly for Great Britain; his efforts to safeguard its survival were faltering.

Physically he was almost inaccessible. During the fortnight from May 14 to May 27 he spent most of his time in bed, with what he claimed was a persistent cold. Robert Sherwood, the playwright, who had become one of the principal writers of his speeches, had a long talk with him in his bedroom and noticed that he never coughed or sneezed or blew his nose. When Sherwood remarked on this to Roosevelt's secretary Missy LeHand, of all those close to Roosevelt the closest, she smiled. "What he's suffering from most of all," she said, "is a case of pure exasperation."[2]

The President had been scheduled to make an address on May 14— Pan American Day, a favorite State Department occasion for hemispheric piety—but had postponed it to the twenty-seventh, adding an element of suspense to what was already anticipation. The news that Sherwood and Judge Samuel I. Rosenman were in Washington, at work on the speech, was reported on the radio, to their discomfort and the President's amusement. In three days, twelve thousand letters came in to the White House, offering advice; from within the government came drafts and requests to be consulted. The two speechwriters found themselves the objects of flattering attention from the many functionaries who wanted to know, or genuinely needed to know, what was in the wind. Everybody wondered what the President was going to say, apparently the President included.

The administration seemed to be stalled on dead center. This was an interlude of equilibrium in which the forces that pushed and pulled at Roosevelt were approximately in balance, heightening his frustration but exposing its origins. In a fireside chat just before year's end, after his triumphant reelection for a third term, he had given every sign of recapturing his sense of purpose, issuing a clarion call for freedom, using the phrase "arsenal of democracy" to describe what America intended to be, and asking the country to supply arms for the Allies "with the same resolution, the same sense of urgency, the same spirit of patriotism and sacrifice as we would show were we at war."

In March, the Lend-Lease Act, hammered out in the heat of debate, had given the President's words the authority of a national resolve. Shortly after the bill was passed, he told the annual dinner of the White House Correspondents' Association that in a democracy decisions may come slowly but, once made, speak with the voice of a hundred thirty million people, so that "the world is no longer left in doubt."[3] Yet there were many doubts.

The power of isolationist feeling in the country at large, reflected and perhaps amplified in the halls of Congress, remained forbiddingly strong. This was a more potent force than it is now easy to realize. Its center was the midwestern heartland, where the world ended with the horizon of the bountiful prairie and there lived people who had never seen the sea. It drew upon abhorrence of war, and the belief—fortified by the findings of historians—that American entry into World War I had been a mistake, if not a trick engineered by the British, the bankers, and the big munitions-makers. It incorporated a mistrust of Europe, viewed as a distant family of quarrelsome nations whose ancient animosities were properly no concern of ours, while it also had ethnic roots among hyphenated Americans whose inheritance predisposed them to mistrust the British and the French. It held that if all else failed, the best defense of America lay on our ocean frontiers, securely guarded by a vigilant navy, and it numbered among its adherents many of the publicly prominent and politically powerful.

At the same time, the aims embodied in Lend-Lease were far short of being realized. Under the mild regime of the Office of Production Management (OPM), the "arsenal" was not producing the goods in sufficient quantity, and in the absence of American naval convoys, not enough of them were getting across the Atlantic. The President seemed not to acknowledge this. For the task of disentangling his industrial controls he had shown no appetite, and to the question of convoys—as contrasted to the euphemistic halfway measure called "patrols," a distinction he insisted on—his answers had been peevish and elliptical. With the nation split in two, he openly took neither side, and on the assumption that his next moves were subject to suasion, public pressures on him mounted. If the isolationists damned him for dragging us to war, the interventionists damned him again for not dragging harder.

Franklin D. Roosevelt has enjoyed, and in some historical accounts still does enjoy, a reputation for either duplicity or impenetrable complexity in his prewar conduct of foreign affairs that hardly seems justified. Perhaps the subsequent unveiling of events he had foreseen, though with no enthusiasm, clothes him with simpler intentions in our eyes. Perhaps he seemed complicated to people who thought his problems were simple, or were trying to sell him simple solutions of their own contriving. At any rate, there is little that now seems baffling or two-faced about his reluctance to lead a parade toward war.

He had in effect made a compact with the electorate that he had every reason for wishing to keep. He had closely observed, and not forgotten, the failure of Woodrow Wilson to reinforce the Executive's foreign policies with congressional backing. He had experimented, in his "quarantine the aggressors" speech of October 1937, with a posture that tried to combine an interventionist distaste for the dictators with an isolationist desire to keep them at a distance, and had been sadly disappointed by the pallid response. There were in his own make-up sentiments of the isolationist that were thoroughly at home there.

"The primary purpose of the United States of America," he had said in 1935, "is to avoid being drawn into war." He had held back in the face of early depredations by the Axis powers, and time and again made clear that he was more interested in preventing war profiteering, and curbing American trade with warring nations through neutrality laws, than he was in collective security with its risk of involvement. "If we face the choice of profit or peace," he said in his Chautauqua speech of 1936, "the Nation will answer—must answer—'we choose peace.' "[4]

If he had since come to believe that the Fascist regimes must be resisted, and that their aggressiveness might eventually reach our shores whether we wished it or not, then he had done so without entirely disavowing his earlier convictions. In 1940, he found himself, even in an election campaign against an opponent so ardently pro-Ally as Wendell Willkie, offering isolationist assurances—"I have said this before, but I shall say it again and again and again: Your boys are not going to be sent into any foreign wars"—that troubled the writers who watched him insert them into his speeches.

In 1941, his awareness that he faced a nation divided as he himself had been divided was all too apparent. Increasingly he seemed to insist on being pushed—by a combination of advisers, newspapers, facts, and general outcry—into doing things, like trading fifty over-age destroyers for

British bases, that his judgment alone might have prompted him to do. Yet it must also be said even now, as his associates had to admit at the time, that Roosevelt demonstrably knew more about American opinion than they did, and that if here he was mistaken, it was among his rare misreadings of the public pulse.

◆

The question of President Roosevelt's "responsibility" for involving the United States in World War II can best be answered by examining his administration in its process of arriving at policy, and for this purpose the "May Crisis" of 1941 is well suited. The long, slow slide down to the moment of truth at Pearl Harbor on December 7 had only imperceptibly begun. This was arguably the last interval of time in which war might have been avoided or significantly stalled, in which the possibilities for peace (if in fact they existed) could have been reached out to and seized by imaginative statesmanship.

What went on in these weeks is also unusually well documented, since virtually all of the participants—the President, as always, excepted—put themselves on record as to what they were doing or thinking or saying to each other. As for Roosevelt himself, if there is any isolable instance where his thought processes about the coming of war can be evoked, and from what he did not do or say as much as from what he did, then it can be sought here.

His speechwriters had their work cut out for them. Contrary to their usual procedure, Sherwood and Rosenman had been given no instructions as to either form or content. Harry Hopkins, then administrator of Lend-Lease, was a semi-invalid too ill to help, though they kept him informed of their progress. (Hopkins had been invited to sleep at the White House, had stayed on, and had been living there in the Lincoln Room for almost a year to the day; he possessed unequaled skill at reading the Roosevelt mind but at this stage could offer them only hints and moral support.) Though the President had dictated some preliminary paragraphs, they were not much use; his first drafts, as he was the first to admit, tended to be rough.

Judge Rosenman arrived in Washington on Friday, May 23, and after dinner he and Sherwood repaired to the Cabinet Room, where they labored, over coffee and sandwiches, until five in the morning. This was their preferred speechwriting spot—it provided quiet and a large table for folders and memoranda—and their routine was well established. Though Sherwood had joined the team only a month before last year's election, Rosenman had been helping with Roosevelt speeches since the first campaign for governor of New York, in 1928. They were both members of the family, at any rate. Rosenman recalled later that when Mrs. Roosevelt maternally rebuked them at breakfast the next morning for having had a light on at 3:00 A.M., and he had replied that she must have been up pretty late herself, she had protested, "I was working on my mail!" and wondered why the others laughed.[5]

A major presidential speech is far more than a speech. It is both a statement and an instrument of executive purpose. Its text will be minutely studied, both at home and abroad, for veiled and buried implications, for hints of omission and carefully calculated turns of phrase, which tell the practiced reader what he wants to know about the government's current cast of mind. Within the administration itself the speech may set a tone, discourage one faction or put another to work, lay down a line of action as firmly as though it were an executive order.

Hence the elaborate attention paid to each word, and the importance, for those who contribute drafts, of what stays in and what goes out. Two examples: In this instance it was desirable to avoid provoking either Japan or Russia, to keep one out of the war as long as possible and encourage the other to hold firm if attacked. (The attack was a month away, as we and the British knew and had told the Russians, though Stalin would not believe it.) This meant that they could not mention either nation, or use "dictatorships," Roosevelt's customary term of opprobrium, but must say only "Axis," and it also meant that in a list of countries overrun by aggression, the name of Finland, after prolonged consideration, would be dropped.

On Friday, to let everyone into the act, there had been a cabinet meeting at which views were canvassed, but like most Roosevelt cabinet meetings, it did not add up to much. The war hawks—Stimson, Secretary of the Navy Frank Knox, and Secretary of the Interior Harold Ickes—came away with the impression that on the critical convoy question the President was balky, playing with the notion that he might be rescued from his boxed-in position by an "incident," like the sinking of an American ship by the Germans.

Such had in fact happened two days earlier when the *Robin Moor*, bound for South Africa with a routine cargo, had been torpedoed in the South Atlantic, the first American merchantman to fall victim to the U-boats, though news of this did not reach the White House until after the speech. Hopkins then sent the President an indignant memo proposing that the Navy be given freedom to react as it saw fit, but Roosevelt refused to issue any such instructions and confined himself to a blustery message to Congress which asked for no action. His thinking about this was not so baldly manipulative of the public as he allowed others (Churchill among them) to imagine.[6]

The cabinet was divided, in any case. Earlier in the month, with the President's prior knowledge, both Knox and Stimson had come out unequivocally for convoys and for repeal of the Neutrality Act. Stimson had even prepared a draft resolution to be sent to Congress, as though such a thing could conceivably be passed, authorizing the President to resort to force. But their counsel had not prevailed, and was not prevailing now.

The secretary of war had long been convinced that war was inevitable and was eager to get into it. Henry L. Stimson was a seasoned product of the Teddy Roosevelt era of upper-class ventures into government, a man of set character accentuated by a look of dogged respectability, with silvering hair parted in the middle and a brisk mustache. His co-workers often called him Colonel Stimson, his rank in a field artillery regiment in World War I; the President called him Harry.

An active career, part in public service and part in private practice as a lawyer, had not prepared him to be comfortable with the tactics of indirection and delay; he thought the second Roosevelt would be a greater politician if only he were a "less artful one," as McGeorge Bundy put it in the memoir he helped Stimson write.[7] Stimson wanted the President to seize the moral initiative, and when he was convinced that a proposed course was necessary, feasible, and morally correct, he did not linger over it.

Nor did he hesitate to speak his mind. At seventy-three, Stimson was no stranger to high office. He had been in charge of the Army before—thirty years before, under President Taft—and he had been urging Franklin Roosevelt to take a strong stand in the Far East as early as 1933, when the President was the Democratic President-elect and Stimson was the outgoing Republican secretary of state. Indeed the American doctrine of "nonrecognition," which involved our refusal to recognize the Japanese conquest of Manchuria in 1931, bore Stimson's name. His years of experience entitled him to be dissatisfied by the President's happy-go-lucky methods, and when he grew impatient he could be brusque. Surely few but Colonel Stimson, faced with a presidential monologue about foreign policy on the telephone, would simply have hung up.[8]

Though still a Republican, by 1940 Stimson had become a fire-eating interventionist. Just before the political conventions of that year he had been brought into the government (along with Knox—publisher of the *Chicago Daily News,* a former Republican vice-presidential candidate, and another rough-riding protégé of the earlier Roosevelt—for secretary of the Navy) in an adroit Rooseveltian maneuver to confound his opponents and create a "coalition" cabinet in defense affairs.

Stimson had taken over the War Department with a will, brought in a group of assistants he described as the best he ever had, and established a working relationship with Chief of Staff George Marshall that was later the envy of civilians in the Navy Department who had to deal with Admiral King. Like everyone else, Stimson had taken his appointment as a tacit endorsement of his views, and he looked forward to the day when he would see them officially adopted. But the President showed increasing signs of being reluctant to go that far, and there had come to be a coolness between them.

On this occasion as on many others, the voice of caution was that of the secretary of state. Not that Cordell Hull was less violently opposed to the dictatorships than Knox or Stimson; but his methods and approach were different. Hull was an old-fashioned southern liberal politician, austere in personal style. Literally born in a log cabin in the foothills of the Cumberland Mountains, he had in him still a strain of the mountaineer's capacity for righteousness and anger.

Hull had been trained in the school of elective rather than (like Stimson) appointive office. Having represented Tennessee in the House and Senate since 1907, he kept Congress ever in the corner of his eye. While much has been made of Roosevelt's preference for running a private State Department of his own, or for favoring subordinates down the line like Under Secretary Sumner Welles, it must be said for Hull that he could see perils his colleagues preferred not to, and in spite of his unfortunate tendency to lisp, to ride hobbyhorses (like reciprocal trade) until they dropped, and to lecture foreign diplomats on the virtuousness of any given American position, he was a fair and practiced bargainer.

Since March of this year, Hull had been engaged in informal conversations with the Japanese ambassador, Admiral Nomura, pursuing a course, in which the President fully supported him, of doing everything possible to avoid war with Japan without sacrifice to what both Hull and Roosevelt saw as basic principles of international conduct. Slim as Hull thought the chances were for a settlement, his determination not to sacrifice them heedlessly reinforced his other reasons for urging restraint. He was aware —as Knox and Stimson, being members of the party out of power, seemed not to be—that any attempt to secure congressional support for an openly interventionist measure was potentially calamitous to the administration.

If it failed, as Hull was convinced it would fail (two months later, the Selective Service Act, the draft, was extended by a margin of only *one* vote), then the President's leadership would have been repudiated, undoing all that had gone before and dealing his aid-to-the-allies-short-of-war policy a blow from which it might not recover. The negotiator with war or peace hinging on his words, and the skilled hand at congressional moods and manipulation, could discern events in prospect that were chilling to contemplate. Hull saw more clearly than the others around him what a tightrope the President, and hence the country, was walking.

"He is so pessimistic . . . ," Stimson noted in his diary after a meeting with Hull. "Today he was about at his worst. 'Everything was going hellward' was the expression he kept using again and again."[9]

◆

American strategy during this period was governed by the iron laws of material insufficiency. Up to the fall of France in May–June 1940, United States military thinking had taken it for granted that France and Britain between them could hold Germany at bay long enough for us to arm them and rearm ourselves. France was considered on nearly all sides but Hitler's to be a formidable military power. Only when this illusion vanished, and German bases were established on the shores of the Atlantic, did the illusion of American invulnerability vanish with it. The possibility then had to be faced of our having to go it alone, and the effect was electric. Congress almost without a murmur had passed a four-billion-dollar construction bill for a two-ocean navy—7 battleships, 18 aircraft carriers, 27 cruisers, 115 destroyers, 43 submarines—and the Army and Navy chiefs had totally revised their plans to take account of the now-immediate threat in Europe.

This redirection of geographical perspective was Hitler's contribution to the American position on Japan. For the two-ocean navy was not scheduled to be operational before 1946, and until then our resources were inadequate to deal with more than one hemisphere at a time. In a meeting at the White House on May 22, 1940, Admiral Stark, General Marshall, and the President had agreed that the United States must not become militarily involved in the Pacific west of the 180-degree meridian—a bit west of Midway Island, which is about a thousand miles west of Hawaii—and soon Stark and Marshall were proposing to go even further in withholding and conserving American strength. On June 22, the day France signed an armistice, they had recommended to Roosevelt that (1) most of the fleet be brought to the Atlantic, and (2) efforts to supply Britain be discontinued.

This was not the last issue to divide the President and his advisers, but it was among the most politically combustible. An equivalent to isolationism was not unknown in the armed services; there were influential senior officers in the War Department, like Major General Stanley D. Embick, who had no confidence in Churchill and thought the sensible thing for the United States to do was stay out of Europe and come to terms with Japan. In the atmosphere of the time, pro-British measures could be construed in a military context as potentially anti-American. Major Walter Bedell Smith, assistant secretary to the General Staff, had told Pa Watson in the White House that if war came and we were found to be short of munitions because of sending them all to the British, then "everyone who was a party to the deal might hope to be found hanging from a lamp post."[10]

The President, in one of his most decisive prewar moves, had rejected both proposals: Aid to Britain would proceed and the fleet would stay at Pearl. The Britain-can't-win school in the War Department had its knuckles rapped; George Marshall admonished his staff, in Secretary Stimson's name, that criticisms of Churchill would not be well received, and General Embick's influence—up to that time considerable—declined. As for the fleet, Roosevelt's reasoning was that the presence of American battleships in mid-Pacific would deter the Japanese from advancing beyond limits we could live with in Southeast Asia. (With France laid low and Holland overrun, there was a danger that Japan might move into French Indochina and the Dutch East Indies, thus putting itself in position to strike against us in the Philippines and the British at Singapore.)

This test of the Theory of Deterrence was not greeted with applause by the American military. Marshall and the Army planners mistrusted it (Marshall was uneasy about the vulnerability of Pearl Harbor), and the commander of the fleet whom it most affected, Rear Admiral James O. Richardson, was especially skeptical. Richardson thought it would lead to a war for which his ships and sailors were unprepared. He had said as much at a luncheon meeting with the President on October 8 and had shortly thereafter been relieved of his command (his replacement was Rear Admiral Husband E. Kimmel). As Stark wrote to Kimmel three months later, about another officer's promotion: "This, of course, is White House prerogative and responsibility, and believe me, it is used these days."[11]

But the President's views on aid to Britain, whether because they were his (and because he won the election) or because they were compelling in their own right, had then matured and flowered as those of the armed forces leadership itself. On November 12, 1940, once the election was out of the way, Admiral Stark had addressed a communication to Secretary of the Navy Knox. It is now remembered as the Plan Dog memorandum, since the option it recommended (strong offensive in the Atlantic, limited defense in the Pacific) was contained in paragraph D, and Louis Morton in his *Strategy and Command* volume in the Army histories calls it "perhaps the most important single document in the development of World War II strategy."[12] Its importance lay in its cogent formulation of the Atlantic-first argument, its acceptability to the Army, and its encouragement of close coordination with the British. Henceforward Plan Dog was to be the cornerstone of American politico-military thought.

The consequences of British defeat were in Stark's judgment so serious for the United States that Britain should be assisted in every way possible, including U.S. Army involvement in a land campaign against Germany. To ensure victory for Britain, Stark believed, "the United States in addition to sending naval assistance, would also need to send large air and land forces to Europe or Africa, or both, and participate strongly in this land offensive." (Remember that he was writing more than a year before Pearl Harbor.) Stark acknowledged the risks of British collapse, or the "possible unwillingness" of the American public to go along with this, but he thought Britain's plight outweighed them. He also conceded that his proposal could not be adopted while, simultaneously, genuine efforts were being made to resist Japan; the United States must be prepared to "do little more in the Pacific than remain on the strict defensive."[13]

In a surprising show of unanimity, the Army with minor reservations had endorsed Stark's paragraph D (the British *not* surprisingly endorsed it), and the Joint Board began preparation of an Army-Navy plan that the two service secretaries could submit to the President. (Roosevelt had asked for an estimate of the situation from the Army, Navy, and State departments combined, but to speed up the process the military wrote theirs first; Hull later approved, but not formally, on the grounds that it was not State's proper business.) This paper was largely the handiwork of Captain Richmond Kelly Turner (director of war plans in Naval Operations) and Colonel Joseph T. McNarney of the Air Corps (representing the chief of the Army War Plans Division); called "Study of the Immediate Problems Concerning Involvement in the War," it was dated December 12, 1940.

Turner's biographer calls it "a remarkable document in many respects," and it is, since it accurately forecast the factors that could provoke Japan to start a war (namely, steps that "seriously threaten her economic welfare or military adventures") and the course such a war might follow in Malaysia (namely, Japan would "make a major effort with all categories of military force to capture the entire area," a campaign that "might even last"—as it did—"several months"). In substance, Turner and McNarney mainly echoed Admiral Stark—"The issues in the Orient will largely be decided in Europe"—and they, too, envisaged "a major offensive in the Atlantic."[14]

Most surprisingly of all, though, when the Turner-McNarney study had gone forward to the President—and a White House conference with Hull, Stimson, Knox, Stark, and Marshall had been convened on January 16, 1941, to discuss it—Roosevelt had drawn back. They might have thought that such a paper was what he wanted, but it wasn't, quite. He authorized exploratory talks with the British to proceed, using this memo as the agenda, but the idea of a land offensive in Europe was not something he was yet prepared to consider. All was well and good as far as *assistance* to the British was concerned, even if distracting troubles came in the Far East, but for anything more than that (according to notes made the next day by Marshall) he desired that "the Army should not be committed to any aggressive action until it was fully prepared to undertake it; that our military course must be very conservative until our strength had developed."[15]

There had been a difference here not only of policy but of basic approach. The senior military kept always in mind that they could not take responsibility for doing something until they had made plans for it; they had to think more about eventualities than about the immediate. This Roosevelt found uncongenial; he disliked the "iffy," he preferred the concrete to the hypothetical. He thought that "we must be realistic in the matter"—Marshall's notes again—"and avoid a state of mind involving plans which could be carried out [only] after the lapse of some months; we must be ready to act with what we had available."[16] They, the generals and the admirals, might be able to contemplate future lines of action the American public would not approve, but he could not. Stark and Marshall might be able to reverse themselves (as they had just done) without anyone being the wiser, but his course (insofar as it might go public) had to be steady. The principle of civil direction of the military was working itself out in practice.

The Plan Dog episode is fairly reflective of the condition of the U.S. means for making strategy by early 1941. Note that the initiative came from the Navy. Note the constant presence and guiding hand of the President; he reread and carefully edited the Turner-McNarney text before turning it over to be used in Anglo-American discussions. Note the arrival of the Joint Board as a body capable of producing such a document. Note the subsequent beginning of regular meetings (on Tuesdays) of Stimson, Knox, and Hull about defense matters, replacing a liaison committee that had lacked their status. Note the essential orientation toward Europe ("if we lose in the Atlantic," Marshall was to say, "we lose everywhere"[17]), and note finally the fact that the United States was approaching the danger of a major war better prepared for it in military thought (though not, plainly, in men and equipment) than it ever had been before.

Thus it came about, a year after France's defeat, that circumstances had altered but the problems had not: American strategy was still polarized around the east-west axis, the rival claims of the two oceans. On one score Stark and the President had been proved correct: Britain stood firm in her island fastness. The Germans had thrown what they had against it, in the air battles of the previous summer and fall, and had failed to knock down the guard of RAF Fighter Command. But the effort to ensure that the Atlantic convoys got through, savaged as they were by German submarines, and at the same time hold off the Japanese by a threat of superior force that was not in fact superior, taxed the U.S. Navy to the utmost. "The situation is obviously critical in the Atlantic," Stark wrote to Kimmel in April 1941, ". . . much worse than the average person has any idea."[18]

It was truly so desperate that to conceal the facts much longer from the public was to betray the expectations aroused by Lend-Lease. The Battle of the Atlantic was going very badly indeed. By the time of the "May Crisis" in 1941, sinkings of British merchantmen by the Nazis had risen to a number *three times* the capacity of British shipyards to replace, and twice the combined British and American capacity. If this continued, aid-to-the-allies was an empty threat.

Here was more than a statistic: It was a statement that an essential element of strategy, forged in political controversy and backed by competent military review, was on the brink of failure. Eventually these sobering figures found their way into the Pan American Day speech, but not until after much discussion—and until they had been cleared by the British, who were beginning to worry that any further information on shipping

losses might be hurtful to their own home-front morale, and with the
American service chiefs, who were opposed on principle to telling "the
enemy" anything.

Part of the President's dilemma was that he had been doing more
than he could admit. How much was it prudent to explain publicly about
decisions he had been compelled to make: whether to occupy Iceland,
what to do about the Germans' westward expansion of their Atlantic
attacks, how heavily to reinforce the Atlantic fleet? In January, there had
begun in Washington the secret conversations between British and American military representatives that the President had authorized, to coordinate a course both countries could follow if the United States became
involved, and from them had emerged two alternative plans for hemisphere defense, of differing degrees of boldness. Which to adopt? In April,
Roosevelt had cabled Churchill an interim summary of added responsibilities that U.S. naval forces might be able to undertake in the North Atlantic,
but there were still unsettled specifics and on some of them the President
had already changed his mind. How much of all this should show itself in
the Pan American Day address?

◆

As before, the central question had come back to those ships at Pearl
Harbor. The Navy was by now insistent that to take pressure off sore-
pressed Britain, some of them would have to be transferred through the
Panama Canal to the Atlantic, but one can almost visualize the ghost of
Mahan or Teddy Roosevelt at the President's elbow, saying: "Never divide
the fleet!" In the era of the battleship, this had been an inviolable axiom
of sea power, and there were those who would still have argued that it
could be disregarded only at great risk.

To complicate the issue, there was this time a new source of reluctance in the State Department, which had come to view the Pacific Fleet
as an essential bargaining chip. How do you deter somebody by weakening
the deterrent? State had argued against the transfer on the grounds that
it would look like an admission of impotence in Japanese eyes, and the
arguments had seesawed back and forth. Finally, a decision had been
reached to send a task force—battleships *Idaho, Mississippi,* and *New
Mexico;* carrier *Yorktown;* cruisers *Philadelphia, Brooklyn, Savannah,*
and *Nashville;* and two destroyer squadrons, about a quarter of the fleet
—and then a second argument began, about how much to tell of this.

Roosevelt seems to have felt that the debit of lending comfort to the
Japanese was worth the credit of materially encouraging the British, and
so early versions of the speech contained the statement: "certain units of
the American Navy have been recently transferred from the Pacific to the
Atlantic." But this and other parts of the text were too much for Secretary
Hull, who strenuously objected and asked to have two men from his

department—Under Secretary Welles and Assistant Secretary Adolf Berle, Jr.—sit in on the further writing, to make sure nothing was said to jeopardize his negotiations. Permission granted, Welles and Berle came over to the White House to join Sherwood and Rosenman, staying all day Sunday and most of Monday, including Sunday lunch with the President. To Sherwood's and Rosenman's relief, Hull's emissaries turned out to be less cautious than Hull himself, and the four of them found no essential disagreements.

But there were other pressures. Sunday, the possibility that the speech was being watered down seems to have been bothering Secretary Stimson, who fired off a note—"I have this morning hurriedly dictated a few paragraphs"—which reached the White House in record time: It had been dictated, typed, delivered, read by the President, and passed on to his speechwriters, all before noon of a Sunday, which says something for the efficiency achievable in those pre-electronic days. Stimson's three pages of suggestions contained even more aggressive phrasings about the fleet transfer and followed them with a threat to "take such further steps as are necessary," which opened the door to convoys.

This, as Rosenman later wrote, was "typical of the kind of material that would arrive from department heads . . . often within a few hours before delivery." Accompanied by both flattery ("I feel confident that the great majority of your countrymen sympathize") and an implied rebuke ("the British disasters in Crete and the North Atlantic have terrifically intensified the necessity of demonstrating that you have already taken command of the situation here"), Stimson's "few paragraphs" amounted to arm-twisting of a professional caliber.[19]

The news they had to draw on, to provide the topical references the President liked to make, was bleakly discouraging. On the island of Crete, the German army and air force, having disposed of Jugoslavia and Greece, had launched a successful paratroop assault. In Africa, during April, the Afrika Korps under General Rommel had crossed Cyrenaica to the Egyptian border in a dazzling twelve-day campaign that wiped out all the previous British gains. Admiral Darlan was in Berchtesgaden, which portended a closer collaboration between France and Hitler, and our ambassador to Vichy was reporting that Marshal Pétain daily expected the Germans to march through France and Spain to take Gibraltar, which would seal up the inland sea for good and cut Britain off from her empire and from Middle Eastern oil.

Lose the Mediterranean and there would be no hope of saving the African coast and the Atlantic islands, a prospect that so alarmed the President that he had given the Navy a minimum of thirty days to prepare an expedition to seize the Azores, in spite of the fact—as the Navy and the Army well knew—that we were pitifully unprepared in troops trained for the operation, ships to transport them in, or suitable landing craft.

In addition, word came in on Saturday that the huge new German battleship *Bismarck,* the most heavily armed warship afloat, had left the North Sea and near Iceland had sunk in one salvo the *Hood,* Britain's heaviest and fastest battle cruiser. The *Bismarck* was headed southwest into the shipping lanes, where there were then ten convoys of British ships carrying Canadian troops and Lend-Lease supplies, not all of which had cruiser or battleship escort, and even those that did were no match for the *Bismarck.* (Earlier, in only two months, two German surface raiders had destroyed 115,000 tons of Allied shipping.) For two days the *Bismarck*'s position was in doubt, and in Washington there was much worried speculation about where she might turn up.

The President thought possibly the Caribbean. "We have some submarines down there," he said to a group in the Oval Office. "Suppose we order them to attack her and attempt to sink her? Do you think the people would demand to have me impeached?"

The scene made a deep impression on Sherwood. Roosevelt was sitting at the desk with his jacket off in the heat. (There was an air conditioner, but he hated it and never, to Sherwood's knowledge, turned it on.) Through the open windows they could smell the blossoms of the big magnolia tree, said to have been planted by Andrew Jackson, and see across the Potomac into Virginia. Sherwood remembered thinking of the contrast between the days when Lincoln lived in this house, and Virginia was enemy territory, and the present atmosphere of oppressive calm in which the President of the United States had to sit, circumscribed by the limitations of his office, "wondering what the next naval dispatch would tell him, wondering what he would be able to do about it . . . wondering whether he'd be impeached."[20]

◆

The final version was of course a blend of its ingredients. The precise wording about the fleet was vague enough to be harmless, while elsewhere there was a reference to "additional measures" vague enough to be ominous. But if Stimson's belligerent proposals were rejected, Hull also—on another, and more important, point—was reluctantly forced to give in, since even his own subordinates were against him. The section in question, which was gradually becoming the highlight of the speech, announced the declaration of an unlimited national emergency.

How it got to be there is somewhat confused, but the confusion is itself illuminating. Sometimes, and this was one of the times, Roosevelt could be devious where deviousness was hardly called for, almost as though he had so accustomed himself to circuitous methods that no others came naturally. What he did in this instance was to let an idea get into circulation without identifying it as his own. Hull claimed to have discussed it with him, and the secretary of the treasury, Henry Morgenthau, Jr., asked

Hopkins about it at lunch on the fourteenth, but no one knew for sure that the President was behind it. He did not even tell his speechwriters that he wanted to declare an unlimited national emergency; Hopkins told them, and told them only as a hunch, and Sherwood and Rosenman went ahead on their own.

They, too, had known for some time that an unlimited emergency was among Roosevelt's thoughts. During the past few days he had kept at his side a Senate document containing a Justice Department memorandum, prepared in 1939, which listed the statutory powers he would acquire if and when he declared such an emergency. Judge Rosenman had noticed him studying it with great care, "picking it up, laying it aside, picking it up again to read, almost wistfully." But he said not a word to them, and after Hopkins relayed his hunch, they could only go downstairs—"somewhat awe-struck," as Sherwood later said—to compose a one-sentence proclamation.

Certain this was no good, they asked the attorney general, again on their own initiative, to draft a proper one. When Welles and Berle came upon the announcement of it in an early version of the speech, not having heard of it before, they naturally asked, "Who drafted this?" Rosenman had to admit that he and Sherwood had, and when asked if the President had seen it, they had to say no. Sherwood thought he could scarcely blame Welles and Berle for thinking that "these were pretty strange goings-on."[21]

During the preparation of an important speech, Roosevelt liked to read it aloud in the evening as it progressed, so that he could settle debated questions and eliminate tongue-twisting phrases that might trip him up in delivery. On Sunday after dinner, the whole clan gathered in his study—Hopkins, Sherwood, Rosenman, Welles, and Berle. Just as the President came to read the final section, Hopkins had to leave the room for some medicine and the two writers, to Sherwood's horror, were left to face it alone.

Let Sherwood tell what happened: "Roosevelt read, 'I hereby proclaim that an unlimited national emergency exists . . . what's this?' He looked up from the typescript with the expression of artless innocence that he frequently put on, and asked very politely, 'Hasn't somebody been taking some liberties?' I managed to explain, in a strangled tone, that Harry had told us that the President wanted something along these general lines. I am sure that Welles and Berle expected Rosenman's and my heads were about to come off."[22]

But Rosenman knew his Roosevelt of old, and was not so easily intimidated. There was much method, if hidden, in the President's apparent lack of method. From his point of view there was always something to be said for considering an idea in its own right, before it was surrounded by conflicting advice, before he had to cope with all the friends and enemies it would acquire in the course of discussing it. Rosenman saw that he was simply trying to make up his mind, and that in good time he would—though he didn't, as a matter of fact, until Tuesday, the very last day.

It was not an easy decision to make. Rosenman remembered him commenting on it, "meditatively . . . as though he were thinking out loud," after he had finished reading their draft that Sunday evening. Here if ever was an exposure of his mind at work. "There's only a small number of rounds of ammunition left to use," the President said, "unless the Congress is willing to give me more. This declaration of an unlimited emergency is one of those few rounds, and a very important one. Is this the right time to use it, or should we wait until things get worse—as they surely will?"[23]

So they plowed on. Sherwood had earlier been over to the War Department for a briefing on strategy, and now on Monday they had breakfast with Hopkins. Later in the day, Sidney Hillman, the labor leader serving as an associate director of OPM, came in to talk. With Hillman, the problem was how to handle the explosive topic of strikes in defense plants, which had been breaking out all through the spring. (Some had dragged on for weeks, as at Allis-Chalmers in Milwaukee, and at the beginning of April, John L. Lewis had threatened to call out the coal miners, which could immobilize the entire economy.) Troubles, troubles.

But if things were bound to get worse, as the President said, in one respect they suddenly got better. The roving *Bismarck* was tracked down and sent to the bottom by the Royal Navy. (The copilot of the Catalina patrol plane that located the fleeing quarry, though this was not revealed until long after, was a U.S. Navy officer on duty as an observer.) The news was phoned over from the Navy Department, the very day Roosevelt was to go on the air, and he turned as soon as he hung up, to shout, "She's sunk!" to Sherwood and Rosenman, who did not need to ask what he meant. "There could not have been more satisfaction in his voice," Rosenman wrote, "if he himself had fired the torpedo that sank her."[24]

Up to the last moment there were revisions, and on Tuesday the President canceled all his afternoon appointments to give his full attention to the speech. By the end, it had been through six distinctly different versions, and the best he could hope for was that there would be something in it somewhere to satisfy everybody who had taken part in the writing. Berle thought it was "calculated to scare the daylights out of everyone," but that was about all.

Roosevelt was concerned lest it scare too many listeners, but he believed it was at least clear and definite. In a cable to Churchill, a few hours before he was to speak, he said that his text "went further than I had thought possible even two weeks ago," and that he hoped it would get "general approval from the fairly large element which has been confused by details." His press secretary, Steve Early, went further in a statement to reporters: "I think you can say that by Wednesday morning there will be no longer any doubt as to what the national policy of this government is."[25]

Mr. Early, as we shall see, was mistaken.

◆

To those who had watched it take shape, the address itself was an anticlimax. Tuesday evening was oppressively hot. While Communist pickets plodded up and down outside the White House, the President spoke from the East Room, seated just inside the main door, at a small desk for the microphones. Around the walls were the newsreel cameramen, for whom he would later repeat selected portions of the speech.

The guests, dressed in black tie and perched uncomfortably on the little gilt chairs used at White House musicales, were the governing board of the Pan American Union and the ambassadors and ministers of the Latin American republics plus Canada (the latter at the President's insistence, for hemispheric solidarity, though the Canadians were unenthusiastic about being treated on a par with Guatemala). There were also a few administration officials and their wives, and Sherwood and Rosenman had asked to bring along their friend the songwriter Irving Berlin.

This was not of course an audience in any strict meaning of the word, but only an excuse for giving the speech to the eighty-five million people who were estimated to be hearing it over the radio. There were few signs of spontaneous reaction from those present until the end, with the unlimited emergency declaration, and their applause was at best polite. Sherwood thought that Roosevelt himself, after the customary acknowledgment of the occasion in the first paragraph, was oblivious to his immediate surroundings and consciously addressing himself to the great world out beyond.

He came quickly to the point, the central proposition the speech had been built around: "what started as a European war has developed, as the Nazis always intended it should develop, into a world war for world domination." The Germans had taken possession of the greater part of Europe and in North Africa were threatening Egypt and the Suez Canal. "But their plans do not stop here." They also had the capability of occupying the "Atlantic fortress" of Dakar and the "island outposts of the New World," the Azores and the Cape Verde Islands. The latter were only "seven hours distance from Brazil" by modern bombers or troop-carrying planes. "They dominate shipping routes to and from the South Atlantic." The war, said the President, was "coming very close to home."

This warning he coupled with an exposition of how military technology had altered the calculations of time and distance on which national defense must rest. He repeated what he had said many times before, "that the United States is mustering its men and its resources only for purposes of defense—to repel attack." But the word "attack" had taken on new meaning in view of "the lightning speed of modern warfare." Some people might wish to think that we had not been attacked until bombs fell on New York or San Francisco, but this was not the lesson of the Nazis' conquests: Their attack on Czechoslovakia had begun in Austria, on Greece in Albania, on Norway in Denmark. "When your enemy comes at you in a tank or bombing plane," the President said, "if you hold your fire until you see the whites of his eyes, you will never know what hit you. Our Bunker Hill of tomorrow may be several thousand miles from Boston." This last phrase was of Roosevelt's own coinage; he had dictated it to Rosenman when he came to the sentence containing "whites of his eyes" in the draft.

Having described what he had previously done to meet this "threat," the President went on to speak of what was going to be done. The government would exert all its powers, he said, to "preserve the democratic safeguards of both labor and management" while seeing to it that the tools of defense were manufactured—a firm and resolute declaration that could offend nobody. The critical passage was the one that dealt with convoys, where he was far more positive. At this point Roosevelt sounded very much as though he were willing and expecting to fight, and for the electorate to endorse their President's words would be to sign him a blank check, for he was saying not that he would do such and such a thing but that he and the military would do what they thought was going to be required.

"Old-fashioned common sense," he said, called for a strategy to prevent an enemy from gaining a foothold from which he could mount a later attack. "We have, accordingly, extended our patrol in North and South Atlantic waters. . . . All additional measures necessary to deliver the goods will be taken. . . . We in the Americas will decide for ourselves whether, and when, and where, our American interests are attacked or our security is threatened." With this statement we have come a long way from aid-to-the-allies-short-of-war.

Underlying the President's argument was a presumed Nazi "plan" for world domination. He referred to it several times, most pointedly when he described the terms that Hitler would be likely to impose in a negotiated peace. "No, I am not speculating about this," he said. "I merely repeat what is already in the Nazi book of world conquest. They plan to treat the Latin American nations as they are now treating the Balkans. They plan then to strangle the United States and the Dominion of Canada." Here the President was indeed indulging in speculation, and this has enabled a revisionist historian like Frederick Sanborn to criticize the Pan American Day speech on the grounds that its central premise was false. Roosevelt, Sanborn wrote, "painted a lurid picture of an imaginary Nazi conquest of the world."[26]

There is something to be said for Sanborn's view, up to a point. It is true that Hitler was at this time trying very hard to avoid or postpone war with the United States (until he had disposed of Russia, as he repeatedly said). He had issued strict orders against the deliberate sinking of any American ship, and he reaffirmed them several times during the autumn. It is also true that he had no "plan" for North and South America. (Hitler's casualness about thinking ahead and his lack of long-term foresight were to undercut him more than once.) That Roosevelt had no proof of any such plan is suggested by the effort he made, unsuccessfully, to acquire it.

Earlier in May, when Hitler's deputy Rudolf Hess startled the world by flying to Scotland in a single-handed attempt to stop the war in the West before the war in the East began, Roosevelt had cabled Churchill, asking that Hess be interrogated about German designs on the Western Hemisphere, "including commerce, infiltration, military domination, encirclement of the United States, etc." The results were disappointing: "Germany had no designs on America. The so-called German peril was a ludicrous figment of the imagination. Hitler's interests were European," etc., etc.[27]

But a reading of Hitler's mind would have to go further than this. He and his naval chief, Admiral Raeder, could see as well as Roosevelt could the importance of the Atlantic islands as the place where German and American interests tangibly collided with one another, and he assumed correctly that the United States was seriously considering a move in that direction. There was indeed a German plan, fully worked out, to forestall this by occupying the Canaries as a part of the attack on Gibraltar known as Operation Felix.

Felix had been intended to get going earlier in the year and had been held up only by General Franco's refusal to let German troops pass through Spain. (Franco was waiting, with encouragement from us, to be absolutely certain that Britain was beaten; his willingness to stall and to ask embarrassing questions so annoyed Hitler, on their meeting at Hendaye, that the Führer said he would rather visit the dentist and have three or four teeth out than go through that again.)

Part of the reasoning behind Hitler's decision to invade Russia was his belief that a Russian defeat would free up Japan, divert American armed commitment to the Pacific, and discourage us from getting involved in Europe. But it is absurd to suppose that his aims, if vague and pragmatic, were peaceable. He told Raeder that he wanted the Azores because they offered "the only facility for attacking America, if she should enter the war, with modern aircraft," and that he was interested in the Cape Verde Islands "with a view to prosecuting the war against America at a later stage."[28] Roosevelt's information may have been inadequate, but his instincts were sound.

◆

When the cameramen had finished with him, the President joined his guests in a garden party under Japanese lanterns on the South Lawn.

(Thinking of the verbal prohibitions they had been observing, Rosenman said to Sherwood, "We've got to be careful and call them 'Axis' lanterns.") When Rosenman had to leave to return to New York, Sherwood took Irving Berlin upstairs to see Harry Hopkins, who had been "lying there in his old bathrobe," listening to the speech on the radio, and soon Mrs. Roosevelt came to invite them to the Monroe Room, where the President was sitting with a few friends and relatives. Roosevelt asked Berlin to play the piano and sing for them, "Alexander's Ragtime Band" and others of his favorites, from the long-ago days when he had been young and not a cripple, and the world a less forbidding place. Mrs. Rosenman told her husband afterward that he had missed a fine party.

Later still, when Sherwood went to the President's bedroom to say good night, he found him surrounded by telegrams (his wont after a speech, so that he would know immediately what the reaction had been). "There must have been a thousand or more of them," Sherwood wrote. "He had looked at them all." Amazingly enough, the vast majority approved of what the President had said. "They're ninety-five per cent favorable!" he told Sherwood. "And I'd figured I'd be lucky to get an even break on this speech."

Further on in the week, with an equally encouraging response from the newspapers, Roosevelt was still pleased and surprised to think he had secured so much more approval—"I should guess at least seventy-five or eighty per cent," he wrote to friends in Scotland[29]—than he had thought possible two weeks before. Even the next day it was apparent that his speech had accomplished everything he could ask. It had encouraged his friends, at home and abroad, without so annoying his foes that they would have to retaliate.

The British, though they would have preferred the announcement of convoys—or better still, as some had rashly hoped, a request that Congress declare war—could reassure themselves that here was a clear preliminary to more forceful steps. The Axis leaders, on the other hand, saw no reason to change their policy (one we liked) of doing nothing but seek to foment Allied disunity and keep the United States on the sidelines. Mussolini, if easily stirred to wrath at Roosevelt—"never in the course of history has a nation been guided by a paralytic"—saw immediately that the speech was "a very strong document" but "not clear as to plans of action," and he made no public response. As for Hitler, his mind had turned entirely to the attack on Russia. He inclined to believe, as he would write to the Duce a few weeks later, that "whether or not America enters the war is a matter of indifference."[30]

The isolationists in Congress were similarly disarmed. Thirty-five of them, who met immediately after the speech to decide what to do about it, issued a statement saying that they had been encouraged to carry on with their antiwar efforts "because the President has not yet been won over by the war party" and had not abandoned the voters "who had preserved their faith in his pre-election pledges." Senator Robert A. Taft consoled himself with remarking that the declaration of an unlimited emergency was meaningless, since Roosevelt had possessed since 1939 all the powers he could legally exercise.

As for the interventionists in the cabinet, disappointed as they were at the absence of concrete proposals, they now confidently expected that these would soon be made. While he felt as he listened to it over the air that the message was "softened down" in delivery, Secretary Stimson went to bed content. The President might still be weak on labor, he noted in his diary, but on freedom of the seas and aid to Britain he was "all right and very praiseworthy."[31]

That was the night before.

Roosevelt's press conference of the following morning, the twenty-eighth of May, has been characterized by two historians of the administration as the "debacle of interventionist hopes." To the questions of reporters, who naturally wanted to know what precise intentions lay behind his generalities of the previous evening, his answers were devastatingly imprecise. Steve Early's expectation of doubt being dissipated was wholly undone by the President himself. He had no plans, he said, to ask Congress to repeal the Neutrality Act; he had no plans to introduce convoys. What would he do if labor and management did not, as he asked them to, reconcile their differences? He brushed that one off as "iffy."

What powers would he exercise under the unlimited emergency? They would require a series of executive orders, he said, to revive various laws that had been enacted over some fifty years. Quite frankly, he had no plans to issue any such orders. Stimson, who never did have a high opinion of the President's press conferences, thought this was "one of the worst and almost undid the effect of the speech." Harry Hopkins had no explanation for this sudden reversal, as Sherwood described it, "from a position of strength to one of apparently insouciant weakness. The fact of Roosevelt's unaccountability was a lesson to be learned over and over again."[32]

◆

Was it really so mysterious? Once again, the President's conduct is puzzling only if one imagines government to consist of simple choices between clear-cut alternatives. Roosevelt did not believe that these existed, but he was surrounded by people who did, who were sure in their own minds of what he should do, and our impression of him has passed through the filter of their preconceptions. He refused, for good and sufficient reasons, to do what either the isolationists or the interventionists wanted him to do. Once a device like this address for Pan American Day had accomplished what he desired of it—brought the people and their government abreast of events, and of each other, at a place where their sense of common purpose would be most strengthened—then that was that as far as he was concerned.

He conceived of foreign policy not as a fixed program but as a process. Five years earlier, in the Chautauqua speech, he had said that the avoidance of war could only be achieved by those who daily charted the nation's course—"Peace will depend on their day-to-day decisions"—and this was still his view. He would do today only what was necessary and fully intended, lest he have to do tomorrow something necessary but not intended.

His most revealing phrase was in the cable to Churchill, where he spoke of the speech as going "further than I had thought possible even two weeks ago." This speaks volumes: about the process of presidential speechwriting as an activity of the whole government, about the President's shared perception with his colleagues of what the public was and was not ready for, about the degree to which the speech had a life of its own independent of his or anyone else's authorship, about his lively awareness of the interplay of forces within his own administration that was shaping his words, about his appreciation of the final product as an affirmation and validation of the procedures that had brought it into existence, and finally —all these elements being combined—of the speech as going before the world through the instrumentality of his own voice, with his authority, bearing his responsibility.

By drawing so fully on what others thought, by sifting and comparing and weaving together so many strands of opinion and conviction, he was able to speak with a force multiplied many times over his own alone. Given the subsequent high percentage of approval from his listeners, the speech thus became in a meaningful sense a statement of where the United States at that moment stood, and with minor modifications would continue to stand, until hostilities broke upon it six months later.

There were those at the time who well understood the President's seeming passivity to be an illusion. One was Dr. Gustav Stolper, an émigré German publisher and former member of the Reichstag, who commented from Wall Street on American political and financial affairs for a British firm that passed on his reports to the Treasury and the Foreign Office. (John Maynard Keynes said of these: "I have read them for a very long time past and attach the greatest importance to them.") On June 13, Stolper wrote to London: "I do not see the slightest reason for the widespread belief that the President is wavering or retracing his steps. Nothing could be further from the truth. I think the President advances steadily and unhesitatingly towards the clear-cut goal of the complete defeat of Hitler and Hitlerism. But he moves with all the caution of a man who is perfectly aware of the complexity of American sentiment. . . . No time is wasted within the limits of the practically possible."

Another was the radio commentator Raymond Gram Swing, who had become an unofficial interpreter of the Americans to the British over the BBC. On May 11, Swing had published an article in the *London Sunday Express* which was widely read in government circles in both London and Washington. Swing had been told that if Roosevelt put on the pressure, he could possibly get a vote supporting convoys through the Senate by a margin of fifty-five to forty, "not a great enough majority to create the national unity needed to support a war."

If the President, Swing wrote, "should assume the leadership now, and appear to be 'taking' the country into war, the public would turn on him later and reproach him for having brought the country to its dark hours. At such times the only possibility of maintaining unity and morale is that the President shall not have whipped up sentiment for war, that he should have yielded to public insistence, and that war should be an enterprise of partnership rather than something entered at his behest."[33]

In his scholarly study of Roosevelt's foreign policy thirty-eight years later, Robert Dallek arrived at very similar conclusions. The President, writes Dallek, "viewed the enthusiasm for his speech as resulting from the fact that he did not go beyond a general discussion of the Nazi threat into controversial details for meeting it. While he believed that the public would strongly line up behind intervention if a major incident demonstrated the need to fight, he did not feel that he could evoke this response simply by what he said or did. . . . In short, if he were to avoid painful wartime divisions, the nation would have to enter the fighting with a minimum of doubt or dissent, and the way to achieve this was not through educational talks to the public or strong executive action, but through developments abroad which aroused the country to fight."

Roosevelt was at the head of a people deeply committed to contradictory purposes. Public-opinion polls conducted between May 7 and May 17 told him that while 68 percent believed it more important to help Britain than to stay out of the war, 79 percent *wanted* to stay out and 70 percent felt that he had either gone too far or already gone far enough on Britain's behalf.[34]

This was the raw material with which the artist in Roosevelt had to work. He molded it into the expression of a common will, put into words for this particular occasion, and so doing, answered to his call of duty as chief executive. One may protest at length that he was overly sensitive to what the public desired, but is a President supposed to be *in*sensitive to this? To take the country into a war it does not have its heart in, as we have learned since and at some cost, can be a far worse irresponsibility.

This was a nation and its government animated by fellow feeling for the British and the vanquished peoples, and by antipathy to Hitler's Germany and Hirohito's Japan, but also constrained by what its political and military leader considered to be imperatives: to prevent our being racked and weakened by internal disunity, to stave off overt hostilities until we had husbanded the strength to prevail in them, and at the same time to forestall potential enemies from gaining such an initial advantage that—should they attack us at some later date of their own choosing—we might be too late and have too little to surmount it.

No wonder Roosevelt knew moments of exasperation. "The President has on his hands at the present time," wrote Admiral Stark in Washington to Admiral Kimmel in Hawaii, "about as difficult a situation as ever confronted any man anywhere in public life."[35]

II

Three weeks later, on Monday, June 16, 1941, Secretary of the Interior Harold L. Ickes unilaterally declared war on Japan by cutting off its oil supply.

Well, almost; he would have done so if he could, and to the extent he could, he did. A telegram had come to him from a Mr. Edward Jobbins, general manager of a plant engaged in defense work and dependent on oil for its operations, complaining that in South Philadelphia a shipment of oil was waiting to be sent to Japan while at the same time there was such a shortage of petroleum products on the East Coast that gasoline rationing was in prospect.

In his capacity as Petroleum Co ordinator for National Defense, Ickes stopped the shipment. He then told his deputy to send telegrams to all the oil suppliers on the Atlantic seaboard, forbidding them to make further shipments to Japan without his permission. Ickes was greatly pleased with this day's work. "The news of the holding up of the shipment was acclaimed generally . . . ," he confided to his diary. "I believe the general sentiment was one of relief that some action was at last being taken."[36]

The thought that he was toying with one of the causes that would eventually drive Japan to war with us never occurred to Harold Ickes, then or later. But it instantly occurred to Franklin Roosevelt. Next day, when Ickes dropped by Steve Early's office at the White House upon another errand, and Early was on the phone to the President, Roosevelt asked Early to ask Ickes if he had cleared his oil order with the State Department.

"I certainly did not!" Ickes indignantly replied, thinking to himself that the oil would have gone all the way to Tokyo before he had any answer from State. Roosevelt asked Early to inform Ickes that this was a touchy matter, that there was a danger of war, and that in any argument on the subject between Ickes and Hull (a politic way of putting it), he would have to back Hull.

On Thursday, Ickes got a letter from the President—"the most peremptory and ungracious communication that I have ever received from him"—reemphasizing, "lest there be any confusion whatever," that the export of oil was at this time so much a part of United States foreign policy that it must not be affected "in any shape, manner or form by anyone except the Secretary of State or the President." Roosevelt was obviously deeply disturbed; Ickes was hurt but unrepentant.

On Friday, Assistant Secretary Dean Acheson came from the State Department, to Ickes's surprise and delight, with the text of a program for legally subjecting oil shipments to export licenses; Acheson had worked it out and the President later the same day approved it, though he issued no enforcing order. "The country does not realize the victory I have won in this matter . . . ," Ickes congratulated himself. "Of course oil and gasoline should not be shipped to Japan from an American port."

Of course? Not necessarily, not if we were negotiating in earnest. Sunday afternoon, June 22 (D-Day for the Wehrmacht in Eastern Europe), the Achesons came to call and the assistant secretary assured Ickes that it was his action at Philadelphia that "had brought matters to a head."[37]

The vital importance of American oil to the Japanese was obscured in the minds of these and other members of the administration who were seeing only the necessity (to their way of thinking) for taking a firm stand, and for responding to each new act of Japanese expansionism with increased tightening of the economic screws. The fact that the latter was inconsistent with a policy of postponing war in the Pacific as long as possible—the fully deliberated policy of the United States, the policy of the President, of the secretary of state, and of the armed services—was not getting the full benefit of their thoughts.

A year earlier, when the Japanese had made the French allow them to move troops into northern Indochina and news of an alliance between Japan and Germany had been confirmed, Roosevelt had responded by ordering an embargo on the export to Japan of all iron and steel scrap. The Japanese had foreseen this and readjusted accordingly; it was a blow but one they could take in stride. Our ambassador to Japan, Joseph Grew, had never believed that measures such as this would fundamentally deter them. "They are a hardy race," he had written in 1938, "accustomed throughout their history to catastrophe and disaster; theirs is the 'do or die' spirit, more deeply ingrained than in any other people. They can live on rice and, if necessary, fight on rice."[38]

By mid-1941, the effect of American and British restrictions on Japanese trade was nonetheless beginning to tell. Few were the Japanese industries that had not been forced by a lack of imports to cut and trim, to substitute raw materials and machinery. Yet with the passage of time, the meaning of the Allied controls that were building up this pressure had lost immediacy in the American perception of them. "They tended to be taken for granted," wrote Herbert Feis, a former State Department economist with full access to departmental records. Eight months had passed and nothing had happened. "The risk had become familiar," Feis went on, "and thereby, perhaps, somewhat forgotten. The State Department, along with the country, rested in the attitude that what was done was done, and that it was up to Japan, not to us, to undo it."[39]

Ickes partook generously of this refusal to picture ourselves as menacing rather than menaced. During the days between June 18 and July 1 (which witnessed the opening in European Russia of the central drama of the war), long and testy letters were exchanged between secretary and President. Ickes reviewed his conduct step by step and found it good, he darkly referred to the political repercussions to be expected from gas rationing, he admonished the President on the desirability of a total and complete embargo on oil to Japan, and finally—in a pet—he resigned.

Ickes at sixty-seven was a redoubtable character: veteran of Chicago reform politics, campaigner for Teddy Roosevelt, conservationist of the old school, and still another link between the second Roosevelt and traditional progressivism; in addition, incorruptible, irascible, pugnacious, a quondam poker-playing crony of the President, an able and energetic organizer, by nature mistrustful of businessmen but capable of gaining their respect.

In his diary, Ickes included the whole correspondence with Roosevelt, apparently under the impression that it revealed himself as long-suffering and in the right, the President as thankless and lacking in courage. It does nothing of the kind; if anything, it shows the President's dexterity and patience in handling his fractious subordinates. Roosevelt, as Arthur Schlesinger, Jr., has put it, "decided early on that he wanted an inventive government rather than an orderly government . . . not a team of reliable work horses, but a miscellany of high-spirited and sensitive thoroughbreds," even at a cost in the time and energy he had to spend in what he called the "hand-holding" of his "prima donnas."[40]

The President politely pointed out to Ickes that this was not a matter of oil conservation but, to repeat, of foreign policy; that the circumstances surrounding it were peculiarly delicate and confidential; and that these could not be known to Ickes or to anyone but the two persons charged under the Constitution with responsibility, namely Hull and Roosevelt. Therefore the latter was required to let Ickes know that his "writ did not run" in the field of oil-export policy.

Period.

When Ickes offered to resign, the President relented and turned on the Roosevelt charm: "Dear Harold: There you go again! There ain't nothing unfriendly about me . . . I guess it was the hot weather . . . You are doing a grand job . . . ," and he casually hinted that Ickes might soon be offered control over "the whole power situation," not only oil but water and coal.

Thus having tendered the olive branch and led Ickes up on a high hill from which a vast new bureaucratic empire was visible, Roosevelt ended by taking him into his confidence: "I think it will interest you to know that the Japs are having a real drag-down and knock-out fight among themselves and have been for the past week—trying to decide which way they are going to jump. . . . No one knows what the decision will be but, as you know, it is terribly important for the control of the Atlantic for us to help keep peace in the Pacific." And finally, in a phrase that has been much quoted since, "I simply have not got enough Navy to go round."[41]

◆

The reason May and June of 1941 represented a last chance to avoid war between the United States and Japan is that for a period of many weeks then, both governments were genuinely divided internally over what course to take and, even more important, each was aware that the other was similarly undecided and perplexed. If the moderates on each side could have neutralized their hotheaded colleagues and reached out to the other, and if each could have managed its government's affairs so as to strengthen the other's hand, then the inertial drift toward open warfare might have been reversed and the peace preserved.

In retrospect it is all too clear that this was a vain hope; the differences were irreconcilable. But it seemed a possibility, no matter how remote, and there were those on both sides who saw it as the only means for trying to avoid, or at the very least postpone, horrors of nearly unimaginable magnitude for the half a world that lay between them.

When Roosevelt told Ickes that "the Japs are having a real drag-down and knock-out fight among themselves," he was writing out of informed knowledge and describing the situation exactly. Cleavages of one kind or another had been common in their government for some years—between civilian and military, between army and navy, between factions within the army—but in the week and a half that preceded the President's letter, these had surfaced to an unprecedented degree. The German invasion of Russia on June 22 shook the foundations on which Japanese official thinking rested, and it brought about what Ambassador Grew described as a "serious disturbance, if not an internal crisis," in the higher levels of the regime.

Meetings and conferences multiplied; Tokyo was rife with rumors. Understanding of what the antagonists were saying to each other was impeded by the complexity of their disagreements, far more varied and interwoven than the relatively simple division in the United States between isolationist and interventionist. But Ambassador Grew had good sources of information, and by July 6 he felt confident enough of their accuracy to summarize in his diary who had been of what opinion, what the arguments had been about, and how they had been (more or less) resolved. Comparisons of his analysis with the surviving Japanese records of the relevant deliberations show that in the main he had it right.[42]

A digression must be introduced at this point. We must step aside and ask what the Japanese had been doing all that time, and this will require looking in some detail at events that had affected them in the 1930s. There can be no evaluation of Roosevelt's dealing with Japan without some understanding of Japanese patterns of thought and action, in particular of the actual processes by which their government worked, as opposed to the theoretical structure of it that was given lip service by the Japanese and widely taken at face value by Americans.

In theory, Japan was an authoritarian country with the emperor as its supreme authority; his will was the paramount principle that animated the nation, to the extent of being almost indistinguishable from it; the government executed his edicts, the armed forces were made up of his fanatically disciplined followers. This picture was for any explanatory purpose almost totally useless.

To anyone brought up in disciplined societies like those of the West, it will be difficult to visualize a society as undisciplined to the edge of crack-up as prewar Japan in fact was, but that is the reality. The government was in practice an indeterminate muddle of shifting rivalries. The young fanatics were not the instrument of the emperor but quite the other way around. When they vowed their devotion to him unto death they meant it, as their conduct in wartime was to prove, but this was not to the emperor as a human being but to an abstract emperor of the imagination, an embodiment of their own often inchoate ideals and animosities. To the emperor who existed as a person they were grossly, systematically, and on principle disobedient.

On many occasions in Japanese history, real power has been hidden behind a figurehead, or a whole series of figureheads. During the Tokugawa period, when for two centuries Japan was sealed off from the world, it is doubtful that most Japanese knew the emperor existed; even in 1945 many did not know his name. By the 1930s, the emperor "ruled" through and was surrounded by a circle of advisers: the imperial household, the cabinet, the privy council, the heads of the armed services, and the *genro*, or elder statesmen, surviving figures from the Meiji Restoration, when Japan reopened its doors and (under the reemergent leadership of Hirohito's grandfather) embraced the West.

There was no supreme coordinating body except the *genro*, ten in number since 1868, and the last of them, Prince Kinmochi Saionji, died in 1940 at the age of ninety-one, desiring that the institution end with him, as it did. National policies were worked out within the competing groups of advisers—who frequently differed—and were then given divine sanction by being stated in the emperor's presence at an imperial conference; he was not expected to comment or reply, and rarely did so. Responsibility was diffuse. Consequently the extreme nationalists who came to dominate Japan in the 1930s saw no contradiction in professing undying loyalty to the emperor while seeking to circumvent, obstruct, or unseat his government.

The idea of power in the hands of one person (other than the unreal "emperor") is inherently unattractive to the Japanese mentality; it implies self-aggrandizement and ostentation. In the hierarchy of reciprocal obligation that knits Japan together, there are rules for the most minute details of behavior, but none for generalized conduct or depersonalized lines of authority. This way of thinking easily lends itself to what the Japanese call *gekokujo,* or "the overpowering of seniors by juniors."

Actual power, especially within the army, rested not in the nominal leadership but in the middle or lower-middle echelons, the *chuken shoko,* or "nucleus group," who intimidated their superiors and were in turn strongly influenced by their own subordinates. In any Western view of efficient organization this makes no sense, but the Tokyo semiofficial newspaper *Nichi-Nichi* explained for doubting readers why it should be so, why "the person who actually handles an affair is best qualified to judge it," and added: "The great propelling force of a strong army emanates from its middle stratum."[43]

True, this is partially the case in every administrative system; staff work and middle management are all-important. But in prewar Japan it was carried to a self-destructive extreme. To read the transcripts of the liaison conferences (preceding an imperial conference and involving the same personalities minus the emperor) can be a puzzling experience unless one realizes that these are not open-ended discussions but a near-ritualistic exchange of views worked out beforehand by staff; if an unexpected subject comes up, it is almost invariably put over until staff have had a chance to study it. They had arrived at a machinery of government in which subordinates not only were setting the agenda and providing the backup material, but were making the decisions.

Nowhere was the phenomenon of *gekokujo* more rampant than in the Japanese Army. General Araki, the minister of war, was said to have suffered a nervous breakdown because of the number of junior officers who woke him in the middle of the night with their complaints. There was even an officer in each division charged with a specific duty which Hugh Byas, correspondent of the *New York Times,* described as that of a "public relations counsel inverted."[44] His job was to report to the War Office and the General Staff on what the young officers were thinking.

What they were thinking bordered on revolution and led to mutiny. It prompted a series of violent incidents in which the few tender shoots of parliamentary civil government that had sprung up in Japan during the 1920s were trampled underfoot, and replaced by a dictatorship of the military, or what Hugh Byas called "government by assassination."

The Japanese Army was a turbulent and potentially explosive force. To the half of Japan's population that still worked the land it was one of the few avenues of upward mobility by which a peasant's son could rise to a position of security and prestige. The conscripts were overwhelmingly rural in their origins, the officers came mainly from the countryside's lower middle class, and rural Japan during the 1930s was deeply impoverished.

The Great Depression struck the Japanese countryside with a special harshness. In 1930, agricultural prices fell sharply until rice and silk, the staples, were at their lowest levels since 1897, and in the northeast, of less fertile soil and less temperate climate, there was famine.

An army filled with men who had seen their parents starve and their sisters sold as geisha girls was a vessel of wrath and resentment against the established order they held to be responsible: a dense net of politicians, industrialists, foreigners, and "evil counselors" around the emperor who must be rooted out if Japan was to recapture its proper greatness and prosperity. There began to be talk of soldiers and farmers forming common cause against capitalism and democracy.

The ideas that fueled this emergent alliance were a strange mixture of nativism, feudalism, anarchism, socialism, and militarism in which somehow there was something for everybody. Its philosophers had made liberal borrowings from Tolstoy and Marx, which they recapitulated in contemporary Japanese terms in such fashion as to make Japanese Fascism a popular, if not populist, movement. Virtue and strength came from the land and the people, but Japan was now ruled by "plutocrats"—the *zaibatsu,* large industrial combines—who denied and betrayed this, hence the low estate into which the nation had fallen. Japan had become drunk on Western ideology.

To counteract this there must be a revival of patriotic spirit, "direct rule" by the emperor, and a harmony of ruler and ruled. Popular rights and the electoral franchise are egotistical and imported foreign notions. The political parties are venal and corrupt (this, regrettably, was true: the Seiyukai or "constitutionalists" were virtually owned by Mitsui, the Minseito or "democrats" by Mitsubishi). Therefore industry should be nationalized and parliament abolished; the capitalists and the politicians must surrender ("restore") their powers to the emperor, who will then rule through the army, the only institution close enough to the people (also true) to be trusted (less true).

Once *Kodo* ("the imperial way") is established it will spread through the world, beginning with the Asiatic nations that are at the outset to be consolidated under Japanese leadership. The army must take the initiative in convincing first the Japanese and then other peoples, by persuasion if possible but by force if not, of the virtues of *hakko ichiu,* "the eight corners of the world under one roof," namely Japan's.

This heady brew of socialistic reform and martial muscle flexing went under the name of Showa Ishin, the Showa Restoration, like *hakko ichiu* one of those catchphrases with multiple meanings and emotional overtones that the Japanese language tends to favor. The Showa Restoration (*showa* means "enlightened peace") was widely preached in the lower and middle ranks of the officer class. Many of its supporters believed in another catchphrase, "direct action," and it was not long before those who held differing views discovered what "direct action" could mean.

◆

To the decade before war began some Japanese gave the name *kurai tanima,* "the dark valley." It was a time of schemes and conspiracies in which appearances were deceptive and purposes concealed; the Japanese talents for indirection and ambiguity were given scope. It also saw the proliferation of secret societies, possessed of truths denied to others and thus devoted to the mission of redeeming Japan at whatever cost. They had names like Sakurakai (Society of the Cherry), Kinkei Gakun (Institute of the Golden Pheasant), and Zen Nippon Aikokusha Kyodo Toso Kyogi Kai (All Japan Patriots' Joint Struggle Society). By far the best known to Americans was the Kokurykai (Amur River Society or Black Dragon Society, from the Chinese name for the Amur), which seems so to have fascinated Western journalists that they attributed a sinister influence to it out of all proportion to its respectable reputation in Japan.

For there were many hundreds of the societies. In 1936, at their peak of enrollment, the police bureau of the Ministry of Home Affairs had identified 747 nationalist and agrarian groups, with a total of 668,787 members,[45] and they constantly came and went; Hugh Byas said that no list of them could be valid for more than a year. Many officers nonetheless belonged to them, they contributed considerably to the conspiratorial tone of public events, and some of them concocted plots which were— albeit clumsily—put into effect.

On the evening of February 9, 1931, as he was entering a hall in the Tokyo suburbs to make a speech, Finance Minister Junnosuke Inoye was shot dead by a country youth of twenty-two. Four weeks later, at the door of his office, Baron Takuma Dan, managing director of the holding company that controlled Mitsui, was shot and killed by another country youth, aged twenty-one. On May 15, a group of naval and military officers whose ages ranged from twenty-four to twenty-eight entered the residence of Prime Minister Tsuyoshi Inukai and shot him down in the presence of his pregnant daughter-in-law. A second group tossed a grenade at the door of the Bank of Japan, while a third threw two bombs, which failed to explode, at the offices of Inukai's political party, the Seiyukai, and three bombs (one of which did explode) at the office of the metropolitan police.

Then they all went to military police headquarters and gave themselves up.

That evening, another group of young officers visited the residence of the war minister to demand that the army rise up in support of the assassins. The vice-chief of the General Staff told them to desist, but he was so disturbed by their visit that he successfully persuaded the leaders of the Seiyukai to forbid statements or speeches that might inflame the moderates in the army and cause them to join the extremists. Two days later, the General Staff sent word to Saionji, who as *genro* would be choosing the new prime minister, that the army would not permit a war minister to be appointed to a political party cabinet.

That was the end of civilian government in Japan.

The murderers were given light sentences, most of which they did not serve; on leaving prison they were met by relatives and representatives of patriotic societies, and were driven to the gates of the Imperial Palace, where they bowed ceremoniously in the direction of the emperor inside.

All were part of a single conspiracy (though it was one of many) to overthrow the government and bring about the Showa Restoration, and their links to agrarian discontent were explicit. The group that killed Inukai threw pamphlets from their cars signed "Farmers' Sympathizers," and another was made up of men known as *nomin kesshitai,* or "death-defying farmers." Many came from Ibaragi province, northeast of Tokyo, a center of nationalist feeling, and were associated with a patriotic academy there called Aiko Juku, or Native-land-loving School.

There, too, at Tsuchiura on Lake Kasumigaura (Misty Lagoon), was the naval air station where in the 1920s then-Captain Isoroku Yamamoto had been second-in-command, learning to fly and introducing regulation crew cuts to the long-haired pilots of the Kido Butai, the carrier striking force. (The naval air arm was the most radical and chauvinistic of that otherwise cosmopolitan and conservative service, and the naval officers in the plot came from Tsuchiura.)

The conspirators appeared to fail in what they had set out to accomplish, but they established a pattern to be repeated many times thereafter, which can only be described as progressive blackmail. Since 1895, the navy and war ministers had been required to be officers on the active list, giving the services an implicit veto on cabinet selection by simply refusing to provide one, and from now on that veto would be exercised. The young officers blackmailed their seniors by threats of "direct action," while their seniors in turn blackmailed the civilians by saying, in effect: You had better do as we say or else these hot-blooded young men, whose violence we of course deplore, might get out of hand.

On August 12, 1935, Lieutenant Colonel Sabura Aizawa went to the War Office in Tokyo, demanded to see the chief of the Military Affairs

Bureau, Major General Tetsuzan Nagata, drew his sword, and killed Nagata with two savage cuts at the neck. Nagata had been arranging army appointments, transfers, and promotions so as to discourage and disperse the Showa Restoration movement. Thus, as Aizawa explained at his court-martial, Nagata was "responsible for the corruption of the Army. . . . Instead of guiding the younger elements in the Army he brought pressure on them."[46]

During the *kurai tanima,* the trials of the various assassins became major public events, not so much judicial proceedings as stage-managed spectacles in which the young officers were given the opportunity to dramatize their cause. The Japanese, fascinated as always by motivation, were genuinely shocked by the murders and the bombings but were endlessly curious about what might have provoked in military men such desperation. Newspapers printed page after page of their testimony; schoolchildren signed petitions on their behalf. Defense counsel submitted bales of letters, some (as evidence of "sincerity") written in blood or (the ultimate in "sincerity") enclosing a severed finger. "They broke the law but their motives were pure," read one such message.

Aizawa's court-martial, held in the barracks of the 1st Division (on orders to be shipped to Manchuria), was no exception to the tendency toward courtroom drama. At its end, his defense counsel, also a lieutenant colonel, made an eloquent summation on the subject of rural poverty and the unequal distribution of wealth. This took up most of the morning. "In the afternoon," wrote Byas, "he gave an address on conditions in the country, the relations between young officers and the young men of the rural villages, the evils of plutocracy, financial panics, the government's inadequate measures to relieve rural distress, the monopoly of capital by the big interests, and the close relations between financial interests and statesmen close to the throne. The court listened stolidly and adjourned at five p.m."[47]

It did not reconvene. That night the Army mutinied.

Sometime before 5:00 A.M. on February 26, 1936, in a blinding snowstorm, fifteen hundred soldiers of the 1st Division led by captains and lieutenants (perhaps 10 percent of the Tokyo garrison) occupied the buildings of the Imperial Diet, the Ministry of War, the headquarters of the metropolitan police, and the newspaper *Asahi,* where they wrecked the presses. (The snow was symbolically significant: it was in just such a storm that the Forty-seven Ronin, the rogue samurai who were made the heroes of the most famous and popular of Japanese dramas, had avenged their dead master in acts of violence inspired by the purest loyalty.)

Meanwhile murder squads with submachine guns in military trucks went in search of the prime minister, the minister of finance, *genro* Saionji, the lord keeper of the privy seal and his predecessor, the grand chamberlain, and the inspector general of military training. Four of the seven, including Saionji—by luck, mistaken identity, or timely warning—managed to escape, but the others were gunned down, again in the presence of their families. Having no further idea what to do, the soldiers then stopped where they were, apparently in the expectation that their superiors would "rise" and take over the country. In that hope they were to be disappointed.

For once, the emperor held firm, calling this a "mutiny" (which no one else dared to do), and he was protected in the palace by loyal troops of the imperial guards division, who controlled its approaches. "I will give you one hour," he told the minister of war, "in which to suppress the rebels." The senior military followed his lead. "Just whose General Staff Headquarters and Army is it?" an outraged Saionji was later to ask.[48]

But executing the imperial order took more than an hour. For four days, the two sides glared at one another, while the rest of Tokyo tried to go about its business in the snowdrifts as though nothing were happening. The fleet came into the harbor, martial law was declared, the mutinous soldiers issued a manifesto, as one by one other army units, brought in from the countryside, ringed them in.

Finally, an appeal in the emperor's name, invoking the supreme Japanese sanction of social disapproval—"your fathers, mothers, brothers, and sisters are all weeping"—brought their resistance to an end. The principal leaders committed suicide and the others surrendered; thirteen of them were tried in secret and executed, as was the unfortunate Aizawa, whose trial had occasioned all this and who otherwise might have got off with a jail sentence. Thus ended what thereafter was known as Ni Ni Roku Jiken—the Twenty-sixth of February Incident.

Ni Ni Roku had the predictable effect of discrediting the more fanatical advocates of the Showa Restoration, but it had other and ultimately more extensive consequences in that it enabled one faction within the army to triumph over another, and the two disagreed not only on army politics but on overall national policy.

It would oversimplify to call them "extremists" and "moderates," though they had that coloration, because both were equally nationalistic and equally committed to Japanese expansion abroad, which was the price the army intended to exact for tranquillity at home. The army was united in favoring expansion, which is to say armed aggression, but what the two factions disagreed about was where to expand.

One was called Kodo-ha, or Imperial Way, and the other Tosei-ha, or Control Group. Adherents of Kodo-ha tended to be rough-and-ready field officers, restless, contemptuous of civilians, impatient of complexity or compromise, and bitterly anticommunist. Those of Tosei-ha were more likely to be suave and businesslike, realists, capable administrators, interested in merit rather than personality, and willing if necessary to cooperate with capitalists and politicians.

More important, the two favored differing strategies, which in Japan were polarized between north and south much as American strategies were polarized between east and west. Kodo-ha wanted to attack Russia in the north, Tosei-ha to strike farther south, in China and Indochina. After Ni Ni Roku, Tosei-ha was able firmly to establish itself in power, and devotees of the strike-north school had to postpone their ambitions.

◆

This digression has been circuitous, but it is drawing to a close, for the "drag-down and knock-out fight" that five years later Ambassador Grew was observing, and President Roosevelt was describing to Secretary Ickes, involved the same argument unexpectedly revived. When Germany attacked the Soviet Union in June 1941, the Japanese were not wholly unprepared, but they were surprised in the military sense of the term, in that questions were raised to which they had prepared no answers. Strict adherence to the Tripartite Pact would have brought them to the aid of their ally Germany, but embarrassingly they had signed a Neutrality Pact with Russia just two months before, by which they were committed to stay out of a war between Russia and anyone else.

This seeming limitation on their freedom to act did not trouble in the least their foreign minister, Yosuka Matsuoka, who had negotiated both agreements and who dreamed of accomplishing Japan's aims by this kind of maneuvering, by his personal diplomacy alone. Ignoring the Neutrality Pact, he now urged on the emperor and the military an immediate, no-holds-barred attack on the Soviet Union, striking north with a vengeance.

Matsuoka's personality was so volatile and egocentric that he alarmed even his fellow countrymen; once when Matsuoka's instability was mentioned, Saionji had said, "It will improve him if he becomes insane."[49] But the admission must be made that if the ultimate advantage of the Axis powers was the aim, on this occasion Matsuoka was right. His was the correct strategy. Attacking Russia was a relatively logical thing for the Japanese to do, and had they done it, we might later have been given cause for regret.

Japanese expansionist thinking long had favored the acquisition of territory on the adjacent Asian landmass, and for many of the extreme nationalists a fervent anticommunism and a desire to take over eastern Siberia went comfortably hand in hand. Again the junior officers were ever ready to arrange matters in their own fashion. The Kwantung Army in Manchuria, thinking itself not without cause to be Japan's finest, had become increasingly impatient and disdainful of higher authority, and had in good part engineered the China "incident" to protect its flank and rear for an eventual showdown with Russia (against that eventuality an immobilized China was a desirable prerequisite). That the China "incident" had resisted resolution was a disagreeable annoyance, but the real enemy was to the north.

For the Kwantung Army had a score to settle with the Soviets. During May 1939, in one of those undeclared wars that the rest of the world ignores, it had in fact taken the field against the Russians in Outer Mongolia near Lake Nomonhan and been badly mauled. There had ensued a full-dress campaign with artillery, aircraft, and tanks over many months and a front of fifty to sixty kilometers, and when the Japanese finally withdrew in September, they had suffered 50,000 casualties (of whom 18,000 were killed) against the Russians' 9,000. (Figures on the Japanese dead at Nomonhan were not released until 1966![50]) Any policy that would keep the Kwantung Army happy, or at minimum lower its level of inflammable discontent, was therefore bound to be welcomed in Tokyo, as Matsuoka knew.

Further, war "between Germany and the Soviet Union," as President of the Privy Council Yoshimichi Hara was later to say, "represents the chance of a lifetime for Japan."[51] This was an opportunity to make a choice that could have gained them at least reasonable odds in winning the war. If there was ever a chance for the Axis powers to coordinate a common strategy, this was it. People on our side, like the President, assumed such coordination to be taking place because it was so obviously what we would have done, what we were doing surreptitiously with the British and would do openly as soon as we could.

But there was no such thing as an Axis strategy. no planning in concert, no agreement on objectives, no pooling of resources, no atmosphere of trust, and very nearly no candid communication. Hitler had not told the Japanese when he was going to invade Russia, and the Japanese, some of them observing that turn about was fair exchange, did not tell the Germans that they were going to court war with Britain and the United States.

A single Axis strategy would have had as its first principle to divide the opposing powers and deal with them one by one, in this case (the issue being joined) *Russia first!* (In comparable circumstances we had the wit to resolve on taking the offensive against Germany first and accepting a defensive posture in the Pacific.) On June 28, the German ambassador to Tokyo, General Eugen Ott, got a cable from Berlin setting forth the reasons he should use in trying to persuade the Japanese to attack Russia. He did not have to be informed that the Russians had large, well-trained, and well-equipped armies in the Far East. "Ott keeps talking about the movement of the Soviet Far Eastern troops to the West," Matsuoka had told a liaison conference on June 25.[52]

The very least the Japanese could have done as faithful allies would have been to engage the Russian armies on their front and keep them occupied while the Germans dealt with the decimated and demoralized Russians facing them. The Japanese could have confronted the Russians with the classic consequences of a two-front war, in which resources must be spread so thin as to be ineffective everywhere at once (the Russian aim was naturally to avoid this). In any case, as Matsuoka unabashedly reminded his colleagues, if Germany should win the war (which they all took for granted), the Japanese could expect slim pickings at the peace table unless they had shed blood in the common cause.

It made for an impressive argument, so much so that foreign observers including our own State Department readily persuaded themselves that strike-north was going to be the ultimate Japanese move. (Admiral Turner in Navy plans thought so too, though Admiral Stark did not.) On June 23 in Washington, the chief of the State Department's Division of Far Eastern Affairs wrote that he believed "the likely development of Japanese thought will be along this line," and on July 2 an internal memorandum within the division conceded that "it seems on the whole more probable that Japan will decide to invade Siberia than continue her southward expansion." On the same day, a cable from Chungking to the White House reported Chiang Kai-shek to have received "reliable information" that Japan would soon abrogate the Neutrality Pact and "declare war on Russia," and the day afterward Sumner Welles conveyed this and other indications of the same tenor to the British ambassador.[53]

The wise money was on the wrong horse.

◆

During the month of June there were nine liaison conferences in Tokyo, which dealt with the possibility, followed by the fact, of Germany's war with Russia and its implications for Japan. These were usually attended by the prime minister, the foreign minister, the war and navy ministers, the army and navy chiefs and vice-chiefs of staff, and by the finance minister, the commerce minister, and the director of the planning board when invited. This group had become the main foreign-policy-making body of the government, or at least the sounding board against which the army and navy could project the decisions they had already made—in this case, their efforts to achieve a unified response to Matsuoka's urging of the strike-north option.

They were having to think harder than had been their custom about a coordinated effort and their nation's capacity for it. The civilian ministers, the navy, and the army all took notes, but only the army minutes seem to have survived the war (and were published in Japan in 1962–63 and in English translation in 1967). These should be understood to reflect an army bias, but they provide an incomparably vivid glimpse into the thought processes of the Japanese leaders as they took the steps leading them to war.

The necessity of their choosing between a north or a south strategy was underscored by the growing realization that they couldn't have both.

"The Empire does not have the materials," the minister of commerce told them at one meeting, ". . . we do not have materials for war on both land and sea." In a postwar analysis, a former director of the planning board wrote that while many may think Japan entered the war despite a lack of resources, exactly the opposite was the case: They went to war *because* their resources were insufficient.[54] To the extent that the army and navy leaders could demean themselves to admit economic constraints, they managed this by rephrasing the proposition to read that they could not fight everybody at once.

"The worst possible eventuality," said Army Chief of Staff Gen Sugiyama, would be "Britain, the United States, and the Soviet Union attacking us simultaneously." According to Navy Minister Koshiro Okawa, the navy was "confident about war against the United States and Britain, but not confident about war against the United States, Britain, and the Soviet Union." He drew a nightmarish picture of American bomber bases on Russian soil and Russian submarines operating from naval bases in the United States. "Don't tell us to strike at Soviet Russia and also tell us to go south," he said. "The Navy doesn't want the Soviet Union stirred up."[55]

The operative issue behind all this was oil. The Japanese filled only a tenth of their oil requirements from domestic and synthetic sources; all the rest came through imports from the Indies, the Caribbean, and the United States, with the last accounting for three fifths to four fifths of the difference. During the 1930s they had been buying more than they needed, and by the end of 1939 their stockpile of petroleum products had reached its peak at about 55 million barrels, enough for a year and a half's consumption. But military use in China and at home for training purposes had increased and, even with restrictions on the civilian gasoline supply, in 1940 and 1941 the stockpile had been shrinking, partly as a result of covert pressure and manipulation by the British and the Americans to obstruct Japanese purchases.[56]

At an imperial conference in September 1940, Director of the Planning Board Naoki Hoshino had been quizzed about the overall supply situation, oil in particular, by then Navy Chief of Staff Prince Hiroyasu Fushimi, cousin of the emperor's wife. It was clear to them all that they could not run the risk of war while depending on oil from the Western Hemisphere. "I would like to know," said Prince Fushimi, "how we will get the additional oil necessary for a long war?" Hoshino's rambling response—"In short," he remarked at one point, "it will be essential to acquire a large amount of oil any way we can"—did not satisfy the prince. "May I interpret this to mean," he asked, "that there is, in general, no assurance that additional oil can be obtained? I will add that we cannot count on supplies from the Soviet Union. In the end, we will need to get oil from the Netherlands East Indies."

This was the reality that stared them in the face. Ultimately it was to convert the navy conservatives, who had no hunger for war with Britain and the United States, into radicals who were willing to consider it. "You cannot carry on a war without oil," as Privy Council President Hara put it, and he added: "I think it will be impossible to obtain oil from the Netherlands East Indies by peaceful means."[57]

The Japanese had been coming on strong at the Dutch in the Indies, where Asia's richest oil fields lay—buying greater amounts than ever before of oil, rubber, tin, and bauxite; demanding concessions for oil drilling and special privileges in port facilities and communications; and attempting to infiltrate military personnel masquerading as engineers. The Dutch were in a bind. If they temporized they would give Japan the weapons to attack with them, and if they held firm they would invite such an attack all the sooner. They chose to hold firm, which was greatly to their credit; but their firmness is what was prompting Privy Council President Hara, despite his own pronounced strike-north leanings, to conclude that in the south, "peaceful means" were not going to be enough.

To take the Indies by force, the navy said it would have to have bases like Camranh Bay in southern Indochina, and to ensure a reliable flow of oil it would have to protect the sea lanes back to Japan, which meant doing something sooner or later about the Americans in the Philippines and the British at Singapore.

The need for oil dictated its own strategy. To seize the Indies they would have to force the French to let them take over the unoccupied parts of Indochina, and then begin to make serious preparations against the possibility of war with Britain and the United States. A war with Russia would have to wait.

So it would be strike-south after all. A document embodying this, entitled "Acceleration of the Policy Concerning the South," had been presented at the liaison conference of June 12, before the German invasion of Russia, and was subsequently challenged and revised, though the essentials remained the same. These had the virtue of involving no basic disagreement between the army and the navy. The army would undoubtedly have preferred to fight Russia, but not too soon, please. They were embarrassed at being bogged down in China and were hoping for better odds in Siberia; their problem was to say this without saying it too loudly.

"There is no difference in importance between North and South," Army Vice-Chief of Staff Ko Tsukada (one of the war hawks) said on June 26. "The order and method will depend on the situation. . . . We will go ahead if we perceive that conditions are extremely advantageous." Army Chief of Staff Sugiyama, pressed by Matsuoka for a strike-north order, said on the twenty-seventh that the Kwantung Army would need forty to fifty days to get ready. "The German-Soviet situation should be clarified by then. If conditions are good, we will fight."

What they meant by "clarified," "good," and "extremely advantageous" were major and indubitable German victories in the West, so as to permit them if not a walkover at least a reasonably promising campaign in the East. "I don't like the 'extreme' in 'extreme advantage,' " said Matsuoka. "I would like a decision to attack the Soviet Union."

"No," said Sugiyama.[58]

As for the navy, they would undoubtedly have preferred no war at all, but the one they liked least was with Russia. Crassly put, there was nothing in it for them of gain or glory, and it would not guarantee them the oil without which they would soon be brought to a standstill. War with Britain and the United States was risky, but the risks could be calculated.

Geography had favored the Imperial Navy, at least insofar as the islands of the Pacific Ocean are largely located in its western half. By capturing or neutralizing them—and, with luck, the isolated eastern Pacific outposts of Midway and Hawaii as well—the Japanese could acquire all the actual and potential naval bases they would need for a prolonged and flexible defense on interior lines. The U.S. Navy would be driven back to the California coast and would lack the forward bases necessary for an effective counterattack or any decisive fleet action in the western Pacific. This was not unrealistic. (The idea of a fleet that put to sea and stayed there, carrying its own base facilities with it—which was germinating and soon to blossom in American minds—did not occur to the Japanese.)

When the "Acceleration of the Policy Concerning the South" memo was presented on June 12, the navy leadership threw aside its traditional conservatism. Under the inexorable sway of oil logistics, the naval moderates came out in support and "strongly recommended using force in case French Indochina did not agree with us, and also in case Great Britain, the United States, and the Netherlands hindered us." When Sugiyama stated the army's position of advancing in the north only "if the situation develops in our favor," Navy Chief of Staff Osami Nagano said, "I agree with the Army Chief of Staff."[59]

That, together with Sugiyama's blunt and untypically Japanese "no" to Matsuoka, did it.

◆

Their final document was called "Outline of National Policies in View of the Changing Situation," and it was read, discussed, and adopted in the presence of the as usual silent emperor on July 2. The crucial paragraph ended with the statement that "various measures relating to French Indochina and Thailand will be taken, with the purpose of strengthening our advance into the southern regions. In carrying out the plans outlined above, our Empire will not be deterred by the possibility of being involved in a war with Great Britain and the United States." Elsewhere there occurred the phrase: "preparations for war with Great Britain and the United States will be made." As for the Russians and the Germans, "we will not enter the conflict for the time being," but as a sop to the Kwantung Army there was an escape clause about "resorting to force" if conditions "should develop to the advantage of our Empire"—i.e., Germany triumphant.

There were also passages about settling the "China Incident" by compelling "the capitulation of the Chiang regime," and there was the necessary conclusion required by all the above, that "we will immediately turn our attention to putting the nation on a war footing." They were "determined to remove all obstacles" to these policies, which were to be followed "no matter what changes may occur in the world situation."[60] Stick to the plan, in other words, and let reality take care of itself—a dangerous if wholly Japanese frame of mind.

Long was the road that led Japan to Pearl Harbor, but surely no turn in it was more fateful than this one. The far-reaching effects of the imperial conference of July 2, 1941, began to be felt almost immediately, if only for the reason (not anticipated by its participants) that the Russians and the Americans knew of the strike-south decision within a matter of days. Report of it is said to have been made to Moscow on July 4 by the Russian ambassador, and to have been confirmed by a dispatch to Berlin by the German naval attaché, which the Russians intercepted.

Further corroboration came from the Soviet spy ring in Tokyo headed by Richard Sorge, whose cover role was that of correspondent for *Frankfurter Zeitung.* Sorge was a confidant and frequent guest of Ambassador Ott's and had an office in the embassy; his associate, Hotsumi Ozaki, a writer for *Asahi,* was a close friend and consultant to the cabinet secretary of the prime minister; between the two of them there was little that happened in high government circles they were not informed about, though Moscow did not entirely trust them.

In any event, the Russians shortly knew they could relax their guard against immediate Japanese attack, and the east-west movement of troops that had so concerned Ambassador Ott began in full flood. Before the end of the year, eighteen divisions and eight armored brigades, seventeen hundred tanks and fifteen hundred aircraft, had been transferred from Siberia westward to face the Germans, whose advance on Moscow they played the critical part in halting and turning back. The Japanese made possible the successful Russian recapture of the initiative in the West. In that sense the imperial conference of July 2 can be said to have sealed the fate not only of Japan but of Germany as well.[61]

A two-part circular summarizing the conference (though deemphasizing war with Britain and the United States) was cabled to Japanese embassies by the foreign ministry. It passed through the hands of Magic and was being read in Washington almost the same day. On the fifth, a high State Department official, Stanley Hornbeck, sent an admonitory I-told-you-so memo to the Division of Far Eastern Affairs to let them know they had been wrong, that "on the basis of excellent evidence received over the weekend" Japan was "sidestepping" the German request to join them against Russia and was instead going to "proceed with operations calculated to strengthen their military position in French Indochina."[62]

The United States government now knew, if it earlier had any doubts, that seeming Japanese willingness to negotiate was a sham, that warnings against further aggression were being systematically ignored, and that new armed interventions into neighboring states would soon follow. Any valid basis there had been for hope in discussion and compromise was fatally undermined.

In Japan, the aftermath of the imperial conference unrolled smoothly. They got rid of Matsuoka by the simple expedient of dissolving the cabinet and then reappointing everyone else. The Kwantung Army was further pacified by being heavily reinforced, doubled in numbers from 300,000 to 600,000, and sent so much equipment that by war's end half of it was still there. What they understood to be a general economic mobilization was begun; orders went out to complete the occupation of Indochina; and operational plans were prepared for invading Malaya, Java, Borneo, New Guinea, the Bismarck Archipelago, and the Philippines.

Not least, the Imperial Navy assembled in Kagoshima Bay at the southern end of Kyushu, and there the pilots of the Kido Butai began to practice coming in low over the mountains, dive-bombing, and dropping torpedoes specially designed for use in shallow waters like a harbor.[63]

In Washington began the preparation of detailed machinery for putting into effect what was by now a considerable determination to halt the flow of war materials to Japan. Even Secretary Hull, who was in White Sulphur Springs, ill and tired, told Assistant Secretary Acheson on the telephone that he wanted "a general tightening up," and at the next day's cabinet meeting, the President—though objecting to an outright oil embargo as too provocative—seemed to agree on a "freezing" of Japanese assets in the United States.

Acheson and his young lawyers (with an assist from the Treasury Department) went to work drafting the appropriate order as Magic continued to pour forth indications of imminent Japanese moves; and on July 23 the President, brushing aside objections (the Navy and the Army, in the persons of Stark and Marshall, were still opposed), agreed to sign it as soon as complementary actions could be worked out with the British and the Dutch, and our own military commanders altered. General MacArthur was recalled to active duty, the Philippine Scouts were incorporated into the Regular Army, and plans were set in motion to reinforce the Philippine defenses. The President accepted a Joint Board recommendation that the United States equip, man, and maintain a five-hundred-plane Chinese air force, and ending a long debate, he approved sending a military mission to China to supervise Lend-Lease.

Roosevelt issued the order on the twenty-sixth, as the Japanese take-over of southern Indochina went forward, and though every effort was made to surround it with vagueness, to keep Tokyo guessing as to what it meant, its effects were not long in becoming clear. This might not be an oil embargo in name, but it was one in fact.[64] If there is any case for the view that the United States "forced" Japan to fight, it rests on this sequence of events and their climax in the "freezing" order.

Ambassador Grew, though he had schoolboy days at Groton in common with the President, had adopted an attitude of "watchful waiting" when Roosevelt was first elected. "I have very little knowledge of Frank Roosevelt's capabilities . . . ," he wrote in his diary. "Frank at least has the background." But within the year he had come around: "We have never had a President who has taken so direct an interest in the Foreign Service; in spite of tremendous political pressure from hungry Democrats after sixteen years on the sidelines, he didn't throw overboard a single career chief of mission." After Roosevelt's reelection in 1940, Grew wrote (addressing him as "Dear Frank"): "You are playing a masterly hand in our foreign affairs and I am profoundly thankful that the country is not to be deprived of your clear vision, determination, and splendid courage."[65]

Grew had read the "arsenal of democracy" speech five times, knew it almost by heart, and had tried to persuade influential Japanese to read the full text rather than the innocuous excerpts that had appeared in Japanese newspapers. Yet he could also see clearly the consequences of an intractable United States policy vis-à-vis Japan. After the freezing order had begun to grab hold, and its full meaning was beginning to be understood in Tokyo, he sensed the mood of coming crisis and concluded that a downward momentum was taking over, of which the only ending could be war. "The vicious cycle of reprisals and counter-reprisals is on," his diary reads in early August and, unconsciously echoing Secretary Hull's words about things going hellward, he added: *"Facilis descensus averni est."*[66]

III

What, then, of Roosevelt's "responsibility"?

Of course he was responsible in the ultimate sense, as every President is responsible for his acts. Roosevelt had framed a foreign policy of which war was the end result. He had made himself the spokesman of American opposition to the Axis. He had urged and adopted measures that were "short of war" by only a shade of meaning, and he had led the nation into a position as the Allies' prime supplier of munitions that enabled the Japanese to argue (as some of them did[67]) that the United States was already in the war anyhow. He had attempted to resolve the dilemmas of a divided people by finding a route between extremes of which the chief merit lay in the things it was not—not actively belligerent, not passively indifferent to danger—and his success in holding the country together was justified in the event by his failure to keep it at peace. All of this could be said either to praise or to blame him, depending on one's viewpoint.

But that is not what many statements asserting Roosevelt's responsibility say. They also include—or, if not include, imply—a further judgment that he deliberately provoked the Japanese into starting a Pacific war and, further still, did so to involve the United States in a European war that most of its citizens wanted to stay out of. This is another assertion entirely. In its most extreme form, it holds that he knew of the Pearl Harbor attack in advance and withheld any warning of it to make sure of having the war he wanted—if true, a most grievous indictment.

Of his guilty foreknowledge of Pearl Harbor it must be said at the outset, and said emphatically, that there is no substantiating evidence whatever. Not one shred of material intelligence has been found, at any level, that points to Hawaii as the immediate target. Without such evidence forthcoming—and after forty years of ardent search, its appearance is most improbable—the attribution must be branded a fiction or a deliberate untruth. The very absence of evidence has in fact reduced the latest exponent of this view to arguing that its nonexistence proves the existence of a conspiracy to suppress it.[68] *Credo quia absurdum.* Anyone who will believe that, to echo the Duke of Wellington, will believe anything.

As to involvement in the European war, if this is what the President intended war with Japan to accomplish, then his own actions cannot be said to have brought it about. After Pearl Harbor he did not ask Congress to declare war on Germany. It was Germany some days later—obligingly, if you like, but also puzzlingly—that declared war on the United States. For the President to have been certain in advance that this would happen is impossible.[69] It is difficult enough even now to know why Hitler did it, why he deliberately minimized Roosevelt's difficulties when by simply doing nothing he could have maximized them. If Germany had *not* declared war on us, the American Europe-first strategy would have been formidably troublesome to implement, and the Anglo-American partnership would have set forth at its first testing on a rocky road. When it comes down to the question of provoking, or goading, or encouraging the Japanese to attack, however, matters become more complicated.

To clear away some of the surrounding underbrush first: There is no doubt that the United States could have had peace with Japan if it had been willing to pay the price. This the Japanese had agreed on among themselves at the imperial conference of September 6, 1941, to the following effect: (1) the United States and Great Britain would not obstruct "the settlement of the China Incident," they would shut down the Burma Road, and they would cease any kind of support—economic, military, political—to Chiang Kai-shek; (2) the United States and Britain would abstain from actions that "threatened the defense of our Empire"—that is, they would not acquire further bases in the Far East or increase their military forces there "beyond the present strength"; and (3) they would "co-operate in the acquisition of goods," restore commercial relations (i.e., lift the oil embargo), and "amicably contribute" to economic cooperation with the Dutch (i.e., make it possible for Japan to get oil from the Indies).

In return, the Japanese were prepared to promise: (1) to refrain from using their Indochinese bases for further advances, except in China; (2) to withdraw their forces from Indochina "after a just peace has been established in the Far East"; and (3) to guarantee the neutrality of the Philippines.[70] This was not an opening bid but (as described in the document) a set of "minimum demands." If by the first ten days of October there was no prospect of their being met by "Bei-Ei" (Japanese shorthand for Britain and the United States), then Japan would "immediately decide to commence hostilities."

Even as an aboveboard basis for negotiation the Japanese terms left a great deal to be desired. When the somewhat modified substance of them was presented to Secretary Hull by Ambassador Nomura on November 20, Hull saw immediately that they were unrealistic; everything the Japanese were asking was specific and everything they were offering was vague. If an agreement along these lines had been put before the bar of American public opinion for approval, it would have been laughed out of court.

There is just as little doubt that those concerned on the American side understood what backing the Japanese into a corner might lead to. In his Pearl Harbor testimony before Congress, Admiral Stark quoted the State Department publication *Peace and War,* which recounts the period 1931–41 from an American perspective and is thus the more impressive for being so definite: "It was the opinion of the responsible officials of the Government . . . that adoption and application of a policy of imposing embargoes upon strategic exports to Japan would be . . . likely to lead to this country's becoming involved in war." Stark, Marshall, Turner, and others were unanimous in this prediction.

There was much talk on both sides about "firmness," quite apart from whatever anyone was going to be firm about. Grew entitled an entry in his diary: "Why America must stand firm in the Far East." In November 1941, Churchill cabled Roosevelt: "The firmer your attitude and ours, the less chance of their taking the plunge." Prince Fumimaro Konoye told the Privy Council in September 1940: "I think it is necessary for us to show a firm attitude, because if we act humbly it will only make the United States presumptuous." Matsuoka told one of the imperial conferences during the same month: "Only a firm stand on our part will prevent a war."[71]

So believing, each side exaggerated, or even misrepresented, the other's firmness. Hull's summary in his memoirs of the terms Japan was offering is the intransigent reading of them, not the necessary one (or so Herbert Feis concluded). The Japanese extremists, to coerce the moderates, doctored the text of Hull's reply to make it firmer, to make it appear as the "ultimatum" it had not been intended to be. Preoccupation with "firmness" induced an approach in both countries that frustrated compromise.[72]

Yet Ambassador Grew believed at the time, and continued to believe in later years, that a compromise was desirable and indeed would have been achievable if only we had measured our own and Japanese interests more accurately (and, as other critics have added, had not been so obsessed with legalistic and moralistic concerns). The argument goes somewhat as follows: America's vital objectives in 1941 were to halt Japanese expansion in Southeast Asia and to avoid a Pacific war. These were reasonable and attainable goals. But to them we had joined another, namely to compel Japan to withdraw its troops from China, and this was neither vital to us nor by us obtainable.

The miscalculation on our side was to think it was both—that a China cleared of Japanese was essential to United States policy and that the Japanese, confronted with American economic and military power, would eventually consent to it (as Churchill thought they would), or hesitate for some time (as Roosevelt hoped they would) before refusing it. This was a profound misreading of the Japanese military preparations known to us through Magic and of the Japanese military character known to us through professional observers of it like Ambassador Grew.

Grew believed that the Japanese had been genuinely taken aback by the oil embargo and that many were having sober second thoughts about making the last desperate move. (This was true; the emperor and the navy leadership were prominent among them.) Grew also believed that we should have accepted the Japanese offer to arrange a summit meeting between Roosevelt and their prime minister, then Prince Konoye, even though Konoye was a slender reed to lean on and the army would not have allowed him much latitude to make concessions.

All the issues did not have to be settled at once. If the China question were set aside, a relaxation of the embargo could have been discussed in terms of assurances about the southward expansion and the Tripartite Pact; a truce or a hold-in-place in China might have followed later. As a temporary measure, and the only alternative to war, a *modus vivendi* or détente might by strong effort have been made acceptable to the publics of both countries. This formulation is by no means a fantasy; George Kennan gave it his considerable support in 1974 in a symposium called "World War II: 30 Years After."

But one essential ingredient was missing: trust. In Feis's felicitous phrasing, "there was no faith—and, as has been said, without faith there can be no works."[73]

◆

On July 8, 1924, the Imperial Japanese Navy had trained its guns on two of its own warships, *Satsuma* and *Aki,* and had shattered and sunk them, thus complying with the Washington Treaty of 1922, which fixed the naval tonnage ratio of Great Britain, the United States, and Japan at 5:5:3. Watching this unwillingly self-sacrificial event was Commander Kanji Kato, who had been an aide at the Washington conference. "From this day on," he was heard to say, "we are at war with the United States."[74]

The Washington conference, followed by the London Naval Conference of 1930—which only modestly increased the Japanese ratio—nurtured a lingering resentment in Japan. It transformed the Imperial Navy from a rational and sophisticated service on the British model into a disturbed organization riven with dissent, in which war with the United States came to be regarded not only as possible but by some as inevitable. Resentment rode down the realism of men like Admirals Yonai and Yamamoto, who had thought primarily in deterrent rather than offensive terms about a Pacific war they believed to be unwinnable.

Commander Kato became a vice-admiral, chief of the navy General Staff, a member of the Supreme War Council, and leader of an enthusiastic pro-German "nucleus group" within the navy. He was an authentic product of the emotionally nationalist mentality. He despised the "poisonous" effects of "materialistic Western civilization" on Japan and was resolved to overcome America's physical superiority by means of Japanese will power.

In 1933–34, Kato engineered a purge of the "traditional" officers who believed Japan's naval potential unequal to that of the Anglo-Americans, and Yonai and his associates declined in influence. Where earlier the top graduates of the naval academy had gone to Washington as naval attachés, after the mid-1930s the majority of them went to Berlin. The restraining influence of the naval ministry was broken and power relocated in the General Staff, which meant in practice the "nucleus group," the fanatical middle-echelon officers with alliances to the radical right in politics, who thought only of what was best for the navy and of how the "fetters" of the "humiliating treaties" could be broken.

In 1934, Kato warned Prince Fushimi, the bumbling royal figurehead they had propped in front of them, that unless the cabinet went along with their demands for naval parity with the United States, "the navy will not be able to control its officers," and Fushimi duly so informed the emperor. Ambassador Grew summarized in his diary a speech about the London treaty given by an army officer at Kobe that same year. "American duplicity during former naval conferences degraded Japan," the officer had said, "and this insult to the Imperial Navy must be *avenged*."[75]

Japanese resentment had many sources, magnified by national self-consciousness. Postwar Ambassador Edwin O. Reischauer, born in Tokyo and as understanding of the Japanese as any American, remarks on their "unquenchable and decidedly morbid interest in every expression of opinion on Japan by any foreigner, no matter how poorly informed or unqualified . . . They feel the eyes of the world are always upon them."[76] Moreover, their resentment was justified. They did not have to look very far, no further than our immigration laws, to find evidences of American racial prejudice and contempt.

Cliché and caricature views of the Japanese abounded in the United States, where everyone knew that they were only imitators, that their cities were made of paper, that they could only manufacture gimcrack goods, and that their poor eyesight prevented them from piloting airplanes. Widely repeated in Tokyo, and deeply rankling, was a remark attributed to Admiral Kimmel: "In the event of war, we shall annihilate the Japanese Navy within four weeks." It all added up to the one thing the Japanese were least able to accept: the sense of not being taken seriously.[77]

Coupled with this was a sense of their own strengths. They well knew that the United States far excelled them in production of material goods, but this did not vitally impress them. It encountered what Reischauer calls "their dogged belief in the superiority of will power over matter." Will power comes from self-discipline and self-denial; in this Japanese image of it there was no room for their conceiving self-indulgent Americans to have any will power at all. They saw no reason to think that we would constrain our abundance, give up our new automobiles and elaborate gadgets, in order to manufacture the instruments of war.

At any rate, their will power was clearly the stronger. One of their military slogans, and very Japanese in spirit, ran: "to match our training against their numbers and our flesh against their steel." They literally believed that they could not lose because they refused to lose; hence their battle reports which consistently substituted determination for results, so that higher headquarters often had no idea of what had actually happened. After the war, General Kawabe Masakazu, who directed the kamikaze attacks at Okinawa, told U.S. interrogators: "The Japanese, to the very end, believed that by spiritual means they could fight on equal terms with you. . . . We believed our spiritual confidence in victory would balance any scientific advantage."[78]

Similarly, American ignorance of Japan was vast and unrelieved by the press. The wire services, the major newspapers, and a handful of others tried to cover Japanese affairs with unprepared and underpaid reporters, most of them "stringers" reimbursed by the word for whatever got printed. (Hugh Byas, a Scotsman with a burr, represented both the

London Times and the *New York Times.*) They were largely ignorant of Japanese history, culture, and language (only two of them tried to learn it), and dependent for their information on the narrow circle that frequented the same bars, clubs, and embassy parties they did. The Japanese did little to help matters, censoring releases, channeling news through "spokesmen," restricting what could be investigated and published, rifling reporters' files, and spying on their movements.[79] The inability of the media to mediate was complete.

To this proud and subtle people, to the land of Prince Genji and the Katsura Imperial Villa, the Americans turned a face of self-righteousness. Hull and Stimson tended to regard the Japanese as wicked folk who had to be chastened. We lectured them; Hull's "four points," which he proposed as a basis of settlement, were not much more than lectures condensed into articles suitable for the preamble of a treaty. We made it abundantly plain that we did not trust what they said (since we were reading their mail through Magic, there was in this some justice).

We did not believe that they genuinely "meant" what they were saying (to the Japanese, a minor consideration) and so we struck postures we had a dubious capacity to carry through on (to the Japanese, a major consideration). Each of us believed the other not to be *sincere,* and it was on the meaning of the word "sincerity"—making allowance for other and obvious factors—that the United States and Japan fatally achieved a mutual miscomprehension.

◆

The closest object the Japanese knew to a sacred text was the 1882 Imperial Rescript to Soldiers and Sailors of the Emperor Meiji. Copies of it were kept in shrines and brought forth for ceremonial occasions, when those who read it aloud had been known to commit *seppuku* if they made a mistake. It was read to the troops on national holidays; they were encouraged to memorize it and meditate on its contents. Its final paragraph, after listing the military virtues, stated that the "soul" of these was sincerity: "If the heart be not sincere, words and deeds, however good, are all mere outward show and avail nothing. If only the heart be sincere, anything can be accomplished."

Count Shinenobu Okuma, in his *Fifty Years of New Japan* in 1909, said that sincerity was "the precept of all precepts; the foundation of moral teachings can be implied in that one word." It was also good Zen Buddhism. The saintly Dr. Suzuki wrote in the between-war years that sincerity, "that is not-deceiving, means 'putting forth one's whole being' . . . in which nothing is kept in reserve, nothing is expressed under disguise, nothing goes into waste. When a person lives like this, he is said to be a golden-haired lion."[80]

For the user of English, "sincerity" means honesty of mind or intention, not feigned or affected, presenting no false appearance; it connotes frankness, the full disclosure of what is in one's heart. But frankness is not a Japanese virtue. It reflects ignorance and insecurity; it reveals an insensitivity to others and to human nature that is more than likely to result in impoliteness. Sincerity as candor is thoroughly un-Japanese; the idea of exposing one's inner feelings is repugnant to them and more than a little ridiculous. They have numerous proverbs embodying this: "Behold the frog who when he opens his mouth displays his whole inside." In Japanese, "sincerity," or *makato,* is a totally different conception.

Sincerity to them, writes Reischauer, "means knowing what is expected of one, or rather what one should expect of oneself to maintain self-respect, and then having the strength of will to do it. It means being too 'big' to act improperly, no matter what the other man does." Someone with *makato* obeys the rules, is not self-seeking, is free of passion and inner conflict. *Makato* is an intensified version of the other virtues; it is the necessary zeal to follow the road mapped out for the Japanese spirit by its code of conduct.

A "sincere" person, as Ruth Benedict put it in her classic study of the Japanese character, *The Chrysanthemum and the Sword,* "never verges on the danger of insulting a person he does not mean to provoke to aggression, and this mirrors their dogma that a man is responsible for the marginal consequences of his acts as well as for the act itself." (Oscar Wilde's definition of a gentleman as someone who is never unintentionally rude comes to mind.) *Makato* has a kind of sleepwalking certainty; it is in-tuneness with oneself and one's obligations to the point where psychic energies are released and, in the Emperor Meiji's words, "anything can be accomplished." It is what Matsuoka meant when he told an imperial conference that it was necessary to "do things sincerely. We need to exercise our influence . . . with our sincerity."[81]

One can readily see that Japanese *makato* and American "sincerity" had little to say to one another that was not bound to be misconstrued. Men like Hull and Stimson, who thought of themselves as virtuous, were totally "insincere" in Japanese terms in that they seemed not to understand, or not to admit, the consequences of what they were doing. How could the Americans go on behaving in such a way as to bring on a war while primly maintaining that their purpose was peace? This was the ultimate in "insincerity" as the Japanese understood it.

They themselves were of course doing something equally reprehensible in American eyes; many of them (Konoye included) were quite ready to make us promises about withdrawing from China that they had no intention of keeping. The readers of Magic were forced again and again to conclude that the Japanese were "insincere" in their attempts to negotiate. Their military leaders had covertly set in motion measures that not merely envisaged war but initiated it and imposed it on their own people, and to do so in secret was a form of insincerity definable as such even to the Japanese; at least one of them who saw it happening was uncomfortable about it. "I do not want to continue this hypocritical existence," Ambassador Nomura cabled home in October, as Magic listened, "deceiving myself and other people."[82]

Could Roosevelt have done anything to break this circuit of faulty communication and clear the air? George Kennan thought he could have. "Had FDR been determined to avoid war with the Japanese if at all possible," Kennan argued, "he would have conducted American policy quite differently . . . than he actually did. He would not, for example, have made an issue over Japanese policy in China . . . where this sort of Americans pressure was not really essential. He would not have tried to starve the Japanese navy of oil. And he would have settled down to some hard and realistic dealings with the Japanese."[83]

This is asking much. Kennan himself would surely be willing to agree that it asked of Americans generally an acceptance of *Realpolitik,* of the cold calculation of national interest, which they have rarely displayed. It would also have had the appearance of "betraying" China. The American public was then busily sentimentalizing China and attributing virtues to Chiang's regime that were quite imaginary, so that Chiang's struggle against Japan was widely envisaged as an integral part of democracy's war against fascism everywhere. Such it was not, but such was the prevailing view, and it would have had to be disavowed before there could have been public approval for seeming to "abandon" China or grant consent to Japan. It may have been a fault in Roosevelt that he contributed to this linkage of otherwise unrelated issues, but if so, he was not alone in it and his political skills would have been sorely tested if he had tried to *un*link them.

Kennan's proposal further asked that both Americans and Japanese be capable of "hard and realistic dealings," and even if we had been, they were not. It was too late: The point of no return had been passed. "I think we could settle with Nomura in five minutes," Stark wrote to Kimmel in October, "but the Japanese Army is the stumbling block."[84] The army was in the saddle in Japan, and it was not in a realistic mood; it and the navy in turn had entered into a dream world of their own in which the "morale" of their young officers was the factor on which the national destiny was to be decided.

The young officers did not want a settlement with America. They did not want terms to be proposed that we could accept. They did not want a Konoye-Roosevelt meeting to be a success. When General Hideki Tojo took over from Konoye as prime minister on October 18, what had previously been implicit was affirmed. Tojo as war minister had been a hard-liner on any withdrawal from China and had urged breaking off negotiations with the United States since they would only give the Americans more time to rearm. The newspaper *Yomiuri* saw his appointment as an inducement for Japan "to rise to the occasion and administer a great shock to the anti-Axis powers." Even the emperor permitted himself a quotation, one that was on the lips of many Japanese during these terminal days of peace: "There is a saying, isn't there? 'You cannot obtain a tiger's cub unless you brave the tiger's den.' "[85]

◆

Roosevelt's idea that the fleet at Pearl Harbor would deter the Japanese from further adventures in Southeast Asia was sound so far as it went, in that the threat was real to them and they recognized it. But the President's reasoning contained a flaw, in that Japanese reasoning went one step further—namely, that if their southern advance was to be successful, then that fleet would have to be eliminated—and this was the logic Admiral Yamamoto used to persuade his reluctant colleagues of the necessity for the Pearl Harbor attack.

It is tempting to speculate that the "sensible" Japanese move would have been to take on only the British and the Dutch, to acquire Malaya and the Indies while leaving Hawaii and the Philippines strictly alone, and thus to confront Roosevelt with the horrendous task of trying to get a declaration of war through Congress when American territory had not been touched. (This is what the President and others in the administration feared was going to happen, which is why their attention was diverted elsewhere, as it was to the Kra Isthmus, when the evidence of imminent Japanese action began to accumulate in late November and early December.)

But the Japanese could not take that risk. As long as the U.S. Pacific Fleet was in position to threaten them—and, so much the more, as long as there were those B-17s at Clark Field on Luzon—then any forces they might commit to the south, and any sources of supply they might gain there, would be at hostage to us. If we should respond by moving to cut them off, then the Japanese would be in bad trouble, and even if this was only a possibility it had to be reckoned with. They were prudently thinking ahead. The President not so much miscalculated as undercalculated, falling short in imagination of that later stage in which the deterrent became the target.

The argument that Roosevelt "forced" the Japanese to fight by imposing the oil embargo, over the protests of his military advisers, has a certain superficial plausibility. The advisers were proved right, in that what they thought would happen did happen. The embargo undoubtedly brought around Japanese holdouts against the war, especially in the navy, to the view that the Americans were irreconcilable and that war was the only way out. But there are several objections to this thesis.

One is that the embargo had more than one effect. It also brought many Japanese to an awareness of how vulnerable they were and of how serious was the course on which they were embarking; it perceptibly slowed them down, and it prompted those very doubts that were a necessary precondition to genuine negotiations along the lines Grew and Kennan envisaged. Without the embargo, the Japanese would have continued with fewer qualms than ever in the direction they were going, which was toward war, and this is the second and more fundamental objection, which is one of chronology.

The basic Japanese strike-south-and-be-damned decision not only had been taken *before* the embargo, but with equal persuasiveness might be said to have brought it about, since reaction to the occupation of southern Indochina, and knowledge of the July 2 imperial conference that authorized it, were the motives behind the President's resolve to draw a stiffer line. The Japanese had consciously chosen to effect a redistribution of power in Asia by force and without regard to our consent, and for us to fuel their military machine for the purpose was not only to consent but to condone; this was not something they could treat as their due once they had determined to make do without it. The first step in the syllogism was theirs; the embargo was not cause but effect.

It may well be that the President (and other Americans) can be faulted for failing to think through a peace-in-the-Pacific policy to its logical conclusion—i.e., that concessions would have to be made to Japan. We tended to think of peace as the natural condition, something that was simply there until someone disturbed it, not as a dynamic equilibrium to which we would have to contribute and in which absence of action on our part was itself a form of action. We were certainly justified in refusing to pay the Japanese asking price, but what price *were* we willing to pay? There is not much indication that extended thought was given to this, and in that sense Kennan is right to say that Roosevelt should have pursued a different line of conduct if peace in the Pacific was what he wanted most of all.

But as a practical matter, criticism in this vein founders on the fact that the Japanese asking price was not really an asking price at all but the final one, a minimum level of accommodation that the military extremists were willing to accept in payment for restraining themselves. There is some indication that the demands were intended to be unacceptable and that a Roosevelt-Konoye meeting would only have been manipulated for propaganda purposes, to demonstrate a failure of negotiations to the Japanese public. For the President to have entered into "hard" bargaining in these circumstances would not have been a tribute to his good sense, since sooner or later the consequences would have been no less, and very probably more, damaging to the United States.

It is possible to imagine a hypothetical American frame of mind in which we would have been more receptive to Japanese overtures, feeble as they were. Paradoxically, we might have been more flexible had we been less knowledgeable, for one of the unintended by-products of Magic was that we knew too much about Japanese intentions to be able to negotiate without constrictive mental reservations on our part. Further, we might conceivably have been more willing to accord Japanese energies and achievements due credit, more willing to draw distinctions between their rampaging military abroad and their relatively temperate government at home, to be realistic about China as beyond our capacity to reinvent in our own image, and finally to bring our government's thinking into line with peace in the Pacific as truly a high priority.

It would also be fair to locate a failure on the part of Americans, since stalling for time was essential to our purpose, in our seeming inability to recognize the pressure of time that the Japanese were under. On the American side, internally, there are repeated references to military preparations intended for completion by April 1942 or even later, as though we would be given all the time we needed. An authoritative Japanese estimate was that by June or July of 1942, even with restricted civilian use, their oil supply would completely have run out and would have immobilized them. Our loose lariat was their hangman's noose.

They were quite aware of our preparations and of our timetable, which powerfully suggested to them that the longer they waited, the worse off they would be. "By the latter half of next year," Navy Chief of Staff Nagano told the imperial conference on September 6, "America's military preparedness will have made great progress, and it will be difficult to cope with her. Therefore, it must be said that it would be very dangerous for our Empire to remain idle and let the days go by." They were not only under the gun but concerned to avoid an American trap, what Nagano called a "winter battle at Osaka Castle," a Japanese historical allusion to an incident in 1614 when an apparently stable settlement led to an overpowering defeat the next year.

This was the imperial conference at which the decision for war was reaffirmed, subject only to the outside chance that America might be brought to terms by the first week of October. Like other such occasions, it followed a rigid protocol: the emperor seated on a dais in front of a gold screen, the others in dress uniform at two long brocade-covered tables, stiffly at attention, their hands on their knees. Each would rise in turn, bow in the emperor's direction, and declaim as if by rote a statement that had carefully been rehearsed at a liaison conference. But this time, to their astonishment, Hirohito at the end drew a slip of paper from his pocket and read aloud in his singsong ceremonial voice a poem by his grandfather the emperor Meiji:

> The seas surround all quarters of the globe
>   and my heart cries out to the nations of the world.
> Why then do the winds and waves of strife
>   disrupt the peace between us?[86]

All present were deeply moved; it was unprecedented. But their minds were untouched. Without the concessions from us that had become necessities for them, they would have to fight or else relinquish everything that honor, national aspiration, and a Japanese sense of destiny better called fatalism would demand. Even their language made peace unattractive. During that last half year of it, a phrase many Japanese used to describe the alternative to war was *gashin-shotan:* "to lie down on faggots and lick gall."[87]

◆

In sum, it cannot therefore be said of Roosevelt with any justice that he "provoked" a war when the Japanese had so thoroughly provoked themselves into undertaking one on their own. The President did not want it and up to the final moments he tried to postpone it, as he was doing in his last-minute message to the emperor on the evening of December 6. If he provoked anything he did so in the North Atlantic, where the strategy of sustaining Britain required him to conduct in effect an undeclared war against the German submarines. Here he might risk open hostilities if he judged, as he did correctly, that Hitler would not; but even here it cannot be demonstrated that he *sought* a formal conflict.

Marshall and Stark had concluded that Germany could not be defeated without unstinted United States intervention and were making plans accordingly. Yet Roosevelt did not approve their plans; he merely did not disapprove them (approval came only after Pearl Harbor). Robert Dallek believes that sometime in the spring of 1941 he had come to a conclusion similar to Marshall's and Stark's but that he nonetheless "refused to force an unpalatable choice on the nation by announcing for war."[88]

The President's conduct bears out this characterization of a man, in Langer's and Gleason's very similar words, "who still cherished the hope that the U.S. could escape with something less than full participation," who "still hoped the American contribution could be restricted to naval and air support and material assistance."[89] He may have talked about an "incident" serving as a cause for war, but with none of the many "incidents" that occurred did he try to make this happen, and if a European war is what he wanted, then he singularly failed to prepare for it.

He did not encourage, and scarcely let begin, the creation of an army capable of fighting it (as late as September 1941 he was actively moving to *reduce* the size of the American ground forces), and he did not press for the full mobilization of a war economy by appointing a "production czar," as many were urging him to do. His antennae told him that the country was not ready, and in the meantime one did what one could to protect the national interest. "After all," he had told the cabinet in 1937, "if Italy and Japan have evolved a technique of fighting without declaring war, why can't we?"[90]

Roosevelt's hopes were rendered null by Japanese resolve and by Japanese and American mistrust and misperception of one another. How much he shared in the latter can be little better than surmised. Over a lifetime, he had been of several minds about Japan. In 1913, not long after he became assistant secretary, there was a Japanese war scare that he seems to have taken seriously; he ordered the submarines at Newport to sea and made a plan to mobilize the Navy if Japan should attack the Philippines. Yet in 1923 he wrote an article for *Asia* magazine titled "Shall We Trust Japan?" in which his answer was decidedly affirmative; he pleaded for abandoning our long-held suspicions of the Japanese since a war between us would produce only a deadlock (then the general public, though not the professional naval, view). In the late 1930s, he was well aware, as he wrote to Cordell Hull, that Japan was not a monolith, that the Japanese Army was so out of control, it and the government were two distinctly different things.[91]

Lodged in that capacious memory, however, were the words of a Japanese student at Harvard in 1902 who had expounded to him a step-by-step program (Roosevelt remembered all the steps) by which Japan over the coming century was going to conquer China, Australia, New Zealand, Hawaii, and so on, though if we behaved ourselves they would leave us alone. He recounted this to Stimson in 1934, and by early 1941 the President's own suspicions of the Japanese had hardened. "They hate us," he said to the journalist Quentin Reynolds in mid-March. "They come to me and they hiss between their teeth and they say: 'Mr. President, we are your friends. Japan wants nothing but friendship with America,' and then they hiss between their teeth again, and I know they're lying. Oh, they hate us, and sooner or later they'll come after us."[92]

One fine day, they did.

II

MARSHALL

IN MUNICH DURING SEPTEMBER 1938, an agreement was signed to dismember Czechoslovakia and satisfy Adolf Hitler; two weeks later, Brigadier General George C. Marshall was appointed deputy chief of staff. Among his first meetings at the White House was a formal one at which the President, disturbed by Munich and by reports of German air strength, proposed a program for building ten thousand airplanes a year (with no increase in supporting forces). Present in the room were the secretary of the treasury, the solicitor general, the assistant secretary of war and his executive, the Chief of Staff and his deputy, the chief of the Air Corps, and the President's two military aides. As the proceedings drew to a close, Roosevelt, summing up, turned to Marshall, whom he scarcely knew, and said, "Don't you think so, George?"

Marshall replied: "I am sorry, Mr. President, but I don't agree with that at all."[1]

He got a startled look from his Commander in Chief and, as they were leaving, expressions of sympathy from the others at so quick an ending to so promising a tour of duty in Washington. They underestimated both the general and the President. He never called Marshall "George" in public again, but five months later, on April 23, as Hitler went on to annihilate what remained of Czechoslovakia, Roosevelt reached thirty-four names down the rank list of senior generals and asked George Catlett Marshall, Jr., to be the next Chief of Staff of the U.S. Army. He had made one of the finest and most consequential choices of his presidency. Marshall took the oath of office on September 1, 1939, the day Hitler invaded Poland and World War II began.

Roosevelt received in May, and kept in his files, a thank-you letter somewhat out of the ordinary:

My Dear Mr. President,

   Ever since your appointment of my husband—as your next Chief-of-Staff—I have wanted to write you [she had been ill]. It is difficult for me to put in words what I really feel. For years I have feared that his brilliant mind, and unusual opinion, were hopelessly caught in more or less of a tread-mill. That you should recognize his ability and place in him your confidence gives me all I have dreamed of and hoped for. I realize the great responsibility that is his. I know that his loyalty to you and to this trust will be unfailing. It is with the deepest feeling of gratitude and happiness that I send you this note of thanks.

Very Sincerely Yours,
Katherine Marshall[2]

   The scene at the White House was not the first in which Marshall's outspokenness had taken his colleagues aback. He had an instinct for the moment to observe the Quaker adage and speak truth to power. In October 1917 in France, American Expeditionary Force commander General Pershing had inspected the 1st Division, of which then-Captain Marshall was a staff officer, and found fault with it to a degree Marshall considered unjust. "General Pershing," Marshall interrupted him, "there's something to be said here and I think I should say it because I've been here the longest," and in front of his "horrified" fellow officers, he proceeded to rebut Pershing's criticisms.[3] Later, when Pershing visited the division, he would take Marshall aside and ask him how things were going; later still, he brought Marshall to the operations section of his headquarters at Chaumont, and after the Armistice he made Marshall his aide, which Marshall remained for five years, one of the longest assignments of his career.

   It was retrospectively a career in which Marshall's abilities had long been noticed. In 1914 in the Philippines, on maneuvers near Batangas, south of Manila, a young infantry lieutenant named Henry H. Arnold (one of the Army's handful of qualified aircraft pilots) was moving up with his company and stopped to rest along the trail. In the shade of a bamboo tree Arnold saw another young lieutenant, with a map spread in front of him. It appeared that this was the acting chief of staff of "White Force," who by accident of others' illness and his seniors' high opinion of him had been put in command of five thousand men. He had successfully organized their amphibious landing at Batangas Bay and was now writing the attack order for their advance on Manila. Following it, White Force won. "When I returned from maneuvers," Hap Arnold wrote in his autobiography, "I told my wife I had met a man who was going to be Chief of Staff of the Army someday." When Marshall was appointed, Mrs. Arnold reminded her husband, by that time chief of the Army Air Corps, of his prophecy.[4]

Lieutenant Colonel (later Major General) Johnson Hagood, who was Marshall's commanding officer at Fort Douglas, Utah, in 1916, had been profoundly impressed by the Batangas maneuvers and wrote in Marshall's efficiency report: "He is a military genius and one of those rare cases of wonderful military development during peace." Hagood thought Marshall should be promoted to brigadier general as soon as possible (this would in fact wait two decades). To the routine question of whether he would like to have Marshall serve under him in battle, Hagood answered, "Yes. But I would prefer to serve *under his command.*"[5] (Marshall's company commander at Fort McKinley said the same.)

Yet Marshall's road was far from smooth. In 1915, he wrote to the superintendent of the Virginia Military Institute, who had been his math teacher when he was a cadet there, of his doubts about remaining in a service where advancement was blocked "by the accumulation of large numbers of men of nearly the same age all in a single grade." Retirement at the rank of major was about all he thought he could look forward to. A decade later, from Tientsin, China, he wrote to another VMI superintendent in the same vein: "I am not unaware that the Army holds limited prospects for the officers in my group."[6]

He was by that time a lieutenant colonel, which he remained for *eleven years,* during that period of early maturity when most men hope to achieve something more tangible than the Army could offer Marshall. No sooner was he promoted colonel than he was assigned to the Illinois National Guard, considered within the service to be a dead end that would bar anyone in it from future high command. He protested in vain to the Chief of Staff who had made the assignment, General Douglas MacArthur. "George had a gray, drawn look," Mrs. Marshall wrote of his first weeks in this duty, "which I had never seen before, and have seldom seen since."[7]

Gerald W. Johnson once observed that the veriest newsboy, seeing Marshall enter the Munitions Building in civilian clothes, might not have known who he was but would have had no question *what* he was: lawful authority. Marshall in command had an aura his contemporaries found quite simply awesome. "Wherever this man goes he inspires reverence," wrote Roosevelt's secretary Bill Hassett, a staunch Catholic, "—may God spare him." Admiral Stark wrote Admiral Kimmel about Marshall, eight months before Pearl Harbor: "he is a tower of strength to us all."

The British reacted to him with an almost touch-sensitive awareness of his powers. "Marshall remains the key," wrote Lord Moran, hardly a week after meeting Marshall for the first time: ". . . neither the P.M. [Prime Minister] nor the President can contemplate going forward without Marshall." And later: "In truth, it was impossible not to trust Marshall. . . . It is what Marshall was, and not what he did, that lingers in the mind

—his goodness seemed to put ambition out of countenance." After dinner with Marshall in July 1945, Churchill said to Moran, "That is the noblest Roman of them all."[8]

He was a tall man, just under six feet, with straight sandy hair turned gray and intensely blue eyes. Moran spoke of his "plain, home-spun countenance," with its long upper lip, stubby chin, and almost pug nose. "A magnificent looking man," wrote Air Marshal Sir John Slessor of the RAF, ". . . superbly confident in himself and the rightness of his opinions . . . there were not many in the British Service to hold a candle to him."[9] He kept in trim during the war years by a daily early-morning horseback ride before returning to Quarters One in Fort Myer, Virginia, for a shower and a hearty breakfast, his car arriving punctually at seven-fifteen (by his instruction, it bore no insignia of rank).

His eyesight required glasses for reading, which his orderly, Master Sergeant James Powder, purchased in quantity at the five-and-dime so as to be able to hand him a new pair whenever the previous one had been misplaced. He had a very poor memory for names, even of close associates, and would call his secretary, Mona Nason, "Mason" and the secretary of the General Staff, Colonel Frank McCarthy, "McCartney." Miss Nason told a Colonel Young in the secretariat that she had corrected the general on this, only to have Young reply, "While you were about it, I wish you had told him that I am Young and not Maxwell Taylor."[10]

From his youth in Uniontown, Pennsylvania, Marshall had liked and lived a life outdoors. He was at bottom a country boy and not a city boy; desk jobs were always distasteful to him. His last tour before becoming deputy chief of staff had been as commander of the 5th Brigade of 3d Division at Vancouver Barracks, Washington, amid the fir trees along the Columbia River in the shadow of Mount Hood, where duty as well as hunting and fishing trips took him into the wilderness he loved. He treasured his and Mrs. Marshall's privacy, shunned social life, and retired early. At their country home in Leesburg, Virginia, he trimmed trees and shrubs, planted and hoed vegetables, and kept a compost heap that Mrs. Marshall said was the pride of his heart.

Among all the high brass he was the favorite of the White House secretaries; they pinned up in their office an envelope bearing his signature, which Hopkins gleefully reported to the President, to Marshall's embarrassment. He could be gravely unbending with animals and small children; a succession of dogs were devoted to him, reaching a peak of sorts in his Dalmatian, Fleet (the gift of a friend), who must be classed among the stupidest works of a prodigal Creator. In Marshall's absence Fleet would go looking for him and invariably get lost; finders would have their pictures taken with Fleet for the newspapers before returning him. "No society belle," wrote Mrs. Marshall, "ever appeared in the paper more often than Fleet."[11] Fleet ended up in the Army K-9 (canine) Corps, where he disgraced the Marshalls by appearing in a training film as the dog who did everything wrong.

Beyond doubt Marshall was a most exceptional and impressive human being; what Mrs. Marshall called his "unusual opinion" covered a wide range of genuine originality. He was also the more impressive for being the more human. His rocklike constancy was not of nature but his own making; he had measured his deficiencies and worked to remove them. "As a youngster he avoided those activities and subjects at which he could not do well," writes his biographer Forrest Pogue. "As he grew older he saw the danger and deliberately set tasks for himself for which he had no special aptitude."[12] While still a young man he discovered—once by falling down unconscious, once by being hospitalized for "neurasthenia"—the physical consequences of overwork; he learned the hard way to teach himself to relax.

A slight pulse irregularity caused by thyroid malfunction could be suppressed by exercise, but the strain of saying "no" and telling others they had failed to measure up took a greater toll on him than his associates imagined. A special danger was his temper, which ranged from white fury to (almost worse for the recipient) cold and quiet contempt. "I cannot allow myself to get angry," he said to Mrs. Marshall, on one of their predinner evening walks when he would unwind; "that would be fatal—it is too exhausting." Immediate co-workers, like Eisenhower, were puzzled by this rapid silencing of an emotion they therefore wrongly thought to be put on. "I've never seen a man who apparently develops a higher pressure of anger at some piece of stupidity than does he," wrote Eisenhower in his diary in 1942. "Yet the outburst is so fleeting . . . he doesn't get angry in the way I do—I burn for an hour."[13]

◆

Strange to believe, there were those at the time who actively disliked George Marshall (in afteryears he was vilified by isolationists and McCarthyites, but this was essentially a postwar political phenomenon). Stimson's predecessor, Secretary of War Woodring, said Marshall "would sell out his grandmother for personal advantage," and Assistant Secretary Johnson (previously Marshall's supporter) faulted Marshall for failing to back him in the running gunfight Johnson conducted with Woodring. Especially bitter were the wives of officers, often long acquainted, whom Marshall refused to promote or place in positions of command. "He was once our dear friend," one of them wrote to Forrest Pogue, "but he ruined my husband."

Marshall was preparing an army for the test of combat, in which lack of ability or the tiredness of age would exact a cost in American lives, and in the weeding-out process he was ruthless. Told that a man he had put on orders to go overseas, another longtime friend, could not leave because his wife was away and his furniture wasn't packed, an unbelieving Marshall took the phone himself. "I'm sorry," his friend said. "I'm sorry too," said Marshall, "but you will be retired tomorrow."[14]

In October 1939, a month after Marshall was sworn in, he was interviewed in the old State, War, and Navy Building by the columnist and commentator Major George Fielding Eliot, who had just come back from blacked-out London. Their conversation turned, as will often happen with the American military in moments of reflection, to the Civil War. In the conflict so obviously coming, Eliot wanted to know, how did Marshall propose to avoid disasters like those that were caused by Lincoln's long search for competent commanders? Marshall said he would answer that question fully, provided Eliot did not for the time being publish his reply, and he leaned back in his chair to collect his thoughts.

"The present general officers of the line," Marshall said, "are for the most part too old to command troops in battle under the terrific pressures of modern war. Many of them have their minds set in outmoded patterns, and can't change to meet the new conditions they may face if we become involved in the war that's started in Europe. I do not propose to send our young citizen-soldiers into action, if they must go into action, under commanders whose minds are no longer adaptable to the making of split-second decisions in the fast-moving war of today, nor whose bodies are no longer capable of standing up under the demands of field service. . . . They'll have their chance to prove what they can do. But I doubt that many of them will come through satisfactorily. Those that don't will be eliminated."

Marshall was as good as his word: of all the senior generals "of the line" at the time he took charge (that is, potential leaders of an army corps or an army in the field), only one, Walter Krueger, was to be given command of U.S. troops in battle during World War II. But the others being "eliminated," where would their replacements come from? Marshall opened a drawer of his desk and handed Eliot a sheet of paper. "I've made a little list," Marshall said. "I've looked over the colonels, lieutenant colonels, and some of the majors of the Army. I've chosen some men who were personally known to me, and some who were recommended to me by others in whose judgment I have confidence." Eliot remembered most of the names: Devers, Hodges, Patton, Eisenhower, Eichelberger, Patch, Collins, Simpson, Clark, Truscott, Crittenberger, Bradley.

"I'm going to put these men to the severest tests which I can devise in time of peace," Marshall went on. "I'm going to start shifting them into jobs of greater responsibility than those they hold now. Then I'm going to change them, suddenly, without warning, to jobs even more burdensome and difficult. . . . I'm going to allow them plenty of room to think that I'm treating them arbitrarily, even unreasonably, that I'm asking of them more than human beings should be required to deliver. . . . Those who stand up under the punishment will be pushed ahead. Those who fail are out at the first sign of faltering."[15]

What eventually became known as Marshall's "little black book" was much feared throughout the Army. "Members of his staff," writes Pogue, "watched with fascination as he took it out from time to time, crossed off one name and moved up or added that of another."[16] Single fine performances were remembered, but so were incidents that had incurred Marshall's disfavor, and woe betide anyone whose name became linked in his mind with the latter. Colonel James A. Van Fleet (who later commanded United Nations forces in Korea) was said to have been held back because Marshall confused his name with another that sounded similar.

But Marshall saw to it that rapid advance, and the test of increasing challenge, went forward for those he had singled out to lead the citizen-soldiers when the time came. The case of Dwight David Eisenhower is representative. Between November 1940 and January 1942, he was in succession executive officer of the 15th Infantry Regiment, chief of staff of the 3d Division, chief of staff of IX Corps, chief of staff of Third Army, and finally assistant chief of the War Plans Division, where he served directly under Marshall's watchful eye until his truly meteoric rise was about to begin. Eisenhower's rapid progress was deserved, but the possibility of it had been planned for.

Marshall liked to have men around him who were willing to make decisions without waiting to be told what to do; they were not only permitted but expected to contradict him when they disagreed. He disliked the telephone and used it as seldom as possible. He did not want to have papers read aloud, or presentations made by anyone who was not prepared to recommend a line of action and defend it. He tired of the inarticulate briefings of his regular staff section officers and told them to go find "three or four bright young men that can talk, lawyers, teachers, or somebody," and have them condense the subjects he needed information about into ten-minute summations to be given in his office every day at 9 A.M. He was proud of these morning show-and-tell sessions, which gave him a sense of being on top of worldwide problems before the full working day began, and he found them useful to convey to visitors the depth and breadth of the Army's responsibilities, the fact (as he put it to one of them) that the "map extends all the way around the world and not to just one corner of it."[17]

He would quickly run through his mail and the contents of his in box, indicating actions to be taken or replies to be drafted. When papers were brought to him for his approval, he would almost automatically reach for a pen and start noting comments and suggestions, an education for those who endured it in how to arrive at direct and simple English, and a way of putting his own mark on whatever bore his signature. Eisenhower once came out of Marshall's office and announced in triumph, "By God, I finally wrote one he didn't change!"[18] If a paper was intended for the President, Marshall took particular pains over it, filling the margins and spaces between the lines with corrections. By the end of the day his desk was clean. In his opinion, no one ever had an original idea after three o'clock in the afternoon, and whenever he could do so he left the office between four and five.

An example Marshall was fond of giving to prove the importance of staff initiative was the day in early 1940 when Major Walter Bedell Smith came in to interrupt a meeting Marshall was having with some generals, and in a minute or so described the plight of a salesman in his office outside, who had been given the runaround everywhere else in Washington. His company had designed a small, compact, lightweight vehicle with a low silhouette that would carry four or five men and could be manhandled out of mud holes by its passengers, which Smith from his days as an instructor under Marshall at the Infantry School knew could be useful.

"Well, what do you think of it?" asked Marshall. "I think it is good," Smith replied. "Well," said Marshall, "do it." Thus did the lowly jeep—the "light truck, ¼ ton, 4 × 4, command," to give its proper name—enter the U.S. Army and its place in history as the most practical, adaptable, and everywhere beloved means of transportation the war produced. By the end of 1945, over 634,000 of them had been delivered to the Ordnance Department that had initially rejected the idea (almost twenty thousand more went to the Allies and the other services, for a wartime total of 653,568).[19]

◆

General Marshall had no officer aide; he did not want one and seemed not to need one, perhaps because Sergeant Powder was so much more than an orderly. Powder was six foot four and three quarters and sturdy. ("Powder" was the anglicization of a Polish original; his great-great-grandfather had gone to Russia with Napoleon and he himself had enlisted in 1914 by lying about his age; he was the assigned driver to the deputy chief of staff when Marshall got the job.) Marshall many times offered Powder a commission as a captain or major and he as often declined, pleading that his lack of education might discredit the general. (He may also have realized that he already possessed in quantity those abilities to get things done outside normal channels that are granted to sergeants but denied to captains.)

Powder smoothed the general's way in innumerable details. He saw to it that Marshall was kept supplied with the paperback books called Armed Services Editions and that there was a candy bar at his bedside; when Marshall could not sleep, Powder doubled as masseur. On trips, Marshall liked to have Powder quartered nearby. Once, in Europe, a major responsible for billeting ignored Powder's suggestion that the general might not approve and located him at a distance with the enlisted men, a mistake shortly corrected by an extremely contrite officer. When Roosevelt died, Marshall put Powder in charge of the men who accompanied the coffin along the route from the White House to the Capitol, and it is Powder who can be seen in the photographs marching tall behind the caisson.

Colonel Frank McCarthy, a reservist and a VMI graduate, was the closest to an aide among Marshall's officers; McCarthy arranged his visits, normally accompanied him, and was in other respects invaluable. Many served with Marshall and then went on to combat assignments overseas: Orlando Ward, J. Lawton Collins, Maxwell Taylor, Matthew Ridgway, and of course Bradley and Eisenhower. At one time or another, Marshall had those on his staff who were known for better or worse as hatchet men. "Beetle" Smith capably filled this role in 1941–42—abrading nerve endings, hacking his way through red tape, tossing out tradition to make room for effective organization—until Eisenhower persuaded Marshall to let Smith come to Europe and do the same there for him.

Another was Colonel (later General) Joseph T. McNarney, a tough-minded Air Corps officer who as deputy chief of staff conspicuously knocked heads together during Marshall's floor-shaking and window-rattling reorganization of the Army in 1942. (At McNarney's first meeting with Marshall, he was astonished to see a subordinate express disapproval of a change Marshall was proposing; McNarney learned the lesson.) A third was Brigadier (later Lieutenant) General Brehon B. Somervell, who became Marshall's G-4 (that is, staff man for supply) in November 1941 and then head of the newly created Army Service Forces. Somervell was an engineer, an empire-builder, and a born expediter, who increasingly relieved the Chief of Staff of the burdens connected with industrial procurement. "He was efficient," Marshall said of Somervell. "He shook the cobwebs out of their pants."[20]

Behind the regular duty assignments that made Marshall's office run smoothly there were others just as necessary but less visible. One officer was routinely assigned to listen to Bernard Baruch, who was not important but had somehow convinced people in high places (Churchill among them) that he was, and thus had to be accommodated. Another was deputized to answer inquiries from Mrs. Roosevelt, who *was* important and often raised questions about the treatment of black troops, which Marshall wanted answered promptly (the rule was that this be done within twenty-four hours).

Still another officer was instructed to keep Pa Watson in the White House happy. Watson had a weakness for trying to end-run Marshall by suggesting to the staff that the President wanted something done they needn't "bother" the general with. Once Watson summoned Colonel McCarthy and said the President would like Fiorello La Guardia to be made a brigadier general and that "if you can just put this through you wouldn't have to worry General Marshall about it." McCarthy sagely replied that he wouldn't dare do such a thing "without telling General Marshall first," and that was the end of the end run.[21]

Many functions were filled by Marshall's own qualities. He was his own best liaison with Congress and the press; no one could have dealt with either better than he. As for his nominal boss, the secretary of war, he and Stimson were cut of similar cloth, matched in character and in sense of duty. Their offices were immediately adjacent and the door between them was never closed; they disagreed on occasion but together they gave a singleness of purpose to the uneasy mix of civil and military rarely seen before or since, and at the end Stimson paid Marshall a tribute that reduced hardened officers to tears. Most critical of all, Marshall formed if not a friendship at least a working truce with Admiral King.

A spirit of intense competitiveness and mistrust between the U.S. Army and the U.S. Navy had been allowed (and even encouraged) to grow beyond a point British observers of it found credible. "The violence of inter-Service rivalry in the United States," wrote Sir John Slessor, who was there, "had to be seen to be believed and was an appreciable handicap to their war effort." (Admiral Cunningham noted the same.)[22] Marshall and King between them tried, at Marshall's initiative, to eliminate this from their own dealings with each other.

Early in 1942, King came to Marshall's office for a talk (Marshall was the senior) and had to be kept waiting; Marshall was closeted with Herbert Evatt, the hot-tempered foreign minister of Australia, who took some handling and more time than had been provided for. King departed in a rage. When Marshall found what had happened, he went immediately to King's office, explained the situation, and assured King that he had no intention of being rude. He went on: "I think this is very important. Because if you or I begin fighting at the very start of the war, what in the world will the public have to say about us? . . . We can't afford to fight. So we ought to find a way to get along together." After a pause, King told Marshall that it was magnanimous of him to have come there. "We will see if we can't get along," said King, "and I think we can."[23]

Eventually, in conversation if not on paper, it was "Ernie" and "George." After the war, King wrote Marshall to reciprocate some "generous" remarks Marshall had made about their four years of association. "We have had our differing points of view," said King, "—even strong ones— but the end-result of our team-work speaks for itself." In 1944, an Army general just back from Iceland sent word to Marshall that on the docks there, Army-Navy cooperation was known as doing "a Marshall-King," which Marshall passed on to King and King returned with the characteristically terse: "Thank you. E.J.K."

Often during the war they seemed to treat interservice squabbling as though they were the benign parents of unruly offspring. Just before the landing in North Africa, one of its commanders, General Patton, wrote to Marshall saying that he had been "shown the utmost co-operation and the finest spirit" by the Navy. "I desire to bring this to your attention," Patton added, "because prior to leaving I had some doubts. These doubts have been removed." Marshall had also sent this to King and it had also been returned with thanks, plus the mocking query: "Why not?!?"[24]

Marshall's quality was invariable. At war's beginning, the Hollywood director Frank Capra (*It Happened One Night, Mr. Deeds Comes to Town, Lost Horizon,* etc.) was commissioned a major in the Signal Corps to make army films. To his surprise, he was summoned to the office of the Chief of Staff and given the usual instructions: Walk in, don't salute, sit down, wait until he's finished whatever he's doing. Marshall then explained the reason for the interview: he wanted the American soldier to understand what the war was about.

He was dissatisfied with "the mediocre and tiresome talks by officers" (as he later described them to the President) that were then intended to serve the purpose, and he sketched out his idea for the documentary films that under Capra's hand were to become the "Why We Fight" series, shown throughout the Army, vivid and realistic recountings of the rise of the dictators. Capra said he would do his best, but the general should know that he was a feature-film director, and had never made a documentary in his life.

"Capra," said Marshall, "I have never been Chief of Staff before."[25]

◆

Why did Roosevelt pick him? The reasons could have been many, and the weight given to each in the President's mind is unknowable, but a cluster of reasonable assumptions can be drawn around them. For one thing, the choice was not so wide as Marshall's low place on the rank list made it appear. Among his seniors, not all were eligible and not all were serious contenders. There was a proviso that no one be appointed Chief of Staff who could not serve out a four-year term before retirement, and this removed all but four of the thirty-three, leaving Marshall fifth. The four ahead of him were Hugh Drum, John DeWitt, Frank Rowlell, and Walter Krueger; of these, DeWitt was overly identified with logistics, Rowlell had no energetic supporters, and Krueger was handicapped by his German birth, which left Drum—the most senior officer in the Army, with powerful political connections in New York—as the strongest competition. There were those—among them, John C. O'Laughlin, publisher of the *Army-Navy Journal*—who thought Drum a shoo-in.

Of course, it was always possible that Roosevelt might name a younger man. When he left for Warm Springs in April, he asked the outgoing Chief of Staff, Malin Craig, to prepare him a list of the eligibles, and Craig added four more, who were junior even to Marshall (Grunert, Benedict, Ridley, and Chaffee), to the first five. Craig thought Roosevelt might reach still further down the line and choose someone like Daniel I. Sultan, whom Craig believed to have Pa Watson's backing (Sultan commanded what was left of the Burma-India theater after Stilwell's dismissal in 1944). Washington throve on the customary rumors, in which Marshall's fortunes seemed to wax and wane. Throughout he conducted himself with shrewdness and tact. He did not press his case and discouraged many from doing so on his behalf where he judged that their approach to Roosevelt might not be welcome (this in contrast to Drum, who promoted himself endlessly and ultimately beyond the limits of the President's patience).

Solidly behind Marshall was General John J. Pershing, by then an invalid but still a figure to be reckoned with if only because of the President's respect for him. Pershing had been advancing Marshall's cause for years. In 1935, Roosevelt had written then–Secretary of War George Dern: "General Pershing asks very strongly that Colonel George C. Marshall (Infantry) be promoted to general. Can we put him on the list of next promotions?"[26] But then–Chief of Staff Douglas MacArthur blocked the idea, arguing that Marshall should wait for an opening as chief of infantry (which never came, though not directly MacArthur's fault). Pershing's part in Marshall's eventual selection may not have been so great as some believed (Drum afterward blamed Pershing for his own losing out), but he was certainly essential in the negative sense; his opposition would have ended Marshall's candidacy. As it happened, Pershing's voice joined others to which the President was disposed to listen.

Of these, the most decisive by far was that of Harry Hopkins. It would not be fair to say (as some of his partisan critics have said) that Marshall was a New Deal general, but it is true that he had a better understanding than most Army officers of the conditions with which the Roosevelt administrations were trying to cope. Chicago at the time he went there with the National Guard in 1934 was in deep depression; in Cook County, 150,000 families were out of work and without help; there were rumblings of violence among the unemployed and panic among the business leaders. Marshall knew that there were other ways of proceeding than panic. He had personally experienced the New Deal in the form of the Civilian Conservation Corps.

When Roosevelt first proposed the CCC in 1933, to get jobless young men out of the cities and into the countryside, at work on conservation and reforestation, it had not been anticipated that the Army would have much to do with them. But only the Army proved capable of receiving, housing, feeding, and organizing the hundreds of thousands of volunteers—their total was ultimately to be 2.5 million—who passed through the CCC camps (most stayed six months to a year, and flourished there). Marshall was one of the few officers who threw himself into the task of running the

CCCs with some sense of the Army's stake in these, its future citizen-soldiers, and of what could be done for the sullen, slouching rejects of urban indifference when they were provided decent food, exercise, medical care, and something worth doing to do in the American outdoors. By the time he was done, Marshall had set up and supervised some nineteen CCC camps throughout the Southeast. He called this "the most instructive service I have ever had, and the most interesting," and expressed his opinion that the CCC was "the best antidote for mental stagnation that an army officer in my position can have."[27]

Marshall was also one of the few who realized how much the Works Progress Administration and the Public Works Administration, the former under Hopkins, had done for the Army. (Parenthetically, PWA funds, at Roosevelt's insistence, had built two aircraft carriers, *Enterprise* and *Yorktown,* for the Navy.) When he became deputy chief of staff, Marshall had asked to be told the total WPA and PWA expenditures on Army projects, which turned out to be $250 million, about equal to the annual War Department budget over the previous fifteen years. Marshall was displeased to discover how little advantage had been taken of the opportunities offered by the relief programs; "but it seemed that some of the aging generals," wrote Hopkins's biographer, Sherwood, "had been too afraid of the Congressional criticism they might incur if they became involved in dealings with such vulgar, radical fellows as Hopkins." Sherwood added: "Marshall himself never had any such qualms."[28]

Marshall and Hopkins really got to know one another in late 1938, when Hopkins was made secretary of commerce and became involved with aircraft production. An officer who had accompanied him on an inspection tour of West Coast manufacturing plants told Marshall that Hopkins was the key to getting more appropriations for the Army into the next relief bill. After Christmas, Hopkins sent word that he would like to come see him, and Marshall, as was his practice, went instead to Hopkins's office.

Their discussion of an hour or more covered the national defense in comprehensive terms and revealed to Hopkins a state of unpreparedness far worse than he had realized; he was shocked. He urged Marshall to go to the President at Hyde Park or in Warm Springs and repeat what he had just said, but Marshall, as again was his practice, declined. (He sensed the hazards in Roosevelt's beguiling informality and shied away from it; he did not go to Hyde Park until the President's funeral.) Hopkins was impressed, however, which proved to be the important thing.

Marshall thought it to his advantage that he was known to the National Guard, the Reserve Corps, the ROTC, and of course the Regular Army, though not to the general public. Probably this was true, but what the President essentially had to go on was his own observation of Marshall's no-nonsense independence of mind plus opinions in which he could place confidence that came from the quintessential New Dealer and from the nation's foremost soldier.

It was an exercise in triangulation of the kind that politics regularly affords. Marshall fell within the angles of favorable judgment by all three, and the fact that he was endorsed by *both* Harry Hopkins and John J. Pershing said something about him that could not be said of any other candidate, certainly not of Hugh Drum. Marshall was the right choice, not that this detracts from the credit Roosevelt deserves for making it. (The thought of what might have happened had he chosen otherwise should be a subject for meditation; Drum would have led a very different Army and fought a very different war.)

Marshall was called to the White House on Sunday, April 23, arriving at 3:25 P.M. and staying for forty minutes in the President's study. Roosevelt had informed no one else, not even the secretary of war. "It was an interesting interview," Marshall said later; it must have been. He told Roosevelt that he would want to speak his mind without hesitation and that this might not always be pleasing.

"Is that all right?" Marshall asked. The President naturally said yes and so Marshall added: "You said *yes* pleasantly but it may be unpleasant."[29] Before leaving, he typically requested that the announcement be delayed until the twenty-seventh so that he would be out of town before the messages of congratulation and the requests for interviews began to pour in. He had intended not even to tell Mrs. Marshall, but she was suffering so miserably from a bad case of poison ivy that he relented.

◆

George Marshall came out of World War I with very clear ideas about what was wrong with the U.S. Army and what should be done about it. These he elaborated over the years in letters, memos, magazine articles, speeches, and finally in testimony before Congress. He began putting them into effect whenever he had the chance, most effectively when he became assistant commandant (i.e., academic head) of the Infantry School at Fort Benning, Georgia.

At Benning, Marshall began the work of metamorphosis on the Army. For the vast forces he was eventually to create, Benning became Mother Church, spinning off disciples and replicate institutions that could carry the Word, center of a True Faith that radiated outward in concentric circles like the ripples on a pond, until they reached every corner of it. The lessons Marshall had learned he taught to his staff and students at Benning, and they in their turn taught the men who taught the men who taught the men who trained the citizen-soldiers in their millions.[30]

In World War I, Marshall had sailed from Hoboken in June 1917 on the first ship of the first convoy of Americans troops. The staff of the 1st Division (on which he served) assembled for the first time on shipboard.

They discovered that the division consisted of units they had never heard of, armed with weapons they knew nothing about, and since radio silence was in effect, they could not communicate with the other ships.

On landing, Marshall found that the various units not only did not have the weapons specified but had even less knowledge of them than he did. The enlisted men consisted of 85 percent recruits who had been issued their rifles on the train to New York. When the division went into action in the fall, it still lacked essential equipment, like field kitchens, and many members of it did not have complete uniforms but were wearing odds and ends they had scrounged from the Allies. These were good men, as Marshall told an American Legion audience in 1938, but "they were not soldiers."[31] If he had anything to do with it, this lack of preparedness would not be repeated.

As a staff officer, Marshall was at the center of American action in France. He wrote the order that first put American troops into the line. He made the dispositions to meet their first German attack and to make the subsequent counterattack. He planned the first American offensive, at Cantigny. He developed plans for the reduction of the Saint-Mihiel salient by seventeen divisions, including artillery preparation; and for a second offensive, on the Meuse-Argonne, sixty miles away, which required him to move 600,000 men and 2,700 field guns over three roads in less than two weeks. (To prepare this last order he was given only a few hours, at the end of which he dictated it—"my best contribution to the war," he later wrote, the only official paper he saved and brought home with him.[32]) He organized the final advance in the Meuse-Argonne, which was followed days later by the Armistice. He then made preparations for marching Third U.S. Army into Germany if the peace negotiations at Paris should fail.

From his vantage point at the right hand of command, Marshall arrived at an "unusual opinion." He perceived something that is obvious once it is stated: The experience of American officers in World War I had been dangerously misleading. They had been given a brief, frantic, and narrowly circumscribed exposure to a very special form of warfare: the final phases of a static or semi-siege campaign.

Everything they encountered was neatly in place: a maze of fixed trenches and gun emplacements in carefully worked out sectors, masses of artillery, huge supply dumps, and miles of narrow-gauge railroad to bring food and ammunition forward. Maps and aerial photographs showed every enemy position; the opposing units, their numbers and their history, were known in detail. All of this spared the Americans the consequences of their ignorance and their worst mistakes, and encouraged that tendency toward the elaborate and the time-consuming which lurks beneath the surface of every military organization. Field orders became long and complicated, and so much care went into their perfecting that they frequently arrived too late to have any effect.

Fortunate indeed were we, Marshall thought, not to have met the Germans in the opening stages of a war of movement, when, with high morale and adequate reserves, they were on the offensive. Mobile warfare belonged to a different universe from that of the trenches. We had no live contact with the conditions of it, in which chaos is normal. "It is," Marshall later said in a lecture at Benning, "a cloud of uncertainties, haste, rapid movements, congestion on the roads, strange terrain, lack of ammunition and supplies at the right places at the right moment, failures of communication, terrific tests of endurance, and misunderstandings in direct proportion to the inexperience of the officers and the aggressive action of the enemy."

Add to this a minimum of information, poor maps, and the constantly changing circumstances brought about by fast-moving troops, and you had a kind of war we knew nothing about, one that had been fought in Belgium and northern France in 1914 (and would be—with a vengeance, of course —in 1940). Marshall thought that Pershing's attempts to train the A.E.F. in mobile warfare tactics, over the opposition of the "battle-wise" British and French, was among his most courageous decisions and a high point in the A.E.F.'s history. But the fact was, as Marshall wrote in the *Infantry Journal* in 1921, that we remained "without modern experience in the first phases of a war."[33]

The conviction grew on Marshall that complexity and formalized thinking, as aftereffects of World War I, were being built into the American Army by the way schools like Benning were training its officers. The standard five-paragraph field order—the essential instrument of command in combat—was the particular object of his dissatisfaction. Once, in China, during a field exercise, he found a young officer sitting on a canal bank trying to draft a formal order for seventy men to attack the flank of a hostile force; the officer had been at this so long that the opportunity for the attack had long since vanished. "The man was no fool," Marshall wrote to a friend, "but he had been taught an absurd system. . . . I learned that he had stood first at Benning, and I then and there formed an intense desire to get my hands on Benning."[34]

Marshall's opportunity came in 1927. In the five years that followed, as assistant commandant he was given substantial freedom to shape Benning's course offerings and methods of teaching, and shape them he did. It was a struggle, writes Forrest Pogue, "against a kind of military scholasticism," against prevailing theory and the even tenor of the ways in which it was embedded. Marshall proceeded slowly, less by edict than by example, but in the end he had transformed the place. Field exercises he set up emphasized the unexpected, the inadequacy of information, the need for prompt decision.

"Study the first six months of the next war" was his dictum, and again and again he preached the lesson of simplicity. A citizen army was not going to have more than a few highly trained officers; the rest must be able to reduce battlefield problems to their essentials, to think about them clearly, and to issue clear orders. "I insist," Marshall wrote, "we must . . . expunge the bunk, complications, and ponderosities; we must concentrate on registering in men's minds certain vital considerations . . . a technique and methods so simple that the citizen officers of good common sense can readily grasp the idea."[35]

In logistics and supply, when Marshall arrived at Benning, the manual of instruction ran to one hundred and twenty pages, and the demonstration of it took three days. He had that cut back to twelve pages and half a day, and the course went from the least to one of the most popular. Open discussion was encouraged regardless of rank. Any student who demonstrated unorthodoxy could be certain of Marshall's approval; by his order, an answer to a problem that ran radically counter to the approved solution but showed creative thought was required to be published to the class. He made Major Omar Bradley head of the Weapons Section and Bradley totally eliminated an elaborate communications system that had previously been thought necessary. The position in charge of the Tactical Section he held open until he could get the hard-driving, imaginative man he wanted, Lieutenant Colonel Joseph W. Stilwell.

All in all, some two hundred future general officers of World War II and after were either students or teachers at Benning during Marshall's time there. Pogue lists only the familiar names: Bradley, Collins, Ridgway, Decker, Stilwell, Bolté, Dahlquist, Almond, Van Fleet, Huebner, Paul, Bedell Smith, Bull, Terry Allen, Leven Allen, Eddy, Cota, Moore, Hull, Cook, Timberman, Hilldring, Lanham, John R. Deane, and William Dean—Marshall's men.[36]

The Benning years were lonely ones for Marshall. His first wife, to whom he was deeply devoted, had died two months before his assignment there. To fill his days, he threw himself into not only the duty but also the off-duty activities of his officers and their wives. He organized hunts, competitive night rides, pageants, games, amateur theatricals; from October to April there were hunts about twice a week. His pageants were held for visiting dignitaries instead of formal military reviews, which he found boring. But diversion for him, writes Pogue, "was only another form of busyness." He lost weight, and a nervous tic that turned up a corner of his mouth grew more noticeable. The pressure on him to relieve emptiness affected others, for whom so much distraction was not always welcome and who, says Pogue, "would gladly have settled for a short period of ennui."[37] Out of his hearing they called him "Uncle George."

Marshall's loneliness ended in 1929. At dinner in Columbus, he was introduced to a widow and sometime actress, Katherine Boyce Tupper Brown, a tall and handsome woman. He offered to drive her home to the house where she was visiting, taking nearly an hour to do so and covering most of the city, which she remarked that he seemed not to know very well. Marshall replied that if he did not know it well he would not have been able to keep going so long without passing her street.

By the spring of 1930, they were close enough to engaged that Mrs. Brown wanted to be certain her children approved, especially twelve-year-old Allen, and she invited Marshall to visit them on Fire Island. He shortly received a note: "I hope you will come to Fire Island. Don't be nervous, it is O.K. with me. A friend in need is a friend indeed. Allen Brown."[38] On October 15, Marshall and Katherine Brown were married, with General Pershing as best man.

On May 29, 1944, Second Lieutenant Allen Tupper Brown, leading a tank platoon in the breakout from the Anzio beachhead, was killed by a German sniper.

II

There have always been conflicting schools of thought about what an American army ought to be like. We came out of our Revolution having learned two lessons: (1) an armed citizenry could stand off European professionals, but (2) it could win victory only by meeting professional standards. One side remembered Concord, Bunker Hill, and Saratoga; the other Brandywine, Monmouth, Yorktown. Afterward Washington, remembering three of these and more, proposed a cadre or skeletal-core system for an expansible army, which in effect is what was used in World War II.

Hamilton wanted a "military university" and made the case for professionalism as ably as it has been put. "May we not," he wrote, "as well calculate to be commodiously lodged, and have the science of building improved, by employing every man in the community in the construction of houses, and by excluding from society as useless, architects, masons, and carpenters?" Jefferson, predictably, wished to rely on the sturdy yeoman farmer for the national defense and said, of the civil-military distinction, "it is for the happiness of both to obliterate it."[39] (Paradoxically, it was Jefferson who founded West Point.)

The difficulty has been that both sides are at least partly right, so that the argument has swung back and forth and refused to resolve itself. The Civil War produced for each view an intelligent exponent with impressive credentials: Emory Upton for the professionals and John A. Logan for the amateurs. Both were brave and experienced veterans who had held high command. Upton argued that the Civil War had been needlessly prolonged by civilian incompetence, Logan that military ability comes not from education but from inherent talent, as countless Americans—Nathanael Greene preeminently—have demonstrated. They tended toward extremes: Upton wanted to remove control by President and Congress over the military, Logan to abolish West Point and Annapolis.

But with the dominance of Germany in late-nineteenth-century Europe, the case for professionalism acquired greater persuasiveness (just as German methods entered American academic life during the same period), and disciples of Upton like John M. Schofield and Elihu Root achieved authority and influence. In 1904, Root while secretary of war had Upton's *The Military Policy of the United States* reprinted as a government document, and Upton's elitist approach became orthodoxy for many American officers. After World War I, however, the debate erupted again, with Marshall in the midst of it.

A good friend of Marshall's was Colonel John McAuley Palmer (he had been on Pershing's staff and had commanded a brigade in the Meuse-Argonne). Palmer was the son of a Civil War officer who had risen from a political appointment by pure ability to command as a general with Thomas at Chickamauga. Young Palmer devoted a career to campaigning for an army of citizen-soldiers like his father. In 1919, he had testified before Congress and so impressed the Senate Military Affairs Committee that they requested his assignment to them as an adviser. Palmer's ideas struck the senators as more politically appealing than the Uptonian elitism then coming from the War Department, and thus Palmer played a major part in shaping the National Defense Act of 1920.

"The form of military institutions," Palmer wrote, "must be determined on political grounds, with due regard to national genius and tradition," a philosophy to which Pershing and Marshall could willingly subscribe. "Palmer," Marshall wrote to the superintendent of VMI in 1929, "is the most exact and painstaking military student in the army today." In a lecture to the Army War College in 1923, Marshall had said, "We are attempting a new mission, a new problem, utterly different from that of the past. . . . [W]e are frankly engaged in creating a citizen force."[40] In 1940, Palmer and Marshall worked together in framing and gathering support for the Selective Training and Service Act, the draft.

The U.S. Army George Marshall took over in September 1939 was a threat to nobody; it stood *nineteenth* in the world, with a meager total of 174,000 men, ahead of Bulgaria but just behind Portugal. Its "divisions" were half under strength and dispersed in scattered posts, with virtually no opportunity to train as units; joint maneuvers were held only every fourth year and lasted two weeks at the outside. "During the lean years . . . ," Marshall wrote in 1940, "the Army's fight for personnel was a fight for its very life."[41]

Marshall could remember commanding a post in which its so-called infantry battalion, in principle consisting of over eight hundred men, could muster only two hundred when all the cooks, clerks, and kitchen police were counted in. Equipment, "modern" by 1919 standards at the latest, was hopelessly obsolete and inadequate. Marshall was himself no interventionist; until the early fall of 1941, he had serious reservations about American entry into the war.[42] But if war did come, it was his responsibility to prepare an army capable of fighting it, and to that task —over the opposition of the Navy, the Air Corps, the Lend-Lease Administration, the British, the isolationists, the newspaper columnists, the Congress, and (by no means last) the President—he gave his best effort.

Incredible as it now must seem, antipathy to Marshall's endeavor remained, until a very late date, the fashionable viewpoint. Less than three months before Pearl Harbor, in September 1941, Walter Lippmann entitled one of his columns for the *Herald Tribune* "The Case for a Smaller Army." Lippmann, who was widely read and respected, argued that "the effort to raise such a large army so quickly is not merely unnecessary but undesirable." It was, he thought, "the cancer which obstructs national unity, causes discontent which subversive elements exploit, and weakens the primary measures of our defense, which are the lend-lease program and the naval policy. . . . [A] surgical operation is indicated—an operation to shrink the Army." Similar sentiments were so widespread that later in the month Roosevelt, wanting more supplies for Russia, asked Marshall to the White House to discuss a possible reduction in the Army's size.[43]

Lack of enthusiasm for a large American army was a matter not only of competition for scarce resources (though that figured in it hugely) but also of principle, of strategy, of doctrine. In some quarters of advanced opinion, the lesson of the German blitzkrieg had been misread to prove that the day of mass land levies was over, that the future belonged to small, mobile, and heavily armed spearheads operating in conjunction with a lightly armed but aroused and rebellious population—the "peoples' war" that Tom Wintringham had forecast in *The Story of Weapons and Tactics.*[44] There would be no "front" as such, no repetition of the murderous and strategically mindless trench warfare of World War I. At the center of British thinking about the war, unstated but incontrovertible, was the proposition that Paschendaele or the Somme in 1916 (where Britain suffered 57,000 casualties, 19,000 killed, in a single day![45]) must never, never be allowed to occur again.

It is useful to recall that during the early stages of World War II, when American belief in the planned concentration of power encountered British belief in indirection and improvisation, the British military had no conceptual image of what George Marshall's handiwork was going to look like, of how armed warriors would spring from the American soil almost on order and an army of 174,000 become, in a handful of years, one of 8.25 million. Neither Churchill nor Eden then wanted a large American army, certainly not at the price of cutting down on munitions supply to the United Kingdom, and British strategy as late as the fall of 1943 included an assumption that a major land campaign on the European continent might not be necessary. Even after that campaign had been fought to its victorious conclusion in 1945, by an Allied force of ninety divisions in which sixty were American, there were still British observers (Churchill among them) who could not fathom where so many trained American formations had come from.

The means that Marshall employed to bring about his miracle were principally four: (1) establishing control over the promotion and retirement of Regular Army officers, (2) generating manpower in quantity by initiating and continuing the draft, (3) teaching new recruits in large numbers through the service schools and the cadre system, and (4) fighting for budgetary increases past the President and the Congress. All four were interrelated, all benefited from Marshall's endless attention to detail, and all required him to enlarge himself and his capabilities in proportion to the mighty military engine he was constructing.

Those who understood the extent to which this was his own personal creation were few; one of them was Dwight Eisenhower. "I think you should make a visit here at the earliest possible moment," Eisenhower wrote to Marshall from his advance headquarters at Rheims in April 1945, "while we are still conducting a general offensive. You would be proud of the Army you have produced . . . you would be struck by the 'veteran' quality of the whole organization. [All] go about their business in a perfectly calm and sure manner . . . you could see, in visible form, the fruits of much of your work over the past five years."[46]

◆

Essential to Marshall's purpose had been the quality of his regular officer corps. "We must have these leaders," he told a congressional committee in April 1940, "and they will not be developed under the present system." Under the National Defense Act, regular officers who failed to demonstrate adequate leadership or physical fitness could be eliminated only by "reclassification," a cumbersome procedure that took over six months and was accordingly shunned by senior commanders (an average of less than eight a year were being reclassified of the fourteen thousand regular officers in 1940). Marshall got a bill through Congress setting up a board to remove the unfit and authorizing the secretary of war to carry out its recommendations.

The Army's prewar promotions policy had operated by seniority, and a special obstacle was posed by the large numbers (more than a third of the total) who had entered the service in World War I and stayed on, filling the middle grades and holding back those beneath them; more than a thousand whose age and length of service qualified them to be lieutenant colonels were still captains. Marshall got a bill introduced in Congress changing this, but it was pigeonholed by the chairman of the House Military Affairs Committee because of pressure from officers Marshall did not plan to promote. With the help of Senator James Byrnes of South Carolina, the bill was redrafted as an amendment to an appropriations act and sailed through without objection. "In Congress nothing just happens," said Byrnes, "somebody must make it happen." Byrnes later recalled Marshall's telling him this was the legislation that enabled Marshall to jump Eisenhower over the heads of more than 350 officers his senior.[47]

With the draft—or conscription, or selective service, or whatever you choose to name it—Marshall adopted a different tactic entirely. He believed it would be a mistake for him to take the initiative (he was also sensitive to the President's disbelief in the likelihood of popular support for a draft, especially in the Middle West). "I wanted it to come from others . . . ," Marshall later said. "If I could get civilians of great prominence to take the lead . . . then I could take up the cudgels and work it out."[48] A civilian of unquestioned prominence did come forward, in the person of Grenville Clark, a New York lawyer and champion of numerous good causes, who had helped set up the Plattsburg training camp for future officers in World War I and now in the spring of 1940 gave his energy and distinction to the cause of universal military training. The outcome of his intervention, without public backing from either the War Department or the White House, was the Burke-Wadsworth bill of June 1940, introduced just as the French signed an armistice with Nazi Germany; it provided for a year of service by 1,400,000 men, plus the incorporation into federal service of the National Guard.

Thus freed up to speak, Marshall testified again and again before Congress on behalf of the Burke-Wadsworth bill. Opposition was intense and the President, preoccupied by his campaign for a third term, held himself aloof. But the stunning German victory over France was having its effect. Public opinion began to swing strongly in the direction of the draft; two weeks before Congress acted, the proportion in favor had reached 71 percent. In July, Roosevelt publicly announced his support; he was followed a few weeks later by the Republican presidential candidate, Wendell Willkie. In mid-September the bill was passed, and two days later, in the appropriate White House ceremony, the President signed it. The thing was done: Marshall would have the men to make his army.

When the time came for the draft to be renewed a year later, Marshall sought still another device to have his influence felt. It had been the custom for the Chief of Staff to make an annual report, a dull document deservedly unread. Marshall converted it into an instrument of advocacy, a forty-page exposition (with clear maps and charts) of how the Army had grown to eight times its size of two years earlier but how this newly acquired strength would vanish if the reservists and the selectees did not remain. This time congressional resistance was even fiercer than before; one of Marshall's liaison officers reported the remark of a congressional secretary that in forty years on the Hill he had never seen such fear of a bill. In the judgment of Marshall's biographer, it was only the high regard in which he was held by congressmen that saved—by a single vote—the draft extension. "Marshall acted and talked the way they believed a leader should . . . ," writes Forrest Pogue; "there was no denying that [his] firmness and personal standing had provided the slim margin of victory."[49]

Marshall's deeply held conviction about training these recruits he had been granted was that it must be sequential and progressive: from individual to organization, from organization to ever larger organization—companies, battalions, regiments, divisions. The citizen-soldiers must be given what they needed in the way of skills to handle weapons and other military equipment with self-confidence, to become soldiers not by rote or automated routine but by understanding of what it was a soldier did. In this he was aided by the existence of a whole series of service schools—one for each of the combat and service arms—and by a teaching tradition that emphasized a hands-on approach long before that phrase became a cliché. There were men in the Army who were not strictly speaking literate, in the more exquisite meanings of that word, but they could teach you how to assemble and disassemble a thirty-caliber machine gun in your sleep.

The old army was somehow gripped in a symbiosis with the new in which its best qualities were preserved and passed on. The peacetime corporals and sergeants, in their faded blue-denim fatigues, bullied and cajoled the baggy-green-suited newcomers into becoming soldiers in spite of themselves.[50] Over this transformation brooded the presence of the Depression, which had given gainful employment (and "three squares a day") some meaning, and had kept men in the service who might otherwise have left it, officers not least. Cohorts of West Point classes in the boom 1920s were decimated as its graduates departed for more lucrative activity, but after 1929 this leakage stopped. Young officers and their families lived simply in plain quarters, and if the circumstances of a bare-bones army post did not directly conduce to integrity of character, they at least did not discourage it. Later the memory of life on those dry parade grounds during the Depression years gave the Army under Marshall a certain dusty dignity that eludes recapture. Marshall was also aided by the man he chose to train his hastily militarized civilians.

Lieutenant General Lesley J. McNair was one of the least noticeable officers that the Army brought to high command. Chief Warrant Officer E. J. Kahn, Jr., labored dutifully in a *New Yorker* profile to make McNair interesting and succeeded only by stressing the *ordinariness* of the man. McNair neither played a spirited game of bridge nor engaged in offhand banter with enlisted men. "Aside from an active dislike of the common fly," wrote Kahn, "against the possible sorties of which he always kept a swatter not only in his office but in his car as well, General McNair had none of these endearing quirks." Mostly he worked, arriving at his office at eight in the morning after a half-mile walk and staying until six-thirty at night, when he packed his briefcase with papers and took them home for further perusal. When he was killed in Normandy, one of our only two lieutenant general casualties, the *Army and Navy Journal* could not even get his name straight and several times misspelled it. "One way is as good as another," McNair had said when this happened before. Marshall described him as "the brains of the Army," and when McNair came upon this in a history being written of the Army Ground Forces, which he commanded, he struck it out.

McNair was a bantam cock of a Scotsman from Minnesota, with more than a usual willingness to define the soldier's job as killing the enemy, an emphasis that did not sit well with civilians for whom the bloody side of war was best left unrecognized. McNair, like Marshall, piously believed in the primacy of the foot soldier. "Our Army is no better than its infantry," said McNair in 1943, "and victory will come only when and as our infantry gains it; the price will be predominantly what the infantry pays. These days the entire nation is following operations on its war maps. It is to be noted that the front lines of these maps are simply where the infantryman is. It is true that he is supported magnificently by artillery and air, but this support is behind and above him. There is nothing in front of him but the enemy." McNair liked to describe himself as no more than a "pick-and-shovel man," but of course he was anything but. One associate said McNair reminded him of a "Presbyterian pulpit speaker—all irony and intellect."[51]

McNair believed in moving from the generalized to the specific. First for the draftee came basic training, a thirteen-week program as simple as the name implied: physical conditioning, close-order drill, day and night marches and bivouacs, rifle practice, elementary map reading, and so on. Then might come the move to a unit or any one of the many noncommissioned-officer schools, according to individual aptitudes or army need. The Infantry School at Benning taught some thirty different courses to over 50,000 officers and 25,000 enlisted men—courses in communications, motor vehicles, air liaison, radio repair, artillery mechanics, sound locating, explosives, mines, booby traps, and so on and on—in addition to the 63,000 officer candidates it successfully converted into second lieutenants: the ninety-day wonders, instant officers and gentlemen (the officer candidate schools had been set up by Marshall, over the objections of his staff).[52] Counting the schools of the other combat arms—Armored, Antiaircraft, Field and Coast Artillery, Cavalry, Parachute, and Tank Destroyer—a total of 138,000 officers, 136,000 officer candidates, and 295,000 enlisted men were graduated. (Similar schools were maintained by the service forces: Engineer, Signal, Transportation, Quartermaster.) On McNair's lead all became mass-production teaching enterprises.

McNair invented the scheme for creating new divisions. Two and a half months before the date of activation, he and Marshall would appoint the commanding general and two brigadiers, who would then report to Washington for instructions. They (with advice from Marshall and McNair) would choose their principal subordinates and staff, and this group would be sent to Command & General Staff School at Fort Leavenworth, Kansas, for a refresher course. A "parent" unit would be picked from among the already existing divisions to provide a skeletal core, the cadre, which might be as many as 185 officers and 1,190 enlisted men for a division of 14,000, the remainder being filled up from the products of basic training and the service schools. Variation on the theme: The 82d, an organized reserve unit that had been activated under Omar Bradley in March 1942, was split neatly in half in August to form the 101st and both were redesignated as airborne (these were the two first-rate outfits that jumped in Normandy on D-day eve). Some divisions were gutted again and again, over the surly protests of their commanders, but when the cadre system got going it could produce an average of three or four new divisions a month.[53]

Marshall tried to show the process at work to Churchill and his colleagues at Fort Jackson, South Carolina, in June 1942. They were polite but skeptical; General Sir Hastings "Pug" Ismay, Churchill's personal chief of staff, told Brooke that he thought it would be "murder" to send these young men against German professionals. Churchill was more admiring, though he never did figure it out. "I think it was a prodigy of organization . . . ," he said to a group of American officers in the courtyard of the Pentagon after the war. "It remains to me a mystery as yet unexplained how the very small staffs which the United States kept during the years of peace were able not only to build up the Armies . . . but also to find the leaders . . . [how] you should have been able to preserve the art not only of creating mighty armies almost at the stroke of a wand—but of leading and guiding those armies upon a scale incomparably greater than anything that was prepared for or even dreamed of."[54]

The probability is strong that President Roosevelt, at least at the beginning, did not grasp General Marshall's conception any better than Churchill did. Marshall had to fight for his army over the President's repeated refusals to concede that it was needed. To be sure, there was little enough attraction for Roosevelt, raked as he was by isolationist-interventionist crossfire, in Marshall's obsession with preparedness and with the costs thereunto accruing, in his insistence that an army could be created only over time and not overnight. Marshall wished that Roosevelt, too, might have a chance to observe the training process, and later tried to arrange a visit for him at Fort Belvoir, Virginia—"only forty minutes' drive from the White House"—but without success.[55] Not only did Roosevelt fall prey to Lippmann's thesis of a diminished army, but he had vigorously resisted increases in the army budget at times when they were vital to Marshall's design and, in Marshall's view, to the nation's safety.

In May 1940, Secretary of the Treasury Henry Morgenthau had arranged for Marshall to meet with the President and present the Army's request for a $657 million appropriation, which Morgenthau supported. Roosevelt turned them down flat. "I am not asking you," he said. "I am telling you." Morgenthau answered, "Well, I still think you're wrong," only to have Roosevelt brush him off with, "Well, you've filed your protest." He started to wave them out of his office. "Mr. President," said Morgenthau, "will you hear General Marshall?" Roosevelt again brushed them off. "I know exactly what he would say," was the reply. "There is no necessity for me to hear him at all."[56]

Speak truth to power.

Marshall walked over to the President's chair, looked down at him, and said, "Mr. President, may I have three minutes?" Roosevelt's tone shifted instantly: "Of course, General Marshall." Pogue describes the scene: "His voice sibilant with frustration, anger, and intense concern, Marshall exceeded his allotted time in pouring forth the Army's critical requirements. More money, better organization of production, effective control of defense developments—these were all set before the astonished President, quiet before the force of an unsuspected torrent." Marshall ended: "If you don't do something . . . and do it right away, I don't know what is going to happen to this country."[57]

Marshall always spoke afterward of the President's response to this as the action that broke the logjam. Roosevelt did not dislike men who stood up to him. He asked Marshall to come back the next day with a detailed list, and Marshall drafted a message for the President to send Congress accompanying a budget request that contained much—though, needless to add, not all—he had asked for. So there would be an army, not because Roosevelt willed it, but because Marshall persuaded him of its necessity.

◆

During the summer of 1941, the War Department began to think seriously about what would be required to defeat Germany. Out of these deliberations came a paper called the "Joint Board Estimate of United States Over-all Production Requirements," known for short as the Victory Program, which General Marshall and Admiral Stark signed on September 11, 1941, and Secretaries Stimson and Knox conveyed to the President on September 25. "It is, in my opinion," wrote Robert Sherwood, "one of the most remarkable documents of American history, for it set down the basic strategy of a global war before this country was involved in it." The Victory Program calculated the number of men and the quantity of armament we would need to fight Germany and Japan both, on the assumption that Germany could be beaten only by a major

European land campaign—a reaffirmation of Stark's Plan Dog of the year before. It proved to be impressively accurate. The Victory Program called for an army of 8,795,658 (the eventual figure as of May 31, 1945, was 8,291,336) and gave "the earliest date when US armed forces can be mobilized, trained, and equipped for extensive operations" as July 1, 1943 (we and the British invaded Sicily on July 10, 1943). To the President's question of whether we had what it took to destroy Hitler, the Victory Program answered: Yes.[58]

Roosevelt had written to Stimson and Knox on July 9, asking them to explore "the overall production requirements required to defeat our potential enemies." This letter of his had a "galvanic effect" on both of the military departments (according to Mark Watson), for it gave planning officers the authority they had previously lacked for assembling detailed information from varied sources. But credit must be given to the several others whose growing concern had reached the President, in particular Under Secretary of War Robert P. Patterson and his executive, General James H. Burns, who had been writing memos during the spring with phrases in them that reappear in Roosevelt's letter. Marshall himself, on May 21, had directed the War Plans Division to prepare a "clearcut strategic estimate of our situation from a ground, air, and naval viewpoint" so as to provide a "base of departure" for "increases and changes in armament," a response on his part to needs that officers on his staff already felt.[59]

The principal authors of the Victory Program as a complete package were two, though they worked apart and in different directions: an Army officer and a government economist. The Army officer was Major (later Lieutenant General) Albert C. Wedemeyer of the War Plans Division and the economist was Robert R. Nathan of the Office of Production Management. Wedemeyer, a protégé of Marshall's and a relative newcomer to WPD, had attended the German *Kriegsakademie* in Berlin during 1936–38 and, ironically, brought to the task of overwhelming the Germans their own analytical methods.

"He assembled estimates of the strength and composition of the task forces," wrote the Army historians, "of the theaters of operations to be established, and of the probable dates at which forces would be committed. He thus became one of the first of the Washington staff officers to attempt to calculate what it would cost to mobilize and deploy a big U.S. Army."[60] In this he was guided by the instructions of his chief, Brigadier General Leonard T. Gerow, to think first in terms of a strategic concept, and the military units required by it, rather than in terms of mere numbers that would exceed those available to Germany. Ultimate munitions production should not be adjusted to capacity but to strategy, an approach that momentarily harmonized with Robert Nathan's.

Given Wedemeyer's success in predicting the size of the Army as a whole, it is surprising—though no fault of his—that he went so far astray with its constituent parts. Having to consider the possibility of Britain and Russia being cut down, he posited the number of divisions we would need to fight Germany and Japan on our own at approximately 215, of which 61 would be armored (we eventually fielded 89, of which 16 were armored). He overestimated the number of men needed for antiaircraft at 464,695, as opposed to the actual May 1945 figure of 246,943. In each case he was responding to prevailing conceptions of how the war would be fought which were later modified by experience. He considerably underestimated the numbers that would be needed for service/supply organizations and somewhat underestimated those for the air force, which he had short by 300,000 at 2,000,000.

The way he got the total right was to start with the best estimates of the nation's able-bodied manpower and subtract those who would be preempted by industry and the Navy, leaving the Army with the remainder, an effective if rough-and-ready technique. But with munitions procurement, a method of that kind would not work, as General Gerow indicated in a letter transmitting Wedemeyer's massive study to Assistant Secretary John J. McCloy on September 10. "Ultimate victory over the Axis powers," wrote Gerow, "will place a demand on industry which few have yet conceived."[61] Here was Robert Nathan's province.

Nathan was a big, burly man who looked (Bruce Catton said) like a professional wrestler or a tackle for the Chicago Bears. He had been a New Deal economist brought into the Office of Production Management by Stacy May, director of OPM's Bureau of Research and Statistics (May was a social scientist from the Rockefeller Foundation). May and Nathan shared the views of Sir Arthur Purvis and of Jean Monnet, who were serving on the British Supply Council in North America, and who had been urging the Americans to set their sights high and make bold plans for the use of their industrial resources to overpower the Axis. On September 17, 1941, Donald Nelson—director of the Supply, Priorities, and Allocation Board and director of priorities of OPM (in each capacity he gave orders to himself in the other)—wrote to the Army, the Navy, the Maritime Commission, and the Lend-Lease Administration, asking for precise statements of their estimated requirements, based on military objectives, over the next two years. Back from the Army came Wedemeyer's bundle of figures. Lend-Lease was less exact and the Navy said they wouldn't know for sure until the war began, but at last Nathan and May had something to go on and they set to work.

What followed was a confrontation between the New Deal mind, the Army mind, and the business mind, in which the New Deal mind came out on top. Nathan had been impatient with the traditionalists in the War Department and the businessmen running OPM, who had been taking the word "defense" literally and refusing to think beyond the limits of their directives. Industry had been giving the Army what it asked for, which was not enough, if only because nobody knew how much "enough" was. "A grim specter haunted these men's minds in those days," writes Catton in *The War Lords of Washington,* "the specter of going back, some day, to ordinary peacetime pursuits and finding the nation equipped with more productive capacity than could profitably be employed. This specter was back of the resistance to the expansion of basic capacity, back of the resistance to a defense program determination that would make such expansion unavoidable. . . . Genuine abundance can be the most horrifying of all concepts."[62]

Nathan's task was to take the stated requirements and translate them into raw materials, man-hours, energy, dollars. So many tanks means so much steel and so many bombers means so much aluminum, and this does what to existing plants and competes with what other items, and so on page after page. Nathan did the job, but in doing so he concluded that OPM and the War Department were using completely unrealistic projections of American industrial potential. OPM said that the production of war goods could be increased to a possible maximum of $33 billion in 1942 and $44 billion in 1943. May and Nathan said those figures ought to be $45 billion in 1942 and $65 billion in 1943—"estimates," writes Catton, "which turned out to be amazingly close to what was actually accomplished."

The figures showed, wrote Nathan, that "the entire program to date must be *doubled and achieved by September 30, 1943,* if the Victory Program objectives are to be fully achieved." (emphasis added). Stacy May handed Nathan's feasibility study to Donald Nelson on December 4, 1941. The powers in OPM and the War Department were displeased, and made their displeasure known, but in a Roosevelt administration there was always more than one way to skin a cat, and Donald Nelson and Vice-President Wallace took the May-Nathan report to the President, who made good use of it in his first wartime State of the Union message, on January 6, 1942, when he set production goals—60,000 airplanes in 1942, 125,000 in 1943; 45,000 tanks in 1942, 75,000 in 1943; 6 million tons of shipping in 1942, 11 million in 1943—far higher than any ever heard of before.[63]

The Victory Program can fairly be said to have provided the base and set the pattern for winning the war, but it had other significant—and utterly unintended—sequelae. On that same December 4, 1941, three days before Pearl Harbor, the substance of it was published in two isolationist newspapers, the *Chicago Tribune* and the *Washington Times-Herald.* Secretaries Knox and Stimson were aghast; Knox described these as "the most secret documents" in the possession of the government and Stimson held a press conference to denounce "persons so lacking in appreciation of the danger that confronts the country, and so wanting in loyalty and patriotism." Wedemeyer was suspected by some of making the leak, because of his intimate knowledge of the program, his German training, his America First views, and his marriage to General Embick's daughter. But Marshall believed him innocent and indeed it appears true that he was; isolationist Senator Burton K. Wheeler later wrote that a copy of the Victory Program had been brought to him by an Army captain and that it was he who had shown it to Chesly Manly of the *Chicago Tribune*.[64] In any event, Pearl Harbor swallowed up the issue, and President Roosevelt called off any further attempts to find a culprit.

The interesting part is what happened in Berlin. The *Tribune* and *Times-Herald* "revelations" were cabled there in full and were carefully studied, as we later learned from a captured German naval staff diary. The German military were inclined to take the Victory Program at face value from the start, but they were absolutely convinced of its genuineness when Knox and Stimson made their protestations of outrage at its disclosure. Hitler believed in it, and absorbed it into whatever were the thought processes that led him to ask the Reichstag for a declaration of war against us on December 11. "A plan prepared by President Roosevelt," he said in his speech, "has been revealed in the United States, according to which his intention [is] to attack Germany in 1943 with all the resources of the United States. Thus our patience has come to the breaking point." The German service chiefs, Admiral Raeder and General Halder, reacted in a dutifully responsible fashion. They saw, with a clarity that does their military acumen great credit, exactly what the Allies could now do.

The German army and navy staff planners professed themselves unable accurately to assess the extent to which the buildup of men and munitions in the United States would proceed, but they thought it necessary to assume the worst—i.e., that the Americans meant what they said and that Germany must anticipate "the concentration of forces of enemy powers in accordance with the now known Roosevelt plans." That the Allies would give priority to a war against Japan was unlikely. Directing their combined forces toward Germany, they would be able during 1942, or 1943 at the latest, to take the Atlantic islands, Dakar, Morocco, and perhaps the whole North African shore. They would threaten the Axis position in southern Europe, would tighten their continental blockade, and would acquire bases for further land and air operations against Italy, the Balkans, Central Europe, and ultimately Germany itself. With the aircraft and shipping contemplated in the Victory Program they would be able "to land at will on various points of the European periphery and thus to reduce the region held by our military power"—than which truer words were rarely writ.

The German professionals, being no fools, put together a strategy for countering the "Roosevelt War Plan," which they summarized for Hitler in a *Vortrags-Notiz* of the *Oberkommando der Wehrmacht*—the German equivalent of the U.S. Joint Chiefs—on December 14. The thrust of it was that everything be done before mid-1943 to make the American objectives unattainable, above all that Britain be ejected from the Mediterranean and the Middle East. To this end they should (1) terminate the Russian campaign, if necessary by going on the defensive (this would release one hundred Axis divisions for use elsewhere); (2) integrate Spain, Portugal, Sweden, and France into Fortress Europe, politically if possible but by force if not; (3) occupy the whole northern coast of Africa and the Suez Canal; (4) give priority to air and naval attacks against Anglo-American shipping in the North Atlantic, on which any future Allied offensive must depend; (5) strengthen air and coastal defenses, cooperate with the Japanese, and prepare for a long war. Hitler had approved their proposals, or so they thought, on December 12 and orders began to go out on the sixteenth.

God help us if they had done it! and there is slight reason to suppose that they could not have. Possibly Franco might have continued to outfox them; possibly the logistic difficulties of Rommel's reaching Egypt (long land distances, inadequate ports) would have proved insuperable; possibly the attempt to build an effective submarine fleet had been begun too late —but they had surmounted worse than this before when they put their minds to it, and concentration of effort along these lines would have opened up possibilities the Allies could ill envisage: no more oil for Britain from the Middle East, no disaster for Germany at Stalingrad, no American landings in North Africa, no prospect of an Allied invasion of Europe until after many years in which the Germans consolidated their strength. How well would the Grand Alliance have borne this? how well, American resolve to spend blood and treasure in Nazi Germany's destruction?[65]

Such dire self-examination we were spared by Adolf Hitler. He returned to *Wolfschanze*, Wolf's Lair, his headquarters at Rastenburg in East Prussia, to discover that his Russian campaign had come upon evil days. The attack on Moscow had been stopped short on December 8— "within sight of the Kremlin towers"—and the Russians, acclimatized to their own winter, had gone over to the counterattack with fresh forces from Siberia, whose presence in the West the Germans had scarcely suspected.

This unforeseen reverse brought out Hitler's mania for territory as such, his determination that where the German soldier set his foot, thence it would never be removed. Generals Halder and von Brauchitsch were summoned for a midnight harangue to the effect that "a general withdrawal is out of the question" and that any talk of "preparing rear positions is just drivelling nonsense." There were those—conspicuously General Günther Blumentritt, no sycophant of Hitler's—who believed that the Führer's hold-in-place orders of December 1941 saved the German Army, that any pullout would have turned into a rout comparable to that of

Napoleon's *Grande Armée.*[66] Be that as it might be, Hitler's rejection of his generals' advice saved the "Roosevelt War Plan." There would be no redirection of effort against the Western Allies. The British could remain in the Mediterranean, where the Americans soon enough would join them.

III

Before dawn on November 8, 1942, American soldiers made their way through the surf toward the shores of French Northwest Africa. They landed on the Atlantic side at Safi and Fedhala, to the south and north of Casablanca, at Mehdia seaward of Port Lyautey, and inside the Mediterranean at three beaches to the east and west of Oran. They included elements of the 1st, 3d, and 9th infantry divisions, the 1st and 2d armored divisions, a battalion of Rangers, and various artillery and engineer units. Farther to the east, the British 11th Brigade and the joint Anglo-American 168th Combat Team landed on either side of Algiers with that center of French colonial administration as their objective. All were under the command of Lieutenant General Dwight D. Eisenhower, making his headquarters inside the honeycombed rock of the British fortress at Gibraltar.

Eisenhower, wave-hopping through bad weather to avoid German radar, had reached Gibraltar two days earlier in a flight of five B-17s from England. There was much for him to think about during that foreboding quiet when an operation has been set in motion and its leader can do nothing but cross his fingers and wait for reports. The Western Task Force from the United States, under Major General George S. Patton, Jr., had been assigned a portion of the Atlantic coast notorious for the heavy breakers that come rolling in from the open sea at heights occasionally reaching fifteen feet. Only twelve days out of the year, according to local informants, would be suitable for debarkation; at other times the light landing craft (we had available only three British *heavy* landing craft) could be tossed about like matchwood and thousands of men might drown. If Patton's convoy of over a hundred ships was unable to land, then it must steam in circles or pass through the strait into the inland sea, becoming in either case a tempting target for German submarines. Aboard cruiser *Augusta,* Patton, fully dressed, had forced himself to sleep; he woke in the early-morning dark and noted in his diary: "Sea dead calm, no swell—God is with us." Shortly before midnight, the BBC in London had begun to broadcast a message certain listeners were waiting to hear: *"Allo Robert. Franklin arrive."*[67]

The French in Africa fought back, though not all of them, and of those who did, not all were clear in their minds whether this "enemy" offshore

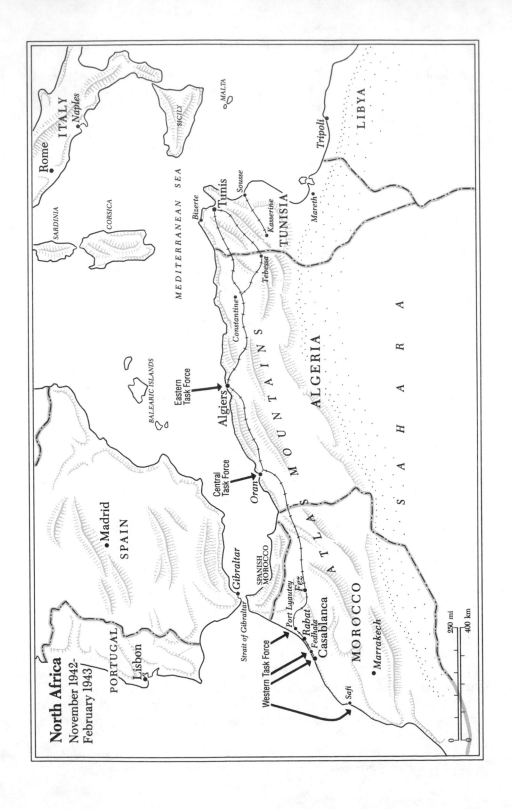

North Africa
November 1942–
February 1943

ITALY
Rome
Naples

SARDINIA
CORSICA
SICILY

MALTA

MEDITERRANEAN SEA

Bizerte
Tunis
Sousse
Kasserine
TUNISIA
Mareth
Tripoli
LIBYA

Tebessa
Constantine

Eastern
Task Force
Algiers

Central
Task Force
Oran

BALEARIC ISLANDS

SPAIN
• Madrid

PORTUGAL
Lisbon

Gibraltar
Strait of Gibraltar
SPANISH MOROCCO

M O U N T A I N S

A L G E R I A

S A H A R A

A T L A S

Port Lyautey
Fez
Rabat
Fedhala
Casablanca
MOROCCO
• Marrakech
Safi

Western Task Force

250 mi
400 km
0

was British, American, or German. At Safi the landing went like clock-work, on a plan the U.S. Navy had contrived that was audacious to the edge of the reasonable. Two destroyer transports ran the gauntlet of French and friendly fire straight into Safi harbor, where *Bernadou* gently grounded and unloaded over cargo nets Company K of the 47th Infantry, followed by *Cole*, which berthed and unloaded Company L (both were specially trained for this work). Battleship *New York* and cruiser *Philadelphia* neutralized shore batteries that had opened up to the north and south; by midafternoon Safi was taken. Snipers continued to fire on the beachhead for several days, and ten Americans were killed, but seatrain *Lakehurst* had moored on Safi quay and was unloading its cargo of Sher-man tanks (Safi, though far to the south, had been picked because it was the only place outside Casablanca where this could be done). By 9 A.M. on the tenth, a fully assembled combat command of the 2d Armored Division had beaten off a French counterattack approaching from Marrakech and was on its way north toward Casablanca under its energetic commander, Major General Ernest K. Harmon.

Back in the States, General Patton had addressed a group of his expe-dition's naval officers with the words: "Never in history has the Navy landed an army at the planned time and place. If you land us anywhere within fifty miles of Fedhala and within one week of D-Day, I'll go ahead and win." He was happily forced to eat his words: all three of his task forces —in the middle of the night, after a voyage of 4,500 miles—had been put on their proper stations almost to the minute. At Fedhala, immediately north of Casablanca, mistakes and delays occurred aplenty, but by sunrise 3,500 men of the 3d Infantry Division (reinforced by artillery and armor) were ashore on the assigned beaches and all their objectives had been secured. French coastal guns again opened fire and again were silenced, this time by cruisers *Brooklyn* and *Augusta;* about a third of the several hundred landing craft were lost to strafing, confusion, and inexperience, which slowed the landings. But by early afternoon, Patton was in Fedhala and its commandant was telling him that the French Army did not want to fight the Americans, and that he should demand Casablanca's surrender —which he accepted, with champagne and toasts of mutual esteem, on the eleventh. ("They drank $40.00 worth of champagne," Patton wrote to Secretary Stimson, "but it was worth it."[68])

The first day off Casablanca itself there was a genuine naval engage-ment. Of all the French armed services, the navy had the least enthusiasm for the Allied cause. An anti-British tradition was of long standing (the great-grandfather of their commander in chief, Admiral Jean François Darlan, died at Trafalgar) and had been exacerbated by Dunkirk and by the reluctant though necessary British destruction of French warships at Mers-el-Kebir in July 1940. So from Casablanca French aircraft rose up, French destroyers and submarines came forth to do battle, and while unfinished and immobilized in the harbor, battleship *Jean Bart* turned loose her fifteen-inch guns. Wildcat fighters and Dauntless dive-bombers from carrier *Ranger* and escort carrier *Suwannee* (a new ship, Jocko Clark commanding) disposed of twenty French planes in the air and many more on the ground. Battleship *Massachusetts,* newly commissioned and on her shakedown cruise, put the *Jean Bart* out of action in sixteen minutes. The French ships were well and ably handled, but American determination and superior firepower did them in. By day's end they had lost four destroyers and eight submarines, 490 killed and 969 wounded. We had suffered one hit each on two destroyers, three cruisers, one battleship— a total of three killed and twenty-five wounded—and commendations had been earned by more than a few Americans, among them Lieutenant Franklin D. Roosevelt, Jr., USNR, gunnery officer of destroyer *Mayrant.*

Port Lyautey to the north is inland from the sea on a winding estuary; we needed it for its airfield. Here French resistance was stiffer and American casualties were higher. The mouth of the estuary is dominated by an ancient Portuguese fort where the French had emplaced six five-and-a-half inch coastal defense guns, surrounded by trenches and machine-gun nests. Naval support fire might have helped in this instance (battleship *Texas,* cruiser *Savannah,* and several destroyers were on hand), but Brigadier General Lucian K. Truscott, Jr., preferred a land assault, which took longer though it eventually succeeded. Of two officers he sent forward to negotiate with the French in Port Lyautey, one was killed and the other made prisoner. Under the guidance of a local pilot who had been smuggled out by the OSS, destroyer *Dallas* then made its way up the estuary, firing on French positions as it went, and landed a raider detachment on the edge of the airfield, which the Americans had cleared by morning of the tenth for the arrival of P-40 fighter planes from escort carrier *Chenango* (many of them, finding the field catered and soft, went on to Casablanca instead). That night, word reached the Port Lyautey garrison from Admiral Darlan, putting a general cease-fire into effect.

The task forces that struck within the Mediterranean at Oran and Algiers had staged in the United Kingdom. Their naval covering group was British—battleships *Nelson, Rodney,* and *Duke of York;* battle cruiser *Renown;* carriers *Victorious* and *Formidable;* light cruisers *Bermuda, Argonaut, Sirius,* and *Phoebe;* and seventeen destroyers—while the transports were a mix of the two navies. The troops were mainly Americans who had been training in Northern Ireland and Scotland, the theory being that they would be more warmly welcomed by the French, especially in Oran (the scene of the British naval attack in 1940). Their convoys had to pass through the Strait of Gibraltar in plain view of Axis agents, which they did on November 5–6. The Germans had no idea where these ships were going, but Hitler demanded their destruction by submarines and torpedo boats: "I await a ruthless victorious attack," his order read. His conviction that "the British" were headed toward Tripoli or Benghazi, to the rear of Rommel fleeing westward after El Alamein, resulted in thirty-odd Axis submarines being all in the wrong place and scoring, for the time being, no hits.[69]

At Oran, the beach landings went smoothly, but of nothing else can the same be said. A plan to deliver up the town intact, by officers loyal to the French general Henri Giraud, misfired and had to be canceled. A paratroop assault on two airfields to the south, scattered by weather and faulty communications, was too small and too late to be effective. The impetuous idea of storming the harbor with two converted U.S. Coast Guard cutters, to capture shore batteries and forestall sabotage, was the failure that senior Royal Navy officers had forecast; both ships were sunk by French fire and hundreds of men were lost. But all was made good on the beaches, at Arzeu to the east and Les Andalouses to the west, where the 1st Infantry Division and half of the 1st Armored (with artillery and engineers) came ashore with little difficulty and fought their way inland to the airfields in a two-pronged pincer movement that enveloped Oran, which they entered against light opposition on the tenth; a capitulation was arranged and a cease-fire issued at quarter past noon.[70]

Algiers was of course the key, a place at which the political side might weigh more heavily than the military. The Anglo-American troops of the Eastern Task Force were to land at three beaches, called Apples, Beer, and Charlie. Once again an attempt to force the main harbor by a frontal attack failed; of two Royal Navy destroyers, one managed to crash through and land an American combat team, but this was quickly pinned down on the dock and surrounded. Fortunately, from Charlie beach the 39th Infantry advanced rapidly on the vital objective of Maison Blanche airdrome, which ceased resistance at 8:27 A.M. and was soon receiving Allied aircraft from Gibraltar; the airfield at Blida, twenty-five miles to the southwest, was taken by the 11th British Brigade and by a regimental combat team of the 34th Infantry Division. Meanwhile, inside Algiers, politics was working its wonders.

"Robert" in the BBC message *"Allo Robert"* meant Robert D. Murphy, a foreign service officer who was U.S. consul and counselor of embassy in Paris during the 1930s, who went along to Vichy as chargé d'affaires in 1940, and had been in North Africa since then as American representative in a policy of cultivating Vichy French officials, gathering intelligence, and trying to arrange a coup d'état that would eliminate resistance when the Allies landed. Murphy (together with Marine Lieutenant Colonel William Eddy of the OSS[71]) was engaged in a delicate maneuver, the essence of it being to persuade the Allies they should come on like lions because the French would give up without a fight (which they couldn't, honorably), while persuading the French they should cooperate because the Allies were going to come on like lions (which they couldn't, militarily). Murphy had to convince Washington and London that the French were eager to welcome us, while at the same time he refused to tell the French where, when, and in what strength our landings would take place. In such soil confusion flowered, and Murphy's conservative French connections led him to offer much bad advice, but in the main he succeeded. The coup in Algiers went forward, faltered, and finally had the desired result.

With the words *"Franklin arrive"* long-prepared plans went into execution. Sympathizers of General Giraud, expecting him momentarily to assume command, took over police headquarters, the radio station, and the telephone system; they locked up top Vichy officials and sent guides to the likely landing places. By 1:30 A.M. they were in control of Algiers, which they held until 7 A.M. But neither Giraud nor the Americans had appeared in the city by that time, and the Vichyites loyal to Marshal Pétain began to reassert their authority. There was sniping in the streets and a comic-opera situation in which each side put members of the other under arrest. Murphy took advantage of the unexpected presence in Algiers of Admiral Darlan, commander in chief of all the armed forces of Vichy France, to impress on Darlan the approach of overwhelming Allied power (Darlan was there quite by accident, to visit his ailing son). This was stretching the truth a little, but by now the Americans and British held the airfields, the principal coastal batteries, the heights west of the city, and the highways approaching it from west and east. Faced with a choice of fighting his way out or waiting to be captured, Darlan gave the overall commander of French forces, General Juin, the authority to surrender Algiers to the Americans. Fighting continued for a time in Oran and Morocco, as we have seen, but shortly before noon on the tenth, Darlan signed a directive in Marshal Pétain's name ordering hostilities to cease in all of French North Africa.[72] A long shot had handsomely paid off; the Allies were there to stay.

A British war correspondent came ashore with the early waves of the 1st Infantry Division near Oran, attended a briefing by General Terry de la Mesa Allen in the concrete schoolhouse at Arzeu, made his first acquaintance with the canned U.S. Army C rations at supper, and bedded down that evening on the schoolhouse roof. There were sounds of distant gunfire; the night was noisy with sentries firing at shadows and shouted exchanges of the password "Heigh-oh Silver" with the countersign "Awa-a-ay!"—delightedly repeated the next morning by Arab children in Arzeu. Dawn brought a splatter of rain. The sentry on the roof, departing when his relief arrived, left behind for the nourishment of the press a slab of emergency D ration chocolate and a bottle of wine. "As far as I know," the correspondent wrote, "he had come direct from the beach with the headquarters company. He had been on duty or in the building all the rest of the day. He had shared the roof outpost all the night—and yet he had vino. Great is the U.S. Army."[73]

◆

The decision to invade North Africa—operation Torch—was nominally made by the Combined Chiefs of Staff but was made in fact by Franklin Roosevelt. General Marshall opposed it, and went on indicating his dissent even after the President's determination was made known. In this first major action of a collaborative effort with the British, the President chose to follow British advice, which meant that in their first operational debate over strategy he and his Chief of Staff confronted one another with diametrically opposing views. The first American offensive against the Germans, the first test in the great enterprise for which Marshall's army was being schooled, would be conducted not as he wished it but as Roosevelt wished it.

"World War II was to see larger operations . . . ," write the historians of the U.S. Army Air Forces about Torch, "but none surpassed it in complexity, in daring—and the prominence of hazard involved—or in the degree of strategic surprise achieved. The most important attribute of Torch, however, is the most obvious. It was the *first* fruit of the combined strategy. Once it had been undertaken, other great operations followed as its corollaries; competing strategies receded or went into abeyance until its course had been run. In short, the Torch operation, and the lessons learned in Africa, imposed a pattern on the war."[74] John Eisenhower, in a book based on a manuscript of his father's, describes the choice of North Africa rather than France for an Allied offensive in 1942 as "the great decision of the European war." His father at the time ardently supported Marshall; he thought that British refusal to accept his and Marshall's plan for invading France would go down as the "blackest day in history." Marshall never changed his mind about it, but later Eisenhower wrote that the decision to invade North Africa instead was probably the correct one.[75]

How George Marshall arrived at the impasse in which he found himself over North Africa, trying to bluff his way out of a no-win box, is not readily understandable, but the logic that led him there was faultless. By early 1943, at least some of his army would be regarded as ready for action. If we remained on the defensive in the Pacific, and he had to go before the public justifying that, then on the Atlantic side we must be visibly and actively engaged against Nazi Germany. Nor could this be, as Marshall well appreciated, by secondary forays around the periphery of the continent at the whim of Winston Churchill. "To demonstrate that the United States," writes Forrest Pogue, "was not in the war merely to furnish men and matériel for any plan the Prime Minister might desire, no matter how advantageous to the British, [Marshall] demanded concentration on the one operation that Americans would list above an offensive against Japan."[76] There must be a serious and substantive Allied campaign in Europe, and everything argued that it be in France.

"It is the only place," reads a War Department draft analysis of April 1, 1942, "in which a powerful offensive can be prepared and executed by the United Powers in the near future. . . . It is the only place where the vital air superiority over the hostile land areas preliminary to a major attack can be staged. . . . It is the only place in which the bulk of the British ground forces can be committed to a general offensive in co-operation with United States forces. . . . The United States can concentrate and use larger forces in Western Europe than [anywhere else], due to sea distances and the existence in England of base facilities. . . . We cannot concentrate against Japan."[77]

This document, though it was written by General Eisenhower and Colonel (later General) Thomas T. Handy, came to be known as the Marshall Memorandum; he read and approved it the day they presented it to him (as usual suggesting changes in language), and later that same day Marshall and Stimson took it over to the White House, where the President also approved it and directed Marshall and Hopkins to hand-carry it to London for approval by the Prime Minister and the British Chiefs.

The Marshall Memorandum envisaged an invasion of France on a six-division front between Le Havre and Boulogne with a combined force of forty-eight divisions (of which thirty would be American) and 5,800 aircraft (of which 3,250 would be American), on a date estimated at April 1, 1943. Parachute troops would be used to delay German reinforcement, and a mobile force of six American and three British armored divisions would serve as the spearhead for a general move on Antwerp. (There was also a contingency provision for an emergency invasion with five divisions in September 1942 if either Germany or Russia should collapse.) If such was acceptable as a generalized objective, then American production, training, scheduling, and allocation of resources could proceed on the basis of an agreed strategy.

Though all this seemed reasonable enough, there were strong streaks of unreality in it, and none saw these more clearly than did the British Chiefs when Marshall made his presentation to them. This was not so much a developed plan as an ideal goal. Sadly enough, Anglo-American relationships were not yet at a stage where easy candor was effortless. Had they known each other better, Ismay later remarked, the British could have taken the Americans out to dinner and said, "Look here, old boy, this sounds lovely but surely we are talking in terms of the end of 1943." Ismay thought the British "should have come clean, much cleaner than we did." They were so eager to reinforce American enthusiasm, on the other hand, that they muffled their denials.

On April 14, the British Chiefs of Staff accepted the Marshall Memorandum in principle and that evening, at a meeting of the War Cabinet Defence Committee, with Marshall and Hopkins present, Churchill officially endorsed the "momentous" American proposal and proclaimed that "our two nations are resolved to march forward into Europe together in a noble brotherhood of arms, in a great crusade for the liberation of the tormented peoples." Ismay was less sanguine. "Our American friends," he wrote, "went happily homewards under the mistaken impression that we had committed ourselves. . . . This misunderstanding was destined to have unfortunate results."[78]

There were misunderstandings of many kinds. Marshall's consisted in attaching to the emergency-contingency invasion of 1942 a weight it had never been intended to bear. His London trip had not deceived him; he saw accurately how tentative the British "commitment" was, but he regarded his duty as one of holding them (and his own Commander in Chief) to the sticking place. The Americans in early 1942 were overwhelmed by the consequences of global war, by demands from every quarter for the plugging of what Stimson called "urgent ratholes." If they continued in this mode, their accumulating potential would be dissipated everywhere at once and never brought to bear. The more thoughtful among them, like Eisenhower, became almost obsessed by the threat of "scatteration," of failure to focus on one goal and bend every effort in its direction. "The struggle to secure the adoption by all concerned of a common concept is wearing me down . . . ," Eisenhower wrote in his diary in January 1942. *"We've got to go to Europe and fight* [emphasis added] and we've got to quit wasting resources all over the world, and still worse, wasting time."[79] (Four months later, he added a congratulatory note of reminder to himself when the British Chiefs approved his and Colonel Handy's plan.)

For Marshall, the threat came primarily from Roosevelt's keeping the alternative of invading North Africa in the corner of his eye, a predilection the President had entertained before Churchill encouraged it, and one that Marshall and Stimson knew had never left his mind even when, in good faith, he sent Marshall and Hopkins to London. Marshall believed that Allied involvement in North Africa in 1942 inevitably meant postponing Allied involvement in France until *later* than 1943. This has since been much debated (the 1943 cross-Channel possibilities may not have been as foreclosed as Marshall thought[80]), but in the outcome he was proved correct: North Africa *did* postpone the main event until 1944, and *did* cause the further diversions of effort (Sicily, Italy, etc.) that he dreaded. The only way he could see to avoid entering this Mediterranean *pis aller* was to insist on the emergency small-scale invasion of France in 1942, which he must have known was a loser, since it would have to be almost exclusively a British show and therefore subject to their veto (Colonel Handy had pointed this out as early as January 1942).[81] Marshall came to think of France-in-'42 as essential to preserving the central strategy of the war, despite its lack of appeal to the British and its very considerable dangers. Pressed by Marshall to justify it, Eisenhower and his staff (in June, Eisenhower had been appointed commanding general of the European theater) came up with only a one-in-two chance of success and, of establishing six divisions ashore, only one in five. Even if successful, "its material effect would probably be of little consequence," they reported.[82] But Marshall persisted, against all the odds.

He was in London once more (with Admiral King) but on a very different errand. The British had by now come clean with a will. In early July, the War Cabinet had declared unambiguously against France-in-'42 and Churchill had cabled Roosevelt that he could find "no responsible British general, admiral, or air marshall" prepared to recommend it. Marshall and King, most unwisely, responded to this by a memo for the President in which they argued that unless there was to be "forceful, unswerving adherence" to the plans for invading France, then they were "definitely of the opinion that we should turn to the Pacific and strike decisively against Japan." This was childish, almost as though (in the President's simile) if you couldn't have everything you wanted you would insist on "taking up your dishes and going away." Marshall said later that he was bluffing, and certainly Roosevelt thought so, for he came down on them hard (from Hyde Park, of a Sunday morning) with a demand to know exactly what their plan was (ships, planes, men, landings, timing, etc.) for the Pacific alternative. Since no such plan existed, they had to cobble one together in a matter of hours, and it did not please the President.[83]

"My first impression," he scrawled in his own hand, "is that it is exactly what Germany hoped the United States would do after Pearl Harbor. Secondly it does not in fact provide use of American troops in fighting except in a lot of islands whose occupation will not affect the world situation this year or next. Third: it does not help Russia or The Near East. Therefore it is disapproved as of the present. Roosevelt C in C." (The original is mounted on display outside the director's office in the Roosevelt Library at Hyde Park, as it deserves to be, an example of his strategic common sense at its most rudimentary and of his relish in his constitutional powers at their most explicit.)

On the fourteenth, Roosevelt told Marshall that he wanted him (with Hopkins and King) to go to London again and settle once and for all the question of where American troops would fight that year. A detailed letter of instruction was drawn up by Roosevelt and Hopkins, in which the President reiterated his opposition to any all-out offensive in the Pacific and his insistence on action somewhere in the West in 1942. "It is of the utmost importance," he wrote, "that we appreciate that defeat of Japan does not defeat Germany and that American concentration against Japan this year or in 1943 increases the chance of complete German domination of Europe and Africa."[84] Marshall in a better moment might have written those words himself. His second London mission he treated as a last-ditch effort to salvage that vital principal by keeping France-in-'42 on the Allied agenda.

It was hopeless. The British held all the cards and their arguments were irrefutable. The major reason the Americans had to fall back on (as Eisenhower did) was that even if the '42 French operation was suicidal, it would at least help the Russians. The British could cogently respond that this was not the case. The Germans had an estimated twenty-five divisions in France, of which six to ten could quickly seal off our beachhead (by then designated as the Cotentin peninsula) at its base, bringing up reinforcements *ad lib* without seriously affecting their operations elsewhere. The Luftwaffe would outnumber our air forces by six to one and resupply would be hazardous; even if our landing was flawlessly executed, it could not survive the winter. The British government's position was that they would not sanction going to France unless we were prepared to stay there, and nothing they were being offered held out that promise.

◆

On July 22, after a meeting which Churchill attended, the Americans gave up and cabled Roosevelt that British opposition to France-in-'42 was unyielding; he replied that he was not particularly surprised. What were the alternatives? Marshall asked himself. "What was the least harmful diversion?"[85] There were only three—North Africa (the British favorite), Norway (Churchill's off-and-on infatuation), and the Middle East (a stepchild)—and of these, North Africa was far and away the "least harmful." Marshall sat down in his room at Claridge's and wrote a North African outline. King came in, read it, and accepted it on the spot (not King's usual behavior with Army proposals); and on the twenty-fourth the Combined Chiefs determined that detailed planning for what was now named Torch should get under way immediately. On the twenty-fifth, before leaving for Washington, Marshall summoned Eisenhower and—scrubbing away in the bathtub—told him that if Torch was implemented, command of it would probably be his.[86] An age-long British way of thinking, tested in the trial of centuries—what Liddell Hart called the "indirect approach"—had triumphed over an American instinct to go for the jugular.

Perhaps there were other attitudes at work. The Americans may have thought the British to be unduly wary of the Germans (some of them characterized British "experience" as experience mainly with defeat), but unquestionably the Americans were not wary enough. They had not yet gone up against the first team, which is what the Germans were, as the British had learned more than once. It took the North African campaign, and setbacks like Kasserine Pass, to acquaint the American soldiery with what it meant to fight the Wehrmacht on halfway even terms.

The German Army of the early 1940s was quite simply the best in the world. At small-scale ground action it had no peer (and all ground action is essentially small-scale), drawing upon skills rooted in a society that gave the foot soldier, in popular literature and statues on the village square, an honored place. Their officers and men were professional to a degree no other nation could match, and this was true not only of the elite units but, toward the end, of the average in a total diluted by Eastern Europeans, older men, sufferers from stomach disorders, and teen-age boys. Even in decline they had a sharp sting, and in their prime, no one who ever met a panzer division in full cry wanted to repeat the encounter. No one who met them on their own terms ever beat them, and to have fought them in France in 1942 would have been on their terms. The trick of it, to which the Russians and we under British tutelage later gave much thought, was to meet them on other terms than their own, but this happy circumstance was still being nurtured in the bosom of time.

Marshall came back to Washington hoping that the decision had not been final and that the buildup for a French invasion could continue. A July 30 session of the Combined Chiefs revealed uncertainty on this score and Leahy insisted on having it resolved by the President. At a White House meeting that evening, resolved it was. "The President stated very definitely," Beetle Smith reported to the Joint Chiefs, "that he, as Commander in Chief, had made the decision that Torch would be undertaken at the earliest possible date. He considered that this operation was now our principal objective and the assembling of means to carry it out should take precedence over other operations. . . ."[87]

Marshall went on being reserved about Torch—as late as mid-August he was telling his staff that "the vicissitudes of war" might intervene— though as a good soldier he did everything he could to back it. He asked Eisenhower and Patton for a "frank estimate" of the chances that Torch would work and on August 17 he relayed their answer to the JCS. They said that if Spain remained neutral and the French offered only token or divided resistance, then "the operation has more than a fair chance of success . . . ," but they thought some of the French *would* resist and that the chances of "overall" success, if that meant reaching Tunisia before the Axis reinforced it, were "considerably less than fifty per cent."[88]

Stimson was angry about the President's decision and, taking his cue, the Army officers tended to speak of it grudgingly as "political," a grab-bag word that could be used for factors they had to acknowledge but neither liked nor understood—a word for everything that was not narrowly defined as "military." Wedemeyer wrote in July that "apparently our political system would require major operations this year in Africa," and after dinner with Eisenhower in London during August, Patton wrote in his diary: "We both feel the operation is bad and is mostly political. However, we are told to do it and intend to succeed or die in the attempt."[89] Before the war was over, Eisenhower and Wedemeyer would become more sophisticated about "politics" (Patton never), so that at this stage one might wish their use of the term to have been more exact: the number of possible meanings is considerable.

The decision for Torch was to them most openly "political" in the sense that it had been arrived at over their objections by political heads of government. It was also political in the sense that it involved foreign relations with neutral powers like France and Spain. It was political for Roosevelt in that congressional elections were coming up in November. (He fastidiously refrained from trying to influence the choice of date— though he held up his hands in mock prayer to Marshall when they discussed it—with the result that the invasion came five days *after* an election in which the Democrats lost forty-four seats in the House and nine in the Senate.) It was political for Churchill in that he had beaten down a vote of censure in the House of Commons on July 2 by 475 to 25, but whether or not his government could survive another major military disaster was problematical.

Most of all it was political in the sense that Roosevelt's analysis found military intervention in the West during 1942 to be necessary for national morale, while the military analysis did not. Marshall's remark that "the leader in a democracy has to keep the people entertained" is symptomatic; he knew better than that, but he knew no better word for it. What Roosevelt knew was that in democratic societies men and women do not go full of purpose to the war factories, nor do soldiers and sailors willingly ready themselves to risk their lives, without some tangible evidence of their government's being in earnest—that war rouses an appetite for action, and that maintaining a level of enthusiasm for it requires real events to feed on. This to Roosevelt was second nature, to Marshall an acquired truth.

Once he gave his will to it, Marshall did not stint in his support for the North African operation. "In the mounting of Torch," he wrote Eisenhower a week before the landings, "I have had the War Department do everything in its power to provide what you have asked for. We have stripped units of men, reduced eight or nine divisions to such low levels of personnel it will require six to eight months to restore them to their proper level of efficiency, and we have scalped the troops in this country [of equipment] to meet your requirements." Equipment that Eisenhower thought was there in England, but could not be handily located in scattered British warehouses, was replaced from the United States. Even so, the divisions were only partially equipped and partially trained. Eisenhower's would-be imposing phalanx of assault was improvised, to say the least. One Army general described the plan for its employment as "fantastic."[90]

No amphibious operation so far from its base had ever before been attempted, let alone on such a scale, and historically—as with the British in the Dardanelles in World War I—a number had been failures. Joint Army-Navy planning was still in its infancy and there were great gaps in our intelligence about Moroccan beaches, their sea approaches and their shore configurations. The Navy was as raw as the Army. The training of landing-craft crews had not begun until June, and of thirty transports only fourteen were in commission by August. On cruiser *Brooklyn,* only nine of its sixty-five officers had been in the service more than three years, and of its fifteen hundred enlisted men, over half were at sea for the first time; none on board had been in combat.[91]

The escort aircraft carriers, obligatory if there was to be air cover, had been included after less than half their normal preparatory training. *Suwannee* had not even been scheduled for completion in time for Torch. Jocko Clark made some quick calculations and went to the Newport News Shipbuilding and Dry Dock Company. "I cannot give away any military secrets," he told them, "but if you can give me my ship two weeks early, I will put her where she will do some good." They said, "That's the kind of talk we like to hear." *Suwannee* was not only finished early but loaded with ammunition (contrary to all the rules) right there in the yard. "You can't *do* that!" yard officials said. "Well, I'm doing it," said Jocko. *Suwannee* sailed with Patton's convoy. On her return to Norfolk afterward, Captain (later four-star admiral) Clark was called to the office of the Chief of Naval Operations in Washington. "You did a good job," said King, not exactly what Clark had expected to be told.[92]

President Roosevelt was fortunate to be spared such detailed knowledge of how makeshift a force he was sending into a deadly test of its readiness; the picture presented to him by the total overview was bad enough. Here was a venture which for every reason of statecraft *must* succeed and yet the men around him most competent to say had told him it might not, that necessary preconditions were wanting or uncertain, that as strategy it was wrong in principle and in practice. He had nonetheless insisted; the responsibility was his not only as chief executive but as final sayer of yea and nay about this opening move in a theater of war to which we were giving first priority. The burden of it was unequivocally his, and he knew it. Normally Roosevelt bore good news and ill about the war with cheerful equanimity, but on this occasion there was no mistaking his anxiety. On the way up to Shangri-La in the car on November 7, Grace Tully could see that he was preoccupied and aware of the tension he was revealing; he told her he was expecting an important message. When the call came the next day from the War Department, his hand shook as she handed him the receiver. The Army was ashore, casualties less than expected.

"Thank God," said the President. "Thank God."[93]

Katherine Marshall was attending a night football game when the news came. The general had been unable to join her and so she had asked

Hap and Bee Arnold to share the Marshalls' box. There had recently been more of this than she cared for—Marshall had canceled a duck-hunting trip down the Potomac she thought he badly needed for relaxation—and she had become a trifle short with him. "Every little thing is important but you!" she had said. The Washington ballpark, packed with 25,000 fans, was floodlit bright as day when the game was interrupted in midplay by a voice on the public-address system calling for attention: "The President of the United States of America announces the successful landing on the African coast of an American expeditionary force."

Now Mrs. Marshall knew why her husband had been detained. "Like the waves of the ocean," she wrote, "the cheers of the people rose and fell, then rose again in a long-sustained emotional cry. The football players turned somersaults and handsprings down the center of the field; the crowd went wild. . . . We had struck back."[94] Readers from the generations since may find this reaction hard to comprehend or credit, but that is how it was—and why the President thought it exigent to take the risk he took.

IV

George Marshall and Franklin Roosevelt were an oddly matched pair. "It is doubtful," writes Forrest Pogue, "that Roosevelt ever enjoyed Marshall's company." Their temperaments and work habits were too unlike for rapport of that kind to develop; Marshall seems almost to have made it a practice not to laugh at the President's jokes. But over the years something else emerged that was deeper and more durable: trust and respect. "It took me a long time to get to him," Marshall said. "When he thought I was not going for publicity and doing things for publication— he liked it." Marshall said that before Pearl Harbor he had doubts about the President's capacity for resolute action. He thought Roosevelt was too easily swayed and too reluctant to make clear-cut decisions, too tolerant of divisiveness and disloyalty among his subordinates. Then the moment came when all that vanished.

In early February 1942, with the inability of the United States to reinforce the Philippines against their Japanese invaders becoming clear, Philippine President Manuel Quezon decided that the time had come for desperate measures. If no aid was going to be forthcoming, then he proposed that both the United States and Japan withdraw their forces and that the islands be neutralized. General MacArthur said later that he opposed this, but he failed at the time to indicate as much; he forwarded Quezon's plan to Washington with a covering telegram to the effect that from a military standpoint it "might offer the best possible solution of what is about to be a disastrous debacle." In some concern at MacArthur's more than halfway endorsement, Marshall and Stimson on February 9 brought these messages to the President, who read them and immediately said, "We can't do this at all." In the face of a tough question—"ghastly in its responsibility and significance," said Stimson—he was resolved without hesitation to do what Marshall believed to be right and necessary: that is, order continued resistance. "I immediately discarded everything in my mind I had held to his discredit . . . ," said Marshall. "I decided he was a great man."[95]

Perhaps it was an advantage for Marshall that Roosevelt did not take the same proprietary interest in the Army that he took in the Navy. It gave Marshall a freer hand, especially in the naming of senior commanders, and it did permit him one opportunity—after a discussion in which the Navy was being favored unrestrainedly—to answer Roosevelt in kind. "At least, Mr. President," said Marshall, "stop speaking of the Army as 'they' and the Navy as 'us.' " This broke up the meeting. And Roosevelt permitted Marshall something he never allowed Ernie King, which was to shake apart the cumbersome machinery by which his service operated and replace it with a streamlined structure. (If the Navy became efficiently organized, this was by the efforts not of Admiral King but of Under Secretary James Forrestal.)

Marshall blamed himself for not having done the job sooner. Pearl Harbor painfully revealed what he had known all along, that the War Department was the least competent command post in the Army. Assistant Secretary of War Robert Lovett said there was enough deadwood in the General Staff to constitute a fire hazard. More than sixty officers had the right of direct access to the Chief of Staff; he was responsible for some thirty major subordinate units and 350 lesser ones. Each of the supply services and the combat arms was headed by a Chief, normally a major general, each of whom had friends, traditions, and political constituencies that gave him the independent power of a feudal baron. In one respect Marshall was wise to bide his time; he waited until the shock would be least, when several of the Chiefs were due for retirement and several others eligible for better jobs.[96] Then he moved with dispatch. He called General McNarney back from London and told him he had sixty days in which to reorganize the War Department; there was to be no talk about this on the outside, and the President would not be informed until a week before it was ready to go. The very audacity of the thing was in good part what got it through.

The plan (an idea urged by Hap Arnold) was to split the Army in three: the Army Ground Forces, the Army Air Forces, and (as they were later called) the Army Service Forces. McNarney called in the Chiefs and told them they were about to be abolished; they would have a week in which to file their protests, after which the new table of organization would take effect anyhow. (Pogue said that the bruises left by this roughshod treatment were still visible when he began doing interviews for his Marshall biography in the 1950s.[97]) There would be an Operations Division to oversee the Army in the field, the General Staff sections would be cut back in size and limited to planning functions, and the number of officers reporting directly to General Marshall would be reduced to six. In his zeal McNarney nearly overdid it. He went to the White House with the draft of an executive order authorizing the changes and insisted so forcefully on his high priority that a secretary took the paper to the President while he was in the dentist's chair in McIntire's office having his sinuses treated. An irate call from his chief soon reached the Chief of Staff. "When I find people who get things done," said Marshall, "I won't fire them." Roosevelt signed the order.[98]

Marshall used his authority to supervise the Army down to the most minute particulars. He traveled widely, usually by air (he relieved officers who refused to fly), moving rapidly from camp to camp across the country (no honors, parades, or parties for him were permitted). On his return to Washington, his staff would receive a checklist. Pogue gives a sampling: "Why was there a shortage of shoes at the Reception Center at Monterey, a shortage of hospital equipment at Fort Sill, a delay in the delivery of laundry machines at Camp Beauregard, a delay in construction of recreational facilities for Negro troops . . . a failure to reply to the 367th Infantry's request for field manuals, a lack of basic issues for the 18th Field Artillery, and no books for the new recreation halls at Camps Livingston and Claiborne?" Any staff officer who wanted to get into Marshall's good graces needed only to satisfy one of these queries on the instant. Nor was the President completely lacking in interest. On one occasion Marshall sent him a two-page single-space memo—"As a result of your comments last Friday"—explaining in detail the methods used by the Army to conserve foodstuffs.[99]

Above all he was concerned about morale. He went in civilian clothes to a small town near a large base, to see what life was like (not very good) for soldiers on a weekend pass. Morale Marshall made a "command responsibility," for which each unit leader would be held accountable. He conceived it as subject to improvement not merely by removing justified causes for complaint (though that must be done) but by infusing organizations with a concept of duty appropriate to a citizen army, based, as he put it, on "respect rather than fear; on the effect of good example given by officers; on the intelligent comprehension by all ranks of why an order has to be."

This he knew was intimately bound up with a sense of national purpose, and before Pearl Harbor it concerned him as much as it did the President that lack of determination "on the home front" was producing the same in the army camps. In September 1941, he had written Roosevelt pleading for "prompt action" about this and the latter had replied that Marshall seemed to be saying, in effect, "Please, Mr. President, do something about this weakness on the part of the civilian population? Got any ideas?" Yet the instinct of each was to deal with the hazards of democracy in a similar fashion, for the essence of George Marshall's army was in fact democratic, the working out—devoid of pomp and pretense—of a unifying principle that combined individual worth and shared purpose. A professor of history at Johns Hopkins, who had heard Marshall speak in Baltimore, later wrote: "If he represents our Army, the American Army is yet a part of the American people."[100]

Marshall's desire to "expunge" the "ponderosities" included the discouragement not only of pompous, authoritarian officers but of everything stilted and artificial that had been connected with them. This down-to-earth approach he shared with Roosevelt and occasionally he would reach out to it as a place where they might find common ground. Once he sent the President what seems at first glance a complicated and not especially relevant page-long disquisition on his old *bête noire,* the five-paragraph field order, explaining how in World War I it sometimes grew to twenty pages and how at Benning he had worked to shorten it. This was actually nothing but an excuse for enclosing a copy of General Terry de la Mesa Allen's order for the 1st Division's attack on Oran, which a delighted Marshall saw might appeal to Roosevelt. Three of the paragraphs were one line each (the first read "omitted") and paragraphs two and three went as follows:

> 2. Div atks at 0715 [10] Nov 1942 (See operation map scheme maneuvers and time of atk). CC [combat command] B atks from S [south] at 0730 in conjunction with 1st Div.
> 3. a. CT [combat team] 18 see operation map 1st Bn [battalion] CT 18 follows CT 18 after mopping up around ST CLOUD
>   b. CT 16 less 1st Bn, see operation map 1st Bn CT 16 (brought forward in trucks follows in Div res [reserve]).
>   x. Civilian snipers caught red-handed will be summarily shot.
>   Nothing in hell must delay or stop this atk.[101]

But there were always potential points of friction. Marshall's attempts to get the President to be more methodical were a failure throughout. Roosevelt wanted no record kept of his conversations. When Marshall had General John Deane bring along a notebook to a White House meeting, "the President blew up." ("Next time Deane brought a book so little he couldn't use it," said Marshall.) Stimson and Knox came back from a cabinet meeting with some notes, but when written out they proved to be so dissimilar as to be useless. Marshall also wanted Roosevelt never to forget (as he himself tried not to) the human cost of what they were about. Every few days he would send a President who can scarcely have welcomed it an accounting of Army casualties, graphically presented, "so it would be quite clear to him . . . because you get hardened to these things."[102]

Further, the two of them continued to encounter differences on substantive issues, as they did in March 1943 when a shortage of shipping appeared to require either closing down military operations or depriving the British of imports they considered a minimum for survival. Marshall and the Joint Chiefs recommended "drastic curtailment of civilian commitments" to Britain, believing these to be based on inflated estimates. There was probably some justice in this, though the American figures may have erred on the side of pessimism too. At any event, the President overruled them. During the months that followed, fortune began to smile on the Battle of the Atlantic; shipping losses dropped while new construction continued to rise, and by midsummer the predicted shortage had failed to appear. The President's impulse to disregard expert fears, and bet on the future, had proved sound.[103]

By a curious turn of events, it was Marshall who ended up doing something the President had originally pressed him to do: namely, to limit the size of the Army. Naturally, the numbers had vastly increased, but it nonetheless remains a striking phenomenon that the calculation of ground forces sufficient to win the war was cut so exceeding fine. At the end on V-J Day, only two divisions—the 13th Airborne in England and the 98th Infantry in Hawaii—had not been committed to action. The cupboard was bare; the McNair division-making machine had been turned off. This had been a conscious decision, and it was Marshall who made it.

The Victory Program, as will be remembered, had called for about 215 divisions, but by the beginning of 1943, with the Russians still very much in the war and prospects brightening for eventual Allied air predominance over Europe, War Department planners with Marshall's support had scaled this down to 120–125. The American reservoir of able-bodied males was turning out, under multiple demands on it, not to be inexhaustible. Marshall wanted even more stringent standards of manpower usage to be met, moreover, and by midyear a committee of the Operations Division had proposed—and Marshall and Stimson had approved—an ultimate goal of only ninety divisions (the final figure of eighty-nine followed the deactivation of the 2d Cavalry in North Africa).

Another force for economy of manpower had been General McNair, who was determined to eliminate from his divisions every man or piece of equipment not essential to their combat effectiveness, every ounce of what he regarded as "fat." After being put through the McNair wringer, an infantry division would have lost 1,261 men and about 20 percent of its motor vehicles, an armored division 3,683 men and 127 tanks. Specialized nondivisional units such as tank destroyer and truck battalions were pooled, and higher headquarters were especially pared down, on McNair's theory that they contributed "a mass of ritual and paperwork" that impeded rapid action. He wanted units that were lean and mean, able to move light and fast, and—against all the internal inertia with which every military organization resists such a principle—he and Marshall applied it with unprecedented zeal.

Stimson was by no means comfortable with so much restraint. He continued to believe, as he wrote Marshall in May of the following year, "that our contribution to the war should include so far as possible an overwhelming appearance of national strength when we actually get to the critical battle." To set a low ceiling seemed to him "to shave the line of sufficiency rather narrowly instead of aiming at massive abundance." Marshall replied three weeks before D-Day in Normandy. "We are about to invade the Continent," he wrote, "and have staked our success on our air superiority, on Soviet numerical preponderance, and on the high quality of our ground combat units." He did believe in those divisions of his. "Our equipment, high standard of training, and freshness," he went on, "should give us a superiority which the enemy cannot meet and which we could not achieve by resorting to a matching of numerical strength."[104] Marshall's "90-division gamble," as it came to be called, ended in a photo finish and has not escaped criticism, both from officers whose operations were affected by it and from historians who have found their complaints to be justified. Of all the calculated risks that accompanied the Allied campaign in Europe, it was exceeded in slender marginality only by the invasion itself.

◆

The realization of Marshall's Grand Design came about in August 1943 when President Roosevelt not only accepted but adopted and gave himself wholeheartedly to the ideas it represented. This was the achievement not merely of Marshall and King, who urged it on the President,[105] but of Henry Stimson, who nailed him down on it. Despite Roosevelt's sidetracking of the secretaries of war and Navy, Stimson did manage to put his imprint on the conduct of the war, in this instance supremely (another was the antisubmarine campaign), and here he did it by taking matters into his own hands and going to the President direct. He was careful to consult Marshall beforehand, to make clear exactly what he intended to ask for, but he did so in such a way that Marshall in good conscience could say he had nothing to do with it.

Stimson's impact on the War Department should not be underestimated. At his age (seventy-six) he sometimes tired easily and was forgetful, and the definiteness with which he pronounced opinions could be intimidating ("I never heard the Lord God speak before," said one officer after a session with Stimson). But he was above pettiness and self-seeking, a living example of an almost forgotten rectitude, and he had able associates like Lovett, McCloy, and Harvey Bundy, who cherished him and ignored his high-handedness; when they went to the Stimsons' for tea, and tried to explain to Mrs. Stimson why her husband was impossible to work with, he would sit there weeping with laughter. Once McCloy was at the White House and took a call from Stimson, who said, "Where are my goddam papers?" McCloy replied, "I haven't got your goddam papers!" and hung up. Navy Under Secretary Forrestal, who was present, could only observe in wonderment that it wasn't done this way in the Navy Department. Stimson's biographer Elting Morison quotes a Pentagon official's attempt to explain Stimson's influence: "You will never get it down on paper, but every day in the War Department people did not do certain things and did do certain other things in a certain way because Stimson was in the office of the Secretary." President Roosevelt said he would trust him with anything.[106]

During July 1943, Stimson spent a fortnight in England. He had intended to visit U.S. troops, but on arrival Churchill took him in charge, and the visit turned into an extended discussion of high policy. Stimson met with Anthony Eden, Lieutenant General Sir Frederick Morgan (head of cross-Channel planning), and repeatedly with the Prime Minister, whom he had long known but with whom he had never before had the chance to talk about Allied strategy so frankly and at such length. Stimson put it bluntly to Churchill and Eden that if Allied troops became so involved in the Balkans, Greece, and the Middle East that no European campaign took place, then this "would be a serious blow to the prestige of the President's war policy and therefore to the interests of the United States"—a notion apparently new to them.

Churchill deployed all his eloquent reservations about the wisdom of invading France. He conjured up images, as he was wont to do more than once, of the English Channel filled with American and British corpses. "This stirred me up," Stimson wrote in a report to the President, "and for a few minutes we had it hammer and tongs." Stimson accused Churchill to his face of trying to back out on an agreement he had made with Roosevelt in May to initiate plans for invading France in 1944. Churchill waffled: He confessed that if he were in total command he would not pursue the project, "yet having made his pledge he would go through with it loyally."

Stimson came home convinced that no attempt to cross the Channel "and come to grips with our German enemy" was ever going to be made under British auspices. The heads of their government opposed it; the shadows of Dunkirk and the Somme fell too darkly across their minds. "Though they have rendered lip service to the operation," Stimson wrote to Roosevelt, "their hearts are not in it and it will require more independence, more faith, and more vigor than it is reasonable to expect we can find in any British commander."

The reason for this was the same divergence of conception that had surfaced in the argument over North Africa. The Americans believed that true victory could be won only by a concentration of the immense power of both allies; the British, that Germany could be defeated by a series of attritions around the edges of its continental fortress. Stimson thought that in the light of postwar problems the British attitude was "terribly danger-ous," since the Russians had been promised a second front and none "of these methods of pinprick warfare can be counted on by us to fool Stalin into the belief that we have kept that pledge."

Stimson woke in Washington the morning of August 10 and, fighting weariness after a sultry night that discouraged sleep, dictated a series of recommendations to the President, "among the most serious I have had to make." Later in the morning they were typed, he signed them and showed them to Marshall, and at one o'clock he took them to Roosevelt in the White House. This was one of their most significant conversations. "I believe . . . ," Stimson had written, "that the time has come for you to decide that your government must assume the responsibility of leadership in this great final movement of the European war which is now confront-ing us. . . . We cannot afford to begin the most dangerous operation of the war under halfhearted leadership." (Stimson proposed a leader in the person of General Marshall, which is why Marshall was scrupulous to disassociate himself.)

The President as he read ticked off point by point for approval and remarked at the end that these were conclusions he had come to himself; Stimson said it was "one of the most satisfactory conferences I have ever had with the President." The Joint Chiefs arrived for a meeting, Roosevelt invited Stimson to stay on, and Stimson listened with mounting satisfac-tion as his own views were reasserted and pronounced with the Presi-dent's authority. "The cross-Channel attack," writes McGeorge Bundy, "had at last become wholly his own."[107]

The plan that had now been named Overlord came in for lengthy debate by Roosevelt, Churchill, and the Combined Chiefs at their subse-quent meetings at Quebec (August) and Cairo-Teheran (November–December). With each reconsideration the familiar arguments were trot-ted out again, but as time went on, the planning and the piling up of forces that led to D-Day gained in mass and momentum. (Properly speaking, "Overlord" referred to the invasion of Europe as a whole, while the landing itself was known as "Neptune," but this is not a distinction much observed by participants then or writers since.) At these meetings with the British, the American chiefs were uneasy lest the President be subject to Churchillian persuasion and change his mind, and yet from this time forward their concern proved groundless. Roosevelt had caught fire, and Churchill (though he never stopped arguing for add-on efforts in the Mediterranean) kept his word and came along. After returning from

Cairo-Teheran, the President lunched with Stimson and was able to say,
"I have thus brought Overlord back to you safe and sound on the ways for
accomplishment."[108]

By now Stimson knew that Marshall would not, as Stimson had devoutly wished, be Overlord's commander.

It was as though the earned fulfillment of a life rich in distinction was
to be, at the very last minute, denied him. Overlord would be the vindication of everything Marshall's career had pointed toward, the operation he
had advocated from the beginning and the one his army was designed for.
The assumption that he would lead in it was so universal as to go almost
unquestioned. No soldier of Marshall's quality could fail to prefer a field
command, let alone one so far above all others in challenge and honor.
Roosevelt was enough of a student of military history to appreciate this.
"You and I," he said to Eisenhower when he stopped in Tunisia on his way
to Cairo, "know the name of the Chief of Staff in the Civil War, but few
Americans outside the professional services do."[109] The wrongness of rele-
gating George Marshall to the status of Henry W. Halleck was apparent
to both of them. Marshall belonged up there with Lee and Grant.

Right as all of the above might be, it was also beside the point. So
general was certainty about Marshall's getting the job that the implications had not been thoroughly examined. Once they were brought out into
full view, the case was no longer so clear and the complexities were
magnified. For Marshall to become a theater commander was in substance
a demotion. If he withdrew from the Combined Chiefs (and Eisenhower
replaced him), then he would thereafter be taking orders from two of his
very recent subordinates. For him to stay on as a member of the Combined Chiefs, on the other hand, would be to render that body superfluous,
since the war in Europe was its principal preoccupation.

When trial balloons about Marshall's appointment were floated in
Washington, the public reaction was strongly negative. Military journals
protested; Republicans accused Hopkins of trying to get rid of Marshall in
order to control Army contracts. At the height of the uproar, a Nazi
propaganda broadcast from Paris announced that Marshall had been dismissed. "President Roosevelt has taken over his command," it went on.
"This occurred two days ago, but has not yet been commented on in
Washington." Marshall sent a transcript to Hopkins, asking him if he was
behind this. It came back with a penciled note: "Dear George—Only true
in part—I am now Chief of Staff *but* you are President. FDR."[110]

Various attempts were made to enlarge the European command sufficiently so that Marshall could suitably occupy it. The rationale of them was
that he should command *all* of the war against Germany, including North
Africa, the Middle East, and the advance up the Italian peninsula. But this
was quite unacceptable to the British. They were willing to give up Overlord to an American, inasmuch as American forces in it would eventually

be the majority, but to relinquish as well the Mediterranean—an area dear to them, about which they believed Americans to be wrongheaded any-how—was asking too much. Once the British position was made known, the conclusion was inescapable. The Americans could not allow Marshall to step down and the British could not allow him to step up. Overlord would have to go to a lesser man, as many in the American military now preferred (King, Arnold, Leahy, and General Pershing, among others, all had decided that they wanted Marshall kept on as Chief of Staff).

But the ultimate choice was Roosevelt's, "one of the most difficult and one of the loneliest decisions he ever had to make," in Robert Sherwood's opinion, "against the almost impassioned advice of Hopkins and Stimson, against the known preferences of both Stalin and Churchill, against his own proclaimed inclination to give George Marshall the historic opportunity which he so greatly desired and so amply deserved." It would be Eisenhower instead. Roosevelt's extenuating aside to Marshall has become part of the legend of them both: "I didn't feel I could sleep at ease with you out of Washington."[111]

◆

Secretary Stimson eventually came around to the conclusion that Roosevelt, in sending Eisenhower to London and keeping Marshall in Washington, had put the right man in each place.[112] Certainly Eisenhower proved to fit the role of Supreme Commander with uncanny exactness, while Marshall, by staying where he was, gave to his post as Chief of Staff an extra dimension it never had under any other occupant.

The near-total backing that the President henceforth provided him, the unmatched esteem in which he was held by Congress, and the subtle (and sometimes not so subtle) dominion he came to exercise over the Combined Chiefs—all conspired to make Marshall a towering figure in the last two years of the war. Brooke and Churchill challenged him again and again, and again and again they failed to break his hold on the shape of the campaign in the West. Stimson believed that Marshall, in refusing to tell the President that he wanted the Overlord command, acted out of a noble effacement of self and self-interest, and if self-denial can be said to increase the magnetic properties of a noble spirit, it did so in the case of General Marshall.

But it should not be considered a criticism to suggest that other thoughts may have been in his mind. He was too intelligent not to be aware of the awkwardness in command structure that his appointment would have created, and he had listened (in silence, at Cairo) to Admiral King argue fervently that the Joint Chiefs had become too good a team to break up, a viewpoint the President also had casually mentioned to Eisenhower. Marshall was too objective to measure his own gifts with any vanity. His essential concerns had been with organization. Field Marshal

Dill had found him less interested in strategy than Dill had hoped, and Marshall—though he was aware of the deficiencies in American weapons —was more tolerant of them than he should have been.[113] Forrest Pogue offers the shrewd perception that Marshall's affection for the military buccaneers—the swashbuckling types like Patton, Wingate, and Terry Allen—might have stemmed from an inner awareness that such was not for him, not for him to ride into battle like some Jeb Stuart with pennants flying.[114]

Indeed he might not have turned out to be as good a field commander as Eisenhower did (saving for a later page consideration of Eisenhower's performance in that capacity). His relish of the unorthodox was still alive, and some manifestations of it are unsettling. Marshall had pressed for an invasion that would have been premature; he now wanted to make the assault landings in Normandy with green troops, saving the seasoned formations for a later stage—an appalling thought (without the Big Red One, the 1st Division, the near-disaster on Omaha Beach might have come far closer to complete failure than it did). He wanted to drop the airborne divisions, not behind the beachhead, but many miles inland near Évreux, halfway to Paris, which would almost surely have imperiled the landing and have sacrificed them in vain. He sent a team of officers to argue for this scheme with Eisenhower, who assembled Generals Montgomery, Bradley, and Ridgway to let them explain why they were dead against it.[115] (Eisenhower was always a skeptic about the employment of airborne units in the mass, since they became immobile on reaching the ground and lacked the firepower and resupply of regular divisions.) And Marshall did not suffer insubordination gladly; the deft handling of Montgomery and British sensitivities that Eisenhower managed to achieve would not have been Marshall's natural style, and the Anglo-American partnership might have suffered accordingly.

As Chief of Staff, on the other hand, he could assert American interests without hesitation, and did so. Marshall himself thought that his major contribution to the war consisted in standing up to Churchill and keeping that errant genius in line. The Prime Minister would sometimes carry along his own chiefs on a proposal they did not truly care for, and then to Marshall fell the necessary task of knocking it down. At Cairo, Churchill was arguing with his usual rhetorical vehemence for a pet project, an invasion of the island of Rhodes in the eastern Mediterranean. "His Majesty's Government can't have its troops standing idle," said Churchill. "Muskets must flame." Finally, Marshall had enough. "God forbid if I should try to dictate," he said, "but . . . not one American soldier is going to die on [that] goddamned beach." The others were stunned but relieved. Marshall said that Churchill did not take it personally but that Ismay had to stay up all night consoling him.[116]

Marshall also took pains to keep Roosevelt in line. Prior to the confer-

ence with the British called Quadrant, he was making the point to the
President that Churchill's way of thinking would lead to a war the American public could not accept, and when Roosevelt departed Hyde Park by
train for Quebec, Marshall sent the chief of the Operations Division, General Thomas Handy, to accompany him and to outline the American case
for Overlord. As Churchill had already discovered, however, the President was by this time squarely in Marshall's camp, and the Quebec conference—while allowing for further limited operations in Italy—agreed on a
substantial strengthening of the buildup for the Overlord forces.[117] The
British viewpoint had prevailed on North Africa not only because it was
sound but because Marshall and Roosevelt were divided. Once they
ceased to be divided, it was their viewpoint that became the core of
conviction.

Further debate over the European war, and determination of how it
would be waged, was controlled in its essentials by the dawning predominance of mobilized American power and the emergent unity of American
strategic thought. Eisenhower was their instrument, almost an extension
of Marshall's mind and purpose, and to that degree the story of Marshall
in good part becomes (as we shall see) the story of Eisenhower, who could
always be sure that Marshall was behind him and that behind Marshall
stood the President. One of the stormiest sessions of the Combined Chiefs
of Staff came toward the end at Malta, when Marshall was nettled by
British nit-picking about Eisenhower and "lit out," wrote Stimson, "so
vigorously that he carried everything before him."[118]

On the evening of the day of victory in Europe, according to Katherine Marshall, the general returned home strangely silent. Only later did
she learn from Colonel McCarthy what had happened. Marshall had been
sent for by the secretary, in whose office he found a seated semicircle of
generals and officials and a vacant chair in the center for him. "I want to
acknowledge my great personal debt to you," said Stimson. They had
passed a milepost in the realization of their work; he himself might not live
to see the end, but he prayed God that Marshall would, for the gaining of
it was his. "I have never seen a task of such magnitude performed by
man," Stimson said. "It is rare in late life to make new friends; at my age
it is a slow process but there is no one for whom I have such deep respect
and I think greater affection.

"I have seen a great many soldiers in my lifetime and you, Sir, are the
finest soldier I have ever known."[119]

III

KING

"WHEN THEY GET IN TROUBLE they send for the sonsabitches." Asked whether he had said this, Admiral King replied no, he had not, but he would have if he had thought of it. They were indeed in trouble when they sent for King, bringing him from the brink of retirement to be Commander in Chief, U.S. Fleet, and King would have been ready to admit that he enjoyed a reputation for toughness and ill temper that had few equals in the upper ranks of the U.S. Navy. He took charge of that navy at the depths of its despair and lifted it to the heights of triumph. He was a hard man in a hard time, well suited to lead a fighting fleet, but he was also a thoughtful man of a breadth and incisiveness that gave him an early and enduring grip on Allied strategy. Much of the war went the way he wished it to. The strongest mind within the American Joint Chiefs of Staff was the mind of Ernest J. King.

King's appointment was not definably Roosevelt's doing, as Marshall's was; to seek the President's favor in peacetime would not have been to King's taste or (given King's abruptness and hauteur) to the President's liking. But they saw one another regularly during the period in 1941 when King commanded the Atlantic Fleet (a post for which Stark and Secretary Knox had recommended him), and in this role he was peculiarly the instrument of Roosevelt's policy—that is, he was conducting an undeclared war against Germany to protect the transatlantic convoys, and doing so with a boldness and determination that the President's concept of that risky venture required.

The admiral's relationship with the President was one that King built, on the basis of blunt speech and demonstrated fitness for the job to be done. King said that eventually his influence with Roosevelt was such that at meetings in the President's study, especially if Churchill was there, King had only to shake his head No ever so slightly when Roosevelt looked in his direction. The President knew what he had in Admiral King. James Roosevelt remembered the President's being asked why he kept King in Washington, rather than let him go "up front" to take command. Roosevelt answered: "The President has to have close to him the shrewdest of strategists. Most critical decisions must be made here. You don't send these men into the front lines where their lives may be endangered."[1]

King himself realized that his place was near the White House. "Where the power is," he once said, "that is where the headquarters have to be." He did not need to fight the President, the Congress, and public opinion to create his navy, as George Marshall had to fight for an army, since the will to bring it into existence was already there, but within the Allied councils where strategic plans were discussed, King had to fight for what he believed to be his navy's proper place in them. Elliott Roosevelt once talked with his father about King. "He's a grand Navy man," said the President. " 'Wars can only be won by sea power; therefore, the Navy's plans must be the best; furthermore, only the Pacific theater is a naval theater; therefore, the Pacific theater must be the most important.' " Elliott said that at this point his father laughed and added: "That's not *exactly* his reasoning, but it's close enough, it'll serve."[2]

The way King's mind worked was characteristically naval in that naval strategy is of its nature aggressive. The "nation that would rule upon the sea," wrote Alfred Thayer Mahan, "must attack." Ships cannot seize a portion of the sea and hold it, as an army can hold a portion of the land. The sea can be held only by crippling any naval force that contests the holding of it with your own. No object is more pressing, as Mahan taught many generations of naval officers of many nationalities, than the destruction of the enemy fleet. The idea of "going on the defensive" in the Pacific, as the corollary of an offensive in the Atlantic, would not have meant the same thing to Admiral King—or, similarly, to the President—as it did to a Brooke or a Marshall. In true naval terms, the only way to defend against the Japanese, as King urged from the beginning, was to attack them.

To do so was not only what King's and Roosevelt's activist temperaments favored, and what the American public desired, but at the same time what sound naval doctrine prescribed. Mahan further said that when you were on the defensive with inferior forces—as we most certainly were in the Pacific in 1942—then an aggressive response was virtually mandatory. "From such a position," he wrote, "there is no salvation except by action vigorous almost to desperation." Mahan's approval was reserved for those who believed in "bringing matters to an issue as soon as possible" —for admirals like Suffren in the Indian Seas during 1782, who always understood that the way to achieve a strategic objective "was not by economizing his own ships, but by destroying those of the enemy."[3]

King was not alone in thinking this way. Nonetheless, as Secretary Stimson's biographer Elting Morison noted, if he may not have been the only officer "who could have retrieved the spiritual and physical disaster" that befell the U.S. Navy at Pearl Harbor, King was the one who did it. "Lord how I need him," Secretary Knox wrote on December 23, 1941. "One of my most important jobs is to transform the mental attitude of a good deal of the Navy from a defensive to an offensive posture."[4] The job of transforming demoralized forces into confident ones was singularly suited to a nature that might have been ill-equipped for a less demanding task. Luckily, King was available for it; he could not have been invented. "Behind the bleak and fixed composure," Elting Morison goes on, "some intense spirit burned away, a spirit fed by incalculable devotions to self and service. Above and beyond all these was resolution—grim, harsh, ruthless and whatever else it is or can be made to seem—but above all, resolution."[5]

Admiral King was a harsh taskmaster; he did not suffer laziness or shoddy performance gladly. He could be publicly abusive of subordinates to an extent the code of military command behavior does not normally countenance; praise he dispensed rarely and in private. One of his daughters said of King, "He is the most even-tempered man in the Navy. He is always in a rage." Sometimes he seemed to go out of his way to find fault. On the bridge of a ship, a junior officer said, "he was meaner than hell." But those who measured up to his exacting standards knew a different King. He could be impulsively considerate and generous; he looked after his own people; officers he relieved would be given obscure but honorable billets; his flag lieutenants were able to humor him and be relaxed about it.[6] "I suppose his reputation was that he was difficult," said an officer who worked closely with him. "I never thought so." And another: "I never had a harsh word from Admiral King. I never met a finer gentleman."[7]

Among King's most conspicuous qualities was competence; aboard a ship he commanded there was likely to be a recognition that no one could do any job better than he could (it took him years to learn, if he ever did completely, that some jobs are better done by others). He had made the Navy his whole existence, and he gave to it every energy except those he reserved for a private life of notable gaudiness. "His weaknesses," writes Professor Robert William Love of the U.S. Naval Academy, "were other men's wives, alcohol, and intolerance."[8] Work hard, play hard, might have been Admiral King's motto. During the between-war years there was no more assiduous partygoer, no more indefatigable (and notoriously successful) pursuer of attractive ladies, than King. He made no secret of this, nor of his liking for liquor; he told one of his officers never to trust a man who didn't drink and enjoy the company of women.[9] It was all of a piece with his hurling himself against existence, to master it, and sometimes existence fought back.

Professor Love describes King's career as "punctuated by great success, devastating failure, and intermissions of torment." His successes were evident. Few could match the diversity of his naval experience: submariner, aviator, staff officer, aircraft carrier commander, salvage director, bureaucrat, leader of a fleet at sea.[10] He had followed a course intended to qualify him for the highest rank, and he expected these qualifications to be acknowledged in their own right, without his having to clothe them in an amiable personality, not least because they included a capacity to deal with politico-military problems of the scope that a global conflict would present. He understood the importance in modern warfare of organization, geography, technology, and industrial production; and from their interaction he drew conclusions of a rigorous order expressed in forceful language. He waged a constant war against paperwork, but he made good use of memoranda in a style unmistakably his own, a mixture of the formal and the colloquial, of the stilted and the pungent, partly the effect of his old-fashioned habit of putting into quotation marks words and phrases of substantive meaning or even remotely idiomatic usage.

King had a retentive memory; he could recall the names of people he had met casually years before. He was devoted to crossword puzzles, which he usually completed without a dictionary, and to playing parlor games like Monopoly with his children (eventually six daughters, one son), though he hated to lose. He had been valedictorian of his high school class in Lorain, Ohio (subject: the "Values of Adversity"), and stood fourth in his class at the naval academy (he was also cadet lieutenant commander, the highest military rank). Technical problems gave him no trouble, and machinery fascinated him (his father, a Scottish immigrant, worked as a foreman in railroad repair shops, which King loved to visit as a child); he disassembled the engine of his first automobile to see how it worked. He made wise investments and over the years accumulated a considerable estate; his uniforms were always from Brooks Brothers.

He well knew his Mahan, but he was interested in land warfare too; he admired Davout and Lannes among Napoleon's marshals, studied the American Civil War, and walked the battlefields of Antietam and Gettysburg with his brother-in-law, an Army officer. In 1909, as a thirty-one-year-old lieutenant, he won a prize (gold medal, five hundred dollars, and life membership) for the first of his many essays for the *Naval Institute Proceedings,* subject: "Some Ideas About Organization Aboard Ship," in which he observed that there was then no "logical system, founded on principles," that shipboard organization could be derived from, the beginning of his lifelong though unsuccessful effort to reorganize the Navy. But it made him a reputation in the fleet as a man to be reckoned with.[11]

He had labored to make his handwriting legible, and his first drafts rarely contained an erasure (in this he resembled the only flag officer he admitted to be smarter than he was, Raymond Spruance). For King, a thought his mind had worked over and accepted cried out for implementation. His acute biographer Thomas Buell, like King a former destroyer commander, said that many of King's ideas "were either so radical or so eccentric that they aroused universal opposition." While instructors at Annapolis, he and his classmate William S. Pye designed a range-finding mechanism for naval guns that the Bureau of Ordnance adopted but refused to give them credit for. When King commanded a submarine division in 1922, he attempted to put into effect principles of submarine deployment that were, in retrospect, sound but far beyond the sea-keeping qualities of the submarines of the time. In 1940, on his flagship battleship *Texas,* he tried to camouflage the white uniforms of the ship's company by having them dipped in coffee, and gave up only when the results (writes Buell) ranged "from ecru to chocolate brown."[12]

Yet some of King's inspirations worked well. In 1920, as head of the Naval Postgraduate School, he wrote straight out the report of a three-man board appointed to consider the problems of officer education: "naval training and career management today"—Buell again—"still conform to the concepts and principles that King set down in one day over a half century ago." He was an attentive and sympathetic observer of the amphibious techniques being developed by the Marine Corps, even though his first ride in an LVT (landing vehicle, tracked) left him stranded on a reef and forced to wade ashore. As chief of the Bureau of Aeronautics, he worked to establish the Naval Aviation Cadet program. As commander of the Pacific Fleet's scouting force, he ranged from Alaska to Panama in tender *Wright,* looking for potential seaplane bases. In 1939, King, who had been the commander of carrier *Lexington,* commanded a division of both *Lexington* and *Enterprise* during Fleet Problem XX in the Caribbean and chafed at his lack of freedom to employ them independently, as he believed should be done. Buell concludes that during World War II, "carriers did operate precisely as King had foreseen," and that King was the "prime mover" in the wartime flowering of naval aviation.[13]

◆

King's greatest disappointment was his failure to be appointed Chief of Naval Operations in 1939, when the post went instead to Harold R. Stark. King was sixty years old. Mandatory retirement came at sixty-four; this had been his last chance. King was present when Stark was informed of the selection and had to repress his feelings to offer congratulations. He reverted to his permanent (two-star) rank and was assigned to the General Board, an advisory group that had deteriorated into a rest home for aging admirals; King regarded it as "a bourne from which no traveler returns." He could reasonably assume that his career was over, and a friend, at a Sunday afternoon cocktail party, saw tears in his eyes.[14]

For 1939, Stark was obviously the better choice. King was not even on the list of candidates that went to the President; his hopes had been illusory. Leahy as outgoing CNO had recommended Stark, and Roosevelt took Leahy's opinions seriously. These were times that called for a blend of diplomacy and strategic foresight, which Stark conspicuously possessed. "Gentle in manner and unobtrusive in personality," writes Admiral Morison, ". . . with his pink complexion, benevolent countenance, rimless spectacles and thick shock of white hair, [Stark] looked more like a bishop than a sailor."[15] More to the point, as it happened, Stark was one of the few people of King's generation in the Navy who not only admired him but liked him. Stark well understood what being put out to pasture on the General Board would mean to a man of King's temperament and ambition; he tried but failed to get King one last seagoing command (he wanted King to take charge of the Pacific Fleet at Pearl Harbor). King immersed himself in his work on the board and spent long hours at it. "They've not done with me yet," he told a junior officer. "I will have another chance." Still, to a former subordinate he spoke of himself as a "has-been."

King's one-year tour on the General Board turned out ultimately to his advantage. His impatience with slowness and low achievement had made a favorable impression on Secretary of the Navy Charles Edison, who recommended to Roosevelt that King be made Commander in Chief, U.S. Fleet. Edison thought that the Navy needed someone who could jar it out of its peacetime ways of thinking. "I believe," the secretary wrote the President, "that Rear Admiral E. J. King, USN, is outstandingly of this type and . . . would do wonders for the fleet and the Service." Roosevelt took no action; there were rumors that he thought King drank too much.[16]

But the war was coming closer. At its outbreak in 1939 in Europe, the President, with Pan-American approval, had established a "neutrality patrol" in the western Atlantic to look out for German submarines and report their locations in the clear, in plain language—that is, intended to be overheard by British ships escorting convoys. In April 1940, after the Germans overran Denmark, the local government in Greenland asked for American protection and Coast Guard cutters were sent there.

In July, Roosevelt had declared that the United States would hold itself responsible for the defense of the Western Hemisphere, and Admiral Stark had sent a Special Naval Observer to London for "exploratory conversations" with the British Chiefs of Staff. The burden of "patrolling" fell on the Atlantic Squadron, a middling force of four old battleships, a division of cruisers, a destroyer squadron, and an aircraft carrier. Stark became dissatisfied with its commander and together he and the Navy secretary (now Frank Knox) persuaded the President to let them offer the post to King. This was implicitly a demotion, since King had last been at sea as a vice-admiral, but he said that it didn't matter and accepted. On December 17, 1940, he broke his two-star flag in battleship *Texas*. He discovered that the war-plans safe contained a single file, for a war with Mexico.[17]

A promotion back to three stars followed shortly, and in February

1941, the Atlantic Squadron was redesignated as Atlantic Fleet; King was appointed to command it, with the rank of full admiral, and Roosevelt extended its mission to include escorting convoys as far as Iceland. In March, the President directed that the Atlantic Fleet be brought to a state of wartime readiness: "patrols" were terminated; King divided his ships into four task forces; they were darkened at night, stripped of superfluous gear, and given their mobilization allowance of arms. In April, King at Roosevelt's behest issued an operational order defining the Western Hemisphere as extending to the twenty-six-degree meridian, west of Iceland but east of the Azores. "Entrance into the Western Hemisphere," it read, "by naval ships or aircraft of belligerents other than those powers having sovereignty in the Western Hemisphere is to be viewed as possibly actuated by unfriendly interests."[18]

Plan Dog, Stark's memorandum to Knox recommending an offensive in the Atlantic, was taking hold. With the transfer in May of the task force from the Pacific (three battleships, four cruisers, one aircraft carrier, two destroyer squadrons), it began to acquire plausibility. By July, the President had decided to put Navy plans for escorting transatlantic convoys into effect. In August, after the conference with Churchill in Placentia Bay, Newfoundland (for which Roosevelt had asked King, in great secrecy, to make the naval arrangements), he ordered King, beginning September 1, to escort convoys two thirds of their way across the ocean.[19] This, in effect, made clashes with the U-boats inevitable.

The condition of the Atlantic squadron at the time patrolling began could have been described in a phrase: old ships, new men. Boats had been wrecked in heavy seas that damaged bulwarks and lockers; there were cracked plates, equipment failures, gun ports that were not waterproof. A destroyer ran onto a reef in Long Island Sound and went to drydock for four months. A young pilot, trying to land on carrier *Ranger*, stalled into the sea and drowned. The lack of bases meant that some destroyers had to be serviced in private yards. The duty was dangerous and exhausting; the men thought the patrols pointless and inefficient, yet the President had insisted on them and subjected the Navy Department to a series of hectoring memoranda. Admiral Stark believed that King was the best possible man in such a situation. "He will lick things into shape," Stark wrote to Kimmel in Hawaii.[20]

King had begun his work by making clear what he wanted, in a series of his own memos in the form of orders to the fleet. The first (December 20, 1940) dealt with the measures necessary to put ships on a war-emergency basis: institution of antimine, antisubmarine, and antiaircraft practices; daily exercises at general quarters or damage control while at sea; "close attention to orders and instructions." Two more (January 21 and April 22, 1941) were devoted to the exercise of command, and constituted a lecture King might well have been giving to himself: delegate, encourage initiative in subordinates, phrase orders so as to specify the "what" but not the "how" of a task. "Initiative means freedom to act," wrote King, "but it does not mean freedom to act in an offhand or casual manner. It does not mean freedom to disregard or to depart *unnecessarily* from standard procedures or practices or instructions."

The fourth, and most fully characteristic of its author, was titled: "Making the Best of What We Have" (March 24). King said that the difficulties and discomforts of the emergency period "must be faced in the same spirit of cheerfulness and willingness with which we would face the hazards and dangers of war—if and when it comes." The fleet did not have the personnel and material resources it needed to carry out its assigned operations while waiting for developments over which it had no control. But that did not excuse anything less than the best performance by all hands. "I expect the officers of the Atlantic Fleet," wrote King, "to be the leaders in what may be called the 'pioneering spirit'—to lead in the determination that the difficulties and discomforts—personnel, material, operations, waiting—shall be dealt with as 'enemies' to be overcome—by our own efforts."[21]

King astonished one junior officer by saying he felt we really were at war in the Atlantic. When the *Bismarck* broke loose in the convoy lanes, he ordered long-range patrol planes based on Newfoundland to make a search, though none found it. When the President declared an unlimited emergency, and said that we would take whatever steps were necessary, King took him at his word. When King asked naval aviators in Bermuda whether they had honored a British request to fly patrols, and they told him they were not allowed to go more than fifty miles out to sea, he asked to see their orders and later appeared pleased when they told him they had done what the British asked for anyhow. His job as commander of the Atlantic Fleet has been described as that of staying "one speech ahead of the President."

For King's officers and men, as Admiral Morison put it, the "strain was not only physical but psychological." They were enduring all the hardships of war but it was not called war, and they could tell nobody about it; when ashore, the crews were forbidden to say where they had been or what they had been doing; they could feel none of the reinforcement that comes from public recognition. Other young men of their generation were still enjoying the perquisites of peacetime. The ships the Navy was escorting flew under foreign flags. Those of them who disapproved of the President's policies, as inevitably some did, wondered whether the mission they had been assigned was constitutionally legitimate. That under the circumstances morale remained relatively high Admiral Morison thought remarkable.[22]

The President was engaged in a complex and hazardous game of nerves. He must do nothing public opinion would not tolerate. Yet it was not in his nature to remain inactive, and the Atlantic Fleet was all he then had to fight with. Patrick Abbazia titles a book about it *Mr. Roosevelt's Navy* and the subtitle refers to that navy's "private war." Roosevelt used the fleet, says Abbazia, "to test the purposes of the German Fuehrer. He soon discovered that his foe lacked the will to give battle at sea. That discovery proved of inestimable value." It momentarily eliminated German naval power from the western Atlantic, releasing Allied warships for employment elsewhere and allowing Allied convoys to assemble safely in American waters. Symbolically it was a halfway house, serving as a warning to the Nazis without unduly alarming the isolationists, who could have no persuasive objection to barring "belligerent ships from the approaches to the Western Hemisphere."[23] Step by step it habituated the American people to the seriousnessness of the German threat.

On September 4, 1941, U.S. destroyer *Greer* was proceeding westward toward Iceland when a British airplane alerted her to the presence of a German submarine some ten miles ahead. *Greer* maintained sound contact with the U-boat for three hours but did not attack, until the latter turned on *Greer* and launched two torpedoes, both of which were dodged. *Greer* counterattacked with depth charges but was unable to reestablish contact and continued on her way. The incident would have been at best a footnote to history but for what the President made of it. He issued a shoot-on-sight order to the Navy and on September 11 delivered a radio address characterizing as "piracy" the attack on *Greer*. "From now on," said Roosevelt, "if German or Italian vessels of war enter the waters the protection of which is necessary for American defense, they do so at their own risk."[24] A *de facto* war had begun for real.

On the night of October 16–17, 1941, a division of five U.S. destroyers was south of Iceland escorting convoy SC-48, some fifty merchant ships in nine columns, when a wolf pack of U-boats made six successful attacks. A burning transport silhouetted U.S.S. *Kearny,* and as she slowed to avoid another ship a torpedo struck on her starboard side, tearing a jagged hole and causing many casualties. *Kearny* was able to reach Iceland unassisted, but first blood had been drawn by the enemy. "I am sure that you realize," Admiral King wrote to a friend, "that the *Kearny* incident is but the first of many that, in the nature of things, are bound to occur."[25] The second came on October 31, when five U.S. destroyers were escorting convoy HX-156 six hundred miles or so west of Ireland. Just at daybreak, a torpedo struck U.S.S. *Reuben James,* which was blown in half and sank. Detonating depth charges killed many in the water; of a ship's company of about 160, only 45, and no officers, survived.

The arrival of actual combat and bloodshed, far from arousing opposition to the President, seemed to strengthen his hand. War in the Atlantic had somehow become politically acceptable. On November 17, Congress revised the Neutrality Act to allow the arming of American merchantmen and their employment in the eastern Atlantic; the Atlantic Fleet took on the job of barring German surface raiders from passage through the Denmark Strait, between Iceland and Greenland. There was a mood of stiffening resolve; even King was affected by it. After the sinking of the *Reuben James* he swore off hard liquor for the duration.

II

It has well been said that building a navy need be only a matter of years, but that building a naval tradition is a matter of centuries. The deeper the tradition, the more likely it is that the navy will have played an instrumental part in its nation's emergence, as did (unlike the German) the American, the British, and the Japanese. The American Revolution was won by a navy—not ours but the French, regrettably, at the Battle of the Chesapeake Capes in 1781—though as Benjamin Franklin said afterward, the real war of independence was yet to be fought.[26] Over thirty years later, it was fought by the U.S. Navy, in the headlong conflict of maritime destinies with Great Britain that goes under the misnomer War of 1812. It must be the least remembered war in American history, the most disparaged as clumsy and inconclusive, yet it forged a national identity the Revolution had only begun to achieve—and the Navy remembers it.

Perry and Decatur, perhaps, but Preble, Porter, Lawrence, Hull, and MacDonough are not exactly household names. They created a naval tradition: seamanship, discipline, fairness, efficiency, courage, originality, a spirit of making do with what you had. The Navy preserves its memories in the names of its ships; names of aircraft carriers made famous in World War II came down from the days of 1812. The first *Intrepid* was a ketch which Stephen Decatur took into Tripoli harbor in 1804 to cut out the captured frigate *Philadelphia* (thirty-eight guns); when he heard of it, Horatio Nelson called it "the most bold and daring act of the age."[27]

The first *Wasp* was a sloop (eighteen guns) which in 1812, between the Delaware and Bermuda, outmaneuvered and so savagely raked H.M.S. *Frolic* (twenty guns) that when the Americans went to board, only three wounded officers were left alive on *Frolic*'s deck; they threw down their swords. *Wasp*'s sister ship was *Hornet*, another eighteen-gun sloop, which under James Lawrence tangled off British Guiana with H.M.S. *Peacock* (eighteen). *Peacock* hauled down the ensign and sank. Later *Hornet* off Tristan da Cunha so smashed up H.M.S. *Penguin*, a brig (eighteen), that she had to be burned.

The first *Essex* was a frigate (thirty-two guns) which under David Porter off Newfoundland gave H.M.S. *Alert* (twenty) a broadside so heavy that *Alert* fired one musket shot and struck the colors. *Essex* went on to round the Horn and eliminate the British whaling industry in the Pacific, taking so many prizes that even little Davy Farragut, the fourteen-year-old midshipman, got to command one. The first *Saratoga* (twenty-six) was the flagship of a force under Thomas MacDonough on Lake Champlain which stopped cold and sent reeling back into Canada the largest invasion of the United States ever attempted.

The first *Enterprise* was a schooner of twelve guns, very fast, which saw more action and captured more enemies than any other American ship; she "moved perpetually through an atmosphere of valor and wonderful good luck," writes Fletcher Pratt,[28] and she survived the war as successfully as did her latter-day namesake, carrier *Enterprise,* the Big E. Only the most illustrious name of all, that of ever-triumphant *Constitution* (forty-four guns), failed to be carried forward, and this because *Constitution* is still in commission, moored to greater glory at her berth in Charlestown, not far from Bunker Hill.

The year 1812 had opened with three contests of ship against ship, each of which ended with an American victory. The President held a ball to celebrate and in the midst of it a mud-stained lieutenant entered a hall resounding with cheers to lay still a fourth British battle flag at the feet of Dolley Madison. In six months the Americans had done more damage to the Royal Navy than all its enemies in nine years of war. This was not the way His Majesty's ships were accustomed to be treated. The London newspapers tut-tutted that it was "an occurrence that calls for serious reflection" and Downing Street observed that comparisons were invidious inasmuch as American frigates mounted forty-four guns while the British had only thirty-eight.

The lion's tail had been tweaked and the lion roared. Twelve battleships, thirty-four frigates, and eighty sloops were sent to put American ports under blockade. Sixty thousand troops were withdrawn from Europe and organized into expeditions to invade the United States from north, east, and south. The upstarts must be taught their place; the coastline was soon defenseless, exposed to pillage and rapine by British squadrons. The blockade intensified, commerce slowed to a halt, and the borning nation faced economic ruin. Then an odd thing happened.

They were called privateers—slender craft with tall, raked masts, beautifully designed and built, manned by sailors bent on a potent mix of revenge and greed. The ships were fast but frail, and many were claimed by the sea, yet American shipyards (notably Baltimore) turned out two for each one lost. Now it was John Bull's turn to be strangled. The privateers ranged the globe, devastating Britain's source of strength, its merchant fleet. By the summer of 1814 the raiders had taken a thousand prizes they admitted to and doubtless more they forgot to mention. British coastwise shipping had to be suspended and the substantial tradesmen whose support a Tory government cannot do without were crying for peace.[29] The northern invasion of America was a failure, the eastern a show of force without conclusive issue, and at New Orleans on January 8, 1815, backed by Navy guns and Navy gunboats, a motley force under Andrew Jackson, made up of U.S. Marines, black refugees from Santo Domingo, swarthy pirates with rings in their ears, and lean mountain men from Kentucky in coonskin caps, annihilated five of the finest regiments in the British Army, men who had faced Napoleon's marshals. The war was won, Jackson was on his way to the presidency, and the U.S. Navy had discovered itself.

Firepower was what had done it, those terrible broadsides from the American frigates that left proud British warships splintered and dismasted. Behind the privateers, writes Pratt, "the cruisers of the American navy . . . did not capture . . . but fought and destroyed everything they met."[30] The lesson was not forgotten: A *guerre de course,* a campaign against commerce, cannot succeed without a war-making fleet behind it, and that fleet must consist of trimly fought ships of which the principal element must be the largest, best protected, and most heavily armed vessels that naval architects can design—which is to say, battleships. Mahan, who published his great work in 1890, made this sacred writ; as a technology of sail and iron gave way to one of steam and steel, he asserted that the principles remained unchanged.

Mahan preached the supremacy of the battle line, the center of every great sea battle since 1655, when the British first employed it against the Dutch in the Battle of Lowestoft—thereafter at Beachy Head, Ushant, the Saintes, Cape Saint Vincent, Trafalgar.[31] In a naval war fought according to Mahan, the battle fleet, screened by cruisers and destroyers, goes forth to sea and there defeats the enemy fleet in a major engagement; thereafter the other objectives of sea power—defending the coastline, guarding the shipping lanes, blockading unfriendly ports—fall into place automatically. Thus Dewey at Manila Bay, Sampson off Santiago, Togo at Tsushima, Jellicoe at Jutland.

The effects of a major success at sea can be all-encompassing. At Tsushima, on May 27, 1905, Admiral Togo met a Russian force sent halfway round the world to lift the Japanese siege of Port Arthur, and in the strait between Korea and Japan he sank eight Russian battleships, five cruisers, and seven destroyers. Japan instantly became the foremost military power in the Far East and arrived at a confident trust in naval preeminence that lasted forty years.

By the same token, failure to reach decision enforces stalemate. Jutland, when the German and British fleets collided off northern Denmark on May 30–31, 1916, was "a story of lost opportunities, misunderstood signals, and questionable leadership . . . ," writes Drew Middleton, "a hazy picture of two giants groping for each other through the North Sea mists, making occasional and bloody contact and then failing to follow fortune."[32] Young officers studied it attentively and drew the moral: Seek at all costs the decisive engagement. Admiral Nimitz could fight the Battle of Jutland on a dining room table with salt and pepper shakers, which his daughter Katy said taught her more about it than she cared to know.[33]

◆

Between World War I and World War II, the U.S. Navy was in a trough of physical inadequacy: not enough sailors, not enough ships, not enough overseas bases. By 1939, the fleet had only 78 percent of the enlisted men its complement called for, the submarine force was short of war strength by 40 percent, the navy yard in the Philippines was totally unprotected, and bases capable of sustaining an adequate flotilla in the Atlantic did not exist. There were latent strengths, a reservoir of doctrine and trained men on whom a thirtyfold expansion could and would be built, but the force in being was insufficient to implement a foreign policy of anything but admonition and delay.

Commodore Dudley Knox, who reviewed this period for Admiral Morison's multivolume history, put the blame for the Navy's low estate on three causes: the constraints imposed by naval treaties, the climate of pacifism and disarmament, and the insistence by air power advocates that navies as such had become obsolete.[34] A contributing factor may have been Rooseveltian overconfidence; at times the President seemed not to realize how far the scales had tipped against us. He told a cabinet meeting in December 1937 that he thought the Navy could "block" a Japanese advance and that Japan "could be brought to her knees within a year,"[35] a misapprehension that it took Pearl Harbor to dispel completely.

As for the naval treaties, the United States had no one else to hold at fault; we imposed them on ourselves. In 1916, Woodrow Wilson had sponsored a naval expansion program that included sixteen battleships and battle cruisers, and when he moved to continue it after the war, there were violent objections from (of all people) the British, whose cherished naval supremacy they thought to be threatened thereby. An international conference was called on the subject in Washington during November 1921, to which we proposed scrapping all the capital ships we had under construction (fifteen) and two already launched (the total that had been spent on these, which as a token of universal amity we were willing to write off, was $300 million). Britain and Japan were to make similar, but much smaller, reductions until the ratio of naval forces among the U.S., Britain, and Japan came out at roughly 5:5:3. We got much the worst of the deal, especially in terms of the comparative modernity of the ships we were giving up in armor, armament, and speed. "Our sacrifice in new tonnage," writes Commodore Knox, "was not matched even approximately by any other power." Perhaps the one fortunate concession we exacted was the right to convert two unfinished battle cruisers into aircraft carriers: these became *Lexington* and *Saratoga*, and were to be invaluable.[36]

A further unfortunate feature of the Washington conference of 1921–22 was its failure to impose a limitation on anything smaller than battleships and battle cruisers—that is, on destroyers and regular cruisers, where Britain enjoyed a superiority she could ill afford to relinquish. If the intention of the conference was to halt naval construction, then its effect was the opposite, for no sooner had the agreement been signed than Japan and then Britain began building cruisers and other "auxiliaries," spending on them all the money they were saving by the moratorium on capital ships. (The United States nobly refrained from following suit, on the grounds that we should set a good example.)

Then there was the question of bases. Japan refused to accept the 5:5:3 ratio unless we agreed to a *status quo*—agreed, that is, not to improve or fortify any naval facilities in the Pacific except for Hawaii. This at one stroke doubled the effectiveness of the Japanese fleet; it left Guam and the Philippines helpless and Alaska vulnerable. An accounting would one day come due, a burdensome cost to be paid for what had been an essentially empty gesture. In 1934, Japan gave notice of her intention to terminate all naval agreements anyway.

The prevailing climate in the United States was set by those who deeply believed in avoiding war. Among their number were of course the isolationists but also pacifists, whose opposition was similarly moral and principled, including clergymen of the major Protestant sects (the Methodists were especially active) and the Federal Council of Churches of Christ in America, which led a successful movement to block naval construction during the Coolidge administration.[37] The belief that armaments led to war, and that weapons-makers were therefore warmongers, was heavily ingrained. It received reinforcement in the 1930s when a congressional committee under Senator Gerald Nye of North Dakota started out to investigate the munitions industry and ended up trying to prove that the economic interest of the European allies, the bankers, and the armaments manufacturers had been responsible for American entry into World War I. The committee's claims were excessive, but that it struck a nerve cannot be denied; even President Roosevelt, who much disliked it, found some of its reasoning persuasive.[38]

More than probably we can now conclude that Navy officers exaggerated the influence of Air Corps propaganda. The latter was strident and annoying, but its more extreme claims had not met the test of battle and its most prominent exponent was to be court-martialed for going too far in criticizing his colleagues. Brigadier General Billy Mitchell, who had commanded a large assembly of fighters and bombers in World War I, put forward in lectures, articles, and books a set of propositions about air power that denied a surface navy any future role: Ships cannot control the sea against aircraft and submarines, land-based aircraft will prevail over aircraft carriers, transport of troops in quantity by surface ships will be impossible, the mere threat of bombing a city will cause it to be evacuated, and thus air power has completely eliminated the traditional function of armies and navies.[39] Needless to add, none of these asseverations survived the war that was approaching.

In 1921, Mitchell arranged to have captured German warships used as targets in a demonstration of what his bombers could do, and on July 21 they sank the "unsinkable" dreadnought *Ostfriesland,* a veteran of Jutland, in what his supporters thought to be a vindication of his views. But there were a number of objections to this interpretation, principally that the *Ostfriesland* had been motionless and was not shooting back, and that no crew was aboard to take measures of damage control. Mitchell ignored an agreement limiting him to six-hundred-pound bombs, loaded his second wave with thousand-pounders, and went on bombing at low altitude until the target rolled over and went under. No attempt was made to analyze the hits or discover where the fatal damage was and what had done it. Interservice rivalry was encouraging a game of public appearances rather than any serious preparation for war, and the game continued for many years, beyond the danger point for national security. This, rather than any threats to the Navy's budget, was the ill outcome of Billy Mitchell's crusade.

The real threat to the budget came from Congress, where isolationism and the lure of neutrality held sway. In December 1938, in the aftermath of Munich, a board under Admiral Arthur J. Hepburn (former Commander in Chief, U.S. Fleet) submitted to the Chief of Naval Operations (then Leahy) a report on naval bases as apt as it was politically ill-timed. The Hepburn board recommended spending $326 million on bases: ten in the U.S., four in the Caribbean, and twelve in the Pacific, of which one was to be on Guam in the otherwise Japanese-held Marianas.

Guam had been inspected by Captain Charles M. Cooke and Commander Forrest P. Sherman, who concluded that it could be made strong enough to defend itself, to reinforce the Asiatic Fleet, to immunize the Philippines, and to serve as a springboard for an American offensive in the western Pacific. Leahy persuaded a reluctant Roosevelt to let him ask for $65 million, of which $5 million was earmarked for Guam, but there were objections on the grounds that a base on Guam would provoke the Japanese. Congress surgically removed the Guam appropriation from the bill before the President could finally sign it in April 1940.[40] Of all the occasions when the United States inflicted future defeats upon itself, this is the most dramatically conspicuous. Perhaps an only partially fortified Guam would have been too vulnerable, another plum for the Japanese to pluck from the tree, but fortifying Guam was the provident thing to do, and it was not done.

In early 1937, the U.S. Navy had fifteen battleships, three aircraft carriers, seventeen heavy cruisers, ten light cruisers, 196 destroyers (162 of them overage) and eighty-one submarines (fifty overage). It counted 113,617 officers and enlisted men, and a Marine Corps of 18,223. When war came four years later, the roster had risen to 312,000 officers and enlisted men, and 64,000 Marines, but the strength in ships was not materially greater except in aircraft carriers. What had fundamentally altered was the future: Under construction was a fleet once again as large, the outcome of the two-ocean-navy bill passed without protest when the fall of France called Congress to its senses. Now the ending was only a matter of time; an eventual victory was no longer in question. Thoughtful officers like Admiral Stark knew that there would be disasters at first, when the Japanese would profit from timing and surprise, but in the long run American losses could be replaced while Japanese could not. "If you attack us," Stark told Japanese ambassador Nomura, "we will break your empire before we are through with you."[41]

◆

At Pearl Harbor, the morning of December 7, 1941, was a brilliant and beautiful one, clear sky with a few puffy clouds. The sound of church bells in Honolulu, ringing for Sunday mass, could be heard across blue water only lightly stippled by sunlight in a gentle breeze. In the U.S. fleet of more than ninety vessels, men of the forenoon watch had been piped to breakfast. Sailors in white uniforms were preparing for the ceremony of hoisting morning colors fore and aft at eight o'clock, when the ship's band assembling on the fantail of battleship *Nevada* would play the national anthem. At seven fifty-five on board minelayer *Oglala,* the senior officer afloat, Rear Admiral William R. Furlong, noticed a plane flying low over Ford Island and heard the *crump* of a bomb exploding on the seaplane ramp; as the aircraft turned up the main channel he could see the red-orange insignia painted on its fuselage. He ordered general quarters and hoisted the signal "All Ships in Harbor Sortie."

What followed was nightmare, as soldiers and sailors struggling to comprehend the incomprehensible—"Hell, I didn't even know they were sore at us," said a seaman on destroyer *Monaghan*—came to life and fought back. Klaxons squawking the alarm mingled with the bark of five-inch antiaircraft and the chatter of machine guns, perhaps one in four of them fully manned. The Japanese—at this stage forty torpedo bombers and twenty-seven dive-bombers, later 353 in all—drove home their assault. Ships shuddered under heavy explosions, lights went out, decks tilted. In the mess hall at Hickam Field, a PFC yelled a warning too late and trays and dishes went flying as a bomb crashed through the roof (thirty-five died instantly). At Schofield Barracks, a bugler, trying to think of what might rouse his regiment, blew pay call. There was much bravery and no little irony. Captain Mervyn S. Bennion of battleship *West Virginia,* disemboweled by a bomb fragment and moved to another part of the bridge, asked only after his ship and its crew until he died. In Waikiki, hearing the distant thunder, war correspondent Joseph Harsch of the *Christian Science Monitor* wakened his wife and said, "Darling, you have often asked me what an air raid sounds like. Listen to this—it's a good imitation."[42]

When the last of the Japanese departed, a little before ten o'clock, they left behind them 2,403 dead and 1,178 wounded, eighteen ships either sunk or seriously crippled, and at the airfields 188 planes destroyed and 159 damaged. (Nearly half of those killed were in battleship *Arizona* when a bomb reached the forward magazine and in fire and smoke she blew up.) The enemy had committed a colossal blunder, accomplishing in moments the goal of American unity for war that had thus far eluded the President, but the battle force had been wiped out, air power in Hawaii decimated, and a stunning blow dealt to the self-respect of the U.S. Navy.

While those ships with their heavy guns so neatly moored on Battleship Row may have been approaching obsolescence, they were nonetheless the pride of the fleet. Now everything they represented of the familiar, the enduring, the unconquerable was gone. Their great base lay bleeding and near-defenseless, many of its men in a state of shock. Their commanders, some still in their Sunday whites, gone wrinkled and grimy, were numbed and bewildered. When Spruance, normally the coolest of admirals, brought cruiser *Northampton* back into Pearl from a mission to Wake Island, saw the shattered, burned-out hulks, and returned that night to his family, they were alarmed at his appearance, his tears, his voice choked with emotion as he tried to describe what he had seen and to talk out his feelings.[43]

There were those who believed that if Admiral King had been in charge of the fleet it would not have been caught so flat-footed. That same Sunday afternoon an officer's wife told King over the telephone from Norfolk that if he had been in command in the Pacific the attack would not have achieved surprise. "There are some that don't think so," said King.[44] But only a man of King's willingness to incur dislike could have broken through the crust of custom and created a state of genuine readiness. The military on Oahu were not careless or complacent, but they were settled in routines and assumptions that no one saw fit to challenge. An officer who tried to increase duty hours, to maintain a full and continuous alert, would have risked a serious morale problem (if then nothing happened); he would have annoyed his fellows and, no less important, their wives. No one saw any compelling reason then for measures later to be taken for granted. "The basic trouble," as King said later, "was that the Navy failed to appreciate what the Japanese could and did do."[45]

Had King been there, he would have confronted the same dilemmas as did Admiral Kimmel and his Army counterparts. Under pressure to prepare for war, and knowing well enough how unprepared they were, they had opted to put training first, not an unreasonable decision. But King would have appreciated (as he already had in the Atlantic) that a state of extreme emergency existed. He would surely not have allowed weekend leaves and liberties to continue (one third of the ships' captains and a third to a half of their officers were ashore when the attack came), and as former commander of the scouting force he would more than likely have ordered extensive seaplane patrolling of the waters around the islands. (That this could have been done is evidenced by the fact that after December 7 it was done.[46]) He could have scheduled fleet movements differently, so that so much of it was not in port on a Sunday, or installed torpedo baffles and moored the battleships differently, so that their antiaircraft would have larger fields of fire. As little as an hour's warning, which they could have had from the report at six forty-five of an enemy submarine off the harbor entrance, would then have made the difference between sporadic and fully mobilized resistance.

The possibility of a carrier attack on Pearl Harbor was a commonplace of the prewar years (mentions of it are innumerable), but King above all others would have been thinking about this, for he himself conducted such an attack from carrier *Lexington,* during Fleet Problem XIII in 1932.[47] Could he have convinced the Army of its likelihood? Their antiaircraft and search radar were also on a "training" basis; many of the guns were not in place and the ammunition was under lock and key. Their aircraft were parked wingtip to wingtip, to forestall sabotage, and their pilots were on only a four-hour alert.

Army-Navy cooperation was believed to be excellent but in fact was less than complete. Each had repeatedly reassured the other: the Army that if given notice it could put up a stiff defense (which was true), the Navy that it knew at all times where the Japanese fleet was (true until recently, when the Kido Butai, the carrier striking force, had imposed radio silence). Even after Washington sent them the "this is a war warning" message on November 27, writes Walter Millis, "the Navy did not know that the Army was totally unprepared for an air attack and the Army did not know that the Navy was quite unable to warn them should one be coming."[48] To unlock this grip of mutual reticence, King would have had to admit to the Army commanders that naval intelligence had lost track of the Japanese carriers, and even had he mastered his pride and done so, would they have understood what this meant and reacted accordingly? Speculation is tempting but conviction impossible.

King was aboard his flagship cruiser *Augusta,* moored in Narragansett Bay, when news came of the attack on Pearl Harbor. Next day he left for Washington and the day after attended a meeting at the White House, which seems not to have impressed him favorably. "We're living in a fool's paradise," he told his aide. On December 15 he was back in Washington, summoned by Secretary Knox to be informed that both the President and the secretary desired King to become Commander in Chief, U.S. Fleet, a position Roosevelt had earlier abolished when he created the Atlantic and Pacific commands.

King was uncertain; he thought that Stark, as senior, was the logical choice. King, Stark, and Knox went that afternoon to see the President. King said he had three conditions: His abbreviated title should be Cominch and not Cincus ("sink us"); he should not have to hold press conferences or testify before Congress unless absolutely necessary; and—most demanding of all—he should have authority over the bureaus of the Navy Department, untouched in their serene independence for a century or more. Roosevelt agreed to the first two but said that the third would require a change in federal law; the best he could offer was to replace any bureau chief King found uncooperative.

To resolve the question of how Cominch King and CNO Stark related to one another, Knox had asked two members of the General Board to draft an executive order defining the duties of each; with minor changes King accepted it, and the President signed it on the eighteenth. King's biographer describes this as "one of the most remarkable documents of the Second World War," and with cause. King in forty-eight hours had been granted powers withheld from any Chief of Naval Operations since the title was created in 1915. King would be responsible directly to the President (what authority the secretary of the Navy retained over him was left obscure). He would exercise "supreme command of the operating forces comprising the several fleets of the United States Navy and the operating forces of the Naval Frontier Command." The CNO would continue to make war plans "from the long range point of view"; King would make the current ones.[49] Truly he was going to have "another chance."

◆

King set up for business in a hastily vacated office on the third floor of the Navy Department building on Constitution Avenue, from which the previous occupant had removed the furniture but not the dirt. King had somewhere located a flat-top desk and two chairs; one of his new deputies borrowed a broken-down table and two more chairs from a friend who was out to lunch. It was, said Rear Admiral Richard S. Edwards, "the most disreputable office I have ever seen." Edwards recalled thinking "that as the headquarters of the greatest navy in the world it fell somewhat short of being impressive."[50]

King had found Edwards in the post of commander of the Atlantic Fleet's submarine force, noted that he had "horse sense," and insisted on bringing him to Washington as his deputy for operations. Another he later insisted on having, as chief planning officer, was Captain Charles M. "Savvy" Cooke, Jr., one of the best brains in the service, then commanding battleship *Pennsylvania* and much preferring to remain there. King asked, Cooke protested; King asked again, Cooke protested again. King replied this time that officers must serve where they can do the most for the Navy, and that the decision was not theirs to make. "It is my considered judgment that you are needed here."[51] Savvy Cooke came, and he and Dick Edwards remained with King throughout the war.

Though King knew his base of operations must be in Washington, he wanted a flagship; he wanted to be able to go to sea whenever he wished or needed to. He found one in the former Dodge family yacht, *Delphine* —257 feet, 1,200 tons—and had it converted to Navy specifications. He asked his staff to suggest a new name (*Unity, Wolverine, Excelsior,* and *Nemesis* were among the contenders) and finally chose *Dauntless.* In mid-1942, *Dauntless* was moored in the Washington Navy Yard, and except for minor excursions, it remained there while King remained in command. Though his official quarters were in the Naval Observatory, where his wife and family lived and he now and then joined them on Sunday afternoons, he preferred the seclusion of *Dauntless* and made it his home throughout the war. A congressman questioned the need to provide King with an expensive ship ($250,000 a year) for an extra bedroom, but did not pursue the matter.

King normally rose at seven, exercised for ten minutes before shaving and dressing, and then breakfasted with any of his officers who might be assigned to *Dauntless* with him (among them at times were Edwards, Cooke, or Rear Admiral Russell Willson, a former superintendent of the naval academy who briefly became King's chief of staff). Willson said that when King read the morning newspaper he turned first to the comic page and "positively roared" over Dagwood and Blondie, which Willson failed to find all that amusing. A Cadillac given King by a vice-president of A & P drove him to the office.

He was an efficient but not a tidy worker; papers were piled six inches deep on his desk and his in-box overflowed, though he always seemed to know where everything was; at the end of the day he walked away and left things as they were, classified documents and all, in the certainty that someone would stand guard when the office cleaners came (someone did). King held no regular conferences; if he wanted to discuss something he simply sent for the officer responsible for it. He kept his staff small and, except for Edwards and Cooke, rotated its members frequently to and from the fleet, so that a seagoing atmosphere would prevail.[52] Around four o'clock he departed, and he did not reappear until time for dinner on *Dauntless;* nobody knew where he went, which could be embarrassing if a call came from the White House. Occasionally he would be away for two or three days at a time, with no explanation other than a need to relax.

Some measure of the strain King imposed upon himself can be found in the means he adopted to relieve it. He had a number of hideaways, one of them a farm in Cockeysville, Maryland, where lived Abby Dunlap and

Betsy Matter, sisters who were both wives of naval officers and had become something of adopted daughters to King (he was godfather to one
of the Dunlap children). The two sisters—"warm, cheerful, beautiful
young women," says Buell—adored King and pampered him. "We were
trying desperately to protect him," Betsy Matter recalled later. There
were times when King would come in, sit on a Victorian sofa with his feet
stretched out and his head back, and not say a word to anyone for a half
hour or more. Sometimes they would cook for him and everyone would
eat out on the terrace, nothing but lighthearted talk. They liked to make
him laugh, and Abby Dunlap told him he should laugh more often. King
sent her the well-known photograph (well-known because it was so
unusual) of him laughing during an Annapolis reunion, with the inscription: "Abby, you see it can be done."

Another refuge was a farm in northern Virginia, overlooking the
Shenandoah Valley, owned by Paul and Charlotte Pihl, friends of King's
since the early 1930s (Pihl was an aeronautical engineering officer who
had served with King; his wife was Wendell Willkie's sister). King would
arrive alone on weekends and go to the guesthouse, a stone building with
bedrooms, a book-lined library, and a large fireplace; King called it his
Shangri-La. He would stay there, even missing meals and asking only for
a sandwich; no one disturbed him, though sometimes he and Charlotte
Pihl talked for hours. Given King's earlier reputation there was the inevitable gossip, but a friend of them both said that anyone who knew Paul
Pihl would realize that if anything were amiss he would throw King out
summarily.[53]

During the months of February and March 1942, King conceived an
American strategy for the conduct of the war. He did not dispute the need
to hold the "citadel and arsenal" of Great Britain, and to support the "line
of British military effort" in the Middle East, "which they—and we—
cannot afford to let go." But he proposed an *offensive* in the Pacific! As he
wrote in a statement he drafted for the Joint Chiefs to send the President,
"No fighter ever won his fight by covering up—by merely fending off the
other fellow's blows. The winner hits and keeps on hitting even though
he has to be able to take some stiff blows in order to be able to keep on
hitting." Whether Roosevelt ever saw King's draft is not known, but in
early March, King addressed a memorandum of his own to the President
in which he sent forth his thinking, and the effect of this document was
profound. "King had embarked," writes Buell, "upon the most important
contribution he would make to victory in the Second World War."[54]

Australia and New Zealand must be held, said King, because they are
"white man's countries," and because of the repercussions their overrunning by Japanese would have "among the non-white races of the world."
We must hold Hawaii and its approaches (i.e., Midway), and maintain the
line of communications to Australia by way of Samoa, Fiji, and New Cale-

donia, where "strong points" (i.e., bases) should be established. Further "strong points" in Tongatapu, Efate, and Funafuti would secure the line and make possible "step by step advances" northwest from the New Hebrides into the Solomon Islands and the Bismarck Archipelago, to draw Japanese forces there and relieve pressure elsewhere (from this proposal came the Guadalcanal campaign). King summoned up his "integrated, general plan of operations" for the President in three lines:

Hold Hawaii.

Support Australasia.

Drive northwestward from New Hebrides.

King believed that the "steps" in "step by step advances" could be made by Marines, who would thereafter be relieved by Army "garrison troops"—an unfortunate term—so that the advance could continue.[55] This did not go down well with the Army's chief Pacific planner, Brigadier General Dwight D. Eisenhower. "The Navy wants to take all the islands in the Pacific, have them held by army troops, to become bases for army pursuit and bombers," Eisenhower wrote in his diary. "Then the navy will have a safe place to sail its vessels. . . . One thing that might help win this war is to get someone to shoot King."[56] But Marshall did not object to King's overall plan and at a meeting of the Combined Chiefs in the White House on March 5 the President approved it. "Roosevelt made it clear . . . ," writes an Army historian, "that the Navy's concept of operations in the Pacific would prevail." In her history of the Joint Chiefs, Grace Person Hayes says of this meeting: "The President stated it as an established fact that activity in the Pacific would follow the Navy's general scheme."[57]

Postlude: On November 11, 1943, *Dauntless* got up steam, engines were tested for the task of getting under way, and the crew reviewed its unfamiliar seagoing duties. Generals Marshall and Arnold with their staffs came aboard, followed by King's principal planning assistants, and *Dauntless* put out into the Potomac. Downstream off Point Lookout, where the river meets Chesapeake Bay, lay at anchor the great gray mass of newly commissioned battleship *Iowa,* Captain John McCrea commanding, about to make her maiden voyage in deep water and carry the President, King, and the others to the Allied conferences at Cairo and Teheran. Next morning the presidential yacht *Potomac* came alongside and transferred the President, Leahy, Hopkins, Ross McIntire, Pa Watson, and Wilson Brown, who had replaced McCrea as Roosevelt's naval aide. *Iowa* hoisted anchor and steamed down the bay to Hampton Roads, where she took on fuel. (This had been McCrea's idea: By lightening ship, *Iowa* could embark the President farther up the bay with greater ease and secrecy; McCrea got on well with King and thought it a pleasure to deal with him, and both King and Roosevelt had approved his scheme.)

One evening during the transatlantic crossing, King and McCrea were in McCrea's sea cabin talking about Mahan and various officers King had known. "You know, McCrea," King said, "I regard you as a good officer, but you could be a lot better. The trouble is, you have one outstanding weakness." What was that? McCrea asked. "Your big weakness, McCrea," said King, "is that you are not a son of a bitch. And a good naval officer has to be a son of a bitch." McCrea said he would rather not have his crew think of him that way: "And besides, Admiral King, you are a good naval officer and universally regarded as such. I must say I have never heard anyone refer to you as a son of a bitch."

"He stomped out of my cabin," McCrea said later, "knowing full well that I was lying."[58]

III

The Battle of the Atlantic was the war's inner core, an only partly visible axle on which other contingencies turned. It was harsh, monotonous, and continuous, from the day hostilities opened until two days before they ceased, five years and eight months later. A "war of groping and drowning," Churchill called it, "of ambuscade and stratagem, of science and seamanship." Its centrality was both obvious and concealed; the menace lay less in open catastrophe than in slow and steady erosion, the leaching away of control over Britain's sea approaches until military and economic strangulation made themselves known too late to be prevented.

"How willingly," wrote Churchill of its progress during early 1941, "would I have exchanged a full-scale invasion for this shapeless, measureless peril, expressed in charts, curves, and statistics." He said that it was the only thing that ever really frightened him during the war. By its end, 4,786 merchant ships of over 21 million gross tons had been sunk, together with 158 British Commonwealth and 29 American warships and a large number of aircraft. On the order of 40,000 Allied seamen—plus several hundred women and children—had lost their lives. But so also had 32,000 German submariners, who went down with the 781 of their U-boats that were sent to the bottom.

Its realities were those of the cruel sea, of small ships in foul weather, heavy wind and wave, lashing rain and sleet; of being tossed about in cramped quarters, with always the prospect of the sudden explosion that sent you into icy waters where none survived for long. Of all the major campaigns of the war, it revolved most vitally around intelligence, around the opponents' penetration of each other's secrets. It was also to a high degree technical, dependent on complex instruments and fine calculations, subject to the hazards introduced by scientific or tactical innovations the adversary had not anticipated. Measure had its immediate effect in countermeasure, producing a seesaw of alternating advantage that went on almost to the very last; "although the turning point had been passed by the end of May 1943," wrote Admiral Samuel Eliot Morison, in his semiofficial history of the Navy in World War II, "it was by no means a foregone conclusion that it would not turn again." An experienced convoy escort commander said to him: "Anything can happen in this war."[59]

Both sides came to it unready, either in equipment or in theory. Neither Hitler nor his navy wanted or expected a submarine war; in September 1939, the Germans had only forty-three U-boats of all types fit for combat and were producing at best four more per month. (By the time they declared war on the United States they had about two hundred of an oceangoing capability and were commissioning twenty per month.) Britain began World War I with 400 destroyers and World War II with 180; in 1939 it had no mines available for defending coastal waters and until mid-1941 could equip only a quarter of its merchant ships with cannon and gun crews. The U.S. Navy had neglected the construction of destroyer escorts—the President repeatedly complained that he could not get the admirals interested in ships under two thousand tons—and had no units or organization specifically responsible for antisubmarine warfare. "My Navy has been definitely slack in preparing for this submarine war off our coast," Roosevelt wrote to Churchill in March 1942, a painful admission.[60]

To make matters worse, both sides committed serious blunders. Hitler was *landsinnig,* a land animal, prone to seasickness and so obsessed with the Eurasian landmass that he failed to see the importance of the Mediterranean or, much as he made bold pronouncements about it, the North Atlantic. "On land I am a hero," he told Admiral Raeder, "but at sea I am a coward." His commander of submarines, Admiral Karl Dönitz, was tactically ingenious and resourceful, but he lacked strategic breadth and steadiness; "he was always chopping and changing," said Air Marshal Sir John Slessor about him. The British, forgetting the hard-earned lessons of World War I, temporarily and disastrously exempted from the convoy system vessels with a speed above thirteen knots; the loss rate of ships operating independently thereupon rose to three times as great, and in June 1941 this mistake was rectified, though the Americans then repeated it. During 1942 and 1943, the latter, unable to agree on what to do or who was in charge, wasted eighteen of the most crucial months of the war in typically Washingtonian wrangling.[61]

When Hitler initiated open warfare against the United States, he rescinded his previous ban on submarine raids in the western Atlantic and authorized Operation *Paukenschlag* (Drum Roll) in the coastal waters of the Americas. Dönitz sent six U-boats under his best commanders and they and those who followed them (probably no more than a dozen at a time) brought off what Admiral Morison called "one of the greatest merchant-ship massacres in history." During the first four months of 1942 they accounted for eighty-two ships (491,000 tons) in the Eastern Sea Frontier and fifty-five more (337,000 tons) near Bermuda. In February, they began to move into the Caribbean, where between March and July they added an additional 160–170 (about 870,000 tons) to this appalling score. "It was," writes Morison, "a fairly desperate situation."[62]

In June, George Marshall gratuitously informed King that the "losses by submarines off our Atlantic seaboard and in the Caribbean now threaten our entire war effort. . . . I am fearful that another month or two of this will so cripple our means of transport that we will be unable to bring sufficient men and planes to bear against the enemy"[63]—as though King did not know this all too well. Coastal shipping carried oil, bauxite, coffee, sugar; coal, iron, concrete, and lumber. At the outset there were no convoys, no escorts, no organized air patrols. By night the seaboard cities were brilliantly lit, silhouetting the ships; soon the emboldened U-boats surfaced even by day and employed their deck guns. Columns of smoke rose in the sight of seaside bathers; oil, debris, and bodies washed ashore. Admiral King had overconfidently placed in charge of the Eastern Sea Frontier his Annapolis classmate Vice-Admiral Adolphus Andrews, whom Secretary Stimson described as a "terrible old fusspocket," and Andrews with a largely administrative headquarters in New York had to depend on the Atlantic Fleet to carry out his often elaborate and ineffectual orders.

When asked to institute convoys, Admiral Andrews pleaded that convoys were useless without escorts, of which he had too few to serve. No German submarines had so far been sunk and King was convinced, contrary to what experience would later demonstrate, that there was a single solution, and that it lay in the as-yet-nonexistent escort ships. "Escort is not just one way of handling the submarine menace," King asserted, "it is the only way that gives any promise of success. The so-called hunting and patrol operations have time and again proved futile."[64] In this unabashed self-assurance he dug in his heels, tried to ignore the cries of anguish and outrage descending on him, and maintained in the face of mounting disbelief that the Navy was doing the best it could.

So the "desperate situation" continued while the Americans argued with each other. King insisted that it made better sense to build escorts that could sink U-boats than to build merchant ships that U-boats could sink, but the Maritime Commission differed with him and nothing was resolved. For the lack of escorts the President blamed the Navy and King (in his postwar memoir) unfairly blamed the President;[65] it was a debate over the size of escort ships in which the essential point, the compelling need for *any* warships appropriate to the task, did not find first place. Roosevelt said that the Navy thought too big, King that the President thought too small.

On July 7, 1942, Roosevelt sent to King a table of successful U-boat attacks accompanied by a memorandum that began: "This furnishes excellent proof of what I have been talking about for many weeks." Losses of ships sailing independently were much greater (118) than those sailing under escort (20). Frankly, said the President, "I think it has taken an unconscionable time to get things going. . . . We must speed things up and we must use the available tools even though they are not just what we would like to have," a sentiment King could or should have echoed.

In his reply, King said that he had mounted as many escorted convoys as he had been able to, using "vessels of every type and size that can keep up with the ships they guard," despite the fact that the former consisted "of a too large proportion of small craft with little fighting power" (fighting power, which depended on size, was the crux of their disagreement). What he needed, said King, was "a very large number—roughly 1000— [of] sea-going escort vessels of DE [destroyer escort] or corvette type. I am doing my best to get them quickly." Merit could be found on either side, but summing up, Admiral Morison concluded that "if the President's wishes and recommendations had been followed, the Navy would have been better prepared to meet the U-boats."[66]

The central fallacy (as Morison saw it) was to suppose that the U-boat war could be won by one method exclusively, whether King's or anyone else's, and suggestions were plentiful—total convoying or total dispersal, more and faster merchant ships or more and faster escorts, forward-throwing contact-bomb launchers like the "hedgehog," improved sound gear and radar, long-range aircraft to patrol or hunt, bombing raids on the home bases in France or the shipyards in Germany, and so on—when in fact the answer would be discovered in a multipurpose approach by a multitude of participants: the navies of four Allies (United States, Britain, Canada, and Brazil), all the bureaus of the Navy Department, the air force, civilian scientists, and the public. The economic and human cost of dealing with a few hundred German submarines was monumental, and the arithmetic favored the enemy side: as a U.S. Navy training manual put it, when a U-boat sinks two transports and a tanker, we lose more matériel than, landed and dispersed, could be destroyed by three thousand bombers. Churchill thought the Germans would have been wiser to stake everything they had on the U-boat.

Dönitz thought in retrospect that the undersea war had been lost before it began, that a "realistic policy would have given Germany a thousand U-boats at the beginning," and it is true, once the Allies got their wits together—and put their air, sea, and scientific power fully to work in tandem with British Admiralty intelligence—that the outcome was not long in doubt. But until his luck turned, Dönitz maneuvered his forces skillfully. When fully escorted convoys began to be extended eastward in the latter part of 1942, and losses dropped while U-boat sinkings rose, he shifted his tactics and returned to *Rudeltaktik* (wolf pack) attacks on the convoy routes, with hideous success. In August 1942, not one transatlantic convoy escaped U-boat assault and in November the number of merchantmen sunk reached 106, for a total of 636,907 tons, the worst month of the Atlantic war for the Allies.

The Germans were still building U-boats faster than the British and Americans could dispose of them; in the last six months of 1942, for 58 sunk 121 new ones were completed.[67] In January 1943, Hitler promoted Dönitz to grand admiral and made him navy commander in chief, in Raeder's place. Their acoustic torpedo, the *Snorchel* breathing device, and the electric-drive type XXI U-boat were expected soon to be available and Dönitz could look back on a record of solid achievement and forward to a prospect of confirming Churchill's worst fears. The latter did not happen, and it was prevented from happening by a convergence of ideas, weapons, and command arrangements that proved King partly wrong but mostly right.

◆

His chief adversary in the dispute that continued over the antisubmarine war was, unexpectedly, Secretary Stimson. Stimson had seen a demonstration of airborne radar's potential for locating ships at sea that powerfully impressed him. A receptiveness to technological innovation was one of his strengths, and he had been instrumental in getting air force planes equipped with the new 10-centimeter radar developed (from British beginnings) by the Radiation Laboratory at MIT. He was convinced that with it, submarines could be located (and destroyed) in the narrow seas where they departed from and returned to their home ports (and in the Bay of Biscay this might have been done), but to convince the Navy proved to be a sore test of Stimson's abilities as a bureaucratic infighter.

He sent a description of radar to the President (whose ideas about it were "hazy"), he called on Secretary Knox, he told Harry Hopkins he was "disgusted" at the Navy, he told Roosevelt that Admiral Andrews (whom he wrongly thought to be the bottleneck) would have to go, and at the end of 1942 he went to the President again, to ask for the latter's personal intervention. At the beginning of 1943, Stimson approached the Navy direct and met with Under Secretary James Forrestal and senior admirals; he rallied his own colleagues behind him. On March 26, 1943, he set out for the White House one more time, carrying charts to prove his case, and receiving carefully qualified presidential consent ("I don't want to go over Knox's head"), he wrote a letter to the secretary of the Navy, proposing a Special Anti-Submarine Task Force under *Army* command.

Stimson might have spared himself these pains; in Admiral King they encountered an immovable object. Antisubmarine warfare was part of the war at sea, and the war at sea was the responsibility of naval officers, to be understood and executed solely by them. There could be friendly discourse, but on this fundamental point there would be no compromise. For two months, King and Marshall tried to find a solution for incorporating Army aircraft into the new command structure, known as Tenth Fleet, that King had instituted to fight the submarines. No way. Finally, the Army gave up and negotiated the so-called Arnold-McNarney-McCain agreement (of which Air Marshal Slessor said, "it could hardly be described as very good from any other point of view than that of Admiral Dönitz"[68]), turning over its antisubmarine aircraft to the Navy. Even here, savoring administrative success, King tried to exact still another concession, and only a final explosion from Stimson ("I am quite unwilling to give my consent") and a threat by Marshall to raise the issue of an independent air force caused King to pull back.[69]

Once the question of jurisdiction had been settled, King showed a creditable if unwonted eagerness to adopt the very ideas (of hunting and patrolling) he had hitherto rejected. New technology made his reservations academic. By the beginning of 1943, seaborne "huff-duff" (a high-frequency direction finder) was standard equipment on escort vessels, and most of them—and more and more of RAF Coastal Command's aircraft—had 10-centimeter radar (which the Germans could not detect). "In the last years of the war," writes Elting Morison, "the stream of new instruments, most of them developed by the Office of Scientific Research and Development, that were fitted imaginatively into a new kind of weapon system by the Navy virtually eliminated the submarine dangers to our shipping and naval forces." One participant in the argument thought that Stimson had been "right on his facts but wrong on his tactics," but Stimson could have responded that what he had done was necessary because (as he wrote in his diary) the President "never dares buck the Navy when the Navy is obstinate." For his insistent pressure Stimson felt that he deserved at least some of "the credit for having accomplished this revolution in submarine warfare."[70]

Credit goes also to King, however, and in greater quantity. His confidence in the destroyer escorts was justified, and with an assist from the President (who had urged their adoption as early as June 1940) and from Under Secretary Forrestal (who put their manufacture on a mass-production basis in February 1943), the DEs finally began to arrive in quantity: 260 were in commission by December 5, and made a massive difference.[71] With them also came the escort aircraft carriers, small and slow by comparison with their stately sisters, but capable of putting air cover over the convoys in the mid-Atlantic gap where land-based planes had been unable to reach, and of engaging in the deliberate hunt-and-destroy pursuit of U-boats that King had at first disparaged. This last came about because of his final and most effective contribution to the antisubmarine war, which was the creation of Tenth Fleet.

King had early appreciated that the British were far ahead of us in naval intelligence, and in June 1942 he had sent a team to London to study their methods, such as the use of "huff-duff" to pinpoint the location of a radio source like a submarine. Beginning in May 1941, the British cryptanalysts at Bletchley Park had been reading every message to and from the U-boats, a copious and informative traffic, so that the Admiralty could plot their locations and route convoys away from them. But in February 1942, the Germans had added a fourth wheel to the Enigma coding machines, and for a time the new key setting (known as "Shark," or "Triton") resisted any effort at decoding. Happily, in December 1942, they broke it, and from then on the Tracking Room of the Admiralty, underground in the somber concrete blockhouse off the Horse Guards Parade, again provided current and exact knowledge of U-boat moves and locations, which they fully and unhesitatingly shared with the Americans. Unhappily, the source was so secret it could not be revealed, and King had seen several instances of the information's being passed on to the fighting forces, only to be ignored because it was not taken seriously.[72] Vital intelligence was being wasted in the process of safeguarding it. "King was obsessed with security," writes his biographer. He came to the conclusion that all U.S. antisubmarine operations ought to be under one roof, where security could be maintained while routing and intelligence were combined, and that the roof would have to be his.

Tenth Fleet had no ships of its own and only about fifty officers and enlisted men and women. It was made up of organizations that had existed previously—the convoy and routing division, the antisubmarine warfare section, Op-20 (Atlantic Section, Operational Intelligence, Cominch) under Commander Kenneth A. Knowles—and put them not only together but in a room near King's office, presided over by Rear Admiral Francis C. Low, a submariner who had served before with King. From here every plane, ship, and merchantman in those parts of the Atlantic under American jurisdiction could be monitored and controlled. The commander of Tenth Fleet should be a naval aviator, Low told King. "He is," King said. "Who?" said Low. "Me," said King.[73] But in practice, Low now ran the American war against Dönitz, and Dönitz lost.

The impact of Tenth Fleet was promptly felt. Escort carrier *Bogue* was assigned to the New York–Gibraltar convoys, which were successfully routed to avoid the waiting wolf packs, and two U-boats were sunk. In July and August, two "hunter-killer" groups built around escort carriers *Core* and *Santee,* operating near the Azores, sank thirteen more. During the same period seven were sunk off Brazil, and five in the Caribbean off the U.S. coast. At the end of August, the Tracking Room reported that the Germans were experiencing such difficulties that there were no U-boats left in the Caribbean or off Brazil, and only three off West Africa. The Allied attackers were having to restrain themselves lest they reveal how accurate their picture of German plans and positions was, but even so, in May 1943, Dönitz had temporarily abandoned the attempt to halt the North Atlantic convoys.

He soon lost another of his weapons. The Germans, too, had some skill at code breaking, and they had made good use of B. Dienst, their naval cryptanalysis service, which had been reading many of the Royal Navy ciphers, among them the one for rendezvousing convoys with their escorts. This was especially useful in the early days, when the number of German submarines was low. During the first few years of the war, writes Patrick Beesly in *Very Special Intelligence,* an account of the Admiralty Tracking Room's accomplishments, "the contribution made by the B. Dienst to Dönitz's success in the Battle of the Atlantic must have been equal to at least an additional fifty U-boats."

It may seem astonishing—in fact, it *is* astonishing—that with each side listening to so much of the other's private conversation, neither was quick to draw the logical conclusion: that its own codes had been compromised. Dönitz and several of his officers, with evidence before them that convoys were being rerouted on the basis of known U-boat locations, were virtually certain that either cryptanalysis, or a spy network in their home bases, was at work. But when they took their concerns to the chief of the Naval Intelligence Service, he assured them that the Enigma codes were unbreakable, or else that so much time would be required to solve them that the results would be too late to use; therefore no change was called for. The Admiralty Tracking Room staff developed a similar suspicion that they were being overheard, and after some reiteration they convinced the joint section responsible for cipher security of its validity. Time was needed to develop new codes and distribute them, but by June 1943 this had been done, and thereafter, writes Beesly, "the B. Dienst was unable to supply Dönitz with more than a trickle of information."[74]

On September 21, 1943, Churchill could announce to the House of Commons that in the third of a year just ending, not one merchant ship had been lost to enemy action in the North Atlantic, and that during the past fortnight no Allied ship had been sunk by a U-boat anywhere in the world. His remarks were greeted by "loud and prolonged cheering," as well they might have been, for it was in so great part a British victory, the cumulative achievement of the Royal Navy, the Royal Canadian navy, the Coastal Command of the Royal Air Force, and the sure direction provided by the Admiralty.[75] But Dönitz was not finished yet.

This was a period of maximum intensity in the preinvasion buildup of American soldiers and equipment in Great Britain, and in early September the first of a new series of relatively fast (14–15 knots) and heavily escorted troop convoys began leaving New York. To harry them both coming and going, Dönitz over the following three months dispatched one offensive after another armed with the *Zaunkönig,* or "Wren," the acoustic torpedo that homed on the sound of a ship's propeller. With these he hoped to break through the escorts and get at the transports.

During September, the "Wrens" did for three escorts and six mer-

and sore. King almost climbed over the table at Brooke. God, he was mad. I wish he had socked him."[78]

It was the conference in Washington of May 1943, called Trident, that put the definitive seal of approval on King's plan for the central Pacific, but his powers of insistence had been exercised to good effect four months earlier at Casablanca, mid-January 1943—the ceremonial conclave at which the Americans discovered how thoroughly outclassed they were by the British, but from which King nonetheless emerged with a prize of great value. The British chiefs came to Casablanca prepared and staffed, and in the harbor they had anchored H.M.S. *Bulolo*, a headquarters and communications ship that Eisenhower's biographer Stephen Ambrose describes as a "floating file cabinet . . . complete with technical details on all possible aspects of any proposed operation." King said that at Casablanca the American Joint Chiefs found "that every time they brought up a subject the British had a paper ready."[79]

The original intention had been to hold the meetings in Marrakech, with the two principals quartered in the villa La Saadia and the others in Churchill's favorite Hotel Mamounia. But Marrakech was filled with Axis spies, and adequate security measures for as long as two weeks proved impossible. Ismay's deputy Sir Ian Jacob settled instead on Casablanca, where five miles out of town, on a knoll overlooking the sea, was a hotel surrounded by comfortable villas and plentiful palm trees, begonia, and bougainvillea, set off against the red soil, the white buildings, and the blue ocean. The area had then been ringed by a wire fence "of immense strength and solidity," as Harold Macmillan described it, forming "a kind of Roman camp with a circuit of about a mile," guarded by Patton's troops. Macmillan said he had "never seen so many sentries armed with such terrifying weapons." He wrote in his letter-diary to his wife that he expected either to be shot or to be saluted with "Present arms!" and that he had difficulty telling which of these drills was being attempted.[80]

When President Roosevelt saw the somewhat frilly bedroom of his villa, he whistled and said, "Now all we need is the madame of the house." Churchill's quarters were fifty yards away. The British planners were installed in another villa near the sea, equipped, Sir John Slessor reported, "with a notable stock of slightly pornographic French literature." Macmillan said the atmosphere of the Casablanca Conference was a cross between a cruise and a summer school, with notices of coming events posted on a bulletin board and field marshals frolicking on the beach after hours. Everything was free, "including most excellent food and quantities of drink." He said he had never seen Churchill in better form: "He ate and drank enormously all the time, settled huge problems, played bagatelle and bezique by the hour, and generally enjoyed himself." Patton was not involved in the formal deliberations, but he shared, if disdainfully, in the

chant ships, yet this was not damage enough, and at the turn of the n
a countermeasure to the acoustic torpedo was installed and in use. (C
"Foxer," it was a towed noise-making device that exploded the torp
harmlessly; no ship towing "Foxer" was ever hit by a *Zaunkönig*.[76]) By
time Dönitz realized that his latest tactic had failed, and that he could
nothing but wait out the availability of better equipment, the snork
breathing submarines that could recharge their batteries without comi
to the surface. In December, he told a conference of flag officers at We
mar that because of Anglo-American electronic research (his favorite e:
planation), Allied sea power had thwarted him.

The war at sea went on, the snorkels were difficult to cope with,
U-boats moved into the South Atlantic and other sections of the sea,
and there was to be no letup in the hunt for them until after V-E Day.
On May 5, 1945, only twenty-eight hours before Germany capitulated,
snorkel-equipped U-853 sank a collier off Narragansett Bay. That night
she was found east of Block Island by destroyer escort *Atherton* (under
Lieutenant Commander Lewis Iselin, USNR, in civil life a sculptor; his
sound-detector man, who located U-853 at rest on the bottom, had an
acute ear because he played the trombone). *Atherton* delivered a
"hedgehog" contact-bomb attack that wrote an end both to U-853 and
to the Battle of the Atlantic in American waters. Dönitz ordered the
U-boats to surrender; 181 did so, 217 were destroyed by their own
crews, and two diehards fled to Argentina—where to their chagrin the
crews were interned and the submarines turned over to the U.S. Navy
representative in Buenos Aires.

At long last it was over. At the close, the Tracking Room knew exactly
what had happened to every one of the 1,170 U-boats built since 1935. On
May 28, convoys were suspended, and the ships were told they could turn
on their lights again after dark.[77]

IV

British perceptions of Admiral King were colored by what appeared to
them his single-minded absorption in the war against Japan. This is not
quite fair to King, who objected not to the Atlantic-first strategy as such,
as MacArthur did, but only to the inference drawn from it that the Pacific
could safely be ignored until Germany had been defeated. He thought this
neither true nor necessary, and said so with a consistency capable of being
misinterpreted to mean that he thought little else. Brooke believed that
to King the "European war was just a great nuisance that kept him from
waging his Pacific war undisturbed." Tempers were on occasion short.
General Stilwell, who was invited to attend the Cairo Conference, wrote
of one Combined Chiefs meeting: "Brooke got nasty and King got good

social life. Coming back from lunch in a car together, he and the President talked about medieval armor, "about which he knows a lot," said Patton. For the first time, Roosevelt seems to have impressed him. "He really appeared as a great statesman," Patton wrote in his diary after an informal dinner.[81]

Marshall, King, and Arnold (Leahy had been running a fever and cut short his trip at Trinidad) were accompanied as staff only by Admiral Cooke and a naval aide, General Wedemeyer, and General Somervell. (Later Wedemeyer was joined by two other officers from the Ops division.) The Americans had no backup for the arguments they were going to be involved in. Jacob said they "had left most of their clubs behind." In the outcome were therefore a number of decisions displeasing to Marshall and the Army representatives. "We came, we listened, and we were conquered," wrote Wedemeyer.[82] But such was not the case for Admiral King.

The British wished to maintain momentum in the Mediterranean by invading Sardinia and Corsica. Marshall as always opposed this, arguing instead for his favored invasion of northern France. Everyone agreed on giving priority to the submarine menace, but from there on the differences multiplied—over what to do in the Indian Ocean, whether or how to invade Burma, which type of bomber offensive to undertake against Germany, or when convoys to Russia might have to be suspended. King took the view that specific operations should not be discussed until a general, overall strategy was settled on, in particular the proportion of effort to be applied in the two main theaters. He estimated that only 15 percent of total Allied resources were going into the war against Japan, a figure he had proposed to the Joint Chiefs on January 5, and no one had disputed. This he did not believe was enough to prevent the Japanese from consolidating their gains and becoming an even more formidable foe later on. He and Marshall were both asking that the percentage for the Pacific be doubled. "He was tough as nails and carried himself as stiffly as a poker," wrote Ismay about King in his memoirs. "He was blunt and standoffish, almost to the point of rudeness."[83]

They were close to deadlock. Brooke became very discouraged and told Sir John Dill, "It is no use, we shall never get agreement with them." Brooke said that he himself did not intend to give an inch. "Oh yes, you will," said Dill. "You know that you must come to some agreement with the Americans and that you cannot bring the unsolved problem up to the President and the Prime Minister. You know as well as I do what a mess they would make of it." Of the many moments during the war when Dill's diplomacy held the Grand Alliance together, this is one of the most telling; Brooke wrote later that his gratitude to Dill for his intervention was "unbounded."[84] Dill told Air Marshal Slessor that he thought the two sides were not so far apart as might appear, and after lunch Slessor went up on the roof of the hotel with a tattered notebook and drafted a compromise statement:

> Operations in the Pacific and Far East shall continue with the forces allocated, with the object of maintaining pressure on Japan, retaining the initiative and attaining a position of readiness for the full-scale offensive against Japan by the United Nations as soon as Germany is defeated. These operations must be kept within such limits as will not, in the opinion of the Combined Chiefs of Staff, prejudice the capacity of the United Nations to take any opportunity that may present itself for the decisive defeat of Germany in 1943. [Later a clause was added authorizing plans and preparations, after the capture of Rabaul, for invading the Marshall and Caroline islands, provided this did not interfere with an invasion of Burma.]

With scarcely ten minutes to go before the afternoon session began, it was typed up, and Dill showed it to the Americans. "I can still see Marshall and King poring over it," wrote Slessor, "exchanging a few words in undertones, Marshall making some notes on it in pencil."[85] After about five minutes, Marshall said that the U.S. Joint Chiefs of Staff were prepared to accept Slessor's draft, and Marshall was delegated by the Combined Chiefs to present it later that afternoon, at a full-dress meeting in the President's villa; Roosevelt and Churchill gave it their blessing. The reference to the Carolines and the Marshalls, while not a binding commitment, meant that King could now assume a central Pacific offensive to be in the cards. He had what he needed to proceed.

The thoughts that King was thinking he had revealed in conversation the previous November to a group of journalists. King's legendary contempt for the press and the public (he was supposed to have said that they should be told nothing until the war was over, and then be told only who won) was not borne out by his behavior. He had been persuaded by his lawyer, Cornelius Bull, that the way to deal with newspapermen was to level with them and rely on them to hold what was said in confidence. King agreed to a meeting at Bull's house in Alexandria, and a reporter and an editor were asked to select the participants. Eventually there were to be fifteen more sessions, after Bull's death in the home of Phelps H. Adams of the *New York Sun* (both Bull and Adams kept notes), and the number of those invited grew to twenty-six. King would arrive at eight in the evening, accept a glass of beer, and then talk to them for three or four hours, his glass periodically replenished. "He told us what had happened, what was happening, and, often, what was likely to happen next," said Adams. "He reported the bad news as fully as the good news. . . . There was never a moment's doubt that his words were gospel; nor was there the slightest suspicion that his statements might be shaded with bias in an attempt to place the Navy or the total war effort in a more favorable light than was justified."[86] King and the gentlemen of the press discovered that they could trust one another, and the benefits of this, though many were intangible, grew as time went on.

At his second "seminar" (as Bull called them), on November 30, 1942, King laid out a strategic assessment as sound as any other Allied leader could have provided. He said that Germany had to be defeated first, that he agreed with the British on clearing the Mediterranean sea lanes from Gibraltar to Suez, and that the capture of Sicily would do this. But he had doubts about invading Italy. The Germans would fight there, and the mountain barrier of the Alps would prevent any further move into Austria and southern Germany. Therefore a cross-Channel invasion was inescapable, though he had an open mind as to when it should take place. He thought that the European war hinged on Russia, and so he favored continuing to send it Lend-Lease matériel. "In the last analysis," King said, "Russia will do nine-tenths of the job of defeating Germany."[87]

This was in large part correct, and thus (Brooke to the contrary) it was King's overview of the European war that underlay his attitude toward the war against Japan. King believed that there was going to be a sufficiency to go round, that American industry could produce enough munitions to equip offensives against both enemies at once. He was certainly first among the Combined Chiefs in perceiving this (among the British, Beaverbrook saw it as early as Arcadia), and once again he was right. No wonder they thought he was stubborn. To him it seemed abundantly plain that a drive across the central Pacific would cut off the Japanese from their source of raw materials in Southeast Asia, and perhaps even starve them into surrender. An increase in the Allied resources allotted to this from 15 to 30 percent seemed to him a modest price to pay for so desirable an eventuality.

It is not clear that King (or anyone else) fully understood what he had accomplished at Casablanca, for in effect he had bargained one theater against the other. If the British were not going to go along with an invasion of France in 1943 (and they weren't), then the Allied armies in North Africa must hold on to the initiative in the Mediterranean. If there was not going to be a French invasion in 1943, then King's request for greater resources in the other hemisphere could not meanwhile be plausibly denied. It was a trade-off. Let the British have their Mediterranean venture (for the time being, Marshall would have added), and let King prepare to implement his Pacific strategy. It was a compromise Americans like Wedemeyer found hard to stomach, but in the long term it shortened the war, and did so more effectively than would any of the alternatives. Casablanca has a poor reputation among students of the Allied conferences; compromise was achieved in some cases through ambiguity, and in the months that followed, the ambiguities were revealed. But it deserves better, and it was at Casablanca that King's title to be called "the shrewd-est of strategists" by the President was validated.

By the end of March, it became apparent that the Casablanca deci-sions had been overambitious (not enough shipping) and that the British and the Americans were interpreting them in different ways. The U.S. Joint Chiefs asked their Joint Strategic Survey Committee for a "clarifica-tion" of Casablanca, and when the British read it—especially a phrase to the effect that we should "maintain and extend unremitting pressure against Japan"—they replied that they saw no need for a clarification, since "the clear decision at Casablanca was that the decisive defeat of Germany came first." King remarked to a meeting of the Combined Chiefs in April that "there was a difference of opinion between the U.S. Chiefs of Staff and the British on the adequacy of forces for the Pacific," and that in his opinion there always would be. In preparation for the Trident Conference, the Joint Chiefs sent a paper to the President recom-mending, should the British refuse to support an invasion of Burma (as they were showing signs of doing), that the United States then "expand and intensify its operations in the Pacific." Whether or not Roosevelt approved it is unknown;[88] Trident would tell the tale.

The Trident meetings opened at the White House on the afternoon of May 12, 1943, with presentations by the President and the Prime Minister of a patently general character, and afterward the Combined Chiefs got down to business. King's opportunity came over a week later, on the twenty-first, when they arrived at the agenda item on operations in the Pacific and the Far East. King began by explaining that nothing he had to say was novel or original with him, inasmuch as the subject had absorbed the attention of the best minds in the Navy Department and the Naval War College for the better part of thirty or forty years. The objec-tive was to sever Japanese lines of communication and recapture the Philippines, and for this the Marianas (Saipan, Tinian, and Guam) were the key. (Planning papers in King's office had not even mentioned the Maria-nas, but no matter: he knew his own mind.) American seizure of the Marianas would isolate the Carolines—where the great Japanese base at Truk was located—and permit further advances, either westward to the Philippines and China, or northwestward to Japan itself. Not least, an American presence in the Marianas would compel the Imperial Navy to come out for a fight, there would occur the major fleet action in which it would be destroyed, and the control of the Pacific would revert to the United States.

If the British delegation had objections to this program, they do not appear in the minutes; Brooke wrote later: "We dealt with the Pacific and accepted what was put forward." Where the hang-up came was over the phrase "maintain and extend unremitting pressure against Japan," which recurred in the American draft for a final agreement. The British argued that this could be construed to permit a diversion of resources away from the war against Germany, and asked for an amendment that allowed for intensification of effort against Japan only if it was "consistent" with the earliest possible defeat of Germany and Italy. Leahy and Marshall urged King to accept this, but King refused; he said it was "a lever" that could be used to stress the European war over the Pacific. This led to what the JCS secretary discreetly referred to as "prolonged discussion," a euphemism for some angry exchanges. Finally, Admiral Sir Dudley Pound, the First Sea Lord, who was not always as sleepy as he sometimes looked, suggested a wording in which the Combined Chiefs would have to give "consideration" to any major Pacific offensive before it was undertaken. Done. That satisfied King, and the next day a text acceptable to all went forward to Roosevelt and Churchill, who approved it.[89] King not only had his mandate; he had it in writing.

◆

Strategy in the Pacific was a more open game than elsewhere: more options, more possible routes to follow. On the American side, the principal constraints were time and geography. There would have to be a period of waiting until the new ships began to arrive, in particular the fast battleships and the *Essex*-class aircraft carriers. The geography was determined by where the islands were and where the Japanese were. The latter had set up a strong perimeter, distant enough from the home country to ensure its safety, and had installed the forces necessary for a vigorous defense. Originally the theory on both sides had been that in order to break through the perimeter we would have to capture their major bases like Rabaul and Truk. Only later did the idea dawn on our side—except, that is, for General MacArthur, who for some time failed to get the point —that Rabaul and Truk could be neutralized or bombed into impotence. The southeastern anchor of the perimeter was what we came to call the Bismarck Barrier, the horseshoe shape of the Bismarck Archipelago formed by the islands of New Britain and New Ireland. At the apex of the horseshoe, at the eastern end of New Britain, lay Rabaul. If the key to the Pacific for the Americans was in the Marianas, King told the newspapermen at Nelie Bull's house in Alexandria, the key for the Japanese was Rabaul.[90]

Rabaul harbor, ringed by disconcertingly active volcanoes, is one of the most beautiful in the world. This had been the capital of New Guinea until signs of restiveness in the volcanoes caused a move to Lae in Papua. The Japanese came in January 1942 and converted Rabaul into a fortress. There had been two airfields; they built four more, with concrete landing strips, taxiways, and revetments for 80 to 120 planes. They dug underground hangars, repair shops, and barracks. They brought in 100,000 men with tanks and artillery, 43 coast defense guns, and 367 antiaircraft. There was an excellent road net and their search radar was effective out to ninety miles. Rabaul was the headquarters of Japanese Southeast Area Fleet and here were based some two hundred aircraft, more than three quarters of them fighters. American carrier pilots who first saw Rabaul described the harbor as "full of cruisers, cans [destroyers], big fat AKs [attack cargo ships] and hundreds and hundreds of barges." They said the ack-ack (antiaircraft) was "so thick you could walk on it" and that Zero fighters were "all over the sky."[91]

Rabaul was a major reason for the advance up the Solomon Islands toward it that Admiral King recommended to the President in March 1942 and the President approved. A direct assault, however, proved unnecessary. The Solomons campaign, beginning with Guadalcanal and ending with Bougainville, permitted the acquisition or construction of airfields from which Rabaul could be reached. From October 1943 to February 1944, when the Japanese abandoned Rabaul as an air base, it was subjected to more or less continuous bombing attacks by American carriers and a land-based organization called Airsols (Air Solomons), made up of about five hundred aircraft from the Army, Navy, Marine Corps, and the Royal New Zealand Air Force. (Marine Major Gregory "Pappy" Boyington, an ace with twenty-six kills, was shot down over Rabaul and captured; he survived.) By the end, we had achieved complete mastery of the air over the Bismarcks, and the Barrier, as King had intended, had been broken. Rabaul, wrote Admiral Morison, demonstrated "the folly of building up a great overseas base and garrison without a Navy capable of controlling the surrounding water and air."[92]

But the U.S. Navy had long believed (and so conducted itself) that the center of the action, the main effort, should be many hundreds of miles to the north. In 1938, Joint Basic War Plan Orange (that is, war with Japan) provided for a stately progress of the fleet westward from Hawaii to the Philippines, though it wisely did not indicate how long this might take. While Plan Orange had since been many times overtaken by events, the logic of it remained dear to the Navy's heart and central (as King set forth at Casablanca and Trident) to his concept of how the war could be won. How to go about it?

Here King displayed a surprising degree of flexibility. His preaching on the delegation of responsibility to subordinates seems at last to have converted the preacher. He initiated a set of gradual moves to shift the making of operational plans from his own headquarters in Washington to that of Admiral Nimitz (Cincpac, or Commander in Chief, Pacific Fleet) at Pearl Harbor.[93] More and more, King—or properly speaking, the Joint Chiefs under the authority of the Combined Chiefs—specified the "what" and not the "how." As King's confidence in Nimitz mounted (at the outset it had not been great), so too mounted his willingness to leave detailed design of operations in Nimitz's hands.

Admiral Morison believed that the planning for the Pacific campaigns was one of the marvels of the war. "The entire process was an intellectual feat of high order worked out under great pressure," he wrote. "Cincpac staff could have used a year from the first directive to prepare for an operation, and would have liked six months; but it never had more than four months, and often not even that." Logistics, communications, and other specialized tasks (weather prediction, landing craft, underwater demolitions, etc.) had to be worked out simultaneously with the plan itself. The fleet commander, the amphibious and ground force commanders, and the land-based air commander all had to participate. Nimitz's staff was genuinely "joint"; two of the section heads, J-2 (intelligence) and J-4 (logistics), were Army officers, and there were many Marines. But the fruit of their endeavors had to be combined by J-1 (plans), a naval officer, and put together into the mimeographed book distributed to the fleet, which allocated the forces and defined their missions.[94] That the Pacific war went so well was a tribute to the skill and dedication of this group of able men, none of whom hesitated to stand up to Nimitz—or to King himself—when they had ideas of their own.

The first operation assigned to them, the seizure of the Gilbert Islands in the fall of 1943, was significantly shaped at Nimitz's headquarters. The timing and sequence had been suggested by Spruance, Nimitz's chief of staff, who (then unknown to Spruance) was to command the fleet when the time for action came. Further, when they received the JCS directive in July, it included not only Tarawa, in the Gilberts, but the island of Nauru, some 380 miles to the west. Neither Spruance nor his Marine commander, Holland Smith, thought well of this—Spruance because he could not cover both islands at once if the Japanese fleet should appear, Smith because he estimated that Nauru would require an entire division of ground troops and because he expected to have his hands full (as he more than fully did) at Tarawa. When King visited Hawaii in September, they gave him a letter Smith had written stating the objections. King read it and asked Spruance what island he proposed to take instead ("Never take only one island" was one of King's maxims). "Makin," said Spruance. After some discussion, King agreed. Tarawa was a bitter battle, but fortunately Makin was not, for the army units assigned to it were inexperienced; they took longer to capture it than Marines thought they should have, an omen of controversies to come.[95]

King's trust in Nimitz grew to be so considerable by January 1944 that he abandoned an idea he had been entertaining, to send Savvy Cooke out to Pearl as deputy Cincpac to keep an eye on things, and instead sent his archrival from days in the Bureau of Aeronautics, Vice Admiral John H. Towers (this was also an acknowledgment by King of the increasingly dominant role of the aircraft carriers). Eventually King acted mostly as a goad; nothing could ever be done as rapidly as he wanted it done. After the capture of Eniwetok in the Marshalls, in February 1944, King became impatient and wrote General Marshall that he thought planning for further advances should proceed "without delay." He always thought MacArthur was slow. When MacArthur's chief of staff, General Sutherland, momentarily inveigled Nimitz and Cincpac staff into going along with MacArthur's proposal to make the main advance up the New Guinea coast to the Philippines, King exploded and wrote Nimitz that the idea was "absurd" and that it filled him with "indignant dismay." In March, Sutherland made a presentation to the Joint Chiefs in Washington but persuaded no one, and the JCS backed King.[96]

MacArthur used the same argument against King that Montgomery used against Eisenhower: that an advance on more than one axis would so weaken both that neither could succeed. King (and Eisenhower) believed that this was not so, that it was more desirable to keep the enemy off balance than it was to let him concentrate against a single thrust. King and Eisenhower were right. The output of American industry was by now so prodigious that there was more than enough for everyone, not only for both Europe and the Pacific but within the Pacific for both Nimitz and MacArthur. King therefore proposed to Nimitz and Halsey (as early as February 1943) a "whipsaw" strategy for the two of them in which each would support the other, and he repeated this recommendation in August at a meeting of the Combined Chiefs in Quebec.[97]

It worked. The Japanese were frequently caught at the wrong place, or the right place at the wrong time. In October, hearing from a midget submarine of forces assembling at Pearl Harbor, Admiral Mineichi Koga (who had succeeded Yamamoto as commander of Combined Fleet) reasoned like the good disciple of Mahan and Yamamoto that he was and took the whole of Combined Fleet from Truk to Eniwetok, where he anchored in the lagoon in readiness to counter the American central Pacific offensive in a "decisive" engagement. When nothing happened, he concluded that no such offensive was coming and on October 24 steamed all the way back to Truk. In early November, informed of the American landings at Empress Augusta Bay on Bougainville, Koga dispatched a strong force of heavy cruisers and destroyers to Rabaul—accompanied by most of his carrier aircraft—on the assumption that *here* was where the blow was going to fall. On November 20, when the Marines landed on Tarawa, Combined Fleet (whose possible presence had been a very real concern at Cincpac) was nowhere to be seen.[98] The principles of war may be immutable but their application is always different, and the secret of successful strategists is that they invariably take account of this.

The argument has been advanced (by Professor Love[99]) that King's Pacific strategy was a strong political factor in causing the Normandy invasion to be attempted in 1944. On the surface, this may appear paradoxical, but a convincing case can be made. The execution of Overlord required the overcoming of British doubts and hesitations inspired by their vivid awareness of how much was perilously at stake. The existence of King's campaign as a potential alternative—and their knowledge of how much American public opinion preferred it—acted as an incentive to action in Europe. The British also knew that the Americans, the President most especially, would not accept some other invasion (such as through the Balkans) as a substitute.

Q.E.D. Either invade Normandy or put the Europe-first strategy at risk, and it was not a risk that could be accepted. Brendan Bracken (minister of information and a close friend of Churchill's) told MacArthur's liaison officer Gerald Wilkinson that MacArthur was important, not because of anything he might accomplish as a general, but because—should he ally himself with the isolationist Republicans, the China Lobby, and the Navy—he could pose a serious threat to American primary emphasis on the European war.[100] King was a threat for similar reasons; he and the Navy made the Pacific alternative real, and if the only way to eliminate the threat was to invade Normandy, then so be it. The reasoning may seem tortuous, but that did not make it any the less persuasive.

To describe King as therefore the architect of not only the Pacific war but the Atlantic as well would be to exaggerate, but there is no denying the accuracy of his perceptions and the skill with which he put them to work. King held a sort of psychological balance of power within the Combined Chiefs, and used it to come down on the right side of the issues that mattered. The picture of him as exclusively Navy and Pacific oriented is misleading; with the exception of President Roosevelt, no other strategist of the war had such a grasp on the relationship of the two hemispheres to each other.

Nor should it be forgotten that King's position depended on the President and the President's confidence in him. Roosevelt, writes Professor Love, was one of King's "few unreserved admirers" and viewed him with "bemused affection." After 1942, the President abandoned his previous insistence on approving senior naval appointments and left them to King. When accused of favoring the Navy, Roosevelt would protest that he was in fact harder on the Navy because of his personal interest in it. Certainly he would not have backed King's proposals because they came from the Navy or because a naval officer was making them; he supported King because he trusted King's strategic judgment and because King's strategies dovetailed with his own. When Roosevelt died, King's influence in the White House abruptly ended.[101] So fully had he completed his task that by then this could not and did not change the course of events.

Praise should also go to King for the relationship he maintained with George Marshall. King responded handsomely to Marshall's gesture of conciliation and shared Marshall's conviction that the two of them must somehow get along. They saw each other at least twice a week at the

Tuesday luncheons of the Joint Chiefs and their Friday afternoon meetings with Dill and the British mission, both held in the Public Health Building, across Constitution Avenue from the Navy Department. Marshall and King between them commanded almost the total of American armed power and spoke with an authority commensurate to this; as a pair they were a formidable combination.

"They probably did not like one another very much," writes Professor Love. Marshall was tactful, reserved, a superb conversationalist; King was easily roused to anger, had little small talk, and hated public speaking. But they both matured during the war, drawn together, in Love's opinion, "by the bond of necessity and the fear that if they did not unite the British would exercise unwarranted influence over the President." King would defer to Marshall even where his staff and (they suspected) King himself might have chosen otherwise. Love adds: "King, the greater strategist, often gave way to Marshall, the greater man."[102]

◆

The President was mildly irritated by King's title of Cominch (he thought there should be only *one* Commander in Chief) and tried without success to get it changed. On another issue, however, Roosevelt flatly refused to let the admiral have his way. This was King's persistent effort to reorganize the Navy Department. The President had casually remarked after King's appointment that the department ought to be "streamlined," and King had taken this to mean that he could reduce civilian authority and eliminate the bureaus, traditionally accountable to the secretary and to Congress but not to Cominch or the CNO. King personally drew up a plan for four "grand divisions"—Material, Personnel, Readiness, and Operations—reporting directly to him, and he proceeded on his own to put this blueprint into effect. "I stumbled on one little pebble," he said later. "I neglected to consult the Secretary and the President first."

When Roosevelt discovered what was happening, he realized that he had unintentionally encouraged not a streamlining but a major work of demolition, and the bureaus made certain that he knew of their distress at being demolished. Summoned, with Knox, to the White House in June 1942, King protested that what had been done was indistinguishable from what the President had permitted Marshall to do in the War Department. Roosevelt was unimpressed; he saw a number of differences, beginning with the legal and congressional ones. On June 12, he instructed Knox to cancel every order King had issued in the past thirty days having to do with reorganization. "There may be more of them that neither you nor I have seen," the President added, in a suspicion born of long exposure to the ways of Washington. Sure enough, a year later King was still maneuvering to gain an administrative edge, in this case over control of naval shipyards, and Roosevelt sent still another note to Knox: "F.K. Tell Ernie *once more:* No reorganizing of the Navy Dept. set-up during the war. Let's win it first. F.D.R." King told Nimitz that he was "sick of hearing" this line of argument, but his cause was lost.[103]

He had stumbled not so much on a pebble as on his own contempt for civilians participating in naval affairs and the President's predictable reaction to his acting on the basis of it. To have informed Roosevelt before-hand would not materially have increased his chances for success. The civilian side of the Navy Department was something the President (from having run it for seven years) presumably knew a great deal about, and one of the things he knew was that its problems were not to be solved by turning them over to admirals. There was no evidence that this was a field in which King had any special competence. King was right in realizing that industrial procurement had become too complex for the creaky pre-war machinery of the bureaus to cope with, but wrong in imagining for a moment that Roosevelt would allow him to replace that machinery with himself.

King had little appreciation for the managerial skills and processes needed to gear up production. He wanted to be able to tell the civilians in the department what he desired in the way of matériel and have them obligingly deliver it; involvement in procurement schedules by civilians, with their niggling concerns over priorities and shortages, he considered tantamount to interference in operations. And he misread the example of the War Department, where Marshall had indeed got rid of the extraneous chiefs of service but had done so without stirring up a bureaucratic hor-net's nest that would embarrass the President, and where Secretary Stim-son (with whom Marshall was in accord, as King and Knox were not) had a team of competent civilian assistants—Patterson, Bundy, McCloy, and Lovett—solidly in place. The Navy would have to find some comparable answer of its own on the civilian side, as it subsequently did.

Under Secretary of the Navy James V. Forrestal was a man profoundly at odds with himself: like the President a Democrat from Republican Dutchess County; a relapsed Catholic, a child of modest background with a taste for luxury, an ardent Princetonian who never received his degree, an intellectual investment banker who had carefully read Marx, a Wall Street insider with an outsider's skepticism about it; self-deprecating at times yet self-advancing at others, drawn to politics yet baffled by politi-cians, dissatisfied by government yet indefatigably immersed in it. Not a bundle of contradictions one might think likely to produce a first-rate public servant, yet that is what it produced in Forrestal. The Navy Depart-ment as he found it was not designed for efficiency—or even designed at all: it had simply accumulated—but he made it work uncommonly well.

Nor was Forrestal himself an orderly administrator. It was not always easy to know what he wanted, since his requests were at times unclear;

he would occasionally send two or three people on the same errand, or answers would be brought him to questions he could not remember having asked. He was slow to make decisions, in part because he wanted to be sure he had considered every aspect of an issue. He liked to talk over all the possible implications; King found him infuriating because he would say, "Now, what do you think of this?" when King had long since made up his mind. For all that, Forrestal produced orderly administration, and the claim has been made that without his contribution to it, the Navy's wartime program could never have been completed.[104]

Forrestal had been recruited into the firm that became Dillon, Read and Company as a bond salesman in 1916. After his service as a naval aviator in World War I, his rise on returning to Dillon, Read was meteoric: a partner by 1923, a vice-president by 1926, and—at the age of forty-six —president by 1938. He had scored a number of spectacular Wall Street triumphs that gave him a reputation as something of a boy wonder. Unlike many of his colleagues, however, he supported the principal New Deal banking and financial reforms, among them the Securities Exchange Act of 1934, and this had brought him to the attention of Harry Hopkins. Forrestal told Hopkins in 1940 that he would welcome the opportunity for government service, and in June he was brought to Washington as an administrative assistant to the President, which he remained for two months. Forrestal was not comfortable in the White House (he found the President difficult to pin down and his own duties inconsequential) and would probably not have continued there, but Congress had meanwhile approved the new position of Under Secretary of the Navy; Forrestal asked for it, and in August—with Roosevelt's approval—he got it. He stayed in the job until 1944, when, with Knox's death, he became secretary.[105]

Forrestal and King did not get on well together. Forrestal was ill at ease with naval officers and tended to approach them with a forced camaraderie, an exaggerated deference, a self-conscious use of naval jargon and Annapolis nicknames which had the opposite effect from that intended. King rarely confided in him any more than was absolutely necessary (and Forrestal often learned of forthcoming operations by lunching with McCloy). King mistrusted Forrestal's devouring ambition and believed that the President "knew what Forrestal really was" (King thought that Roosevelt had allowed him to continue in the titles of both Cominch and CNO—where he had replaced Stark in 1942—because otherwise Forrestal "would have tried to manage the whole thing.") Forrestal for his part seems never to have expressed anything but deep respect for King—as a strategist; it was King's ability to "manage the whole thing," the administration of the Navy Department, that Forrestal (and others, including the President) doubted.[106]

When Forrestal first took office he was inundated every morning with cartloads of contracts and letters of intent requiring his signature. He expressed a strong wish to know what he was signing, and discovered that the methods of preparing contracts—mostly by clerks in the various bureaus filling out standard forms—did not include an evaluation of financial soundness or value to the Navy. Forrestal brought in H. Struve Hensel (a partner in the law firm of Milbank, Tweed) and W. John Kenney (a Los Angeles attorney who had worked with the Securities and Exchange Commission) to straighten out the contracts. He discovered that amortization certificates (permission to write off the costs of constructing new war plants in five years instead of twenty) were piling up in the Office of the Judge Advocate General—a dignified admiral with a pince-nez on a black ribbon who was possessive of his prerogatives—because the OJAG lacked officers competent to process them. Hensel and Kenney set up a Certificatory Supervisory Unit under Forrestal and straightened that one out.

Forrestal found that there was no overall organization within the department responsible for coordinating the procurement activities of the bureaus, which lacked trained people competent to deal with questions of research, design, purchasing, production, and transportation. There was no general counsel's office staffed with lawyers competent to pass on the legal and commercial aspects of procurement contracts once they had been drafted. Forrestal in July 1941 established a Procurement Legal Division to advise him on contract negotiation, preparation, and performance, and he put Hensel in charge of it. (Hensel later became general counsel to the Navy and, in 1945–46, assistant secretary; he was followed in the latter post by Kenney.)

Early in 1942, Forrestal established the Office of Procurement and Material (OP&M as opposed to OPM) to deal with planning, statistics, and resources—one of the soundest and most productive measures that he initiated during his tour as under secretary. Forrestal saw that if the Navy was to compete for scarce materials and manpower with the Army, the Merchant Marine, Lend-Lease, and the civilian economy, then it must have some way of making an accurate and documented statement of its needs—in ships, guns, trained men, supply depots, and all the rest. "Without OP&M," write Albion and Connery in *Forrestal and the Navy*, "this would have been impossible. . . . The creation of this office proved a master stroke."[107] King would not have been capable of it.

Forrestal was never fully satisfied that he had arrived at an optimum structure for the Navy Department, and he and Knox had to expend time and effort in fending off King's ceaseless conniving to impose on them his own antic notions. Forrestal was a compulsively hard worker; even his social calendar presents a frightening picture of the intensity with which he pursued some inward but elusive goal. (There were demons in him, and they eventually drove him to take his own life.) As under secretary, he did not enjoy frequent contact with the President; he seems to have seen Roosevelt more often in 1941 on Lend-Lease affairs (six appointments, one dinner, in a single month) than he did later on, though sometimes he would sit in for Knox at cabinet meetings. During the early period, the questions Roosevelt was asking Forrestal were highly technical—about weather conditions on North Atlantic flight routes, the use of carriers to ferry light aircraft, or the availability of "sea sleds with pompom and Y-gun"[108]—but the answers appear to have been satisfactory, for thereafter in the disagreements with Admiral King the President consistently backed Knox and Forrestal, and it was this support of his that made possible the streamlining of the department rather than the reducing of it to administrative rubble.

The wartime growth of the U.S. Navy was a prodigy, an essential condition of victory; never before in history was a naval war won by a fleet that did not exist when that war began. This was the work of many hands (Rear Admiral Edward L. Cochrane, a brilliant naval architect Forrestal managed to have appointed as head of the Bureau of Ships, ranks high among them), but to rationalize and accelerate the process was the work of James V. Forrestal. The Navy as he took over its material development bore little resemblance to the one that witnessed war's end. Between July 1940 and June 1945 it increased from 1,099 vessels to 50,759, in personnel from 160,997 to 3,383,196. There were to be 8 new battleships, 92 new aircraft carriers, 35 new cruisers, 148 new destroyers, 365 new destroyers escorts, 140 new submarines, and 43,255 new landing craft.[109] Their creation was in Forrestal's care. The presence of King ensured that this would be a fighting fleet, but the presence of Forrestal ensured that it would be there in the first place for King to command.

The subdivision of labor effected here was the work of Franklin Roosevelt. He rarely exposed to others the sum of his thinking about appointments, least of all to military posts. Here as elsewhere he held his cards close to his chest; he liked to keep more factors in mind than others might be willing to consider (he always, said King, "had two strings in his bow"). Thus the only verifiable way to analyze his choices is to observe their end result; the thought processes that went into them can be evoked from the consequences that followed. Here were two men he had been given the opportunity to study closely; one had plans for what to do with a Navy that someday soon would be, the other had plans for bringing that Navy into being. Roosevelt arranged matters so that each was freed up to do what he did best: The organizer was put to organizing and the fighter was put to fighting. To suppose that this had not been a conscious decision strains credulity. The journalist Quentin Reynolds once addressed himself in a speech to the American war effort. "This enormous program," he said, "must have been thought out and planned by someone. Could it have been the President?"[110]

◆

Admiral King never quite escaped from a boyish tendency to thumb his nose and tell the world to go hang. Buell thought that his eccentricity and administrative clumsiness were notably in evidence during the notorious Affair of the Gray Uniform. King had always liked to tinker with uniform regulations and it annoyed him, the dark double-breasted blues being somewhat severe for ordinary daily use, that so many officers preferred the khakis that (to King's taste) too closely resembled the Army's. He wanted a permanent "working" uniform, both dignified and utilitarian and yet the Navy's own—a commendable impulse—and this led him to conceive a single-breasted variant in bluish-gray, with black insignia and buttons, which he himself wore at the Trident Conference.

Secretary Knox gave his approval to King's new uniform in April 1943. "Everyone loathed it," writes Buell. Outside Washington, officers refused to wear it, and in the Pacific it was virtually banned. Only in his own headquarters was King able to enforce its adoption. The principal outcome was inconsistency; a photograph of the Combined Chiefs at Quebec reveals Leahy in gray, King in blue, and Captain Forrest B. Royal (secretary of the JCS) in khaki. King must have recognized the inevitable on a visit of Admiral Halsey's to Washington, when a photographer, mistaking the gray-clad King for an enlisted man, asked him to get out of the way. When King retired, the gray uniform was retired with him.[111]

King still showed quirks of character. One of them had to do with decorations, which at heart he did not believe in. He thought that special commendation for doing what was no more than one's job was quite wrong, and that awarding too many medals cheapened their value. For him, the phrase "beyond the call of duty" was meant to be taken literally. "I sincerely hope," he wrote to Nimitz, "that there will be no repetition of certain awards made during the last war when people were, in effect, decorated when they lost their ships." The Navy began the Second World War with no clear policy on decorations, and King's negative attitude, combined with his stubbornness, meant that no clarification could come about. Nimitz prodded him to bring Navy policy into line with that of the other services (the air force was egregiously generous), but King would do nothing. He relented slightly when he discovered that Rear Admiral Alan G. Kirk had not been given the DSM for the Normandy landings, in which he commanded (an award to Kirk was soon forthcoming), but the Navy ended the war as confused about medals policy as it began.

Another of his vagaries had to do with rank, about which King's feelings were the reverse. It galled him that the British, having lost their place as senior partners in the Alliance to the Americans, who were now making the major contribution to the war, still outranked the American chiefs and at times, in King's view, behaved accordingly. He wanted five-star rank for himself and Marshall, but Marshall balked (he may have felt reluctant to share that honor with Pershing while Pershing was alive). One of the problems was what the title would be; King disliked "Admiral of the Fleet" because it followed British usage, and the awkwardness of "Field Marshal Marshall" was self-evident. King came forward with the characteristically oddball proposal of "Arch Admiral" and "Arch General," which he was annoyed to discover some thought to be facetious. (Secretary Knox gently reminded him that the word "arch," while technically correct, had ecclesiastical overtones.) President Roosevelt was said to favor "Chief Admiral" and "Chief General." Eventually they settled on "Fleet Admiral" and "General of the Armies," with Leahy, King, Nimitz, Halsey, Marshall, MacArthur, Eisenhower, and Arnold so designated. King and Marshall were photographed posing self-consciously with their new insignia.[112]

But King still took an active part in determining the character of the fleet in the Pacific, and in appointing its senior commanders, conspicuously during his visits to Hawaii and Saipan during July 1944, when assignments were substantially reshuffled. Some officers were promoted, others sent home; when it was over, a transformation had taken place and the controlling power of the Gun Club—the battleship admirals who had been in charge ever since anyone could remember—had been broken. The aviators had not yet totally taken over (one age dying, the other as yet powerless to be born), but the outlines of Ernie King's Navy, in which the aircraft carriers would assume the independent role he had long before envisaged for them, were beginning to take shape.

He still kept non-aviator generalists like Nimitz and Spruance in overall command, and he knew he did not have enough competent carrier admirals to go round (he told Nimitz not to waste them on the command of atolls), but those they had—Marc Mitscher, Ted Sherman, Monty Montgomery, Jocko Clark, Ralph Davison, Gerry Bogan—were brought forward. Many of the decisions involved were group decisions, and King sometimes played favorites in a way that recalled W. S. Gilbert's lines about polishing the handle of the big front door; but by and large, King and his colleagues arrived at sound judgments of men, and their Navy in action showed it.[113]

That Navy had also changed character in becoming amphibious, another development not fully anticipated. King did not at first appreciate how essential experienced amphibious officers were going to be; he held back on allocating scarce manpower to transports, cargo ships, and landing craft, though he correctly recognized that the Army greatly exaggerated its competence in this field. (Marshall in the early days, perhaps remembering his youthful exploit at Batangas, seemed to think of landings from the sea as easily managed; he learned better.) King was saved from his lapse of foresight by a piece of blind luck that dropped into his hand, without so much as a pretty-please on his part—the most gifted amphibious commander the war produced, a man too little understood in his lifetime and too little remembered now: Admiral Richmond Kelly Turner, "Terrible Turner," of whom the Japanese said he was like an alligator ("Once he bites into something he will not let go") and their news agency added, inaccurately, "This man Turner shall not return home alive."[114]

It was said by Americans that Halsey was a sailor's admiral, Spruance was an admiral's admiral, but Turner was a fighter's admiral. The news that he had assumed command was universally interpreted to mean that violent action was in prospect. He had been King's classmate at Pensacola in 1927 and was even then notorious for being brainy and aggressive. He was one of the Navy's most brilliant prewar planners; he wrote, among much else, the early drafts of Rainbow Five, the U.S. war plan that went into effect after Pearl Harbor. But he was not permitted to continue in that useful function. King would sometimes tease Turner by addressing him as "the Army's greatest single contribution to the war in the Pacific," and Turner would reply, "Greatest favor that anyone ever did me." It was a secret between them that in March 1942, Turner had been sacked as King's assistant chief of staff for plans because George Marshall persuaded the President that Turner, as a member of the joint planning staff, was too difficult to get along with. So King sent him to the Pacific, where Turner made a greater name for himself than he could ever have done in Washington. When King told Turner that he was to command amphibious forces for the landing on Guadalcanal, Turner protested that he did not know enough about amphibious warfare. "You will learn," said King.

Turner became amphibious warfare's unchallenged master. He commanded the successful invasions of Guadalcanal, the Russells, New Georgia, Tarawa, Eniwetok, the Marianas, Iwo Jima, and Okinawa. He instructed cohort after cohort of younger officers. He had a capacity for hard work that those who observed it found unbelievable, and his attention to detail was forbidding; he knew offhand the number, dimensions, and cube footage of every item of equipment in a Marine division. He was always conscious to near-obsession of his responsibility for keeping casualties low, and by the end of the war he was very tired. Sometimes he drank too much, especially at the end of day when his part in an operation was over and he grew bored. But others echoed Lincoln's words about Grant and wondered what his brand of whiskey was, and both Nimitz and Spruance insisted that alcohol never affected the clarity of Turner's mind during duty hours; "the man had tremendous resilience," Spruance said. Holland Smith, the Marine general who served alongside Turner, and argued with him more or less continuously, said: "We [the Marines] would rather go to sea with him in command than any other admiral under whom we have served."[115] Fate had given King a fine appointment, and the amphibious capability Turner perfected—plus the fast carriers under the air admirals' guidance—made inexorable the central Pacific offensive and the annihilation of Japanese sea power.

There was another subject on which King held pronounced opinions, and that was how the war should end. He had all along believed that an invasion of the Japanese home islands would be unnecessary (though he said privately after the war that he "didn't like the atomic bomb or any part of it"[116]), and the dismissal of Stilwell dampened his enthusiasm for landing in China (King admired Stilwell). King and Leahy were both reluctant to consider invasion inevitable, because of their traditional naval confidence in a blockade, but JCS planners doubted whether a blockade would produce unconditional surrender or rather might lead to a negotiated peace. In the end, King went along with planning for an invasion of Kyushu on the grounds that preparation for contingencies did no harm. (If there had to be an invasion, he thought the battle for the Tokyo plain on Honshu would be the decisive one.[117]) Where King's views were even more decided, however, was on two questions subsidiary to ending the Pacific war: (1) should the British be involved in it? and (2) should the Russians be involved in it? King's answer to both was No.

British participation was a touchy topic because Churchill had insisted on it at Second Quebec (September 1944). "I was determined that we should play our full and equal part . . . ," he wrote. "We had to regain on the field of battle our rightful possessions in the Far East, and not have them handed back to us at the peace table." Churchill forced the issue at the first plenary session by repeating his offer of the British battle fleet to serve in the Pacific under an American commander. "The offer has been made," Churchill said. "Is it accepted?" Roosevelt replied, "It is."[118] But King was of contrary mind, and at the Combined Chiefs meeting the next day he kept interposing objections and insisting (contrary to fact) that no presidential commitment had been made.

He did not believe that the British had sufficient logistical backup to stay at sea for long periods, and felt that such assistance as they might offer would be more than offset by the drain on American resources if he had to support them. King was in the impossible position of appearing to humiliate what had been the greatest naval power in history by saying, not only that he didn't need its help, but that he considered it a liability. Fortunately, the other American chiefs did not stand behind him on this, and he had to give in, though he did so with ill grace. In April 1945, a self-sufficient British task force—four fast carriers, two battleships, five cruisers, and eighteen destroyers—joined Fifth Fleet for the assault on Okinawa, neutralizing Japanese airfields and fending off *kamikazes* with fighter-direction techniques demonstrably superior to the American.

(British carriers also had armored flight decks, which ours did not.)[119] King's haughtiness had been without justification.

The Russians were another matter. King was brisk and categorical in his assertion that Russian entry into the Far East war was no longer something to be sought after in its own right. The point would not be worth laboring had it not become a postwar political football, with numerous contenders vying for the title of having been first to recognize that the Russian bear was not a friendly but a dangerous animal. MacArthur, for example, later maintained that he had been opposed to Russian entry when "Washington" pressed him to welcome it. This is doubly untrue.

King had earlier believed that Russia was entitled to warm-water ports, and he had therefore been willing to concede Soviet acquisition of the Baltic states and internationalization of the waterways of the Kattegat, the Skagerrak, and the Bosporus. (He had nonetheless opposed giving the Russians information as long as they gave us so little: "Under no circumstances," he told his combat intelligence officer, "are you to tell that Russian anything important.") Also, as a member of the Joint Chiefs, King had participated in the JCS evaluation of a Russian campaign against Japanese armies in Manchuria as an essential precondition of a successful U.S. invasion of Japan. This had long been the conventional wisdom. Marshall had communicated it to Roosevelt on the Joint Chiefs' behalf in January 1945, for the President's guidance during the forthcoming conference at Yalta.[120]

MacArthur shared it, and since he would command any land invasion of Japan, his opinions had to be respected. After Yalta, a group of planning officers was dispatched to inform the Far East commanders of the relatively few military decisions reached there, most having to do with arrangements for coordinating future American and Russian actions; comments on these were to be invited. MacArthur was interviewed on February 25, 1945, a few days after the recapture of Bataan, by Brigadier General George A. "Abe" Lincoln, who reported as follows: "General MacArthur considers it essential that maximum number of Jap divisions be engaged and pinned down on Asiatic mainland, before United States forces strike Japan proper." To another officer MacArthur had "emphatically stated that we must not invade Japan proper unless the Russian army is previously committed to action in Manchuria," and had astonishingly gone on to add that Russian seizure of all of Manchuria, Korea (!), and part of North China was "inevitable," but that she should "pay her way."[121]

MacArthur retroactively attempted to withdraw from this position. Eight years later, in early September 1953, he was queried by former President Herbert Hoover about the facts surrounding Yalta, and on the ninth replied: "My views on the entry of Russia into the war against Japan were frequently expressed in the negative after our recapture of the

Philippines." He said that at Tarlac, north of Clark Field, when Navy
Secretary Forrestal told him "of a projected plan which was being discussed in Washington to bring in the Soviet," subsequent newspaper accounts had reversed this and warped it "into my suggestions to him,"
which MacArthur said was "a prevarication and a complete misrepresen-
tation of the facts." Forrestal's diary unfortunately does not bear this out.
MacArthur, Forrestal wrote, "felt that we should secure the commitment
of the Russians to active and vigorous prosecution of a campaign against
the Japanese. . . . He expressed doubt that the use of anything less than
sixty divisions by the Russians would be sufficient."[122]

All of which makes it the more remarkable that MacArthur's views
were then either rejected or set aside by many in Washington, King
conspicuously among them. At a special meeting of the Joint Chiefs at the
White House on June 18, 1945, King told President Truman that the
Russians "were not indispensable and he did not think we should go as far
as to beg them to come in." (In Moscow, Ambassador Harriman at that
time believed "Russia would come into the war regardless of what we
might do.") King let Truman know he had no doubt "we could handle it
alone," and he thought realization of this would "greatly strengthen the
President's hand" in the conference soon to be held at Potsdam with Stalin
and Churchill.[123] King once again was right. In the event, when the Soviet
Union finally declared war and invaded Manchuria on August 9 (four days
after Hiroshima), the military consequences were minimal; the Japanese
were profoundly shocked, but mainly because this eliminated their last
hope that Russia might serve as an intermediary between them and the
Anglo-Americans.

King had come to have a finer feel for political leaders than he for-
merly had; he saw the inner metal in Truman far sooner than did anyone
else. At Potsdam, King was seated next to Lord Moran and whispered to
him: "Watch the President. This is all new to him, but he can take it. He
is a more typical American than Roosevelt, and he will do a good job, not
only for the United States but for the whole world."[124]

King was not all stiffness and intransigence. Buell has commented on
"the amazing ability of the [Combined] chiefs to leave their differences on
the doorstep" after their daily sessions were finished. This was true at
Cairo, after King's nearly climbing over the table at Brooke (according to
Stilwell), when they observed King's birthday with "good food, good conversation, and good fellowship," and had been true at Casablanca, when
Roosevelt invited everyone to dinner after the first day's meeting. King
encountered a difficulty those who swear off hard liquor sometimes experience with its milder forms. "King became nicely lit towards the end of the
evening," wrote Brooke in his diary, with only a drop or two of acid. "This
led to many arguments with P.M. [Prime Minister] who failed to appreciate fully the condition King was in. Most amusing to watch."[125]

Yet the British paid him handsome amends after the last of the arguments was over. Oxford gave him an honorary degree, presented by Lord Halifax: *"neque Glauci regno nec Neptuni nec ipsius Iovis Tonantis intemerato"*—"You have invaded alike the realms of Glaucis [a merman], of Neptune, and of Jove the Thunderer." From the British chiefs, on King's retirement as CNO in 1946, came an illuminated manuscript in handsome calligraphy, bound in blue morocco—"We are anxious that you should know how deeply we have appreciated, throughout our association in the higher direction of the war, your keen insight, your breadth of vision and your unshakeable determination to secure the defeat of our enemies in the shortest possible time"—and signed "Alanbrooke, Cunningham of Hyndhope, Portal of Hungerford."[126] They do these things well, bless them. We should not forget.

King had mellowed. When the Japanese overtures toward surrender became serious—in August 1945—he sent a message to Nimitz that began: "This is a peace warning."[127]

IV

ARNOLD

HAP ARNOLD WAS TAUGHT TO FLY by the Wright brothers. The course lasted eleven days (it would have taken ten except that the Wrights did not fly on Sunday). A two-seater Wright model B weighed 750 pounds and had a four-cylinder engine that delivered twelve horsepower; it could go above four thousand feet (Arnold set the military record at 4,167 on April 18, 1911), but when he tried to race an interurban trolley car with it, the trolley, making forty-five miles an hour, won. By the time of Arnold's death in 1950, from the last of his many heart attacks, the British had a jet-propelled transport, the de Havilland Comet, that could carry commercial passengers at 42,000 feet and 490 miles per hour, while the U.S. F-86 Sabrejet was doing 675 mph at 48,000; soon an advanced version of the F-86 would break the sound barrier. Arnold's career had spanned the dawn of manned flight from its bold inception to the routine acceptability in which we experience it today.

He was a pioneer among pilots. He was the first to fly the U.S. mail. He piloted the first plane from which a rifle was fired. When a bug caught in his eye he introduced the practice of wearing goggles. He was the first to win the Mackay Trophy for "outstanding aerial achievement" (on a reconnaissance flight over Virginia he successfully spotted a troop of cavalry on a country road), and in 1934 he won it a second time for flying nonstop from Juneau to Seattle (which also earned him a Distinguished Flying Cross). He and a friend developed the first system of aircraft nomenclature and maintenance. For a time they were the only two qualified pilots in the U.S. Army.[1]

Those who flew in the early days did not enjoy a high life expectancy. Of the twenty-four Army officers who were qualified between 1909 and 1913, eleven were killed in training and seven others subsequently died in crashes; many are the U.S. military airfields named after men who then

206

and later perished in their aircraft: Selfridge, Kelly, Rockwell, Scott, Hickam, Westover, Andrews. On November 5, 1912, Arnold's Wright Flyer went into a flat spin from which he managed to recover only seconds before it would have hit the ground. He landed safely but came away with a classic case of fear of flying, which lasted four years. He overcame it by pure will power and on December 16, 1916, flew a Curtiss Jenny for forty minutes, putting it (and himself) through every test he could think of.[2]

Arnold had great affection for Wilbur and Orville Wright, unpretentious men who never (he wrote) "took themselves half so seriously as we took them." Their father was a United Brethren bishop, who made his first flight at eighty-two and at 320 feet shouted to Orville, "Go higher, higher!" The Wright family would invite Arnold to Sunday dinner (not unwelcome for an impecunious second lieutenant) and he sat there marveling as the brothers told their quiet stories of the miracle he thought they had accomplished—"and it is a miracle to me today," Arnold wrote years afterward. "More than anyone I have ever known or read about," said Arnold, "the Wright brothers gave me a sense that nothing is impossible. I like to think —and during World War II often did think—that the Air Force has rooted its traditions in their spirit."[3]

What the Wrights had invented was of course not so much a machine as a principle: By repeated trials with a glider they had arrived at an understanding of the need to compensate for an aircraft's tendency to slew leftward when you tried to bank it to the right. Once this was established, the addition of a controllable vertical tail fin did the trick. True, they had also designed better wings and propellers than anyone else, but it was the discovery of the relationship between a rudder and the warping of the wings to bank that made possible the first true sustained level flight, and the phenomenally rapid development in aircraft design that followed. On a Wright plane, the warping of the wings and the turning of the tail were controlled by a single stick, the handle of which you pushed forward or back (wings) and twisted to the right or left (rudder). Learning to do this instinctively—and given the instability of the early aircraft it *had* to be instinctive—was what pilot training was about, and why not everyone could master it.[4]

Aviation was for many years rooted in the military (if you wanted to fly you joined the Army), and military aviation was a dedicated fraternity. Its members saw a different world from that of sailors or other soldiers; their perceptions of time and space had been so radically altered that they spoke a different language (the view of the ground from above at two hundred miles per hour is not communicable to someone who covers it on foot at two). They tended to become somewhat fanatical about their faith in air power, especially when it was greeted elsewhere in the services —as it almost invariably was—by incomprehension and obstructionism. For men like Arnold, the twenties and thirties were years of bitterness and frustration, of hopes dashed and a future wrapped in doubt. The observation was made of the Army Air Corps before World War II that it was fueled on ego, and there was truth in this. It took a degree of passionate conviction merely to keep the enterprise going.

Also, from the beginning, the pilots entered into a peculiarly intimate relationship with the machines they flew, inasmuch as their lives were linked with this aircraft and the mechanics who serviced it. The sea can be a treacherous medium but not half so menacing as the air, with its turbulence and pressure pockets. (The gallows humor of the air service songs, with their explicit references to going down in flames and having one's innards tangled up with the crankshaft, were ways of coping with this.) Arnold saw it from the start. His report to the chief of the Signal Corps, during his first week with the Wrights, records eleven flights for a total of one hour, forty minutes, and adds: "During weather not suitable for flying I have been studying the construction of the machine."[5] He learned how to disassemble and assemble its wood and canvas frame; he had to: the Wright planes were packed in boxcars for a move from one field to another. The only instrument was a piece of string tied to a strut; if it pointed straight to the rear, you were flying properly.

Henry H. Arnold seems to have been picked for this duty almost at random. (The nickname "Hap" was attached to him later, when he commanded March Field in California; his family called him Harley, from his middle name.) He was Pennsylvania Dutch, son of a doctor in Ardmore whose own father had been the first of the Arnolds in two centuries to abandon the family's Mennonite faith and become a Baptist. (Dr. Arnold remained a stern and uncompromising parent; he was a medical reserve officer who had served in the Spanish-American War and ran his household like an army barracks.) It had been intended that the older son, Tom, go to West Point, but he declined, and second son Henry—who had planned to go to Bucknell and become a Baptist minister—inherited the obligation. To everyone's astonishment he passed the exams and on July 27, 1903, found himself in a plebe's uniform on his way to a career, so he now hoped, in the cavalry.[6]

It was not to be. He became a proficient horseman, but otherwise his performance at the academy was lackluster; in a class of a hundred and ten, he usually stood somewhere between sixty-second and sixty-sixth, and he never made higher than cadet corporal. Much of his time there he seems to have spent walking punishment tours for being the ringleader in a series of ingenious pranks that culminated in a fireworks display on the barracks roof. To his deep disappointment, on graduation he was commissioned not in the cavalry but in the infantry. In despair, he requested duty in the Philippines, where he spent two years. (His memorable encounter near Batangas with George Marshall came on a later assignment there.)

During the summer of 1909, his regiment was reassigned to Governors Island in New York harbor; he had saved enough of his pay to make an extended trip home (partly in pursuit of the young lady who became his wife) by way of Singapore, Suez, Genoa, and Paris, where he heard a noise in the sky and looked up to see "a queer contraption overhead," in which, only a few weeks before, Louis Blériot had flown the English Channel. Arnold at the time felt no great desire to fly, but he did remember wondering what would happen to England's island defenses if a lot of men in a lot of machines crossed the channel by air. If he was ever going to be promoted to first lieutenant, he would have to find some kind of angle. At Governors Island he applied for "aeronautical work" with the Signal Corps; on April 21, 1911, he was detailed to it and ordered to report for instruction with the Wrights in Dayton, Ohio.[7]

Hap Arnold fathered the American air force. In six years, beginning in 1938, when he took command, he led it from an unimpressive twenty thousand men and a few hundred semi-obsolescent aircraft to a total of 2.4 million men and eighty thousand modern planes. "Never before or since," writes his biographer, Thomas M. Coffey (himself a World War II pilot), "has a military machine of such size and technical complexity been created in so short a period." Arnold did this less by intellect or organizational ability than by driving energy; he drove everyone else as relentlessly as he drove himself, at a pace that eventually punished his physical constitution beyond its ability to bear. He demanded, he cajoled; he was unreasonable and sly (he told manufacturers they would have to make planes faster because he had more pilots than planes, and he told the schools they would have to train pilots faster because he had more planes than pilots[8]). By asking the impossible, he worked his own miracle.

That Arnold ever ended up in senior command was of itself remarkable. Time and again he overstepped the bounds, taking actions on his own that his superiors neither had authorized nor were willing to countenance in retrospect. After one such he was sent to Panama, after another to Fort Riley, Kansas, widely regarded as the most disagreeable facility in the air service. When he attempted to send food and blankets to victims of the Long Beach earthquake in 1933, he was accused of giving away government property without permission and was nearly court-martialed. In 1940, he gave a congressional committee testimony displeasing to the President, and a gathering of notables was summoned to the White House on March 12, at which Roosevelt, looking pointedly at Arnold, observed that officers who were unable to "play ball" with the administration might be found available for duty on Guam. Many months passed before Arnold was asked to the White House again.[9]

Arnold hated Washington and had been miserable on previous tours of duty there. For all that—for all his often headstrong, tactless impatience with those who failed to share his vision—he had risen through the ranks to become, in September 1938, chief of the Air Corps. "He must have been doing something right," his biographer remarks. Though he sometimes broke with discipline, he knew how to maintain it; though he was tough and exacting with those who worked for him, he had their respect and, often enough, affection. His boyish good spirits were so engaging that, whatever the President's momentary annoyance with him, he ultimately became the one member of the Joint Chiefs whose company Roosevelt genuinely seemed to enjoy (Leahy, Marshall, and King were stiff sticks by comparison). As time passed, Arnold polished his political skills, learning to play the game of compromise until he could make the case for air power without upsetting the congressional-military applecart on which its achievement depended, and hold his more extreme colleagues in check until that extraordinary day, November 14, 1938, when he entered a meeting in the President's office and came out of it with a mandate to create an American air force.[10]

Exactly how Roosevelt arrived at the conclusion that World War II would be an air war must remain obscure, but regarding the why and when there is little question. He was a relatively late convert. Earlier he had straddled the issue; though no enemy of aviation, he was no enthusiast, either. He admitted the possibility that in the long perspective, aircraft might make surface vessels obsolete, but for the present and immediate future he held traditional Navy views. In May 1921, he told the Kiwanis Club of New York that "it is highly unlikely that an airplane or a fleet of them could ever successfully attack a fleet of navy vessels under battle conditions."[11] Some change may have been in prospect when he perceived, as a political candidate, that air travel was an aspect of the innovative spirit he wanted to exemplify. In 1932, breaking all precedent, he flew from Albany to Chicago in a Ford trimotor (making fuel stops in Buffalo and Cleveland) to accept the Democratic nomination for President. But he did not enjoy flying, and years later, on his return from Casablanca, told reporters that the more he did of it the less he liked it.[12]

The precipitating event was Munich. For at least a year, the President had been getting reports on the threat of growing German air power (a letter to him from Ambassador Hugh Wilson in Berlin had been "emphatic" on the subject[13]), and no great prescience was needed to see its connection with the reluctance of European statesmen to stand up to Hitler. On September 12, 1938, in his private railroad car on a siding in Rochester, Minnesota (where his son James was undergoing an operation in the Mayo Clinic), Roosevelt had listened on the radio to Hitler's speech at a party rally in Nuremberg, the Führer's voice filled with hatred and his audience shouting back at him, *"Sieg Heil! Sieg Heil! Sieg Heil! Sieg Heil!"* (The capitulation of Chamberlain and Daladier in dismembering Czechoslovakia was two weeks away.) The President could understand German and much else besides; Harry Hopkins (who was present) thought this was the moment when he arrived at some certainty that the Nazis were bent on war. He thereupon sent Hopkins on a tour of inspection to investigate the capacity of aeronautical manufacturers on the West Coast for producing military aircraft. "The President," Hopkins wrote, "was sure we were going to get into the war and he believed that air power would win it."[14]

◆

In World War I, as executive officer and then assistant director of military aeronautics, Arnold was the youngest colonel in the Army, principally because he was one of the few experienced air officers they had. The job involved him in every possible aspect of the attempts, many of them far too slow for his liking, to develop and procure aircraft, set up schools and airfields, recruit and train personnel. When he finally managed to get himself sent to Europe (to brief General Pershing on the invention of a pilotless aircraft), he arrived at the front just in time for the Armistice.

On the way, he met an American flier who had actually fought in the air and shot down German fighters, Major Carl "Tooey" Spaatz.[15] After the war, when Arnold was sent to command Rockwell Field near San Diego, he asked for Spaatz as his exec; as adjutant they were assigned a square-jawed Texan, Lieutenant Ira Eaker, who thought that Colonel Arnold was about the most impressive officer (with the exception of General Pershing) he had seen, tall and erect, wearing the uniform with dash and grace, possessing an engaging smile but also "a reserve and dignity of bearing which did not encourage familiarity." Eaker decided to stay in the Army. He thought Arnold and Spaatz "were going places and this would be a good team to join."[16]

Arnold thought an air offensive that Brigadier General Billy Mitchell had launched in the Saint Mihiel salient was "the first massed air striking power ever seen," and that Mitchell was badly needed at home to be chief of the air service. The job went instead to another man, and an infantryman at that, with Mitchell downgraded to be his assistant. It was the beginning of a series of assignments, demotions, insults, budget cuts, and general humiliation with which the ground-minded officers in high position in the War Department exerted themselves to bring the air service to heel and hamstring its growth. Their cause was advanced in September 1925 with Billy Mitchell's court-martial. He always talked too much, and this time, after the crash of the dirigible *Shenandoah,* he had accused the Navy and War departments of "incompetency, criminal negligence and almost treasonable administration of the National Defense."

Arnold, Spaatz, and other air officers testified eloquently on his behalf (Captain Ira Eaker had been detailed to provide Mitchell with documentation), but the verdict was never really in doubt. In December, Mitchell was found guilty of bringing discredit upon the military service and sentenced to five years' suspension from duty without pay, an obvious move to force him to resign his commission, which he soon did. Arnold was so cast down that he considered leaving the Army and becoming president of Pan American Airways, a company he and Spaatz had helped to found. Arnold and others distributed a pamphlet suggesting that pro-air pressure be put on Congress, and when his role in this was discovered he was offered a choice between resignation and a court-martial; he chose a court-martial and the offer (thus shown to be a bluff) was withdrawn. (It was after this that he was sent to Fort Riley.) He wondered whether he should remain in a service that had so little future, and he in it even less.[17]

The air officers mainly had each other to fall back on. They all knew one another and their careers were intertwined. Arnold and Spaatz—a brisk, sardonic man who was well described as looking like a rusty nail— became not only the good team Eaker anticipated but close friends (they served together again when Arnold commanded March Field in California). Other names begin to appear. Eaker came to Arnold at Rockwell to report that there was a man at an auxiliary airfield to the south whose conduct was so reprehensible it required Arnold's personal attention: This was Second Lieutenant James H. Doolittle, who had won a five-dollar bet that he could sit on the landing gear of a plane while it landed. (Arnold grounded him for a month but remembered the name.) When Spaatz flew a Fokker trimotor called the *Question Mark* in a test to see how long it could stay aloft by in-flight refueling, he chose as relief pilot a man who had shown some gifts at flying, Lieutenant Elwood Quesada. (They stayed up there a total of 150 hours, 40 minutes, 15 seconds.) Later Arnold was to learn that a commander has no friends, and he dealt impersonally and at times brusquely even with Spaatz and Eaker when Eighth Air Force did not live up to his expectations for it.[18]

Elliott Roosevelt—who had been a civilian pilot, had worked in the aviation industry, and had been aviation editor of the Hearst newspapers —spotted Arnold early (in 1934, when he was at March Field) and sent a note to his father recommending Arnold for promotion to brigadier general. But that would wait several years. Arnold's upward progress when it came owed a lot to positioning, to being at the right place at the right time with the right position. Some of the more fanatic air advocates thought that he temporized because he was ambitious, but one could as well conclude that the fanatic argument—immediate and complete independence for an air force, on the British model—was in practical terms unworkable. The Army Air Corps simply did not have the backup—administration, budget, housekeeping, personnel—to go it alone, to train and pay not only the pilot, the air crew, the mechanic, but also "the cook, baker, military policemen, signal personnel, medics—all of it," as Arnold wrote. Like it or not, these the Army provided, and Arnold realized sooner than did many of his co-workers that they "didn't want an independent

Air Force until we could sustain it properly."[19] Their problem meantime was to maintain some kind of doctrinal independence until the day came when they could prove that air power worked. It was not an easy row to hoe.

This was a period of constant improvement in aircraft technology—higher speed, higher altitude, better instrumentation—and given its step-child status and low priority, the Army air service was barely able to keep up. Put to the challenge, as happened in 1934 when President Roosevelt in a misguided moment gave them the job of delivering the U.S. mail, they seemed to demonstrate that the critics were right. Of the 281 pilots available for the task, only 31 had more than fifty hours of night flying, and the rest had fewer than twenty-five hours on instruments. None of the planes was properly equipped; they had too few directional gyroscopes and artificial horizons, and few of those they had were mounted in aircraft. Inevitably there were crashes and deaths, and a very angry President. Actually they did not do too badly in the seventy-eight days they worked at it—one and a half million miles flown, 777,000 pounds of mail carried, close to 75 percent of flights completed, and not a letter lost—but the incident mainly had the effect of highlighting the weaknesses of the air service.

The doctrinal opponents continued to be obdurate. Their views were well expressed by General Hugh Drum, a senior and influential officer, when he said that antiaircraft would shoot down all attacking planes and that he saw no reason why any of them should be designed to fly farther than three days' march by the infantry.[20] He and those like-minded did everything they could to sabotage the development of any but light and medium bombers, on the grounds that the national policy—as deputy chief of staff Major General Stanley D. Embick put it in May 1938—was one of "defense, not aggressiveness," that defense of sea areas was "a function of the Navy," and that the effectiveness of a heavy four-engine bomber like the B-17 "remains to be established."[21] When they punished, they could be mean. Major General Frank Andrews was rewarded for having successfully trained and organized a General Headquarters Air Force by being reduced to his permanent grade of colonel and dispatched to Fort Sam Houston, Texas, where he was assigned an office in a latrine. The men who sent him there were not only individually unintelligent and vindictive, they were collectively dangerous; had they prevailed, we would have entered the war ill-equipped indeed to fight it.

The reason they did not prevail was the arrival of George C. Marshall. "I found everyone on the [General] Staff hostile to Air," he later told Forrest Pogue, "and the young air officers were going to Congress and stirring up everything—and the [situation] was in a general muddle. They had something to complain about because they were not getting recognition." While he was still acting chief of staff, Marshall brought Andrews back from Texas, promoted him to permanent brigadier general "of the line," and made him assistant chief of staff, G-3 (operations), this over the strong objections of Secretary Woodring, Assistant Secretary Johnson, and Chief of Staff Craig, who thus had the privilege of being among the first in the upper administration to feel the force of Marshall's personality.

Some thought that making Andrews a line officer was a devious maneuver to get him out of the Air Corps, but Andrews said, "George Marshall doesn't work that way." (He had earlier taken Marshall on a tour of air bases, during which Marshall had been impressed by the potentialities of air power and the qualities of Andrews as an officer; Andrews would have gone on to high command if he had not died in a crash in Iceland during May 1943.) His restoration to favor and greater authority than an airman had been granted before revived the flagging spirits of the air officers; one of them wrote him: "What was due to happen has happened."[22] They could feel a fresh breeze blowing.

Arnold, however, thought it had been the meeting at the White House on November 14, 1938, that gave the Air Corps its Magna Carta. (This was the occasion in the aftershock of Munich on which Marshall told the President he was sorry but he didn't "agree with that at all.") Roosevelt did most of the talking. He told them that he didn't want to hear about ground forces, that a new barracks at some post in Wyoming would not scare Hitler one goddamned bit. What he wanted was airplanes! and lots of them! He wanted an Army Air Corps of 20,000 planes and an annual production capacity of 24,000, but since Congress wouldn't give him that, he intended to ask for 10,000, of which 2,500 would be trainers, 3,750 line combat, and 3,750 combat reserve. He had much to say on the subject of mass production, about which he seemed to have been well briefed (long talks between Arnold and Harry Hopkins were having their effect). To be kept in mind: Boeing was at this time geared to produce thirty-eight B-17s a year, and other manufacturers were no different.

Mark Watson wrote that with this meeting, "the effective rearming of the nation's ground and air forces took its start."[23] Earlier there had been Army plans aplenty, but now for the first time the initiative was coming from the President. From his lack of interest in anything but the aircraft themselves it can be assumed that the idea had not left his mind of selling them to the British and the French, but Arnold, Marshall, and Craig managed to get him to change his mind on that. There were to be many vicissitudes, revisions, and arguments with Congress, but Roosevelt "had started a momentum," writes air historian DeWitt Copp, "and the momentum once started could not be stopped, orchestrated as it was by a determined leader and the onrush of climactic events."[24]

Arnold sent for Tooey Spaatz and put him in charge of a three-man board (the other two members were Joseph McNarney and Claude Duncan; all were lieutenant colonels). They had no idea why they had been summoned until he told them, in effect: Boys, this is it! They were to draw up an expansion plan that would total 10,000 aircraft over two years. Since 2,320 already existed or were on order, that meant an additional 7,680, of which 2,000 would be built in two government-owned plants and the remainder by the aircraft industry. The President had appointed a board to rewrite the procurement laws so that they could award split contracts. They were to provide Arnold with arguments for the necessary expenditures so that he could defend a budget to Congress. They had a month in which to do this. Any questions? "The grin was wide," writes Copp, "and the sparkle in his eye must have been an inner reflection of the sun rising after twenty years of overcast."[25]

II

Arnold had the dream and the inner drive to undertake a great mission, but neither the brains nor the organizing capacity to carry through on it. His idea of administration, writes Thomas Coffey, "was to think of something that ought to be done and tell somebody to go do it right away."[26] Fortunately, he also had the good sense to recognize his limitations and to form an alliance that compensated for them. A combination of luck and business-world enterprise sent him an ally in the person of Robert A. Lovett as assistant secretary of war for air (later he was assistant secretary of state and later still, secretary of defense). A man of commanding ability who deserves to be even better remembered than he is for his part in forging American air power, Lovett, wrote Arnold, "possessed the qualities in which I was weakest, a partner and teammate of tremendous sympathy, and of calm and hidden force."[27]

Arnold and Lovett took to one another from the start and eventually (like Marshall and Stimson) had adjacent offices. Lovett saw that Arnold could be "very bouncy" but then have fits of depression: "He'd think things weren't going well. He needed help. He was a young boy in many ways. Not sophisticated." Arnold said that Lovett knew exactly how to handle him: "When I became impatient, intolerant, and would rant around . . . [he] would say with a quiet smile, 'Hap, you're wonderful! How I wish I had your pep and vitality! Now . . . let's get down and be practical,' and I would come back to earth with a bang."[28]

Robert Lovett was nothing if not sophisticated. A well-to-do investment banker, he lived with style. He and his wife, Adele, moved with ease in the New York worlds of theater, literature, and journalism. He knew Arthur Krock, C. L. Sulzberger, Walter Lippmann, Henry Luce; to the Lovetts' town house near the East River on Eighty-third Street, or to their summer home in Locust Valley on Long Island, came Robert Benchley, Archibald MacLeish, Tallulah Bankhead, Philip Barry, Lillian Hellman, Robert Sherwood, Greta Garbo, Dorothy Parker. Lovett was described as likely to quote Dorothy Parker and George Santayana in the same paragraph.[29]

His urbanity and tact made him the perfect foil to Arnold's bull-in-a-china-shop impulsiveness. But Lovett also possessed the understanding of air doctrine and skill at expounding it that enabled him to argue the merits of air power with Marshall, Stimson, and the President; and he further possessed the detailed familiarity with the aircraft industry, the feel for how it worked, that enabled him to organize the processes of procurement which alone could make air power a reality. To a degree unparalleled among other major actors in the American drama of World War II, he combined the functions of strategist and industrial czar in the same person. It was also said of Lovett (by *Time* magazine) that unlike Billy Mitchell, he "gets things done by pressing the right button instead of wrecking the keyboard."[30]

Lovett was a flier, a decorated Navy pilot in World War I (lieutenant commander and recipient of the Navy Cross). He belonged to a group of Yale undergraduates who had learned to fly on their own in aircraft provided by one of their number's father, a Morgan partner; they had then been inducted into active service through the good offices of Assistant Secretary of the Navy Franklin Roosevelt. (Another member of the group was Artemus Gates, who in World War II was to be Lovett's opposite number in the Navy Department.) Lovett served for a time with a British unit based in France, flew bombing missions over Belgium and Germany, and was promoted to command of the Navy's northern bombing group. (It was during this period that Assistant Secretary Roosevelt inspected his airfield and wrote home that Lovett was "the son of Judge Lovett" and "seems like an awfully nice boy.") Lovett came away from his World War I experience persuaded of the offensive potentiality of bombers against enemy industry, an opinion on which he was later to act with some effect.

The fact that men like Lovett were welcomed into the wartime administrations, though this was an aggravation to pure-in-heart New Dealers, was not fortuitous. The President's attitude toward free enterprise and a market economy had always been far more conventional than his political rhetoric might at times have implied. Patterson, Bundy, McCloy, Lovett, Forrestal, Gates (and, of course, Averell Harriman), were the kind of people he knew, and he knew he needed them. That they were willing to put aside their often considerable antipathies to the New Deal in order to serve the nation struck him as commendable, if not a prior condition of his appointing them to their jobs. As a group they formed "the essential link," so writes Jonathan Fanton in a Yale Ph.D. thesis about Lovett's war years, "between Roosevelt's conception of the national interest in wartime and the many specific assignments and sacrifices imposed on American industry. . . . At the same time, their instinctive respect for business values and their restraint in exercising authority maintained the perception of the voluntary co-operation of business."[31]

"Judge" Lovett was a self-made Texas lawyer who acquired the judicial honorific after a brief stint on a state bench. He represented a railroad that was bought out by E. H. Harriman and before long had become legal counsel for the Harriman interests in Texas. By 1906, he was vice-president of the Union Pacific, and on Harriman's death, in 1909, he became its president. The family had moved to New York and young Lovett went the approved route: Hill, Yale (Elizabethan, Skull and Bones, but also Phi Beta Kappa). After the war he tried Harvard Law School but found it stifling; in 1919, he married the daughter of James Brown, senior partner of Brown Brothers, investment bankers, a neighbor and family friend. Brown, who had no sons, found one in his son-in-law. In 1921, he took Lovett into the firm that later became Brown Brothers Harriman, and by 1926, Lovett was a partner, "a lifetime association," writes Fanton, "to which he would return after each tour of public service." (The merger with the Harrimans took place in 1930; Lovett and the Harriman brothers, Roland and Averell, had been friends from boyhood.)

The business of Brown Brothers was international, as it had been from its beginnings in the importation of Irish linens to Baltimore toward the end of the eighteenth century. Four generations of the family had engaged in financing every aspect of the flourishing transatlantic trade, and so diversified were its activities that at the time of the merger *The World's Work* could speak of Brown Brothers as "a venerable banking house whose history is closely linked with American history."[32]

His work required Lovett in the years between the wars to make two trips annually to Europe, visiting the bank's correspondents in as many as twenty cities. He watched the coming of World War II and on his final trip in 1940 became more than ever aware of the resurgence of German air power. He returned home on a refugee ship, convinced that neutrality was a chimera and that America must rearm. In October 1940, he organized for himself a private inspection tour of manufacturing plants on the West Coast, most of whose managers he knew personally. They confirmed for him what he already suspected—that the American aircraft industry as then organized was incapable of meeting the demands war would impose upon it.

This conviction he imparted to his friend James Forrestal, recently appointed under secretary of the Navy, and Forrestal induced him to say the same to Assistant Secretary of War Robert Patterson, who asked him to put it in writing. Lovett's report of November 22, 1940, tried to avoid undue criticism of the manufacturers (he said it should be read "with the same sympathy which would be extended to a hen if she were asked, on short notice, to produce an ostrich egg"), but he left no doubt where the difficulty lay.

"This is a quantitative war," Lovett wrote. "The airplane industry has, so far, been qualitative." He argued for better procurement procedures, greater geographic dispersal, stronger measures to meet the shortages of machine tools and skilled workers, closer attention to special military requirements, and above all, more standardization and mass production. Patterson showed the report to Secretary Stimson, who also knew Lovett and decided then and there to hire him as a special assistant. Two weeks later, President Roosevelt approved and Lovett reported for duty ("the more I see of him," Stimson wrote in his diary, "the better I like him"[33]). Four months later, Lovett was named assistant secretary of war for air.

Lovett said that air matters in the War Department as he found them were "a hell of a mess."[34] Even making an allowance for New Broom Syndrome, it does not seem an unfair assessment. Lovett could scarcely believe the stacked-up hierarchies that seemed to surround every action, the rotation policies that snatched away officers as soon as they learned anything. "Private industry," as he wrote to an air force commander some years later, "would curl up in the corner and die after such practices." He was especially astonished at the absence of reliable data; he couldn't understand how anyone was willing to arrive at decisions without trustworthy facts. He set up his own reporting system on the numbers of planes, pilots, ground crews, and bombs available each day. "Mr. Lovett has lost faith in our figures," General Arnold reported to his staff in August 1942, admonishing them henceforward to "be accurate."[35]

Lovett's primary and most exhausting task, one in which he never quite succeeded, was to persuade the President to be realistic. Roosevelt believed that people can always do more than they think or say they can. He liked to set ambitious goals, often by plucking figures out of the air, on the theory that this would ensure a maximum effort. Lovett did not think that in aircraft production the theory applied. He believed, as he wrote Arnold in October 1942, that an "extravagant target figure is likely to produce less planes than more." The pushing of panic buttons diverted resources and upset the orderly development of increased capacity. It encouraged the continuation of obsolete models, tempting manufacturers (as Lovett had written Hopkins in January) "to fall into the trap of the old numbers racket and build the easy types and forget about the spares." (Failure to make enough spare parts had for a time grounded part of the RAF.) It led to a concentration on fighters, which could be made more quickly, rather than on heavy bombers, which took more time. It invited a crisis in credibility if, as Lovett believed, the President's goals could not be met.

Roosevelt had told Stimson within a month after Pearl Harbor that he wanted 60,000 aircraft (45,000 combat type) produced in 1942 and 125,000 (100,000 combat type) in 1943. Lovett pointed out to Hopkins that this was incapable of realization, if only because the lead time required for materials and machine tools meant that 1942 production was "largely past history already."[36] He was still making the same point to Arnold later in the year, when accumulating evidence of shortfalls indicated how right Lovett was. In August, the President had gone to Arnold direct, asking (through Marshall) for his estimate, not of predicted production, but of how many aircraft *should* be produced in 1943 "in order to have complete air supremacy over the enemy," a characteristic Rooseveltian device for avoiding unwelcome statistics. (When shown figures he did not like, the President was known to ask that he not be shown them again.) Arnold, sharing the same psychology of provocation and prodding as Roosevelt's, was inclined to go along with him on the figure of 100,000 for combat aircraft alone, and it was this that produced Lovett's two-and-a-half-page memorandum to Arnold of October 14, 1942, which reveals his intelligence and integrity (and fluency of expression) at their best.

What purported to be a schedule of 1943 aircraft production, wrote Lovett, was not a schedule at all: "It is a fantasy." No responsible person in the Material Command, the Bureau of Aeronautics, or the War Production Board would consider it credible. "In giving currency to such a program we are kidding no one but ourselves, the public, and the President." Ten months of 1942 had already passed. Material was already going into the forging, fabricating, and other primary processes that would determine the rate of production through at least the second quarter of 1943. An achievable total figure for all types, combat included, would be 100,000 overall and probably less. If there were delays in reaching decisions, that number would have to be reduced still further, to between 92,000 and 96,000. "I do not feel that I can have any part," Lovett wrote, "in supporting a program which, in my opinion, . . . is likely to cause false hopes initially and bitter disappointment later. Therefore, I feel compelled to disassociate myself."[37]

Arnold was not deterred. He believed that his duty was to raise the banner and shout Onward!; to state the needs and make every effort to meet the President's program. He replied that future possibilities should not be judged by past performance. "The negative assumption that requirements cannot be met," he wrote Lovett on October 19, "supported by facts as they are and not as we are capable of making them, too often has characterized thinking on this entire subject."

The Wright brothers lesson: Nothing is impossible.

But Lovett had by this time mastered the techniques of Washington maneuver and had mustered an imposing phalanx of allies: Stimson, Knox, Marshall, King, Forrestal, and—not least—Under Secretary of War Robert P. Patterson, who had written Arnold on October 17 that the 100,000 combat total was "utterly unattainable" and that no informed person he knew had any confidence in it. Arnold finally retreated, and forwarded Patterson's letter (in which he recommended a program of 82,000 combat and 25,000 training, for a total of 107,000) to the Joint Chiefs, who met on October 21 and approved it, as then and reluctantly did the President, though he continued to insist that this should not be regarded as "a goal to shoot at" but as a "program [to] be carried out in toto."[38]

There *were* delays, caused by an aluminum shortage and a decision to replace two obsolete models with improved designs, and by March 1943 Lovett was warning Hopkins that a total of 88,000 was now a more likely 1943 figure. The WPB supported him, but Arnold prevailed with the Joint Chiefs and they stuck with the 107,000 target. They were wrong and Lovett was more than right: Total U.S. aircraft production for 1943 turned out to be 85,898, of which about 60 percent were combat types, little more than half of what the President had begun by demanding.[39]

◆

Arnold tended to go a bit overboard when he talked about air power; Lovett did not. The mission of the Air Forces, Arnold wrote in his reply to Lovett's memo, was "to destroy the capacity and the will of the enemy for waging war." He was confident that the mission could be carried out, and that *"no other offensive effort open to us can bring us this success"* (his emphasis). Lovett never went that distance; his position was strong but judicious. "While I don't go so far as to claim that air power alone will win the war," he had written to Hopkins in March 1941, "I do claim that the war will not be won without it."[40] Lovett's view had many merits, among them that of containing the truth, but it also was better calculated than Arnold's to convince the skeptical.

When Lovett first arrived in the War Department, he found it still at odds with the President over quotas that allocated the planes we produced equally between ourselves and the British. Roosevelt had begun by thinking of aircraft manufacture largely as an aspect of Lend-Lease, appreciating as he did (and Arnold and Secretary Woodring did not) that foreign orders were a politically acceptable device for increasing American productive capacity, an appreciation Lovett as a civilian had shared. It took time for the President entirely to abandon this perspective, and in dealing with it, Arnold, Marshall, and Stimson had become entangled in a wearing fight. Lovett came to the fray afresh, and produced ingenious arguments to use with Roosevelt—e.g., that a shortage of training planes was crippling the expansion of our own forces, that there were three pilots for every available plane, so that the pilots were not gaining familiarity with up-to-date equipment. For the moment nothing happened, but Lovett was on the right track.

His central endeavor was to create a climate of informed opinion. He began with Secretary Stimson, giving him in February 1941 what amounted to a tutorial on how air power had been employed in the present war up to that time, with an emphasis on British experience with granting air a large measure of self-governance. Stimson, as was his practice, summarized in his diary what he had learned that day. "Air warfare involves not merely a new auxiliary weapon for the ground troops," Lovett had convinced him, "but it is becoming clear now that it involves independent action quite divorced from both the land and the sea." Lovett was no advocate of full independence for the airmen, but he impressed on Stimson that it would be the secretary's responsibility to strike a balance in "just how far to go in freeing them."[41]

Next came Marshall, who Stimson feared might be unreceptive, a needless worry; Marshall proved to be an almost ideal channel through which Lovett's (and Arnold's) ideas could enter the Army mind. Lovett at Stimson's request made a presentation to Marshall, and Stimson could see that it made "a good and strong impression." Marshall and Lovett between them achieved a compromise in which Marshall granted the Air Corps increased autonomy while Lovett opposed the public and congressional pressures that in 1940 began building up for a separate air force. Lovett drafted the letter for Stimson to send to the Senate Military Affairs Committee (with the President's approval) in which this mutually acceptable position—autonomy but not independence—was set forth. Forrest Pogue said that Marshall "highly prized" Lovett's calm appraisals, and that by the end Lovett was as close to Marshall as to Stimson.

"I tried to give Arnold all the power I could," Marshall told his biographer after the war. "My main difficulties came from the fact that he had a very immature staff. They were not immature in years, because they were pretty old, but I used to . . . say [they were] antique staff officers or passé airmen—passé fliers, I guess—because they were not trained at that kind of staff work and they were busy taking stands . . . about promotions." Marshall much preferred able young officers like Lauris Norstad and Laurence Kuter, and urged Arnold to promote them, but Arnold said that he couldn't because if he did so the rest of his staff would quit; Marshall promoted them anyhow.[42] Marshall's and Lovett's work came to a climax in June 1941 when the President approved the revision to Army Regulation 95-5 that established the Army Air Forces (formerly Corps), with its own air staff and with Arnold both as its chief and as Marshall's deputy. It had been well done; the pieces were in place.

What Lovett had badly wanted the President to accept was the need for increased production of heavy bombers. "If there is one lesson this war has taught," Lovett wrote Stimson in the period following Pearl Harbor, "it is that defensive weapons will not win the war." Offensive weapons meant to Lovett, as for the most part they did to Arnold, heavy bombers. Stimson encouraged Lovett to take his case to Hopkins in the White House; on February 28, 1942, Lovett did so and Hopkins's response was sympathetic. He took a memo of Lovett's to the President, who found it persuasive and accepted a Lovett draft for a presidential directive. On

May 4, Roosevelt wrote to Stimson establishing a monthly goal of 500 heavy bombers as opposed to 4,500 other types. It had been Lovett's first great success in influencing overall policy.[43]

Another subject much on his mind was personnel and pilot training. Initially Lovett had shared the elitism (for which read snobbery) of Air Corps recruitment procedures, in which, for example, only college graduates were accepted as prospective pilots. But by early 1941 Lovett had come to realize that this and other arbitrary requirements were going to produce a chronic shortage, both in air and ground crews. He secured copies of one of the entrance tests, and he and the president of MIT took it; both failed (high scorer among MIT students taking it was "a young girl from Flatbush whose family were a bunch of musicians"). Eventually Lovett favored dropping what was by then the minimum acceptable level for pilots of two years of college. His own experience, he wrote to Arnold in November 1941, was that "the gilded son who has spent two years in the ivy-clad halls of Yale, can come out at the end of that time uneducated, uncultured, and unintelligent. . . . In my short life, some of the worst boors and most complete stinkers I have met were college graduates." The system was revised, and within a year air force enrollment had increased fivefold.[44]

But Lovett's most critical function was to rule over the aircraft industry like a sympathetic but demanding father confessor. He did not hesitate to intervene; as a banker he was accustomed to being listened to by management. If it performed poorly it was scolded or, in some cases, replaced. "The government always has to step in in some form or other," he told a senator who wanted to investigate one company. Yet he was on a first-name basis with most of the executives and kept their confidence. His office, writes Fanton, "served as an informal court of appeals" for the industry. Lovett did not want it to suffer unfairly and did want it to emerge from the war healthy and competitive. Under his guidance it expanded five times in plant space and ten times in manpower; by V-J Day it had produced over three hundred thousand aircraft.[45]

If Lovett had flaws, they were those of his time and place. Like Stimson, he never quite shed the antilabor bias of the prewar business community; working people were meant to work and be content with their lot, unrest was the work of agitators (if Stimson had had his way, labor would have been conscripted and strikers sent to jail). The President tended to see labor troubles in the light of labor-management relations, where for Lovett they were complicated by other factors, like declining unemployment, the lack of skilled workers, and geographic disparities in pay; he found the failure to arrive at a national manpower policy very annoying. During 1943, three million people were involved in strikes of one kind or another and yet Roosevelt, as so often where a "solution" would only have made the problem worse politically, was content to let things drift. Lovett was flexible enough to advocate an expanded role for women, yet on racial questions he remained indifferent, and the air force record in its treatment of qualified blacks continued to be disgraceful.[46]

If Lovett had an influence on grand strategy, it was less in his own right than through others: Arnold, Marshall, Stimson, the President. Most of all this concerned heavy bombers (though Lovett later intervened decisively to increase the range of fighter planes). Roosevelt's approval in May 1942 of increased production of the heavies had not settled the issue, for when the Navy found out what the implications were for their own programs, they carried their complaints to Congress, where the House Committee on Naval Affairs lent a sympathetic ear. Lovett wrote a letter for Stimson's signature to committee chairman Carl Vinson, Stimson's first systematic statement of the air force stand. Lovett got Air Chief Marshal Charles Portal to write a letter, intended for public consumption, stating that "the heavy bomber in the offensive sphere still transcends all other requirements in importance." (Eventually Lovett worked out a deal with Forrestal in which the two of them jointly pressed OPM for critical items *both* services needed.) Marshall had come to rely on him for daily briefings, and Stimson's trust in him was complete. "The next time anybody asks you . . . what your authority is," Stimson said to Lovett, "you just tell them that whatever authority the Secretary of War has, you have."[47]

Gradually the struggle to prevent aircraft production from being swallowed up in Lend-Lease had been going Arnold's and Lovett's way. Force of circumstance, and the perilous straits Britain was in, brought it home to the President that we could not go on forever aiding our allies at the expense of weakening ourselves. At a White House meeting on September 27, 1940 (Arnold was still in disfavor for arguing the cause of the Air Corps too insistently and was not present), Roosevelt urged that our B-17s be made available to the British. Stimson let Marshall do the talking, and Marshall (well advised by Arnold) pointed out that, setting aside a few squadrons in Hawaii and the Philippines, the United States had presently available for its own defense the sum total of forty-nine bombers. Stimson said that "the President's head went back as if someone had hit him in the chest." Stimson thought that Roosevelt "finally saw the situation we were in."[48]

Arnold's appointment as deputy chief of staff, the highest position any airman could have aspired to, followed in October. The absence of presidential objection to it has been variously explained by, among other contributing causes, the commissioning of Roosevelt's son Elliott as an Air Corps captain in September. (Arnold maintained, in the face of public complaints, that Elliott Roosevelt was well qualified,[49] and whether or not such was the case, the President's favor was not that easily purchased.) More likely Roosevelt now realized that Arnold and Lovett had been right, that we badly needed an effective air force and could not defer indefinitely the labor of assembling it.

A few weeks before Christmas 1940, Arnold was invited to a small dinner at the White House and arrived to discover that he was early and that the President awaited him with a tray of cocktail mixings set out. "Good evening, Hap," said Roosevelt, as though there had never been the slightest difference between them. "How about my mixing you an Old Fashioned?"

To the extent that Arnold indulged, which was sparingly, Old Fashioneds were among his favorite drinks. Someone had gone to the trouble of finding this out. It also occurred to him that he had nearly been turned down for chief of the Air Corps in 1938 because of a rumor that he was a drunk. He decided to permit himself a slight exaggeration.

"Thanks, Mr. President," said he. "I haven't had one for about twenty years, but I assure you I will enjoy this one with you, tremendously."[50]

III

On October 8, 1938, less than two weeks after he became chief of the Air Corps, Arnold wrote a personal letter to Charles A. Lindbergh, who was then living with his family on the island of Illiec, off the coast of Brittany. Arnold explained that he felt the need, and felt that the U.S. government had a need, for an exact evaluation of the present and potential air power of other nations. "I realize," Arnold wrote, "that you have had an opportunity which has been available to no one else to observe the aviation industry the world over. . . . I shall count it a great personal favor, and believe you will be performing a patriotic service, if you can supply me with any data on this subject."[51]

Lindbergh replied on November 2: "This is the third consecutive year during which I have had the opportunity of watching the German aviation development. . . . Germany is undoubtedly the most powerful nation in the world in military aviation and her margin of leadership is increasing with each month that passes. . . . In a number of fields the Germans are already ahead of us and they are rapidly cutting down whatever lead we now hold in many others. . . . I wish that you yourself could make a trip to Germany in the near future to see what is being done in that country."[52]

Lindbergh had already been providing information on the German air force and its equipment for American military intelligence. His first visit to Germany, in July 1936, had been arranged by Major Truman Smith, military attaché in the Berlin embassy. Lindbergh was shown the Heinkel and Junkers factories; he piloted two German aircraft and inspected others, including the Ju 87 Stuka dive-bomber. Smith said that Lindbergh's visit vastly improved his own access to the Luftwaffe and the quality of his reports to Washington. In October 1937, Lindbergh and his wife were invited back to Germany. He was shown the Focke-Wulf, Henschel, and Daimler-Benz factories, and was permitted to examine closely the Dornier 17 twin-engine bomber and the Messerschmitt 109 fighter. (Later he was allowed to fly the Me 109 and to inspect their best and newest bomber, the Junkers 88.) Before leaving, he helped Smith prepare a "general estimate" of German air power, which went back to the War Department over Smith's signature but contained data and ideas that were Lindbergh's, often set forth in the latter's language.[53]

Arnold answered Lindbergh on November 17; he had indeed contemplated a German trip three months earlier, he said, but had canceled it "for diplomatic reasons." (The annexation of Austria took place in March; the Czech crisis began in May, reaching its height in early September, and the Munich agreement was signed at the end of the month.) Arnold invited further comments on the "refinements" of German design and Lindbergh obliged. "It seems to me," he wrote in part on November 29, "that we should be developing prototypes with a top speed in the vicinity of 500 miles per hour at altitude. . . . I have no way of checking [the] figures, but the trend over here seems to be toward very high speed, both for bombers and fighters. Apparently, range and bomb load are sacrificed considerably for speed."[54]

In April 1939, Lindbergh publicly returned to the United States for the first time since the kidnapping and death of his son, which had caused him so much pain and so heightened his already considerable antagonism to journalists. Lindbergh arrived on the *Aquitania* (his wife and family followed shortly) and had to be escorted by a flying wedge of police through the crowd of shouting newspapermen and photographers awaiting him. That evening he telephoned Arnold, as Arnold had asked him to do. To escape the ravening press, Arnold suggested that they meet in the Hotel Thayer at West Point, where the dining room was cleared for their use. Later they continued several hours of conversation in the grandstand on the Plain, where the Army baseball team was playing Syracuse, and were seated immediately behind a row of reporters who would have given much to know where Lindbergh was.

Lindbergh, Arnold later wrote, "gave me the most accurate picture of the Luftwaffe, its equipment, leaders, apparent plans, training methods, and present defects that I had so far received."[55] Lindbergh was well aware that the most serious German deficiency lay in a shortage of trained personnel, but he missed (as did virtually everyone else) another defect that in the long run proved more debilitating—the failure to develop an effective capacity for strategic bombing. He had seen the factories and he had seen bombers with enough range to reach anywhere in Europe. He drew the seemingly logical conclusion that a potential capacity had in fact been realized. "If she wishes to do so," Lindbergh told Ambassador Joseph

Kennedy in London during September 1938 (and Kennedy reported to Washington), "Germany has now the means of destroying London, Paris, and Prague." He believed that German factories were "capable" of producing 20,000 aircraft annually, though he admitted uncertainty as to what actual production was; he thought perhaps 500 to 800 a month. Others, more alarmist than he, gave higher numbers. (Average monthly output was in fact 691 for 1939, but the total for the year was only 8,295; given losses, attrition, and obsolescence, this was not enough to fight a major war; total Luftwaffe operational strength in September 1939 was only 4,204 planes, of which 3,609 were serviceable.[56])

Charles Lindbergh has not been dealt with charitably by time and reputation. He was a ploddingly rational and indefatigably earnest young man who was trying to remain true to his beliefs, while at the same time coping with the most punishing consequences of fame to have descended on any unfortunate in the twentieth century. An apostle of teamwork and technology, he had been idolized as the epitome of individualism and heroic adventure (when he titled his first book *We*, the point did not get across).[57] An admirer of German industriousness and technical competence, he was vilified for admiring (as he did not) everything else about Nazi Germany. For reporting truthfully on what he saw, he is now condemned for having sowed defeatism, as indeed he had done with isolationists like Ambassador Kennedy, whatever his intentions.

Lindbergh was himself an isolationist but no pacifist. "Of course," as he wrote Arnold, "war can not, and should not, always be avoided." Yet always in his mind was the image of those fleets of Ju 88s he envisaged (range 1,553 miles, maximum bomb load 5,510 pounds) flying over London, Paris, and Prague. Like so many others among his contemporaries (Arnold included), he exaggerated not only Luftwaffe actual strength but the effects of aerial bombardment as such; he thought of it in terms of total destruction. His attitude toward Germany—his desire to "understand" it—was based on a conviction that another general European war would be a disaster for mankind and, as he had written Arnold from Brittany, "might result in the loss of Western civilization as we know it."[58]

The odd thing is that Lindbergh's carefully gathered figures and erroneous conclusions drawn therefrom had exactly the opposite effect on Hap Arnold from the one they had on an advocate of appeasement like Ambassador Kennedy; they only steeled Arnold's resolve to accelerate the development of an American air force to match and overpower Germany's. One could further indulge the irony and say that a significant motive force behind the creation of the USAAF was the misunderstanding of German mobilization that Lindbergh encouraged. He was not alone in it, but Arnold took his opinions very seriously, and it can be said with some justification that their interview on the playing fields of West Point was an important step in Arnold's forward progress, that it earns Lindbergh more credit for his contribution to the American war effort than he usually receives. At conversation's end, Arnold asked Lindbergh if he would be willing to serve on a board to review American wartime requirements, and Lindbergh said yes—a response with consequences that will appear when we come to consider LeMay and the B-29s in a later chapter.

When war in fact came, and Lindbergh's strenuous efforts (through speeches for the America First Committee) to keep this country out of it were shown to be pointless, he offered Arnold his services. "I fully realize the complications created by the political stand I have taken . . . ," wrote Lindbergh on December 20, 1941. "However, I want you to know that if the opportunity should arise during this crisis, I am ready and anxious to be of service. . . . May God strengthen you for the ordeal ahead." When rumors of this letter leaked out, and Arnold was asked by the INS wire service if they were true, he diplomatically replied that if Lindbergh had volunteered, then "it indicated that he had changed from a non-interventionist status to one in which he desired to participate in activities for which his years of experience had best qualified him."[59]

Arnold's statement did not have the mollifying effect he had hoped for; it generated a substantial outcry. Arnold saved, and filed in his papers, all the letters he received about the possibility of Lindbergh's recall to active duty (just as Marshall, probably for similar reasons, saved all the letters he received about George Patton), and what is remarkable about them is their venom. There were by this time many Americans who hated Hitler with a smoldering hatred, and it rubbed off on Lindbergh; a medal Göring had conferred on him, an incident magnified out of proportion, made him appear a conscious Nazi sympathizer. When Lindbergh in January 1942 sought a meeting with Arnold, Arnold's aide advised him to go directly to the secretary of war, and there followed two sessions, first with Stimson and Lovett and then with Lovett and Arnold, in which they expressed doubt about his ability to serve "loyally"; Lindbergh got the impression they were under instruction from higher authority and not wholly comfortable about it. There is no direct evidence for the President's hand in this but every reason to suspect it.

In political matters Franklin Roosevelt was not a forgiving man, and in matters of principle Charles Lindbergh was not a yielding one. Lindbergh had served since 1931 on the National Advisory Committee for Aeronautics, and in 1938, when the Civil Aeronautics Authority was set up, he was approached about becoming its chairman (he declined, and resigned from NACA in 1939). In September 1939 of that year, when he was preparing his first major noninterventionist radio address, an offer was made to him (through Arnold and Truman Smith) to the effect that if he would cancel his speech and not publicly oppose the President's policies, a cabinet post, secretary of air, would be created for him.

Neither Arnold nor Smith thought that Lindbergh was the kind of man to be bought off so blatantly, and he was not. He again declined; if anything, the incident strengthened his mistrust of the administration. When he met with Arnold and Lovett in 1942, he told them that he had "very little confidence in the President," that he had not changed his prewar views, but that if he returned to uniform he "would follow the President of the United States as Commander-in-Chief of the Army." They did not feel that went far enough, and their response convinced him that further efforts to rejoin the Air Corps would be a mistake.[60] Millions of others (including many who were equally ardent America Firsters) took identical positions without having their loyalty questioned, and served without incident.

But Lindbergh was not an ordinary American.

The President's attitude is unappealing but comprehensible. He had been trying to guide the nation on a course beset by real and menacing hazards, and to his mind the opposition of people so prominent as Lindbergh seriously compounded the danger we were in. He used—and, in judicious hindsight, abused—every instrumentality of his office to counter them. He authorized the attorney general to employ wiretapping and asked him to explore the possibility of a grand jury investigation into the America First Committee's finances. He turned over to the FBI telegrams critical of his own position, and to the Secret Service letters supporting Lindbergh. Even if Lindbergh was a guileless innocent, he was aiding those the President considered to be subversive. And Roosevelt did not think Lindbergh to be innocent. "If I should die tomorrow," he told Secretary Morgenthau, "I want you to know this. I am absolutely convinced that Lindbergh is a Nazi."[61]

Lindbergh's attempts to serve his country in a civilian capacity were at first frustrated. When he sounded out friends at Pan American and Curtiss-Wright about such a possibility, they told him there were objections from the White House. Four months passed before he received an offer from Henry Ford—who could not have cared less what the White House thought—to join him at the Willow Run plant, where Ford was building B-24 Liberator bombers (eventually 6,791 of them and 1,893 "knock-down" units for assembly elsewhere; Willow Run's total output, after some teething troubles, was the largest of any aircraft plant in the country).[62] Lindbergh accepted Ford's invitation and bought a house in Bloomfield Hills. He made high-altitude flights in the P-47 Thunderbolt and worked to improve the engine in the Navy's Corsair F4U. In April 1944 he went to the Pacific as a technical representative of United Aircraft and showed pilots how to get increased range out of the P-38 Lightning by using low revolutions per minute, high manifold pressure, and an auto-lean mixture-control setting. He flew the Corsair with heavy bomb loads, to prove it could be done. He flew fifty combat missions, on one of which he shot down a Japanese fighter.[63] Medals are given for less. That his President should have believed him a Nazi is a sad sidelight on the bitterness that political passion can arouse, and a reaffirmation of the rule that true tragedy should be inevitable, as this one was not.

Fortunately, it had no effect on Lindbergh's friendship with Hap Arnold, which continued throughout and after the war. In 1945, Lindbergh went to Germany as a member of a technical mission to study advanced German aircraft, in particular those with jet or rocket propulsion. In 1949, after Arnold had retired and finished the manuscript of his book, *Global Mission,* Lindbergh one day encountered him in the Pentagon, and wrote him some days later: "I wish there had been more opportunity to talk. I have thought of you often as I traveled around the Air Force establishments you took such a large part in creating. It was a great privilege to serve under you and to know you. My best wishes always travel with you."[64]

◆

In 1941, Arnold was still having trouble persuading President Roosevelt that an air force in prospect was not the same thing as an air force in being, and that there was no point in sending everything we had to the British unless we knew exactly what they needed. In the spring he decided to go to London to see for himself (this Arnold did often, as in the trips he made to the Pacific in 1943 and 1945). He planned to meet with Air Marshal Portal (who headed the RAF) and with—he hoped—Lord Beaverbrook (who was in charge of aircraft production), but he still thought of himself as a minor league player in the major league of senior Allied commanders, and he had little expectation of anything special in the way of a reception. Here Arnold was mistaken; he was given a welcome of warmth and great regard. Every door was opened; there were dinners with the high brass and cabinet ministers, a weekend with Churchill and family at Dytchley Park, and—to top it off—an audience with the king.

Arnold found himself confronted with a basic disparity in scale; a number of his listeners seemed to have no clear picture of what American industry would be able to produce. When he told Portal that we would need bauxite for the aluminum in 75,000 airplanes, he realized that Portal was having difficulty with so large a figure, and when Arnold talked about storage for two million gallons of gasoline in Newfoundland, the idea was treated as "somewhat staggering." Arnold's aide, now-Major Elwood P. "Pete" Quesada, said that the British "would talk about squadrons whereas we would talk about groups" (a difference in terminology: RAF "squadron" meant U.S. "wing"). Both Arnold and Quesada thought that our future allies were setting their sights too low, and that in order to win the war they were going to have to do "a hell of a lot more" than they seemed to have in mind.[65]

The evening of Arnold's third day in London, he witnessed his first air raid; he and Quesada went up on the roof of the Dorchester to watch. Sirens began to wail, searchlights to probe the sky, and the antiaircraft guns to open fire. Arnold could hear the bomb bursts coming closer as the horizon reddened with burning buildings. Soon the German planes were directly overhead. "The noise was deafening," wrote Arnold, "with the firing of the guns and the bombs dropping—and then, almost as quickly as the raid had started, the noise rapidly receded and all was silent again, leaving the sky bright from the fires."

The scene made a profound impression on Arnold and Quesada, primarily because as air officers they thought the raid had been less than what the Luftwaffe was capable of delivering, "not—according to my mind—in any way a display of Air Power," Arnold wrote. When he was surveying damage to London later in the week, the thought occurred to him that it had been caused by no more than five hundred bombers. What if (the terms in which Americans were thinking) there had been eight hundred or a thousand or more? "Air power," wrote Arnold, "means employment of airplanes in numbers large enough to secure complete destruction."

Quesada said that the two of them "came to a sort of opinion, an intuitive opinion, that the British didn't know what they were in for. We sold them short, in other words." If the Germans really turned loose the power Arnold thought they possessed, then there could only be one outcome. He believed "the British were actually in an awfully tight spot, and knew it." He came home so discouraged about the chances for Britain's survival that at the President's request a speech he had intended to give to some of his officers was canceled, and he asked Quesada to speak in his place.[66]

Why was Arnold so wrong on a subject of such importance for air warfare? This is another way of phrasing a related question, one of the seemingly simple yet in fact complex puzzles of the war—namely, why had the Luftwaffe lost the Battle of Britain when by all rights it should have won? The Germans in 1940 possessed numerical superiority in aircraft and in bases that ringed Britain from the east and south. Had they achieved control of the air, nothing could have prevented their invasion of the British Isles. Had this succeeded, Europe and the Middle East would have been abandoned and America isolated, the undivided weight of Germany would have fallen upon Russia, and German and Japanese armies would have met on the borders of India. Yet the Luftwaffe failed, and none of the somber events noted above came to pass. Why? Those who have offered answers, from both the Allied and the enemy sides, are uncommonly united in agreeing that the Germans lost because they were stupid beyond belief, while the British won because they were unbelievably resolute—and not in the least bit stupid.

One reason for Arnold's error was the American overestimation of German strength; he discovered in London that he had been crediting the

Luftwaffe with 2,000 more aircraft than the British did, and they in turn (as was later learned) had the total too high—at the outbreak of war, 4,320 as opposed to the actual 3,647, and the error accumulated.[67] But another error lay in the fact that the picture of German air power as painted by someone of Lindbergh's familiarity with it had a great deal of plausibility. When the Luftwaffe was unveiled before a startled world in 1935, it offered alarming evidence of the superiority Hitler and Göring claimed for it. The prohibitions of the Versailles Treaty against a German air force were shown to have been farcical. Planes built as transports reappeared as bombers, and "sport" aircraft as fighters; men appeared as pilots who had trained on gliders or in a secret school south of Moscow. With the success of the campaigns in Poland, Scandinavia, and the West in 1939–40, a theoretically overwhelming instrument of war, when put to the test, gave every appearance of being all that Lindbergh and others had said it was.

The evidence was misleading, however. The test had not been a genuine one; the Luftwaffe was riddled with weaknesses. There had been considerable bluff involved, and the bluff had not been called by air combat against opponents whose own air forces were weak or ineffectual. German air theory had been identical to that of the hidebound American Army General Staff in the between-wars years; the difference was that the Americans succeeded in disembarrassing themselves of it, while the Germans did not. The Luftwaffe was fully and consciously designed for ground support, and for ground support in a short, limited European war. When it had to face a broader and more extended challenge, its inner flaws were revealed. The Battle of Britain faced it with that challenge.

From the start, the German air force encountered serious shortages, especially in middle-grade staff, which meant that army and navy officers, who lacked air background, had to be brought in. There was a shortage of aluminum, which meant pressure to concentrate on light and medium bombers. (The Luftwaffe had once possessed a confirmed believer in long-range heavy bombers in the person of its chief of staff, Major General Walther Wever, but Wever died in a crash in 1936 and the four-engine prototypes he had been encouraging—the Dornier 19 and the Junkers 89 —were abandoned.[68]) There were not enough fighter planes, and the standard model, the Messerschmitt 109, had too short a range, which meant that it could not escort bombers over England much beyond London.

Germany's true capability in the air resided in its scientists and technicians, who were justly well-regarded. Had their talents been properly employed, the end product would have been a powerful adversary. Fortunately for our side, their talents were not properly employed, but rather were dissipated in irrelevant projects or frustrated by feuding bureaucrats. A case in point was Professor Willy Messerschmitt himself, the gifted owner and chief designer of the Bayerische Flugzeugwerke near Augsburg, where postponed delivery dates seem to have been a permanent condition. No one had the authority, or tried hard enough, to get Messerschmitt to concentrate on standard and reliable lines. His designers were far more interested in brilliant innovation than in testing what came off the production line, and their wishes were indulged, with the result that during 1942 they were working on forty new models in addition to twenty-two prototypes with six variations, while Messerschmitt aircraft were still undergoing accidents from faulty landing gears.[69]

Luftwaffe organization was top-heavy and sluggish. The enormous Air Ministry building in Berlin's Leipzigerstrasse has been suggested as being one of the causes of Germany's defeat, inasmuch as it filled with a steady stream of sections and bureaus in furious rivalry with one another, and with "engineer generals" absorbed in infighting and intrigue. When the Air Ministry was asked to choose between the Me 109 and the Heinkel 112 fighters, no one could agree, so they ordered both. "There was hardly a decision," writes Luftwaffe bomber pilot Werner Baumbach, "that was not reversed several times and then finally restored." A state of chronic indecisiveness ensured that the production of obsolete types continued and that the Luftwaffe entered the Battle of Britain with models that had essentially been in the advanced design stage in 1933.[70]

At the top of this busy ant heap was a total incompetent. Hermann Göring was a World War I hero who had promoted all his former comrades and, at least until late 1941, enjoyed Hitler's full confidence. He was monumentally uninterested in technical matters of any kind yet thoroughly persuaded of the Luftwaffe's technical superiority. Confronted with the chaos of too many designs and too few effective aircraft, at a conference on February 7, 1940, which he chaired, he firmly settled the question in classic authoritarian style. "Only those projects will be considered absolutely essential," reads the conference report, "which will be completed in 1940 or promise to be producing by 1941 at the latest."[71] This substantially set back the development of new prototypes, on the grounds that they would not be needed after a war soon to be over. It was among Göring's most successful contributions to Allied victory. If the Me 262, a jet fighter of truly advanced design that was operational by October 1944 and took a worrisome toll of Allied bombers, had been available earlier in sufficient numbers, Allied mastery of the air over Europe would have been a doubtful prospect.[72]

There could be no better illustration of the colossal inefficiency of Nazi Germany, or of the Nazis' success in concealing it from others (and, at times, from themselves). Two myths coincided: Everyone knew that Germans are efficient and everyone knew that dictatorships are efficient; therefore, if Hitler says Germany is totally mobilized for war, Germany must be totally mobilized for war. Werner Baumbach saw something quite contrary. He remained a German patriot even in defeat, but experience had taught him that a totalitarian system, "thanks to the rigid dogmatic thinking of its leaders and the clumsiness of its organization," is incapable of adapting to the volatile conditions of modern warfare. He knew what weakness the Nazi bombast concealed. "They knew abroad that we were not bluffing," boasted Göring in 1939. "And yet how often we bluffed!" said Baumbach ten years later. At the time of the Rhineland reoccupation in 1936, they had only one Potemkin squadron of Arado biplane fighters, unarmed, which they moved from field to field, changing the insignia each time to reveal a "new" squadron to foreign observers.[73]

I have dilated at this length on the inherent faults of the Luftwaffe, not because it was a less than formidable foe, but because they serve as a useful object lesson, because they help in part to explain much of what happened in 1940, and because they stand in such sharp contrast to the relative sanity and system with which the emergence of air power was managed from Washington. The matters Roosevelt, Arnold, and Lovett had to deal with may seem to the reader to have been theoretical and abstract when in fact they were not. High management, like high command, if well done will often be invisible; if badly done, its effects will litter the landscape and crop up underfoot at every turn.

Luftwaffe pilots like Werner Baumbach were able and dedicated men (he held the Oak Leaves with Swords to the Knight's Cross of the Iron Cross, highest decoration awarded to a bomber pilot), but they were helpless against the incompetence, corruption, and viciousness that flowed over their country from the top like a gray, molten, volcanic tide. Two of Göring's most devoted generals, Ernst Udet and Hans Jeschonnek, committed suicide when he deceived and betrayed them. ("Iron Man, you deserted me!" Udet scrawled on the wall before he shot himself[74]). Seeing how something was done wrong can be helpful in appreciating how it was done right.

The British did everything right—well, nearly everything.

The Battle of Britain was fought on their side by a singular concurrence of well-crafted solutions to the problem of how to defend an island. Out of disparate elements—thirty thousand ground observers in a thousand posts, clever Oxbridge dons who were reading German ciphers, countrywide communication lines operated and maintained by the Post Office, two excellent aircraft in steady production and several hundred high-spirited young men to fly them, a gadget of tall steel towers and dancing lights on a cathode-ray tube, and above all two commanders of genius—was spun a web in which the Luftwaffe ensnared itself in victories never quite attained and defeats not clearly acknowledged. Some Germans went on insisting after the war that there had never been any such thing as the Battle of Britain, but their pilots thought otherwise. Told again and again that RAF Fighter Command had statistically ceased to exist, the

German fliers over England saw the swift formations rising up against them. "Here they come again," said one, "the last fifty Spitfires."[75]

The RAF fighter pilots occupy center stage and deserve to, if only for their humor. (Listening on the radio to Churchill's great tribute— "Never in the field of human conflict has so much been owed by so many to so few"—one among them was heard to remark, "That must be a reference to mess bills.") But in the wings was a multitude. When the German missions formed up over their bases, the low-grade radio traffic they generated was read and understood, so that their origin and composition—sometimes their destination—were known even before radar picked them up and the trim WAAF girls in the sector stations with their croupier rakes began moving colored counters on the plotting tables (for most of the battles they were never more than four minutes, or fifteen miles, behind the event[76]).

Then the squadrons were "scrambled," the whine of the engines began, and the gladiators of this incomparable struggle climbed into the sky. Radar lost the enemy when he crossed the coast, which was when the ground observers took over, but most vital of all was the command control by leaders who must husband every resource and spend it only where justified: Air Chief Marshal Sir Hugh Dowding, chief of Fighter Command, and Air Vice-Marshal Keith Park, commander of 11th Group in southeast England, of whom it was justly said that he was the only man who could have lost the war in an afternoon.[77]

The Germans never quite took the measure of their opponent and the calculated economy of his tactics. They knew, vaguely, that the British had radar (the tall steel towers on the coast were visible for miles), but they disparaged it as ineffectual and Göring, after an attack on the towers more successful than he knew, called off any continuation. They could hear the ground-to-air conversations of RAF fighter control with the pilots, but this they interpreted as only a manifestation of British "rigidity." Their invasion plans were impromptu and they seemed at times to think that the Luftwaffe could accomplish the defeat of Britain single-handed. Lacking any air staff that could plan or execute a strategic offensive, they wobbled about from one objective to another, abandoning one to take up something else just at the moment when the first of the two, if pursued with consistency, might have succeeded.

They began with attacks on coastal convoys in the Channel, and continued these well into mid-August, allowing their opponent a precious month in which to recuperate and prepare. (Can you fill "the unforgiving minute?" asked Kipling, a question George Patton often quoted to himself and others.) The next stage consisted of a major effort to destroy Fighter Command and achieve air supremacy over Britain, but they were ill prepared for this and there were those in the Luftwaffe high command who knew it. They did not know, except from pilots' reports, which were the airfields the British fighters were flying from, and they did not know which were the all-important sector stations in the command net, nor that these—because of parsimony on the part of the Air Ministry—were located aboveground and highly vulnerable.

How close, how close the Germans came to winning! In the battle of fighter versus fighter, by early September the Luftwaffe seemed on every evidence to be ahead. Fighter Command was on the ropes. Pilot reserves were seriously depleted. Morale was beginning to show wear and tear; some squadrons avoided contact with the Germans and at one field (Manston, in Kent, the most exposed and heavily bombed) men went into the air-raid shelters and refused to come out. By the beginning of September the defense of Great Britain depended essentially on two sector airfields, Tangmere near Portsmouth and Kenley near London, and if these had been attacked to the exclusion of all else, neither you nor I would be sitting where we are at this moment.[78] What it came down to was not a coterie of superheroes in Spitfires but the consummate maneuvering of Park and Dowding, and the average quality of the average pilots (many flying Hawker Hurricanes, with which the battles were mainly fought)—and even some of the Germans admitted that the British average was better than theirs.[79] What it came down to was who cracked first, and it was not RAF Fighter Command that cracked.

On September 7, Göring personally took charge of the campaign and made the decision that determined its subsequent course and outcome. He switched the attack from the airfields to London; Fighter Command was spared destruction and what Londoners called "the blitz" began. It was an impulsive and irrevocable blunder. In London that day, 306 died and 1,337 were seriously injured, but this was to be the last of the daylight raids; thenceforward the bombers came mostly by night and slowly the balance began to swing toward the defenders until September 15, the day so glowingly described by Churchill in his war history, when the Germans lost sixty bombers and the RAF lost only twenty-six fighters, thirteen of whose pilots were saved. On October 26, the cryptanalysts at Bletchley Park decoded a Luftwaffe message indicating that a special administrative unit attached to the invasion forces had been disbanded.[80] The conquest of Great Britain had been indefinitely postponed.

Drew Middleton had been in the House of Commons in June when Churchill delivered his speech, with its matchless peroration, announcing that the Battle of Britain was about to begin. The words form ranks in the back of every mind in which they echo: "Let us therefore brace ourselves to our duties, and so bear ourselves that, if the British Empire and its Commonwealth last for a thousand years, men will still say 'This was their finest hour.'" There was a moment of silence and then the cheering began. "Somehow from the recesses of the British spirit the challenge was going to be met, the duty done," wrote Middleton. "Somehow these incredible people were going to do it." He came out into a sunshine that seemed brighter than it had been before.[81]

From end to end that island burned with a white flame in those days, and it lit the world.

Coming as early in the war as it did, the Battle of Britain caused three nations to draw conclusions from it that were consequential in being both true and not true. The Americans concluded, since German bombers were too lightly armed (true), that therefore our own bombers, which were heavily armed (true), could with ease break through fighter defenses of the kind that had partially stopped the Germans (not true). The Germans concluded that bombers could be hurt by swarms of fighters (true), but neglected to notice, as they themselves had very nearly demonstrated, that swarms of fighters could be hurt by other swarms of fighters (also true, and later our salvation). Some but not all Germans concluded that they had delivered such a knockout blow (almost true) that the British were really defeated anyhow (not true) and merely didn't know it (neither true nor relevant). Finally, in rhythm with their leader's prose, the British concluded that in the skies over their green hills and valleys during the summer of 1940 had been fought the battle that saved everything.

True.

◆

Arnold's realization that he had finally reached the major leagues came in August 1941, when he attended the meeting between Roosevelt and Churchill that produced the Atlantic Charter. At the time he had no notion why he had been invited, and only later did he discover that it had been Harry Hopkins's idea, to match the British representation by all three services. Marshall had told him only to bring heavy clothing and expect to be away about ten days. At New York, Arnold was embarked aboard *Tuscaloosa*, Marshall and Stark in Admiral King's flagship, *Augusta*. Screened by four destroyers, they proceeded eastward down Long Island Sound. Arnold was on the bridge when he noticed a burst of signal-flag activity from *Augusta*, two or three halyardsful. He asked a Navy friend what the message meant. The answer, after a pause: "That's Admiral King asking the Captain of *Tuscaloosa* just what the hell he thinks he's doing, anyway."[82]

They anchored off Martha's Vineyard on the afternoon of the fourth. That night a blinking light appeared and a signalman on *Augusta* reported: "Tell the Admiral that the *Potomac* has just entered the anchorage with President Roosevelt aboard." The President's yacht had put out from South Dartmouth, Massachusetts, where Roosevelt had been visibly vacationing with Princess Martha of Norway, her two daughters, and Prince Karl of Sweden. Never was Roosevelt's delight in minor royalty and deception more evident. Early that morning he was transferred to *Augusta* and later that day *Potomac* passed through the Cape Cod Canal with persons vaguely resembling the President and his party waving at onlookers ashore. *Augusta, Tuscaloosa,* and the destroyers meanwhile steamed past Nantucket Shoals Lightship and headed north at a brisk twenty-two knots, through dense fog in heavily traveled fishing grounds and shipping lanes. "It was a serious misjudgment," writes King's biographer. Radar was not yet all that reliable and King was very lucky there were no collisions.[83]

They reached Placentia Bay, Newfoundland, on August 7. Arnold was thoroughly enjoying himself, though one aspect of *Tuscaloosa*'s plumbing facilities puzzled him. "One starts to wash one's face or hands in clear crystal water," he wrote in his diary, "but when one uses soap—bingo the water turns blue. Investigation reveals that there are two ships in the Navy that have that particular peculiarity." He wrote out a set of three principles he believed they should follow in the meetings he now knew to be forthcoming—(1) a plan to be made for developing U.S. Army and Navy strength; (2) aid to Britain and China only in items effectively usable and not needed for such a plan; and (3) no commitments to be made until our experts had studied them—and he was pleased when Marshall, Stark, and the President accepted these. On the basis of his London trip he anticipated that the British would be well prepared, while as far as he knew, "we were going into this one cold."[84] We were not sufficiently ready for war and the men who would become the Joint Chiefs were not so far functioning as such.

Churchill had not yet arrived and the President went fishing. According to Arnold, ho caught onc toad fish, one dog fish, and one halibut; according to Elliott Roosevelt, he caught one what-is-it that nobody could identify and he suggested it be sent to the Smithsonian. (At the President's request, Arnold had arranged for Captain Roosevelt, then stationed at Gander Bay, to join them; King, similarly, had ordered Lieutenant [jg] Franklin D. Roosevelt, Jr., from destroyer *Mayrant* to report to the "commander in chief," which young Roosevelt thought meant King, and wondered what mistake he could have made that was *that* bad.[85]) The President held a conference with his military leaders aboard *Augusta* and presented them with an overall statement of policy (Arnold afterward made notes).

Our line of responsibility ran east of Iceland and the Azores, the President said, and in this area we must ensure the safe passage of the goods we produce. Hostile craft entering it must be assumed to have hostile intent, and if they come within shooting distance, "we must start shooting first." We must do everything possible to provide for delivery of aircraft to England: establish weather and radio stations, help train ferry pilots. We should put ten thousand soldiers into Iceland. We should put more forces into the Philippines, principally B-17s and P-40s, to give some "bite" to any ultimatum we might have to send Japan. If Japan goes into

Thailand, "The United States will not be overly concerned," but if she goes into the Dutch East Indies, "then we are vitally interested, and must do our utmost to get them out"[86]—one of the best summations to be had of the American position in the summer of 1941, with war four months away.

On the morning of August 9, H.M.S. *Prince of Wales* broke through the mist into sunshine, the crew manning the rails and the Prime Minister standing on the bridge in the uniform of an Elder Brother of Trinity House. After an exchange of ceremonies, there began four days of conferences (Arnold thought two days too many, in view of the live danger from German submarines) among the principals and their subordinates, in which no matters of great moment were resolved but much groundwork was built for the combined efforts that lay ahead. Marshall and Sir John Dill here discovered one another.

Arnold in retrospect believed the meetings "invaluable" in giving the two prospective partners a better understanding of each other's problems, though what he chiefly came away with was a vivid impression of how much the British were willing to ask of us. His grandiose use of large numbers in London seemed to have backfired. They were asking for four thousand heavy bombers immediately when our total production had not yet reached five hundred a month. "All they want is our birthright," said one American officer. Arnold was relieved that the Americans "were able to get away without promising or giving away everything we had," and he thought that his opposite number, Air Chief Marshal Sir Wilfred Freeman, "accepted our refusals gracefully."[87]

The first evening had been spent in "a family dinner," Roosevelt's physician, Ross McIntire, called it, aboard *Augusta:* broiled chicken, spinach omelet, chocolate ice cream. "I have never seen a happier group," McIntire said, "meeting on such a serious subject." (British fare was more elegant: Arnold said that lunch aboard the *Prince of Wales* consisted of caviar, vodka, mock turtle soup, grouse, champagne, port, coffee, and brandy.) After dinner on *Augusta* that first day, Churchill, at Roosevelt's invitation, gave one of his *tour de force* summations of the world situation. Elliott Roosevelt said that normally his father dominated every occasion as though that were his natural due. "But not tonight. Tonight Father listened. Somebody else was holding the audience, holding it with grand, rolling, periodic speeches." Roosevelt listened, fiddled with his pince-nez eyeglasses, rubbed his eyes, doodled on the tablecloth with a burnt match. "But never an aye, nay, or maybe," wrote young Elliott, "came from the Americans sitting around that smoke-filled saloon."[88]

They were not being persuaded. The British strategic plan "did not include our Army and Air Force playing more than a very secondary role," Arnold wrote in his diary. "Hence, it did not mention nor did the British representatives bring up point of our building up our Army or Navy for active participation in the war." This was of a piece with a British approach contrived to minimize the risks of American involvement and maximize American willingness to allocate the fruits of our industrial production to Britain. If the Americans needed aircraft, Arnold wrote, "then they said—we will give you planes to operate when you arrive."

To this casual brush-off was coupled the idea that Germany could be defeated without an Allied landing on the Continent, or even if there was to be a land campaign, that it would be one of armored spearheads and armed resistance groups in which large infantry forces would be unnecessary. How much of this was meant to make intervention palatable to Americans, and how much was the consequence of British realistic appraisal of their inadequate resources, one cannot tell. At any event, it was absurd, and the Americans recognized its absurdity. Marshall knew that there would have to be large ground armies, and Arnold felt instinctively that an apparently hopeless set of circumstances was not to be accepted as long as the air power eventuality was open.[89]

It was a confrontation that foreshadowed many of the Anglo-American conferences to come: British awareness of the deadly war they were in, American awareness of how much deadly force would be needed to win it. The Americans were sensitive to the fact that they were talking to people who had actually been doing the fighting (the *Prince of Wales* still bore the scars of its battle with the *Bismarck*), and to the symbolic significance of holding these conversations in the first place. To the President, the latter consideration was all-important, and therefore he devoted much of his time to working out the text of a declaration he and the Prime Minister could sign together, not least to protect himself against any accusation that some secret commitment had been made ("we wished to God there *had* been," said one of the British officials later to Robert Sherwood[90]).

The Americans were astonished at the speed and complexity of British communications. Churchill took no step without consulting the War Cabinet in London, with whom in three days he exchanged some thirty messages. Churchill sent a draft of the joint declaration at 1:50 P.M. (local time) on the eleventh and received an answer within twelve hours. The draft reached London around midnight, when many cabinet ministers were asleep, but they promptly convened, discussed it, and cabled their approval (plus a suggested additional point that Roosevelt readily accepted) at 4:10 A.M. (London time). "Please thank Cabinet for amazingly swift reply," Churchill answered.[91]

If what Roosevelt wanted was a symbol, he surely got one at the Atlantic Charter meeting. The photographs of the religious services held on the *Prince of Wales*'s quarterdeck, the military of the two nations intermingled, the pulpit draped with their two flags, communicated more meaning than did the charter. The lesson was from the first chapter of Joshua: "There shall not any man be able to stand before thee all the days of thy life: as I was with Moses, so will I be with thee: I will not fail thee, nor forsake thee. Be strong and of good courage." Churchill had picked the hymns himself: "For Those in Peril on the Sea," "Onward, Christian Soldiers," and "O God, Our Help in Ages Past," of which he wrote in *The Grand Alliance,* "Macaulay reminds us the Ironsides had chanted as they bore John Hampden's body to the grave."[92]

"We live by symbols and we can't too often recall them," Justice Felix Frankfurter wrote to the President some days later. "And you two in that ocean . . . in the setting of that Sunday service, gave meaning to the conflict between civilization and arrogant, brute challenge, and gave promise more powerful and binding than any formal treaty could, that civilization has brains and resources that tyranny will not be able to overcome."[93]

Footnote to the future: The President put ashore in Maine and to his train at Portland was delivered a message by a young special assistant to the secretary of the Navy identified in the naval log as "Adelai Stevenson," who at some risk had been chasing the train in a small aircraft. The message, deemed highly secret, was that a reliable source reported Stalin to be negotiating with Hitler. "Adlai, do you believe this?" said Roosevelt after he read Stevenson's handwritten scrawl (here was the first and the last time two of the great Democrats of their age were to meet). Stevenson said he wasn't sure. "I don't believe it," Roosevelt said. "I'm not worried at all. Are you worried, Adlai?" Stevenson said he guessed not, and on turning to leave, by his account, bumped into the door. Stevenson's stories about himself tended to be self-deprecatory and to improve in the telling. Thus ended what he described to his wife as, with the exception of their marriage and the birth of their three sons, "the most exciting day of my life."[94]

IV

The first and severest test of American air power came in August 1943 with the raid on Ploesti, Rumania, by 178 B-24 Liberators based in North Africa. The Ploesti raid stands apart from the rest of the war in the air. The idea for it, and the unusual tactics involved, came from the top; it was conceived in Arnold's headquarters and approved by the President. It was not an element in some other campaign but regarded as worthwhile in and of itself. It was thought through and planned in meticulous detail, to be executed by the best-prepared and most experienced force we then had available, and it was fought with incomparable bravery, the only single action of the war for which five Congressional Medals of Honor (three of them posthumous) were awarded. It was also the worst disaster in the history of the USAAF, and considered as a test, it brought in an inconclusive verdict.

Ploesti, a small town north of Bucharest, was the dream target of all time—fragile, concentrated, vital. It was the source of 60 percent of Germany's crude oil supply. Hitler's Chief of Staff, General Jodl, said that no success the Russians could achieve on the eastern front would be "directly disastrous" as long as they did not capture the Rumanian oil fields, and Hitler himself conceded that if the Ploesti refineries were destroyed, "the damage will be irreparable."[95] Germany had little natural oil, but Rumania's was plentiful and of high quality; it was piped or otherwise transported to the processing plants in or around Ploesti, for conversion there into fuel oil, lubricants, and high-octane gasoline, of which Ploesti produced the best the Germans had. Some forty refineries were located near Ploesti, among them the six catalytic crackers that made the aviation fuel, all netted together by pipelines and railroad yards, dotted with thousands of combustible storage tanks. Power plants, distilling units, and boiler houses were equally vulnerable—a total of delicate and complex units that were producing some 400,000 tons of refined petroleum a month for Hitler's war machine. No wonder Allied air commanders looked at Ploesti and longed to destroy it.

The bombing of Ploesti had early on appealed to Franklin Roosevelt. In May 1942, he had approved the diversion to it of a project even more appealing to him, which was the bombing of Japan. In the hasty extemporization of the post–Pearl Harbor days, a scratch force of B-24s under Colonel Harry A. Halverson had been trained in great secrecy to attack Tokyo from bases in China, but by the time they reached Khartoum in the Sudan, the situation in Burma had deteriorated so badly that their original mission was canceled. General Marshall persuaded the President to send them instead against Ploesti, which twelve of them reached at dawn on June 12 and bombed through overcast at 10,000 feet. Though damage was negligible, no aircraft were lost to enemy action and no one was killed; four B-24s landed in Turkey, where they and their crews were interned (within a year all were released and rejoined their outfits). But the Germans had been alerted. Luftwaffe Colonel Alfred Gerstenberg, who was responsible for the defense of Ploesti, told his staff, "This is the beginning."[96]

The Russians had bombed Ploesti during the summer of 1941, with indifferent success. American studies of the feasibility of striking it had begun less than a month after war came, and in April 1943—with the ground campaign that would give us North Africa nearly completed—General Arnold had ordered the project revived (it was meaningful to him; he had relinquished for it officers and aircraft dearly needed elsewhere). Detailed planning was entrusted to Colonel Jacob E. Smart of Arnold's staff, who flew to England for consultation with a British officer formerly the manager of the Ploesti plant. It appeared that most of the refineries were in a circle around Ploesti about six miles in diameter.

Smart could not hope to have available more than two hundred bombers, and he therefore must not waste bombs. Somehow he would have to find a way of attacking only the outer ring. "It was like trying to bomb an atoll," write James Dugan and Carroll Stewart in their book about Ploesti, "without dropping anything into the lagoon. . . . The Allied chiefs had given Jacob Smart a strategic mandate with no tactical solution."

Then Colonel Smart had a smart idea. What if the B-24s went in low, *very* low, on the deck? This would permit the greatest possible selective targeting and the most accurate bombing. It would reduce civilian casualties. It would present the enemy antiaircraft gunners with only close-in and fleeting targets, and also would allow the B-24 gunners to fire back. It would deprive the enemy fighter planes of half their normal sphere of attack, and it would bring the mission in on Ploesti underneath the lowest level reached by German radar. B-24s that were hit would have a better chance of surviving a crash landing. Most of all, the Americans were well known to be wedded to the idea of flying heavy bombers at high altitude. For them to do the opposite would come as a complete surprise. The more he thought about it, the more it seemed to Colonel Smart the only sensible answer.[97]

Arnold and his colleagues were convinced, and in May they presented Smart's plan to Roosevelt, Churchill, and the Combined Chiefs at the conference in Washington called Trident, which gave its approval. In June, a delegation was sent to Algiers for a meeting with Eisenhower, who commanded the theater from which the operation would be mounted and whose consent was desirable. Eisenhower wrote after the war that he had doubts. He mistrusted plans worked out (as he put it) on an "academic basis" of "mathematical possibilities." He and his advisers (Spaatz and Air Chief Marshal Sir Arthur Tedder) questioned the efficacy of a single strike; too often factories reported as destroyed had turned out to be back in operation after only weeks or even days.

Further, it was their understanding that the Germans had a surplus of refinery capacity (true, unfortunately) and could quickly expand production to make up for damage (which was what did happen at Ploesti). Tedder reckoned that there was a 10 percent chance of eliminating 50 percent of the plant and that they might suffer 40 percent losses (the former pessimistic, the latter only 10 percent too high). But such reservations were not decisive, Eisenhower wrote, "because the air units to be used were specially sent to us for the execution of this particular mission."[98] If Ploesti was what the Air Forces and the Allied leadership at the highest level believed essential to hit, then hit it would be. The low-level attack was on.

Colonel Smart acknowledged a flaw in his reasoning in that the B-24 was only in part designed for this kind of task. It had high speed (315 mph), enormous range (then 3,500 miles, later more), a high ceiling (35,000 feet), and a relatively light bomb load (7,000 pounds). Bombers reflect national character and objectives. British bombers like the Halifax, Lancaster, or Stirling tended to have two thirds the range and two to three times the bomb load of the B-24 (they were intended to pulverize the Ruhr from British bases). American bombers were intended to deliver swift, sharp blows at great distance. (The differences in design reflected themselves in the controversy over British-night-area vs. American-daylight-precision bombing, which must wait for more extended treatment on a later page.)

A force of two hundred B-24s could not carry enough bombs to obliterate Ploesti from high altitude in one attack, and of all aircraft there was none less suited—in its big, boxcar-like configuration—to the low-level flight Smart's plan required. The commander of Ninth Air Force, who would have to give the order, Major General Lewis Brereton, studied the target folders for two weeks before making up his mind that he had to go through with it. He wrote in his diary on July 26 that "best planning indicates that it will take a minimum of eight attacks with an average strength of 136 bombers to complete the job at high altitude."[99]

There were intangibles here specific to that time and stage of air force development. For years the believers in air power had been waiting for an opportunity to show in action what they could do (Brereton had been a distinguished combat pilot in World War I and an aide to Billy Mitchell). The USAAF, writes Leon Wolff in *Low Level Mission*, "was a muscular, energy-packed adolescent looking for trouble and confident that he could lick his weight in wildcats. . . . The youngster was spoiling for a fight, anxious to demonstrate his mocked-at theory that unescorted U.S. heavies were a match for any number of fighters, could go almost anywhere, could smash almost anything to smithereens." The Ploesti assignment had magnetized the air force planners and high command. "Now they had a chance," adds Wolff, "to prove their point by means of an episode of unparalleled glamour and high drama." Brereton's subordinate commanders, too, had doubts (several of them never believed until the last moment that the talk about going in at low altitude was serious), but they suppressed them and Brereton tolerated no discussion. "You should consider yourself lucky to be on this mission," he told the crews, adding rather tactlessly that destruction of the target would be worth the loss of all 178 aircraft. Tact, as Wolff and others have noted, was never one of Brereton's strong points.[100]

He had five bombardment groups: the 376th (thirty B-24s under Colonel Keith K. Compton), the 98th (forty-six, Colonel John Kane), the 44th (thirty-six, Colonel Leon Johnson), the 93d (thirty-six, Lieutenant Colonel Addison Baker), and the 389th (thirty, Colonel Jack Wood). Colonel Compton's and Colonel Kane's groups had been based in Palestine and the Nile Delta to reinforce British Eighth Army by bombing shipping and harbors in the Mediterranean. Colonel Johnson's and Colonel Baker's groups had been the B-24 component of U.S. Eighth Air Force in Great Britain, heavily cannibalized to reinforce the invasion of North Africa.[101] Colonel Wood's group was newly arrived in Britain from the United States. In late June, they had all been assembled at fields near Benghazi and had been flying missions during July and August in support of the invasion of Sicily, 1,183 sorties (twice the normal) against seventeen targets. Then they were pulled off this duty and set to training for Ploesti.

The men lived under tents in the desert, with furniture made out of bomb-fin casings and oil drums; sand flies and scorpions shared their quarters. In the afternoon the wind came, blowing a reddish dust the consistency of talcum powder, which got into everything: food, clothing, and, worse, the aircraft guns and engines (each round of 50-cal ammunition in the machine-gun belts had to be wiped off individually to prevent jamming). Food was dreary and monotonous, no fresh vegetables or fruit, though Libyan locals found their way unescorted through the bases selling melons and grapes, which had to be carefully washed (in the weeks before the Ploesti mission, about a third of the combat crews were weak from dysentery and two extreme cases had been grounded). Drinking water was tepid and had a chlorine taste that the Army's ubiquitous lemonade powder could only thinly disguise. Entertainment consisted of swimming in the Mediterranean or watching sixteen-millimeter movies that had known better days and many a previous showing.[102]

Yet their spirits were not unduly low.

They were being well briefed; the intelligence they were getting was excellent in every respect but one. They had detailed maps of each of the refinery targets, accompanied by an oblique sketch of what it would look like to them as they made their final approach. (The sketches were the work of a former architect from Connecticut, discovered by their operations officer wandering around Eighth AF headquarters trying to sell the idea.) South of Benghazi in the desert, a full-scale plan of Ploesti was painted on the ground with whitewash and for two weeks they bombed it with practice bombs. (In the final dress rehearsal, with live bombs, they destroyed the desert Ploesti in less than two minutes.) A special training film had been made for them in England, the first of its kind, with an exact scale model and a sound track by newspaperman Tex McCrary, and it was at this point that the accuracy of the information being offered them broke down. McCrary's text emphasized the weakness of Ploesti's defenses— "nothing like as strong here as they are on the Western front"—many guns and aircraft believed to be manned by Rumanians lacking enthusiasm for the war.[103]

It was not quite so. Luftwaffe Colonel Gerstenberg had done his work well; Ploesti was one of the most heavily defended targets in Europe. It lies in a shallow valley between two ridges, and along the ridges had been placed 237 flak (antiaircraft) guns, many of them heavy 88s and 80 percent of them manned by German crews; within the refinery areas were barrage balloons, light-flak towers, and hundreds of machine guns. The main German air base was twenty miles to the east at Mizil, where there were four wings of Messerschmitt 109s, of which almost half were flown by German pilots; another base nearby held night-fighting Me 110s. In addition, Gerstenberg could count on Luftwaffe bases in Greece and Italy, and various Rumanian and Bulgarian units spread out between Bucharest and Sofia. Most menacing of all, and unknown to the Americans, he had an efficient radar detection net, together with a Signals Interception Battalion near Athens which could read Ninth Air Force codes, all reporting to Luftwaffe Fighter Command five miles north of Bucharest, where flights of both friend and foe were plotted by *Luftnachrichtenhelferinnen* (Luftwaffe air women) on a huge glass map.[104]

◆

The Ploesti mission took off at dawn on Sunday, August 1, Colonel Compton's group in the lead, followed in order by Baker's, Kane's, Johnson's, and Wood's, all under the command of Brigadier General Uzal G. Ent, flying with Compton. (By General Arnold's order, Brereton, Smart, and other high-ranking officers had been forbidden to accompany them, on the grounds of knowing too much.) Heavily laden, the B-24s seemed hardly able to get off the ground, yet they managed it and headed north over the blue Mediterranean toward Corfu. They flew in V's, each successive group a little higher than the one ahead of it. Except for the newcomers from the States, these men had flown an average of fifteen raids over Western Europe; three hundred of them had done more than twenty-five missions and long since worn out their odds for survival. This was one mission it would be nice to be able to tell about someday.

The Germans picked them up almost immediately. An informational message to other Allied forces in North Africa announcing their departure from Benghazi was decoded in Athens and relayed to Luftwaffe Fighter Command, which assumed at first that this was a training exercise, to take advantage of the cool, early-morning hours. General Ent bore a German name, from the Palatinate (he was sometimes called "P.D." for "Pennsylvania Dutch"), but the German in charge at Luftwaffe Fighter Command bore a thoroughly non-German one; he was an East Prussian pilot who had fought in Spain, in Russia, and in the Battle of Britain, and his name was Douglas Pitcairn (his family had migrated from Perthshire in 1830 after quarrels with Catholic neighbors). When a later report came in from Salonika that the Americans were still headed north at two to three thousand feet, Major Pitcairn concluded that prudent measures were called for. "All right, everyone," he said to the *Luftnachrichtenhelferinnen* in his war room. "Let's have a big breakfast. We may be here quite a while." He ordered a first-stage alert.[105]

The Americans were beginning to have mechanical difficulties. Planes would develop engine trouble, feather propellers, and abort—that is, return to base. In all, eleven B-24s aborted, which some thought too high a figure, especially since seven of these came from Colonel Kane's group. He was not universally liked, a hulk of a Texan with a square jaw and cold eyes. He was known as "Killer Kane," from the villain of the Buck Rogers comic strip (at least one naval pilot in the Pacific, though better beloved, bore the same nickname). "His desire for inflicting harm on an opponent was almost psychopathic," writes Leon Wolff. Kane pressed his men to fly beyond their operational limit; he had delayed the stateside leave of crews who were entitled to it, which may further have lowered the pitch of their enthusiasm.[106] At any rate, as each B-24 dropped out, its place was filled by another and the groups remained intact. Then bad luck struck them, twice.

As Colonel Compton's group came in toward Corfu, the lead plane began to stagger, nose rising in the air, until it slid over on its back and dove vertically into the sea, no one knows why. With it went the mission navigator, Lieutenant Robert W. Wilson, and when a second B-24 went down to investigate (contrary to orders), it found itself unable to regain altitude and had to turn back; with the second plane went the deputy mission navigator. Now lead navigator for the 165 B-24s, as Colonel Compton and General Ent moved up to lead position, was a relatively inexperienced second lieutenant named William Wright. Compton and Ent doubted Wright's ability to handle the assignment, in which they were much mistaken; he did better at it than they did.[107]

The mission swung northeastward across Albania and Jugoslavia, the groups already somewhat stretched out, and at a range of mountains they ran into a heavy bank of cumulus clouds. Four of the group commanders elected to fly over it, Kane to go under. When they came out on the other side, near the Bulgarian border, their sequence had been mixed up. Compton's group was the first to break through, but Wood had overrun both Baker and Johnson, and Kane was far behind[108] (his B-24s were older, and needed to nurse fuel). Brereton thought a wise decision might have been to hold for a moment and reassemble at the Danube, before going on together as planned, but to do so would have required breaking radio silence and the theory still held that this would mean sacrificing surprise, which had of course long since been lost.

As the B-24s passed over the mountains between Jugoslavia and Bulgaria, German radar was tracking them and reporting: "Big wings! Zone Twenty-four East, Sector Twenty-two." When they crossed the Danube and came down to five hundred feet the radar lost them—"The devils have vanished"—and Major Pitcairn was momentarily puzzled. He signaled "Stand by" to the fighter bases and told the Rumanian squadrons they were at liberty to defend Bucharest if they wished (the Germans did not have great respect for the Rumanians). Then he ordered a full alert and fifty-two Messerschmitts were airborne within five minutes. Lieutenant Werner Gerhartz closed his cockpit canopy, then on second thought opened it and handed out his dog, Peggi. (Aboard a B-24 in Colonel Johnson's group was Lieutenant Robert Patterson's dog, Rusty; his ship was called *D for Dog* and both Patterson and Rusty were to make it safely home that day to Benghazi.) Peggi died later of anoxia in a high-altitude battle over Italy; Lieutenant Gerhartz made a forced landing behind Soviet lines during the battle for Berlin and survived five years in Russian labor camps.[109]

Inexperienced Lieutenant Wright led them straight and true down the flight path to the initial points at Pitesti, Targovisti, and Floresti, where (minus Colonel Wood's group, gone north to Campina for a special target) they were supposed to turn to the southeast toward Ploesti. But at Targovisti, Colonel Compton and General Ent—over Wright's objections and shouts of "not here!" and "mistake! mistake!" over the command channel from the other pilots—made the wrong turning and took two groups (Compton's and Baker's) in the wrong direction, not toward Ploesti but toward Bucharest, into the heart of Gerstenberg's heaviest flak concentration.

When Pitcairn pressed the red button for full alert, an order went out to the heavy 88s: "They're flying very low. Change your fuze settings for point-blank fire!" So, writes Wolff, "the worst of all possible nightmares was now a definite reality: surprise was lost, the defenders were 100 percent alert, the bombers were stranded twenty feet above ground without escort and were about to be hit by fighters . . . 'flak, small arms, everything but slingshots.' "[110] On they flew. Were it not for the photographs of those enormous B-24s almost literally scraping the cornstalks, one would not believe it.

We are shortly before noon Greenwich mean time (three o'clock Benghazi base time, two o'clock Rumanian time). What happened in the next hour does not lend itself to tidy summary. In the pages of their book, *Ploesti*, Dugan and Stewart have somehow managed to put together a convincing narrative of the battle from German, Rumanian, and surviving American accounts (A. J. Liebling in *The New Yorker* called it "the very model of a war book"[111]), but only by treating the bomb run of each group as though it were almost a separate event.

Colonel Baker's was the first to rectify the wrong turn; he saw the smoke of Ploesti to the left and swung his unit ninety degrees toward it, himself (as was his preference) in lead position. Haystacks and the roofs of cottages flew open, revealing flak guns. By the time they closed the target, several B-24s were trailing smoke from damaged engines; one plane took a direct hit and exploded; another snapped the cable of a barrage balloon, which drifted lazily upward, and still another grazed the tip of a church steeple. Colonel Baker's plane caught fire; he pulled it up and held course, but then it faltered and he crashed and died. An oil storage tank exploded, the first of many; a B-24, both wings sheared off, was seen sliding down a street. Ribbons of tracer bullets seemed to form a curtain in front of them. A veteran copilot went berserk and the navigator had to sit on him. Of Colonel Baker's group, thirty-nine planes left Benghazi that morning and thirty-four reached the target area; fifteen emerged from it, only five of them relatively undamaged, and the others carried dead and wounded. Then the Me 109s came after them.

Colonel Compton and General Ent corrected their mistake not long after Baker did, and approached Ploesti from the south, but the flak was so murderous they veered eastward to try a different tactic. General Ent gave an order to attack targets of opportunity, which was surely a mistake, since many of the pilots could see no targets; they turned north of Ploesti and jettisoned their bombs. Except, that is, for one section of five aircraft, led by Major Norman Appold, a chemical engineer from Michigan, whose short stature and collegiate style concealed his considerable abilities as a bomber pilot and his conviction that the way to save one's life was to risk it at every opportunity. Appold spotted a refinery north of the town and headed his slender force in its direction. They flew in at ten feet and dropped three dozen 500-pounders fuzed at forty-five seconds. They had hit one of the major cracking plants and eliminated 40 percent of its capacity. But by this time some of the other groups were beginning to arrive from other points of the compass and their major problem was to avoid hitting each other. Ploesti, write Dugan and Stewart, "was roofed with three layers of interweaving Liberators." Now-General Gerstenberg stood in the street below, "in awed admiration of the galaxy of bombers maneuvering precisely at top speed without colliding." He had no idea that he was witnessing a monumental snafu.

Colonel Wood's greenhorn group from the States delivered one of the best performances. At one point they, too, made a wrong turning but quickly discovered it and found their way down a valley toward Campina, their propellers chopping treetops like lawnmowers. As they went in, the flak opened up and one B-24 caught fire, crash-landing with wings aflame (the top turret gunner escaped); in another, the pilot's head was blown off by a 20-mm shell. The plane piloted by Lloyd D. Hughes began to leak gasoline and then became a flying blowtorch as it first released its bombs and then tried for a belly landing in a dry riverbed; the aircraft cartwheeled and exploded, but two of the crew came out alive. Hughes's posthumous citation for the Medal of Honor read: "Rather than jeopardize the formation or success of the attack, he unhesitatingly entered the blazing area, dropped his bombs with great precision, and only then did he undertake a forced landing." The Wood group's refinery targets were totally destroyed, not to be back in production for six years, and losses were only six planes out of twenty-nine, among the lightest of those that were attacking selected targets.[112]

Another precision demonstration was turned in by Colonel James T. Posey, commanding twenty-one B-24s of Colonel Johnson's group of thirty-six. As Johnson and Kane (having avoided Compton's and Baker's error) wheeled southeast over their proper turning point at Floresti, Colonel Posey's force was on the right. They had been assigned Blue Target, an isolated high-octane plant at Brazi, five miles north of Ploesti, which was the most modern of all. Though spared the worst agonies of Johnson's and Kane's men, they had to deal with flak towers as they came in (one of their number was *D for Dog*). Their orders were so precise that one aircraft was given as an aiming point "the near wall of Building G." Another had been told to aim at the southwest corner of the boiler house; the plane's three thousand pounders put it permanently out of business. They came out at low level. "People ask me what I mean by low level," said one pilot. "I point out that on the antennas on the bottom of my airplane I brought back sunflowers and something that looked suspiciously like grass." They lost two planes; their target was out of operation for the rest of the war.

Colonel Kane's and the remainder of Colonel Johnson's group were coming south abreast on either side of a railroad leading to Ploesti. As they did so they overtook what seemed to be a train of boxcars. It was not; it was one of General Gerstenberg's most ingenious measures, a flak train. The tops and sides of the boxcars unfolded to reveal antiaircraft, perfectly sited to fire on both of the flights as they went down the track together to either side. B-24 gunners managed to shoot up the locomotive, but not before eight of the fifty-seven bombers had been hard hit.

Over Ploesti hung what seemed to Colonel Johnson to be a dark curtain of smog. As they came closer he saw that it was not smog at all but a billowing cloud of heavy black smoke lit by fires within it. This was when he realized that someone had already bombed his target. The success of Baker's group in setting fire to storage tanks (which were trivial in importance compared to the refineries) now had a most adverse effect. Inside the smoke were balloon cables and towering smokestacks. Delayed-action bombs were still going off; updrafts from the fires would toss the heavy aircraft about like bits of paper. They plunged on in.

Some of the most dramatic photographs of the Ploesti mission come from this episode within it, B-24s silhouetted against openings in the smoke as they tried to find their way through. Many did not. Colonel Johnson lost five aircraft over the target area, Colonel Kane fifteen. "We had expected to take losses," said Kane later, "but I never will forget those big Libs going down like flies."[113] His group was the largest to attack Ploesti; he was piloting its flagship, wearing a World War I helmet and a Colt automatic. (The Germans knew about him; the first question asked a pilot who survived the later crash of his B-24 was "Where is Killer Kane?") He went into the black clouds so low that flames singed the hair off his left arm, and he came out of the smoke with one engine down and a maximum speed of 185 mph. But he and his men, while at appalling cost, had destroyed half the productive capacity of the largest oil refinery in Europe.

A happy combination of circumstances had so far spared the bombers the attention of enemy fighters. (The Messerschmitts had been waiting to the north, and the wrong turning they thought to be a clever feint at Bucharest.) But as the B-24s came away from Ploesti, the fighter planes swarmed above them. The bombers were scattered, nearly all were damaged, many contained dead or wounded gunners and had exhausted their ammunition. The marvel is that more of them were not shot down by the Me 109s. Partly it was the low altitude (as planned) that protected them; a fighter would make a dive, be unable to pull out, and plow into the ground (after this happened to a few, the others desisted). But the bombers were running a gauntlet of fire, anxious now to save every drop of fuel and lighten loads to get back over the mountains.

"The crews threw out everything that was loose or could be yanked loose," said one of them, "and we left behind us a long, wobbling trail of seats, tanks, belts, shoes, boxes, and first-aid kits with gauze bandages unrolling in great circles, figure-eights, and curious, sometimes beautiful designs."[114] They took care, insofar as they could, of their wounded. It was going to be a long way home.

Eventually ninety-three of them reached Benghazi, nineteen landed at other Allied airfields, seven landed in Turkey, and three crashed at sea. The final figures showed that fifty-four planes had been lost, forty-one of them in action; of their crews (1,726 men), 532 were either dead, prisoners, missing, or interned.[115] This was a high price to pay for a single mission. Was it worth it?

General Brereton attached to his diary a report, based on post-strike photographs, of the British officer who had been a prewar Ploesti plant manager. The latter concluded with careful conservatism that one of the targets would require at least six months' work to resume operation, that another could be considered "immobilized" for six months or more, another cut by 30 percent of capacity, but still another likely to be repaired quickly and two untouched (some damage had of course been much greater).

The air force historians, many years later, concluded that Ploesti as a whole had lost 42 percent of total capacity, that cracking plant production had been cut by 40 percent, and that the production of lubricating oils had been "considerably reduced." Sadly, none of this made very much difference. Ploesti had been running at only 60 percent of capacity, which meant that the effective long-term loss was not 42 but 2 percent. Idle plants were activated, others repaired, and within weeks Ploesti was producing at a higher rate than before the raid.[116]

Thus the verdict on the Ploesti raid has to be a mixed one, and it contained lessons not all of which could have been read at the time. If all its bomber missions had come in on schedule from the right direction, and had been accomplished with the same finesse as Colonel Wood's, Colonel Posey's, and Major Appold's, then there is no question that fatal damage would have been done to Ploesti, which is to say that all (rather than only two) of its nine major refineries would have been largely incapacitated for some time (which is also to say that Smart's plan had been theoretically sound). What was wrong with it was the burden of necessity it carried; it demanded too much: perfect timing, perfect coordination, perfect luck. The real world does not vouchsafe these bounties routinely, and this is not a matter for blame so much as for subdued reflection.

The lesson to be learned from Ploesti was that air power could be a potent weapon against precision targets, but that the idea it could guarantee to deliver single knockout blows was mistaken. (A veiled lesson that bombers without fighter escort were vulnerable was not yet visible to USAAF observers.) It would take the remainder of the air war, in 1944–45, for the dialectic between these several propositions to work itself out.

V

Hap Arnold was unusual among the Allied leaders in his absolutely open-ended attitude toward the future. Perhaps because he had witnessed so much technological change in his own lifetime, he was at ease with the certainty that more of it was to come. Unlike many air officers, even today, he was not wedded to the idea of manned flight as the *sine qua non* of air power. For many years he had known how simple it would be for the bomber to be replaced by a flying bomb, and after the war he wrote an article called "Our Power to Destroy War," in which he argued that airmen must be prepared to give up the airplane. "We must bear in mind," he wrote in *Global Mission*, "that air power itself can become obsolete."[117] When you think of it, coming from a man who never had or wanted any reputation as a great brain, this is quite remarkable for its freshness and flexibility of mind.

In 1917, Arnold had worked with Charles F. Kettering—"Boss Ket," one of the great American technologists, inventor of the automobile self-starter and no-knock gasoline—on the development of a pilotless aircraft they called the Bug, theoretically capable of hitting within a hundred yards of its target after a forty-mile run. The project, twenty-five years ahead of its time, was well in process when the war ended. In 1941, they revived it, in a version controlled by radio, and flight-tested it at a range of two hundred miles. Arnold and Kettering reviewed every factor they could think of, and concluded that from bases in England they would only be able to reach northern France, Belgium, and Holland, and not the interior of Germany. They scrapped it. Arnold later reflected that if we had been on the Continent and the Germans in England, then Bugs by the thousands would have crossed the Channel long before the date when the Germans unleashed the V-1, their version of it, in 1944.[118]

Arnold insisted on staying in touch with scientists and engineers who could think far ahead of his own people. In 1939, he sent for Theodor von Kármán, a physicist and aeronautical engineer, and asked him what the Air Corps needed in the way of equipment for experimentation. Von Kármán said a forty-thousand-horse-power wind tunnel. Arnold said that was just what he wanted and they built it. Von Kármán thought that Arnold was "the greatest example of the American military man—a combination of complete logic, mingled with far-sightedness and superb dedication." (In 1944, Arnold engaged von Kármán to come to the Pentagon and head a committee to examine air force research needs for the next fifty years.) But this side of Arnold came as a surprise to many who knew him. One day Arnold invited George Marshall to lunch with a number of his scientist acquaintants. "What on earth are you doing with people like that?" asked Marshall. "Using their brains," said Arnold.[119]

Arnold was one of the very few for whom Marshall had, and was willing to show, real affection. General Kuter, who saw them together often, said that the way they treated one another "defied description by usual categories." There was none of the "banter or chit-chat that you'd expect between old pals." He could not remember their using first names or nicknames. "They were simply two senior officers who had known each other for thirty years with mutual friendship." Marshall was the senior, but Kuter never saw him pull rank. "Arnold was free to announce his plans or intentions," said Kuter. "I never heard of him asking Marshall's permission. Theirs was a unique top-side relationship."[120]

Actually, in correspondence, it was sometimes "Hap" and "George," sometimes "Arnold" and "General Marshall," as though neither of them thought it important enough to be consistent. In December 1942, Marshall writes "My dear Hap" to express his "deep appreciation for the splendid support you have given me during the past year," and for the "magnificent job" Arnold had done in coping with rapid expansion and with "air operations in various corners of the world." Marshall adds: ". . . you have taken these colossal problems in your stride but still have managed to retain some remnants of a golden disposition." And further adds: "P.S. Incidentally, Merry Christmas."[121] Many of the Arnold files in the Marshall papers, however, show nothing so much as Marshall's concern with Arnold's health and his unsuccessful efforts to get Arnold to slow down and take it easy.

Arnold routinely worked a seven-to-seven day. "He was always a step ahead of everybody," said one aircraft manufacturer. He would come into a plant, summon all the designers and engineers, and say, "I want four hundred miles an hour. Why in hell can't somebody give it to me?" and they would go away wondering why somebody couldn't. Arnold's pilot, Gene Beebe, said of him that his idea of a good time was "to work all day, then go to Bolling Field, fly all night to Los Angeles [in a DC-3], arrive in the morning, visit about five aircraft plants, and then go to someone's house for dinner that night."[122]

Eventually all this caught up with him and he was hauled off to Walter Reed Hospital, from which (on May 10, 1943) he sent the Chief of Staff a handwritten note (addressed "Marshall" and signed "Arnold"): "This is one Hell of a time for this to happen. My engine [pulse rate] started turning over at 160 when it should have been doing 74 to 76. For this I am sorry. Back to normal now. . . ." (There follow suggestions on who should take over what duties in his absence.) "Maybe within a day or two the medicos will be able to keep the R.P.M. under control."

Marshall's reply, only slightly delayed, gives details on various affairs he had been immersed in and adjures Arnold, firmly, not to cut short his Oregon vacation in order to make a speech Arnold had planned to give at West Point. "Your Army future is at stake," wrote Marshall, "and I don't think you should hazard it with a matter of such trivial importance. . . . It is vastly important to you, and it certainly is to me, and to the Air Force, that you make a full recovery. . . ." He advised Arnold not to fly west and put him on orders, "so that you can avoid the expense of a rail journey," something officers of their generation always thought about. Marshall ended: "Please be careful," and signed himself: "Affectionately."[123]

Arnold was not corrigible. In May 1944, he had his third heart attack in fourteen months but bounced back, and in June, four days after D-Day, took off with Marshall for a meeting of the Combined Chiefs in London and followed it with a visit to the Normandy beachhead and a tour of the front in Italy. His fourth attack came in January 1945, but in February he improved and by March was plotting another trip to Europe. In April, a cable from Marshall found him in Paris: "I read of your presence and statements with various active commands. Where is the Bermuda rest, the lazy days at Cannes, the period of retirement at Capri? You are riding for a fall, doctor or no doctor." Arnold countered with a suggestion that he "continue leisurely and restfully" to visit Switzerland, Italy, the CBI, MacArthur and Nimitz, and return to Washington by way of San Francisco.

Marshall responded: "The crux of your message is in the third paragraph. I quote: 'or if I continue leisurely and restfully.' Each statement you have given me regarding leisurely and restful movements has not been in accord with your subsequent movements and I assume that the same will happen in this case. . . . I am rather depressed at seeing you start on another of your strenuous trips, this time carrying you around the world. It may demonstrate to the Army and the public that you certainly are not on the retired list but also it may result in your landing there."[124] This time the message sunk in, a little, and Arnold cut short his itinerary in Italy. Not for long; in June he flew to Hawaii, Guam, Iwo Jima, the Philippines, and Okinawa, and he attended the Potsdam Conference after victory had been won in Europe.

On V-J Day, the Arnolds were giving a reception for Air Marshal Sir Arthur Harris, and after dinner, when the news was official, friends began to drop by. One of them was George Marshall, whose quarters were only a few doors away. He thanked the officers present for their help and then he and Arnold solemnly shook hands. Robert Lovett said that he thought Marshall recognized in Arnold "this warm-hearted, loyal, mercurial, flamboyant belligerent fellow who didn't care who he took on in battle." Arnold once told Ira Eaker: "If George Marshall ever took a position contrary to mine, I would know I was wrong."[125]

In January 1948, at the Valley of the Moon, his retirement home in Sonoma, California, Arnold had still another heart attack, and Marshall wrote him: "I have just heard that you are temporarily laid up, but according to my informants, and I quote directly from a message I received, you are 'threatening to get up and cursing and swearing at everyone.' There is the clear implication that there really was nothing wrong with you except that you are getting too much care and attention." And again, "Affectionately." In the fall of the following year Lovett came to visit and found Arnold noticeably thinner and "slowed up."[126] He died on January 15, 1950.

Arnold's part in the formulation of Allied strategy was determined by his service interests, which were precise but limited. He opposed the North African invasion, and he opposed Marshall and King in the summer of 1942 when they seemed to be serious about turning to the Pacific—in both cases because he saw a threat to his European air offensive. (He thought the Navy was not strong enough for the Guadalcanal campaign, in which he was of course partly right.[127]) He supported the invasion of the Marianas because they would provide him with bases for the B-29s.

But his straightforward and uncompromising desire was that air power in its fullest form be visited upon Germany and Japan, and how this was done in detail turned out to be more of a tactical than a strategic question, one over which he did not have a great deal of direct influence; his role was to set the goals and demand their accomplishment. No one could have done this better than he, but someone else *could* have done it, and in that sense he was not central and essential to the war in the way King and Marshall were. So much having been granted, he gave the President the air force Roosevelt wanted and had to have, and he fitted to perfection his niche in the Joint Chiefs of Staff, neither trying to stretch its limits nor trying to expand it into something it was not and did not need to be.

Air Marshal Sir John Slessor wrote of him: "He was an intensely like-able person was 'Hap' Arnold, transparently honest, terrifically energetic, given to unorthodox methods and, though shrewd and without many illusions, always with something of a schoolboy naïveté about him. . . . No one could accuse him of being brilliantly clever but he was wise, and had the big man's flair for putting his finger on the really important point."[128]

Let that stand beside his name.

V

VANDEGRIFT

THE PRESIDENT LIKED TO IDENTIFY with the Marine Corps. Talking to its commandant, General Holcomb, at a White House dinner, he used the pronoun "we" in referring to the Marines' lack of participation in the high command. "First thing you know," he said to Holcomb, "we are going to be left out of things. We are not represented on the Joint Chiefs of Staff" —Rooseveltian banter at its frequently disingenuous. "How would you like to be a member of the Joint Chiefs of Staff?"[1] Holcomb tactfully replied that he would like that very much but had no idea what the Joint Chiefs might think, and nothing came of it.

In July 1914, in his capacity as acting secretary of the Navy, Franklin Roosevelt had ordered seven hundred Marines moved to Guantánamo in readiness to invade Haiti, which was undergoing one of its periodic revolutions. The Marines did occupy Haiti and in January 1917 Roosevelt was sent there for a tour of inspection, sailing on a destroyer and joining some fifty ships of the Atlantic Fleet in the bay of Port-au-Prince. Dressed in a cutaway and top hat, he addressed the Haitian president and his cabinet in French and made a graceful attempt to represent the presence of massive American force as a "visit of courtesy." But the Navy and the Marines controlled Haiti and he was there as their senior official. After several days of ceremony, during which he made more speeches in French —larded with anecdotes and references to Haitian customs, almost as though he were running for office—he started out by horseback into the hills, where bandits were still active, on a 160-mile trek from Port-au-Prince to Cap Haitien.

His party of American and Haitian troops and pack animals included Marine General George Barnett, then commandant of the Corps. "The road was very mountainous," Barnett told a newspaper reporter, "and in places was exceedingly rough, and nothing but a mountain trail."[2] They took in scenes of Marine skirmishes, talked to local officials and parish priests, and combined duty with generous amounts of sightseeing.

Toward the end, Roosevelt left most of his exhausted companions behind and climbed the four-thousand-foot peak of the Citadel of the Emperor Christophe. (Flying to Trinidad on his way to Casablanca in 1943, he asked the pilot to circle the Citadel so he could point it out to his fellow passengers.) "When I die," he said a quarter century later, "I think that 'Haiti' is going to be written on my heart," so much did the associations of this visit mean to him. In the course of it, he came to know many of the Marine officers, among them a thirty-year-old captain named Alexander Archer Vandegrift.[3]

In June 1942, in his capacity as Commander in Chief, Roosevelt took a hand in initiating—and later strongly reinforcing—a predominantly Marine operation commanded by Archer Vandegrift, now a major general. This was the Guadalcanal campaign, which began on August 7 with landings on Guadalcanal and Tulagi in the Solomon Islands, and ended on February 9, 1943, with the elimination of the last organized Japanese resistance on Guadalcanal. Of the countless battles in the war, it is one the President seemed to feel personally involved in, one that he spoke of often and with concern, for not only was he among those responsible for its inception, but time and again it nearly failed.

Strategically speaking, the Guadalcanal campaign was a stepchild. It led nowhere, except to the port and harbor of Rabaul in New Britain, where, as it happened, we never went. It had no geographical relation to the course the war would later follow, neither to Nimitz's central Pacific campaign nor to MacArthur's return to the Philippines. The plan for it was impromptu, a compromise that satisfied no one, and it developed on a pattern its planners had not foreseen and the men who fought it had not been prepared for. Several of the senior commanders involved either disapproved or gave it halfhearted support, and there is some question how many of them really understood it. The logistical backup was at first so mismanaged that essential weapons and equipment were lacking or in short supply. Our losses—in men, in aircraft, and in ships—were hideous. Yet victory when it came—and victory rarely wore so strange a guise—was decisive.

The Solomon Islands were anything but the ideal place for an opening test of arms against the Japanese Army. Lovely to look at, they are on close inspection miserably inhospitable—dank, fetid, malarial. The annual rainfall averages 164 inches, and a change in rainfall is the only way of telling the seasons apart. We would be coming in the "fine weather," when there are only eight inches of rain a month, humidity is only 80 percent, and temperatures range from 75 to 80 degrees. Jack London hesitated to wish a visit here on his worst enemy.

But the Solomons extend about halfway along the thousand miles or so that separated the Japanese base at Rabaul from the Allied bases in the New Hebrides. If the Japanese controlled them, then the populous eastern coast of Australia would be exposed to raids and the lifeline to the western coast of the United States could be cut. If we held them, the defensive perimeter of the Japanese Empire around the Bismarck Archipelago could be punctured. Neither side could comfortably afford to let the other have them, and to a discerning eye like Admiral King's it had long been evident that an armed encounter hereabouts was sooner or later bound to occur; for King, the sooner the better.

The administrative center of the Solomons was at Tulagi, a tiny but relatively healthful sliver of land two miles long and a half mile wide just off the south shore of Florida island, where Lever Brothers maintained a coconut plantation. The British had established themselves here because this was the best deep-water anchorage in the islands. Inspecting Tulagi after World War I, Admiral Jellicoe had urged that it be developed into a principal bastion of the British Empire.

Not having become anything of the kind, Tulagi now boasted a single street, a few Chinese shops, a hotel, a wireless station, and a British residency with scattered bungalows rising up the hills. In early May of 1942, the Japanese had driven out the Australian garrison and occupied Tulagi, as a seaplane station in support of their campaign to capture Port Moresby on the southern shore of New Guinea, which the Battle of the Coral Sea had fatally cut short.

In June, the Japanese seaplane base commander had wandered over to nearby Guadalcanal and spotted a level strip of land, where, apparently as his own idea entirely, he ordered construction of an airfield. This act of individual enterprise was to have long-term effects, for it was duly reported by the "coastwatchers," the efficient corps of British and Australian planters and civil servants who stayed behind after the Japanese advance and—concealed and aided by loyal Melanesians—relayed word of Japanese moves by radio. Confirmation from an Allied reconnaissance plane on July 4 of an airfield being built on Guadalcanal, when it reached Washington, set alarm bells ringing and added impetus to an operation for invading the Solomons which was already in the works.

After the Battle of Midway in June—when the Japanese lost four aircraft carriers and their ability to stay on the offensive—it could be argued either way: that we should now relax in the Pacific (as Army planners would have preferred) or else (as King preferred) recapture the initiative, in which case a move to defend communications to Australia made sense. Beyond that, there was not much agreement. Even before Midway, Admiral Nimitz had proposed attacking Tulagi with the 1st Marine Raider Battalion, but Marshall, MacArthur, and even King demurred, on the grounds that the force would be too small. (It would have been; Tulagi was eventually assaulted by six battalions—the 1st Marine Raiders included—and all the same the action was sharp and bloody.) Moreover, the Pacific theater had been carved up in such a way that Tulagi and Guadalcanal fell within MacArthur's area, and he had assumed as a matter of course that he would be in overall command of any move in that direction.

MacArthur's plan, propounded in preliminary form before Midway and elaborated afterward, was to drive directly on Rabaul. But since the three infantry divisions available to him (one of them Australian) were not trained in amphibious operations, and since the objective lay beyond the reach of land-based fighter planes, he said he would have to have a division of Marines and two aircraft carriers, plus an increase in his force of heavy bombers, to ensure success. Marshall endorsed this, and sent to King on June 12 a proposal which his own staff had spelled out in the particulars.

The Navy was having none of it. The seas around the Solomon Islands are full of foul ground, and many of the charts of them were a century old. To risk the few carriers here, within range of Japanese land-based air, did not strongly recommend itself. To do so under the command of Douglas MacArthur, whose headquarters the Navy rightly or wrongly believed to regard aircraft carriers as expendable, was flatly out of the question. Since the forces involved would be largely naval, they should be under naval command; in any event, Tulagi would have to be taken first, to draw the sting of its seaplane patrols.

King's natural gifts for obduracy came to the fore. His mind had been focused for some time on a step-by-step drive into the Solomons, as his letter of March 5 to Roosevelt had made evident, and he was not to be deflected from it by foot soldiers with grandiose schemes. In vain did MacArthur plead that his proposal had been misunderstood, that what he meant was a progressive advance to capture airfields. In vain did Marshall and King exchange further memoranda. Forcing the issue, King took matters into his own hands and instructed Nimitz to prepare an attack on Tulagi by the Navy and Marines, going it alone.

◆

King's single-handed *démarche* was a puzzle to his biographer. Was it just pure gall, as given King's personality it might well have been? Was he behaving like a sea lawyer, having said what he intended to do and not being told to stop, and therefore driving ahead on an assumption of tacit consent? Did he believe that the executive order authorizing him to command the Navy and Marines meant what it said, and that by God he was at liberty to do just that? Or none of the above? There is a better explanation.

A recent study of King in his role as Chief of Naval Operations concludes that he went forward with his unilateral proposal because he had been prompted to do so by the Commander in Chief. "King clearly discussed the Guadalcanal operation with Roosevelt *before* he revealed his plan to Marshall," writes Professor Love of the U.S. Naval Academy. "He also apparently had the President's approval of the plan."[4] Roosevelt wanted action, his beloved Navy was now urging it, and the place proposed was a logical choice. This offers a much more illuminating perspective on the confidence with which King, on June 25, went to the Joint Chiefs and asked for their concurrence in what threatened to be a *fait accompli.*

So there had to be a compromise. Dropping at last the formality of paper exchanges, Marshall and King got together, and by July 2 they had hammered it out. The boundary between South and Southwest Pacific would be moved slightly to the west and Tulagi-Guadalcanal brought under Nimitz's jurisdiction. The offensive in its entirety would be in three stages: Tulagi-Guadalcanal first, the rest of the Solomons and the north coast of New Guinea second, and third and finally Rabaul. Nimitz would command stage one, MacArthur two and three, though MacArthur would be asked to contribute support to Nimitz for stage one (King doubted that this would amount to much in air and ground forces and he was right, it didn't).

Marshall later tried to put on record the Army's willingness to go along with stage one as such, since the danger of an operational Japanese airfield on Guadalcanal was just as clear to him as it was to King. "The Marines went to Guadalcanal at my urging in a way," Marshall told Forrest Pogue, "because if we lost that field down there we were pushed way to the south in trying to move troops to Australia . . . and so we went ahead and made do with what we had."[5]

Under Nimitz, the local theater commander would be Vice-Admiral Robert L. Ghormley, who was instructed to meet MacArthur forthwith in Melbourne and coordinate efforts. Ghormley had been serving as a naval observer in London; he was highly regarded by the President, among others, but he suffered from severe dental problems and had less experience of seagoing command than those who picked him for this billet may have thought. His conference with MacArthur, in the words of Nimitz's biographer, "seems to have generated little more than funk."[6] Each of them took counsel of the other's caution. They jointly recommended delay, shelving stage one until enough strength had been accumulated for two and three to follow in a continuous sweep (the suspicion that such was not necessary is reinforced by subsequent events, in which stage three never came about at all when Rabaul was bypassed). In any case, this did not satisfy King's sense of urgency.

He took the satisfaction of pointing out to Marshall that MacArthur's position was inconsistent. "Three weeks ago," he wrote (or Savvy Cooke wrote and King signed), "MacArthur stated that, if he could be furnished amphibious forces and two carriers, he could push right through to Rabaul.

Now he feels that he cannot undertake this extended operation but not even the Tulagi operation." In private, King thought MacArthur was sulking. "He could not understand that he was not to manage everything," King later said. "He couldn't believe that. Of course he was absolutely against going into Guadalcanal, and he said so."[7]

The Joint Chiefs backed King: The Tulagi-Guadalcanal landings, though granted a week's delay, would proceed. This is what Marshall meant by their deciding to go ahead and make do "with what we had."

It was a casual way at best of mounting a great enterprise, and a price was paid for extemporizing so much of it. But Roosevelt, King, and Marshall (if each for his own reasons) all saw the need to act, and the idea was not unfamiliar to any of them that in war, audacity can have a weight equal to the more material factors. Though none of the three perceived what taking Guadalcanal would ultimately cost, their impulse to strike first proved in the end to be sound. Guadalcanal fatally eroded Japanese strength. Atypical in so many respects, it became a prototypical battle, serving as a model for tactics in later Pacific island campaigns and occupying a special place in the history of the war for the intensity that both sides, if at first with hesitation, would eventually put into it. For those who were there, wrote Admiral Morison, Guadalcanal "is not a name but an emotion."

When two military forces are maneuvering against one another and graze into contact, it may come about that each will feel compelled to commit itself and then bring in reinforcements, until a full-scale contest ensues at a place and time neither side had initially intended. In military parlance this is called a meeting engagement. Gettysburg was a classic meeting engagement, with important consequences. So, as Admiral Morison was one of the first to remark, was Guadalcanal.[8]

This was not so much a battle as a cluster of battles, knit together by a common theme. For six months, we and the Japanese contended for possession of the same ninety-by-twenty-five-mile oblong of jungle, mud, kunai grass, mountains, and mosquitoes. In the doing there took place six major naval engagements, scores of ground actions involving thousands of men, and air combat that was almost continuous, yet all were connected to a single outcome.

For control of a patch of ocean a battalion of Marines clung doggedly to an inland ridge, for a ground victory weeks in the future pilots nursed aloft their worn-out aircraft against all odds, and for possession of their landing field warships miles distant pounded at one another in a darkness fitfully lit by searchlights, gunfire, and flaming wreckage. No episode in World War II better illustrates than Guadalcanal the interdependence of the three services that is characteristic of "modern" war. Any one of the military arms of land, sea, or sky could have thrown away the issue; none alone could gain it.

had not heard there was a war on; the map went astray in shipment and never arrived in time to be of use.

Marines had their first opportunity to see Guadalcanal when an Army B-17 carrying two of Vandegrift's staff officers traversed the coast and made photostrips of it. Just as they approached Lunga Point, where the Japanese airfield was supposed to be, three float-equipped Zero fighters from Tulagi came up at them and further observation was interrupted by a melee in which the B-17 fended off the Zeros; the "turn-back" point had long since been passed and the pilot necessarily headed for home. Their photostrips nonetheless showed the Lunga beaches suitable for landing, and Goettge managed to obtain a few high-quality photographs of the defenses on Tulagi and its neighboring islets from the Navy, which had raided them with planes from carrier *Yorktown* on May 4. Otherwise the Marines landed on Guadalcanal with a "map" of their own manufacture on which rivers had the wrong names, the airfield was barely roughed in, and the high ground that commanded it—known as Mount Austen—was two miles out of place.

More serious still, in view of what transpired, was the lack of confidence and sense of common objective in the high command. Several in important positions either had not given their hearts to this endeavor or else entertained purposes in conflict with it. MacArthur's and Ghormley's doubts we have observed. Ghormley was nominally theater commander, but his orders were ambiguous in that they allowed for task forces to be sent to him with their missions (as in this case) already laid on by the Joint Chiefs; how much of a voice he had in their employment was unclear. Command of the task force assigned to Guadalcanal he thus had delegated to Vice-Admiral Frank Jack Fletcher, who before leaving Pearl Harbor in his flagship, aircraft carrier *Saratoga*, had expressed his opposition, and certainty the operation would fail, to the commander of the landing forces, Rear Admiral Richmond Kelly Turner.

Fletcher was the most battle-seasoned of the senior officers involved, but he was an unlucky admiral; two aircraft carriers had already been sunk while under his flag, and he was understandably reluctant to let this happen again. The importance of clear missions and clear lines of authority was not yet fully appreciated. Fletcher had no previous experience in amphibious operations, the forces he would command had never worked together before, Ghormley had issued him no instructions, and he had submitted no plan to Ghormley for approval. A recipe for trouble could hardly have been better brewed.

Somehow order was caused to appear out of the chaos on Aotea Quay in Wellington and the Marines, leaving nonessentials behind and taking only what they would need to live and fight, sailed on schedule. The rehearsal on Koro Island in the Fijis was a mixture of mechanical breakdowns, demonstrated inadequacies, and badly chosen beaches in which only a third of the Marines got ashore. But valuable lessons were learned and procedures revised. Vandegrift and Turner could at worst fall back on the adage that a poor rehearsal foretells a great performance.

Sunday, July 22, they had met with Fletcher on board *Saratoga*, the first time all the commanders (except for the absent Ghormley) had conferred face to face, and of this occasion the best that can be said is that it plumbed new depths of the unwelcome for Vandegrift. The meeting was described as "stormy" by one participant, but this may have been because he was unaccustomed to the bluntness of senior naval officers in their dealings with one another. Asked by Fletcher how long it would take to land the troops, Turner said five days, to which Fletcher replied that he would keep his carriers there no more than two days; to stay longer would endanger them.

Rear Admiral Daniel J. Callaghan, who was attending as Ghormley's representative and was taking notes, put an exclamation point after this statement by Fletcher, but he was in no position to speak up against it. (Callaghan had been naval aide to President Roosevelt from 1938 to 1941; he was to command the support group of cruisers and destroyers in the naval battle of Guadalcanal five months later and die in the confused and violent night action of November 13.) There has been speculation that if he had been present, Ghormley might have overruled Fletcher, but given his limited view of his own authority this seems unlikely. Turner and Vandegrift did the best they could.

Vandegrift tried to explain that this was no hit-and-run affair but an attempt to effect a full lodgment on a hostile shore by an entire division, which would have to have air cover until the Marines fully possessed the Guadalcanal field and could fly their own fighters in. Fletcher was unconvinced; he gave the impression of blaming Turner for "instigating" the whole idea (this was true only in that Turner, as director of war plans in King's office, had done the staff work for the landing he was now being sent to carry out). Turner repeatedly replied that "the decision has been made; it's up to us to make it a success." Fletcher would not be dissuaded. Afterward Turner asked Vandegrift, "How did I do?" and Vandegrift replied "all right," though neither could have been particularly pleased or reassured. With these auguries, on the last day of July the ships weighed anchor, took up antisubmarine formation, and set course for the Solomons.[13]

In sheer quantity they were an impressive sight, over eighty of them, stretching to the horizon: the three groups of cruisers and destroyers built around the carriers *Saratoga*, *Wasp*, and *Enterprise*; the new battleship *North Carolina*; and finally the Amphibious Force itself: eight cruisers, twenty destroyers, and twenty-three transports under Admiral Turner in *McCawley*, a command transport that had once been the Grace Line passenger ship *Santa Barbara*.

This was the largest Allied invasion fleet to be assembled thus far. The weather had been gale-force stormy before the Fiji rehearsal, but afterward it turned fair and then, D-Day minus one, favored them with a heavy overcast that hid the fleet from Japanese eyes. On board the transports the Marines sharpened bayonets, skimmed half dollars they saw no further use for across the waves, and indulged in the offhand bravado men under pressure find reinforcing at such times. They needed no reminding that this was the first American descent on enemy-held beaches of the war.

General Vandegrift roamed transport *McCawley,* trying to get the measure of his men, how much he could ask of them. He liked what he saw. On the afternoon of August 6, the carriers peeled off to the south and that evening the Amphibious Force rounded Guadalcanal from the southwest and came to on its staging and support areas. On *McCawley*'s deck, Vandegrift peered into the murk, lamented his poor night vision, marveled that they seemed to have achieved the surprise he knew they so badly needed; then he groped his way below to finish a letter to his wife.

Early next morning in the Guadalcanal highlands, coastwatcher Martin Clemens awakened to the roar of cruiser *Quincy*'s guns, leapt out of his hut with field glasses in hand, and surveyed the armada in the sound below him. Coming down from the hills, his Melanesian sergeant major, Vouza (later Sir Jacob Vouza, O.B.E., and holder of the Silver Star), found him happily listening to the chatter of American pilots on his radio. "Calloo, callay," shouted Clemens, "Oh what a day!"[14]

◆

It dawned clear. "Guadalcanal is an island of striking beauty," wrote an awestruck Marine press officer. "Blue green mountains, towering into a brilliant tropical sky or crowned with cloud masses, dominate the islands. The dark green of jungle growth blends into the softer greens and browns of coconut groves and grassy plains and ridges." Even Admiral Turner was impressed: "a truly beautiful sight that morning," he later recalled.[15]

For a first effort this one went well. The fog and haze of the day before had grounded their patrol planes and the Japanese had no warning until the shells from *Quincy* burst at just before quarter past six. Dive-bombers from *Wasp* disposed of the nineteen seaplanes moored off Tulagi, then of their storage tanks and maintenance shops on shore. The landings went off smoothly; only one, on the little islet of Tanambogo east of Tulagi, was repulsed. At Tulagi itself, the landing craft hung up on a coral reef but the Marines waded ashore. Ten minutes after eight o'clock, the Japanese garrison on Tulagi radioed its final message to Rabaul: "Enemy troop strength is overwhelming. We will defend to the last man."[16] On this promise they made good.

Here for the first time the Marines met the intricate defense of caves and connecting tunnels honeycombing the coral that they would later find

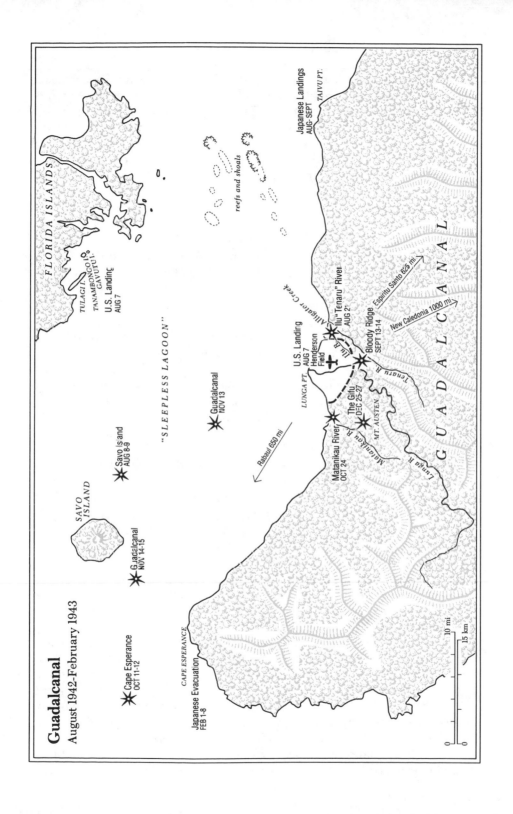

Guadalcanal
August 1942–February 1943

FLORIDA ISLANDS

TULAGI
TANAMBOGO
GAVUTU
U.S. Landing
AUG 7

"SLEEPLESS LAGOON"

Japanese Landings
AUG–SEPT

TAIVU PT.

reefs and shoals

Cape Esperance
OCT 11-12

Guadalcanal
NOV 14-15

SAVO
ISLAND

Savo Island
AUG 8-9

CAPE ESPERANCE

Japanese Evacuation
FEB 1-8

Guadalcanal
NOV 13

Alligator Creek

Ilu "Tenaru" River
AUG 21

Espiritu Santo 625 mi

New Caledonia 1000 mi

Bloody Ridge
SEPT 13-14

LUNGA PT.

U.S. Landing
AUG 7
Henderson
Field

Ilu R.

Tenaru R.

The Gifu
DEC 25-27

Matanikau River
OCT 24

MT. AUSTEN

Matanikau R.

Lunga R.

Rabaul 650 mi

G U A D A L C A N A L

10 mi

15 km

again and again on Japanese-held islands. The cave openings covered each other with interlocking fields of fire and were suicide to approach directly. To deal with them the Marines on Tulagi lacked the special equipment (flamethrowers and the like) it was eventually routine to employ. Naval gunfire would have helped, but the Navy had not yet been convinced that this was ineffective at the distance from shore they then believed it necessary to maintain ("ships can't fight forts" was the conventional wisdom).

So the Marines improvised demolition charges and began the slow, nasty work of closing cave openings or flushing out the occupants. It took them three days of gruesome fighting. "For some," wrote Lieutenant Colonel Samuel B. Griffith II, executive officer of the 1st Marine Raiders, "this first encounter with death by violence was a brutal shock."[17] (Griffith later received the Navy Cross, became a brigadier general, and took a doctoral degree at Oxford in Chinese history.) Over six hundred Japanese were killed, perhaps a hundred more were buried in their caves, and as many as seventy or eighty may have escaped to Florida Island—but this at a cost to us of 144 killed and 194 wounded. Tulagi was a foretaste of how bitter warfare in the Pacific islands was going to be.

The situation on Guadalcanal could not have been in greater contrast. The landing, on a beach several miles east of where the Japanese were thought to be concentrated, was unopposed. The boat pool Vandegrift had organized after the fiasco at Koro Island functioned to perfection and the Marines came in standing up. It soon developed that the Japanese, many of them construction workers, had departed when the cruisers opened fire. The Marines began to work their way inland through the jungle and the tough, tall, saber-edged kunai grass.

Discovering that Mount Austen was much farther away than had been supposed, Vandegrift, who was ashore by midafternoon, canceled the mission to seize it, but all the other first-day objectives were secured. (Mount Austen was not taken until six months and many casualties later, by the U.S. Army's 25th Division.) That night it rained. Trigger-happy sentries fired off hundreds of rounds at imaginary enemies in the dark, sometimes hitting each other. Miles away, the fleeing Japanese wondered what all the noise was about.

During that first day the only real misadventure on the Guadalcanal beaches was the pileup of supply. Having to assume there would be a fight once they were ashore, Vandegrift had been unwilling to assign more than a minimum of his men to the task of tote and carry. Most of the landing craft were of the early Higgins-boat type that lacked a down ramp in front, so that bales and boxes had to be manhandled over the sides. The new amphibious tractors turned out well, but there were not enough of them and the versatile DUKWs and LSTs were still in the future.

Though the landing crews worked to exhaustion, the matériel continued to come in from the ships faster than it could be disembarked and dispersed; at times as many as a hundred boats were beached while fifty more waited offshore. The men labored on, but before midnight the shore party commander had to report that things were completely out of hand, and unloading from the ships was halted till morning. Fortunately, the Japanese took no advantage of the tempting target this mass of exposed food and ammunition provided. Though some bombers flew over Sealark Channel in the afternoon, they confined their attention to the transports and did little damage.

Come daybreak, the 5th Marines began a careful advance to enlarge their beachhead toward the west. (Vandegrift thought it was *too* careful; he gave a stiff lecture to the battalion commander and later replaced a number of colonels and lieutenant colonels with younger men.[18]) They overran the nearly completed airfield and by midafternoon had come upon the main Japanese encampment, where they found every indication of how surprised its occupants had been. Tables were set with dishes still full of food, chopsticks propped against them or dropped in haste on the matting floor. No attempts at demolition had been made; quantities of food, ammunition, and equipment were captured intact.

The INS correspondent Richard Tregaskis encountered several Marines riding shiny new Japanese bicycles; in a motor pool were a hundred trucks and a complete repair shop. The Marines were at first inclined to scorn this windfall, but later, when their own supply conditions worsened, they were grateful. Japanese bombers appeared again at midday, preceded by warning of their approach from a coastwatcher on Bougainville, and this time crippled a destroyer and set fire to a transport, which burned for hours. Further and more vigorous Japanese reaction was not long in coming.

◆

In Tokyo, reports of the American landing were received with equanimity. The army general staff was surprised to learn that the navy had been building an airfield on Guadalcanal (nobody had told them) but an intelligence dispatch from Moscow said this was only a reconnaissance in force, and besides, everyone knew the U.S. Navy had been shattered (nobody had told them to the contrary).

The navy general staff knew slightly better, but nonetheless regarded the American move as a heaven-sent opportunity for a counterstroke. Its chief, Admiral Osami Nagano, instructed Admiral Yamamoto and Combined Fleet to begin preparations for the recapture of Guadalcanal, and Yamamoto, as could be expected from so resolute an officer, saw this as a chance for returning to the attack and making up for Midway. Guadalcanal was unimportant to him, but if the American fleet was rash enough to gather there, then there would it be annihilated.

At Rabaul, news of the early-morning action at Tulagi was quick to reach Admiral Gunichi Mikawa, commander of Eighth Fleet. Five heavy cruisers were at sea and he ordered them posthaste to join him. He dispatched the bombers whose arrival over Sealark Channel we have noted, and sent with them eighteen Zero fighters which would be operating at extreme range, six hundred miles out and as many on return. Assembling a scratch force of naval landing troops, he embarked them in the transport *Meiyo Maru*, which did not get far before it had the misfortune to encounter U.S. submarine S-38, take two torpedoes, and go down, ending for the moment any prospect of Japanese land reinforcements for Guadalcanal.

But by nightfall, when Mikawa sortied from Rabaul in cruiser *Chokai*, he had brought together a flotilla of five heavy and two light cruisers plus one destroyer and was headed for the Solomons. Permission had been asked of Tokyo and granted (despite some reservations on Nagano's part) for what would be the samurai stroke, too sudden to parry, the quick and fatal stab to the vitals—and very nearly it was.

Mikawa and his cruisers were spotted repeatedly as they came: by a B-17 from Australia, by vigilant submarine S-38, and twice on the morning of the eighth by Australian planes flying patrol from the New Hebrides. But their reports were either late or misleading when received and did not induce the proper state of alarm in the Amphibious Force, or in Fletcher and the three carrier groups on station south of Guadalcanal.

Fletcher was thinking less about Mikawa than Mikawa was thinking about him. The American carriers had done enough damage to call an alarming amount of attention to their presence. An hour before sunrise on the day of the landings, *Enterprise, Wasp,* and *Saratoga* had launched Wildcat fighters and Dauntless dive-bombers in support of the Marines, flying combat air patrol over the screening cruisers and destroyers, and bombing shore targets on call. The formation of twin-engine Mitsubishi bombers and its escort of Zeros seeking out the transports were repeatedly jumped by Wildcats from *Enterprise* and *Saratoga*, and many on both sides went down.

All in all, of the sixty-odd Japanese aircraft which attacked that day, the Japanese themselves admitted a loss of sixteen. (Among the Zeros that astonishingly managed to make it back to Rabaul was that of Saburo Sakai, at sixty kills Japan's ace of aces, so badly wounded he did not fly again until the final days of the war.) But Fletcher, too, had taken punishment—his fighter strength was down from ninety-five to seventy-eight—and at the end of the afternoon on the eighth he asked Ghormley's permission for a withdrawal of the carriers to safer seas.

Mikawa came on. As dark descended, he increased speed to twenty-six knots and blinked a Nelsonian signal to his sailors: "May each one calmly do his utmost." The Japanese possessed no radar, but for a night action they had something almost as good, a corps of lookouts specially trained to pick up targets at long distances even on a black, squally night like this one. Their cruisers had torpedo tubes, as ours did not, and a torpedo appropriately called the "long lance," more reliable by far than the ones we went on using well after their faults had been demonstrated. The Japanese also had courage. They were headed into the channel between Savo Island and Guadalcanal's Cape Esperance, where anything might be waiting for them; their patrol planes had reported many Allied cruisers and, inaccurately, a battleship to be present.

At 12:43, a Japanese lookout spotted a vessel at more than five miles distance crossing their course from starboard to port. It proved to be an American destroyer on patrol, which, incredibly, turned back on its path and ignored them, as did another destroyer, sighted at twenty degrees to port, also headed away. Thus they silently passed between the watchdogs, so one writer about the battle puts it, "as smug as a fox already in the henhouse."[19] Their lookouts now picked up a cruiser at eighteen thousand yards (nine miles!) and then three more (one actually a destroyer) at eight thousand yards. Parachute flares lit the sky at 1:33 A.M. as Mikawa ordered "All ships attack!"

He had found the Allied cruisers and destroyers guarding the transports posted in two separate forces and on less than full alert. At 1:43, destroyer *Patterson*—"the only American ship that was properly awake," comments Admiral Morison[20]—signaled "Warning! Warning! Strange ships entering harbor!" but it was too late. Mikawa made a leisurely circuit of Savo Island, sowing havoc as he went. In the southernmost of the two Allied groups, Australian cruiser *Canberra* took two torpedoes and twenty-four shells, her captain and gunnery officer were killed, and fires spread uncontrollably (*Canberra* listed, dead in the water, and was subsequently abandoned and destroyed). Cruiser *Chicago*, her bow knocked off by a torpedo, staggered erratically out of the fight, unfortunately failing to alert the northern group, whose turn came moments later.

Round after round of eight-inch shells from *Chokai* raked *Astoria*, heavy with wooden fittings and soon aflame, though its last salvo in reply hit one of *Chokai*'s turrets. (*Astoria* had to be abandoned, and went down the next day; Admiral Turner, who had once commanded *Astoria*, wrote that watching "that brave, lovely little ship burn and sink" was a "memory that will never leave me."[21]) *Quincy* was framed in *Aoba*'s searchlights with her guns innocently pointed fore and aft, was caught in crossfire, and soon heeled over and sank, but not before her turrets had swung about and given the Japanese the heaviest return fire they received, one round hitting *Chokai*'s operations room and killing thirty officers and men. *Vincennes* also managed to strike back at *Kinugasa*, but the Japanese shells and torpedoes poured in, the airplanes on her afterdeck exploded, and she went under not long after *Quincy*.

Within a half hour the Japanese had destroyed four heavy cruisers and heavily damaged another, and in departing they sighted and savaged a destroyer. At 2:23, Mikawa gave the order to withdraw, re-formed his line, and set course for home. Behind him he left 1,023 Allied dead and 789 wounded, perhaps a thousand clinging to oily wreckage in the shark-infested sound, of whom about seven hundred were subsequently saved.

◆

Thus ended the Battle of Savo Island, news of which was taken to the President at Shangri-La on Sunday by Captain McCrea. It was the worst defeat at sea ever suffered by the United States Navy; reports of it gave Admiral King his worst day of the war. In the aftermath, under pressure to find out what had caused it, there was some agreement that of the many contributing factors, faulty reconnaissance would be high on any list. Admiral Turner had noticed a gap in the air coverage of The Slot between Santa Isabel and New Georgia, through which Mikawa came, and had put in a request for closing it to Rear Admiral John S. McCain, the theater air commander. But McCain reported to Ghormley, so that Turner had to ask Fletcher to ask Ghormley to ask McCain. In this laborious grinding of gears nothing got done, and nobody told Turner that nothing had been done.

"If I had known of any 'approaching' Jap force," said Turner after the war, "I would have done something—maybe the wrong thing, but I would have done something." There is a feeling that more unified command might have generated a greater urge for action in the reconnaissance apparatus. One pilot, instead of maintaining contact after sighting the enemy, as his orders read, returned to base and had tea before turning in a report that should have been radioed instantly.[22]

A phrase that recurs repeatedly in the postmortems is "lack of battle readiness," and it seems fair. This is not, as might be supposed, so much a question of how often you have your nose bloodied as it is of paying attention and not making unwarranted assumptions. There had been more assumptions made that night than fate permits: If we were in danger the high command would have told us and they haven't, so we aren't. Those airplanes would not be flying around out there if they weren't friendly, therefore they are friendly. Maybe some Japanese have been sighted but so far away and coming at such a speed that they won't get here until tomorrow afternoon, therefore we have until tomorrow afternoon to get ready.

The possibility that the Japanese had other ideas and would increase speed, that the planes were *not* friendly, and that danger was very real and immediate—all this simply was not at the forefront of anyone's attention. Also, they were all tired; many had not yet learned the lesson that you cannot stay awake forever and that steady attention to duty is more effective than bursts of energy. "Battle readiness" is a state of mind that sometimes only the shock of experience can bring about. Pearl Harbor was shocking, but there you could argue that we were excused because the enemy had cheated. This time we were supposed to be awake and were not. Perhaps it took Savo Island to bring all hands bolt upright in awareness that we were dealing with a skillful and audacious foe, armed with weapons that could hit hard and hurt.

Looked at from the Japanese side, Admiral Mikawa's withdrawal is less easy to excuse. He had it in his hand to end the Guadalcanal campaign there and then, and he let it escape him. If he had pressed on and wiped out the transports waiting helpless off Tulagi and Lunga Point—which was, after all, his mission—he would have written finish to our chances. There *were* no more transports in the South Pacific. As it was, these fled, but they came back later and often, and in the end this made the difference. The Japanese said we won at Guadalcanal because we reinforced faster than they did, and their testimony should carry weight. A failure to follow through on their part, like Mikawa's, recurred throughout the war—from Nagumo's at Pearl Harbor to Kurita's at Leyte Gulf—until eventually people wondered if there was not some consistent pattern.

On the other hand, from his own perspective Mikawa's decision was not unreasonable. He had just brought off a stunning victory, by the apparently miraculous luck of getting into the sound undetected, and Lady Luck is notorious for abruptly withdrawing her favors. As far as he knew, there were still American carriers roving out there somewhere (there were not, but news of Fletcher's departure had been denied him), and if he were still within their aircraft range by morning he would invite the fate that overtook Nagumo at Midway and his victory could go a-glimmering. Best play it safe: One never knows.

The same applies with far less force to Fletcher's haste in pulling out the carriers. The reasons he gave to Ghormley at the time were the depletion of his fighter strength, the presence of enemy torpedo planes and bombers, and the low state of his fuel supply; and Ghormley read his orders in such fashion that he was loath to overrule the man on the spot. Yet Fletcher's fuel was not low.

Later examination of the ships' logs showed that the carriers had enough oil for seventeen days, *North Carolina* for eighteen, the cruisers for eleven, and even the thirsty destroyers for seven (they could have been refueled from the others). As for enemy air, Fletcher had no reason to suppose that the Japanese had spotted him, and they hadn't. "His force could have remained in the area with no more severe consequences than sunburn," was Admiral Morison's verdict.[23]

Fletcher later maintained that fuel had not been among his major concerns, which were: the low ebb (four) of American carrier strength, Japanese ability to bring more carriers to this vicinity than we could, the fact that no U.S. carrier replacements were coming for at least nine months and that Magic decoding indicated Japanese submarines coming south in his direction. Knowing that many of his officers would have preferred otherwise, he still thought that on August 8 a defensive decision was in order.[24]

You never know. Two times already the carriers alone had stood between the Allies and major defeats, and there was every reason to expect similar times to come again. But as Nimitz later put it, the carriers were only precious because they could be used—as they might have been to prevent Mikawa from getting away scot-free—and the ultimate flaw in Fletcher's argument was that in safeguarding the carriers he risked losing the Marines, which might have been a setback of greater magnitude than he seemed to recognize.

"He's left us bare arse," Turner is supposed to have said when told of Fletcher's decision. He himself had no choice but to follow suit and pull out the thin-skinned and unprotected transports, as he had determined to do even before catastrophe at Savo Island eliminated any doubts. The slowness and delays in unloading now assumed a monstrous importance.

The ships had cleared New Zealand with only two thirds of the food and ammunition Marine doctrine would consider normal, and of this less than half had so far made it to the beaches—that is, about enough for Vandegrift's men to eat and fight for a month. No radar, no coast defense guns, no heavy construction equipment had been disembarked, as had very little of the sand bags, barbed wire, and entrenching tools the Marines would soon want badly for their own defense.

When the last transports left, late in the afternoon of the ninth, the Marines required no expert strategist to read the meaning of the empty water between Tulagi and Guadalcanal. They were on their own.

III

The Marine Corps as Roosevelt encountered it in Haiti in 1917 was undergoing an experience that profoundly shaped its character. In the years between the Spanish-American War and World War II, the Caribbean was its training ground. During this period the United States intervened repeatedly in the islands and in Central America, the so-called banana wars, and the Marines did the intervening—in Cuba, in Panama, in Santo Domingo, in Nicaragua, at Vera Cruz in Mexico, as well as in Haiti. American involvement to protect American business interests was defended on the grounds that the region was inherently revolution-prone and would benefit from the imposition of civic order, sanitation, and the forms if not the substance of democracy—a view Roosevelt shared at the outset with his contemporaries though he renounced it in his Latin American policies as President. Vandegrift, too, became skeptical. Writing later of that earlier time, he used the phrase "protect the lives and property of American citizens" only with irony.

But Caribbean service was the education of the Marines. A tour of duty there was commonly part of a young officer's career, and not uncommonly a stepping-stone to advancement, as it was for Vandegrift. Born and raised in Charlottesville—his grandfather, a Baptist deacon who had been wounded at Antietam and Gettysburg, habitually prayed to "the God of Abraham, Isaac, Jacob, Robert E. Lee, and Stonewall Jackson"[25]—he early leaned toward the military, but he failed his physical exam for West Point. He was then told by one of Virginia's senators, a family friend, of a chance to become an officer in the Marine Corps, which he had never heard of. He passed the exams, received his commission, and after a brief assignment at the Portsmouth Navy Yard shipped to Panama to join a battalion led by Major Smedley D. Butler.

The entire corps at that time consisted of about 350 officers and less than 10,000 men. Butler was one of its legendary figures, a hero of the Boxer Rebellion, slightly round-shouldered, with a beaked nose and a sharp tongue. He later became a public character; his assertion in 1931 that Mussolini was a hit-and-run driver who had killed a child was a cause of much scandal and nearly resulted in his court-martial. He was a fine troop commander and one of a handful of Marines to have been twice awarded the Congressional Medal of Honor.

Butler took a liking to Vandegrift, which did no harm, and favorable appointments followed in due course. In Nicaragua, Butler dispatched him with a corporal to ride the cowcatcher of a locomotive and look for mines along the tracks. Vandegrift reported back with a grin on his face, causing Butler to refer to him thereafter as "Sunny Jim" (from the commercials of a contemporary breakfast cereal) until his promotion to captain, whereupon Butler modified it to "James" in deference to his new rank. He called Vandegrift "James" to the end of his life, as did some of Vandegrift's friends.

Sent to the Caribbean, the Marines had to teach themselves to fight irregular warfare in a tropical climate. They learned to live and stay healthy in jungle country, engaged against fast-moving and sometimes savage antagonists ranging from bandits in a literal sense of the word to guerrilla forces under able leaders like the Nicaraguan Augusto César Sandino, who eluded them for six years and was never decisively defeated. They learned to stay mobile, to avoid ambush, and to master the tactics of patrolling and small-unit combat.

Conspicuous among them were Marines like Lewis B. Puller, who by the time he left the Caribbean had fought in over a hundred actions and earned two of his five Navy Crosses, the Marine record. (Puller, as a sergeant, served in Haiti under Vandegrift, who described him as "headstrong," about the mildest term anyone ever applied to Chesty Puller; on

Guadalcanal, Lieutenant Colonel Puller commanded the 1st Battalion of the 7th Marines.) Here also they began to develop the techniques of amphibious warfare which revolutionized the conflict that came in 1941. "If the Battle of Waterloo was won on the playing fields of Eton," wrote Marine General Holland M. Smith, "the Japanese bases of the Pacific were captured on the beaches of the Caribbean, where the problems involved were worked out in Marine maneuvers."[26]

It should be remembered that in those days an assault landing on a defended shore was regarded in most professional military circles as worse than folly. The example of the British in the Dardanelles in 1915 was frequently, if misleadingly, cited. Even Liddell Hart, who was right about so much else, was wrong about this. "A landing on a foreign coast in face of hostile troops," he wrote in 1939, "has always been one of the most difficult operations of war. It has now become much more difficult, indeed almost impossible." (Admiral Turner had read and well remembered this passage from Liddell Hart, and it came into his mind on board *McCawley* the night before the Guadalcanal landings.)[27]

The Marines did not agree. They had always made contested landings, ever since two hundred of them under Captain Samuel Nicholas took Fort Montague in the Bahamas on March 3, 1776, but now they began to apply themselves to the study of attack from the sea as their primary mission. Though it became so officially in 1929, the operative date as Marines saw it was 1933, with the withdrawal in January of their last detachment from Nicaragua and the creation in December, at least on paper, of what was called the Fleet Marine Force, permanently attached to the fleet for the purpose of seizing advance bases.

In the years when Holland Smith attended Naval War College, there was no such thing as a doctrine of Marine landings. As he put it in his customarily sardonic language, "Assault forces were stowed in boats 5,000 yards off the beach and given a pat on the back [*sic!*], with the hope that all would go well. Warships threw a few shells into the beach and that was all. Nobody took these landings seriously, because the mere appearance of a large naval force off shore was supposed to inactivate the enemy."[28] Thus an equally critical event was the publication in 1934 by the staff and students of the Marine Corps School at Quantico of a *Tentative Manual of Landing Operations,* which was to become the bible of amphibious tactics for years thereafter.

To the nonmilitary reader it may seem strange that doctrine should be so significant in war, but it is. There must be agreed-upon understandings, fully shared and uniformly interpreted, about who is in charge where and when, and who does what in what sequence, so that some kind of order can be sought behind the chaos of the actual event. Such doctrine the "tentative manual," drawing on nothing but the experience and intuition of its authors, laid out in detail—for command relations, naval gunfire, aerial support, ship-to-shore movement, securing the beachhead, and the logistics of loading and unloading supplies. With a few revisions, the Navy subsequently adopted it as *Fleet Training Publication 167,* and the Army put a new cover on it and called it *Field Manual 31-5.*

The consequences of this endorsement by the other services should not go unnoticed. Much later, in the *U.S. Naval Institute Proceedings* of 1948, Archer Vandegrift emphasized the point: "Despite its outstanding record as a combat force in the past war, the Marine Corps' far greater contribution to victory was doctrinal; that is, the fact that the basic amphibious doctrines which carried Allied troops over every beachhead of World War II had been largely shaped—often in the face of uninterested or doubting military orthodoxy—by U.S. Marines, and mainly between 1922 and 1935."[29]

◆

Then equipment had to be developed and tested: transports and destroyer-transports adapted to Marine needs, radios that could survive the passage to the beach and still perform, and—above all—landing craft. Fortunately, there was a man named Andrew Jackson Higgins in New Orleans who had been building shallow-draft boats that could beach and retract easily, for use by fur trappers and oil drillers in the Louisiana bayous (at least that's what Higgins said; during Prohibition his boats were also well suited to rumrunning). Holland Smith believed that the Higgins boat, to be known in action as the LCVP(R), "did more to help win the war in the Pacific than any other single piece of equipment." It was adopted as standard only after prolonged and angry argument with the Bureau of Ships. Typical objection: The boats must not be longer than thirty feet. Why? Because davits on most Navy ships are spaced for thirty-foot boats.[30]

But Higgins was a fighting Irishman who had political access to the President and did not easily accept defeat; besides, his landing craft were rated superior in every test to which they were repeatedly subjected. Eventually he was asked to design a boat for bringing tanks ashore, and this—again over the Bureau of Ships' drawn-out and wasteful touting of its own inferior version—became the LCM(3). Higgins got on well with the Marines and with Holland Smith, who was not noted for amiability; Smith's nickname "Howlin' Mad" was earned. In 1942, when he was pressing for a combat command, Smith was erroneously reported to have diabetes and thus be headed for retirement. Higgins got so steamed up he went to Roosevelt and told him what he thought "about some four-flushy Admirals and Generals I had met, and what I thought about the Marines by comparison."[31] Smith was not diabetic and went on to lead amphibious landing forces in the Pacific, though he said the whole episode should have given him high blood pressure.

Then both doctrine and weapons had to be tried out in actual use. In 1932, Holland Smith rented Culebra Island off Puerto Rico, and until war came the Marines held annual training exercises either there or on San Clemente Island near San Diego. Larger and larger units, and more and more complex maneuvers, were exposed to the test of practice. In 1936, someone had the bright idea of hanging cargo nets over the side of the transports, in place of the old-fashioned gangway, for transferring men to the boats, and this worked so well it was used generally throughout World War II. Many who joined in the trial runs were later to be part of the real thing. In 1939, Fleet Exercise XX was held off Culebra, with battleship *Mississippi* commanded by Captain Raymond A. Spruance and carriers *Lexington* and *Enterprise* commanded by Vice-Admiral Ernest J. King. The President came, aboard cruiser *Houston*, to watch.

Houston was Roosevelt's favorite ship for Caribbean cruises; he had been on it there in 1934, 1935, and 1938 for his customary combination of inspection visits and deep-sea fishing. This time his party included Admiral Leahy, White House physician Ross McIntire, Pa Watson, and naval aide Dan Callaghan. On February 26, *Houston* joined "Black" Fleet for Exercise XX. The wind was fresh, says the ship's morning news summary, and the sea choppy. When the exercise was over, *Houston* anchored off Culebra near *Pennsylvania* and the senior officers of the fleet were invited aboard to meet the President. On Culebra's Flamingo Beach, the Marines staged a landing for him with Higgins boats. When he left *Houston* at Charleston in early March, Roosevelt sent a thank-you message to the crew: "Another happy cruise—and for me a very instructive one."[32]

When nothing much was going on after the exercise ended, Captain Spruance asked a junior officer he knew was interested in amphibious technique to join him in one of his well-known strenuous walks along Flamingo Beach. Shortly they came upon a group of other ranks and a man in bathing trunks, splashing about in the surf with what the young officer described as "two of the strangest looking small craft I had ever seen." Spruance, watching attentively as the man in the bathing trunks put the boats through their paces and explained their characteristics, broke in to say, "By the way, you two have not met. Lieutenant Oliver this is Kelly Turner."[33] (Oliver wondered what the commanding officer of cruiser *Astoria* was doing messing around with experimental landing craft; Turner became Spruance's principal subordinate in command of amphibious forces; Oliver was his flag lieutenant at Midway.)

A number of Marine officers had already been thinking about the duties that might devolve on them in the event of a war with Japan. Among the most prescient was a major named Earl H. Ellis, who had submitted a plan of operations to the commandant of the Corps in 1921 which foresaw amphibious invasion of the Japanese-held islands and, in some cases, the exact number of Marines that would be required. Pete

Ellis wandered the Pacific as an agent of naval intelligence until the Japanese finally caught up with him and he disappeared in 1923, under suspicious circumstances, while on Palau in the Carolines, then in Japanese hands.[34]

The streams all converged on a single conclusion: The Marines were going to be shock troops. Setting aside their first-to-fight mystique, they had engaged in more recent and more vigorous (albeit specialized) combat than the other services, and they alone had developed the capability—that is, the combination of theory, hardware, and hard conditioning that they put together in the twenties and early thirties—for landing on enemy-held shores. Marines like Howlin' Mad Smith and Chesty Puller were bellicose, opinionated, and at times outrageous, but they had a refreshing contempt for garrison soldiers, gold braid, and tradition gone moldy from disuse. Their ideas about fighting were rooted in some genuine encounter with it and their professionalism took precedence over even their own tough-guy rhetoric.

The Marines' goal had more and more come to be one of violent assault on short-term objectives, taking the losses this implied. Prodigal expenditure in lives would be made up for by the economy of decisive effect. The Marines would storm the beach and eliminate its defenders; all would be done quickly. Then the Army would come in, mop up any last-ditch resistance, and take over the long-term jobs of occupation and defense against counterattack—a thoroughly sound approach in view of the Marines' past, their existing state of readiness, and the future their most thoughtful prophets could foresee.

Consciously and unconsciously this grew to be the Marines' prevailing state of mind. It was the governing principle in which their employment was envisaged. When naval strategists like King and Nimitz thought of using the Marines, this is what they thought about. All of which made it the more disquieting that in their first major engagement of the war the Marines should find themselves in a situation exactly the opposite from the expected, one for which their organization and approach were unsuited and their doctrine inapplicable. On Guadalcanal in August 1942, they were not only stranded and seemingly deserted, but left with the prospect of at best preparing to withstand a siege, and not likely a short one.

◆

Vandegrift called in his officers. "Singly or in pairs," he wrote, "they straggled to my CP [command post], the colonels, lieutenant colonels, and majors on whom so much depended." He had to confess they were a sorry-looking crew—tired, in dirty dungarees, some with bloodshot eyes and "embryonic beards." They sat on the wet ground in the drizzle, sipped coffee from canteen cups that scalded the lips, and watched the beach where survivors of Savo Island, black with oil and burns, were still being brought ashore. Nobody talked much.

Vandegrift believed there were times when a commander should hold back information but that this was not one of them. He wasted no words: The carriers had gone, the transports were going, with more than half their supplies still aboard. No one knew when our aircraft or the Navy would be back. Japanese attention would now be concentrated on the Marines. Vandegrift asked them to report all this frankly to their men, but he told them to say something else and to stress it hard. Marines had been in tough spots before and survived, and this one, too, they would survive. There would be no Bataan, no Wake Island, if everyone did his utmost.

Three immediate objectives were announced and delegated: Set up a main line of resistance, finish the airfield, and bring the supplies in from the beaches to dispersal dumps under the coconut palms. As before, Vandegrift simply stated the tasks to be accomplished and assumed that his staff was capable of converting these into missions for specific units and their detailed orders. Privately his greatest worry was over an enemy landing from the sea, or an attack from the west, the direction in which the Japanese had retreated, and to prepare against these he had to hold his force together and leave much of the jungle to the south and east covered by outposts and aggressive patrols.

There would be no fuss about parade-ground etiquette, but correct if informal uniform and clean shaves where possible would be required. When Vandegrift called a second conference several days later, his staff and command officers were looking somewhat better, and he posed with them for a photograph—"a morale device that worked because they thought that if I went to the trouble of having the picture taken then I obviously planned to enjoy it in future years."[35]

First casualties on Guadalcanal were suffered on August 9, when a patrol across the Matanikau River to the southwest ran into a Japanese force and lost one officer killed and several men wounded. At midday came the first of the air raids that were to continue more or less day and night thenceforward. Japanese submarines and surface ships controlled the sound, lobbing in a shell now and then, and cutting all but radio communication with the Marines under the assistant division commander still on Tulagi and Florida, victorious but momentarily out of the action. An aide to theater air commander McCain flew in a PBY amphibious patrol plane, evacuated two wounded Marines, and pronounced Henderson Field—which they had decided to name after Major Lofton Henderson, a Marine pilot killed at Midway—fit for use.

On the twelfth, everyone went on rations of two meals a day, and another patrol to the west, led by Colonel Goettge, under the mistaken impression that a group of Japanese wanted to surrender, was almost totally wiped out and Goettge was killed. Next day a Catholic priest in a native village reported rumors of a Japanese force assembling to the east, and on the fourteenth Martin Clemens and Sergeant Major Vouza came through the lines with news of a Japanese radio station which seemed to confirm this.

Clemens, an athletic Cambridge graduate, put his constabulary at Vandegrift's service as scouts, an offer gratefully accepted. (Vouza and his friends also taught the Marines how to husk a coconut with three blows of the machete, the beginning of a long and amicable relationship between Melanesians and Marines.) A patrol to the east encountered and virtually eliminated an arrogantly careless force of four enemy officers and thirty men carrying documents which showed that the Japanese, evidently from observation posts on Mount Austen, had pinpointed Marine positions with disconcerting accuracy.

For Vandegrift, the most eventful day was the twentieth. In late afternoon, flying from the east into the setting sun, "came one of the most beautiful sights of my life." Admiral McCain, on receiving the report of a usable airfield, had sent U.S.S. *Long Island,* a motorship converted to an escort carrier, close enough in on Guadalcanal to fly off Marine air squadrons VMF-223 (nineteen Grumman fighters) and VMSB-232 (twelve Douglas dive-bombers). Vandegrift at last had an air force, however small. There was a glimmer of light in the dark future he had been contemplating. "Thank God you have come," he said to the first pilot who jumped to the ground, and he was not the only one with tears in his eyes. Eight hours later, all hell broke loose.

The Japanese made the same mistake repeatedly: They underestimated the Marines and overestimated themselves. Not long after the American landings, Tokyo transferred responsibility for Guadalcanal ground operations from the navy to the army, and General Harukichi Hyakutake, commanding Seventeenth Army at Rabaul, gave the honor of retaking the island to Colonel Kiyono Ichiki, who had been slated to capture Midway.

Ichiki thoughtfully filled out his diary in advance: "17 Aug. The landing. 20 Aug. The march by night and the battle. 21 Aug. Enjoyment of the fruits of victory."[36] He sailed from Truk with over nine hundred men in six destroyers and, undetected by the Marines, landed at night to the east of them near Taivu Point. At three-ten on the morning of the twenty-first, two hundred shouting and screaming Japanese came pouring across a sandbar at the mouth of a river then incorrectly known as the Tenaru. The Marines were waiting for them.

Sergeant Vouza, on patrol, had been captured by Japanese, who found a miniature American flag in his possession. When he refused to give information they tied him to a tree, used him for bayonet practice, and left him for dead. Vouza chewed through his bonds and crawled to the American lines at the Tenaru, where he warned the battalion commander of the

Japanese presence and described their numbers and weapons. For his heroism Vouza was awarded the Silver Star by the United States and the George Cross by Great Britain. He was twelve days in the Marine hospital: "there they done the treatment," he wrote to an English friend, "and the wounded was healthed up."[37]

The fight lasted sixteen hours. The Japanese showed all the ferocity, skill at deception, and willingness to sacrifice themselves that their patriotism required. Their wounded would wait until a Marine came to inspect them, then explode a hand grenade ("You can readily see the answer to that," Vandegrift wrote to the corps commandant, General Holcomb; from here on with the Japanese, the Marines asked and gave no quarter.)

But it was useless. The attack across the sandbar was stopped short, and Vandegrift ordered a flanking movement that pinned the rest of Ichiki's men against the sea and left no escape. A platoon of light tanks was sent in to finish them off; some of the Japanese were literally chewed up in the tank treads. A few stragglers escaped to the hills; fifteen were taken prisoner, but otherwise casualties were total: over eight hundred dead, at a cost of thirty-five Marines dead and seventy-five wounded. Colonel Ichiki fled, tore up and burned his regimental colors, and shot himself. "The attack of the Ichiki Detachment," General Hyakutake reported to Tokyo, "was not entirely successful."[38]

There were many acts of bravery and selflessness on the Tenaru that day. For Vandegrift, this was a triumphant vindication of his confidence in his men, a victory far transcending the numbers involved. "In but hours," he wrote, "its psychological effect grew out of all proportion to its physical dimensions." The Japanese were not supermen but fallible if fanatic human beings. The Marines on Guadalcanal had won their first battle; now they felt unbeatable. "These youngsters," Vandegrift ended his letter to Holcomb, "are the darndest people when they get started you ever saw."[39]

◆

Initially neither the Japanese nor the American command seemed quite to understand what was at stake on Guadalcanal. The Imperial Navy's misconception was well illustrated by their next effort to land a handful of troops, this time some fifteen hundred strong, another corporal's guard sent to do a job beyond its capacity. But they came incongruously accompanied by much of Combined Fleet: three carriers, three battleships, eight cruisers, a seaplane tender, and many auxiliaries—a sledgehammer sent to drive a thumbtack.

Yamamoto was looking for his major sea battle, which he did not find. Warned of the Japanese approach, Ghormley sent Fletcher north again and there ensued the inconclusive carrier-versus-carrier engagement called the Battle of the Eastern Solomons. *Ryujo* was sunk, *Enterprise* badly hit (some of its aircraft landed on Henderson Field and temporarily joined the Marines, causing one cynical officer to observe that what "saved Guadalcanal was the loss of so many carriers"). In any event, the Japanese transports were turned back and their troops had to be landed later, at night, by destroyer.

The Americans, too, were still uncertain as to which mission came first. Amphibious doctrine had not sunk in to that level of the mind where it became automatic, and there were still functional relationships between marine, naval, air, and army forces that had not been fully worked out. Fletcher had not concerned himself enough with the protection and support of the Marines for which doctrine said he was responsible. Turner fully understood that supply of the Marines was now first charge on his resources, but he did not have the backup he needed to effect it. Logistics were poorly organized. There was a monumental mess on the docks and in the harbor at Nouméa for which Ghormley, though it was not his fault, was blamed; the fault was in Hawaii and Washington.

Turner's biographer, Admiral Dyer, wrote that he thought "the biggest bottleneck was the basic lack of know-how by the Navy concerning logistical support for a big operation six thousand miles away from a United States source of supply."[40] Even Turner was not wholly settled in his mind that doctrine meant what it said when it defined the ground commander as the best judge of ground requirements and objectives. Turner liked to move troops around and kept proposing diversions, such as the originally scheduled landing on Ndeni in the Santa Cruz Islands to the east, or further landings elsewhere on Guadalcanal. Vandegrift had to remind him that the principle of concentration of force was in effect, that holding Guadalcanal was first priority and that first priority on Guadalcanal was Henderson Field.

General Vandegrift seems to have perceived this instinctively. He was one of the earliest to arrive at a balanced understanding of how land, sea, and air power interrelate; at least he was the first in a command position to make sequential decisions in which that understanding is always apparent. The presence of active American air power on Guadalcanal (gas, ammunition, and maintenance crews having been snuck in by sea) transformed the set of conditions he was dealing with, as he plainly saw. No longer could Japanese planes or ships approach the island during daylight with impunity. Guadalcanal bristled with the implicit threat of its fighters and dive-bombers, however few. The Marines who had been left behind across the sound on Tulagi could now rejoin their comrades; reinforcement and support by sea, though tentative at first, could now recommence (two transports came back with supplies on September 7).

All of this stemmed from the handful of aircraft on Henderson Field, and reciprocally the defense of that field now became Vandegrift's primary concern as ground commander. It is far from certain that his superiors saw this as clearly as he did. Major General Millard F. Harmon, a former chief of air staff who commanded Army forces in the South Pacific, thought that the reason the situation on Guadalcanal became so critical— and critical it did become—was the Navy's failure to move rapidly with airfield construction. (Not surprisingly, some of the Japanese thought their own difficulties stemmed from a failure of the same kind on their side.) Harmon's representations to this effect, he wrote to General Arnold, were greeted with smiles of assent, but "the positive action was not taken . . . the plan did not have as its first and immediate objective the development of Cactus *as an airbase*" (Cactus was the code name for Guadalcanal).[41]

Cactus Air Force, as it came to call itself, was a miscellaneous lot. It achieved a semblance of unity on September 3 when a DC-3 brought in as its commander Brigadier General Roy S. Geiger, a "cold white grizzly bear," as one Marine who was there described him.[42] (Geiger was a veteran Marine aviator who had trained with Vandegrift and served with him in Haiti, where he and Chesty Puller improvised air raids by dropping bombs attached to a rope from the cockpit of a de Havilland Jenny; he went on to be, on Okinawa, the first Marine to command an army.) But the Marines were soon joined by some Army Air Forces P-400s, by various Navy groups, which came and went from the carriers, and by more Marine squadrons. Units were scrambled together and there was little time or inclination for paperwork, with the result that no one really knows who was flying from Henderson Field at any given moment.

Methods for fueling and arming the aircraft were makeshift; wear and tear on the planes and their crews was considerable. "Nobody cared about lineage," Admiral Morison wrote. "If it had wings it flew; if it flew it fought; and if it fought very long something was certain to happen to it." Henderson Field was the continuous object of Japanese attentions: bombs from the air and shells from ships offshore and, eventually, from artillery inland. "Marines who had occasion to spend a night at Henderson Field," Morison adds, "were always glad to get back to the comparative quiet of the front lines."[43]

But the pilots were getting the hang of it. One on one, the Grumman was no match for the Zero, which was faster and more maneuverable, but with mutual support, two Grummans were equal to four or five Zeros. The Grumman was sturdier and more heavily armed. Saburo Sakai encountered his first Grumman on that flight out and back from Rabaul on which he returned so badly wounded. "For some strange reason," he said after the war, "even after I had poured five or six hundred rounds of ammunition directly into the Grumman, the airplane did not fall, but kept on flying."[44]

Another legend, that of the invincible Zero, was crumbling. Before long the Americans were scoring about five Japanese planes destroyed for every one of their own. When Marine Fighter Squadron 223, which had been the first to arrive, was finally withdrawn and returned to San Francisco, its score stood at 111 Japanese aircraft, of which nineteen had been shot down by its commander, Captain John L. Smith, Guadalcanal's first ranking ace, who received the Medal of Honor. After some weeks of press interviews and bond rallies in the States, Smith asked to be sent back to combat. "Not," he was told, "until you have trained 150 John Smiths."

"Grumman," Under Secretary of the Navy Forrestal was to say, "saved Guadalcanal."[45] Well, not exactly. What saved Guadalcanal was the inability of the Japanese to recapture Henderson Field. Heaven knows they tried, but not with enough until too late. Their second attempt was executed with the greatest energy and came the closest to success, but on balance it was again less strong than the task required. This was the attack of the Kawaguchi Detachment, otherwise known as the Battle of Edson's Ridge, or Bloody Ridge, or just The Ridge.

There had come to be a seesaw situation in which control of the sea around Guadalcanal changed hands every twelve hours; the Americans dominated it in daytime, but at night the Japanese brought their destroyer-transports down The Slot with supplies and reinforcements, the so-called Tokyo Express. On it late in August came Major General Kiyotake Kawaguchi, commander of 35th Infantry Brigade, with the advance party of a body of troops eventually to number six thousand.

He landed as Ichiki had done at Taivu Point, east of the Marines, and set his engineers to work clearing a jungle path southwestward through the hills and ravines to a point on the high ground south of Henderson Field, from which he intended to assault and capture it. Kawaguchi's plan, which he had confidently drawn up even before he left Rabaul, was to surprise the Marines with attacks from east, west, and south (the latter, led by himself, would be the main effort), the three supported by aerial bombing and naval gunfire on the airfield to distract its defenders. Before long his brigade would be ready.

But Vandegrift acted first. His notion of defense had never been passive; he always ordered active patrolling and encouraged aggressiveness in his commanders. Among the Marines who had come over to Guadalcanal from Tulagi were the First Marine Raider and Parachute battalions, jointly under the command of Colonel Merritt A. "Red Mike" Edson. Hearing of Kawaguchi's presence to the east, Vandegrift sent Edson's men by sea to investigate; they struck pay dirt.

Kawaguchi's main body of several thousand had departed into the jungle on their long circuit to the south, and the Raiders, with very light losses, devastated a rear echelon and an artillery depot that had been left behind. The depot was reduced to rubble: Shell fuzes and the breech mechanisms of guns were thrown in the sea, food tins punctured with bayonets, and other stores treated with whatever indignities the Marines could contrive. Kawaguchi had now lost both his base and the factor of surprise on which he was overly depending. Another curious Japanese characteristic emerged: insistence on following to the letter a plan from which essential elements had been removed.

When the Raiders returned from the raid (somehow managing to bring with them twenty-one cases of Japanese beer and seventeen half-gallon flasks of sake), there was a conference at division headquarters. The Japanese were obviously coming, but where? "This looks like a good approach," said Edson, tracing on an aerial photograph an open ridge perhaps a thousand yards long which overlooked the airfield and pointed in its direction, with jungle on either side. Edson's men took up positions on the ridge, not far from a new headquarters Vandegrift had moved to in the hopes of getting a decent night's sleep. "Too much bombing and shelling here close to the beach. We're moving to a quiet spot," said Red Mike. "Some goddam rest area," one of his corporals said later. Most significantly for what was to come, division artillery—105-mm howitzers of the 11th Marines—was sited and registered in on likely Japanese assembly areas and jungle trails leading to the ridge.

Kawaguchi had the same idea as Edson; the ridge was going to be his avenue down on Henderson Field, not far below it. He decisively outnumbered the Raiders and parachutists who faced him, but his own account reveals something of his frustration. The destruction of his base had hampered communication with higher headquarters. Cutting through the road had taken longer than expected, and his troops were strung out all along it. "Because of the devilish jungle," he wrote, "the Brigade was scattered all over and completely beyond control. In my whole life I have never felt so helpless."[46] Japanese warships, transports, and aircraft were standing by, waiting for his word that the airfield had been taken. He was under pressure to move too soon.

For this we can be grateful, for when they came on the nights of September 12 to 14, his attacks were of a fury that nearly broke the Marines' defense: calcium flares, mortar barrages, infiltration behind our line, and wave after wave of Japanese screaming *"Totsugeki!"* (Charge!) or "Ma-line you di-e-e-e!" ("You'll eat shit first, you bastards!" one Raider is said to have replied.) It was among the most bloody and brutal of the battles on Guadalcanal. Some Marine positions had to be pulled back, and men in the last stages of exhaustion rallied to fight again; they stumbled like sleepwalkers, lifting their feet high. One Japanese got as far as General Vandegrift's tent before he was gunned down.

Edson reestablished his line on the last knoll between the ridge and Henderson Field, his own CP less than ten yards behind the most forward machine gun; he lay on his stomach, raising himself occasionally to use his hand phone. That night the Japanese attacked twelve times. The Raiders were stunned and glassy-eyed but they held, and the Marine artillery put down a murderous curtain of fire. Edson would call for a concentration only a hundred yards ahead of his men and then, seeing the shells burst in place, would whisper, "Closer! closer!"[47]

When Kawaguchi began a grim march of withdrawal to the west, without adequate food or medical supplies, he left the bodies of 600 of his men on the ridge. His total casualties were 1,213 killed, wounded, or missing—about a fifth of his force. Edson, with around 700 present on the ridge, lost 49 killed, 204 wounded, and 10 missing—more than a third of his valiant Marines. Many are the candidates, as there should be, for the credit of "saving" Guadalcanal, but few will deny that the loss of Edson's Ridge could have lost it.

◆

"At least the half of generalship," said Günther Blumentritt, who served as chief of staff to von Rundstedt and Model, and later commanded German armies in Holland and Germany, "is the ability to cope with the unexpected and incalculable, the other half being common sense and staff work."[48] By this measure, Vandegrift's generalship was first-rate. His trusting and confident use of staff has been noted; the common sense with which he handled the unexpected and incalculable deserves further comment. Not only were the Marines fighting a different war from the one they had expected, but they were doing so by using highly unusual tactics designed by Vandegrift to fit the unusual circumstances.

To protect Henderson Field, the Book (orthodox doctrine) would have said "defense in depth," but Vandegrift threw away the Book and wrote his own text. On Guadalcanal, defense in depth was possible only on exposed high ground like Edson's Ridge; elsewhere the wet, low-lying jungle "restricted visibility to a few yards" and made defense in depth "out of the question" (thus Lieutenant Colonel Griffith, who took command of the raider battalion when Red Mike was promoted to regiment[49]).

Vandegrift's reinforced division of about twenty thousand men occupied a roughly oval-shaped area four and a half miles long and less than three miles wide between the ridge and the sea, bounded on the west by the Japanese encampment area and on the east by the Tenaru, now more properly known as Alligator Creek. Once the threat of a counterlanding had been reduced by Cactus Air Force, Vandegrift had strung his main line of resistance around the perimeter of the oval, with barbed wire, fields of fire cut through the foliage, and dug-in positions similar to those with which the Marines had greeted Colonel Ichiki. A thin single line like this around a large area—technically a cordon—has a poor reputation among students of tactics, as Fletcher Pratt put it, because of being "the type of defense whose unsoundness Napoleon Bonaparte spent most of his career in demonstrating."[50]

Orthodox theory said, as Napoleon had proved, that artillery would punch a hole in the cordon through which a spearhead column could pass and strike about *ad lib* at everything in the rear. But Vandegrift did not think that on Guadalcanal the theory applied. He doubted that the Japanese could bring up that much artillery through the jungle, while his own field guns could be concentrated on whatever sector the enemy chose to attack. Further, the Japanese seemed to be imprisoned, as they had been before and would be again, within a fixed and unchangeable set of plans. A force of theirs would be landed nearby, make an overland march, and then hurl itself against Vandegrift's wired-in perimeter. This they did again and again.

Vandegrift, says Pratt, had "invented a new system of war—the system of seizing a beachhead on which an airfield could be constructed, setting up a cordon perimeter defense around it, and then proceeding to the next step. The process was repeated in endless variations throughout the southwest Pacific—at Bougainville, Cape Gloucester, Hollandia, Aitape, Geelvink Bay, Mindoro. The Japanese never did succeed in fathoming it."[51] Of course, it could only be used where you had strong naval support and a particular kind of island, one with a coastal plain and jungle-covered mountains; the coral atolls of the central Pacific, like Tarawa and Kwajalein, were another matter entirely. But the ability to recognize special conditions and adapt to them is what distinguishes a gifted general from the run of the mill, and what has earned Vandegrift his high place among the gifted.

Not everyone at first had confidence in Vandegrift's perimeter. Years later, Kelly Turner was still toying with the idea that the Marines should have gone on the "offensive" and chased after Japanese concentrations elsewhere on Guadalcanal. When Turner flew in on September 11, he brought with him a copy of a dispatch from Ghormley to Washington, indicating the imminence of a major Japanese attack, the meager resources for meeting it, and Ghormley's opinion that Guadalcanal could not be held. (Vandegrift handed the paper to his operations officer, who put it in his shirt pocket and carried it with him until the Army took over from the Marines three months later.) Then Turner broke out a bottle of Scotch and told Vandegrift that he did not share Ghormley's dire view.

But to Vandegrift's dismay, Turner was still contemplating thoughts of scattering reinforcements all over the island. The experience of an evening's "rest" on Guadalcanal persuaded him otherwise; for two hours that night, Japanese ships shelled the ridge nearby. "You know," Vandegrift later said, "Kelly thought we were 'trigger happy,' but when those shells began coming in he changed his mind. The Japanese made a Christian out of him. Before he left the next day, he told me he would bring the Seventh Marines up and land them wherever I wanted him to."[52]

A week later, Turner brought in a convoy of five transports and two supply ships—with carrier, cruiser, and destroyer escort—to anchor off

Lunga Point in the sound, by now known to Marines as "Sleepless Lagoon." They had come at heavy cost: Japanese submarines had caught them in the waters northwest of Espíritu Santo that sailors called "Torpedo Junction," destroyer *O'Brien* and battleship *North Carolina* had been badly damaged, and aircraft carrier *Wasp* was set incandescently afire and had to be sunk. (What Admiral Fletcher dreaded had come to pass; there was now only *one* American carrier, *Hornet,* left in the South Pacific.)

But Turner brought with him tanks, artillery, motor transport, medics, aviation ground crews, PX supplies (mysteriously including free contraceptives), and the 7th Marines, commanded by a colonel known as "Gentleman Jim," who came ashore wearing whipcord riding breeches and highly polished low-quarter shoes. (Vandegrift's face on observing this is said to have been a study; Gentleman Jim was soon sent home.) With them, too, came Chesty Puller, who asked to be told where the Japanese were. Someone handed him an elaborate map, which he held upside down. "Hell, I can't make head or tail of this," said Puller, "just show me where they are [and] let's go get 'em."[53]

Bit by bit, Admiral Turner's efforts to support Vandegrift had been bearing fruit. On September 1, Higgins boats loaded with men and gear had come in toward the beach and curious Marines had gone down to investigate. To their astonishment, out came "old" men in their forties, some with gray hair, which led to the obvious remarks: "Hey, pop, you get your wars mixed up or somethin'? They running out of men at home?" But the Marines' derision quickly turned to respect. This was the 6th Naval Construction Battalion, first to arrive of the Seabees (CBs), professionals at construction work who had volunteered for combat duty and before they were done would substantially remodel many islands in the Pacific. (The Seabees were the invention of Rear Admiral Ben Moreel, a man with little use for red tape, who had been discovered by Roosevelt in the Azores during World War 1 and appointed chief of yards and docks, over the heads of the bureau's own candidates.)

Among much else, the Seabees took over completion of Henderson Field, drained it, laid down Marston metal matting, made revetments for the aircraft, and started a second landing strip, followed by a third. They built roads, put concrete walls around the command post, replaced the Japanese bridge across the Lunga with a new one that could bear a medium tank, and made an oven out of an old Japanese safe (fresh bread!). They found a beached Japanese torpedo, disassembled it, and sent the parts home, which should have improved the quality of American torpedoes more than it did. They are also said to have conducted certain experiments in the fermenting and distilling of coconuts, which the official record does not show.

On October 13, scuttlebutt brought the strangest news of all: "The doggies are here. It's the straight dope. They're out in the bay." It was true: The Army had arrived. This was the 164th Infantry Regiment, a National Guard outfit from the Dakotas, Scandinavian-American farmers, "big burly men, a little slow on the uptake," wrote Fletcher Pratt. They came with lavish supplies by Guadalcanal standards, and a brisk trade developed in Japanese souvenirs. A "meat ball" flag went for a dozen Hershey bars, and when the Marines ran out of the authentic article they became adept at replenishing their flag supply.

Of necessity, the new arrivals were at the outset put into the line piecemeal to strengthen thinly spread Marine units, a fortunate arrangement in that their fighting qualities thus counted for the most and their lack of experienced leadership the least. They may have been slow to wrath, but they were formidable when aroused, and exceptionally heavy Japanese shelling on their second day ashore aroused them considerably. "An annoyed Swede"—Fletcher Pratt again—"is a very good fighting man indeed and this lot reached their peak irritation just as the occasion arrived." In the course of the next all-out Japanese assault, another Marine prejudice had to be abandoned. After the night of October 24, the correct form of address was no longer "doggie" but "soldier." Colonel Clifton B. Cates, USMC, composed a letter to Colonel Bryant Moore, USA. "The officers and men of the First Marines," he wrote, "salute you for a most wonderful piece of work. . . . We are honored to serve with a unit such as yours."[54]

IV

During mid-October, conditions on Guadalcanal became so desperate that on the twenty-fourth President Roosevelt intervened personally. "My anxiety about the southwest Pacific," he wrote to the Joint Chiefs, "is to make certain that every possible weapon gets into that area to hold Guadalcanal, and that having held it in this crisis that munitions and planes and crews are on the way to take advantage of our success. . . . I wish therefore that you would canvass over the weekend every possible temporary diversion of munitions that you will require for our active fronts and let me know what they are."[55] (The original, in Roosevelt's hand, drafted with Hopkins's help, is reproduced in Sherwood's *Roosevelt and Hopkins.*)

Stiff language, but one of the most positive and precise of his military directives of the war: *Hold Guadalcanal* and prepare to profit from success in so doing. Note the words "temporary diversion" (that is, don't fatally compromise long-term purposes) and "active fronts" (that is, don't forget where the bullets are flying). These were carefully chosen, as was the word "crisis," no exaggeration.

For Guadalcanal, October was the month of despair; the President's combination of determination and optimism was not widely shared. "It now appears that we are unable to control the sea in the Guadalcanal area . . . ," Admiral Nimitz, normally cheerful, reported on the fifteenth; "The situation is not hopeless but it is certainly critical." Secretary Knox, another congenital optimist, when asked at a press conference on the sixteenth whether he thought we could hold Guadalcanal, said he "would not make any prediction, but every man will give a good account of himself."[56]

A sea battle named after Cape Esperance on October 11–12, though tactically an American victory, had not prevented the Japanese from landing the major part of their 2d (Sendai) Division with its full equipment, including heavy guns that outranged the Americans'. They now at long last had forces on the island equal to those of the Marines and were planning a large-scale effort to recapture it. The day before Admiral Nimitz made his somber report was among the worst, one those who went through it called "the bombardment," as though there had been no other. Supplementing the routine air raids and artillery shelling, that night the Japanese brought in battleships *Kongo* and *Haruna,* and for an hour and a half, under the light of air-dropped flares, subjected the Americans to almost a thousand rounds of concentrated fire from fourteen-inch naval batteries, which throw a shell far larger and heavier than ground troops normally encounter.

To the Japanese crews who were watching, Henderson Field seemed to erupt in a sea of flame, and they shouted and cheered. On Guadalcanal, men hugged the shaking earth, aircraft and storehouses were shattered, fuel dumps exploded, a command post received a direct hit, forty-one died and many more were wounded. Some who survived "the bombardment" moaned and cried aloud in their sleep for months afterward. Next morning, out of ninety aircraft on Guadalcanal only forty-two could fly, and aviation gasoline was almost gone. Henderson Field, its metal matting ripped and torn, closed down. There was a limit to how much of this we could take.

From the Joint Chiefs' point of view, Roosevelt's was no easy request to answer. Available resources were stretched. The decision in July to invade North Africa in November had preempted troops, supplies, and transports, while Marshall and Arnold—with backing from Secretary Stimson—were as always sensitive to any reduction in the commitment of force to England for the eventual invasion of France. MacArthur in Australia, asked to help the beleaguered Marines, had taken the occasion to predict the worst, congratulate himself, snipe at the Navy, and ask for the moon.

MacArthur said that he could do no more, that what he had done so far was having a "vital effect," but that "unless the Navy accepts successfully the challenge of the enemy surface fleet," we must prepare "for possible disaster in the Solomons," after which "the entire Southwest

Pacific will be in gravest danger." Therefore he urged "that the entire resources of the United States be diverted temporarily to meet the critical situation; that shipping be made available from any source; that one corps be dispatched immediately; that all available heavy bombers be ferried here at once"[57]—in short, a total redirection of Allied strategy to his theater on his request; not likely. But Admiral Cooke, on King's staff, and Generals Handy and Deane, on Marshall's, must have spent a busy Sunday, for on Monday the separate Army and Navy replies were ready for the President.

They had already been doing much. Admiral King said that substantial forces were being reallocated: one battleship, six cruisers, two destroyers, and twenty-four submarines, plus torpedo boats and dive- and torpedo-bombers. General Marshall said that Army troops of the Americal Division in New Caledonia plus part of the 43d Division, totaling approximately fifteen thousand men, were "available for immediate reinforcement of Guadalcanal." In the air, three heavy bombardment squadrons under orders for Australia had been redirected, and a squadron of pursuit planes in Hawaii made available for transfer. Both he and King agreed, and Marshall explained in detail, that shipping was the main issue. Marshall sent his report to the President by way of Admiral Leahy, noting that he wished the Joint Chiefs could talk it over first. They all must have done so during the day, inasmuch as later that afternoon, on Roosevelt's authority, Leahy ordered the War Shipping Administration to "provide without delay twenty additional ships . . . for use in the South Pacific."[58]

General Vandegrift was then unaware of this presidential pressure on his behalf, but later, when he learned of it, he recorded his satisfaction at having "gained a powerful ally in my fight to save Guadalcanal." In his view, what Roosevelt had done was to override "the supreme strategy which was giving priority . . . to the European theater," an interpretation that of course needs some sifting to save the grain of truth in it. He also understood that the President had encouraged *Time* magazine to do a cover story on him, which in soldierly fashion he professed to like "because it seemed to bring the real meaning of the campaign home to the American public." After that, said Vandegrift, he "doubted if the authorities in Washington would permit us henceforth to continue operating on our only too familiar shoestring."[59]

There is every reason to believe that Guadalcanal was very much on Roosevelt's mind. His son James was fighting there, as a lieutenant colonel in the First Marine Raider Battalion. The surmise that the President had encouraged Admiral King to initiate the campaign in the first place is substantiated by the number of times he referred to it in communications, press conferences, and conversation. Not long after Captain McCrea brought him news in the Blue Ridge camp of the debacle at Savo Island, he cabled Stalin: "We have gained, I believe, a toehold in the Southwest

Pacific from which the Japanese will find it very difficult to dislodge us. We have had substantial naval losses there but the advantage gained was worth the sacrifice and we are going to maintain hard pressure on the enemy."

He made no such attempt to put a fine face on things later in October. Several days before his memorandum to the Joint Chiefs, he told the Pacific War Council of Allied representatives "that in the Solomons it was no use saying that we were not in a hole." The attack in August had been brilliantly carried out, he said, "but, looked at now, it seemed questionable whether it was not too far from a supply base to be permanently tenable . . . the Japanese had launched a major operation with far greater forces than we could put there or maintain." And on the twenty-fourth he cabled Churchill: "I have no additional news here about Guadalcanal but you of course know that we are hard pressed there."[60] Between August 1942 and November 1943 he commented on the Guadalcanal campaign at six separate press conferences, more often than he mentioned any other battle.

Nor did the President often discuss individual military actions with his civilian staff: Guadalcanal was the exception. In mid-August, when the landing had just taken place, his secretary Bill Hassett described Roosevelt's mood in his diary: "Worried about fight for Solomon Islands. Said that official communiqués are all right but that newspaper interpretations are too optimistic." On November 1, Hassett noted: "The President was really apprehensive about Guadalcanal Island and our losses there, particularly the loss of our fourth airplane carrier, announced last night by the Navy Department" (this was *Hornet*, sunk in the Battle of the Santa Cruz Islands on October 27). In July of the following year, Hassett wrote of the President, who was just finishing a late Sunday breakfast at Hyde Park: "Pleased with the news of another naval victory over the Japs in the Solomons; said he would talk with the Map Room in the White House as soon as he got downstairs for further details. . . . 'Our war of attrition is doing its work,' he said with satisfaction."[61]

"War of attrition" is a curious phrase for Roosevelt to have used, and he used it again at a press conference in November. Among readers of military history like himself, it is not always a term of approval, having closer ties to the tactics of a deadly head-on slugging match associated (not always correctly) with Ulysses S. Grant rather than with those of deft thrust-and-parry maneuvers associated (not always correctly) with Robert E. Lee. "Attrition" implies a willingness to let lives be lost, which may not be altogether creditable. To be consciously engaged in a war of attrition, as Hitler eventually was in Russia, can be close to an admission of strategic bankruptcy, or at best of inability to think of anything better to do. But this was not the case with Guadalcanal, and from his use of the phrase it appears that Roosevelt knew it.

Very much as Admiral King intended, we had found a place where

admirals were dead. But tactical success concealed strategic defeat. The U.S. Navy had succeeded in what it set out to do, the Japanese had failed. If any one action convinced them that further efforts to regain Guadalcanal were hopeless, this was it.

We and they had an objective in common—that is, we both intended to bring in reinforcements. But beyond that there was a vital difference. Since Cactus Air Force was the bar between their troops and dry land, the Japanese were under an obligation to eliminate Henderson Field once and for all, the Americans to forestall them. This time there would be no stinting on Japanese ground troops. They had eleven fast transports filled with 13,500 men of the Hiroshima Division and their equipment. Four battleships and two aircraft carriers, ample cruisers and destroyers, would cut a path for them. All were under the command of Admiral Yamamoto himself, in superbattleship *Yamato* at Truk.

The Japanese plan was as usual complex, with separated forces on interrelated missions. The American plan was simplicity itself: Convoy in the men and supplies with as many cruisers and destroyers as we had on hand. The 8th, Admiral Turner in overall command under Halsey, left Nouméa with four transports and a support group that eventually numbered five cruisers and eight destroyers, led by Rear Admiral Dan Callaghan. The 9th, Rear Admiral Norman Scott in cruiser *Atlanta,* sailed from Espíritu Santo with three attack cargo ships and four destroyers. All had closed Lunga Point by the twelfth, but word from a coastwatcher of bombers coming south caused Turner to break off unloading and get his ships under way, which he did so skillfully that none was lost and all but one of the attackers were removed from the sky, by antiaircraft and by Wildcats from Henderson Field.

Now Turner had news of two Japanese battleships, four to six cruisers, and ten to twelve destroyers, coming down from the north. There was nothing for it but to send away the transports (this time 90 percent emptied) and order Callaghan and Scott, outnumbered and outgunned, to block the Japanese, who would be trying to repeat the performance of *Kongo* and *Haruna* in October and unlimber their wide-mouth guns on the airfield. Callaghan and Scott, on the night of Friday the thirteenth, accomplished this desperate mission.

At ten o'clock, Uncle Dan Callaghan bade Turner "bon voyage" over the TBS (talk between ships) voice radio and turned his five cruisers and eight destroyers to face the coming foe. "Austere, modest, deeply religious . . . There was something a little detached about this man," writes Admiral Morison. He formed his force in line, cruisers in the center, destroyers divided fore and aft, and here he may have erred, for the ships that mounted up-to-date radar were not in the lead; his flagship, *San Francisco,* was comparatively blind, and this would be fatal in a fight where everything depended on surprise, on who fired first. At 1:24, radar on *Helena* reported contact with the Japanese, reconfirmed at 1:30; the two forces were closing at forty knots and with every minute the American advantage dropped toward zero. The Japanese came on oblivious, but at 1:41 their lead destroyer, *Yudachi,* almost crossed the path of American destroyer *Cushing,* and too many precious moments had ticked away before Callaghan gave the order to open fire.

So began what Admiral Morison called "the wildest, most desperate sea fight since Jutland." Ships of opposing nationality mingled together, barely avoiding collisions; nobody quite knew which target to fire at or when. A Japanese searchlight would blink open and bathe American ships in an eerie glow that signaled shells and torpedoes on the way. *Atlanta* sent round after round into the Japanese, but they responded in kind, and Admiral Scott and all but one with him on the bridge were killed. Morison called it "fifteen minutes of raw hell," and his description of it beggars imitation:

"The greenish light of suspended star shell dimmed the stars overhead. Elongated red and white trails of shell tracers arched and crisscrossed, magazines exploding in blinding bouquets of white flame, oil-fed conflagrations sent up twisted yellow columns. Dotting the horizon were the dull red glows of smoldering hulls, now obscured by dense masses of smoke, now blazing up when uncontrolled fires reached new combustibles. The sea itself, fouled with oil and flotsam, tortured by underwater upheavals, rose in geysers from shell explosions."[67]

Around 2:00 A.M., the adversaries disengaged, and the stricken survivors limped apart. Daylight revealed eight crippled ships, five of them American, scattered in disorder between Savo Island and Guadalcanal. On the starboard side of the flag bridge of *San Francisco* they found the body of Dan Callaghan, a trail of cigarettes leading from an opened pack in his hand to the emergency cabin, whence he had come forward when battle was joined and the furies descended. But he had saved Henderson Field.

There was to be only the briefest of interludes; the Japanese were far from finished. Another major force of theirs was yet to be heard from, and it arrived the following night, the fourteenth, consisting of Vice-Admiral Nobutake Kondo with battleship *Kirishima,* five cruisers, and nine destroyers. This time there was no blocking force in place, no Scotts or Callaghans there to stop him. Patrolling off Guadalcanal that evening was the sum total of three PT (motor torpedo) boats, gnats to an elephant.

The surface of the sound was calm, a quarter-moon was settling, and across the water—instead of the island's normally foul smell—came an odor vaguely suggestive of honeysuckle. There were shapes looming out there and the PTs could be heard exchanging alerts on the TBS. "There go two big ones, but I don't know whose they are," said one. "Let's slip the bum a pickle," said another (i.e., a torpedo). Suddenly out of the clear came words as dramatic as any scriptwriter could have contrived:

"Refer your big boss about Ching Lee. Chinese, catchee? Call off your boys."[68]

Ching Lee. Big boss Vandegrift knew the nickname. That would be Rear Admiral Willis Augustus Lee, Annapolis '08, commanding Task Force 64 with *Washington* and *South Dakota*.

Battleships.

So the boys scurried out of the way, Ching Lee came on through, and soon the Marines on Guadalcanal heard American guns speak with a louder voice than they had heard before. Halsey had sent in the battleships despite doctrine that deplored their use in narrow waters, where they lacked sea room to maneuver. There was a tangle of destroyers in which the Americans were badly mauled, but then the big ones met in a battlewagon duel straight out of the textbooks, one of the few such of the war. *South Dakota* was mangled topside but stayed afloat and managed to withdraw under its own power. *Washington* was unscathed. Nine sixteen-inch shells and scores of five-inch from *Washington* hit home on *Kirishima*, wrecking the steering gear, damaging the engines, and setting many fires; after midnight her captain ordered Abandon Ship, the departing crew opened the seacocks, and she sank off Savo as Kondo gave up thoughts of bombarding any airfield and withdrew.

Meanwhile, what of the Japanese transports? Once again, with *Hornet* gone, there was only one American carrier left in the South Pacific, and Halsey had used it with care. This was *Enterprise*, in a task force under Rear Admiral Thomas C. Kinkaid, from which Lee had been detached for his spectacular running charge at Kondo. *Enterprise* had a jammed forward elevator, left over from damage at Santa Cruz, and was functioning at something less than customary dash, but her Wildcats and Avengers had immobilized battleship *Hiei* (which later sank), dealt a mortal blow to cruiser *Kinugasa*, and heavily wounded three other cruisers and a destroyer before they came upon Admiral Raizo Tanaka and the eleven transports, at midday of the fourteenth, coming down The Slot.[69]

What followed can only be called a massacre. *Enterprise* pilots, joined by Marines, shuttled to and from Henderson Field, which became a tense and furious turnaround point for fueling and rearming the planes. Kinkaid sent off everything that *Enterprise* had, and when they were done, only four of the eleven troopships were still steaming on their way toward Guadalcanal.

The other seven had literally been blown apart. Kondo insanely ordered Tanaka to continue, to beach and unload the remainder, and there the next morning Cactus Air Force found them and came in low on what were soon blazing hulks. Perhaps two thousand Japanese got ashore, with 260 cases of ammunition and 1,500 bags of rice, more a liability than an asset to their compatriots.

Vandegrift, who in moments of impatience had sometimes wondered how hard the Navy would fight, sent a dispatch to Halsey: "We believe the enemy has suffered a crushing defeat—We thank Lee for his sturdy effort of last night—We thank Kinkaid for his intervention yesterday . . . but our greatest homage goes to Scott, Callaghan and their men who with magnificent courage against seemingly hopeless odds drove back the first hostile stroke and made success possible."[70] Only hours later did Vandegrift learn that Scott, Callaghan, and seven hundred Navy officers and men had perished in that endeavor.

"We've got the bastards licked!" said Halsey to his staff when the reports came in. In Washington, President Roosevelt, urged by Sherwood and others to say that the tide had been turned, resisted raising hopes, but he did tell the *Herald Tribune* forum on the seventeenth: "it would now seem that the turning point in this war has at last been reached." There was good news not only from the Solomons but from Papua, from North Africa, and from Stalingrad. In London, Winston Churchill called it not "the beginning of the end" but "the end of the beginning." Lying badly wounded in the Marine hospital at Lunga Point, Chesty Puller heard that the big Japanese convoy had been smashed and knew that the battle for Guadalcanal had been won.[71]

V

After a while, everybody on Guadalcanal got to be a little flaky. One lieutenant put on his dress uniform and stood by the side of the road, saying he was waiting for the Poughkeepsie bus, until other men shyly came up to him with names and phone numbers, asking him to call home when he got there. Another man carried on conversations with an imaginary dog, which so annoyed his buddies that he was summoned to the company dugout, where the first sergeant raged at him, "Now don't bring that flea-hound of yours in here or my bull-dog will chew its damned head off!" and the conversations stopped.

It wasn't just the war, it was Guadalcanal: the rain, the mud, the humid air in which nothing ever dried out and clothing rotted, the abundant animal and insect life underfoot, and in the trees strange birds that would now and then emit an unearthly screech. Flies attracted by the Japanese corpses were so thick that you had to brush them off the food with one hand while eating with the other. Then there was disease: malaria and dengue fever, jaundice and dysentery, fungus and tropical ulcers that ate away the flesh.

Men turned inward on themselves, turned tribal and clannish, each to his own squad or platoon. If for two months you had been in the same foxhole by the same river on the same ridge and had survived—well, you didn't exactly feel like leaving it, even if you had the strength.

opening for the charge that the Marines were "duplicating" the Army and could without loss be abolished. In some quarters there was surprising bitterness. A lingering resentment left over from World War I prompted even the normally levelheaded George Marshall to remark, "I am going to see that the Marines never win another war." Through all this Vandegrift held his course and his temper, knowing that the Marines' best defense was their record and that he needed only to recount it. Secretary of the Navy Forrestal, for whom Vandegrift had unmatched respect, told him that the photograph of the flag being raised on Iwo Jima would alone ensure the continued existence of the Marine Corps for five hundred years.[78]

Vandegrift adapted himself to giving and attending dinners, making speeches (a chore for such an undemonstrative man), and testifying before Congress. In late December 1944, he persuaded President Roosevelt to visit Camp Lejeune in North Carolina. "He loved excursions of this nature," wrote Vandegrift. "Inevitably his spirits rose when he left Washington." Roosevelt told Vandegrift that he still thought the base should have been located somewhere else, but privately he told Ross McIntire that the Marines should be proud of Camp Lejeune. McIntire told Vandegrift that he had never seen the President more enthusiastic about a military installation.[79]

On February 4, Vandegrift was summoned to the White House and there, with his wife and son attending, the President pinned on his tunic the Congressional Medal of Honor and read aloud the citation: "His tenacity, courage and resourcefulness prevailed against a strong, determined and experienced enemy, and the gallant fighting spirit of the men under his inspiring leadership enabled them to withstand aerial, land and sea bombardment to surmount all obstacles. . . ."

From time to time, Vandegrift saw Roosevelt at official functions, but the last exchange of words they had was in January 1945, after a White House dinner, when host and guests retired to a drawing room. "He relaxed easier than most men," Vandegrift wrote, "but there was no missing the fatigued and drawn face." For a few moments the general and the President sat together on a sofa, reminiscing about the old days, with the Marines, in Haiti.[80]

VI

MACARTHUR

ONE DAY IN AUGUST 1932, two months after the Democratic party in its convention in Chicago had nominated him for President, Governor Roosevelt of New York was sitting at lunch in Albany with friends and family. A phone call came from Senator Huey Long of Louisiana, who began a tirade so loud the others could not help but overhear. Roosevelt was betraying the people who nominated him, said Long; he was consorting with Wall Street types like Bernard Baruch and Owen D. Young. The governor heard him out, with a generous application of hearty bonhomie. "It's all very well for us to laugh over Huey," he said after hanging up. "But actually we have to remember all the time that he really is one of the two most dangerous men in the country." Who was the other? a listener asked. Father Coughlin?

"Oh, no," said Roosevelt. "The other is Douglas MacArthur."

The governor elaborated on what he meant. Not far beneath the surface of American life, given the stress of economic collapse and the threat of public disorder, he felt there was a latent sense that democracy had run its course, that the totalitarians had a point, and that some measure of liberty would have to be sacrificed to strong leadership. Sentiments of this kind were to be heard among prominent industrialists and at business gatherings. (In this Roosevelt was correct; he might have added Congress and a number of national magazines, where demands for dictatorship and martial law were also being aired.) All that was lacking was the familiar figure of the man on horseback, a symbol for the Fascist-minded among Americans to rally around, and who better qualified for this role —who came better equipped with charm, tradition, and majestic appearance—than Douglas MacArthur? "We must tame these fellows," said Roosevelt, "and make them useful to us."[1]

Roosevelt and MacArthur had first come to know one another fifteen

305

years earlier, when the former as assistant secretary of the Navy and the latter as a major from the War Department had worked together on economic mobilization. MacArthur had been appointed Chief of Staff by President Herbert Hoover in 1930 and had labored conscientiously to defend the Army and its appropriations during a period of deepening depression and widespread pacifism. But the incident that truly made his name one to conjure with on the political far right—and that prompted Roosevelt's remarks—was the so-called Battle of Anacostia Flats, when in July of that same year MacArthur and troops under his command had dispersed a group of unemployed veterans who had marched on Washington.

They called themselves the Bonus Expeditionary Force, drawn to the capital by the vain hope of persuading Congress to vote them immediately a bonus that had been promised them for 1945. They numbered at their peak some fifteen thousand, camped with wives and children in shacks, packing cases, and secondhand army pup tents on the marshy flats across the Anacostia River. They were for the most part peaceable; the Communists who attempted to take them over had failed repeatedly but finally did succeed in provoking a scuffle with police that gave President Hoover and Secretary of War Patrick Hurley the excuse to invoke military force. MacArthur complied, with more enthusiasm than his superiors had in mind.

His several hundred infantry and cavalry (and a handful of irrelevant light tanks) used tear gas and weapons at the ready to drive about three thousand members of the B.E.F. down Pennsylvania Avenue and past the Capitol. (The veterans had no arms and defended themselves with brickbats and profanity.) There had been no injuries, as MacArthur proudly told a reporter, and this might have continued to be so if only MacArthur had been willing to leave well enough alone. Secretary of War Hurley twice sent him the message that President Hoover did not want him to pursue the B.E.F. across the Eleventh Street bridge over the Anacostia. "In neither instance," wrote one of MacArthur's staff officers, Major Dwight D. Eisenhower, "did General MacArthur hear these instructions. He said he was too busy and did not want either himself or his staff bothered by people coming down and pretending to give orders."[2]

After several hours' interlude of warning, MacArthur, in disregard of the wishes of his Commander in Chief, ordered his men to cross the river. They drove the B.E.F. from its shantytown, which caught fire and burned with a glow visible across the city, while the veterans and their families fled into the night. (Many homes in nearby towns were opened to them.) Believing that this "was the focus of the world today," MacArthur then took another unnecessary step. Against the advice of Major Eisenhower, he issued a statement to the press.

He said that no one had been seriously injured. Not strictly so: One man had his ear cut off by a cavalry saber; a seven-year-old boy who ran back for his pet rabbit was bayoneted in the leg; two score more were hurt by bricks, clubs, bayonets, and sabers; and an eleven-week-old baby exposed to the tear gas died. MacArthur said that they were not really veterans, he thought probably no more than 10 percent of them were. Not so: An extensive check of the B.E.F. by the Veterans Bureau concluded that 94 percent of them were *bona fide.* He said that the "mob down there was a bad-looking mob . . . animated by the essence of revolution," and that they were about to take over the government. "Had [the President] let it go another week," said MacArthur, "I believe that the institutions of our Government would have been severely threatened."[3]

If this forecast had any substance whatever, it has escaped the attention of historians who have studied the episode since. These were bewildered, hungry, unarmed men and women seeking help; the violence directed at them was wholly uncalled for, far out of proportion to any threat they posed. MacArthur magnified their hostility in order to justify his own. In his comments to reporters he could not resist a rhetorical flourish: "I have released in my day more than one community which had been held in the grip of a foreign enemy." What communities and what foreign enemies he was referring to, his biographer has been unable to discover. "These remarks were destined to sear his reputation for years to come," writes Clayton James in *The Years of MacArthur.* "I think," added Eisenhower, "this meeting [with the press] led to the prevailing impression that General MacArthur himself had undertaken and directed the move against the veterans and that he was acting as something more than the agent of civilian authorities."[4]

The taming of Douglas MacArthur went on over many years, but it began not long after a new President took office. Hoover's last budget had cut the Army back, but the Roosevelt administration proposed to cut it even further. MacArthur and the new secretary of war, George Dern (former governor of Utah), went to the President in an attempt to get the cuts restored. Dern argued that with Germany rearming and Japan becoming aggressive, it would be "a fatal error" to economize on defense, and MacArthur said the country's safety was at stake, but Roosevelt poured scorn on them.

Emotionally exhausted, MacArthur said "something to the general effect that when we lost the next war, and an American boy, lying in the mud with an enemy bayonet through his belly and an enemy foot on his dying throat, spat out his last curse, I wanted the name not to be MacArthur, but Roosevelt." The latter turned livid with rage, and shouted, "You must not talk that way to the President!" MacArthur realized at once he had been at fault, apologized, offered his resignation, and turned to leave. As he reached the door, Roosevelt, self-composure quite restored, said, "Don't be foolish, Douglas; you and the budget must get together on this."[5] MacArthur, sometimes subject to fits of nausea, was physically ill on the White House steps outside.

Contrary to expectations, Roosevelt did not replace MacArthur as Chief of Staff but kept him on for an additional year. There were complex reasons for this (he told Jim Farley that he wanted to eliminate MacArthur's candidate for successor by letting the man become a year too old for the job), but the extension did have the effect of allowing MacArthur to put through a better appropriation and thus go out on a note of triumph. He had been accustomed to have his own way in the War Department and, according to one account, was not pleased to discover that Roosevelt "would be no mere nominal Commander-in-Chief, but would exert the final authority in regard to the peacetime Army."[6]

Once it was established who was master, however, the President showed no inclination to undercut the general's successful cultivation of Congress for his budget and in fact gave MacArthur many indications of trust and confidence. "Tame these fellows, and make them useful to us." At one point he invited the general to dinner at Hyde Park and offered him the post of high commissioner of the Philippines, which MacArthur would have accepted if the affair had not become a political hassle that caused the President to renege. Roosevelt read his man aright. He would ask MacArthur to the White House for informal chats and sound him out on varied matters, including New Deal legislation, that had nothing to do with the military. Why was this? MacArthur asked. "Douglas," said the President, "you are my American conscience."[7]

Waving flags. Organ tones. Fade.

◆

Douglas MacArthur's first conscious memory was the sound of bugles. He was born on an Army post in Little Rock, Arkansas, in 1880, of a father who had won the Congressional Medal of Honor in the charge up Missionary Ridge at Chattanooga—one of the most gallant and headstrong assaults by the Federals in the Civil War—and a mother four of whose brothers were Confederate veterans (several shunned the wedding). Arthur MacArthur led a brigade in the Philippine insurrection of 1899, rose to command a division, and later became a lieutenant general; those who knew both said that so far as ego was concerned, he almost matched his son. It never occurred to young Douglas that he would be anything but a soldier; the Army was his home and the military panoply, the regalia and the accoutrements, never lost their romance for him. He stood first in his class at West Point and his devotion to the corps, to the "Long Gray Line," was lifelong. "In the evening of my memory," he told the assembled cadets six decades later, "always I come back to West Point."[8]

In World War I, MacArthur's record was outstanding. He went to France a colonel as Chief of Staff of the 42d (Rainbow) Division, the first

American division to take over a sector of the front on its own (near Baccarat). MacArthur was promoted to brigadier, the youngest in the Army, and to command of the 42d's 84th Brigade. During the Champagne-Marne defensive he was awarded his second Silver Star (eventually he won seven of them, an A.E.F. record, in addition to two Distinguished Service Crosses, the Distinguished Service Medal, two Purple Hearts, and a number of French decorations). The Rainbow was in the line 162 days and suffered 14,683 casualties; the Germans rated it one of the few American divisions on a par with the elite of the British and the French. MacArthur was recommended for promotion to major general and, the day before the Armistice, was made commander of the division. He came out of the war with a reputation as one of the few general officers who actually accompanied their troops into action. On returning to Washington in 1919, he was told, to his surprise, he would be the new superintendent of West Point.[9]

By this time he had already manifested many of the characteristics that were to mark him in later life. His acute sensitivity on points of personal honor had shown itself at West Point when he was a cadet and challenged (successfully) a professor who refused to grant him an exam exemption he thought he deserved. He was reluctant to undertake assignments he did not like (as a lieutenant of engineers in Milwaukee in 1907 he was absent from duty so often his superior reported this to the War Department) and he indulged an idiosyncratic taste in uniforms (in France in 1918, he removed the wire grommet from his service cap—as Air Force pilots did in World War II, the "fifty-mission crush"—and wore a brightly colored sweater with a knit muffler). He bridled under criticism and took it personally. After a dressing-down from Pershing no different from Pershing's normal practice, MacArthur wondered aloud what Pershing had against him, perhaps some ancient grudge against his father? (MacArthur conceived the idea that a "Pershing faction" was persecuting him and later associated George Marshall with it.[10])

As West Point superintendent he was regarded as a liberal reformer. He tried to modernize the curriculum, to give cadets more freedom, to broaden their horizons by bringing in guest lecturers, and even to eliminate the worst excesses from the hazing of plebes by upperclassmen. He ordered each professor to spend at least a month a year visiting civilian institutions of higher learning. He would periodically visit classrooms and afterward make suggestions on how to improve teaching methods. All this was much resented by the elder faculty, with whom he had little in common but devotion to the football team. The old guard wanted to train technical specialists, MacArthur wanted generalists; MacArthur wanted more contact with the outside world, they wanted less. MacArthur suspected that whatever he had accomplished would be discarded as soon as he departed and this proved true, though in the long run the times were on his side. "Slowly his innovations would be restored, his ideas accepted," writes one historian. His biographer found that among West Pointers MacArthur was generally credited with bringing the academy into the twentieth century.[11]

As Chief of Staff he had less success. Under his administration the Army reached rock bottom in numbers and budget. Yet this was hardly his fault. In the climate of the early 1930s it would have taken a miracle worker to wring money out of Congress for the military, and for all MacArthur's eloquence, he could not manage a miracle. He tried to protect the personnel, the officers and men, their pay and allowances, with the result that development of new weapons suffered. MacArthur disbanded the experimental armored force that had been organized by Major Adna Chaffee at Fort Meade. He opposed extra funds for the Air Corps and said of military aviation in 1932 that "its value as an instrument of war was still undemonstrated[!]" He thought more could be done "for economy and for civilization" by giving up army and navy aviation entirely. The mobilization plans drawn up during his tenure failed to take technological progress into account and were accordingly useless when war came, though MacArthur did argue for giving "educational" orders to manufacturers and for stockpiling critical raw materials, again without result.

During this period his politics seemed to have been neither especially intense nor extensive; they followed the upper-middle-class norms of the time, those of a conservative Hoover Republican. His deeply held convictions were moral and patriotic rather than political, though there was in him a streak of midwestern populism that surfaced from time to time, to the surprise of opponents and supporters alike. (Clayton James aptly remarks that MacArthur and the Populists shared "a phobia toward Europe in general and Great Britain in particular.") He disliked the New Deal and was visibly uncomfortable in the atmosphere it brought to Washington. "No one spoke his language," said a friend. "No one wanted to." Secretary Ickes thought MacArthur a toplofty type and said it gave him "a great kick to . . . break the news" to the Chief of Staff that the President had denied some of his budget requests.[12] It must have come as a relief both to MacArthur and to Roosevelt when MacArthur departed for the Philippines in October 1935 to be military adviser to the Philippine Commonwealth.

He is frequently described as possessing a brilliant mind, though the signs of this are to be seen mainly in his West Point record and the testimony of observers (like Hap Arnold) whose own modest mental pretensions predisposed them to be generous. MacArthur had a fluent and rhetorical intelligence rather than a probing or analytical one; if an idea could be warped into language it became valid for him. He had an excellent memory and a well-stocked fund of verbal ornaments like anecdotes and quotations, but vast stretches of the contemporary universe of discourse were a blank to him. In its essentials his range was narrow and his interest short in subjects other than military history, athletics, nationalist lore, and the background of events against which he saw himself projected. He had no small talk, no gift for the dialogue of give-and-take, no use for the company of equals. These are intellectual limitations. His natural instrument was the monologue, often lengthy, and in it he unquestionably excelled. All witnesses agree as to the power of his personality and his ability in conversation, preferably one on one, to make a formidable impression. No doubt about it: He could charm the most disinclined listener.

The instigation of his appointment as military adviser came from Philippine president Manuel Quezon, who was in an unenviable position. The commonwealth had been promised complete independence by 1946, at which time it would find itself alone in a hostile world, and until then no one in the War Department seriously believed (and MacArthur well knew this) that the islands could be saved in the event of a war with Japan. In 1938, Quezon made a supposedly secret trip to Tokyo in which he was suspected of having sought Japanese recognition of Philippine neutrality (Quezon denied this). Quezon needed MacArthur as a visible token of American military commitment. MacArthur, having reached the top of his profession, faced the dreary alternatives of either retiring at fifty-five or accepting a lowlier command. The post of military adviser would be prestigious and well paid (his combined salaries would be greater than those of either the Philippine president or the high commissioner). As for President Roosevelt, it can reasonably be surmised that he took no dissatisfaction in getting MacArthur safely out of the country. Everybody came out ahead.

MacArthur's affection for the Philippines was genuine and of long standing. He had served there as a young lieutenant in 1903, when he first met Quezon, a recent law school graduate. In 1928, MacArthur returned to Manila as a brigadier general and commanded the Philippine Department, leaving only to become Chief of Staff. Between 1928 and 1930, his friendship with Quezon deepened and he developed a warm acquaintanceship with the then-governor general, Henry L. Stimson. His days in the islands passed pleasantly. On his departure he was given a dinner at the Manila Hotel by Quezon, Manuel Roxas, and other governmental leaders and was highly praised. "Leaving the Philippines," he said in response, "is severing the threads of connections which have linked me with this country for thirty years. During that span of time the world has changed more rapidly than in any other period, and one of the notable features of that change is the shift of the center of interest from the Atlantic to the Pacific."[13]

This MacArthur profoundly believed. During World War II, when his insistence on the importance of the Pacific had such obvious overtones of self-interest, it often went unnoticed how long he had held such views and whence they came. He was that rarity among Americans, a truly Far Eastern–oriented man. In 1905–1906, MacArthur had accompanied his father as an aide (his mother came too) on an eight-month, twenty-thousand-mile mission to inspect military installations in Japan, Malaya, Java, Burma, India, Siam, and China. They traveled twelve hundred miles in the interior of Java by train and carriage, went by river-boat up the Irrawaddy in Burma as far as the Chinese border, in India journeyed northward to the Himalayas and the Khyber Pass, and in Bangkok were treated like visiting royalty. (MacArthur replaced a fuse when the lights went out during a royal banquet and barely avoided being decorated on the spot.) Later MacArthur said of this tour that "the experience was without doubt the most important factor of preparation in my entire life. . . . It was crystal clear to me that the future and, indeed, the very existence of America were irrevocably entwined with Asia and its island outposts."[14]

MacArthur's nature alternated between exhilaration and despair. "He was conspicuous in the matter of temperament," said George Marshall, in one of the few comments on MacArthur that Marshall seems ever to have made. The prospect of defending the Philippines aroused MacArthur's enthusiasm; therefore it was not only possible but certain to enjoy fortune's favor. "General," Quezon asked him, "do you think that the Philippines, once independent, can defend itself?" MacArthur replied: "I don't *think* that the Philippines can defend themselves. I *know* they can." MacArthur's plan was for a force of 11,000 regulars, a five-and-a-half-month training period annually for 40,000 citizen soldiers, a fleet of fifty torpedo boats, and an air force of 250 planes. This was expected to cost $8 million a year and produce an adequate defense at the end of a decade; "in the world today," MacArthur told Quezon, "there is no other defensive system that provides an equal security at remotely comparable cost to the people maintaining it."[15]

◆

MacArthur's thinking was not then applauded in Washington. Contingency plans of 1936 against the possibility of war with Japan provided for the Army to defend Manila Bay (i.e., the island of Corregidor at the harbor entrance) until the Navy worked its way across the central Pacific with reinforcements, which might require two to three years. This scenario was revised in 1938 to retain the defense of Manila Bay but omit any reference to reinforcements or the time they might take to get there, a tacit admission that the planners had decided the Philippine position was untenable. Congress in 1939, as we have seen, rejected a proposal to fortify Guam in the Marianas, a vaunted guarantee of Philippine immunity to attack, on the grounds that this would offend the Japanese. "The nation would not abandon the Philippines," reads the Army history, "but neither would it grant the Army and Navy the funds to ensure their defense."[16] This was the vacuum MacArthur was seeking to fill; it is to be wondered not that he failed but only that he thought he could succeed. By the fall of 1941, astonishingly, he had managed to bring around many in the War Department to join in his optimism.

The reason for their turnaround was not only that he insisted so strongly but that air power had shifted the apparent balance of strength. In September 1941, a squadron of nine B-17s under Major (later General) Emmett "Rosie" O'Donnell had flown from Hawaii to Manila by way of Midway, Wake Island, New Guinea, and Australia—the first flight of land-based bombers across the Pacific, accomplished with primitive service facilities and inadequate weather information, a convincing demonstration that the Philippines could be reinforced by air.[17] The buildup continued until the Air Corps had more modern aircraft in the Philippines than anywhere else and MacArthur had persuaded the War Department and the Joint Board to accept a revision of their plans to include his own more aggressive ideas. He intended not merely to hold a "citadel" at Manila Bay but to make an active defense on the beaches of all the islands in the Philippines. "The strength and composition of the defense forces projected here," he wrote to Washington, "are believed to be sufficient to accomplish such a mission." In September, he had declined the offer of a national guard division, saying that with the one U.S. division he had and the ten Philippine he was mobilizing, he did not need it.[18]

The capabilities of air bombardment were at that time vastly overrated. At a secret briefing of Washington correspondents in November 1941, a War Department official assured them that our position in the Philippines was "highly favorable," that we were preparing not only to defend the commonwealth but to conduct an air offensive and set the "paper" cities of Japan on fire.[19] That our bombers were in fact highly vulnerable was obvious to Air Corps officers on Luzon, but they lacked the means to do much about it. Antiaircraft was almost nonexistent, there was no radar, and communications were primitive. There were not enough pursuit planes and they had no oxygen for fighting at high altitude.

At Clark Field north of Manila, the major base, attempts had been made to secure construction equipment for making dispersal pens, but to no avail. An RAF officer who visited in the spring from Singapore pointed out that lack of dispersal was our greatest weakness and that in his opinion a sudden air attack, pressed with determination, could virtually wipe out our air force on Luzon. The B-17s themselves were early versions, without the power turrets, heavier armor, and tail guns of later models, and had difficulty protecting themselves when they flew (as they had to) in small numbers. The pilots might just as well, said Rosie O'Donnell, "have been flying spotted ponies."[20]

MacArthur's sanguine mood was no different from that of most

Americans who underestimated the Japanese, merely more sanguine. The correspondent John Hersey visited him in May 1941, to be told that "if Japan entered the war, the Americans, the British and the Dutch could handle her with about half the forces they now have deployed." The Philippine situation "looks sound," with twelve Filipino divisions already trained. A war between Japan and America was unlikely because Japan was helping Germany more by tying down Allied forces than she would by engaging them.[21] When MacArthur was recalled to active service in July and appointed commander of U.S. Army Forces in the Far East, he cabled Marshall his thanks to Stimson and the President, and went on: "I would like to assure you that I am confident of the successful accomplishment of the assigned mission." Shown this by Pa Watson, Roosevelt said he was "very much pleased." On September 9, an assurance followed from MacArthur that "the development of a completely adequate defense force will be rapid."[22]

MacArthur's return to duty was in part his own doing. On March 21, he had written to White House secretary Steve Early, a longtime admirer of his, offering his services "to the President." Early replied on April 14 that Roosevelt, on being told of the offer, said, "Isn't that fine? It's just what I would expect Douglas MacArthur to do," and the next day Pa Watson, another admirer, wrote MacArthur that as for the Far East, Roosevelt "wants you there in your military capacity rather than any other." MacArthur answered: "This would naturally be my choice and I am gratified beyond words that that is his decision." Stimson and Marshall talked it over, and on June 20 Marshall wrote MacArthur that Stimson "at the proper time . . . will recommend to the President that you be so appointed," that is, as Army commander in the Far East. "It is my impression," Marshall added, "that the President will approve [this] recommendation"—and so he did, when Japan's intended southward moves became known, the following month. "The Secretary of War and I were highly pleased," Marshall radioed MacArthur the week before Pearl Harbor, "to receive your report that your command is ready for any eventuality."[23]

MacArthur and his second wife (his first marriage had not worked out) lived in an air-conditioned penthouse atop the Manila Hotel. From the dining room and its terraces there were striking views of the waterfront and of Manila Bay, with the harbor and Bataan peninsula beyond, in the often-magnificent sunsets. If Douglas MacArthur ever came to rest in his peripatetic life, he did so here; here in the Philippines was his finding place. Here was his library of seven to eight thousand volumes, mostly history and biography, notably about the Civil War. Here he settled into his consistent but unusual working habits. His aide, Major Eisenhower, said that MacArthur would arrive at the office about eleven, stay until two, return about three-thirty, go home two hours later, but sometimes come back in the evening—and this was repeated seven days a week. Here, on

February 21, 1938, was born his son, Arthur, the joy of his days, who remained with him through much of the war. His ties to the Philippines, and to their president Manuel Quezon, became so firm and abiding that his biographer finds much of the rest of his life incomprehensible apart from them.[24]

In later years it developed that the relationship between Quezon and MacArthur had been far more complex than was imagined. In 1979, a doctoral candidate at Rutgers, Carol M. Petrillo, published the incredible but thoroughly documented discovery that Quezon, on January 3, 1942, one month into the war, had given MacArthur personally a half-million dollars out of the Philippine treasury (three staff officers—Sutherland, Richard Marshall, and Huff—got sums totaling $140,000). MacArthur was at that time receiving an $18,000 salary and $15,000 in allowances from the Philippine Commonwealth in addition to his suite in the Manila Hotel and his pension as a U.S. major general. The transfer was arranged by the Chase Bank with the assurance that the President of the United States and the secretary of war had been informed. (Secretary Ickes also knew about it and complained sourly in his diary.) The whole affair was conducted with the utmost discretion; none of the principals involved (except for Ickes) ever committed any comment to paper beyond the flowery text of the executive order in which Quezon made the gifts and expressed his country's gratitude to MacArthur and the military mission: "the record of their services is interwoven forever into the national fate of our people," etc.

Army regulations then as now state that "every member of the Military Establishment, when subject to military law, is bound to refrain from [acceptance] of a substantial loan or gift or any emolument from a person or firm with whom it is the officer's duty as an agent of the government to carry on negotiations." What can have possessed them all, President and secretary of war included? The entire transaction was appallingly improper; if it had come to light, the impact on all concerned would have been enormous. The unanswered questions fall all over themselves in the asking: Did MacArthur actually believe there was no impropriety? Would he have answered, if asked, that he acted as a Philippine and not an American officer? Why did Roosevelt and Stimson allow it? Did they feel they had an angry and unruly general on their hands who needed pacifying? How much effect was there on MacArthur's subsequent favoring of Quezon's departure to Australia? What was the role of Manuel Roxas, who countersigned the order as Philippine treasurer and later received much-needed support from MacArthur in his campaign to become Quezon's successor? We will never know.[25]

On June 20, 1942, Quezon appeared in General Eisenhower's office in Washington and offered him a similar honorarium. Eisenhower, exercising as much sensitivity as he could to the importance of gifts in the Far East, politely but firmly declined it.[26]

II

At twelve-forty on December 8, 1941, fifty-four Japanese bombers from Formosa, in two V of Vs at eighteen thousand feet, one behind the other, appeared over Clark Field. They came in perfect order, as though on drill, and to intercept them only four pursuit P-40s managed to get aloft before the bombs began to fall with practiced accuracy. Afterward, through the fire and smoke, came Zero fighters to strafe with their 20-mm cannon the parked American aircraft. By the time the Japanese departed, Clark Field as a tactical air base had ceased to exist; as at Pearl Harbor ten hours earlier, the Japanese at a single stroke had removed one of the major obstacles to their southward advance. A hundred Americans were dead, more than twice that number wounded, and no plane left was fit to fly. Our air offensive capability in the Philippines—thirty-four B-17s, at that time the largest concentration of American heavy bombers in the world —had been cut in half. (The Japanese also raided Iba airfield to the north and totally destroyed it.) In the first day of the war, despite many hours' advance warning, the American air power in the Philippines from which so much was anticipated had been crippled beyond repair—"on the ground!" as President Roosevelt was to say incredulously, "on the ground!"[27]

So impervious to political criticism did General MacArthur become that the disaster at Clark Field was never officially investigated, never subjected to the exhaustive congressional examination lavished on Pearl Harbor, with the result that contradictory statements about what caused it were allowed to go unchallenged. General Lewis H. Brereton, the Air Corps officer in command, said that MacArthur's chief of staff, General Richard K. Sutherland, called around 4:00 A.M. to tell Brereton the fleet at Pearl Harbor had been bombed and a state of war existed between the United States and Japan. (7:55 A.M. December 7 Hawaiian time was 2:55 A.M. December 8 Manila time.)

Brereton reported in person to MacArthur's headquarters around 5:00 A.M. and (he said) asked permission to make an attack on the Japanese Formosan bases after daylight with the B-17s on Clark Field, to be followed by more of them staged from Del Monte Field on Mindanao. He said he was told by Sutherland to proceed with preparations but to wait before loading bombs for MacArthur's authorization, which did not come until 11:00 A.M., too late to mount the mission before the Japanese preempted it. MacArthur after the war denied this. He said that no recommendation from Brereton to bomb Formosa had been received and that he knew "nothing of such a recommendation having been made."[28]

Brereton returned to his own headquarters at Nielson Field and told his staff that "we couldn't attack until we were attacked" (interview by Air

Force historians of Colonel Harold Eads, who was there and like everyone else was puzzled and unbelieving, inasmuch as they were unanimous in wanting to strike at the Japanese without delay; the Japanese themselves were dreading precisely that possibility). The file of a daily Summary of Activities by this headquarters has survived and contains the following entries: "07:15 General Brereton . . . requested permission of General MacArthur to take offensive action. He was informed that for the time being our role was defensive" and 9:00 A.M.: "In response to query from General Brereton a message received from General Sutherland advising planes not authorized to carry bombs at this time." Target information on Formosa had been prepared by the intelligence officer, Lieutenant Allison Ind, who recorded that during that morning he was told, "It's all off . . . General Brereton has ordered us not to send bombers."[29] The testimony of everyone but MacArthur is that Brereton asked MacArthur for permission to bomb Formosa immediately and that MacArthur refused it.

MacArthur's subsequent explanation was unsatisfactory. He said that "the over-all strategic mission of the Philippine command was to defend the Philippines, not to initiate an outside attack." Not true. His most recent orders (Rainbow 5 revised, November 19, 1941) required him in the event of war to "conduct air raids against Japanese forces and installations within tactical operating radius of available bases."[30] Why else were those B-17s there? He further said: "Our air forces in the Philippines were hardly more than a token force . . . hopelessly outnumbered . . . never had a chance of winning. The date of April 1 . . . was the earliest possible date for the arrival of the necessary reinforcements which would make a successful defense of the Philippines possible."[31] This is in contradiction with everything he had been saying up to the outbreak of war, with his often reiterated assurances to President Quezon and the War Department that an all-out defense of the Philippines not only could but would be carried through.

MacArthur's paralysis of will is explicable only if he believed that for him the war had not yet begun, that, in Brereton's words, "the Pearl Harbor attack might not have been construed as an overt act against the Philippines." MacArthur wore two hats as both American and Philippine commander. The desirability of having Japan commit the "first overt act" was American policy, a phrase drawn from the War Department's "final alert" sent to him on November 27, but to argue that it was somehow still in effect as far as the Philippines were involved was ludicrous, as though the sinking of the American battle fleet did not constitute an "overt act."

MacArthur seems to have assumed that war as it applied to the United States and war as it applied to the Philippines were two different things. If this is how he thought, then that would also explain his otherwise baffling support of Quezon's later proposal that both the United States and Japan withdraw and the Philippines be neutralized, a counsel of despair. It was as though the war defined itself in terms of MacArthur; it began only when he was drawn into it, and when it went against him, he could invoke an escape clause by proposing to end it. This was an illusion cleared from his mind by the Japanese bombers on December 8 and by the President on February 9, when Roosevelt rejected the Quezon plan and ordered MacArthur to fight on without surrender "as long as there remains any possibility of resistance."[32]

MacArthur's conduct of the Philippines' defense does not compel admiration. His idea of fighting on the beaches contained strategic weaknesses, since the islands form an archipelago with many times more miles of coastline than could conceivably be manned by the forces their population could raise. These in any event proved inadequate. Not a single division of the Philippine Army had been fully mobilized when war came and no unit was at full strength. Training facilities were almost nonexistent and there were serious shortages in every kind of equipment, including weapons and clothing. MacArthur had tried to put a good face on this in glowing reports to Quezon that his own aides, like Eisenhower, thought were "far too optimistic." When the Japanese came, landing in Lingayen Gulf on December 22, the Philippine troops facing them broke "at the first appearance of the enemy," writes the U.S. Army historian, "and fled to the rear in a disorganized stream."[33]

The problem of defending the Philippines had been long and carefully studied by American officers, but all their labors came to nothing. With the absorption of the Philippine Department into MacArthur's command, the department reverted to a service status and "the headquarters which had made the plans and preparations for war"—the Army history again—"had no tactical control when war came." MacArthur—with 20,000 Americans, 12,000 Philippine Scouts, and eight Philippine Army divisions—could muster from 75,000 to 80,000 men on Luzon, substantially more than the 43,000 the Japanese landed. The latter were new at amphibious operations and made several blunders, but we made more of them and ours were irreversible. Eisenhower, observing from the War Plans Division in Washington and making every effort to reinforce MacArthur, thought that the latter could have used the men he had more effectively. "I still think he might have made a better showing," Eisenhower wrote in his diary on January 13.[34]

The sidestep movement into Bataan peninsula was skillfully executed, but the logistics of it were not. Though an earlier war plan had provided for stockpiling of supplies on Bataan, with MacArthur's fight-on-the-beaches order this was changed and supplies were located in the Luzon plain; to retrieve them quickly proved an arduous exercise, even though valiant attempts were made. Hard lessons of war had not yet erased a peacetime mentality. Philippine Commonwealth regulations forbade moving rice or sugar from one province to another, and permission to move ten million pounds of rice into Bataan was held up so long that it arrived too late. One American officer who asked permission to commandeer two thousand cases of canned food belonging to a Japanese firm was told by MacArthur's headquarters that he could not do so and would be court-martialed if he did. Much that might have been saved was abandoned in the retreat. These and dozens of other difficulties meant that the shortage of food on Bataan was severe from the earliest days and soon was demanding almost as much attention as the advancing Japanese. The lack of supplies, and of food in particular, had a greater impact on the somber outcome of the siege of Bataan than any other factor.[35]

Bataan was where the legends all began, the good and the bad. The good tells of a MacArthur whose vital presence "gave his troops the lift they needed," according to his former staff officer General Courtney Whitney, a MacArthur who energized these severely tested soldiers, doomed as they were to surrender under General Wainwright and to barbarous treatment by their captors. "Unexpectedly, at a front-line position they looked up and there he was . . . ," wrote Whitney, "he flashed his wide smile of reassurance and his men smiled back." The bad was a MacArthur whose real self could not match this description, whose hopes had proved illusory, whose poor planning had brought them there so badly supplied, and whose sense of his own flawed image made him uncomfortable in their presence.

MacArthur seems in fact to have left his tunnel headquarters on Corregidor and gone to Bataan only once; it was here that he acquired the nickname "Dugout Doug." Of his personal bravery there were still to be many instances, but somehow his once-exemplary capacity for shared experience at the point of action had been lost; thenceforward he is a distant and reclusive leader. On January 30 he sent Roosevelt a message which for its rhetorical excess would be difficult to equal: "Your birth anniversary comma smoke begrimed men covered with the muck of battle comma rise from the foxholes of Bataan and the batteries of Corregidor comma to pray reverently that God may bless immeasurably the President of the United States."[36]

MacArthur's apologists have made the charge that he and his men were deliberately sacrificed by the Roosevelt administration. "Not only were no large reinforcements sent to the Philippines," wrote General Whitney, "but, more important, the administration never intended to send them and concealed the fact that they would not be sent."[37] Is this indictment justified? If what Whitney referred to was the Europe-first strategy beginning with Admiral Stark's "Plan Dog" memorandum and continuing in its many reaffirmations, and if by "large" he meant a reversal of that strategy leading to an American concentration on the Pacific war, then yes; there was no intention of any such reversal. (MacArthur, throughout the war, never reconciled himself to the Europe-first strategy and constantly complained about it.) But Whitney's implication was that no serious reinforcement efforts were made, which is not the case, nor is it fair to the President to imply that he was not behind those that were made.

The day war began, a convoy of seven ships accompanied by cruiser *Pensacola* was in mid-Pacific on its way to Manila. On board were the pilots of an air bombardment group, two regiments of artillery, and large quantities of ammunition. The Joint Board (at the urging of General Gerow and Admiral Turner) recommended recalling the *Pensacola* convoy to Hawaii if not the United States. Three days later, at a White House meeting, the President indicated his desire that the convoy continue to the Far East and the Joint Board reversed itself (the vessels went to Brisbane, Australia). Stimson and Marshall were determined to support MacArthur in every way they could and on December 14 they found the President more than willing to order the Navy to do likewise. On the seventeenth, Stimson told his aides McCloy, Lovett, and Bundy that a policy of making "every effort possible in the Far East" had "been accepted by the President."[38]

The man in charge of putting this policy into effect was Dwight Eisenhower. He had been brought into the War Plans Division at least in part because he had previously served with MacArthur. "I've been insisting the Far East is critical," he wrote in his diary on January 1, 1942. On January 4: "we're getting some things on the road to Australia." January 12: "We'll get off twenty-one thousand men on January 21 to Australia; but I don't know when we can get all their equipment and supplies to them. Ships! Ships! All we need is ships! Also ammunition, antiaircraft guns, tanks, airplanes, what a headache!" Former colonel and secretary of war Patrick Hurley was reinducted as a brigadier general and sent to Australia with an open checkbook for one million dollars and instructions to organize blockade-running to MacArthur.

Ten submarines made the run to reach the Philippines, yet the most they were able to land was 53 tons of food, 3,500 rounds of three-inch antiaircraft ammunition, 37 tons of fifty-caliber and 1 million rounds of thirty-caliber, and about 30,000 gallons of diesel fuel. Nothing else got through; all the other efforts failed. The Roosevelt administration was not the cause of this, it was the Japanese; and even over the long haul the Pacific war did not suffer the starvation MacArthur so often claimed. By the end of 1942 there were more U.S. troops in the Pacific than in the Atlantic and by the end of 1943 the number of Army divisions deployed against Germany (seventeen) was not that much greater than those (thirteen plus three Marine) deployed against Japan.[39]

The decision to bring General MacArthur and his family out to Australia was made by President Roosevelt on February 22, at a time when

Bataan's defenders—though driven down to the peninsula's southern end —had inflicted heavy casualties on the Japanese and were still a combative force. Marshall, who had sent preliminary alerts, radioed MacArthur the President's order for him to proceed by way of Mindanao to Australia, where he would assume command of a new theater of operations in the Southwest Pacific.

MacArthur, his wife and child, a nurse, and seventeen staff members left Corregidor on the night of March 12 in four PT boats and reached Darwin in three B-17s on the morning of the seventeenth. "This hazardous trip by a commanding general and key members of his staff through enemy controlled territory," MacArthur reported to Marshall, "undoubtedly is unique in military annals." Eisenhower had other thoughts. "I'm dubious about the whole thing," he wrote in his diary. "He [MacArthur] is doing a good job where he is, but I'm doubtful that he'd do so well in complicated situations. . . . If brought out, public opinion will force him into a position where his love of the limelight may ruin him."[40]

III

General MacArthur was ill-served by his admirers, who enveloped him in a cloud of exaggerated claims that have to be dispelled before anything like reality is visible. He himself contributed to the process of overstatement. A year after the fact, he said that defending Australia by attacking the Japanese in the island of New Guinea to the north had always been his intention since the moment of his arrival from the Philippines in March. Prime Minister John Curtin of Australia, who saw him often then, doubted this and thought it was some considerable time before MacArthur went over "to a defense of the [Australian] mainland from a line of the Owen Stanley ridge" in New Guinea.[41] As late as June, very little had been done to strengthen New Guinea defenses, even though the 41st American Division had been brought from Melbourne to near Rockhampton on the northeast coast of Australia and the 32d from Adelaide to near Brisbane, where MacArthur now made his headquarters. He struck many observers as tired and depressed. Clark Lee, a sympathetic correspondent who had also come out from Corregidor, said that MacArthur "was hard to get along with in those early Australia days."[42]

Except for Greenland, New Guinea is the largest island in the world. Before the war, the eastern half of it, called Papua, was under Australian administration; but in March 1942, the Japanese occupied Lae and Salamua on the north coast and the Allies were left with nothing but positions on the south coast at Port Moresby (the closest contact with Australia) and on the eastern tip of the island at Milne Bay. (In August, the Japanese tried

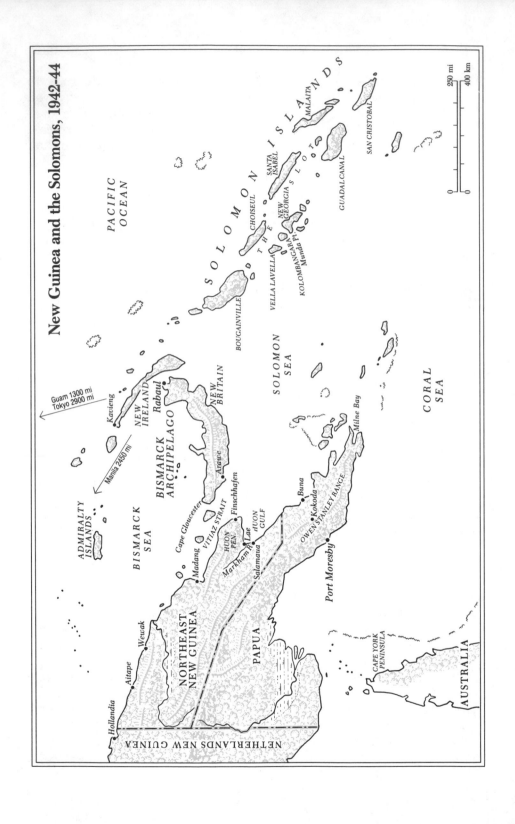

New Guinea and the Solomons, 1942–44

PACIFIC OCEAN

SOLOMON ISLANDS

MALAITA

SANTA ISABEL

THE SLOT

CHOISEUL

NEW GEORGIA

SAN CRISTOBAL

KOLOMBANGARA
Munda Pt.

VELLA LAVELLA

GUADALCANAL

BOUGAINVILLE

SOLOMON SEA

CORAL SEA

Milne Bay

Kavieng

NEW IRELAND

Rabaul

Guam 1300 mi
Tokyo 2900 mi

Manila 2450 mi

NEW BRITAIN

BISMARCK ARCHIPELAGO

Arawe

Cape Gloucester

ADMIRALTY ISLANDS

BISMARCK SEA

Buna

Kokoda

VITIAZ STRAIT

Finschhafen

HUON PEN.

HUON GULF

Lae

Markham R.

Salamaua

OWEN STANLEY RANGE

Madang

Port Moresby

Wewak

Aitape

NORTHEAST NEW GUINEA

PAPUA

Hollandia

NETHERLANDS NEW GUINEA

CAPE YORK PENINSULA

AUSTRALIA

250 mi
400 km

to capture Milne Bay but failed, driven off by a combined force of seven thousand Australians and a thousand Americans.) Between the Allies and the Japanese there was little but jungle and the formidable Owen Stanley range, rising sawtooth sharp to heights above thirteen thousand feet; across it from Port Moresby on the south shore to Buna Mission on the north ran no roads but only a jungle track called the Kokoda Trail, which rose and plunged precipitously across the ridges. This was miserable country to fight in, a fact at first insufficiently appreciated at MacArthur's headquarters.

General Marshall and Admiral King, as has been told, agreed July 2 on a directive that included a landing on Guadalcanal under Nimitz and an attack on Lae and Salamua under MacArthur. The key to the latter lay in acquiring an airfield somewhere along the north coast of New Guinea well to the east of Lae, and attention for this purpose fell on Buna Mission, the prewar center of government in the area, three houses, a few native huts, and an airstrip. On July 10–11, a recon party of three American and three Australian officers flew to Buna from Port Moresby in a Catalina flying boat, encountering no Japanese.

They found the Buna airstrip to be unusable for military purposes, but fifteen miles to the south at Dobodura was a grassy plain that could support large-scale air operations (as eventually it did). When the recon party reported this, a decision was quickly reached to occupy Buna Mission, if possible in secret, and to establish a major air base at Dobodura, an excellent plan that should have succeeded if the Japanese had not forestalled it. They, too, had their eyes on Buna Mission, though their motivation was different; they wanted it as a base to launch an attack down the Kokoda Trail on Port Moresby, which indeed they did come within a hair's breadth of reaching.

Leaders of the Allied Buna task force were to be General Robert Van Volkenburgh of the 40th Artillery Brigade and Lieutenant Colonel David Larr of MacArthur's staff. They set about assembling troops and writing the movement orders. On July 18, however, they received the disquieting news that twenty-four Japanese ships, some of them quite large, were gathering in Rabaul harbor and they concluded (correctly) that these were destined for Buna. Larr called General Sutherland and (speaking for Van Volkenburgh) urged that the largest number of troops the flying boats could carry be flown in to Buna at once, and that the entire operation be accelerated.

Both Larr and Van Volkenburgh thought that the element of surprise had already been lost. "We may be able to hold Buna," Larr concluded, "if we get there first." MacArthur's headquarters thought otherwise; they did not believe the Japanese were headed for Buna or that surprise had been lost; the original plan would be adhered to as drawn. On July 22, the Japanese convoy hove to offshore about nine miles northwest of Buna and began unloading; Allied aircraft tried to break up the landing, but the weather was bad and the results were disappointing. We had lost the race for Buna, and would pay dearly for having done so.

General Tomitaro Horii of the Nankai Shitai, or South Seas Detachment (which had captured Rabaul), ordered a group of about nine hundred men to head south from Buna. They first encountered a thin screening force of Australians near Kokoda, drove it back, and waited for the main body of the Nankai Shitai to come up behind them. General Horii had a total of about eight thousand troops (he would have had more if things had not been going badly on Guadalcanal). On August 12, he came forward to lead an advance with about five thousand of them through a gap in the Owen Stanleys to Port Moresby. On that same day, MacArthur's intelligence officer, General Charles Willoughby, issued an estimate to the effect that any such thing was most unlikely: "an overland advance in strength is discounted in view of logistic difficulties, poor communications, and difficult terrain."[43]

Not quite. By September 16, the Japanese, steadily driving the under-strength Australians before them, were in the southern foothills of the Owen Stanleys at Ioribaiwa, almost within sight of their goal, thirty-five miles away. Horii issued a proclamation: "We will strike a hammer blow at the stronghold of Moresby."[44] Not quite. Willoughby had been wrong about the enemy's capabilities and right about their logistics; the Japanese at Ioribaiwa had run out of rice. (Much of their trouble came from Allied airpower, which constantly interdicted the Kokoda Trail, especially the wire-rope bridge at the place therefore known—in pidgin English—as Wairopi.) Further, their higher headquarters was losing its nerve. The failure at Milne Bay had unsettled them, a small Australian force was still holding out at Wau near Salamua, and on Guadalcanal things were going even worse than before; Horii was instructed to fall back on Buna. The Japanese had lost their race for Port Moresby, and would pay dearly too.

As the Japanese withdrew, the Australians—now consisting of 25th and 16th Brigades of the 7th Division—kept close on their heels, and sharp actions took place in October and early November at Templeton's Crossing, Eora Creek, and Oivi-Gorari. Between late July and mid-November, the Japanese committed at least 6,000 men and the Australian casualties were 103 officers (39 killed) and 1,577 enlisted men (586 killed). During the fight at Templeton's Crossing they had been none too pleased to receive a message from the Allied ground commander, Australian General Sir Thomas Blamey: "General MacArthur considers quote extremely light casualties indicate no serious effort yet made to displace enemy unquote."

MacArthur, quite without justification, was contemptuous of his allies. "The Australians," he informed Marshall, "have proven themselves unable to match the enemy in jungle fighting. Aggressive leadership is lacking." Australian Major General A.S. Allen, a brave and capable commander, later told MacArthur how distressed he had been by messages indicating a lack of confidence. MacArthur said: "But I've nothing but praise for you and your men. I was only urging you on." Allen replied: "Well, that's not the way to urge Australians."[45]

On October 1, MacArthur had issued a cautious plan for a three-pronged advance on Buna (it was cautious in that it contained specific provisions for retreat). The Australians would continue along the Kokoda Trail. The Americans (126th Infantry Regiment of the 32d Division) would come up a similar jungle track to the southeast from Kapa Kapa to Jaure, and at the same time we would move forward along the northeast coast by sea and air from Milne Bay. There was a general expectation both at MacArthur's headquarters and that of the 32d Division that Buna would be a pushover. Very little thought had been given to the supplies and equipment necessary for jungle warfare—not enough machetes, no insect repellent, no waterproof containers for personal effects and medical supplies.

MacArthur's staff seemed wholly unaware of what New Guinea was actually like; no senior officer had come forward along the Kokoda Trail farther than the point where the motor road ended at Ower's Corner, about ten miles short of the point of farthest Japanese advance. Lieutenant General Robert L. Eichelberger, commander of the corps to which the 32d Division belonged, had told MacArthur and Sutherland that he considered the 32d, through no fault of its own, insufficiently trained and "barely satisfactory" in combat efficiency.[46]

The trail the Americans followed was far rougher and more precipitous than the one to Kokoda, so narrow they had to climb in single file and there was no place at either side to sleep or eat. They stumbled over vines and roots in the ever-present mud and slime. Rain was heavy and continuous; swollen mountain streams could knock a man over when he tried to cross. The only way up and down the ridges was on hands and knees; four or five ridges meant a day's march. Their rations were Australian: hardtack, bully beef, tea, and rice. (Some of the beef became contaminated; most of the battalion soon had acute diarrhea and dysentery.) "It was one green hell to Jaure," said the first sergeant of E Company.

It was also unnecessary. At the initiative of a local missionary who came to Port Moresby with the information, usable airfield sites were found on the other side of the Owen Stanleys at Fasari and Pongani on the coast, and by November 2 Blamey had persuaded MacArthur that the rest of the 32d should be brought across the mountains by air.[47] By the middle of the month, a combined force of two Allied divisions was closing in on Buna.

◆

The Americans, writes the official Australian army history, "could have had little idea . . . of the country into which they were moving."

as "mopping up." It took three weeks and cost 3,500 casualties, roughly seven hundred more than Buna and two hundred more than Tarawa. The intelligence estimate of the number of Japanese at Sanananda had been five hundred when there were in fact five thousand. Eichelberger was justifiably disconcerted at the inference "that when the Sanananda campaign is concluded it was of such unimportance that the high command did not need to give it its personal attention." He thought that the term "mopping up" should be stricken from the military and journalistic vocabulary; it was not, he said, "a good enough phrase to die for."[52]

MacArthur's tendency to report victories before they were achieved continued throughout the war. Eventually his communiqués became notorious for their boastful inaccuracies—costly actions dismissed as minor and skirmishes magnified into major engagements—and these could not be blamed on an overzealous staff; his own press officer said that MacArthur wrote many of the communiqués himself and heavily edited the others. Perhaps the worst was issued in December 1942, when the fighting at Buna was at its height: "On Christmas Day our activities were limited to routine safety precautions. Divine services were held."

That was the day eight companies of the 127th Infantry, after a "thunderous" mortar and artillery barrage, attacked through a Japanese position in what were called the Government Gardens. The commander of C Company was killed leading an assault on a Japanese bunker. General Eichelberger said "the fighting was desperate and the outcome of the whole miserable, tortured campaign was in doubt." The probability is low that many there even knew what day it was, although an AP correspondent wrote that he had seen a "tall, gray-haired general" walking among the sick and wounded saying, "Good morning, lads. I only hope you will all be home next Christmas." When Mrs. Eichelberger read this she learned for the first time where her husband was, since she knew of no other general in the Army who addressed his men as "lads."[53]

But the most astonishing of all MacArthur's statements, for those who had been there, was the one he made afterward about the Papuan campaign as a whole. "There was no reason to hurry the attack," he said, "because the time element was of little importance." Eichelberger records not one but repeated instances of MacArthur's urging him to make haste, telling him that time "is fleeting . . . Hasten your preparations . . . time is working desperately against us." MacArthur said: "The utmost care was taken for the conservation of our forces with the result that probably no campaign in history against a thoroughly prepared and trained Army produced such complete and decisive results with so low an expenditure of life and resources." This, after ordering attacks "regardless of losses." General Whitney, too, writes of "surprisingly small losses" in Papua and makes a comparison with Guadalcanal in MacArthur's favor.[54]

Very well then, compare.

There were about 60,000 Americans fighting on Guadalcanal and they suffered 5,845 casualties, of whom 1,600 were killed. There were about 33,000 Americans and Australians fighting in Papua and they suffered 8,546 casualties, of whom 3,095 were killed. One man in eleven died in Papua compared to one in thirty-seven on Guadalcanal. Papua was *three times* more exacting in loss of life than was Guadalcanal. The official U.S. Army history of the Papuan campaign sums up an analysis of the human cost: "the conclusion is inescapable that the fighting in Papua had been even costlier than at first thought, and that the victory there, proportionate to the forces engaged, had been one of the costliest of the Pacific war."[55]

◆

Defeat in the Philippines had been followed by apotheosis at home. Streets were renamed after him; between March 1 and April 8, 1942, thirteen babies born in New York City were given the first and middle names of "Douglas" and "MacArthur." Honorary degrees and honorary memberships were showered on him; the Blackfeet Indians adopted him into their tribe and called him "Chief Wise Eagle." General Marshall and President Roosevelt arranged for him to be given the only high decoration he did not already have, the Congressional Medal of Honor (Marshall wrote the citation and the President approved it on March 25). The National Father's Day Committee named him "Number One Father for 1942." He replied that he hoped his son, when he was gone, would remember him in repeating the simple prayer "Our Father, who art in Heaven"—a lapse in sense of the appropriate that staggers the imagination.[56]

Eisenhower observed all this with further distaste. His diary for March 19, 1942, reads: "MacArthur is out of the Philippine Islands. . . . The newspapers acclaim the move—the public has built itself a hero out of its own imagination." May 6: "Corregidor surrendered last night. Poor Wainwright! He did the fighting . . . another got such glory as the public could find. . . . General MacArthur's tirades, to which TJ [Captain T. J. Davis, MacArthur's aide] and I so often listened in Manila, would now sound as silly to the public as they then did to us. But he's a hero! Yah."[57]

Now begins the stream of suggestions that MacArthur be brought home and placed in supreme command of all American forces (Walter Lippmann called him "a great commander," with "vast and profound conceptions") or—this from Republicans desperate for an alternative to Roosevelt—that he become a candidate for President in 1944. Congressman Hamilton Fish came out for him in March 1942 and told MacArthur the following year that he expected to be a convention delegate and to vote for MacArthur's nomination. "We need an Army man at the head of the government . . . ," wrote Fish. "The people will be overwhelmingly for you and I believe at the present time you are the only person in the country that can decisively defeat the fourth-term candidate."[58]

MacArthur's biographer Clayton James properly points out that during these years (later was different) MacArthur himself never indicated and constantly denied any desire for high political office, let alone for the role of dictator that some of his overly eager friends like Major General George Van Horn Moseley would have liked to thrust upon him. But James and others have described how MacArthur's officers (Sutherland, Kenney, and Willoughby) met with Senator Arthur Vandenberg in Washington during 1943 and so praised the general that Vandenberg organized an informal MacArthur-for-President committee involving newspaper publisher Frank Gannett and Robert E. Wood, chairman of the board of Sears Roebuck. MacArthur was unable to stop listening when others cast him as a presidential possibility. The siren song had caught his ear, for all his protests; he was an innocent besought by others not so innocent, a party to maneuverings he neither understood nor could convert into practical political advantage. (At the Republican convention in Chicago in June 1944, MacArthur received one vote to Dewey's 1,056.[59])

In late 1942 and early 1943, MacArthur had a number of interviews in Brisbane with his British liaison officer, Lieutenant Colonel Gerald Wilkinson, in which he spoke his mind with expansive candor. (MacArthur got on well with Wilkinson, who had a certain respect for him, and Wilkinson kept a careful journal.) MacArthur thought, wrote Wilkinson, "that, if Roosevelt gains strength politically, it is quite possible that he will find some pretext to relieve MacArthur altogether of his Command." Wilkinson questioned MacArthur closely as to whether he really believed in such "an absurdity," but MacArthur "stuck to it and thinks that Roosevelt might well pull it off . . . that Presidential prerogative might be enough." (Wilkinson added: "All this sounds a day dream to me.")

MacArthur said "that the recent Northwest African campaign was a real blunder and would bog down in a mess from which it would be very difficult to go forward or backwards." He was aware that Marshall and Eisenhower had opposed it and he "considered the thing inspired by Roosevelt—with Churchill's assistance—primarily to save Roosevelt from growing feelings against him." Wilkinson asked MacArthur if it would not be possible for us to drive up through Italy after taking North Africa, "to which his comment was that Germany was operating on interior lines and could hold us, that they [directors of Allied Strategy] were just plain wrong."

MacArthur told Sir Campbell Stuart (according to Wilkinson) that "Roosevelt and Churchill were dominating the whole war direction" and refusing to heed professional advice, the "Chiefs of Staff mere pawns, etc.," and that "Japan, not Germany, is our main enemy." Germany could not now defeat Britain, "and even if she won a partial victory, or only half lost the peace," said MacArthur, "life under a civilized race, or with a civilized people, would be tolerable." (This was too much for Wilkinson, who thought the Nazis something less than "tolerable" and characterized MacArthur's views as "the most superficial wrong-headed biased stuff.") If the Germany-first strategy goes wrong, as MacArthur "seems always to infer that it must," then he believed that "two men [Roosevelt and Churchill] may yet have to answer to the Anglo-American people," since there "is 'another' element (the fighting services) whose voice may one day have to be expressed (MacArthur did not say by whom)." The tenor of all this was unmistakable: hatred and fear of Roosevelt, resentment of Allied strategy and his subordinate part in it, simmering political ambitions to get out from under both.

In February 1943, MacArthur, knowing that Wilkinson through British Intelligence had direct contact with Churchill, tried another stratagem. He told Wilkinson that because of "the jealousy of Washington and the U.S. Navy" Churchill was "his only ally." Should Churchill ever want his advice, MacArthur would be glad to convey the same provided this was *to him alone.*" It was evident, Wilkinson noted, that "MacArthur feels that he can by-pass the Washington instructions which confine his military reports to Washington" and "that he can justify communication with Churchill—if caught at it—by the fact that, as an Allied Commander in Chief, he owes allegiance not only to the United States but also to Curtin, Queen Wilhelmina, and Churchill." This was a clumsy and insubordinate gesture, of a dubious patriotism; Washington did catch on to what MacArthur was up to and in April MacArthur, as he wrote to Churchill, was put under direct orders to report only to Washington.

MacArthur nonetheless managed to make his views known to Churchill in June through Major General R. H. Dewing (who was serving as a military observer at his headquarters), insisting that they were "to be communicated to the Prime Minister and not to the British Chiefs of Staff." After reviewing the situation in the Pacific, which he described as centering on Japanese bases at Rabaul and Wewak, which in fact were later bypassed, he had given Dewing his plan for the war in Europe. To assault the Continent from the seas was to invite "a costly failure." There was only one practical solution: "to throw all the reserves of America and Great Britain on the Russian front[!]," taking over a sector on the southern flank where we would have a secure [!] line of communications through the Caucasus. Churchill appended a note for Ismay to this extraordinary proposal: "The General's ideas about the European theatre are singularly untroubled by considerations of transport and distance."[60]

MacArthur did not, moreover, function as an Allied commander. His headquarters remained monochromatically American despite two admonitions from Marshall on this score, to which MacArthur paid no attention; no major staff position of his was held by a Dutch or an Australian officer. For the remainder of his New Guinea operation he set up something called Alamo Force, which was Walter Krueger and his Sixth Army headquarters thinly disguised, a transparent measure designed to circumvent the authority of General Blamey as commander of Allied Land Forces. This was disturbing to Australians, as was MacArthur's habit of referring to Australian troops as "Allied" and to Allied troops as "American." MacArthur was heavily dependent on Australia; during the latter half of 1942, from 65 to 70 percent of his supplies came from Australian sources. Yet he seemed not to regard American-Australian relations as worthy of his concern and rejected a proposal by Blamey for improving them. "Shortly after I arrived in Australia," said Eichelberger, "General MacArthur ordered me to pay my respects to the Australians and then have nothing further to do with them."[61]

The wonder is that Australo-American relationships worked as well as they did. With the increasing arrival of American soldiers in large numbers, there occurred inevitable incidents of friction and even violence, and the strong-arm methods of American military police were not welcomed; one Australian commented that while a display of armed force might stop a riot in the United States, in Australia it was a good way of starting one.

As a country, Australia was in an unusually malleable state, just coming out from under (but only partway) its sense of inferiority to Britain, never having known complete success in conquering its empty spaces, and opting instead for the living-wage security of its cities. Suddenly to be overrun by these hordes of blithe and bouncy young men with their miraculous profusion of equipment produced a shock with aftereffects, one of the few refutations to be found of Aldous Huxley's dictum that armies are almost perfect nonconductors of culture.

That the Americans thought of them as "foreigners" was for the Australians "a cram course in international living," writes John Hammond Moore in a book about the American invasion. "For the first time," he goes on, "Australians saw the composite produced by a melting-pot world, watched great machines at work, and marveled at the actions and thoughts of men to whom nothing seemed impossible." Moore notes that Eichelberger did not obey MacArthur's order to ignore the Australians; at Rockhampton he set up his office in the city hall and arrived at understandings with the mayor, Henry Jeffries, that made Rockhampton a demonstration case of how well the two nationalities could get along together. After the Americans had gone, many Australians discovered that life was less eventful but somehow less interesting. Their emergence into their own nationhood had been hastened. At a highway intersection south of Brisbane, on the site of what was once a bustling encampment, can be seen today a small monument with a brass plate that bears one of the nicest compliments ever paid to the U.S. Army: "U.S.A. They Passed This Way. 1942–44."[62]

MacArthur's headquarters was shaped to his needs and personality, made up of men whose principal qualification was fidelity and who were united by little else than their determination to "protect" the General against adversaries real and imagined; of his eleven senior staff, eight were officers who had served with him in the Philippines, the "Bataan gang." As a rule, according to Clark Lee, "MacArthur did not select the brightest, most capable, and most promising officers in the Army to serve under him. Most of the men on his staff were never heard of in the Army before they joined him, and never will be again."

Lee, who accepted much of the MacArthur legend without cavil and is a *favorable* witness, wrote of these men: "it is frequently (and largely truthfully) said that they share several characteristics—each carries a chip on both shoulders, is highly and sometimes childishly sensitive, and is convinced that the General is the greatest man who ever lived," not to be judged "as an ordinary mortal . . . but as if he existed in some perfect idealistic vacuum." Anyone who refused to accept the concept of a flawless MacArthur was for them an enemy; "everyone in the world is either 'for' or 'against' the General." When George Marshall visited MacArthur on Goodenough Island in December 1943 and MacArthur used the phrase "my staff," Marshall said, "You don't have a staff, General. You have a court."[63]

The two of MacArthur's officers who have since most notably put themselves on record as to their high opinion of him are Charles Willoughby and Courtney Whitney. Whitney, Maryland born, served in the Army during World War I and left it to practice law in the Philippines from 1927 to 1940. John Gunther described him as having "a sharp, fluent mind." As a lawyer in Manila, writes Clark Lee, Whitney "was shrewd, aggressive, and acquisitive, and before long had purchased or lawyered his way into extensive holdings." He reentered the Army in 1941, and in 1943 MacArthur called him to Australia, where he began to organize and direct Philippine guerrilla resistance to the Japanese. Clayton James describes Whitney as "the pompous, opportunistic officer who was probably the most despised by other members of the GHQ staff. . . . on his way toward becoming MacArthur's alter ego." Whitney was said to think interchangeably with MacArthur. His book, *MacArthur: His Rendezvous with History*, is the most extreme exemplar of tendentious writing on MacArthur's behalf, a work not of biography but of hagiography, and unreadable as a serious text.[64]

Willoughby, according to John Gunther, was "tall and stout as an ox, with what seems to be a square yard of decorations on his cask-like chest . . . a man of the world, gay, clever, irreverent." After dinner with the

Gunthers one evening, Willoughby proposed a toast to "the second great-est military commander in the world, Francisco Franco," which Jane Gunther with dignity declined to drink. He spoke with a German accent and claimed to be the son of a baron—Freiherr T. von Tscheppe-Weiden-bach—by an American mother whose maiden name he had adopted when he became an American citizen. Willoughby enlisted in the U.S. Army in 1910 under the name of Adolph Charles Weidenbach. He briefly left the service to take a college degree and do graduate work; commissioned a second lieutenant, he served on the Mexican border and in France during World War I, later attended the Infantry School, the Command and Gen-eral Staff School, and the Army War College. MacArthur met him at Leavenworth in the thirties, took a liking to him, and in 1941 brought him to the Philippines as his G-2 (intelligence officer).

In 1951, the German magazine *Der Spiegel* became curious about Willoughby and looked into the Heidelberg register for March 8, 1892, the day he claimed to have been born there, finding the birth only of one Adolf August Weidenbach, son of August Weidenbach, ropemaker, and Emma née Langhäuser. A General Franz Erich Theodor Tülff von Tschepe und Weidenbach did exist, but he was not a baron and of his five children none was born in 1892. Willoughby's book, *MacArthur 1941–1951*, is far more temperate than Whitney's, but it leans heavily on the so-called MacArthur Histories (prepared in MacArthur's headquarters by Willoughby), which in turn draw copiously on MacArthur communiqués and are thus about as reliable historically as Willoughby's account of his own origins.[65]

The object of these admiring works had by mid-1942 experienced a recovery of self-confidence, and the operative agent was again air power. Clark Lee dates MacArthur's "restoration to full health and activity" by the arrival in August of Major General George H. Kenney to command what eventually became Fifth Air Force. Kenney was a short, vigorous Nova Scotian whose highly original mixture of pugnacity and good nature enabled him to be the one "outsider" among MacArthur's subordinates to win his complete trust. When Sutherland made drastic changes in Ken-ney's first attack order, Kenney informed him that he (Sutherland) was a total ignoramus about air power, that he (Kenney) intended not to have his authority tampered with, and that if there was any question about this, they (Kenney and Sutherland) had better go right now to MacArthur and have it out. (Sutherland backed down; Kenney never thought very much of him anyhow.) Kenney worked so effectively at MacArthur's right hand that the Southwest Pacific theater became an almost classic, textbook illustration of what air power—with limited means and over vast distances —can do. Kenney was a free spirit; his favorite expression was "Hell, let's try it."[66]

This was a poor theater for aircraft to perform in. Maintenance was an unremitting trial; in the never-ending damp, electrical equipment grew fungus, and in the heat, ordinary lubricating oil seemed to evaporate. (Kenney knew about maintenance: A graduate of MIT, he had been for two years Army representative at the Curtiss plant and then head of production engineering in the Air Corps Matériel Division.) Kenney made airstrips turn into bomber bases; he cannibalized wrecked aircraft for spare parts; he patched up B-17s with old tin cans. He instituted the "parafrag" bomb (dropped from a few hundred feet by parachute so that the bomber was safely out of range when it burst) first used at Buna, and encouraged adoption of the skip-bombing techniques (invented by the British) for low-level attack on Japanese shipping, employed with such effectiveness at the Battle of the Bismarck Sea in February 1943.

MacArthur in his communiqué on this engagement characteristically claimed twenty-two vessels to have been sunk, as opposed to the actual twelve, and threatened to take "appropriate steps" against anyone who challenged his inflated figures, but the fact was that a major convoy had been wiped out and that Japanese attempts to reinforce Lae thereafter ceased. Kenney in his realism pressed Washington for P-38s, the twin-tailed high-flying fighters that were more than a match for the Japanese Zero. From a strength at the beginning of 1942 of 13 heavy bombers and 101 fighters, Fifth Air Force had grown by the end of the year to 81 heavy bombers, 83 medium bombers, and 238 fighters (by 1944, these numbers had doubled). Before late 1943, MacArthur was writing Arnold: "The Air Force has been magnificent and is the very hub of our success."[67]

He was in fine fettle now, with a winning campaign and an adoring entourage; his friends were always limited to his immediate staff. In Brisbane, the MacArthurs lived a monastic life in an apartment in a private section of Lennon's, the only hotel in town with air-conditioning; except for his daily limousine ride to and from the nine-story AMP Insurance Building, which had been taken over for his use, he was rarely seen. When he moved to Port Moresby in November, he lived in Government House, a rambling white structure on a knoll overlooking the harbor, in similar seclusion. A soldier who saw him strolling before breakfast in his dressing gown thought this so eventful that it was reported in *Time* magazine; another claimed to have seen him walking the grounds with some messages in one hand and a head of lettuce in the other. Though he never allowed himself to be medically examined, he was in excellent physical condition, which he attributed to a daily nap and abstemious habits. (When John Gunther later asked MacArthur's doctor whether the general was a good patient, the answer was: "I don't know. He's never sick.") He took no exercise but did a great deal of pacing to and fro, some associates estimated as much as several miles a day. Eichelberger noted with interest that he never appeared to perspire.[68]

What are we to make of this strange man, so endowed by nature with the stuff of greatness and with faults that should have been trivial but instead turned sour and disabling? He had the need to disturb the universe, which is a great gift, but too often he ended by disturbing other people, whose needs and achievements he seemed not to recognize. He had no generosity in sharing the stage of history, no easiness in the presence of other actors. Always there was the inability to leave history alone; the record must be rewritten—at whatever cost to truth—until there was only one major figure, one guiding genius, one hero. He had the hunger that can never be satisfied: always to have been right, always perfect, always admired. There is a hollowness here, a lack of centrality, of commitment and conviction beyond the self that could have redeemed what is otherwise empty posturing. As a human being he was a shell of tarnished magnificence, a false giant attended by real pygmies.

IV

For the Army, water is a forbidding barrier, for the Navy, a broad and inviting highway, and these are habits of mind engendered from earliest training. If by geography alone, war in the Pacific opposed the two services to one another. MacArthur and the Army, looking northward from Australia, saw the many-islanded land route to the Philippines and victory beyond laid out before them. Nimitz and the Navy, at Pearl Harbor, saw the almost empty ocean leading to the west and to the inexorable crushing of Japanese sea power, followed by blockade and economic strangulation. Each sensed the capability of realizing his vision to be within reach; each sensed the other as an unreasonable and uncomprehending rival who might prevent that, and each believed in the principle of unity of command provided it was his unity and not the other's. The result was that "unity of command" over the Pacific war as a whole was never attained by either the Army or the Navy, and the odd thing was that it turned out not to matter very much.

At the beginning of 1943, with the Guadalcanal and Papuan campaigns winding down to a close, there was much discussion in Washington about what to do next. At the Casablanca Conference with the British in January, where King began to achieve his aims, agreement was reached on further operations in the Solomon Islands, New Guinea, and the area around Rabaul, together with encouragement for the further advance the Navy wanted into the central Pacific to the Marshall and Caroline islands (Tarawa would be the first target among them). But this was at best a general outline intended to satisfy everybody and keep them all moving. There was as yet no focused strategy, no thought-through proposal for how Japan was ultimately to be defeated. After repeated requests from the Joint Chiefs, MacArthur put together a plan to satisfy his part of the Casablanca directive, and in February he sent General Sutherland to

Washington to make the argument for it. He had at that time about fifteen divisions, eleven of them Australian (of which only three were trained and equipped for offensive operations) and four American (one of them Marine), and about a thousand aircraft, of which a quarter were Australian.[69] He wanted more, much more.

MacArthur had long insisted that he needed aircraft carriers. In April of the previous year, he had encouraged Prime Minister Curtin to request a British carrier (and two British infantry divisions) from Churchill, prompting a tart inquiry from Churchill to Roosevelt as to "whether General MacArthur has any authority from the United States for taking such a line." The President's reproof of MacArthur was gentle and invited his views, to which MacArthur responded by saying that he needed *two* carriers, *three* more divisions, and five hundred to a thousand more aircraft.

Carriers were a case in point of the divergence between MacArthur and the Navy. He thought of them as a highly desirable device for giving air cover to his amphibious landings until a field had been acquired ashore and his own land-based aviation could be brought in. The Navy saw the carrier as the most potent offensive weapon they had, provided it stayed in motion and had sea room to maneuver. To confine any of the precious few carriers we then possessed to a secondary and heavily risk-attended role made no sense to them. As late as 1954, MacArthur was still professing not to understand why the carriers had been denied him.[70]

The MacArthur plan Sutherland brought to Washington called for him to have five more divisions, 1,800 more aircraft, and more cruisers, destroyers, and PT boats. The Joint Chiefs had a clear choice among giving MacArthur what he asked, getting him to scale down his requests, or canceling his offensive and substituting something less ambitious. After two weeks of at times heated debate, and some pressure from the President, a solution emerged that was somewhere in between. MacArthur's mission was modified to end short of Rabaul and he was allocated but two more divisions, more heavy bombers, and six and a half Army air groups. Between them he and Admiral Halsey, commander of the South Pacific theater adjacent to his, would have 2,500 planes, 240 of them heavy bombers.[71] It was a realistic compromise, but its most remarkable feature —and something of a puzzle in the light of previous history—was that the new directive issued by the Joint Chiefs straightened out, at least on paper, the question of command.

The Solomon Islands campaign (under Halsey) and the New Guinea campaign (under MacArthur) were of necessity closely interlinked, since both were directed at Rabaul and Rabaul was the base from which resistance to both would come; Japanese ground forces consigned to fight off one could not be used in the other. Who should be in command on our side was discussed by Leahy, Marshall, King, and Hopkins with the President on February 13 and continued to preoccupy the Joint Chiefs for many of the weeks that followed. Drafts of possible ways of relating the two offensives (MacArthur in charge? Halsey in charge? mutual coordination?) were exchanged by Army and Navy planners, principally General Handy and Admiral Cooke. The latter in March produced a list of seven reasons why the top direction should be naval, and in a similar situation, where Guadalcanal had been at issue, the Navy in the person of Admiral King had been almost immovable in its resistance to supervision by MacArthur. Thus the final phrasing accepted by the JCS will come as a surprise, in that it provided for Admiral Halsey to have "direct command" of the Solomons operation under the "general directives" of General MacArthur. In the final stages of discussion, writes the historian of the Joint Chiefs, "no consideration was given to the possibility of assigning over-all command to anyone but General MacArthur."[72]

This was the work of George Marshall, whom MacArthur so unjustly believed to be hostile to him. The new instructions sent out at the end of March 1943 were in all essentials what Marshall had been arguing for since December 1942 and the Navy for four months had been powerfully and sometimes angrily opposing. What had happened was that Marshall had consistently spoken up for MacArthur's integrity of operation in the South Pacific and had finally persuaded King. "I have come to the conclusion," writes an unnamed naval officer quoted in the Army history, "that Admiral King considers his relations with General Marshall on such a successful plane . . . that there are some matters in which he will not proceed to their logical accomplishment believing that even if he succeeded he would damage the relationship mentioned beyond repair. One of these items is the unification of command in [the Pacific], including the efforts of General MacArthur up the New Guinea coast." The arrangement they had settled on may appear an awkward one—the distinction between "general" and "direct" command is not always bound to be clear—but the thing worked, essentially because Halsey and MacArthur hit it off when they met, and were able to argue amiably over issues that divided them, as Halsey put it, "until one of us changed his mind."[73]

Lae and Salamua are on the gulf of New Guinea's Huon peninsula, about 140 miles northwest of Buna. Of the two, Lae was the more important, since it had a good anchorage and was the entrance to the Markham River valley, where there were many fine sites for airfields. During July and August 1943, the Japanese had been focusing their attention not on Lae and Salamua but on resisting (effectively but without final success) landings under Halsey in the Solomons by the American 43d Division and the 1st Marine Raider Battalion near Munda Point on New Georgia. Meanwhile, during late July, the 3d Australian and 41st U.S. divisions had been marching overland on Salamua, causing the Japanese to transfer thence four times as many troops as they left behind in Lae.

Whereupon, September 4, the Australian 9th Division landed seventeen miles east of Lae and next day 1,700 men of the U.S. 503rd Parachute Regiment jumped in the Markham Valley and captured an airstrip. (General MacArthur flew over them in a B-17 to provide, as he said, "such comfort as my presence might bring to them.") In twenty-four hours, a field was ready for Kenney's transports to fly in Australian 7th Division, which converged with its compatriots on Lae; they entered the town from both sides on September 16, to discover that the Japanese had departed. Salamua fell the same day, and on October 1 the Australians added Finschafen on the Huon peninsula's eastern tip. A well-conceived and well-executed operation, for which Australian General Blamey deserves at least some of the credit; "it was a honey," MacArthur radioed his wife in Brisbane.[74]

MacArthur's own touch could still be a bit unsteady. Two of his amphibious assaults in December, on Arawe and Cape Gloucester in New Britain, were not in strategic terms required. The ostensible purpose was to open the Vitiaz Strait between New Guinea and New Britain, but effectively the capture of the Huon peninsula had already done that. Neither Arawe nor Cape Gloucester ever became an air or a naval base and neither contributed to the advance on the Philippines (which was in the opposite direction) or to the reduction of Rabaul (which was accomplished by airpower, some of it Kenney's and a hefty part of it on November 5 from Halsey's aircraft carriers *Saratoga* and *Princeton;* thereafter no Japanese heavy ships ever came again to Rabaul). General Whitney justified the casualties at Arawe and Cape Gloucester (428 dead and 1,435 wounded) on the grounds that this was a feint, intended to make the Japanese "expend all their resources preparing the strongest possible defenses against an attack that would never come"—i.e., on Rabaul. His explanation has the odor of an afterthought; the record does not support it. The official Army history says that Arawe and Cape Gloucester were "first planned by GHQ on the assumption that Rabaul *would* be captured" (emphasis added).[75] Leaving Rabaul as it was made these operations superfluous.

◆

MacArthur's major claim to fame in the strategy of the Pacific war was the technique of "leapfrogging," or bypassing centers of Japanese resistance and going on to capture weaker ones at a lower cost in lives. He is often credited with the principle of "hit 'em where they ain't," a baseball phrase attributed to "Wee Willie" Keeler of the Baltimore Orioles for batting into the emptiest parts of the outfield. In his postwar statement on the subject, MacArthur managed to concede that this was a system "as old as war itself" and simultaneously to claim his own priority in applying it to World War II. "Immediately upon my arrival in Australia . . . ," he wrote, "I determined that such a plan of action was the sole chance of fulfilling my mission. . . . The first actual physical bypass was probably when I had Halsey's forces . . . bypass the lines of Guadalcanal along the west coast of Bougainville. Probably the first time it attracted general public attention was the Admiralty landings."[76] To say that this exposition fails to fit the facts is to deny not MacArthur's eventual enthusiasm for leapfrogging but only his predating of when it began.

MacArthur was quite right in remarking that the notion was obvious, so much so that it occurred to many people and more than once. The one thing that can safely be said, though, is that whoever had the idea first, it was not Douglas MacArthur. The first major Japanese base to be bypassed was Rabaul, and MacArthur went on insisting that he would have to take Rabaul long after the Joint Chiefs had concluded this to be unnecessary. Admiral King suggested outflanking Rabaul by going to the Admiralties in November 1942, but in January 1943 MacArthur rejected this. In May 1943, the planning committee of the Joint Chiefs recommended invading the Admiralties; in July, the Joint Chiefs approved and Marshall told MacArthur that they believed he should "isolate" Rabaul rather than assault it. But MacArthur again replied that capturing Rabaul was a "prerequisite" to his New Guinea campaign. Fortunately, his opinion was ignored. Rabaul's garrison of 100,000, well dug in and spoiling for an attack, might have been all too successful in repulsing it.[77]

General Arnold said that at a meeting of the Joint Chiefs with the President (it would probably have been sometime in late 1942), Roosevelt commented on the slowness of our progress and remarked that at this rate it would take us two thousand years to reach mainland Japan. "We talked about various methods," wrote Arnold, "and finally the 'leapfrog' technique was suggested, I believe by General Marshall." (At a plenary session with Churchill and the Combined Chiefs at Casablanca on January 23, 1943, the President stated his view that "an island-to-island advance across the Pacific would take too long to reduce the Japanese power. Some other method of striking at Japan must be found.") Admiral Morison credits Admiral Theodore Wilkinson, amphibious commander under Halsey, with the idea and with the "hit 'em where they ain't" phrase. Leapfrogging had been suggested by Naval War College staff planners as early as 1940 and was revived by an article in the Naval Institute *Proceedings* in May 1943. During that same month, Admiral Thomas Kinkaid, in the Aleutians, bypassed Kiska to take Attu. The Combined Chiefs, meeting at Quebec in August, decided to bypass Rabaul despite MacArthur's protests; Halsey did not invade Bougainville until November and he bypassed not Guadalcanal but Kolombangara, by landing on Vella Lavella in August.[78]

What it comes down to is the Admiralties. MacArthur's decision to land there on February 29, 1944, with a "reconnaissance in force" (which he personally and at some risk accompanied), displays him at his best: bold, resourceful, effective. It shortened the Pacific campaigns by at least a month. It enabled us to acquire what became (again over MacArthur's protests) the major naval base of Seeadler Harbor and it went a long way toward convincing the Combined Chiefs that MacArthur's much-desired return to the Philippines was feasible. Most of all, it made a convert of MacArthur. The first dramatic leapfrog proposal genuinely his own—to bypass Hansa Bay and Wewak and go all the way to Hollandia in Netherlands New Guinea—he made on March 5, when it was clear to him that the Admiralties operation was going to succeed and naval (decoding) intelligence had told him that Hollandia was weakly held.[79]

The original initiative for the Admiralties, as will be remembered, came from Admiral King and was signed and sealed into Allied strategy at Quebec, whereupon planning began to go forward in General Krueger's headquarters near Finschafen in New Guinea. MacArthur's air force commander, General Kenney, was eager to speed things up, and on February 23 he went to MacArthur with a report that three B-25s had just spent an hour and a half over the Admiralties, had not been fired on, and saw no Japanese, no motor vehicles, and no laundry hanging out to dry; airfields were pitted and overgrown with grass. (The impression of no Japanese being present was unfortunately mistaken; MacArthur's intelligence officer, General Willoughby, estimated the number there at 4,500 and for once he had it just about right; they had been ordered to lie low during daylight.)

Kenney's recommendation of a "reconnaissance in force" by several hundred men to seize an airfield was almost instantly accepted by MacArthur. A scratch group from the 1st Cavalry Division joined by artillery and antiaircraft was put together in a day, about a thousand in all, and loaded in twelve destroyers. MacArthur and Admiral Kinkaid would accompany them in cruiser *Phoenix* to make the on-the-spot decision whether to remain ashore. They sailed from Oro Bay at 6:45 A.M. on February 28 and landed in the Admiralties a little more than twenty-four hours later—less than a week from inception to event, a marvelous display of flexibility and improvisation.

Four and a half hours after H-Hour, the entire force had disembarked and overrun the airstrip, against light opposition and with light losses, two dead and three wounded. (Navy casualties were the same, when shore guns fired on landing craft.) General MacArthur came ashore at two in the afternoon, decorated the first man to land, reconnoitered areas still under fire, and gave the order to hold what had been taken. "It seemed too good to be true," reads an Army account.[80] It was. Reduction of the Japanese Admiralties garrison in its various strongpoints eventually took a month and a half and cost 326 Americans killed and 1,189 wounded. But Japanese losses were almost ten times greater and the gain in time—and in the number of Japanese bases like Kavieng that could now be ignored—was the prize the American casualties had paid for. The quick exploitation of an unforeseen opportunity was MacArthur's.

The strategy that won the Pacific campaigns, however, was not MacArthur's but Admiral King's, the "whipsaw" idea of attacking the Japanese from two different directions at once, so that they would have to shift their forces from one side to another and could never concentrate, which King proposed to Nimitz in February 1943. There is no indication that MacArthur ever understood this or did anything but object to it. In November 1943, when General Sutherland again went to Washington to make MacArthur's case, he argued that attempting a major effort on more than one axis "would result in weakness everywhere in violation of cardinal principles of war, and . . . in failure to reach the vital strategic objective at the earliest possible date, thus prolonging the war." MacArthur wanted *his* axis to be the only one. In February 1944, he cabled the War Department: "All available ground, air and assault forces in the Pacific should be combined in a drive along the New Guinea–Mindanao axis supported by the main fleet."

He said it was "impossible" to move through the central Pacific "due to the lack of adequate land areas" for fleet and air bases, a view that recalls the traditional Army attitude toward sea and sky, and that reveals his incomprehension of the means by which the Navy and the B-29s were to prove him wrong.[81]

And yet, paradox of paradoxes, it was MacArthur's insistence on his return to the Philippines, his success in persuading President Roosevelt and the Joint Chiefs to endorse it, that kept the whipsaw strategy alive at a time when many were prepared to abandon it, and it was his landing at Leyte Gulf that brought about the major sea battle the Navy so ardently desired.

◆

MacArthur was in Brisbane when he received a message from Marshall summoning him to Hawaii on July 26, 1944, for an important conference. He assumed this to involve the President, in which he was quite right, and it displeased him. He felt that he was being exploited as part of a presidential election campaign. (On July 20 in Chicago, Roosevelt had been nominated for a fourth term; he delivered his acceptance speech from San Diego, where he was inspecting the Marine base, and then put to sea in cruiser *Baltimore*.) MacArthur brought with him no planning papers and no senior staff. Striding up and down the aisle of his B-17, he did not attempt to conceal his anger. "The humiliation," he said, "of forcing me to leave my command to fly to Honolulu for a political picture-taking junket! In the First War I never for a moment left my division, even when wounded by gas [he had refused to wear a mask] and ordered to the hospital. In all my fighting days I've never before had to turn my back on my assignment."[82] His assignment now, as surely he must have realized, was to defend his strategy.

Baltimore stood up the channel at Pearl on the twenty-sixth, flying the presidential flag, while every ship in the harbor manned the rails. As will happen on such occasions, security was not perfect and a large crowd had collected on the dock, where several dozen generals and admirals in their dress whites were lined up to greet the President. As *Baltimore* moored, Nimitz's chief of staff, Vice-Admiral "Soc" McMorris, gave them the order "Right face!" but they had not been doing much close-order drill lately and two of them turned left, to cheers from the crew of *Baltimore*. On board, they were presented to the Commander in Chief in the flag cabin. (Nimitz and the Army Pacific commander, General Richardson, had come aboard earlier from a tug outside the harbor.)[83] There was a conspicuous absentee. No MacArthur. Embarrassed silences. Judge Rosenman, who was in the presidential party (Admiral Leahy, Ross McIntire, Pa Watson, Fala, and others), has left a lively picture of what followed.

Suddenly a piercing siren was heard. There raced onto the dock and screeched to a halt a motorcycle escort followed by what Rosenman described as "the longest open car I have ever seen"; it bore four stars. In the back was a lone figure wearing a leather flight jacket and the by-now-familiar battered khaki field marshal's cap. MacArthur acknowledged the cheers of the crowd and strode up the gangplank alone, stopping midway to acknowledge the cheers again. To a chorus of boatswain's pipes, he smartly saluted the quarterdeck and disappeared below. "Hello, Douglas," said Roosevelt. "What are you doing with that leather jacket on?" MacArthur explained that he had just come in from Australia (he had landed an hour or so before *Baltimore* docked) and "It's pretty cold up there." Returning to General Richardson's quarters, where he was staying, MacArthur unburdened himself that evening to his colleague and long-time friend Colonel Bonner Fellers about "his long years of struggle and his many defeats and frustrations."[84]

The President, confirming MacArthur's worst suspicions, spent the next day traveling about Oahu with Leahy, MacArthur, and Nimitz, inspecting Army and Navy installations. Roosevelt and MacArthur monopolized the conversation, reminiscing about their work together early in World War I. They talked, according to MacArthur, "of everything but the war—of our old carefree days when life was simpler and gentler, of many things that had disappeared in the mists of time." That evening the President had MacArthur, Leahy, and Nimitz to dinner in the cream stucco house on Kalaukau Drive in Waikiki (normally a rest center for naval aviators) where he had been quartered. Afterward they sat in the living room before a large map of the Pacific. Roosevelt tapped the map with a bamboo pointer and said, "Well, Douglas, where do we go from here?"

MacArthur rose and began to speak, by all accounts one of his best performances. "Leyte, Mr. President," he began, "and then Luzon!"[85]

This meeting has taken on a symbolic significance that professional historians are loath to concede it. No minutes were kept and no document confirms any decisions being reached at the end; Marshall, King, and Arnold took no part in it and the subjects discussed continued to be debated in Washington for weeks thereafter. The author of the Army history devoted to this, Robert Ross Smith, observes in a footnote with a touch of asperity that all statements attributing great importance to the Hawaii conference have been made by people who were not there.[86]

True, but the participants talked about it freely to others; Roosevelt described it to Admiral Morison, MacArthur described it to his staff, to John Gunther, and to Eichelberger (who said he heard about it from "several persons who were present"). While some accounts may be secondhand, and others confuse the order of events, they do not differ as to material substance. The consensus is that the discussion was amicable, that the President conducted it analytically and impartially, and that when it was over he and Leahy had been brought around to MacArthur's viewpoint. Even Robert Ross Smith admits that from this time forward Leahy took MacArthur's side, and that because of "his intimate contact with President Roosevelt," his opinion was respected by the other Joint Chiefs.[87] The matter at hand has passed into the literature under the general heading Formosa versus Luzon, with Luzon coming out ahead.

We will have to backtrack a bit in seeking for the reasons why a choice between the two was of such moment. To begin with the U.S. Navy, as of July 1944 its offensive arm under Admiral Spruance constituted "the most powerful battle fleet the world has ever seen," so says Clark Reynolds—a force of fifteen fast carriers and a battle line of seven new fast battleships, supported by a train of fuel, supply, and repair vessels that enabled it to stay at sea for months on end. In June, Fifth Fleet had invaded the Mariana Islands, the "key" to the western Pacific as King believed, and off Guam in the Battle of the Philippine Sea on the nineteenth the Japanese lost 315 aircraft to our 23, a savaging of their naval air capability from which they never recovered.[88] Fifth Fleet (renamed Third Fleet when Halsey commanded the same ships) could go virtually where it chose on the wide expanse of the unharvested sea, and where it *ought* to go had therefore to be thought about at length.

As for MacArthur, his venture into leapfrogging had been rewarded. The Joint Chiefs believed that the central Pacific was the best route to follow, but they also believed in the whipsaw of both routes at the same time and in the probability that Australia would react unfavorably to an advance in the central Pacific only. Accordingly, at Cairo in December 1943, the Combined Chiefs had approved MacArthur's further progress along the north coast of New Guinea. In March 1944, the Joint Chiefs authorized him to jump to Hollandia, bypassing Wewak and Hansa Bay, and in June they asked him (as they often had to do) for detailed information about his plans. He replied on July 8 to a further inquiry from Marshall with a proposal for seizing the western end of New Guinea, called the Vogelkop because of its bird's-head shape, and then bypassing Halmahera and Davao to reach Morotai and thence the southern Philippines. (As usual, he asked that his be the main effort, supported by the entire Pacific Fleet, a prospect Admiral King did not find pleasing.)[89]

But by July, the 41st and 24th U.S. Divisions of Krueger's Alamo Force had occupied Hollandia and elements of the 41st and the 32d had landed at nearby Aitape, where they and reinforcements from the 43d beat off a fierce Japanese counterattack along the Driniumor River by two divisions of Japanese 18th Army, one of those cutthroat and forgotten encounters. Said Eichelberger of the Driniumor, "it was a famous, if insufficiently reported, battle." The march northward from Australia was beginning to gather momentum; Krueger now had ten American divisions. General Marshall wrote, in his biennial report: "In a little over twelve months, American forces in the southwest Pacific, with the assistance of Australian units, had pushed 1,300 miles closer to the heart of the Japanese Empire, cutting off more than 135,000 enemy troops beyond the hope of rescue."[90]

Formosa versus Luzon was unusual among the strategic debates of the Pacific war in that it involved not two opposing schools of thought but many, and these did not divide exclusively along Army-Navy lines; within each service there were significant disagreements. The Formosa–Luzon–China coast triangle had been the overall objective of the Joint Chiefs for some time past; possession of it, as King believed, would cut Japan off from the riches of Southeast Asia and the Indies, perhaps starving it into submission without an invasion of Japan proper. The logic of this was that taking Luzon was probably a prerequisite to taking Formosa, and that Formosa was a prerequisite to landing on the China coast. But then things started to get complicated.

The success of the Japanese Ichigo offensive in overrunning the American East China air bases made a landing on the coast seem less attractive, and as the persuasiveness of bypassing took hold, it began to be liberally applied. If we did not have to go to the China coast, then perhaps we did not have to go to Formosa, either; perhaps the whole triangle could be bypassed by going directly to Japan. But the idea that established itself most firmly in Washington minds was that of bypassing Luzon, or even the entire Philippine archipelago. The very mention of it produced explosions of outrage from Brisbane. For MacArthur, returning to his "second homeland" had by now become an obsession.[91]

The principal exponent of the going-to-Formosa school was Admiral King; he clung to the need for it tenaciously long after the Roosevelt-MacArthur meeting, long after everyone else had given it up. (The arguments that finally did it in were logistical; Army studies showed that invading Formosa would lead to a major land campaign for which resources would not be available until the war in Europe was over.) At the moment MacArthur was departing for Hawaii, however, the planning committee of the Joint Chiefs was still assuming that Formosa came first and that the purpose of acquiring the southern Philippines (Mindanao and Leyte) was only to reduce Japanese air power on Luzon, in order to ensure success for the Formosa operation; a message to this effect arrived in Brisbane while MacArthur was away.

The War Department was not fully behind him this time. General McNarney was strongly in favor of bypassing the Philippines, and so, it appears, was General Arnold; General Marshall at one point favored bypassing *both* the Philippines and Formosa. Backing for the go-to-Luzon school came mainly from General Somervell, from senior Army officers in the Pacific, and—just for variety—from Admirals Halsey, Spruance, and Turner.[92] For MacArthur to be on his own at Waikiki had therefore a certain poetic justice.

MacArthur's position was frankly a mixture of the military and the political, with the latter having a distinct edge. On the military side, he maintained that possession of *all* the Philippines would achieve the purpose of severing the Japanese lifeline more economically than what he described as "the naval concept of frontal assault against the strongly held island positions of the enemy in the Western Pacific." He saw the Philippines as a secure base for further advances, whereas the Pacific islands were too small (the *land* mode of thought again) and Formosa had too "hostile" a population.

The Philippines were "American" territory where our "unsupported" forces had suffered a crushing defeat; to sacrifice them a second time "would not be condoned or forgiven." The Philippine people were still loyal despite our failure to "succor" them. If we were to bypass the islands, this would have the "gravest psychological reactions," confirming Japanese propaganda that pictured Americans as unwilling to shed blood for an Asian ally, incurring Philippine hostility and a "loss of prestige among all the peoples of the Far East," and causing "extremely adverse reactions" in the United States. "We have a great national obligation to discharge . . . ," MacArthur had radioed Marshall on June 18. "The American people I am sure would acknowledge this obligation."[93]

Later, when he had a moment alone with Roosevelt, MacArthur seems to have been even more explicit. "Mr. President," General Whitney reports him as saying, "if your decision be to bypass the Philippines and leave its millions of wards of the United States and thousands of internees and prisoners of war to languish in their agony and despair—I dare to say that the American people would be so aroused that they would register most complete resentment against you at the polls this fall."[94]

That has the authentic MacArthurian ring to it; it is in character. MacArthur's propensity for writing indiscreet letters to Republican congressmen was already well known; if he chose to make an issue of this— and he came as close as language allows to implying that he would, without actually saying so—then the President would face unpredictable hazards in the fall campaign, a loose cannon on the deck. Mr. Roosevelt did not like unpredictable hazards in elections. One could put it bluntly and say that MacArthur was stating his price for participating in this "political picture-taking junket," for permitting himself to be assigned the part of loyal lieutenant to his Commander in Chief.

The case for Formosa was made by Admiral Nimitz, who had met recently with King and was fully conversant with King's convictions. The second and final session ended at noon the next day. Eichelberger says that MacArthur bowed and started to leave under the impression that his cause was lost, but that Roosevelt said, "Wait a minute, Douglas. Come back here," and assured MacArthur that the Philippines would not be bypassed. Frazier Hunt's version has Leahy plucking at MacArthur's sleeve and saying, in a stage whisper, "I'll go along with you, Douglas." Morison quotes "a source close to MacArthur" as recounting that when his plane left Oahu, the general told an aide: "We've sold it!" That afternoon, Roosevelt insisted that MacArthur accompany him on another inspection tour, and MacArthur took the opportunity to ask the President what he thought were Dewey's chances in the coming contest. Roosevelt said he had been too busy to think much about politics. MacArthur later said: "I threw back my head and laughed. He looked at me and then broke into a laugh himself."[95] But the President laughed last.

The Pacific war *did* figure in the fall campaign: Governor Dewey claimed that Roosevelt was willfully withholding support from MacArthur. He had the misfortune to do this several days before the Philippine invasion began in Leyte Gulf, on October 20. On the twenty-seventh, Roosevelt spoke at Shibe Park in Philadelphia, calling attention to the fact that in the past year we had made twenty-seven successful landings in force on enemy-held soil, two of them thirteen thousand miles apart, in Europe and the Philippines. "And," he added, "speaking of the glorious operation in the Philippines—I wonder whatever became of the suggestion made a few weeks ago, that I had failed for political reasons to send enough forces or supplies to General MacArthur?"[96] He had not practiced this art thirty years for nothing.

Before the President left Oahu, he visited a hospital and asked to be conducted slowly through the wards of men who had lost one or more arms or legs. "He insisted on going past each individual bed . . . ," wrote Rosenman. "He wanted to display himself and his useless legs to those boys who would have to face the same bitterness. This crippled man in the little wheel chair wanted to show them that it was possible to rise above such physical handicaps." Rosenman had seen Roosevelt do the same thing with polio patients at Warm Springs; there were smiles to be distributed at large and a pleasant word at the bedside of a score or more. Rosenman said that he never saw Roosevelt with tears in his eyes, but "that day as he was wheeled out of the hospital he was close to them."[97]

◆

The Philippine campaign was MacArthur's vindication, the culminating event of the Southwest Pacific war. The Japanese recognized possession of the Philippines as vital to them and fought in that conviction; by the end, their Fourteenth Army—which included nine of their very best, first-class divisions—was no more and their fleet had been shattered beyond recall. The event was neither brief nor inexpensive. MacArthur had promised the Joint Chiefs that he would have hold of the Central Luzon–Manila Bay area within four to six weeks of landing in Lingayen Gulf and he almost made it (by dint of pressuring Walter Krueger), but the fighting in the islands as a whole went on, and on; the equivalent of three and two thirds American divisions was still actively engaged against the Japanese in northern Luzon on V-J Day.

Roosevelt had queried MacArthur about casualties, only to be assured that "my losses would not be heavy. . . . The days of the frontal attack are over. . . . Only mediocre commanders still use it. Your good commanders do not turn in heavy losses." As so often before, MacArthur was confusing intentions with performance. Total U.S. Army casualties in the Philippines were about 47,000 (10,380 killed, 36,550 wounded), not a great deal lower than Okinawa's 49,151 (12,520 killed, 36,631 wounded), by common consent the bloodiest action in the Pacific. (Nonbattle casualties in the Philippines were the *highest* of the war, 93,400 lost to sickness or injury, of whom 260 died.)[98]

Manila was a city of some 800,000, more venerable than any in the United States save Saint Augustine. MacArthur in recapturing it almost obliterated it. General Willoughby had estimated that there were about 152,500 Japanese troops on Luzon (the actual figure was some 250,000), and MacArthur did not believe that they would fight for Manila. He was wrong. They fought, and hard, street by street, building by building. MacArthur forbade the use of aerial bombardment as "unthinkable," since it "would result beyond question in the death of thousands of innocent civilians." The difference between an air raid and heavy artillery is not all that great; American artillery leveled much of Manila to the ground and an estimated 100,000 civilians died.

The city was left a shambles: the university, hospital, and government buildings were rubble, there was no public transportation or electric power, water and sewage were erratic, twenty-nine of a hundred bridges had been knocked out, and residential and industrial areas alike were in ruins. On February 25, 1945, MacArthur climbed the damaged stairway of the Manila Hotel to what had been his penthouse apartment. His possessions, his library and the rest, had been scattered or destroyed; a dead Japanese officer lay between two smashed vases given MacArthur's father by the emperor in 1905. "It was not a pleasant moment . . . ," MacArthur said later. "I was tasting to the last acid dregs the bitterness of a devastated and beloved home."[99]

How much of the Philippine campaign was military necessity is still debatable. MacArthur's staunchest defender is Eichelberger, who believed—"with, to be sure, the advantage of hindsight," he said—that the landings on Formosa or the China coast without clearing the Philippines and Borneo first "would have been almost disastrously costly," since Japanese air power could have "made our position untenable." As late as the landing on Mindoro, two months after the Leyte invasion and our unceasing attacks on their airfields, the Japanese were still strong enough in the air to keep Mindoro harbor clear of Allied shipping. "If the enemy could do that with our Army planes already cozily based on Leyte," wrote Eichelberger in 1950, "it gives any reasoning man a shudder to envisage what might have happened at Formosa."[100] If Eichelberger was right about Luzon versus Formosa, then so was MacArthur. But was Formosa necessary?

Other questions arise concerning the operations to recapture the bypassed islands of the central and southern Philippines, which began even before the Luzon landing was a month old. The Joint Chiefs had not authorized these; they were MacArthur's own idea, and they seemed to reflect a preoccupation with repossessing Philippine real estate for its own sake (the remaining islands "had no strategic importance," says the U.S. Army history). Between Leyte and V-J Day, Eichelberger's Eighth Army made fifty-two amphibious assaults; in one forty-four-day period there was a landing every day and a half. The Army history attributes this juggernaut to "pressing political considerations"—that is, liberating the Philippine population and reestablishing lawful government. The cost in Army casualties was 7,880 (1,910 killed and 5,970 wounded). Neither the War Department nor the Joint Chiefs objected. By the time the JCS got around to approving the southern Philippine battles, most of them were already over.[101]

As a professional military performance this was not topnotch. MacArthur's intelligence was frequently poor and the Leyte campaign went on much longer than anticipated. When Eichelberger's Eighth Army took it over from Krueger's Sixth on Christmas Day 1944, Eichelberger was told there were only 6,000 Japanese left on Leyte; before his men were done, they had killed 27,000. MacArthur told Eichelberger he did not believe there were more than 4,000 Japanese left alive on Mindanao; at war's end, 23,000 surrendered. On the basis of wrong information from MacArthur's headquarters about Manila's water supply, 38th Division attacked the wrong dam. Sound strategy was sacrificed to MacArthur's devouring passion to redeem himself. His unauthorized move into the central and southern Philippines with Eighth Army meant that Sixth Army on Luzon was seriously weakened. According to Clayton James, "Krueger's forces were, time after time, severely handicapped in the execution of their mission for want of the units MacArthur had peremptorily decided to assign to Eighth Army."[102]

The fact is MacArthur sometimes gives the impression of having wandered into World War II by mistake. He disapproved of its overall conduct, and except for defeating Japan and restoring American hegemony in the Pacific, he had little empathy with its aims. In his theater he gave the directives; every operation was set up by his order. But he was not interested in tactical specifics and left these largely to his Army and Navy commanders, such as Krueger, Eichelberger, Kenney, and Admiral Kinkaid; he interfered with them only when they failed to give him a quick enough victory. Clayton James concludes that he could never be considered a major contributor to military thought.[103] His heart lay elsewhere, in the distant skies of glory.

MacArthur was an essentially thespian general whose position required constant backstage handling by the President to prop it up. Roosevelt and MacArthur needed each other, but the latter's need was the greater. John Gunther was the first writer about him to notice how completely MacArthur's World War II career had depended on Roosevelt's conscious interventions: keeping him on for an extra year as chief of staff, enabling him to go to the Philippines as military adviser, bringing him back into active service as ranking general officer in the Far East, stiffening his resolve when he wanted to give up the fight, ordering him out from Bataan to command the Southwest Pacific theater, and finally preferring his return to the Philippines over the Joint Chiefs' alternatives. Clayton James believes that in the long term, MacArthur will be more appreciated as an administrator (of postwar Japan) than as a military figure.[104]

What was MacArthur's contribution to the war? Not much, really. He mishandled the defense of the Philippines, by imposing an unsound plan and failing to train a Philippine army. He allowed his air force to be wiped out on the ground. He was slow to move in New Guinea and lost an opportunity to take the initiative away from the Japanese. He was a late convert to leapfrogging and for a time resisted it; his first bold move, in the Admiralties, was urged on him by others. He rejected the whipsaw strategy that made his amphibious landings work. His advance from Hollandia to Morotai was sound and well done, but the overall shape of it was determined by the Joint Chiefs and the detailed plans and execution by his subordinates. His final campaign in the Philippines he forced on a reluctant President by a political threat, and in reconquering the islands he nearly destroyed what he set out to save. Throughout he misrepresented his own achievements, surrounded himself with nonentities, patronized and disparaged his allies and the Navy, tampered with the historical record, tried to undercut concerted Allied strategy, and flirted with political opponents of his Commander in Chief. Where, in all this, is there anything to justify his reputation as a great commander?

Franklin Roosevelt was not a bad judge of character, and with MacArthur he seems to have been almost preternaturally perceptive. MacArthur would sacrifice a great deal to ego, and Roosevelt saw to it that MacArthur's ego was gratified, that he was offered a number of roles pleasing to him even where they were those of an *enfant terrible,* not on the face of it pleasing to the President. MacArthur's endless teeterings on the edge of insubordination I suspect bothered Roosevelt not in the slightest. There was nothing in the general's character patterns that did not suit the President's need for an idol his enemies could worship at without damage to him, so long as MacArthur was fighting a war within the Roosevelt consensus. This resonant figurehead was a political hopeless cause, and the more of Roosevelt's opponents who could be persuaded to join it, the safer the President became from serious attack—up to a point, that delicate point where the general roiled the political waters sufficiently to require that he be neutralized, as was done at the Hawaii conference, leaving MacArthur to stomach his wrath at having to play spear-carrier in Roosevelt's 1944 reelection.

The President's conduct was not above reproach; to lay on a major military campaign for such ulterior motives would hardly be admirable even where it was understandable. But the choice was not clear-cut; MacArthur's case had *some* military merit despite his clothing it in considerations of domestic votes and postwar prestige. And Roosevelt whether he liked it or not had to do *some*thing about MacArthur and the far-right Republican forces for which MacArthur had been let to serve as rallying point. Had the President lived longer, he might one day have savored the irony of solving one problem only to create another, for he was trapped by his own success. Having invented the MacArthur legend, he could not *dis*invent it; MacArthur would have to be allowed to reach even greater heights as ground force commander in any invasion of Japan, though Roosevelt believed that no invasion would be necessary, because of the atomic bomb.[105] The President and his successor would have to permit the MacArthur phenomenon to go full course, down to its triumphant climax on the deck of battleship *Missouri* in Tokyo Bay.

The Japanese surrender ceremony ennobled MacArthur to a degree that observers of his progress to date might never have anticipated. It enabled him to make a simple statement, divested of bluster and rodomontade; he rose to the occasion. There had always been something abstract about MacArthur's attitude to the war, his odd way of distancing it, that shows up now in his remarks on board *Missouri.* "The issues," he said, "involving divergent ideals and ideologies, have been determined on the battlefields of the world and hence are not for our discussion or debate." Ours not to reason why. These are the words of someone largely untouched by the war's political passions, someone who could think of a Nazi victory as "tolerable," and this now stood him in good stead. He did not hate the Japanese for their "ideals and ideologies"; he regarded them as a mean and merciless foe because they were his enemy, and MacArthur's enemy must always be the worst, the gravest menace. Now that there was no need for an enemy, a generous peace was in order, one that restored the Japanese to a healthy society, tutored them in American democracy, and persuaded them to abandon their bloodthirsty habits.

It is not, said MacArthur, "for us here to meet, representing as we do a majority of the people of the earth, in a spirit of distrust, malice, or hatred. But rather it is for us, both victor and vanquished, to rise to that higher dignity which alone befits the sacred purposes we are about to serve, committing all our people to faithful compliance with the obligation they are here formally to assume. It is my earnest hope and indeed the hope of all mankind that from this solemn occasion a better world shall emerge out of the blood and carnage of the past—a world founded upon faith and understanding—a world dedicated to the dignity of man and the fulfillment of his most cherished wish—for freedom, tolerance, and justice."[106]

The Japanese surrender party, nine in number, formed up in what was left of Tokyo and was driven to Yokohama in four limousines. They included Foreign Minister Mamoru Shigemitsu and Army Chief of Staff Yoshijuro Umezu, together with assistants like Toshikazu Kase of the Foreign Office, who had been delegated to write a report of the proceedings for the emperor. No Japanese ships remained afloat capable of carrying them the eighteen miles down the bay to *Missouri,* so they were embarked in destroyer *Landsdowne* and after about an hour came abreast of the huge gray battleship, flanked by line on line of American warships and flying the flag that had been hoisted over the White House on Pearl Harbor Day.

The Japanese were apprehensive; some had sent their women and children to the hills.[107] Kase said that as he and the others came up to the deck of *Missouri,* he had never before been conscious of how "staring eyes could hurt so much." Kase looked up and saw on the ship's side an array of painted miniature rising suns, representing the planes and ships shot down or sunk by *Missouri,* and he thought of the young men who had manned them as cherry blossoms, "emblems of our national character, swiftly blooming into riotous beauty and falling just as quickly."

When MacArthur spoke, Kase was mesmerized. "Here is the victor announcing the verdict to the prostrate enemy," he later wrote. "He can exact his pound of flesh if he so chooses. He can impose a humiliating penalty if he so desires. And yet he pleads for freedom, tolerance, and justice. For me, who expected the worst humiliation, this was a complete surprise." Kase in his report to the emperor raised the question "whether it would have been possible for us, had we been victorious, to embrace the vanquished with a similar magnanimity." Kase noted that the paper in MacArthur's hands trembled in the wind. As the proceedings ended, the cloudy sky parted, the sun broke through, and fleets of B-29s and carrier planes flew over them. The Japanese had not been beaten on the battlefield merely by superior arms, Kase found himself thinking. "We were defeated in the spiritual contest by a nobler ideal."[108]

It was Douglas MacArthur's finest hour.

VII

NIMITZ

"TELL NIMITZ TO GET THE HELL OUT TO PEARL and stay there til the war is won." Thus the President to the secretary of the Navy on December 16, 1941, with that war nine days old. A week beforehand, Knox had flown to Hawaii for an on-the-spot assessment of the state of the Pacific command, physical and psychological, and had returned in the conviction that Rear Admiral Husband E. Kimmel would have to be replaced by a fresh and unimplicated officer. After he and Roosevelt had given it a night's sleep, they settled on the choice of Rear Admiral Chester W. Nimitz, at that time head of the Bureau of Navigation. Nimitz went with Knox to the White House the same afternoon and then walked home to his apartment on Q Street, where he told his wife—with a demeanor that indicated his disquiet—that he was to be the new Commander in Chief in the Pacific. "You always wanted to command the Pacific Fleet," she said. "You always thought that would be the height of glory."

"Darling," said Nimitz, "the fleet's at the bottom of the sea. Nobody must know that here, but I've got to tell you."

Admiral Nimitz stood high in the President's estimation. Earlier that year, Roosevelt had offered him the second-highest post in the Navy, that of Commander in Chief, U.S. Fleet, but Nimitz had asked to be excused, pleading that such an advance by a junior over so many officers his senior would generate ill will. "Between the two men," writes Nimitz's biographer, "there developed a curious bond." Perhaps this came about because Nimitz, as Chief since 1939 of the Bureau of Navigation (later Bureau of Personnel, or Bupers), was concerned with the assignments and promotions of the top naval commanders, a subject in which the President took an inordinate interest.

One admiral who had a run-in with Roosevelt when the latter was assistant secretary said he still felt the repercussions a quarter century later; another had his name crossed off for a fleet command by the President with the words, "Why, I do not even know Admiral ———." Nimitz thought Roosevelt not quite natural, more than a little the actor, but respected him, especially for his mastery of politics. "I for one feel a deep sense of personal loss," Nimitz wrote to his wife when the President died. "Whether or not we liked *all* the things he did, and stood for—he was always for a strong Navy and was always most cordial and friendly to me."[1]

Nimitz was a Texan of German stock on both parental sides (Nimitzes fought with the Teutonic knights). The family household was bilingual. His father died before he was born, but he was greatly attached to his white-bearded grandfather, who had built a hotel near the Pedernales River with a marquee shaped like the prow of a ship and told his adoring grandchildren fantastic tales of his youth at sea in the German merchant marine. "The sea—like life itself—" grandfather Nimitz would say, "is a stern taskmaster." The military were familiar figures; to the Nimitz Hotel had come as guests Robert E. Lee, James Longstreet, and Phil Sheridan. An encounter with two recent West Point graduates almost as young as he was persuaded young Chester that in the Army lay the road to wider horizons, and he sought out his congressman, to be told that all the military academy places had been filled but that there was an opening at the naval academy, which Nimitz until that moment knew nothing of. Swallowing his disappointment, he buckled down to study for the exams, came out on top, and at Annapolis on September 7, 1901, was sworn in as a cadet.[2]

Nimitz at fifty-six was trim and vigorous, with a fair complexion and very blue eyes; only his silvering hair betrayed his age. His was not a demonstrative personality; he rarely raised his voice. "Possesses that calm and steady Dutch way that gets to the bottom of things," said his naval academy classbook of him. Admiral Spruance, perhaps his closest colleague, said that Nimitz had so many good qualities it was impossible to single out one of them and say, "Here is the key to the man." Among his characteristics seem to have been a fondness for dogs, classical music, and pitching horseshoes, at which he showed some skill: "he could always beat me with either hand," said Spruance. Nimitz made atrocious puns and had a seemingly endless stock of slightly off-color stories. His doctor recommended pistol practice as a relief from tension and a range was constructed behind his headquarters on Makalapa Hill above Pearl Harbor; Nimitz often repaired there after his morning conferences and could be heard firing away to clear his mind.[3]

This quiet man fought the Pacific war—not, to be sure, all by himself. In a sense, he served the indispensable purpose of standing as a buffer between Admiral King and the men like Spruance, Halsey, Turner, and Holland Smith who commanded in combat. King was at the outset uneasy about Nimitz, as he was about everybody connected with the Bureau of Personnel; he regarded them all as "fixers," always ready to "work things out." King mistrusted Nimitz's judgment, thought he took bad advice and was too willing to compromise. "If only I could keep him tight on what he's supposed to do," King once said to a friend. "Somebody gets ahold of him and I have to straighten him out"—which may have contained a germ of truth but says as much about King as it does about Nimitz. King always wanted to do everything himself, believing as he did that he could do it better. He insisted on frequent meetings with Nimitz (a total of eighteen during the war, usually in San Francisco) and sent him admonitory letters. According to King's biographer, "King would never allow anything or anyone to come between him and Nimitz."[4]

But King could not have achieved what Nimitz did and there were virtues in Nimitz that fell entirely outside King's range of comprehension: humility, diplomacy, accessibility. Nimitz's judgment was no worse than King's and sometimes better, and he had at least an equal ability to make prompt and firm decisions. His estimates of men were acute and he got their best work out of them, partly because he worked so hard himself. "No more fortunate appointment to this vital command could have been made," wrote Admiral Morison. "He restored confidence to the defeated fleet. He had the patience to wait through the lean period of the war, the capacity to organize both a fleet and a vast theater, the tact to deal with sister services and Allied commands, the leadership to weld his own subordinates into a great fighting team, the courage to take necessary risks, and the wisdom to select, from a welter of intelligence and opinion, the strategy that defeated Japan."[5] The President, once again, had chosen well.

Among the cadets at Annapolis while Nimitz was there were most of the U.S. naval leaders of World War II: Stark, Kimmel, Halsey, Fletcher, Spruance, Turner, McCain, Fitch, and many more; the total enrollment never exceeded seven hundred and everyone knew everyone else. Nimitz's own career began in submarines; he successively commanded three of them—*Plunger, Snapper,* and *Narwhal*—eventually rising to be chief of staff to the commander of submarine forces, Atlantic Fleet. He campaigned for the elimination from submarines of gasoline engines, because of escaping fumes and a tendency to explode, and their replacement by diesels. In 1913, Nimitz and his wife, Catherine, visited Germany, so that he could study diesels in the German plants where they had been developed, and before long he had become the Navy's most skilled diesel expert. The Nimitzes had an apartment with a balcony and a green backyard in Hamburg, a city he thought more beautiful than any he had known, with its gardens, parks, and *Bierkellers.* "Certainly none of our cities can equal it . . . ," he wrote to his mother in Texas. "I never saw so much beer consumed in my life."

Nimitz built the submarine base at Pearl Harbor, as he liked to say in afteryears, out of "stolen materials" (meaning that he and his chief petty officers were adept at cadging and somehow getting their hands on lumber and equipment other commanders were reluctant to give up). But neither submarines nor marine engineering was the route to high rank. Nimitz was also executive officer of battleship *South Carolina* and commanded cruisers *Chicago* and *Augusta* (flagship of the Asiatic Fleet). He attended Naval War College, which he credited with teaching him the strategy and tactics of the war against Japan: "nothing that happened in the Pacific war was strange or unexpected . . . ," Nimitz wrote forty years afterward; "we were well prepared for the fantastic logistic efforts required." He commanded cruiser and battleship divisions and introduced a number of tactical innovations; the idea of the circular formation (which became standard and remains so) was his, and he was instrumental in the integration of aircraft carriers into the hitherto battleship-dominated fleet. As chief of Bunav, he made the farsighted ruling that regular and reserve officers wear the same uniform (contrary to British practice), a powerful incentive to a unity he thought essential.[6]

The Nimitzes (there were to be four children) lived the life of nomadic naval families that follow the fleet where they can. In the summer of 1934, when Nimitz commanded *Augusta*, Mrs. Nimitz and the girls lived in the Japanese town of Unzen, in the hills above Nagasaki. (The Marine detachment on *Augusta* was headed by Lieutenant Chesty Puller, whom Nimitz would meet again on Guadalcanal.) In San Diego, they lived aboard tender *Rigel*, which had been made over for family quarters, and ashore then-Captain Nimitz went for long walks with Captain Raymond Spruance, then chief of staff to the commander of destroyers, Scouting Force. (Nimitz's daughter Anna, known as "Nancy," hung around the *Rigel*'s machine shop and a petty officer told Mrs. Nimitz that Nancy could run a better acetylene weld than any of the men.)

One time when they were living in the Q Street apartment in Washington, they went for a Potomac cruise on the yacht *Sequoia* as guests of the secretary of the Navy and met downstream the President's yacht *Potomac*, flying his flag. Everyone went on deck to salute him but Nancy, who said she wasn't sure she wanted to salute Roosevelt. "Whether you want to salute Roosevelt is your business," said her father, "but you are going to salute the President." (Anna Nimitz commented later, "It sunk in"; she studied Russian at Harvard and became a Soviet expert with the Rand Corporation.)[7]

When Nimitz took command as Cincpac—on the deck of submarine *Grayling*, December 31, 1941—morale in the Pacific Fleet was at an all-time low. It had not been improved by the withdrawal at the very last moment, on orders of the acting commander in chief awaiting Nimitz's arrival, Vice-Admiral W. S. Pye, of a task force, which included carrier *Saratoga*, sent to relieve the siege of Wake Island. Pye reasoned that conserving carriers was more important than saving Wake—and who can say he was wrong?—but his decision did little to lessen the sense of helpless rage that many Americans felt. One senior admiral, hearing of *Saratoga*'s recall, said he used to think "a man had to be both a fighter and know how to fight. Now all I want is a man who fights." They soon found that this was what they had in Chester Nimitz. "The one big thing about him," said Spruance, "was that he was always ready to fight. . . . And he wanted officers who would push the fight with the Japanese. If they would not do so they were sent elsewhere."[8]

Nimitz quickly reached two conclusions. One was that Cincpac could not be a seagoing command; the theater was too large and too complex for him to leave its communication center at Pearl Harbor and sail with the fleet, much as he would have preferred to. The second was that the disaster of December 7 was not so devastating as he had supposed. The carriers, being at sea, were still intact. The machine shops, the submarine base, and the tank farm—with its 4.5 million barrels of fuel oil—were untouched. (Had these been lost, Pearl would have become useless and what was left of the fleet would have had to retreat to California.) In any event, the eight battleships the Japanese sank or damaged were too old and slow to operate with carriers, and they were not "at the bottom of the sea," as Nimitz had told his wife; five of them were salvaged and lived to fight another day, at the Philippine Sea and Leyte Gulf. Had they been forewarned and sallied out to do battle, the Japanese carriers would have run rings around them and many would have gone down in deep water, taking thousands of men with them. "It was God's mercy that our fleet was in Pearl Harbor on December 7, 1941," Nimitz said later.[9]

One of Nimitz's first acts was to tell the Cincpac staff that he had complete confidence in them, did not blame them for what had happened, and hoped that they would all stay on. If any wished other assignments, he would do what he could to help them, "but certain key members of the staff I insist I want to keep." Morale "now rose several hundred per cent," Admiral Morison wrote. Nimitz was under pressure from King to make raids on Japanese-held islands using all available forces, including the half-dozen battleships then on the West Coast, but Nimitz insisted on thorough study and discussion beforehand. Spruance, who participated, said that the change in atmosphere in Cincpac conferences was "like being in a stuffy room and having someone open a window and let in a breath of fresh air." Nimitz sent Admiral Pye to Washington to dissuade his classmate King from an attempt to use the old battleships. The Marshall and Gilbert raids, carried out by Halsey with carriers *Enterprise* and *Yorktown,* did not do great damage to the Japanese, but they helped to mollify King and had the side effect of lifting spirits among sailors, soldiers, and civilians at home. They were the first hesitant steps on the road that led to Midway.[10]

Midway was Nimitz's great battle. He planned it, he picked its commander, he ordered it into execution. He proceeded thus because he had decided to accept as valid an intelligence estimate that forecast the time, location, and strength of a Japanese attack (there were senior and staff officers, especially in Washington, who did not share Nimitz's confidence in the prediction). Nimitz's reading of the crystal ball was the right one. By having the proper riposte prepared in advance, he was able to spring a trap of classic elegance. The Japanese plan was segmented, complex, synchronous; his was simple and flexible, timed only for lying in wait and striking when opportunity came.

There was a clarity about the American preparations that reflected itself in their implementation, a sequence of motions in which mistakes were made but none that flawed the central purpose, so that tasks followed one another in what seems like predestined order only because they were so well conceived and so well performed. By all rights this should not have been expected, and the Japanese did not expect it; they had abundant reasons to anticipate success and we had more than a few to be prepared for failure. Thus the victory when it came was not only one of inferior forces over superior but a stunning reversal in the tides of fortune, one of those passages at arms that turn the world around and send history off in a new direction.

II

Commander Joseph J. Rochefort, Jr., was not your sharp and trimly turned out naval officer. His working uniform was red smoking jacket and carpet slippers; his office was a mess, stacks of folders piled up on desks and chairs and spilling out over the floor. He was quartered in a windowless basement of the naval district administration building at Pearl Harbor, along with about a hundred co-workers and exotic equipment like key punchers, collators, and machine tabulators. Visitors were not welcome; they had to buzz two locked steel doors and show proper credentials before being admitted. Inevitably there was speculation about what went on down here, even amused suggestions that "Rochefort was trying to break the Japanese code."[11]

Rochefort presided over the local branch office, sometimes known as "Hypo," of Op-20-G, the Communications Security Section of the Office of Naval Communications in Washington. There was an arc of radio receiving stations with direction finders spread across the Pacific, recording Japanese transmissions and sending them to Op-20-G for analysis. Hypo specialized in the Imperial Navy's operational code, known to the Americans as JN25, a system of some 45,000 five-digit groups, each of which meant a word or phrase and was further encrypted by additive five-digit groups, changed periodically, taken from two volumes of 50,000 random numbers.[12]

In principle, the additives rendered the code invulnerable; in practice, the Japanese used it so heavily—up to a thousand messages a day—that the same random and code groups were bound to recur. This made possible a mathematical process called "stripping the additives," which is what the machine tabulators were there for. After that it was merely the formidable art of cryptanalysis, which is what Joe Rochefort and the others were there for. With its other stations in the United States, the Philippines, and (with the British) Singapore, Op-20-G had been breaking deeply into JN25.

Intelligence in general and decrypting in particular make up a chancy business. Rarely is there any such thing as a perfect solution; there are only bits and pieces, and the skill of the intelligence trade consists in matching these in a pattern so that each illuminates the others, and with luck allows an outline to emerge of what the enemy is doing and thinking. At Hypo, the source of the message, the frequency of traffic, the location of ships, the characteristic "fist" of the operators, information from submarine sightings and the like—all had to be taken into account.

Only a fraction (perhaps a third) of the 45,000 five-digit groups in JN25 was ever identified, but these were the most frequently used, and by May of 1942 Rochefort was reading perhaps 90 percent of the average Imperial Navy messages. His decodings were passed on to Lieutenant (later Captain) W. J. "Jasper" Holmes, an Annapolis graduate who had been retired for disability (arthritis) and then recalled to active duty and assigned to the Hawaii Combat Intelligence Unit. He in turn reported to Commander Edwin T. Layton, Nimitz's intelligence officer.

On May 5, 1942, Imperial Naval Headquarters issued Navy Order Number 18, instructing Combined Fleet to occupy Midway Island and the western Aleutians. The Japanese intention had been to distribute and begin using new codebooks on May 1, but their ships were so scattered and their confidence in their own security so great that the changeover had been postponed another month. This was only one of the interventions by Divine Providence in the Midway battle, but it was most fortunate, for it meant that Joe Rochefort could read some 85 percent of the detailed orders that followed. The missing parts had to do with dates, times, and places, which were in separate codes. For example, one of the objectives was designated only as AH; though Rochefort was reasonably certain that "AH" meant Midway, he did not know for sure.

Hypo normally put in long hours, but now it really turned on. After standing one twelve-hour watch, Lieutenant Commander Wesley A. "Ham" Wright stayed over all night and into the next day, working on the time-date cipher, which David Kahn in *The Codebreakers*, with no intent to make it sound easy, describes as "a polyalphabetic with independent mixed-cipher alphabets in two different systems of Japanese syllabic writing."[13] They broke it: The Japanese would strike what Hypo had concluded to be the Aleutians on June 3, and "AH" on June 4.

Then Jasper Holmes had a bright idea. There was an undersea cable from Hawaii to Midway that enabled the two to communicate directly safe from Japanese ears (this turned out to be important in other respects). Midway was instructed by cable to broadcast, in the clear, a radio message to the effect that it was running short of fresh water. Sure enough, the Japanese on Wake Island picked this up, and Wake radioed Tokyo that "AH" was short of fresh water. Now they knew. On May 24, when Nimitz sent for him—and he arrived, somewhat disheveled, a half hour late—Rochefort was able to give Nimitz what only commanders favored by Providence have enjoyed, the enemy's order of battle and plan of operation. Nimitz's staff was skeptical—the whole thing was too pat: it must be a ruse—and so the admiral instructed them (Commander Layton included) to keep checking the supposed Japanese plan against all other sources of information.

Layton brooded over charts, studied the Pacific winds and weather, and conferred constantly with Rochefort. Nimitz finally called for Layton and asked to be given a detailed and specific estimate. Layton as a cautious intelligence officer said he did not like to be specific. Nimitz would not be denied. "All right then, Admiral . . . ," said Layton. "They'll come in from the northwest on bearing 325 degrees and they will be sighted at about 175 miles from Midway, and the time will be about 0600 Midway time." If there were a prize for prescience, Commander Layton should have it: He was off by five degrees, five miles, and five minutes. On June 4, the Japanese carriers were first sighted bearing 320 degrees, 180 miles from Midway, at 5:55 A.M. Midway time.[14]

For some weeks now, conviction had been growing both in Hawaii and in Washington that the Japanese were up to something big; Nimitz and King had been reading the same enemy messages but interpreting them differently. Nimitz had thought all along that the attack would come in the central Pacific, but King and his own intelligence officers had not; a month earlier he had instructed Nimitz to keep at least two of his carriers in the South Pacific. Nimitz as a matter of course had been concerned about Midway. On May 2, he had flown there in a PBY (Catalina flying boat) to inspect defenses and to get the feel of them. He subsequently reinforced the island with antiaircraft, two companies of Marine Raiders, Marine dive-bombers and fighters, and Army B-26s and B-17s; he alerted the Navy and Marine commanders and promoted each of them one grade. ("I sent you the flowers before the funeral," Nimitz told them later.)

He thought of summoning the battleships from the West Coast but once again decided against it, on the grounds of their relatively slow speed and his inability to spare them sufficient air cover. But by mid-May, Nimitz had become convinced that he must somehow persuade King to let him bring back from the South Seas the two carriers (*Hornet* and *Enterprise*, under Halsey) and he determined to resolve the issue by ordering them back and letting King cancel the order if he didn't like it. King thought the matter over, concluded Nimitz was right, and indicated consent. On May 17, Halsey in *Enterprise* received the laconic message: "Expedite return."[15]

Halsey had arrived in the South Pacific one day too late to participate in the Battle of the Coral Sea (May 7–8, 1942), the first naval engagement to be fought by forces that never came in sight of one another and traded blows by air. The Japanese had launched a seaborne invasion of Port Moresby in southern New Guinea, accompanied by a task force built around large carriers *Shokaku* and *Zuikaku*. But Op-20-G had alerted Nimitz and Nimitz had sent carriers *Lexington* and *Yorktown* under Admiral Frank Jack Fletcher to head them off. The two-day action was a tactical victory for the Japanese; they lost only light carrier *Shoho* in exchange for U.S. oiler *Neosho*, destroyer *Sims*, and carrier *Lexington*, gallant Lady Lex, which took two torpedoes and two bombs. (*Lexington* might have been saved if a motor generator had not been left running; this ignited gasoline fumes and caused internal explosions that did her in.)

Yorktown and *Shokaku* were both damaged, the latter heavily, and both limped home. Yet the strategic victory went to the Americans, for the convoy of troops intended for Port Moresby was turned back, never to come again, and neither *Shokaku* nor *Zuikaku* (the latter having lost too many aircraft) was available for the coming carrier duel to the northeast. Admiral Morison believed that for us, the experience gained was alone invaluable: "call Coral Sea what you will," he wrote, "it was an indispensable preliminary to the great victory of Midway."[16]

Yorktown, trailing an oil slick ten miles long, returned to Pearl Harbor on May 27 and was warped into drydock. Marine engineer Nimitz put on his hip boots and went down with the inspection party to see how bad the damage was. He told them: "We must have this ship back in three days." They glanced at one another uneasily and said, "Yes, *sir.*" The legend is that repairs normally requiring ninety days were done in two, but that is an exaggeration; *Yorktown* was not made good as new but only acceptably seaworthy. (The legend also tells that power was turned off in Honolulu residential districts to provide electricity for the welding torches, but Jasper Holmes said he was never able to verify this.)[17]

Workmen swarmed over *Yorktown*, propping bulkheads with timber, restoring watertight integrity, replacing damaged equipment. The worst harm had been done not by a bomb that exploded amidships but by two near-misses that burst the seams of the portside fuel tanks, and these had to be welded closed. Three inoperative boilers were left as they were, so that *Yorktown* could only make twenty-seven knots, but at 9:00 A.M. on the morning of May 29, water was let back into the drydock and she floated out with hundreds of men still hammering away at her, took on fuel and replacement aircraft, and made ready to sortie next day.[18] Nimitz now could count his carrier strength as three against the probable Japanese four.

Hornet and *Enterprise* had reentered harbor on the twenty-sixth; they were to be in port only one full day. Nimitz came aboard *Enterprise* to award Distinguished Flying Crosses to Lieutenant Commander Clarence "Wade" McClusky, Lieutenant Roger W. Mehle, and Lieutenant (jg) James G. Daniels of VF-6, "Fighting Six" (Grumman Wildcats), for work they had done in the Marshall and Gilbert raids, the first of many decorations to be won by *Enterprise* pilots. As he pinned the medal on Mehle, Nimitz remarked, "I think you'll have a chance to do it again in a couple of days." The bad news was that Bill Halsey was ill, down with severe skin irritation compounded by sheer exhaustion; Nimitz saw immediately that he was in no shape to fight a major battle. Halsey suggested as his replacement a man who had never before commanded carriers, an old friend of his from destroyer days who had led the cruisers in his recent task force, Rear Admiral Raymond Spruance. His advice was taken. "It was a choice I never regretted," said Nimitz.[19]

Nimitz called in his commanders and gave them their orders, to which he appended a Letter of Instruction containing language of an austere clarity: "In carrying out the task assigned . . . you will be governed by the principle of calculated risk, which you shall interpret to mean the avoidance of exposure of your forces to attack by superior enemy forces without good prospect of inflicting, as a result of such exposure, greater damage on the enemy." *Hornet* and *Enterprise* filed down the channel on May 28, joined up with their cruisers and destroyers, and took aboard their aircraft groups flown out from the naval air stations at Ford Island and Kaneohe. At last the staff of Spruance's Task Force 16 could be shown Nimitz's operational order, in its wealth of detail (though the origins were concealed) about a Japanese stroke they were being sent to parry, and where, and when. Faced with this unusually precise preamble to action, Commander Richard Ruble, navigation officer of *Enterprise*, could only say, "That man of ours in Tokyo is worth every cent we pay him."[20]

◆

Nimitz's opponent was the Commander in Chief of Combined Fleet, Admiral Isoroku Yamamoto, not only the ablest of Japanese war leaders but the most attractive and appealing as a person. We made a great mistake to hate him so, and it is sad that we should have taken such pains to shoot down a bomber in which he was flying. He had spent almost three years in the United States and knew something of America and Americans. He despised the Japanese Army and the extreme nationalists. In 1939–40, he argued against the Tripartite Pact and said that war with the United States would be "a major calamity for the world." He accepted war's approach as "the will of Heaven," but the thought of it depressed him. "I find my present position extremely odd," he wrote to a friend, "obliged to make up my mind and pursue unswervingly a course that is precisely the opposite of my personal views."

Yamamoto was short of stature (five foot three) and earthy, sentimental, mischievous, blunt in speech, professional to the core, highly intelligent. He disliked pomposity and people who talked too much. Two fingers of his left hand were missing from a gun explosion in the Russo-Japanese War; the geisha in the Shimbashi district of Tokyo called him "Eighty Sen," because a manicure normally cost a hundred sen. ("I may be 'Eighty Sen,' " said Yamamoto, "but I can play the great man when I have to.") He passionately loved all forms of gambling and dearly liked to eat, especially sardines, broiled dumplings, or anything sweet. He was a good father to his family (two boys, two girls), but he and his wife were no longer close; his two loves were geisha, Chiyoko Kawai and Masako Tsurushima, whom he wrote often and saw when he could. He was no philanderer; one of his staff officers, Captain Yasuji Watanabe, said he was "extraordinarily innocent where women were concerned" (Watanabe was not).[21]

Yamamoto believed that in any war with the United States, "the outcome must be decided on the first day." In 1940, Prime Minister Konoye asked him what the navy's prospects were in such a war. "If we are ordered to do it," said Yamamoto, "then I can guarantee to put up a tough fight for the first six months, but I have absolutely no confidence as to what would happen if it went on for two or three years. . . . I hope at least that you'll make every effort to avoid war with America." He spoke with special intensity about the horror that would accompany American air raids, and he predicted that the naval tactics of a Pacific war would consist in capturing islands and building airfields.

The idea for the Pearl Harbor attack seems not initially to have been his, but he embraced it wholeheartedly as the only possible device for achieving a decision "on the first day," and it bothered him until his death that the late delivery of the Japanese ultimatum made him seem guilty of a "sneak" attack. His constant concern was for an early peace and for bringing about conditions that might favor it (his mistake, of course, lay in thinking that a crushing American defeat would create such a situation). His famous prewar statement about the war ending with "a capitulation in the White House" was the distortion of a letter to a friend in which he was suggesting the impossibility of any such thing, the impossibility of winning a total victory over the United States.[22]

The original Pearl Harbor plan called for "repeated attacks"; it aimed at no less than the complete destruction of the U.S. fleet. Japanese naval air officers like Commander Mitsuo Fuchida were frustrated and disappointed by the decision to withdraw after the first (successful) strike. Asked twenty years afterward whether he had any regrets about Pearl Harbor, Commander Minoru Genda conceded that he had. "We should not have attacked just once," he told a journalist in London. "We should have attacked again and again."[23] After Pearl Harbor, Yamamoto concurred in the belief that before the end of 1942 he must eliminate American sea power in the Pacific entirely or face eventual defeat.

During the early months of the year, with the job only half done, Yamamoto and the staff of Combined Fleet worked on plans for finishing it off, and in the first days of April, Captain Watanabe took these to the Navy General Staff in Tokyo, where they met numerous objections. Combined Fleet's scheme was the two-pronged seizure of Midway and the Aleutians, and the objections were well taken; Midway was too small to be a staging point for a major invasion of Hawaii, and even if the Japanese captured it, the demands of maintenance and supply would be great. But Yamamoto insisted; as he had done before, with Pearl Harbor, he made an issue of it, threatening to resign, putting his prestige on the line, and the General Staff backed away from him.[24]

The incident that finally forced a resolution was an unexpected one: American aircraft bombed Tokyo. This was the Doolittle Raid, by a force of sixteen Army B-25s under the leadership of Lieutenant Colonel James H. Doolittle and launched from the deck of aircraft carrier *Hornet*. The genesis of it is attributed by Army Air Forces historians to President Roosevelt, though no documentation links him to it directly. Admiral King said that the conception came from his operations officer, Captain Francis C. Low. Apparently what happened is that during the months after Pearl Harbor, the President kept pressing the Joint Chiefs for some way of bombing Japan, and Admiral King sent word to General Arnold asking him whether or not he could arrange for Army bombers to fly from a Navy carrier (no carrier planes had sufficient range). Arnold took on this mission with enthusiasm and plans proceeded apace; the B-25s were adapted to carry extra fuel tanks and were assembled at Eglin Field in Florida, where a group of pilots who had volunteered for a risky mission then practiced taking off from a 750-foot runway with heavy loads. Arrangements were made for them to land in China. "President Roosevelt," wrote Arnold, "was kept constantly advised on the details."[25]

It is conventional to disparage the Doolittle Raid as militarily pointless and carried out mainly for morale purposes, and this is justified insofar as the damage done did not match the cost in the loss of the eastern Chinese airfields that the Japanese promptly overran. But what the President wanted was to bring the war home to Japan, and this the raid accomplished. Though we did not fully appreciate the fact, there was acute sensitivity among the Japanese military to their duty in protecting the sacred person of the emperor and the inviolability of the homeland.

"In Admiral Yamamoto's mind," writes Commander Fuchida, "the idea that Tokyo, the seat of the Emperor, must be kept absolutely safe from an air attack amounted almost to an obsession."[26] The raid gave men like Yamamoto a premonitory shiver at what the future might hold, and it hardened his resolve that any similar penetration of the empire's defensive perimeter, as Fuchida put it, "must not be allowed to happen again at any cost." Opposition to his Midway plan within the General Staff now vanished; even his most vociferous opponents could no longer deny the reality of the threat from the east and the necessity of eliminating for once and all the American carriers. Viewed in that light, the Doolittle Raid was a pronounced success, and Roosevelt's instinct for audacity was thus a contributory cause of the Midway battle.

Yamamoto's object was to lure the Americans out to fight. If he could succeed in this, then an overpowering possession of superior strength should secure him the advantage. Midway was ideally suited to the purpose by being so close to Hawaii that in Japanese hands it would pose a serious threat. (Some American officers, like Spruance, doubted that if the Japanese took it they would be able to hold it,[27] in which some Japanese concurred, but that did not obviate the need for an American response.) The Japanese believed that we had two to three carriers, which was true, though on May 15 they had spotted (and correctly identified) *Hornet* and *Enterprise* in the South Pacific and the General Staff in Tokyo doubted the likelihood of these having returned to Pearl (the Japanese intelligence net on Oahu was of course no longer operative).

They thought we had four to five heavy and three to four light cruisers, about thirty destroyers, and twenty-five submarines (we had in fact seven heavy and one light cruisers, fourteen destroyers, and—yes—twenty-five submarines). Against us Yamamoto was bringing ten battleships, eight aircraft carriers, twenty-four heavy and light cruisers, seventy destroyers, fifteen submarines, eighteen tankers, and about forty transports and miscellaneous other craft, 185 ships in all. If the Japanese seem overimpressed with themselves, it should be remembered that this, as a U.S. naval writer about Midway describes it, was "one of the most prodigious displays of naval power in modern times."[28]

Yamamoto flew his flag in the new *Yamato,* with its sister ship, *Musashi,* the largest battleship ever built, carrying nine eighteen-inch guns capable of throwing a 3,200-pound projectile twenty-five miles. He had divided his fleet into several task forces. To the Aleutians would go two light carriers with cruisers, destroyers, and transports to take and occupy Kiska and Attu. To capture Midway there was an Occupation Force (with transports, cruisers, destroyers, and two battleships), flanked by the two most important groups of all: the Carrier Striking Force, the Kido Butai, and the Main Body of battleships, with Yamamoto personally in command. The carriers would be in the van, to soften up Midway for occupation, while the Main Body would come up when the U.S. fleet emerged. Yamamoto was popular with the carrier pilots and their officers, for he had been a pioneer of naval aviation, but this was not an airman's plan. The carriers were being used to screen the battleships rather than, as it should have been, the other way around; the surface engagement was still assumed to be the decisive one. Also, like all Japanese plans, it was too tricky, and it rested squarely and unequivocally on the misapprehension that the enemy was unaware of it.

◆

Carrier Striking Force departed Hashirajima anchorage south of Hiroshima on May 27, 1942, Navy Day, the anniversary of Admiral Togo's great victory over the Russians in the Battle of Tsushima in 1905. It included carriers *Akagi* (Red Castle), *Kaga* (Increased Joy), *Hiryu* (Flying Dragon), and *Soryu* (Green Dragon), two battleships, three cruisers, and twelve destroyers—twenty-one ships in all, under the command of Vice-Admiral Chuichi Nagumo in *Akagi.* They headed in single file through Bungo Channel toward the open Pacific; a fishing fleet waved and cheered them as they passed.

Their officers and men were full of confidence; another great victory was surely in the making. "Through scattered clouds the sun shone brightly on the calm blue sea," wrote Commander Fuchida. "For several days the weather had been cloudy but hot in the western Inland Sea, and it was pleasant now to feel the gentle breeze which swept across *Akagi*'s flight deck."[29] Mitsuo Fuchida was one of Nagumo's two air commanders; it was he who had led the attack on Pearl Harbor. His friend Minoru Genda was First Air Fleet operations officer. Both were pilots, and leading spirits in Japanese naval air. ("Is Genda all right?" was Yamamoto's first question when news was brought to him of *Akagi*'s loss.[30]) Not long after the sortie of Nagumo's task force, the two of them fell ill, Fuchida of appendicitis and Genda of pneumonia, a bad omen.

The Japanese carriers drew near Midway on June 3 through a blanket of heavy fog that resisted the most powerful searchlights. That day and night, as the skies began to clear, they anxiously awaited indications that their approach had been detected, but none came. Nagumo decided to launch the Midway air strike, one of their two mutually contradictory missions, the other being to destroy the enemy fleet. As the aircraft engines revved up in *Akagi* at 3:00 A.M. on June 4, both Fuchida and Genda, unable to sit by while action impended, came out from their sickbeds to *Akagi*'s bridge. (They thus saved their lives; all the patients in the sick bay were later killed by fire.) A force of seventy-two bombers and thirty-six fighters was launched from all four carriers; it circled the fleet and headed for Midway at 4:45. Fuchida was uneasy and inquired about fighter cover. He was told that nine planes had been launched from *Kaga*, while nine more were standing by on *Akagi,* and he thought, "just eighteen fighters as combat air patrol for our force of twenty-one ships"![31] That made him even more uneasy.

At 6:15, the Japanese air strike on the way to Midway encountered its first Americans, a gathering of twenty-five Marine Brewster and Grumman fighters sent out to stop them. Soon there were five Zeros on the tail of every outclassed American aircraft, and seventeen of ours were lost, but they had blunted the sharp point of the Japanese attack by perhaps as many as nine bombers and four fighters shot down (three bombers and one fighter were later downed over Midway by its defenders). The surviving Japanese hit Midway between 6:30 and 6:50. They destroyed the oil tanks, the seaplane hangar, the Marine command post and mess hall; badly damaged the powerhouse and gasoline system; set the hospital and storehouses ablaze; and killed twenty men. But they had been met by antiaircraft fire Admiral Nagumo after the battle described as "vicious," and they had not done away with Midway's ability to strike back. At 7:00, their leader, Lieutenant Joichi Tomonaga of *Hiryu,* radioed Nagumo: "There is need for a second attack wave."[32]

Admiral Nagumo's troubles were about to begin. (Fuchida thought he was showing his age and that "his once-vigorous fighting spirit seemed to be gone.") Between 5:30 and 6:00, American patrol planes shadowed them and at 7:05, just after they received Lieutenant Tomonaga's request for a second strike, the first American attack arrived: six TBF Avengers and four B-26 Marauders from Midway, armed with torpedoes. All but one of the TBFs and two of the B-26s were shot down and none of the torpedoes struck home, but their appearance convinced Nagumo that Tomonaga was right: Midway must be hit again.

The admiral had been holding back ninety-three aircraft aboard *Akagi* and *Kaga,* the bombers armed with torpedoes for an attack on enemy ships, in the event that the U.S. fleet should show itself. At 7:15, he issued the order Genda had drafted for him to change the mission: "Planes in second attack wave stand by to carry out attack today. Re-equip yourself with bombs." This meant at least an hour of hard work; planes would have to be lowered to the hangar, their torpedoes removed and replaced with land bombs, the planes raised to the flight deck once again. The assumed absence of American ships was leading to irrevocable actions.

Nagumo has been much faulted for that decision, yet it is hard to see how he could have made it differently. He had sent out patrol planes (not enough of them, and not quickly enough, but that was less his mistake than one of routine Japanese practice), and they had reported no enemy ships. Only the previous day, Tokyo had informed him: "There is no sign that our intention has been suspected by the enemy." This latter message may have been a by-product of the Hawaii-Midway cable, which carried many routine communications that if broadcast might have indicated a major fleet movement to the intelligence analysts in Japan. (Also, on Nimitz's order, a cruiser in the South Pacific had been broadcasting on frequencies normally assigned to air groups, in the hope the Japanese would pick them up.)[33] Yamamoto's staff in *Yamato*, six hundred miles to the rear, had received indications of increased radio traffic in Hawaii, but they had not informed Nagumo, partly because they wanted to keep radio silence and partly because they assumed that Nagumo, being closer, would have picked up the same signals (he had not). On the basis of all he knew, setting consequences aside, he did the only thing he could.

But it was the wrong thing, and its wrongness was soon made evident. At 7:28, a Japanese patrol plane catapulted from cruiser *Tone*, coming to the end of its outward leg and turning back, sent a message that seems to have reached the bridge of *Akagi* at about 7:40: "Sight what appears to be 10 enemy surface ships, in position 10 degrees distance 240 miles from Midway. Course 150 degrees, speed 20 knots." Fuchida said this report struck Nagumo and his staff "like a bolt from the blue"; it was not part of the plan; it was "unexpected," that quality so disagreeable to the Japanese.

Genda recalled that they "were at a loss how to make an accurate judgment of the situation." A quick plotting on the navigation chart showed that the enemy was within carrier aircraft range, about two hundred miles away. But did the American force include carriers? Some on *Akagi* thought it must; all hoped not. Nagumo had to make another less than premeditated choice. At 7:45, he ordered: "Prepare to carry out attacks on enemy fleet units. Leave torpedoes on those attack planes which have not as yet been changed to bombs." Two minutes later, a message went to *Tone*'s patrol plane: "Ascertain ship types, and maintain contact."[34]

The sailors sweating to rearm the planes can be forgiven if not much later in the morning they concluded, as soldiers and sailors everywhere have always done, that higher authority had gone out of its mind. Each new change in information was going to compel a change in orders. Before long the aircraft that attacked Midway would be returning, and meanwhile three more flights of American land-based planes were coming after them: sixteen Marine Dauntless dive-bombers and eleven obsolete Vindicators (known to their pilots as "wind indicators"), followed far above at 20,000 feet by fifteen B-17 Flying Fortresses, which unloosed on them 8,500 pounds of bombs per plane. Eight of the Dauntlesses, nine of the Vindicators, and all of the Fortresses returned safely to Midway and reported many hits, but alas, they were succumbing to the failure of accurate perception inherent in air combat and evidenced by pilots of all nationalities. There had been no hits, period; no damage and only a few casualties from strafing had been experienced by the Japanese.

Yet the bridge of *Akagi*—surrounded by chattering antiaircraft, buzzing fighters and dive-bombers, and exploding near-misses—was no place for calm reflection, and calm was called for. At 7:55, *Tone*'s patrol plane radioed: "the enemy is on course 80 degrees, speed 20 knots." This was ominous: The Americans had turned into the wind, which is what carriers do before they launch. Nagumo again asked for the types of ships, and at 8:09 came the reassuring answer: "Enemy is composed of 5 cruisers and 5 destroyers." Universal relief, which lasted about ten minutes. At 8:20, the message was received they had been dreading: "The enemy is accompanied by what appears to be a carrier in a position to the rear of the others." This was not merely disturbing to the Japanese, it was a profound shock; and it called for a third unappetizing decision by Nagumo.

Circling overhead and waiting to land were Lieutenant Tomonaga and the returnees from Midway. Armed and on deck, ready to take off, were only thirty-six dive-bombers on *Hiryu* and *Soryu*, and the torpedo bombers on *Akagi* and *Kaga* that had been rearmed with heavy land bombs. This was not the right mix of aircraft and armament to send against an American carrier and there were no fighters available to accompany it. If the flight decks were kept full, Tomonaga's force would have to ditch in the sea, with the loss of the planes and perhaps of pilots. Nagumo did again what he thought he had to do; he ordered the decks cleared for Tomonaga to land and the bombers prepared for a strike with torpedoes and less-heavy bombs (there was not time to return the heavy ones to the magazine, so they were stacked on the hangar deck, a risky procedure).

The admiral and his officers on *Akagi* were still in a cheerful frame of mind. "We had by this time," wrote Fuchida, "undergone every kind of attack by shore-based planes—torpedo, level bombing, dive-bombing— but were still unscathed. Frankly, it was my judgment that the enemy fliers were not displaying a very high level of ability, and this evaluation was shared by Admiral Nagumo and his staff. It was our general conclusion that we had little to fear from the enemy's offensive tactics." They knew themselves to be a well-balanced force superior in numbers to their opponent. Genda said that they realized they had been ambushed but that this only "made us make up our minds to have a decisive engagement with the enemy." At 8:35 A.M. on June 4, Nagumo signaled all his ships: "After completing homing operations, proceed northward. We plan to contact and destroy the enemy task force."[35] They were going to their final encounter with the principles of air power they so deeply believed in.

◆

Naval warfare is abstract; it is played out on the flat chessboard of the ocean, where there are no mountains, no rivers, no obstacles of mud or jungle, no accidents of bridge or roadway to confine or liberate the tactician. The only variables are wind, weather, fuel, or volume and range of fire; the ships, like chesspieces, can be moved forward and back according to a refined calculation. This is the natural domain of an almost mathematical mentality, one that can factor in purpose, time, and circumstance until a correct course of action is manifest. It is intolerant of error; if the course of action is *not* correct, retribution will follow. It calls for a commander who does not make mistakes.

As Task Force 16 steamed on its way northwestward, officers on board *Enterprise* speculated about their new admiral. An intense loyalty to Halsey inclined them to be hard to satisfy. Virtually all they knew of Spruance was that he had come to them from cruisers, that he was not an airman —and this was important. The day of the battleship was dying and that of the aircraft carrier dawning, but not everyone knew that. To be led in battle by someone who thought in obsolete terms was not only a discouraging prospect but a potentially dangerous one.

Some years into the war, the carrier admirals ("brown shoe") would continue to mistrust the battleship admirals ("black shoe") and to believe that the new fast *Essex*-class carriers were not being properly—which is to say, aggressively—employed unless an airman was in charge. During the first meal in Spruance's mess, his staff was so unsure of him and of themselves that the silence was palpable. He began to talk, about nothing in particular, and then raised his voice until it could be heard the length of the table. "I want you to know," he said, "that I do not have the slightest concern about any of you. If you were not good, Bill Halsey would not have you." That was their last silent meal.

They began to get to know him. He wore no cap or necktie and went around with his sleeves rolled up, and soon so did they. An officer who found him in the flag mess, sitting in an easy chair reading the radio news, froze and turned to leave. "Come in and relax," said Spruance. "This is our home. We have nowhere else to go." He walked a lot on the flight deck, always with a companion from the staff or the ship's company, engaged in earnest conversation; it was part of his method, to talk things out, to listen, to consider as many possibilities as he could from as many points of view as possible.

His breakfast routine was invariable: toast, coffee of his own mix that he brewed himself, and a bowl of canned peaches (Spruance said he had adopted the habit because in his early Navy days these were always available). Wherever he went he carried a twenty-inch-square chart called a maneuvering board—a printed form with a compass rose and a distance scale, used to calculate relative positions at sea—which he had rolled up and fastened by a paper clip. When he entered a cabin or the bridge he would put it down, but he always retrieved it when he left.[36]

Nimitz's order was that the carriers should rendezvous, refuel, and then take up position to the northeast of Midway. Here they would be able to strike at the Japanese carriers if these came on Layton's schedule or to block them if, instead, they headed for Oahu. From here on, it was up to

Fletcher in *Yorktown* and even more so to Spruance, who had already determined in his own mind that when the Japanese carriers were located he would hit them with everything he had.

He signaled his task force what the plan was and added, not an eloquent or inspiring phrase, but a characteristic piece of understatement: "The successful conclusion of the operation now commencing will be of great value to our country." In Washington, the President had been following the course of developments thus far, though his information was colored by the views of others there who did not share Nimitz's confidence in Joe Rochefort. "It looks at the moment," Roosevelt wrote to MacArthur on June 2, "as if the Japanese Fleet is heading toward the Aleutian Islands or Midway and Hawaii, with a remote possibility it may attack Southern California or Seattle by air."[37]

On the top of the superstructure of *Enterprise,* Halsey had established a command post, called the flag shelter, equipped with a chart table, two settees, metal book racks, a voice-radio handset, and phone outlets. To the flag shelter early on the morning of June 4 came Spruance to join his staff, carrying as always his rolled-up chart; a radio loudspeaker was tuned to the frequency of the Midway PBY patrols. The day promised well: fair skies, puffy white clouds, cool temperature, smooth seas, though the wind was so gentle they would have to make speed to launch aircraft. *Yorktown,* ten miles to the north, had sent off search planes and fighter cover at 4:30 A.M., and at 5:34 the loudspeaker on *Enterprise* spoke the words they waited for: "Enemy carriers."

But where? An answer did not come until 6:03, when the loudspeaker spoke again: "Two carriers and battleships bearing 320° distant 180 [miles from Midway] course 135 speed 25." Spruance's officers fell all over themselves getting to the chart table, while his flag lieutenant, Robert Oliver, watched Spruance calmly unroll his "maneuvering board," which to Oliver's surprise was totally blank. Spruance entered on it his and the Japanese position and then, using his thumb and forefinger as a compass, swept off the distance between the two: about 175 miles, within torpedo-bomber range. He tossed the chart aside. "Launch the attack," said Spruance.

This makes it sound easier than it was. His decision involved many risks, but Spruance being Spruance, they had been put through the calculator of a fully prepared mind and balanced against our own strengths. Only two carriers had been reported. Where were the others? Would the Japanese continue to close Midway or come after him? Their search planes might find the Americans at any moment, perhaps had already done so. Those risks Spruance discounted. Later he refused to accept Japanese praise for our cleverness in figuring the time and distance so finely that we caught them at their most vulnerable moment, flight decks full of aircraft.

"All that I can claim credit for, myself," wrote Spruance in 1955, "is a very keen sense of the urgent need for surprise and a strong desire to hit the enemy carriers with our full strength as early as we could reach them." *Enterprise* went to general quarters; the task force turned into the wind and bent on twenty knots. A message came from Fletcher, the senior and in tactical command, that Spruance should "proceed southwesterly and attack enemy carriers when definitely located," which is what he was already doing. *Yorktown* would "follow as soon as planes recovered."[38]

An aircraft carrier is an ungainly object. "A carrier has no poise," wrote Ernie Pyle. "It has no grace. It is top-heavy and lop-sided. It has the lines of a cow. It doesn't cut through the water like a cruiser, knifing romantically along. . . . It just plows." Yet Pyle caught the poetry. He also wrote (in 1945) that an "aircraft carrier is a noble thing . . . a ferocious thing. . . . I believe that every Navy in the world has as its No. 1 priority the destruction of enemy carriers. That's a precarious honor, but it's a proud one."[39] Admiral Morison recognized life aboard a carrier to be so unto itself, and so unfamiliar to his readers, that he had his colleague Commander James C. Shaw write a separate foreword to one of his volumes about what it was like (Shaw was gunnery officer of carrier *Bunker Hill,* Marc Mitscher's flagship in the later justly famous Task Force 58).

Commander Shaw spoke of a carrier as a "giant aircraft hatchery" in which time is measured by strikes—so many weeks since Rabaul, so many more before Tarawa—and every carrier strike day brings death to someone aboard. He writes as a man who remembered: the bugle blast of reveille two hours before dawn; the "big chow" breakfast of steaks, eggs, fried potatoes; the cry of "Pilots, man your planes"; the snarl of the engines as they cough into life, miss, and settle down to a steady roar; the ballerina-like motions of the flight deck officer as he twirls his hand for full throttle and brings down his flag for takeoff, fighters first, then dive-bombers, last the heavy torpedo planes; the rising and sinking of the elevators as a new flight is spotted, fueled, and chocked in place; the radar screens glowing with departures and returns; the waiting, the waiting, and the anxious counting of noses as the pilots come back into the landing circle and one by one are waved down to the deck, caught in the arresting gear, and signaled—hand drawn sharply across the throat—"Cut the engine!"[40]

Enterprise and *Hornet* began launching at 7:02 A.M.—twenty Wildcat fighters, sixty-seven Dauntless dive-bombers, and twenty-nine Devastator torpedo bombers, every operational aircraft they had except those needed for combat air patrol above the carriers. Spruance was going all-out; he had wanted a coordinated effort, but the torpedo planes were slow to get off and after a half hour he got word of a "bogey" (unidentified aircraft) on the horizon (this was the float plane from cruiser *Tone* that had spotted them), which meant there could be no lingering: He ordered Lieutenant Commander McClusky, leader of the *Enterprise* air group then circling overhead, to proceed to the attack with the fighters and bombers already aloft. Fletcher had delayed *Yorktown*'s launching in case another Japanese carrier should turn up, but none had done so and at 8:38 the *Yorktown* strike force—seventeen Dauntless dive-bombers, twelve Devastators, and six Wildcats—was also airborne, with orders to head east of the last reported Japanese position, a most opportune piece of timing and instruction.[41]

Let us look briefly at some of these young men, now winging their way toward *Akagi, Kaga, Hiryu,* and *Soryu.* Let us look specifically at Torpedo Squadron 8 of *Hornet,* fifteen pilots and fifteen crewmen. Their "skipper" was Lieutenant Commander John C. Waldron, a veteran naval aviator and Annapolis graduate from Fort Pierre, South Dakota, one of whose great-grandparents was a Sioux Indian. His pilots were that cross-section of Americans beloved of journalists: the Kansas City meat packer, the Harvard Law School graduate, the insurance man from upstate New York, the former track star from Oregon State, the Texan who had been at A & M, the Virginian who had enlisted as a seaman and worked his way to Annapolis. The Navy had taught them to fly at Miami or Pensacola and then sent them to Norfolk, where Waldron had welded them into a unit. He drove them and drilled them, until they knew exactly what he wanted them to do.[42] But aside from Waldron, only one of them had so much as six years' experience as a navy flier; none of them had been in combat before or even flown with a live torpedo.

Before they left the ready room, Waldron told them to ignore navigation and follow him; he would take them to the enemy, and he did no less than that. "We went just as straight to the Jap Fleet as if he'd had a string tied to them," said one. Waldron also told them that if there was only a single plane left to make the final run, he wanted that man to go for a hit, and this is what happened, though unhappily there was to be no hit. *Hornet* completed launching at 7:55. Waldron formed up, together with his fighter cover of ten Wildcats, and headed southeast, but their differences in altitude and speed—and a layer of cloud between them—caused the two flights to separate. When the point came where Waldron's Sioux intuition told him to turn northwest, Torpedo Eight went on alone.

Cruiser *Chikuma* saw them coming at 9:18; she and a destroyer laid down smoke screens and opened antiaircraft fire. Then *Akagi* saw them and began evasive maneuvering. Commander Genda was on deck and said that Torpedo Eight looked to him "like waterfowl flying over a lake far away." At last they have come! he thought. What a funny approach they are making! Genda wondered why they were flying so low and without fighter protection, for about thirty Zeros were swarming down on them.

On the American side, the only witness who survived to record the final moments of Torpedo Eight was Ensign George H. Gay, who watched as one by one the Zeros felled his companions in a burst of flame, a cloud of smoke and spray, and then the debris swirling by to the rear. Gay, writes Walter Lord, "could only think of the time when he was a boy and tossed out orange peels from the back of a speeding motorboat."[43] He saw Waldron standing up in a blazing cockpit and then Waldron, too, was gone. Soon there were only three Devastators left, then two, then Gay's was the last.

Gay released his torpedo at *Soryu* by hand (the electric release wouldn't work) and pulled up over the carrier, trying to get a shot at it, but his gun jammed so he made a flipper turn over the fantail and then five Zeros came after him. (Gay thought it impossible for his torpedo to have missed, but he had not seen *Soryu* shift course at the last moment and his "pickle" pass it by.) The Zeros shot away his rudder controls and killed his crewman. Then a wing fell off and his Devastator dropped like a stone; he had just time enough to grab his seat cushion and a bag containing his rubber life raft before it sank. By hiding under the cushion he escaped Japanese attention and, though wounded, managed to survive, to inflate his life raft, and to be picked up next day by a PBY and flown to Pearl Harbor, where he gave Admiral Nimitz an eyewitness account of the Battle of Midway as seen from a front-row seat.

At 9:40, another torpedo attack (fourteen planes from *Enterprise*) was made on *Kaga* and at 10:00 (fifteen from *Yorktown*) on *Soryu;* of these, only four returned to *Enterprise* and only two to *Yorktown,* and again there were no hits. The Japanese would have been thoroughly entitled to think that the Americans had shot their bolt and that the verdict was as good as won. Genda concluded that the Japanese now did not need to fear enemy aircraft no matter how many there were. All that remained was to destroy their carriers and then mount a devastating attack on Midway Island tomorrow morning. Preparations for the counterstroke had been going on aboard all four carriers throughout the torpedo run-ins, planes being hoisted to the flight deck, fueled, and armed. At 10:20, Admiral Nagumo gave them the order to take off when ready and *Akagi* slowly began turning into the wind. "Within five minutes all her planes would be launched," thought Fuchida.[44]

There were black specks in the sky. The lookout on *Akagi* shouted, "Hell-divers!" For three Japanese carriers northwest of Midway at the hour of 10:20, June 4, 1942, five minutes of further effective operation were not to be granted.

◆

Wade McClusky came to the moment of decision. The air group from *Enterprise* that he commanded had been given a vector—a direction and a distance—supposed to bring them over the Japanese fleet, and at 9:20 they had reached the end of it. From twenty thousand feet, McClusky could see to the horizon almost as far as Midway itself, sixty or so miles away to the south across the empty blue Pacific. Repeat empty: scattered clouds, no Japanese.

Question: Had they increased speed toward Midway, withdrawn to the west, or turned to the northeast? McClusky's falling fuel gauge was not going to give him much time to make up his mind; he would have been justified in jettisoning bombs and heading back to *Enterprise*. McClusky, short and stocky, was a fighter pilot who had never before dropped a bomb from a dive-bomber, but he was determined to find and strike the Japanese, and reviewing all the information available to him, he reasoned that they had turned northeast. Good thinking, McClusky.

Nimitz, Captain George Murray of *Enterprise*, and nearly all who have examined the battle since agree that no other chess-game choice at Midway can match McClusky's for its fatefulness. (Observe that others made it wrong: Confronted with the same dilemma, *Hornet*'s air group chose to go south and played no part in the ensuing drama.) McClusky kept his flight on course for another thirty-five miles and then turned northwest, to make a box search. At 9:55, he spotted a Japanese "cruiser" hightailing it northeast (this would have been destroyer *Arashi,* which had been chasing a U.S. submarine), and figuring that it was rejoining the fleet, he headed toward the direction in which it pointed. Good thinking again. Ten minutes later, they saw the first foamy wakes about thirty-five miles ahead and a little to port, looking like "curved white slashes on a blue carpet," as one pilot said; another said he had never seen so many ships at one time in his life.[45]

Providence was intervening with a vigor the Americans had no right to rely on. The staggered times of launching and the varied routes they had taken conspired to bring McClusky's thirty-seven Dauntless dive-bombers and Lieutenant Commander Maxwell Leslie's seventeen of the same from *Yorktown* directly on top of the Japanese at almost the same instant, approaching at right angles to one another and each oblivious of the other's presence. Pure accident produced the coordinated attack that Spruance had hoped for.

What amazed McClusky is that no one was shooting at him: no fighters, no antiaircraft. The Japanese carriers had been making tight turns, probably to avoid torpedoes, he thought (correct: another miraculous piece of luck). He assigned one of the flattops to each of his two squadrons, lowered wing flaps, and pushed over into a screaming dive. (His shout of "Tally ho!" was audible over the air on *Enterprise,* to the great relief of everyone in the flag shelter.) Within minutes, Max Leslie —patting his head, the sign for "Follow me!"—had done the same. "I saw the huge orange disk of the rising sun painted on the vessel's flight deck . . . ," said one pilot. "It seemed as though they'd painted a bull's eye for me to aim at." Seen from below, said Lieutenant James Thach of *Yorktown*'s fighter group, the descent of the Dauntlesses "looked like a beautiful silver waterfall. . . . I'd never seen such superb dive bombing."[46]

Now all the Japanese chessboard blunders fall into the pattern that exposed them to a mating move. They were nearly unprotected, because the covering Zeros had been down on the deck coping with the last of the torpedo bombers. Torpedo Eight had not sacrificed itself in vain (the Japanese were preoccupied by torpedo bombing, perhaps because they were so good at it). In addition, they were in a highly vulnerable state. The confused mission, the changes in orders, and the hesitation to strike immediately had brought it about that their carriers were at maximum flammability, like tinderboxes waiting to be lit: rank on rank of aircraft filled with gasoline and explosives, fuel hoses lying about, all those bombs in the hangar not yet stowed away. One thing had led inexorably to another, and a demonstration would follow that the god of naval battles does not forgive mistakes.

The first three bombs that fell on *Kaga* missed, but the fourth hit starboard aft in the midst of the planes grouped for launching, which burst asunder and burned. *Kaga*'s power went off, passages below were aflame, and most of the crew was trapped. The next two bombs missed, but the seventh and eighth struck near the forward elevator, one of them crashing through to the hangar deck and letting go among the armed aircraft there. A gasoline truck near the superstructure blew up, killing everyone on the bridge. The hangar was an inferno; the paint on the starboard side began to catch fire. All that day *Kaga* drifted and burned, as bucket brigades vainly fought the flames, until at 4:40 in the afternoon the surviving senior officer ordered her abandoned. At 7:00, *Kaga* seemed to leap out of the water, racked by two heavy internal detonations, and slowly she began to sink, going down for good a half hour later.

A plane was just taking off when the first hit landed on *Soryu* and blew that unfortunate aircraft into the ocean. The second bomb broke through the flight deck just forward of the forward elevator and burst in the hangar, the third falling aft in the middle of the planes awaiting takeoff. Within minutes, *Soryu* was ablaze from stem to stern; belowdecks the heat was so intense it melted and warped the hangar doors. Communication, power, and water mains were out; when the fire reached the torpedo storage room, the subsequent blast nearly tore *Soryu* apart. Abandon Ship was ordered at 10:45. Around sunset, the fires seemed to die down and a brawny petty officer was sent aboard to persuade her captain to leave the bridge, which he would not do. A pillar of flame shot up, the stern dipped, the prow rose, and *Soryu* sank at 7:13. Minutes later came the shudder of an explosion deep undersea.

Akagi's first bomb was a near-miss that sent up a geyser of water off the port bow and drenched everyone on the bridge. The second struck the amidship elevator and the third hit the edge of the port flight deck. More than a hundred men were blown over the side; superheated air sucked down through the exhaust system killed everyone in the starboard engine room. A Zero parked near the bridge caught fire and started a blaze that soon spread to the bridge itself, and when the flames reached the large bombs stacked in the hangar, they were set off in a chain reaction. By 10:42, steering and communication were out of operation and the engines had stopped.[47]

Akagi lasted longer than *Kaga* or *Soryu,* but she was a doomed and helpless ship. Admiral Nagumo was with great reluctance persuaded to transfer his flag to cruiser *Nagara. Akagi* was abandoned at 6:00 and at 3:30 next morning the order was given to scuttle: Four destroyers turned their torpedoes on *Akagi* and sent her down a few minutes before sunrise. Again there was what Fuchida described as "a terrific underwater explosion." When the attack began, he had sought out Genda, his sharer of joy and sorrow for so many years, who looked at him and said, *"Shimmatta,"* which Gordon Prange and his collaborators, in their detailed study of Midway, translate as "We goofed!"[48]

Opinions differ radically as to what relative positions the Japanese carriers were in and who hit what when. Not only did impressions blur in the stress of the moment but the American pilots had recognition cards that were out of date and they all thought *Soryu* to be smaller than it was (by their accounts, nobody hit *Soryu* at all). Historians have consequently been divided among themselves. Admiral Morison has McClusky attacking *Akagi,* Lieutenant Richard Best of *Enterprise*'s Bomber Six attacking *Kaga,* and Leslie attacking *Soryu;* Commander Tuleja has McClusky attacking *Soryu,* Dick Best attacking *Akagi,* and Leslie attacking *Kaga;* Walter Lord has McClusky attacking *Kaga,* Best attacking *Akagi,* and Leslie attacking *Soryu.* Prange et al. pretty much throw up their hands and declare "the point of little interest to anyone but a unit historian . . . there is plenty of credit to go around."[49] On the whole, Walter Lord's reconstruction—based on the conclusion that Nagumo had changed the carriers' course ship by ship rather than as a formation, and that the positions where they sank approximate those where they were hit—seems to this writer the most reasonable.[50]

That left *Hiryu,* exempted from the Dauntless hurricane by being farther north and under clouds. *Hiryu* promptly retaliated. A flight of eighteen Aichi dive-bombers and six Zeros took off twenty minutes after McClusky, Best, and Leslie began their textbook-perfect exercise. The Japanese found the American task force by homing on the signal of the scout plane from *Tone* that had spotted it. Our combat air patrol met them, and cruisers and destroyers put up a curtain of antiaircraft, but six managed to bore through and bomb *Yorktown,* registering three hits that started fires and sent up clouds of smoke.

Three Zeros and five Aichis were all that returned to *Hiryu,* which at 12:45 launched a second strike of six fighters and ten torpedo bombers. At 2:30, they came upon what they thought was a second American carrier, since it seemed to be untouched, but this again was *Yorktown*, whose damage control was so efficient that the fires had been put out, the boilers were back on line, and she was making twenty knots. *Yorktown* managed to evade all save two of the torpedoes, but these breached once more the portside fuel tanks, jammed the rudder, severed power connections, and caused a heavy list. At a few minutes before three o'clock, her captain, fearing that she might capsize any moment, ordered her abandoned.[51]

(*Yorktown* refused to give up, and belatedly there was genuine hope of saving her, but the afternoon of June 6, Japanese submarine I-168 appeared on the scene and torpedoed not only *Yorktown* but destroyer *Hammann*, which broke in two and sank in four minutes; *Yorktown* stayed afloat until dawn and then, with a hollow rattle of the loose gear inside her, rolled over and went under in two thousand fathoms.)

Hiryu was not to be spared. At 3:30, Spruance sent off twenty-four Dauntlesses, ten of which had come over from *Yorktown* and all of them piloted by veterans of the morning's encounter. They found *Hiryu* an hour and a half later, came in from the southwest so that the sun was behind them, and scored four hits, all near the bridge. The forward elevator was twisted upward, the planes on board were set afire, and the men belowdecks cut off from rescue. During the night, *Hiryu* slowed to a halt and began to list. The order to scuttle her was given, the torpedoes went home, at 5:10 she seemed to be done for and they left her, though apparently *Hiryu* went on burning and did not actually sink until nine o'clock in the morning of June 5. With her at their own insistence went the captain and Admiral Tamon Yamaguchi, one of the most competent and beloved of Japanese officers, who had been expected to succeed Yamamoto. With her, too, went the best hope of retrieving any solace from what even the normally cheerful Genda now referred to as "a calamity."[52]

Yamamoto was at first unwilling to admit defeat. If there was only one American carrier, as initially indicated, then his force was still substantially the stronger. The reports of pilots returning from *Hiryu*'s first strike disabused him of this; they had seen all three, which they correctly identified as *Hornet, Enterprise,* and *Yorktown*—*Yorktown*, which they were sure they had disposed of at the Coral Sea! Even so, coming north to Nagumo's aid on the afternoon of the fourth was the covering force from the invasion transports—two battleships, four heavy cruisers, a light carrier, and a destroyer squadron—under Vice-Admiral Nobutake Kondo, and not far behind him were ten more destroyers and another light cruiser.[53]

There would be a quarter moon, which would partly make up for the Japanese lack of radar. If the Americans could be drawn into the kind of night action the Japanese excelled at—in which the U.S. carriers (not yet having radar-equipped night fighters) would be helpless and Japanese heavy guns would count for the most—then the balance might yet be tipped back in reverse. By midnight, Kondo was about 125 miles away; Yamamoto had relieved Nagumo and put Kondo in command, and Kondo had ordered all ships prepared for a night engagement. But the Americans failed to oblige him and Yamamoto was having second thoughts.

When the first attack on *Yorktown* knocked out her radar, Admiral Fletcher had sensibly shifted his flag to cruiser *Astoria* and then, even more sensibly, had relinquished tactical command to Spruance. After recovering aircraft from the *Hiryu* strike and getting their reports, Spruance decided to reverse course, take *Enterprise* and *Hornet* back to the east until midnight, when they would steam north for an hour, and then again head westward. This order has been much criticized by the air admirals, on the grounds of "allowing the enemy fleet to escape." Then-Captain Marc Mitscher, commander of *Hornet,* thought it was wrong.[54]

But Spruance's logic was pellucidly clear. "I did not feel justified in risking a night encounter with possible superior forces," he wrote in his after-action report, "but on the other hand I did not want to be too far away from Midway the next morning. I wished to have a position from which either to follow up retreating enemy forces or to break up a landing attack on Midway."[55] And Spruance was right. It is apparent now that had he continued westward that night, he would have collided head-on with Kondo, whose battleships were just as fast as Spruance's carriers, and Yamamoto would have had his night fight, with an outcome that can only have been devastating for the Americans.

As the night wore on, and intelligence reports made it increasingly clear to Yamamoto that his four carriers were lost irretrievably and at least one and possibly two American carriers were still operational, he could see that continuing eastward in search of a night battle (in Admiral Morison's words), "he was likely to get a dawn air attack instead." This was not desirable. At five minutes to three on the morning of the fifth, he ordered cancellation of the Midway occupation and a general retirement to the northwest. At 8:15 A.M., Kondo's force rejoined him and together, with Nagumo trailing behind, they headed homeward. The mood on board *Yamato* was not of the best. Admiral Yamamoto sat on the forward bridge, face ashen, eyes glittering, and sipped rice gruel.[56]

◆

This is not all there was to Midway, by any means. Included also were the Aleutian operations, which our side bungled in such fashion as to lose two islands without a fight, though to no great effect one way or another. (From their location, the Aleutians ought to have been important, but the weather was so atrocious that neither we nor the Japanese made a major effort there.) Then there were the adventures and misadventures of U.S. submarines, such as *Nautilus,* which thought that it had scored with three torpedoes on the burning *Soryu* while in fact this was *Kaga,* and of the three, two missed and the third was a dud; or *Grayling,* which was proceeding on the surface when B-17s dropped twenty thousand-pound bombs on her from ten thousand feet and *Grayling* had to crash-dive. (The bombers returned to base and reported sinking a "cruiser" in the record time of fifteen seconds; *Grayling* came into Pearl several days later, manned by a most indignant crew.)[57]

Nor was this the only one of repeated demonstrations that level high-altitude bombing is ineffective against moving ships. The Flying Fortresses from Midway attacked not only the carriers but the invasion fleet, claiming "five hits, one probable hit, and four near misses" on two battleships and two transports. Again, sorry, but the Japanese had not been so much as scratched. In fairness, there was to be an exception that proved the rule in August off Guadalcanal, when Fortresses from Espíritu Santo sank destroyer *Mutsuki,* their first genuine warship victim. *Mutsuki* was not in motion at the time, however, and her commander, when fished from the water, is reported to have said, "I suppose even a B-17 has to hit something sometime, but why did it have to be me?"[58]

Properly speaking, the battle was to last two more days. Spruance pursued the Japanese to the northwest, but his search planes failed to find the main force. They came instead upon two cruisers, *Mogami* and *Mikuma,* that had crippled one another in a night collision and could no longer keep up with the rest. Dauntlesses from *Hornet* and *Enterprise* went after them, severely mauling *Mogami* and sinking *Mikuma.* The dialogue of the pilots as they made their dives, rich in profanity, violated every rule of radio discipline and Spruance's communications officer was apprehensive when the admiral requested an exact transcript (it turned out he wanted to send a copy to Nimitz, who he thought might enjoy it).

Yamamoto was still trying to bait Spruance by making a diversion near Wake Island, with its Japanese land-based air, but no such luck. Nimitz briefly ordered Task Force 16 northward to deal with the withdrawing Aleutians invasion force but then thought better of it; no one considered it pusillanimous when the order was canceled. On the way home to Pearl, *Enterprise*'s chief medical officer brought four gallons of bourbon into the wardroom. It was a great relief, said a squadron commander, "to see that in war time the old Naval Regulations go by the board in favor of a little human good sense."[59]

Understanding of it all would wait for many years, until Japanese records and testimony became available, and (as we have seen) much is still in dispute. But the Japanese revealed their awareness of a catastrophic upset in the efforts they made to conceal it from their own public. Survivors from the lost carriers were isolated under guard. Fuchida was brought into the hospital at Yokosuka Naval Base (he had a leg wound) at night on a covered stretcher; no nurses or corpsmen were allowed in his room and he was forbidden communication with the outside.

After-action reports were classified "top secret," and following the surrender many of them were burned. Fortunately, Fuchida on his recovery became an instructor at the Naval War College in Tokyo, where he was one of the few authorized to examine Midway records and to interview those who had been present there; it was he who drafted a study based on this research and managed to preserve his copy of the manuscript.[60] After the war, he and Commander Masatake Okumiya, also a naval aviator, expanded it into a book telling the full story insofar as it was known to them; it was published in Japan in 1951 and in English translation four years later, with a foreword by Admiral Spruance.

The benefits of hindsight are many, despite its unfairness to those who at critical moments must act without its help. Since Yamamoto did not survive the war, there is no way of judging what was in his mind, but even giving him credit for having known better than he performed, there were fundamental flaws in his plan. These would have been present from the beginning even if the outcome had not so pitilessly revealed them. They are principally five:

(1) An assumption of American ignorance of it should not have been made an essential feature of the Midway operation. To do this was not only unwarranted but unnecessary. Their preponderance of power so far exceeded the requirements that the Japanese could have anticipated that every available American warship would be lying in wait for them and still have enjoyed a comfortable margin of safety. To count on surprise is to invite being surprised in one's turn.

(2) Yamamoto should not have split up his huge armada into penny packets, five separate units some of which were then subdivided further. To do this wasted his numerical advantage, resulted in only a fraction of his force being engaged, and ensured that at the point of contact he would have only marginal rather than overwhelming superiority. Had he moved on Midway with the bulk of Combined Fleet, it is hard to see how the Americans, even with their prior knowledge, could have withstood him.

(3) The heavy carriers should not have been placed where they were and given two missions. The job of "softening up" Midway could better have been done by battleships, which should have been in the lead, and light carriers could have provided them with air cover. The proper job of the heavies was to deal with their American counterparts, and to maintain readiness for this until they were absolutely certain that no American carriers were present or on their way out from Pearl Harbor.

(4) Provisions for reconnaissance should have been more generous. A red flag should have gone up when they discovered that the submarine cordon had been late in getting on station east of Midway, and that seaplane patrols to cover Hawaii could not be refueled at French Frigate

Shoal because the Americans were already there. This meant that they were not only ignorant of the U.S. fleet's location but *knew* they were ignorant, which compounded the folly of presupposing American unawareness of their approach.

(5) It may seem a minor point, but Yamamoto need not personally have been present. The commander of an entire fleet needs communication more than he needs mobility or physical proximity to the action; his place, as Nimitz had realized, is where the communications are. So long as he imposed radio silence on himself, Yamamoto could have no immediate influence on events. Radio silence prevented his headquarters in *Yamato* from informing Nagumo of suspiciously brisk communications they were picking up from the Hawaii area, which caused them to suspect an enemy sortie.[61] Had Yamamoto anchored at Truk, he would have been in better touch with Nagumo, he would have been just as well informed of Nagumo's losses, and he could just as well have issued the order to withdraw—or any alternative order—from there.

As for Nagumo, his errors were of a lesser order of magnitude but just as grievous:

(1) He should have launched patrols on a two-phase rather than a one-phase search, or so Fuchida argued. Each plane was sent out to reach the end of its radius at dawn, so that half of its arc was covered in darkness; a second search of the missing segment should have been sent out an hour or so later (apparently one of the Japanese patrols *did* fly over the American carriers in the dark without seeing them). But Japanese doctrine, emphasizing the offensive, allowed only 10 percent of total aircraft strength to be spent on searches, "which had proven detrimental to our purposes before this," wrote Fuchida, "and would again."[62]

(2) Nagumo should not have made the Midway strike with a force drawn evenly from all four of his carriers. If he had assigned only two of them to the job, he could have kept the other two armed and ready for his second mission, which was in fact the primary one of attacking American ships, and thus have avoided all the mix-up over arming and rearming aircraft when the call came for a second bombing of Midway.

(3) Even as it was, he should have sent out a strike on the instant (as Spruance did) when an enemy carrier was located. Admiral Yamaguchi thought as much at the time; he signaled Nagumo from *Hiryu:* "Consider it advisable to launch attack force immediately," which was going pretty far for a subordinate Japanese commander.[63] Yamaguchi was notoriously aggressive; Nagumo preferred the wiser course. After all, his experience of American attacks during the previous hour and a half could be said to have proved that bombers without fighter escort would be wiped out, and so for all the right reasons he made the final wrong decision in the Battle of Midway.

Everything that had gone amiss for the Japanese had in common the element of overconfidence, what some of them later called the "victory disease." After an uninterrupted string of triumphs—sinking or disabling the American battle fleet, sinking British battleship *Prince of Wales* and cruiser *Repulse,* capturing "impregnable" Singapore, overrunning most of Southeast Asia, and making a successful foray into the Indian Ocean as far as Ceylon—Japan was in the position of a scrappy little fighter who has just floored the two biggest bullies on the block, and the Japanese are not to be begrudged the savor of their satisfaction. But it led them into miscalculations that could (and should) have been avoided, and they were duly called to account.

As for Nimitz and Spruance, it does the truth no disservice to say that they did nearly everything right. Nimitz saw where the attack was coming sooner than King did, he assembled on his own the forces to meet it, and he gave them concise and correct orders. That Spruance rather than Halsey should have been in command at Midway was another example of the providential, since Spruance proved supremely suited to a task that called for a balance of carefulness and boldness rarely found in the same man, and certainly not in Bill Halsey.

Spruance observed Nimitz's measured injunction as to "calculated risk" with scrupulous precision. When it was time to attack he attacked, when it was time to withdraw he withdrew, and he went on doing this throughout the battle, maneuvering his ships with an almost unerring sense of where they ought to be. "Midway paved the way for victory in the Pacific," wrote Captain Gilven M. Slonim, USN, in a study of seagoing command decisions for the *U.S. Naval Institute Proceedings.* "But, it also was the inception of the greatness of Admiral Raymond Spruance. Fortune smiled upon him again many times as our war progressed westward, but he always beckoned her with sound judgment and his uncanny ability to be one thought ahead of his adversary. . . . Midway gave evidence that he was to become the greatest tactician in the history of our Navy."[64]

Midway broke the back of Japanese naval striking power; the Kido Butai never rode again in the attack. They had suffered more than mere numbers indicate. When the four carriers went down, 280 aircraft went with them, in addition to the forty-two lost to combat in the air, but with them too went irreplaceable pilots and technicians. The number of pilots recovered varied from carrier to carrier, as survivors were picked up from the water by destroyers; *Akagi* lost only six, but *Soryu* lost thirty and *Hiryu* sixty (these were men with over seven hundred hours' flying experience). The air groups were reorganized and sent to Rabaul, where they suffered even deeper attrition in the campaign to recapture Guadalcanal.

The Japanese program of training was unable to keep up. It had concentrated on producing an elite; it made small allowance for recuperation from losses, since losses were unthinkable. (Eventually training fell off even further as American submarines sank their tankers and they ran short of aviation fuel.) Captain Watanabe, in a postwar interrogation, said they had suffered a total of about seven hundred missing from each of the carriers, "which weakened the Navy Air Force."[65]

After Midway, Combined Fleet was still in being, more carriers were there or being built, but the elite had been hard hit and the heart had gone out of their air offensive capability: no further advances in the southeast; invasions of New Caledonia, Fiji, New Zealand—all canceled. Any threat to Pearl Harbor or the American continental bases had been removed; the initiative had passed to the U.S. fleet. For the Americans, Midway meant, even more, the gift of time, time in which to wait out the arrival of the new fast carriers the following year: *Essex* in May 1943, a new *Yorktown* (Jocko Clark commanding) in July, and a new *Lexington* later that summer; by the end of 1943, four more—*Intrepid, Bunker Hill,* a new *Wasp,* and a new *Hornet*—were in commission, and there were ten more on the way to come before the spring of 1945. The fast carriers were the progeny of Midway.[66]

Enterprise and *Hornet* returned to Pearl Harbor—"almost unnoticed and without fanfare," says Spruance's biographer—late of a Saturday afternoon. They did not really appreciate what they had done. At that stage, writes Captain Slonim, "the full impact of the victory was not completely recognized by most of its participants." Both Nimitz and Spruance said that no one at Pearl had any "feeling that we had won the war,"[67] and they hadn't: Savo Island was still to come. They knew only that they had sunk at least three carriers and turned back a superior force; months of analysis would be needed before the true import sunk in and the thought began to dawn on both Americans and Japanese that this single battle had permanently altered the odds.

Perhaps the easiest way to visualize Midway's significance is to imagine what might have happened had we lost. Yamamoto planned next to cut the supply line to Australia and the South Pacific; he could then have raided Hawaii and the West Coast with impunity. The American reaction would surely have been to demand a redirection of the war toward the Pacific. No landings in North Africa, no buildup for an invasion of Europe. Without Nimitz's battle, Roosevelt's strategy would have been deeply imperiled. Defeat at Midway would have brought about exactly that concentration of the major effort against Japan that the President was so firmly seeking to avoid, and would have postponed victory—if total victory was still within reach—for an unpredictable period of harsh and costly fighting. That Midway spared us those painful and sorrow-filled years was its ultimate triumph.

In the aftermath there were contretemps. Never averse to publicity, the air force claimed credit for Midway it did not deserve. To repeat, not a single one of the 322 bombs dropped by the B-17s found its target. But their pilots were unaware of this, and they returned to Pearl Harbor before *Enterprise* and *Hornet* did, quite naturally proud of themselves and persuaded that the victory had been theirs. They had attacked an approaching force, the carriers had been sunk, and the Japanese had turned back. ARMY FLIERS BLASTED TWO FLEETS OFF MIDWAY ran a *New York Times* headline of June 12, and Army Secretary Stimson's diary records his impression that "our big bombers have played a decisive part in the battle . . . they have hit and injured capital ships of the enemy."

It wasn't so. The Navy pilots knew it wasn't, and they scuffled in the Royal Hawaiian Hotel with Army pilots more boastful than the true victors were prepared to tolerate. But Spruance and Nimitz, who also knew better, held their peace. (Naval officers of their generation could remember all too well the Sampson-Schley affair of their youth, which had tarnished everyone involved and had made Nimitz in particular traumatically sensitive to the corrosive effects of public controversy.) So the image of Midway as a demonstration of land-based, high-altitude air power was let to persist, and as late as 1949 General Arnold was still maintaining: "To this day, I haven't the faintest idea whether the B-17s we had in the battle of Midway hit any Japanese ships or not." This was less than straightforward: He knew.[68]

Worse had been narrowly avoided. The secret of Midway—the intelligence source that had made it possible—was very nearly compromised. On June 7, the *Chicago Tribune* published a story under the title "Navy Had Word of Jap Plan to Strike at Sea," which revealed to any informed reader the breaking of the Japanese code. (It was simultaneously printed in the *New York Daily News* and the *Washington Times-Herald.*) It had been written by Stanley Johnston, a *Tribune* correspondent who while on his way from Nouméa to Pearl Harbor aboard cruiser *New Orleans* had seen left open on the captain's desk (and had memorized) a classified document on which his dispatch was based. A grand jury was convened in Chicago to investigate, but no naval officer would testify and the head of the government's legal staff, former Attorney General William G. Mitchell, had to tell the press that "no violation of the Espionage Act had been disclosed."

A congressman denounced the *Tribune* on the floor of the House for handing the Japanese a priceless piece of information and enabling them to change their code, but, incredibly, this was not the case. The Japanese were either uninterested in American newspapers or not paying attention, for they went on using JN25 without essential changes until the end of the war—with dire consequences to themselves and happy ones for us. There are those who feel, had full testimony been given, that Johnston, the *Tribune*'s editor, and its publisher—whose virulent hatred for Roosevelt overcame any patriotic scruples he possessed—would have been indicted for treason.[69]

Nor did the Navy do justice by Joe Rochefort, one of the most deserving of all to be honored and recompensed. Nimitz was warm in praise of him and recommended him for the Distinguished Service Medal, but King disapproved this and dissolved Hypo into a larger organization of his own contrivance. Rochefort was summoned to Washington, accused of "squabbling" with Nimitz's staff and failing to keep King sufficiently informed, and assigned sea duty—a chilling example of King's vindictiveness. This was Rochefort's reward for the greatest intelligence achievement in the history of the U.S. Navy. Jasper Holmes, recounting it, was barely able to contain his disgust. "It was not the individual for whom the bell tolled," he wrote, "but the Navy died a little." Scripture speaks truly: "the race is not to the swift, nor the battle to the strong . . . nor yet favor to men of skill; but time and chance happeneth to them all."[70]

III

When a new ship joined the Pacific Fleet, its commander, whether a young lieutenant from an LST or a senior captain from a battleship, was invited to Cincpac headquarters for an eleven o'clock interview with Admiral Nimitz. These morning meetings lasted fifteen minutes. The admiral would open them with a few remarks about what he was doing, operations planned or in prospect, and then say, "Now tell me what you are doing." He would ask if anything bothered them, if there was anything he could do for them, and then shake hands with each as they filed out. It was, however brief, a contact with "the lords of the ships and the ships' numbers"—as Homer puts it in the roll call of the Greeks at Troy—who were under his jurisdiction. If a visitor overstayed the time allowed, as might sometimes happen, Nimitz would accompany him down the hall to the office of Admiral Spruance, since Midway his chief of staff, where no one lingered long; Spruance worked at a stand-up desk and there were no chairs.

Nimitz's headquarters in the compound on Makalapa Hill was a white concrete building with two stories above ground and one below, the two upper stories surrounded by wide verandas that gave access to the rooms within. (The belowground floor contained air- and water-pumping equipment and was in fact a self-sufficient fortress.) Nimitz's corner office looked out on a part of Pearl Harbor and the Koolau mountain range in the distance. It was a light and airy place, with split-bamboo furniture and flowered cushions that matched the drapes; there were maps thumbtacked to the walls and a barometer behind the admiral's desk, which held a few ashtrays and mementos and—surprisingly—a framed photograph of General MacArthur clipped from a newspaper. Nimitz would not allow the offhand disparagement of MacArthur that was commonplace in Washington naval circles, but he once admitted to a friend that he kept the picture there as a reminder not "to make Jovian pronouncements complete with thunderbolts." Under the desk could usually be found Makalapa, a schnauzer who was amiability itself with Nimitz and surly with everyone else.

Nimitz's working day started around seven-thirty, with a reading of reports that had arrived during the night. Staff officers like Commander Layton would bring him questions that were too pressing or confidential for the general briefing, which began at nine, attended by principal staff, fleet and task force commanders present at Pearl, and senior officers just returned from an operation or about to depart on one. These conferences were informational rather than intended for decision, and the atmosphere was informal. After visiting time at eleven, Nimitz would normally see anyone with legitimate business and some without. One sailor from *Enterprise* turned up on a bet with his shipmates that he could get in to meet the Commander in Chief; Nimitz sent for the staff photographer and had a picture taken as evidence on which to collect.

Cincpac staff worked seven days a week and often into the evening, but Nimitz believed in exercise and relaxation, and on a slack day no one objected if you knocked off for a game of tennis in the afternoon. Nimitz himself organized frequent afternoon excursions to Kailua, on the eastern shore of Oahu, for a several-mile walk down the beach and a swim back. (These were strenuous, and invitations to join him were not so sought after as he may have thought; some officers are said to have hidden under their desks when the call went out.)

For Nimitz, working afternoons ended around four or four-thirty, with a walk (often accompanied by Spruance) or a horseshoe match, followed by a bath and dinner. Nimitz kept a good table; his young officer guests were offered bourbon or the potent Hawaiian okolehau—two per man, mixed by Nimitz himself or sometimes by Spruance, though the latter was abstemious—and a meal prepared by an excellent chef who grew his own vegetables, topped off by ice cream in unusual flavors such as avocado. Afterward Nimitz might show a movie or play records of classical music, with lights out and the blackout curtains open, to a not always enthusiastic audience.

The center and focus of his existence was the planning of future operations, and here he concentrated his greatest attention, picking draft plans to pieces and sending them back for revision. This was a group enterprise, much of it done orally, at gatherings in the corridor or in front of maps, since both Nimitz and Spruance shared a predilection for what Spruance called thinking aloud, preferably on their feet. Nimitz would indicate a course of action he preferred, which would then be staffed out as papers setting forth the details passed up and down the echelons. Three questions Nimitz always insisted on having answered about any proposal, and they were in fact lettered in a sign on the wall of his office. Is it likely to succeed? What are the consequences of failure? Is it practicable in terms of materials and supplies? Under the glass top of his desk was a card listing factors to be kept in mind: "Objective, Offensive, Surprise, Superiority of Force at Point of Contact, Simplicity, Security, Movement, Economy of Force, Co-operation"—an abbreviated textbook in the principles of war.

One of his officers spoke of Nimitz as "rather easygoing . . . [a] sort of old shoe type," but this runs the risk of giving a very false impression. His simplicity and almost folksy style concealed both intellect and determination from those—Spruance at first included—who had met him only casually. "The better I got to know him," said Spruance, "the more I admired his intelligence . . . and, above all, his utter fearlessness. . . . He is one of the few people I know who never knew what it meant to be afraid of anything."[71] King's flag secretary, Captain George L. Russell, told Nimitz's biographer, Professor E. B. Potter, chairman of naval history at Annapolis: "Admiral Nimitz was a lot tougher than he's ever been given credit for." The Central Pacific campaigns were not the handiwork of an easygoing old-shoe type; Nimitz when he wanted to be was hard as nails.

In December 1943, when the invasion of the Marshall Islands was being discussed, Nimitz overrode the recommendations of Spruance, Turner, Holland Smith, and other Fifth Fleet commanders by assigning Kwajalein as the objective. (They all wanted to take the nearer islands of Wotje and Maleolap first, the safer course.) Spruance and Turner stayed on after the meeting to state their case and Turner turned vehement. "He argued and argued and became very determined," said Nimitz later. (Turner's biographer calls this the "fateful, decision-making conference.") Finally, Nimitz said: "Sitting behind desks in the United States are able officers who would give their right arms to be out here fighting the war. If you gentlemen can't bring yourselves to carry out my orders, I can arrange an exchange of duty with stateside officers who can. Make up your minds. You have five minutes. Do you want to do it or not?" Turner's knit brows unknit and he smiled. "Sure I want to do it," he said, and do it they did, going on to capture Eniwetok without a break in stride.[72] Theirs was not the only advice Nimitz was getting, as we shall see, but his was the command and the responsibility.

Nimitz had found in Spruance so close to what he wanted in a chief of staff that he was reluctant to give it up. "There are going to be some changes in high command of the fleet," he told Spruance one morning as they walked to work. "I would like to let you go, but unfortunately for you, I need you here." Spruance replied diplomatically that the war was the important thing, that he personally would like another crack at the Japanese, "but if you need me here, this is where I should be." (Curiously, an

refused to censure him. Halsey had been a strong proponent of the offense in the early days of defeatism at Cincpac, and Nimitz never forgot it. "Bill Halsey came to my support and offered to lead the attack," he said. "I'll not be party to any enterprise that can hurt the reputation of a man like that."[77]

The criticisms that lingered over Spruance's head had to do with the fact that he was lazy (which he was the first to admit) and with his handling of the carriers at the Battle of the Philippine Sea, the invasion of the Marianas (Saipan, Tinian, and Guam) in June 1944. When the Japanese fleet came out to oppose him, Spruance held the carriers back and let the Japanese aircraft come to them, rather than turn the carriers loose to send their own air groups after the Japanese. The result was a slaughter of over three hundred Japanese planes and the utter failure of their attack (only one nonfatal hit on *South Dakota*), but the Japanese fleet was not dealt the demolishing blow that the air admirals believed they could have delivered.

"It was the chance of a century missed," Jocko Clark told Morison ten days later. Spruance, who saw his primary mission as safeguarding the invasion, said that he wanted to avoid an "end run" by part of the Japanese force, and air-minded commentators have pounced on the phrase as indicating his failure to understand that in the age of the aircraft carrier there is no such thing as an "end run"; the sky is open over every quarter of the compass.[78] Yet an "end run" is precisely what happened to Halsey at Leyte Gulf, when he went impetuously after a decoy of empty Japanese carriers and left the invasion transports exposed to a surface attack.

Spruance himself acknowledged eight years later that he had been conscious of letting pass a great opportunity, and the carrier admirals were at the time convinced that this was what came of letting a non-aviator command them. But both Morison and Potter take the view that Spruance "through luck or intuition" (Potter) had put Task Force 58 "in about the optimum position to inflict the greatest damage on the enemy" (Morison). Postwar analysis showed that the Japanese fleet had been divided in a fashion no one on our side expected, with their heaviest antiaircraft vessels formed in three groups around the light carriers and placed a hundred miles in advance of the heavy carriers. In order to attack the latter, writes Potter, the Americans "would have had to pass through the intense antiaircraft fire and air attacks of the van force, fly a hundred miles farther to the main force, attack it and defend themselves there, fly back another hundred miles and again pass over the enemy van force before returning to their own carriers." Morison thought the outcome would have been "anyone's guess," Potter that American losses would have been "catastrophic."[79] What Captain Slonim called Spruance's "uncanny ability to be one thought ahead of his adversary" had once again been demonstrated.

Clark Reynolds, writing from the airman's perspective, pays tribute to Spruance as a brilliant coordinator of large naval forces afloat, but considers him one of "the last inheritors of battle line [i.e., battleship] formalism," who misused the carriers in a defensive mode on the two occasions (the Gilberts and Saipan) when he took them under his own command. "Military men," as Admiral Morison wisely noted, "never get any credit for guarding against dangers that might occur yet do not." Spruance lacked Halsey's glamour and gift for publicity; he never received either the adulation or the fifth star that Halsey did; quiet and unassuming, he slipped into obscurity. But the Japanese held him in esteem. "He had air admiral's best character," said Captain Watanabe in 1964, "—strong, straight thinker, not impulsive fluctuating thinker; he aims right at main point and go, no stop. That is good admiral."[80]

Morison called Spruance "one of the greatest fighting and thinking admirals in American naval history,"[81] and to say that Roosevelt appointed Nimitz and Nimitz appointed Spruance is to say much of what needs to be said about the way the war was fought in the Pacific hemisphere. Victory over Japan came much sooner than anyone anticipated at least in part because the fleet so thoroughly prevailed, and to lead at sea so large a naval aggregation in a series of attacks so unprecedented in aggressiveness and complexity was a task for which no one else demonstrated the capacity. It can be said of Spruance as of no other American high commander in the war that he did not make mistakes.

Outside of the professional purposes to which he put it, Spruance's mind was a half-formed instrument. Like many of his time and place, he was a Social Darwinian, contemptuous of democracy and welfare measures that encouraged "low grade" elements in society to propagate. He read widely but indiscriminately; as an agnostic, he revered the Bible for its language though his other bible was Henry George's *Progress and Poverty,* which led him when he was later ambassador to the Philippines into the "populist" position of opposing the large landowners and the Quirino regime. If he had any sympathy for the liberal objectives of the war, however, he never expressed it, with the possible exception of his comments when Mrs. Roosevelt visited Cincpac and was seated next to him at dinner. "She is very simple, charming, and has a delightful sense of humor," Spruance wrote to his wife. "Whatever we may think of the possibility of achieving her ideals, she certainly has them and she has a deep faith in the underlying goodness of the ordinary human being. She is certainly a very fine person."[82]

◆

One of the salient features of American participation in the Second World War was the incorporation of the unexpected. None of the three services had planned for the manner in which it eventually performed. The air force did not anticipate the dependence of the heavy bomber on the long-range fighter; it set out to destroy German industry and, instead, destroyed the Luftwaffe; it set out to destroy Japan's industry and, instead, burned down its cities. The Army generals were fond of saying that the war in Europe was going "just the way we did it at Leavenworth," but in fact their successes were coming from an integration of the infantry/tank/artillery/fighter-bomber team that was extemporized rather than provided for in the Tables of Organization. The navies of both the United States and Japan desired and looked forward to a surface fleet action that eluded them, while the task force organized around the aircraft carrier replaced the battle line as the backbone of the fleet. (The Marines, similarly, landed on Guadalcanal to conduct a completely different campaign from the one doctrine had prepared them for.) To repeat, the war in the Pacific was the first in history (and probably the last) to be won by a navy that did not exist when that war began. The ships were new, their crews were new, and their weapons were new; inevitably they confronted old problems with new solutions, and the marvel was that the new solutions worked.

The fast carriers were a phenomenon beyond compare, a combined product of training, tactics, and technology that changed the syntax of naval warfare. Richard Rodgers's instincts did not betray him when in providing a musical score for the television series *Victory at Sea* he wrote the "Theme of the Fast Carriers," with its strumming undertone of confidence and its soaring assertion of mastery. Well before war's end, the fast carriers dominated the Pacific; in them the dream of successfully patrolling that vast expanse of emptiness was realized. After the surrender, General Tojo told MacArthur that the three main factors in Japan's defeat had been the American submarines, the fast carriers, and the bypassing and neutralizing of major bases that the fast carriers permitted.[83] In them was achieved that rare triumph, the perfecting of a weapon at its moment of most effective use.

President Roosevelt was knowledgeable and inquisitive about carrier technology. After Coral Sea and Midway, he asked King and King asked Nimitz whether catapults had been used in either battle; answer: no.[84] After Midway, three of the Navy's leading pilots—Lieutenants O'Hare, Thach, and Flatley—were invited to the White House and told the President that what they needed was "something that will go upstairs faster." During the Aleutians operation, a Zero had been recovered almost intact, repaired, flight tested, and carefully studied; Grumman set out to design a plane specifically intended to outperform it. The result (in production within half a year) was the F6F Hellcat, which could outclimb and outdive the Zero and had twice the power, higher speed, a higher ceiling, and heavier armament. Commander Okumiya, a staff officer of the carrier force from which the captured Zero came, thought that the loss of that single aircraft, in causing the Hellcat to be created, "did much to hasten our final defeat."[85] The first Hellcats arrived at Pearl Harbor with the new carriers.

Essex, first of her class (there were ultimately seventeen), displaced 27,000 tons and carried a hundred aircraft (*Enterprise* displaced 20,000 and carried eighty). Fourth Navy ship to bear the name, *Essex* was launched in August 1942. She fought in sixty-eight engagements over a period of two years, seventeen months of it in continuous action. *Essex* was rugged; no *Essex*-class carrier was ever sunk. Her air groups destroyed 1,531 Japanese aircraft plus 800 "probables" and her antiaircraft shot down 33 more. *Essex* sank 25 warships and 86 merchant vessels, hit and damaged 308. Commander David McCampbell of *Essex,* with thirty-four kills, was the Navy's leading ace. When a civilian visitor saw the number of rising suns painted on *Essex*'s bridge, he asked, "Is that the record of Task Force 58?"[86]

Essex and her sister ships came with advanced communications equipment Clark Reynolds thought "held the key" to their success: multi-channel, very-high-frequency, short-range radio and new radar like the PPI (Position Plan Indicator) that enabled a many-carrier force to maintain high speed at night or in foul weather without its ships bumping into each other. (Previous debates about the wisdom of using carriers together were ended by the technological answer.) Antiaircraft had been beefed up; on *Essex,* twelve five-inch dual-purpose guns fired a shell with the proximity (or posit) fuze, which had a small radar in its nose that caused it to explode not at a preset altitude but on coming close to an attacking plane. With the introduction of high-velocity rockets in 1944, the fire-power of individual aircraft was significantly increased, until a single squadron packed a punch equivalent to a volley from a division of three cruisers.[87]

And the quality of the pilots was improving. By the Battle of the Philippine Sea, every U.S. aviator considered fit to fly from a carrier had at least two years' training and three hundred hours' flying time (by comparison, the best Japanese carrier division in the same battle had six months' training and the others, three or only two). With new capabilities came new ways of employing them. "Carriers were no longer an expensive weapon for dealing single sharp blows," reads an official analysis prepared at Cincpac in June 1944, "but had become efficient machines for keeping aircraft constantly in motion against enemy targets from dawn to dusk."[88]

When Task Force 58 went on the prowl in February 1944, it assumed the form and facility it would have for the remainder of the war: nine fast carriers with nearly six hundred aircraft—ever-faithful *Enterprise,* four of the *Essex* class (*Essex, Yorktown, Intrepid, Bunker Hill*), and four of the new light *Independence* class, with half the tonnage and half the hangar capacity of *Essex* (*Belleau Wood, Cabot, Monterey, Cowpens*)—six new fast battleships, ten cruisers, thirty destroyers, and nine submarines, all under Spruance in *New Jersey* and Mitscher in *Yorktown*. This was the "first team" thought one officer aboard *Enterprise* as he surveyed the ships that filled the ocean as far as he could see. The invasions of Kwajalein and Eniwetok completed, they had left Majuro atoll on February 12 and 13 in the first large-scale independent carrier strike to be attempted. Its target was Truk in the Carolines, "impregnable" Truk, the "Gibraltar of the Pacific," since July 1942 the main forward base of Combined Fleet, the linchpin in Japan's defensive perimeter.[89]

Truk is a collection of a dozen volcanic islands and over thirty smaller ones, ringed by a coral reef; it contained the fleet anchorage, a bomber airfield, three fighter strips, seaplane bases, docks, supply installations, and plentiful antiaircraft. We knew very little about it, other than that its importance for the Japanese was similar to that of Pearl Harbor for us. Marc Mitscher said that most of his information about Truk came from the *National Geographic;* an air group commander, told that Truk was the objective, said that his first impulse was to jump overboard.

They wrecked the place. A fighter sweep of over seventy blue Hellcats was sent in first, an idea of Marc Mitscher's, to clear the air of Japanese. (The Hellcat was much appreciated; said a pilot, "If they could cook, I'd marry one.") There followed a total of thirty strikes in sequence, each of them larger than the Japanese attack on Pearl Harbor (one, using radar, was made at night, a most efficient innovation). They destroyed 250 Japanese aircraft and 200,000 tons of shipping: two auxiliary cruisers, a destroyer, two submarine tenders, an aircraft ferry, six tankers, and seventeen transports. They bombed the airfields, hangars, ammunition dumps, and oil storage tanks (the last sent up a column of black smoke to eight thousand feet).

Spruance and the battlewagons made a circuit of the island to catch any vessels that tried to escape, and sank a cruiser, a destroyer, a subchaser, and a trawler. When the Hellcats went back the second day, no Japanese fighters left the ground to greet them. We lost seventeen planes and twenty-six crewmen; *Intrepid* took a torpedo that put it out of action for months, but the usefulness of Truk as an anchorage or advanced naval base had ended; the flagship of Combined Fleet was never seen there again.[90]

The Truk operation set the pattern for the future. It showed what the carriers, given a chance, could do, and the men who commanded them began to feel with some justification that their time had come. In 1943–44, the number of air admirals increased from thirty-four to fifty-four, from 20 to 26 percent of the total. In Washington they had a good friend in Forrestal, a naval aviator in World War I, who on Knox's death in April 1944 became secretary of the Navy. They had to be assuaged, accommodated, and accepted, and it was Nimitz—with considerable pushing

from King—who presided over the process in which a surface navy became an air navy.

King sent him Vice-Admiral John H. Towers—naval aviator number
3, a pioneer from before World War I—to be deputy Cincpac; more ardent
an airman was there none. King in January 1944 put through a ruling
(suggested to him by his own air deputy, Slew McCain) that any fleet or
task force commander who was not an aviator must have a chief of staff
who was, and vice versa. Nimitz disliked Towers (as did others) and would
never give him a seagoing command, but Towers and Rear Admiral (later
Admiral and CNO) Forrest Sherman as Cincpac assistant chief of staff for
plans had gained Nimitz's confidence in air matters. It was Sherman, in
the planning for Kwajalein, who convinced Nimitz that the carriers could
knock out any opposition in the outer islands and thus allow going to
Kwajalein direct, causing Nimitz to overrule Spruance and the others.
Nimitz made Marc Mitscher, greatest air admiral of them all, commander
of the fast carriers, despite Spruance's initial lack of enthusiasm for him.
Perhaps because, as a submariner, he belonged to neither faction, Nimitz
was able to keep the peace between them.[91]

The submarines were another of the surprises. They took on work of
great variety: Among much else they sank warships, put out picket lines,
ran supplies to guerrillas in the Philippines, and did noble duty in air-sea
rescue after carrier strikes. (By the end of 1944, a total of 224 pilots and
crewmen had been plucked from the drink and brought safely home by
submarines.) But their most incontrovertible achievement—one so total
and invisible to the normal newspaper reader that common understanding has never quite caught up with it—was the elimination of the Japanese
merchant marine. By the time the American submarine fleet was finished
with their economy, the Japanese no longer had the capability of waging
offensive warfare, and the argument can be made with some plausibility
that they had been defeated by the submarines alone.

Nimitz had a strong interest in this. Not only did his career begin in
submarines, not only was he responsible for converting them to diesel
engines, not only did he build the Pearl Harbor submarine base, and not
only did he assume command as Cincpac on board a submarine, but his
son was a submariner too. Chester, Jr., was an officer aboard *Sturgeon*
operating out of the Philippines when war began. He became exec of
Bluefish, which on two patrols from Australia in late 1943 sank six ships,
for a total of 39,000 tons. In August 1944, as commander of *Haddo* outside
Manila Bay, he sank a destroyer and with companion *Ray* sank three coast
defense vessels and four big transports. (Rear Admiral Chester W. Nimitz,
Jr., retired from the Navy in 1957, dissatisfied with the cold-blooded im-
personality of intercontinental ballistic missiles. "I think," said his father,
"he felt that the kind of person required by the armed forces was no longer
the kind of person . . . he had tried to be.")[92]

Under Nimitz, Sr., there were more than a hundred and fifty U.S. submarines operating in the Pacific by the end of 1943, forty of them based on Australia; they were commanded by Rear Admirals Charles A. Lockwood in Hawaii and Ralph Christie in Fremantle. Though generally speaking only about fifty were in action at any given time, and of these twenty or more would be en route to and from a patrol, they nonetheless ranged from the South China Sea to eventually as far north as the Sea of Japan, and despite a disgraceful delay in repairing deficiencies in their torpedoes, they strangled Japan's war effort.

By early 1944, the Japanese were so alarmed at their losses in oil tankers (twenty-five in the month of February) that they made drastic changes in their shipbuilding program to convert cargo ships to tankers. But their naval strategy had become a function of a dwindling oil supply, their tanker routes from the Indies were crowded up against the China coast, and they were under a virtual blockade. By the end of the year, they had abandoned all attempts to move dry cargo from Southeast Asia in a desperate (and unsuccessful) effort to keep enough oil flowing to the home islands.[93]

There was a spiral effect: less iron ore meant fewer ships, fewer ships meant less oil, less oil meant less ore and less gasoline to train pilots, and fewer trained pilots meant greater losses and less of everything. In the latter months of 1944, American submarines, as Jasper Holmes put it, "ripped the Japanese merchant marine to shreds." Between September and November alone they sank 34 warships and 170 transports, for a total of 868,361 tons; by the end, Japan had little left but small wooden ships in the Inland Sea. Examination of Japanese records after the war showed that submarines had sunk 1,314 of their vessels, for a total of 5.3 million tons. Another way of putting it would be to say that a force representing less than 2 percent of the U.S. Navy had accounted for 55 percent of Japanese maritime losses. The cost had been great: 375 officers and 3,131 enlisted men out of the 16,000 who went out on submarine patrols, a casualty rate of 22 percent, highest of any branch in the American military.[94]

The victory again owed a debt to intelligence. British practice in the use of decoded material was extremely strict; the information could not be used as the basis of action if it was the *only* source. The Americans in the Pacific violated this rule at every turn and, *mirabile dictu,* got away with it. The Japanese regularly radioed the origin, destination, composition, and estimated noon positions of their convoys, and after decoding, these were passed on to the submarine commanders by Frupac (Fleet Radio Unit, Pacific, the successor to Hypo). Jasper Holmes said that messages to the submarines "were of almost nightly occurrence, too many to enumerate." In a wide ocean, this narrowing of attention made a deadly difference. Holmes gives one example: On the night of July 16, 1944, a wolf pack of three—*Piranha, Guardfish,* and *Thresher*— was coached by Frupac into contact with a ten-ship convoy in the Luzon Strait, and sank six of them.[95]

◆

The climax of the Pacific war occurred in late October 1944 at Leyte Gulf, when the two axes of our advance (Nimitz in the center, MacArthur from the southwest) met together in the Philippines, two U.S. fleets (Nimitz's Third under Halsey, MacArthur's Seventh under Vice-Admiral Thomas C. Kinkaid) fought the greatest sea battle of all time, and the final curtain fell for the Imperial Japanese Navy. Leyte Gulf was an engagement unlike any other, not only in size but in variousness, in confusion, and in closeness of decision. Even at this late date the Japanese fleet was a formidable force; for this occasion it emerged in full strength, and it came within a cat's whisker of winning a major victory. What prevented our defeat was the fighting quality that the U.S. Navy in the Pacific had by this time achieved, a combination of numbers, skill, and bravery that compels not only admiration but awe.

The Battle of Leyte Gulf included naval action of practically every type, between fighting craft of every kind then in use, with weapons from machine guns to the huge eighteen-inch rifles fired here in combat for the first time, at distances ranging from point-blank to fifteen miles, and including one extraordinary episode in which some of the lightest warships involved were matched against some of the heaviest—and the former prevailed. It was marked by the first appearance of the Japanese *kamikaze,* the suicide pilots who crashed into American ships and were to do much painful damage before they were through. It was also distinguished —ironically, given the widespread conviction that carriers were now the dominant naval arm—for the last appearance on the stage of history by a classic battle line of battleships and cruisers, engaged in the often sought but rarely seen maneuver of "crossing the T" and bringing their concentrated fire to bear on an advancing enemy line.

Admiral Morison thought that the Japanese would have been wiser not to seek action at Leyte but to have waited until we invaded Luzon, where they might have been able to inflict even heavier losses on the Americans.[96] But the Japanese did not see it that way; they regarded the Philippines as vital to their continuation in the war and hence they considered an American presence there to be insupportable. "Should we lose in the Philippine operations," said Admiral Soemu Toyoda, who had replaced Koga in command of Combined Fleet, "even though the fleet should be left, the shipping lanes to the south would be completely cut off so that the fleet, if it should come back to Japanese waters, could not obtain its fuel supply. If it should remain in southern waters, it could not receive supplies of ammunition and arms. There would be no sense in saving the fleet at the expense of the loss of the Philippines."[97]

The Japanese plan was as usual intricate, fragmented, and overly dependent on successful deception, but it was not unintelligent and it rested on a number of strategic advantages that the Japanese enjoyed. The closer we came to Japan, the shorter would be their lines of communication and supply, while ours were increasingly strung out over many thousands of miles of open sea. In previous operations it had been possible for us to neutralize enemy airfields, but in a Philippine invasion we could no longer do so; they were far too numerous—some seventy were operational—and reinforcements could be staged to them from Formosa and the home islands. Our nearest airfield was five hundred miles away and the soil of Leyte valley was unsuitable for airfield construction during the monsoon, which meant that we would have to rely on the carriers for air cover and support, and continue to rely on them far longer than usual. The winding water passages of the Philippine archipelago, probably mined and guarded by land-based air, would be denied to us but available to the Japanese. These were not favorable odds.

The American planners recognized this, with the result that their schedule for a Philippine campaign to begin with a landing in Leyte Gulf had been a conservative one, providing for five preliminary operations in September, October, and November—Peleliu, Morotai, Yap, Talaud, and Mindanao—before a Leyte invasion was attempted on December 20. On September 15, the 31st Infantry Division (MacArthur's axis) landed unopposed on Morotai and the 1st Marine Division (Nimitz's axis) assaulted Peleliu, one of the bloodiest actions of the war, in which it suffered 6,526 casualties, of whom 1,252 died.[98]

Meantime, in support of these, Halsey and Third Fleet had launched air strikes on Mindanao and the Palau Islands against unexpectedly light opposition. Some 2,400 sorties were flown and 200 Japanese aircraft shot down or destroyed on the ground. Halsey and his staff reasoned that the Japanese air arm was close to extinction; they recommended that the Yap, Talaud, and Mindanao landings be canceled and the one on Leyte advanced to October 20, a two-month speed-up. Their conclusion that Japanese air resources were nearly exhausted was mistaken (planes and pilots were deliberately being held back, and were not truly devastated until Third Fleet attacked Formosa in early October), but the Joint Chiefs—summoned from dinner at Quebec—instantly approved Halsey's suggested acceleration in timing for Leyte Gulf.

Considering that the plans of two large fleets had to be largely rewritten, and complex preparations made in one month for which three months had been expected, the degree of coordination attained was remarkable —C. Vann Woodward calls it "one of the greatest achievements of the

Pacific War." But routines were further dislocated by the simultaneous more-than-thousand-mile displacement forward of the main base from Eniwetok to Ulithi, and by a typhoon that struck the latter on October 3. The changes in schedule upset the delicate logistic balance and created unexpected shortages; forces intended for Yap were not necessarily well suited to Leyte. Third Fleet had not only been at sea since the previous year but had just finished two months of intensive operations in which it stood off the heaviest Japanese air strikes hitherto experienced. Medical officers were reporting symptoms of fatigue; Marc Mitscher said that his crews' reactions were slowing down and that they were "not completely effective against attack."[99] He himself was closer to exhaustion than many realized. American abilities were going to be dangerously stretched.

The Japanese frame of mind was complicated by the worst example yet of their inability to secure accurate after-action reports and their eagerness to provide their own public with overly optimistic information. When Third Fleet struck Formosa, the Japanese air arm struck back and damaged two cruisers, *Canberra* and *Houston,* which were taken under tow. Japanese pilots turned in such enthusiastic accounts that the two cruisers and their escort appear in Japanese reports as "the crippled remnants of the Third Fleet" and Imperial General Headquarters issued a communiqué claiming that eleven carriers, two battleships, three cruisers, plus one destroyer had been sunk and damage done to dozens more. A special session of the cabinet was called to advise the emperor of a "glorious victory."[100] This was the occasion for Halsey's famous dispatch to Nimitz saying that the ships reported sunk by Tokyo radio had been salvaged and were "retiring at high speed toward the enemy." *Canberra* and *Houston* came safely home to the States for a total overhaul.

Certainly there were many Japanese naval officers who knew better than to believe their own propaganda, but something of the home-front elation rubbed off on the plan for meeting the Philippine invasion; Woodward calls it "the most daring, not to say the most desperate, attempted by any naval power during the war." Three Japanese forces would converge on the beaches five days after the landing, when the Americans would still be vulnerable and dependent on seaborne support. (They were in fact far more vulnerable and dependent than the Japanese realized, with only a few days' supply ashore and no airstrips operational.)

Southern Force under Vice-Admiral Shoji Nishimura consisted of two battleships, a heavy cruiser, and four destroyers; it was to enter the gulf from the south through Surigao Strait. Center Force under Vice-Admiral Takeo Kurita consisted of five battleships (including the giants *Yamato* and *Musashi*), twelve cruisers, and fifteen destroyers; it was to approach through the Sibuyan Sea, round Samar through San Bernardino Strait, and attack from the north. Northern Force under Vice-Admiral Jisaburo Ozawa was referred to as the Main Body, though this was misleading. It consisted of four carriers, two converted battleship-carriers, three cruisers, and ten destroyers. But Halsey's Formosa attack had done the job of reducing the quantity and quality of Japanese pilots and aircraft to near-ineffectuality; the carriers were in good part empty; their air groups totaled little more than a hundred planes and their pilots were green. Northern Force was a fake, a decoy, intended to prowl off Luzon and bait Halsey into coming after it with Third Fleet while Central and Southern Forces dealt with Seventh Fleet, which had made and accompanied the landings. Not only was this plan sound, it nearly succeeded.

Leyte found Admiral Halsey not at his best but rather at his all too characteristic: impetuous, careless about staff work, not wholly at ease with tactics that had changed in the years while he was ashore. Nimitz and King had clearly sent him on the Leyte mission because they wanted boldness; Nimitz told King at San Francisco in late September that he hoped Halsey would here draw out the Japanese fleet and finish the job Spruance had begun in June. To be certain there was no doubt about this, Nimitz gave Halsey explicit orders that had previously been only implied: "In case opportunity for destruction of major portion of the enemy fleet is offered or can be created, *such destruction becomes the primary task*" (emphasis in original).[101] To a man of Halsey's disposition this was a license to disregard if he chose his other mission, of safeguarding MacArthur's landing, an invitation to judge for himself how and where Third Fleet should operate. It was not the counsel of prudence.

Third Fleet and Mitscher's task force (now renamed 38) were virtually identical, three groups totaling eleven attack carriers, six fast battleships, fifteen cruisers, and fifty-eight destroyers under air admirals Gerald F. Bogan, Frederick C. Sherman, and Ralph E. Davison. (A fourth group, under McCain, had been sent on its way back to Ulithi to refuel and refit.) As we have noted, this was a concentration of the heaviest striking power in the U.S. Navy; in regular cruising formation at sea it filled an area forty miles long and nine miles wide. Task Force 38 was nominally under Pete Mitscher's command, but when Halsey took charge of Third Fleet (in battleship *New Jersey*) it was often his practice to assume tactical command as well, leaving Mitscher as little more than a passenger in carrier *Lexington*. Mitscher had suffered a bout of malaria and more than one heart attack ("He doesn't look a day over eighty," another admiral said) and probably should not have been at sea, but one cannot help wishing that somehow better use could have been made of this wiry aviator's wisdom and experience. His chief of staff, Commodore Arleigh Burke, noted his discontent and tried to alleviate his burdens.[102]

First blood was drawn during the night of October 23 when Kurita and Central Force in the Sibuyan Sea encountered U.S. submarines *Darter* and *Dace,* which reported the Japanese approach and toward dawn, with conspicuous effect, made an attack that sank two Japanese cruisers at great loss of life and damaged a third. One of the two to go down was Kurita's flagship, *Atago,* from which he had to transfer to *Yamato,* losing half of his communications personnel. (Poor communications bedeviled both sides at Leyte, but the Japanese the more, and the loss of *Atago* contributed thereto.) *Darter* and *Dace* continued to pursue Central Force, but *Darter* ran aground on Bombay Shoal and had to be abandoned, its men rescued by *Dace. Dace* set course for home at Fremantle in Australia and reached it after eleven days in which the doubled-up crews were reduced to the only rations *Dace* had in sufficient quantity, mushroom soup and peanut butter.

Alerted by the submarines, Third Fleet moved against Kurita. Planes from the fast carriers cleared what little air cover there was over Central Force and then, against heavy antiaircraft, went to work on its capital ships. Greatest harm was done to superbattleship *Musashi,* which took seventeen bomb and nineteen torpedo hits, became unmanageable, flooded uncontrollably, and trailed the main force by twenty miles. At seven thirty-five in the evening of the twenty-fourth she rolled over and sank, taking with her 112 officers and 984 men of her 2,287 complement. Returning U.S. pilots made reports of many hits on other ships as well, to which Halsey gave greater credence than Mitscher did, for in fact Kurita still had *Yamato* and his remaining battleships, cruisers, and destroyers undiminished in speed and hitting power. Our scouts reported them as headed west, as though in retreat, but they were only milling around to reorganize, and about an hour before sunset Kurita turned them back to the east and headed toward San Bernardino Strait, on course, unknown to Halsey, for a rendezvous with Nishimura in Leyte Gulf.

Fortune did not smile that night upon Admiral Nishimura. He was being joined by a second force (three cruisers, four destroyers) under Vice-Admiral Kiyohide Shima, but both had been spotted in the Sulu Sea and Kinkaid had concluded without much hesitation that they were headed for Surigao Strait. He assigned the task of intercepting them to Seventh Fleet's Bombardment and Fire Support Group under Admiral Jesse B. Oldendorf. "We didn't want them to pull another Savo Island on us," said Oldendorf, and so at the head of the strait he placed his line of old and slow battleships (five of them salvaged survivors of Pearl Harbor), with two cruiser forces (seven in all) on either side, both screened by destroyers and by a picket line of destroyers and PT boats farther forward. The Japanese appeared not to realize what they were getting into. Oldendorf's theory, as he said, was never to give a sucker an even break.[103]

Nishimura was met before and after midnight south of Leyte by the PT boats, thirty of which attacked him in sequence with commendable verve, releasing torpedoes and retiring under smoke. But they scored only one, nonfatal hit and from Nishimura's point of view they had been easily driven off by gunfire. So on up the strait came he and his doomed ships.

"Their strategy and intelligence," said one American officer, "seemed to be inversely proportional to their courage."[104] Nishimura's sharp-eyed lookouts spotted the first of the destroyers 4.3 miles away just before three o'clock in the morning, but his searchlights could not reach them and he held his fire. The destroyers came after him in three groups, the first of which released forty-seven torpedoes with phenomenal success; they scored five hits and eliminated three vessels, including battleship *Fuso* (which dropped out of line and later sank). By the time Nishimura came within range of Oldendorf's battle line, he was down in effectiveness to a single battleship, a single cruiser, and a single destroyer, and not one of the American destroyers had suffered a scratch.

Of Nishimura's entire force, only destroyer *Shigure* survived the Battle of Surigao Strait. Oldendorf's battleships and cruisers opened up on him just before four o'clock. "The devastating accuracy of this gunfire," said one of the destroyer commanders, "was the most beautiful sight I have ever witnessed. The arched line of tracers in the darkness looked like a continual stream of lighted railroad cars going over a hill."[105] At four-nineteen, battleship *Yamashiro,* brightly aflame, capsized and sank, taking with her Admiral Nishimura and all but a few members of her crew. When Shima came on after at four-thirty, he passed what seemed to be two ships on fire (actually the two halves of *Fuso*). He sent off torpedoes at two small islands he wrongly identified as the enemy, and prudently retired.

The Japanese had left behind them two battleships and three destroyers on the bottom of the strait, and two of their cruisers were so badly crippled that they were later found and disposed of without difficulty by escort-carrier and Army Air Forces bombers. We had taken heavy casualties only aboard destroyer *Albert W. Grant,* which was caught between friendly and hostile fire; the twenty-eight Liberty ships, Amphibious Force flagships, and cruiser *Nashville* (General MacArthur aboard) in San Pedro Bay were for the moment safe; and an era in naval warfare had come to an end. This was the last battle in which air power played no part, the last broadside fired by a battle line in action.

A good many hours before Nishimura met his demise, the most critical decision on the American side had been made. Ozawa with his half-empty carriers to the north had been trying every way he could think of to attract Halsey's attention, and finally he got it. In midafternoon on the twenty-fourth, pilots from Ralph Davison's task group found him off Cape Engaño and Halsey now had the one piece of information he had been lacking about the Japanese dispositions. He believed that Third Fleet had so heavily damaged Center Force in the Sibuyan Sea as to leave Kurita no longer a serious threat. He believed it was "childish" (as he later wrote MacArthur) "to guard statically San Bernardino Strait" when by steaming north with his full force he could finish off the carriers that *were* a real threat and that represented Japan's last offensive capability at sea. At ten-twenty-two in the evening, he ordered Task Force 38 to concentrate and go after Ozawa. He had taken the bait.

Another unusual feature of the Battle of Leyte Gulf was the closeness with which it could be monitored by higher headquarters, by Nimitz in Hawaii and by King in Washington. Radio communication was slow (especially in code), but there was a lot of it; since the weather was clear and created little static, listening stations picked up most of the messages and relayed them to Cincpac, which in turn relayed them to Cominch. Halsey cared not in the slightest about maintaining radio silence; he had no direct link with Kinkaid and MacArthur, but Kinkaid was intercepting the bulk of Halsey's traffic and decoding it. Unfortunately, fallibility and mischance were also playing their parts; messages were not always clearly worded, some were misunderstood, and one of them was accidentally corrupted in such a way as to convey an unintended slur.

The first and most serious misunderstanding came about when Halsey turned north. Two of his radioed instructions and advisories had been so phrased as to give the impression that he was detaching his fast battleships under Ching Lee, designating them as Task Force 34, and leaving them behind to guard San Bernardino Strait. This was not the case—Lee and the battleships were with Halsey—but it was a logical assumption for others to make, since it was what nearly everyone but Halsey thought should be done. Lee thought so, Mitscher thought so, task group commander Admiral Bogan thought so, Kinkaid thought so, Nimitz thought so, and King thought so.[106]

The overpowering need to block Kurita was underscored the evening of the twenty-fourth, when patrols from carrier *Independence* reported his Center Force to be still very much in being and headed east. Navigation lights in San Bernardino Strait, previously blacked out, were now brilliantly lit. When the *Independence* sightings were confirmed, Arleigh Burke and Commander James Flatley decided to waken Mitscher and recommend that Third Fleet turn around and go south. "Does Admiral Halsey have that report?" asked Mitscher. "Yes, he does," Flatley replied. "If he wants my advice," said Mitscher, "he'll ask for it," and he rolled over and went back to sleep.[107]

Halsey did not want anyone's advice. When Admiral Bogan got the *Independence* reports, he called Halsey on the TBS and the "rather impatient voice" of a staff officer told him, "Yes, yes, we have that information." Admiral Lee, whose opinions commanded respect, had concluded that the Northern Force they were going after was a decoy. (U.S. naval intelligence knew that the Japanese had such a plan, but no one had taken it seriously.) Lee sent Halsey a message stating his views and got only a perfunctory "Roger" (that is, "received") in reply. When he learned of the *Indepen-*

dence sightings, Lee sent Halsey word on the TBS that he was certain Kurita was coming out; thereafter he said nothing.[108] Kurita was indeed coming out, and there was no one there to stop him, or even to report his progress.

Kinkaid's Seventh Fleet was vastly different in composition from Halsey's Third: no fast carriers, no fast battleships. It was strictly an invasion fleet. Aside from Amphibious Force and Oldendorf's battle line, its one other major component was a group of eighteen escort carriers, loaned to MacArthur by Nimitz to provide air cover for the landing. Escort carriers had been built on hulls originally meant for tankers and freighters; they were slow, thin-skinned, lightly armed, and in this instance the ammunition for the thirty-odd aircraft per carrier was primarily for supporting ground troops rather than fighting a fleet action. At sunrise on the morning of the twenty-fifth, four escort carriers under Rear Admiral Clifton A. F. "Ziggy" Sprague were steaming off Samar. They had just launched combat air patrol for Amphibious Force in Leyte Gulf and were settling down to breakfast when their lookouts saw the unmistakable pagoda-like masts of Japanese ships on the horizon and heavy shells began to splash in the water around them. Kurita had arrived.

It would be difficult to say who was the more surprised, the Americans or the Japanese. Kurita had not expected to come upon carriers, and these he mistook for Halsey's; some of his officers thought they even saw cruisers and battleships (of which there were none) among the Americans. Ziggy Sprague reacted with marvelous calm and adroitness; he turned east, increased speed, began making smoke, launched all his aircraft, and sent off a message in the clear giving his and the Japanese positions and asking for all the help he could get.

He would need it. He had a screen of three destroyers and four destroyer escorts, and each of his "jeep" carriers mounted only 40-mm antiaircraft and a single five-inch gun. Coming down upon him were six heavy cruisers and four battleships (*Yamato* being one), with two destroyer squadrons flanking them. Of Sprague could be said what Robert E. Lee said of Chancellorsville, that he was too weak to defend and so he attacked (a favorite quote of George Patton's). "The most admirable thing about this battle," wrote Admiral Morison, "was the way everything we had afloat or airborne went baldheaded for the enemy."[109] The pure courage of it, and the impact this had on the Japanese, were beyond equal.

Sprague noted that Kurita's battleships and cruisers were closing on him with disconcerting rapidity and that the volume and precision of their fire were increasing; his chances of surviving the next five minutes did not look promising. At 7:06, he ordered the ships in his screen to attack the enemy with torpedoes, and at that very moment luck favored the jeep carriers with a rain squall which concealed them from Kurita for about a quarter hour. Sprague took advantage of this to change course to the southwest, opening the range between him and the Japanese, whose fire turned less heavy and less accurate. Kurita was becoming confused; he thought that he had already sunk a "cruiser." By this time he was under air and surface attack himself.

Sprague's destroyer screen consisted of *Hoel, Heermann,* and *Johnston,* the latter under the command of Ernest E. Evans, a Cherokee Indian like Jocko Clark: barrel-chested, leather-lunged, iron of resolve. As soon as Kurita was sighted, Evans had given orders to "prepare to attack major portion of Japanese fleet." As *Johnston* went forward on her mad and magnificent course, she opened fire on heavy cruiser *Kumano* with rapid salvos of two hundred rounds from her main battery, which scored numerous hits. *Johnston* closed to within ten thousand yards and launched ten torpedoes, all she had, and one of them hit *Kumano,* flagship of the Japanese cruisers, which dropped astern and out of the action. *Johnston* was not to get off lightly. At seven-thirty, she was struck by three fourteen-inch shells from a battleship and three six-inch from a cruiser. "It was like a puppy being smacked by a truck," said one of her officers. The heavy shells knocked out the after fire and engine rooms, cutting down speed and electric power. Commander Evans lost two fingers of his left hand and the clothing above his waist was blown off. But steering was shifted to manual and all gun stations were still operative. *Johnston* was not finished yet.

Hoel took on battleship *Kongo.* She opened fire at fourteen thousand yards, received a hit on her bridge, and at nine thousand yards launched four torpedoes at *Kongo,* which evaded them. *Hoel* received many more hits, losing the use of three guns and, temporarily, of rudder control. At about seven-fifty, she came back into the battle and got off the rest of her torpedoes at cruiser *Haguro.* Following close behind her, *Heermann* launched seven more torpedoes at *Haguro,* though whether any of these struck home is disputed. The confusion was considerable; sometimes as many as four Japanese ships would be firing on a single American destroyer. *Hoel* was punctured with over forty holes by heavy shells that plowed through her without exploding, and at eight-thirty she went dead in the water with number 1 magazine on fire. "Abandon ship" was ordered, the Japanese continued firing, and at eight fifty-five *Hoel* went down.

Sprague ordered a second attack by the destroyer escorts, and *Johnston,* torpedoes expended but still full of fight, joined with them. *Johnston* opened five-inch fire on *Kongo* and observed many rounds landing, but "it was like bouncing paper wads off a steel helmet," the same officer said.[110] Then *Johnston* sighted an entire squadron of Japanese destroyers approaching and went for them, firing at one after another and totally disorganizing a torpedo attack the Japanese were intending to make on the carriers. "Now I've seen everything," Commander Evans was heard to say. But the Japanese destroyers, their attack completed and (they wrongly thought) successful, concentrated on *Johnston*. This time it was too much. At nine-forty she was dead in the water; "Abandon ship" was ordered, and at ten-ten she sank. Of her crew of 327, only 141 survived, and Evans was not among them. As *Johnston* went down, the commander of a Japanese destroyer was seen standing on his bridge, saluting.

Since the American ships were so willing to engage, the Japanese assumed these must be equals or better, and identified the destroyer escorts as destroyers and the destroyers as cruisers. (*Johnston* they reported at one point to be a "heavy cruiser," a nice compliment; "all the ducks that day," as Admiral Morison wrote, "were swans to the enemy."[111]) We lost two destroyers and one destroyer escort and sank no Japanese, but the contribution of this supremely aggressive performance was substantial nonetheless. The evasive actions the Japanese were compelled to take created such disorder that Kurita momentarily lost tactical control and needed badly to regroup. During the same two hours, of course, he had also been experiencing an onslaught of similar ferocity by a bewildering variety of American aircraft.

The escort carriers—including the two other groups to the south and east, who heard Sprague's call for help—launched virtually every plane they had aboard. As many as possible were armed with torpedoes or, if not possible, with antipersonnel bombs or even depth charges; others carried no bombs at all and merely made machine-gun strafing runs on the enemy or, when their ammunition ran out, "dry" runs to distract Japanese attention. Torpedo hits were scored on *Chikuma* and *Chokai*, both of which subsequently sank. Further help was coming from McCain's fast carriers, which had been refueling on their way to Ulithi, but we were running out of any other resources for response when the incredible happened. Ziggy Sprague could not believe his eyes, or his ears when one of his signalmen shouted, "Goddammit, boys, they're getting away!" The Japanese were withdrawing; Kurita was pulling out of the fight and retiring north.

He left a sufficiency of destruction behind him. One of the escort carriers, *Gambier Bay*, had been riddled with heavy shells and sank. Another, *Kalinin Bay*, was hit but successfully fought off a cruiser with her single gun. Later in the morning, a third, *St. Lo*, was rammed into by one of the first *kamikaze* and blew up. But there is no question whatever that Kurita could have done far more. There was nothing left to prevent him from wiping out the escort carriers entirely and proceeding south to do the same, as he was supposed to, with the transports in Leyte Gulf. Not for the first time, but for the last, the Japanese had success within their grasp and let it slip away. Sprague in his after-action report attributed his survival to "our successful smoke screen, our torpedo counterattack, continuous harassment of enemy by bomb, torpedo and strafing air attacks, timely maneuvers, and the definite partiality of Almighty God."

Kurita was rattled but not irrational. No message had reached him from Ozawa to indicate that the decoy was succeeding and that Halsey had fallen for it. The boldness of the Americans persuaded him that there must be more to them than met the eye. The radio pleas for assistance in the clear that Kinkaid, too, was soon making convinced him that assistance was in fact on the way. The smoke and confusion, and the constant evasive actions of his own ships, prevented him from getting an accurate fix on the speed with which the escort carriers were running from him, which he thus wildly overestimated at thirty knots—that is, the speed of a fast carrier. (Top speed of an escort carrier was eighteen knots. "I knew you were scared, Ziggy," said another admiral when he later read of Kurita's estimate, "but I didn't know you were that scared!")[112] Kurita thought he was facing a massive force that included fast carriers; he thought he was facing Third Fleet, and if that was the case, then his chances of doing any harm to the transports in the gulf were minimal and his mission might sensibly be abandoned.

In Pearl Harbor, Admiral Nimitz had been puzzled by the absence of reports indicating the night fight he expected would take place when Kurita coming through the strait encountered Task Force 34, made up, as Nimitz believed, of Lee and the fast battleships, lying in wait. He was beginning to think Task Force 34 might not be where he thought it was, and when Kinkaid's report of being attacked by cruisers and battleships was received in Hawaii, Nimitz was even more concerned and authorized a query to Halsey. The practice then was to insert nonsense phrases in coded messages, to make decoding more difficult, and that was done, but one of them—"the world wonders"—failed to be nonsensical enough. October 25 was Balaklava Day, and this echo of Tennyson's "The Charge of the Light Brigade" may have been in the mind of the ensign who prepared Nimitz's question for coding.

At any rate, when the dispatch reached *New Jersey,* the ensign who prepared the decoded text thought the added phrase just possibly made sense, and left it in. What came to Halsey on the bridge was therefore the following: "From Cincpac Action Com Third Fleet info Cominch CTF Seventy-seven X Where is rpt where is Task Force Thirty-four RR The world wonders." Halsey was so furious at what seemed to him heavy sarcasm, with King and Kinkaid invited to be witnesses, that he slammed his cap on the deck and one of his officers had to tell him to pull himself together.[113] To the end of his days Halsey insisted that his mistake had been not in going north but in going back, for by the time he turned around it was too late to make any difference.

Jocko Clark was in Admiral King's office in Washington when the news came that San Bernardino Strait had been left unguarded, and Clark said he had never seen King so angry—which must have set some kind of record in anger. But King never criticized Halsey publicly, and when Halsey later admitted to King that he had made a mistake, King told him to say no more about it. (King also believed that Kinkaid should have sent out air searches of the strait on his own.) Nimitz was equally restrained; when his analytical section prepared a report critical of Halsey, he sent it back to be toned down. Perhaps they both realized that the orders Halsey had been given were in part responsible and that Halsey, if piqued, might assert as much. Nimitz's son thought that the "primary task" wording had given Halsey *carte blanche* to abandon the beachhead, and said to his father, that night at dinner in Pearl Harbor, "It's your fault." The table went quiet. The elder Nimitz gave his son a bleak look and said, "That's your opinion."[114]

And anyhow, Leyte Gulf was a great victory. The evening of the twenty-fifth, Halsey radioed Nimitz: "The Japanese Navy has been beaten and routed and broken by the Third and Seventh Fleets," and next day President Roosevelt jubilantly summoned reporters to his office to tell them of this. It was true. Ozawa's carriers, their purpose served, had not escaped. Before turning back, Mitscher's pilots had done for all four; only the converted carrier-battleships got away. This brought the total of Japanese losses to three battleships, one large carrier, three light carriers, six heavy cruisers, four light cruisers, and nine destroyers. (The Americans lost one light carrier, two escort carriers, two destroyers, and one destroyer escort.) The Japanese still had carriers—and, amazingly, were building more—but with rare exceptions these hereafter stayed in port, and in March 1945 they were deactivated. The B-29s were hitting the fighter plants, and such planes and pilots as could be scraped together were assigned to the defense of the homeland, as *kamikaze*. "The Imperial Japanese Navy," writes Clark Reynolds, "was dead as a fighting fleet."[115] Nimitz had won his war; he could come home now.

Halsey sounded off long and loud about his role in the battle—in dispatches afterward, in his autobiography in 1947, and in a *U.S. Naval Institute Proceedings* article in 1952—but Kinkaid for many years kept silent. Only when Hanson Baldwin wrote an account of Leyte Gulf, and sent copies to Kinkaid and Halsey for comment, did Kinkaid speak up. His reply (printed as an appendix to Baldwin's *Battles Lost and Won* in 1966) is clear and pensive. Halsey had done exactly what the Japanese wanted him to do, said Kinkaid, and as a result Lee's fast battleships played no part in the last decisive engagement where they might have done so. If Kinkaid had erred in trusting Halsey too much, then many others (Mitscher included) had erred with him. "Divided command" was not the fault, but rather Halsey's ignoring of his mission to cover the landing. And, finally, the headlong onslaught of Sprague's destroyers and destroyer escorts "was the most courageous and also most effective incident brought to my attention during the war."[116] History will I think stand with Kinkaid.

Nimitz did not, of course, stay in Pearl Harbor "til the war was won." He came back to Washington for a meeting of the Joint Chiefs in March

1944 and went to lunch at the White House on the eleventh with Leahy and King. The President was not well; his face was pale and his hands trembled, but he brightened at their plans and command arrangements and approved them. He began making conversation and asking random questions, including those to which they thought he must know the answers, such as why Nimitz after the powerful raid on Truk had gone on to raid the Marianas. Nimitz tried to lighten the occasion by telling the story of the hypochondriac, after an appendectomy, who complained of a sore throat. His doctor explained that his colleagues had so applauded the operation that he had removed the patient's tonsils as an encore. "So you see, Mr. President," said Nimitz, "that was the way it was. We just hit Tinian and Saipan for an encore." Roosevelt threw back his head and laughed, and the visit ended.

A year later, the President had Fleet Admiral Nimitz and Secretary Forrestal to lunch and spent an hour and twenty minutes discussing the imminent Japanese defeat. Nimitz thought that Roosevelt's health had deteriorated further; his jaw was slack and he slurred his words. That was the last time they met.[117] Five weeks afterward, the President was dead and Nimitz was writing his wife to express his deep sense of personal loss.

VIII

EISENHOWER

DWIGHT DAVID EISENHOWER GRAVITATED UPWARD as naturally as a sunflower seeks the sun. Partly it was a matter of personality, of an open and transparent fairness that immediately impressed itself upon the observer, and of a disarming grin that alone—said his colleague Lieutenant General Sir Frederick Morgan—was "worth an army corps in any campaign."[1] Partly it was a matter of prior preparation, of study and self-discipline over many a superficially empty year. But mostly it was a quality that Eisenhower himself went to some lengths to conceal from the public: intelligence, an intelligence as icy as has ever risen to the higher reaches of American life.

Eisenhower moved into the upper levels of national policy-making as though he had always belonged there. Within weeks of his arrival in Washington in December 1941, as deputy chief of the War Plans Division for the Pacific and Far East, he was drafting messages and memoranda not only for Marshall and Secretary Stimson but for the President himself. He wrote Roosevelt's reply to Quezon when the Philippine president blamed the Americans for providing the islands with inadequate defenses, and he wrote Roosevelt's reply to MacArthur when MacArthur forwarded with a favorable endorsement Quezon's proposal that the Philippines be neutralized. He wrote, and personally took to the President, the latter's cable to Chiang Kai-shek about command arrangements in Burma, and he wrote Roosevelt's cable to Churchill on the same subject.[2]

On June 21, during Churchill's second visit to Washington, Harry Hopkins said to him, "There are a couple of American officers the President would like you to meet," and that afternoon at five, Eisenhower and Mark Clark were brought to Churchill's quarters in the White House. "I was immediately impressed," he wrote, "by these remarkable but hitherto unknown men. . . . We talked almost entirely about the major cross-Chan-

412

nel invasion . . . on which their thoughts had evidently been concentrated.
. . . I felt sure that these officers were intended to play a great part in it,
and that was the reason why they had been sent to make my acquaintance.
Thus began a friendship which across all the ups and downs of war I have
preserved with deep satisfaction to this day."[3]

On the day of Pearl Harbor, Brigadier General Eisenhower had been
at Fort Sam Houston, Texas, where he was chief of staff of Third Army
under Walter Krueger. The next week was filled with the feverish extemporization of means to move troops and guns to the West Coast as rapidly
as possible. On the morning of the twelfth, a direct-line phone to the War
Department rang and the voice of Colonel Walter Bedell Smith asked, "Is
that you, Ike?" It was. Thus Smith: "The Chief says for you to hop a plane
and get up here right away. Tell your boss that formal orders will come
through later."

Eisenhower's heart sank. During World War I his every effort to get
into action had failed; he had since put in eight years' duty in Washington,
and he wanted to stay away from it, to stay with troops. He reported to
Marshall on Sunday morning, the fourteenth, to be given one of Marshall's
masterly twenty-minute summations, in this case of the military situation
in the western Pacific, followed by the abrupt question: "What should be
our general line of action?" Hoping that he was showing a poker face,
Eisenhower asked for a few hours' time. "All right," said Marshall.

This was the fourth time the two had met, and the first occasion on
which they had exchanged more than a few dozen words. But Eisenhower
had heard enough about Marshall to know that his answer had better be
short, emphatic, and to the point. He typed out notes for himself, triple
space, on a yellow sheet of paper, which began, "Build up in Australia a
base of operations . . . ," the first official proposal that this be a priority.
He returned to Marshall and said that in his opinion it would be a long time
before reinforcements could reach the Philippines, but that everything
humanly possible should be done to get them through, to establish the
Australian base and secure communications to it. The peoples of Asia will
be watching us. "They may excuse failure but they will not excuse abandonment. . . . We must take great risks," he ended, "and spend any amount
of money required."

"I agree with you," said Marshall. "Do your best to save them."[4]
Eisenhower was now in charge of the program he had just proposed. He
had passed the test, by arriving at a conclusion Marshall had already
reached. Now all he had to do was make good on it, which apparently he
did to Marshall's satisfaction, for on February 16, Marshall made Eisenhower chief of the Plans (later renamed Operations) Division and a month
later, promoted him.

An episode preceded this last that delightfully embroiders Marshall's
methods and the relationship, formal yet strong, that was building be-

tween these men. One day the subject of an officer's promotion came up and Marshall took the opportunity to expound his theory that promotions should go only to field commanders and not to staff officers who clutter up the headquarters. "Take your case," said Marshall. He knew that Eisenhower's superiors had recommended him for divisional or even corps command. "That's all very well. I'm glad they have that opinion of you, but you are going to stay here and fill your position, and that's that."

Eisenhower got a little angry. "General," he said, "I'm interested in what you say, but I want you to know that I don't give a damn about your promotion plans as far as I'm concerned. I came into this office from the field and I'm trying to do my duty. I expect to do so as long as you want me here. If that locks me to a desk for the rest of the war, so be it!" He got up and started to leave the room, but at the door he stopped and turned, a bit ashamed of himself for this outburst, and saw pass across the face of George C. Marshall the shadow of a smile. Three days later, there arrived on his desk a copy of Marshall's recommendation to the President that he be made a major general.[5]

The man who had told Eisenhower about George Marshall was a major general named Fox Conner, a hard-bitten Mississippian with whom Eisenhower served in Panama in the early 1920s. Conner had been Pershing's operations officer in France and spoke to Eisenhower often about Marshall's "genius," his fine judgment and integrity. Even after Eisenhower retired from the presidency in 1961, he said that Conner was the ablest man he had ever known, which covers a lot of territory. Conner was Eisenhower's graduate school, his first true military education. As a boy, Eisenhower had been an omnivorous reader, but at West Point in his day military history was taught by rote, as a memory course, with no attempt to explain why battles happened or what their commanders were trying to do, and he had acquired an aversion to it.

Conner started him off on historical novels and then asked him if he wouldn't like to know what the armies were up to during the same stretch of time. Before long, Eisenhower was borrowing one history book after another from Conner's well-stocked library, and after he finished each, Conner would quiz him about it: Why had such and such a decision been made? What would have happened if it had been made otherwise? Eisenhower read Clausewitz's *On War* three times. Conner gave him the courage to apply to Command and General Staff School at Leavenworth and the background that enabled him to graduate there first in his class. Eisenhower said later that it took him years to appreciate the value of what Conner had led him through.[6]

Conner also drummed into Eisenhower a set of convictions about the future: (1) the Treaty of Versailles made another war with Germany inevitable and it would come within thirty years; (2) it would be a coalition war and America would enter it; and (3) it would be won by the Western allies under a unified command. Eisenhower governed himself accordingly, so much so that some of his fellow officers called him "Alarmist Ike." During one of Eisenhower's early tours of duty in Washington, a friend noticed in his apartment a number of books about Luxembourg, Belgium, and the Low Countries, and asked why they were there. Because, said Eisenhower, that was where the next war was going to be fought and he intended to know more about it than anyone else. Conner must also have warned him that coalitions can be frustrating, for he noted on his desk pad in February 1942: "Conner was right about allies. He could well have included the Navy!"[7]

Eisenhower was always interested professionally (much more so than Marshall) in the technical side of warfare, especially tanks. In the early 1930s, he worked for the office of the assistant secretary of war on problems of industrial mobilization, involving such recondite subjects as synthetic rubber, and after consultation with Bernard Baruch, he drafted the War Department's mobilization plan. He was one of the first in the General Staff to sense the importance of landing craft, and his papers during the months he headed the Ops Division are filled with indications of his strong feeling that not enough was being done to produce them. He was concerned about antitank weapons and he foresaw the need for army divisions to be equipped with a small "puddle-jumper" type of aircraft. Tanks he came to be familiar with when as a major he commanded a tank battalion in World War I (though it never got overseas), and in 1919 at Camp Meade, Maryland, he and a colonel named George S. Patton entirely disassembled a tank, including the engine, and put it back together again. (P.S. There were no parts left over and it was still in running order when they finished.)[8]

The association with Patton is noteworthy: "you are about my oldest friend," Patton wrote Eisenhower in early 1942, after a visit to Washington. At Camp Meade, the two of them had been the center of a group of young officers, tank enthusiasts, who were trying to rewrite the doctrine for employing armor and to redesign the tanks that would execute it. The well-to-do Patton had his own stable of horses, and Eisenhower shared his devotion to riding and shooting, though a knee injury acquired playing football at West Point prevented him from indulging in Patton's other passion, which was polo. "From the beginning he and I got along famously," wrote Eisenhower. They had come to the conclusion that current infantry-oriented theory, and tanks that could go only three miles an hour, were all wrong. "We believed that they should be speedy," Eisenhower wrote, "and that they should attack by surprise and in mass . . . [to] make possible not only an advance by infantry, but envelopments of, or actual breakthroughs in, whole defensive positions"—fairly unorthodox stuff for 1920—and these heretics had found a tank designer who thought as they did.[9]

J. Walter Christie is an unsung hero of American military technology. He was a builder and driver of fast motorcars, ranking with Barney Old-field; he designed the standard turret track for battleships and the first four-wheel-drive mobile gun mounts. He has justly been called the father of the modern tank, for he was the first to realize that an ability to cover rough ground rapidly was a desirable characteristic. This is a function of compression amplitude, or the degree to which the wheels within the tank tracks can move up and down. World War I tanks had a compression amplitude of two to three inches at the most; a Christie tank had one of *twenty-four* inches, could do sixty miles an hour on tracks (faster with the tracks removed), and could climb a two-and-a-half-foot wall and jump a seven-foot trench.

Christie like many military pioneers believed that his inventions "would make war too costly for civilization to withstand," but Eisenhower and Patton recognized what Christie had to offer them, and they were delighted when the Ordnance Department in June 1920 signed a contract with him for a prototype chassis. Eisenhower wrote that Christie "was designing a model we thought had many advantages over those of the war vintage." Patton said he understood that "in the Christie [tank] we are buying a principle not a vehicle." Patton went on supporting and working actively with Christie over the next ten years, and may even have provided him with funds—which Christie badly needed.[10]

For this man's way was not an easy one. Engineers respected his ideas but not his personality; he thought he could do everything better than they could, which was not always so. Ordnance purchased a total of seven tanks from him but then refused to declare the model standard or to pay him further. (It was a time of wait and see on American arms development.) Christie began investing his own money in his product, including an airborne variant, and in 1928 he sold two Christie tanks to the Soviet Union, where they became known as the "Christie-Russki" and were copied by the thousands. Over the years, the Russians beefed up the "Christie-Russki" in the heaviness of the gun and the thickness of the armor, until eventually it became the T-34, by common consent the best tank of World War II, bearing a recognizable configuration clearly derived from Christie's original.[11]

It was with the T-34 that the Russians fought the Battle of Kursk in July 1943, greatest tank battle of all time—*Todesritt,* the Germans called it, the death ride of the panzers, the defeat from which they could not recover. Russian T-34s in the hundreds charged at full speed across the open country of the upper Donets valley—"streaming like rats across the battlefield," said one German Tiger tank commander—and on August 5, Moscow celebrated its first "victory salute" of a hundred and fifty guns. "The Tigers are burning," reads a Russian dispatch.[12] The Germans in Russia never again took the offensive; the vision of the young Eisenhower at Camp Meade two decades before—surprise, mobility, mass—had been realized. Christie lived to survive, though unhappily not to savor, this victory; he died—destitute, facing eviction, and suing the government—on January 11, 1944.[13]

That Eisenhower knew Patton so well, and inhabited a common universe of tactical discourse with him, was one of the more fortunate circumstances of the war. Eisenhower, as a stranger might not have been able to, could see Patton's strength and understand his weakness, preserving him from the consequences of his loudmouth indiscretions for the performance of tasks that no one else could carry out so well as he. We are the better off for that, by many lives and many victories Patton spared others the burden of winning (the present author was a minute quantity among that multitude), and we have Eisenhower to thank. Behind Patton's blood-and-guts personality was an absolute professional, one of the most competent army commanders our side put into the field; the Germans were painstaking in their analysis of the leaders who faced them in battle, and Patton was the only Anglo-American who seriously troubled them. They could never predict what he was going to do next. Yet it was not in him to accept Eisenhower's magnanimity with good grace; Patton's diaries and letters to his wife reveal his discomfort in references to Eisenhower as "Divine Destiny" and in reflections on how much better the war would be fought if he and not Eisenhower were supreme commander.[14]

Something similar happened to Eisenhower's relationship with MacArthur, with whom he served in both Washington and Manila during the 1930s. For a time they had worked closely and harmoniously together, and as a writer Eisenhower may even have been at least a co-inventor of the florid MacArthurian prose style. "You know that General MacArthur got quite a reputation as a silver-tongued speaker when he was in the Philippines," Eisenhower wrote to a friend. "Who do you think wrote his speeches? I did." MacArthur was Eisenhower's first exposure to a senior officer who chose not to draw a clear-cut distinction between the military and the political in Washington's commingling of the two, who had a wide acquaintance with people in every branch of government. "Working with him brought an additional dimension to my experience," said Eisenhower.[15]

MacArthur was aware that Eisenhower had been directing the War Department efforts to reinforce him but ignored this, and his reaction to Eisenhower's progress toward eminence in Europe was a mixture of envy and something close to paranoia. MacArthur told his British liaison officer, Gerald Wilkinson, that Eisenhower had not been "wholly loyal" and that for this reason MacArthur had not kept him on in the Philippines when his term was up. (Eisenhower says the opposite: that he requested to be let go and that MacArthur tried to persuade him to stay on; given the choice, belief inclines toward Eisenhower.)[16] MacArthur told Wilkinson that he thought Eisenhower, "spotting White House jealousy of himself (MacA) has enhanced his own position by feeding the White House with anti-MacA data"—a delusion on MacArthur's part, to say the least.

MacArthur described Eisenhower to Wilkinson as "the ablest officer he has ever known at absorbing 30 minutes detailed description of an idea (or plan or strategic conception?) and getting the whole thing out on paper —orders, arrangements etc etc—in *10* minutes." According to Wilkinson's journal, MacArthur said that Eisenhower was "ambitious, clever, hardworking (an excellent bridge player) . . . a brilliant executive of someone else's original thought but *not*—as far as MacA knows—in any way an original mind—and *no fighting experience.* . . . MacA thinks (and possibly almost hopes) that commanding real fighting British officers will shew up E's ~~defeets~~ [*sic*] true proportions."[17]

Eisenhower in turn had no illusions about MacArthur but acknowledged the power of the man's personality and his capacity for leadership. When Eisenhower took command in the European theater, an off-the-record dinner was arranged for him in London to meet a group of American correspondents, who quizzed him about MacArthur. Eisenhower described the now-familiar characteristics—the ego, the love of the limelight, the self-dramatization, the unstable temperament—and then added: "Yet, if that door opened at this moment, and General MacArthur was standing there, and he said 'Ike, follow me,' I'd get up and follow him."[18]

Of Eisenhower's respect for Marshall there can be no doubt; he told Beetle Smith that he wouldn't trade Marshall for fifty MacArthurs. ("My God," the thought came to him, "that would be a lousy deal. What would I do with fifty MacArthurs?") Eisenhower wrote to a friend that Marshall was "a great soldier . . . quick, tough, tireless and a real leader. He accepts responsibility automatically and never goes back on a subordinate." Eisenhower said that he had conceived "unlimited admiration" for Marshall because of the burden Marshall bore without complaint, being at the same time "rather a remote and austere person." Eisenhower had been known in the Army as "Ike" since the day he entered West Point, but Marshall (except on one occasion) always called him "Eisenhower." The one exceptional lapse into "Ike" so embarrassed Marshall that Eisenhower said he used "Eisenhower" five times in the next sentence to make up for it.[19]

The American military have a wise custom allowing officers in a high command relationship to exchange not only formal reports but personal letters in which they unburden their thoughts to one another (as before the war Admiral Stark did to Admiral Kimmel). It is an admirable if not always foolproof device for avoiding misunderstandings. The letters of Eisenhower to Marshall (published separately from the Eisenhower papers under the title *Dear General*) are of singular interest in the picture they provide of the way these two men interacted, with Eisenhower exposing his judgments on men and events so that Marshall, if so he wished, could offer corrections or suggestions. There seem to have been few of either.

Marshall had a very large respect for Eisenhower's mind; he wanted it kept in trim, for he well knew that a sharp mental edge can be a wasting asset. When he visited Algiers in January 1943, Marshall had a long post-breakfast chat with Eisenhower's naval aide, Commander Harry C. Butcher, in which he virtually "ordered" Butcher to make Eisenhower relax, get him outdoors as much as possible, get him home early, get him to take regular exercise. Marshall did not like working with people whose ideas went no further than his own; he had enjoyed Eisenhower's alive and inventive approach but wanted it preserved for future challenges to come. "You must keep him refreshed," Marshall told Butcher. "It is your job in the war to make him take care of his health and keep that alert brain from overworking, particularly on things his staff can do for him." Eisenhower might think he had encountered troubles thus far, Marshall said, but he would have so many more before the war was over that those up to now would be nothing.[20]

As he had done before becoming deputy chief of the plans division, Eisenhower designed the next job he would hold. He wrote for Marshall the basic strategy of a European war and in May 1942 Marshall sent him to London, ostensibly to study command arrangements for an invasion but actually to let the British have a look at him (Eisenhower met Brooke, Montgomery, and Mountbatten, among others[21]).

On his return, Eisenhower revised a directive he had written outlining the role of Commanding General, ETOUSA (European Theater of Operations, U.S. Army) and showed it to Marshall, asking him to read it carefully because it was likely to be an important document in the subsequent course of the war. "I certainly do want to read it," said Marshall. "You may be the man who executes it. If that's the case, when can you leave?" Eisenhower professed his astonishment in a desk-pad note;[22] on June 24, he arrived in London to take charge.

This was a most unusual man, a veiled man, so seemingly forthright, so ready to volunteer his thoughts, yet in the end so secretive, so protective of his purposes and the hidden processes of an iron logic behind them. A reviewer of his published diaries commented on his "closed, calculating quality" and went on: "Few who watched him carefully indulged the fantasy that he was a genial, open, barefoot boy from Abilene who just happened to be in the right place when lightning struck."[23] Another perceptive comment was made by the war correspondent Don White-head, who covered the European theater and the invasion for the Associated Press. "I have the feeling," Whitehead wrote years later, "that he was a far more complicated man than he seemed to be—a man who shaped events with such subtlety that he left others thinking they were the architects of those events. And he was satisfied to leave it that way."[24]

Eisenhower conveyed warmth but there was a chill inside him. An early sorrow, the death of his first son, had seared his emotional nerve endings. "This was the greatest disappointment and disaster of my life," he wrote, "the one I have never been able to forget completely. Today when I think of it, even now as I write of it, the keenness of our loss comes back to me as fresh and terrible as it was that long dark day." He came to question whether passionate attachment to another person was a luxury that could be afforded. In 1947, he was told of the crack-up over personal loss of a wartime associate and wrote in his diary: "makes one wonder whether any human ever dares become so wrapped up in another that all happiness and desire to live is determined by the actions, desires—or life —of the second." The associate in question was Kay Summersby, his driver and secretary, to whom he himself appears for a time to have been attached, and his words bear the mark of a steely will.[25]

Not the least of the paradoxes is that Eisenhower wrote such lucid and at times almost elegant prose. (The impression he later gave as President, of waffling vagueness and wandering syntax, was contrived for presidential purposes; Roosevelt himself was no less guilty of similar obfuscations when required.) During the 1920s in France, Eisenhower wrote the guidebook of the American Battle Monuments Commission and among the many speeches he wrote for MacArthur was a much-admired one called "Farewell to the Army," which MacArthur delivered when he resigned as Chief of Staff. Eisenhower dictated *Crusade in Europe* in seven weeks. For years, he kept Fowler's *Modern English Usage* at close hand, and he was said to have fired an aide who couldn't master the difference between "shall" and "will." He told John Gunther that he thought very few officers knew "how to use the English language." After V-E Day, when he was made a citizen of London, he gave a speech at the Guildhall that Gunther accurately describes as "pithy, vivid, not a word wasted, no false oratory, and moving in the extreme."[26]

The Guildhall speech is the capstone of Eisenhower's conduct of the war and the keystone, to preserve the metaphor, of his postwar career as Allied leader and as President. It was an impressive achievement; even Brooke was awed ("I had never realized that Ike was as big a man," he wrote in his diary, "until I heard his performance today"[27]). As far as can be proved, Eisenhower did write it himself (he told Gunther that he had worked on it for three weeks; no one else has published a claim of authorship).

In it he said that he could receive the honor of London's citizenship only as representative of all the Allied men and women who had served with him, and that no commander could contemplate with anything but humility and profound sorrow the blood that had been shed and the sacrifices that had been made. He wove together the theme of his rural American origins with the historic grandeur of London, with the admiration Americans felt for British endurance, with the readiness of free men to defend their freedom, with the success of the Allied partnership, and with the hope that it would continue on into a world where wars would not be necessary. This was a political speech in the best sense of the word, drawing people together and, as though accidentally, offering himself as symbol of their unity.[28]

Eisenhower disliked excessively rhetorical flourishes because they betrayed a desire to be ingratiating, or overly persuasive, or too eager for promotion. Fox Conner had drilled him in the army mystique of never seeking or refusing an assignment, and Eisenhower always managed matters so that the assignments sought him. His gift for being offered jobs he had not asked for would appear almost magical if one did not keep in mind "that alert brain" at work. One of the most tedious and revealing sections of his "diaries" deals with the self-examination he went through to persuade himself to run for President in 1952. Couldn't the man *see?* the reader keeps asking himself. No, he could not. It was not in his nature to appear to want something; his nature was to be *wanted*. And so he progressed from obscurity—he first appears in the White House Usher's Diary at two-thirty on February 9, 1942, as "P. D. Eisenhauer"—to greatness. His rise was rocketlike. Within less than two years he went from lieutenant colonel to full general.

His exposure to politics in the raw came as rapidly as his promotions. When he was appointed to command the North African expedition, Eisenhower was briefed by Robert Murphy, our diplomatic representative there, on the "bewildering complexities" of the quarrels among not only French factions but Spanish, Arab, Berber, German, and Russian as well. "Eisenhower listened with a kind of horrified fascination," wrote Murphy, "to my description of the possible complications. . . . The General seemed to sense that this first campaign would present him with problems running the entire geopolitical gamut—it certainly did."[29] What he could not have realized was that it would also place him in the crossfire between two towering political personalities, Franklin Roosevelt and Charles de Gaulle.

Say this, too, for Eisenhower: He was able to confront himself, in words and on paper, with the harsh unpleasantness of the work that lay ahead. "The actual fact is," he wrote in a note to his desk pad on May 5, 1942, "that not 1 man in 20 in Govt. (including the W. and N. Depts) realizes what a grisly, dirty, tough business we are in!"[30]

◆

Roosevelt knew France and considered himself well conversant with it. From the age of seven to fifteen he annually traveled several months in England, France, and Germany with his parents. On his first visit, in

1889–90, he played in the parks and gardens of Versailles and the Tuileries, walked the Champs Élysées and the Bois de Boulogne, and climbed to the top of the Eiffel Tower with his father. "Furthermore," as de Gaulle shrewdly observed, "he felt a genuine affection for France, *or at least for the notion of it he had once been able to conceive*" (emphasis added). Roosevelt from age five to eleven had been tutored by European governesses and he spoke French (as opposed to the fractured Harrovian Franglais Churchill invented for himself) well enough to be proud of it. "He is affronted and insulted," reads a memo to Herbert Bayard Swope signed with Grace Tully's initials, "by your suggestion that his French is 'as good' as that of Winston . . . the President's accent is not only infinitely superior but his French profanity is so explosive that you had better not be within a half mile of him when it goes off."[31]

De Gaulle thought it was Roosevelt's very attraction to France that caused him to be "at heart disappointed and irritated by yesterday's disaster among us [the defeat in 1940] and by the mediocre reactions the latter had aroused among so many Frenchmen, particularly those he knew personally." The France Roosevelt observed was the prewar Third Republic, which provided the world such an unedifying picture of hooded Fascists, decadent aristocrats, sullen proletarians, and left-wing intellectual politicians tearing one another to bits in the aftermath of historic arguments that had never been resolved but only postponed. Roosevelt described to de Gaulle with bitterness what his feelings had been "when before the war he watched the spectacle of our political impotence unfold before his eyes." It was not to be wondered that the President's expectations for postwar France were set so low, that he thought it would take ten or twenty years to reestablish France as an important power, and that in the meantime he felt himself to be in some measure a custodian of her fate. "It seemed to me," wrote Anthony Eden, "that Roosevelt wanted to hold the strings of France's future in his own hands."[32]

In this the President reckoned without Charles de Gaulle, who knew the flaws in the French character as well as or better than Roosevelt did but knew also that the way to redeem it was to ennoble it. De Gaulle intended to purify France in the process of saving her. He instinctively appreciated that to distract his countrymen's attention from each other one must keep their eyes on the flag—"France cannot be France without greatness"—and hold before them an embodiment of national aspiration and unity even if that had to be, *faute de mieux*, oneself. He must yield nothing, nowhere and to no one, in this endeavor; obstinacy must become his armor. And so he undertook what he called the "perpetual bondage" of symbolizing "the image of a France indomitable in the midst of her trials."

De Gaulle by sheer determination and force of character (and British help) established the existence of a "Free" France apart from and opposed to the defeated and past-enshrouded government in Vichy, and he did it over Roosevelt's prolonged and strenuous obstructions and objections. Gaullism as a faith made the President uncomfortable because it challenged faith in himself and his convictions, but it was nonetheless very wrong of him to put down and disparage as mere ego what he of all people should have recognized as self-identification with destiny, at a level so high that the word "ego" becomes meaningless (perhaps that is why it made him so angry); and he continued to make this mistake even after—on de Gaulle's visit to Washington in July 1944—Roosevelt began to treat de Gaulle as someone to be taken seriously. De Gaulle was a far better and more fair-minded judge of Roosevelt than Roosevelt was of him, and it is depressing to have to record that the President seemed never to assimilate this.[33]

The President, Secretary Hull, and Admiral Leahy as our ambassador there were all more comfortable with Vichy France than they had any call to be. The State Department's striped-pants affinities, and the President's preference for the company of well-bred foreigners, combined to disastrous effect. Leahy had moments of admiring Pétain. In his first report, he spoke of the marshal's "vigor and strength of character," and of his "personal appreciation of the friendly attitude of America." Leahy thought that by discouraging de Gaulle we would stiffen Pétain's resolve to take a stronger stand against the Germans, an absurd hope. (State Department officials like Roy Atherton, acting chief of the Division of European Affairs, strongly subscribed to this same anti-Gaullist argument.)

Roosevelt sent Pétain a letter of "sympathy and understanding" for his "steadfast courage and determination" in fighting for a "free and independent France," an absurd characterization of Pétain's conduct in office. The President seemed almost to feel that France and Pétain deserved one another, and that the marshal was thus a logical figure on whom to base American policy. Roosevelt was convinced that once the Germans withdrew, France would undergo a revolution in which its myriad political factions, unable to arrive at stability, would end up with a "federal form of government" on the American model, an absurd vision of a France not renewed but merely put on hold in the President's imagination.[34]

Roosevelt clothed his policy toward the Vichy regime in a mantle of high principle. He said that he had a sacred duty to the French people not to impose a government on them against their will. He would not recognize "any one person or group as the Government of France," as he told Robert Murphy, "until a liberated French population could freely choose their own government." Though these feelings were no doubt genuine, they happily accorded with his less elevated motives—his plain dislike of de Gaulle, his mistaken belief that in a free election de Gaulle would lose —and the line he followed in practice was one of outright expediency:

hoping that Pétain and his colleagues could be kept from coming totally under German domination, hoping to detach or at least immobilize the French fleet at Toulon, hoping that Vichy-appointed officials in North Africa would welcome an American invasion.

Of this last point the President was particularly persuaded. His government, wrote Harold Macmillan (who was sent to Algiers in December by Churchill with the rank of minister, to advise Eisenhower), "suffered under the delusion, to some extent shared by the American people, that they were especially popular in France." Roosevelt on invasion's eve thought he could convince Pétain that his sending of troops to North Africa had no other purpose in view than "to support and aid the French and their administration." He had confidently written Churchill in September that an "American expedition led . . . by American officers will meet little resistance from the French army in Africa. . . . I have several experienced civilians who would be persona grata to accompany the landings and be charged with getting French civil co-operation."[35] There was unseemly condescension here.

Eisenhower's policy was one of expediency pure and unalloyed. An element of bluff still attended the Allied enterprise and he was charged with sustaining it. He simply did not have enough troops to maintain a military occupation of Morocco and Algeria while at the same time fighting the Germans in Tunisia, his most immediate task. That being so, the French would have to govern for him; he had neither any choice in the matter nor any way of explaining this without giving the game away.

The result was the so-called Darlan-Clark Agreement—literally wrung out of Admiral Darlan by General Mark Clark and later signed in its full form on November 23—which established the right of the Allied forces to be in North Africa at the price of retaining the existing (Vichyite) administration. Once made known, it produced howls of outrage from the press and politicians in both Britain and the United States. It was denounced as "a sordid nullification of the principles for which the United Nations were supposed to be fighting." De Gaulle expressed his contempt by asserting that elimination of the "guilty men" who had taken their orders from Vichy was an essential precondition for Gaullist cooperation with any French North African authority.[36]

There was no little virtue in the negative reaction. Among the French of North Africa, the *colons*, were many if anything more admiring of the Germans and antipathetic to the Allies than the Vichy government they professed to serve. The large landowners of Morocco were so sunk in greed, so contemptuous of democracy, so pro-Fascist and anti-Semitic— thus spoke A. J. Liebling of them—that they "had not really collaborated with the Nazis; the Nazis had come along belatedly and collaborated with them."[37] Since the armistice in 1940, they had happily exported to Germany their grain, their fruit, and the alcohol made from their brandy, which the Germans had paid for in paper francs of dubious value. Then we came along, pegged their currency, and made *real* millionaires out of them—and still they hated us. There were many unpleasant incidents of Vichy-appointed officials, with our apparent blessing, continuing to persecute and imprison Jews and the pro-Allied French who had expected us to come as benefactors. It took some time to undo all this, though undone it eventually was.

In the process, the general educated the President as often as the latter the former. Eisenhower was aided by events that mercifully cleared the air. Vichy did not bend before our windy puffs of goodwill. The day after the Allied landings, the Germans, with Vichy's consent, began to send troops to Tunisia. In violation of the Armistice, and throwing all pretense aside, they moved their army into that part of France they were not occupying already. Pétain repudiated Darlan's cease-fire, and Darlan's order that the fleet leave Toulon to join the Allies was ignored.

When the Germans tried to seize the ships, however, in a glorious if tardy gesture, the French Navy—one battleship, two battle cruisers, seven cruisers, twenty-nine destroyers and torpedo boats, and sixteen submarines—scuttled itself in port. (Few who were present will forget the performance that evening of the Boston Symphony, which opened its concert not with "The Star-Spangled Banner" but with the *Marseillaise;* there was scarcely a dry eye in the house.) Then on Christmas Eve, irrelevantly but providentially, Darlan was assassinated by a young anti-Nazi royalist.

Eisenhower had started the exercise that led to his ascendancy over misguided superiors by establishing his credentials. When the furor over the "Darlan Deal" broke around his head, he had written a cable to the Combined Chiefs (dated November 14) asserting his competence to judge local conditions and to take action on the basis of them. He began by stating bluntly that what he had been told to expect was not borne out by what he had found: "The actual state of existing sentiment here does not repeat not agree even remotely with some of prior calculations." The idea that French affection for Americans would overpower their sense of loyalty to their legally constituted government—or cause them to take orders from the figurehead we offered them, General Henri Giraud—was self-deceptive.

The French stopped fighting because Darlan, as their legitimate leader, had told them to; they would obey no one else. An early conquest of Tunisia would be impossible without his aid. No one who was not there on the ground could have any clear appreciation of what Eisenhower called "the complex currents of feeling and of prejudice that influence the situation." If the two governments were dissatisfied with the measures he had taken, then they should send British, American, and even Gaullist representatives to Algiers, "where, in ten minutes, they can be convinced of the soundness of the moves we have made."[38]

On receiving Eisenhower's communication, the Combined Chiefs sent it to the President at Hyde Park. Sherwood has recounted how Roosevelt then declaimed it aloud to him and to Hopkins, giving it the full treatment, almost as if it were one of his speeches; "he sounded as though he were making an eloquent plea for Eisenhower before the bar of history," wrote Sherwood. Well might the President be impressed. Here was an extraordinary thing: a general who could think politically, with cool realism, and then act with an amorality worthy of the Old Master himself. He was discovering a man who would one day reveal gifts for handling "complex currents of feeling and of prejudice" to rival his own.

Two days later, at a press conference, the President read a public statement backing Eisenhower's "temporary arrangement" and privately he sent the general a message of support, adding that Darlan was not to be trusted or kept in civil power "any longer than is absolutely necessary." To his press conference Roosevelt quoted what he said was an "old Bulgarian proverb of the Orthodox Church: 'My children, you are permitted in time of great danger to walk with the Devil until you have crossed the bridge.' "[39]

Darlan's death spared Eisenhower the eventual task of discarding him, but it raised the embarrassing question of who would be his replacement. Giraud filled the bill briefly but ineffectually; he had by now shown himself clearly to be no long-term answer. By the time of the Casablanca Conference, in January 1943, Eisenhower was being advised politically by Murphy and Macmillan, whom he trusted, and they had formed common cause. They were agreed that there must be a merger of Giraud's North African administration and de Gaulle's French Committee for National Liberation in London, under Giraud's and de Gaulle's joint leadership.

Macmillan liked Murphy and sympathized with the vulnerable position in which he had placed himself, having had to make contact with Frenchmen both reputable and disreputable, and to incur obligations that had become difficult to fulfill. "Murphy," wrote Macmillan, "was inexorably caught in the meshes of a past which everybody now wished to forget." Murphy's French acquaintances were aristocrats, Roman Catholic (like himself), and authoritarian in politics; for the job next needing to be done they were the wrong allies. Macmillan thus admired Murphy all the more for being willing to support a policy and program that would not please his friends nor be welcomed in the State Department and the White House, and he admired Eisenhower in turn for having the fortitude to give the two of them authority and let them carry out their notion of a Giraud–de Gaulle binary regime.

It was an unequal partnership, bound to advance the cause of one at the expense of the other. "De Gaulle was strong, but uncertain," wrote Macmillan. "Giraud was reliable, but weak." Steadily during the spring, the influence and popularity of de Gaulle grew, the Americans became increasingly disenchanted with Giraud's stupidity, and pressure built up for the formal recognition by Britain and the United States of de Gaulle's French Committee for National Liberation. This was resisted every inch of the way by President Roosevelt, who protested and repeatedly expressed his inalterable opposition. In June, Roosevelt proposed to Eisenhower and Churchill that they break with de Gaulle entirely, and Eisenhower (with Macmillan's strong encouragement) had to calm him down.[40]

"More clearly than Roosevelt . . . ," writes Eisenhower's biographer Stephen Ambrose, "Eisenhower recognized de Gaulle's strength. . . . [He] also realized—as Roosevelt did not—that de Gaulle could not be intimidated or bribed." Eisenhower remained patient and steady through weeks of tedious and complicated argument. "If the President knew how much [his] policy is disliked and even despised by the American Army here," Macmillan wrote in his letter-diary to his wife on July 27, "I think he would get a rude shock." On August 4, Churchill cabled Roosevelt calling attention to Macmillan's and Murphy's view "that extreme bitterness and resentment will be caused among all classes of Frenchmen by continued refusal" to recognize the FCNL.[41]

Losing interest, and with fewer and fewer on his side, the President backed away. By August 26, a compromise had been worked out for parallel (American and British) statements of recognition of the FCNL, differing slightly in formula but each acceptable to the other and, unexpectedly, to both de Gaulle and Giraud. A milestone had been passed in the politico-military conduct of the alliance in its relations with a major once and future ally. Roosevelt to the contrary, de Gaulle was now in effect prime minister of a provisional government of France.

It was a solution generally along the lines Eisenhower had recommended, and it secured tranquillity in the rear-area base of the military operations he was conducting in Sicily and would open soon in Italy. Over the intransigence of his Commander in Chief, he had achieved what the military necessities required, and had built the foundation for a political accommodation with the French future that the President's policy would have frustrated.

Eisenhower, too, had grown. He and Omar Bradley, though West Point classmates, had seen one another scarcely a half-dozen times in the years since, and when Bradley reported to Eisenhower at the St. Georges hotel in Algiers, he found a larger human being than he had remembered. "Ike had matured," he wrote, "into a charming man with a first-class mind." John Eisenhower noticed the change in his father. "Before he left for Europe in 1942," young Eisenhower said, "I knew him as an aggressive, intelligent personality." Then there had been a transformation "from a mere person to a personage . . . full of authority, and truly in command."[42]

Eisenhower was not yet in Roosevelt's full confidence, but he was gaining a place there. At the Casablanca Conference, he had dined with the President and given him details that had not earlier reached Washington on Darlan's actual position (Roosevelt had not realized the degree to which the admiral had been virtually an American prisoner). He took the opportunity to explain why he had proceeded in the "Darlan Deal" without Washington's permission; it was central to Eisenhower's thinking that generals can be replaced if they make mistakes, governments cannot. This pleased the President, but he still held back when later in the conference Marshall urged him to promote Eisenhower to full general. Roosevelt wanted to wait until there was some "damn good reason."[43] He wanted a victory.

◆

The Tunisian campaign was the education of the Americans, and of their commander. Eisenhower had never before led troops in combat; those units under him of his own nationality had never before fought the Germans, let alone Rommel, the Desert Fox. They would do so under rain and leaden sky, in a hilly, bare, and rock-strewn country, far at the end of tenuous supply lines, fragmented and at times confused in command, and in company with allies they did not particularly like, who heartily disliked them in turn. When it was over, the enemy would have suffered a greater loss in men than the Germans did at Stalingrad, the Americans would have absorbed and surmounted the experience of failure, and the groundwork would have been built for that uneasy but firm coordination between them and the British that won battle after battle to come.

Eisenhower and Patton had been right in their estimate that the odds of reaching Tunisia before the Germans did were no better than fifty-fifty. Eisenhower ordered a British force called an army but in fact consisting of scarcely two divisions to move eastward as rapidly as possible. Communications were miserable—the four hundred miles from Algiers to Tunis were covered by a rudimentary single-track railroad and a two-lane dirt road—and the weather was worse, turning the ground into mud that engulfed vehicles and aircraft. Eisenhower ordered Combat Command B (CCB) of the 1st Armored Division to go forward with the British, over the objections of George Patton (help the *British*!) and of a staff officer obsessed by regulations who said that driving half-tracks that far would wear them out. On Christmas Eve, Eisenhower was forward at "army" headquarters in Medjez-el-Bab. About thirty feet off the road, he saw four soldiers struggling to get a motorcycle out of the mud; by the time they gave up, it was in deeper than when they started. That convinced him; he called off the attack. The race to Tunis from the west had been lost.[44]

As the British under General Sir Harold R. L. G. Alexander approached Tunisia from the east, there arose a delicate question of command. It was resolved at Casablanca. Somewhat to Marshall's surprise, the

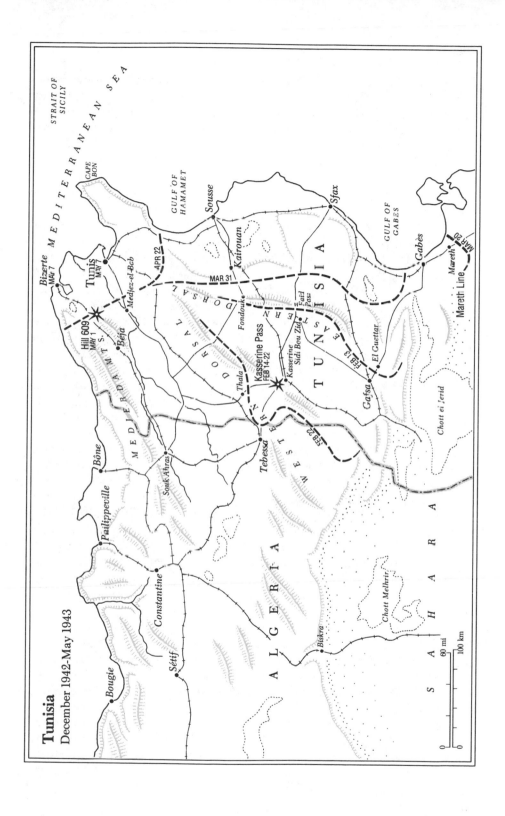

Tunisia
December 1942-May 1943

MEDITERRANEAN SEA

STRAIT OF SICILY

CAPE BON

GULF OF HAMAMET

Bizerte
MAY 7

Tunis
MAY 7

Medjez-el-Bab

APR 22

Sousse

Kairouan

Sfax

GULF OF GABÈS

Gabès

MAR 20

Mareth

Mareth Line

Hill 609
MAY 1

MAR 31

Béja

Fondouk

DORSAL

Faïd Pass

EASTERN

MEDJERDA MTS.

Thala

Kasserine Pass
FEB 14-22

Kasserine
Sidi Bou Zid

FEB 13

El Guettar

Bône

Tébessa

WESTERN DORSAL

FEB 22

Gafsa

Chott el Jerid

Philippeville

Souk Ahras

ALGERIA

Constantine

SAHARA

Bougie

Sétif

Chott Melrhir

Biskra

60 mi

100 km

TUNISIA

British members of the Combined Chiefs proposed that Eisenhower continue as Supreme Commander, with three British deputies: Alexander for land forces, Air Marshal Sir Arthur Tedder for air, and Admiral Sir Andrew B. Cunningham for sea—all of whom were one grade senior to him! There were good reasons for this: Eisenhower got on well with Tedder and Cunningham and he had already established the only genuinely Allied headquarters in North Africa. The move was flattering to the Americans while preserving the British "committee" approach to command, which was their normal practice and preference. Yet British intentions were complex. "We were pushing Eisenhower up into the stratosphere and rarefied atmosphere of a supreme commander," wrote Brooke, "where he would be free to devote his time to the political and inter-allied programs."[45] The day-to-day conduct of the campaign would be handled by the triumvirate of Britons, or so he thought. They misread their man.

Eisenhower did not believe that in modern warfare such a fragmentation of authority would work, and in retrospect there is much to be said for his—i.e., the American—viewpoint. He was delighted to be Supreme Commander, but to him that did not mean just sitting in Algiers receiving dignitaries, worrying about de Gaulle, and announcing victories. He intended to *command*. When the Combined Chiefs sent him directives in mid-January spelling out organizational procedures in a detail he thought to be his business and not theirs, he dictated a scorching reply that Beetle Smith persuaded him to tone down. Marshall had clearly counseled Eisenhower at Casablanca not to let British conceptions of organization prevail, and he did not. "As far as I am concerned," he wrote Marshall on February 8, "no attention will be paid to such observations. . . . I believe that I have grasped your idea and that I will be constantly on my guard to prevent any important military venture depending for its control and direction upon the 'committee' system of command."[46]

Eisenhower was dissatisfied with the way things were going. He wanted the 1st Armored Division to operate as a unit, concentrated, not scattered around the countryside, and he was angry when he discovered —despite his orders—that this was not being done. He wanted supply to be better organized, and pressed the Joint Chiefs for more trucks (five thousand, with Admiral King providing convoys, were soon on the way). He was dismayed to discover that the overall American commander, Major General Lloyd R. Fredendall of II Corps, was digging his headquarters into caves near Tebessa, some hundred miles behind the front, and he pressed Fredendall to make commanders go forward (to no avail, in Fredendall's case).

Most of all he was concerned about the poor performance of American soldiers. Air and ground force coordination was inadequate; the physical condition of the men left much to be desired. "Troops must be hard," he wrote to his commanders, ordering cross-country runs and something

better than perfunctory calisthenics. Combat exercises must be continuous, especially at the level of squad, platoon, and company. "I cannot urge
too strongly," wrote Eisenhower, "that emphasis be placed on individual
and small unit training."[47]

The test that Eisenhower anticipated was soon to come, in a composite of battles that are grouped together under the generic name Kasserine
Pass. The German Afrika Korps under Generalfeldmarschall Erwin Rommel had been retreating westward through Libya, with British Eighth
Army, commanded by Lieutenant General Sir Bernard L. Montgomery,
in not exactly ardent pursuit. (Montgomery was a week or so behind the
Germans and was not doing them much damage.) Rommel, safely beyond
a prepared position in the Mareth Line, decided the opportunity had been
offered him to turn in the other direction and teach the Americans a
lesson, to strike them a blow so savage that it would thereafter linger in
their memories, would establish the same kind of moral ascendancy Robert E. Lee achieved by similar means—and relied on to fuddle the minds
of his opponents—would (in Rommel's own words) "instil in them from the
outset an inferiority complex of no mean order."[48] In this he failed, though
not for lack of effort on his part.

Eisenhower, informed by British (Ultra) intelligence that an attack
impended but not sure where, spent the afternoon of February 13 consulting with his officers at corps and Combat Command A of the 1st Armored.
He came as far forward as the front lines at Sidi Bou Zid, where a little
after midnight he went for a walk in the desert under a shining moon. To
the east he could just make out the gap in the black mountains at Faid Pass;
all was quiet. He returned to his car and the long drive back to II Corps
headquarters, which he reached around five-thirty in the morning, to
learn that the Germans were attacking through Faid Pass. This was the
10th Panzer Division, which had come over from France. It wiped out an
American tank battalion, overran a battalion of artillery, isolated two large
pockets of American troops, and drove Combat Command A out of Sidi
Bou Zid, back toward Sbeitla. CCA lost ninety-eight tanks, fifty-seven
half-tracks, and twenty-nine field guns. "It had," writes Stephen Ambrose,
"in effect, been destroyed."[49]

The German onslaught was in two spearheads, of which this was the
northernmost, and it was the other, to the south, that on February 19
arrived at Kasserine Pass, which was held by a mixed bag of American and
British infantry, artillery, engineers, and tank destroyers. The Germans
had achieved a deep penetration into the Allied front; it would eventually
go twice as deep as the Bulge, the similar counterattack they later
launched in Europe, but it was similarly unsuccessful in reaching its goal.
Rommel broke through at Kasserine Pass. He himself was present on the
nineteenth, urging 10th Panzer forward against what he described as
"extremely well placed American artillery and mortar fire from the hills."

By 5:00 P.M., the Germans held the pass and were pressing forward toward Thala and the road to Tebessa. Thus far and no farther.

Rommel thought that the Germans had committed a tactical error. Their first attack at Kasserine had been made not by 10th Panzer but by a task force of Afrika Korps veterans from the desert, and it failed. They had relied on their skills in using armor to push through on the valley floor, even though the Americans held the heights above and called down on them that "well placed" artillery fire. They should have "combined hill and valley tactics," Rommel wrote, "and should have taken possession of the hills on either side of the pass," as under his angry goading they before long did. "The Americans had fought extremely well," Rommel added, "and [German] losses had been considerable."

When they pressed on through Kasserine Pass, the desert veterans, to Rommel's annoyance, again held to the valley bottom and again the British and American artillery brought them to a halt. The next day, Rommel concluded that the enemy had grown too strong for him and broke off the offensive. American losses in the Kasserine battles had been heavy—over two hundred tanks shot up and four thousand men captured—and the American commanders, as Rommel surmised, had been shaken in their confidence. But for the American soldiery as a whole, it had been a humiliation rather than a major defeat. They had learned a great deal, and they would come out of Tunisia stronger than they entered it.

Eisenhower had been very busy: ordering the 9th Division artillery forward, stripping 2d Armored and 3d Infantry of equipment to send II Corps, cannibalizing other units intended for the invasion of Sicily, to get trucks, tanks, and ammunition—not the distant "chairman of the board" commander Brooke had in mind and others have pictured him as being. Above all, a sense of "inferiority" had turned upon those who had planned to "instil" it. The Americans, wrote Rommel, "made up for their lack of experience by their far better and more plentiful equipment and their tactically more flexible command . . . we could look forward with but small hope of success to the coming mobile battles."[50]

Eisenhower had established an advance headquarters at Constantine under the direction of Major General Lucian K. Truscott as his deputy chief of staff (Truscott later commanded Fifth Army during the drive into northern Italy). Truscott was dismayed, as Eisenhower was, at the bickering between allies at the senior level and the bickering even of American commanders among themselves. Fredendall had been put in charge of II Corps at Marshall's behest, so that Eisenhower was reluctant to relieve him, but gradually it became apparent that Fredendall would have to go. "Small in stature, loud and rough in speech," wrote Truscott of Fredendall, "he was outspoken in his opinions and critical of superiors and subor-

dinates alike. . . . He rarely left his command post . . . yet he was impatient
with the recommendations of subordinates more familiar with the terrain
and other conditions than he was."[51] Fredendall was promoted to lieutenant general and returned home to a hero's welcome, but he never commanded in combat again. To replace him, Eisenhower turned to George
Patton.

Patton was to lead II Corps for forty-three days (before returning to
his more important task of preparing for the invasion of Sicily), and it was
during this period that he acquired his reputation as a rigid disciplinarian
in trivial things. He needed some way of making every member of II Corps
aware that they had a new commander and that the days of sloppiness and
defeat were over; casting about, he hit upon the regulations concerning
uniform. Helmets, neckties, and leggings *would* be worn; violators would
be fined, and they were frequently rounded up by Patton himself. "Every
time a soldier knotted his necktie, threaded his leggings, and buckled on
his heavy steel helmet," wrote Omar Bradley (who had become Patton's
deputy), "he was forcibly reminded that Patton had come to command the
II Corps, that the pre-Kasserine days had ended, and that a tough new era
had begun."[52] Patton led them in an attack intended to relieve pressure
on Montgomery and British Eighth Army, coming ponderously in the
other direction—"with the majestic deliberation of a pachyderm," says
the U.S. Army historian—and they won the battles of Gafsa and El Guettar. (Eisenhower thought Patton could have done even more if Alexander
had not held him back.)[53]

When with Patton's departure Bradley took over II Corps, its mission
was an unsatisfactory one. Alexander proposed to have the two British
armies converge on Tunis, in which case the Americans between them
would be pinched out and play no part in the conclusion of the campaign.
(American suspicions that the British were trying to hog the limelight
began around that time and later grew to epic proportions.) Eisenhower
made it plain to Alexander that this was to risk the loss of American public
support for the Europe-first strategy, and Alexander got the point. At
Eisenhower's order, II Corps was assigned a new sector to the north,
opposite Bizerte, and using the trucks the Joint Chiefs had sent him,
Eisenhower moved 100,000 troops and their supporting units around the
rear of British First Army in two days—"an operation," writes Ambrose,
"that showed the Americans at their logistical best."[54]

The terrain to which Bradley was now assigned (he says at his request[55]) was far from promising, filled with hills and unsuitable for armor,
yet here he began to demonstrate the tactical flair and the capacity to
inspire confidence that led him to greater heights in Europe. He avoided
the mistake of the Germans at Kasserine Pass; he told his commanders to
shun the valleys and move through the hills. "I told them to stay off
obvious routes of approach such as macadam roads . . . ," he wrote, "and

first take the high ground." (This was the way to go; the Germans had covered all the "obvious routes" with batteries of 88-mm guns.)

The highest ground in Bradley's front was a rocky knob known as Djebel Tahent, or Hill 609 (the height in meters). Bradley gave Hill 609 as an objective to the 34th Division, believing that success would restore its sagging morale. (The 34th had taken a beating at Fondouk not entirely its fault, and been subjected to scorn from the British, Alexander included; there was talk in high quarters of sending it back to the States for retraining.) The 34th took Hill 609 in stride on May 1, rejuvenated itself, and went on to be in Bradley's judgment "one of the finest infantry outfits of World War II."[56] A. J. Liebling, who as a war correspondent was just getting to know Bradley, wrote of this: "Many generals, in the course of history, have taken a hill at the cost of a division, and as many have lost a division without taking a hill. Bradley took a key hill and saved a division."

Liebling first encountered Bradley at a press briefing on a brush-covered hillside near a place called Béja. Bradley arrived in his jeep, carrying a map and accompanied by an aide with an easel and a pointer. The general was wearing his helmet, a regulation field jacket, leggings, and pants—"thus qualifying," wrote Liebling, "as the least dressed up commander of an American army in the field since Zachary Taylor, who wore a straw hat." In contrast with Patton, "the new general, lanky and diffidently amiable, seemed a man of milk."[57] Thus the correspondents assumed that the Americans were going to have little to do with the final drive and they were suitably skeptical when Bradley unrolled the scheme for a major attack—with all the panache of "a teacher outlining the curriculum for the next semester," said Liebling—and seemed to take it for granted that his plan would succeed on the same ground where in late November the British 36th Infantry Brigade had failed. Bradley was right; his plan worked. At three-thirty in the afternoon on May 7, the Americans were in Bizerte, only twenty minutes later than the British arrived in Tunis.

The same things tended to happen to Bradley. He would be given a subordinate mission and a secondary supply priority. Then when the end came, the closing in for the kill, there would be Bradley delivering a decisive blow—in this case, foreclosing the possibility of a last-ditch German defense on the Tunisian tip. It happened in Tunisia, it happened in Sicily, it happened on the Rhine: After a while you begin to wonder. This was one of the great tacticians, and he had absorbed from Marshall at Benning a taste for the unorthodox. "I never saw that one in the book," he said after one of his maneuvers on the march to Bizerte, "but it seemed like a good idea so I did it."[58] Eisenhower gave him highest marks. "There is very little I need to tell you about him," Eisenhower wrote to Marshall in the fall of 1943, "because he is running absolutely true to form . . . in my opinion the best rounded combat leader I have yet met in our service. While he possibly lacks some of the extraordinary and ruthless driving power that Patton can exert at critical moments, he still has such force and determination that even in this characteristic he is among our best."[59]

President Roosevelt had not waited for a victory before promoting Eisenhower to full general, but had accepted Marshall's recommendation after the British chiefs agreed to keep Eisenhower on as Supreme Commander (in order, at least, to put him on a par with his British deputies). The news came through (and Eisenhower promoted all the enlisted men in his headquarters one grade) just before Kasserine Pass. Two years later during the Bulge, when the same thing happened again, Eisenhower said to Patton, "Every time I get a new star I get attacked." Patton replied, "And every time you get attacked, I pull you out."[60] In December, Eisenhower had written Handy: "I think the best way to describe our operation to date is that we have violated every recognized principle of war, are in conflict with all operational and logistic methods laid down in textbooks, and will be condemned, in their entirety, by all Leavenworth and War College classes for the next twenty-five years." He wrote to a friend: "I think sometimes that I am a cross between a one-time soldier, a pseudo-statesman, a jack-legged politician and a crooked diplomat."[61] But he won Tunisia and 275,000 enemy troops surrendered.

In August 1943, Eisenhower's Allied Force Headquarters published a document called "Lessons from the Tunisian Campaign"; when Marshall read it he had it republished and distributed throughout the Army "for the information of all concerned" (this author's copy was issued to him at the Tank Destroyer School in Camp Hood, Texas). It is an absorbing example of how experience can be condensed and made accessible (it was carefully read at Camp Hood, as I can testify, because the Tank Destroyers had performed in Tunisia quite contrary to the doctrine we were being taught in Texas). It was filled with obvious advice: emphasize scouting and patrolling, better map-reading, defense in depth, closer coordination between infantry and tanks, and so on—but the best thing about it was that it had been written by men no greatly different from ourselves, products of the same training as ours, who had survived, and who said that the "myth of the invincibility of the German army and its equipment has been exploded."[62] This may have been overstated, but it carried a tone of conviction.

Many among the Americans looked back on Tunisia as the place where they discovered themselves and each other. "Hundreds of company and battalion officers," writes George F. Howe in the U.S. Army history's volume on North Africa, "were sifted by situations in which they showed what they could give and how much they could take. Regimental and division officers were winnowed by the same process." Some went back to the United States to start and train new units; others stayed on to carry forward their achieved self-possession in their own organizations. Indirectly, this is a validation of Roosevelt's decision to invade North Africa first, over Marshall's objections. To have moved into Western Europe against German veterans without attaining this military maturity beforehand would have been an ardent exercise but an adolescent one, and who knows what would have come of it? We needed a place to be lousy in, somewhere to let the gift for combat and command be discovered, to let at least a few of our divisions be "blooded"—a harsh if apposite word.

George Howe wrote that another among the "fruits of victory" in Tunisia was an integrated international Allied headquarters as "a successful going concern," able to take on the campaigns in Sicily and Italy to come. "Anglo-American co-operation had survived some hard tests during the preceding months," wrote Howe. "If the coalition, with the disappointments, frustrations, and recriminations inherent in such a union, could survive the initial and struggling phases, it seemed certain to remain effective as the war . . . proceeded."[63] Eisenhower thought that the great lesson of Tunisia was the necessity for commanders to put Allied unity ahead of the frictions inevitable when men are fighting for their lives, abnormally sensitive to newspaper headlines and radio broadcasts that appear to favor one nationality over another, and to observe this principle scrupulously not only in public but "in the confidence of the personal contacts of subordinates and staffs."[64] If such appears obvious now, one must remember that it did not appear so then to many American and British officers.

American antipathy toward the British, as Eisenhower observed to Marshall in April 1943, came from seeds of discord "sown, on our side, as far back as when we read our little red school history books." There was an undercurrent of Americans-coming-to-the-rescue that went back to World War I, when there had been references to the A.E.F. as "After England Failed." Each military system assumed its own to be the only proper way of doing things, and the two differed in countless details. (General Sir Frederick Morgan said that when he received the American operational order for the North African invasion, "a weighty document," he had to read it several times before he could admit to himself that he didn't understand a single word.)

Styles of behavior that seemed normal to the British seemed supercilious to Americans, and British remarks about the Americans as "our Italians" didn't help much, either. Ismay's deputy, Sir Ian Jacob, thought that the U.S. Army was "a mutual admiration society, [so that] any failings in this theater can be comfortably blamed on the British." Alexander in particular acquired a low opinion of the Americans that overcame his customary suavity. He wrote to Brooke that they "simply do not know their job as soldiers . . . the junior leadership . . . just does not lead with the result that their men don't really fight . . . they are soft green and quite untrained"—in which there was, of course, some truth, though Rommel and Bradley thought otherwise—and he showed his lack of confidence by giving them limited missions lest they get in trouble.[65]

Eisenhower devoted his considerable gifts to preventing the damage all this might have done. One of his reasons for dismissing Fredendall was Fredendall's constant disparagement of the British. In Eisenhower's head-quarters, every major subordinate or staff head of one nationality had a deputy of the other, and descriptions of particular plans or positions as "British" or "American" were not allowed. A story was later told and retold throughout the European theater, though it is not clear where and when it happened, which so perfectly epitomizes Eisenhower's influence that it deserved its wide circulation. He was supposed to have sent an American officer home for getting into an argument with his British "op-posite number," in the course of which the former had called the latter a son-of-a-bitch. "As far as I can see you were justified," Eisenhower is said to have told the man, "but you called him a *British* son-of-a-bitch, and for that I'm sending you home."

Much the same story of the stormy but enduring Anglo-American marriage could be told of the campaigns in Sicily and Italy, but it would add little to what we have already seen. Sicily, in particular, saw the further exploits and excesses of George Patton, the steady performance of Omar Bradley (as a corps commander under Patton), and the emergence of Colonel (later Lieutenant General) James M. Gavin of the 505th Para-chute Infantry Regimental Combat Team as one of the youngest and ablest of the American battlefield commanders, and among them by far the best writer (his account of the action on Biazza Ridge in Sicily will reward the reader who wishes realism and clear explication in war writ-ing[66]).

In Sicily and Italy, on the British side as well, realization grew that this was no longer the main show (as Marshall had all along insisted) and that nothing lay ahead here but hard fighting to no great gain. Montgomery and British Eighth Army, the heroes of El Alamein, felt downgraded; the Americans, loyal to the priority of invading France, saw themselves becoming partners to a stalemate. J. F. C. Fuller, in his history of World War II, divided the Italian campaign into three stages: the reasonable (securing Naples and the Foggia airfields, the political (taking Rome), and "The Daft, from the occupation of Rome onwards."[67] More must be said of this later.

At the first Cairo Conference, Eisenhower made a presentation to the Combined Chiefs on the war in the Mediterranean that confirmed their good impression of him. He told them that in Italy he wanted to reach the Po Valley but that without more matériel, especially landing craft—which would mean delaying Overlord sixty to ninety days—the best he could do

in the spring was take Rome and establish a defensive line. By this time
he was trying to reconcile himself to a return to Washington as Chief of
Staff when Marshall, as everyone expected, went to London to command
the invasion. (Eisenhower thought that he himself was temperamentally
unsuited to be Chief of Staff.) At Cairo, Marshall gave a Thanksgiving
dinner and discovered that Eisenhower hadn't realized it was Thanksgiving. He ordered Eisenhower to take a vacation. "Just let someone else run
that war up there for a couple of days," said Marshall. "If your subordinates
can't do it for you, you haven't organized them properly."[68]

President Roosevelt had been stalling on the Overlord appointment,
but the pressure on him had been building up, especially after Stalin
repeatedly asked at Teheran who the commander was going to be. As we
have seen, the decision was largely shaped by negative reasons—why the
choice could not be Marshall—but there were positive factors as well in
the President's mind as he weighed the alternatives. During the second
Cairo Conference (after the return from Teheran), Churchill persuaded
Roosevelt to take a drive with him out to see the Sphinx, and on the way
the President casually remarked that General Marshall could not be
spared and would Eisenhower be acceptable? Churchill said that it was for
the President to decide but that the British would gladly entrust their
fortunes to Eisenhower's direction. The two of them gazed at the Sphinx
for some minutes in silence. "She told us nothing," Churchill wrote, "and
maintained her inscrutable smile."[69] On December 7 they parted, Roosevelt by plane for Tunis, where Eisenhower met him. When they were
seated in the car, Roosevelt turned to Eisenhower and said, "Well, Ike, you
are going to command Overlord."

Roosevelt had examined the job and the man and found them compat-
ible. Many months later, James Roosevelt asked his father why, in view of
his obvious respect for Marshall, he had chosen as he did. "Eisenhower is
the best politician among the military men," replied the President. "He
is a natural leader who can convince other men to follow him, and this is
what we need in his position more than any other quality."[70]

II

There was never anything before like D-Day and there will never be
again. Stalin, no easy judge, said that "the history of warfare knows no
other like undertaking from the point of view of its scale, its vast conception, and its masterly execution." It was surrounded by risk; many who
made it happen were anticipating the worst. Ismay wrote in March that
"a lot of people who ought to know better are taking it for granted that
Overlord is going to be a bloodbath." Brooke, up to the very last moment,
feared that "it may well be the most ghastly disaster of the whole war."[71]

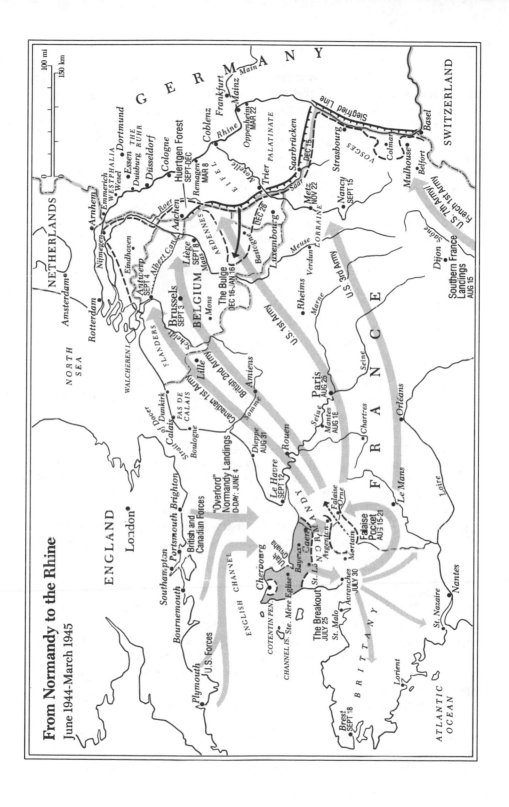

From Normandy to the Rhine
June 1944-March 1945

100 mi
150 km

GERMANY

Frankfurt
Mainz
Main
Coblenz
Rhine
Oppenheim
MAR 22
Trier PALATINATE
Saarbrücken
DEC 15
Saar
Moselle
Metz
NOV 22
Nancy
SEPT 15
Strasbourg
Colmar
Basel
VOSGES
Mulhouse
Belfort
SWITZERLAND

Dortmund
Essen THE RUHR WESTPHALIA
Emmerich
Duisburg
Düsseldorf
Cologne
Huertgen Forest
SEPT-DEC
Remagen
MAR 8
Roer
Aachen
EIFEL
Arnhem
Nijmegen

NETHERLANDS

Amsterdam
Rotterdam

Eindhoven
Antwerp
SEPT 4
Liège
Maas
Albert Can.
Brussels
SEPT 3
Mons
BELGIUM
Bastogne
DEC 26
Luxembourg
The Bulge
DEC 16-JAN 16
ARDENNES
LORRAINE
Verdun

WALCHEREN I.
Schelde
FLANDERS
Lille
Scheldt
Canadian 1st Army
British 2nd Army
U.S. 1st Army
U.S. 3rd Army

NORTH SEA

Str. of Dover
Dunkirk
Calais PAS DE CALAIS
Boulogne
Somme
Amiens
Dieppe
AUG 31
Rouen
Le Havre
SEPT 12
Seine

Meuse
Rheims
Marne
Mantes
AUG 18
Paris
AUG 25
Seine
Chartres
Orléans
Le Mans

Dijon
Saône
Southern France
Landings
AUG 15
U.S. 7th Army
French 1st Army

ENGLAND

London

Southampton
Portsmouth Brighton
British and
Canadian Forces
Bournemouth
"Overlord"
Normandy Landings
D-DAY: JUNE 4
Plymouth
U.S. Forces

ENGLISH CHANNEL

Cherbourg
COTENTIN PEN.
CHANNEL IS. Ste. Mère Eglise
The Breakout
JULY 25
St. Malo
Utah
Omaha
Bayeux
St. Lô
Caen
NORMANDY
Avranches
JULY 30
Mortain
Argentan
Falaise
Orne
Falaise
Pocket
AUG 15-21

FRANCE

Loire

BRITTANY

Brest
SEPT 18
Lorient
St. Nazaire
Nantes

ATLANTIC
OCEAN

Siegfried Line

Britain was sending into Normandy its only remaining army; after this there was nothing left. If the invasion failed, it was not likely to be repeated; all was being wagered on a single throw.

Force of every form that ingenuity could then contrive would be concentrated upon a single fifty miles of gravelly seashore. We would have to breach the Atlantic Wall, Hitler's vaunted ring of steel and concrete fortifications that circled the coast. Behind the vanguard would come the ranked array of Allied formations, which envisaged nothing short of the total destruction of the most formidable military power of the twentieth century. On all sides the invasion was awaited with hushed expectancy and repressed anguish: this enormous venture, this event of infinite complexity and guile, of bravery beyond measure, of sorry mistakes and unbidden initiatives, of humor and pathos, of Americans on its eve making a show of confidence for their commander and of British officers quoting Shakespeare's *Henry V* to one another.

> *He that outlives this day, and comes safe home,*
> *Will stand a-tiptoe when this day is named . . .*

There will be no more D-Days; the atom bomb will see to that. It was the last great continental exercise in "conventional" military arms: preliminary air and naval bombardment, an armada of landing craft debouching armor and infantry, and infantry most of all—the hapless foot soldiers who must slog their way inshore with nothing but their rifles, their grenades, and with luck a mortar or machine gun or two. A major amphibious operation runs the gamut from the macro to the micro in scale, from the vast numbers in which it must be visualized down to the relative paucity of human beings who at the moment of "Down ramp!" wade forward bearing the weight of decision. D-Day is the monumental plan, but it is also the few scores of men on Omaha Beach who reached out and plucked the flower victory from a nettle of smashed ships, drowned tanks, dead and mangled comrades, blood-running tide, and punishing gunfire from the bluffs above them.

If the will behind it was American, the mind was British. The decision where to land was British, the design of the landing craft and other special equipment was British, the skill in combined operations that underlay it was British, and above all the deception plan—the most successful manipulation of an enemy's mind in modern warfare—not only was British in origin but was resisted and misunderstood by Americans who grumpily participated in it.[72]

More than a million and a half American soldiers, sailors, and airmen had been assembled in Britain, an encounter between cultures which mixed warmth, inconvenience, and disbelief that people who spoke the same language could behave so strangely. The British had become accustomed to the presence of foreign military—Dutch, Polish, Czech, the

Dominions—but the Americans were more numerous, more exasperating, more generously paid and supplied, more rambunctious.[73] British pubs resounded with American voices and British homes were opened to them; many American memories of that time are nostalgic. They trained in British fields and valleys, and they would march down British country lanes to their ships. They would go forward in company with British fighting men and with the hopes and anxieties of a Britain that had been through five years of war, with more than its share of loss and sorrow, of which this enterprise was to be the climax and redemption.

Five Allied divisions would make the first assault. On the American beaches alone the first day we were planning to land the equivalent of two hundred trainloads of troops. These would be followed, in the next two weeks, by twice as many American soldiers as there had been in the entire U.S. Army in 1939 and by enough vehicles to form a double line from Pittsburgh to Chicago. They would be taking with them everything that modern war requires, from 120-foot steel-span bridges to sulfa pills, not to mention fresh drinking water (300,500 gallons of it for the first three days). General Bradley likened the transit of the Channel to disassembling a giant jigsaw puzzle and then putting it back together on what he and others now referred to as the Far Shore. The process was so complicated that an early operational order of First U.S. Army had more words in it than *Gone With the Wind*.[74]

The debarking schedule was literally minute by minute. On the American beach between Vierville and Colleville, which had been code-named "Omaha," at H-Hour minus one, would land thirty-two floatable tanks of the 743d Tank Battalion, and on their left at H-Hour, LCTs (landing craft, tank) would bring in twice as many more. At H+01, twenty-four LCVPs (landing craft, vehicle and personnel) would land four companies of the 116th Infantry of the 29th Division, and at H+03, twelve LCMs (landing craft, mechanized) would follow with demolition experts of the 164th Engineer Combat Battalion to clear the beach of German mines and obstacles. Wave would come after wave: H+30 and H+40 (headquarters detachments and more engineers), H+50 (four more companies of the 116th Infantry). Between H+60 and H+90 would arrive the first artillery and antiaircraft. The real influx of vehicles and supply would begin at H+180, and by H+240 there would be cranes, tank-recovery vehicles, half-tracks and every possible kind of truck, in particular the rugged amphibious version called the DUKW.[75]

The invasion plan in all its intricacy was the handiwork of a joint Anglo-American staff that had been assembled in early 1943 under the command of Lieutenant General Sir Frederick Morgan, who had led a British corps in North Africa. He bore the title of COSSAC, Chief of Staff to the Supreme Allied Commander (designate), meaning that he served a boss who had not yet been appointed, and eventually COSSAC came to be the usual name for the Allied group around him. Morgan was an ideal choice and COSSAC did its job well. At the outset he insisted on two points, which the British chiefs were wise enough to accept: (1) this was not to be a paper exercise but the real thing, the plan actually to be executed, and (2) there was to be a complete amalgamation of American and British "staff, effort, troops, and everything else from the very beginning," on the model of what he had seen work so effectively under Eisenhower in Algiers.

Morgan said later that very little original work turned out to be needed, since so much had already been accomplished in the way of study and preparation: "The more we became aware of what had been done, the more we came to realise that we were heirs to a considerable fortune" (without it, he doubted that they could have finished their labors in time). "From all kinds of unexpected quarters," he wrote, "men of all ranks and all services came into Norfolk House [COSSAC headquarters] telling us of the bits and pieces on which they had been working and suggesting how they might be fitted into the broader picture."[76]

The first steps to solve the problem of invading Europe had been taken two and a half years earlier with the creation of Combined Operations, the "commandos," for the purpose of conducting small-scale attacks on the Nazi-held coast: the Lofoten islands, Vaagso, Dieppe, Bruneval, Guernsey, Saint-Nazaire. Goebbels referred to them contemptuously as "Red Indian" raids,[77] and in stealth and ferocity, that they were, but they gave the German sentries something to think about and they provided the all-essential test-in-action for Combined Operations' organization, tactics, training, and equipment. In the fall of 1941, Churchill had brought in Captain Lord Louis Mountbatten to head Combined Operations and had instructed him: "You are to prepare for the invasion of Europe. . . . You must devise and design the appliances, the landing craft and the technique to enable us to effect a landing against opposition and to maintain ourselves there. . . . The whole of the south coast of England is a bastion of defence . . . you've got to turn it into the springboard for our attack."[78]

COSSAC's most elemental decision was where the landings should take place. Actually this did not prove to be so difficult a question as might have been thought. Given the need for air coverage by fighter planes, there were only two serious possibilities: the Pas de Calais—that is, the coast of France immediately across the Strait of Dover between Dunkirk and Boulogne—or Normandy, between the mouth of the Seine and the Cotentin peninsula. The Pas de Calais had much to recommend it, so much so that many German military professionals assumed it to be the necessary choice. (Hitler's intuition, for once in working order, told him they were wrong.) It was the shortest crossing and the most direct route to Germany; behind it was open country leading to Brussels and the great port of Antwerp.

But there were many objections to the Pas de Calais, in sum persuasive. The coast was more exposed and the weather would predictably be
worse than in the sheltered bay of the Seine. The beaches, though adequate in themselves, did not have as good exits as there were in Normandy, and it would be vital to get the battle off the beaches as rapidly
as possible. The ports in the Pas de Calais were meager; how could a
lodgment area be built around them for the massive buildup needed for
a breakout? Where did you go from here, anyhow? From Normandy you
could go to Brittany, and Brittany had ports large enough for major reinforcement. Not least, since the Germans expected us in the Pas de Calais,
that was where their defenses—in guns, divisions, and concrete—were
concentrated. All in all, Morgan and his co-workers began with a preference for Normandy and never abandoned it.

COSSAC was by no means unaware of the hazards. "The prospect of
launching an invasion out of England was little short of appalling," writes
Morgan. "There was no precedent in all history for any such thing on such
a scale." They could hope at best for a slender margin of superiority. In
the early planning stages, they lacked the landing craft for more than a
three-division assault, which meant they would have to concentrate on the
beaches opposite Bayeux and might not have the strength to cut the
Cotentin peninsula and capture the major port at Cherbourg. It was
doubtful that tactical surprise could be achieved. An early COSSAC estimate was that the scheme could succeed only if there were no more than
twelve fully mobile German divisions in reserve in France. (Told of this
by Churchill at Teheran, Stalin asked what would happen if there were
thirteen.) Ringing in Morgan's ear was the parting admonition he had
received from Brooke, the chief of the Imperial General Staff: "Well, there
it is. It won't work, but you must bloody well make it."[79]

Gordon Harrison, in the official U.S. Army history of D-day, tries to
provide an explanation for what he calls "this ready agreement to mount
the cross-Channel invasion on a shoestring." The Americans wanted a firm
decision on action with a definite target date, even if this meant making
do with less than ideal conditions. "The British," he writes, "were not
likely to take serious issue." They attached little importance to long-range
planning and were mainly interested in the next operation to come.[80]
Morgan agrees: "the British authorities," he adds, "had at this time no real
plan for the day when they would have to stop being flexible." Years of
cheese paring and parsimony had ill prepared them to visualize the immense resources that D-day would require and that the United States
would be bringing to bear. "I fancy it is little exaggeration," writes Morgan, "to say that the sheer size of Overlord was not appreciated by some
of the British higher-ups until very late in the day."

Within the British services generally, COSSAC encountered resistance to the concept of any invasion at all being possible. From what

threatened to become a deadlock they were saved by Admiral Mountbatten, who organized a combination seminar and demonstration on the subject at Combined Operations headquarters at Largs, on the Firth of Clyde in Scotland. A course routinely given there was subtly altered in enrollment and content to include the principal skeptics and the principal points at issue. Mountbatten's showmanship could not have been better: On sentry go were commandos of impressive bearing, the weather was Scotland's finest, and from time to time bagpipers of the local Home Guard appeared to offer what Morgan called "the indigenous substitute for music." By the end, the doubters had come around. "For the first time," said one of them, "I really believe in this operation." Morgan wrote that Mountbatten "rescued" Overlord—and certainly some such idea was in George Marshall's mind, for later, when he and the other Combined Chiefs visited the Normandy beachhead on D+6 (and dined that night on Churchill's train returning to London), Marshall drafted a cable of acknowledgment to Mountbatten and they all signed it.[81]

Landing craft soon became the principal preoccupation: "the destinies of two great empires . . . ," Churchill was to complain, "seemed to be tied up in some god-damned things called LSTs." The story is a wretched one, from which few emerge with much credit. The U.S. Navy had not been interested in landing craft. By 1937, they had developed nothing but an unsuccessful tank lighter; they did not start ordering Higgins boats until September 1940, nor did they order them in quantity until the spring of 1942. "During the first years of the war," writes Harrison, "the majority of naval leaders resisted the development of landing craft as a foolhardy gamble with an untried weapon and a waste of resources badly needed for naval construction." President Roosevelt, as late as early 1942, told Captain McCrea that he thought building landing craft was a mistake.[82]

The British, meantime, had done what had to be done. As far back as 1920, they had produced a tank lighter which, with few changes, became the LCM. In 1938, deciding that special-purpose ships were going to be important, they developed the LCA (landing craft, assault), and in 1940—at Churchill's insistence—they came up with the LCT, which could carry three forty-ton tanks and disembark them in three and a half feet of water on steep beaches. Finally, seeing the need for a larger, oceangoing equivalent, they contrived the LST (landing ship, tank), with a bow that unfolded like a sideways clamshell to disgorge tanks and trucks, one of the simplest-seeming yet most fundamentally transforming technical innovations of the war. The LST, 328 feet long, with a 50-foot beam and twin-diesel screws, could carry a deadweight load of 2,100 tons; its deckload could even include a fully loaded LCT; diving tanks similar to a submarine's enabled it to reduce the seagoing draft of the bow for beaching. The United States undertook the entire production of LSTs and in the spring of 1942 began a program of mass-producing landing craft intended for the 1943 invasion of France proposed in the Marshall memorandum.[83]

However, the production of landing craft had to be superimposed on top of already jam-packed American production schedules. Contracts had to be let to small boatyards and manufacturing companies on the inland waterways, which had never made anything like this before. LSTs were built along the Ohio River, for example, at Pittsburgh and Ambridge, Pennsylvania, at Jeffersonville and Evansville, Indiana; they were slid sideways off rough ramps and sailed down to the sea by green crews. (One of them from the Great Lakes missed the turning into the Erie Canal in the Niagara River at night and would have gone over the falls if it hadn't run aground.) During 1942, landing craft were built on priorities established by emergency directives, but once the heat was off—with the successful landings in North Africa—they fell back into competition with other compelling needs (e.g., for destroyer escorts). In October 1942, they had been in second place on the Navy Shipbuilding Precedence List (aircraft carriers were first), but by November they had slid down to twelfth. Landing craft were not included in President Roosevelt's "must" list of programs for 1943.[84]

In March 1943, the British pointed out to the American Joint Chiefs that the prospect of an invasion in 1944 was being jeopardized by a shortage of LSTs and LCTs; they said that British production was at its peak and could not fill the gap. This was met with a mean and sullen suspicion. The Americans thought the British were rigging the figures; they thought the British were trying to make an invasion appear impossible in order to get out from under the obligation of undertaking it. Admiral King stated flatly that any increase in landing-craft production would cause serious dislocation in other and more important programs; one Navy spokesman said it "would be disastrous from a standpoint of all other Naval construction."[85]

Many British believed that the shortage in landing craft arose because Admiral King was diverting them to the Pacific for his own campaigns. Brooke was especially resentful of what he saw as the Americans' use of landing craft as bargaining chips to get their own way in strategy. "History will never forgive them," he wrote in his diary. Chester Wilmot, in *The Struggle for Europe*, stated that at the end of 1943, "by far the greater part of the U.S. Navy's landing-craft was in the Pacific," and he gave a table of landing craft "on strength" as of May 1, 1944, to prove his case. A necessary distinction must be made, however, between those "on strength" (American: "on hand") and those serviceable and operational, as Admiral Morison cogently argued in rebuttal. Morison's figures (as of June 1) show that many landing craft were in the United States and not yet serviceable, that the number both operational and in the Pacific was far less than

Wilmot implied, and that in actuality, "the war in the Pacific was not a drag on the war in Europe."[86]

In retrospect, one marvels that this snarl of misperceptions was ever disentangled, but somehow—after a fashion—it was. Morgan was unrelenting in his realism, in giving the indifferent what he called "a proper earful," and the Americans increasingly realized that if they wanted Overlord so badly, then there was a cost to be paid. Admiral King did relent; at the Quebec Conference in August 1943, he said that a halt in constructing 110-foot subchasers might increase landing-craft production by as much as 25 percent, and in September he raised this to 35. When General Morgan visited Washington in October, at Marshall's invitation, he had hopes of getting it raised still further, though they went unfulfilled.[87]

Morgan's mission to Washington was a high point in his friendly acquaintance with Americans. He was met at La Guardia Airport by a guard of honor and "a platoon of general officers," then put up in what after years of British austerity "seemed like paradise itself, the visiting general officers quarters at Fort Myer," which appeared "to entail a standard of living slightly higher than that portrayed by Hollywood as befitting a multimillionaire." The Marshalls had him to lunch *à trois,* and Marshall enjoined on him that he must take time off and see something of the country, go wherever he pleased.

Where would he like to go? Morgan decided to obey Mark Twain and, when in doubt, tell the truth. Since the days he started soldiering he had admired Stonewall Jackson and longed to visit the Shenandoah Valley. They looked at him unbelievingly. "If you had thought it out for a hundred years," said Mrs. Marshall, "you couldn't have given a more tactful answer. We love the place. It is where we live." Morgan had his tour, with Marshall's friend Brigadier General John MacAuley Palmer (retired), now military historian to the Library of Congress, as guide.

He was taken to inspect amphibious training on the Gulf of Mexico, to the infantry at Fort Benning, the airborne at Camp McCall, the artillery at Fort Bragg, the air force at Miami, and the Port of Embarkation at New York, where he saw for himself "profusion on an unlimited scale," provision for dealing with everything from locomotives to lice-infested German prisoners. "A liberty ship was fully loaded, it seemed, almost before our eyes." And he spent an hour, in the President's study, with Franklin Roosevelt. "Never before had I been," wrote Morgan, "and seldom in future can I possibly be, lucky enough to encounter so immediately and powerfully attractive a person." Their conversation ranged widely over the shape of things to come. To Morgan's amazement, Roosevelt seemed to be entertaining odd ideas about invading France, whose source Morgan thought he could detect, and this led to a discussion of the relationship between President and Prime Minister.

"The things that man has called me," said Roosevelt, "you wouldn't believe. But don't think he has it all his own way. No, sir. You know perhaps the clearest indication of the strength of our alliance is that we can call each other every name we can lay our tongues to and yet remain good friends. Once we start being polite to each other it won't be anything like the same thing."[88]

◆

Eisenhower came to Overlord as though born for it. His mentor had predicted it. He was one of the principal designers of the strategy that led to it; he had written many of the directives from which the driving power behind it came. He had commanded three successful amphibious invasions and he had the confidence of men (or *most* of the men) from the several arms, services, and nationalities he would be working with. He had successfully set up a functioning Allied headquarters that would serve as model for the one he must now create. He got along well with Churchill. He and Marshall were virtually as one, Marshall and Roosevelt were in harmony about his mission, and Roosevelt had picked him because of strengths he saw in Eisenhower that he thought the task required. More than this would not be reasonable to ask.

Churchill once wrote of Eisenhower that "he supervised everything with a vigilant eye, and no one knew better than he how to stand close to a tremendous event without impairing the authority he had delegated to others."[89] It is a just assessment, and it puts Eisenhower in the proper context of a role which had not existed before and which he must therefore invent. Eisenhower was later to be criticized, and not only by British observers, for failing to take a more vigorous part in the direct supervision of the battle, yet it must be kept in mind that he guided himself by a thought-through and tested conception of what it was a supreme commander did, and did not, do. (One may argue that the conception was wrong, but preferably by proposing a better.) He did not go out of his way to explain his reasons. This was not the kind of thing Eisenhower talked about except in abstractions; when it came to his own motives and methods he expected to be judged on the outcome, and otherwise left alone. Eisenhower did not mind in the slightest, as Don Whitehead suggested, if others believed that *they* were the active and initiating agents—provided the thing got done, and done with a will, and done the way he wanted it done.

When Eisenhower first saw the early COSSAC plan in North Africa, even before he knew he would command it, his immediate reaction was that the number of divisions in the first wave must be increased, and he pointed this out to Montgomery when he encountered the latter at Marrakech visiting a convalescent Churchill. (Churchill at Quebec, four months before, had also urged Marshall that the landings be in greater force.) Montgomery, characteristically, later said that it was he who had pointed out the flaws in the plan to Eisenhower. Montgomery's biographer Nigel Hamilton goes further and insists that Montgomery was "alone" in having the "courage and conviction" to replace COSSAC's scheme with a better one, a claim more legitimately belonging to the field of hero worship than of history.[90] Montgomery, as ground force commander in the opening phase, was a major asset to Overlord, but it was Eisenhower who fleshed out the total plan, who secured the necessary landing craft to enlarge the assault, who fought for the additional landing in southern France over British objections, who approved any proposals for the landing itself, and who had the courage to order employment of the American airborne divisions despite the repeated assertions of his air commander that they would be massacred.

Eisenhower established SHAEF—Supreme Headquarters, Allied Expeditionary Force—in London on January 16, 1944. SHAEF was located first at 20 Grosvenor Square, but Eisenhower wanted to get away from the city, with its endless distractions, and on March 5 moved to Bushy Park, near Kingston, under tents and camouflage. He was able to secure the out-of-the-way rural retreat he had enjoyed before, Telegraph Cottage, a tiny slate-roofed house in a ten-acre wooded tract near Richmond Park, between Coombe Hill and Coombe Wood golf courses, with a lawn in back and a small rose garden. Here he could lounge around in an old shirt, GI slacks, a half-suede, half-leather jacket, and a pair of straw sandals left over from his days in Manila. Here he could work, relax, play a little golf, and read Western magazines to his heart's content. (Asked by Kay Summersby why he enjoyed cheap cowboy fiction, Eisenhower said, "I don't have to *think.*"[91])

"Our only hope," German General von Thoma was overheard to say as a prisoner, "is that they come where we can use the Army upon them."[92] In France, Belgium, and Holland, the Germans had fifty-eight divisions, of which ten were panzer, sixteen were "attack" and thirty-two "static" infantry, under Generalfeldmarschall Gerd von Rundstedt as *Oberbefehlshaber West* (Commander in Chief in the West) and Erwin Rommel as commander of Army Group B, reporting directly to Hitler and the army high command. If they could concentrate at the point where the landing came, either before or after it, then the landing could with good probability be shattered. To fight on the beach was Rommel's idea, to counterattack the lodgment area was von Rundstedt's, but either would have worked had it been implemented in sufficient force.

Our prime and overriding object was therefore to cause the Germans to disperse their strength, and this could be done by (1) keeping them in doubt as to where the landing would be, and (2) convincing them that the first assault was not the main one but would be followed by another and larger somewhere else. After the landing, a further means of preventing a German concentration of force was by (3) isolating the battlefield, and this could be done through air attacks on bridges, railyards, and moving columns, and through sabotage by the French Resistance. All these methods were used, and all of them—to the great relief of the Allied commanders—worked.

The British had been sharpening their skills at deception for some time, and had scored notable triumphs in North Africa. (A fine effort, though its success is disputed, was the planted false "going" map intended to lead Rommel at Alam Halfa into ground unsuitable for tanks.) They invented twenty-six imaginary divisions, and no less than twenty-one showed up in German intelligence estimates as genuine. By May 1944, the Germans thought there were seventy-one Allied divisions in the Mediterranean theater when there were actually only thirty-eight. The invasion of Sicily achieved tactical surprise in part through deceptions—like the celebrated "man who never was," the corpse left floating in the sea off Spain with false credentials and false documents—which caused them to keep substantial forces in the Balkans and divide their resources in Italy equally between Sicily, Sardinia, and Corsica.

The main preinvasion deception plan consisted of two parts, the first of which threatened an invasion of Scandinavia. This the Germans took very seriously indeed; they had twelve divisions in Norway and five in Denmark. These, as a result of what they thought were vigorous training exercises in Scotland by a nonexistent "Fourth Army," were put on a state of readiness in May 1944; an additional first-class division was sent to Norway and a reduced one to Denmark (that many more who would not be available in France). The second part of the plan, however, and the most important, was the threat of a massive attack on the Pas de Calais, two hundred miles east of the true landing place. Charles Cruikshank, in his *Deception in World War II,* describes it as "the largest, most elaborate, most carefully planned, most vital, and most successful of all the Allied deceptions."[93]

The base of it was an imaginary army group, theoretically commanded by George Patton, stationed in East Anglia and ready to pounce across the Channel. Its existence was confirmed by dummy installations, false radio traffic, and reports from the numerous German spies in England, who were all (conveniently) under British control. A bonus was provided by the breaking of the German codes that has come to be called Ultra, which enabled the British to monitor the progress of the deception measures by watching the German reactions. This was all beneficial beyond belief to the Allies. German Fifteenth Army, fifteen divisions in all, was in the Pas de Calais and it stayed there, waiting for an assault by fifty-seven divisions (forty-two were fictitious) that von Rundstedt believed he lacked the resources to resist. The Germans went on believing in a second invasion for weeks after the real one began, to our great gain in preponderance at the point of contact.[94]

The decision had yet to be made as to the invasion date. There were a number of constraints on this. We should ideally land at or near dawn, to allow the fleet to approach under cover of darkness and give the men ashore a full day to establish a beachhead. Since the Germans had covered the beaches between the high- and low-tide marks with steel obstacles, to rip apart the landing craft, it was compulsory to land at low tide despite the hazards of crossing the intervening sands under fire. A full moon would expose the fleet, but a partial one was needed by the paratroopers. The date should be late enough to permit maximum preparation but early enough to leave four months of campaigning before winter came. All these conditions could be met only three times in the spring of 1944: the first days of May and two periods of a few days each in the first and third weeks of June.

Eisenhower as always insisted on an atmosphere of confidence and optimism in his headquarters. He operated on the assumption that this was *the* major operation of the war and that if he stated his needs plainly and cogently enough, then they would be met. He insisted on having officers in the major commands whom he knew and trusted, even at the cost of denuding the Mediterranean (one he wanted but failed to get was Lucian Truscott as a corps commander). Eisenhower demanded that the bomber forces in England, both British and American, be used in support of the invasion during the months preceding it, though this contravened the deeply held convictions of their commanders, Harris and Spaatz. Eisenhower had his way, though he had to use the threat of resignation to get it, and he ordered Harris and Spaatz to concentrate on isolating the battlefield—the "transportation plan"—despite the latter's insistence that it would not work. The "transportation plan" *did* work; the battlefield *was* significantly isolated. Eisenhower had been right, and the fact that he held firm, writes Stephen Ambrose, "was perhaps his greatest single contribution to the success of Overlord."[95]

He had more than one occasion to exercise firmness. Among the most energetic arguments thus far provoked between the Americans and the British was that on the question of whether or not to support Overlord by invading southern France as well. Eisenhower badly wanted this done (Marshall's feelings were even stronger, and substantially reinforced Eisenhower's). Brooke and Churchill were opposed, bitterly opposed, to subordinating the Mediterranean—with what Churchill called "all its dazzling possibilities"—to an operation they believed to be hazardous and unnecessary. They argued (correctly) that it would not draw as many German divisions away from Eisenhower's front as would an active campaign in Italy, that (incorrectly) the Germans would fight an effective delaying action in the Rhone Valley and southern France would thus become a dead end.

The differences caused what Eisenhower said was "one of the longest-sustained arguments that I had with Prime Minister Churchill throughout the period of the war." At one point Churchill threatened "to go to the King and lay down the mantle of my high office." When it was over, and Eisenhower had prevailed, U.S. Ambassador John Winant said of Churchill that he had "never seen him so badly shaken."[96] For Churchill, this was a premonition of what it would feel like to be no longer senior partner in the Grand Alliance, to be no longer able to work his will.

The American reasoning was so far apart from the British that the two positions scarcely came into contact. In Marshall's view, this was the moment to put on the brakes at last in what he had always regarded as a waste of resources in a subsidiary theater. He and Eisenhower both believed that the port of Marseilles was essential to Overlord for at least three reasons: for supplying the armies that would otherwise be dependent on the Normandy beaches, for bringing fresh American formations more rapidly and directly from the United States, and (this was much in Eisenhower's thoughts) for enabling the French divisions we had at some expense been equipping in North Africa to participate in the liberation of their homeland. President Roosevelt supported Marshall and Eisenhower—"I always think of my early geometry," he cabled Churchill; "a straight line is the shortest distance between two points"—and Churchill had to give ground.

Eisenhower's intelligence sources told him that German defenses in southern France were weakly held and would be easily penetrated, which proved to be the case. As for the importance of Marseilles, the Americans again were right. It became SHAEF's major source of supply, and remained so until Antwerp came into full operation in January 1945. Between September and December 1944, more tonnage came in through southern France than through any other Allied port, and during the last three months of 1944 this amounted to over a third of the total unloaded by the Allies in Europe.[97] In standing up to the Prime Minister, Eisenhower had saved for Overlord the extra increment of power it would need.

But by far the most burdensome of Eisenhower's preinvasion decisions came in the final week. It concerned the employment of the two American airborne divisions, the 82d and the 101st. The exits from the westernmost American beach, code-named "Utah," led over causeways the Germans could easily interdict. General Bradley, commanding First U.S. Army in the assault, believed that an air drop behind Utah Beach to seize the exits from the causeways was central to the success of the landing. On May 29, Eisenhower got a letter from his air commander, Air Chief Marshal Sir Trafford Leigh-Mallory, recommending that the American parachute drop and glider landings be canceled as too dangerous.

The British airborne operation east of Caen Leigh-Mallory thought still to be sound, but he said that recent intelligence information indicated a German buildup in the American drop zone. He did not think that the results there would justify the cost, which he estimated as high as 70 percent in casualties, and the next day he called on Eisenhower to make his plea personally, speaking of the "futile slaughter" of two fine divisions. "It would be difficult," wrote Eisenhower, "to conceive of a more soul-wracking problem."[98]

He went to his tent alone to think it through, concluded that the American airborne attack must proceed, and called Leigh-Mallory to tell him so. (When the air drop took place, it was scattered by clouds and antiaircraft, but it accomplished its mission and casualties were only 5 to 8 percent; partly in result of it, on Utah Beach two regiments of the 4th Division had casualties of less than 4 percent.)[99]

Eisenhower had set the Day for early June, and throughout May his forces began to assemble in southern England. It required 54,000 men merely to maintain housekeeping for their marshaling areas, which were sealed off from the rest of the world and guarded by 2,000 counterintelligence agents; 4,500 new Army cooks had to be trained in order to feed them; 3,800 trucks transported them and hauled their supplies. Final rations and ammunition were issued, maps distributed, briefings completed, and units broken down into boatloads for the move to the ships. This last began on May 30, and by June 3 nearly all the troops had been loaded. Eisenhower used a figure of speech to describe his armed host that others have adopted since: "a coiled spring . . . a great human spring coiled for the moment when its energy should be released and it would vault the English Channel."[100]

> For now sits expectation in the air
> And hides a sword, from hilts unto the point . . .

◆

Southwick House, a mansion with extensive grounds, lay in the lee of the downs above Portsmouth. This was the headquarters of Admiral Sir Bertram H. Ramsay, naval commander for the invasion, and here on the first of June, in tents and caravans under the trees, Eisenhower established SHAEF Advance, where he would stay until the decision to go or not to go was made. Weather was the concern that demanded attention above all else. Twice daily, Eisenhower and his commanders met with the meteorologists, headed by Group Captain James M. Stagg, whom the general described as a "dour but canny Scot."[101]

The weather conferences took place in the senior officers' mess of Southwick House, a room Stagg said remained vivid in his memory a quarter century later. It had once been a library but now the bookshelves were bare, the tables had been pushed aside, and easy chairs and couches were arranged in roughly parallel arcs. Two or three other chairs faced them, the one nearest the door invariably occupied by the Supreme Commander. Eisenhower would call them to order and then say, "Well, Stagg, what have you for us this time?"

Stagg was in a quandary. The forecasters who reported to him were organized in a half-dozen centers, differing in nationality, in branch of the service, and in technique; not surprisingly, they more often than not differed in their predictions, which it was Stagg's duty to reconcile. The Americans had more confidence in long-range forecasting than he did and, worse, at first the U.S. team at strategic air force headquarters was determinedly optimistic about the critical period ahead.

Stagg was not. He decided to conceal the divided nature of the counsel he was receiving and stick to his own convictions. "There goes six foot two of Stagg," said an admiral, "and six feet one of gloom." Since mid-April, Eisenhower had been asking for weekly forecasts, so that he could get a feel of what to expect and then test it against the outcome, and his confidence in Stagg's restraint and precision had been growing. This was well, for when Stagg looked at his charts in the first days of June—with their isobars, their fronts, their highs and lows—he did not like what he saw, not in the least.

The weather situation over the British Isles and the northeast Atlantic was very disturbed and complex. A series of three low-pressure depressions was strung out between Scotland and Newfoundland, and an anticyclone it had been hoped might act as a bumper against them was weakening and giving way. At the moment Stagg reported this (the 9:30 P.M. conference of Saturday, June 3), the skies over Portsmouth were clear and the air calm, but Stagg expected heavy clouds, low visibility, high winds, and drenching rain to arrive soon and remain through Wednesday.

Even the American optimists had come around to this dark view and Stagg, for once, was able to report unanimity. Though D-Day had been scheduled for June 5, after hearing Stagg out and consulting the others, Eisenhower postponed it for twenty-four hours. (Stagg thereby earned his pay and the honors he was later given; Monday morning the weather along the French coast was just as bad as he had predicted: Strong onshore winds would have made the landings almost impossible and a continuous sheet of low cloud would have obscured the targets of bombing and naval gunfire—well done, Stagg!)

Yet Eisenhower was born to be lucky and his luck was holding. When Stagg rose to face them Sunday night, he had a surprise to share; "since I presented the forecast last evening," he said, "some rapid and unexpected developments have occurred over the north Atlantic." The rain that was at that moment lashing their windows would stop in two or three hours. A vigorous cold front from one of the depressions had pushed east more quickly and farther to the south than could have been foreseen. It would pass through the Channel that night and early Monday, and be followed by an interlude of only partly cloudy skies and decreased winds.

They questioned him closely about what would happen later in the week and how great his confidence was (he was firm about the latter but insisted that the former was still beyond calculation) and they met again on Monday at 4:30 A.M., all in battle dress except Montgomery, who was wearing a fawn-colored turtleneck sweater and light corduroy trousers. The room was quiet, faces grave. "Go ahead, Stagg," said Eisenhower.

"Gentlemen," said Stagg, "no substantial changes have taken place since last time but as I see it the little that has changed is in the direction of optimism." The "interlude" would extend into Tuesday afternoon, winds would be moderate, visibility good. "The relief that statement brought into the room was a joy to behold," wrote Stagg. "Immediately after I had finished the tension seemed to evaporate and the Supreme Commander and his colleagues became as new men."[102]

Now sits the wind fair, and we will aboard . . .

But it was up to Eisenhower. If there was to be any further postponement, it would have to be for two weeks, until a favorable condition of tides and moonlight would recur; security might be compromised, morale dampened. (Two weeks later came the storm in the Channel that irreparably damaged the American artificial port—Eisenhower luck.) Finally, after polling them again, he spoke the words only he could speak: "O.K. Let's go." The subordinates leapt to their tasks and within less than a minute the room was empty except for their commander.

"The outflow of the others and his sudden isolation were symbolic," writes Stephen Ambrose. "A minute earlier he had been the most powerful man in the world. Upon his word the fate of millions of men, not to mention great nations, depended. The moment he uttered the word, however, he was powerless. For the next two or three days there was almost nothing he could do that would in any way change anything. The invasion could not be stopped, not by him, not by anyone. . . . He could now only sit and wait."[103]

There was something in the air that D-Day eve, something akin to confidence yet beyond it, something felt by the soldiers, sailors, and airmen in their thousands, something more resembling an awareness—in the words of General Morgan—"that there was arising a surge that would not be denied," something that "spoke through the lips of General Eisenhower when at dead of a June night he said, 'Go,' and it went."[104]

Ambrose believes that by this time the Supreme Commander had become more adept at killing time. Eisenhower after breakfast visited Portsmouth to see British soldiers board their landing craft. He played checkers with his aide Harry Butcher and got a draw out of what had looked like a certain loss. They told each other dog-eared political stories and in the afternoon he met with the press. "The nonchalance," wrote were hearing the largest airborne armada hitherto assembled, and that it was headed south.

In the west country, in a small town in Devon, a ten-year-old boy named John Keegan had been making the acquaintance of the Americans, with their astonishing equipment and their carefree way of driving a jeep with one booted foot hanging casually over the side. He came down into the garden with his parents when the roar began. "It seemed as if every aircraft in the world was in flight," Keegan wrote years later, "as wave followed wave without intermission. . . . Long after the last had passed from view and the thunder of their passage had died into the stillness of the night . . . we remained transfixed on the spot where we stood, gripped by a wild surmise at what the power, majesty and menace of the great migratory flight could portend.

"Next day we knew. The Americans had gone."[108]

In Wiltshire, near towns with names like Chilton Foliat and Crooked Soley, there was an airfield that had filled them with the noise and bustle of the Americans who made practice parachute jumps in the nearby parks. But that night the bar of the Stag's Head in Chilton Foliat was strangely silent, nobody but the local regulars nursing a mild and bitter; the bottled ale and the rationed whiskey stayed on the shelves. At closing time, the landlord locked up, washed a few glasses, and went outside to shut in his chickens. Suddenly the airfield came to life as the transports rose up over the elms of the park in twos and threes, then dozens, and then joined others coming from the north in hundreds. He called to his wife to come listen. "This is it," he said.

Down on the Channel, at Saint Alban's Head, a coast guard watcher named Percy Wallace had come off duty after an extraordinary day. For weeks now, the panorama he could survey with his field glasses—from Weymouth and Portland in the west past the mouth of the Solent and the Isle of Wight to the east—had been filling with ships. Portland harbor was black with them, until they began to overflow into Weymouth Bay and destroyers were sent out to screen them while hundreds more came in.

Then that morning they had all departed, more than a thousand of them, together with battleships and heavy cruisers that steamed up from the west, and still another fleet from Southampton emerged from the Solent and turned south past the Isle of Wight. "Wallace stood on the head of the cliff," wrote David Howarth, "entranced and exalted by a pageant of splendor which nobody had ever seen before, and nobody, it is certain, will ever see again. Before evening, the last of the ships had gone, hull down on the southern horizon, and once more the sea was empty."

Wallace was making his way homeward when the sound in the sky began. "This is it," he said to his wife.

Butcher, "with which he announced that we were attacking in the morning and the feigned nonchalance with which the reporters absorbed it was a study in suppressed emotion which would interest any psychologist."

Eisenhower got a phone call from Beetle Smith at SHAEF Main that de Gaulle was acting up again and refusing to make a broadcast tomorrow. Before dinner he wrote out for himself, as he had done before each of his previous invasions, a statement to be issued if it should not succeed: "Our landings in the Cherbourg-Havre area have failed to gain a satisfactory foothold and I have withdrawn the troops. . . . If any blame or fault attaches to the attempt it is mine alone."[105] And at six o'clock he drove to an airfield near Newbury, where men of the 101st Airborne Division were loading up. These were the paratroopers Leigh-Mallory had told him were going to suffer 70 percent casualties.

Goronwy Rees of *The Spectator*, who was there, said that over the years he had watched many generals address their troops before battle and had noted the various styles—flamboyant, belligerent, mock simple—none of which had seemed to him really successful in overcoming the uneasy awareness that some of these men were going to die and the general was not. Eisenhower walked among them, talking and listening; one from Texas, who owned a ranch, offered him a job after the war. They told him not to worry. Rees realized later that the led were reinforcing their leader as much as the other way around.

"General Eisenhower spoke to each of the crews individually," Rees wrote, "joked with them and almost always asked them where their home was, and as one heard them say, 'Kansas, sir,' 'Iowa, sir,' 'Missouri, sir,' and the States of the Union answered in turn, like a roll of battle honours, one was suddenly aware that this general and these men were intimately associated in some great romantic enterprise, whose significance could not be wholly grasped by an Englishman, and yet one felt it to be of profound importance, in ways one could not quite penetrate then, to oneself as well as to them."[106]

Eisenhower waited until the last C-47 had left the runway and then turned with a sag in his shoulders and, so one reporter thought, tears in his eyes. "Well," he said, "it's on."[107]

> *O God of battles! steel my soldiers' hearts;*
> *Possess them not with fear; take from them now*
> *The sense of reckoning . . .*

All over southern England that night people wakened to a sound that filled the sky; over London it lasted two and a half hours. They had by that time become practiced at distinguishing the noises airplanes make, but this was different, not the Germans, not Bomber Command outward bound at dusk and returning at dawn. Some knew or guessed that they

And gentlemen in England now abed
Shall think themselves accurs'd they were not here . . .

By morning everyone knew. Berlin radio began broadcasting frag-
mentary reports at six-thirty, though in London the first formal announcement, and a guarded one at that, did not come until nine. Services were
held in St. Paul's and Westminster Abbey. "Some people had a sense of
anticlimax," writes Howarth; "it seemed wrong that life should go on as
usual." In the factories, where the workers were mainly women—few of
whom did not have husbands, lovers, sons, or brothers they had not heard
from recently—many wept over their work.

The House of Commons was packed, but tradition must be served.
First, question time: A Communist member called for the abolition of
banks; an independent asked the secretary of the treasury to make certain that "office cleaners" be referred to thenceforward as such and
not as "charwomen" or "charladies." Finally, Churchill rose and, savoring the suspense, talked for ten minutes about Rome's fall the day before.[109]

Then he proclaimed the invasion.

"I have also to announce to the House," said Churchill, "that during
the night and the early hours of this morning the first of the series of
landings upon the European continent has taken place. . . . So far the
commanders who are engaged report that everything is proceeding according to plan. And what a plan!" He described the vast size of the fleet
and the air umbrella over it; he mentioned the airborne landings, the
silencing of shore batteries, the probability that surprise had been
achieved, and the probability for the enemy of many surprises in store.
"The battle that has now begun will grow constantly in scale and intensity
for many weeks to come, and I shall not speculate upon its course. This
I may say however. Complete unity prevails. . . . There is a brotherhood
in arms between us and our friends of the United States."[110]

President Roosevelt had spent the weekend at Pa Watson's home near
Charlottesville, Virginia. Grace Tully again noticed his tenseness and
preoccupation. He fingered his Book of Common Prayer, looking for
words appropriate to the occasion. Monday he returned to Washington
and that evening made a broadcast about the fall of Rome, the great city,
embodiment of Christianity and now of Allied victory. During the night
he kept in touch with the Pentagon. At three-thirty the news was official,
and at four the White House operator began waking staff members to tell
them of it. By the time of his regular press conference Tuesday morning,
the President was cheerful, if "a little sleepy," he said. That night on the
radio he led the nation in prayer for its sons—"Lead them straight and
true; give strength to their arms, stoutness to their hearts, steadfastness in

their faith"—and for those at home who would have to bear the travail and sorrows to come.[111]

◆

Sorrows on Omaha Beach there were aplenty. Let us follow two companies of the 116th Infantry, Able and Baker, as they came in on their assigned sector opposite Vierville, known as Dog Green. At 4:30 A.M., Able unloaded from the British transport *Empire Javelin* into LCAs and LCVPs and began the two-hour, eleven-mile run in to the shore. The sea was choppy; they were drenched with spray, many became seasick, and the landing craft took in cresting waves that had to be pumped or bailed out in helmets. They passed men in the water with life preservers or on rafts, fortunate to have escaped from the floatable tanks that had failed to float in the rough seas (if a tank went down, the crew had twenty seconds in which to abandon it). At about five thousand yards out, they came under artillery fire and at a thousand yards Boat No. 5 of Able Company was hit dead on and foundered; six men drowned and the other twenty-one paddled around until picked up by the Navy. They were the lucky ones. At a hundred yards, a shell hit Boat No. 3 and killed two men; taking to the water as it sank, another dozen drowned. That left Able Company with five boats.

Boat No. 6 simply disappeared. No one knows what happened to it; there were no survivors, only corpses of about half its complement found next day along the beach. When Boat No. 7, carrying a medical section, lowered its ramp, two German machine guns opened up and every man aboard was killed instantly. The men in Boat No. 1 jumped off in water over their heads and, weighed down by equipment, many drowned; the others clung to the sides of the boat to stay afloat. Same story with Boat No. 4. From Boat No. 2, Lieutenant Edward Tidrick took a bullet in the throat as he left the ramp and staggered onto the beach, ordering PFC Leo J. Nash to advance with wire cutters. Nash had no wire cutters. Giving the order had caused Tidrick to raise up on his hands, and Nash watched as machine-gun bullets ripped through Tidrick's body. By the end of ten minutes, all the sergeants of Able Company were either dead or wounded and only one officer was alive, Lieutenant Elijah Nance, who had two bad wounds, in the heel and stomach. Not a shot had been fired at the Germans. The right wing of the assault, as Gordon Harrison put it, had "all but disintegrated."

Baker Company was supposed to come in on the same part of the beach a half hour later. Smoke and dust raised by mortar fire and gunfire obscured it from them until the last moment, when the landing-craft coxswains—seeing the debacle ashore and the blood, dead, and dying in the water—wanted to veer aside. Captain Ettore V. Zappacosta drew his Colt .45 and said, "By God, you'll take this boat straight in." Gallant but foolhardy; within minutes he was dead; only one man from his boat got out of it unharmed, and managed this mostly by crouching in the water for two hours behind a piece of driftwood in the advancing tide. He and a rifleman from Able Company dragged ashore the bodies of men they could recognize; the unrecognized they left to the sea. Only one other boat from Baker Company came in straight on Dog Green. It foundered and all aboard—a British coxswain and thirty American infantrymen—were killed. Of them nothing more is known.

Other Baker Company boats turned to the left and right. Those on the latter landed in a cove under the promontory called Pointe du Hoc and joined a ranger battalion whose mission was to neutralize the heavy coastal defense guns on top of it. (They succeeded; the guns had been moved inland, where the rangers found them unguarded and destroyed them.) Those who turned left did relatively well; some encountered gaps in the intensity of German fire and worked their way through it. Seven men under Technical Sergeant William Pearce—whose lieutenant, badly wounded, had handed him a map and compass, the symbols of authority —had wiped out a German hedgerow line beyond a draw in the bluffs and walked, exhilarated with success, into Vierville, where they found Baker Company's Lieutenant Walter Taylor. Taylor had come in on a beach opposite Hamel-au-Prêtre, miraculously free of fire. Pearce told him that his own officer was out of action. "I guess that makes me company commander," Taylor said. He took a head count: twenty-four, including himself. "That ought to be enough," said Taylor. "Follow me."

There are such men, and by no other sign shall you know them except that in combat they show no fear and seemingly without hesitation go forward. "We followed him," said Pearce later, "because there was nothing else to do." As far as they could have known, the invasion was a failure and they were advancing on their own. Taylor took them inland. Joined by fifteen rangers, they beat off three truckloads of German infantry who suddenly appeared and deployed in the fields around them. By dark they were near the village of Louvieres, a mile and a half from the beach and almost a half mile out in front of the rest of the U.S. Army, and a runner had to be sent to tell them that what remained of their battalion was reassembling closer to the sea, and that they should fall back. There are such men.[112]

The situation was not quite so bad elsewhere on Omaha Beach as it was on Dog Green, but it was bad enough. The coast here is a shallow crescent almost four miles long and there was a tidal current pulling eastward that caused boats to land in the wrong places, off by as much as a hundred to a thousand yards. Maps had been made and descriptions given of the German fortifications in each sector, but they were useless anywhere else. The heavy naval gunfire was comforting, but the men in the first waves quickly discovered that it had done little damage to the enemy defenses. Neither had the aerial bombardment a half hour earlier by over three hundred Liberators from Eighth Air Force; of their thirteen thousand bombs, all had fallen inland, some by as far as three miles. Only five of the thirty-two floatable tanks made it ashore (the rest were swamped), which together with losses to the sixty-four loaded in LCTs meant that strength in tanks had been reduced by a third even before they landed.

Only a third of the engineer demolition teams arrived on their proper locations, and these had lost much of their equipment (of their sixteen bulldozers, only three became operational on the beach). Their marking buoys and poles were missing, so that when by heroic efforts they cleared six lanes through the obstacles, only one of these could be marked. (This meant that landing craft of the successive waves would not know where to come in on the rising tide and might be torn open by the obstacles now underwater.) Fifteen officers and men of the engineers, from colonel to private, were awarded the DSC for what they did this day: They had suffered 41 percent casualties, most of them in the first half hour.

Surveying Omaha Beach from its western end, the German commander of the fortifications on Pointe et Raz de la Percée concluded that the invasion had been halted in its tracks. He could see ten tanks and many other vehicles burning. He could see the dead and wounded lying on the sand; those of the Americans who were still unhurt could be seen huddled behind the gravel shingle, or any other piece of cover they could find. He thought the fire from his own position and from the artillery had been excellent, and had caused the heavy American losses. The German 916th Regiment, in the center of the division whose responsibility included the beach, reported to higher headquarters that the landing had been repulsed, though they added that their own losses were mounting and that they needed reinforcements.[113]

Omaha Beach hung on the edge of disaster but did not fall over it, and the reasons why are worth assessing. Partly it was a matter of pure weight; men and machines were being sacrificed but there were many more of both behind them. Partly it was the thinness of the German line; the reinforcements they needed did not get to them, or not in time or in sufficient numbers. Some landing craft in the later waves bravely tried to ram their way through the obstacles, and enough of them made it. The naval gunfire was critically important, as it became increasingly accurate and daring.

Nine U.S. and three British destroyers under Captain Harry Sanders, USN, decided on their own to close the beach until their bottoms scraped and to blaze away with their gun batteries at every target they could see. (One group of Germans, waving a white flag, accomplished the unusual feat of surrendering to destroyer *McCook*.) Inspecting the concrete pillboxes and gun positions after they had been overrun, the chief of staff of the 1st Division (which landed left of the 29th) concluded that without the naval gunfire we could never have crossed the beaches.[114] But there was another factor that made a difference, and it is less easy to explain.

One by one, first as individuals and then as groups never larger than a company, the men pinned down and lying prone behind the shingle began to get on their feet and move inland. Leaders of uncommon valor urged them on. No one knows how many groups failed to make it, but it is clear that many tried, and that roughly a dozen succeeded. A lieutenant stood up and said, to no one in particular, "Are you going to lay there and get killed, or get up and do something about it?" A private tried to blow a gap in the barbed wire and died in the attempt; the lieutenant who followed him detonated the charge. The first man to enter the gap was killed, but then others followed, in twos and threes, until what was left of their company had passed through.

The intention had been to leave the beach by way of the draws, but these the Germans still covered with fire, so that making a virtue of necessity, handfuls of Americans went up over the bluffs and attacked the German positions from the flank and rear. These men deserve a special place in memory. They had few heavy weapons and no artillery support, but they put a crack in the Atlantic Wall that could not be closed.[115]

During the afternoon, German artillery and automatic-weapons fire continued but with diminished fury. As the tide receded, the engineers went to work again on the obstacles and cleared five large and six small boat channels. By evening, while still being shot at, they had bulldozed five exits from the beach and built a new road inland. Later waves of landing craft followed apace. Tanks began to move south, artillery was being landed in strength, and by dark the better part of five infantry regiments from the 29th and 1st divisions was ashore and had formed a continuous line from southwest of Vierville to east of Colleville. This was short of their planned objectives, and unloading was behind schedule, but momentum had been regained and casualties and matériel losses, if still high, were falling. Omaha Beach had been secured.

I have taken this single action to stand for what happened on D-Day because it was so fiercely fought and so narrowly won, but of course it was only a stanza in a poem of epic proportions. The American airborne drop had been an epic in its own right: 13,000 paratroopers in 822 transport planes, coming in across the Cotentin peninsula from the west to jump between 1:15 and 1:30 A.M. on drop zones behind the second American beach, called Utah.

Flying in the lead serial, Jim Gavin—now a brigadier general and assistant division commander of the 82d—could see from the open door the stream of aircraft behind him as far as the eye could reach. Sporadic antiaircraft fire came up at them from the Channel Islands; it increased in intensity when they passed the coast, and one minute inland they ran

into a heavy cloud bank that obscured landmarks and broke up the formations. The 82d jumped on schedule but in disarray; some ended up miles
distant. Fortunately, the greater portion came down near one of their
objectives, the village of Sainte-Mère-Église. Lieutenant Colonel Edward
C. Krause hit the ground on exactly the spot he had picked from an aerial
photograph for his CP. But the most reassuring thing that night was to
land, as General Gavin did, near a group of cows, whose benign presence
indicated that the field you were in had not been mined.

In the little village of Azeville, a German soldier named Erwin Müller
was standing guard near a garden gate when the whole sky to the south
and west filled with parachutes, and he knew in a moment that Germany
had lost the war. During the night, a friend of his was killed and another
wounded; somewhere he could hear a man screaming. After dawn, he and
his sergeant captured two Americans, one of whom said, "Say, how far is
it to Paris, fella?" and offered him a piece of chocolate. A third American
was badly wounded; when he died they folded his arms across his chest
and a small group of Germans and Americans said the Lord's Prayer for
him in their respective languages. A week later, Müller himself was captured, and so returned alive after the war to his wife in Denmark, where
he lived.

The paratroopers identified themselves to each other in the dark by
snapping small toy crickets, and this way groups began to form. The
largest from the 82d was gathered by General Gavin, who from a scout's
report of a railway embankment now knew where he was and what to do
next, which was hold the bridges on the Merderet River, across which the
Germans would have to come if they counterattacked, as they surely
would. Sainte-Mère-Église had meanwhile been occupied by a group
under Colonel Krause, first town in France to be liberated, an honor it still
celebrates in an annual fête on the sixth of June. Krause found the cable
that connected Cherbourg to Paris and cut it. He sent a report—"I have
secured Ste. Mère-Église"—and distributed his forces to organize a defensive position around it. By the end of D-Day, the 82d controlled about 40
percent of its infantry and 10 percent of its artillery, and was strongly
positioned around Sainte-Mère-Église, but it was not yet in contact with
the 101st or with the seaborne landing at Utah Beach.[116]

These two, however, were in contact with each other. The drop of the
101st was almost as badly scattered as the 82d's, but they had somewhat
better luck in assembling large groups. The Germans had dispersed their
own units, small packets in isolated villages and strongpoints, so that there
took place numbers of individual and confused firefights, further broken
up by the ubiquitous hedgerows of the Normandy *bocage* country. On
both sides, immediate knowledge was limited to a few hundred yards. The
Americans had at least the advantage of knowing their missions, and how
these fitted together, and they set about accomplishing them. Within

hours they had seized or cleared the exits from the causeways across an inundated marsh behind Utah Beach, and before dawn they had captured the lock that controlled the flow of water into the flooded area. By the end of D-Day, the 101st had assembled only about 2,500 of its 6,600 men who had jumped, but they had accomplished the essential mission of clearing the way for the assault from the sea. The airborne and the seaborne forces met at 11:05 A.M.[117]

It can be argued that the scattering of the paratroopers all over the landscape had a useful side effect: It thoroughly confused the Germans, and it brought about what David Howarth called "a gigantic and lethal game of hide-and-seek," fought out over ten square miles between ten thousand Americans and perhaps five thousand Germans. "In this unique contest," writes Howarth, "the Americans knew what was happening, but few of them knew where they were; the Germans knew where they were, but none of them knew what was happening."[118] German communications broke down; their telephones would go dead, their dispatch riders would drive off into the night and disappear. If a kind of torpor seems to have overcome the initial German reactions to the invasion, one reason for it was their inability to get a clear picture of what was going on.

The landings on Utah Beach—by the 4th Division in column of regiments on a two-battalion front—went comparatively well. Smoke and dust from the naval bombardment again obscured the landmarks, and the boats came in two thousand yards south of where they were supposed to, which was that much to the good, since the place they did land at was less heavily defended. By H+3 hours, the beach was clear and the later waves of landing craft were coming in routinely, harassed from time to time by sporadic German artillery fire. Though not all the D-Day objectives had been reached by day's end, the backup forces from the transports were coming ashore virtually unhindered and on schedule. Eisenhower's "soul-wracking" decision to commit the airborne divisions had been handsomely rewarded.

◆

Forty years afterward, the Normandy campaign is still being argued over. Was it well or badly done on our side? Did the Allied planners have any awareness of what they were getting into in the *bocage,* the hedgerows in which the Americans entangled themselves? (Each side believed the hedgerow country to favor the other, but both agreed it was a miserable place to fight.) Could the Germans, had it not been for their demented Führer's reluctance to commit reserves, have conducted an even more resourceful defense than they did? Was it a "failure" on Montgomery's part not to capture Caen promptly, as he had asserted he would do? Did the eventual American breakout to the west proceed according to Montgomery's prior design, or had he seriously meant his own attack east of

Caen to be the major effort? When subsequently the Germans were very nearly surrounded near Falaise, could the gap have been closed and their entire Seventh and Fifth panzer armies have been trapped? Ultimate success has not prevented these points from remaining in dispute.

This was Montgomery's battle and he won it, but reading his mind on such questions as the above is made difficult by two of his psychological quirks that did not accord well with one another. Before an action began, he liked to make bold predictions as to its outcome; this was part of his way of gingering people up, of creating an aura of victory to come. In the aftermath, however, he liked to claim that everything had gone exactly as he had intended. When the two did not jibe, as ofttimes happened, the observer was compelled to conclude either that Montgomery's original plan had not been what he said it was, or that something other than the original plan had been followed. On occasion, the documentation permits either or both interpretations, and in whichever case Montgomery comes out looking the worse for it.

On D-Day he looked just fine; his own airdrop and landings had been near letter-perfect. The mission of the British paratroopers was to wipe out a coastal defense battery that commanded the British beach near Ouistreham, to protect the beachhead flank by destroying five bridges over the Dives River, and to capture intact two bridges over the Orne that would be needed in the advance. All were accomplished with finesse, casualties few. The three British (one Canadian) seaborne landings were somewhat more expeditious than the American and at lighter cost—partly because they employed specialized armor (which the Americans had spurned) to clear minefields and reduce pillboxes—but the fine-grain detail was no different: landing craft disabled, trucks and tanks set afire, bodies riddled and blown apart.

There was no easy way ashore that morning. By nightfall, the British penetration was wider and farther inland than the American, and a heavier body of armored formations was building up, but Caen had not fallen and already there were signs that attempts to take it would be hotly contested. By the end of the first week, despite their grievous losses, the Allies had linked up and achieved a bridgehead fifty miles long and eight to ten miles deep. In the week that followed, the Americans—VII Corps under Major General J. Lawton Collins—cut across the base of the Cotentin and by the end of the month they had occupied Cherbourg.

To have secured a large and continuous lodgment and a major (though heavily demolished) port in a matter of weeks was a fine thing and a great victory, but from long back the SHAEF staff and commanders had realized that the period ahead would be even more alive with dangers than the landing itself. They *must* somehow find a way out of the beachhead, for it could contain only a certain amount of troops and stores, and as time passed, an inescapable arithmetic would increase the number of

Germans who could be brought to face them. Most to be feared was "stabilization," a stalemate degenerating into fixed-position warfare on the mind-chilling model of World War I, and this was a very real possibility taken seriously by, among others, Omar Bradley and George Patton.[119]

The Allied advantage lay less in infantry than in air power and mobility, and to exploit these there must also be a breakout somewhere. But where? Logic said to the east, in the British sector, where lay open country usable by tanks and roads that led to Paris. But logic said the same thing to the Germans, who considered the British to be the more menacing opponent anyhow, and so the Wehrmacht put the bulk of its power there and fought with grim determination. Montgomery made three attempts to crack through and encircle Caen; all failed.

His chief, Brooke, did not believe that the Americans could achieve what Montgomery had been unable to. "I know the bocage country well from my boyhood," Brooke wrote to Tedder, "and they will never get through it." Brooke was wrong. The breakout when it came was a revelation in the Word According to Liddell Hart, the "expanding torrent" of his between-the-wars writing and lecturing,[120] a brilliant exercise in blitzkrieg that determined the outcome of the European war and still dominates the maps of it, a great branching tree of American divisions rampaging through France, an exultant Patton at their head. But sight should not be lost of Bradley, who planned it—Bradley, pacing the wooden floor of a tent at his headquarters near Colombières, in which he had mounted an eight-foot map of the beachhead, "scribbling boundaries, penciling roads, coloring the river lines,"[121] until the outlines emerged of a detailed scheme in which Collins and VII Corps, aided by a massive air bombardment, would punch a hole in the front, and the rest of First Army, fifteen divisions strong, would stream through it behind him. There are some battles that might have been lost and victory still won, but not this one: This one tipped the balance that could not be restored, and afforded Rundstedt his famous reply to Hitler's headquarters when they asked him what to do now: "Make peace, you idiots! What else can you do?"[122]

The air bombardment on July 25 was a mess (it killed General McNair and many other Americans), but it stunned and disoriented the Germans, and that afternoon—even though the infantry at first bogged down and Bradley grew discouraged—Collins made the critical decision to commit the armor; two days later, one of his division commanders reported: "This thing has busted wide open."[123] On August 1, two entire corps (VIII and XV) of the newly activated Third Army under Patton were pouring through Avranches at the base of Brittany and across a single bridge at Pontaubault—"one of those things which cannot be done," wrote Patton, "but was"—and riding with them in his jeep, he shouted with delight each time he ran off one map and had to start using another. "Compared to war," he wrote in his diary that day, "all [other] human activities are futile, if you like war as I do."[124] He was in his element and on his way, and nothing would stop him now until, quite literally, he ran out of fuel.

Bradley believed, and according to his posthumously published memoir went on believing to the end, that this had all along been Montgomery's object: to draw the Germans toward his left flank so that the Americans could deliver an overwhelming blow on the right; if such is so, it was self-denying on Montgomery's part, and all honor to him for carrying through on it. But Bradley—who now commanded an American army group containing the armies of Patton and Hodges—suspected that Montgomery had several other purposes in sight, among them the possibility that his own third and final attack might in fact become the breakout, and this eventuality Montgomery had clearly underscored to others at the time with his customary sauciness. The "others" included Brooke, whom he had no reason to deceive, and most inopportunely Eisenhower, who took Montgomery's professions of high intent at face value and got up hopes for decisive results which then faded and dissolved in the absence of their realization.

Montgomery later claimed that Eisenhower's aroused expectations were caused by military inexperience and incomprehension of the Plan, which is tantamount to saying that Eisenhower was a fool to have believed him, not a firm base on which to build a command relationship. Eisenhower was more than a little angry at being let down—Bradley says "red as a hot coal"—and Bradley believed that the Supreme Commander would have dismissed Montgomery there and then if he thought Churchill and Brooke would have allowed it.[125]

Liddell Hart thought that the one American general who really understood deep armored exploitation and the importance of speed better even than Patton did was John S. Wood—"P" Wood, for "professor," from West Point days when he tutored other cadets—commander of 4th Armored Division, the first to drive through Avranches and on into Brittany. Wood wanted to pivot eastward to Chartres or Orléans, and beyond them to Paris, but his assigned mission was to take the port at Lorient, which was the wrong job for an armored division, and the Allied command could not readjust quickly enough to turn him loose from it. Both Montgomery and Eisenhower realized by this time that Brittany was not going to require more than a corps of Patton's Third Army, the rest of which should do as Wood wanted, but the realization somehow failed to be converted into orders, Wood was immobilized, and not until mid-August was 4th Armored—among the most reckless, confident, and aggressive of divisions —set free and headed east. "It was," Wood told Liddell Hart later, "one of the colossally stupid decisions of the war."[126]

By then, Patton had turned his XV Corps east and told its commander not to be surprised if orders came to go northeast or even north. Patton, whose battlefield nostrils were as sensitive as any known, could smell the chance to trap the Germans west of the Seine by a wide envelopment, and so could Bradley, who told a visitor (Secretary of the Treasury Morgenthau): "This is an opportunity that comes to a commander not more than once in a century."

It had been brought about by Hitler's determination not only to keep his Seventh Army in Normandy but also to have Fifth Panzer Army attack from Mortain toward Avranches and cut Patton off, a decision that cost Hitler his hold on France. Ultra picked up and decoded his order on August 3 and both Bradley and Patton knew of it, so that when the counterattack came on the night of August 6–7, it ran into fierce U.S. resistance and the encirclement continued. By the eleventh, the Germans were beginning to pull back, and by the sixteenth, Hitler had (with great reluctance) been persuaded to authorize both armies' withdrawal from an exposed salient in which they were being gripped from three sides at once.[127]

Should they—or *could* they?—have been prevented from escaping? Much ink has been spilled over this issue. Bradley ordered Patton, who was coming from the south, to halt at Argentan, and Patton told his diary that he believed this order to have originated with Montgomery, who was coming from the north. (Bradley said not so: It was his idea.) Some hundred thousand Germans were being caught in the Falaise Pocket, as it came to be called, and the first fact to be noted is that not all of them did escape, at best from twenty to forty thousand, of whom most were service and not combat troops, and they left behind virtually all of their equipment (not only tanks and artillery but machine guns and radios and field kitchens). The Germans surrendered in droves (one of their sergeants shot a company commander who tried to halt this), thousands a day, so many the Allies could not count them, perhaps fifty thousand in all, including three general officers. Inside the pocket, the devastation caused by Allied artillery and fighter-bombers was awesome: Approximately ten thousand German dead were counted amidst the smoldering wreckage of their guns and vehicles—"as if," wrote one American officer who could compare this with World War I, "an avenging angel had swept the area bent on destroying all things German."[128]

The Americans thought Montgomery's move from the north to close the gap a poor performance; he did not give it his best effort, and he seemed more intent on squeezing the Germans out of the pocket than on containing them within it. But Bradley never denied that the decision to halt Patton was his, and over the years he offered a number of explanations for it (misleading intelligence, lack of sufficient force, need to avoid friendly units' firing on each other). All are somewhat short of satisfactory, since they fail to include the more probable possibility: namely, that Bradley did not want to tangle with a buzzing swarm of angry Germans.

"I much preferred," he wrote, "a solid shoulder at Argentan to the possibility of a broken neck at Falaise." The experienced British combat writer Max Hastings gives Bradley credit for having the good sense not to move in precipitately on a trapped, desperate, and deadly enemy. "If the man outside the thicket," writes Hastings, "knows that the wounded tiger within it is bleeding to death, he would be foolish to step inside merely to hasten the collection of the trophy. If this was indeed Bradley's reasoning, he was almost certainly correct."[129]

The two opponents had taken each other's measure thus far, and the phenomenon had to be faced—as men so far removed from one another as Patton and Churchill both faced it—that the Americans and British were not as good infantry fighters as the Germans. "The Germans *liked* soldiering," said one of Montgomery's officers. "We didn't." An American statistical study showed that man for man, the Germans inflicted at least 50 percent more casualties on us than we did on them, and this was true whether they were attacking or defending, whether they won or lost. It is what General von Thoma meant by wanting to "use the Army" upon us; his was not an idle boast. They seemed to have an inexhaustible supply of colonels who could form battle groups out of whatever soldiers they found at hand, and of noncoms and junior officers who could lead them in platoons and companies. Not always, but again and again, a small group of Germans with a tank and a field gun or two would hang in there beyond the point of reasonableness or necessity and bring a well-organized Allied attack to a halt. To repeat, this was the best army in the world.

Also, their weapons were better. Their light machine gun, the Spandau MG-42, was more portable than our Browning 30-caliber and had a far more rapid rate of fire. Their mortars were more numerous and more murderously accurate, accounting for as much as three quarters of Allied casualties in Normandy. Their *Nebelwerfer*, multibarreled rocket projectors for which the Americans had no equivalent whatever, threw a bomb fitted with a siren almost as unnerving as the explosive it contained. Their tanks—the Mark V Panther and the Mark VI Tiger—were more heavily gunned and armored than our M-4 Sherman, the Allied workhorse; a Tiger's 88-mm gun could knock out a Sherman at four thousand yards, while the Sherman's 75-mm could not get through a Tiger's frontal armor at all.[130]

The penetration of armor is a function of muzzle velocity, to which the Germans had devoted great attention, developing long, tapered barrels that sent shells popping out like steel champagne corks at thousands of feet per second. The alternative is a shaped charge, which literally burns a hole through a tank's armor and sprays red-hot particles around inside it, but here our "bazooka" was a toy popgun compared to the German *Panzerfaust*. The 82d Airborne captured truckloads of *Panzerfäuste*, Gavin had translations made of their instruction manuals, and training was conducted in their use.[131] Of the American carbine the less said the better; in action it was worthless, and it jammed at a dirty look.

If so, how did we manage? The answer was a combination of things or, rather, *combination* was the answer. The Americans, summoning up a native talent for on-the-job training, learned how in ways that had not been foreseen to combine their strengths. Of these, the greatest was artillery, which the Germans had neglected; they had counted on the Stuka dive-bomber as a substitute, as for a time it was, but when the air filled with high-speed Allied fighter planes, the slow Stuka vanished from the skies, not to be replaced. They had nothing comparable, for example, to our 155-mm Long Tom, prince among long-range rifles, of which we had twelve per division and as many more per corps as need required.

Nor did they have anything approximate to the American volume and organization of fire; artillery, as the American military historian Russell Weigley puts it, was "the outstanding combat branch of the American ground forces." The Americans could bring to bear the artillery of an entire corps (perhaps two hundred guns) on a single target, a so-called serenade, and sometimes they fired it TOT (time on target), a calculation of each shell's trajectory so that all arrived at the same instant. Survivors of a TOT serenade were unhesitating witnesses to its devastating efficacy.

The great discovery was that infantry, tanks, artillery, and fighter-bombers form a team, each member of which needs the others, and the total of which is greater than the sum of their parts; together they composed a military instrument of a kind the Germans had once wielded to deadly effect but no longer possessed, at least not on a comparable scale, and mainly because they had lost control of the air. The Luftwaffe had destroyed itself in the great air battles over Germany of earlier in the year, and had ceased to exist as a fighting force. The British Typhoons and the American P-47 Thunderbolts roamed the battlefields with impunity. During the breakout, a tank column would call its group of P-47s to ask: "Is the road safe for us to proceed?" and get the reply, "Stand by and we'll find out," followed by the destruction of four German tanks and the message: "All clear. Proceed at will."[132]

None of this had been carefully thought through in advance; it was extemporized by individual ground and air commanders rather than provided for in tables of organization and manuals of tactics (a field manual on the subject was not published until later in the war). The air force bomber barons had given ground support scant attention and Bradley said the Americans "went into France almost totally untrained in air-ground co-operation." The lack of it was made up for by experience gained in Italy and by a single man, thirty-six-year-old "Pete" Quesada, now a major general, who had caught Eisenhower's attention in North Africa and been made commander of IX Tactical Air Force, Bradley's air arm. Breezy and untrammeled, Quesada brought to ground support the same intensity of conviction and determination to prove the worth of air power that Spaatz and Eaker had for strategic bombing.

Quesada landed on the Far Shore in a P-38 Lightning on D+1, set up his tent next to Bradley's, and by the end of the month had established sixteen fighter-bomber groups at fields in Normandy. He hung heavier and heavier bombs under the wings of fighter aircraft. He found Bradley willing to let him have a few tanks, in which he installed air force radios, so that tank and fighter-bomber could talk to each other. He created units called Forward Air Controllers, who rode with the ground troops to keep the air in contact with them, and later he urged the use of radar to vector the fighter-bombers in on target. "This man Quesada is a jewel," Bradley wrote to Hap Arnold; "he was not only willing to try everything that would help us, but he inspired his whole command with this desire."[133] Tactical air became so effective that during the breakout it took over the task of protecting Patton's southern flank.

Whatever else you say of the Normandy campaigns, they unlimbered the muscles of mobility in the Allied armies, especially in the American, whose zest for motion seemed to echo some innate national impulse. When Churchill visited Bradley's CP at Saint-Sauveur Lendelin on August 7, Bradley showed him a map on which it could be seen that twelve U.S. divisions had already passed through Avranches. "Good heavens," said Churchill. "How do you feed them?" Bradley explained that trucks ran bumper to bumper night and day, a way of warfare new to the Prime Minister.[134]

Even Montgomery, whose lack of interest in the exploitation phase of a battle had been noted by Liddell Hart as early as 1924, was about to break loose in a spirited pursuit of the fleeing Germans that impressed his most convinced critics. These were many, and it is perhaps the aftereffect of Normandy most ominous for what was to come that they had been given something they considered to be just cause by his combination of boastfulness and plodding performance. The preliminaries were in place for the confrontation between Montgomery and Eisenhower that would provide the latter with his most severe test as Supreme Commander.

III

Lieutenant General Sir Bernard Law Montgomery was the object of such overpowering veneration by the British public that it was impossible then (and is little less difficult today) to arrive at any balanced view of his merits and defects. With one success in October 1942 he had swept clean the memory of a past littered with failures. El Alamein was less of a decisive battle than an icon; it was a triumphant reassertion of national valor, a recapture of ongoing self-confidence summed up in Churchill's observation that before Alamein they never knew a victory, after it they never knew defeat. Montgomery became a cherished symbol of this return to familiar commerce with an almost foregone glory; he walked in the company of the great captains, his every step a vindication of their living presence. Crowds followed him, yearned to touch his sleeve. He had become a rule unto himself and could do no wrong. He wore his nonregulation uniform of sweater and beret even in the presence of the monarch, who smiled. He was known to be arrogant, puritanical, eccentric; numerous anecdotes told of this. They were greeted with chuckles. Good old Monty.[135]

Behind the public personality was a private one of considerable interest, and thus of fascination to biographers who would rather grant their subject human failings than military ones, who would rather have him dismaying than mistaken. His supporters are prickly; one of them refers to a reputable British writer's study of Montgomery's North African campaigns as an "attempted character assassination." Some—beginning with Brooke, who noted it in his diary in June 1943—have emphasized the personal animosity Montgomery aroused in Americans,[136] as though this explained away American misgivings about his generalship. Agreed that arguments abound around him, but what were they all about? For purposes of acuity in this regard, one might wish it were possible to ignore Monty the personality—the warmth that endeared him to his staff officers, the conceit that drove Americans up the walls—and try to focus instead on Montgomery the professional soldier. But human beings, alas, are of a piece.

For an American to write about the military Montgomery is an awkward exercise, since there is a wrenching disproportion between the legend and the reality as Americans perceive it. The transatlantic view is not only less charitable than the homegrown one but alien, in a literal sense, to the world Montgomery inhabited, in which public approval was confirmed by that of his service superiors—Brooke preeminently but also the director of military operations, Major General Frank Simpson, and the secretary of state for war, Sir James Grigg—who strongly and steadfastly supported him. He breathed an atmosphere of professional reinforcement in what he was about. To admit of doubt was not in his nature, and no reason to doubt was brought to his attention. British discussion of his leadership accordingly tends to begin with an assumption of his "greatness" and then go on to admit certain deplorable faults, while the American begins with an assumption of unproven merit and goes on to admit certain strengths.

Strengths, then: force of character, singleness of mind, fidelity of purpose, the self-assertion essential in a field commander. "He was a magnificent master to work for," said his chief of staff. "He never got excited, never lost his temper, gave you the task and then left you to carry it out without interference." His headquarters ran smoothly and he took meticulous care in appointing subordinates, many of whom he knew personally, down as far as battalion level; during battles he visited his commanders every day. He communicated well with troops (including American troops), infusing them with his conviction of success and making them feel a part of a sound plan. At a "set-piece" operation he excelled. When he took command of the ground forces for the invasion, they acquired a vigor and sense of direction few others could have imparted, and this earns him credit that his subsequent blunders and misbehavior do not deface. Both Beetle Smith and Eisenhower told Drew Middleton after the war that the invasion would not have been possible without Montgomery.

For many Americans, however, his "greatness" is only another example of an inflated military reputation, of a halfway competent general mistakenly elevated to a level above his capacity, where he could no longer cope with either a mobile battlefield or the complexities of an Allied relationship. Montgomery reciprocated in kind. He believed that the British and the Germans understood warfare in a way the Americans did not. "The real trouble with the Yanks," he wrote to Grigg, "is that they are completely ignorant of the rules of the game we are playing with the Germans. You play so much better when you know the rules."[137] He not only had a low military opinion of Americans but found them incomprehensible professionally—in their silences, their maddening politeness, their stubborn refusal to accept the subordinate position in which they so evidently belonged. All of this would be of interest merely as a case history in how military ability is formed and judged, and in Anglo-American disparities of perception, were it not for the contest in which Montgomery and the Americans were engaged, which had to do overtly with the conduct of the war and covertly with the future of the world.

Montgomery believed that if he had been allowed to have his way, the war would have been won before the end of 1944, hypothetically with the capture of Berlin by Allied armies. "The point to understand," he wrote in an entry for his diary-log the week after V-E Day, "is that if we had run the show properly the war could have been finished by Xmas 1944. The blame for this must rest with the Americans." Here is a heinous charge, not to be lightly made or lightly discounted, inasmuch as the "blame" encompassed is not only for the deaths of thousands of British and American soldiers and airmen but the prolonged sufferings of a prostrate Europe. Montgomery's biographer Nigel Hamilton includes within it the deaths of Anne Frank and the "millions of Jews, political opponents, and ordinary people" subject to the Nazis, for whom the Allies "arrived too late."[138] A further extension of the thesis holds that had we met the Russians sooner and farther east—on the Oder, say, rather than the Elbe—the postwar Soviet domination of Eastern Europe might have been forestalled or mitigated. If Montgomery was right, the Americans and their President have much to answer for, since Eisenhower's views prevailed at Roosevelt's insistence.

The problem as Eisenhower had to face it was primarily one of logistics. The breakout from the beachhead had encountered supply difficulties by mid-August, and by mid-September it had reached the end of its logistical tether. Patton and others lavished reproach on the supply moguls of Supreme Headquarters for allowing this to happen. The support apparatus of SHAEF, known as Com Z (Communications Zone), was commanded by Lieutenant General John C. H. Lee (sometimes called "Jesus Christ Himself" Lee), and Com Z personnel were alternately loathed and envied by the frontline units. After Paris was liberated, Eisenhower wanted it reserved for combat troops on furlough, but without his knowledge Lee moved 8,000 officers and 21,000 men into Paris and filled up so many hotels that a French satiric magazine referred to SHAEF as *Societé des Hôteliers Américains en France.* [139] Eisenhower was furious but did not, as he should have done, send Lee home.

Yet it is hard to see how the shortages of August 1944 could have been relieved even by prodigies of foresight and energy on Com Z's part. In truth, the planners had little choice. It must not be forgotten that Overlord, for all its majesty and might, was a marginal enterprise. Only a phased progress, contingent on the availability of port facilities, had been possible for supply officers to consider, and they had been given no margin of safety; they might have been more flexible but hardly could they have been more generous. Then reality had outrun the plan.

The conservative calculators had figured that by D+90 (September 4), they could support twelve American divisions at the Seine River barrier; when D+90 came, sixteen U.S. divisions were already operating 150 miles beyond the Seine, and by D+98 they had reached a line they were not supposed to get to until D+350! Neither the Brittany nor the Seine River ports had been opened and the liberation of Paris had imposed a demand for civilian relief (2,400 tons a day) that had not been anticipated until much later. Operational reserves had been exhausted and the whole system was strained to the breaking point. Well aware of this, but equally aware that the initiative had to be tightly held—"we must now as never before," he wrote Marshall on a critical day, September 4, "keep the enemy stretched everywhere"—Eisenhower had accepted the risk of ordering the advance to continue. [140]

For the Allies, late August and early September 1944 were heady times to be alive. Montgomery—as though to dispel his reputation for slowness—was speeding with his British and Canadian armies across the Flanders battlefields of World War I, covering in hours distances that had then taken months and tens of thousands of lives. Hodges's First (U.S.) Army went over the Seine on August 27 and within a week had taken 25,000 prisoners at Mons. Patton's Third Army was racing for the Meuse, which he crossed on August 30. Patch's Seventh Army (U.S. and French) had landed in the south of France and driven north beyond Lyons. Alexander's Fifteenth Army Group (U.S., British, and other allies) was successfully attacking in Italy north beyond Florence. The Germans had withdrawn from Greece; the Russians had reached Jugoslavia; Rumania had surrendered and Bulgaria was trying to. Those whose memories went back to November 1918, when Germany capitulated with her armies still in the field, could only wonder whether this might not be about to happen again.

In this ambience of all-pervading optimism, during the month between August 15 and September 15 (when the Allies closed along the German border), decisions were made that determined the way the war would be fought, harshly contested, and finally won. August was a climacteric, marking as it did the end of the road for British predominance in the Grand Alliance. "It was in August," writes the able British analyst R. W. Thompson, "that the unbalance in strength between the U.S.A. and Britain began to assert an overwhelming influence on the campaign. Neither the [British] Chiefs of Staff, nor even the voice of Churchill, could any longer prevail in matters of major strategy or policy. The design, henceforth, was the design of Roosevelt. . . . In the mid-summer of 1944, Britain, having withstood the siege and contrived at last the springboard into Europe, was denied the chance to be the architect of the victory she had made possible." These elegiac and autumnal words are profoundly apt.

After five years of war, Britain was harried and worn. For the second time in three decades she had given of her life's blood and it was ebbing away. The production peak of 1943 had been passed and could not be regained. The labor force was declining and new age groups were not enough to fill the army's needs; some divisions were two thousand men under strength and the replacement pool was nearly dry; five divisions and four armored brigades would have to be disbanded unless more men could be found.[141] In December, Churchill would have to order the last call-up of 250,000 men. If Montgomery was unaware of all this, the War Office regularly reminded him of it.

With the bright victories of July and August a sense of urgency came to prevail: now or never, the last chance for British arms to win the laurels they deserved. With every day the Americans were becoming more numerous, their new divisions queued up in quantity, waiting only to land and fight; with every day the Germans seemed further beyond hope. Victory beckoned: so near, so inviting. It was a moment of destiny and to deal with it Britain made a sorrowful miscalculation: She sent the wrong man with the wrong scheme of action.

◆

The original SHAEF plan—set forth in an internal staff paper a month before the invasion and signed, be it noted, by British officers—had been for a careful advance on a broad front that would push the enemy back to the German frontier by May of 1945. It was considered dangerous to attack by a single route, which would invite concentration against it, and therefore the planners envisaged a main axis from Amiens to the Ruhr, with a second one south of the Ardennes in the direction of Metz and Verdun. The Ruhr, Germany's industrial heartland, was the one essential goal—Berlin was "too far east to be the objective of a campaign in the West"—but a two-pronged offensive on a wide front would give the Allies an ability to maneuver and shift to exploit opportunities. It was taken for granted that General Eisenhower would assume personal command as soon as there were both American and British army groups in operation.[142]

Montgomery had other ideas; on August 17, he met with Bradley and unveiled them. The two Allied army groups would move together in a "solid mass" of forty divisions toward the northeast, north of the Ardennes, capturing the Channel ports and the V-1 flying-bomb sites, establishing airfields in Belgium, and heading no farther south than Aachen and Cologne. Montgomery came away from this meeting with the impression that Bradley had agreed "entirely" with this conception, as he informed Brooke the next day, though this was not the case. It happened again and again. Montgomery's self-confidence led him to interpret a vague or temporizing response to his demands as consent. He would deliver a schoolmarmish lecture that discouraged discussion and then conclude from the absence thereof that everyone agreed with him. Later, discovering his mistake, he would accuse the Americans of bad faith. He further assumed that he would continue to be the ground commander, despite the fact that Eisenhower's eventual occupancy of that post had long been known to be demanded by Roosevelt and agreed to by Churchill.[143]

Montgomery gave the same lecture to Eisenhower on August 23, at his headquarters in a Normandy apple orchard, and got part—but only part—of what he wanted. Eisenhower made it clear that the command arrangements were settled, and that he would take over on September 1, but he agreed to issue a directive giving Montgomery the mission of clearing the Channel coast, overrunning the Belgian airfields, and taking Antwerp; Bradley's mission would be to clear Brittany and advance in the center to support the main effort to the north—in short, the original SHAEF plan somewhat modified in Montgomery's favor.

Bradley objected, as did many SHAEF officers, and the directive as finally issued on the twenty-ninth did not give Montgomery "operational control" of Bradley's army adjacent to him (the First, under Hodges), but only "authority to effect the necessary operational co-ordination"—a distinction Montgomery considered to be basic. Eisenhower was not willing to abandon entirely the possibility of Bradley—which is to say, Patton—advancing south of the Ardennes on Metz and Verdun.

Montgomery's rapid progress at the turn of the month, in the un-grudging words of Eisenhower's biographer, was "one of the most extraor-dinary campaigns of the war."[144] His two armies covered two hundred miles in less than a week and by September 4 he had taken Antwerp (though not its water approaches, which turned out to matter more than anyone then imagined). But Patton had been moving too, the whole Ger-man front seemed on the verge of collapse, and Eisenhower still believed that the two-pronged approach was possible. He met with Patton and Bradley at Chartres on the second of September and on the fourth he issued a directive that allowed Bradley (Patton) to continue going forward through the Saar toward the Rhine.

This order precipitated a collision between British and American pride and priority; it caused Montgomery to make his most complete challenge to the Supreme Commander's conception of the Allied effort. On that same day, the fourth, the day his men reached Antwerp, Mont-gomery sent the following message to Eisenhower:

> (1) I consider we have now reached a stage where one really power-ful and full-blooded thrust towards Berlin is likely to get there and thus end the German war.
> (2) We have *not* enough maintenance resources for two full-blooded thrusts.
> (3) The selected thrust must have all the maintenance resources it needs without any qualification, and any other operation must do the best it can with what is left. . . .

Here is the heart of it, of Montgomery's conviction then and later that if the Allies "split our maintenance resources so that neither thrust is full-blooded we will prolong the war."[145] The seriousness with which this charge has been taken by American military historians is indicated by the number of detailed studies (three) devoted to it by the principal authori-ties: Forrest Pogue, Roland Ruppenthal, and Stephen Ambrose.[146] Their work has been supplemented by that of Martin van Creveld of the He-brew University of Jerusalem, who published in 1977 a scholarly book on "logistics from Wallenstein to Patton" called *Supplying War*. Creveld devotes an entire chapter to the situation in Europe in August–September 1944 and points out first of all that Montgomery's mention of Berlin was "unfortunate," in that Berlin was four hundred miles away and far beyond either ally's reach at this stage.

No reallocation of resources, as Eisenhower bluntly informed Mont-gomery the following day, "would be adequate to sustain a thrust to Berlin" (privately, in his diary, the word Eisenhower used for the idea was "crazy"). Montgomery must later have realized the justice of this, for when he came to publish his memoir *From Normandy to the Baltic* in 1946 he had modified the wording: "My own view, which I presented to the Supreme Commander, was that one powerful full-blooded thrust across the Rhine and *into the heart of Germany*, backed by the whole of the resources of the Allied Armies, would be likely to achieve decisive results" (emphasis added).[147]

Montgomery should have phrased his proposal that way in the first place. The true issue is whether—given first priority on supplies and genuine "command" of First U.S. Army—he could have reached and encircled not Berlin but the Ruhr, without which further German war-making in the West was beyond the realm of the real, and *that* (as Creveld remarks) in fact involves two questions: (1) was the logistical arithmetic such as to make it possible, and (2) did it offer Eisenhower a significant choice over and beyond the original two-pronged strategy? To the first question Creveld answers, "it could have been done, but only just." To the second he answers No.[148]

We should not suppose that the SHAEF planners had been idle. In late August, they considered a quick drive to the Rhine by Patton with twelve divisions, all other armies halted, and concluded that he could get there but not much farther, certainly not beyond Frankfurt, which was not an objective of any importance. (Patton was at a greater distance from his supply sources than Montgomery was.) There seemed to be an assumption behind this plan that it would frighten the enemy into surrendering, and Eisenhower with good reason rejected it. In early September, they looked into Montgomery's "full-blooded thrust" to Berlin and decided that it might work (even though it wouldn't be full-blooded when it got there) but only if Antwerp were open, certain railheads repaired, ten U.S. divisions immobilized and twelve others "quiescent," and the main body of both Allied army groups on the Rhine by September 15. Since these prior conditions could not be met, the proposal had to be regarded as unworkable.[149]

Creveld's analysis is more realistic in its set of prerequisites and choice of objective. He assumes that we are talking about an attack (Montgomery plus Hodges) in mid-September with a combined total of eighteen divisions headed for Dortmund, on the far side of the Ruhr, 130 miles away. He assumes that the port of Antwerp would *not* have been opened but that trucks would be taken from three American divisions immobilized in Normandy, from the corps (American) attacking Brest, and from Patton. Figuring a total requirement of 11,700 tons a day (650 per division), he arrives at his solution of marginal feasibility, with even a little left over for the Canadian army to continue clearing Antwerp.

Creveld adds the caution, however, that the supply apparatus as a whole might not have been able quickly to readjust itself for another extreme effort, especially under the auspices of statistics-minded staff officers who considered the advance over the Seine to be impossible even while it was being carried out. "That SHAEF logisticians were not cast in the heroic mould," Creveld writes, "it seems impossible to deny." The mathematical equation included neither the human element nor the reality principle. Therefore his conclusion: "In the final account, the question as to whether Montgomery's plan presented a real alternative to Eisenhower's strategy must be answered in the negative."

Eisenhower, of course, had a great many other factors to consider. He must ask himself at the outset whether Montgomery's proposal, even if adopted, could be executed by a commander of Montgomery's known methods and style. In Eisenhower's experience of him in Sicily, Italy, and Normandy, Montgomery had been systematic, determined to wait until he had accumulated preponderant strength, until everything was "tidy," before launching a set-piece frontal assault, a "colossal crack." Was this the man to entrust with an operation that above all else required speed and audacity? Eisenhower doubted it; he ascribed the request for First Army's support in the northeastward advance to Montgomery's "usual caution."[150] Moreover, he must keep in mind the implications of halting Patton on Montgomery's behalf in the light of its effect on Marshall, on Roosevelt, and on the American public—none of whom, to put it conservatively, would applaud.

British critics have seized upon this deference of Eisenhower's to "American public opinion" as unworthy, as insufficient grounds for making what should on its merits have been a military decision. (Later they reverse themselves and criticize Eisenhower for making on military grounds what they feel should have been a political decision—i.e., whether or not to take Berlin.) But one may ask whether Churchill, Parliament, and British "public opinion" would have stood for it if Eisenhower had turned Patton loose and held Montgomery back in a "quiescent" posture. The question answers itself. It all depends on *whose* politics are being taken into account.

A conviction that Montgomery was mistaken has not been confined to Americans. Even his own chief of staff thought he was wrong and said so, to Eisenhower, on repeated occasions during August and September. "It is only fair to say," wrote Major General Sir Francis de Guingand, "that throughout the war, this was the only major issue over which I did not agree with my Chief." De Guingand thought that without Antwerp, even with resources taken from Patton, a force of a dozen divisions could not have been sustained on a full scale east of the Rhine. Bridging equipment was not yet ready to move up and winter was coming; only a few weeks remained of weather good enough for mobile operations. Even assuming a successful crossing of the river, de Guingand wrote, "I cannot see how it would have produced a German capitulation."

He believed that the Wehrmacht, after a period of crisis, could mobilize the necessary troops to strangle the spearhead, and events bear him out; it took eight more months of air bombardment, a Russian offensive with 160 divisions, and our own massive attacks, to bring the Third Reich down. "My own conclusion is, therefore," de Guingand wrote, "that Eisenhower was right when in August he decided that he could not concentrate sufficient administrative resources to allow one strong thrust deep into Germany north of the Rhine [Ruhr?] with the hope of decisive success. . . . I think it possible that we might have obtained a bridgehead over the Rhine before winter—but not more."[151]

Montgomery was wrong. His indictment must be dismissed and his superiors (especially Brooke and Grigg) faulted for encouraging him.

Eisenhower's ability to ride down Montgomery's provocations with the force of his own forbearance is well illustrated by an incident that occurred during this same period. It fixed the shape of a balanced tension between the two in a form it retained for the remainder of the war, although Montgomery continued to bristle and Eisenhower at the end (with Churchill's consent) reduced his mission to a comparatively minor one. Regrettably the episode was also the occasion for Montgomery to propose, and Eisenhower to approve, the greatest mistake of the campaign and of Montgomery's career—a single mistake with two sides to it, one of them called Antwerp and the other called Arnhem.

In his crucial message of September 4, Montgomery had asked Eisenhower to come meet with him for a discussion, and on the tenth Eisenhower obliged. (This was Montgomery's habit; he would not go meet with others if they could be persuaded to come meet with him, and if not he sent a deputy, an annoying and unnecessary piece of self-protection.) Eisenhower had wrenched his right leg (his "good" one) in an accident and so they met inside his aircraft on Brussels airfield.

Montgomery insisted that his own chief administrative officer, Major General Miles Graham, should be present but that Eisenhower's (Lieutenant General Sir Humphrey Gale) should not, another needless affront. What we know of the meeting is therefore Graham's account, given by him to the Australian journalist Chester Wilmot. Montgomery leafed through a file of recent signals to him signed by the Supreme Commander and asked Eisenhower if he had written them. The latter said yes.

"Well, they're balls," said Montgomery, "sheer balls, rubbish!"

Eisenhower let the tirade continue for a time, then leaned forward and put his hand on Montgomery's knee. "Steady, Monty," he said. "You can't speak to me like that. I'm your boss."

Montgomery bit back the next word he had intended to utter, and replied, "I'm sorry, Ike."[152]

◆

Antwerp—answer to a supply officer's prayer, high alongside Hamburg, Rotterdam, and New York among the world's great ports: with its twenty-nine miles of docks and quays, more than six hundred hydraulic and electric cranes, nine hundred warehouses, pipelines to five hundred fuel storage tanks, five hundred miles of track and marshaling yards, and direct access to the railroads and waterways of northwestern Europe. Antwerp, in the words of a U.S. Army historian, "had a potential capacity which completely dwarfed that of all the other ports the Allies had thus far captured and put to use."[153] In 1938 alone, it had registered twelve thousand vessels and handled sixty million tons of freight. There was only one catch: Antwerp was fifty-five miles from the sea down the estuary of the Scheldt, and who controlled the banks of the Scheldt controlled Antwerp.

When the British 11th Armoured Division rolled into Antwerp on September 4, it was riding a wave of triumph. Miraculously the enemy had departed in a state of such disorder that the port (unlike Cherbourg and Marseilles, which the Germans demolished with assiduous care) was taken almost intact: some damage to locks, three railroad bridges destroyed, and two coasters sunk in the Scheldt, but otherwise the quays and the crane machinery were in working condition. It was an unbelievable windfall, and it contributed to the general euphoria.

Notice that important objectives were not far away. There were bridges over the wide and deep Albert Canal on the northern edge of the city, and less than twenty miles to the north was an inviting terrain feature, the Beveland Isthmus, a narrow neck connecting the Beveland and Walcheren Island to the mainland, command of which would cut off any Germans who were trying either to escape or to block the Scheldt estuary. But the men of 11th Armoured were exhilarated, tired, and ready to enjoy success. In the absence, so reads their division history, of "any indication [having] been given that a further advance to the north was envisaged," nothing was done. A three-day halt was ordered on Montgomery's authority to "refit, refuel, and rest."[154]

Russell Weigley is sardonic in his characterization of this delay, and rightly so: It was one of the most disastrous blunders of the campaign. When the British XXX Corps tried to seize the Albert Canal bridges three days later, the effort barely succeeded; the Germans had rallied and recovered their balance. By failing to take the Beveland Isthmus, we missed the chance to trap the German Fifteenth Army, which had been retreating up the Channel coast and was now being ferried across the Scheldt. While XXX Corps rested and refitted, 86,000 German soldiers, 600 artillery pieces, 6,000 vehicles, and 6,000 horses crossed the Beveland Isthmus back into Holland, where they would be encountered again at Arnhem. Worse, Fifteenth Army left behind it sufficient force to hold Walcheren Island at the mouth of the estuary against anything but the most determined assault—and for this we paid dearly indeed, not only in the ultimate cost of capturing Walcheren but in the cost to all the Western armies of the failure to open Antwerp in September.

Eisenhower began emphasizing the prime significance of "a secure base at Antwerp" to Montgomery on August 24 and went on doing so with increasing pertinacity during September and October. But Montgomery's mind was elsewhere, on the Rhine and the Ruhr, on the war-winning victory he thought within his grasp. He was not enthusiastic about clearing Antwerp. "To him it was not an interesting military operation . . . ," said his intelligence officer, Brigadier Sir Edgar Williams; "whatever the result the Scheldt attack could not fit into the series of victories on which his reputation was based at the moment."

This was not just vanity. Montgomery wanted to save lives, and if he could finish the war a costly Scheldt operation would be unnecessary. He did not need Antwerp for his own supply; it was the Americans to the south for whom it was a sink-or-swim affair. There are those (Brigadier Williams included) who have suggested that if Eisenhower wanted a functioning Antwerp port so much, he should have sent Montgomery a peremptory order to give the Scheldt first priority (as he eventually did). "But you must remember," said Williams, "at that time Ike was in no position to contradict Monty, because the incredible victory in Normandy and the swift advance had established Monty as a brilliantly successful commander in the field."[155]

That an opportunity was missed by the Allies in the fall of 1944 seems beyond denying. The German "front" was so full of holes that it scarcely deserved the name, the Rhine bridges had not been prepared for demolition, and a breakthrough at nearly any point (according to General Siegfried Westphal, then Rundstedt's chief of staff) would have succeeded. But what was the opportunity and who missed it? Liddell Hart in a postwar analysis agreed with Montgomery that a "single thrust" was called for, but denied that Montgomery could then have executed it or that he was deprived of the chance because supplies were going elsewhere. Liddell Hart concluded that Montgomery was essentially handicapped by failures in his own sector: by that four-day delay after reaching Antwerp, by reluctance to open the Scheldt, by the excessive allocation of supply to ammunition rather than fuel, by the discovery that 1,400 British trucks had faulty pistons, and by a six-day stoppage of air supply to mount an air drop on Tournai which never took place because the land forces, as Bradley had predicted, got there first.

The Germans themselves were in little doubt as to where they dreaded an attack the most, not on Montgomery's front but on Bradley's. General Westphal told Liddell Hart after the war that "the most vulnerable part of the whole Western Front was the Luxembourg sector, leading to the Rhine at Coblenz." Westphal's predecessor, General Blumentritt, said that a "swerve northward" by Patton "in the direction of Luxembourg and Bitburg would have met with great success" and would have cut off at least one German army "before it could retreat behind the Rhine."[156]

Here was the opportunity, yet it was not to be seized while Eisenhower continued—as to Bradley's and Patton's frustration and despair he did—to designate Montgomery's as the "main thrust" and to commit First U.S. Army in support of Montgomery. Much bitterness flowed, and still flows, from this decision to let Montgomery (who was unequal to it) lead the way into Germany. "It seems to me overwhelmingly clear," wrote General Gavin thirty-four years later, "that Patton should have been given the task."[157]

When First Army received the role of protecting Montgomery's southern flank, it also was saddled with terrain to fight in that might better have been avoided: the Peel Marshes, sixty square miles of swampland and innumerable canals, traversed by inadequate roads; the fortified coal-mining area around Aachen, filled with slag heaps and pillboxes; and the Huertgen Forest, the ultimate nightmare, a thick mass of tall, dense fir trees and spongy soil, twenty miles long and ten miles wide, that became the scene of one of the worst American reverses of the European war.

Liddell Hart thought that the sector First Army had been assigned was strategically a "blind alley," an "entanglement" with little room for maneuver, which consumed three quarters of the American supply tonnage without significantly helping Montgomery or gaining any objective worth having—except for the Roer River dams, which should have been approached from a different direction (the Monschau corridor) rather than through the dark and bloody labyrinth of the Huertgen Forest. Liddell Hart places responsibility for the clumsy positioning of First Army on Montgomery's insistence that it support him.

Easy enough it is in the aftermath to prescribe what should have been done, but unless the exercise is attempted, the past can become a graveyard of unexamined errors, enough of which were made in this instance to call attention to themselves. An open port at Antwerp was far too essential for sensibilities to be spared. If Montgomery didn't appreciate its importance the Germans did; they fired more V-2 rockets at Antwerp (1,610) than they did at London (1,190), and 734 Allied soldiers and 2,900 Belgian civilians lost their lives.[158] Eisenhower in late August (assuming that he could risk a divisive row and make this stick) should have *ordered* Montgomery to clear the Scheldt and block the retreat of Fifteenth Army. Montgomery should most certainly not have been allowed to undertake the Arnhem venture first, if at all.

What Bradley and Patton might have been asked to do is less clear. If First Army had not been pushed to the north, it could have covered the Ardennes in greater force, which would have been helpful in December, and Bradley with adequate strength and supply might have been able to organize earlier the drive to the Rhine near Mainz that later succeeded so spectacularly. But whether Patton could have broken loose again before winter is uncertain. He believed that an enemy left alone is a dangerous enemy (which is why he was apprehensive about the Ardennes), and he put the same driving energy into frontal assaults as he did into what he called "broken field running."[159] His siege of Metz and his Saar offensive, though they drew German divisions away from the north, turned into slugging matches much criticized as wasteful of men and munitions. Yet he was beginning to appreciate that taking territory as such was less important than eliminating German units, and when he eventually grabbed onto the idea wholeheartedly (in the Palatinate), what had by then become Eisenhower's plan to destroy the German armies *before* they retreated over the Rhine was put into powerful execution.

Most of all to have been avoided (or at least better conceived) was the series of ill-omened battles that together make up the Winter War of 1944–45, beginning with Arnhem in mid-September and ending with the elimination of the Colmar pocket in late January 1945. At their center symbolically stands the German counterattack of late December in the Ardennes, which goes under the name of the Battle of the Bulge. First and last they do not reveal the Allied high command at its sagest but rather testify to the tactics that come of frustration. It was a bitter and depressing period, made worse by weather of unusual severity, torrential rains, falling temperatures, and a land covered in snow and slush. Only in March 1945, with the capture of the Remagen bridge and the Bradley-Patton campaign in the Eifel-Palatinate, does the momentum pick up again, the gift for mobility and maneuver reassert itself, and the final march into Germany begin which never slackened in pace thereafter.

Arnhem—the wrong turning in the road, the place where things begin to go sour, the operation that should never have been. Churchill, Montgomery, and Eisenhower all tried to extenuate it after the war, but not with great success. Eisenhower in *Crusade in Europe* downgraded its importance by referring to it as "merely an incident and extension of our eastward rush to the line we needed for temporary security." But it was the largest airborne assault ever made and total casualties were greater than on D-Day. Montgomery and Churchill both argued that but for the weather it would have worked, but Montgomery's operations officer, Brigadier David Belchem, said that this was not so, that weather "was not the principal shortcoming." Montgomery in his *From Normandy to the Baltic* insisted that Arnhem had been "ninety percent successful," and Churchill described it as "a decided victory."[160] But it was neither.

Three airborne divisions (two of them American, the 82d and the 101st) were to be dropped in advance of British XXX Corps along a corridor sixty-five miles long leading to the Arnhem bridge over the Lower Rhine; XXX Corps would then join up with them and establish a bridgehead on the far bank of the river (Montgomery of course hoped for much more, for a collapse in enemy resistance that would open the way for him into northern Germany). The planning was hurried and overconfi-

dent; when General Gavin heard that the commander of 1st British Airborne intended to drop six to eight miles away from his objective at the
Arnhem bridge, Gavin said, "My God, he can't mean it." Intelligence
indicating that German forces were building up in the area, and that these
included tanks, was disregarded. When Beetle Smith told Montgomery
that German armor near Arnhem meant that the Allied forces landing
there must be increased, "Montgomery ridiculed the idea" (so Smith
subsequently said) and "waved my objections airily aside."[161]

The 101st jumped northwest of Eindhoven, opened the road for the
British to proceed northeast, and successfully kept it open against repeated counterattacks. But the 82d (now under Gavin's command) outdid
itself. Frequently outnumbered, it won every engagement. The men of
the 82d took the bridge over the Maas River at Grave and two bridges over
the Maas-Waal canal. They took the high ground southeast of Nijmegen
that commanded the area and held it against three German attacks.
(Gavin had foresightedly included a parachute artillery battalion in the
first drop, which proved useful in breaking up enemy formations; "that's
what generals are for," said a friend of Gavin's later.)[162] Finally, in an
improvised river crossing with British folding canvas boats, they captured
the big bridge over the River Waal at Nijmegen, and tanks of the Guards
armored division that had joined them from the south moved over and
across it. (In the lead tank was Captain the Lord Carrington, who would
one day be foreign secretary and then head of the North Atlantic Treaty
Organization.)

A German commander who opposed them in this action said they
were better at night and forest fighting than the Germans were. The
British journalist Richard Lamb said of the 82d's river crossing that "it was
undoubtedly one of the finest feats of arms of the Second World War." The
commander of British Second Army, Lieutenant General Miles C. Demp-
sey, greeted Gavin at Nijmegen with the words, "I am proud to meet the
Commanding General of the finest division in the world today."[163]

But the men of the 82d soon discovered to their disquiet that they
were being denied public credit for what they had done. Newspaper
accounts emphasized only the British at Arnhem. *Washington Post:* "Arnhem hereafter will be a prouder name in British memories than Agincourt
or Waterloo, or even Trafalgar." *New York Times:* "There will be no
prouder men in years to come than those qualified to wear the Arnhem
badge or ribbon."[164] No mention had been allowed of either the 101st at
Eindhoven or the 82d at Nijmegen. This malodorous example of self-
serving manipulation of the news, for which Montgomery's headquarters
must bear the blame, will live in memory but not in honor.

The men of the 1st British Airborne who fought at Arnhem did not
and do not need to have their courage magnified, but they had been sent
on a disastrous errand. The drop zones, as Gavin had recognized, were

placed too far from the objective. Of the three groups of paratroopers who tried to reach the bridge, two ran into stiff German opposition and only the third got there. They took one end of the bridge and disarmed its demolition charges, but they could not hold it. The Germans reacted in force and 1st Airborne was savagely mauled; of the 9,500 men who had landed from the sky at Arnhem, only 2,000 made it back across the Rhine and south to Nijmegen, where the 82d gave them blankets, food, and shelter. "Thus," wrote Gavin, "the great gamble to end the war in the fall of '44 came to an end."[165]

How explain the impetus for Arnhem? How explain, above all, Eisenhower's willingness to go along with it? Setting aside the still-magnetic grip of Montgomery's reputation, it may be that Eisenhower was adhering too rigidly to the original SHAEF plan, with its inherent location of the main effort in the north. This might have been treated as slightly less sacrosanct. The value of the Ruhr was unquestionable, but the idea that the plains of Westphalia offered the most satisfactory route into Germany was not. Bradley never shared it, and pointed out to Eisenhower that this was a region of innumerable rivers, streams, and canals ripe for bridge-blowing and stalling tactics. (The more hilly route from Frankfurt to Kassel that Bradley eventually took had fewer obstacles and turned out to be just as passable.)

But the influence of George Marshall must not be ignored, either. Marshall was still thinking of using the airborne divisions in the daring manner he had proposed for the invasion, and had to be dissuaded from. Eisenhower, writes Gavin of the Arnhem decision, was "under considerable pressure from both General Marshall and General Arnold to be much bolder and more imaginative in his employment of the new and fledgling [airborne] arm."[166] Eisenhower's tactical instincts—and his doubts about the isolated use of airborne units in the mass—were here the better, and he would have been the wiser to have heeded them. The 1st, the 82d, and the 101st were SHAEF's strategic reserve and to squander them here deprived him of it. The Allies had a precious resource in their airborne capability, but they never quite figured out how to get the best from its unique potentialities.

And then, too long postponed, the opening of Antwerp. Walcheren Island, like so much of the Netherlands, is below sea level. Over centuries its people had driven the waters back and built their farms and villages. Then the Germans came and made Walcheren a fortress, filled with pill-boxes and coastal batteries to stop any Allied ship that dared enter the Scheldt. There was an answer to that, and so in October the RAF came, smashed the dikes, and gave Walcheren back to the sea. By October 21, the only dry land on Walcheren was a patch to the east, the two main towns, and the German batteries. Canadian 2d Corps had been condemned to fight a battle of the polders, of mud and water and a cold gray

an overall plan by Bradley, and not one of his best, to make a final two-pronged stab at breaking through the fortifications of the Siegfried Line and reaching the Rhine before winter closed in. It failed. The weather was egregious: rain was heavy, cold, and continuous; rivers flooded, mud was everywhere. Bradley's northern attack, by Collins's VII Corps, ran into the Huertgen Forest and ground to a stop, with terrible losses. Patton's went forward, but slowly; he raged at his commanders, and at Bradley. On November 22, Metz was declared taken, though pockets of Germans in the forts around it continued to hold out until mid-December. Patton drove his army forty miles forward to the Saar River, crossed it, and came to a halt at the Siegfried Line. "Each day the weather grew colder, our troops more miserable," wrote Bradley. "We were mired in a ghastly war of attrition."[172]

When the German counterattack came in the Ardennes on December 16, Patton got wind of it in his early-morning briefing, and began making preparations for a move north to meet it. Two German panzer armies of twenty-four divisions and over two hundred thousand men were moving on a sixty-mile front in an American sector thinly held by divisions newly arrived from the States or battered ones being given a rest. The attack would eventually drive a deep wedge into the front that gave the battle its name. The German (that is, Hitler's) objective was no less than to split the Allies apart and destroy the supply base at Antwerp. Eisenhower called a meeting of his commanders at Verdun on the morning of the nineteenth, in a dank stone barracks heated by a single potbellied stove.

He had already (on the sixteenth) ordered two divisions moved from the north and south to strengthen the shoulders of the salient, and had alerted his only reserve—the 82d and the 101st, still recovering from Arnhem—in readiness for a move. At Verdun, he said that the situation was to be regarded "as one of opportunity for us and not of disaster," and he asked Patton when he would be able to attack. "On December 22," said Patton, "with three divisions." Less than seventy hours away. It was his supreme moment. The reaction around the table was a mixture of pleased surprise, skepticism, and outright disbelief. "Don't be fatuous," said Eisenhower.[173]

Patton was proposing to disengage an entire army from the front, wheel it to the left by ninety degrees, and make a lateral march in the presence of an attacking foe—not a maneuver that would find favor in the Command and General Staff School at Leavenworth. He would have to move some 133,000 tanks and trucks over a network of small roads, already heavily used, while keeping them out of each other's way. Gavin called it "an amazing performance" that no one but Patton could have carried out. Bradley said later that any other commander would have asked for twice the time and still have thought that he was taking a chance.[174]

Patton was not being fatuous. He had worked it all out beforehand, with a set of alternatives his staff was meanwhile preparing to which code numbers had been assigned. (When Eisenhower discovered that Patton's plan had been thought through, he approved it.) When the Verdun meeting broke up, Patton needed only to phone the appropriate code number, send Codman to Nancy to get headquarters moving, and then take off in a jeep with his driver, Master Sergeant John L. Mims, to visit his commanders, straighten out details, and generally animate the enterprise. He made other phone calls too, about tank and tank destroyer battalions, hospitals, ammunition, bridging equipment, cannibalizing some units to form others, and all the rest of the particulars that go with a complex operation. At the end of the afternoon, Sergeant Mims said, "General, the government is wasting a lot of money having a whole General Staff. You and me has run the Third Army all day and done a better job than they do."[175]

His three divisions jumped off as he had said they would at 6:00 A.M. on December 22, and four days later the 4th Armored relieved the siege of Bastogne, kingpin and defiant center of American resistance. At the beginning of January, the counteroffensive began and by the end of the month the Bulge had been erased as though it never existed. Montgomery, who took command of the northern side of it at Eisenhower's request, had told Bradley that this was impossible, that First Army could not return to the offensive for three months, that Patton was "too weak" to attack, and that the Allies should retreat to the Saar-Vosges line or the Moselle. His desire to fall back was described to Patton by Bradley at dinner on Christmas: "We both considered this a disgusting idea," wrote Patton. On January 7, Montgomery, confidence restored, issued a statement to the press so self-congratulatory in tone and patronizing of the Americans that Churchill had to disavow it and remind the House of Commons that "the United States troops have done almost all the fighting, and have suffered almost all the losses."[176] Too late. Montgomery's days as a commander of American troops were numbered.

He had sent Eisenhower another message, totally misapprehending the position he was in, accusing Eisenhower of being unable to do the job of land commander, and demanding that he (Montgomery) be given "full operational direction, control, and co-ordination" for a northern advance; otherwise there would be another failure. British newspapers had taken up a similar cry so loudly that Marshall (knowing of the President's desire that Americans serve only under American commanders) cabled Eisenhower: "My feeling is this: under no circumstances make any concession of any kind whatever . . ."[177] and Eisenhower drafted a cable to the

Combined Chiefs, which he showed to de Guingand, saying that he and Montgomery could no longer work together and that the Combined Chiefs would have to choose between them.

Realizing that if one of the two must go it would not be Eisenhower, de Guingand flew through heavy weather to Montgomery's headquarters, with some difficulty convinced his chief that an ax was about to fall, and got him to sign an "eyes only" letter of apology, asking Eisenhower to tear up his previous communication and ending: "Your very devoted servant, Monty." Eisenhower relented, his cable was never sent, and the worst crisis of all had been passed. When the Combined Chiefs met in Malta at the end of January, and Brooke made one more effort to undercut Eisenhower's authority, Marshall demanded that they go into a "closed session" (no stenographers), in which Marshall unleashed his fury, made it clear what he thought of Montgomery, and stated his inalterable opposition to Montgomery or anyone else as land commander under Eisenhower—and that issue was momentarily put to rest.[178]

Which meant that Bradley and Patton would sooner or later have their chance. Neither man especially liked the other: Bradley thought Patton's bombast superfluous and his impetuosity in need of restraint, while Patton thought Bradley timid and referred to him in diary entries and letters as "Omar the tent maker." But together they made a team in which nonredundant virtues overlapped and complemented one another. Bradley thought the long thoughts; Patton said that his best ideas came into his mind intact, "like Minerva," and were not laboriously worked out on paper "as historians attempt to describe." He awoke for no reason at 3:00 A.M. on February 6, 1945, and there it all was in his head, the Palatinate campaign.[179]

Montgomery had unlimbered another of his "colossal cracks," this time *south*east from Nijmegen: Canadian 1st Army with thirteen divisions, four armored brigades, and immense quantities of artillery, a total of more than four hundred thousand men echeloned to pass through the slot between Nijmegen and Grave, then overrun the Reichswald Forest and close the Rhine from Emmerich to Wesel. (As at Alamein, Montgomery was trying to push too many units under too many different commanders through too narrow a space.) In this sodden maelstrom of undulating woods, interspersed with marshes, swamps, backwaters, and flooded streams, the best of British arms—with names, writes Thompson, "like the music of tradition sounding down the years"—gave of themselves in a struggle that once again slowed down but once again drew German strength away from the Americans. U.S. Ninth Army, under Lieutenant General William H. Simpson (but under Montgomery's overall command), broke through to the Rhine and craved Montgomery's permission to cross it near Düsseldorf. Permission denied. "It was a stratagem that hardly could have failed," writes the U.S. Army historian, but it did not fit within

Montgomery's grand plan. His spacious overview had room for only *one* Rhine crossing, and guess whom he proposed to have make it?[180]

◆

Montgomery's attack across the Rhine (scheduled for March 24) rivaled the Normandy invasion in massiveness of force and of the buildup behind it. He had three armies of thirty divisions (six of them armored and two of them airborne) and over five thousand artillery pieces. (He had demanded, and been promised, ten divisions from U.S. First Army as a reserve in case he suffered a reverse.) The British alone had brought up sixty thousand tons of ammunition, thirty thousand tons of engineering equipment, and twenty-eight thousand tons of other supplies in addition to their normal daily requirements. Sixty-nine thousand engineers would be involved; the Royal Navy would provide landing craft; during the three days before the assault, Allied air forces would drop forty-nine thousand tons of bombs.[181] Both Eisenhower and Churchill would be present.

But Bradley had been thinking. As usual, he was fighting a poor man's war and was supposed to remain on the "aggressive defense," but he interpreted this to mean that no one would object if First and Third armies cleared the Germans out of the Eifel triangle between the Moselle and the Rhine, and no one did. It was flawlessly done. "No other campaign of the war brought me greater professional pride," Bradley wrote. Then on March 7, Company A, 27th Armored Infantry Battalion of 9th Armored Division, captured the railway bridge over the Rhine at Remagen almost intact and when he learned of it Bradley turned to Eisenhower's operations officer—who was visiting him in another effort to deprive Bradley of three more of his divisions—and said, "There goes your ball game."[182] With Eisenhower's strong assent, Bradley poured across the Rhine three corps of seven divisions and established a bridgehead thirty miles wide and ten miles deep. Now all he needed was to get Patton across.

Bradley's thought was that Third Army was now in a position from which it could surround the German armies in the Palatinate west of the Rhine with two pincerlike moves that would meet at Mainz, opposite the Frankfurt "corridor" into central Germany. Like the star performers among Bradley plans, this one made use of the means available while simultaneously it fitted into a larger purpose whose success it made possible—in this case the double envelopment of the Ruhr, by Ninth Army from the north and First and Third armies from the south, that had been in his and Eisenhower's minds all along.

Bradley made his case to the Supreme Commander, who approved. (Eisenhower had by this time abandoned his exclusive devotion to a single thrust in the north and firmly, and in writing, returned to the two-thrust strategy.) Bradley drove to Luxembourg, where he found Patton in a home for the aged, having his hair cut; Bradley joined him and under steaming towels they worked it out. Earlier Bradley had asked Patton whether he had his bridging equipment well forward. No, said Patton, but he had "a helluva lot of it stashed away." Bring it forward, said Bradley. He wanted Patton to "take the Rhine on the run," or as Patton put it, "pass through the gate with the crowd."[183]

The Saar-Palatinate, to give it the more descriptive name, is a three-thousand-square-mile oblong lying between the Rhine, the Moselle, and the French-German border to the south. It produced seven million tons of coal annually, 40 to 50 percent of Germany's chemicals, and 10 percent of its iron and steel. Filled with mountains and deep valleys, it would have been a military obstacle of the first order even if it had not also contained some of the most heavily fortified portions of the Siegfried Line. Defending it were two German armies, First and Seventh, which had asked to be allowed to withdraw or at least fight a delaying action, and had been told No: the Saar-Palatinate must be held. Patton disposed of it in ten days.

The Saar-Palatinate campaign was Patton at his most elegant and economical. Knowing him well, Bradley did nothing to dispel the notion that they were putting something over on the Supreme Commander. When he turned 4th Armored loose on March 15, Patton—like Nelson at Copenhagen, putting his telescope to his blind eye—failed to report where it was for twenty-four hours, under the impression that if SHAEF found out they might tell him to stop. After Mortain, Third Army headquarters had learned to appreciate the value of Ultra; there were daily morning briefings and Patton attended them. According to Commander Winterbotham, author of *The Ultra Secret*, Patton in the Palatinate took advantage of Ultra's location of German units and methodically "worked his way around them." Twelve of his divisions, each trying to outdo the other, were running wild through the German rear areas. What Bradley called Patton's "uncanny feel for the front" showed itself at Bad Kreuznach, where Patton told 4th Armored to stop and wait for reinforcement, causing Bradley's staff to wonder what had possessed the old man; Bradley told them not to worry. When the counterattack Patton had anticipated arrived, 4th Armored was ready and brushed it off.[184]

By the end, two German armies had lost 75 to 80 percent of their infantry—well over a hundred thousand men, of whom ninety thousand were prisoners—the Siegfried Line had been unhinged, and the war had been won west of the Rhine just as Eisenhower, Bradley, and Patton had intended. Patton issued an order of the day congratulating Third Army for conquering 6,482 square miles and 3,072 cities, towns, and villages: "History records no greater achievement in so limited a time." His chief of staff wrote in his diary: "It can safely be said that . . . [this] has been the greatest campaign of Third Army. . . . Students of military history will study [it] for years to come." Patton wrote in his own diary: "I really believe this . . . is one of the outstanding operations in the history of war."[185] And then at the end—in the middle of the night, when no one was looking, where it was least expected, totally without the elaborate preparations Montgomery was making in the north, and two days ahead of him—Third Army crossed the Rhine.

"Uncanny" is the right word. The previous summer, while he was still in England, Patton had picked the exact spot for his Rhine crossing (near Oppenheim) where it actually happened. (His son later informed him that Napoleon had crossed in the same place.) The terrain on the near side dominated the other and the Frankfurt hills were too far away for artillery fire to be directed on the bridges. There was a bright moon the night of March 22 when Company K, 3d Battalion, 11th Infantry, of the 5th Division, crept down to the Rhine and climbed into assault boats. When they landed on the other side, seven surprised Germans surrendered and helpfully rowed themselves back to the west bank. Elsewhere there were firefights, but by midnight the whole regiment had crossed over with only twenty casualties.

Bradley was eating breakfast when Patton phoned: "Brad, don't tell anyone but I'm across." (He wanted to be sure he was there to stay.) But at Bradley's briefing later in the morning, the Third Army liaison officer reported, in an allusion that needed no explanation: "Without benefit of aerial bombing, ground smoke, artillery preparation, and airborne assistance, the Third Army at 2200 hours, Thursday evening, March 22, crossed the Rhine River," and that night, his voice trembling, Patton called Bradley again: "Brad, for God's sake tell the world . . . I want the world to know Third Army made it before Monty starts across."[186]

The consciousness of making history possessed him. Driving to Trier from Luxembourg, the day his Saar-Palatinate offensive opened, Patton was reminded that Caesar's legions had trod this same road before him (he had been reading the *Gallic Wars*), and he wrote that he "could almost smell the coppery sweat and see the low dust clouds where those stark fighters moved into battle." Coppery sweat? For Patton, the past was so real that he sometimes seemed to believe that he had lived it in some earlier incarnation. Coming up to the great river, two days after the crossing, he paused in the middle of the pontoon bridge his engineers had built and according to Codman (who retreated into a French quotation to describe it) *a fait pipi dans le Rhin.* Arriving at the other shore, he feigned to stumble, and rising let sift to the earth a handful of German soil. Thus Scipio Africanus, thus William the Conqueror, thus George Smith Patton, Jr.[187]

A personal aside: XXI Corps of Seventh Army, to whose headquarters I belonged, had been in position opposite the deep sector of the Siegfried Line near Saarbrücken. Patton was right about Lorraine; it is a gloomy part of France, and from French Renaissance history I associated it only with the Guise family, a disreputable lot. This war had dealt harshly with

Lorraine; shattered buildings and the stench of destruction were every-where. The weather was monotonously grim. On March 15, the 63d Division of our corps tried to bypass Saarbrücken but ran into heavy going in the fortified areas. On the seventeenth, my diary reads: "Patton moving." On the nineteenth, with Third Army attacking it from the rear, the German front opposite us began to break up. On Wednesday the twenty-first, the sun came out and we prepared to move into Germany. We were never held up for long thereafter until we reached the Alps south of Munich and the war in Europe was over. To say that we had a high opinion of General Patton is a large understatement.

On Palm Sunday, the sun still shining, a convoy I was in made its way to Neustadt down a road from Pirmasens that Michelin describes as "hilly, with many declines," as indeed it was. There, in a defile between a wooded ridge and a ravine, a mainly horse-drawn German supply column had been caught by a company of tanks from Patton's 10th Armored Division. For two miles along the road there was a scene of desolation almost beyond bearing. Dead horses, some disemboweled, their legs stiff in the air in angular attitudes, lined the ditches. Some had been marked by the treads of the tanks and the powder burns of guns fired at point-blank range. The shattered German trucks and wagons, with their dead, had simply been bulldozed off the road and into the ravine by the American tanks. German soldiers, unattended, were still wandering dazedly through the wreckage. This had been too much, when he had come the same route two days before, even for George Patton. He had viewed it for a time in silence. "That," he finally said to Codman, "is the greatest scene of carnage I have ever witnessed. Let's go home."[188]

IV

When R. W. Thompson wrote that after August 1944 the European war followed "the design of Roosevelt," he did not say what he thought that design was, but he did go on to contrast "American innocence, naive idealism, bigotry and good intentions" with the mature and complex vision of Winston Churchill, who would presumably have done it differently. For all his adherence to British worldwide interests, Churchill was a European; the rich tapestry of his mind was filled with European images. After all, had he not been born in Blenheim Palace, named after the great victory over France won in Bavaria by his illustrious ancestor the Duke of Marlborough? When in 1940 he is writing to Roosevelt about the Battle of Taranto against the Italians and mentions the date October 21, he automatically adds "(Trafalgar Day)," never to be forgotten, when (in Mahan's lovely sentence) "Those far-distant storm beaten ships, on which Napoleon's soldiers never looked, stood between them and the dominion of the world." Thompson writes that Churchill's was "a mind nurtured in the political and historical background of Europe, aware instinctively of the subtle balances of power, the nuances of ambition, the underlying hatreds, the national chicaneries, and the genuine aspirations of the European peoples. All this was in his blood."[189]

Churchill's own account of the war's end is a curious work, marred by ominous foreboding and a sense of dismay that seems authentic but also forced, as though in part got up for the occasion. This, the sixth and final volume of *The Second World War,* he calls *Triumph and Tragedy,* the "tragedy" being the tale of "How the Great Democracies Triumphed, and so were able to Resume the Follies Which Had so Nearly Cost Them Their Life." An important element in the story is necessarily his own ejection from office by the British public while Japan was still undefeated, which it would be understandable for him to regard as a personal tragedy or a tragic folly on the part of his countrymen. But otherwise the tragedy seems mainly to be the emergence of Soviet Russia as a major power and its presence "in the heart of Europe," which he calls "a fateful milestone for mankind." How this parallels the prewar "follies" of the democracies —appeasement, irresolution, unpreparedness—he does not make completely clear, and if he believed that the westward expansion of Soviet power should have been resisted, then it was distinctly an afterthought on his part. The British official history of the war concludes that even if Churchill and Eden had decided in the spring of 1945 to act on an assumption that Soviet Russia was a potential enemy, there was no likelihood of such a policy being adopted in Britain or America. "But secondly," writes John Ehrman, *"they did not so decide. . . .* They did not despair of a solution with the Russians: indeed they expected it." (Emphasis added.)[190]

Up to the end of the European war, no one had gone further to conciliate Soviet Russia than Churchill. In early 1942, he pressed Roosevelt to join him in recognizing the Soviet acquisition by force of the Baltic states—Estonia, Latvia, and Lithuania—which the President resolutely refused to do. In Jugoslavia in 1944, Churchill shifted his support to Tito and the Partisans, and away from Mihailovich and the Chetniks, even though he was well aware that Tito would install a Communist postwar government in Belgrade. Churchill went along wholeheartedly with Russian claims to territory in Poland, and leaned heavily on the exiled Polish government in London to make it accept them, though Roosevelt resisted at every step of the way but the last, at Yalta.

In October 1944, Churchill did intervene against the Communists in Greece (whom he believed to be "Trotskyites") but with the understanding that Russia would not protest (and it didn't). Earlier in the month, during an extraordinary scene at dinner in the Kremlin, Churchill had proposed to Stalin that they carve up eastern Europe into spheres of influence in which Russia would control Rumania and Bulgaria, with a fifty-fifty split in Hungary and Jugoslavia, and British control in Greece. "It was all settled," writes Churchill of so cynical and offhand an episode, "in no more time than it takes to set it down." (The Yalta agreement tried to undo this mésalliance by making provision for freely elected governments in the liberated countries, but Russia—preferring the *realpolitik* of Churchill's proposal—failed to observe it and Yalta has passed into mythology as a "sellout" while Churchill's willingness to yield up Eastern Europe is forgotten.) He told Stalin at Potsdam that he welcomed Russia as a great power at sea, and he prided himself on being able to talk to Stalin "as one human being to another."[191]

All of which makes Churchill's discovery that the "Soviet menace . . . had replaced the Nazi foe" look like a case of rather belated illumination. He unquestionably wanted the Allied armies, as he put it, to "join hands with the Russian armies as far to the east as possible," and he did not want the Americans to pull back from the areas they had overrun in Germany and Czechoslovakia while there was still a possibility of renegotiating the postwar zones of occupation. But once again it is not clear how he thought "the future peace of Europe" could be assured by rejecting agreements already reached and hitherto regarded as acceptable. The Russians could have asked with some justification why we hadn't thought of that before, and thus have put the blame for obstructing the restoration of a tranquil Europe on us.

Churchill's real cause for concern was that "the bond of common danger"[192] which united the Grand Alliance had vanished, that the ties of comradeship were loosening, and that the realities of British exhaustion and impoverishment could no longer be glossed over. He was too honest to rewrite his own record, and all his hopes were focused on preserving the very special and intimate relationship with the Americans, so that he could not blame or overly criticize them. (What his private thoughts were about the "design of Roosevelt" replacing his own can only be guessed.) The "Soviet menace," which was real but as yet unrecognized in the West, came to his rescue.

Other critics of Roosevelt, Marshall, and Eisenhower have had no such inhibitions as Churchill's. There has come in fact to be a body of belief that puts responsibility on their shoulders for having won the war but lost the peace. In fullest extension it attributes to Churchill military plans he did not propose and foresight he never claimed to possess, but it must be conceded to have been the single most successful revisionist interpretation of World War II. For convenience it may be called the Wilmot thesis, since it was first and most skillfully advanced by Chester Wilmot in his book, *The Struggle for Europe,* which was warmly praised in the British press on its publication in 1953. Wilmot's viewpoint has found many adherents (Hanson Baldwin and General Mark Clark among Americans), and echoes of it can be heard in American popular histories of the war's ending, such as John Toland's or Cornelius Ryan's.[193]

The "Wilmot thesis" runs roughly as follows: Because of American determination to employ military power in Western Europe rather than the Balkans, "Stalin succeeded in obtaining from Roosevelt and Churchill what he had failed to obtain from Hitler," namely Russia's position as "the dominant power on the Continent." The Americans were "militarily unsophisticated" and lacked "subtlety and skill in strategy." They believed in a "head-on assault" by an accumulation of massive strength, by the "sheer smashing power of superior force." Therefore they failed to perceive the "golden opportunity" (as Alexander called it) of an attack from northern Italy through the Ljubljana gap to Vienna, which Alexander proposed in a cable to Churchill on June 19, 1944. By rejecting this, by their aversion to action in the Balkans of any kind, and by a naive disinclination to annoy the Russians, the Americans threw away the chance of reaching Vienna ahead of the Red Army, of shortening the war, and of reducing postwar Russian influence in Eastern Europe. Similar American obtuseness accounts for their refusal to make a final drive on Berlin and get to the German capital first. The end result was "the destruction of the European balance of power which Britain went to war to maintain."[194]

As a military proposition this devolves on what Eisenhower called "that gap whose name I can't even pronounce." Alexander and others drew a picture of Allied armies pouring through it to spread out irresistibly into the Danubian plain. But the Ljubljana gap, as anyone who has been there knows,[195] is not a gap at all but a heavily forested, narrow, ascending defile nearly two hundred miles long, wound through by a double-track railroad and a single, poorly surfaced road twenty feet wide, with many tunnels, steep gradients, and two mountain passes at about two thousand feet dominated by higher mountains on either side. Room for maneuver is there none; only one way through. It would be difficult to imagine a battleground more made to order for those masters of demolition and defense, the Germans, who were there in strength and in Italy had already demonstrated their capacity for fighting in mountainous terrain.

The Russians reached Bucharest on August 31, 1944. Even assuming that we could have stormed our way through the "gap," and reopened its road and railroad in time—a considerable assumption—our chances of reaching Vienna in any strength ahead of the Red Army were minimal. This was no route for ample supply. The number of divisions that could have been provisioned on the other side of Ljubljana, as Roosevelt pointed out to Churchill on June 29, was six at a maximum and more likely two, as Admiral Morison believed.[196] The idea of such a force overawing the Russians, while at the same time marching triumphantly through Austria and southern Germany, is and was a fantasy.

Churchill knew this. "In his postwar memoirs," writes Maurice Mat-loff, "Churchill steadfastly denied that he wanted a Balkan invasion." So did Wilmot, who wrote: "At no time did the Prime Minister or his Chiefs of Staff suggest that the major offensive against Germany could, or should, be launched through Southern Europe." The trouble is that Churchill (and Wilmot) wanted to have it both ways. Churchill advocated at most a limited, diversionary effort with armor in company with Jugoslav guerril-las (he said he believed we could "slip through"), and yet he twice com-plains in his book that the failure to mount a *major* effort—because of invading southern France instead—had deprived us of the opportunity "to reach Vienna before the Russians, with all that might have followed there-from."[197]

Such as what? When it comes to the tangible benefits to be derived from an Allied presence on the Danube, the proponents of the same turn silent. We are in the domain of appearances, of the pyschology of national preeminence. To Churchill—for whom the terms "power" and "prestige" were, if not synonymous, at least correlative—the answer was self-evident. Power in postwar Europe would come from prestige, and prestige would consist in how visibly one had been the victor. No illusion was to be more brutally dispelled. When the iron curtain came down, the fact that Allied soldiers had been the first in Lübeck or Pilsen turned out not to matter very much to their inhabitants.

The charge of failure to demonstrate military sophistication is difficult to rebut, since sophistication resides so largely in the eye of the beholder. Of American inexperience there is no question, but it has its equivalent in that form of institutionalized amateurism that the British sometimes mistake for professionalism. The prewar British Army was idea-resistant to a degree (read Liddell Hart's memoirs), and it had no George Marshall to weed out deadwood and nurture the gifted. The strategy of poking at the perimeter of Europe and hoping for the best was not sophisticated; it was merely the acceptance of the inability to do anything else. One British historian has suggested that there was really no coherent British strategy but only a blend produced by pressures, opportunities, and personali-ties.[198] As for reliance on "sheer smashing power," none could have mani-fested this more consistently than Montgomery. Bradley's and Patton's campaigns were deft rapier thrusts compared to the heavy blunderbuss blows Montgomery insisted on delivering. There *was* an American strat-egy for ending the war—the strategy of Eisenhower, Marshall, and Roose-velt—and it was thoroughly sophisticated to the extent of being political, rooted in hardheaded realism, and calculated to preserve the Anglo-American alliance in the postwar world.

The politics of it were in the order of things American. Roosevelt domestically confronted a necessity: The European war must be ended as quickly as possible and the Army redeployed against Japan. His electorate would be content with nothing else. At the first plenary session of the Yalta Conference he therefore said that the United States could not keep a large army in Europe after the fighting ended or maintain an occupation force in Germany for longer than two years. For the same reason he could not indulge in "diversionary" efforts if they involved any risk whatever to the main enterprise. "I could never survive even a slight setback in Overlord," he wrote Churchill in June 1944, "if it were known that fairly large forces had been diverted to the Balkans." As for the Jugoslav partisans, Roosevelt had doubts about the value of insurrectionary movements in general.[199]

Further, the President's military advisers believed that the high cost of a Balkan operation, given the poor terrain and poor communications, was not being acknowledged and they had arrived at a strategic assessment of the postwar international scene in which any British desire to cut a large figure there had no place. On July 28, 1944, the American Joint Chiefs of Staff addressed a paper to the secretary of state on the military background of postwar diplomacy as they saw it at the time. This is a dark document in its recognition of Russia's rise and Britain's decline.

"Both in an absolute and relative sense," said the Joint Chiefs, ". . . the British Empire will emerge from the war having lost ground both economically and militarily." The termination of hostilities would find the world undergoing a change more profound than any in the fifteen hundred years since the fall of Rome, among the causes of which were the development of aviation, the mechanization of warfare generally, and a "marked shift in the munitioning potentials" of the major victorious nations. "After the defeat of Japan, the United States and the Soviet Union will be the only military powers of the first magnitude. . . . While the U.S. can project its military power into many areas overseas, it is nevertheless true that the relative strength and geographic positions of these two powers preclude the military defeat of one . . . by the other, even if that power were allied with the British Empire."[200]

It is unfortunate that this document is not better known (only Maurice Matloff has paid much attention to it), for it explains so abundantly why the American military thought and acted as they did before the fog of cold-war posturing obscured their earlier clarity of perception. They were thinking globally; the "European balance of power which Britain went to war to maintain" did not strike them as any longer relevant, and its revival seemed to them neither necessary nor feasible. (Eventually a balance would be restored, but only by a revived West Germany and American arms on semipermanent station there, two thoughts unthinkable in the climate of 1944.)

The Joint Chiefs were motivated not by desire to placate Soviet Russia so much as by awareness of their inability to make it disappear from the world scene, of British inability to dominate Europe, and of the inability of either the U.S. or the U.S.S.R. to destroy the other. (This is still true, if only in that both can now destroy the other many times over, which amounts to the same thing.) For an analysis of the controlling military factors on foreign policy to resist obsolescence for forty years is no mean achievement. Nor was it any mean achievement for Eisenhower, having provided the military concept that won the campaign, to have provided the political concept of Allied unity that built the basis for the peace.

◆

Eisenhower was misunderstood by many among the British military because he represented an American way in war, which they misconstrued. It is not simply a matter of mass, or of organization, or of industrial plenty, though these play a part. The American way was a war of voluntary combination, the war by which the North beat the South and thus the war that fixed itself in the minds of Americans for generations to come. Fletcher Pratt said that it constituted "this nation's one outstanding contribution to the science of human relations, a contribution not even yet thoroughly understood."[201] American combination is for certain purposes, while maintaining perfect freedom in all others, the individual in suspension within the group: the husking bee, the ridgepole raising, the wagon train westward, the jazz band, the street gang, the naval task force, the Army of the Potomac. From the many, one.

Once the purpose is accomplished the combination disbands. Yet while in existence it is everything: infantry with tanks and artillery, then all three with air—and ultimately with allies, as Fox Conner had taught the young Eisenhower. It must be voluntary, willed by all, for no other way can the force of the combination be realized and the generous energies liberated. It is sometimes considered to be a mechanical way of doing things, when this is in fact quite wide of the mark. It is political.

Eisenhower and Churchill genuinely liked one another, but they had a more lasting bond in the high importance both attached to Allied unity. Churchill dreamed of an Anglo-American partnership continuing into the postwar world. "Still," he ended his speech to Congress in December 1941, "I avow my hope and faith, sure and inviolate, that in the days to come the British and American peoples will for their own safety and for the good of all walk together side by side in majesty, in justice, and in peace."[202] He would do nothing that might darken this fair prospect and would even, on occasion, take Eisenhower's side against his own chiefs, to their chagrin.

Eisenhower in turn had long since arrived at a conviction that Allied differences must in no circumstance whatever be allowed to get in the way of victory. He repeated this again and again. After Casablanca, when many American officers felt outmaneuvered and overpowered by the British, he pleaded with General Handy in the Ops division *not* "to deal with our military problems on an American vs. British basis." He wrote Handy in

January 1943 that "one of the constant sources of danger to us in this war is the temptation to regard as our first enemy the partner that must work with us in defeating the real enemy."[203]

The principle of an Allied unity that might supersede national and imperial considerations, however, was not endorsed by the British high command. Montgomery wanted British unity. "The senior British officers at SHAEF," he wrote to Brooke in August 1944, "must realise that, in addition to being good allied chaps, they have definite loyalties to their side of the house; and, in our side of the house, we must all pull together." Now and then the pangs were felt of a latent hunger for a purely British victory. Brooke, in April, had written of a Far Eastern attack in Borneo that it "might give us a chance of running an entirely British Imperial campaign instead of furnishing reinforcements for American operations."[204]

Thoughts of a similar nature fueled the intensity of discourse about Italy, southern France, the Balkans, and the drive into Germany. Alexander at one point proposed to Brooke that Italy be made an all-British theater by sending the American divisions there to France and replacing them with British ones. Even Churchill succumbed. In July 1944, he wrote Ismay of his desire to have the "chance to launch a decisive strategic stroke with what is entirely British and under British command." He said he was not going to give way about this: "Alexander is to have his campaign." The Americans must understand "that we have been ill treated and are furious" (about southern France). "Do not let any smoothings or smirchings cover up this fact," Churchill ended his memo. "After a little we shall get together again; but if we take everything lying down there will be no end to what will be put upon us." In January 1945, Brooke wrote in his diary that Churchill was still proposing "strategies based on ensuring that British troops were retained in the limelight, if necessary at the expense of the Americans."[205]

It was not to be. The "design of Roosevelt" was in effect, and in essentials had been for some time. It can be briefly summarized: that a major invasion of Europe take place during 1944, that Eisenhower command it and that his authority be uncompromised, that a supplemental invasion of southern France be made using divisions from Italy, that we stay out of the Balkans, that American soldiers serve under American leaders,[206] that Nazi Germany be defeated as rapidly as possible (so that American troops could be redeployed), and that the United States not involve itself in postwar national rivalries.

What needs to be emphasized, however, is the validity of Roosevelt's design and its close-call success. If the President had *not* put himself completely behind Overlord in 1944, it would almost certainly have been postponed until 1945 or later; Brooke was all along reluctant about it and Churchill's doubts are notorious. In that event, Hitler would have been able to open the barrage of the V-weapons on Britain (from France, Belgium, and the Netherlands) without hindrance, inasmuch as we would not have had the ability to overrun their launching sites. The V-1 flying bomb could have been countered, up to a point, but for the V-2—the first genuine ballistic missile—there was at that time no answer. The consequences for London are sobering to think about. The same applies to a Balkan campaign, even assuming its success. The invasion of southern France was in every way preferable, and gave Eisenhower a superiority of force only a little more than adequate to his task.

A policy of backing Eisenhower in his arguments with the British about strategy was demonstrably the right one; the President's confidence in him was justified many times over. To suggestions that the war in Europe should have been ended sooner, the proper answer is: *It was*. It had all been done in less than a year. It had been won by the time its planners had expected merely to have reached the German border, and none of the proposals for a quicker or easier victory are convincing. An appearance of delay came from disillusionment after the headlong race across France, from the discovery—at the little-noticed tank battle at Arracourt in September 1944—of how quickly and vigorously the Germans had recovered. They had to be beaten at their own game.

But none of the setbacks slowed the progressive destruction of the Wehrmacht, which was achieved on a faster timetable but virtually without change (except for the abandonment of the Brittany ports) in Eisenhower's original intentions. Beetle Smith has described how in May 1944 at Bushy Park, a month before D-Day, Eisenhower penciled in on a map for his staff the course he expected the fighting to follow. "I doubt that there has ever been a campaign in history," wrote Smith, "where actual operations fitted so closely the initial plan of a commander, adopted so far in advance."[207]

So much having been said, it should also be emphasized that the strategy that won the European war overall was not exclusively Marshall's and Eisenhower's (backed by Roosevelt) but a compromise with the British which the President also encouraged. At a meeting before the Quebec Conference in August 1943, Roosevelt pressed Marshall to send more divisions to the Mediterranean and thus make possible an advance in Italy north of Rome, even though Marshall feared this could not be done without weakening Overlord, then still under debate. At the conference itself, the Combined Chiefs adopted a plan for a "limited" Italian campaign of the kind the President wanted, partly on the strong recommendation of Brooke, who wrote in his diary that it took him hours to get past American suspiciousness and incomprehension: "finally I had to produce countless arguments to prove the close relation that exists between cross-Channel and Italian operations."[208]

The long ordeal of the Italian campaign, together with disparage-ments of it like General Fuller's, have combined to minimize the degree to which it did, and did effectively, what it was intended to do. Unlike Churchill, Brooke had always regarded it as a means to an end rather than an end in itself, and the argument he made for it at Quebec was that it would divert German divisions away from the campaign in France and, for that matter, the Russians. This it did. It was not the "daft" absurdity Fuller thought it was.

At one time or another, the Allies employed the equivalent of thirty-three divisions in Italy, the Germans thirty-six (of which three were Italian and one Russian). Since there were only six German divisions in Italy when the Allies landed, the latter would therefore seem to have drawn some thirty enemy divisions away from other (and more critical) fronts. Moreover, the thirty Allied divisions assembled in Sicily and North Africa could not have been transferred to northern Europe (because of limited British port capacity) without slowing down the arrival of new divisions from the United States, whereas the Germans, with interior transportation lines over shorter distances, could have moved their units to either the east or the west with relative ease.[209] Brooke would later reassure himself that his strategy had been the correct one, and had proved itself in practice; but he might have added a footnote of thanks to Roosevelt for bringing the Americans into the Mediterranean in the first place and then, sooner than Marshall, seeing the merits of Brooke's Italian campaign.

The same cannot be said for Brooke as far as the double envelopment of the Ruhr is concerned. He stated flatly that it would not work, on December 12, 1944, at a meeting in London of Eisenhower and Tedder with Churchill and the British chiefs. Brooke was brutally outspoken. He said that Eisenhower's plan violated the principle of concentration of force—"which had resulted in the present failures"—that a double invasion of Germany was impossible with the limited resources Eisenhower had, and that it would lead only to a dispersal of effort into two inadequate thrusts. Eisenhower said that Brooke later recanted, when they were standing together on the bank of the Rhine during Montgomery's crossing, but Brooke denied this. He said that he went on thinking to the end that Eisenhower had been wrong—and thus Montgomery right.[210] None of them ever really changed his mind.

The surrounding of the Ruhr was executed with a dispatch that conceals how well it had been planned. Industrially speaking, the bombers had left the Ruhr not much of an objective, but German soldiers were there prepared to defend it, which is what mattered. Bradley's Eifel and Palatinate campaigns, exactly as anticipated, had put Hodges and Patton in position to wheel together in a wide right hook to the north, to Paderborn and Kassel. The Germans had little enough to meet this with, and what they had was positioned in anticipation of something different. Field Marshal Albert Kesselring, who had replaced Rundstedt as C. in C. West, said that he felt "like a concert pianist who is asked to play a Beethoven sonata before a large audience on an ancient, rickety and out of tune instrument," and four times he tried to arouse in Hitler some awareness of what was actually happening.

An American task force was formed in 3d Armored Division and given the order, "Just go like hell!" toward Paderborn. They were slowed down less by opposition than by overrunning a champagne warehouse; one German general managed to escape the lunging American columns only by joining one of them in the dark.[211] On Easter Sunday, 3d Armored coming from the south and east met 2d Armored coming from the west at Lippstadt and the trap was closed. The Ruhr had been encircled by three American armies, and the two more southern—coming by way of Bradley's Frankfurt corridor—had traveled the fastest and farthest of the three. So much for the single-thrust strategy.

Enemy resistance by now was unpredictable. Some American units went for miles and encountered nothing but white sheets hung from bedroom windows. But then a fanatical last-ditch Nazi might organize a group of teen-age SS cadets from a nearby school, or the crews of heavy antiaircraft guns might man them as antitank weapons, and there would be heavy fighting. The formula of "unconditional surrender" adopted at Casablanca seemed to have little to do with it; Heinrich Himmler's decree of September 10, 1944, that the family of a deserter "will be summarily shot" probably did as much or more to keep German soldiers in the line. Beetle Smith said that in general, Germans under frontal attack continued to fight, while when surrounded, attacked from the rear, or deserted by their officers, they would willingly enough give up.[212]

Certainly they did so in the Ruhr; in early April, American divisions began taking them in at the rate of one thousand, then two thousand, then five thousand a day. Some had to walk for miles to find an American not too busy to accept their surrender; one U.S. soldier started out marching sixty-eight prisoners to the rear and on arrival found that he had twelve hundred. "In every conceivable manner . . . ," writes Charles B. Mac-Donald in The Last Offensive, "they presented themselves to their captors: most plodding wearily on foot; some in civilian automobiles, assorted military vehicles, or on horseback . . . some carrying black bread and wine; others with musical instruments—accordions, guitars; a few bringing along wives or girl friends in a mistaken hope they might share their captivity. . . . There was nothing triumphant about it; it was instead a gigantic wake watching over the pitiable demise of a once-proud military force." The final count in the Ruhr was 317,000, including twenty-five generals and an admiral. Their commander, Field Marshal Walter Model, who believed that field marshals do not surrender, walked off into the woods near Düsseldorf and shot himself.[213]

On April 4, the 4th Armored Division reached Ohrdruf, first of the death camps to be uncovered, first direct encounter with a bestiality and sadism beyond the comprehension of Americans nurtured for the most part in a bucolic innocence by comparison. The Supreme Commander, when shown Ohrdruf, turned pale; Patton vomited. The burgomaster of the town and his wife, when compelled to view the corpses and the living dead, went home and hanged themselves. The evening my organization overran its first concentration camp, the officers' mess was a silent place; some simply stared at their plates. I think it fair to say that for many this was their first realization of what it was we were fighting against.

This was a strange experience to witness, the collapse of a monumental despotism and the exposure of its inward rottenness and banality: to move in mechanized columns along the parallel strips of an *Autobahn* while German soldiers slouching toward captivity a dozen or more abreast filled the grass in between; to watch civilians who had been told that the Americans were starving and wearing paper shoes as their eyes followed the blur of truck after truck moving past them; to see a concentration-camp inmate with shaved head and striped pajamalike suit standing by the side of the road, eyes closed, kissing his hand in blessing to the sky; to hear once too often the plaint, *"Ich bin kein Nazi, ich bin nur deutscher Arbeiter,"* and to wonder what the plaintiff had thought ten years—or even ten days—before; to occupy offices of the German security service whose bookcases seemed to be lined with spy novels about the diabolically clever British; to read the pages-long counterintelligence lists of newly remonstrant bureaucrats denouncing one another; and to live briefly in German houses where army uniforms were still in the closet and dirty dishes were still in the sink, even in the Twilight of the Gods.

Endgame: Do we, or do we not, try to beat the Russians to Berlin? It was the same old argument between the same protagonists; only the subject was different. Montgomery wanted to be given U.S. Ninth Army and Berlin as an objective, to take his final bow in the spotlight as bringer of triumph. Churchill wanted Berlin, so he told Eisenhower, because its fall "would have a profound psychological effect in every part of the Reich . . . while Berlin remains under the German flag it cannot, in my opinion, fail to be the most decisive point in Germany." Eisenhower was not interested in psychological effects; he was interested in destroying "German resistance in every part of the Reich," in employing his now-abundant armies to make certain there were no holdouts, no postponement of the inevitable. Montgomery, being in the north, would be given the mission of reaching the Baltic and denying the Russians any entry into Denmark, a consideration Eisenhower was one of the first to entertain and one that Churchill was compelled to acknowledge. Ninth Army was no longer Montgomery's; it would revert to Bradley, where it belonged, despite Churchill's outrage at this "withdrawal." Bradley now commanded the largest single force the United States had ever fielded: four armies, twelve corps, forty-eight divisions, more than 1,300,000 men.[214]

But should it—or *could* it?—win a race to the German capital? The evidence is fairly clear that it could not have done so and therefore should not have tried. By mid-February, the Russians had reached the Oder and Neisse rivers, thirty-five miles from Berlin, where they halted and began building up their strength. By April, they had concentrated 1,250,000 men and 22,000 field guns, which Stephen Ambrose (in his book on Eisenhower's decision about Berlin) calls "the greatest armed force in so small an area in the whole of military history."[215] In early April, the Americans were still engaged in cleaning up the Ruhr pocket, but they were also moving east, and by April 11, advance points of Simpson's Ninth Army had reached the Elbe at Magdeburg. Berlin was fifty miles away.

Could the effort to capture it have been successful? General Simpson thought it could, and went on thinking so after the war, but his commander who would have been stuck with the job—Major General Raymond S. McLain of XIX Corps—did not think so. The Americans had a small bridgehead over the Elbe, perhaps fifty thousand men in the area, and very little artillery. XIX Corps was strung out over the countryside, its rear 150 miles from its front, and Germans were still harassing its flanks. To supply it for a further advance would have required every transport aircraft SHAEF possessed. Present at McLain's headquarters happened to be one of the shrewdest of American military analysts, the chief historian of the theater, Brigadier General S. L. A. Marshall. The two of them reviewed the problem and concluded that it was insoluble. McLain thought that at best he might be able to get a few patrols into the outskirts of Berlin by the time the Russians had taken the city. Marshall agreed.[216]

When Eisenhower asked Bradley how many casualties it would cost us to get to Berlin first, Bradley said 100,000. (The cost to the Russians was eventually more than three times that number.) Eisenhower, if he had not already done so, at that moment wrote Berlin off. Incurably romantic to the last, Patton remonstrated with the Supreme Commander and got nowhere. Eisenhower was not a sentimental man. To him Berlin had become, as Bradley put it, nothing but a "prestige objective," whose postwar occupation by the Allies jointly had already been decided on (an agreement the Russians honored without argument at this stage), and thus was not worth an American life. Eisenhower was the first to admit, as he informed the Combined Chiefs, that wars are fought for political purposes, and if they instructed him to drive on Berlin for political reasons he would cheerfully comply. No such instructions came.[217]

Eisenhower's truly astonishing accomplishment was swallowed up in the victory itself. Not many really noticed, as he so often arranged it, the piece of legerdemain that had been performed. The conduct of the war had been removed from British hands so deftly that they had no legitimate cause for complaint. His policy was simplicity itself: "he would not let either a British or an American general win the war singlehandedly," writes Martin Blumenson; "both British and Americans had to win it together." There was going to be no mean-spirited haggling over honor or glory; victory was going to be shared.

The very simplicity of the idea seems to have been what prevented Montgomery or Brooke from ever grasping it; their endless variations on the theme of let-Monty-do-it broke over the bar of Eisenhower's logical consistency. He saw to it that American armies stood forth at the close in proportion to their numbers and their contribution to the fighting, but without denigration to their comrades in arms. "His real achievement," writes Ambrose, "was that he had won without alienating the British."[218] The word "indispensable" should be used with care, but no candidate has been proposed for the role of doing what Eisenhower did.

Churchill understood. "Let me tell you what General Eisenhower has meant to us . . . ," he wrote to President Truman after Roosevelt had died and the European war had ended. "In his headquarters unity and strategy were the only reigning spirits. . . . At no time has the principle of alliance between noble races been carried and maintained at so high a pitch. In the name of the British Empire and Commonwealth I express to you our admiration of the firm, far-sighted, and illuminating character and qualities of General of the Armies Eisenhower."[219] And lastly, which no one much noticed either, the design of Roosevelt had been supplanted by the design of Eisenhower. America was not going to withdraw from European concerns as the President wished but would embrace them as Eisenhower had learned to do. In the figure of this man we were in Europe to stay, and on this rock would be built the Truman Doctrine, the Marshall Plan, the North Atlantic Treaty Organization, and the world we have lived in since.

On May 7, I was in Augsburg, quartered in an apartment complex south of the city and taking the sun in its garden. A little girl appeared, perhaps eight or nine years old, with a rubber ball she bounced in my direction and I bounced back. It developed that my name was Eric and hers was Hilda. She had a younger brother, who became very agitated and shouted, *"Terror! Terror!"* when a P-47 flew by. Through an open window I could hear a radio tuned to the Armed Forces Network when the announcement came. *"Hilda,"* I said, *"der Krieg ist auf. Um Mitternacht heute Abend der Krieg ist auf."* She clapped her hand to her mouth and she and her brother ran away home.

Beetle Smith has described the closing scene. In SHAEF advance headquarters at Rheims, after the surrender ceremony, a group gathered with the Supreme Commander to compose a victory message to the Combined Chiefs. They all tried their hands at putting together portentous and resounding phrases, until finally Eisenhower thanked them all and dictated the cable that was sent:

"The mission of this Allied force was fulfilled at 0241 local time, May 7, 1945."[220]

IX

STILWELL

SOMETIMES IT SEEMED AS THOUGH HIS FATE was to be the only sane person in a madhouse. When war came on December 7, 1941, responsibility for defending the western shore of the American continent from San Luis Obispo to the Mexican border rested with Major General Joseph Warren Stilwell, commanding III Corps of Fourth Army at Monterey, four miles from Stilwell's home in Carmel, where he had invited his officers and their wives for coffee and sandwiches that Sunday morning. A day or so later, his higher headquarters helpfully informed him: "The main Japanese fleet is 164 miles off San Francisco"—not 160 or 170, but 164.[1]

The area now in Stilwell's unwonted keeping, within range of battleship guns from the sea, held five million people, three quarters of the American heavy-bomber industry, major oil wells and refineries, and the home ports of the Asiatic and Pacific fleets. To protect this three-hundred-mile frontier he had available seven regiments of infantry (more than half of them on guard duty), four battalions of coast artillery, and what he described to his diary as "almost a hatful" of ammunition, enough for a few hours' combat.

On the thirteenth came another warning from Fourth Army: "Reliable information that attack on Los Angeles is imminent. A general alarm being considered." San Francisco had already experienced an "air raid" by "enemy" planes that had turned back, so a senior officer informed Stilwell, because the radio broadcasts on which they were "homing" had been silenced. ("If turning off the radio broadcasts will win the war," wrote Stilwell, "there will be no objection from me.") A colonel had observed suspicious signaling with flashlights. A captain and his wife and daughters had seen three Japanese aircraft silhouetted against the crescent moon. A coast artillery sergeant had been "fired on" by a passing motorist.

509

All of this was of course a product of the purest panic, and through it moved Stilwell, dispensing calm and common sense. He and his aide, Major Frank "Pinky" Dorn, set up headquarters at the California Hotel in San Bernardino. Stilwell roamed the coast, inspecting outposts, sorting out his forces, badgering Washington for more men and matériel. He went to see components of the 1st Marine Division at San Diego and found their commanding officer, much to his reassurance, a "solid citizen" more than willing to help. He kept to himself his own "sinking feeling" at the paucity of his resources, the magnitude of his mission, and the idiocy of so many of his military fellow professionals.

On December 22, a phone call at six-thirty in the morning summoned Stilwell to Washington; higher duty was at hand. He was to command the first American offensive of the war and should expect to "be away for some time." His family gave him a premature holiday send-off ("Not a tear in the crowd—just smiles and waves for good luck," his diary reads), and he and Dorn reached Washington, after a storm-tossed and bumpy flight, on an icy sunlit late afternoon of Christmas Eve. A skidding taxi ride took them to the Munitions Building, where they were kept waiting in his office by a general deeply engaged in a phone conversation about whether dinner that evening was or was not black tie.

They went to the War Plans Division and talked to the deputy chief, Stilwell's classmate from Command and General Staff School at Leavenworth, Brigadier General Eisenhower. ("I'll bet he's not worried about wearing a tuxedo to any damned party tonight," Stilwell told Dorn.) By this time they knew the assignment: an invasion of either Casablanca or Dakar. "Pretty gloomy," Stilwell and Dorn went out to eat at a "dog wagon" on Pennsylvania Avenue. The following day they spent at the War College, being briefed at greater length than they cared to be about French West Africa; afterward they had Christmas dinner—this time "a good one," Stilwell wrote his wife, "at a restaurant"—and indulged themselves in a movie, Walt Disney's Dumbo, which Stilwell enjoyed so immoderately that they stayed through it twice.[2]

Plans for an expeditionary force in the South Atlantic had been prepared, at President Roosevelt's request, many months before Pearl Harbor and later grew to include the Dakar operation, which the President urged on his service chiefs at a White House meeting on December 21, hence the call to Stilwell. The presence in Washington of Churchill and the senior British military was adding further pressure, since Churchill wanted full American involvement in the war, saw North Africa as the logical place for it, and found a ready audience in a President whose instinct was all for the attack.

The more the Americans looked at the idea, the less they liked it. They thought the British estimates of the force required were too low, the lines of communication too vulnerable, and the possibilities of reinforcement far better for the Germans than for us. Stilwell, whose job it was to put together plans he would have to execute, early on perceived their futility. He soon had ample company. "All agree," he wrote after a meeting of Army brass with Secretary Stimson, "that any move we make *must* go. All agree that the means are meager, the transport uncertain, the complications numerous, the main facts unknown, the consequences serious."[3]

Again he was trying to nourish sanity in an atmosphere unconducive to it. "My impression of Washington," he wrote Mrs. Stilwell, "is a rush of clerks in and out of doors, swing doors always swinging, people with papers rushing after other people with papers, groups in corridors whispering in huddles, everybody jumping up just as you start to talk, telephones ringing, rooms crowded, with clerks all banging away at typewriters. . . . Six months of this and I'd be screaming in my sleep." Nor did he think there was much hope for a reasoned strategy at the highest level. "The moving agent of all this"—thus to his diary on December 29—"is of course the President."

Stilwell held a view of Roosevelt shared by many Army officers at the time—that he was a rank amateur in military matters and that he was vacillating, impulsive, too easily influenced by the last person to see him, especially if that person was British or, worst of all, Churchill. Stilwell thought that a lack of sound and steady thinking in Washington came from the top, and the side of the President that was gradually revealing itself to George Marshall was unknown to Stilwell. "Events are crowding us into ill-advised and ill-conceived projects," he wrote, echoing what Eisenhower, too, was then thinking.[4] Eventually reality took hold. There was simply not the shipping to mount an assault strong enough to overcome resistance in North Africa while at the same time continuing to supply Britain.

The only plan "within the joint capabilities of the United States and the British," General Marshall flatly informed the President on January 9, "is one which contemplates a *French invitation* for a direct occupation of French Morocco, with a reasonable assurance that the troops in Spanish Morocco would not cooperate with the Axis powers."[5] There was no such invitation and no such assurance. Q.E.D. For the moment, North Africa was out.

But then another prospect beckoned. Marshall had asked Stilwell, as someone who had served in China for almost a decade, to recommend an officer for duty there as the overall American military representative, and Stilwell (Dorn says it was his idea) suggested Lieutenant General Hugh A. Drum of First Army, stationed at Governors Island in New York harbor, who was already in fact first choice (though neither Dorn nor Stilwell knew this) of Secretary Stimson and his assistant John J. McCloy. "Since Drum was the senior officer in the whole army," writes Dorn, "and proba-

bly its biggest stuffed shirt, it occurred to me that he might impress hell
out of the Chinese. Stilwell agreed."

The thought was in both their minds that it would be better to have
Drum go to China than be sent there themselves; they had no desire to
miss out on being where the action was, in the Atlantic, for which so far
they had seemed to be at the head of the line. "Drum will be ponderous
and take time through interpreters"—Stilwell to his diary. "He will decide
slowly and insist on his dignity. Drum by all means." So Drum, too, was
called to Washington, arriving with observable alacrity ("quick work,"
Stilwell noted) and a staff contingent of fifty officers, apparently expecting
to be given the top field command in Europe, to be the Pershing of this
war. His self-confidence was his undoing, for it led him into two serious
mistakes.[6]

The first was to pick a fight with George Marshall. When Drum discovered what post they had in mind for him, and when conversations with
staff officers revealed how hazy was the mission and how few were the
resources behind it, he conceived the notion that the offer was a trap,
intended to sidetrack him into a dead end in a distant theater, with little
authority and a hopeless task (he was not the only one by whom this
possibility had been noticed). Worse, he said as much to Marshall, and
Marshall's temper, normally so well contained, flared in fury; heated
words were exchanged that would be difficult to retract.

Next Drum decided to take his case to Secretary Stimson, and here
his blunder was to couch it in terms not of what was best for the country
but of what was best for Hugh Drum, an unpromising tack to take with
Henry Stimson. "He had brought me a paper which he had drawn," wrote
Stimson, "in which he virtually took the position that he did not think the
role in China I had offered him was big enough for his capabilities. The
paper said a good deal more than that but that was what it boiled down
to." Finally realizing what might be at stake, Drum made frantic efforts
to indicate his willingness to comply, but the damage had been done. Four
days later, Stimson addressed him a friendly letter containing the deft,
surgical sentence: "I don't think I will ask you to make that sacrifice."[7]
There ended Drum's chances for overseas command in World War II.

Which left open the question of who should go to China. "Me?"
Stilwell asked his diary. "No, thank you. They remember me as a small-fry
colonel that they kicked around. They saw me on foot in the mud, consorting with coolies, riding soldier trains." On January 14, Stilwell was asked
to appear in the evening at Woodley, Stimson's house and capacious
grounds overlooking Rock Creek Park, where the secretary had been
accustomed to take his daily twelve-mile horseback ride. Stilwell discovered that he was the only guest.

For an hour and a half, before the fire in Stimson's library, they talked
about China. Stilwell, Stimson wrote, "gave me a better first-hand picture

of the valor of the Chinese armies than I had ever received before." Asked how he felt about duty there, Stilwell said he would go where he was sent, in the secretary's book a creditable reply. Stimson retired that night "with a rather relieved feeling that I had discovered a man who will be very useful."[8]

Stimson promptly communicated his "discovery" to Marshall, who had naturally arranged all this. Stilwell's diary completes the story: "Next day Henry said he had been stimulated, and that George should keep his eye on me, because I might be a commander. So George told him, Hell, that's just what he'd been telling Henry." To Stilwell, "George said how about it and who else is there. . . . So I said, 'What's the job?' and he gave me the paper. Co-ordinate and smooth out and run the road [i.e., the Burma Road], and get the various factions together and grab command and in general give 'em the works. Money no object."

Asked by Marshall what the chances were of success, Stilwell said they were good if he could have command. So then Marshall asked Stilwell to put in writing what he would mean by "command," and Stilwell's terms were cabled to Chiang Kai-shek by way of T. V. Soong, Chiang's brother-in-law, who was ambassador to Washington. (Soong was not a reliable channel of communication with Chiang, but the Americans did not discover this until much later.) Within the week, Chiang had accepted and Soong said he thought "the best man in the Army for the job had been chosen." Stilwell was not allowed until some days later to tell his wife, but he did write her now: "I am going where I believe you would want me to go."[9] Indeed they had found their man.

◆

Marshall and Stilwell had soldiered together in China in the 1920s. Their tours of duty there overlapped only by eight months, but these were enough for two kindred spirits to recognize one another. When Lieutenant Colonel Marshall became assistant commandant of the Infantry School at Fort Benning in 1927, he asked for Lieutenant Colonel Stilwell as head of the tactical section, and he subsequently wrote in Stilwell's efficiency report that the latter was "qualified for any command in peace or war," not language used lightly by George Marshall.

The Chinese post the two of them shared was Tientsin, southeast of Peking, the principal port and business center of northern China, where the United States maintained the 15th Infantry Regiment under the terms of the Boxer Rebellion protocols, to "safeguard the lives and property" of American missionaries, diplomats, and business entrepreneurs amid the disorders of a China making its painful way toward contemporary nationhood. Marshall was the regiment's executive officer, Stilwell one of its battalion commanders.

Stilwell was already an Old China Hand. He had been selected for military intelligence language training in 1919 and, all the Japanese slots being filled, had opted for Chinese as his second choice. His studies had commenced at Berkeley and continued for three years in Peking, where the Stilwells and their three children lived in a Chinese-style house outside the Legation Quarter and began to acquire the Chinese furnishings and *objets d'art* that later filled their home in Carmel. (The other two Stilwell children were born in Peking and Tientsin.) He had been in China once before this, for a period of weeks in 1911 after service in the Philippines, and in Shanghai and Canton had witnessed the revolution against the Manchu dynasty which made China a republic and brought Sun Yat-sen, the son of a peasant, to its presidency.

Stilwell had a gift for languages—he stood number one in French at West Point, later taught French and Spanish there—and he had the requisite military intelligence background as chief intelligence officer of IV Corps in France during World War I. In Peking he was given his Chinese name, Shih Ti-wei—*shih* having the possible meaning "history" and *ti-wei,* "lead in the right direction." From Peking he had been sent out into the countryside to supervise construction of a road in Shansi province and there to immerse himself in Chinese life to a degree unknown by Westerners in the sheltered compounds of the treaty ports.

Stilwell brought his family to join him, in a beat-up truck, and along the road his wife, Win, nursed the baby, surrounded by friendly Chinese curious to know whether foreigners did it the same way. In Shansi, they "settled in a mill with large airy, whitewashed rooms, rough beams and morning glories climbing the walls," writes Barbara Tuchman. "Outside were trees and songbirds, a spring of clear drinking water, grass spotted with buttercups, and flocks of sheep and goats."[10] During such years as these began for Joseph Stilwell his affection and respect for *lao-pai-hsing,* "old hundred names," the common folk of China, which never left him.

In July 1935, Stilwell returned to China for the fourth time, in the job he had always wanted, military attaché to the U.S. Embassy. He and the family lived in a century-old house built for a viceroy, avoided the social life of the diplomatic set, but cultivated the friendship of many and varied Chinese. His duties were to observe and report. Under insistent Japanese pressure, control of North China by the Nationalist government of Chiang Kai-shek and his Kuomintang party was crumbling, and Chiang was showing little readiness for determined resistance. (America, having twice as much trade with Japan than with China, was no more interested in provoking Japan than he was.)

With China in turmoil and information about it confused, Stilwell set out on a series of trips into the interior to see for himself, ranging from South China (which he disliked) to Manchuria (whose Japanese custodians he liked even less), traveling not by rail but by roundabout routes on bus, on boat, and on foot—a *huang-yu,* "yellow fish," that is, someone who cadges rides and haggles over prices, as foreign service officer Jack Service was to do a decade later in Honan and elsewhere in China on Stilwell's behalf.[11]

Stilwell came back with little confidence in Chiang's generalship or the government's determination to hold against the Japanese. "No evidence of planned defense . . . ," his notes read. "No troop increase or even thought of it. No drilling or maneuvering." Of Chiang: "He can have no intention of doing a thing or else he is utterly ignorant of what it means to get ready for a fight with a first class power . . . it looks as if the Japs have told him they wouldn't go any further just now."

Of the Communists: "They have good intelligence work, good organization, good tactics. They do not want the cities. Content to rough it in the country. Poorly armed and equipped, yet scare the Government to death." A Chinese colonel came to him with a proposal to set up a joint Sino-American staff in Washington. "It looks," Stilwell reported, "like another manifestation of the Chinese desire to get somebody else to do something they are afraid to do themselves . . . possibly an intimation that they have no intention of offering resistance unassisted."[12]

In July 1937, after an "incident" on the venerable Marco Polo Bridge twelve miles west of Peking, the war began in earnest. (When Stilwell drove out to investigate, both sides opened fire and his driver turned back "on two wheels" without stopping.) After a few weeks of trading accusations as to who was responsible, the Japanese military moved in and took over the whole Peking-Tientsin region, it would seem without the whole-hearted consent of their own government. At last concluding that he had more to gain by resisting than by knuckling under, Chiang Kai-shek ordered his 87th and 88th divisions (trained and equipped by the Germans) to Shanghai, where there was soon a genuine battle with the at-first-outnumbered Japanese.

The brave and hopeless defense of Shanghai brought China's struggle against the Japanese to the world's attention. On October 5, President Roosevelt delivered his "quarantine the aggressors" speech and a day later the League of Nations adopted a report describing Japanese actions in China as "out of all proportion to the incident that occasioned the conflict,"[13] tough talk for the tired League. But Chiang's hopes of intervention by the Western powers were to go unrealized. Shanghai fell and then Nanking, to be brutally ravaged. In October 1938, the Japanese landed in South China and within a week took both Hankow and Canton, China's then-capital and its chief port of entry for foreign supplies. Chiang and his government retreated to Chungking, far to the west, beyond the gorges of the Yangtze River.

When the time came for Stilwell to return to the United States, he could fairly be said to know China and the Chinese better than any other American officer. He spoke their language and had lived and traveled widely in their country, not as an encapsulated *lao-mao-tze* ("old hairy one"—that is, foreigner) but as one of them, sharing their hardships and admiring their indomitable spirit. He had seen at first hand the consequences for China of subjugation by Japanese who could be, in the wake of battle, extremely unpleasant conquerors (he had seen more than his fill of the mutilated corpses they left behind them).

He had seen at first hand, in the field and at the front, the durable fighting qualities of the Chinese soldiers and the pervasive incompetence of their officers. He had seen opportunities squandered, initiatives lost, lives sacrificed in vain through the mismanagement of its military potential by the Kuomintang regime. If his judgment on Chiang and his government seems harsh, this was not through personal animosity but as the result of direct observation by a seasoned intelligence officer with no stake in the matter, since he was on his way home in the expectation at best of some sinecure in which to wait out retirement.

By a curious irony, Stilwell made what he thought were final visits to three personalities who would be principal figures in the drama about to enfold him. Toward the end of 1938, he found his way by car over the mountains to Chungking and paid his farewell respects to Generalissimo and Madame Chiang. "Very cordial," he noted. "Both looked extremely well. They were quite frank. Gave me a photo and their blessing." Then he flew to Kunming for dinner and a long talk with Captain Claire L. Chennault (USA-ret.), with whom he would one day contend over the nature and employment of American forces on Chiang Kai-shek's behalf. "Had I but known . . ." would have been the only appropriate ending to this chapter in Stilwell's life.

He and his family sailed homeward in May 1939, by way of Indochina, Malaya, and Java. As they approached Hawaii, the ship's radio brought a message so stunning that Stilwell had to walk the deck for a time to digest it. George Marshall was going to be the new Chief of Staff, and one of his first acts had been to recommend Stilwell for promotion to brigadier general. By the time the Stilwells reached their new post in Texas, Hitler had invaded Poland and the American giant was stirring to life. The future career of Joseph Stilwell was not going to be so uneventful as he had thought.

◆

In 1942, Stilwell was fifty-nine years old and half blind. The explosion of an ammunition dump in World War I had damaged his left eye so severely that with it he could not count the fingers of a hand at three feet, and his right eye needed constant correction. In a gallery of types, he would be the shrewd Yankee pedlar, lean and wiry. (In China, he had been handball champion of the Orient, and at Benning he kept in shape by strenuous running.) His squint, his strong nose and scrawny neck, gave him the look of a wise and ancient turtle, and the fact is that like a turtle, under his shell he was soft inside. He doubted himself and took things hard; thoughts of home and family were never far away. His diary on his daughter's birthday reads: "a rainy, windy night just like December 2, 1916, at West Point, when I went for the nurse."[14]

Stilwell has been the unintended victim of the publication in 1948 of *The Stilwell Papers*, a collection from his wartime journals and letters so colloquial and pungent in expression that they have been heavily drawn on since by everyone who writes about him. An assumption is almost irresistible that what someone sets down at nightfall in the privacy of the bedchamber is the "real" person, the authentic individual concealed from others during working hours. The assumption is quite unwarranted. Diaries, too, have their distortions, especially when they are used—among World War II leaders, by Stilwell and, for another, Brooke—as an emotional outlet, a dustbin for the psychological *dreck* that accumulates during a day of putting up with ignorance and folly.

Doubly is this so when the diarist is a sensitive man (again like Stilwell or Brooke) in a position of high responsibility, daily surrounded by intractable problems and frustrations that would drive a lesser human being to despair. Both Stilwell and Brooke have suffered from the availability of extracts from their diaries before more balanced study of their lives began; indeed Brooke's most recent biographer goes to some length in trying to undo impressions left by Brooke's own words.[15] Similarly the Stilwell of conventional image—acidulous, mean-spirited, devoured by various hatreds—is a Stilwell that can be found in the diaries, but is by no necessity the "real" Stilwell.

"Vinegar Joe" he had been called at Benning and "Vinegar Joe" he became to the American public. It is a caricature and not a portrait. Too few descriptions of Stilwell's intense and often profane reactions take sufficient account of what he was reacting against; there was a real world out there which no amount of tact would have caused to vanish. The suggestion has been made[16] that someone of, say, Eisenhower's gifts for the politic handling of ego and dissent would have been better fitted to the job Stilwell was sent to do. But Eisenhower was dealing with people of a shared tradition with a common goal; Stilwell was not. His world of striving against deceit and sloth was one few others even tried to enter. His story as theater commander is therefore one of continuous conflict between the unpleasant truth and a roseate distortion of it, and the task fell to him of pointing out the contrast. His duty was not only to bear evil tidings but to rebuke delusion, and by that route no one ever won popularity. Given what Stilwell had to cope with, as Jack Fischer once wrote, if Saint Francis of Assisi had been put in charge of the China-Burma-India theater he would now be known as Vinegar Frank.[17]

Stilwell was, to the hilt, a professional soldier. To lead Americans in battle was the as-yet-unrealized purpose of his existence. He had not only mastered the trade in its obvious aspects but had demonstrated that rare ability to direct large formations, and to do so with imagination and drive. In the army maneuvers of the prewar years, he regularly led the "enemy" forces with such verve and competence that he was given a division and promoted to major general.

He was one of the few American field commanders who seemed able to achieve the combination of rapidity and surprise that had come to be called the blitzkrieg. Later, when Stilwell headed a corps, General Marshall asked his staff officer Major Mark Clark to prepare a list of the nine corps commanders in order of merit, and Stilwell's name led all the rest. Considered in the abstract, it might have been thought a needless waste of talent to assign such a man as this to a part of the world where American soldiers in any numbers were not likely to be sent.

Before 1940, American sympathy for China had expressed itself largely in loans for civilian purposes, despite requests for arms that became ever more insistent after the Japanese occupation of northern Indochina closed down foreign access except by the Burma Road. Finally, on December 19, 1940, President Roosevelt approved military aid for the Nationalist Chinese and asked the State, War, Navy, and Treasury departments to work out a program. (It is interesting to note that at this stage the idea was already current in the War Department of threatening to bomb Japan with B-17s from Chinese bases, though this proposal was not approved.)

After the passage of Lend-Lease in March 1941, China presented a list of its requirements, which included an air force of a thousand planes (with American training and maintenance), arms and equipment for thirty divisions, a railroad from China to Burma, and trucks, repair shops, and resurfacing for the Burma Road. Though dismayed by an air of the imprecise and dreamy in the Chinese requests, the War Department provided a listing of items already on hand that were not vital to U.S. or British programs, and on May 6 the President approved the first shipment (three hundred two-and-a-half ton trucks), which was on its way within a fortnight from New York to Rangoon.[18]

Technically not a part of Lend-Lease, but very much an enterprise of the U.S. government, was the American Volunteer Group, the Flying Tigers, set up in April 1941 to take advantage of the availability for use in China of a hundred P-40 fighter planes. Pilots were recruited from both the Navy and the Army on one-year contracts, and they and their aircraft sailed in June (escorted through the Japanese-mandate islands by American warships, in violation of the neutrality laws). The AVG was the brainchild of Claire Chennault, with whom Stilwell had dined and talked in Kunming in 1939, a former American Air Corps pilot who had become an adviser to the Chinese and a colonel in their air force. By August, the P-40s were based in Burma near Toungoo, and Chennault had begun training his men in tactics he had worked out over years of studying the Japanese in action in the air.

The instrument of Lend-Lease on the Chinese side was an organization called China Defense Supplies, which by May was presenting a steady stream of requisitions intended to implement the thirty-division program. There now appeared a feature of Chinese demands that for some time to come would dog the American effort to satisfy them: an insistence on the newest and biggest equipment regardless of availability or appropriateness. The agents of China Defense Supplies, in the words of U.S. Army historians, "not only had no idea of what was actually needed for war in China but were ignorant of the inherent limitations and qualities of the weapons desired."

They insisted on being sent the standard U.S. light tank, which weighed thirteen tons and could not cross the majority of bridges in Burma and China. One Chinese ordnance expert refused to accept anything but the most modern rifles because to do so "would jeopardize his reputation."[19] Incident after incident of this kind built up a demand in the War and Treasury departments for greater control over Chinese Lend-Lease, and the military mission approved by the President in July (on word of further Japanese moves in Indochina) was the result. Headed by Brigadier General John Magruder, it arrived in Chungking on October 10, "Double Ten Day," the thirtieth anniversary of the Chinese Republic, in an atmosphere of joyous Sino-American amity.

In principle, China was fully mobilized for war against Japan. It had three times as many formations in the field as the United States would have on V-J Day; there were 316 Chinese divisions and 47 brigades, a total of almost four million men under arms. On paper this was power indeed, but on the ground it was pitiful. Only thirty to forty of the divisions could remotely be described as medium effective militarily, and of these none were in fact fighting the Japanese. The rest were large but lightly armed hordes of poorly trained men, with a loyalty not to Chiang's government but to their own leaders, whose despotic rule over the local countryside they served to maintain. A Chinese division was its commander's personal property; he conscripted and equipped his men; he received the division's food and pay allowances and dispensed them as he saw fit (if more came in than had to go out, so much the better for him).

The question of who would obey whom was always open; the Ministry of War would not think of ordering certain divisions to leave their provinces. Loyalty to the Generalissimo rather than success in battle was the key to advancement, yet even so, no more than thirty divisions (those the Germans had trained) were personally loyal to Chiang Kai-shek, and these had to be stationed in the rear to keep the others in the line. None were in action any more than they had to be, which in 1942 was not much. The

Japanese controlled the major cities, the seaports, the principal lines of communication, and such areas in the north as were not held by the Communists, but elsewhere there was stalemate, an extensive and undeclared truce, and any Chinese impulse to break it by taking the offensive was invisible to American observers.

As for the Burma Road, it was less the lifeline of freedom than a highly profitable racket. There was no central control; no less than sixteen Chinese agencies supervised it, all of them heavily overstaffed with relatives and hangers-on. Lend-Lease supplies had to compete for road space with private truckers carrying bazaar goods; and trucks were overloaded, recklessly driven, and poorly maintained. Even the official statistics showed that the contents of the lifeline were somehow vanishing along the way and never reaching their destination. British traffic figures at the starting point were greater than those at the Chinese border, which were in turn 50 percent greater than those on arrival at Kunming. One estimate was that fourteen thousand tons had to leave Burma in order for five thousand to get to Chungking. Attempts to reveal this to the American public were not welcomed. When Leland Stowe of the *Chicago Daily News* tried to tell the truth about the Burma Road in a series of seven articles, only three of them reached print; under pressure from Washington, the remainder were suppressed.[20]

None of this would have come as any great surprise to Stilwell as he made his preparations to depart. He read the relevant files in the War Department, paid a brief visit to his family in Carmel, was inoculated against a battery of diseases and promoted to lieutenant general. He and Dorn assembled a staff of officers from III Corps at Fort Ord and those they knew with experience (as Dorn also had) in China. Dorn won twenty-seven free games at pinball.

Stilwell called at the White House for interviews, which struck him as pleasant but unimpressive. He got off on the wrong foot with Roosevelt and Hopkins, or they with him. The presidential monologue failed to break through Stilwell's fairly conventional family Republicanism (his brother was a Roosevelt-hater of the first water), and when Stilwell finally interrupted to ask whether there was any message he could take to Chiang Kai-shek, Roosevelt seemed to him to be groping for something world-shaking to say. Finally, the President came up with: "Tell him we are in this thing for keeps, and we intend to keep at it until China gets back *all* her lost territory," and he told Stilwell he thought it best for Madame Chiang not to make a U.S. visit. ("He's right on that," Stilwell noted.) But somehow the values and ideas they shared failed to find expression between them.

Hopkins Stilwell found to be "a strange gnomelike creature" wearing an old red sweater, beat-up shoes, and falling socks, eager to help but tending to be vague. "You are going to command troops, I believe," said

Hopkins, and he talked about taking planes off commercial airlines or using the French liner *Normandie* for transport to India. ("Great stuff," wrote Stilwell, though at that very moment *Normandie* was burning at her pier in New York and about to capsize.) Hopkins told Stilwell that his room had been Lincoln's study, where Lincoln met Grant, and Stilwell thought the parallel overdrawn. It again was the beginning of a failure to connect that would later assume fatal proportions.

Stilwell read with mounting dismay the news from Burma, where the Japanese were on the move. By the time he got there, Marshall told him, he might find himself commanding in Australia. There was the usual last-minute confusion: "We go Thursday. We go Wednesday. No, Thursday. No, Wednesday. To New York on Tuesday. 5 go . . . No, 7 go . . . No, 5 . . . No, no, no . . . 14 go. What the hell, let's all go."

II

Once upon a time there was something called the British Empire. Indubitable handiwork of an insular people—who had planted their flag around the globe and sent their sons to rule the far-flung lands, pacify the inhabitants, and administer their commerce—it was an enterprise of limitless diversity that was somehow all one and the same. Its masters marched to the same drumbeat, wore the same tropical kit, took tea with the same tinned biscuits, read the same back issues of the *London Illustrated News,* and drank the same warm gin and quinine water as they watched the sun go down.

Wherever they went the English recapitulated England. For every colony with a lowland in its dusty heat, disease, and torpor there was up-country a cool and healthful hill station of graceful bungalows and trim lawns, polo and cricket grounds, and an outpost of the established church. Some families had lived out here over generations in a kind of double exile, dreaming of that moist, green island always known as "home" even to those who had never seen it, and should one of the masters retire and return there—to grow boring and dyspeptic in a second-rate club on a reduced income—he would always dream of empire: of the vibrant exercise of command, of distant mountains, deserts, and the sea.

Jewel in the crown of the king-emperor was the British Raj, India, the vast subcontinent of forty human families and four hundred languages where the wisdom of an inscrutable deity had placed a population of 300 million Indians in the care of 75,000 Englishmen. The guardians of civilization had built roads, canals, railroads, and telegraph lines; they had turned barren wastes into prosperous provinces. One of them discovered the etiology of malaria.

But aside from extirpating a few customs they found too revolting to stomach—ritual murder, child sacrifice, the immolation of widows called suttee—they had left the Indian society, its religions and its caste system, pretty much intact, and had brought about a blending of East and West that was historically close to unique. In 1835, English had replaced Persian as the official language of government, diplomacy, and law, and there had begun to emerge "a class of persons" like those Macaulay had imagined, "Indian in blood and color, but English in taste, in opinion, in morals and intellect."[21] Eventually they would begin to think English thoughts about government, as Macaulay foresaw, but few others of his countrymen shared his prescience.

Most effective of all in its mixing of the races was the Indian Army. Since the mid-eighteenth century it had taken part in 131 actions in eighteen wars and its members had won 127 Victoria Crosses, on the list of whom can be found the names of Havildar Kulbir Thapa, Subadar Khudadad Khan, and Lieutenant Ishar Singh, along with many more of their compatriots. Still alive in British memory was the Great Mutiny of 1857–58, which began over the use of animal fats to lubricate cartridge papers, a sacrilege to Hindus and a defilement to Moslems; the mutiny had spread through north and central India and had been suppressed only with brutal ferocity, but the Indian Army as an institution had survived it.

Of all armies in the world, this was the most truly multinational, and by 1942, of all volunteer armies it was the largest. Its private soldiers, the sepoys, were drawn from what the British called the "martial races": Baluchis, Pathans, Rajputs, Sikhs, and above all the formidable Gurkhas. The bulk of its commissioned and many of its noncommissioned officers were British, and in its heyday, for a young subaltern out from England, this could be an agreeable life.

"If you liked to be waited on and relieved of home worries," wrote one of them, "India thirty years ago was perfection. All you had to do was hand over all your uniforms to the dressing boy, your ponies to the syce, and your money to the butler, and you need never trouble any more. . . . For a humble wage, justice and a few kind words there was nothing they would not do. . . . Princes could live no better than we." These were the words, in *A Roving Commission,* published in 1930, of Winston Churchill.

Yet it did not escape thoughtful Englishmen that they were sitting on a volcano. Churchill himself, during World War II, still spoke with emotion of the bloodbath that followed the Great Mutiny. Empire affected all who were a part of it, not always for the best; even the author of *Lives of a Bengal Lancer* wrote of the "hysteria which seems to hang in the air of India."[22] Endemic illnesses took their toll, especially among the women and the children.

The Indian culture itself, an erotic stew of unrestrainable fecundity, mocked British stiffness and restraint (the theme of Forster's *Passage to India* and Orwell's *Burmese Days*). Drink and one depravity or another found their victims among the guardians. The venting of frayed tempers on the guarded was not unknown, and not likely to prolong the tranquillity young Churchill had enjoyed, while some (like Orwell's colonial agent John Flory) cracked up under the strain of enforcing an imperial presence they no longer believed in.

Power was spread paper thin, and self-assurance was its principal underpinning. In August 1943, the American correspondent Eric Sevareid was compelled to parachute out of a stricken C-46 over northern Burma and landed among tribesmen in Naga country, on the edge of the unknown. (Stilwell's political adviser, foreign service officer John Paton Davies, tucking classified documents into his shirt front and smiling, jumped first.) Supplies were air-dropped to them and ten days later out of the misty forest came a "tall slim young man wearing a halo of shining fair hair . . . garbed in a soft blue polo shirt, blue shorts and low walking shoes. . . . He was Philip Adams, the Sahib of Mokokchung, king of these dark and savage hills."[23] With Adams came the emblems of authority: his Naga guards, his hand-crank radio, his cook, his peppermints, his jug of rum, and his chess set. Sevareid and Davies were saved.

The corner of the empire that first and last would concern Stilwell the most was Burma, an appendage to India that for defensive purposes occurred to many British as an afterthought. Roughly as large as Texas, Burma is a shallow dish of rivers and valleys running southward to the Bay of Bengal, ringed by jungle-covered mountains. It was then a rich country by Asian standards, annually exporting 3.5 million tons of rice (mostly to India) and containing abundant petroleum (in the oil fields at Yenangyuang) and tungsten in the mines at Mawchi (35 percent of the commonwealth's prewar supply). The population stood at about seventeen million, defined as the Burmese (about two thirds of the total) and the others. Of the Burmese, John Masters wrote: "They are a sophisticated, intelligent, hot-tempered people with beautiful women, a high state of civilization, and a long history, most of it spent in warfare against Siam, China, or both."[24]

The Burmese did not particularly like the British, who had conquered them in 1882 and then ruled them as a part of the Raj. The "others" were the tribal people of the hill country—Shans (east), Chins (west), Kachins (north), and Karens (south)—who generally did like the British on the grounds that they were not the Burmese. Further to complicate matters, around a million Indians lived in Burma, allowed there by the authorities and attracted by higher pay than in India. They had worked their way into manual labor, retail trade, government administration, and moneylending (where they had come to own most of the rice lands), and they were much resented.

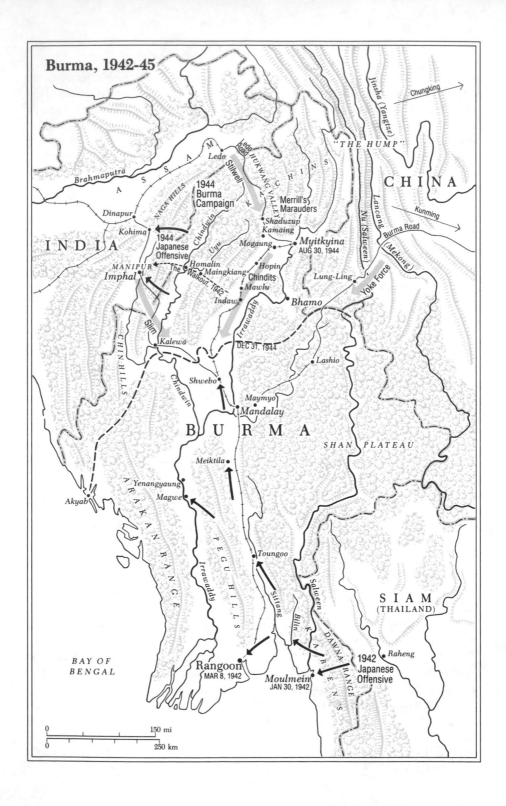

Burma, 1942-45

Chungking

Jinsha (Yangtze)

"THE HUMP"

CHINA

Brahmaputra

A S S A M

Ledo

Stilwell

HUKWANG VALLEY

Ledo Road

K A C H I N S

Kunming

Lancang (Mekong)

Nu (Salween)

Burma Road

1944 Burma Campaign

Merrill's Marauders

Dinapur

NAGA HILLS

Kohima

Shaduzup

Kamaing

Myitkyina
AUG 30, 1944

INDIA

1944 Japanese Offensive

Chindwin

Uyu

Mogaung

Hopin

Lung-Ling

Yoke Force

MANIPUR

Imphal

The Walkout, 1942

Homalin

Maingkiang

Chindits

Mawlu

Bhamo

Slim

Indaw

Irrawaddy

DEC 31, 1944

CHIN HILLS

Kalewa

Chindwin

Lashio

Shwebo

Maymyo

Mandalay

BURMA

SHAN PLATEAU

Meiktila

Yenangyaung

Magwe

Akyab

ARAKAN RANGE

Irrawaddy

PEGU HILLS

Toungoo

Sittang

Bilin

K A R E N S

DAWNA RANGE

Salween

SIAM
(THAILAND)

Raheng

1942 Japanese Offensive

BAY OF
BENGAL

Rangoon
MAR 8, 1942

Moulmein
JAN 30, 1942

0 ____ 150 mi

0 ____ 250 km

The Burmese looked forward to independence. In 1935, they had been given a constitution that separated Burma from India and set up (though granting little real authority) two houses of a legislature, a council of ministers, and a premier—in 1941 an amusing but unsavory scoundrel named U Saw. In the fall of 1941, U Saw went to London on a losing errand to convince Winston Churchill that Burma should be independent. On his way home, he stopped off in Lisbon and held indiscreet conversations with the Japanese ambassador there, assuring him that Burma would rise against its British overlords if the Japanese invaded. This was twisting the lion's tail too hard. His words were reported to Tokyo in a code the British had broken, and when U Saw landed in Haifa he was arrested, then interned in Uganda.

This episode prompted one of Roosevelt's rare outbursts of ethnic prejudice. "I have never liked Burma or the Burmese," he cabled Churchill on April 16, 1942, "and you people must have had a terrible time with them for the past fifty years. Thank the Lord you have HE-SAW, WE-SAW, YOU-SAW under lock and key. I wish you could put the whole bunch of them into a frying pan and let them stew in their own juice."[25]

Burma was isolated and its transportation system rudimentary. Since Rangoon was so accessible from Calcutta by sea, no effort had been made to link Burma to India by land. Through the hills, other than a few jungle paths, there was only an unfinished track that lacked bridges and was impassable in wet weather (the heavy rains of the monsoon begin in mid-May and end in mid-October). Of Burma's three great north-south rivers, the greatest was the Irrawaddy, navigable for nine hundred miles, almost to the Chinese border, with its westernmost tributary the Chindwin, navigable for three hundred and fifty miles; river steamers carried their principal traffic. From Rangoon a railroad ran north through the valleys to Mandalay, about midway, and thence farther north to Myitkyina (pronounced Mitchinah and better known to Americans as "Mitch"), at the base of the Moguang and Hukawng valleys and the Naga Hills, which Americans were to come to know all too well. Roads were few and unimproved, the most important being the fabled Burma Road, which left the railroad at Lashio and wound its way northeast to China, through the mountains and all its hazards of mismanagement and graft.

Against Japanese attack Burma was absurdly unprepared. Singapore was the bastion of the East and known to be impregnable, protecting the territories to its flank and rear. Thus no one had told anybody to organize the defense of Burma, and anyhow there was nothing to defend it with: no antiaircraft, no reserves of rifles or machine guns, and no stocks of other weapons that were better than inadequate. The only British air squadron consisted of sixteen obsolete fighter planes; the naval force was a flotilla of five motor launches. The army troops (seasoned and officered as always by British regulars) were made up into two "divisions," 1st Burma and

17th Indian, which by bravery and good leadership managed to survive the coming campaign; but they were no match for the Japanese in training, numbers, or equipment and they were incapable of a major operation.[26]

The only battleworthy unit was the British 7th Armoured Brigade, two companies of light tanks recently transferred from the Middle East; they had fought Rommel and quickly adapted themselves to Burma, though they lacked high-explosive (as opposed to armor-piercing) ammunition and their tracks were too narrow to navigate the rice paddies. These sketchy forces were organized into 1 Burma Corps, or Burcorps, soon to come under the command of a remarkable general named William J. Slim, of whom more will be heard in this narrative. Overall army commander in Burma was to be Lieutenant General Sir Harold Alexander, reporting in turn to General Sir Archibald Wavell, then supreme commander in the Southwest Pacific, whose headquarters was over two thousand miles away in Java, where he had his hands full and was not always aware of how badly the situation in Burma was deteriorating.

Least of all had everyone been prepared for the possibility that the Japanese would invade Burma from the southeast, which is of course precisely what they did.

◆

In the first weeks of war, the Japanese Fifteenth Army was kept busy occupying Siam and the isthmus leading down to Malaya and Singapore. But by January 24 they had secured three airfields on the Bay of Bengal coast and were able to give fighter protection to their bombers over Rangoon, which they had raided for the first time on December 23 and proceeded to do liberally thereafter. Already their 55th Division had concentrated across the Burma-Siam border at Raheng, and on January 20 it had come through a pass in the Dawna Range and begun a drive to the sea at Moulmein, which a battalion of Gurkhas and a brigade from 17th Indian Division were vainly trying to protect. By the end of the month, Moulmein had fallen and another Japanese division, the 33d, had crossed the range and was striking northwest toward Rangoon.

The only hope of stopping them lay in holding the river lines—the Salween, the Bilin, and the Sittang—which is what Wavell wanted Burcorps to accomplish, but 17th Division was spread so thin over a front of eighty-five miles that the best it could do was set up blocks at key points on the road net. This was not enough. By February 11, the Japanese were across the Salween in force and, though the defense of the Bilin held them up four days, they were over it by the nineteenth and racing toward the Sittang, where the order to demolish the bridge was given too soon, and for the British and Indian troops left on the eastern bank there was nothing but to swim for it, carrying as many arms as they could on improvised rafts. As a fighting force the division had momentarily ceased to exist. The road to Rangoon lay open.[27]

Rangoon was by this time a half-deserted city. Much of the Indian population had fled, decimating the ranks of manual labor and administration that operated the port and essential services. Public order disintegrated. Looting and murder were commonplace as disaffected Burmese roamed the streets, joined by thirteen hundred criminal lunatics from a local asylum (released by an official who later committed suicide in horror at what he had done). On the docks, the riches of American Lend-Lease intended for China were fair game to all who cared to take the trouble, and one man who went down for a look said that he doubted anyone he saw there was sober.

An empire coming unstuck is not a pretty spectacle; the stiff upper lip can quickly become indistinguishable from fatuous pretense. In the Strand Hotel, a mess of dirt and broken glass, Leland Stowe saw two Englishmen in dinner jackets and a lady in an evening gown sweep into the bar for their evening *chota peg*, for all the world oblivious to the fact that Rangoon was burning and its hospitals were filled with wounded. At Government House, where once had been *chaprassis* in long white coats and red-and-gold waistcoats, there were only a cook and a butler when the governor, Sir Reginald Dorman-Smith, entertained two journalists from London, over mutton and the last bottles of claret, in order as the phrase went to "deny comfort to the enemy." They repaired to the billiard room for a desultory game, surrounded by portraits of the former governors of Burma, until finally Dorman-Smith's aide could stand it no longer, picked up a billiard ball, and let fly at one of the portraits. Others joined in until all was a shambles.[28]

Those who could fight fought. The 7th Armoured Brigade was still intact and parts of three British regular battalions—7th Hussars, 1st West Yorkshire, and 1st Cameronians—had come over from India to provide what they could in the way of a rear guard. In the air, wonders had been accomplished by the British in their Brewster Buffalos and by the Flying Tigers, who had been transformed by confronting the Japanese from a group of overcocky fly-boys, grousing about their aircraft and their pay, into effective professionals. The tactics Chennault taught them worked: Stay in pairs; don't dogfight with the Zero; dive in for one pass, shoot, and break away. The AVG and the RAF between them shot down so many Japanese that they achieved air superiority over Rangoon, and maintained it until March 6, when the decision was made to demolish port facilities and oil installations, and pull out. The Japanese entered without opposition on the eighth.

That day, Stilwell was in Chungking, discovering to his somewhat astonishment that Chiang Kai-shek had placed him—nominally—in command of two Chinese armies in Burma. He and his staff had come in flying boats and air transports by way of Brazil, Africa, the Middle East, and India, arriving in New Delhi on February 25 and marveling at the enormous size of the headquarters—"big enough to run our War Department" —needed to command a relatively small number of men in the field. Stilwell's interviews with Chiang were little more inspiring. The Generalissimo lectured him on the perfidy of the British, the reasons why Chinese troops in Burma should not take the offensive, why they must be careful to avoid defeat because it would be "a disastrous shock to morale," and so on. But Stilwell was impressed by Chinese willingness to send men to Burma at all and to admit a foreigner even this far into their counsels. "It must be a wrench for them," he wrote, "and they should be given due credit."[29]

When Chiang first offered two armies for use in Burma, Wavell had seemed at least in part to decline. He was unable to provide the independent lines of communication the Chinese asked for, and he thought at the time that reinforcements from India were going to be sufficient. Regrettably, he also thought "it was advisable that a country of the British Empire should be defended by Imperial troops rather than foreign,"[30] and Chinese readiness to take offense was by this slight activated and reinforced. What Wavell considered to be a "qualified acceptance" they interpreted as a racist slur, and reports of the Magruder mission to Washington emphasized Wavell's "refusal," so that when the Chinese forces did arrive in Burma their three-way relationship with the British and the Americans was flawed from the outset by suspicion and mistrust. The British, moreover, were not overjoyed to encounter Stilwell in a command they had expected to exercise themselves. Alexander, when Stilwell met him at Maymyo, said "Extrawdinery!" and looked at Stilwell (in the vivid image of the diary) "as if I had just crawled out from under a rock."[31]

A Chinese "army" was comparable in size to an American reinforced division. Chiang Kai-shek said of the ones he offered Stilwell that they were his best, and this is not wholly inaccurate, at least of the Fifth, which had a few dozen Lend-Lease 75-mm howitzers and contained a division (the 38th) commanded by Sun Li-jen, a graduate of VMI and the Chinese officer Stilwell esteemed the most. (Sixth Army was less prepossessing; one American uncharitably described it as a third-rate warlord's levy.) The Chinese soldiers were as Stilwell had known them, cheerful and adaptable in adversity and, when properly supplied and led, brave and perdurable in action. They would steal anything that was not nailed down, but it must be said that this was how they had survived in life thus far and was by them considered normal practice. All in all they numbered about 27,500. (Sixty-sixth Chinese Army arrived later, and one division of it fought well, but too late to affect the outcome.)

For with few exceptions these men were not well led. Some of their officers were as competent and dedicated as Sun Li-jen, but not enough of them, and it was the others who set the tone and controlled the action. They believed in conserving strength and in trading territory for time. They came of an ancient culture that had conceived the Taoist principle of *wu-wei erh wu pu-wei* (which is to say, "through not doing all things are done"), and had admitted it into the innermost of their thought processes. They had no conception of timely and unexpected attack as the best defense, an axiom that was to Stilwell so obvious as to need no argument, and the idea of aggressive action on their own part was quite literally beyond their comprehension. The worst of the Chinese officers were simply corrupt, with their eyes on the main chance until circumstance distracted them with the more pressing problem of saving their own skins.

Add to this the highly qualified nature of the "command" that Chiang Kai-shek had granted Stilwell. What he had told Stilwell was not what he had told his subordinates. He continued to carry on a vast correspondence with them, countermanding Stilwell's instructions and directing the disposition of units down to the battalion level, according to his own antic conception of the campaign. He believed Mandalay to be a walled city (it was not) and hence the "key" to central Burma (as it was not), and accordingly he consigned Sun Li-jen's division to its defense when this made no tactical sense whatever ("poor Sun," Stilwell noted).

Not until many weeks had passed did Chiang give Stilwell the "chop," the *kwang-fang,* the seal of authority required to validate an order, and even so it was not that of commander in chief, as he had promised, but only that of chief of staff, so that any Chinese was free to disregard a Stilwell "order" as merely advisory, as many freely did. "Ah, Your Excellency," said Tu Yu-ming, commander of Fifth Army, when Dorman-Smith commented on the discrepancy of rival claims to command, "the American general only thinks that he is commanding. In fact he is doing no such thing. You see, we Chinese think that the only way to keep the Americans in the war is to give them a few commands on paper. They will not do much harm as long as we do the work."[32]

◆

Had Stilwell led an expedition to Casablanca or Dakar, the commander of any British forces involved would have been Alexander. Roosevelt mused on this in a message to Churchill: "Strange that these two, who were originally intended to meet in 'Super-Gymnast' [i.e., French North Africa], should in fact meet in Maymyo." This thought was occasioned by the President's urging Churchill, who was distinctly reluctant, to accept a dual command in Burma shared between Stilwell and Alexander, as the best means of ensuring Chinese cooperation. "Stilwell is not only an immensely capable and resourceful individual," said Roosevelt, with doubtless some prompting from Marshall and Eisenhower, "but is thoroughly acquainted with the Chinese people, speaks the language fluently, and is distinctly not a self-seeker." Churchill commented: "I did not press the point at this difficult moment."[33]

The two commanders were not well matched. Alexander had what the British call "presence," a degree of panache that did not go down well with Americans like Stilwell, while Stilwell was "intense," as one British writer puts it, and Alexander "did not care for intense chaps." Perhaps we are fortunate that they did not meet at Casablanca, and that they managed to get on as well as they did despite the disparity of temperaments. But the British general whom Stilwell was instinctively drawn to, trusted, and worked with in harmony was William Slim. "Good old Slim," reads Stilwell's first diary entry about him.[34]

Slim was a midlands Englishman of middle-class parentage, a Birmingham boy, who had come up through the ranks and, even after he became chief of the Imperial General Staff, "never forgot the smell of soldiers' feet." Churchill did not cotton to him ("I cannot think that a man with a name like Slim can be any good"), but he was the greatest general that Britain produced in the war—he forged an army, skillfully directed it in the great battle of Imphal-Kohima, and led it in the flawless return to Mandalay and Rangoon—and he was incomparably the best writer. His *Defeat into Victory* is the only commander's account from World War II that can stand on the same shelf with Grant's *Personal Memoirs.*

Slim genuinely liked Stilwell and understood him, seeing the private person and the sense of humor behind the Vinegar Joe persona. "He had a habit," wrote Slim, "which I found very disarming, of arguing most tenaciously against some proposal and then suddenly looking at you over the top of his glasses with the shadow of a grin, and saying, 'Now tell me what you want me to do and I'll do it.' " When the two of them later fought the successful campaign to recapture northern Burma, Stilwell (though he was far senior) voluntarily placed himself under Slim, in order to simplify the structure of command. When it was over, Stilwell proudly pointed out to Slim that he had been a dutiful subordinate and had obeyed all of Slim's orders. "Yes, you old devil," Slim replied, "but only because the few I did give you were the ones you wanted."[35]

But neither Alexander, Slim, Stilwell, nor all three together, could halt the advancing Japanese. The latter had worked out a tactical system admirably suited to Burmese conditions: that is, to a sympathetic population and a roadbound foe. When they encountered opposition the Japanese would hold in place, then swing wide through the countryside led by local guides and set up a roadblock in the Allied rear, offering the defenders the seemingly inescapable choice between stand-and-die or a fighting retreat (normally the latter was preferred). Later Slim invented the counter to this, but for the time being it was uncannily effective. The sense of being cut off, coupled with a reminder that the Burmese people were unfriendly, turned a simple maneuver into a powerful propaganda weapon. With each successful application the psychlogical impact grew, until finally the very words "road block" could induce alarm even in seasoned British regulars.

Every fiber of Stilwell's being rebelled against this reactive form of warfare. He thought the Japanese might be weaker than they appeared and that boldness would pay off. He saw that the Japanese were making mistakes of which the professional in him ached to take advantage. At Toungoo, about 150 miles north of Rangoon, the Chinese 200th Division under a resolute major general named Tai An-lan held off the Japanese for twelve days, the longest and most successful action by any of the Allied troops in Burma. A counterattack would have caught the Japanese off balance and outnumbered. "Here's our chance," wrote Stilwell in his diary.

All he had to do was persuade Tu Yu-ming to order his 22d Division into action. *"Mei yu pan-fa,"* said Tu (It's impossible). Attack, said Stilwell. "Tomorrow *tsai shuo,"* said Tu (We will discuss it again). Tu retreated into his own room and would not come out. Eventually a message from Tai An-lan at Toungoo produced from Tu an uncompromising *"Ming T'ien i ting kung chi"* (Tomorrow we certainly attack). But the next day there were more excuses: the Japanese had 105-mm howitzers, the Japanese had forty-nine tanks. Would he attack? "Well, don't know. Must *shang liang"* (think it over). There never was an attack. General Tai An-lan, having lost a thousand casualties but inflicted four times that number on the Japanese, extricated his men from Toungoo. Later he told INS correspondent Jack Belden that if the 22d had attacked, he could have held Toungoo indefinitely.[36]

Stilwell tried to fire two Chinese generals (Kan of Sixth Army and Ch'en of the 55th Division) on the grounds of incompetence, inability to command their troops, and unwillingness to obey orders, but Chiang Kai-shek refused to sanction this. Perhaps the best insight into the Chinese military mind was provided at Toungoo by General Tu Yu-ming himself, when General Alexander asked him what had become of the field guns there the day before, expertly sited and camouflaged, but now gone. They had been withdrawn, said Tu. Then what use were they? asked Alexander. "General," said Tu, "the Fifth Army is our best army because it is the only one which has any field guns, and I cannot afford to risk those guns. If I lose them the Fifth Army will no longer be our best."[37]

The Chinese armies had no medical service, but the Lord had favored them and sent a substitute, Dr. Gordon Seagrave, the "Burma Surgeon." Trained at Johns Hopkins, Seagrave was the fourth generation of his family to be a Baptist missionary among the Karens; he spoke Karen before he spoke English, later learned Shan and Burmese. (He refused to learn Kachin because he thought there were no words in it for anything important.) Seagrave had been running a hospital in the

Shan states until war overcame him with the task of mending and patching together its victims.

Seagrave had a remarkable group of nurses, referred to by the press as "Burmese" though in fact only one of them was; the others were Karen, Kachin, Shan, and a smattering of the really minor tribes like Hkamti, Padaung, Tangthu, Lahu, Maru, Atsi, Lashi, Pwo, Bghai, and Paku. There were two Indians and one genuine princess, who spoke impeccable English. Seagrave insisted only that they be gentle with their patients and submerge their tribal identities (this he preached to them on Sundays in Burmese, their lingua franca). He and Stilwell took an instantaneous liking to one another, and Stilwell commissioned him almost on the spot a major in the Medical Corps.

Seagrave operated hundreds of times a day, as truckload after truckload of the wounded were brought to him. Once he looked up to see Stilwell watching and they exchanged grim smiles; "he always has time," wrote Seagrave, "for anyone who is trying to do a good job."[38] Seagrave said his nurses immediately saw through Stilwell's gruff exterior and began calling him "Granddaddy Joe." Most of them were five feet tall and weighed about a hundred pounds, but—as the Walkout was soon to prove—they were in better physical condition than most of the Americans.

In late March, they lost their air cover. The airfield at Magwe had been given a nasty going-over in a Japanese air raid and the RAF withdrew, first to Akyab and then to India. "Oh, you independent air force," wrote Stilwell. He had set up headquarters of a sort at Maymyo, above Mandalay, the summer capital of Burma, a pleasant enough hill station with English houses, as Slim described them, "in the best Surrey stockbroker style." But no sooner did Stilwell make a new plan than it would be overtaken by events and he would have to contrive another, each being more hopeless than the last.

The Chinese divisions would retreat without his permission, and often without even informing him; one of them simply disappeared, melting away into the hills. Burcorps pulled back to Meiktila, then Kalewa, then Tamu. They destroyed the oil fields at Yenangyuang, much to Stilwell's disgust, though it is difficult to see what else they could have done. Jack Belden thought that by this time the inevitability of defeat had "fixed itself in the minds of military and civilian officials alike."[39] The railroad repeatedly failed; equipment wouldn't work or there were breaks along the line (sabotage?). Life began to reduce itself to the rudiments of staying alive and getting out.

Through all this the official British communiqués kept up a steady manifestation of sangfroid. After the loss of Moulmein, one of them read: "our troops inflicted such heavy casualties on the enemy, he was unable to pursue us when we withdrew." They were the handiwork of Dorman-Smith's son-in-law, a major who had been a lieutenant six months before.

He reported "widespread offensive activity of RAF bombers" when only two of them were capable of getting off the ground, and shortly before the fall of Rangoon he produced the following: "Well-informed quarters are not inclined to admit any question of an immediate, or even distant, threat to Rangoon at present. . . . Our forces are in very good heart and are only anxious in so far as they are counting the days until the time comes for an advance."

Eventually the level of pumped-up nonsense disgusted even British observers of it; the government had failed to take the most rudimentary precautions and was sunk in indecision. "I don't trust them," said the wife of one British officer then fighting with Burcorps. "I simply don't trust them." A British general told an American officer: "I wish somebody would shoot the Governor." No supplies had been stockpiled along routes to the north now jammed by refugees as the British and the Indians in Burma fled homeward. "Thousands will die," said Stilwell to Belden. And he was right: Thousands did.[40]

Stilwell and his staff, including Dr. Seagrave and the nurses, headed north in a convoy of about twenty jeeps, sedans, and trucks. Their goal was Myitkyina, where Stilwell expected to find most of the Chinese troops. At Shwebo, with Japanese twenty miles away, a C-47 flew in on direct orders from General Arnold to fly Stilwell out. He declined. That was simply not within Joe Stilwell's code: You stayed with your men until they ceased to exist as coherent fighting entities. (He sent part of his staff instead; Barbara Tuchman believes that feelings were hurt and that this may have been the beginning of the conviction, in air force circles, that Stilwell did not "understand" air power.)

At Indaw, there was a bloody riot of starving refugees and helpless British that Stilwell said was the worst sight he had seen in Asia. "You're looking at the end of an era, Dorn," said Stilwell. "The fall of an empire."[41] It was now increasingly clear that the road to Myitkyina was blocked and that they would have to head west toward India. Stilwell had in mind a difficult but less traveled route, which would keep them ahead of the mass of refugees and north of the Japanese: west to Homalin on the Chindwin and then over the hills to Imphal, about two hundred miles from Indaw. At Mansi, they came to a deep ravine with a bridge over it made of rope and bamboo, which could not carry their trucks. End of the line.

◆

Stilwell's Walkout from Burma may not belong among the great epics, but surely in World War II no other exploit on so small a scale has managed to contain so large a symbolic meaning. Everything about it gives a sense of fitness, as though someone groping for the reality principle at last had found it and a single sharp blow of ill fortune had caused vast patterns of confusion and inconclusiveness to tumble into proper place. "This is war now, you know," Belden heard Stilwell say to a British general. "This is serious business."[42] When the worst came, you marched on your own two feet, you carried your own weapon (Stilwell's was a Thompson submachine gun), kept it cleaned and oiled, and you were ready to fight. If walking out of Burma was the only way to remind people of these essentials, then walk he would and gladly. Other essentials: Share and share alike, nobody gets left behind, the boss gives the orders and they *will* be obeyed. There have been less edifying epics.

Stilwell called them into a circle, over a hundred by now, from nine nations: Americans, British, and a generous sampling of Asians; soldiers of all ranks, doctors, nurses, missionaries, mechanics, cooks, a journalist (Belden), and a Tamil boxer named Sterling. An important addition had been the Reverend Breedom Case, who spoke the dialects of the hill country they were about to enter. Two British officers, a Sikh lieutenant, and an enlisted man had joined when Stilwell found them on the road and discovered that they were trying, with five days' rations, to make Imphal on their own. As the circle drew together he noticed two Eurasian girls standing shyly apart, discovered the drivers had given them a lift, told them he didn't care where they came from, that they were part of the group and should move over there with the nurses. Several British soldiers caught his eye: dirty, unshaven, utterly fatigued. "Where the hell did you come from," said Stilwell. "Got any rations?" No answer. "I didn't think so," said Stilwell. "That can't be helped now. Stay with the British group. Colonel Huston, get those men shaved and cleaned up. They'll feel better and so will I."[43]

To business. This was henceforward a unit under Stilwell's command. Anyone not willing to accept his orders without question had a last opportunity to say so and leave. All food would be pooled; anyone discovered to have held food back would be run out of the party by Stilwell personally. Weapons and ammunition would be kept, all heavy baggage and bedrolls thrown away. Personal belongings would be limited to what the individual could carry; those who had extra clothing and shoes should share with those without.

Breedom Case lowered his head in prayer. A sharp breeze swept through the clearing and suddenly all of them, egged on by the Seagrave nurses, were falling all over themselves throwing things away. Just before noon a skinny, short-haired mongrel dog, its tongue lolling with thirst, came up to Stilwell, who grinned and asked it, "Got any food?" Furious tail-thumping greeted a friendly voice. "Well, you need some, boy," said Stilwell. "Water, too. Stick around with us."[44]

They hired porters and by pure blind luck they acquired a pack train of twenty scrawny mules headed in the direction they were going, on what dubious errand of cross-border illegal trade (probably opium) they did not inquire. The odds of running out of food were thus reduced but not far enough. They had to get through by radio to somebody, in either India or Chungking, and arrange for provisions to be stashed along the way.

Late into the night the communications sergeant tapped out message after message, but no acknowledgment came. Dorn drafted the final one, giving their numbers and route (Maingkaing, Uyu River, Homalin, Imphal), and urgently requesting food and medicine to be put on the other trails into India from Sittaung to the Hukawng valley, since tens of thousands of troops and refugees would soon be coming along them. "We depart early morning," it ended. "Should reach Maingkaing in three days. This is our last message repeat our last message. Stilwell."[45] Then they smashed the radio beyond repair.

Stilwell said later that without the nurses he didn't think the group could have made it. Their effervescent spirit enlivened everyone and their energy on the trail matched his. ("I thought we'd have to gear the march to *their* short steps," said Stilwell.[46]) They were flirtatious but chaste; at evening camp they would disappear, chattering and giggling, to wash their *longyis.* Seagrave would lead them in singing "Onward Christian Soldiers" or "Nearer My God to Thee," and the whole column would quiet.

Stilwell led off, tommy gun over his shoulder, at a regulation pace of 105 steps per minute. Nothing broke his stride; on the hour, a five-minute break, then back to the trail. Two or three of the American officers collapsed in the heat and fell behind. "Christ, we're a poor lot," said Stilwell (they caught up that evening). He drove them: reveille at three-thirty, on the march by five. He found a bedroll one officer had concealed and tongue-lashed (in private) its guilty owner. He sacked the mess officer for allowing delays and put Dorn in his place. He drove them, by a combination of example, self-possession, and scorn. At the Uyu, they made rafts and floated down it under leaf-thatch awnings the nurses made, their own idea. "We know how," they explained. "You don't. So we do it."

On a sandbar, an RAF bomber spotted them (for a terrible moment they thought it was Japanese) and dropped welcome packages of British Army corned willy and hardtack. Stilwell called a weapons inspection and growled at the dirt and rust he found, guns that couldn't be fired. At the Chindwin, they luckily encountered a flotilla of dugouts which got them across the otherwise impassable river. The little dog was nearly left behind, disconsolate on the shore, until someone remembered him and they went back. Stilwell cradled in his lap and scratched the wet ear of what Dorn described as "a frenzied bundle of gratitude."

Now came the hard part. The trail led up into the hills. Stilwell had been told it was "steep," but they had not reckoned on how steep that might mean. He kept the killing pace as one by one his officers told him it was more than the group could stand. A crowd of disheveled mountain folk materialized out of the forest, and after an exchange of insults with the Shan and Kachin porters, it was agreed through Breedom Case that the two groups change places.

The Shans and Kachins said the mountain folk were savage headhunters but that the trail was too steep and besides they wanted to go home; the "headhunters," when offered payment somewhat beyond the usual, said that the American general was a great and noble lord, that they would serve him as long as life remained, and that he would be relieved no longer to be dependent on lowland scum like the Shans and Kachins. Deal.

The trail led upward and the rains began; their food, down to tea and rice, was running out. Gnarled roots tripped them up and breath came short; feet turned to lead and legs to rubber. "It was all a man could do," wrote Dorn, "to drag himself up those murderously steep climbs." After a few days of agonized progress, the monsoon came down for real and Stilwell halted them at a village where there seemed to be enough *bashas* to get everyone under cover. In the doorway of one hut, arms akimbo and smiling, stood a tall, blond Englishman.

"Who the hell are you?" said Stilwell. "I'm Tim Sharpe," said this apparition. "President of the Manipur Durbar." He had been sent from Imphal to meet the American general's party. Coming up were five hundred porters and hundreds of pack ponies; a doctor with medical supplies was one day behind him. "Come in out of the rain, sir." Stilwell's messages had been received. Breedom Case fell on his knees in the mud, face raised to the darkening sky, and offered thanks.

In a nearby hut, pigs were being roasted and they dined that night on barbecued pork, every mess tin full; the little dog gnawed bones and, said Dorn, "groaned with pleasure." The rest of Stilwell's message had also been heeded; British army depots in Assam and Manipur had mounted a massive relief operation and stocks were being placed on every route from Burma into India. For Stilwell's people there would be five more days on the trail to Imphal, but no more worries about food, and those too ill or footsore to walk would be carried.

That mean old man had brought them through and not a one had been lost, to anyone in the military calling a statement of consequence. Even Stilwell was tolerant the next morning when the sun broke through and they were late getting started, and he laughed when told that the British food supplies included large quantities of oatmeal. Only one shadow had fallen across their sleep. Starved for news of the outside world, they had been told by Sharpe of the loss of Bataan and Corregidor. Most of the Americans had friends there, for Dorn five West Point classmates.

Stilwell was now all eagerness for the next stage. He must get in touch with Wavell. He must get to New Delhi and Chungking, report to the Generalissimo, start making plans for training and reequipping Chinese troops for the reconquest of Burma. Gradually he reconciled himself to patience and the routine of the days that followed, the chieftains of each

Naga village coming forward in their red blankets to greet him, proffering clay jars of ceremonial rice beer, which the abstemious Stilwell actually grew to like.

Endlessly he questioned Sharpe about the Nagas, their customs and their history; the intelligence officer in him was awake. On May 20, they reached Imphal: two weeks, 150 miles, 114 people and a small dog—no big deal, really, but for the remarks Stilwell was to make about it when they reached New Delhi. Dinner in Imphal was at the quarters of the provincial administrator, a fat and red-faced pillar of inconsequence who served them half-cold mutton, boiled potatoes, brussels sprouts, and soggy pastry. Stilwell whispered to Dorn: *"Che-keh Ying-kuo fan. T'ai pu-hao. K'e liao pu-teh"* (This English food! It's awful. It can't be helped).[47]

By staff car to Kohima and Dimapur, where Stilwell commandeered a train and left an Indian official spluttering until his palm was crossed. From Tinsukia they flew to New Delhi in General Brereton's private plane, Stilwell noting with displeasure ("pure vandalism!") that a Persian carpet had been cut to fit the floor. Stilwell dozed and wakened only long enough to be shown Mount Everest and the Taj Mahal ("Can't hold a candle to the Temple of Heaven in Peking"). At New Delhi, they waved off newsmen and checked in at the Imperial Hotel, where Dorn discovered on the bathroom scales that he had lost thirty-two pounds; even the lanky Stilwell had lost twenty. (Stilwell was coming down with jaundice, caused by faulty serum in his predeparture shots.)

A telegram from George Marshall awaited him, conveying the commendation of the President, Secretary Stimson, and the entire War Department for what he had done, to which Stilwell could attach only the one-word comment "why?" He felt nothing but failure. That evening there was a press conference, a packed house, and one tenacious British reporter kept after Stilwell to comment on statements by Wavell and Alexander describing the evacuation of Burma as "a glorious retreat" and "an heroic, voluntary withdrawal." Finally, the hatred of hypocrisy that had been building up in Stilwell burst forth and he spoke the words that made him famous:

"In the first place, no military commander in history ever made a *voluntary* withdrawal. And there's no such thing as a *glorious* retreat. All retreats are as ignominious as hell. I claim we got a hell of a licking. We got run out of Burma, and it's humiliating as hell. I think we ought to find out what caused it, go back, and retake Burma. That's all, gentlemen. Good night."[48] And he left the room. New Delhi censors tried to stop or emasculate his statement, but truth had been spoken and it would prevail.

The exodus from Burma held all the horrors that Stilwell had feared. The Chinese exerted themselves to hold their armies together. The men of General Sun Li-jen's 38th Division, though weak and emaciated, came out in good order, with each soldier carrying more weapons than he had been assigned. The greatest suffering was that of the refugees, especially those who took the northernmost path through the Hukawng valley, two hundred and fifty miles of malarial jungle. Not enough prepared camps or food stocks were in place when the monsoon began, which meant mud to the knees and nights in soaking clothes in addition to the dysentery and the leeches.

The route was terrorized by roving Chinese deserters, and each mile or so along it was a corpse, usually a victim of cholera, pneumonia, or total exhaustion. Everyone was a little bit insane; husbands deserted wives, parents deserted children. Under such circumstances the heroes were those who risked their lives for others: fourteen-year-old Norman Richardson, who brought out three of his five brothers and sisters after their mother died; or B. W. North of the Burma Frontier Service, who stayed on in the valley until the very last of the twenty thousand who survived had been rescued.[49]

At least one other military leader besides Stilwell and Sun Li-jen came out with his force intact. General Slim stood by the side of the road at Tamu and watched Burcorps straggle back into India. "All of them," he wrote, "British, Indian, and Gurkha, were gaunt and ragged as scarecrows. Yet, as they trudged behind their surviving officers in groups pitifully small, they still carried their arms and kept their ranks, and they were still recognizable as fighting units. They might look like scarecrows, but they looked like soldiers too."[50] Out of these scarecrows he would make an army.

III

Chungking, capital of "free" China. It was, wrote Eric Sevareid, as though the United States had been walled in from the east and south—New York, Charleston, New Orleans, and Galveston sealed off—so that travelers from the outside world had to come in through Alaska to find the seat of government in Helena, Montana. Leland Stowe thought Chungking looked "like a large Pennsylvania mining town, transplanted and stuck hit-or-miss upon a half-crumbling section of the Hudson River's Palisades." It hung on to the many-headed bluff that rose hundreds of feet from the confluence of two rivers, where the Yangtze met the Chialing. "The bluff is scarred by innumerable ravines and gullies," Stowe wrote, "and its limestone cliffs and hillsides sheer off and fall with startling sharpness. Yet on all sides and in every crevice drab dwellings, some with slate roofs and others of new or fading thatched straw, cling to the sudden slopes like colonies of swallows' nests."

High on one hill stood Chialing House, where for a time the corre-

spondents lived, the only hotel in Chungking to have survived three years
of Japanese air raids. Its windows had long since been blown out, its
spartan rooms of cracked plaster and missing ceilings (with one communal
washroom) were either too hot in Chungking's searing summer or too cold
in its frigid winters, but from the hotel balconies there were striking vistas
of the river valley as it spread out into a undulating plain of greens and
browns, eternal China.

From Chialing House a rutted lane, thick with mud or dust depending
on the season, led up and around the cliff to the main road, which then
twisted crazily and laboriously downward into the heart of Chungking
until it came to the head of the three hundred and seven stone steps that
descended to the Yangtze ferry. The streets had a raw vitality, a constant
jostling of ricksha boys, noodle vendors, soldiers, men with merchandise
on their backs beating blocks of wood or leather tom-toms, and the coolies
dragging their heavy two-wheel carts and chanting "Hai-*toh!* Hai-*tah!*
. . . Hai-*toh!* Hai-*tah!*" as they must have done for centuries. Everywhere
the smells; a metropolis of smells, Stowe called it: enough smells to last a
lifetime.[51]

To this dirty, foggy provincial backwater Chiang Kai-shek at the end
of 1938 had brought his government; within two months the population
of 200,000 had doubled and in a half year it was crowding a million. In May
1939, the Japanese had methodically begun to bomb Chungking, driving
its people into caves and, for once, uniting them. The raids gave the city's
polyglot populace something in common, if only the experience of bur-
rowing underground—workshops, living quarters, everything—and carrying on. A spirit of fierce resistance lasted as long as the raids lasted; it
diminished only with America's entry into the war, which paradoxically
had the effect of a great letdown. Now someone else would bear the
unbearable and win the victory. "Pearl Harbor Day in America," said one
American, "was Armistice Day out here."

The Americans were ill prepared for China: for its poverty, its ubiquitous filth, its acceptance of corruption, its obsession with "face," its utter
disregard for Western notions of time, coordination, or exactness. Surrounded by armed guards, the correspondents lived a drab existence, only
slightly alleviated by poker games and local vodka, as they sought to find
their way through a maze of official propaganda and get anything worth
writing about past the censors.

They were daily confronted by a China in violent contrast to their
American readers' idea of it: a single-party police state with all the attributes of dictatorship but none of its authority, ruled by a "party" that was
in practice a cluster of slippery alliances, headed by a "national leader"
who rather more resembled top man on a pyramid of nervous acrobats—
a tyrant in many matters and more narrow, more the peasant, more
ignorant of and indifferent to the outside world than they could possibly

have imagined. Sevareid said he was familiar with dictatorships that used suppression of information and secret-police terror to conceal what they were doing, but that this was the first he had encountered using the same methods to conceal the fact that it was doing nothing.

To this well-remembered Chungking came Stilwell, to climb the stone steps and set up one of his two headquarters (the other was in New Delhi) in a modernistic hillside villa designed and built for T. V. Soong and staffed by twenty-nine servants in the employ of Tai Li, Chiang's head of secret service (Stilwell found one of them rifling his papers). From the terraced roof there was a spectacular view of the cleft between the mountains through which the Chialing swept in from the north. The cook, regarding Stilwell as only slightly lesser than God, served spectacular Chinese-American dishes. Dorn acquired a foul-tempered monkey that bit everyone but Stilwell, who lived in a suite on the first floor with a gloomy bedroom and a small office where he did most of his work. In the basement was the map room, which doubled for showing movies. "Of the two and a half years in the CBI theater," wrote Theodore H. White, "Stilwell probably spent no more than eight months in this house; but it was more home than any other spot in Asia, and to it he always returned from his long trips."[52]

Here he set about the task of obeying his orders: to increase the effectiveness of United States aid to China for the prosecution of the war and to improve the combat efficiency of the Chinese Army. The tale of Stilwell's efforts to carry out his mission is a long one (two thick volumes of the U.S. Army histories are devoted to it), filled with twistings and turnings, comings and goings, doings and undoings; now sinister, now comic; now lighted by a prospect of success, now darkened by awareness that success was impossible. Yet for all its tangled involution, the essentials —the controlling background, the array of forces and their bearing on one another—remained very much the same throughout; it is all a single story. One caution: The central theme of it is not, as sometimes may appear, the tortured relationship between Stilwell and Chiang Kai-shek. Chiang and eventually Roosevelt labored mightily to make this appear to be the case, but they did so for reasons of their own.

As time passes, it grows more and more difficult to find anything good to say about Chiang Kai-shek. He was not an intelligent man, though he had a certain cunning, and he lacked the abilities called for by the national leadership to which he aspired. His military gifts were insignificant, and as for administration, he seems not to have known what it was; his government had by his indifference been incapacitated for managing either the economy or the currency, its two most pressing tasks. In Honan in 1942–43, it could not feed its own people (what food there was went to the large but useless army) and there was famine in which four million died. (When the Japanese invaded Honan in 1944, the peasants were still so filled with hatred of Chiang's government that they helped the Japanese disarm the Kuomintang soldiers.)

Chiang was not a believer in democracy and made no pretense of being so. His book *China's Destiny* (1943) combined tolerance of fascism and attacks on liberalism with racist views of China's past and future so unacceptable to Westerners that, wisely, it was never translated or distributed abroad. (Jack Service read it and made a digest of the revised edition, which he sent to Washington in 1944.[53]) Chiang's singular achievement was to maintain himself in power, which he accomplished by playing off one faction, interest, clique, or warlord against another, an art at which he did demonstrate some skill.

President Roosevelt's picture of Chiang Kai-shek was at very large variance with that of the American correspondents in Chungking. It was a product not of observation or of reading foreign-service-officer reports but of his "policy," such as it was, toward China—his usual blend of idealism and realism, tempered on this occasion with a dash of wishful thinking. Roosevelt wanted postwar China to be a "great power" and he believed, quite properly, that the first step in making it one was to treat it like one. Japan's Asia-for-the-Asians propaganda would be counteracted by our having this massive Asian ally, drawn into the alliance and then strengthened after the war was over by the promised "return" of Formosa and Manchuria.

But the President's sense of realism told him that China was an unfathomable and resilient civilization highly resistant to change, that the Kuomintang and the Chinese Communists despised and mistrusted each other, and that—in any case—China did not and could not have a high priority in the war. Hence he temporized, adopting a posture of hanging in there and looking pleased, a policy that was really no policy at all. Having no answer, he tended to evade the question. Repeated attempts by Stilwell and others to get him to state a China policy produced only a change of subject or a stream of reminiscence about the Delano family in the China trade.

Nor was he inattentive to the cherishing of China, by much of the American public, as an especially favored ally, an affection he saw no cause to contest. He was in a frame of mind—publicly positive, privately doubtful—that easily disposes to overstatement, and overstate is what Roosevelt at the outset did. In his own characterization of Chiang Kai-shek, elements of the genuine were dramatically rearranged into a pattern of hopeful imagining.

"All of us must remember," he wrote to Marshall in 1943, "that the Generalissimo came up the hard way to become the undisputed leader of four hundred million people—an enormously difficult job to attain any kind of unity from a diverse group of all kinds of leaders—military men, educators, scientists, public health people, engineers, all of them struggling for power and mastery, local or national, and to create in a very short time what it took us a couple of centuries to attain . . . one cannot speak sternly to a man like that or exact commitments from him the way we might do with the Sultan of Morocco." (Scarcely a year would pass before he would find himself addressing words to Chiang that were more than stern.)

When a shortened version of this memo was cabled to Stilwell by Marshall (with the reference to the Sultan of Morocco bowdlerized to "tribal chieftain"), John Paton Davies read it with his worst fears confirmed and wrote of it later as "this nearly irrecognizable description of China."[54] All the crucial phrases—"undisputed leader . . . any kind of unity . . . what it took us a couple of centuries to attain"—were wildly out of focus.

The President in his memo was seeking to shape Stilwell's method of dealing with Chiang. He was trying, as he had tried so often in the past with such success, to impose his will on the flow of events. He perceived this as a test of his will. The memo ends with a pointed reminder to Marshall that had not Roosevelt insisted, they would not now be in North Africa. But it was a fatal misapplication of that formidable force. It misperceived the responses the Chinese would make to whatever the Americans did. It led in application toward goals quite contrary to those the President's realism about China would have recommended. Most fatally of all, it failed to appreciate that he had, in Stilwell, the one instrument capable of bringing those goals within reach.

Chiang's position was shrewdly calculated to make the most of the President's commitment to his cause—a commitment, be it said, diluted when Roosevelt (1) met Chiang in person and (2) encountered directly Chiang's stubborn refusal to order his forces into action. Chiang relied first of all on the assumption that the Americans would totally defeat the Japanese no matter what he did or did not do. Second, he assumed that his real problem was to beat the Chinese Communists in the civil war that would follow the peace. For this he badly needed military supplies which would not be forthcoming if their purpose were revealed, and therefore he must maintain the myth of China's struggle to the death with Japan while squirreling away his American equipment against the postwar showdown with Mao Tse-tung.

Chiang went this one better and successfully employed—not once but time and again—a threat to "leave" a war he was not fighting in the first place and could not have "left" even had he wished to. This transparent piece of blackmail astonishingly persuaded numbers of Americans (Marshall and Morgenthau were honorable exceptions) to go on urging that money and munitions be poured down the rathole for the purpose of "keeping China in the war." This may not have been an admirable policy on Chiang's part, but it was at least a policy, from his perspective it was necessary, and—for a time—it solved his problems.

◆

American military planners were beguiled by China for a variety of reasons. Its legendarily limitless manpower offered the possibility (to the Army) of tying down Japanese troops that might otherwise be turned against us. Its coastline offered (to the Navy) potential bases from which to blockade Japan and, if such should be necessary, invade it. (Admiral King, almost to the end, insisted that a Chinese base at or near Amoy was a major objective of the Navy's drive across the Pacific.) Finally, it offered (to the air force) airfields within bombing range of the Japanese home islands, then thought to be peculiarly accessible to this form of attack. The three in combination, some believed, might render an actual invasion unnecessary.

"Keeping China in the war" was thus imagined to be self-evidently desirable, and the best means of achieving this (so thought Marshall and King) was to reopen a land route into China through northern Burma, without which China's contribution would be limited to nominal by the limited tonnages that could be flown from India over the Himalayas, "the Hump." One thing with another, China could be regarded as a key to the Pacific war, and it would have been a rash analyst, in the Washington of 1942 and early 1943, who dared suggest that China might prove to be, as ultimately it did, almost irrelevant.

The British had doubts about it from the start, and never ceased to wonder at the Americans' fixation on such a flimsy goal. Churchill had an instinctive abhorrence of fighting in northern Burma, which he classified as "jungle," a place where the modern arms of sea and air power could not be productively employed (though the same might equally have been said of places where he *did* want to fight, such as Sumatra). He saw no functional connection between sending supplies to China and any increase in the effectiveness of its fighting forces (in this, if Stilwell were left out of the equation, he was correct).

He had no objection to the reconquest of Burma (of course one must restore the honor of the empire), but his mind like that of many of his countrymen was bent on Singapore, where the greatest dishonor had been incurred and the greatest prize could be rewon. Statistics about the significance of the Chinese as a large portion of the human race failed to captivate him ("four hundred and twenty-five million pigtails," he was heard to mutter). Discussions about China struck him, so he pithily recorded of the Cairo Conference, as "lengthy, complicated, and minor." With such lack of enthusiasm at the top, a state of lethargy in the middle echelons was almost automatic, and Stilwell necessarily surmised that efforts on his part to assist China through India might be greeted with indifference or outright hostility.[55]

It is frequently said, and not only by British writers, that Stilwell hated the British as such. This is not true, as several of his comments over many years attest. What he disliked was a particular British type—arrogant, self-important, out of contact with reality, dubiously disposed toward fighting—and of these India in 1943–44 contained an inordinate number. For too long the empire had been a dumping ground for unemployables. For too long they had enjoyed there deference and luxury beyond anything they could have commanded elsewhere. For too long they had cultivated the form and ignored the substance. When a plane landed at New Delhi, a young officer would come aboard and announce: "You will now leave the aircraft in the order of your rank." Hearing this, Turner Catledge of the *New York Times* said, "I assume that means American taxpayers first," and stepped to the door.

At British headquarters in Burma, Dorn had counted one full general, one lieutenant general, five major generals, eighteen brigadiers, and 230 other officers "all floundering through red tape they themselves had set up" to direct 16,000 troops. New Delhi was worse. "The Limey layout is simply stupendous," Stilwell wrote to this wife, "you trip over lieutenant generals on every floor, most of them doing captain's work, or none at all."

They were a race apart, independent of London, possessed of India as their own private affair, and certain that they were right and India, in its desire for self-government, wrong. The very mention of the name Gandhi or Nehru (both were in jail) would turn them apoplectic and incoherent, table-pounding in their wrath. "The moral climate was poisoned," wrote Sevareid; "the place was neurotic and sick." Though no liberal himself, Stilwell can be excused for recognizing unpromising allies.

The approach had been to paper over the fundamental divergences in American, British, and Chinese national interest by giving Stilwell grandiose titles. He was (1) Chief of Staff to the Generalissimo as Supreme Allied Commander in the China Theater, and commander of such Chinese forces as Chiang chose to place under him. He was (2) Commanding General of American forces in the China-Burma-India theater, including air forces, the three thousand infantrymen who came to be known as Merrill's Marauders, the distribution of Lend-Lease, and (until Roosevelt took it away from him) the allocation of supply tonnages over the Hump. When Lord Louis Mountbatten was appointed Supreme Commander, South-East Asia Allied Command, Stilwell became (3) his deputy commander.

Efforts to rationalize this administrative chamber of horrors were sought and eagerly welcomed by Stilwell, but the only real solution—that the conflicts in national purpose be acknowledged and dealt with at a level higher than his—was seldom attempted. At levels lower than his, the ensuing complexities were enormous beyond belief. "I'm working now," one of Stilwell's staff officers told Jack Fischer, "on a three-dimensional organization chart with a wire framework and five shades of colored ribbon, which ought to indicate at least the simpler relationships."[56]

One further hazard, perhaps least avoidable of all, was presented by Claire Chennault. Chennault had been promoted to brigadier general when the Flying Tigers were incorporated into the U.S. Army as Fourteenth Air Force, and he enjoyed great favor with the Generalissimo and Madame Chiang. He had access to the White House through Soong and Hopkins (after May 1943, he was authorized to communicate directly with the President, outside of channels), and his amanuensis, Joseph W. Alsop, Jr., was a noted newspaper columnist cultivated by Roosevelt, and first cousin of the President's wife.[57] Between Chennault and Stilwell there seems to have been no personal animosity, but in character and conviction they were worlds apart. Both were fighters, both loved China, and both wanted to defeat Japan; there the similarities ended.

Stilwell was a Yankee, Chennault a southerner. Stilwell loved the China of the common people; Chennault's China was that of the governing class. Stilwell was a West Pointer, a regular of regulars, who expected to obey and be obeyed; Chennault was a military iconoclast who had achieved success only outside the establishment and by disregarding accepted doctrine. Stilwell was focused inward and given to self-questioning; Chennault was an extrovert with a high opinion of himself, accustomed from childhood to having his own way. "I early developed very fast mental reactions [and] was always impatient with anyone who required more time," he wrote. "This trait produced unfortunate results in later years because I was seldom able to explain my plans in detail to my superiors . . . and I suffered a defensive complex if required to do so."

Chennault believed that he and he alone knew how to win the war. In October 1942, he wrote to the President that if given an air force of 150 fighters, 30 medium bombers, and 12 heavy bombers, he could "accomplish the downfall of Japan." He would destroy the Japanese air force and bomb the Japanese home islands, after which the way would be clear for MacArthur in Australia, the Chinese in China, and the U.S. Navy in the Pacific to advance on Japan "with comparatively slight cost." His stated needs were to increase as time went on, but the central conviction remained. "My entire above plan is simple," he informed the President. "It has been long thought out. . . . I have no doubt of my success."[58]

Stilwell did not believe that Chennault's plan would work. He was convinced—as he put it in a meeting with Chennault, Marshall, and Stimson in Washington—that "any attempt to bomb Japan is going to bring a prompt and violent reaction on the ground." If we stung the Japanese enough to hurt, they would retaliate by overrunning the bases from which the bombers flew (which is in fact what happened). Chennault's answer to this was that air power could stop a ground attack, a conclusion he had erroneously drawn from a single, unrepresentative instance. Further, on his behalf Chiang Kai-shek had promised the President that the bases would be defended. "The Generalissimo also wishes me to transmit to you," Soong wrote by way of Hopkins in April 1943, "his personal assurance that in the event the enemy attempts to interrupt the air offensive by a ground advance on the air bases, the advance can be halted by the existing Chinese forces"—a vaporous bluff the Japanese would have no trouble in calling.

But Chennault's plan had a powerful appeal both to Chiang Kai-shek and to Roosevelt. For Chiang, it would bring American power to his side with the least possible disruption to his regime, relieving him of Stilwell's annoying determination to reform his army and risk it in combat; Chennault would take over the war and produce an effortless triumph. For the President, Chennault's plan had the initial merit of being what Chiang Kai-shek wanted. It promised high return on a low investment and, best of all, it would be highly visible. Roosevelt told Marshall on May 3, 1943, "that politically he must support Chiang Kai-shek and that in the state of Chinese morale the air program was therefore of great importance." By his own decision, without discussion with either Churchill or the Joint Chiefs, Roosevelt approved Chennault's plan and instructed Marshall to put it into effect.

The President had made a mistake of the first magnitude and the airman had won a hollow victory. The latter's (and Chiang's) indifference to logistics and ground defense had led them into commitments they could not keep. For ground transportation from the air terminus at Kunming to his forward bases Chennault had relied on the Chinese, who failed him, and Kunming became a bottleneck. Even when Chennault was given the highest priority over the Hump and received twelve thousand tons a month (he had claimed ten thousand would do the job), neither he nor Chiang was able to stop the Japanese when they finally became annoyed enough to invade East China in 1944, and the bases, as Stilwell had predicted, were lost.[59]

The ultimate irony is that Stilwell and not Chennault might have saved Chiang Kai-shek. All Stilwell wanted to do, over Chiang's persistent foot-dragging, was create for him the two things he needed most: a government that could govern and an army that could fight. Had Stilwell succeeded, Chiang would have come out of the war in a far stronger position vis-à-vis the Communists than he actually did; he still might not have survived, but his chances would have been markedly improved. Stilwell asked nothing in return; he had no personal postwar ambition other than going back to Carmel and watching his children bring up his grandchildren. All he wanted was to carry out his orders, and he and others knew that to do just that was well within his capacity. "If the

Chinese Army is to be regenerated," wrote John Paton Davies in a memo to the American ambassador (Gauss) in March 1943, "it must be through General Stilwell."

Davies later concluded that Stilwell was asking the impossible of Chiang, that Chiang accurately perceived the consequences for him of a reformed army—namely, that it would no longer be his. Officers who became competent would become rivals and the incompetent would become rebels. "Confronted with a purge," Davies wrote in 1972, "most Chinese generals would have ceased to take orders and either have turned on the Generalissimo or simply assumed the character of warlords, their troops staying with them. The system was therefore inalterably opposed to its reformation." Davies in later years believed that Stilwell had been "sent on a self-defeating mission."

But that is not what Davies believed at the time. He thought then that the Chinese were badly in need of the Puritan spirit Stilwell exemplified, that showering them with munitions while pleading with them to fight was pointless, that any American who compromised with Chinese politics would be useless in the role he had been assigned, and that many among the Chinese military understood this and sympathized with Stilwell. "More than a score of Chinese officers," Davies wrote to Gauss, "have come to him privately telling him that he was doing China a great service by his forthrightedness [sic], that he is needed, and to keep on going straight down the road."[60] Many of them (Chiang Kai-shek included) had been watching attentively what Stilwell had already achieved at Ramgarh in India, where he had begun to reconstitute on his own the Chinese Army he would one day soon lead back into Burma.

IV

Lorna Wingate is remembered as very beautiful, almost Oriental-looking, with dark eyes and black hair. At sixteen, on a P. & O. steamship in the Mediterranean, she had introduced herself to an army officer fourteen years older than she by saying, "You're the man I'm going to marry," and a year later she did. At twenty-six, staying with her parents near Aberdeen during August 1943, she was sent on her way to London by a phone call from a husband she had believed to be in India, and more mysteriously still, at Edinburgh she was whisked off the train under orders from the highest authority by transportation officers as much in the dark as she was.[61]

Next morning she was reunited on a suburban railway platform with Brigadier General Orde C. Wingate, D.S.O., wearing the same bush jacket and sun helmet in which he had departed New Delhi four days before, and by evening the two of them were aboard the blacked-out *Queen Mary*, slipping down the Clyde and out to sea. They had joined several hundred high-ranking officers and staff, on the way to a conference with their American counterparts in Quebec. The long arm of Winston Churchill had reached out, and the Wingates' unexpected journey was to change the course of the war in Burma.

It was Churchill, to whom Wingate had originally been introduced by Liddell Hart, who summoned him to London. At dinner in 1938, Wingate held forth about irregular warfare in Palestine, and Churchill had silenced a woman who tried to interrupt. In early 1941, Major and later Colonel Wingate led a column of sixteen hundred Sudanese and Ethiopians offic- ered by one hundred British into Ethiopia, killed or captured an Italian force of over eighteen thousand, and returned Emperor Haile Selassie to his homeland. In early 1943, now-Brigadier Wingate had taken troops he himself had organized—the first Chindit expedition—deep into Japanese- held Burma, disrupting enemy communications and proving the feasibil- ity of what he had chosen to call "long range penetration." In a time of troubles, Wingate's exploit had been seized upon by the press and had made him a celebrity. His report of it, characteristically outspoken, reached Churchill in late July and prompted the Prime Minister's desire to see more of its author.

Wingate arrived in London August 4 and was taken that day to meet with Brooke, who quizzed him about his needs for future operations, indicated a willingness to have them met, and instructed him to report his arrival to 10 Downing Street. Churchill's account of the episode picks up there: "I was about to dine alone . . . when the news that [Wingate] had arrived by air and was actually in the house was brought to me. I immedi- ately asked him to join me at dinner. We had not talked for half an hour before I felt myself in the presence of a man of the highest quality. . . . I decided at once to take him with me [to Quebec]. . . . He was of course quite ready to go, but expressed regret that he would not be able to see his wife. . . . However, the resources of my Private Office were equal to the occasion. Mrs. Wingate . . . had no idea what it was all about until, in the early hours of the morning, she actually met her husband. . . . They had a very happy voyage together."[62]

Orde Charles Wingate was born at Naini Tal, a hill station in the Himalayas, of an ancestral line that followed the Bible and the Sword, ministers and soldiers. His father was a colonel in the Indian Army and his mother came of a military family. Both parents were convinced members of the Plymouth Brethren, a sect of nonconformist piety and missionary zeal, and their son was reared in that strenuous faith. He was educated in England, at Charterhouse and the Royal Military Academy at Woolich, where he showed a gift for horseback riding and a streak of unconvention- ality—"something of a clown, something of a rebel," writes his biographer, Christopher Sykes.

In 1923, he was commissioned in the Royal Artillery and posted to a brigade near Stonehenge, where he rode to hounds with a fellow officer, his friend Derek Tulloch, later his chief of staff in Burma. Wingate attended a War Office course at the School of Oriental Studies, learned Arabic, and was sent to the Sudan Defence Force in Khartoum. In 1936, destiny took him in hand and he was appointed intelligence officer to the 5th Division in Haifa, Palestine, a region to whose future he would deeply devote himself.

There is a breed of Englishmen who under the spell of Islam and the desert go slightly daft and begin believing themselves to be Arabs; Wingate's distant cousin T. E. Lawrence, of whom he strongly disapproved, is the archetype. Wingate was cast in a similar mold, though what he desired to be was not an Arab but a Jew. Within months of arrival in Palestine, he had become more Zionist than the Zionists. Asked why, he said he had been looked down upon at school and that here was a people who had been looked down upon for centuries. To a Jewish acquaintance who asked what he had read of Zionism, he replied: "There is only one important book on the subject, the Bible, and I have read it thoroughly."

Lorna joined him and they lived in Jerusalem; he began to learn Hebrew and became a friend of Chaim Weizmann. To his uncle Sir Reginald Wingate, the "Sirdar," former high commissioner of Egypt and one of the last empire-builders of the old school, he wrote: "Islam in reality cares little for the Arabs of Palestine. . . . The potential military strength of the Jews . . . is equivalent to at least two army corps when trained and organized. . . . I tell you that the Jews will provide a better soldiery than ours."[63]

Wingate started a training school for Jewish officers and noncoms at Ein Harod. "Our purpose here," he would say to them, "is to found the Jewish Army." He dreamed of creating such an army and leading it into battle. His hero was Gideon of Ophrah, to whom the Lord commended three hundred men out of twenty-two thousand, and with these few by guile and boldness Gideon totally defeated the Midianites and the Amalekites, who "lay along the valley like grasshoppers for multitude" (Judges 7:12). Wingate organized "special night squads" of Jewish reservists to counteract Arab terrorists; with them he saw his first of many actions and in one of them he was badly wounded. He was never to behold the fulfillment of his vision, the Israeli Army of the Sinai War in 1956, but its birth was there in the patrols of scarcely a dozen men or more that Wingate mounted twenty years earlier.

Wingate was a gifted fighter, a born leader in the field, and—when he pulled himself together—an impressive and even a handsome presence. "To see Wingate urging action on some hesitant commander," General Slim said of him, "was to realize how a medieval baron felt when Peter the Hermit got after him to go crusading." But strain bore down heavily

Pirates. He had commanded a fighter squadron in North Africa and been known to post a notice on his bulletin board that said: "To all personnel: Look, sports, the beards and attempts at beards are not appreciated by visitors." After their first meeting, Wingate protested that as head of his air force they had sent him "the hero of a comic strip." Cochran said that when he asked Wingate about flying conditions in Burma, he got "a lecture on Buddhism."

Cochran had trouble with British accents; he thought Wingate had a speech defect. But Cochran, as Christopher Sykes puts it, did not take himself as seriously as he took his profession. After their second encounter, it dawned on him that Wingate wanted to use guerrilla columns "in the same way that fighter-control headquarters directs planes out on a mission. I saw it as an adaptation of air to jungle, an application of radio-controlled air-war tactics to a walking man in the trees and weeds. . . . I realized that there was something very deep about him." These two in combination could do much.

When Alison, Cochran, and No. 1 Air Commando arrived in India the second week of November 1943, they found Wingate recovering from a bout of typhoid and arguing with everyone in sight—including Stilwell, who happened to be in New Delhi—to get the airlift Wingate wanted for a second penetration of Burma. He was even trying to persuade Stilwell to allocate him transports from the Hump, which was like asking a victim of suffocation to blow up a balloon. "All my planning has gone for nothing," Wingate told Cochran. "They have done this to me deliberately. Why do I have so many enemies?" Cochran is said to have replied: "Look, sport, that's like asking why Hitler hates Churchill. Now tell me everything, and stop feeling sorry for yourself." Alison and Cochran managed to convince Wingate, who was still unfamiliar with the capabilities of his air weapon, that the gliders they had brought along for equipment supply could also carry troops. "Since our talk after lunch," Wingate wrote Stilwell on November 17, "I have had a good discussion with Colonel Cochran. . . . What it amounts to is that we need not put the strain on your Air Forces that I was suggesting."[67]

Wingate and the Americans were back in harness.

◆

At about this time, the high-level American attitudes toward China began to change. The increasing strength of the fast carriers was making possible a more rapid advance across the Central Pacific than had been anticipated, and on November 20, Marines landed at Tarawa in the Gilberts, the first—and one of the costliest—of the Navy's giant steps forward from Pearl Harbor, some two thousand miles to the rear. (The Marines staged at Efate, in the New Hebrides.) The potentialities of the B-29 were about to be more fully appreciated and the possibility was beginning to occur to staff planners that Japan might be defeated without any land campaign in China at all.

On November 23, there opened in Cairo the first plenary session of the Allied conference called Sextant, to which (with no encouragement from Churchill) Roosevelt had insisted on inviting the Generalissimo and Madame Chiang. What had been hoped for was consensus on the future course of the war in Southeast Asia; what emerged was something else again. The Chinese generals presented a spectacle of ineptitude from which even generous displays of shapely leg by Madame Chiang could not distract attention, and the President, the Prime Minister, and the Combined Chiefs of Staff got their first full exposure to Chiang's unique combination of vacillation and inertia, his constant readiness—once agreement had been reached—to reverse himself the following day. "They have been driven absolutely mad," wrote Mountbatten with ill-concealed satisfaction.[68]

More important by far, the Russians had made a move. On October 30 in Moscow, Stalin had told Secretary Hull that once Germany was defeated, he would enter the war against Japan. Hull thought this momentous news (though there had earlier been premonitory hints), so much so that he cabled it to the President with the message divided in two, half in the Army's code and half in the Navy's. The Russian commitment was reiterated when Roosevelt and Churchill met for the first time with Stalin in Teheran at the end of November, and when they returned to Cairo (with Chiang absent), the President was in even less of a mood to humor the Generalissimo. Russian intervention could provide bases for an attack on Japan far superior to anything Chiang might offer, and Russian armies could be relied upon to give the Japanese in Manchuria rough handling. (John Paton Davies viewed this expansion of Russian power in the Far East as a mixed blessing, but most Americans—including those like MacArthur, as we have seen, who were later volubly anti-Communist—thought of it at the time as highly desirable.) The preconditions were now in place for writing China off.

Immediately at issue was a proposed seaborne invasion of the Andaman Islands in the Bay of Bengal, a preliminary to invading southern Burma, on which Chiang was placing great emphasis. Roosevelt had told him it would go forward, but the British held back, repeatedly reminding the President that the landing craft required would have to be withdrawn from Western Europe. Under their importunities, the logic of numbers, and his disenchantment with Chiang, Roosevelt consented to canceling the Andaman operation, despite warnings by Marshall, King, and Leahy that breaking a promise to the Chinese would have unhappy consequences. In a sense it did; it gave Chiang an inarguable, multipurpose excuse for inaction that he regularly invoked thereafter.

At second Cairo, Davies and Stilwell had a meeting with Roosevelt at

554 COMMANDER IN CHIEF

which they found him willing to envisage a world without Chiang but not yet willing (or able) to formulate concrete plans about what to do next, considering the obvious fact that to call off the Andaman action was to put Stilwell in a next-to-impossible position. Davies asked the President what we should do if the Chiang regime collapsed, and Roosevelt immediately replied that we should bolster the next in line, whoever that might be. Davies and Stilwell both agreed that it was less likely to be a person than a group, and Stilwell added that we need not go looking for them: They would come to us.

Dorn says that Roosevelt told Stilwell to prepare a contingency plan for having Chiang Kai-shek assassinated. This is on the face of it improbable; the President, of all people, would have regarded any such plot as certain to be exposed sooner or later and to damage him irreparably. Rapport between general and President was not of the best, and it is far more likely that Roosevelt made an offhand, indirect, and ambiguous remark that Stilwell in his direct fashion interpreted unambiguously. "If you can't get along with Chiang and can't replace him," Dorn says that Roosevelt told Stilwell, "get rid of him once and for all. You know what I mean. Put in someone you can manage." Stilwell told Dorn that Roosevelt was fed up with Chiang and his tantrums. But still, Stilwell added, *"this* is not the solution for the China problem . . . the United States doesn't go in for this sort of thing."

Davies and Stilwell had the usual difficulties in getting the President to stay on the subject, and Stilwell's impressionistic reconstruction of this conversation makes Roosevelt sound frothy. He rambled off into family anecdotes, stories about loan negotiations with Chiang's finance minister, and speculations about the postwar period. Stilwell concluded, as his notes read, that all he could get out of this was: "Policy: 'we want to help China.' —Period." Hopkins wandered in and they talked about Japan, in particular the status of the emperor. "At no point," Davies wrote, "did either give the general a coherent statement of what they wanted him to do." As Davies and Stilwell were leaving, the President said, "Remember, you're both ambassadors, both ambassadors." On their way to their quarters, Stilwell held his head in his hands.[69] Two weeks later, he was back where he preferred to be, in the field, commanding troops in the attack.

The Burma campaign of 1944 is an unsung saga of the war, in part because it had so little effect on the war's outcome and in part because it consisted of actions so different in character and separated by geography that on first impression they seem unrelated. At the turn of the year, the two Chinese divisions from India, with Stilwell leading them, began a drive down the Ledo Road toward Myitkyina. In early March, Wingate and the Chindits were flown in to the area around Indaw to cut the railroad and other routes on which Myitkyina's defense depended. Later in that month, however, to the west, the Japanese opened a very strong offensive against Slim's Fourteenth Army at Imphal and Kohima that threatened to cut off both Chindits and Chinese from their Indian sources of supply. Participants in any one of these battles had little idea what was happening in the others, which led to violent misunderstandings and sorely tried tempers, but when it was all over the Japanese had suffered a major defeat. Burma broke the Japanese Army as it had never been broken before.

Two factors had been decisive in altering the Burmese circumstances. Of these, the first was the enlarged presence in India of Allied air power, and Allied it was, American and British commingled. Backbone of it was the C-47, by the British called Dakota, the DC-3, the Grand Old Lady, most rugged and dependable of air transports. Reinforcing it was an improvised but highly efficient system of supply technique: standardized loads, production-line packaging, simultaneous fueling and loading, with their result in round-the-clock performance. In Burma, air supply came into its own, and both Stilwell and Slim saw its importance. What Slim saw more clearly than most was that with this instrument the Japanese tactics of encirclement could be counteracted. Let them encircle, and then let them waste themselves against defenders supplied from the air and no longer intimidated. The Japanese could neither match nor answer this; their own air power was being spread too thin (of their four bomber groups in Burma, two had to be sent to New Guinea in January 1944). After the war, one Japanese officer said that the "difference in ground-air co-operation between the Japanese Army and the Allies was the difference between victory and defeat."[70]

All of this was above and beyond the achievements of India-China Wing of Air Transport Command in flying the Hump, a saga in itself. The direct route from Ledo to Kunming in CAVU weather (ceiling and visibility unlimited) was 520 miles across the mountains at sixteen thousand feet, for forty-five minutes over an area the Japanese controlled. But in bad weather, which was mostly, detours were frequent and minimum altitude was twenty thousand feet, or two thousand feet higher than Pikes Peak. In the monsoon on the India side there were turbulent storms with winds up to 100 mph and air pockets that could lift or drop a plane thousands of feet in a minute; during one such in January 1945, nine aircraft were lost. All in all, from January 1944 to August 1945, every 340 tons carried over the Hump cost one American life. But the number of flights and the total tonnages kept going up. In December 1944, a plane took off for China every eleven minutes, heavier traffic than La Guardia Airport carried, and by the end the Hump had carried more freight than the Burma Road. President Roosevelt (who had ordered the operation) insisted that India-China Wing be given a Presidential Unit Citation, despite objections from the adjutant general's office that these went only to "combat" troops, and for the first time in history it was done. (When a supply officer inquired how many ribbons should be shipped, he was startled to be told eleven thousand.)[71]

The second of the two decisive factors was Admiral Mountbatten. When he arrived in New Delhi as supreme commander, he was solemnly assured by the deskbound lieutenant generals that air supply was impossible, that it was impossible to fight during the monsoon, that Japanese infiltration was impossible to stop, that an offensive from Assam was impossible because of inadequate communications, and that Wingate was—well, impossible. All such expert advice Lord Louis in characteristic fashion ignored. He let it be known that he took his authority as supremo seriously and intended to exercise it. Battles would not be governed by weather and there would be no more retreats. Liking what he saw in Slim, he offered him command of Fourteenth Army, and when Slim asked whether it might not be a good idea to consult New Delhi first, Mountbatten politely said no, that would not be necessary. He came to Slim's headquarters near Barrackpore and spoke to his officers. "We began to feel," Slim wrote, "that we belonged to an efficient show, or what was going to be one, and that feeling spread."[72]

Slim had three anxieties: supply, health, and morale—all of which he proceeded to deal with in his patient and methodical way. Given the creeping inanity of New Delhi, supplies where they existed did not always reach the men they were intended for, and not enough of them existed; even ammunition was short. Measures were taken to repair this. As for health, Slim's army was melting away. For every man wounded he was losing 120 to disease; the malaria rate was 84 percent, followed by dysentery and jungle typhus. Measures were taken. The curves of hospital admissions began to bend downward, until by 1945 the sickness rate of Fourteenth Army had dropped to one per thousand per day. As for morale, Slim gave it his fullest and best-rewarded attention. His weapon was the spoken word.

From a platform that was normally the engine hood of his jeep, Slim talked to his multilingual army, sometimes three or four times a day. He said the cockneys laughed at his jokes before he finished them, the north country men took longer but roared louder. The Welsh, the Scots, and the Irish (unlike the English) could be reached on subjects involving emotion or the spirit, as could the Indians and (he hoped but wasn't sure) the Africans. Many of the new Indian recruits knew no Urdu or Hindustani; he thought it was only their innate good manners that caused them to ignore his mistakes. Once, after giving what he thought had been a particularly eloquent harangue in Urdu, he asked his aide if that hadn't been rather a good effort. "Quite, sir," was the reply, "but I suppose you know that after the first two sentences you relapsed entirely into Gurkhali."[73]

Slim talked to them about their homes, their traditions, the importance of the jobs they were doing. He would talk about the material things

—food, pay, leave, beer, mail—before he moved on to the foundation of their effort in ideals. The Fourteenth might be the Forgotten Army, but its goals were no less worth achieving. He told them what was going on, what was happening and what was going to happen. He told them they were going to defeat the Japanese, and how and why they would do it: how man for man they could best the enemy at the jungle game and, with intelligence and skill, excel and outwit him. He insisted on discipline— saluting, good turnout, personal cleanliness—and to instill self-confidence and keep his men active, he sent them out on constant patrols into Japanese-held territory. A group of Gurkhas proudly brought their general three Japanese heads they had detached with their *kukris*.

One day in Burma during the retreat, Slim and Stilwell had been sitting on a hilltop in a state of some discouragement. Well, said Stilwell, at least the two of them had an ancestor in common. Who was that? Slim asked. "Ethelred the Unready," said Stilwell. This time they would be ready.[74]

◆

Wingate's first Chindit expedition into Burma had produced an unexpected reaction from the Japanese. They, like Churchill, had thought ill of fighting their way through jungle-covered mountains and had concluded that from Burma an invasion of India's easternmost provinces (Manipur and Assam) was not worth the trouble. Wingate changed their minds; if he could do it in their direction, they could do it in his. They were well aware that the Allies were preparing a stroke against them and they reasoned soundly that the best way to parry it was to strike first. If they could seize the bases on the Indian side of the border from which an attack must come, then that attack would be indefinitely postponed. In consequence, on January 7, 1944, Imperial General Headquarters in Tokyo ordered Burma Area Army to "occupy and secure" the area in the vicinity of Imphal, the capital of Manipur, "at the opportune time."

The Japanese plan was excellent except for one large gaping flaw: It depended on instant success. Three full divisions plus a scratch force of Indian turncoats would cross the Chindwin in early March to cut the Imphal-Kohima road, take Kohima, and enter the Imphal plain from north, east, and south. They would travel light and fast, resupplying themselves from the great base they would acquire at Imphal. (This was the flaw: If Imphal's capture was delayed, their supply problems would mount geometrically.) To distract Slim's attention—and cause him to shift forces away from Imphal—there would be a diversionary attack in February on the Arakan front down near the Bay of Bengal. But Slim refused to be distracted.

His plans had been long and carefully prepared. He assumed that Imphal was the objective (a conclusion confirmed by Ultra intelligence) and that it would probably be surrounded. His instructions read that when the Japanese were detected crossing the Chindwin in any numbers, his divisions should fall back on Imphal and concentrate there, ready to withstand a siege with the largest force he could muster. He persuaded Mountbatten to loan him thirty C-47s, on Mountbatten's own authority, and with them he flew 5th Indian Division into Imphal from Arakan. (Technically, such a transfer of aircraft could be made only by the American Joint Chiefs; fortunately, they and President Roosevelt agreed with Mountbatten and approved his decision.) Slim made one mistake. His figures showed him that the trail up to Kohima from the Chindwin could support only one Japanese regiment, and he garrisoned Kohima accordingly. The figures were correct but the Japanese disregarded them, assaulted Kohima with their entire 31st Division, and very nearly took it.

The battle for Imphal lasted three months. The plain and its complex of headquarters, hospitals, and storehouses was cut off as Slim had expected, and Japanese efforts to break into it were driven home from every quarter of the compass. All were blocked by the four Indian divisions of 4th Corps—5th in the north and northeast, 20th in the southeast, 23d in the south, and 17th in reserve—which fought with a tenacity and valor that earned them seven Victoria Crosses, four Indian and three British. Japanese air was ineffectual and always the C-47s flew, bringing in supplies and taking out the wounded. By mid-June, 4th Corps was beginning to drive the Japanese back, and on the twenty-second, the road to Kohima was reopened. That night the first truck convoy from Assam drove through to Imphal, headlights blazing.

At Kohima, the Japanese had run into a rock. Three battalions of 2d British Division stood off constant Japanese headlong charges in numbers greater than their own for sixteen days! Kohima is on the spur of a ridge, a cluster of hills wound through by the Imphal-Dimapur road on its way back to Assam. It had to be held and held it was. At Kohima now there is a cemetery of 1,287 graves and a monument with an inscription that recalls Thermopylae: "When you go home/Tell them of us and say,/For their tomorrow/We gave our today." The stone was cut from a local quarry and dragged up the hill by Naga tribesmen from their village nearby.

The retreat of Japanese Fifteenth Army back into Burma was a sordid rout: no ammunition, no food, no medical care. Their casualty rate was somewhere between 85 and 90 percent. The pursuing British and Indians found scene after scene of rotting, emaciated, and half-naked corpses surrounded by abandoned equipment. Years later in Mandalay, a Buddhist monk told Drew Middleton that the exhausted survivors he met had only two words of explanation, "Imphal" and "Kohima," and when they heard the sound of aircraft they dove for cover.[75]

Wingate and the Chindits in the Railroad Valley around Indaw fared less well than 4th Corps at Imphal. They did the necessary; they made the capture of Myitkyina possible (just as Stilwell and the Chindits between them made victory at Imphal possible). But there was a lack of concentration and clarity in what the Chindits did, in some part compounded by the death—in midcampaign—of Wingate himself. Wingate always had more than one plan, at a minimum the official one put forward to conceal a second of his own, and perhaps in this instance one or two more drifting half formed in that restless mind. None of these but the first did he discuss with others, but more than likely his conception of the Chindits was changing toward the more ambitious, and thoughts were reaching him of playing not a supplemental but a major role in the reconquest of Burma.

The Chindits were of course not "special forces" in the sense that Merrill's Marauders were, men self-selected for the task. They were made up of units of the regular Indian Army that Wingate had been able to co-opt. Their name was his own invention, a word he derived from the Burmese *chinthé*, for "lion" or the griffin-like beasts that sometimes adorn pagodas. While Wingate lived, the Chindits were magnetized by his energy and many of their officers—among them John Masters—fully comprehended and applauded the principle of mobile columns in the enemy rear. But the Chindits' mobility was strategic rather than tactical; once committed to action, they were no more mobile than any other body of marching men, and with Wingate absent or no longer alive they tended to behave no differently. A plausible idea might be that Wingate in the Railroad Valley should have been like Stonewall Jackson in the valley of the Shenandoah: moving all the time, turning up where least expected, keeping his opponent ever off balance. But it did not work out quite that way.

Their departure was inauspicious. When the Chindits and their commanders, their gliders and their C-47 tugs, were assembled at Lalaghat airfield in Assam on March 5, they were headed toward three carefully selected landing grounds, code-named Broadway, Piccadilly, and Chowringhee. Wingate had unwisely forbidden aerial reconnaissance of these fields for the past week, to avoid arousing Japanese suspicions, but Colonel Cochran (wisely) had on his own initiative ordered photographs to be made and a half hour before takeoff they were brought to Wingate, showing Piccadilly to be covered by what looked like anti-glider obstacles.

A nightmare became real—that security had been compromised and the Japanese would be waiting for them. Wingate went into a moody rage and Slim drew him aside to calm him. To go or not to go? Slim says the decision was his, one of those moments when a general earns his pay: The operation (with the Piccadilly force diverted to Broadway) would proceed. Cochran summoned the Piccadilly pilots and told them, "Say, fellas, we've got a better place to go."[76] The anti-glider "obstacles" proved to be logs of teak laid out in the sun to dry by foresters.

Once in place, the Chindits roamed northern Burma in fair freedom, destroying stores, shooting up vehicles, inflicting random casualties on the Japanese. It was not always clear to the Japanese (or to anyone in the Allied command, either) where they were or where they were going. Some of their blows were struck against the empty air. They tried to take Indaw and failed. They established several strongholds—one called "White City" near Mawlu and another called "Blackpool" north of Hopin—but both were later abandoned. They did succeed, and quickly, in cutting the roads and the railroad, but the Japanese had stockpiled and this did not have the immediate impact on their logistics that Slim had hoped for. By March 24, Wingate had a division-sized body of ten and a half battalions deployed in Burma as he had wished them to be and ready to execute his subsequent intentions, but whatever they were will never be known, for on that day the B-25 bomber in which he was flying crashed in the mountains west of Imphal and all aboard it were killed.

Less than a month after Wingate died, one of his brigade commanders, Bernard Fergusson (later the Lord Ballantrae) wrote from the field in Burma to his mother and father about the Chindits' leader: "I think he really was a genius . . . a superman, because he was able to invent, persuade, plan, train, *and* execute. He was thoroughly hated by almost everybody. . . . He had no instincts of kindness or charity at all. . . . He loved publicity although chiefly because it furthered his ideas. In conversation he was almost hypnotic. I have heard him lecture for 4 hours and more without a break and hold everybody's attention. His physical courage sometimes failed him but his moral courage never. . . . [W]hen all is said and done, he was one of the best soldiers and certainly one of the greatest men I have met. In a word, he was mad."

The most generous tribute paid to what the Chindits had accomplished was that of the Japanese officers in the postwar interrogations. In their opinion, the Imphal-Kohima operation had by the Chindit activity been substantially weakened. The main force of a division in overall Burma reserve and a battalion each from two others, plus half their air strength, had been diverted to cope with the Chindit raids. Moreover, the cutting of the supply line to their 18th Division in the north, facing Stilwell and the Chinese, meant that in the long run its holding operation there would be hopeless.[77] More elaborate justifications than these are not required. But the employment of the Chindits did not end when Wingate was lost, and thereafter the style and substance of it were modified.

The conclusion was becoming inescapable that the only way to effect a permanent stoppage of Japanese freight along the railroad was to set up a block on it and stay there, something the Chindits had not originally been intended to do. The creation of the strongpoint at Blackpool by 111th Brigade in May marked a signal change in Chindit strategy. Gone was the quasi-guerrilla practice of independent columns weaving a net of harassment around the Japanese, striking here, vanishing there. Blackpool was to be a fortress. If the Japanese attacked it, they would be counterattacked in turn by other Chindit brigades. (A flooded river and some monsoon-soaked mountains prevented this part of the plan from being carried out.) Blackpool turned instead into a three-week agony that occupies a special place in the list of bloody actions of the Burma campaign.

The fight at Blackpool is the subject of one of the best and most harrowing pieces of battle writing of the entire war, the work of a talented novelist (*Bhowani Junction,* etc.) who was not only present there but in command, John Masters. When Wingate died, Slim had replaced him with the 111th's leader, Brigadier Joe Lentaigne, and Lentaigne had chosen Masters (then only a major) as his successor. Masters established the brigade not directly on the railroad but nearby, where his guns could interdict its traffic (as they did with great success) and where there was room for an airstrip to accommodate the C-47s. But Masters anticipated trouble at Blackpool and trouble came, in the form of Japanese attacks, supported by their own artillery, that doubled and redoubled in fury.

Masters fought 111th Brigade with desperate economy, sending his best officers and men to patch holes in his defenses until one by one they were killed or wounded and finally he heard the sound he had been waiting for with dread—the *pom-pom-pom* of Japanese antiaircraft—and knew that the C-47s would now be at hazard and the end was not far off. The pilots continued to fly regardless and to make parachute drops when they could no longer land, but then the monsoon weather closed in and the flying had to stop. On May 25, Masters decided to save his men to fight another day, and a withdrawal under fire commenced. Three days later, they reached safety at Mokso Sakkan and Masters radioed Lentaigne that he had brought with him 130 wounded and 2,000 men organized and under arms.[78]

Stilwell was outraged by the abandonment of Blackpool, and by what he regarded as the Chindits' refusal to obey his orders (they were now nominally under his command). British doctrine did not include the destruction of a unit by asking too much of it, as Stilwell would ask too much of the Marauders. He had sensed victory at Myitkyina almost within his grasp until the Imphal-Kohima offensive threatened it, and here was another threat from the possibility that Myitkyina could now be reinforced.

He was in one of his worst Vinegar Joe moods, lashing out at Americans and British alike, and his staff did him no service by catering to his prejudices. Slim, trying to patch things up, discovered that Stilwell was refusing to meet with Lentaigne. "There was too much of the siege of Troy atmosphere," wrote Slim, "with commanders sulking in their tents." Slim got them to meet. Later one of the Chindit officers reported to Stilwell with a straightforward accounting of what they had done and how many casualties it had cost them, and Stilwell at least partially realized that he had been at fault. "Why wasn't I told?" he said to his staff, and he author-ized some American decorations—small comfort!—for the Chindits.[79]

◆

Stilwell's advance from the north had been begun by two Chinese divisions plus Merrill's Marauders, but these "divisions" were unlike any-thing the Chinese Army had seen before. In numbers they were compara-ble to American in strength, three regiments each, from 11,000 to 12,000 men, with service troops that included antiaircraft, transport, engineers, and later artillery. They were the 22d, commanded by Sun Li-jen, and the 38th, commanded by Liao Yao-hsiang, a graduate of Saint-Cyr and judged by Americans to be "a good field soldier, courageous and determined . . . a capable commander."[80] Under Liao, the 38th had come up rapidly to rival the 22d. Both divisions were products of the training Stilwell had given them, overcoming by main force Chinese and British recalcitrance, at Ramgarh in India.

The 23,000 Chinese troops assembled at Ramgarh (in what was for-merly a camp for Italian prisoners of war) had been fed, clothed, housed, and paid—this last a source of astonishment. (They were paid exactly what they were owed and couldn't figure out where their American paymaster was getting his "squeeze.") They were medically examined, treated for their routine sores and diseases, and taught the rudiments of sanitation; field hospitals were trained and equipped for them by Seagrave, and veterinary, dental, and paramedical units set up. They were taught by American Army methods—through a corps of hard-working interpreters —to fire rifles, light and heavy machine guns, light and heavy mortars, hand grenades, grenade launchers, rocket launchers, and the 37-mm an-titank gun. A course in jungle warfare was given after the weapons train-ing had been completed. "And in return," one of the Chinese was heard to say in wonderment, "all the Americans want us to do is fight."[81]

Fight they did, and they were fighting—to their great credit—first-class Japanese troops, the 18th Division, based on Kyushu and heir to its martial past, veterans of the conquest of Burma and bearers of a special unit citation for their valiant part in the storming of Singapore. The two forces met first at Yupbang Ga in an action planned by Stilwell and Sun Li-jen. (Stilwell's sketch for it is reproduced in the Army history.) It was a modest battle at best but a memorable one for the Chinese because they won it, and this made a heavy imprint. "The Chinese soldiers talked of it over and over again," write the Army historians; "the first victory is never forgotten." A profound pattern of mental set was being reversed. It might not be a miracle, said an American officer who observed it, but "anyone who has known Chinese troops in the past . . . will regard it as a miracle."[82]

It was Stilwell who made them advance. Sun Li-jen said the Chinese wanted to do a good job for *lao-hsien-sheng* (the old gentleman), but even

Sun disappointed Stilwell by his lack of initiative. Stilwell suspected (with reason) that both Sun and Liao Yao-hsiang were being subjected to constant admonitions from Chiang Kai-shek to stay where they were. Stilwell would rise at dawn and hike forward three or four miles to the Chinese command posts, where he would quietly hang around until orders were given to attack. Once he told them that if they didn't fight he would go stand in the trail up front. "This makes them move," he wrote in the diary, "and is the only thing that does." On his sixty-first birthday, they crossed the divide between the Hukawng and the Mogaung valleys and in tandem with the Marauders were driving the Japanese back: "double birthday present," Stilwell wrote.[83] On June 16, Sun's division took Kamaing, and four days later a neck-and-neck race between Liao's division and the Chindits ended with the Chindits' capture of Mogaung.

Originally the intention had been that the north Burma campaign would consist not of three battles but of four. To the east across the Salween River in Yunnan, Chiang Kai-shek had eleven American-equipped divisions, collectively known as Y- (Yoke) Force, faced by Japanese who had been weakened to support the defenses against Stilwell. Mountbatten and Stilwell had been urging that Y-Force take the offensive, but Chiang had replied that this was "impossible." Following the Burma fighting in the White House Map Room, President Roosevelt could see the massed array of pins that represented Y-Force and the scattered few for the Japanese on the other side of the river. He could not understand, according to Marshall, why such an obvious chance was being missed. His confidence in China as a military power was at last being put to the test, and under it that confidence crumbled. On April 3, 1944, he radioed Chiang in language (drafted by Marshall) that even the Sultan of Morocco might have considered "stern."

"It is inconceivable to me," part of Roosevelt's message read, "that your Yoke Forces, with their American equipment, would be unable to advance against the Japanese Fifty-sixth Division in its present depleted strength. . . . A shell of a division opposes you on the Salween. Your advance to the west cannot help but succeed. To take advantage of just such an opportunity, we have, during the past year, been equipping and training your Yoke Forces. If they are not to be used in the common cause our most strenuous and extensive efforts to fly in equipment and to furnish instructional personnel have not been justified. . . . I do hope you can act." Whether this rocket ever reached Chiang Kai-shek is unclear; Madame Chiang told one of Stilwell's officers that the tone of it would displease the Generalissimo, which conveyed the impression that she had not delivered it. At any rate, it was never answered.[84]

Meanwhile Marshall had sent Stilwell a complementary communication even more directly to the point. All along, Stilwell had been arguing that we should deal with the Chinese on a *quid pro quo* basis (that is, we should "exact commitments," as the President had been opposed to doing). At long last, Stilwell's policy was being recommended by the Joint Chiefs. Marshall on their authority instructed Stilwell to inform the Chinese military that if Yoke Force did not attack, all Lend-Lease shipments to it would cease, and at long last, the withdrawal of the carrot proved to be more effective than the application of the stick. The Chinese war ministry issued an order for the move, accompanied by a radio message to Washington with the bland, face-saving declaration that the decision "to move part of Yoke Force across Salween was made on initiative of Chinese without influence of outside pressure."[85] Sure. The crossing of the Salween in mid-May was unopposed and Yoke Force made slow but steady progress until the Japanese counterattacked at Lung-ling and hopes ended of a breakthrough to Myitkyina from the east. By September, Chiang Kai-shek was threatening to pull Yoke Force back into China.

But by that time the Marauders had taken Myitkyina.

◆

The Marauders were a hard-luck outfit from the start. They were the first American ground troops to take the field in Asia since the Boxer Rebellion and they were the only Americans between Italy and New Guinea who were actively engaged with the enemy; sometimes they had the feeling that the War Department and the nation had lost track of them and they had been forgotten. Moreover, they were all volunteers, and an old army adage holds that the only thing stupider than volunteering is asking for volunteers; in any well-run unit, no one gets to "volunteer" for duty elsewhere unless he can be spared. "We've got the misfits of half the divisions in the country," said one Marauder officer.

Some of them were there because they could think of nowhere better to be, and yet some others were there because they actually *liked* combat. Charlton Ogburn, a Marauder himself, tells of the 1st Battalion commander who suggested, in a lull between battles, that if nothing else was going to happen, they might cross the ridge and start a fight with 2d Battalion. "He gave a half-laugh," writes Ogburn, "and of course he was joking, but all the same . . . the idea *had* occurred to him."

They were conceived in haste, with no past and a dubious future, as an outcome of Marshall's offer at Quebec to let Americans serve with Wingate. (His generosity was undercut by Stilwell, who insisted on keeping the Marauders to himself, and got his way.) They did not even have the consolation of a glamorous name, like the Queen's Own Royal West Heathshire Rifles or whatever, since "Merrill's Marauders" was the subsequent invention of a journalist. They knew only that they belonged to something called the 5307th Composite Unit (Provisional), which sounded, as one Marauder said, like an address in Los Angeles, and led another, in a moment of stress, to inquire what the hell had become of the other 5,306 composite units (provisional)?

After the Marauders made their approach march down the Ledo road from Assam into northern Burma, they pitched camp on an island in the Tarung River and General Stilwell waded across to greet them. He made a good impression, but there had already been an ill omen. When they had passed his headquarters, having marched over a hundred miles in full kit, they thought he might at least have come out to take a few salutes from his only American combat troops, specially spruced up for the occasion. He did not do so, and thus he missed—as Ogburn writes in his book about the Marauders—"the chance for an inexpensive gesture that could have repaid him in days to come."[86]

Later their disappointment turned to unrelieved bitterness. Rightly or wrongly, the heavy moral pressure ("just short of outright orders") from his headquarters, to keep in the firing line every American who could pull a trigger, was associated by the Marauders with Stilwell personally. They thought him a small man in a job too big for him, utterly bloodless and lacking in human kindness; and only when the war was long over, and the story of Stilwell's own frustrations began to be published, did Ogburn himself realize how badly they had misjudged their commander.

The trouble was that he took them for granted. All his career, Stilwell had looked forward to leading Americans in war, but now that the chance had come to him, there was too much else to be done. Surrounded as he was by skepticism and indifference on the part of the British and Chinese, he was filled with a considerable mistrust of either's enthusiasm for fighting. The one thing in his universe of baffled intentions and thwarted hopes he thought he could count on was American infantry. The Marauders at least he could trust—they were after all "picked" men, led by one of his own best officers, Frank Merrill—and so he gave them the dirty jobs to do, and pushed them beyond their limit, and wore them out.

Between February and May 1944, the Marauders fought in five major and thirty minor actions against the veteran Japanese. The records of these engagements are sketchy. On their second mission, a Japanese artillery shell hit the mule carrying the headquarters maps and files, and at Myitkyina their intelligence officer was killed and his papers washed away in the rains before anyone could collect them.[87] What remains is properly legend. The scheme was that Stilwell and the Chinese would advance down the main river valleys while the 5307th Composite Unit (Provisional) made wide left hooks through the mountains and hit the Japanese from the flank and rear. This the Marauders did at Walawbum; at Shaduzup, Nhpum Ga, and Inkangatawng; and finally at Myitkyina—always with success. Eventually they were given the recognition they deserved—a Presidential Unit Citation, six Distinguished Service Crosses, four Legions of Merit, and forty-four Silver Stars—but at the time they had little sense that anyone cared.

On the trail, the Marauders' worst enemy was their own apprehension, the condition of uninterrupted suspense imposed by a jungle march in enemy country. There is nothing on either side of you and ahead there is only the next bend in the trail, and after that the next bend, and so on for another hundred miles. Sooner or later, or any moment now, the silence is broken by the sudden *pup-pup-pup . . . pup-pup-pup-pup* of a Japanese machine gun, and the column comes to a halt. There is a cry of "Weapons platoon forward . . . clear the trail!" Then perhaps there is the sound of mortar fire—ours? theirs?—and, shortly, "Medics forward!" until the trail-block has been cleared and the column can move on again. The Marauders lived through this, as Ogburn writes, "not just when it happened but a hundred times a day" in anticipation of it. "Ahead the view was always closed by a bend in the trail. Always there was a bend to be rounded. Each one had to be sweated out. From first to last that was probably the worst part of the campaign for those who had to endure it: *what was around the next bend?*"[88]

Disease was their other enemy, the sores and fevers and dysentery that incapacitated more of them than Japanese gunfire. In all, the Marauders suffered 93 killed and 293 wounded in action, but their medical casualties were nearly five times as great. Less than half of the Marauders reached Myitkyina, and these were soon being withdrawn from combat by the medics as unfit to fight, at a daily rate of seventy-five to a hundred (to be considered unfit, a man had to be running a fever of over 102 degrees for three consecutive days), until finally only two hundred could be classed as fit. During their last battle, several fell asleep from sheer exhaustion and their commanding officer lost consciousness three times while directing it. "For in the end," wrote the medical historian of the CBI theater, "amoebas, bacteria, rickettsiae and viruses, rather than Japanese soldiers and guns, vanquished the most aggressive, bravest and toughest outfit that fought in the Far East in the Second World War."[89]

A sad threnody of that war is the viciousness, compounded of envy and shame, with which rear-echelon authorities treated frontline troops. Victory won, the Marauders were retired to a so-called rest camp in India, a totally unprepared pasture surrounded by *bashas* they considered unfit for cattle. They had been told to expect shower baths. One morning, some lengths of rusty pipe and a few oil drums were kicked off a truck, and those were their showers, while a few miles away clerks in uniform who had never heard the whine of a hostile's bullet enjoyed comfortable quarters and concrete shower stalls, and in New Delhi officers had electric fans and refrigerators. The Marauders blew up. With the aid of a local product called Bull-Fight Brandy (unsuccessfully proscribed by the medics), they began to tear apart hospitals, Red Cross canteens, and their own quarters.

Orders were impossible to enforce, threats meant nothing, and men went AWOL in quantity. The strain of the disreputable, which had been part of their strength, now did them in and the Marauders were disbanded.

General Slim had never really been convinced that special-purpose organizations like the Marauders or the Chindits could justify their moral and physical cost. "Both forces . . . ," Slim wrote, "had been subjected to intense strain, both had unwisely been promised that their ordeal would be short, and both were asked to do more than was possible." Slim believed that such *corps d'élite*, while they may give a magnificent account of themselves, are wrong in principle. "The level of initiative, individual training, and weapon skill required in, say, a commando, is admirable; what is not admirable is that it should be confined to a few small units. . . . Armies do not win wars by means of a few bodies of super-soldiers but by the average quality of their standard units. Anything, whatever short cuts to victory it may promise, which thus weakens the Army spirit, is dangerous."[90] Hard but seasoned counsel.

And yet, and yet. Surveying their largely deserted camp with a wave of his hand, a Marauder lieutenant had said to Ogburn: "The time will come when you will realize that you were with the Green Mountain Boys and Mad Anthony Wayne's Indian fighters and Morgan's Raiders. And being as big an idiot as I am, you will wonder how anyone as fearful and unworthy as you could have been included in such glorious company."[91] Whatever else is said, they had given Stilwell Myitkyina. Whatever else is said, they had done what the lieutenant generals in New Delhi said could not be done. Whatever else is said, they, the Chinese, the Chindits, and Slim's army had reconquered northern Burma.

Myitkyina's fall was agonizingly prolonged. The initial capture of its airfield had been followed by tenacious Japanese defense of Myitkyina town. Sick Marauders were recalled, engineers were converted to riflemen, and green replacements were thrown into vicious firefights in which some of them panicked. But the Chinese divisions were brought forward and the outcome was never seriously in doubt. On the afternoon of August 30, Myitkyina was declared officially secure. Stilwell had foreseen British displeasure and he was not far wrong. Mountbatten was annoyed at not having been informed in advance and was further discomfited by a sharp inquiry from Churchill as to how "the Americans by a brilliant feat of arms have landed us in Myitkyina."[92] It was shocking; it was not supposed to have happened.

It was a triumphant vindication of everything Stilwell stood for. Not only had he carried out his mission—to reopen the land route to China—but he had proved the truth of his contention that the Chinese were potentially victorious soldiers, that they could achieve what in a letter to his wife he put into capital letters, the "FIRST SUSTAINED OFFENSIVE IN CHINESE HISTORY AGAINST A FIRST-CLASS ENEMY." He did not have to add that this was largely his doing. "He may yet perform what has seemed impossible—cause the launching of a Chinese offensive against the Japanese," John Paton Davies had written Ambassador Gauss in 1943. "If it happens it will have been a one-man achievement." Bill Slim accorded him a similar accolade: "Yet, when all was said and done, the success of the northern offensive was in the main due to the Ledo Chinese divisions—and that was Stilwell."[93] His faith had accomplished the work.

V

On the subject of China the effective teamwork of George Marshall and Harry Hopkins broke down. Hopkins's role was to represent the President, and the President and Marshall were not in harmony. Marshall told Forrest Pogue that while he and Hopkins did not "disagree violently" about China, there came a time when the two of them by mutual consent avoided the topic entirely. On one occasion Marshall was summoned by Roosevelt and in the presence of presidential aide Lauchlin Currie, sprawled in an armchair, was told of a decision about the Army in the CBI theater that had gone against Marshall and in favor of Currie, a needless indignity. Years later, Marshall was still angry at the way he had been treated in the White House on matters pertaining to China.[94]

President Roosevelt's attitude toward China revolved around a sense of familiarity. His grandfather Warren Delano had been partner in a trading company with branches in all the Chinese treaty ports, and his mother for several periods of her life lived in a family house in Hong Kong. The Roosevelt home in Hyde Park was filled with Chinese memorabilia, including the dinner gong, and the President's stamp collection had begun with Hong Kong and Chinese issues given him by his mother when he was ten years old. China was something he had always *known* about. "Please remember," he wrote to Secretary Morgenthau in 1934, "that I have a background of a little over a century in Chinese affairs. China during the past hundred years has not changed very much."[95]

China not only *had* changed but was in the grip of changes to come. The China Stilwell knew was unknown to the President and, having confidence in his own "background," Roosevelt did not know what it was he did not know. It seems unlikely that Stilwell could have given him the picture Stilwell gave Stimson of "the valor of the Chinese armies" and made any deep impression. They were not on the same wavelength; Stilwell never "made his number," as Stimson put it, with the President. Roosevelt told Hopkins that Stilwell "obviously hated the Chinese," a ludicrous misreading of Stilwell's acute perceptions of the Kuomintang.

The President showed no signs of being ill-disposed toward Stilwell personally, though he had for some time considered withdrawing him

from China (as, for that matter, had Marshall). In early 1944, one of Stilwell's officers was in Washington and, after an interview with Roosevelt,
was able to radio Chungking that the President "revealed complete sympathy with Stilwell's efforts to advance in Burma," the first indication
Stilwell had received in almost two years that his Commander in Chief
supported him.

But by summer of 1944, Roosevelt was not putting China at the top
of his list of concerns.[96] In June we had launched two major invasions at
opposite ends of the earth, of Normandy in France and of Saipan in the
Marianas, and in July the President was going to meet in Hawaii with
Nimitz and MacArthur to settle the substantial differences between the
two on future strategy in the Pacific. In September there would be another meeting with Churchill and in November a presidential election.
For Stilwell's determination to bring about "change" in China the President cannot have cared much one way or the other, and into this vacuum
stepped three men who did care: Harry Hopkins, T. V. Soong, and Joseph
Alsop.

Even before Pearl Harbor, in the course of his work on Chinese
Lend-Lease, Hopkins had become "very warm friends" (according to
Sherwood) with T. V. Soong, who had honed for many years his skill at
making Americans feel guilty about China. Despite Soong's outlandish
proposals for supplying Chiang, such as by way of Tibet or Siberia—he
assured Roosevelt that the air route over the Hump was one of "comparatively level stretches"—Hopkins became a convert. When Madame
Chiang was in Washington, Hopkins told her that he was "in sympathy"
with her husband's views "and would do everything I could to get them
accomplished." For a time Soong was in disgrace with Chiang, but recently he had been restored to favor and was now advising the Generalissimo on his dealings with the West. Advising Soong was Alsop. "Davies was
the political adviser of Gen. Joseph W. Stilwell," Alsop wrote in 1951. "I
was the adviser of Dr. T. V. Soong and Maj. Gen. C. L. Chennault."[97]

Alsop had employed his White House entrée to address to Hopkins
lengthy letters arguing the case for Chennault. Later, when Alsop was
drafting Chennault's letters to Roosevelt, the same officer courier would
deliver both missives "by a safe hand," a British phrase, characteristic of
Alsop in its overtones of conspiracy. Alsop's attempts to sabotage Stilwell
begin to show up in the record as early as March 1943, when he is writing
Hopkins (twenty-one pages, double-spaced) that the "key" to the situation
in China is "the personality of General Stilwell" and that "General Stilwell's approach to the problem can only end in something very close to
disaster for all of us." Alsop thought that American aid should be given
Chiang with no strings attached, to be used (or, presumably, not used) as
Chiang saw fit. "If Stilwell is removed," Alsop ended, "and a properly
instructed man sent out, that will clean the matter up entirely."

Four days and two letters later, Alsop was writing Hopkins: "The Chennault effort will be immediate; the Stilwell effort cannot produce its first military results until a time now far distant. The Chennault effort has the complete confidence of every airman with China experience . . . while the fruitfulness of the Stilwell effort is dubious in the extreme." Two other letters (seven pages, single-spaced) soon followed to the same effect, accompanied by a seven-page memo on Chennault's requirements.[98]

In July, Alsop followed on with a six-and-a-half-page single-spaced letter to T. V. Soong, listing various complaints about Stilwell's command. This bill of indictment opened with Alsop's feelings about Stilwell—"I dislike the old gentleman so much that I hardly trust my own judgment where he is concerned"—and closed with an abject protestation of loyalty to Soong: "I'm now your man." This was the letter Soong showed to Mountbatten and Somervell in New Delhi, as the basis for his and Chiang's first attempt to have Stilwell recalled. In September, after that attempt failed, Soong sent a copy of Alsop's letter to Hopkins and Alsop wrote Hopkins that Stilwell in his plan to recapture Burma was "arrogantly courting disaster."[99]

In late December 1943, Chennault wrote to General Arnold asking to have Alsop, at that time an air liaison agent with China Defense Supplies, commissioned a first lieutenant in the Army Air Forces. Arnold talked this over with Marshall during January and Marshall's staff drafted a stiff refusal. But on February 8, Chennault wrote to Hopkins, his second letter on the subject, saying "it will really mean a lot to me to have [Alsop] on my staff" and on the fourteenth, Colonel McCarthy in Marshall's office received a phone call from Steve Early in the White House, directing him in the President's name to have Alsop given his commission.

Marshall the next day indicated his compliance, but he did so in a memorandum to the President stating in no uncertain terms why he would not have recommended this action. Marshall had Alsop's July letter to Soong, a copy of which he attached. "It means to me," Marshall wrote Roosevelt, "that Alsop is either more competent as a commander than Stilwell or as a General Staff expert than the officers we have out there (which would continue him in the class with some other columnists and commentators), or that he is a seriously destructive force. . . . I am of the opinion that we will be placing our command and control in the Burma-China theatre on a foundation of sand if we accept subordinates who are determinedly critical and disloyal to the commander whom we charge with the responsibility for our soldiers and operations in that theatre."[100] How Roosevelt took this stern rebuke is not so far as I know recorded.

The latter part of 1943 and early 1944 had been a good period for Alsop and Chennault. After some delay, reinforcements had begun to flow in and Hump tonnages to approach and then surpass Chennault's requests. Though Arnold forbade him to attack Japan proper, he began to do real damage to Japanese coastwise shipping and to a Formosan air base. But later in 1944, everything went awry as one by one the defects of Chennault's conception revealed themselves. Chinese transport, on which he had too casually relied, proved incapable of bringing up to his forward bases in the Hsiang valley all the supplies that were being landed at Kunming. He still dismissed the possibility of a Japanese ground attack, but the Japanese thought otherwise; on January 17, 1944, Imperial General Headquarters in Tokyo had ordered China Expeditionary Army to move into East China and eliminate this nuisance. The Japanese attacked in April; by mid-May, Chennault was pleading for help (including the B-29s) and his intelligence officer was admitting to him that the Chinese had shown "only slight evidence of either plan or capability to hamper Japanese movement or to regain lost territory." So much for Chiang's promise to the President that Chennault's bases could and would be defended.

Reading Chennault's dispatches and requests, Stilwell concluded that a paper case was being built to provide excuses for an imminent defeat. "Chennault has assured the Generalissimo that air power is the answer," Stilwell wrote in notes to his file. "Now he realizes it can't be done, and he is trying to prepare an out for himself by claiming that with a *little more*, which we won't give him, he can still do it. He tries to duck the consequences of having sold the wrong bill of goods, and put the blame on those who pointed out the danger long ago and tried to apply the remedy." Alsop made several trips to Chungking, wrote John S. Service, trying to make a case for still more Hump tonnage by "painting the situation in the most catastrophic terms . . . and no one was more gloomy and pessimistic than Joe Alsop—'The end has come!'—in his usual apocalyptic sort of way."[101]

It had not been long before Marshall and Stilwell became aware that a steady stream of misinformation and special pleading was being fed to the President through Hopkins. Until the point was reached where they could no longer talk about it, Marshall did his best to break the grip on Hopkins that Soong and Alsop had acquired. By the time Roosevelt approved Chennault's plan in May 1943, Stilwell too had become alert to what was going on and drew up a memo to Marshall (possibly never sent) that listed second among "preventive measures" the need to "close the White House back door."[102] Too late.

◆

The dismissal of General Stilwell in October 1944 came at the end of a series of individual events none of which had such an outcome in view, a step-by-step sequence that in retrospect gains a spurious inevitability while in fact much of it was fortuitous or unrequired. Several links in the chain have been disputed and on others the President's recollection afterward became highly selective, but the main outlines are clear. It all began when the Japanese invaded East China with far greater success than had been anticipated, not only devastating Chennault's pretensions and menacing the B-29 bases near Chengtu but arousing a high level of anxiety in Washington, where a keep-China-in-the-war mentality still prevailed and the Japanese offensive was believed to threaten that thesis. Hence the so-called China crisis.

It is illuminating to observe that Chiang Kai-shek did not take the Japanese successes so seriously as did Marshall and the Joint Chiefs, and that in the outcome his instincts—and the doctrine of *wu wei,* or "not doing"—proved the sounder. Marshall queried Stilwell, who was finishing up the Burma campaign, whether he could return to China and retrieve disaster, and Stilwell sensibly replied that he lacked enthusiasm for the job, which he doubted could be brought off unless someone was given genuine overall command of the Chinese armies. Stilwell thought the only course that could possibly succeed was to strike southeast into the Japanese rear with the relatively competent divisions Chiang had been sequestering in the north to contain the Chinese Communists in Yenan, something Chiang could be relied on to oppose. So far, so good.

The Joint Chiefs endorsed Stilwell's analysis and on July 4, 1944, passed on to the President a proposed draft for him to send to Chiang Kai-shek and a memo reinforcing it that was "candid almost to bluntness,"[103] as the Army historians put it, in reminding Roosevelt of their long-held views on China that he had for so long disregarded. The memo is in effect a scorecard totting up Chennault's failures and Stilwell's triumphs, and ending with the recommendation that the President urge Chiang "to place General Stilwell in command of all Chinese armed forces" and that, as an indication of confidence in Stilwell, he be promoted to four-star general (a rank then shared by only Marshall, MacArthur, Eisenhower, and Arnold). Roosevelt accepted these recommendations and signed the message to Chiang Kai-shek. By now he realized that Soong and Madame Chiang had been watering down or suppressing his communications with Chiang, so that on his order this one and all others thenceforward were delivered in person by the highest-ranking American general in Chungking, at that time Brigadier General Benjamin G. Ferris.

The wisdom of this JCS paper and its sequel can be questioned. The logic of it was not internally coherent. The points scored against Chennault were doubtless justified, but they did not have anything to do with compelling Chiang to accept Stilwell as commander. No policy basis for this demand was developed. There was something doctrinaire about asking for such an unprecedented appointment if the principal argument for it was largely that Stilwell had been right. It amounted to forcing a disconnected issue in a way that revealed Americans to entertain submerged thoughts about "face" not readily distinguishable from those of the Chinese.

Moreover, there was no reason to suppose that giving Stilwell "command" over incompetent armies would make them competent, or that he could persuade the warlords to come out of their provinces any more readily than could Chiang. If catastrophe was coming, why put in charge and make responsible for it an American, in this case one who had sought so vainly to prevent it? (This consideration emerged later, after Stilwell was relieved, but at the time it was muted.) At any event, why wasn't more consideration given to the position in which the JCS request put Chiang Kai-shek? Whether they knew it or not, the Americans had overreached themselves, and there was always the possibility that Chiang might instinctively perceive this. His immediate response was predictable: He agreed in principle and stalled on the details.

There matters might have rested for a while if Chiang had not demanded full control over American Lend-Lease and threatened to withdraw all Chinese troops from Burma. Major General Patrick J. Hurley, the Oklahoma politician, secretary of war under Herbert Hoover, who was in Chungking as Roosevelt's personal representative, believed that he had made praiseworthy progress in getting Chiang to accept a letter of appointment for Stilwell that Hurley had drafted. (Whether there was any substance here can be doubted; it suited Chiang's purpose for Hurley to believe so, and Hurley was a stranger to Chinese subtlety.)[104] But all surmise was rendered nugatory by Chiang's demand to Stilwell that either the Chinese divisions at Myitkyina support his stalled Salween offensive or else he would abandon it.

"The Gmo says," Stilwell reported to Marshall on September 15, "that if I do not attack from Myitkyina towards Bhamo within a week, he will withdraw the Y-Force, thus throwing away the results of all our labors." This dispatch reached the President, Churchill, and the Combined Chiefs at Quebec and did not, to put it mildly, produce a favorable reaction. Here was Chiang Kai-shek, after two and a half years of strained effort to succor him, indicating that he held the reopening of the Burma Road as of no account compared to the safety of a parcel of his own bogged-down troops. It was too much.

The document Chiang Kai-shek received from Roosevelt and the Joint Chiefs in response was the occasion for Chiang's demand that Stilwell be recalled. It has been described as harsh and perhaps it was; it was also just. Perhaps Chiang had been spoon-fed for too long by Soong's and Madame Chiang's sugared versions of Roosevelt's thinking. Perhaps it was offensive to him that this message was delivered, in accordance with the President's express wish, by Stilwell personally. Perhaps also Chiang,

Soong, and Alsop gauged that the moment had come for suitably modulated outrage. (Hurley had turned against Stilwell; his correspondence with Washington was passing through insecure channels and being read by Tai Li.) Chiang had convinced himself (with Soong's hearty help) that Roosevelt's message had been written by Stilwell or dispatched at Stilwell's behest. Neither was true, but it no longer mattered.

"[I]f you fail to send reinforcements to the Salween forces and withdraw these armies," the President's message read, "we will lose all chance of opening land communications with China and immediately jeopardize the air route over the Hump. For this you must yourself be prepared to accept the consequences and assume the personal responsibility. . . . Only drastic and immediate action on your part alone can be in time to preserve the fruits of your long years of struggle and the efforts we have been able to make to support you. Otherwise political and military considerations alike are going to be swallowed in military disaster. . . . In this message I have expressed my thoughts with complete frankness because it appears to all of us here that all your and our efforts to save China are going to be lost by further delays." To this Chiang replied, "I understand."[105] He did not understand: He struck.

Chiang's reply was an *aide-mémoire* conveyed to Hurley on September 25, demanding to have Stilwell recalled and recounting a list of grievances against Stilwell as a field commander that can be charitably described as unjustified where they were not totally distorted. According to Alsop, this document was drafted by Alsop. Twelve years later, he was still congratulating himself on having "saved China for a while," though he did admit that what he had done was "unconventional" or even an "impropriety." He had aided a foreign power in undercutting the authority of his constitutionally designated superior officer, whom he had sworn an oath to obey. Marshall's choice of words—"a seriously destructive force . . . a foundation of sand"—had proved to be the more precise.

In Washington, there surfaced belatedly an impulse to stall that could usefully have been enjoined earlier. Marshall prepared a number of drafts for the President supporting Stilwell, none of which was accepted. (Michael Shaller, in *The U.S. Crusade in China, 1938–1945,* has published one of them.) Marshall conveyed to Leahy on October 4 Stimson's view of "the evil result, catastrophic as he phrased it, that will come from Stilwell's relief."[106] There had developed an eyeball-to-eyeball situation of a kind that should never have been permitted, since the President's heart was not in it and the American side blinked first.

At a dinner party in Washington, Hopkins told Chinese Finance Minister H. H. Kung that the President was prepared to sacrifice Stilwell, and Kung promptly conveyed this tidbit to his brother-in-law T. V. Soong in Chungking, who relayed it to Hurley on October 1.[107] The next day, Chiang Kai-shek went before a meeting of the Central Executive Committee of the Kuomintang and told them that he had refused to appoint Stilwell. The fat was in the fire; after this there could be no turning back. On October 18, Roosevelt capitulated and ordered Stilwell's relief.

◆

Soong, Alsop, Hurley, Chiang, and the President (in a press conference following Stilwell's return) all insisted that the sole issue had been one of personality differences between Stilwell and Chiang Kai-shek. This is not true. The issue had been the same from the beginning and remained the same after Stilwell's departure, namely the extent of China's participation in the war against Japan. Chiang was determined that it should be minimal and by getting rid of Stilwell he ensured that it would continue to be. Major General Albert C. Wedemeyer was brought in to replace Stilwell in China on the assumption that he would be tactful and conciliatory where Stilwell had been acerb and intransigent, yet within two months Wedemeyer was reporting to Washington in the same tone of exasperation at the same exasperating features of Kuomintang China. Chiang had made a few palliative gestures, but nothing had changed.

"The Chinese have no conception of organization, logistics, or modern warfare," Wedemeyer wrote to Marshall on December 16, 1944. "The Gissimo will not decentralize power to subordinates . . . he is vacillating —in fact, he has ordered movements of divisions from the Kunming area without my knowledge. . . . It is the influence and chicanery of his advisers, who have selfish, mercurial motives and who persuade him when I am not present to take action which conflicts with agreed plans. . . . [M]any high-ranking Chinese officials are asking me to facilitate their evacuation to America by air. . . . Self-sacrifice and patriotism are unknown. . . . The Chinese soldiers are starving by the hundreds. . . . If only the Chinese will co-operate!"[108]

President Roosevelt told both Marshall and Hurley that he had no alternative but to support Chiang Kai-shek. This also is not true. An alternative had been fully worked out by John Service in a memo he wrote for Vice-President Henry Wallace on the latter's visit to China in June. Wallace never read it, but Service sent a copy to Washington, where it was widely distributed by OWI, OSS, the Army, the Navy, and the State Department.

Service's program had the virtue of being applicable in stages and offering the least possible affront to Chinese sovereignty. It was based on his own unexampled knowledge of China rather than on distant dreaming and it was open-ended toward the future rather than grimly wedded to a dying past. It required only that there be *one* American policy toward China rather than the hodgepodge of overlapping and inconsistent variants so far prevailing, and it went somewhat as follows:[109]

First, we should deal with the Chinese as fair-and-square bargainers rather than merely upend the American cornucopia over their heads. We should take a firmer stand in financial negotiations and stop making unconditional promises about postwar economic assistance. We should restrict Lend-Lease and cut down on training the Chinese Army until it showed a willingness to engage in action against the Japanese.

Second, we should discontinue active collaboration with the Kuomintang secret police. This was a reference to U.S. Naval Group China, under Commander (later Vice-Admiral) Milton E. Miles, a pet of Admiral King's that had turned into a most disreputable animal. Miles had formed an alliance with Tai Li, whom other Americans rarely mentioned without the adjective "infamous"; yet Miles found him to be a decent sort, devoted to his mother, and between them they had set up an organization—formally approved by the President on April 1, 1943—to train Tai Li's men in "modern" police methods. (At the end of the war, Miles had a spectacular, and very public, nervous breakdown and had to be returned to the States in the care of Navy doctors.[110])

Third, we should acknowledge the existence of other elements in China than the Kuomintang, especially those that were genuinely democratic, and recognize them publicly—as, for example, by honors and awards, or by inviting Madame Sun Yat-sen to Washington. Service thought the Kuomintang and the Communists were equally unacceptable as a long-term government, but he believed we should continue to show an interest in the Communists, above all in their military operations, and should insist on American observers being allowed at the fighting fronts. Consideration might be given to training or equipping provincial or other Chinese armies elsewhere.

Last but important, we should begin educating public opinion in the United States for a more realistic though constructively sympathetic attitude toward China. Background material to that end should be made available to writers, commentators, and research workers. (The fact that this had *not* been done meant that disillusionment when it came was all the more extreme. After Stilwell's recall, American correspondents in Chungking like Brooks Atkinson of the *New York Times* came home with blood in their eye and a determination to tell all. Atkinson's series for the *Times* opened the floodgates and there began what Joseph C. Harsch of CBS called "the long delayed washday for China's dirty linen.") Essentially Service was saying that we should use Chiang's dependence on us to make him pay attention and "stop building up the Generalissimo's and the Kuomintang's prestige internationally and in the United States. . . . Our inclusion of China as one of the 'Big Four' served a useful purpose in the early stage of the war as a counter to Japanese racial propaganda but has now lost its justification."[111]

The chances of the President approving such an approach were mi-

croscopic, but at the same time it is evident that he did realize how far
out on a limb he had gone. Part of what was on his mind is revealed in a
document drawn up in the White House during the weeks after Stilwell
had been dismissed. Roosevelt's political radar told him that if Chiang's
regime went down, he himself would be subject to partisan attack for
having "lost" China (as his successor subsequently was). To prepare against
this eventuality it would be prudent to have at hand an analysis of the
historical record showing how hard the President had labored to sustain
Chiang Kai-shek despite the latter's failings.

Such a paper (running to over sixty pages) was prepared by a young
naval officer in the Map Room named George M. Elsey and sent to the
President's naval aide in mid-November. It drew solely on Map Room files
and reflects a thorough knowledge of them; it is polite toward the Generalissimo and the President, and dutifully optimistic about the current situation, but it reveals no illusions about Chiang (the detailing of Roosevelt
messages that went unanswered is damning) and in general is sympathetic
to Stilwell. Concluding sentences read: "Conferences are continuing but
there has been little progress yet. . . . The Chinese will move slowly in their
reforms, no matter how badly needed, if there is not a Stilwell to goad
them." On December 4, the President returned the manuscript to his
naval aide with a note: "I have read this Lend Lease report in regard to
Chiang Kai-shek by Elsey and think it is excellent. Please thank him for
me. F.D.R."[112]

Stilwell had come home to be treated like a pariah. He was met in
Washington neither by Marshall nor by Stimson but by two generals from
the War Department who told him that he was under orders to make no
comment about China whatever. A presidential election was coming up
and Franklin Roosevelt did not take unnecessary risks with elections. On
the way to Carmel, Stilwell was literally kept under armed guard and only
after a few days of seclusion at his home were the press and photographers
permitted to see him. He obeyed his orders: Not a word about China was
spoken. Winifred Stilwell's account of this disgusting performance by
Roosevelt and Marshall is in The Stilwell Papers.[113]

Roosevelt's China strategy had been a bad one—bad in conception,
bad in execution. No wonder he didn't want it discussed. Lives had been
lost and millions spent to no good effect and the objective was as far off
as ever. From the closing of the Burma Road until June 30, 1944, some
$380,584,000 in Lend-Lease supplies had been sent to China ($867,000,-
000 more to India) and we had nothing to show for it but a country more
weak, more divided, and more heavily overrun by Japanese than when we
started. Chinese strategy on the other hand had been to play the game of
national self-interest in its most cynical form. Their realism persuaded the
Kuomintang leaders to exploit American idealism for all it was worth, and
in this they succeeded. But having no other object than survival, they paid

the price, which was failure to survive. History in the postwar years discarded them. No tears need be shed.

But even so, the President's treatment of General Stilwell remains the darkest blot on his record as Commander in Chief. It was all so *unnecessary!* His other theater commanders he left largely alone, but with Stilwell he continually meddled, undermining Stilwell's efforts and compromising his authority by sending a stream of "presidential representatives"—Lauchlin Currie, Wendell Willkie, Henry Wallace, Patrick Hurley, Donald Nelson—whose chief qualifications were their ignorance of China or, in some cases, Roosevelt's desire to get them out of the country. An Eisenhower or a MacArthur would have blown his stack; Stilwell patiently put up with it. "More than any other American theater commander in the war," in Secretary Stimson's view, "Stilwell required the constant and vigorous political support of his own government, and less than any other commander did he get it." The President, thought Stimson, "never gave to Stilwell the freedom of action and automatic backing which he so courageously accorded to his commanders in other theaters."[114]

As for Joseph Stilwell—what can one say? Marshall tried to find jobs for him commensurate with his four-star rank (he would have preferred to revert to permanent grade and go with a combat division). He commanded Army Ground Forces, then Tenth Army on Okinawa. He was given the Legion of Merit and an Oak Leaf Cluster to his DSM. He was present at the Japanese surrender ceremonies on board the *Missouri* in Tokyo Bay and he attended the atomic bomb tests at Bikini atoll as an observer. The one decoration he had always wanted, the Combat Infantryman Badge, was awarded him in October 1946 as he lay dying of stomach cancer, blessedly free of pain. He woke briefly to ask the nurse, "Say, isn't this Saturday?" and then returned to a sleep from which he did not wake again. "The trouble was largely one of posture," he wrote in an undated entry in his papers. "I tried to stand on my feet instead of my knees. I did not think the knee position was a suitable one for Americans. . . . If a man can say he did not let his country down, and if he can live with himself, there is nothing more he can reasonably ask for."[115]

He did not let his country down.

X

LEMAY

THE ISLANDS OF JAPAN ARE SMALL, their populations dense, their cities vulnerable to fire, and they lay within 1940s' aircraft range of the mainland. An idea that the Japanese might be bombed into submission from the air had therefore showed itself in American military thinking well before war began. It underlay President Roosevelt's endorsement in December 1940 of a scheme proposed by Secretary Morgenthau for moving bombers to China, though Marshall ruled this unworkable.[1] It underlay the President's approval in July 1941 of a plan for equipping China with five hundred planes to be ready for offensive action by November, though this project fell through. It underlay Roosevelt's acceptance of General Chennault's assertion in October 1942 that with twelve heavy and thirty medium bombers flying from Chinese bases he could "accomplish the downfall of Japan," though Chennault's hopes proved illusory and his bases indefensible. It underlay the intense presidential interest a year later in the full development of the VLR (Very Long Range) bomber, to be known as *Bikko* to the Japanese and "Dreamboat" in U.S. Navy code, the Superfortress, the B-29.

While the Dreamboat would be able to reach Kyushu from safer and more distant bases northwest of Chungking, it too had frustrated Roosevelt by its slow emergence from promise into reality. He badly wanted it, as a means not only of scourging Japan but of supporting Chiang Kai-shek's morale. On October 15, 1943, we find him writing Marshall to express his vexation at B-29 production delays, and on November 3, Hopkins is urging the Joint Chiefs to press the matter; "this B-29 business has been an awful headache," Hopkins writes to Leahy, "and surely is a very important instrument."[2] Eventually the mission the President wished for would be accomplished, in a fury of destruction, by a force of many hundred B-29s led by a thirty-nine-year-old air force major general named Curtis E. LeMay.

The B-29 was the greatest U.S. gamble of the war—greater even than the atom bomb ($3 billion invested, as opposed to $2 billion for the bomb, on a similar absence of hard evidence). The B-29 was conceived in self-confidence and purchased on faith. "Innocence built the B-29," said one of its creators. "We could not have done it if we had known what we were getting into."[3] Six months before a single prototype had left the ground, Boeing had been authorized to make 250 of them; when the first B-29 did fly, in September 1942, over 1,600 were already on order.

The B-29 was at that time the heaviest high-speed aircraft ever designed, with twice the weight and bomb load of the B-17 and almost twice the horsepower; and its configuration was unorthodox, with a thin, narrow wing and a bulbous, pressurized cabin. Aside from its enormous size, by prevailing standards it was a handsome piece of aerodynamics: silver, smooth, and sleek. Soldiers and sailors who saw it for the first time were often prompted to speculate that this supreme weapon would end the war—as, in a sense, it did.

The B-29s prefigured the future. They made up the first aggregate of air power that was truly global, bound to no single theater of operations, subordinate to no single theater commander; in principle they could operate anywhere. They came directly under the orders of General Arnold as representative of the Joint and Combined Chiefs. This was in the nature of their range and bomb capacity, of their "strategic" mission; they were a war-winning weapon or they were nothing. They had to be treated as an independent entity, for reasons General Arnold explained in his book, *Global Mission.* "I could not give them to MacArthur," he wrote, "because they would operate ahead of Nimitz's command; I could not give them to Nimitz since in that case they would operate in front of MacArthur's advance. So, in the end, while everybody wondered why I kept personal command . . . there was nothing else I could do."[4]

This also meant that the commander on the spot, General LeMay, would have considerable latitude in the tactics by which they were employed, and would on his own responsibility make a drastic change in those tactics, one that reversed the theory on which American air power had been founded (and of which he, in Europe, had been one of the foremost exponents), that contravened the deeply held convictions of his civilian superior the secretary of war, and that went against the grain of his experienced pilots and crews. The independence inherent in the B-29 was not a quality Curtis LeMay was reluctant to exercise.

Like many pilots, LeMay remembered vividly the moment when the idea of flight captured his imagination. He could not have been more than four or five years old, and he knew it must have been winter because he had on his red stocking cap: Columbus, Ohio, 1910–11, in the garden outside his family's modest house. "Suddenly, in the air above me, appeared a flying machine," LeMay wrote many years afterward. "It came from nowhere. There it was, and I wanted to catch it. It would be a wonderful thing to possess—that mysterious fabrication which was chortling through the sky, its few cylinders popping in a way far different from any automobile or truck which went past our place."

He ran after it as fast as he could, across vacant lots and neighbors' lawns, until it disappeared from sight and he stomped his way home, fighting tears of disappointment. He had wanted to possess not only its substance but also its speed and energy, had wanted to *understand* it, "to possess the reason and purpose." LeMay wrote later that he had never been able to turn his back completely on the tender and the trivial, and that the image had never left him of that child in Ohio, "trying to catch up with something which moved faster than I could run."

His first experience of flying came in the early 1920s. During the summers of his high school years he worked as an apprentice in structural ironwork, but one Sunday he and a friend pooled their resources—$2.50 each—and made a deal with a barnstorming pilot who flew out of a field in East Columbus long since swallowed up in subdivisions and shopping centers: five dollars for five minutes. The aircraft was a Waco three-seater biplane. LeMay recalled the grind and roar and sputter as the engine caught, then taxiing and bumping and the ground dropping away as though it had sunk on an elevator.

Familiar places seemed squeezed together in miniature, not familiar at all but recognizable, and then they all went slanting off at a different angle. It was over much too soon. The young LeMay thought: "Some day I'm going to go up in an airplane . . . I'll be flying it. I'll just ride around wherever I want to go—fly wherever I want to, stay up as long as I please."[5] When he came to write his memoirs, the older LeMay realized that this ambition had never been fulfilled, that whenever he got airborne there had always been something he had to do, something to keep him busy.

LeMay saved enough to enroll at Ohio State for a degree in civil engineering and worked nights setting cores in an iron foundry to pay for his education. (One of his fellow students was Milton Caniff, creator of *Terry and the Pirates* and a wartime comic strip called *Male Call,* who was also working his way.) LeMay joined the Reserve Officers Training Corps. He would have applied to West Point if he had known a congressman, but he didn't and knew no one who did; this seemed like the second-best way. Not that he wanted to join the service for its own sake. He wanted to fly, and the Army was where you learned; of civilian flying schools there then were none.

He did not get the engineering degree until later, but he was an honor graduate of ROTC, received a reserve commission, transferred to the National Guard, and applied for admission to the Army Flying School at March Field near Riverside, California. He kept after people, telegraphed Washington, passed the physical, and finally he and his friend Francis H. "Butch" Griswold (later lieutenant general and deputy commander, under LeMay, of Strategic Air Command) found themselves on a Pullman (the Army generously provided them with one berth, but they cadged another), headed west as designated flying cadets. Late October 1928.

They learned on PT-3s (primary trainers) and then moved up to pursuit planes (P-1s) at Kelly Field near San Antonio, Texas. There wasn't much difference then among the single-seaters; they all had the same thing: a stabilizer, a stick, a rudder, a throttle, and a spark control. "That was it," said LeMay. "You just got in and flew." LeMay served in the CCCs, he was sent to Navigation School, he was one of the pilots who flew the mail in 1934, he got married, and he was assigned to a pursuit squadron at Wheeler Field in Hawaii. In January 1937, he reported for duty with Second Bomb Group at Langley Field, Virginia, and began to make the acquaintance of a flying machine that became a part of his life, the first —"and, in many ways, the greatest," said LeMay—of the four-engine bombers, the B-17, the Flying Fortress. "I fell in love with the 17 at first sight," LeMay said. Six years later, he would be leading an entire air division of B-17s over France and Germany.[6]

LeMay at the start made a name for himself as a navigator, notably on several "goodwill" flights to South America that called public attention to the B-17's range and speed. He plotted course in the lead plane of a group of seven B-17s that in August 1937 "bombed" (with practice water bombs) the battleship *Utah*. This was a joint Army-Navy exercise that had been laid on at the President's personal request. (He wanted to know, even if the Navy did not, what land-based bombers could do against a fleet.) On July 10, after a meeting with Roosevelt, Chief of Staff Malin Craig and CNO Leahy settled on arrangements to conduct the test at sea off the West Coast.

Sad to confess, the Navy was playing with a stacked deck; *Utah*'s approach was to be detected by naval scout planes, which would then report the location to the Army. Twice *Utah*'s position was given by the Navy one degree off (sixty miles), but twice the B-17s found her nonetheless, scoring three hits on the first mission and thirty-seven on the second. Internal Navy accounts failed to mention any bombing whatever and an attempt to clamp a lid of secrecy on the whole affair might have succeeded if someone had not leaked the story, complete with photographs, to radio newscaster Boake Carter. Straight-faced officers at Langley Field professed innocence; next time they would try to make sure beforehand that their side got a hearing.[7]

For the purposes of May maneuvers the following year, the Italian

liner *Rex* was to simulate an attacking enemy fleet and three B-17s were
to attempt the interception; no Navy involved, it would be an open challenge to the Air Corps's efficiency. On board the bombers would be Hanson Baldwin of the *New York Times* and a three-man team from the
National Broadcasting Company; lead navigator was again to be Lieutenant LeMay, who had been given the *Rex*'s noontime position of the day
before. Takeoff would be at eight-thirty. LeMay's estimate was that they
would find the *Rex* about six hundred miles off Sandy Hook at twelve-
thirty on May 12, and arrangements had been made for the NBC an-
nouncer to go on the air at that moment over a coast-to-coast hookup—
if the *Rex* held course and speed, *if* the weather was good enough, *if*
LeMay's calculations were correct. The Air Corps was determined to go
public in a big way, and either success or failure was going to be very
conspicuous indeed. LeMay wanted to go somewhere and hide.

They took off from Mitchell Field on Long Island in a driving rain and
headed into a succession of thunderstorms. LeMay said that in thirteen
thousand hours of military flying he had seen his share of turbulence, but
nothing to match this. He hunched over his charts, soaked with rain
through a leak in the plexiglass window, as the B-17 heaved and bucked
in the air pockets and downdrafts; the pilot wrestled with the control
column as though a giant had hold of the other end. Now and then they
skimmed the water and LeMay had a chance to figure a correction for
their drift. A dark wall loomed up before them, the cold front, and they
slammed into it, coming out ten minutes later into bright sunshine. Then
came another line squall. LeMay looked at his watch: Twelve twenty-
three. "Columns of murky clouds split, staggered aside . . . ," said LeMay;
"we could even see the ocean." Twelve twenty-five: There, dead ahead,
was the *Rex*.

"It was all a movie," LeMay wrote. "It was happening to someone
else." Next day there would be the headlines—FLYING FORTS, 630 MILES
OUT, SPOT ENEMY TROOP SHIP—and a classic photograph, taken from one
of the planes, of the other two passing the *Rex* at masthead level. Her
captain radioed an invitation to lunch, which they declined with regret.
Hundreds of passengers, wrapped in raincoats and scarves, lined the rails
and waved at them. On the afterdeck was a group apart from the others.
They were Americans, and they were singing "The Star-Spangled Banner."

LeMay's success provoked the Navy's wrath. The next morning his
boss, commander of Second Bomb Group Colonel Robert Olds, was put
under orders by the Chief of Staff never to fly Army bombers again more
than a hundred miles out to sea. Olds said he wanted that in writing, and
the circumstances were well known to many officers, but when Tooey
Spaatz some years later tried to locate Craig's letter, no copy could be
found. LeMay believed it had been removed from the Army files. "I won't

attempt to guess *who* snuck it out of there," he wrote. "But I think I know *why.*" (Ironically, after the *Rex* episode, the Navy made discreet inquiries as to whether two of its officers might be permitted to attend the Air Corps's navigation school.[8])

LeMay was stocky and tough or, more to the point, he *looked* tough. An attack of Bell's palsy had temporarily paralyzed half of his face, leaving him with a right upper lip that refused to smile when the left lip did, and leading to the legend that he never smiled at all. When the B-29s were stationed on Guam, he took up the habit of smoking cheap PX cigars, which further increased his bellicose presentation of the self. Somewhere along the way, his men had begun to refer to him as "Iron Ass."[9]

In the stratosphere of high command, where what would pass for dross below can be transmuted into manly virtue, and, worse, in the labyrinth of the Pentagon, where backbiting and bureaucratic maneuver seem to take up as much of the day as winning a war—in those ambiences human character is not always easy to discern. But there was a chiel amang them takin' notes, Major James Gould Cozzens, later to be the author of *Guard of Honor,* in the judgment of many readers besides this one the best novel to deal with American participation in the war, though there are no scenes of combat in it. Cozzens was a writer of speeches and confidential reports in the Air Force Office of Information Services, and one day his novelist's eye lit on General LeMay.

"He had a dead cigar in his mouth when he came in," wrote Cozzens in his diary on June 18, 1945, "and he never moved it for three quarters of an hour, though talking around it well enough when occasion arose. The superficial first impression was that he was dumb or gross; but he has one of those faces that grow on you—a real intelligence and even a kind of sweetness—as though he would not do anything mean, or even think anything mean, though he is well known to be a hard man, and you can see that too—becoming more apparent the longer you look at him. Around the motionless cigar he spoke sensibly."[10]

II

The first bomb dropped from an aircraft is said to have been a gas pipe filled with black powder, at San Francisco in January 1911, as a fairground stunt. The Germans bombed Compiègne in France a few weeks after World War I began, and by 1915 both sides had incorporated aerial offensives into their strategies, but the first truly massed bombing campaign did not occur until September 1918, when Brigadier General Billy Mitchell assembled a force of 1,500 Allied planes of all types and in relays of 500 each struck at the sides of the Saint-Mihiel salient. By the end of the war, the United States had accumulated air forces of 190,000 men, more than

11,000 pilots in 45 combat squadrons, and had flown 150 bombing missions[11]—the potential beginnings of a formidable power.

Yet the doctrine of its employment was uncertain and the years between the wars did little to remove the uncertainty. Not only did the Navy
resist any encroachment by Army Air over its own watery province, but
within the Army there was basic disagreement between the War Department and the Air Corps over what the purpose of the latter and its proper
role should be. Mitchell himself in books and public statements varied
between extravagant claims and lesser ones adjusted to the temper of the
times, but in either case he remained far out ahead of the Army leadership, which had persuaded itself (in the words of a board convened by
Pershing in 1919 to review the lessons learned in 1916–18) that "nothing
so far brought out in the war shows that aerial activities can be carried on,
independently of ground troops, to such an extent as to materially affect
the conduct of the war as a whole." Since the Air Corps believed otherwise, there came about a doctrinal standoff, an unacknowledged persist-
ence of mutually irreconcilable views within the same establishment.

The official bible of Army orthodoxy was the Field Service Regulations, revised by the General Staff and reissued on November 2, 1923. In
them, the message was made clear that the chief mission of aviation was
the close support of ground operations. While conceding that no one of the
arms can alone win battles, and that their combined use is essential to
success, the FSR went on to state that the "co-ordinating principle which
underlies the employment of the combined arms is that the mission of the
infantry is the general mission of the entire force." The other arms derive
their missions from their power to support the infantry.

Air bombardment targets lie "beyond the effective range of artillery,"
but they consist of objectives "vital to the functioning of the enemy's line
of communication and supply"—*not*, be it noted, of the industrial base
from which that supply comes. The Field Service Regulations were still in
effect when World War II began, and their intent had been reaffirmed in
January 1926 by the publication of Training Regulation 440-15, "Fundamental Principles of Employment of the Air Service," which asserted that
the organization and training of air units was to be "based on the fundamental doctrine that their mission is to aid ground forces to gain decisive
success."

No true disciple of Billy Mitchell could accept this, and there were
many such in the Air Corps. By 1935—with the creation of the GHQ Air
Force and the flight of the first B-17—they were beginning to assert
themselves (the perfecting of the Norden and Sperry bombsights comp-
leted their weapons package). Their pulpit and forum was the Air Corps
Tactical School, moved in 1931 from Langley Field to Maxwell Field in
Alabama. There in the mid-1930s, instructors who would later be generals
—Captain Harold L. George, Lieutenants Laurence S. Kuter and Hay-

wood S. Hansell—expounded their faith and philosophy in a series of lectures that, taken together, provided a coherent alternative to the exclusively ground-force orientation of the Field Service Regulations.

The objective of war was to break the enemy's will to resist, they said, which incorporated destroying the power to resist. The air arm was uniquely equipped to do so by attacking the "enemy national structure," in particular its "industrial web." This requires more than random strikes at targets of opportunity, rather a deliberate and sustained interruption of the complex and delicate balance of the enemy economy, which alone might be sufficient to force a surrender.[12] The idea was analogous to a traditional naval blockade, which aims to strangle an entire nation, and bears down with equal brutality on all its people alike. But the reader will see the looming shadow here of unequivocally brutal events to come.

Even at the time there were objections made to strategic bombing on humanitarian grounds, and the European war was to be opened by solemn promises from both sides that they would never engage in any such thing. "I want no war against women and children," Hitler told the Reichstag on September 1, 1939, "and I have given the Luftwaffe instructions to attack only military objectives." Two weeks later, Neville Chamberlain assured the House of Commons: "Whatever be the lengths to which others may go, His Majesty's Government will never resort to the deliberate attack on women and children, and other civilians for purposes of mere terrorism."[13] Hitler seems conveniently to have forgotten the raids on Madrid in August 1936 during the Spanish Civil War, the first of their kind, by Junkers 52 bombers of the German Condor Legion, not to speak of the destruction of Guernica on April 26, 1937, by waves of German aircraft —Ju 52s and Heinkel 111s—dropping heavy bombs and incendiaries, and machine-gunning the population that had gathered there for market day; 1,654 died and 889 were wounded. (Göring himself later admitted that Guernica had been regarded in Germany as a test of bombing effectiveness.[14]) The British too, under the stress of a struggle to survive, would soon forget Chamberlain's pledge.

In June 1941, there arrived in Washington, accompanied by his young wife and eighteen-month-old daughter, Field Marshal Sir Arthur Travers Harris of the Royal Air Force, to head the RAF's permanent delegation. Born in Britain but raised in Rhodesia, Harris was a blunt-faced and blunt-spoken advocate of all-out air attack on Germany. He got on well with Americans, in particular with Hap Arnold and Ira Eaker, and became "a frequent and welcome visitor at the White House," writes Dewitt Copp, "where his fierce determination to bring down Hitler at all costs appealed to Roosevelt and Hopkins." Hopkins and Bert Harris worked together to circumvent the rules in getting more planes and equipment to the RAF, and one day Roosevelt asked Harris whether there was anything "within reason"—meaning without risk of impeachment—the President could do for him. Harris said he was short of pilots on the Atlantic ferry run. Arnold sent Harris a blond aviatrix named Jacqueline Cochran, and that was the beginning of the RAF women's ferry command.

Brigadier General Ira Eaker was a pursuit pilot who had pioneered in instrument and long-distance flying (the President knew of this and had congratulated him); Eaker had collaborated with Arnold on several books, including one called *Army Flyer,* a handbook for the newly inducted. Arnold called him to Washington after Pearl Harbor, while Churchill was there for the Arcadia meetings, and told Eaker he was posting him to England to command the bombers we would soon be sending over. "Bombers, hell!" said Eaker. "I've been in fighters all my service!" Arnold said that didn't matter, that perhaps Eaker could infuse bombers with some fighter spirit, that he himself was going to a dinner that evening where Bert Harris would be present, and that Eaker had better come along too. Arnold at dinner explained, as Eaker and Harris listened, how the Americans planned to work, how important to them was coordination with the British, but how they did not propose to be absorbed by the RAF. He also described the tactics they were determined on using: daylight precision bombardment. "I bloody well don't think you can do it," said Harris.

At the first official session of Arcadia in the White House on December 23, 1941, with Harris and Arnold present, Roosevelt told them that he had already discussed with Churchill sending a small number of bombers to Britain right away, an advance guard of what would become Eighth Air Force. When asked how large a unit was proposed, Arnold said at least a group (forty aircraft), since it was the smallest that was self-sustaining and self-contained. When asked when, Arnold said March. Later Hopkins pressed Arnold to set a goal of eight hundred bombers in England by the end of the year, and later still the President quizzed Arnold on whether that goal could be met, what the obstacles were, and what kind of cooperation he was getting from the RAF. "One hundred per cent," said Arnold, and he explained that an agreement had been reached that no planes would be held back waiting for something to happen, but all would be sent across to fight. "That's an excellent thing to do," said Roosevelt.[15]

Easier said than done, however. One by one, the obstacles began to appear. First was Churchill. By early March, worried over Japanese advances in Asia and British reverses in the Middle East, he proposed to Roosevelt that the Eighth Air Force buildup in the British Isles be postponed. (Arnold objected vigorously at a White House meeting on the sixth, but the President cabled Churchill the next day that the "American contribution to an air offensive against Germany in 1942 would be somewhat curtailed.") Second was the North African invasion, which Arnold along with the other Joint Chiefs opposed and which, by consuming planes and crews intended for the Eighth, effectively ended any immediate American participation in the air war the RAF was by then waging in earnest. Third came the South Pacific, to which in July the Combined Chiefs diverted fifteen combat groups that had been earmarked for Britain.[16] The high hopes aroused at Arcadia seemed to recede more rapidly as each month passed.

Arnold had excellent reasons for not wanting to expose his air force to the Luftwaffe (and to British skepticism) piecemeal, in dribs and drabs. He was bringing to bear a new weapon (the daylight high-altitude bomber) and a new technique (precision attack), neither of which had been tested in action against the Germans, and he perceived correctly that the effectiveness of his B-17s and B-24s would not be demonstrated until he could deploy them in massive formations. (To reveal them prematurely could also facilitate German countermeasures, and in fact did.) The delays and diversions were therefore doubly upsetting to his purpose, especially because he was one of the pioneers and true believers. In 1935, when Arnold commanded 19th Bomb Group at Rockwell Field, California, he had noted on a chart (and saved it) that with the early B-10s and B-12s, using a Norden bombsight, the crews' proficiency increased until at the end of seven weeks, from fifteen thousand feet they were putting their bombs within fifty-five yards of an aiming point no bigger than a woodshed; "for 1935," wrote Arnold, "a near bull's-eye from almost three miles up struck us as pretty good."[17]

What the British knew, on the other hand, was that trying to bomb accurately through bad weather, exploding flak (antiaircraft), and a cloud of persistent Messerschmitt 109s flown by seasoned pilots is a very different dish of tea from hitting a white circle in the desert on a clear day with no one bothering you. By the end of 1941, they had discovered that their attempts to strike specific factories, bridges, railway centers, and the like were simply not succeeding. "There was reason to believe that these small targets had seldom been hit," wrote Air Marshal Sir Robert Saundby, then the senior air staff officer of RAF Bomber Command. In early 1942—under the passionate and uniformly stubborn leadership of Bert Harris, recalled from Washington to become Bomber Command's chief—they consciously shifted to a policy of "area" night attacks, which is to say the demolishing of German cities as such: Lübeck, March 28–29; Rostock, April 23–26; followed by the first of the thousand-plane raids: Cologne, May 30, and Bremen, June 25. "Give me 20,000 bombers," said Harris, "and I will finish Germany in a week."[18]

Against this serried array of principle entwined with practice the Americans, given their inevitably jejune efforts, were unable to make much headway. Also, the old ways died hard. When Ira Eaker arrived in London on February 20, he found an American Army headquarters already there, with officers so wooden-headed that staff work containing references to Army Air Forces was returned with a request that it be rewritten to eliminate the word "Air."

The first B-17 landed in Prestwick, Scotland, on July 1, 1942, and on August 17—a historic date for American proponents of strategic bombing —eighteen of them attacked the marshaling yards at Rouen, General Eaker riding in the lead: all bombs on or close to target, no American casualties (Harris sent Eaker a congratulatory telegram). Fourteen more missions followed in the next few months, against France and the Low Countries, generally at 22,000 to 26,000 feet under heavy RAF fighter escort, in which results were mixed: relatively accurate bombing, no losses, but not much damage done, either.

In October through January, at the suggestion of President Roosevelt, there was an ill-advised effort to use the American heavies (now capable of ninety-plane missions) against the German submarine pens in Brittany and the Bay of Biscay, but the thickly reinforced concrete roofs proved impervious even to one-ton bombs and the casualties among French civilians were not appreciated. The overall results were unimpressive and by January 1943, at Casablanca, Churchill was to complain that after a year of preparation the Americans had five hundred bombers "all laid out in East Anglia" (not true! more like a hundred) and had not bombed Germany once (true, though not their fault).[19]

Casablanca was the crux. By the President's instruction, a comprehensive plan had been prepared for an American daylight effort to complement Britain's at night, but Churchill came to Casablanca convinced that daylight bombing would not work and prepared to ask Roosevelt that Eighth Air Force abandon its independent mission and join the RAF in night bombing. When Arnold saw that he was (as the British say) batting a sticky wicket, he sent for Eaker, who came from Britain accompanied by his aide, Captain James Parton (a journalist by profession, later a publisher and Eaker's biographer) and between them they worked out a twenty-three-page position paper. Eaker presented a single-page summary of it to the Prime Minister on the morning of January 20 in an hour-long session of the two of them alone. Eaker's brief memorandum is worth quoting:

1. Day bombing is more accurate and can destroy obscure but important targets night bombers can't find.

2. Being more accurate, day bombing is more economical because a small force concentrating its bombs is more effective than a large force scattering its bombs.

3. By bombing the devils around the clock, we can prevent the German defenses from getting any rest.

4. If the R.A.F. works by night and we work by day, we can prevent airdrome and airspace congestion.

belly gunner to curl up in. The tail held barely enough room for the rear gunner to maneuver his weapons and change their ammunition belts. "It's a good spot for praying," said one. "You're on your knees all the time." It was cold up there, and noisy; a "musician type" told LeMay that the engines "sang a steady song . . . over two octaves in the lower register . . . A-E-A-E."[25]

On the ground a B-17 did not look like much; taxiing, with its high dorsal fin in back, it resembled, said one navigator, "a humpback hawk." But in the air it was slender, graceful, and alive. "A Fort lives in the sky," wrote Bert Stiles, "from three to six miles up, and the only real things up there are the throttles and the feathering buttons, the engine gauges and the rudder pedals, an oxygen mask full of drool, and a relief can full of relief. The flak is real," Stiles added, "when it clanks on the wings and knocks out your number one oil cooler. The rest of the time it is only a nightmare of soft black puffs and yellow flashes outside the window. The [Focke-Wulf] 190s are real enough when they swing in from one o'clock high and start blinking their landing lights. They're plenty real when the top turret opens up, and the nose guns start shooting, and the 20-millimeters blow away half the tail of the ship."[26]

The B-17 was unbelievably rugged, with what Edward Jablonski in a book about it called "an almost human will to live." Credibility would be strained if photographs did not exist of the B-17s that brought home their crews with engines smashed, gaping holes in wing and tail assembly, or—in one spectacular instance—a fuselage almost cut in half by an Me 109 that sheared into it out of control. "Home is when the props stop spinning," said Bert Stiles. One pilot brought home so many mortally wounded B-17s that by the end he used up seven of them; to all he had given the same name: *Hang the Expense,* I through VII. Men could be torn apart and killed up there, too, as LeMay did not forget. "You have always complained about my not being sentimental enough," he wrote to his wife. "I think sometimes I'm too soft to properly fight a war."[27]

On their first mission, he flew in the top turret of the lead element (three planes), to keep the whole group in sight. He had begun by trying to assess bomb damage. Not many aerial photographs had been taken during strikes, but when he put together the few he could find with the post-strike photos, the evidence was unassailable; "the bombing was stinko," he wrote, almost useless. The B-17s had been bobbing and weaving so much they hadn't been able to see what they were trying to hit. "It was SOP [standard operating procedure] to use evasive action over the targets," wrote LeMay. "Everybody was doing it. And everybody was throwing bombs every which way." This was what came of Frank Armstrong's ten-seconds-straight-and-level-and-you're-dead thesis, to which LeMay's attention had next been turned.

From his artillery schooling in ROTC at Ohio State, LeMay remembered the formulas for calculating how many rounds the Germans would have to fire—given normal dispersion, scattering, and inaccuracy—to hit an object the size of a B-17 at a distance of 25,000 feet. The number came out at 237, which seemed like rather a lot; "it was worth a try," LeMay thought. "We're going to fly formation," he told his pilots. (An apocryphal legend holds that one of them replied, "Sir, shall we go to the stockade *now*, or wait for the MPs to take us?" Some may have thought that, but none said it.) There must exist, LeMay believed, a "master" formation that would be simple enough for average pilots to maintain, that would provide the opportunity for optimum bombing, and that would place the planes in relation to one another so that their machine-gun fire in the forward hemisphere of flight would be at its most copious.

They tried it. From his viewing point in the top turret, LeMay talked the other aircraft into the positions he had in mind, stacked and echeloned —Lead, High, Low—in elements of three, an eighteen- or twenty-one-ship unit. He had invented the Combat Box, later adopted as standard by the other American bomber units in England. It worked. On their first mission over Saint-Nazaire on November 23, 1942, the 305th flew straight and level for eight minutes, put more than twice the number of bombs on target than any other group, and had no planes hit by antiaircraft (two were lost, but to fighters, another story).[28]

Formation flying is not easy on the pilots. "Eighth Air Force," wrote Bert Stiles, "allowed about an hour of every mission for flubbing around" —that is, for getting the planes into position. "Every wing man circled around looking for his element leader, while he looked for his squadron leader, and the squadron leader tried to stay in sight of the group." From a distance the formation may seem static and beautiful, "deadly and simple and easy," since the constant effort required to hold it together is invisible. "You don't hear the pilots screaming at the co-pilots," said Stiles, "and the element leaders bitching at the squadron leaders," as they try to stay out of each other's prop wash and get neither too far ahead nor behind. "It is always work," Stiles said, "and nine hours of it on a Berlin trip knocks you flat."

From the day he started out in B-17s, Stiles had been told that formation flying was the secret of getting back alive. "The Luftwaffe is always looking for a mangy outfit that is strung out halfway across Germany." When the enemy lies low for a time, there is a temptation to loosen up and take it easy—"then one day the 190s come moaning down out of the clouds and the whole low squadron blows up and the high squadron piles into the lead squadron, and three or four ships out of a whole group come home. After that some pretty fair formation is flown for a while."[29] (Lieutenant Stiles completed the requisite thirty-five bomber missions and then, instead of returning to the United States on leave, as he was entitled to, he requested transfer to fighters; on November 26, 1944, he was shot down and killed in a P-51 on an escort mission over Hannover; he was twenty-three years old.)

◆

Air strategy in World War II was necessarily surrounded by a certain amount of guesswork. Battles of this size and complexity had never been fought before, and in their early stages the outcome was rarely clear-cut. Bombing "results" consisted of aerial photographs that sometimes made the extent of damage seem greater than it was, and the contests of plane versus plane in the air above were attended by the degree of uncertainty about gains and losses which permitted those German claims that the Battle of Britain had never happened. Air "supremacy" or "command" of the air is a vital but elusive concept. An air battle does not conveniently end with the victors in possession of the field and the vanquished in retreat. After an engagement in which both sides have taken heavy losses, the air is as empty as it began.

U.S. Air Forces planners and commanders thus had to deal with relationships between their own and enemy power that resisted accurate assessment. Where the weaknesses were in both antagonists would not be discovered until there was a real test. Before August 1943, the Americans had not tried to penetrate deeply into Germany, and their experience up to that time had tended to convince them—or, rather, to confirm them in a belief they already held—that the B-17s could not be stopped by the German defenses. General Eaker at first had realistic reservations about this; after the Rouen raid in August 1942, he pointed out to Spaatz that its success did not necessarily prove long-range missions into Germany to be possible without either fighter escort or punishing cost. But overall the bomber offensive had begun in a mood of high confidence.

In the months that followed, there were aircraft shot down that might have served as a warning, but these could be discounted on the grounds that we were still disposing of insufficient numbers. Once the total of bombers in flight went over three hundred, so Eaker could argue and so he wrote to General Arnold in October 1942, they should be able to "attack any target in Germany with less than 4 per cent losses."[30] A going theory held that fighter escort was needed only to break through a "fighter belt" believed to be concentrated forward along the coast of France and the Low Countries; once the bombers were safely past it, long-range fighter escort would not be essential. During the latter half of 1943, these two propositions were put to the challenge, and both of them proved to be dismally invalid.

For the Germans had not been passive. They had captured at least one B-17 intact, flown it, tested its guns, and constructed a chart of the cones of fire in order to find the most vulnerable directions of approach. Luftwaffe Leutnant Heinz Knocke, Messerschmitt 109 pilot and commander of a *Staffel* of Second Fighter Division based on Holland, has recorded how carefully they studied the B-17. "Bit by bit we are able to familiarize ourselves with every technical detail . . . ," he wrote on January 27, 1943. "I have spent hours in lectures and discussions with the other pilots. . . . Every minute of our spare time is occupied in an infinite variety of calculations of the various speed allowances for different forms of attack . . . the spell is broken: the myth that these monsters are invulnerable is ended." An Oberleutnant Egon Meyer, on the day of LeMay's Saint-Nazaire mission, is credited with developing the head-on attack that found an opening in the B-17's armament.[31]

At first the Germans had not taken daylight bombing seriously and had shown a marked disinclination to tangle with the Fortresses. But as the threat became more real and their self-confidence grew, the Luftwaffe worked out a whole battery of tactics—and an elaborate system of fighter control—for coping with the American offensive. There *was* no "fighter belt" but, rather, a grid laid out over all Germany on which fighters could be vectored to intercept the "bomber stream" once it had been picked up on radar and its direction plotted. Me 109s or FW 190s would repeatedly fly parallel but out of range as the approach to the target began, and then pull ahead and make a U-turn back for an overhead pass to knock out the lead bombardiers or upset their aim.

The Germans developed the *Zerstörer* (destroyer), a twin-engine Messerschmitt 410 equipped at first with cannon and later with 21-cm rockets, to break up the formations and allow the survivors to be dealt with singly. The fighters would make vertical dives from above or indeed any angle, sometimes with three or four planes coming on abreast and firing simultaneously. They would wait until the Allied fighter escort had to turn back, because of its limited range, and then would attack in waves, a new one arriving as each departed.[32] Their energy and resourcefulness reached its apogee in an event recalled by Eighth Air Force, for its extent of commitment and its punishing cost, as Second Schweinfurt, or "Black Thursday," October 14, 1943.

The initial step in American air strategy was targeting. If the purpose (as had been taught at Maxwell Field) was to upset the delicate balance of an industrial web, then everything depended on choosing the right place to assault, on finding the pressure points in the body economic. Energy sources were an obvious candidate, one that eventually turned the trick. The British had provided an exemplary demonstration of how to go about this in May 1943, when with nineteen Lancasters carrying special bombs they cracked open the Möhne Dam, one of four that supplied hydroelectric power to the Ruhr. (Albert Speer put seven thousand men to work and had it repaired by September, in time to catch the autumn and winter precipitation.)[33] Other possibilities were there in real and potential bottlenecks: to wit, tanks and aircraft cannot run without engines, engines cannot run without ball bearings, and German ball-bearing production was highly concentrated. Over 40 percent of it was in a single plant in Schweinfurt, on the Main River northeast of Würzburg in Bavaria. (Speer pointed out Schweinfurt's importance to Hitler in September 1942, and Hitler had ordered its antiaircraft defenses to be heavily strengthened.)

The first attack on Schweinfurt (August 17, 1943) was the deepest into Germany yet attempted and it involved the largest American air fleet (376 B-17s) hitherto dispatched. More bombers arrived over their targets (315) and they dropped a bomb load of greater size (724 tons) than ever before. The tactical plan included an effort to divert and confuse the Germans by dividing our force; part of it—led by Curt LeMay, still a colonel but now commanding an entire division, a major general's job—would first attack the complex of Messerschmitt aircraft factories at Regensburg, a hundred miles farther into Germany than Schweinfurt, to draw off fighters from the larger force coming on behind. Speer thought this a mistake on our part and it may well have been, for at any rate the decoy did not decoy; the Schweinfurt mission was delayed in getting off by bad weather, and when it flew in over Germany it was met by the largest force of fighters the Luftwaffe had so far managed to put together. Both the onslaught of August 17 and the air battle it precipitated were without parallel.

The bombing was impressive, especially at Regensburg, where every important building in the plant was struck and a number of finished fighter planes parked on the ground were destroyed. At Schweinfurt the accuracy was not so great, but there were eighty hits on the two main bearing plants and Speer estimated that ball-bearing production had been cut by 38 percent. (He was not worried about the Regensburg damage, which could be repaired, and he was reassured that the Americans—by failing to concentrate their attentions on Schweinfurt—seemed not to appreciate how crucial it was.) But the cost in B-17s had been staggering. The Regensburg mission lost thirty-six, the Schweinfurt mission twenty-four, for a total of sixty, or 19 percent of those making the attack, a toll in men and machines nearly five times greater than Eaker had forecast to Arnold the previous year.

One of LeMay's officers was reminded that Regensburg was the Ratisbon of history, and of the Browning poem generations of schoolchildren have had to memorize, which ends, "Smiling, the boy fell dead." He told LeMay that the night after, thinking of the Fortresses he had seen explode or go down in flames, a body dropping from one of them with no parachute opening, the lines kept coming back to him and he could not get them out of his mind:

> . . . And his chief beside,
> Smiling, the boy fell dead.[34]

It was the second Schweinfurt raid, however, that opened the eyes of even the most devout believers in the B-17's invulnerability. October 14 in Schweinfurt was a lovely autumn day, trees in color from yellow to red; dahlias and asters were still blooming, trucks were bringing in grapes from the nearby vineyards, boats were plying to and from on the river. But people had learned to refer to this as *Schweinfurt Wetter,* the kind of clear, crisp weather when the Americans came in their terrible silver aircraft, and at about two o'clock in the afternoon the sirens began to sound.[35]

A total of 291 B-17s were moving on them in two streams abreast, thirty miles apart. (LeMay was not along this time; he had been promoted to brigadier, and generals were not encouraged to fly missions on which they might be captured.) An escort of P-47 Thunderbolts, known to airmen as "Jugs," accompanied them as far as Aachen, some 240 miles from the British coast, but from there on and back they were subjected to the full impact of the German response.

The Luftwaffe, write the American air force historians, "turned in a performance unprecedented in its magnitude, in the cleverness with which it was planned, and in the severity with which it was executed."[36] Wave after wave of fighters came after them, the "destroyers" lobbing rockets into the center of formations and then coming back to open fire with their cannon and machine guns. One combat wing was almost completely wiped out; LeMay's old outfit, the 305th, lost thirteen out of fifteen of its aircraft and their crews; the German countryside from Schweinfurt to the border was littered with the fall of Fortresses. Hitler came on the phone personally to tell Speer the news of a great triumph.

It was not quite that one-sided. In all, 228 B-17s succeeded in bombing Schweinfurt and in scoring 88 hits on factory buildings, 143 more within the factory area, and Speer reckoned that this time 67 percent of his ball-bearing capacity had been lost. (He could not understand why the blow was not repeated; had the Americans come back again, they would have given him real problems; "the Allies threw away success," he wrote, "when it was already in their hands.")[37] But the Americans did not come back because the weather had turned against them and they had taken punishment not easily borne. Only 197 Fortresses returned to England, and of these only thirty-three were unharmed. Five were abandoned or crashed on landing, and seventeen were badly enough damaged that they had to be written off, so that the total number lost was 82 out of 291, or nearly 30 percent, and of these sixty had again gone down with all their men. Casualties were 642 out of 2,900, over 18 percent, and of these 594 were missing, many of them dead.

Moreover, it was not merely "Black Thursday" but "Black October." There had been four great raids between the eighth and the fourteenth (Bremen, East Prussia, and Münster were the others), with a total of 1,342 heavy-bomber sorties. During the month, 214 had been lost (10 percent) and the damage rate was running at 42 percent; losses and damages were amounting to more than half of the sorties. If the attrition continued at this rate, an entire new bomber force would be required every three months. The morale of the air crews had dropped to the vanishing point. "It has come to be an accepted fact," wrote one of their number after Second Schweinfurt, "that you will be shot down eventually ... that it is impossible to complete a full tour of duty."[38]

President Roosevelt, in a press conference on the fifteenth, was queried about the Schweinfurt losses and attempted, not altogether convincingly, to put them in a larger context. "We couldn't afford to lose sixty bombers every day," he said, "but we are not losing sixty bombers every day"—true, but small comfort. He balanced this against the score in downed German fighters—a hundred, "let us say" (possibly not far wrong) —and, "on the credit side ... the probability that we put out of commission a very, very large industrial plant, or plants, in Germany." A passable try, but not wholly satisfactory from Arnold's point of view, and on the sixteenth he published a statement amplifying it and claiming "not merely a spectacular air raid" but "a major campaign," in which Schweinfurt's ball-bearing plant had been rendered "completely useless."

Not so; Arnold was obviously uncomfortable. Three days later, he held a press conference of his own and went further, saying "Now we have got Schweinfurt!" Some of his air crews would have said it was the other way around. Second Schweinfurt had marked the end of a chapter in the American offensive. After mid-October, the fog closed in over southwestern Germany and precision bombing became problematical. Eaker believed that but for the weather, they could have gone back to Schweinfurt in greater numbers and with proportionately lower losses,[39] but the fact remained that for the moment, the American air force had gone up against its German adversary and suffered a tactical defeat.

One incident lightened an otherwise pervasive gloom. After a raid on Kassel, *Tondelayo* returned with eleven unexploded 20-mm shells in its fuel tanks, any one of which should have been enough to blow it out of the sky. The shells were sent to Ordnance to be examined, and when they were opened, each was found to be empty, no explosive charge—all but one, which contained a rolled-up slip of paper on which was written, in Czech: "This is all we can do for you now."[40]

◆

No strategic enterprise of World War II has produced, in the aftermath, such divergence of professional opinion about its wisdom as the bomber offensive over Germany. Bert Harris believed that it had been the most important single element of the fighting, not only in the air but on land and sea. The ground forces that faced the Allies on the Continent were substantially reduced in numbers and striking power because of the bombing, and more German ships were sunk by Bomber Command— through mining channels and attacking submarine bases—than by the Royal Navy.

Yet recognition of this was never vouchsafed by His Majesty's Government. The combat crews of Bomber Command were never given a campaign award but given only a "defence" medal, in contrast to back-area personnel overseas who had not heard a shot fired in anger. Harris himself never received the hereditary peerage accorded to Montgomery, Alexander, Cunningham, and Tedder, though it could be argued that he had made their achievements possible. Those who had ordered the bombing seemed to want to forget it.[41]

The contrary to Harris's position, most recently and earnestly advocated by Freeman Dyson, holds that the bomber offensive was a costly blunder. Dyson classes it with what he calls "technical follies" and asserts that if it had not been allowed to absorb "almost one-quarter of the entire British war effort" (a conservative estimate) the war in Europe "would probably have ended at least a year sooner." Bomber Command, writes Dyson, "had the three salient characteristics of a technical folly. First, it was incapable of doing the job—paralyzing the enemy's production—for which it had been designed. Second, it was incapable of adapting itself effectively to any other job. Third, it was inordinately expensive."[42]

Under the rain of bombs, German production steadily increased, reaching its peak in July 1944. They proved able to rebuild and expand factories faster than we, until near the end, could destroy them. Under the direction of Speer, who took over as minister of armaments production in February 1942, output trebled, while the cost of our ineffective effort to hinder this was a somber one in Allied dead and wounded. Harris gives the number of lives lost by Bomber Command as 60,000; General Marshall gave the total casualties ascribed to strategic air forces in the European theater (minus Italy) as 37,500. The Combined Bomber Offensive was undeniably vicious. Major General J. F. C. Fuller, in *The Second World War,* writes of it as "a war of devastation and terrorization unrivalled since the invasion of the Seljuks," and worse, "a grotesque failure."[43]

The extent of German civilian casualties caused by the bombing is difficult to evaluate, since so many records were lost and authorities tended to understate the numbers. The statistical office of the West German government, in its *Wirtschaft und Statistik* for 1962, put the dead at 593,000, which is remarkably close to the 600,000 arrived at independently by Hans Rumpf, for his book *The Bombing of Germany* (Rumpf has the "seriously injured" at 800,000). A large proportion of these were necessarily women, children, and the elderly. One civilian died for every four combatants. "In some towns," writes Rumpf, "the casualties amongst those who stayed at home were greater than amongst the men who went to the front." And their homes were laid waste. The loss in living space was figured by the statistical office at around 50 percent for Berlin, Hamburg, Essen, Düsseldorf, or Hannover; 58 percent for Kiel, 61 for Darmstadt, 64 for Duisberg and Kassel, and 70 for Cologne. Dead figures, live horror; it had been an inferno down there. Flying over Berlin on his way to Moscow in May 1945, his last mission to Stalin, Harry Hopkins said, "It's another Carthage."[44]

On the moral issue, military judgment (*pace* General Fuller) must stand mute, for in this war conspicuously an accusation of inhumanity from one side prompts a *tu quoque* from the other. War is war. The Germans had sown the wind, and they reaped the whirlwind. When Churchill visited the bombed-out sectors of London, the cries of "Give it 'em back, Winnie" were authentic voices of British will, and he heeded them. The bomber was the only instrument at hand for accomplishing that compelling purpose, and it was wielded.

To call this a failure, because it could not achieve the success advertised by its enthusiasts, is to scant what it *did* achieve, which was not the same but no less vital. Bert Harris insisted that "the customer is always right," and that the only witness worth listening to in this matter is the principal customer, who was Albert Speer. Speer said that the bomber offensive opened up a new air front over Germany, that it consumed essential strengths needed elsewhere, and that eventually it "meant the end of German armaments production." The repeated bombings of Hamburg, in late July and early August 1943, he wrote, "put the fear of God in me."

Speer said that the barrels of ten thousand dual-purpose 88-mm guns pointed skyward as antiaircraft could have been employed in their other role to kill Russian and Anglo-American tanks. Hundreds of thousands of soldiers were tied down in manning them; a third of the optical and a half of the electronics industry had to be engaged in producing their gunsights, radar, and communications.[45] He might have added that hundreds of thousands of skilled tradesmen were not called up for military service because they were required to repair bomb damage and that, most important of all, in responding to the bomber offensive the Luftwaffe encompassed its own downfall. One mission of the Allied air leaders was to achieve command of the air over Europe before an invasion was attempted, which they proposed to do by eliminating the factories from which the German aircraft came. They failed in the latter and succeeded in the former; they set out on one route to their goal and arrived at it by another.

During February and March 1944, it was the turn of the Luftwaffe to suffer a bitter defeat at the hands of Eighth Air Force. The critical events were a series of air battles beginning on February 20, to which press officers then and historians since have given the name "Big Week." During it, a total of 3,800 bombers dropped almost 10,000 tons of bombs and damaged or destroyed 75 percent of the buildings in plants that accounted for 90 percent of German aircraft production.

Yet this was not the victory; as before, the recuperative powers of German industry had been seriously underestimated. Two months' production had been lost, but the number of planes delivered—as measured by single-engine-aircraft "acceptances"—continued to rise rapidly until September. It was not the bombing but the air battles the bombing provoked that made the difference. The German fighter squadrons rose to the challenge, and were decimated. American claims of German fighters downed in Big Week amounted to over 600, and surviving German records suggest—astonishingly—that this may not have been far off the mark. Over 700 Luftwaffe flying personnel were dead or missing, 277 wounded.[46]

Pilot training was the weak point of the German air force. They had skimped on it in order to conserve fuel, and when the all-out attack came on their oil industry, they lacked the pilots to protect it. On March 8, 1944, Heinz Knocke wrote in his diary that he had been sitting with one of his men in the squadron crew room staring at photographs on the wall of companions who were gone: Sergeant Wolny, Lieutenant Steiger, Warrant Officer Kolbe, Lieutenant Gerhard, Sergeant Kramer, Sergeant Dölling, Lieutenant Killian, Flight Sergeant Führmann . . . Dolenga . . . Nowotny . . . Raddatz . . . Arndt . . . Reinhard, Zambelle, Weingerber, Hetzel, Krueger, Veit, Höfig, Trockels, Tröndle . . . "Now only Jonny and I remain." (Knocke, though badly wounded, survived the war; he had completed over four hundred combat missions and was credited with shooting down fifty-two Allied aircraft; he had been awarded the Knight's Cross of the Iron Cross.[47]) The Germans lost air supremacy not because they ran out of fighter planes but because they ran out of trained fighter pilots like Heinz Knocke.

There is no question what had been responsible for the turnaround in Eighth AF's favor: It was the development of an American fighter plane with extended range. Nor is there any question why it had been so long and so deplorably delayed: The need for it had not, at the outset, been acknowledged. A popular view holds that the solution came in mid-1944 with the arrival in quantity of the improved P-51, the Merlin Mustang, which showed itself to be the best all-around fighter of the war. (The beautiful Mustang—an American design that enjoyed little favor until a British engine gave it added power—was not what pilots call a "forgiving" aircraft; it was difficult to fly but, once mastered, could outperform not only the Messerschmitt and the Focke-Wulf but even the Spitfire.)[48]

Before the Mustang replaced it, however, the workhorse of VIII Fighter Command had continued to be the stubby P-47 Thunderbolt, the "Jug," and it was the P-47s that fought the great air battles of February

1944, a point most persuasively made by a former Jug pilot, William R. Emerson, in a lecture at the Air Force Academy in 1962 (he was at that time a professor of military history at Yale). What had enabled the P-47 to prevail was a device so simple that matériel experts had tended to ignore it: the droppable fuel tank.

Emerson in his Air Force Academy lecture reviewed the faultless logic by which thoughtful and experienced airmen, in both the United States and the United Kingdom, had over the years repeatedly arrived at the certainty that the long-range fighter was a bad bet. To defend a bomber successfully, a fighter would have to fly faster, ideally by as much as 40 or 50 percent. But the pioneering American bombers up to and including the B-17 were little if any slower than the fighters of their day. A suitable escort for them would have to be high-powered and heavily armed—that is, bigger than the bomber itself! The bomber was the primary offensive weapon and, being capable of its own defense, would have no need to defeat the enemy air force before going on to accomplish its primary mission, destabilizing the enemy economy. There would be no big air battles.

The idea of a fighter escort was therefore probably unnecessary, technically impossible, and anyhow incapable of doing the job. Only a bomber could escort bombers. So Portal believed and so the Americans conceded by the creation of the YB-40, a heavily armored B-17 with added gun turrets. (It was a failure, and Eaker scrapped it.) This conclusion was reached by board after board of experts who studied the problem between 1935 and 1942. With the exception of mavericks like Captain Claire Chennault, who persistently argued the case for fighters but with no success, American and British airmen qualified to speak were unanimous in the opinion that for a combination of mechanical and tactical reasons, fighter escort of bombers was out of the question. "On no point was American doctrine more clear-cut," said Emerson. "On no point was it to prove so wrong."[49]

◆

The disillusionment in the bomber's self-defensive prowess that came in 1943 was at first veiled by the innate optimism of Eighth AF leaders, and by their reading of the climate in higher headquarters; pessimism was not a quality in his commanders that appealed to Hap Arnold. "There is not the slightest question," Eaker determinedly wrote to Arnold on the very day after Second Schweinfurt, "but that we now have our teeth in the Hun Air Force's neck." The savage German reflex of the day before had only been "the last final struggle of a monster in his death throes." But within the week, on thinking it over, Eaker cabled Arnold that he saw no evidence of an early Luftwaffe collapse. The evidence on the need for fighter escort, on the other hand, was by now overwhelming. A study by

Eighth AF's Operation Research Section showed that an unescorted bomber mission sustained *seven times* the losses and two and a half times the damage of a mission with full fighter escort. The men who flew the planes knew. At the debriefing after Second Schweinfurt, when comments were invited, one crew member said, "Jesus Christ, give us fighters for escort!"

Significantly, too, the cause of the long-range fighters had at last acquired a friend in high places. After a visit to England in June 1943, Assistant Secretary of War Robert Lovett had returned to Washington convinced that something had to be done, quickly, and for the first time there was a real sense of urgency behind efforts to give longer legs to the P-47. Eaker, as a fighter pilot himself, had not questioned the value of fighter escort in principle; he merely acknowledged the limitations imposed on it by a limited fuel supply. As early as October 1942, Eighth Air Force had been asking to have the P-47 equipped with lightweight, expendable auxiliary fuel tanks, but nothing had happened; Air Materiel Command at Wright-Patterson Field didn't seem to get the point, and it wasn't until December 1943 that supply of the fuel tanks started to come anywhere near demand.[50]

Once produced, their effect was to rewrite the rules. The P-47s began to rove deeper and deeper into the Reich, to the dismay of German pilots and fighter controllers. On September 27, the Jugs took the B-17s all the way to Emden and back, half again as far as they had initially been able to go, and bomber losses were only 3 percent of the total attacking. By January 1944, most of Western Germany lay under the wings of the long-range P-47s, flying either from East Anglia or (Fifteenth Air Force) from the Mediterranean.

Even before Big Week, a subtle transformation had come about in the way the American fighters behaved. They had begun to think more about the attack than about the reply to it; they wanted not merely to protect the bombers but to go after German fighter aircraft wherever encountered. This is what fighters should have been doing all along; it was not so much a change in strategical plans as one in tactical performance, even though it did acquire sanction from at least one of the senior commanders. In charge of Eighth AF was now Jimmy Doolittle (Eaker had gone to the Mediterranean and Spaatz had been promoted to command of all U.S. strategic air in the European theater), and one day he visited fighter headquarters at Bushy Hall, northwest of London. On a wall was the motto of VIII Fighter Command: "Our Mission Is to Bring the Bombers Back." When he saw it, Doolittle said, "That's not so. Your mission is to destroy the German Air Force," and on leaving he added, "Take that damn thing down."[51]

Destroy it they did, in a markedly short span of time. Between January and June, control of the air over Europe passed to the American fighters. They not only accompanied the bombers but went hunting for the German fighters and attacked the fighter fields. Outnumbered seven to one, the Luftwaffe went over to the defensive. In April 1944, General der Jagdflieger Adolf Galland, inspector general of German fighter forces, wrote in a report: "The standard of the Americans is extraordinarily high. The day fighters have lost more than 1000 aircraft during the last four months, among them our best officers. These gaps cannot be filled. During each enemy raid we lose about 50 fighters." When the invasion came in June, the commander of German fighters opposing it was down to 160 planes, of which only half were operational. On that day of days, the entire German air force managed to make only 250 sorties, and the overpowering American 8,722 flown against them endured losses of less than 1 percent. "By April the Luftwaffe was defeated," said Emerson. "By June it was impotent."[52]

A consequence of fighter success was to free up the bombers. There had been an argument about whether they should focus on isolating the battlefield (the "transportation plan") or on eliminating German fuel sources (the "oil plan"); in the event, the solution had been to do both, and both worked. The battlefield was made perilous of access and transportation was wrecked, until by the end railroads and canals were useless and Germany was reduced to the foot and horseback level. Speer dated the beginning of the end from May 12, 1944—"On that day the technological war was decided"—when over eight hundred American heavies hit the German synthetic-oil industry in six or more cities and daily fuel output dropped 18 percent.

"The enemy has struck us at one of our weakest points," Speer told Hitler. "If they persist at it this time, we will soon no longer have any fuel production worth mentioning." They did persist. On June 22, nine tenths of airplane fuel output was knocked out, and by July 21, 98 percent of aircraft fuel plants were out of operation—"virtually done for," said Speer. By prodigies of exertion they were able to work back up during the fall to 28 percent of where they started, but it was a bootless task. The inexorable pressure continued on every aspect of the war economy and by "the end of February," write the American air force historians, "Nazi Germany was no longer an industrial nation."[53] It was strangled and paralyzed before the Allied ground troops overran it.

In the concluding months of the war, there was a frenzy of bombing, a spasm of unbridled ferocity. It was almost as though, having acquired the capacity to annihilate, we knew not how to refrain from using it. The American leaders like Spaatz and Eaker continued to maintain allegiance to the doctrine of precision, but in fact Eighth Air Force had for some time been engaging in radar bombing (where its margin of probable error was two miles!)[54] and increasingly it participated in missions with the RAF—especially against Berlin—that were more vindictive than purposeful. The worst of the destruction was done when it was no longer necessary. "In its final stages," wrote Hans Rumpf, "the air offensive seemed almost to take charge on its own and to develop apocalyptic forms. . . . It was like an elemental irruption which could no longer be controlled and localized, but which emptied itself over the country like a natural catastrophe."[55]

Dresden, on February 13, 1945, was one of the most beautiful cities in Germany, filled with refugees fleeing from the Russian advance. Dresden, on February 14, 1945, was a shattered ruin filled with countless corpses. For the first time in the war there were not enough able-bodied survivors to bury the dead. It was, writes David Irving, "the biggest single massacre in European history." The sack of Magdeburg in May 1631, from which the whole continent recoiled in shock, did not even approach it.[56] The reasoning behind the Anglo-American raid on Dresden is obscure. The appropriate directives had been issued, memos exchanged; but they reveal nothing so much as a fatal combination of vagueness and momentum. Dresden was not a military target of any importance, and its obliteration did not significantly assist the Russians, though this was one of the reasons given. The rationale was to deal a massive blow to some East German population center other than Berlin, on the theory such would hasten victory, and Dresden was on the list. So the ponderous machinery ground on. The bombing had become its own justification.

The lessons to be learned from all this are many, but among them is that the strategic air offensive over Europe in World War II was not what either its defenders or its detractors have claimed. Few generalizations about it can stand without qualification. Harris's fantasy of finishing Germany "in a week" proved a delusion, yet the bomber offensive was not the "grotesque failure" General Fuller called it. Freeman Dyson's characterization of Bomber Command as "incapable of adapting itself . . . to any other job" was strictly speaking accurate, yet that did not prevent another job from being accomplished, which was the diversion and dissipation of German energies, for which Speer gave due credit. An effect of bombing on morale was assumed, for the good reason that it has such an effect (especially on the battlefield), but area bombing did not lower German national morale on the scale anticipated, perhaps because it was a case (as the air force historians put it) "of trying to lower the morale of a people who had no morale,"[57] at least as we understood it. The Germans endured and went on fighting for a number of reasons, but one of them was that they had no choice, and that to fight and endure was what a German was expected to do.

The American bomber commanders vastly overrated their weapon (until very late in the day, both Spaatz and Eaker continued to believe that if given the full opportunity they could make the invasion superfluous[58]) and they had to reverse themselves, as far as doctrine was concerned, about fighter escort. Yet their trust in precision bombing was not proved to be misplaced simply because it seemed at the time not to work. If any moral can be drawn from Speer's testimony, it is that a modern military machine consists of precisely that delicate web the air force planners at Maxwell Field had visualized; only the right series of karate chops was needed to bring it down. "The idea was correct," wrote Speer, "the execution defective."[59]

Until the final phase, we failed to concentrate and follow through. (Speer thought this was because we assumed that a dictatorship must be efficient and that, as an example, ball-bearing production, once attacked, would instantly be dispersed; the Third Reich didn't work that way.)[60] We assumed that we could wear them down, failing to realize that Germany in the early stages was not fully mobilized and that production would necessarily go up as soon as (under Speer) it was mobilized. Instead of putting the principle of precision to work in its pure form, we diluted it with the principle of attrition. Tooey Spaatz, writes Dewitt Copp, "was, in a real sense, the Ulysses S. Grant of the air war. . . . He had the force, and he used it whatever the immediate cost . . . so long as it damaged the enemy's capacity to fight back."[61] Eventually he removed that capacity, but the cost had been high.

Among the American officers whose confidence in precision bombing had been shaken was Curtis LeMay. He was proud of the accuracy 305th Group had attained in the Regensburg strike, and kept photos of it in his personal file. On them the Messerschmitt plant looked to be completely out of action. Only later did he realize that such was not the case. "To be utterly frank," LeMay wrote, "this was true in all our bombing of Germany. The recovery capability was infinitely better than we had imagined it to be."[62] In June 1944, he was ordered to go to Asia and take command of the B-29s, where his thoughts on this subject would have a direct and critical impact on the remaining course of the war.

III

After Hap Arnold met with Charles Lindbergh on the playing field at West Point in May 1939, and asked him to serve on a panel to determine what kind of aircraft we would want for the next five years, Arnold convened what came to be called the Kilner Board, after its chairman, Brigadier General Walter G. Kilner, who had commanded an air base in France during World War I. (Arnold called it the Kilner-Lindbergh Board; Tooey Spaatz was also a member.) For the next two years, Lindbergh worked with Arnold. "The value of the findings of that Board was inestimable," Arnold wrote. "I can still see poor stolid Lindbergh being trailed through the halls of the Munitions Building by excited clerks and predatory newspapermen as he did his job." The Kilner Board shaped the matériel procurement policies of the air force as war approached, and among its recommendations was the development of a heavy bomber with a 2,000-mile radius and a high speed of 375 miles per hour above 20,000 feet. The aircraft that eventually came closest to fitting these specifications was called by its designers at Boeing the Model 345 and by the air force (at first) the XB-29, X being for experimental.[63]

The Boeing company had been giving the idea of a "super-bomber" considerable thought. In mid-1939, their most promising product, the B-17, had not yet been ordered into full production and they were borrowing from the banks to meet the payroll. They fully appreciated that the airplane the military were buying in the B-17 and the one really needed were two different things; every reason argued for producing something bigger and better. During the summer they held exploratory conversations with Arnold and with Materiel Command at Wright Field, and by July they had on the drawing boards a Model 334-A, which was the first "blood ancestor" of the B-29, with a pressurized cabin and the characteristic long, tapering wing.

In August, as a result of the Wright Field conversations, it had become Model 341, and toward the end of the year, at their own expense, they began to make a full-scale wooden mock-up of it. On February 5, 1940, when they received specific requirements from the air force and a request to submit a competitive proposal, they were able to meet the thirty-day deadline. By June—with the Germans overrunning France—they had been given funds to start designing an even larger, heavier, and more powerful version.[64]

By force of circumstance, the relationship between the air force and its prime suppliers was a close one. From the perspective of a later era, in which the phrase "military-industrial complex" has come to have unfortunate connotations, the admission must be made that in those earlier days it served us well. Daring, innovation, rapid results, and quality achieved in quantity were made possible essentially because the two parties to the arrangement trusted and understood one another. If sometimes the military seemed too demanding, it helped that the Boeing executives could put themselves in the place of the aircrews who would have to fly the damned thing. If sometimes Boeing seemed too stubborn, it helped to be reminded that they did have a demonstrated capacity to bring large new aircraft into existence. One day Brigadier General Oliver P. Echols, head of Materiel Command, asked Boeing's chief engineer, Wellwood E. Beall, to come to Washington. "The United States government," said Echols, "is about to spend more money on [this] one project than any other project of the whole war. . . . We haven't even flown the airplane. . . . We want to know, really—the survival of the whole country may depend on this— we want to know what you really believe in your heart, whether that will be a good airplane or not."

After taking a deep breath, Beall replied: "Yes. It's really going to be a good airplane. If you'll give us first priority on test facilities and let us do all the testing we want, when we want to do it . . . I'll guarantee that we'll get you successful operating airplanes."[65] Echols went with this answer to General Arnold, who with Lovett's and the President's backing said to go ahead. The thought was not absent from their minds that the B-29 would have to be built in plants that didn't exist by people who hadn't ever worked on aircraft before. The problem wasn't money but resources; more than one company would have to be involved. (The Boeing plant at Wichita, Kansas, would be enlarged, but then Bell Aircraft would build a plant at Marietta, Georgia; North American, one at Kansas City; and Fisher Body Division of General Motors, another at Cleveland.) Further, the B-29s were wanted in time to affect the outcome of the war and in very large numbers. (Boeing delivered the first seven production models in July 1943; by August 1945, the air force had received and accepted a total of 3,763 of them.)[66]

During the design process, Boeing and the air force argued a lot. They argued about the ball turrets, whether the machine guns in them should be locally or remotely controlled (air force wanted local, Boeing wanted remote; Boeing won the point). They argued most of all about the tapered wing, and its effect on the factor of wing loading (the amount of aircraft weight per square foot of wing surface) and thus on stability at slow speeds and the ability to reach high altitude. The B-29's wing loading was by prevailing standards excessive, but Boeing again persisted. Wellwood Beall was asked into the Wright Field office of General George Kenney (Echols had been transferred to Washington), who wrote on a blackboard: "Plane X—wing loading fifty-three pounds per square foot, ceiling 28,000 feet. B-29—wing loading sixty-nine pounds per square foot, ceiling . . ." and then he drew a big question mark. Beall said they were going to get a 33,000-foot ceiling. "We're counting a lot on your word, my friend," said Kenney. (The Superfortress was eventually credited with a ceiling of 38,-000 feet.)[67]

The first completed XB-29 left the ground at four-thirty in the afternoon on September 21, 1942—a clear, hot day in Seattle, with a light north wind—at the controls, Edmund T. Allen, one of the greats among test pilots. It cannot have been an emotionless moment for those who watched this gleaming giant, its four engines turning over at a then-unequaled 8,800 horsepower, thunder down the runway and then aloft, up, up, and up. Seventy-five minutes later, Allen touched down and taxied to a halt. He was a stoic, methodical man, a bit of an actor and a poker player, now expressionless until finally a broad smile broke through. "She flies," he said. Wellwood Beall drafted a telegram to Washington: "Eddie Allen reports that we have an excellent airplane."[68]

Not right away, and not before delay and disaster intervened. Even for an entirely original and unproved design the XB-29 was full of bugs, especially in its engines, which had an unpredictable tendency to overheat, blow cylinder heads, and catch on fire. "If you ever saw a buggy airplane, this was it," said Curtis LeMay of his first experience at flying the B-29, in the summer of 1944. "Fast as they got the bugs licked, new ones crawled out from under the cowling." Fuel tanks leaked, propellers would not feather properly, bomb-bay doors opened and closed at some whim of their own, gun-sighting blisters frosted up or blew out at high altitude. Aerodynamically she performed well at any height they went to, but minor defects continued to multiply until February 18, 1943, when Eddie Allen, taking off with XB-29 Number 2, reported minutes later that he was coming in with a wing on fire. Control tower could hear their intercom: "Allen, better get this thing down in a hurry," and it crashed, killing all aboard.[69] The same had happened before, with an early B-17, but it was hard to take, a heaviness in the heart; the three-billion-dollar bet was being called. Arnold persevered regardless, and sent General Kenneth B. Wolfe from Wright Field to make sure that no pains were spared in bringing the B-29 through to fruition.

Arnold's concern had presidential pressure behind it. Roosevelt's interest in having Japan bombed did not let up after the Doolittle Raid. He encouraged two proposals to send bombers to China by way of the Middle East during 1942, one task group under Colonel Caleb V. Haynes and another under Colonel Harry A. Halverson, but the latter was diverted against the Germans from North Africa and the former arrived in India with insufficient force to accomplish the mission. In April 1943, Arnold set up a special B-29 project, with General Wolfe in charge not only of production but of training crews and forming them into units, and Wolfe brought forward a plan responding to the President's reiterated demands for the employment of American air power in China, the only area from which the B-29s could then reach Japan.

The planes would be based near Calcutta and staged through advance fields around Chengtu; they would carry their own supplies with them. On October 13, 1943, Arnold endorsed Wolfe's proposal in his own hand: "I have told the President that this will be started (in China to Japan) on March 1. See that it is done. H.H.A." Roosevelt had not been pacified, however, and his annoyance can be assumed to underlie much of Arnold's subsequent hounding of his own subordinates. On the fifteenth, the President wrote to General Marshall: "I am still pretty thoroughly disgusted with the China-India matter. The last straw was the report from Arnold that he could not get the B-29s operating out of China until March or April of next year. Everything seems to go wrong."[70]

Arnold tried to have the B-29 given "over-riding priority over all other aircraft," but King objected that other programs were important too, and the Joint Chiefs agreed with him. Actually, priority would not have helped much; delays were inherent in the unorthodox practice of testing component parts on the plane itself, rather than separately and over years of trial. Design changes had grown into the thousands; eventually they would number thirty thousand.

In January 1944, ninety-seven B-29s came off the assembly lines but only sixteen were flyable. Arnold went to the Boeing plant at Wichita, picked out a bomber farther down the line than their monthly production, and said, "This is the plane I want this month." They named it the "General Arnold Special" and delivered it on time, with appropriate ceremony. (In November 1944, the "General Arnold Special" ran out of fuel on a mission over Japan and made an emergency landing in Vladivostok; after much delay, the crew was returned to Allied hands in Iran, but the aircraft itself vanished into the obscurity of Russian secretiveness and indifference to American protests.)[71]

The attempt to meet Arnold's deadline produced an episode of extemporized and concentrated effort called the Battle of Kansas, March 10 to April 15, 1944. In order to keep the planes coming out of the plants, it had been necessary to refrain from incorporating design changes during production; these were to be made later, at "modification centers" run by the air force. The "mod centers" for the B-29 were at bases near Salina, Pratt, Walker, and Great Bend in central Kansas, where the backlog of aircraft waiting to be worked on piled up alarmingly during February.

The job had to be done outdoors (no hangars were big enough for the B-29) and this was Kansas in midwinter: snow, sleet, subzero temperatures. Arnold put in charge a cigar-chomping major general named Bennett E. Meyers, who set up headquarters with a battery of telephones and a cot by his desk at the base hospital at Salina, where he dispensed coffee and doughnuts to all comers at any hour of the day or night. (Benny Meyers got in trouble after the war for using his position as a procurement officer to increase the value of stock he secretly held in manufacturing companies, an aspect of the "military-industrial complex" in its less attractive form, but Arnold in his book defended him; "when he was given a task, he did it," Arnold wrote.[72])

They pulled mechanics from all over the country; Boeing sent six hundred of their best production men. Against the cold they commandeered sheepskin-lined high-altitude flight suits from the quartermaster, no questions asked; boxload after boxload of equipment came in, to be stacked in the open; every man on his own, if you needed a part you grabbed a jeep and went after it; no nonsense about receipts, no records of anything but what needed to be done and what had been done: new flat glass in the nose section, revised nose ring cowling, prop feathering pumps to be relocated, new engine generators to be installed, electrical circuits to be rewired, limit stops to be changed in the tail turret, and on and on. Each plane was to be flown off by its combat crew, modified, fully armed, carrying a spare engine and a complete set of spare parts. Four or five of them departed every dawn for India. On the morning of April 15, the last crew, in boots and leather jackets, arrived in the officers' mess at Salina and silently ate a substantial breakfast. Finally, the pilot stood up and said, "Well, let's get going." Somehow the thing had been done.[73]

The men and women who built the B-29 were legion. One of Bert Stiles's girlfriends was among them; another was a spry little lady who came to the gates of the Bell plant in Marietta the day it opened, having walked from the cottage down the road where she lived. She was vague about her age, but it must have been around seventy-five. She was the the widow of a Confederate officer and her name was Mrs. James Longstreet. Her husband had commanded First Corps in the Army of Northern Virginia, the "good right arm" of Bobby Lee. Mrs. Longstreet worked the 7:00 A.M. shift, never late, never absent; she was there two years.[74]

The gun crews of a destroyer in the Pacific were at their stations when a formation of B-29s passed overhead, the first they had seen. "Are they ours?" asked one of them, somewhat awestruck. "Yes, they're ours," said another. "Nobody else could build anything as big and pretty and make it work."[75]

◆

LeMay thought that Arnold had never really believed in the "China-India matter," which reinforces the impression that without the President's insistence it would never have been attempted. The logistical arithmetic was against it; the idea that the B-29s could supply themselves was unrealistic. *Seven* flights from India to China were required to build up enough fuel for *one* flight staged through China to bomb Japan. Hope of achieving significant results against such odds as these should never have been great, and for many in air force headquarters it was not.[76]

In November 1943, President Roosevelt informed both Churchill and Chiang Kai-shek of the B-29 China project and asked for their help in securing airfields; both replied promptly and favorably. Formal approval was given at the Cairo Conference in December. In February 1944, Roosevelt cabled Churchill, to persuade him that two fighter groups should be sent from the Mediterranean to China for the defense of the B-29 bases. "I have always advocated the development of China as a base," the President cabled Churchill later in the month.[77]

In southern Bengal, by the time the B-29s began to arrive in April, four airfields had been built near Kharagpur, with concrete runways and hardstands, and with a pipeline connecting them to a tanker dock on the Hooghly River downstream from Calcutta. In China, four B-29 bases and three fighter fields were built, literally by hand, by hundreds of thousands of Chinese farmers and their families, in the fertile Min River valley near the Szechuanese capital of Chengtu. Each B-29 field in China had a 8,500-

foot runway with a surface a foot and a half thick, and fifty-two hardstands, on a base of rocks set in sand and gravel, topped with a sort of native adobe made of crushed rock, sand, clay, and water, packed down by stone rollers.

"Materials were carried from nearby streams," write the air force historians, "in buckets or baskets slung from yokes, in squeaky wooden-wheeled wheelbarrows, or infrequently in carts. Excavation was by hoes. Crushed rock was patiently beat out with little hammers and stones were laid individually by hand. Rollers were drawn by man (and woman) power, the slurry puddled in pits by barefoot men and boys."

It was a prodigious display of traditional Chinese strength—paid for by the United States but in the complete absence of modern machinery —of the sturdy abilities and goodwill of her indestructible people. "The project was to challenge credulity by the magnitude of the force involved," the air force historians write. "Western witnesses sought analogies in the building of the Great Wall of China or in Herodotus' account of the building of the great pyramid of Cheops." Work began on January 24, three months to a day later the first B-29 set down, and by early May the runways were finished and the fields were operational.

On June 15, 1944, the first B-29 mission against Japan took off from China. Ninety-two battle-loaded B-29s had left Bengal, of which seventy-nine reached the Chengtu bases. After refueling, seventy-five were dispatched, of which sixty-eight got airborne. Their target was the steelworks at Yawata, responsible for 24 percent of Japan's production. Forty-seven of the Superforts arrived over Yawata, against light opposition; only three fighter planes attacked them and the flak was inaccurate, doing at best minor harm. But photos taken on the fourteenth showed that the raid had done very little harm too. Only one hit had been scored on the Yawata plant and what other damage there was had been to an arsenal, to miscellaneous industrial buildings, and to business-industrial areas in Yawata itself. The prime target, Japan's steel production, was unhurt.

The second major mission, on July 29, was against the Showa steelworks in Anshan, Manchuria, specifically its coke ovens, which produced about a third of Japan's supply. Seventy-two B-29s got aloft and fifty of them bombed Anshan, while sixteen—too late for Anshan—bombed a supplemental target, Taku harbor near Tientsin. Again opposition was almost negligible, and this time results were better; post-strike photos taken in early August showed substantial damage at both Anshan and Taku. On the night of August 10–11, thirty-nine B-29s staged through Ceylon bombed the Pladjoe oil refinery at Palembang in Sumatra, source of 22 percent of Japan's fuel oil and 78 percent of her aviation gasoline. Crewmen reported having seen explosions and fires, but the strike photos were too hazy to show much, and later observation in mid-September indicated that only the destruction of a small building could be definitely credited to the mission. This was the way things had been going when, on

August 29, General Curtis LeMay arrived in Kharagpur to take command.[78]

LeMay had characteristically insisted on being taught "the correct way to fly the 29, if there was any such way," before he left the United States, and he had announced that he intended to fly at least one combat mission when he got to India. Washington at first refused to allow this, but he insisted and finally—his total ignorance of the atomic bomb project, he later concluded, gave them an excuse to relent—permission was granted. September 8, he went on the second strike against Anshan; his aircraft was hit by flak and two crew members were wounded. He wanted to set up lead-crew schools and teach them to fly formation, as he had done in Europe. He wanted them to cruise at speeds that would consume the least fuel. He wanted to take this impossible job and get it done, to catch something flying faster than he could run.

He wanted maintenance tightened up; he was convinced that they were losing more B-29s to undetected causes than to known ones, let alone to enemy action. Engines still overheated, cylinders blew, power failed. "The instrument wasn't ready, the people weren't ready, nothing was ready," LeMay wrote.[79] The B-29 accident rate was so visible that in the Pentagon, Major James Gould Cozzens several times referred to it in his regular informational memos to his chief, including the report of one officer's conviction that failures resulted from the planes' being built by "dim-witted Georgia crackers" and flown by inexperienced pilots. "I gather," wrote Cozzens, "that as soon as all the pilots who can't manage to learn how the fly the brute are killed, attrition by crack-up will go to normal."[80] He was wrong about the reason, but pilots, aircraft, and engines did improve.

In early January 1945, LeMay was summoned to Guam, to meet with Brigadier General Lauris Norstad, chief of staff to Arnold in Arnold's capacity as overall B-29 commander. Since the capture of the Marianas in July and August, a force of B-29s had been building up there—on Saipan, Guam, and Tinian—but there was room for improvement in their performance. Norstad told LeMay that the "China-India matter" was going to be abandoned. "Someone," wrote LeMay, "had finally tumbled to the fact that there was no profit in trying to supply the Chengtu Valley with gasoline for attacks on Japan." As soon as new fields were available, the B-29s in India would be moved to the Marianas. The new commander there would be LeMay, whose reaction was that they had found another great big bear for him to grab by the tail.

Looking back on the China operation, LeMay and others have concluded that it didn't amount to a great deal. Thus far, LeMay wrote, the B-29s "hadn't made much of a splash in the war."[81] The title for the China plan had been "Early Sustained Bombing of Japan," and the bombing had in fact been neither early nor sustained. "No one has ventured to endorse

he was all "vividly articulate Irish-American Brooklyn-born lighthearted-ness, humor, and spiritual gaiety," wrote McKelway, "except for an inner toughness and thoughtfulness which the pale face subtly intimates." McKelway asked Possum Hansell where his nickname came from, only to have Hansell half-smile, half-close his eyes and say, "I have no accurate information as to the explanation of its origin." McKelway revered Hansell and concluded, nonetheless, that "Possum looks like a wide-awake, smart, kind, somewhat preoccupied, and very efficient possum."[86]

McKelway was therefore considerably upset when Hansell told him that LeMay was coming to command the B-29s in the Marianas and that he (Hansell) was going back to the States. McKelway said that he tried to respond as a lieutenant colonel should, but what he wanted to say was, "Holy God, Possum! They can't do this to you!" The bad news had been brought by Lauris Norstad (aged thirty-eight), who later tried to explain to McKelway that all those involved were close friends and there was nothing personal about it. "The reason is," said Norstad, "that General Arnold—and all of us, including, I think, Possum—now know that this LeMay is the best man in the Air Forces right now for this particular job, the job of carrying out what Possum and the rest of us started. LeMay is an operator, the rest of us are planners. That's all there is to it."

McKelway first began to take note of LeMay at a ceremony McKelway had arranged for the transfer of command, and he noticed mainly that LeMay was smoking a pipe, which he seemed to be trying to hide in a hopefully fireproof hip pocket. "General," said McKelway, "please let me hold your pipe for you while the picture is being taken." LeMay quietly asked where to stand. McKelway had been up all night and was tired. He was also desperately afraid that he was about to be impressed again, that he had caught "something deeply, bottomlessly disturbing in this stocky, plain-looking new commanding general." Why were they doing this to *him?* Why couldn't he have "a lousy, easygoing, mediocre general for just a few weeks?" He didn't want another leader he *liked!* "Dear God," thought McKelway, "don't tell me this LeMay is as good as he looked just now!" After the photographing, LeMay came up to McKelway and in a barely audible voice said, "Better get some sleep. Thanks for holding my pipe."[87]

McKelway's experience with general officers and public relations was that those who eventually used and understood it best were those who began with a lack of enthusiasm for it, and this proved to be the case with LeMay. Before long, LeMay decided that McKelway should be briefed on the highly classified details of a forthcoming operation. These were star-tling, to say the least, the consequences of a conclusion LeMay had come to that broke with every possible precedent. Norstad had told him that General Arnold wanted results and that if LeMay didn't get results he would be fired, that there would be no strategic air forces in the Pacific, and that Japan would have to be invaded at a cost of half a million lives. The three-billion-dollar bet was being called again.

LeMay had been thinking long, hard thoughts. He stayed up nights, studying intelligence reports and strike photos. The key to the thing was altitude—we were still going in too high and fighting the jet stream—and the big question was whether the Japanese had low-altitude antiaircraft. LeMay couldn't find any; he began to believe that they didn't. What if we went in low, nine or even five thousand feet? What if we stripped the planes of guns, gunners, and bomb-bay fuel tanks, so as to load them with the maximum weight of bombs, and what if we made all the bombs incendiaries, both napalm and phosphorus? What if the B-29s flew singly, not in formation, with the best crews first to start a fire the others could bomb on? What if . . . ?

He decided not to tell Arnold what he was thinking of doing. If Arnold okayed it beforehand and it didn't work, then Arnold would be stuck with some of the responsibility; this way the responsibility would be all LeMay's. Voices of history and guilt ran through his head: "Dear General Burnside. This is the anniversary of the death of my son Sam, whom you killed at Fredericksburg. Dear General Hancock. Twenty years ago today you killed my son Benjy at Chancellorsville. . . ." He asked Norstad, "You know General Arnold. I don't know him. Does he ever go for a gamble? What do you think?" Norstad then had no idea of what LeMay had in mind, but an interest in area incendiary bombing of major Japanese cities had been growing for some time in Arnold's headquarters, and his Committee of Operations Analysts had formally recommended it on October 10, 1944.[88]

He called in his antiaircraft experts and asked them what would happen if the B-29s flew in over Japan at five or six thousand feet. Almost to a man, they told him that he would lose 70 percent of his aircraft. He talked to his commanders, many of whom liked the idea, among them Brigadier General Thomas S. Power, the man LeMay had in mind to lead the mission, and Power's operations officer, now-Colonel Hewitt T. Wheless of Menard, Texas, whom we met earlier when the President mentioned him in a speech and invited him to the White House. LeMay thought about the two incendiary attacks he had made from Chengtu, on Nanking and Hankow, and how the buildings hit had burned. He thought about civilian casualties, an appalling thought that only the comparable nightmare of an invasion persuaded him to accept. He would do it. The target would be Tokyo, the night of March 9–10; 334 B-29s would take off with about two thousand tons of incendiary bombs. "This B-29 is a wonderful airplane," LeMay said to McKelway.

To say that the pilots and their crews were shocked at the briefing session for this operation puts it very mildly; one writer describes them as "dumfounded . . . frightened." Here was LeMay, the apostle of high-altitude, formation-flying precision bombing, and he was tossing aside every rule in the book of which he was a principal author. Someone composed a couplet that became a slogan of the Superforts:

> Throw your oxygen mask away,
> General LeMay is here to stay.

But on thinking it over, they began to realize that the proposition made a certain crazy sense. For each of the elements in it there was a valid reason. The absence of guns would prevent them from hitting each other (which was known to happen), and the absence of extra fuel tanks would be made up for by flying low and saving fuel. The low altitude was possible because the Japanese had been observed to lack barrage balloons, low-level automatic weapons, and a sufficient number of night fighters. So large a bomb load of incendiaries could start a very large fire. Most of all, there was the factor of surprise. They might just be able to pull it off.[89]

LeMay and McKelway both stayed up that night in the operations room and sweated it out. "A lot could go wrong," said LeMay. He was sitting on a wooden bench smoking a cigar. "If this raid works the way I think it will," he said to McKelway, "we can shorten this war." He looked at his watch. "We won't get a bombs-away for another half-hour," he said. "Would you like a Coca-Cola? I can sneak in my quarters without waking the other guys and get two Coca-Colas and we can drink them in my car. That'll kill most of the half-hour." They sat in the dark drinking the Cokes and looking at the jungle that surrounded their headquarters. For some reason they talked about India. "The way all those people are in India gets you down," said LeMay. "It makes you feel rotten."

They got back to the operations room a few minutes before the bombs-away message came in. It read: "Bombing the primary target visually. Large fires observed. Flak moderate. Fighter opposition nil." Other officers who had been sleepless or awakened on call began to gather in the room. "It looks pretty good," said LeMay. "But we can't really tell a damn thing about results until we get the pictures tomorrow night. Anyway, there doesn't seem to have been much flak. We don't seem to have lost more than a few airplanes."[90] (Actually they lost fourteen, a ratio of 4.2 percent, as opposed to the 5.7 percent for the month of January, and the crews of five of them were picked up by air-sea rescue.[91]) LeMay shifted his cigar and creased his face in the grimace McKelway by this time recognized as a smile.

The post-strike photographs were ready the next evening at about midnight. Five or six jeeps full of staff officers alerted for the occasion came racing up to the general-officer quarters just as the pictures were brought in. LeMay and Norstad were in pajamas, rubbing sleep from their eyes, and LeMay was lighting a cigar (wrote McKelway) "in a dogged manner that seemed to indicate that anybody, or anything, that interfered with his lighting this particular cigar at this particular moment would be noiselessly and totally obliterated." The photos were spread out on a well-lit table. There was a full minute of silence. Large parts of Tokyo were tinted a whitish gray. "All this is out," said LeMay, running his hand over several square miles. "This is out—this—this—this." He stood up and looked at the rest of them, his face expressionless. Norstad bent over the table. "It's all ashes," he said, "all that and that and that."[92] More than sixteen square miles of Tokyo had gone up in fire and smoke.

"It was," wrote General Power later, "the greatest single disaster incurred by any enemy in military history. It was greater than the combined damage of Hiroshima and Nagasaki. There were more casualties than in any other military action in the history of the world." The Japanese called it the Raid of the Fire Wind. "It was like a silver curtain falling," said Father Gustav Bitter, German-born rector of Sophia University in Tokyo, "like the *lametta,* the silver tinsel we hung from Christmas trees in Germany long ago. And where these silver streamers would touch the earth, red fires would spring up." Father Bitter, who was interviewed after the war by Marine Lieutenant Harold H. Martin, described how the B-29s had set one central fire and then other fires radiating out from it like the ribs of a fan.

"And the big fire in the center," Father Bitter said, "sent up a rising column of air which drew in toward the center the outer circle of flame, and a hot, swift wind began to blow from the rim toward the center, a twisting wind which spread the flames between all the ribs of the fan, very quickly. Thus, everywhere the people ran there was fire, in front of them and in back of them, and closing in on them from the sides. So that there were only a very few who escaped."[93]

Tokyo's fire chief reported that within thirty minutes the blaze was out of control; it consumed 95 fire engines and killed 125 firemen. The destruction of light buildings was total; very little rubble was left and only here and there a fire-resistant wall, scarred by the heat. The police records indicate that 267,171 buildings were destroyed, about a quarter of Tokyo, and over a million people were homeless. Removing the dead from the ruins took twenty-five days. Many had perished in the panic of seeking to flee from the fire wind by jumping into rivers or canals, but in some of the smaller canals the water boiled. "The official toll of casualties," write the air force historians, "listed 83,793 dead and 40,918 wounded. . . . No other attack of the war, either in Japan or Europe, was so destructive of life or property."[94]

With the second fire raid two days later, on Nagoya, LeMay and the B-29s methodically began the destruction of urban and industrial Japan. Osaka was struck on the thirteenth, Kobe on the sixteenth, and Nagoya for a second time on the nineteenth. They had run out of incendiaries. After an interlude in April, while the B-29s supported the invasion of Okinawa, they took up where they had left off. In mid-May, Nagoya was hit twice again and scratched from the target list. Tokyo was hit twice again and scratched from the target list. Five more raids on Osaka, Kobe, and Yokohama followed, until by mid-June the six major industrial centers of Japan were in ruins, their factories destroyed or heavily damaged, feeder units burned out, casualties in six figures, and the homeless in the millions.[95]

That was only the beginning. The horror that fell from the skies upon Japan during the spring and summer of 1945 exceeded Admiral Yamamoto's worst imagining. General LeMay had not abandoned precision targets and these continued to be hit, with improved accuracy as the B-29 crews grew in competence and resistance slackened: Otaka oil refinery on May 10 ("completely inoperative"), electric power center at Kofu ("permanently eliminated"), Sumitomo Light Metals at Osaka and Kawanishi Aircraft at Takarasuka (both three-quarters knocked out), followed by a series of nine oil installations ending with the Nippon refineries at Amagasaki ("completely destroyed") and at Tsuchizaki ("100 per cent destroyed"). The B-29s mined the harbors and ship channels of the Japanese islands until waterborne traffic from the mainland slowed to a trickle, no more raw materials and only a fraction of the food that was required, and Admiral Nimitz congratulated them on their "phenomenal results."[96]

Between mid-June and mid-August, having disposed of the major cities, the B-29s of XXI Bomber Command turned their attention to the minor ones and struck sixty of them, ranging in population from thirty thousand to three hundred thousand. Rate of destruction averaged slightly more than 50 percent of the urbanized totals. By the end, about 178 square miles of built-up area were leveled and civilian casualties had reached 806,000, of whom 330,000 were dead. The fast carriers eliminated the Japanese Navy, the submarines eliminated the Japanese merchant marine and strangled their commerce, but the B-29s eliminated Japanese industry and Japanese willingness to resist.

By the time of the surrender, 64 percent of the Japanese people felt "personally unable to go on with the war," and the most important reason for this was the pre-atom-bomb air attacks, the effects of which pervaded all Japan as evacuees from the bombed cities spread their pessimism elsewhere and the American aircraft flew far and wide with hardly a challenge. Prince Konoye said: "Fundamentally the thing that brought about the determination to make peace was the prolonged bombing by the B-29s." Prime Minister Baron Kantaro Suzuki, who played a signal and hazardous part in bringing hostilities to a close, said that "merely on the basis of the B-29s alone I was convinced that Japan should sue for peace."[97]

Most vividly remembered by Father Bitter and the people of Tokyo for its eerie beauty was the night of April 15, named by the Japanese the Raid of the Dancing Flames. Father Bitter was returning to the university after trying to buy food on the black market for his starving priests, when the sirens sounded and from a radio in a nearby house he heard the words *su hentai,* "many squadrons." Father Bitter said: "Ach Gott, those words. They put blood into the veins of the people. Even the dead get up and walk when the radio says those words." He was ringing an alarm on the chapel bell when he heard people in the streets below shouting, *"Bikko! Bikko!"*

"They came in majesty," said Father Bitter, "like kings of the earth. The flak from the ground poured up toward them, but they held their course, proud and regal and haughty, as if they said 'I am too great for any man to do me harm.' I watched them as if I were in a trance." There were 303 of them, they were dropping 1,930 tons of incendiaries, and they were burning out 6 square miles of Tokyo, 3.6 miles of Kawasaki, and 1.5 of Yokohama. Father Bitter's university caught fire and he spent the night in fighting to save, by extravagant exertion, the monastery, the chapel, and the precious library. But what lingered in his mind was not the struggle against and victory over the flames, but what had happened when the first bomb landed.

"I heard the huzzle-huzzle of something falling," Father Bitter said, "and I ducked and crouched in a corner. It struck beside me, with a noise like a house falling, and I leaped a fine leap into the air. I must have shut my eyes, for when I opened them again I was in a world of fairyland. On every tree in the garden below, and on every tree so far as the eyes could see some sort of blazing oil had fallen, and it was dancing on the twigs and branches with a million little red and yellow candle-flames. On the ground in between the trees and in all the open spaces, white balls of fire had fallen, and these were bouncing like tennis balls, high in the air to the tree tops, and down and up again."

XXI Bomber Command came to deal Tokyo its death blow on the nights of May 23 and 25. The second of these was the most devastating of all in terms of square miles burned, and this one the Japanese called the Raid of the Leaping Tigers of Flame. Its target was an area north and west of the Imperial Palace, which was a convenient aiming point though the Americans were under strict orders to spare it and for the most part succeeded in doing so. This time there were no silver streamers but shining cylinders, and from each when it came to earth there grew a tree of fire that broke and flowered at the top into banners of flame which the Japanese said "bounded across the rooftops like leaping tigers."

Father Bitter was watching as the tongues of fire "seemed only to touch the roofs so lightly" and pass on, but then the house left behind would glow, envelop itself in arms of fire, and *foof!* it would vanish. He heard shouts of *Banzai! Banzai!* "Ach Gott," said Father Bitter. "It was Lucifer himself running across the heavens. It was a *Bikko,* a B-29 all in flames from wing tip to wing tip, from nose to tail. But even in dying it flies with majesty. It sweeps in a circle over the city, a circle that seems

ten minutes it takes to complete. And I think 'What courage!' " Marine
Lieutenant Harold Martin wrote that in an internment camp to the north,
a Belgian priest named Father Van Overmeeren watched the same plane
burning and gave absolution to its crew: "Under condition that it is valid,"
the proper qualification, "I absolve you of your sins in the name of the
Father, and of the Son, and of the Holy Ghost."[98]

The *Bikko* did not come in wrath to Tokyo again. The imperial city
was a city no more.

EPILOGUE

AN ESSENTIAL THEME OF THIS BOOK has been leadership, the intangible quality that empowers human beings to influence events through their influence on each other. It is instantly recognizable in the present yet arduous to reconstruct when the present has faded into the past. The record of what a leader did does not necessarily tell us what he (or she) was. Least of all does it convey their aura, the halo of intensity that caused their contemporaries to listen when they spoke. It is not definable in any other terms than that. Ulysses Grant is the prime exemplar; all observers of him agreed that everything about his personality was undistinguished except for the fact that in his presence men behaved differently. When Grant was there a current flowed. Roosevelt as President conveyed a similar electricity.

All of his principal military subordinates possessed the same quality in some measure, though they were utterly unlike one another in training and temperament, applied themselves to dissimilar challenges, and did so with highly individualistic styles: Marshall for making an army, King for reanimating a navy, Arnold for inventing an air force, MacArthur for symbolizing a cause, Eisenhower for forging an alliance, and so on. The suitability of each to his task makes him seem in hindsight almost indistinguishable from it, as though no other choice were imaginable. But these were *picked* men, either by conscious presidential design (Marshall, MacArthur, Nimitz) or by having survived Roosevelt's scrutiny (King, Arnold, Eisenhower) or by being suited to his intentions (Vandegrift, Stilwell, LeMay). Together the Joint Chiefs and their theater commanders gave a cohesion and decisiveness to the American high command that allowed the President when it suited him to maintain, as far as the conduct of the war was concerned, that they were in charge. This was not the case: He was in charge.

Leadership of the kind Roosevelt practiced required him to devote himself to detail while rising—or appearing to rise—above it. The cardinal rule is: *Pay attention!* Few other occupants of the office in our time can so attentively have minded the store, and been so minutely committed to being the master of any given situation. Yet the machinery of this was largely invisible to any but his immediate staff. The thousands of day-to-day decisions, minor as well as momentous, that make up the full texture of administration are precisely those that he went to the greatest lengths to conceal. He did not want anyone to know how he did it. "All the hard things were made to seem easy," wrote his onetime colleague Rexford Tugwell. "He left nothing to help us see how magnificent his achievement was. On the contrary, he put every possible obstacle in the way. . . . There are carloads of papers, records galore, correspondence in reams; and re-markably little of it is of much essential use . . . There is hardly a dependable record of a conversation in Franklin Roosevelt's whole life."

He enjoyed seclusion, and relished the atmosphere of secrecy with which wartime security requirements permitted him to surround his comings and goings. "Mr. Roosevelt," said White House correspondent Merriman Smith, "made a fetish of his privacy during the war." His departures for Hyde Park mainly took place from a basement railroad siding under the Bureau of Engraving and Printing on Fourteenth Street, where he would not be seen; Hyde Park phones were connected to the White House switchboard so that callers often did not know which location they had reached; White House staff accompanying him were put up not in Pough-keepsie hotels (as previously) but in the Vanderbilt mansion nearby, where the President insisted that "Hackie"—Louise Hachmeister, the chief switchboard operator of legendary competence—be quartered in Mrs. Vanderbilt's boudoir and that it be decorated with blue ribbons. He drove over in his Ford sedan equipped with hand controls to visit them.

Insofar as possible he protected the process by which he arrived at conclusions from unnecessary outside interference, and surely this is why so many who knew him found him so baffling. "His character was not only multiplex," wrote Robert Sherwood, "it was contradictory to a bewildering degree." His purposes were best served if their point of origin was obscure, located somewhere in what Sherwood called "his heavily forested interior."[1] The conversion of intention into action was too important to be exposed to manipulation by others. Yet one wonders if he was really so complicated as he managed to appear. Sherwood himself believed that Roosevelt would eventually be less of a mystery to his biographers than he was to his co-workers, and this is true. Out of complexity he achieved simplicity, and it is the simplicity that now comes through so clearly. The clues are scattered, but they can be reassembled.

Contradictions did not greatly matter so long as he was in command, and in command he always was, of every occasion, of every condition with which the presidency could confront him. The possibility that something might turn up he could not deal with seemed never to cross his mind. He greeted each day in anticipation of enjoying it to the full. His memory for particulars was unpredictable but wide-ranging; he would now and then astonish, as he did Patton at Casablanca or Kenneth Pendar at Marrakech, by the breadth and perception of his knowledge, even though equally often he might display a surprising gap of incomprehension, equally shrouded in self-assertiveness. But any omissions were more than re-deemed by his ability to tie it all together; his intelligence was adhesive and synoptic. The fact that things relate to other things was not merely a condition of his thinking but its guiding principle—and this enabled him not only to perceive the war as a whole but to convey that perception of it to his constituency, to provide the sense of purpose his nation and its people had to have if their generous energies were to be liberated.

President Roosevelt's style of national leadership was both warm and lofty, both intimate and distant. It has often been noted that by his voice alone, through the medium of radio, he was able to convince people in the millions that he was speaking directly to them (whether he would have done better or worse with television, the more mercilessly demanding medium, is a subject for reflection). For many of the young men and women in the armed services he was *the* President, the only one they had ever been consciously aware of. He was quite simply *there,* a part of their lives, and he exuded confidence, a sense of being on top of the world; the idea of anyone else being President did not naturally come to mind. That —and the buoyancy, the hat brim turned up in front, the cigarette holder at a jaunty angle—made him an unbeatable politician and a reassuring Commander in Chief. It contributed to the widespread sense of depriva-tion and emptiness when he died.

He was also an emblem of the war's objectives, the expression of a continuity between the humane impulses of the New Deal and those implied by a determination to defeat the dictatorships. He put great store by the Atlantic Charter—with its promise, only slightly qualified, of self-determination for all peoples—though it came from a British draft (by Sir Alexander Cadogan), was never issued as anything but a press release, and seems to have had little impact on public opinion. Of his own authorship, however, were the Four Freedoms—of speech, of worship, from want, and from fear—enunciated in his State of the Union message to Congress in January 1941, an address so impressive that the Third Inaugural following it was something of an anticlimax.

In the military, the Four Freedoms were not on every tongue; a survey of American soldiers in 1943 showed that over a third had never heard of them and only 13 percent could name three or all four. But the spirit got through. Another survey (in 1942) showed that 65 percent believed that they were fighting to "guarantee democratic liberties to

all peoples of the world." If a sense of elevated motive was not obligatory in World War II, it was permissible. After V-J Day, Bernard
DeVoto, stalled in a railway club car somewhere in Indiana, listened to
a group of soldiers arguing. One of them was defending the corruption
and storm-trooper brutalities of Huey Long on the grounds that he had
done a lot for Louisiana and that graft was just "business." Finally, one
of the others said, "Where you spent the war, Mac, didn't you hear
what it was about?"[2]

German interrogators of American prisoners in Tunisia were quick to
discover how little "motivated" many of the latter were in German terms
(reports of this were pleasing to Hitler). But Pearl Harbor had provided
the American soldiers, sailors, and airmen with all the motivation they
needed: We had been attacked, therefore we must reply in kind, and win.
Civilians thrust into uniform were skeptical about the military—its drill,
its makework, its pretensions and formalities—but by and large they put
up with it as an unpleasant necessity. If there was no extravagant zeal—
so conclude Samuel Stouffer and his collaborators in their monumental
study *The American Soldier*—neither was there defeatism. The mood was
one, with few illusions, of Let's get it over with. GI humor was sardonic,
and it did not spare the President.

I have a memory that could probably be duplicated by others a hundred times over. I was riding in the back of an army truck full of soldiers,
somewhere in the middle of England in the middle of the night, going
where or why I have long since forgotten, a moment suspended in time.
Mimicking the familiar accent, a voice out of the dark said, "I hate wa-
ahr." Pause. Then another voice: "Elean-or hates wa-ahr." Pause, and
another: "Fala hates wa-ahr." Finally, "Sistie and Buzzie [Roosevelt grand-
children] hate wa-ahr." It was not vindictive, it was mocking: a manifestation of the "black" humor common to many armies, which surfaced later
in Joseph Heller's *Catch-22*. Like the Marine on Guadalcanal shouting
"Blood for Franklin and Eleanor" at the Japanese, it reflected a view that
incorporated the presidential presence without being overawed or intimidated by it.

He was thus the right kind of leader for that kind of war. There was
a sense of fitness in his being at the head of armed forces that remained
essentially nonmilitaristic in nature, a sense that under his direction they
would not be given over to pomp and gold braid but put to practical
purposes, and purposes that he as leader of two liberal-democratic administrations had embodied. (One reason he won the 1940 election was
that voters, when surveyed and asked to assume that war was coming,
preferred Roosevelt to Willkie as a potential Commander in Chief by a
margin of 18 percent.[3])

For many Americans, as Studs Terkel has reminded us, it was "the
good war," though no war can possibly be called "good" that kills and

maims so many of the helpless, so many women and children, as did World War II. It was "good" only in that it gave many who participated in it a feeling of being lifted outside themselves, of performing at a higher pitch than ever before, of being fully engaged in a transcendent cause. In any large and complex organization, let alone a nation, the last of these convictions comes only from the top.

What did Roosevelt attempt and what part of it did he achieve? On Christmas morning, the President liked to read aloud to his children and grandchildren (there were thirteen of the latter) from Dickens's *Christmas Carol*. Perhaps we may imagine him then, on Christmas Eve of December 1941, visited in his sleep by the Ghost of Christmases to Come, who offers to be questioned.

"Will Hitler be beaten?"

"Hitler will die by his own hand in the ruins of Berlin. The Anglo-American and Russian armies will link arms across the fallen body of a devastated and defeated Germany."

"And Japan?"

"The emperor will surrender even before your soldiers reach his homeland. His cities will be in ashes, his industry wrecked, his navy sunk beneath the sea. The scientific experiment Einstein has commended to you will prove successful, and Japan will feel the searing heat of its incandescence, rivaling the sun's."

"Will the war be long and painful?"

"It will be won in less time than a presidential term. No enemy bomb will have fallen on continental American soil. American dead will be no more than a few hundredths of those in uniform."

"And afterward, will there be a new and better world?"

"There will. The ancient empires will crumble as you expect, the colonial peoples will be free, and they will join in the parliament of man you will have convened."

"Shall I live to see this?"

"That alone I may not tell you."

"Well enough. I rest content."

President Roosevelt accomplished in essentials what he set out to do, nearly everything he might have hoped for. Not only was his victory total but he left behind him a nation grown to a wealth and strength never before seen. Its gross national product had risen from $91 billion to $166 billion; its index of industrial production, from 100 to 196; its merchant marine, which stood in 1939 at 17 percent of the world total compared to Europe's 63 percent, now exceeded that of all European nations combined.[4] Its navy and strategic air forces were without peer, and it was the sole possessor of the Absolute Weapon. The United Nations were being formed under its aegis; their headquarters would be located—where else? —in its world capital, New York. Merely as a by-product of fighting the war, without initially intending to or fully understanding it, the United States had become the foremost international power.

To this amazing performance the President greatly contributed, but how much? The view could be advanced that the genie was already in the bottle and that all he had to do was pull the cork. An ability to win the war was latent in the America of 1939: in the oil fields, the bauxite mines, the Mesabi range, the pent-up waters of the Tennessee and the Columbia; in an unexploited industrial potential and an underemployed work force; in a Navy with a venerable sea-fighting tradition, in a Marine Corps teaching itself techniques no one else believed in, in an Air Corps yearning to stretch its wings, in the citizen Army dreaming in the mind of George C. Marshall. It was Roosevelt's first and foremost strength that he knew all this—out of seven years' having steered the ship of state, out of a lifetime's immersion in American politics and an absorptive curiosity about every aspect of American life, out of an instinct for optimism and action, out of the mixture of all these together that was singularly his—and he knew he could put his trust completely in this awareness.

If fault were to be found in his prewar conduct of affairs, it might be for his failure to mobilize the national energies sooner. A precious year was lost in 1940 that could have been spent in speeding up preparedness and bringing preponderant military force into existence earlier than 1944. He judged it impossible to do this and win a third-term election at the same time; he judged that the New Deal was still a sure thing politically while a war was not, and who is to gainsay him? Although by 1942 he was able to put the New Deal into temporary storage, in 1939 his one chance of preparing for war at all was to go on functioning not as a harbinger of conflict to come but as the New Deal's presiding genius. "By one of the most far-reaching and meaningful paradoxes in history," writes Eliot Janeway, "he survived the New Deal by continuing to symbolize it during the war years; and, because he symbolized the New Deal when there could be none, the New Deal in turn survived him."[5] It was, if you wish, an exercise in chameleon-like political expediency, but it was phenomenally effective.

Roosevelt stretched the boundaries of executive authority (as Lincoln did) and let precedents accumulate for single-handed presidential action that would later prove susceptible to abuse. The White House during his tenure had no ostentation and very little class (Ickes claimed never to have had a decent meal there and abominated the champagne), but he gave the office glamour and hence in part contributed to the "imperial presidency" that in subsequent years acquired ornamental trappings beyond reason or need; and he allowed the war to fortify the position of the corporate giants without whom he could not fight it (as Woodrow Wilson and Josephus Daniels might have warned him would happen). Both in the New Deal and above all in the war, he acculturated American businessmen to the idea that government need not be their enemy but can in fact undergird the economy, and in so doing he helped bring about that intermingling of industry with the military that has become so forbiddingly durable a feature of American life, threatening to impede a more peaceable quest after the public good.

Roosevelt thought of armaments as a drain on the nation. He had once calculated that over 90 percent of all national deficits from 1921 to 1939 were caused by payments for past, present, and future wars. "Don't forget that the elimination of costly armaments is still the keystone," he wrote to Adolph Berle, Jr., in connection with postwar planning, "for the security of all the little nations and for economic solvency."[6] Since he intended that the peace should be maintained by American armed force, he cannot have thought to eliminate it, but that he would have worked to *increase* it is difficult to conceive. The idea of an arms race, or of the United States as dispenser of munitions to the smaller nations, who then might use them on one another, would have been abhorrent to him.

When the war came, he could be criticized for doing the opposite of his temporizing on preparedness. He pushed the military into action before they were ready for it: in the Doolittle Raid with its unanticipated by-product at Midway, in the landings at Guadalcanal and on North Africa. By what close calls these enterprises avoided failure the reader will have seen, but their success produced the *annus mirabilis* of 1942 for American arms, the base on which everything that followed was built. It is my contention that this second only to the wisdom of his appointments to the major commands—was Roosevelt's most significant contribution to the war. It perceptibly shortened that war and lowered its cost in American lives. If ever Danton's precept *"de l'audace, encore de l'audace, et toujours de l'audace"* was proved in practice, it was so here. "I was too weak to defend," said Robert E. Lee, "so I attacked." It was not prudent, it was not even, except by generous interpretation, a "calculated" risk, but it was militarily and politically sound. It made the completeness of the victory certain far sooner than would otherwise have been.

Not to say that others of his strategies were without consequence. High among them in effect on the outcome would be his insistence on the full delivery of Lend-Lease to Russia. The President had to prod and prod to get this done. "Nothing would be worse than to have the Russians collapse . . . ," he told Secretary Morgenthau in March 1942. "I would rather lose New Zealand, Australia or anything else than have the Russians collapse." By midsummer, deliveries were beginning to catch up with promises and thereafter the outpouring continued, with interruptions caused mostly by the hazards of the Murmansk convoy run. "It is no exaggeration," wrote German General Siegfried Westphal, "to say that, without this massive American support, Russia would scarcely have been able to take the offensive in 1943." The ultimate tribute was paid by Stalin at Teheran when he said that without American production the war would have been lost.[7] It was Roosevelt who put the American arsenal behind Russia's otherwise strained and spartan resistance to the German onslaught.

Aid to Britain went without saying; it began early and was sustained throughout by the President, as it was in June 1940 over the opposition of Marshall and Stark, at a time when it mattered, and again in March 1943 over Marshall's and the Joint Chiefs' objections, at a time when the health and vitality of the British people still depended on it. Aid to Britain was necessary not only because the self-interest of the United States required the continued existence of Great Britain as a major power, but because Nazi Germany was the number one enemy and Britain was already clenched in mortal conflict with it. The principle of Atlantic-first was the fulcrum on which the success of American strategy rested; the choice was by no means Roosevelt's alone, but he was one of the first in it, eloquent and thoroughly understanding in its defense, and unfailing in its firm assertion against Marshall and King when in July 1942 they proposed to abandon it.

Aid to China was a fruitless goal, one that beckoned the President into futility. It is odd—and perhaps a salutary lesson—that the two countries he most conspicuously mishandled, China and France, were those he thought he knew best. (He was rescued from his dead-end French policy by Eisenhower and Churchill.) Roosevelt was pressured by American opinion to accord China in his public pronouncements a greater role in the war than he privately knew it could have. Perhaps he allowed his China "policy" to go astray because he believed it didn't matter very much. "There are forces there which neither you nor I understand," he wrote to a friend in 1935, "but at least I know that they are almost incomprehensible to us Westerners. Do not let so-called facts or figures lead you to believe that any Western civilization's action can ever affect the people of China very deeply."

He had a point (it is the same conclusion Barbara Tuchman comes to at the end of her book about Stilwell)[8] and it is a useful corrective to naïveté about the transplantation overseas of American attitudes. But it is also an excuse for inattention and inaction, and the theory that at least one intractable Chinese institution (the army) could not be changed by a Westerner was proved wrong by Stilwell at Ramgarh and on the Ledo Road. "By not doing, all things are done," say the Taoists. By Roosevelt's not doing, a number of things were done in China, many of them bad, but he saw that Chiang's demise would precipitate more problems foreign and domestic than he cared to think about, and that the Chinese Communists were by no means a preferable alternative. So he clung to his ideal of a coalition government under Chiang, an objective his successor (with the able assistance of George Marshall) continued vainly to strive after.

But on the whole, so well conceived were Roosevelt's strategies, so complete their realization, that he might not unfairly be regarded as a contributor to the overconfidence of the postwar years, to what Denis Brogan in 1952 called "the illusion of American omnipotence." The experience of a victorious global war fostered the belief that every American objective must be readily attainable, and encouraged that tendency to resort prematurely to pure power, to prefer military solutions over diplomatic ones, which in recent years George Kennan has spoken out against with his usual cogency and force.

Whether the President, had he lived out his fourth term, would have put a curb on this jingoistic excess we cannot tell, but there are grounds for guessing that he might have tried. He had too good a sense of history, of human fallibility. He knew that there are limits, that a nation cannot be roused to high endeavor (as Woodrow Wilson had taught him) more than once in a generation, and that "you cannot," as on one occasion he told a younger man, "just by shouting from the housetops, get what you want all the time."[9]

◆

A subtheme of this book has been the interaction of war with politics, which I trust the text has managed to demonstrate is more complex than is often assumed. Note first of all that the permeation of the GIs' war by a certain New Deal spirit did not necessarily extend to the high command. Roosevelt's lieutenants were not drawn from his political supporters. Only rarely—as in the case of Fiorello La Guardia, who was blocked by Stimson and Marshall—did he attempt to secure a military appointment for a political ally, or—as in the case of Joseph Alsop—grant an officer's commission to a friend over military reluctance.

What would now sound like a reactionary and racist undertone would not then have been considered offensive within the professional officer class. Admiral King was contemptuous of the democratic process and, at least in his early encounters with it, unable to hide his annoyance when testifying before Congress.[10] Lack of sympathy for the President's domestic policies finds an extreme in MacArthur, whose anti–New Deal bias was so notorious as to constitute a strength, a reason for Roosevelt to pacify him. Stilwell seems at times to lapse into a conventional Roosevelt-hating posture similar to his brother's, and various degrees of anti-liberal-Democratic belief can be found in Nimitz, Spruance, and—with his own characteristic extravagance—Patton. Men like Marshall, Bradley, and Vandegrift managed to achieve a common-man touch without in any way identifying themselves with its political manifestation.

But "politics" can cover too many meanings to be used as a simple, self-evident noun, and the military in their professional conduct were never as spotlessly apolitical as advertised. Eisenhower is the preeminent example of a general whose mission drew him into the political sphere whether he wished to be there or not, and he demonstrated such skills in the process that the momentum of it took him to the presidency. Moreover, neither MacArthur, Marshall, nor King hesitated to use political arguments with President Roosevelt when they felt the need: MacArthur for the Philippine campaign (we have a national obligation), Marshall for Overlord (the American people will not tolerate further diversions), and King for defending Australia and New Zealand (they are "white man's" countries); while in turn there were none of the President's "military" strategies, even though they made military sense, that did not also have a heavy political component.

Roosevelt concentrated American power on the destruction of the enemy before all else rather than on the creation of what others thought to be favorable postwar circumstances, and this has earned him criticism for a lack of geopolitical savvy, for lack of appreciation of war as a means to political ends. But it should be understood that postwar circumstances favorable to others did not therefore look favorable to him, and that a world cleared of the two towering adversaries was to him a slate wiped clean, a blank page of history on which he then could write. His political objectives did not end with total victory, as has been implied, but began there. His goal was a postwar world in which peace would be secured by a multinational organization dominated by the United States and enforced by American military power. It did not need the intricate prewar structure of "political" affiliations and alliances that had so obviously failed, now so obviously lay in ruins, and could now so obviously be superseded.

There was always a streak of the isolationist in Roosevelt. He was fully determined that the United States not be enmeshed in the restoration of colonial rule, and since this was inconsistent with maximum support for Britain, it produced much friction and some heated exchanges with Churchill on the subject of India. The anticolonialism of Americans in the Far East—especially in its sometimes feckless, knee-jerk form—raised many British hackles. (Christopher Thorne has written an admirable and copiously documented book about this, called *Allies of a Kind*.) But the President was equally standoffish about Europe. He liked to tease Churchill about France and Italy being Britain's postwar responsibility, yet behind this was a serious (and, as it turned out, unfounded) belief that after the war European countries would revert to their historic squabbles among themselves, from which the United States should remain aloof. And of course he hoped that American avoidance of involvement would prevent a falling-out among the victorious allies, especially Russia.

Too much has been made of Roosevelt's chatty way of saying that he thought he could "get along" with "Uncle Joe," as though this somehow epitomized an attitude of naive innocence about Soviet communism (Churchill's very similar words are forgotten) or a belief that Soviet-American understanding would guarantee the peace. Such was not the inner trend of Roosevelt's thoughts about Russia, and his record of hatred and contempt for the Soviet dictatorship, while not the equal of Churchill's, was a long and valid one (see, for example, his speech to the American Youth Congress of February 1940, which earned him boos and hisses from that organization's leftist members).

Examples of Russian ham-handed behavior were multiplying in the months before the President died and were beginning to anger him, as he indicated to Senator Arthur Vandenberg in March, just before the senator departed for the United Nations Conference in San Francisco.[11] Harriman, who saw more of both men than anyone else, thought that Stalin was afraid of Roosevelt, of his worldwide popularity,[12] and this would not be in conflict with Stalin's oft-quoted remark to Milovan Djilas that Churchill was the kind of man who would go into your pocket for a kopeck but that Roosevelt went only for the larger denominations. De Gaulle said that Roosevelt thought he could fool the Russians.

It need not come as a surprise, since there were good reasons for it, that Roosevelt was more cynical in exposing his view of the postwar world to de Gaulle than he seems to have been with anyone else. The President could recognize a realist when he saw one and he wished, after such a history of antipathy on his own part, to pay de Gaulle the compliment of confiding in him. De Gaulle spent five days in Washington during July 1944 and received the first-class VIP treatment. He was met at the door of the White House by the President personally. He held meetings with the Vice-President and several cabinet members, with the Joint Chiefs, and with the chairmen of the House and Senate committees on foreign affairs. "I observed with admiration the flood of confidence that sustained the American elite," he wrote, "and discovered how becoming optimism is to those who can afford it."[13] This was an astute observer.

The Roosevelt who revealed himself to de Gaulle was a very different man from the liberal internationalist we have come to expect. A streak of the World War I imperialist was still alive in him too, and shows itself here in a clear connection with military power in its rawest and most naked form. The President's vision of a postwar international organization, said de Gaulle, required "the installation of American forces on bases distributed throughout the world and of which certain ones would be located on French territory."

This was not just idle talk. In January 1945, Roosevelt blandly argued to the State Department that the United States should establish a base on Clipperton Island, off the coast of Mexico, inasmuch as title to Clipperton was disputed between France and Mexico (not true: Mexico acknowledged French sovereignty), and in "the utmost secrecy" he ordered that a weather station be set up there, guarded by American troops. The State Department disagreed, and the President's death ended the matter.[14]

"In his mind," wrote de Gaulle, "a four-power directory—America, Soviet Russia, China, and Great Britain—would settle the world's problems." An assembly of the other Allied nations would give "a democratic appearance" to the authority of the Big Four, and of that four, two (China and Britain) would be beholden to the United States and in need of its cooperation. The "horde of small and middle-size states" could be influenced by offers of American aid. "Roosevelt," de Gaulle wrote, "thus intended to lure the Soviets into a group that would contain their ambitions and in which America could unite its dependents." (So indeed did the United Nations operate during its early years, though no longer.) In any such global prospect as this, questions relating to Europe—which were uppermost in de Gaulle's thoughts—seemed to the President "quite subordinate." De Gaulle adds: "As was only human, his will to power clothed itself in idealism."

The "monumental conception" Roosevelt "dreamed of turning into reality" seemed to de Gaulle full of danger. It risked the loss of the Western civilization the war had been intended to save. He promptly answered the President by saying that the restoration of the West was what mattered, and that if this could be accomplished, the rest of the world would take it for an example.[15] How right he was! By comparison, Roosevelt's scheme seems flawed by an unwarranted assumption that American world hegemony would be harmless because its purposes were benign, and certainly there was some substance to the widespread European suspicion that Americans contemplated dismembering the colonial empires politically in order to take them over economically. De Gaulle's vision of a resurgent West was realized by Roosevelt's successors, by Truman and Acheson, and not by their predecessor's foresight.

But to picture Roosevelt as a closet imperialist goes too far. There is I think a better explanation in the book that saturated his thinking in his youth. The voice we are hearing here is that of Alfred Thayer Mahan, the Mahan whose *The Influence of Seapower upon History* so powerfully exposed the young Roosevelt to the proposition that by looking after its own self-interest, a great power (in Mahan's example, Britain between 1660 and 1783) can keep an unstable world in balance. The application of that stabilizing principle to a turbulent world of newly emerging nations would readily have commended itself to the mature Roosevelt.

For all his residual avoidance of compromising foreign entanglements, the President made clear to de Gaulle that he knew the war had ended American isolationism forever, and it had. His postwar military vision was tolerably prescient; his worldwide network of American bases has been in existence now for forty years. If one rewrites the Mahan formula to read "two" great powers, and makes allowance for the brutal domineering of its neighbors together with grandiose world ambitions by one, and the sometimes necessary, sometimes disastrous interventions in

Asia by the other, then so the balance has been (more or less) preserved. It is not peace, but neither is it the war that would consume both superpowers and all else besides, and the deployment of American force—including those bases that Roosevelt visualized—sustains it.

◆

Another subtheme of these pages—and a major one—has been the decline of British preeminence and the replacement of Churchill by Roosevelt at the head of the Grand Alliance. This is a subject that both British and American writers, for their several reasons, approach with diffidence; it is embarrassing for the one, and immodest for the other, of the two surviving partners from a tempestuous relationship. Once again de Gaulle is a student of the phenomenon who proves attentive, since it vitally affected his interests—indistinguishable as they were from those of France—and since he preferred Britain's competitive cunning to America's splendid indifference. He noted British discomfort at their country's diminished position almost as soon as the Americans began to arrive in England, and London streets to fill with "good-natured, bad-mannered" American soldiers. "The British," wrote de Gaulle of the spring of 1942, "did not conceal their gloom . . . at finding themselves dispossessed of the leading role they had played—and so deservingly!—for the last two years."[16]

The degree of cultivation—genuine, be it added—among educated Englishmen made it almost inevitable that they should perceive Americans as shallow and backward. "The fact is," wrote Harold Nicolson to his wife, Vita, in November 1943, "that the United States are the only really Tory power in the world. We are far more advanced. I despair sometimes about the Americans. They have no keel and veer in every wind."[17] To these British products of sound classical schooling the analogy was bound to occur between themselves as ancient Greeks and the Americans as early Romans, needing to be rescued from their clumsy muscularity and introduced to their obligations and duties as inheritors. This makes for good literary small talk but bad history, for the fact is (to echo Nicolson) that the Americans did have a keel, however immature and moralistic their opinions, and that the British were becoming disconnected from their own moorings in a sequence of events that American bumptiousness could neither account for nor arrest.

With the best will in the world the Americans could not have restored to British prestige those sources of its strength that were still the interior landscape of so many British minds, in which centuries of victory and conquest were not to be erased from memory overnight. The military moves that the masters of empire longed to make as the war wound down (and that the American "keel" resisted) were rooted in prewar perceptions that now exposed themselves as delusory. A military presence on the

Danube was a will-o'-the-wisp. In Germany, the importunate Montgomery could have been allowed to ride into Berlin on a white horse and the history of the ensuing years would not have been changed by so much as a comma. To exert "leadership over the countries of Western Europe" (which Sir Alexander Cadogan said was an "accurate assessment" of British aims) was beyond their reach. In the Mediterranean, of which so much had been made, Britain ended the war with more prominence than power, and the power was leaching away. Less than two years would pass before the Foreign Office, on February 21, 1947, informed the State Department that His Majesty's Government could no longer carry the load of its obligations in Greece and Turkey, and the transfer of responsibility that had been implied became explicit.

American pretensions to a greater nobility of purpose were nonetheless aggravating to bear. Observing Roosevelt and Churchill at Cairo, Cadogan noted that the latter "had to endure much with a good grace, including explanations from the President of other powers' higher morality." What occasioned this sour aside was Roosevelt's remarking to Churchill that national acquisitive instincts for territory as such were out of date, that a "new period has opened in the world's history and you [Churchill] will have to adjust yourself to it."[18] One may agree that the President's anticolonialism smacked of the doctrinaire, that his worldview was not inherently superior to Churchill's in depth or subtlety, or that the British imperial presence in the world had done much good that Americans either knew nothing about or chose to disparage. But—and it is a necessary but—Roosevelt was essentially right. Churchill's world could not be prolonged, not by him, not by the President. Whatever else one says of Roosevelt's views, they proved to have a better fit with circumstance, to be in better tune with actuality, and to be open-ended toward a future of human possibilities thus far unattainable but now on the edge of realization. The "revolution of rising expectations," as it came to be called, was one that the President could clearly see coming.

Yet the solidity of the Anglo-American compact surpasses that of any alliance known to history. There was continuous tension and disagreement, especially in the Far East, where conflicting national purposes could not be reconciled, but never on either side was the possibility allowed to arise of a break that would have imperiled the solemn march together, side by side, of their divergent interests. The vigorous arguments merely brought their leaders closer together. This we owe to the men they were, but above all to the principals, those two majestic egos who chose to subordinate vanity and short-term advantage to a long-term unity. One has only to compare the Grand Alliance with the Fascist Axis, "the Pact of Steel," which presented a facade of shared ideology and protestations of undying loyalty, but never achieved a common strategy and crumbled at the touch of adversity. The

Grand Alliance was in contrast unequivocally grand.

◆

Another subtheme has been flexibility, the same openness of mind that Roosevelt routinely showed, in its relation to the readiness with which all three of the services managed to adapt themselves in midwar to conditions they had not prepared for: the air force by changing its targets and by accepting the need for fighter escort, the Navy by making the aircraft carrier the major weapon, the Army by absorbing the fighter-bomber into the tank-artillery-infantry team. The first and third, and to some extent the second, were advanced from the bottom up rather than the top down, out of reactions to reality rather than theory. (All three also had in common the element of air power, the availability of which had its origins in Roosevelt's prewar realization that if war came it would be an air war.) This willingness to innovate, in the experimental mode of General Kenney's "Hell, let's try it," is too diffuse a characteristic to have a single source, but surely some influence on it can be seen in the examples the New Deal provided—the way the CCCs did for George Marshall, for instance, as an "antidote for mental stagnation"—and the presence of the Great Pragmatist himself in the presidency.

His armed services showed a remarkable capacity to learn from experience, especially about how to employ the components of amphibious warfare that in the beginning nobody knew how to coordinate properly. At Guadalcanal, command arrangements were confused and missions unclear, reconnaissance was ineffective and naval protection withdrawn at a crucial moment; unloading of supplies was incomplete, air power and reinforcement slow in being brought forward, and organized logistic backup at the start nonexistent. When the Solomons campaign ended, with the invasion of Bougainville little more than a year later, a degree of teamwork and efficiency had been reached that was almost reflexive.

The plan for Bougainville (under Halsey) was hazardous but continually revised in the light of emergent intelligence. All the Japanese airfields on the island were bombed out of commission beforehand and kept that way. A task force of submarines was assigned to screen the Bismarck Archipelago and another of carriers to raid nearby Japanese bases. Land-based air provided reconnaissance and support for the landings (under Vandegrift, now a lieutenant general and corps commander), which went off smartly, with lighter casualties than expected (78 killed, 104 wounded). By the end of the first day, a division was ashore and by the end of the second, all the cargo ships had been unloaded. A week later, the substantial buildup began to establish an airfield ringed by a perimeter on the model Vandegrift had invented at Guadalcanal.[19]

"Flexibility" is what Roosevelt liked in his loose structuring of the

Joint Chiefs of Staff, and in them he had found an effectively functioning instrument, primarily because Marshall and King pragmatically worked out their differences (with the exception of that over unified command in the Pacific, where Marshall was bound by the President's policy of keeping MacArthur inside the administration's camp and King chose not to make an issue of it). Otherwise each supported the other in the other's theater of primary concern. The President's advocacy of air power (and the need to parallel Britain's independent air force) brought Arnold to the Joint Chiefs, and enabled the Air Forces to operate independently in virtually everything but name. The system of theater commanders, and a principle of granting them flexible responsibilities, linked the JCS to the armed forces in action. Leahy, in turn, linked the Joint Chiefs to the President. During the latter half of 1942 and most of 1943, Roosevelt's first appointment of the day was always with Leahy, the JCS connection. As for the Combined Chiefs, John Gunther once asked a "high authority" how they worked in practice and received the answer: "In essence the Combined Chiefs are the White House."[20]

Then there is the aspect of flexibility called timing, where the President's intercessions were decisive. The Mediterranean strategy was properly speaking Brooke's, but Roosevelt, too, had a Mediterranean strategy (as he showed at Quebec), unlike the Joint Chiefs' and very like Brooke's. Kent Roberts Greenfield believed that Roosevelt saw "sooner and more clearly than his military advisers" that the determining fact about the cross-Channel invasion was the date when it took place, that we should make "maximum and aggressive use of what we had [i.e., in the Mediterranean] until we had accumulated enough power to deliver a knock-out punch [i.e., in France]."[21] Since this precluded Overlord in 1943, it made possible King's acceleration of an advance in the Pacific far faster than either the British or the U.S. Army would have liked. The President did not have to argue for this; all he had to do was allow it—which he did. The notion that the United States could successfully fight wars in both hemispheres at once, or that the two wars could come to an end within months of one another, would have seemed outlandish in 1942. It was done, and it was the President's setting of the pace that made it doable.

The theme of flexibility should not be let to obscure that of constancy. The means might vary, the ends did not. For a man who made so much of his determination to keep his options open, to take advantage of opportunities as they arose, and to sabotage any other decision-making machinery than his own, President Roosevelt was almost rigidly consistent in his overall geopolitical strategies for waging the war: in his support of Britain, Russia, and China; in his insistence on crushing Germany first; in his resolve on unconditional surrender by all his enemies; in his intent to establish a postwar "united nations" directed by a firm (which is to say, U.S.-controlled) union of the major victors. Nothing was allowed to get in the way of these aims, and military objectives were subordinated to—or, fortunately, coincided with—their attainment. It was a package program, in which war and politics were united to a degree rarely seen, and he stuck with it from start to finish.

Second only to the President's encompassing perspective was his concentrated focus on the war's *point d'appui,* on the one sector of the globe he could not afford to lose, the North Atlantic. His prompt and continued efforts to acquire bases that dominated it, to push the Navy into fighting there, testify to his acute perception of its overriding significance. In May 1941, eight months before Pearl Harbor, we find him reading a lesson in strategy to Churchill: "My previous message," Roosevelt writes, "merely meant to indicate that should the Mediterranean prove in the last analysis to be an impossible battleground [not admissible by Churchill] that I do not feel that such fact alone would mean the defeat of our mutual interests. I say this *because I believe the outcome of this struggle is going to be decided in the Atlantic* and unless Hitler can win there he cannot win anywhere in the world in the end" (emphasis added). Hence also Roosevelt's pressure for landings in the Atlantic islands, and on the African Atlantic coast, long before these were in any way feasible.

The more the American war is looked at in its entirety, the more fully the conclusion emerges that the invasion of North Africa was the pivotal move. None was more risky, none more extemporized, or none more unquestionably made at the President's demand over the opposition of his service chiefs. It put the Axis powers on the defensive; by opening the Mediterranean theater, it made possible the capture of 275,000 Axis troops in Tunisia and in Italy the diversion of thirty divisions away from France and Germany; by postponing Overlord a year, it ensured that operation's success and gave King his breathing space in the Pacific. That Roosevelt should have had all these benefits precisely in view ahead of time is asking too much, but it was his decision, it was the right one, and he sensed its criticality at the time. "I cannot help feeling," he wrote Churchill a few days after he had made it, "that the past week represented a turning point in the whole war."[22] Conversely, failing to prevent the North African landings was among the worst of Hitler's blunders.

Hitler and Roosevelt were the great antagonists; Roosevelt knew this from the beginning, Hitler not until too late. When the President sent Hopkins to London in early 1941, and Churchill tried to cultivate the arch–New Dealer by making one of his best welfare-of-the-people speeches ("he's more left than you are," Hopkins told Roosevelt later), Hopkins was said to have cut the Prime Minister short by saying, "The President didn't send me here to listen to any of that stuff. All he wants to know is: how do you propose to beat that son of a bitch in Berlin?" Hitler in the delirium of his defeat paid Roosevelt the compliment of calling him "the greatest war criminal of all times," but in the early days, when he should have known better, he brushed Roosevelt off as a "tortuous, pet-tifogging Jew" and Mrs. Roosevelt as someone whose "completely negroid appearance . . . showed that she too was half-caste."[23] If ever there was "the greatest war criminal of all times" it was Hitler, and it was Roosevelt above all others who accomplished his downfall, who brought him down to his tawdry end.

◆

A word must be added here about the war between Germany and Russia. In violence, in magnitude, and in human cost it dwarfs the rest of World War II; it was a battle of titans, a struggle that has seared the minds of the Russians who experienced it, and awed the Western historians who attempt to plot its course. More was at issue there than elsewhere, more was saved by resolute Russian endurance than could have been won (up to the Normandy invasion) by the Anglo-Americans in all their combined endeavors. A statement is apocryphally attributed to Stalin that the war was won by British brains, American brawn, and Russian blood (surely the Russian language would not produce that alliteration), and it rings true. Without the Russian absorption of the Wehrmacht in the east, the Anglo-Americans could never have overcome it at so little cost in the west. At the same time, however, a Russian offensive—after the Battle of Kursk had broken the backbone of the panzers in 1943—*might* have reached and reduced the Reich, but it could not have done so if the threat of war in the west had been absent. Without Roosevelt—that is, without a "second front" and Lend-Lease—a Russian offensive would (on German and Russian testimony alike) for some years have been unlikely or unachievable.

The Anglo-American European campaign of 1944–45, which still prompts admiration for its economy and decisiveness, does not find the President conspicuously standing forth as its author or directing its execution, but his influence is apparent in the determination that made it happen, the choice of its commander, and the shape imposed on it by sustaining the latter's plan for southern France and rejecting a Balkan alternative. The concentration of Allied armies in Western Europe that came about as a result proved to have been an essential precondition of victory. The fact that by this time the President is becoming a figure in the military background should not conceal his position as the European war's strategist in the word's best meaning, as the one who sees to it that power is brought to bear at a time and place most favorable to the tactical exploitation of its superiority. A straight line, as he told Churchill, was still the shortest distance between two points. The extent of Roosevelt's control is evidenced by the complaints of those who wished to control the campaign themselves, and discovered that they were unable to do so.

The planning of the Pacific war was a creature of circumstance that did not, except for its opening and closing phases, find Roosevelt calling every signal, inasmuch as the predominant element in it was that advance across the central Pacific the Navy had been thinking about for years. The thinking had been sound, and once again the accomplishment is impressive for its boldness and skill. King was right to insist that the Marianas were the key, though they would have been so for him even if Arnold had not wanted them as an air base, and though King was wrong to continue maintaining for so long that the final objective was the China coast. By early on encouraging King in the Solomons, and by allowing MacArthur to have his place in history, the President permitted the almost accidental evolution of the double-axis, "whipsaw" strategy that King favored and that proved to work so well. But should it have led to the Philippines in the form it did? If the Battle of Leyte Gulf was the object, then yes. If the sensible and nondestructive liberation of the Philippine Islands was the object, then no. The Philippine land campaign in its totality can be characterized as wasteful and inept, and Roosevelt went along with it for reasons that reflect great credit on him not as a strategist but only as a politician.

Lastly, the President's long-standing desire to have Japan bombed from the air bore its grim fruit in the Marianas with the B-29s and the Fire Raids. No application of military force ever achieved so total and so horrible a success. In the shadow of the cloud over Hiroshima the Fire Raids have tended to fade in memory, yet they were far more destructive, more deliberately calculated, more primitive in conception and more intimate (if the word will serve) in the interaction between weapon and victim. "Guilt" is a term that must be used with restraint in contemplating the evils wrought by war, so long as nations continue (as they still do continue) to believe that war is an appropriate instrument of policy. Tragic sorrow at *all* of war's gutting waste is more appropriate, and within that "all" the Fire Raids must not be forgotten. "Offhand it always seemed like a sort of sick way of doing things," as the young Bert Stiles wrote of strategic bombing before he died, "and when the day turns up that we can start using other methods, I'm going to be one of the gladder people in the world."

Necessarily, there has been little emphasis in these pages on the domestic aspects of Roosevelt's wartime presidency, despite their evident impact on the creation and deployment of military power. The national base had to be secure. Industry had to be mobilized, priorities set, manpower allocated, rationing instituted, prices held down, labor relations harmonized, the machinery of government kept agile and alert, and all this against a political background in which a shared goal of victory had by no means eliminated criticism and dissent. The publication of Isaiah Berlin's literate and perceptive dispatches from Washington to the British Foreign Office has served as a reminder of how numerous and troublesome Roosevelt's enemies still were. In nonmilitary and economic affairs, a potential coalition of Republicans and anti-administration (mostly southern) Democrats threatened the President's authority in Congress and often seemed less intent on prosecuting the war than in using it as an opportunity for dismantling the New Deal.

Especially in its early stages, before American fighting men became heavily involved, the war was not universally popular and complaints that it was being mismanaged were common. In May 1942, the Office of Facts and Figures estimated that 17 million Americans (out of 130 million) were opposed to it in one way or another, and that 30 percent would be willing to talk peace with the German Army if it would get rid of Hitler.[24] There was a somber side—racial tensions persisted; violence broke out in Detroit, Los Angeles, Newark—and an illusory one: The picture of the war presented by advertising, the media, and sometimes government itself struck the men in uniform as boastful and false, its overtones of piety and assumed American superiority as grotesquely in contrast with the boredom of military life and with the viciousness and risk of combat. The war was just as revealing of American vices as it was of virtues. But the home front held, and Roosevelt held it all together in a balance that was steady even when it looked precarious.

Throughout, the President generated around himself an atmosphere of calm; his office was well organized and ran smoothly. "Although hell might be popping all around Roosevelt," wrote Sherwood, "it was rarely audible in his immediate presence, where tranquility prevailed." Hopkins was struck by the contrast with Churchill: "the guns were continually blazing in his [Churchill's] conversation"; Sherwood said, "wherever he was, there was the battlefront." But to read through the President's wartime press conferences you would hardly know that battles were being fought, victories lost and won; the reporters were not prepared to ask military questions and there was naturally much that Roosevelt could not have told them had they done so. From this restraint and absence of bravado on the President's part comes much of the misapprehension that he refrained from involving himself in the war's direction. He marched to his own internal rhythms. In the midst of everything else, he remained town historian of Hyde Park and found time to carry on a correspondence with a lady neighbor in Poughkeepsie about the pressing affairs of the Dutchess County Historical Society.[25]

Of course, he made military mistakes. It took him time to appreciate the fact that air power does not consist merely of aircraft but also of trained pilots, bases, and maintenance crews; and he seemed not always to be completely clear in his mind as to how various types of bomber differed from one another in range and load. He had no developed feel for the Army and how it worked, as he did for the Navy, and he therefore at first gravely underestimated how long it takes to produce trained ground-force units and how many of them would eventually be required (he was saved from this only by Marshall). As for the Navy, he shared some of *its* mistakes—for one, on the supposed lack of need for landing craft—and added another of his own in a misplaced enthusiasm for the "Sea Otter," a small, shallow-draft, gasoline-driven freighter intended to be mass-produced, which proved to be impractically noisy and un-seaworthy.[26] And also, until far too late, he was profoundly wrong about the military potential of China, both as a combatant and as a base for the B-29s.

One way of judging Roosevelt as Commander in Chief is to compare him with that ultimate standard in presidential military performance which is Abraham Lincoln. Their situations were vastly different: Lincoln dealt with his commanders seriatim, as one by one he had to recognize their inadequacies and replace them. He possessed no general staff but had to invent it in his own person. The image of him in the War Department telegraph office—looking into space and forming the words with his lips, as he wrote some of the most thoughtful and concise of military instructions—is not one in which Roosevelt can be imagined in his stead. But then, Lincoln was a natural, a born military mind, one of the finest his country has produced.

Here was this rustic country lawyer, with no military education, no experience with operations in the field, no knowledge of the theaters of war except through maps, and no prior acquaintance with his army and navy leaders. Yet he instituted the blockade, kept the border states in line, mobilized the northern armies, read each day's dispatches, and gave both overall and specific guidance to the campaigns. His messages to McClellan were lessons in strategy and tactics McClellan was too self-infatuated to heed. Lincoln's youth in the central valley prepared him to accept (when Winfield Scott suggested them) the possibilities it offered for isolating the Confederacy. Lincoln saw as his generals failed to that the objective was not Richmond but Lee's army, and when he found in Grant a man who understood this he put him in charge and left him largely alone. Had he lived, the peace would have been more magnanimous.

Roosevelt was no Lincoln, if one is looking for Lincoln's penetrating grip on what was wrong, say, with Meade's failure to pursue Lee after Gettysburg. Roosevelt did not have to concern himself at that level; he did have a general staff, and one he could rely on; he could get some elements wrong and the general propositions right, as he did at Guadalcanal, the campaign he especially cared about, where he wrongly thought that we had overreached ourselves but rightly saw that the point of it was attrition, wearing the enemy down.

Roosevelt did not critique his field commanders in particulars, as Lincoln did. Again, he did not have to; in Marshall, King, and Arnold—as he told Hopkins—he had men "who really like to fight" and would see to it, without having to be needled by the President, that fighting was done. Roosevelt did not have Lincoln's tactical gift, but he had something comparable to it in his ability to identify the essentials and place them in a balanced relationship with each other. Measured against Lincoln, Roosevelt had a mind of similar strategic capacity, and put it to work with similar effect. Churchill told Moran that Roosevelt was "the most skillful strategist of them all." Better than Marshall? Moran asked. "Yes, better than Marshall."[27]

Trying to follow the President's thought processes could be a wearing task. Stimson, in a memorable phrase, said it was "very much like chasing a vagrant beam of sunshine around an empty room." John Gunther once asked Mrs. Roosevelt, "Just how does the President *think?*" She replied, "My dear Mr. Gunther, the President never 'thinks'! He *decides.*"[28] Roosevelt was undeniably forceful, able, and intelligent to a degree, but his was not a syllogistic or logical mind, given to sequential reasoning, not a linear mind in McLuhan terms but a mosaic one, suited for the discerning of patterns and syntheses, "for knowing all kinds of diverse things at once in a flash," at which, as Secretary of Labor Frances Perkins put it, he could be "almost clairvoyant."

Madame Perkins's biographer George Martin believed that while this talent "would be useful in any period . . . its application is particularly obvious in wartime." Martin thought that "the approach of war gave [Roosevelt] an extraordinary opportunity to display it," and that the war itself was an arena in which he could give it full rein; "as a wartime leader in the four years from 1940 through 1943, mobilizing the country for war and leading it to a point where victory was assured, he was brilliant. *There were evidently many, many times when he truly could see it all:* men, guns, ships, food, the enemy, the Allies, the war aims and finally the peace" (emphasis added).[29]

The verdict is compelling: More than any other man, he ran the war, and ran it well enough to deserve the gratitude of his countrymen then and since, and of those from whom he lifted the yoke of the Axis tyrannies. His conduct as Commander in Chief, on a par with or perhaps even above that as President in peacetime, bears the mark of greatness.

◆

On October 11, 1939, the President was called upon by Alexander Sachs, a financier he had relied on in the early New Deal days, who read aloud to him a letter signed by Albert Einstein, calling his attention to recent developments in physics that might lead to a weapon of enormous destructive power. The letter had been drafted by Sachs and by two Hungarian refugee scientists, Eugene Wigner and Leo Szilard, who had persuaded Einstein to sign it. Szilard was deeply disturbed at reports from Europe which indicated that the Germans were already pursuing the "possibility in principle of the release of a chain-reaction in uranium," followed by the menacing news that they had forbidden further export of

EPILOGUE

645

uranium ore from Joachimsthal in Czechoslovakia, one of the two principal sources of supply. The other source was the Belgian Congo. Szilard wanted the United States to make certain that the Congo ore was kept beyond Hitler's reach.[30]

Roosevelt's concern was not at first aroused; he thought government involvement in a scientific matter like this would be premature. Sachs, despairing, managed to arrange an invitation to breakfast the next day and spent the evening trying to think of a way to get the President's attention. He found it. At breakfast, he told Roosevelt about Napoleon's rejection of Robert Fulton when Fulton tried to interest the emperor in the steamboat, so that England was saved only by the shortsightedness of her adversary. The President was silent for a few moments, and then said, "Alex, what you are after is to see that the Nazis don't blow us up." He sent for General Watson. "Pa," said Roosevelt, "this requires action."[31]

Many British and American scientists had been thinking along similar lines about the potentialities of atomic power, but the action the President would eventually ask for was not instantly forthcoming. He did soon appoint an Advisory Committee on Uranium, chaired by Dr. Lyman J. Briggs, to investigate the separation of uranium isotopes. In June 1940, the committee was placed under the newly formed National Defense Research Committee, headed by Dr. Vannevar Bush, and in April 1941, Bush asked the National Academy of Sciences to appoint a committee of prominent physicists to review progress thus far. Its chairman, Dr. Arthur Holly Compton, reported favorably to Bush, urging "a strongly intensified effort" and closer contact with British scientists, who were at that time further ahead than the Americans. On October 11, Roosevelt sent Churchill a letter suggesting that British and American efforts be jointly conducted.[32]

By November 1941, Vannevar Bush had in hand both a British report and the final report of the Academy committee under Compton, and on November 27 he transmitted the latter to President Roosevelt with his comments. This time, writes Compton, "action was immediate." (He was among the American scientists who had been most intent on something being done.) Bush, Briggs, Compton, President James B. Conant of Harvard, and Ernest O. Lawrence (a founding father of atomic research) were asked to meet with the President. He told them to go ahead, to do everything possible to find out whether atomic bombs were feasible, and to report back within six months. If their report was favorable, they should expect all the resources the nation could spare to be made available. Meanwhile he would commit several millions of dollars to them out of a fund Congress had put at his disposal. The date was December 6, 1941.

Compton had never met or even seen Roosevelt before, and had never voted for him. "Yet," Compton wrote later, "as I see it, we were rarely fortunate to have at the helm during these critical years a man of

ACKNOWLEDGMENTS

Grateful acknowledgment is made for encouragement and fruitful advice to Arthur M. Schlesinger, Jr., and to William R. Emerson of the Franklin D. Roosevelt Library in Hyde Park; to the Guggenheim and Sybil and William T. Golden Foundations; to John Jacob of the George C. Marshall Research Library in Lexington; Edward J. Boone of the MacArthur Memorial in Norfolk; Evelyn M. Cherpak of the Naval War College in Newport; John E. Taylor of the National Archives in Washington; Correlli Barnett of the Churchill College Archives Center in Cambridge; Michael Reeper of the Public Record Office in Kew; and Patricia Methuen of the Liddall Hart Center for Military Affairs, Kings College, in London; also for help of every kind to Simon Michael Bessie, George Brockway, Matt Clark, Clifton Daniel, Arthur T. Hadley, Lewis Iselin, Jim Jones, Wilson Kierstead, Dan Lacy, Russell Lynes, Dan M. Martin, Drew Middleton, Robert Moskin, James Parton, Forrest C. Pogue, John M. Russell, and Grant Sanger, with a final bow to the shade of Fletcher Pratt.

E. L.

NOTES

PROLOGUE

1. Watson, *Chief of Staff: Prewar Plans and Preparations,* pp. 5–6.
2. Neustadt, *Presidential Power,* pp. 154–5.
3. In Janeway, *The Struggle for Survival,* p. 58.
4. *Public Papers and Addresses (1941),* pp. 522–30.
5. Perkins, *The Roosevelt I Knew,* p. 380.
6. Lee to John B. Hood, May 21, 1863; in Freeman, *Lee's Lieutenants,* vol. I, p. xvii.
7. Greenfield, *American Strategy in World War II,* p. 1.
8. *Public Papers and Addresses (1942),* pp. 235–7. Both Wheless and Wassell were later invited to the White House to meet the President (White House Usher's Diary, MS, FDR Library). Wheless's own account of the Legaspi mission is quoted in Sheean, *Between the Thunder and the Sun,* pp. 411–13; in Mansfield, *Vision: A Saga of the Sky,* p. 199.
9. See Riefler, "Our Economic Contribution to Victory," in *Foreign Affairs,* October 1947, pp. 90–103.
10. See Fuller, *The Conduct of War,* Ch. II, "The Rebirth of Unlimited War."
11. In Pogue, *Ordeal and Hope,* p. 330.
12. Bureau of the Budget, *The United States at War,* Ch. 16, "Assaying the Record," pp. 510–19; and Greenfield, op. cit., pp. 11–12.
13. Klein, *Germany's Economic Preparation for War,* pp. 76–205.
14. Even George Kennan, surely of all Americans one of the least misled by wartime passions, said in an internal State Department memorandum in 1943: "Let the impact of defeat, therefore, be as tremendous as possible. Let the immediate impressions of failure be so vivid and unforgettable that they become a part of the national consciousness of the German people for all time" (Kennan, *Memoirs 1925–1950,* p. 178); he went on to disparage the concept of "punishment."
15. Strongly argued examples are in Baldwin, *Great Mistakes of the War,* pp. 1–4, 8–9, 44–5, 58, 107–8.

16. In Pogue, "The Wartime Chiefs of Staff and the President," pp. 69–70, in *Soldiers and Statesmen.*
17. Notes made after dinner with the President, January 24, 1942; in Sherwood, *Roosevelt and Hopkins,* p. 492.
18. By Gaddis Smith, during a military history symposium at the Air Force Academy in 1970; in *Soldiers and Statesmen,* pp. 100–1.
19. In Pogue, loc. cit.; in Matloff and Snell, *Strategic Planning for Coalition Warfare 1941–42,* p. 52.
20. In Morison, *Turmoil and Tradition,* p. 601; Hull, *Memoirs,* p. 1111.
21. Huntington, *The Soldier and the State,* p. 315; Vagts, *Militarism,* p. 475; Churchill, *Closing the Ring,* p. 346; Ehrman, *Grand Strategy,* Vol. VI, p. 343; Bryant, *Turn of the Tide,* p. 335; Harrison, *Cross-Channel Attack,* p. 92; Sherwood, op. cit., p. 446.
22. In Sherwood, op. cit., p. 948; Leahy, *I Was There,* pp. 103–6.
23. In Thompson, *Generalissimo Churchill,* p. 93; see also ibid., pp. 90ff., and Lewin, *Churchill as Warlord,* pp. 23ff.
24. Greenfield, op. cit., pp. 53, 80–4.
25. In Middleton, *Crossroads of Modern Warfare,* p. 170.
26. Matloff, "Mr. Roosevelt's Three Wars: FDR as War Leader," p. 3, Harmon Memorial Lecture 6, Air Force Academy.
27. Davis, "Origin of the Joint Chiefs of Staff," p. 40, MS, FDR Library.
28. See Emerson, "F.D.R.," pp. 136–9, in May, ed., *The Ultimate Decision: The President as Commander in Chief.*
29. In Bryant, op. cit., p. 234.
30. Moran, *Churchill Taken from the Diaries of Lord Moran,* pp. 21–2.
31. *Foreign Relations of the United States,* Conferences at Washington and Casablanca, p. 207; see also Davis, loc. cit., Ch. V, and Sherwood, op. cit., pp. 471–2.
32. Moran, op. cit., p. 23.
33. Davis, loc. cit., pp. 256, 191; Cline, *Washington Command Post: The Operations Division,* p. 101n.
34. Davis, loc. cit., p. 237.
35. Ibid., p. 254.
36. *Complete Press Conferences,* Vol. 20, p. 19.
37. Davis, loc. cit., p. 255; in Buell, *Master of Sea Power,* p. 186.
38. Churchill, *The Grand Alliance,* p. 663.
39. May, op. cit., pp. 94, 117; Chandler, "Lincoln and the Telegrapher," *American Heritage,* April 1961.
40. Tully, *F.D.R. My Boss,* p. 262.
41. Elsey, "The Map Room Papers of President Franklin D. Roosevelt 1941–45," MS, in Elsey Papers, Truman Library.
42. In Rosenman, *Working with Roosevelt,* p. 353.
43. McCrea, Memoir and Oral History, MSS, FDR Library.
44. According to Admiral Morison, Rodman was a man of "powerful voice and commanding personality," who in 1903, as a lieutenant commander, single-handedly claimed the island of Midway for the United States; Morison, *Coral Sea, Midway, and Submarine Actions,* p. 71.

45. McCrea also remembered, though he did not remind the President at the time, that he had helped Roosevelt out of a stalled elevator at the Stewart Hotel in San Francisco during the Democratic convention of 1920, where Roosevelt had been nominated for vice-president; McCrea MS.
46. Hassett, *Off the Record with F.D.R.*, pp. 36, 143, 175, 176, 277; McCrea MS.
47. In Buell, *Master of Sea Power*, p. 101.
48. Roosevelt, *My Parents: A Differing View*, p. 166; Gunther, *Roosevelt in Retrospect*, p. 45.
49. King and Whitehill, *A Naval Record*, p. 412; Buell, op. cit., p. 187.
50. In Bryant, op. cit., p. 242n.
51. In Pogue, *Ordeal and Hope*, p. 26.
52. Stimson, Diary, March 5, 1941, in Stimson and Bundy, *On Active Service*, Vol. II, p. 334.
53. Rosenman, op. cit., p. 542.
54. Roosevelt, ed., *F.D.R. His Personal Letters 1928–45*, Vol. II, p. 1343.
55. Daniels, *The Wilson Era: Years of Peace, 1910–17*, pp. 124, 126, 127.
56. In Freidel, *Franklin D. Roosevelt: The Apprenticeship*, p. 157; Daniels, op. cit., pp. 127, 129.
57. Tugwell, *The Democratic Roosevelt*, pp. 99, 105.
58. Freidel, op. cit., p. 312; Albion and Connery, *Forrestal and the Navy*, p. 161.
59. In Eccles, *Beckoning Frontiers*, p. 336.
60. Halsey and Bryan, *Admiral Halsey's Story*, p. 18.
61. Text as delivered, in *Franklin D. Roosevelt and Foreign Affairs*, Vol. III, p. 380.
62. In Loewenheim et al., eds., *Roosevelt and Churchill: Their Secret Wartime Correspondence*, p. 89.
63. The subtitle of his book *Roosevelt and Churchill 1939–41*.
64. In Loewenheim, op. cit., pp. 242–50.
65. See Thompson, *Winston Churchill's World View*, passim; in Moran, op. cit., p. 790.
66. Tugwell, op. cit., p. 295n.
67. Churchill, *The Grand Alliance*, p. 663.
68. In Martin, *Madame Secretary*, pp. 435–6.
69. In Loewenheim, op. cit., p. 326; in Dallek, *Franklin D. Roosevelt and American Foreign Policy*, p. 470; Churchill, *Their Finest Hour*, p. 558.
70. Churchill, op. cit., p. 566; Sherwood, op. cit., p. 224.
71. De Gaulle, *Memoirs*, p. 165; in Churchill, op. cit., p. 569.
72. Moran, op. cit., p. 90.
73. Harriman and Abel, *Special Envoy to Churchill and Stalin*, p. 191.
74. Pendar, *Adventures in Diplomacy*, pp. 152–3.
75. Moran, op. cit., p. 90. The painting has had a curious history: In 1950, it was sold by Elliott Roosevelt for $7,500 to a Nebraska farmer named George W. Woodward; later John Spencer Churchill saw it in the window of an Omaha art shop and alerted a New York collector, Norman G. Hickman, who purchased it for the same price and is the present owner; it has been exhibited twice, in the lobby of the Daily News Building in January 1965 and in the Churchill Memorial in Fulton, Missouri, in the summer of 1970; *New York*

Daily News, January 25, 1965, p. C5, and letter, Virgil Johnston to James E. O'Neill, May 12, 1970, MS, FDR Library.

76. In Pendar, op. cit., p. 154.

I. ROOSEVELT

1. Stimson Diary, May 10, 1941, in Langer and Gleason, *The Undeclared War,* p. 455.
2. In Sherwood, *Roosevelt and Hopkins,* p. 293.
3. *Public Papers and Addresses (1941),* p. 63.
4. See Divine, *Roosevelt and World War II,* pp. 8–9.
5. Rosenman, *Working with Roosevelt,* p. 279.
6. See Bailey and Ryan, *Hitler vs. Roosevelt,* p. 141 and passim; Dallek, *Franklin D. Roosevelt and American Foreign Policy 1932–1945,* p. 285.
7. Stimson and Bundy, *On Active Service,* Vol. II, p. 369.
8. Gunther, *Roosevelt in Retrospect,* p. 26; Ed Flynn, the Democratic boss of the Bronx, hung up on the President once in 1940; see Schlesinger, *The Coming of the New Deal,* p. 525.
9. Stimson Diary, May 27, 1941, in Langer and Gleason, op. cit., p. 515.
10. Smith to Marshall, June 11, 1940, in Watson, *Prewar Plans and Preparations,* p. 312.
11. Stark to Kimmel, January 31, 1941, in *Pearl Harbor Attack Hearings,* Part 16, p. 2144.
12. Morton, *Strategy and Command,* p. 81.
13. In Matloff and Snell, *Strategic Planning for Coalition Warfare, 1941–42,* p. 28; and in Morton, op. cit., p. 82.
14. Dyer, *The Amphibians Came to Conquer,* pp. 158–9, and in Watson, op. cit., p. 123.
15. Marshall, memo for ACofS WPD, January 17, 1941, in Watson, op. cit., p. 125.
16. Ibid., p. 124.
17. In Major, "The Navy Plans for War, 1937–41," Hagan, ed., *In Peace and War,* p. 253.
18. Stark to Kimmel, April 4, 1941, in *Pearl Harbor Attack Hearings,* Part 16, p. 2161.
19. In Rosenman, op. cit., p. 281.
20. Sherwood, op. cit., p. 295.
21. Ibid., pp. 296–7.
22. Ibid.
23. In Rosenman, op. cit., p. 284.
24. Ibid., p. 283.
25. Berle Diary, May 26, 1941, in Berle, *Navigating the Rapids,* p. 369; Roosevelt to Churchill, May 27, 1941, and Early in the *Christian Science Monitor,* May 27, 1941, both in Langer and Gleason, op. cit., p. 459.
26. Sanborn, *Design for War,* p. 259.
27. In Langer and Gleason, op. cit., pp. 528–9n.
28. A translation of the German "Felix" plan, and British comment thereon, is in WO 106/2793 and 2794, MS, Public Record Office, Kew; Bullock, *Hitler,* pp. 555–6; in Hinsley, *Hitler's Strategy,* p. 113.

29. Roosevelt to Colonel and Mrs. Arthur Murray, June 2, 1941, in Roosevelt, ed., *F.D.R. His Personal Letters, 1928–1945*, Vol. II, p. 1165.
30. Hitler to Mussolini, June 21, 1941, in *Nazi-Soviet Relations*, p. 351.
31. Langer and Gleason, op. cit., p. 462.
32. *Complete Press Conferences*, Vol. 17, pp. 358–70; also Langer and Gleason, op. cit., p. 463, and Sherwood, op. cit., p. 259.
33. Stolper in FO 371/26244, MS, Public Record Office, Kew; Swing in Lash, *Roosevelt and Churchill*, pp. 303, 316–17.
34. Dallek, op. cit., p. 267.
35. Stark to Kimmel, April 19, 1941, in *Pearl Harbor Attack Hearings*, Part 16, p. 2164.
36. Ickes, *Secret Diary*, Vol. III, *The Lowering Clouds*, p. 544.
37. Ibid., pp. 546–51.
38. In Grew, *Ten Years in Japan*, p. 272.
39. Feis, *Road to Pearl Harbor*, p. 206.
40. Schlesinger, *The Coming of the New Deal*, pp. 544, 540–41.
41. Ickes, op. cit., p. 567.
42. Grew, op. cit., pp. 401–13.
43. Byas, *Government by Assassination*, p. 77.
44. Storry, *The Double Patriots*, p. 141n, and Byas, op. cit., p. 78.
45. Ito, "The Role of Right-Wing Organizations in Japan," in Borg and Okamoto, eds., *Pearl Harbor as History*, pp. 491–3.
46. In Byas, op. cit., pp. 111, 103.
47. In ibid., pp. 42, 118.
48. In Storry, op. cit., pp. 187–8, 284.
49. To Harada, in Feis, op. cit., p. 120.
50. Butow, *Tojo and the Coming of the War*, pp. 127–8, and Ienaga, *The Pacific War, 1931–45*, p. 82.
51. In Ike, ed., *Japan's Decision for War: Records of the 1941 Policy Conferences*, p. 86.
52. In ibid., p. 59.
53. *Foreign Relations of the United States, 1941*, Vol. IV, pp. 276–7, 288–9.
54. Teiichi Suzuki, in Ienaga, op. cit., p. 132.
55. In Ike, op. cit., p. 74.
56. Feis, op. cit., pp. 268–9.
57. In Ike, op. cit., pp. 7–8, 10.
58. Ibid., pp. 61–2, 67.
59. Ibid., pp. 51, 69.
60. Ibid., pp. 78–9; see also Butow, op. cit., p. 220.
61. Reports to Moscow are described by Farago, in "Secret Agent," *New York Times Book Review*, May 8, 1966; Maclean, *Take Nine Spies*, pp. 162–5; Clark, *Barbarossa*, pp. 149, 170, 180; and Salisbury, "Moscow," in Frankland and Dowling, eds., *Decisive Battles*, p. 138.
62. In *Foreign Relations of the United States, 1941*, Vol. IV, p. 290.
63. Feis, op. cit., p. 217, and Butow, op. cit., p. 220; on the pilots practicing at Kagoshima Bay, interrogation of Admiral Osami Nagano, March 21, 1946, in Trefousse, ed., *Pearl Harbor Documents*, p. 255.
64. Acheson, *Present at the Creation*, pp. 24–7.

21. In Pogue, "Marshall and His Commanders," loc. cit., p. 82.
22. Slessor, op. cit., p. 494; Cunningham, *A Sailor's Odyssey*, pp. 466–7.
23. In Pogue, *Ordeal and Hope*, p. 372.
24. King to Marshall, November 30, 1945, MS, Box 73, Folder 39, Marshall Library; Grogan to Marshall, with endorsements, January 26, 1944, MS, Box 73, Folder 18, Marshall Library; Patton to Marshall, with endorsements, November 6, 1942, MS, Box 79, Folder 11, Marshall Library.
25. Marshall to Roosevelt, November 23, 1942, MS, Box 80, Folder 38, Marshall Library; Capra, *The Name Above the Title*, p. 362.
26. For O'Laughlin's support of Drum, see Copp, *A Few Great Captains*, pp. 480–1; Roosevelt to Dern in Pogue, *Education of a General*, p. 295.
27. In Bland et al., eds., op. cit., p. 659; and Pogue, op. cit., p. 311. The CCCs provide both a parallel and a contrast with Nazi Germany, where a similar problem prompted the creation of the *Hitlerjugend*, in which youths 14–18 were conscripted for what became in effect paramilitary training; by 1938, after the annexation of Austria and the Sudetenland, they numbered over four million; see Koch, *The Hitler Youth*, pp. 101, 114.
28. Sherwood, *Roosevelt and Hopkins*, p. 76.
29. Pogue, op. cit., p. 330.
30. When the author was an officer candidate at the Tank Destroyer School in Camp Hood, Texas, two of his tactical officers were Benning graduates; nothing was said about this, nothing needed to be said. For Marshall's philosophy during the 1930s and 1940s, see DeWeerd, ed., *Selected Speeches and Statements of General of the Army George C. Marshall*.
31. In Bland et al., eds., op. cit., p. 647.
32. Ibid., p. 160.
33. Ibid., pp. 335, 205; it might be noted that British uneasiness about mobility still persisted in World War II; see d'Este, *Decision in Normandy*, p. 356.
34. In Pogue, op. cit., p. 250.
35. In ibid., p. 251.
36. Ibid., p. 248.
37. Ibid., pp. 262, 261.
38. In ibid., p. 267.
39. In Weigley, *Towards an American Army*, pp. 25, 26–27.
40. In ibid., p. 231; in Bland et al., eds., op. cit., pp. 340, 241.
41. In Watson, *Chief of Staff: Prewar Plans and Preparations*, p. 25.
42. Pogue, *Ordeal and Hope*, p. 120.
43. Pogue, op. cit., p. 76.
44. Wintringham, *The Story of Weapons and Tactics*, p. 228; Wintringham was a Communist who served in the RAF in World War I, commanded the British International Brigade in the Spanish Civil War, and helped found a training school for the Home Guard in England during World War II.
45. Taylor, *English History 1914–1945*, p. 60.
46. In Hobbs, ed., *Dear General*, pp. 223–4.
47. In Watson, op. cit., p. 249; ibid., pp. 241–4, 247; Pogue, op. cit., p. 98.
48. In Pogue, op. cit., p. 58.
49. Ibid., pp. 148, 149, 154.
50. How this was done, as well as the atmosphere of a training camp, is beauti-

fully conveyed by John Cheever in his short story "Sergeant Limeburner," *The New Yorker,* March 13, 1943.

51. Kahn, *McNair: Educator of an Army,* pp. 40, 44, 13, 4, 10.
52. Palmer, Wiley, and Keast, *The Procurement and Training of Ground Combat Troops,* pp. 327–8.
53. Greenfield, Palmer, and Wiley, *The Organization of Ground Combat Troops,* pp. 53–4; Palmer et al., op. cit., pp. 308, 489ff, 493. In July and August of 1942, *six* new divisions a month were activated.
54. Pogue, op. cit., p. 335; Churchill, *The Hinge of Fate,* p. 387. See also Churchill to Marshall, after V-E Day: "Not only were the fighting troops and their complicated ancillaries created but, to an extent that seems almost incredible to me, the supply of commanders capable of maneuvering the vast organisms of modern armies and groups of armies and moving these with unsurpassed celerity were also found wherever they were needed"; in Marshall, *Together,* p. 250.
55. Marshall to Roosevelt, May 6, 1942, MS, Box 80, Folder 33, Marshall Library.
56. Blum, *From the Morgenthau Diaries,* Vol. II, pp. 140–1.
57. Pogue, op. cit., p. 31.
58. Sherwood, op. cit., p. 410; Watson, op. cit., pp. 352, 344; Matloff and Snell, *Strategic Planning for Coalition Warfare 1941–1942,* p. 61n.
59. In Watson, op. cit., pp. 338–9; ibid., pp. 339, 340; in ibid., p. 335; in Cline, *Washington Command Post: The Operations Division,* p. 60.
60. Matloff and Snell, op. cit., p. 59; Cline, op. cit., p. 61.
61. Watson, op. cit., p. 344; in ibid., p. 350.
62. Catton, *The War Lords of Washington,* pp. 42, 49, 46; Civilian Production Administration, *Industrialization for War: History of the War Production Board and Predecessor Agencies 1940–1945,* pp. 134, 139.
63. Catton, op. cit., p. 83; *Industrialization for War,* p. 140.
64. Wheeler, *Yankee from the West,* pp. 32–6.
65. Kittredge, "A Military Danger: The Revelation of Secret Strategic Plans," in *U.S. Naval Institute Proceedings,* July 1955, pp. 731–43.
66. In Freidin and Richardson, eds., *Fatal Decisions,* p. 78.
67. In Blumenson, ed., *The Patton Papers 1940–45,* Vol. II, p. 103; John Eisenhower, *Allies,* p. 183.
68. In Morison, *Operations in North African Waters,* pp. 41–2; in Blumenson, op. cit., p. 112.
69. Craven and Cate, *The Army Air Forces in World War II,* Vol. II, p. 77; Morison, op. cit., p. 223; Howe, *Northwest Africa: Seizing the Initiative in the West,* p. 186.
70. Howe, op. cit., pp. 188–9, 212–13, 223–4; Morison, op. cit., pp. 225–30.
71. See Smith, *The Shadow Warriors,* pp. 145–57.
72. Howe, op. cit., pp. 250–1, 263.
73. "Rame" [Divine], *Road to Tunis,* p. 22.
74. Craven and Cate, op. cit., Vol. II, p. 41.
75. John Eisenhower, op. cit., p. 107; in Butcher, *My Three Years with Eisenhower,* p. 29; Eisenhower, *Crusade in Europe,* pp. 70–1.
76. Pogue, op. cit., p. 314.
77. In Matloff and Snell, op. cit., p. 185.

78. In Pogue, op. cit., p. 320; in Sherwood, op. cit., p. 535; Ismay, *Memoirs*, pp. 249–50.
79. Eisenhower diary, January 22, 1942, in Ferrell, op. cit., p. 44.
80. See Grigg, *1943: The Victory That Never Was;* Dunn, *Second Front Now— 1943*.
81. Cline, op. cit., pp. 149–50.
82. Steele, *The First Offensive: Roosevelt, Marshall, and the Making of American Strategy*, p. 168; Ambrose, op. cit., p. 71.
83. In Loewenheim et al., eds., *Roosevelt and Churchill: Their Secret Wartime Correspondence*, p. 222; in Matloff and Snell, op. cit., p. 269; Stimson diary, July 15, 1942, in Stimson and Bundy, *On Active Service*, p. 425; in Pogue, op. cit., pp. 340–1. Roosevelt told Marshall that he wanted the record "altered" to eliminate any appearance of proposing the "abandonment" of the British. Marshall to King, July 15, 1943, Box 73, Folder 12, Marshall Library; see also Hayes, *The History of the Joint Chiefs of Staff in World War II*, p. 786, note 53.
84. Complete text of the letter is in Sherwood, op. cit., pp. 603–5.
85. Matloff and Snell, op. cit., p. 235; Steele, op. cit., pp. 171–2; in Pogue, op. cit., p. 346.
86. John Eisenhower, op. cit., p. 107.
87. In Matloff and Snell, op. cit., p. 283.
88. In ibid., p. 294; Marshall to Leahy and King, August 17, 1942, MS, Box 74, Folder 4, Marshall Library.
89. In Matloff and Snell, op. cit., p. 272; in Blumenson, op. cit., pp. 81–2.
90. Pogue, op. cit., p. 410; in Morison, op. cit., p. 47.
91. Morison, op. cit., pp. 23–33, 45–7.
92. Clark, *Carrier Admiral*, pp. 96–7, 102.
93. Tully, *F.D.R. My Boss*, pp. 263–4.
94. Marshall, *Together*, pp. 129–30.
95. Pogue, op. cit., pp. 23, 247–8.
96. Morison, *Turmoil and Tradition*, p. 504; Pogue, op. cit., pp. 22, 289–90, 295.
97. Pogue, "Marshall and His Commanders," loc. cit., pp. 80, 90.
98. Pogue, *Ordeal and Hope*, p. 296.
99. Ibid., pp. 87–8, 114–15; Marshall to Roosevelt, March 29, 1943, MX, Box 80, Folder 44, Marshall Library.
100. Pogue, op. cit., pp. 113, 118; Marshall to Roosevelt, September 6, 1941; Roosevelt to Marshall, September 22, 1941; MSS, Box 80, Folder 30, Marshall Library.
101. Marshall to Roosevelt, March 27, 1943, with attachment, MS, Box 80, Folder 44, Marshall Library.
102. Pogue, *Organizer of Victory*, pp. 70, 316.
103. Leighton, "U.S. Merchant Shipping and the British Import Crisis," in Greenfield, ed., *Command Decisions*, p. 218. See also Hancock and Gowing, *British War Economy*, pp. 432–3: viz. "some evidence which is already available suggests that the country was not quite so close to the margin of danger as the War Cabinet at that time believed."
104. Matloff, "The 90-Division Gamble," in Greenfield, ed., op. cit., p. 377; Greenfield, Palmer, and Wiley, op. cit., pp. 261–382; in Matloff, loc. cit., p. 378.

105. Love, "Ernest Joseph King," in Love, ed., *The Chiefs of Naval Operations*, p. 165.
106. Morison, *Turmoil and Tradition*, pp. 506, 495, 494, 560.
107. In Stimson and Bundy, op. cit., pp. 430, 432, 436, 437, 435, 439.
108. In ibid., p. 443.
109. In Eisenhower, *Crusade in Europe*, p. 197.
110. In Sherwood, op. cit., pp. 761, 763.
111. Ibid., pp. 802–3; Roosevelt liked this figure of speech and used it more than once, though the testimony suggests that he was in fact a sound eight-hour-a-night man who never lost sleep over anything.
112. Stimson and Bundy, op. cit., p. 443.
113. Pogue, op. cit., p. 120; Marshall sometimes appeared overconfident about the quality of American weapons; see DeWeerd, op. cit., p. 42.
114. Pogue, op. cit., pp. 406–7.
115. Ambrose, op. cit., pp. 299, 395; Hastings, *Overlord*, p. 98; Evans and Bidwell to Marshall, March 1, 1944, and McCarthy to Leahy, March 2, 1944, MSS, Box 74, Folder 10, Marshall Library.
116. Pogue, *Organizer of Victory*, pp. 331, 307.
117. Pogue, op. cit., pp. 243, 245; Matloff, *Strategic Planning for Coalition Warfare 1943–1944*, pp. 223–4.
118. In Pogue, op. cit., p. 516.
119. In Marshall, *Together*, pp. 250–1.

III. KING

1. Buell, *Master of Sea Power*, p. 172; in Roosevelt, *My Parents: A Differing View*, p. 166.
2. In Roosevelt, *As He Saw It*, p. 82.
3. Mahan, *The Influence of Seapower upon History 1660–1783*, pp. 68, 351, 369, 377.
4. In Lobdell, *American Secretaries of the Navy*, p. 711.
5. Morison, *Turmoil and Tradition*, p. 567.
6. In Holmes, *Double-edged Secrets*, p. 142; in Love, "Ernest Joseph King," in Love, ed., *The Chiefs of Naval Operations*, p. 140; in Buell, op. cit., pp. 402–3.
7. Vice Admiral George L. Russell and Rear Admiral John D. Bulkeley, in Previdi, "Fleet Admiral Ernest J. King," MS, Naval War College.
8. Love, "Fighting a Global War, 1941–45," in Hagan, ed., *In Peace and War*, p. 264.
9. In Buell, op. cit., p. 89.
10. Love, in Love, ed., loc. cit., p. 137.
11. Buell, op. cit., pp. 9, 5, 7, 12, 19, 42, 48, 34, 27, 29, 35; Love, loc. cit., pp. 137–8.
12. Buell, op. cit., pp. 130, 111, 356; Buell, *The Quiet Warrior*, p. 111; Buell, *Master of Sea Power*, pp. 29, 35–6, 62, 130.
13. Ibid., pp. 55, 100, 102–3, 110, 374.
14. King and Whitehill, *Fleet Admiral King, A Naval Record*, p. 294; Buell, op. cit., pp. 118–19.

15. Morison, *The Battle of the Atlantic*, p. 41.
16. Buell, op. cit., pp. 123, 127; Love, loc. cit., p. 141.
17. Morison, op. cit., pp. 58, 61, 40, 41.
18. Abbazia, *Mr. Roosevelt's Navy: The Private War of the U.S. Atlantic Fleet, 1939–1942*, pp. 144–5; in Morison, op. cit., p. 61.
19. Abbazia, op. cit., p. 216; Love, in Love, ed., op. cit., p. 142.
20. Abbazia, op. cit., pp. 66, 79, 68; in ibid., p. 236.
21. In King and Whitehall, op. cit., pp. 311–12, 313, 316, 325–6.
22. Morison, op. cit., p. 98; Buell, op. cit., p. 140; Albion and Connery, *Forrestal and the Navy*, p. 90.
23. Abbazia, op. cit., pp. 80–1.
24. Morison, op. cit., pp. 79–80.
25. In Abbazia, op. cit., p. 278.
26. See H. A. Larrabee, *Decision at the Chesapeake;* Franklin in Pratt, *Preble's Boys*, p. 393.
27. In Pratt, pp. 94–5.
28. Pratt, *The Heroic Years*, p. 232; *Preble's Boys*, p. 304; *The Heroic Years*, pp. 291–2; *Preble's Boys*, p. 209.
29. Pratt, *The Heroic Years*, pp. 235, 236, 237, 285, 288, 290.
30. Ibid., pp. 322–7, 291.
31. Morison, *Leyte*, p. 241.
32. Middleton, *Crossroads of Modern Warfare*, p. 37.
33. Potter, *Nimitz*, p. 146.
34. Major, "The Navy Plans for War, 1937–1941," in Hagan, ed., op. cit., p. 247; Knox, "The United States Between World Wars," in Morison, *The Battle of the Atlantic*, p. xxxiv.
35. In Ickes, *The Inside Struggle 1936–1939*, p. 274.
36. Knox, loc. cit., p. xxxvii.
37. Ibid., pp. xlii–xliii.
38. Leuchtenburg, *Franklin D. Roosevelt and the New Deal*, p. 218n.
39. Knox, loc. cit., p. xlvi.
40. Major, loc. cit., p. 244.
41. In Morton, *Strategy and Command: The First Two Years*, p. 125n.
42. Lord, *Day of Infamy*, pp. 74, 79, 82, 85; Morison, *The Rising Sun in the Pacific*, p. 106.
43. Buell, *The Quiet Warrior*, pp. 97–8.
44. Buell, *Master of Sea Power*, p. 151.
45. In Morison, op. cit., p. 129.
46. Millis, *This Is Pearl!*, pp. 333–4; Morison, op. cit., p. 136.
47. King and Whitehill, op. cit., p. 228.
48. Millis, op. cit., p. 272.
49. Buell, op. cit., p. 153; in ibid., pp. 526–7.
50. In King and Whitehill, op. cit., p. 353.
51. In Buell, op. cit., p. 51.
52. Ibid., pp. 157, 161, 418, 178, 228, 156, 178.
53. Ibid., pp. 302–3, 305–6.
54. In King and Whitehill, op. cit., pp. 384–5; in Buell, op. cit., p. 193; ibid., p. 189.

55. In King and Whitehill, op. cit., pp. 385, 383.
56. In Ferrell, ed., *The Eisenhower Diaries*, pp. 48, 50.
57. Morton, op. cit., p. 292; Hayes, *The History of the Joint Chiefs of Staff in World War II*, pp. 138, 782.
58. McCrea, Memoir and Oral History, MSS, FDR Library; also Buell, op. cit., pp. 420–1.
59. In Morison, *The Atlantic Battle Won*, p. 11; Churchill, *The Grand Alliance*, p. 115, *Their Finest Hour*, p. 598; Martienssen, *Hitler and His Admirals*, p. 22; Morison, op. cit., pp. 363, 11.
60. Morison, *The Battle of the Atlantic*, pp. 4, 11; Baxter, *Scientists Against Time*, pp. 39, 37; in Loewenheim et al., eds., *Roosevelt and Churchill*, p. 196.
61. In Martienssen, op. cit., pp. 2, 128; Slessor, *The Central Blue*, p. 521; Kemp, *Key to Victory*, p. 160; Hinsley, *British Intelligence in the Second World War*, Vol. II, p. 169; Morison, op. cit., pp. 244–6.
62. Morison, op. cit., p. 128, *The Atlantic Battle Won*, pp. 7–8.
63. Marshall to King, June 19, 1942, MS, Marshall Papers, Box 73, Folder 12, Marshall Library.
64. Stimson in Morison, *Turmoil and Tradition*, p. 569; Buell, op. cit., p. 284; in ibid., p. 288.
65. Buell, op. cit., pp. 185–6; King and Whitehill, op. cit., pp. 446–7.
66. Roosevelt to King, July 7, 1942, and King to Roosevelt, July 9, 1942, MSS, King Papers, Manuscript Division, Library of Congress; Morison, *The Battle of the Atlantic*, p. 230.
67. Morison, pp. 203–4, 127–8; Churchill, in *The Hinge of Fate*, p. 125; Dönitz, in Morison, op. cit., p. 4; ibid., pp. 322, 315, 317, 410.
68. Morison, *Turmoil and Tradition*, pp. 561–74, 577; Slessor, op. cit., p. 534.
69. Stimson to McNarney, June 25, 1943; Marshall to King, June 28, 1943; Handy to Marshall, June 28, 1943; Marshall to King, July 15, 1943; MSS, Marshall Papers, Box 73, Folder 15, Marshall Library; Fanton, "Robert A. Lovett: The War Years," MS, doctoral dissertation, Yale University, 1978, p. 190.
70. Morison, op. cit., pp. 579, 580; in ibid., p. 579.
71. Morison, *The Atlantic Battle Won*, pp. 32, 35–6.
72. Love, in Love, ed., loc. cit., p. 167; Hinsley, op. cit., Vol. II, pp. 170, 179; Love, loc. cit., pp. 167–8.
73. In Buell, op. cit., p. 294.
74. Beesly, *Very Special Intelligence*, pp. 197, 55, 168–70; also Hinsley, op. cit., Vol. II, pp. 553–5.
75. In Morison, op. cit., pp. 135–7; ibid., pp. 133, 138, 361–2.
76. Baxter, op. cit., p. 34; Hinsley, op. cit., Vol. III, p. 223.
77. Morison, op. cit., pp. 146, 177, 356–7, 360–1; Beesly, op. cit., p. 262.
78. In Bryant, *The Turn of the Tide*, p. 446n; White, ed., *The Stilwell Papers*, p. 245.
79. Ambrose, *The Supreme Commander*, p. 158; in Hayes, op. cit., p. 363.
80. Macmillan, *The Blast of War*, pp. 192–3.
81. In Burns, *Roosevelt: The Soldier of Freedom*, p. 317; Slessor, op. cit., p. 443; Macmillan, op. cit., pp. 193–4; Blumenthal, ed., *The Patton Papers 1940–1945*, Vol. II, p. 157.
82. In Ambrose, op. cit., p. 158; Wedemeyer, *Wedemeyer Reports!*, p. 192.

83. King and Whitehill, op. cit., p. 417; in Buell, op. cit., p. 274.
84. In Bryant, op. cit., p. 274.
85. Slessor, op. cit., p. 446.
86. King and Whitehill, op. cit., p. 656; in Buell, op. cit., pp. 260–1.
87. Bull, "Record of Meetings," MS, Naval War College; also Buell, op. cit., p. 265.
88. Hayes, op. cit., pp. 358, 360, 361, 376.
89. Ibid., p. 403; Buell, op. cit., pp. 338–9.
90. Bull, loc. cit., p. 27.
91. Morison, *Breaking the Bismarcks Barrier,* pp. 393–4, 396, 25.
92. Ibid., pp. 395, 398, 409.
93. Love, in Love, ed., loc. cit., p. 166.
94. Morison, op. cit., pp. 12–13.
95. Buell, *The Quiet Warrior,* pp. 164, 179–80, 199–201. Marine dissatisfaction with the Army flared up on Saipan in June 1944, when Holland Smith relieved Army general Ralph Smith; for the Army side, see Love, "Smith vs. Smith," *Infantry Journal,* November 1948.
96. Love, loc. cit., p. 170; in Hayes, op. cit., pp. 554, 558–9; Buell, *Master of Seapower,* p. 440.
97. Buell, op. cit., p. 359; Hayes, op. cit., pp. 310–11, 432.
98. Morison, op. cit., pp. 286, 323; Dyer, *The Amphibians Came to Conquer,* Vol. II, pp. 638–9.
99. Love, loc. cit., pp. 178, 173; Love, in Hagan, ed., loc. cit., p. 279.
100. Wilkinson Diaries, MS, Churchill College, Cambridge.
101. Love, in Love, ed., loc. cit., pp. 161, 146, 177; Love, in Hagan, ed., loc. cit., p. 286.
102. Love, in Love, ed., loc. cit., pp. 162–3.
103. Albion and Connery, op. cit., p. 132; Buell, op. cit., pp. 325–37.
104. Albion and Connery, op. cit., pp. 17, 25, 31–2, 96.
105. Rogow, *James Forrestal,* pp. 66–8, 81–2, 88–92.
106. Ibid., p. 105; Buell, op. cit., p. 239; Albion and Connery, op. cit., pp. 91–2.
107. Albion and Connery, pp. 63–4; Rogow, op. cit., pp. 93–7, 100–1; Albion and Connery, op. cit., p. 96.
108. Albion and Connery, p. 134.
109. Ibid., pp. 287–8.
110. In Buell, op. cit., p. 239; in Perkins, *The Roosevelt I Knew,* p. 387.
111. Buell, op. cit., pp. 379, 396, 380.
112. Ibid., pp. 380–3, 149, 382, 383–6.
113. Reynolds, *The Fast Carriers,* pp. 233, 234–5, 237, 239, 236.
114. Dyer, op. cit., pp. 215–16; King and Whitehill, op. cit., p. 321; Buell, op. cit., p. 443; Dyer, op. cit., pp. xx, 1, 1035.
115. Ibid., pp. 1168, 1145, 1143, 1161, 1160, 1146.
116. In Ibid., op. cit., p. 497.
117. King and Whitehill, op. cit., p. 605n; Hayes, op. cit., pp. 702, 704.
118. Churchill, *Triumph and Tragedy,* pp. 146–7; Burns, op. cit., p. 519.
119. Buell finds the minutes of this Combined Chief's meeting so "unusually revealing" that he prints them in full: Buell, op. cit., pp. 471n, 535–9; ibid., pp. 470–1; Cunningham, *A Sailor's Odyssey,* p. 612; Reynolds, op. cit., p. 316.

120. Buell, op. cit., pp. 415, 417; Marshall to Roosevelt, January 23, 1945, MS, National Archives, Leahy file, #125.
121. War Department, "The Entry of the Soviet Union into the War Against Japan," MS, FDR Library, pp. 49–50.
122. Hoover to MacArthur, September 3, 17, 1953; MacArthur to Hoover, September 9, 1953; MSS, MacArthur Archives; entry for February 28, 1945, Millis, ed., *The Forrestal Diaries*, p. 31.
123. In Morton, "The Decision to Use the Atomic Bomb," in Greenfield, ed., *Command Decisions*, pp. 503–4; also King and Whitehill, op. cit., p. 606.
124. Moran, *Churchill Taken from the Diaries of Lord Moran*, p. 303.
125. Buell, op. cit., pp. 428, 275; in Bryant, op. cit., p. 446.
126. In King and Whitehill, op. cit., p. 5; in Buell, op. cit., pp. 505–6.
127. In Millis, ed., op. cit., p. 84.

IV. ARNOLD

1. Arnold, *Global Mission*, p. 19; Coffey, *Hap*, pp. 49, 48, 42, 58–9, 160, 52.
2. Copp, *A Few Great Captains*, p. 491; Coffey, op. cit., p. 87.
3. Arnold, op. cit., pp. 27–8.
4. Langewiesche, "What the Wrights Really Invented," *Harper's Magazine*, June 1950; Wescott and Degen, *Wind and Sand: The Story of the Wright Brothers at Kitty Hawk*, passim; Coffey, op. cit., p. 44.
5. In Coffey, op. cit., p. 48.
6. Ibid., p. 12.
7. Arnold, op. cit., pp. 7, 15; Coffey, op. cit., pp. 37, 40, 41.
8. Coffey, pp. 11, 224.
9. Ibid., pp. 4, 6, 10; Arnold, op. cit., p. 186.
10. Arnold, p. 11; Copp, op. cit., pp. 432, 455.
11. Coffey, op. cit., p. 103; in Hinton, *Air Victory: The Men and the Machines*, p. 41.
12. Schlesinger, *The Crisis of the Old Order*, p. 312; *Complete Press Conferences*, Vol. 21, pp. 140–2 (February 2, 1943).
13. Watson, *Chief of Staff: Prewar Plans and Preparations*, p. 132.
14. Bullock, *Hitler*, p. 414; Copp, op. cit., p. 445; in Sherwood, *Roosevelt and Hopkins*, p. 100.
15. Coffey, op. cit., pp. 90, 93–5; Copp, op. cit., pp. 27–8.
16. Coffey, op. cit., pp. 96–7.
17. In ibid., p. 99; in Copp, op. cit., p. 40; ibid., pp. 45, 47, 49–51; Coffey, op. cit., pp. 4, 122.
18. Coffey, pp. 100, 257; Copp, op. cit., pp. 83, 310.
19. Roosevelt, *As He Saw It*, p. 9; E. Roosevelt to F. D. Roosevelt, April 18, 1934, MS, PPF 8559, FDR Library; Arnold, op. cit., p. 161.
20. Copp, op. cit., pp. 167, 220, 47; Coffey, op. cit., pp. 156–7, 161.
21. In Watson, op. cit., p. 36.
22. In Coffey, op. cit., p. 205; ibid., p. 205; Copp, op. cit., p. 483.
23. Arnold, op. cit., pp. 179, 177, 178; Watson, op. cit., pp. 136–7, 126.
24. Watson, pp. 130, 138; Copp, op. cit., p. 456.
25. Ibid., p. 457.

26. Coffey, op. cit., p. 222.
27. Arnold, op. cit., p. 196.
28. In Coffey, op. cit., p. 222; Arnold, op. cit., p. 195.
29. Fanton, "Robert A. Lovett: The War Years," MS, doctoral dissertation, Yale University, 1978, pp. 12–13; Pogue, *Ordeal and Hope*, p. 44.
30. In Craven and Cate, *The Army Air Forces in World War II*, Vol. VI, p. 15.
31. Fanton, loc. cit., pp. 7–8, vii, viii.
32. Ibid., pp. 12, 14; in Kouwenhoven, *Partners in Banking*, pp. 10–11.
33. Fanton, loc. cit., pp. 17, 18, 21; in ibid., pp. 20, 24.
34. In Craven and Cate, op. cit., Vol. VI, p. 15.
35. Fanton, op. cit., p. 32; Lovett to Eaker, January 28, 1945, in ibid.; in ibid., p. 33.
36. Lovett to Arnold, October 14, 1942, MS, Arnold Papers, Manuscript Division, Library of Congress; Fanton, loc. cit., pp. 79, 76, 75; in ibid.
37. Roosevelt to Marshall, August 24, 1942; Arnold to Roosevelt, October 8, 1942; MSS, Arnold Papers, Manuscript Division, Library of Congress; Lovett to Arnold, loc. cit. in note 36.
38. Arnold to Lovett, October 19, 1942; Patterson to Arnold, October 17, 1942; Arnold to Joint Chiefs of Staff, October 19, 1942; Roosevelt to Stimson and Roosevelt to Nelson, October 29, 1942; MSS, Arnold Papers, Manuscript Division, Library of Congress.
39. Fanton, loc. cit., pp. 84–5; Craven and Cate, op. cit., Vol. VI, p. 350.
40. In Fanton, loc. cit., pp. 40–1.
41. Ibid., p. 37; in ibid., pp. 48–9.
42. Ibid., pp. 51, 54; Pogue, op. cit., pp. 44, 290–1.
43. Fanton, loc. cit., pp. 39–42.
44. Ibid., pp. 45–6, 107–8; in ibid., p. 110; ibid., p. 111.
45. Ibid., pp. 85ff.; in ibid., p. 91; ibid., pp. 92, 102.
46. Ibid., pp. 126, 103–5, 132–3, 115.
47. Ibid., pp. 141–2, 64, 55; in ibid., pp. 142, 56.
48. Pogue, op. cit., p. 64; Stimson Diary, September 27, 1940, in ibid.
49. Coffey, op. cit., p. 219.
50. Arnold, op. cit., p. 194.
51. Arnold to Lindbergh, October 8, 1938, MS, Arnold Papers, Manuscript Division, Library of Congress.
52. In Coffey, op. cit., p. 190.
53. Cole, *Charles A. Lindbergh and the Battle Against American Intervention in World War II*, pp. 32–3, 39, 36.
54. Arnold to Lindbergh, November 17, 1938; Lindbergh to Arnold, November 29, 1938; MSS, Arnold Papers, Manuscript Division, Library of Congress.
55. Cole, op. cit., pp. 65–7; Arnold, op. cit., pp. 188–9.
56. Kennedy to Hull, September 22, 1938, MS, Arnold Papers, Manuscript Division, Library of Congress; Wood and Dempster, *The Narrow Margin*, p. 478.
57. See Ward, "The Meaning of Lindbergh's Flight," in Ward, *Red, White, and Blue*, pp. 21–37.
58. Lindbergh to Arnold, November 29, 1938, loc. cit. in note 54; Wood and Dempster, op. cit., p. 446.
59. Lindbergh to Arnold, December 20, 1941; Arnold, memorandum of record,

December 30, 1941; *New York Times,* December 31, 1941; MSS, Arnold Papers, Manuscript Division, Library of Congress.

60. Cole, op. cit., pp. 216–17, 73–4.
61. Ibid., pp. 129, 128.
62. Ibid., p. 218; Craven and Cate, op. cit., Vol. VI, pp. 329–30.
63. Cole, op. cit., pp. 222–3.
64. Lindbergh to Arnold, June 7, 1949, MS, Arnold Papers, Manuscript Division, Library of Congress.
65. Arnold, op. cit., p. 215; Coffey, op. cit., p. 227.
66. Arnold, op. cit., pp. 220–1, 227; in Coffey, op. cit., p. 229; Arnold, op. cit., p. 235; Coffey, op. cit., p. 232.
67. Arnold, op. cit., p. 224; Hinsley, *British Intelligence in the Second World War,* Vol. I, pp. 75, 228, 299–300.
68. Jablonski, *Airwar,* Vol. I, p. 13, Kesselring, *A Soldier's Record,* p. 28.
69. Baumbach, *The Life and Death of the Luftwaffe,* pp. 28–9, 49; Deighton, *Fighter,* p. 72.
70. Wood and Dempster, op. cit., pp. 44, 47, 42; Baumbach, op. cit., p. 48.
71. Baumbach, pp. 25, 30; in ibid., p. 42.
72. Jablonski, op. cit., Vol. IV, p. 103.
73. Baumbach, op. cit., pp. 39, 25.
74. Deighton, op. cit., p. 244.
75. Ibid., pp. 4, 215.
76. Ibid., p. 99.
77. Johnson, *Wing Leader,* p. 46. The outrageous treatment Dowding and Park were subsequently accorded by small-minded men not fit to black their boots is fortunately not my tale to tell; the thought of it still rankles.
78. Klee, "The Battle of Britain," in Jacobsen and Rohwer, *Decisive Battles of World War II: The German View,* pp. 74, 93, 77; McKee, *Strike from the Sky,* pp. 211–12; Middleton, *The Sky Suspended,* p. 142; Deighton, op. cit., p. 208.
79. McKee, op. cit., p. 126.
80. Wood and Dempster, op. cit., pp. 339, 353–4; Hinsley, op. cit., Vol. I, p. 189.
81. Middleton, op. cit., p. 11.
82. Arnold, op. cit., p. 247.
83. Buell, *Master of Sea Power,* pp. 142–3; Burns, *Soldier of Freedom,* p. 125.
84. Arnold, "Notes Relative to President Roosevelt's and Prime Minister Churchill's Conference held aboard ship in Placentia Bay, Newfoundland," August 9–12, 1941; MS, Arnold Papers, Manuscript Division, Library of Congress; Arnold, op. cit., p. 248.
85. Arnold, MS, loc. cit. in note 84; Roosevelt, *As He Saw It,* pp. 20, 17.
86. Arnold, MS, loc. cit. in note 84.
87. Ibid., Arnold, op. cit., p. 253; Roosevelt, *As He Saw It,* p. 28.
88. In Buell, op. cit., p. 144; Arnold, op. cit., p. 253; Roosevelt, *As He Saw It,* pp. 28, 30.
89. Arnold, MS, loc. cit. in note 84.
90. In Sherwood, op. cit., p. 355.
91. Ibid., p. 361; in Churchill, *The Grand Alliance,* p. 446.
92. In Sherwood, op. cit., p. 353; Churchill, op. cit., p. 432.

93. In Dallek, *Franklin D. Roosevelt and American Foreign Policy 1932–1945*, p. 284.

94. Martin, *Adlai Stevenson of Illinois*, pp. 191–3.

95. In Wolff, *Low Level Mission*, p. 7.

96. Craven and Cate, op. cit., Vol. II, pp. 9–10; Matloff and Snell, *Strategic Planning for Coalition Warfare 1941–42*, p. 246n; Dugan and Stewart, *Ploesti*, pp. 14, 20, 15.

97. Craven and Cate, op. cit., Vol. II, p. 477; Dugan and Stewart, op. cit., pp. 36–9.

98. Matloff, *Strategic Planning for Coalition Warfare 1943–44*, p. 151; Copp, op. cit., p. 415; Eisenhower, *Crusade in Europe*, pp. 160–1.

99. Wolff, op. cit., pp. 196–7; Brereton, *The Brereton Diaries*, p. 197.

100. Wolff, op. cit., pp. 166, 67–8, 97–100, 114; Copp, op. cit., p. 274.

101. Craven and Cate, op. cit., Vol. II, p. 235.

102. Wolff, op. cit., pp. 100–1, 103; Dugan and Stewart, op. cit., p. 81.

103. Dugan and Stewart, illustration following p. 184, p. 45; Wolff, op. cit., pp. 110–11.

104. Dugan and Stewart, op. cit., pp. 71–4, 77, 86–7.

105. Ibid., pp. 86, 88–9.

106. Wolff, op. cit., pp. 131, 119–20.

107. Dugan and Stewart, op. cit., pp. 93–4; Wolff, op. cit., p. 132.

108. Wolff, p. 185.

109. Dugan and Stewart, op. cit., pp. 97, 99–101, 161, 164, 389; Wolff, op. cit., p. 117.

110. Wolff, pp. 136, 141; Dugan and Stewart, op. cit., pp. 107–8.

111. Liebling, "Ploesti," *The New Yorker*, October 20, 1962, p. 228.

112. Dugan and Stewart, op. cit., pp. 129, 139, 30, 142, 182, 187–8; Craven and Cate, op. cit., Vol. II, p. 481.

113. Dugan and Stewart, op. cit., pp. 159, 161, 164, 147, 146; Kane in Wolff, op. cit., p. 151.

114. Dugan and Stewart, op. cit., pp. 165, 166, 174; Wolff, op. cit., pp. 160–1; in ibid., p. 165.

115. Craven and Cate, op. cit., Vol. II, pp. 481–3.

116. Ibid.; Wolff, op. cit., pp. 177, 183.

117. Coffey, op. cit., pp. 376–7; Arnold, op. cit., p. 615.

118. Arnold, pp. 74–6, 259–60, 261.

119. Coffey, op. cit., pp. 207–8, 350–1; Arnold, op. cit., p. 165.

120. In Coffey, op. cit., pp. 209–10.

121. Marshall to Arnold, October 1, 1940, MS, Marshall Papers, Box 56, Folder 39, Marshall Library.

122. In Coffey, op. cit., p. 223.

123. Arnold to Marshall, May 10, 1943; Marshall to Arnold, May 14, 1943; MSS, Marshall Papers, Box 56, Folder 41, Marshall Library.

124. Marshall to Eisenhower for Arnold, April 8, 1945; Arnold to Marshall, April 14, 1945; Marshall to Arnold, April 16, 1945; MSS, Marshall Papers, Box 56, Folder 43, Marshall Library.

125. In Coffey, op. cit., p. 346.

126. Ibid., p. 387.

127. Ibid., p. 284.
128. Slessor, *The Central Blue*, p. 387.

V. VANDEGRIFT

1. In Hough et al., *History of U.S. Marine Corps Operations in World War II*, Vol. I, *Pearl Harbor to Guadalcanal*, p. 86n.
2. In FDR scrapbook, Assistant Secretary of the Navy file, FDR Library.
3. In Freidel, *Franklin D. Roosevelt: The Apprenticeship*, p. 270.
4. Miller, *Guadalcanal: The First Offensive*, p. 14; Love, "Ernest Joseph King: 26 March 1942–15 December 1945," in Love, ed., *The Chiefs of Naval Operations*, p. 402, note 40.
5. Zimmerman, *The Guadalcanal Campaign*, p. 7; in Pogue, *Ordeal and Hope*, p. 382.
6. Potter, *Nimitz*, p. 179; Miller, op. cit., p. 20.
7. In Buell, *Master of Sea Power*, p. 219; for MacArthur's opposition, see letters, Marshall to King, June 6, June 29, July 1, 1942, Marshall Papers, Box 73, Folder 12, Marshall Library.
8. Morison, *The Struggle for Guadalcanal*, pp. 373, 116.
9. Commander Yasumi Doi, United States Strategic Bombing Survey, *Interrogation of Japanese Officials*, Vol. I, p. 211.
10. In USSBS, op. cit., Vol. II, p. 331; also Vol. I, p. 68.
11. In McMillan, *The Old Breed: A History of the First Marine Division in World War II*, p. 21.
12. Nick Polifka's is a name remembered by those like the present writer who were involved in photo intelligence during World War II; he made aerial reconnaissance interesting to pilots by showing that it could be daring and dangerous; he commanded the First Photo Recon Unit in the Southwest Pacific and flew 347 combat missions; he died in Korea; *New York Times*, July 9, 1951, p. 7, col. 2.
13. See Dyer, *The Amphibians Came to Conquer*, Vol. I, pp. 300–2; Vandegrift, *Once a Marine*, pp. 120–2; Griffith, *The Battle for Guadalcanal*, pp. 35–6.
14. In Leckie, *Challenge for the Pacific*, p. 67.
15. In Dyer, op. cit., p. 328.
16. In Zimmerman, op. cit., p. 28.
17. Griffith, op. cit., p. 50.
18. Vandegrift, op. cit., pp. 125, 162.
19. Newcomb, *Savo: The Incredible Naval Debacle Off Guadalcanal*, p. 43.
20. Morison, op. cit., p. 37.
21. In Dyer, op. cit., Vol. I, p. 151.
22. In ibid., pp. 371–2, and Morison, op. cit., p. 25.
23. See Zimmerman, op. cit., p. 50; Morison, op. cit., p. 28.
24. Fletcher in 1963, in Dyer, op. cit., p. 395.
25. In Vandegrift, op. cit., p. 25.
26. Smith, *Coral and Brass*, p. 19.
27. Liddell Hart, *The Defence of Britain*, 1939, in Isely and Crowl, *The U.S. Marines and Amphibious War*, p. 5; Dyer, op. cit., p. 318.
28. Smith, op. cit., p. 49.

29. Vandegrift, "The Marine Corps in 1948," in Isely and Crowl, op. cit., p. 4.
30. Smith, op. cit., p. 90–1.
31. In ibid., p. 101–2.
32. *Houston Morning Press News,* March 2, 1938, Trips of the President file, FDR Library.
33. In Buell, *The Quiet Warrior: A Biography of Admiral Raymond A. Spruance,* p. 81.
34. Isely and Crowl, op. cit., pp. 25–7; also Dorwart, *Conflict of Duty: The U.S. Navy's Intelligence Dilemma, 1919–1945,* pp. 33–5.
35. Vandegrift, op. cit., pp. 132, 135.
36. In Pratt, *The Marines' War,* p. 43.
37. In Zimmerman, op. cit., p. 67.
38. In Pratt, op. cit., p. 44.
39. In Vandegrift, op. cit., p. 144.
40. Dyer, op. cit., p. 419.
41. In Miller, op. cit., p. 85.
42. Leckie, op. cit., p. 153.
43. Morison, op. cit., pp. 74, 78.
44. In Okumiya and Horikoshi, *Zero!,* p. 188.
45. Sherrod, *History of Marine Corps Aviation in World War II,* p. 83.
46. In Griffith, op. cit., p. 117.
47. Ibid., p. 117.
48. In Freidin and Richardson, eds., *The Fatal Decisions,* p. 38.
49. Griffith, op. cit., p. 133.
50. Pratt, *Eleven Generals,* p. 285.
51. Ibid., p. 294.
52. Turner in Dyer, op. cit., Vol. I, p. 397; in Griffith, op. cit., pp. 114–15.
53. In Davis, *Marine! The Life of Lt. Gen. Lewis B. (Chesty) Puller,* p. 122.
54. Pratt, *The Marines' War,* p. 88; in Griffith, op. cit., p. 174.
55. In Sherwood, *Roosevelt and Hopkins,* pp. 624–5.
56. In Morison, op. cit., p. 178.
57. MacArthur to Marshall, October 17, 1942, with letter of transmittal to Roosevelt, October 19, 1942, MSS, Box 80, Folder 36, Marshall Library.
58. Morton, *Strategy and Command: The First Two Years,* pp. 341–5.
59. Vandegrift, op. cit., p. 191.
60. In Sherwood, op. cit., p. 622.
61. In McCarthy, *Australia in the War of 1939–1945: South-west Pacific—First Year,* pp. 259–60; in Loewenheim et al., *Roosevelt and Churchill: Their Secret Wartime Correspondence,* p. 260.
62. Hassett, *Off the Record with F.D.R.,* pp. 104, 129, 192; *Complete Press Conferences,* Vol. 20, pp. 74–5, 178–9, 196–7, 242–5; Vol. 22, pp. 134, 199–200.
63. In Halsey and Bryan, *Admiral Halsey's Story,* p. 116.
64. In Leckie, op. cit., p. 168; Davis, op. cit., pp. 118, 111.
65. Leckie, op. cit., pp. 263, 265, 267; in Pratt, *The Marines' War,* p. 93.
66. In Morison, op. cit., p. 287.
67. Ibid., pp. 236, 258, 250.
68. The story of Lee's arrival was soon being told and retold, so that there are many versions of his message. Pratt gives: "This is Ching Chong Lee. Get out

of the way; I'm coming through" (*The Marines' War*, p. 113). I have used Morison's, which is based on ships' logs and Lee's own recollection (Morison, op. cit., p. 273).

69. See Stafford, *The Big E*, pp. 182–207.
70. In Vandegrift, op. cit., p. 199.
71. In Halsey and Bryan, op. cit., p. 130; in Sherwood, op. cit., p. 656; Puller in interview of January 1946, in Zimmerman, op. cit., p. 153.
72. McMillan, op. cit., pp. 115–16, 118; Leckie, op. cit., pp. 301–2.
73. Vandegrift, op. cit., pp. 175–6.
74. Halsey and Bryan, op. cit., p. 123; Leckie, op. cit., p. 315.
75. Roosevelt, *This I Remember*, p. 308.
76. Leckie, op. cit., p. 341; Churchill, *Closing the Ring*, p. 21.
77. Vandegrift, op. cit., pp. 235–6, 242.
78. Marshall in Buell, *Master of Sea Power*, p. 360; Vandegrift, op. cit., p. 283.
79. Vandegrift, pp. 279–80.
80. Ibid., pp. 212, 280.

VI. MACARTHUR

1. Schlesinger, *The Crisis of the Old Order*, pp. 417, 268; Tugwell, *The Democratic Roosevelt*, pp. 348–50.
2. Eisenhower, *At Ease*, p. 217.
3. In James, *The Years of MacArthur*, Vol. I (1880–1941), pp. 403–4; also ibid., p. 680, note 28.
4. Ibid., p. 404; Eisenhower, op. cit., p. 218.
5. MacArthur, *Reminiscences*, p. 101; James, op. cit., pp. 428–9.
6. James, op. cit., pp. 429, 493–4.
7. Hunt, *The Untold Story of Douglas MacArthur*, p. 158.
8. James, op. cit., pp. 23–4, 84; Gunther, *The Riddle of MacArthur*, p. 24.
9. James, op. cit., pp. 164, 239, 240.
10. Ibid., pp. 76–7, 98, 156, 169; Hunt, op. cit., pp. 74–5; "MacArthur has always been convinced that his opinions and views would have had more sympathetic consideration in Washington if almost anyone except Marshall had been in charge" Lee and Henschel, *Douglas MacArthur*, p. 124.
11. James, op. cit., pp. 272–3, 282–3, 289.
12. Ibid., pp. 356, 379, 380, 469, 57–8, 4, 442–3; Ickes, *The First Thousand Days 1933–36*, p. 71.
13. James, op. cit., pp. 475, 535, 482; in ibid., pp. 345–6.
14. Ibid., pp. 91–3; MacArthur, *Reminiscences*, pp. 30–2.
15. James, op. cit., pp. 481, 504.
16. Morton, *Strategy and Command: The First Two Years*, pp. 39, 43.
17. Craven and Cate, *The Army Air Forces in World War II*, Vol. I, pp. 178–9.
18. In Morton, *The Fall of the Philippines*, p. 65; ibid., p. 32.
19. Baldwin, *Great Mistakes of the War*, pp. 64–5.
20. Edmonds, *They Fought with What They Had*, pp. 13, 27, 71; Craven and Cate, op. cit., p. 187.
21. Hersey, *Men on Bataan*, pp. 287–91.
22. MacArthur to Marshall and Watson to Marshall, July 30, 1941, MSS, Box 74,

Folder 47, Marshall Library; in Marshall to Roosevelt, September 5, 1941, MS, Box 80, Folder 30, Marshall Library.

23. Early to MacArthur, April 14, 1941; Watson to MacArthur, April 5, 1941; Marshall to MacArthur, June 20, 1941; MSS, MacArthur Archives; Marshall to MacArthur, November 28, 1941, MS, Box 74, Folder 48, Marshall Library.

24. James, op. cit., Vol. II (1941–1945), pp. 90–9. "There he could prove himself in ways unavailable elsewhere. There, also, he could find solace and support when failure on other fronts seemed imminent. For forty years, the Philippine Islands provided both safe haven and appropriate center stage for Douglas MacArthur" (Petillo, *Douglas MacArthur: The Philippine Years*, p. vii).

25. Petillo, "Douglas MacArthur and Manuel Quezon," *Pacific Historical Review*, February 1979, pp. 107–17.

26. Ferrell, ed., *The Eisenhower Diaries*, p. 63.

27. Edmonds, op. cit., pp. 100, 108; Gunther, *Roosevelt in Retrospect*, p. 324.

28. Brereton, *The Brereton Diaries*, pp. 38ff; MacArthur in *New York Times*, September 27, 1946; see Baldwin, op. cit., p. 70, and Morton, op. cit., p. 83–4.

29. Craven and Cate, op. cit., pp. 206–7, 687–8 note 31; Edmonds, op. cit., p. 81; Ind, *Bataan*, p. 93.

30. In Hayes, *The History of the Joint Chiefs of Staff in World War II*, p. 17; also in Morton, *Strategy and Command*, p. 67.

31. In Baldwin, op. cit., p. 70.

32. Brereton, op. cit., p. 39; Morton, op. cit., pp. 119, 190.

33. James, op. cit., Vol. I, p. 504; Morton, *The Fall of the Philippines*, pp. 26, 28, 136.

34. Morton, op. cit., pp. 23–5, 162n; Eisenhower in Ferrell, ed., op. cit., p. 43.

35. Morton, op. cit., pp. 256, 259.

36. Whitney, *MacArthur: His Rendezvous with History*, p. 25; Manchester, *American Caesar*, pp. 266–7; MacArthur to Roosevelt, January 30, 1942, MS, FDR Library.

37. Whitney, op. cit., p. 27.

38. Morton, op. cit., pp. 145–6; Stimson and Bundy, *On Active Service*, pp. 395–7.

39. Eisenhower in Ferrell, ed., op. cit., pp. 40–3; Morton, op. cit., pp. 399, 400; Morton, *Strategy and Command*, p. 537; Matloff, *Strategic Planning for Coalition Warfare 1943–44*, pp. 392–3.

40. Morton, *Fall of the Philippines*, pp. 359–60; Eisenhower in Ferrell, ed., op. cit., p. 49.

41. Milner, *Victory in Papua*, pp. 24–5. "If MacArthur had a radical change of policy in mind after his arrival Austen and Blamey were not made aware of it, and the steps taken to reinforce Port Moresby were singularly cautious" (McCarthy, *South-West Pacific Area—First Year: Kokoda to Wau*, p. 112). Also James, op. cit., Vol. II, pp. 181–2.

42. McCarthy, op. cit., p. 120; Lee and Henschel, op. cit., p. 165.

43. Milner, op. cit., pp. 51, 53–4, 60–71; in ibid., p. 70.

44. In Willoughby and Chamberlain, *MacArthur 1941–1951*, p. 88.

45. McCarthy, op. cit., p. 334; also Milner, op. cit., p. 124n; in McCarthy, op. cit., pp. 274, 225, 307.

46. Milner, op. cit., p. 134; McCarthy, op. cit., pp. 308, 141, 175; Eichelberger, *Our Jungle Road to Tokyo,* pp. 11–12, 50.
47. In Milner, op. cit., pp. 113–14; ibid., pp. 115, 118.
48. McCarthy, op. cit., pp. 356; Milner, op. cit., pp. 126, 195; in McCarthy, op. cit., pp. 370, 359.
49. McCarthy, op. cit., p. 371; Milner, op. cit., p. 204; in Eichelberger, op. cit., pp. 20–1.
50. Eichelberger, op. cit., pp. 21–2.
51. Ibid., pp. 17, 29, 48, 49.
52. In Luvaas, ed., *Dear Miss Em,* pp. 64–5; James, op. cit., p. 430; Eichelberger, op. cit., p. 99; Milner, op. cit., p. 368; in James, op. cit., pp. 271, 272; Eichelberger, op. cit., p. 182.
53. James, op. cit., p. 90; Milner, op. cit., pp. 298–9; Eichelberger, op. cit., pp. 47, 51.
54. In James, op. cit., p. 279; in Eichelberger, op. cit., pp. 42–3; Whitney, op. cit., pp. 86–7.
55. James, op. cit., pp. 279–80; Milner, op. cit., pp. 100–2.
56. James, op. cit., pp. 133–5, 129–31; in Whitney, op. cit., p. 100.
57. In Ferrell, ed., op. cit., pp. 51, 54.
58. James, op. cit., p. 137; Fish to MacArthur, June 5, 1943, MS, MacArthur Archives.
59. James, op. cit., p. 251; Vandenberg, ed., *The Private Papers of Senator Vandenberg,* pp. 77–89; the one vote was not Hamilton Fish's but that of a member of the Wisconsin delegation named Ritter (ibid., p. 89).
60. Wilkinson Journal, MS, Churchill College, Cambridge (a photocopy of some but not all passages relating to MacArthur is in MacArthur Archives); Thorne, *Allies of a Kind: The United States, Britain, and the War Against Japan, 1941–1945,* p. 367; MacArthur to Churchill, April 12, 1943; Churchill to Ismay, May 7, 1943, with enclosures, MSS, PREM 3/158 and 3/159/4, Public Record Office, Kew.
61. McCarthy, op. cit., p. 28; James, op. cit., pp. 176, 254–5; in ibid., p. 256.
62. In James, op. cit., p. 254; Thorne, op. cit., p. 276; Moore, *Over-sexed, Over-paid, and Over Here: Americans in Australia 1941–1945,* pp. 277, 257, 277, 271; Moore is an American writer who for three years taught American history at Macquarie University in Sydney.
63. Lee and Henschel, op. cit., pp. 188, 180.
64. Ibid., p. 183; Gunther, op. cit., p. 73; James, op. cit., p. 598.
65. Gunther, op. cit., p. 74; declining the toast, Gunthers in conversation with the author; "Willoughby's Troubles," *U.S. News & World Report,* December 15, 1950, pp. 39–40; Kluckhohn, "Heidelberg to Madrid—The Story of General Willoughby," *The Reporter,* August 19, 1952, pp. 25–6; Willoughby and Chamberlain, op. cit., p. *vi.*
66. Lee and Henschel, op. cit., p. 167; James, op. cit., pp. 200–1; Haugland, *The AAF Against Japan,* p. 154; "Hell, let's try it," Kenney obituary, *New York Times,* August 11, 1977.
67. Craven and Cate, op. cit., Vol. IV, pp. 101, 106–7, 146–50; James, op. cit., pp. 295–9; Arnold, *Global Mission,* p. 383; in Craven and Cate, op. cit., Vol. IV, p. 345.

68. James, op. cit., pp. 194, 245, 248, 452, 664; Gunther, op. cit., p. 49; Eichelberger, op. cit., p. 107.

69. Morton, *Strategy and Command,* pp. 389-91.

70. Churchill to Roosevelt, April 29, 1942, in Loewenheim et al., eds., *Roosevelt and Churchill: Their Secret Wartime Correspondence,* p. 213; in Hayes, op. cit., pp. 126-7; in James, op. cit., p. 360.

71. Morton, op. cit., p. 395.

72. King and Whitehill, *Fleet Admiral King: A Naval Record,* p. 429; in Hayes, op. cit., pp. 330-1, 332, 333.

73. In Morton, op. cit., p. 399; Halsey and Bryan, *Admiral Halsey's Story,* p. 155.

74. Morison, *Breaking the Bismarcks Barrier,* p. 258ff; in Willoughby and Chamberlain, op. cit., p. 130; in Whitney, op. cit., p. 105.

75. Miller, *Cartwheel: the Reduction of Rabaul,* pp. 289, 294-5; Reynolds, *The Fast Carriers,* pp. 97-101; Whitney, op. cit., p. 106; Miller, op. cit., p. 272.

76. In Willoughby, op. cit., pp. 100-2.

77. Morison, *Strategy and Compromise,* p. 94.

78. Arnold, op. cit., p. 372; Morison, *Strategy and Compromise,* pp. 92-3; Morison, *Breaking the Bismarcks Barrier,* p. 226; Reynolds, op. cit., p. 116.

79. Miller, "MacArthur and the Admiralties," in Greenfield, ed., *Command Decisions,* pp. 301-2.

80. Ibid., pp. 298-9; Historical Division U.S. War Department, *The Admiralties,* pp. 12-22, 29, 31, 27.

81. Hayes, op. cit., pp. 310, 432, 549; in James, op. cit., p. 365.

82. In Hunt, op. cit., pp. 331-2.

83. Morison, *Leyte,* p. 9.

84. Rosenman, *Working with Roosevelt,* pp. 456-7; James, op. cit., pp. 527-9.

85. James, op. cit., p. 529; Morison, *Leyte,* p. 9.

86. Smith, *Triumph in the Philippines,* p. 8n.

87. Ibid., p. 15.

88. Reynolds, op. cit., p. 161; Morison, *New Guinea and the Marianas,* p. 277.

89. Smith, *Approach to the Philippines,* p. 5; Morton, *Strategy and Command,* p. 605; Hayes, op. cit., pp. 605, 608.

90. Krueger, *From Down Under to Nippon,* pp. 56ff., 71-3, 75-6; Millis, ed., *The War Reports,* pp. 225-6.

91. James, op. cit., p. 509.

92. Smith, "Luzon versus Formosa," in Greenfield, ed., *Command Decisions,* pp. 471, 468; Hayes, op. cit., p. 610.

93. In Willoughby, op. cit., p. 235; in Hayes, op. cit., p. 606.

94. In Whitney, op. cit., p. 125.

95. Eichelberger, op. cit., p. 166; Hunt, op. cit., p. 337; Morison, *Leyte,* p. 10n; in James, op. cit., p. 532.

96. Tugwell, op. cit., p. 660n; in Rosenman, op. cit., p. 487.

97. Rosenman, pp. 458-9.

98. Smith, *Triumph in the Philippines,* pp. 140, 651, 652; in Hunt, op. cit., p. 336.

99. Smith, op. cit., pp. 237-9, 141; in ibid., p. 294.

100. Eichelberger, op. cit., p. 166.

101. Morison, *The Liberation of the Philippines,* p. 214; Smith, op. cit., pp. 584-5; Eichelberger, op. cit., p. 200; Smith, op. cit., pp. 584, 597, 599, 618, 647.

102. Eichelberger, op. cit., pp. 171, 181, 264; James, op. cit., Vol. II, pp. 690, 677–8.
103. Morison, *New Guinea and the Marianas*, p. 48; James, op. cit., Vol. II, pp. 591–2; James, op. cit., Vol. I, p. 572.
104. Gunther, op. cit., p. 9–10; James, op. cit., Vol. I, p. viii.
105. So he told his son James, though without mentioning the bomb; Roosevelt, *My Parents*, pp. 169–70.
106. In Whitney, op. cit., p. 221.
107. Craig, *The Fall of Japan*, pp. 299–300, 261.
108. Kase, *Journey to the Missouri*, pp. 7–8; in Whitney, op. cit., pp. 221–4.

VII. NIMITZ

1. Potter, *Nimitz*, pp. 9–10, 373; Albion and Connery, *Forrestal and the Navy*, p. 131.
2. Potter, op. cit., pp. 22, 24, 26, 30.
3. In Prange, Goldstein, and Dillon, *Miracle at Midway*, pp. 11–12; Potter, op. cit., pp. 176–7.
4. In Buell, *Master of Seapower*, pp. 108, 315, 361, 197.
5. Morison, *The Rising Sun in the Pacific*, pp. 256–7.
6. Potter, op. cit., pp. 52, 62, 122, 123; in ibid., pp. 123, 133, 136; ibid., pp. 139, 141–2.
7. Ibid., pp. 155, 152, 151, 456; in ibid., p. 169.
8. Morison, op. cit., pp. 249–54; in Prange et al., op. cit., p. 12.
9. In Prange, p. 9.
10. Potter, op. cit., pp. 18, 41, 34, 42.
11. Lord, *Incredible Victory*, p. 17; Holmes, *Double-edged Secrets*, p. 14.
12. Potter, op. cit., p. 64; Kahn, *The Codebreakers*, p. 301; for a view of Op-20-G from the Washington side, see Van der Rhoer, *Deadly Magic*.
13. Kahn, op. cit., pp. 307–8, 306–7; Holmes, op. cit., p. 83; Kahn, op. cit., p. 310.
14. Holmes, op. cit., p. 90; Potter, op. cit., pp. 82–3, 93.
15. Potter, p. 104; Sherrod, *History of Marine Corps Aviation in World War II*, p. 54; Buell, op. cit., p. 201; Morison, *Coral Sea, Midway, and Submarine Actions*, p. 82.
16. Morison, pp. 33–63, 64.
17. Potter, op. cit., p. 85; Holmes, op. cit., p. 94.
18. Frank and Harrington, *Rendezvous at Midway*, pp. 95, 104, 107.
19. In Stafford, *The Big E*, p. 72; in Prange et al., op. cit., p. 386.
20. In Morison, op. cit., p. 84; in Potter, op. cit., p. 87.
21. Agawa, *The Reluctant Admiral*, pp. 186, 231, 60.
22. Ibid., pp. 220, 189, 127, 220, 259, 283, 291.
23. Fuchida and Okumiya, *Midway: The Battle That Doomed Japan*, pp. 32–4; Lord, *Day of Infamy*, pp. 180–1; Genda in *New York Post*, September 10, 1961.
24. Prange et al., op. cit., pp. 22–3.
25. Craven and Cate, *The U.S. Army Air Force in World War II*, Vol. I, p. 438; King and Whitehill, *A Naval Record*, p. 376; Arnold, *Global Mission*, p. 298; see also King to Quentin Reynolds, March 19 and 25, 1952, MS, King Papers, Library of Congress.

26. Fuchida and Okumiya, op. cit., p. 65.
27. Buell, *The Quiet Warrior*, p. 121.
28. Prange et al., op. cit., p. 53; Fuchida and Okumiya, op. cit., pp. 79, 108; Tuleja, *Climax at Midway*, p. 52.
29. Fuchida and Okumiya, op. cit., p. 4.
30. In Morison, op. cit., p. 138.
31. Fuchida and Okumiya, op. cit., p. 154.
32. Morison, op. cit., pp. 104–5; in Prange et al., op. cit., p. 206.
33. Fuchida and Okumiya, op. cit., p. 117; Prange et al., op. cit., pp. 214, 215; Morison, op. cit., p. 71; Potter, op. cit., p. 88.
34. Fuchida and Okumiya, op. cit., pp. 165–6; Prange et al., op. cit., pp. 216–17.
35. Fuchida and Okumiya, op. cit., pp. 168–71, 163; Prange et al., op. cit., pp. 232–6.
36. Buell, *The Quiet Warrior*, pp. 126–8; Stafford, op. cit., p. 75.
37. In Buell, op. cit., p. 128; in Burns, *Roosevelt: The Soldier of Freedom*, p. 226.
38. In Fuchida and Okumiya, op. cit., p. v; in Morison, op. cit., p. 103.
39. In Reynolds, *The Fast Carriers*, p. ii.
40. In Morison, *Aleutians, Gilberts and Marshalls*, pp. xxix–xxxvi.
41. Buell, op. cit., p. 133; Morison, *Coral Sea, Midway, and Submarine Actions*, p. 114; Prange et al., op. cit., p. 254.
42. James, "Torpedo Squadron 8," *Life*, April 31, 1942, pp. 70–80.
43. Prange et al., op. cit., pp. 242, 246; Lord, *Incredible Victory*, p. 144.
44. Fuchida and Okumiya, op. cit., p. 177.
45. In Lord, op. cit., pp. 162–3.
46. In Buell, op. cit., p. 133; in Powers, "Incredible Midway," in *U.S. Naval Institute Proceedings*, June 1967, pp. 64–73; Thach in Spector, *Eagle Against the Sun*, p. 174.
47. Prange et al., op. cit., pp. 262–3, 270, 264–5.
48. Lord, op. cit., p. 183; Fuchida and Okumiya, op. cit., pp. 183–4; in Prange et al., op. cit., p. 265.
49. Prange, p. 262n.
50. Lord, op. cit., pp. 289–9.
51. See "Comment and Discussion," in *U.S. Naval Institute Proceedings*, September 1967, pp. 106–7; Morison, op. cit., p. 135.
52. Fuchida and Okumiya, op. cit., pp. 196–200; Morison, op. cit., p. 137; in Prange et al., op. cit., p. 274.
53. Morison, op. cit., p. 142.
54. Taylor, *The Magnificent Mitscher*, p. 135.
55. In Morison, op. cit., p. 142.
56. "Yamamoto's Yeoman's Story," in ibid., p. 144.
57. Ibid., p. 151.
58. In Prange et al., op. cit., p. 173; in Pratt, *The Marines' War*, p. 55; cf. Leckie, *Challenge for the Pacific*, pp. 137–8.
59. In Prange et al., op. cit., p. 355.
60. In Fuchida and Okumiya, op. cit., pp. xiv–xv.
61. Ibid., p. 129.
62. Ibid., pp. 147–8.
63. Ibid., p. 170.

64. Slonim, "A Flagship View of Command Decisions," in *U.S. Naval Institute Proceedings,* April 1958, pp. 80–9, 86.
65. Testimony of Captains Ohmae, Ohara, Kawaguchi, Tsuda, and Watanabe, United States Strategic Bombing Survey, *Interrogation of Japanese Officials,* Vol. I, pp. 176, 168, 6, 269, 66, 68.
66. Reynolds, op. cit., pp. 72, 75, 411.
67. Buell, op. cit., p. 149; Slonim, loc. cit., p. 84; Prange et al., op. cit., p. 395.
68. In Morison, op. cit., p. 159n; in Prange et al., op. cit., p. 365; Lord, op. cit., p. 288; Potter, op. cit., pp. 52–3, 104–5; Arnold, *Global Mission,* p. 483; cf. Arnold, pp. 378–9.
69. Sanger, "Freedom of the Press or Treason," in *U.S. Naval Institute Proceedings,* September 1977, pp. 96–7.
70. Prange et al., op. cit., p. 384; Potter, op. cit., pp. 211, 104; Holmes, op. cit., p. 116; Ecclesiastes 9:11. In November 1985, the Navy Department announced that Rochefort would be posthumously awarded the Distinguished Service Medal (McDowell, "Officer Who Broke Japanese War Codes Gets Belated Honor," *New York Times,* November 17, 1985).
71. Iliad, II, 493; Potter, op. cit., pp. 223, 176, 221–6; 228–9.
72. Potter, "The Command Personality," in *U.S. Naval Institute Proceedings,* January 1969, p. 22; in Dyer, *The Amphibians Came to Conquer,* Vol. I, p. 741; Potter, loc. cit., p. 23; Potter, *Nimitz,* p. 265.
73. Buell, op. cit., pp. 165, 168, 177; in ibid., p. 179.
74. Potter, op. cit., p. 293; Halsey and Bryan, *Admiral Halsey's Story,* p. 197; in Potter, op. cit., p. 331.
75. Morison, *Aleutians, Gilberts and Marshalls,* p. 107; Nimitz, Thesis: Tactics; Naval War College, Class of 1923; MS, U.S. Naval War College Archives, p. 35.
76. Buell, op. cit., p. 185; in Potter, "The Command Personality," loc. cit., p. 25.
77. Halsey and Bryan, op. cit., p. 198; Reynolds, op. cit., p. 387; in Potter, *Nimitz,* p. 35.
78. Reynolds, op. cit., pp. 205–6.
79. Potter, op. cit., pp. 303–4; Morison, *New Guinea and the Marianas,* pp. 316, 265.
80. Reynolds, op. cit., p. 386; Morison, op. cit., p. 315; in Prange et al., op. cit., p. 386.
81. Morison, *Coral Sea, Midway, and Submarine Actions,* p. 158.
82. Buell, op. cit., pp. 33–4, 183.
83. Morison, *Leyte,* p. 412.
84. King to Roosevelt, July 12, 1942, MS, King Papers, Library of Congress.
85. In Reynolds, op. cit., p. 56; in Okumiya and Horikoshi, *Zero!,* pp. 162–3.
86. Motley and Kelly, *Now Hear This,* pp. 42–4.
87. Reynolds, op. cit., pp. 54–5, 225–6.
88. Morison, *New Guinea and the Marianas,* p. 235; in ibid., p. 34.
89. Reynolds, op. cit., p. 133; Stafford, op. cit., p. 282; Morison, *Aleutians, Gilberts and Marshalls,* pp. 316–19.
90. Reynolds, op. cit., pp. 137–8; Morison, op. cit., p. 325; Stafford, op. cit., p. 297.
91. Reynolds, op. cit., pp. 214–16; Buell, *Master of Seapower,* p. 137; Potter, op. cit., p. 265.

92. Potter, op. cit., p. 6; Blair, *Silent Victory,* pp. 461–2; Holmes, *Undersea Victory,* p. 361; Potter, op. cit., p. 461.
93. Morison, *Leyte,* p. 412; Holmes, op. cit., pp. 310–11, 424.
94. Holmes, p. 351; Morison, op. cit., p. 413; Blair, op. cit., pp. 853, 851.
95. Van der Rhoer, op. cit., p. 140; Holmes, op. cit., pp. 185–6.
96. Morison, op. cit., p. 338.
97. In USSBS, *Interrogations of Japanese Officials,* Vol. II, p. 317.
98. Hough, *Peleliu,* p. 183.
99. Woodward, op. cit., pp. 10, 43.
100. Ibid., pp. 18–19; Morison, op. cit., pp. 108–9.
101. In Morison, p. 58.
102. Taylor, *The Magnificent Mitscher,* pp. 160, 157, 261.
103. In Morison, op. cit., pp. 199, 202.
104. In Woodward, op. cit., p. 102.
105. In Morison, op. cit., p. 228.
106. Morison, op. cit., p. 195; Potter, op. cit., p. 334.
107. In Taylor, op. cit., p. 262.
108. Morison, op. cit., pp. 195, 160.
109. Ibid., p. 255.
110. In ibid., pp. 257, 267.
111. Ibid., p. 266.
112. In ibid., pp. 288, 297, 298.
113. Potter, op. cit., p. 340.
114. Clark and Reynolds, *Carrier Admiral,* p. 201; King and Whitehill, *A Naval Record,* p. 580; Reynolds, op. cit., pp. 343–4.
115. Burns, *Soldier of Freedom,* p. 540; Reynolds, op. cit., p. 285.
116. In Baldwin, *Battles Lost and Won,* p. 477.
117. Potter, op. cit., pp. 288–9, 366.

VIII. EISENHOWER

1. Morgan, *Overture to Overlord,* p. 8.
2. Chandler, ed., *The Papers of Dwight David Eisenhower,* Vol. I, pp. 83–4, 104–5, 180–2, 194–5.
3. Churchill, *The Hinge of Fate,* pp. 384–5.
4. Eisenhower, *Crusade in Europe,* pp. 13–22.
5. Eisenhower, *At Ease,* pp. 248–9.
6. Chandler, ed., op. cit., p. 130n; Eisenhower, op. cit., pp. 185, 187.
7. Gunther, *Eisenhower,* p. 60; Wilson Kierstead to the author, 1985; Chandler, ed., op. cit., pp. 100–1.
8. Eisenhower, op. cit., pp. 210–12; Gunther, op. cit., p. 64; Chandler, ed., op. cit., pp. 70, 148, 283, 53, 419.
9. Chandler, ed., op. cit., p. 142n; Eisenhower, op. cit., pp. 169–70.
10. Eisenhower, op. cit. pp. 169–170, Blumenson, ed., *The Patton Papers 1940–1945,* Vol. II, pp. 795, 931, 947.
11. Morris et al., *Weapons and Warfare of the 20th Century,* pp. 238–9.
12. Clark, *Barbarossa,* p. 337; Werth, *Russia at War,* p. 685.
13. On Christie: Jones et al., *The Fighting Tanks Since 1916,* pp. 161–71, 190;

United Press dispatch, January 10, 1944; *New York Times* and *New York Herald Tribune,* January 12, 1944; correspondence of David C. Prince with author, January 1944; for Liddell Hart's efforts to secure a Christie tank for the British, see *The Liddell Hart Memoirs,* Vol. I, pp 390–1; the Russians credit Major General Aleksandr A. Morozov with the design of the T-34 (*New York Times,* June 15, 1979).

14. Blumenson, ed., op. cit., pp. 411, 511.
15. In Rhodes, "Ike: An Artist in Iron," *Harper's Magazine,* July 1970, p. 73; Eisenhower, op. cit., p. 213.
16. Eisenhower, op. cit., p. 231.
17. Wilkinson Journal, MS, Churchill College, Cambridge.
18. Daniel, *Lords, Ladies, and Gentlemen,* p. 88.
19. In Ambrose, *The Supreme Commander,* pp. 105, 50; Eisenhower, op. cit., p. 248; Ambrose, op. cit., p. 21.
20. Ambrose, p. 35.
21. Ibid., pp. 30–1, 44–6; Pogue, *Ordeal and Hope,* p. 339.
22. Eisenhower, *Crusade in Europe,* p. 50; Chandler et al., eds., op. cit., Vol. I, p. 333.
23. Roche, "Eisenhower Redux," *New York Times Book Review,* June 28, 1981, p. 12.
24. Whitehead, "A Correspondent's View of D-Day," in *D-Day: The Normandy Invasion in Retrospect,* p. 52.
25. Eisenhower, *At Ease,* pp. 181–2; in Ferrell, ed., *The Eisenhower Diaries,* p. 145.
26. Gunther, *Eisenhower,* pp. 25–8.
27. In Bryant, *Triumph in the West,* p. 408; Gunther, op. cit., p. 26.
28. Complete text of the Guildhall speech is in Gunther, pp. 158–62.
29. Murphy, *Diplomat Among Warriors,* p. 104.
30. in Chandler et al., eds., op. cit., p. 282.
31. Dallek, *Franklin D. Roosevelt and American Foreign Policy 1932–45,* p. 3; De Gaulle, *Complete Memoirs,* p. 575; in Burns, *Soldier of Freedom,* p. 299.
32. De Gaulle, op. cit., p. 575; Feis, *Churchill, Roosevelt, Stalin,* p. 68; Avon, *The Reckoning,* p. 372.
33. De Gaulle, op. cit., pp. 3, 130, 576.
34. Viorst, *Hostile Allies: FDR and Charles de Gaulle,* pp. 54–6, 105–8; see also White, *Seeds of Discord: De Gaulle, Free France, and the Allies,* Ch. XXIV, "Sum and Substance."
35. In Murphy, op. cit., pp. 101–2; Macmillan, *The Blast of War,* p. 160; Roosevelt to Churchill, September 2, 1952, in Loewenheim et al., eds., *Roosevelt and Churchill: Their Secret Wartime Correspondence,* p. 248.
36. In Dallek, op. cit., p. 364; Macmillan, op. cit., p. 162.
37. Liebling, *Liebling Abroad,* p. 181.
38. In Ambrose, op. cit., pp. 128–9; Sherwood gives Eisenhower's message in paraphrase, *Roosevelt and Hopkins,* pp. 651–2.
39. Sherwood, p. 651; in ibid., pp. 653–64; *Complete Press Conferences,* Vol. 20, pp. 243–7.
40. Macmillan, op. cit., pp. 190, 284, 282–3.

41. Ambrose, op. cit., p. 199; Macmillan, op. cit., p. 291; in Loewenheim et al., eds., op. cit., p. 361.
42. Macmillan, op. cit., p. 295; Ambrose, op. cit., p. 204; Bradley, *A Soldier's Story*, p. 29; Bradley, *A General's Life*, p. 132; Eisenhower to Herbert Mitgang, in Mitgang, "Eisenhower Manuscript Used by Son for a Book," *New York Times*, May 29, 1982.
43. Eisenhower, *Allies*, pp. 230–1.
44. Ibid., pp. 199–203, 212.
45. Ambrose, op. cit., pp. 160–1; Eisenhower, op. cit., p. 231; in Bryant, *Turn of the Tide*, p. 455.
46. Ambrose, op. cit., pp. 161–2; in Hobbs, ed., *Dear General*, p. 100.
47. Eisenhower, op. cit., pp. 267–8, 256; Ambrose, op. cit., pp. 168, 154.
48. Ibid., p. 166; in Liddell Hart, ed., *The Rommel Papers*, p. 398.
49. Ambrose, op. cit., pp. 170–1.
50. Howe, *Northwest Africa: Seizing the Initiative in the West*, pp. 460–4; Ambrose, op. cit., p. 172; Liddell Hart, ed., op. cit., pp. 403–8.
51. Truscott, *Command Missions*, p. 144.
52. Bradley, *A Soldier's Story*, p. 44.
53. Howe, op. cit., p. 521; Ambrose, op. cit., p. 183.
54. Ambrose, pp. 183–4.
55. Bradley, op. cit., p. 59.
56. Bradley, *A General's Life*, pp. 156–7.
57. Liebling, op. cit., pp. 313–14.
58. In Pratt, *Eleven Generals*, pp. 313–14.
59. In Hobbs, ed., op. cit., pp. 121–3.
60. In Blumenson, ed., op. cit., Vol. II, p. 600.
61. In Ambrose, op. cit., pp. 143–4.
62. War Department, *Lessons from the Tunisian Campaign*, p. 37; on the inapplicability of Tank Destroyer doctrine, see Gabel, *Seek, Strike, and Destroy*.
63. Howe, op. cit., pp. 674–5.
64. Eisenhower, *Crusade in Europe*, p. 158.
65. In Ambrose, op. cit., p. 179; Morgan, *Overture to Overlord*, p. 17; Eisenhower, *Allies*, p. 271; in Ambrose, op. cit., p. 681; in Lamb, *Montgomery in Europe 1943–1945*, p. 446.
66. Gavin, *On to Berlin*, pp. 18–42.
67. Fuller, *The Second World War 1939–45*, p. 268.
68. Ambrose, op. cit., pp. 304–5, 296; in Eisenhower, *At Ease*, p. 266.
69. Churchill, *Closing the Ring*, pp. 385, 419.
70. In Roosevelt, *My Parents*, p. 176.
71. In Churchill, *Triumph and Tragedy*, p. 9; in D'Este, *Decision in Normandy*, pp. 108–9.
72. Cruikshank, *Deception in World War II*, pp. 213–15.
73. On GIs in Britain, see Calder, *The People's War 1939–1945*, pp. 307–11.
74. Bradley, *A Soldier's Story*, p. 224.
75. War Department Historical Division [Taylor], *Omaha Beachhead*, pp. 31–3.
76. Morgan, op. cit., pp. 21–2, 64–5.
77. In His Majesty's Stationery Office, *Combined Operations*, p. 154.

78. In D'Este, op. cit., p. 21.
79. Morgan, op. cit., pp. 128, 145, 63; Stalin in Churchill, *Closing the Ring,* p. 371.
80. Harrison, *Cross-Channel Attack,* pp. 67–8.
81. Morgan, op. cit., pp. 70, 135, 137–9; Fergusson, *The Watery Maze,* p. 281; Churchill, op. cit., pp. 13–14.
82. In Harrison, op. cit., p. 64; ibid., pp. 60–1; Morison, *Operations in North African Waters,* p. 267.
83. Harrison, op. cit., pp. 61–2.
84. Walton, *Miracle of World War II,* pp. 442, 436; Harrison, op. cit., p. 62.
85. In Harrison, op. cit., p. 63.
86. In Bryant, *Triumph in the West,* pp. 132–4; Wilmot, *The Struggle for Europe,* pp. 177–8, 180; Morison, *The Invasion of France and Germany,* p. 57, and *Strategy and Compromise,* p. 80.
87. Harrison, op. cit., pp. 101, 104, 105.
88. Morgan, op. cit., pp. 192–6, 207, 209, 200; in ibid., p. 201.
89. Churchill, *Triumph and Tragedy,* p. 31.
90. Harrison, op. cit., p. 99; Lamb, op. cit., p. 60; Hamilton, *Master of the Battlefield: Monty's War Years 1942–1944,* pp. 489, 485.
91. Butcher, *My Three Years with Eisenhower,* pp. 76, 477; Ambrose, op. cit., pp. 58–9, 345.
92. In Churchill, *Closing the Ring,* p. 312.
93. De Guingand, *Operation Victory,* pp. 146–8; Cruikshank, op. cit., pp. 156–7, 59, 170.
94. Cruikshank, Ch. 12, "The Crucial Deception"; Wilmot, op. cit., pp. 332–3; in Cruikshank, op. cit., p. 189.
95. Ambrose, op. cit., pp. 333, 372, 367.
96. In ibid., p. 453; Eisenhower, *Crusade in Europe,* pp. 283, 281; in Ambrose, op. cit., p. 457; in Thorne, *Allies of a Kind,* p. 379.
97. In Ambrose, op. cit., p. 453; Eisenhower, op. cit., p. 283; Ambrose, op. cit., p. 458.
98. Eisenhower, op. cit., pp. 246–7; Ambrose, op. cit., pp. 406–7.
99. Harrison, op. cit., p. 300; Weigley, *Eisenhower's Lieutenants,* pp. 75, 93; Brereton, *The Brereton Diaries,* p. 278; War Department Historical Division [Ruppenthal], *Utah Beach to Cherbourg,* p. 55.
100. Harrison, op. cit., pp. 269–70; Eisenhower, op. cit., p. 249.
101. Eisenhower, p. 249.
102. Stagg, *Forecast for Overlord,* pp. 96, 97, 120, 112, 116, 117–18.
103. Ambrose, op. cit., p. 417.
104. Morgan, op. cit., p. 289.
105. Ambrose, op. cit., p. 418; Butcher, op. cit., p. 562; in ibid., p. 610.
106. Rees, "Supreme Commander," in *The Spectator,* January 7, 1949, p. 6.
107. Ambrose, op. cit., pp. 418–19.
108. Keegan, *Six Armies in Normandy,* p. 15.
109. Howarth, *D-Day,* pp. 22–7, 243–4, 247–8.
110. In Churchill, *Triumph and Tragedy,* pp. 5–6.
111. Burns, *Soldier of Freedom,* pp. 475–6.

112. Marshall, "First Wave at Omaha Beach," in *The Atlantic Monthly,* November 1960, pp. 67–72; Harrison, op. cit., p. 313.
113. Ibid., pp. 300–21.
114. Morison, *The Invasion of France and Germany,* pp. 142ff.
115. War Department Historical Division [Taylor], op. cit., pp. 58–62; Howarth, op. cit., pp. 153–5.
116. Howarth, pp. 73–4, 63–5, 85; Marshall, *Night Drop,* pp. 22–30.
117. Harrison, op. cit., pp. 301–4.
118. Howarth, op. cit., pp. 85–6.
119. Bradley, *A General's Life,* p. 272; Liddell Hart, *History of the Second World War,* p. 557n.
120. Brooke to Tedder, c. July 20, 1944, in Tedder, *With Prejudice,* p. 563; see Liddell Hart, *The Liddell Hart Memoirs,* Vol. 1, pp. 220–1.
121. Bradley, *A Soldier's Story,* p. 329.
122. In Shulman, *Defeat in the West,* pp. 120–1.
123. Bradley, *A General's Life,* pp. 280–1; Blumenson, *Breakout and Pursuit,* pp. 246, 251.
124. Patton, *War As I Knew It,* p. 98; Blumenson, ed., *The Patton Papers 1940–45,* Vol. II, pp. 499, 496.
125. Bradley, op. cit., pp. 273–5; Hastings, *Overlord: D-Day and the Battle for Normandy,* p. 231; Lamb, op. cit., p. 126; Weigley, op. cit., pp. 117–18; Bradley, op. cit., p. 277.
126. In Liddell Hart, *History of the Second World War,* p. 557n; Blumenson, *Breakout and Pursuit,* pp. 362–8, 431–2; in Liddell Hart, ibid.
127. Blumenson, op. cit., pp. 432–3; Bradley, *A Soldier's Story,* p. 375; Weigley, op. cit., p. 192; Blumenson, op. cit., pp. 486, 523.
128. Weigley, op. cit., pp. 206–9; Blumenson, op. cit., pp. 555–8.
129. Bradley, op. cit., p. 377; Hastings, op. cit., pp. 314–15.
130. Patton in Blumenson, ed., *The Patton Papers 1940–45,* Vol. II, p. 521; Churchill in Moran, *Churchill Taken from the Diaries of Lord Moran,* pp. 41, 56–7, 387–8; in Hastings, op. cit., p. 192.
131. Gavin, op. cit., p. 52.
132. Weigley, op. cit., p. 127; Craven and Cate, *The Army Air Forces in World War II,* Vol. III, p. 240.
133. Bradley, op. cit., p. 249–50; on the development of tactical air in Italy, Greenfield, *American Strategy in World War II,* pp. 108–11; on the structure Quesada set up, memoranda, IX Tactical Air Command, January 28, 1945, "Standing Operating Procedure for Air-Ground Cooperation Officers"; February 21, 1945 ("To: All Air Ground Co-operation Officers"); March 7, 1945 ("Armored Division Liaison Quota"), MSS, Quesada Papers, Manuscript Division, Library of Congress; Bradley in Weigley, op. cit., p. 166.
134. Bradley, op. cit., p. 368; Liddell Hart, *The Liddell Hart Memoirs,* Vol. I, pp. 55–6.
135. Churchill, *The Hinge of Fate,* p. 603; Thompson, *Montgomery: The Field Marshall,* p. 21.
136. Hamilton, op. cit., p. 225; Bryant, *Turn of the Tide,* p. 525.
137. De Guingand, op. cit., pp. 189–91; personal communication, Middleton to

the author, May 1985; Montgomery to Grigg, January 6, 1945, MS, Grigg Papers, Churchill College, Cambridge.

138. In Lamb, op. cit., p. 394; Hamilton, op. cit., p. 835.
139. Ambrose, op. cit., pp. 487–8.
140. Ruppenthal, "Logistics and the Broad-Front Strategy," in Greenfield, ed., *Command Decisions*, p. 422; in Chandler, ed., op. cit., Vol. IV, p. 2119.
141. Thompson, *The Battle for the Rhineland*, pp. 12–14; Lamb, op. cit., p. 291.
142. In Pogue, *The Supreme Command*, pp. 249–50; Ambrose, op. cit., pp. 504–5.
143. Lamb, op. cit., p. 180.
144. Ambrose, op. cit., pp. 505–8.
145. In Lamb, op. cit., pp. 207–8.
146. Pogue, op. cit., Ch. XIV, "The Pursuit Stops Short of the Rhine"; Ruppenthal, loc. cit.; Ambrose, in Chandler, ed., op. cit., Vol. V, "Eisenhower as Commander: Single Thrust Versus Broad Front," pp. 39–48.
147. Creveld, *Supplying War*, pp. 224–5; in Ambrose, op. cit., p. 515; Montgomery, *From Normandy to the Baltic*, p. 193.
148. Creveld, op. cit., pp. 226, 230.
149. Ruppenthal, *Logistical Support of the Armies*, Vol. II, pp. 8–10.
150. Creveld, op. cit., p. 230; in Chandler, ed., op. cit., Vol. IV, p. 2122. Eisenhower did not permit himself open criticism of Montgomery until many years after the war, when he was prompted to do so only by Ismay's writing him that publication of Montgomery's memoirs was making it impossible, as Ismay had hoped, for Montgomery to "go down in history as one of the great British captains of war." Eisenhower replied, from the White House, that he had never thought Montgomery "stood much chance" of doing so:

"I recall the impatience with which we waited for any northern movement of Montgomery's out of the Catania Plain [in Sicily] and the long and unnecessary wait before he stepped across the Messina Strait. Do you remember the great promises that he made during the planning for OVERLORD about moving quickly to the southward beyond Caen and Bayeux to get ground fit for airfields, and his post-war assertions that such a movement was never included in the plan? Next consider his preposterous proposal to drive a single pencil-line thrust straight on Berlin, and later his failure even to make good his effort for a lodgment across the Rhine, and this after I had promised and given him everything he requested until that particular operation was completed.

"I cannot forget his readiness to belittle associates in those critical moments when the cooperation of all of us was needed. So, I personally believe that, on the record, historians could never be tempted to gild his status too heavily, even if his memoirs had not revealed traits far from admirable." (Eisenhower to Ismay, January 14, 1959, MS, Ismay Papers, IV/Eis/130B, Liddell Hart Centre for Military Archives, Kings College London)

151. De Guingand, op. cit., pp. 411–13.
152. Butcher, op. cit., p. 659: Wilmot, op. cit., p. 489. Montgomery's words about the signals, published here for the first time, are in "Interview with Major General Sir Miles Graham," London, January 19, 1949, Wilmot Papers, Liddell Hart Centre for Military Archives, Kings College London.

153. Ruppenthal, op. cit., Vol. II, p. 104.
154. Weigley, op. cit., pp. 293–4; Lamb, op. cit., p. 203.
155. Eisenhower in Chandler, ed., op. cit., Vol. IV, pp. 2090ff.; in Lamb, op. cit., pp. 278, 216.
156. Liddell Hart, *History of the Second World War,* pp. 563–6.
157. Gavin, op. cit., p. 202.
158. Jones, *Most Secret War,* p. 578; MacDonald, *The Siegfried Line Campaign,* p. 230.
159. Blumenson, ed., op. cit., Vol. II, p. 552.
160. Eisenhower, *Crusade in Europe,* p. 307; Bradley, op. cit., p. 332; in Lamb, op. cit., p. 249; Montgomery, op. cit., p. 243; Churchill, *Triumph and Tragedy,* p. 200.
161. Gavin, op. cit., p. 150; in MacDonald, op. cit., p. 122.
162. Gavin, op. cit., p. 160; Arthur T. Hadley in conversation with the author.
163. Gavin, op. cit., p. 191; Lamb, op. cit., p. 233; in Gavin, op. cit., p. 185.
164. In Gavin, op. cit., pp. 186–7; the caption to an illustration in the British official war history credits the capture of the Nijmegen Bridge to the "British Second Army" (Ellis, *Victory in the West,* Vol. II, *The Defeat of Germany,* opp. p. 55).
165. Lamb, op. cit., p. 233; Gavin, op. cit., p. 183.
166. Bradley, *A Soldier's Story,* p. 513; Gavin, op. cit., p. 136.
167. Thompson, *The Eighty-five Days,* pp. 13, 15; Den Doolaard, *Roll Back the Sea,* p. 429.
168. Roosevelt to Shipman, December 18, 1942, MS, PSF file, FDR Library; *Complete Press Conferences,* No. 927, December 17, 1943.
169. Phillips, "The Ordeal of George Patton," *New York Review of Books,* December 31, 1964, p. 3: "There is no doubting his sincerity, and no doubt that compared to the dreary run of us, George Patton was quite mad."
170. Thompson, *The Battle for the Rhineland,* p. xii.
171. Blumenson, ed., op. cit., Vol. II, pp. 588–9; Codman, *Drive,* pp. 203–8.
172. Bradley, *A General's Life,* pp. 342–3.
173. Eisenhower, op. cit., p. 350; in Codman, op. cit., p. 230.
174. Gavin, op. cit., p. 246; Bradley, *A Soldier's Story,* p. 472.
175. In Patton, op. cit., p. 196.
176. In Blumenson, ed., op. cit., Vol. II, p. 606; Patton, op. cit., p. 606; Churchill, op. cit., p. 282.
177. In Pogue, *The Supreme Command,* p. 386.
178. Bradley, *A General's Life,* p. 377.
179. In Blumenson, ed., op. cit., Vol. II, p. 636.
180. On Montgomery's tactics at Alamein, see Barnett, *The Desert Generals,* p. 270; Thompson, op. cit., p. 160; MacDonald, *The Last Offensive,* p. 178.
181. Bradley, op. cit., p. 408; Montgomery, op. cit., pp. 314, 321–2.
182. Bradley, op. cit., pp. 401, 406.
183. Ibid., p. 408; Bradley, *A Soldier's Story,* p. 519.
184. Church, "Ultra and the Third Army," May 28, 1945, MS, Public Record Office, Kew; Winterbotham, *The Ultra Secret,* p. 184; Bradley, op. cit., p. 519.
185. MacDonald, op. cit., p. 264; Patton, op. cit., p. 269; in Bradley, op. cit., p. 410; in Blumenson, ed., op. cit., Vol. II, p. 659.

186. MacDonald, op. cit., pp. 269–70; Bradley, op. cit., pp. 521–2.

187. Patton, op. cit., p. 258; Codman, op. cit., p. 269.

188. Patton, op. cit., pp. 272–3; Codman, op. cit., p. 268.

189. Churchill, *Their Finest Hour,* p. 545; Mahan in Pratt, *Empire and the Sea,* p. xvii; Thompson, op. cit., p. 12.

190. Churchill, *Triumph and Tragedy,* p. 609; Ehrman, *Grand Strategy,* Vol. VI, p. 150.

191. Feis, op. cit., pp. 58–60, 332–3; Churchill, op. cit., pp. 227, 634–5, 214.

192. Ibid., pp. 569, 601, 569.

193. Schlesinger, "Wilmot's War, Or, 'Churchill Was Right,' " *The Reporter,* April 29, 1952, p. 35; Baldwin, *Great Mistakes of the War,* pp. 37–45; Clark, *Calculated Risk,* pp. 368–72; Toland, *The Last 100 Days,* p. 386; Ryan, *The Last Battle,* pp. 199–200.

194. Wilmot, op. cit., pp. 12, 128–9, 449, 691–5; in Nicolson, op. cit., p. 259.

195. In Butcher, op. cit., p. 644; Morison, *The Invasion of France and Germany;* pp. 227–8. The present author went through the "gap" by train from Ljubljana to Trieste in the winter of 1963. See also Kassabring, *A Soldier's Record,* p. 261.

196. In Churchill, op. cit., p. 721; Morison, *Strategy and Compromise,* p. 55.

197. Matloff, "Wilmot Revisited: Myth and Reality in Anglo-American Strategy for the Second Front," in *D-Day: the Normandy Invasion in Retrospect,* p. 124; Wilmot, op. cit., p. 130; Churchill, op. cit., pp. 120, 100, 504–5.

198. Michael Howard, quoted by Matloff, loc. cit., p. 121.

199. In Churchill, op. cit., p. 723; Chandler, ed., op. cit., Vol. II, pp. 304–5.

200. In Matloff, *Strategic Planning for Coalition Warfare 1943–1944,* pp. 523–4.

201. Pratt, *Ordeal by Fire,* p. 279.

202. In Churchill, *The Grand Alliance,* p. 672.

203. In Ambrose, op. cit., p. 159.

204. In Lamb, op. cit., p. 431; in Fraser, op. cit., p. 414.

205. In Churchill, op. cit., p. 691; in Bryant, op. cit., pp. 282–3.

206. Roosevelt to Stimson, in Lamb, op. cit., p. 273.

207. Smith, *Eisenhower's Six Great Decisions,* p. 157.

208. Matloff, loc. cit., pp. 211–12; in Bryant, op. cit., pp. 579–80.

209. Ibid., p. 190; Fisher, *Cassino to the Alps,* pp. 535–6.

210. Bryant, op. cit., p. 266; Eisenhower, op. cit., p. 372; Bryant, op. cit., p. 333.

211. MacDonald, op. cit., pp. 351, 354.

212. In Shulman, op. cit., p. 218; Smith, op. cit., pp. 130–1; see also Armstrong, *Unconditional Surrender,* whose author treats the Casablanca formula, I think correctly, as the reflection of an attitude toward war that ruled out the possibility of a negotiated peace.

213. MacDonald, op. cit., pp. 370–2.

214. Churchill, op. cit., p. 463; MacDonald, op. cit., p. 367.

215. Ambrose, *Eisenhower and Berlin,* p. 67.

216. Ibid., pp. 93–4, 97.

217. Erickson, *The Road to Berlin,* p. 622; Bradley, *A Soldier's Story,* p. 98; Pogue, *The Supreme Command,* p. 446.

218. In d'Este, op. cit., p. 470; Ambrose, *The Supreme Commander,* p. 588.

219. In Churchill, op. cit., p. 547.
220. In Smith, op. cit., p. 229.

IX. STILWELL

1. Stilwell, diary, December 11, 1941, in White, ed., *The Stilwell Papers*, p. 4.
2. Ibid., pp. 5–12.
3. Churchill, *The Grand Alliance*, pp. 648–9; Matloff and Snell, *Strategic Planning for Coalition Warfare 1941–42*, pp. 102–8.
4. In White, op. cit., pp. 15, 16, 28; Ferrel, ed., *The Eisenhower Diaries*, p. 44.
5. Marshall to Roosevelt, January 9, 1942; MS, Box 80, Folder 31, Marshall Library; see also Marshall to Roosevelt, December 26, 1941; MS, Box 80, Folder 29, Marshall Library.
6. Dorn, *Walkout*, p. 11; in White, op. cit., pp. 19–20; Pogue, *Ordeal and Hope*, pp. 355–9.
7. Stimson diary, January 13, 1942, in Stimson and Bundy, *On Active Service*, Vol. II, p. 529; Stimson to Drum, January 17, 1942, in Pogue, op. cit., p. 360.
8. In White, op. cit., p. 19; Stimson, diary, January 14, 1942, in Stimson and Bundy, op. cit., Vol. II, p. 530.
9. In White, op. cit., p. 26; the text of messages exchanged with Soong is in Department of State, *United States Relations with China*, pp. 468–9; in White, op. cit., p. 30.
10. Tuchman, *Stilwell and the American Experience in China*, p. 75.
11. Kahn, *The China Hands*, p. 85.
12. In Tuchman, op. cit., pp. 153, 158, 156.
13. Collier, *The War in the Far East*, pp. 38, 41, 43.
14. In White, op. cit., p. 174.
15. Fraser, *Alanbrooke*, passim. A would-be biographer of Stilwell told Viscount Slim, on the authority of Riley Sunderland, that *The Stilwell Papers* had been edited to remove anti-Russian and pro-British remarks. Hart to Slim, October 1, 1960; MS, RLEW 4/10, Slim Papers, Churchill College, Cambridge.
16. "Strategicus" [H. C. O'Neill], *A Short History of the Second World War*, p. 240.
17. Fischer, "Vinegar Joe's Problem," *Harper's Magazine*, December 1944, p. 91.
18. Romanus and Sunderland, *Stilwell's Mission to China*, pp. 15–16.
19. Ibid., p. 26.
20. Ibid., p. 45; Stowe, *They Shall Not Sleep*, pp. 74–7.
21. For Major Ronald Ross's discovery of the malaria cycle, see Harrison, *Mosquitoes, Malaria, and Man*, Chs. 3, 12; Macaulay in Spear, *India: A Modern History*, p. 257.
22. In Beaumont, *Sword of the Raj*, p. 88.
23. Sevareid, *Not So Wild a Dream*, pp. 252–4, 282–3.
24. Masters, *The Road Past Mandalay*, p. 142.
25. In Loewenheim et al., eds., *Roosevelt and Churchill: Their Secret Wartime Correspondance*, p. 206.
26. Kirby, *The War Against Japan*, Vol. II, pp. 9–11; Lewin, *Slim: The Standard-bearer*, pp. 84–5.

27. Kirby, op. cit., pp. 23–46, 59–77.
28. Collis, *Last and First in Burma,* pp. 92–3; Stowe, op. cit., p. 89; Collis, op. cit., p. 104.
29. In White, op. cit., pp. 45, 55–6.
30. Kirby, op. cit., pp. 18–19; in Lewin, *The Chief,* p. 159.
31. Romanus and Sunderland, op. cit., pp. 55–6; in White, op. cit., p. 60.
32. In Collis, op. cit., p. 122.
33. Churchill, *The Hinge of Fate,* pp. 169–70.
34. Collis, op. cit., p. 123; in White, op. cit., p. 75.
35. Lewin, *Slim,* pp. 9, 3; Slim, *Defeat into Victory,* pp. 51, 279.
36. In Romanus and Sunderland, op. cit., p. 108; in White, op. cit., pp. 72–4; Belden, *Retreat with Stilwell,* p. 53.
37. Romanus and Sunderland, op. cit., p. 130; Tuchman, op. cit., p. 289.
38. Seagrave, *Burma Surgeon,* pp. 210–11.
39. In White, op. cit., p. 74; Slim, op. cit., p. 10; Belden, op. cit., p. 196.
40. In Eldridge, *Wrath in Burma,* p. 54; in Stowe, op. cit., pp. 103–4, 109, 117, 129; in Belden, op. cit., p. 304.
41. Tuchman, op. cit., pp. 292–3; in Dorn, op. cit., p. 145.
42. In Belden, op. cit., p. 215.
43. In Dorn, op. cit., pp. 152–3.
44. Ibid., pp. 154–5.
45. In ibid., p. 159.
46. In ibid., p. 164.
47. In ibid., pp. 163, 180, and ibid., pp. 198, 206, 209, 211, 237.
48. In ibid., p. 243.
49. Collis, op. cit., pp. 177, 178n.
50. Slim, op. cit., p. 110.
51. Sevareid, op. cit., p. 311; Stowe, op. cit., pp. 21, 23, 25.
52. Sevareid, op. cit., p. 316; White, op. cit., p. 112.
53. Esherick, ed., *Lost Chance in China: The World War II Dispatches of John S. Service,* pp. 9–19, 88–90.
54. Roosevelt to Marshall, March 8, 1943, in Romanus and Sunderland, op. cit., pp. 278–80; Davies, *Dragon by the Tail,* p. 264.
55. In ibid., p. 280; in Churchill, *Closing the Ring,* p. 328. Numerous evidences of covert British opposition to Stilwell's endeavor are in WO 106/3547, MS, Public Record Office, Kew, typically a draft telegram, Brooke to Wavell (undated, September 1942), suggesting that a response to Chinese troops at Ramgarh should be "ostensibly a warm acceptance," followed by pointing out practical difficulties.
56. Sevareid, op. cit., p. 238; Dorn, op. cit., p. 49; in White, op. cit., p. 113; Sevareid, op. cit., pp. 240, 239; Fischer, loc. cit., p. 92.
57. "I wish I could go with you to Chennault," the President wrote in November 1942 to "Dear Joe"; in Roosevelt, ed., *F.D.R., His Personal Letters, 1928–1945,* Vol. II, p. 1361.
58. Chennault, *Way of a Fighter,* p. 5; in Romanus and Sunderland, op. cit., pp. 252–3.
59. Romanus and Sunderland, op. cit., pp. 322, 253; in ibid., pp. 320, 325; Romanus and Sunderland, *Stilwell's Command Problems,* p. 403.

60. In *Foreign Relations of the United States, 1943 (China)*, p. 29; Davies, op. cit., p. 424; in FRUS, loc. cit.
61. Rolo, *Wingate's Raiders*, p. 16; Sykes, *Orde Wingate*, pp. 87, 448.
62. Mosley, *Gideon Goes to War*, pp. 125–7; Sykes, op. cit., pp. 192–3; Churchill, *Closing the Ring*, pp. 67–8.
63. In Sykes, op. cit., pp. 110, 122, 123.
64. In Evans, *Slim as Military Commander*, p. 127. Slim, op. cit., p. 162.
65. Matloff, *Strategic Planning for Coalition Warfare 1943–44*, p. 240; Hayes, *The History of the Joint Chiefs of Staff in World War II*, p. 451; Sykes, op. cit., p. 455.
66. Mosley, op. cit., pp. 213–14; Bidwell, *The Chindit War*, p. 64; Sykes, op. cit., p. 467.
67. Mosley, op. cit., pp. 217–18, 222; Sykes, op. cit., pp. 467, 486.
68. In Romanus and Sunderland, op. cit., p. 65.
69. In Dorn, op. cit., pp. 75–6; in Romanus and Sunderland, op. cit., p. 72n; in Davies, op. cit., p. 281.
70. See Glines and Moseley, *Grand Old Lady;* Romanus and Sunderland, op. cit., pp. 86, 90.
71. See La Farge, *The Eagle in the Egg*, pp. 109–28.
72. Lewin, *Slim*, pp. 130–2; in Slim, op. cit., p. 192.
73. In Slim, op. cit., p. 186.
74. In Lewin, op. cit., p. 141.
75. Winterbotham, *The Ultra Secret*, p. 170; see Evans and Brett-James, *Imphal*, and Swinson, *The Battle of Kohima;* Middleton, *Crossroads of Modern Warfare*, p. 168.
76. Bidwell, op. cit., p. 104; Slim, op. cit., pp. 261–3.
77. In Romanus and Sunderland, op. cit., pp. 222–3; Ballantrae to Lewin, August 14, 1975, with enclosures, MSS, Churchill College, Cambridge.
78. See Masters, op. cit., pp. 227–76.
79. Slim, op. cit., p. 279; Bidwell, op. cit., p. 274.
80. In Romanus and Sunderland, op. cit., p. 32.
81. In Bidwell, op. cit., p. 49.
82. Bellah, "Stilwell's Chinese Offensive," *Infantry Journal*, July 1944, pp. 41–2.
83. In White, op. cit., p. 295.
84. See Romanus and Sunderland, op. cit., pp. 309–10.
85. In ibid., p. 314.
86. Ogburn, *The Marauders*, p. 86.
87. War Department Historical Division, *Merrill's Marauders*, p. iv. A war diary survives containing the dialogue: a Marauder, "Tojo eats shit!" a Japanese, "Roosevelt eats shit!" Marauder, "Tojo eats corned beef!" Japanese, "Eleanor eats powdered eggs!" (MS, WO 203/4868, Public Record Office, Kew).
88. Ogburn, op. cit., p. 97.
89. In ibid., p. 218.
90. Slim, op. cit., pp. 280, 547.
91. In Ogburn, op. cit., p. 285.
92. In Tuchman, op. cit., p. 448.
93. In White, op. cit., p. 313; in FRUS, loc. cit., p. 29; Slim, op. cit., p. 281.
94. Pogue, op. cit., pp. 354–5.

95. In *F.D.R and Foreign Affairs,* p. 306.
96. Stimson and Bundy, op. cit., p. 535; in Sherwood, *Roosevelt and Hopkins,* p. 739; Romanus and Sunderland, op. cit., pp. 163–4; ibid., p. 385.
97. Sherwood, op. cit., pp. 408, 513, 706–7; in Romanus and Sunderland, op. cit., p. 385n.
98. Alsop to Hopkins, March 1, 3, 5, 26, and April 5, 1943, MSS, FDR Library.
99. Alsop to Soong, July 12, 1943, MS, Box 56, Folder 21, Marshall Library; Soong to Hopkins, September 25, 1953, and Alsop to Hopkins, September 1, 1943, MSS, FDR Library.
100. Chennault to Arnold, December 28, 1943, and Marshall to Roosevelt, February 15, 1944, MSS, Box 56, Folder 21, Marshall Library; Chennault to Hopkins, December 27, 1943, and February 8, 1944, MSS, FDR Library.
101. Romanus and Sunderland, op. cit., pp. 316, 327, 326; in Esherick, op. cit., p. 133.
102. In Romanus and Sunderland, *Stilwell's Mission to China,* p. 325.
103. Romanus and Sunderland, *Stilwell's Command Problems,* pp. 381–2.
104. Romanus and Sunderland, op. cit., p. 443; for a sympathetic view of Hurley's mission, see Lohbeck, *Patrick J. Hurley.*
105. In Romanus and Sunderland, op. cit., p. 452.
106. Alsop and Alsop, *The Reporter's Trade,* p. 168; in Shaller, *The U.S. Crusade in China, 1938–1945,* pp. 357–61; Marshall to Leahy, October 4, 1944, MS, Box 74, Folder 15, Marshall Library.
107. Soong to Hurley, October 1, 1944, in Romanus and Sunderland, op. cit., p. 456. Hopkins later denied this (to Hurley; see Elsey MS, p. 48), but it would not have been the first time he conveyed such a message and Kung's account is consistent with the predilections of the participants.
108. In Romanus and Sunderland, *Time Runs Out in the CBI,* pp. 165–6.
109. Service, "The Situation in China and Suggestions Regarding American Policy," June 20, 1944, in Esherick, op. cit., pp. 138–57.
110. Miles, *A Different Kind of War,* pp. 115–16 (this source should be used with care; it was published posthumously and has been heavily edited); on Miles's breakdown, see Shaller, op. cit., pp. 248–50, and Wedemeyer to Marshall, September 14, 22, 1945, MSS, Box 73, Folder 37, Marshall Library.
111. In Tuchman, op. cit., p. 506; in Esherick, op. cit., p. 153.
112. Elsey, "The President and U.S. Aid to China," p. 53, with attachment from Roosevelt to Brown, MSS, FDR Library.
113. In White, op. cit., pp. 351–4.
114. Stimson and Bundy, op. cit., pp. 535–6.
115. In White, op. cit., pp. 348–9.

X. LEMAY

1. Blum, ed., *From the Morgenthau Diaries: Years of Urgency 1938–1945,* pp. 366–8.
2. Craven and Cate, *The Army Air Forces in World War II,* Vol. V, pp. 17, 760; Patterson to Hopkins, October 24, 1943 (with attachment), Hopkins to Leahy, November 3, 1943; MSS, RG 218, Records of the United States Joint Chiefs of Staff, Leahy File #137, National Archives.

3. In Collision, *The Superfortress Is Born*, p. 44; on A-bomb cost, see Groves, *Now It Can Be Told*, p. 360; Craven and Cate, op. cit., Vol. V, p. 209.
4. Arnold, *Global Mission*, p. 348.
5. LeMay, *Mission with LeMay*, pp. 13–14.
6. Ibid., pp. 33–7, 66, 131.
7. Copp, *A Few Great Captains*, pp. 392–8; LeMay, op. cit., pp. 140–52.
8. Copp, op. cit., pp. 418–26; LeMay, op. cit., pp. 183–93.
9. Ibid., p. 218.
10. In Cozzens, *A Time of War: Air Force Diaries and Pentagon Memos 1943–45*, p. 307; LeMay, op. cit., p. 59.
11. "The Strategic Bomber," *Air University Quarterly Review*, Summer 1955, Vol. I, No. 1, pp. 89–91.
12. In Craven and Cate, op. cit., Vol. I, pp. 43, 44–45, 50–2.
13. In Rumpf, *The Bombing of Germany*, pp. 19–20.
14. Thomas, *The Spanish Civil War*, pp. 255–6, 419–21.
15. Copp, *Forged in Fire*, pp. 222–6.
16. Craven and Cate, op. cit., Vol. I, pp. 561–2, 574; in Loewenheim et al., *Roosevelt and Churchill: Their Secret Wartime Correspondence*, p. 189.
17. Craven and Cate, op. cit., Vol. I, p. 575; Arnold, op. cit., p. 150.
18. Saundby, *Air Bombardment*, p. 108; Harris quoted by Middleton, *New York Times*, April, 7, 1984.
19. Craven and Cate, op. cit., Vol. I, pp. 585, 644, 661–2, 665; Copp, op. cit., pp. 310, 345, 346.
20. Parton, *"Air Force Spoken Here," General Ira Eaker and Command of the Air*, pp. 188, 212–22; in Coffey, *Decision over Schweinfurt*, p. 187.
21. Ibid., p. 188; Churchill, *The Hinge of Fate*, p. 679; Arnold, op. cit., p. 397.
22. LeMay, op. cit., pp. 228–31.
23. Stiles, *Serenade to the Big Bird*, pp. 20–1, 94.
24. Jablonski, *Flying Fortress*, pp. 308–9, 310–11.
25. Bendiner, *The Fall of Fortresses*, pp. 40–2, 131; LeMay, op. cit., p. 227.
26. In Jablonski, op. cit., p. 35; Stiles, op. cit., p. 133.
27. Jablonski, op. cit., pp. xiii, 109, 206; Stiles, op. cit., p. 52; LeMay, op. cit., pp. 245, 283, 259.
28. Ibid., pp. 231, 238–9, 241, 243, 245.
29. Stiles, op. cit., pp. 106–8.
30. Parton, op. cit., p. 177; in Emerson, "Operation Pointblank," Harmon Memorial Lecture, Air Force Academy, 1962; p. 23.
31. Knocke, *I Flew for the Führer*, pp. 88–9; Galland, *The First and the Last*, pp. 180–1.
32. Craven and Cate, op. cit., Vol. II, pp. 225, 669, 685–6.
33. Speer, *Inside the Third Reich*, pp. 280–1.
34. Craven and Cate, op. cit., Vol. II, pp. 682–3, 686; Speer, op. cit., p. 285; LeMay, op. cit., pp. 294–5.
35. Coffey, op. cit., p. 309.
36. Craven and Cate, op. cit., Vol. II, p. 702.
37. Ibid., p. 703; Speer, op. cit., p. 286.
38. Emerson, loc. cit., pp. 5–6; in ibid., p. 7.

39. *Complete Press Conferences*, Vol. 22, pp. 160–1; *New York Times*, October 16, 1943, p. 16; Parton, op. cit., pp. 324–5.

40. Bendiner, op. cit., pp. 138–9.

41. See Cameron, "In the Dropping Zone," *Times Literary Supplement*, August 12, 1983, p. 850.

42. Dyson, "Weapons and Hope, II," *The New Yorker*, February 13, 1984, pp. 89–93.

43. Craven and Cate, op. cit., Vol. III, p. 788; Harris, *Bomber Offensive*, p. 268; Marshall in *The War Reports*, p. 275; Fuller, *The Second World War*, pp. 222, 226. The Seljuk Turks, who established an empire in Asia Minor during the eleventh century, were ferocious in war but surely do not merit this use as an epitome of barbarism; they were also patrons of art and literature, and supported the reform of the calendar by the astronomer-poet Omar Khayyám (died about 1123).

44. Rumpf, op. cit., pp. 164, 163; in Sherwood, *Roosevelt and Hopkins*, p. 887.

45. Harris in Cameron, loc. cit.; Speer, op. cit., pp. 346, 284, 278–9; Craven and Cate, op. cit., Vol. III, p. 792.

46. Ibid., pp. 43, 59–60, 46–7, 62–3.

47. Knocke, op. cit., pp. 144, 168–9, 209.

48. Freeman, *Mustang at War*, p. 5; Emerson, loc. cit., pp. 34, 31.

49. Ibid., pp. 10–21; on Chennault see Copp, *A Few Great Captains*, pp. 105–6, 259–60, 318–22, and Parton, op. cit., pp. 97–8.

50. Craven and Cate, op. cit., Vol. II, p. 711; Emerson, loc. cit., p. 27; in ibid., p. 8; ibid., pp. 27–30.

51. Copp, *Forged in Fire*, pp. 456–7.

52. Galland, op. cit., p. 250; Craven and Cate, op. cit., Vol. III, p. 58; Emerson, op. cit., pp. 9, 39.

53. Craven and Cate, op. cit., Vol. II, p. 176, Vol. III, pp. 754, 729; Speer, op. cit., pp. 346, 350.

54. Craven and Cate, op. cit., Vol. III, p. 723.

55. Rumpf, op. cit., p. 149.

56. Irving, *The Destruction of Dresden*, pp. 158, 234; Wedgwood, *The Thirty Years War*, pp. 278–81.

57. Craven and Cate, op. cit., Vol. III. p. 735.

58. Copp, op. cit., p. 476.

59. Speer, op. cit., p. 352.

60. Ibid., pp. 280–7.

61. Copp, op. cit., p. 475.

62. LeMay, op. cit., p. 295.

63. Coffey, *Hap*, p. 200; Arnold, op. cit., p. 189; Craven and Cate, op. cit., Vol. VI, pp. 178–9.

64. Mansfield, *Vision*, pp. 150–1, 153; Collison, op. cit., pp. 34, 36–7, 21.

65. Mansfield, op. cit., pp. 196–7.

66. Craven and Cate, op. cit., Vol. VI, p. 209.

67. Mansfield, op. cit., p. 181; Craven and Cate, op. cit., Vol. V, p. 9.

68. Collison, op. cit., pp. 138–41.

69. LeMay, op. cit., pp. 321–3; Collison, op. cit., pp. 146–8.

70. Craven and Cate, op. cit., Vol. V, p. 17; Vol. I, p. 493; Vol. V, p. 21; in ibid.

71. Coffey, op. cit., pp. 334–5; Hinton, *Air Victory: The Men and the Machines,* p. 227; Arnold, op. cit., p. 482.
72. Arnold, op. cit., p. 479; see also Coffey, op. cit., pp. 342–3, 381.
73. Collison, op. cit., Ch. 6, "The Battle of Kansas," pp. 175–88.
74. Walton, *Miracle of World War II,* p. 381.
75. Haugland, *The AAF Against Japan,* p. 416.
76. LeMay, op. cit., pp. 322–5; Craven and Cate, op. cit., Vol. V, p. 94.
77. Ibid., p. 60; Loewenheim et al., eds., op. cit., pp. 439, 454.
78. Craven and Cate, op. cit., pp. 60ff, 71, 68, 99–101, 105, 107–10, 115.
79. LeMay, op. cit., pp. 328, 330–3, 324.
80. Cozzens, op. cit., pp. 157, 143, 91.
81. LeMay, op. cit., pp. 338, 333.
82. Craven and Cate, op. cit., pp. 175, 170–3; LeMay, op. cit., p. 322.
83. Craven and Cate, op. cit., pp. 546, 558.
84. LeMay, op. cit., pp. 342–3, 340, 341–2.
85. Haugland, op. cit., pp. 442, 445; LeMay, op. cit., p. 345; Craven and Cate, op. cit., p. 568; McKelway, "A Reporter with the B-29s, III. The Cigar, the Three Wings, and the Low-level Attacks," *The New Yorker,* June 23, 1945, p. 27.
86. McKelway, loc. cit., "I. Possum, Rosy, and the Thousand Kids," June 9, 1945, pp. 33, 28–9. (O'Donnell's nickname has a variety of spellings; I have used LeMay's.)
87. McKelway, loc. cit., "II. The Doldrums, Guam, and Something Coming Up," June 16, 1945, pp. 36–7.
88. LeMay, op. cit., pp. 347–9; Craven and Cate, op. cit., vol. II, pp. 568–613.
89. Gurney, *Journey of the Giants,* pp. 208–9, 215, 216–17; Snyder, *General Leemy's Circus,* p. 111.
90. McKelway, loc. cit., III, June 23, 1945, pp. 36–8.
91. Craven and Cate, op. cit., Vol. V, p. 616.
92. McKelway, loc. cit., p. 38.
93. In Martin, "Black Snow and Leaping Tigers," *Harper's Magazine,* February 1946, p. 153.
94. Craven and Cate, op. cit., Vol. V, p. 617.
95. Ibid., p. 643.
96. Rust, *Twentieth Air Force Story,* pp. 35–8; Nimitz in Craven and Cate, op. cit., Vol. V, p. 674.
97. Ibid., pp. 674–5, 750, 755, 756; other Japanese attributions of defeat to the B-29s are quoted in Morrison, *Hellbirds,* p. 180.
98. Martin, loc. cit., pp. 153, 154, 155; Craven and Cate, op. cit., Vol. V. pp. 636, 638–9.

EPILOGUE

1. Tugwell, *The Democratic Roosevelt,* p. 14; Hassett, *Off the Record with F.D.R., 1942–45,* pp. vii, 126–7, 23, 8; Sherwood, *Roosevelt and Hopkins,* p. 9.
2. Stouffer et al., *The American Soldier,* Vol. I, pp. 432–3, 81; DeVoto, "The Easy Chair," *Harper's Magazine,* January 1946, p. 39.
3. Dallek, *Franklin D. Roosevelt and American Foreign Policy 1932–1945,* p. 250.

4. Wright, *The Ordeal of Total War, 1939–1945*, p. 265.

5. Janeway, *The Struggle for Survival*, pp. 20–1.

6. In Roosevelt, ed., *F.D.R. His Personal Letters 1928–1945*, Vol. II, p. 1175.

7. In Blum, *From the Morgenthau Diaries: Years of War, 1941–1945*, p. 85; in Freidin and Richardson, eds., *The Fatal Decisions*, pp. 87–8; Sherwood, *Roosevelt and Hopkins*, p. 793.

8. Roosevelt to Fred I. Kent, July 26, 1935, in Dallek, *Franklin D. Roosevelt and American Foreign Policy*, p. 94; Tuchman, *Stilwell and the American Experience in China, 1911–1945*, p. 531.

9. Brogan, "The Illusion of American Omnipotence," *Harper's Magazine*, December 1952, pp. 21–8; in Schlesinger, *The Coming of the New Deal*, p. 529.

10. Buell, *Master of Sea Power*, pp. 95, 98–100.

11. Vandenberg, ed., *The Private Papers of Senator Vandenberg*, p. 155.

12. In Terkel, *"The Good War,"* p. 328.

13. De Gaulle, *The Complete War Memoirs of Charles de Gaulle*, p. 572.

14. Ibid., p. 573; Thorne, *Allies of a Kind*, pp. 666–7.

15. De Gaulle, op. cit., pp. 571–4.

16. De Gaulle, op. cit., pp. 307–8.

17. Nicolson, ed., *Harold Nicolson, Diaries and Letters: The War Years, 1939–1945*, p. 328.

18. Dilks, ed., *The Diaries of Sir Alexander Cadogan 1938–1945*, pp. 727–8, 578.

19. Miller, *Cartwheel: The Reduction of Rabaul*, pp. 222–50, 256.

20. In Gunther, *Roosevelt in Retrospect*, p. 326.

21. Greenfield, *American Strategy in World War II*, p. 79.

22. In Loewenheim et al., eds., *Roosevelt and Churchill: Their Secret Wartime Correspondence*, pp. 141, 227.

23. In Sherwood, op. cit., p. 242 (Sherwood disbelieved this anecdote; I find it highly plausible); in Bracher, *The German Dictatorship*, p. 462; in Burns, *Soldier of Freedom*, p. 68.

24. Nicholas, ed., *Washington Dispatches 1941–45*, p. 37.

25. Sherwood, op. cit., p. 241; Gallagher, "The President as Local Historian: The Letters of F.D.R. to Helen Wilkinson Reynolds," *New York History*, April 1983, pp. 137–70.

26. Morison, *The Battle of the Atlantic*, pp. 290–1.

27. Ballard, *The Military Genius of Abraham Lincoln*, p. 3; Williams, *Lincoln and His Generals*, pp. 264–70; Moran, *Churchill Taken from the Diaries of Lord Moran*, p. 142.

28. In Morison, *Turmoil and Tradition*, p. 510; Gunther, op. cit., p. 7. (In his book, Gunther did not identify Mrs. Roosevelt as the source of this remark, nor give it in full, but he did so in conversation, among others with Simon Michael Bessie, to whom I am accordingly indebted.)

29. Martin, *Madame Secretary*, p. 435. (The importance of this passage was pointed out to me by William R. Emerson.)

30. Jungk, *Brighter Than a Thousand Suns*, pp. 89–93.

31. Burns, *Soldier of Freedom*, p. 250.

32. Baxter, *Scientists Against Time*, pp. 423–5; Churchill, *The Hinge of Fate*, pp. 378–9.

33. Compton, *Atomic Quest*, pp. 63–4.

34. Churchill, op. cit., pp. 379–80.
35. In Sherwood, op. cit., pp. 667–8; in Rosenman, *Working with Roosevelt*, p. 512; in Burns, op. cit., p. 456.
36. Groves, *Now It Can Be Told*, p. 63.
37. Roosevelt to Oppenheimer, June 29, 1943, and Oppenheimer to Roosevelt, July 9, 1943, MSS, Oppenheimer Papers, Manuscript Division, Library of Congress; the Roosevelt letter is marked "Secret" in the President's hand; it is filed with a card reading: "This letter was reviewed by Dr. James Beckerley for declassification purposes. It is now declassified; but it was felt undesirable to mar the letter with declassification stamps and cross markings."
38. Davis, *Lawrence and Oppenheimer*, pp. 227–8.

WORKS CITED

Abbazia, Patrick, *Mr. Roosevelt's Navy: The Private War of the U.S. Atlantic Fleet*, Naval Institute Press, Annapolis, 1975.

Acheson, Dean, *Present at the Creation: My Years in the State Department*, Norton, New York, 1969.

Agawa, Hiroyuki, *The Reluctant Admiral: Yamamoto and the Imperial Navy*, Kodansha International, Tokyo, 1979.

Albion, Robert G., and Robert H. Connery, *Forrestal and the Navy*, Columbia University Press, New York, 1962.

Alsop, Joseph, and Stewart Alsop, *The Reporter's Trade*, Reynal & Company, New York, 1958.

Ambrose, Stephen E., *The Supreme Commander: The War Years of General Dwight D. Eisenhower*, Doubleday, Garden City, 1970.

Ambrose, Stephen E., *Eisenhower and Berlin: The Decision to Halt at the Elbe*, Norton, New York, 1967.

Armstrong, Anne, *Unconditional Surrender: The Impact of the Casablanca Policy upon World War II*, Rutgers University Press, New Brunswick, 1961.

Arnold, Henry H., *Global Mission*, Harper & Brothers, New York, 1949.

Avon [Anthony Eden], *The Reckoning*, Houghton Mifflin, Boston, 1965.

Bailey, Thomas A., and Paul B. Ryan, *Hitler vs. Roosevelt*, Free Press, New York, 1979.

Baldwin, Hanson W., *Battles Lost and Won*, Harper & Brothers, New York, 1966.

Baldwin, Hanson W., *Great Mistakes of the War*, Harper & Brothers, New York, 1950.

Ballard, Colin R., *The Military Genius of Abraham Lincoln*, World Publishing, Cleveland, 1952.

Barnett, Correlli, *The Desert Generals*, Pan Books, London, 1962.

Baumbach, Werner, *The Life and Death of the Luftwaffe*, Coward-McCann, New York, 1949.

Baxter, James P., *Scientists Against Time*, Atlantic Monthly Press, Boston, 1946.

Beaumont, Roger, *Sword of the Raj: The British Army in India 1747–1947*, Bobbs-Merrill, New York, 1977.

Beesly, Patrick, *Very Special Intelligence: The Story of the Admiralty's Operational Intelligence Center 1939–1945*, Doubleday, Garden City, 1978.

Belden, Jack, *Retreat with Stilwell*, Knopf, New York, 1943.

Bendiner, Elmer, *The Fall of Fortresses*, Putnam, New York, 1980.

Benedict, Ruth, *The Chrysanthemum and the Sword: Patterns of Japanese Culture*, World, Cleveland, 1967.

Berle, Adolf A., Jr., *Navigating the Rapids*, Harcourt, New York, 1973.

Bidwell, Shelford, *The Chindit War: Stilwell, Wingate, and the Campaign in Burma: 1944*, Macmillan, New York, 1979.

Blair, Clay, Jr., *Silent Victory: The U.S. War Against Japan*, vols. I and II, Lippincott, Philadelphia, 1975.

Bland, Larry I., and Sharon R. Ritenour, *The Papers of George Catlett Marshall*, vol. I, Johns Hopkins University Press, Baltimore, 1981.

Blum, John M., *From the Morganthau Diaries, Vol. II, Years of Urgency, 1938–1941; Vol. III, Years of War, 1941–1945*, Houghton Mifflin, Boston, 1965–1967.

Blumenson, Martin, *Breakout and Pursuit*, Office of the Chief of Military History, Department of the Army, Washington, 1961.

Blumenson, Martin, *The Patton Papers, Vol. I, 1885–1940; Vol. II, 1940–1945*, Houghton Mifflin, Boston, 1972, 1974.

Borg, Dorothy, and Shumpei Okamoto, eds., *Pearl Harbor as History*, Columbia University Press, New York, 1973.

Bracher, Karl D., *The German Dictatorship*, Praeger, New York, 1970.

Bradley, Omar, *A Soldier's Story*, Holt, New York, 1951.

Bradley, Omar, and Clay Blair, *A General's Life*, Simon & Schuster, New York, 1983.

Brereton, Lewis H., *The Brereton Diaries*, Morrow, New York, 1946.

Bryant, Arthur, *A History of the War Years Based on the Diaries of Field-Marshal Lord Alanbrooke, Chief of the Imperial General Staff, Vol. I, The Turn of the Tide; Vol. II, Triumph in the West*, Doubleday, Garden City, 1957, 1959.

Buell, Thomas B., *Master of Sea Power: A Biography of Fleet Admiral Ernest J. King*, Little, Brown, Boston, 1980.

Buell, Thomas B., *The Quiet Warrior: A Biography of Admiral Raymond A. Spruance*, Little, Brown, Boston, 1974.

Bullock, Alan, *Hitler: A Study in Tyranny*, Harper & Brothers, New York, 1952.

Burns, James M., *Roosevelt: The Soldier of Freedom*, Harcourt, New York, 1970.

Butcher, Harry C., *My Three Years with Eisenhower*, Simon & Schuster, New York, 1946.

Butow, Robert J. C., *Tojo and the Coming of the War*, Princeton University Press, Princeton, 1961.

Byas, Hugh, *Government by Assassination*, Knopf, New York, 1942.

Calder, Angus, *The People's War: Britain 1939–1945*, Pantheon, New York, 1979.

Capra, Frank, *The Name Above the Title*, Belvedere, New York, 1982.

Catton, Bruce, *The War Lords of Washington*, Harcourt, New York, 1948.

Chandler, Alfred D., ed., *The Papers of Dwight D. Eisenhower: The War Years*, vols. I–V; Johns Hopkins Press, Baltimore, 1943.

Chennault, Claire, *Way of a Fighter*, Putnam, New York, 1949.

Churchill, Winston S., *The Second World War, Vol. I, The Gathering Storm; Vol. II, Their Finest Hour; Vol. III, The Grand Alliance; Vol. IV, The Hinge of*

Fate; Vol. V, Closing the Ring; Vol. VI, Triumph and Tragedy, Houghton Mifflin, Boston, 1948–1953.

Civilian Production Administration, *Industrialization for War: History of the War Production Board and Predecessor Agencies;* U.S. Government Printing Office, Washington, 1947.

Clark, Alan, *Barbarossa: The Russian-German Conflict, 1941–45,* Morrow, New York, 1965.

Clark, J. J., with Clark G. Reynolds, *Carrier Admiral,* McKay, New York, 1967.

Clark, Mark W., *Calculated Risk,* Harper & Brothers, New York, 1950.

Cline, Ray S., *Washington Command Post: The Operations Division,* Office of the Chief of Military History, Department of the Army, Washington, 1951.

Codman, Charles R., *Drive,* Atlantic Monthly Press, Boston, 1957.

Coffey, Thomas M., *Decision over Schweinfurt,* McKay, New York, 1977.

Coffey, Thomas M., *Hap: The Story of the U.S. Air Force and the Man Who Built It,* Viking, New York, 1982.

Coles, Harry L., ed., *Total War and Cold War,* Ohio State University Press, Columbus, 1962.

Cole, Wayne S., *Charles A. Lindbergh and the Battle Against American Intervention in World War II,* Harcourt, New York, 1974.

Collier, Basil, *The War in the Far East: A Military History,* Morrow, New York, 1969.

Collis, Maurice, *Last and First in Burma,* Macmillan: New York, 1956.

Collison, Thomas, *The Superfortress Is Born: The Story of the Boeing B-29,* Duell, Sloan & Pearce, New York, 1945.

Compton, Arthur H., *Atomic Quest,* Oxford University Press, New York, 1956.

Copp, Dewitt S., *A Few Great Captains: The Men and Events That Shaped the Development of U.S. Air Power,* Doubleday, Garden City, 1980.

Copp, Dewitt S., *Forged in Fire: Strategy and Decisions in the Air War over Europe 1940–1945,* Doubleday, Garden City, 1982.

Costello, John, *The Pacific War,* Rawson, New York, 1981.

Cozzens, James G., *A Time of War: Diaries and Pentagon Memos 1943–45,* Bruccoli Clark, Columbia, 1984.

Craig, William, *The Fall of Japan,* Dial, New York, 1967.

Craven, Wesley F., and James L. Cate, *The Army Air Forces in World War II, Vol. I, Plans and Early Operations; Vol. II, Europe: Torch to Pointblank; Vol. III, Europe: Argument to V-E Day; Vol. IV, The Pacific: Guadalcanal to Saipan; Vol. V, The Pacific: Matterhorn to Nagasaki; Vol. VI, Men and Planes; Vol. VII, Services Around the World,* University of Chicago Press, Chicago, 1948–1958.

Creveld, Martin van, *Supplying War: Logistics from Wallenstein to Patton,* Cambridge University Press, Cambridge, 1977.

Cruikshank, Charles, *Deception in World War II,* Oxford University Press, New York, 1979.

Cunningham, Andrew B., *A Sailor's Odyssey: The Autobiography of Admiral of the Fleet Viscount Cunningham of Hyndhope,* Dutton, New York, 1951.

Dallek, Robert, *Franklin D. Roosevelt and American Foreign Policy 1932–1945,* Oxford University Press, New York, 1979.

Daniel, Clifton, *Lords, Ladies and Gentlemen,* Arbor, New York, 1984.

Daniels, Josephus, *The Wilson Era: Years of Peace 1910–17*, University of North Carolina Press, Chapel Hill, 1946.

Davies, John P., *Dragon by the Tail*, Norton, New York, 1972.

Davis, Burke, *Marine! The Life of Lt. Gen. Lewis B. (Chesty) Puller*, Little, Brown, Boston, 1962.

Davis, Nuel P., *Lawrence and Oppenheimer*, Simon & Schuster, New York, 1968.

Deighton, Len, *Fighter: The True Story of the Battle of Britain*, Knopf, New York, 1978.

Department of State, *Peace and War: United States Foreign Policy 1931–1941*, U.S. Government Printing Office, Washington, 1943.

Department of State, *United States Relations with China*, Division of Publications, Office of Public Affairs, Washington, 1949.

D'Este, Carlo, *Decision in Normandy*, Dutton, New York, 1983.

De Gaulle, Charles, *The Complete War Memoirs of Charles de Gaulle*, Simon & Schuster, New York, 1955–1960.

De Guingand, Francis, *Operation Victory*, Scribner, New York, 1947.

DeWeerd, H. A., ed., *Selected Papers and Speeches of General of the Armies George C. Marshall*, Infantry Journal, Washington, 1945.

Dilks, David, ed., *The Diaries of Sir Alexander Cadogan, 1938–1945*, Putnam, New York, 1972.

Divine, Robert A., *Roosevelt and World War II*, Penguin, Baltimore, 1970.

Doolard, A. Den [C. Spoelstra], *Roll Back the Sea*, Simon & Schuster, New York, 1948.

Dorn, Frank, *Walkout: With Stilwell in Burma*, Crowell, New York, 1971.

Dorwart, Jeffrey M., *Conflict of Duty: The U.S. Navy's Intelligence Dilemma, 1919–1945*, Naval Institute Press, Annapolis, 1985.

Dugan, James, and Carroll Stewart, *Ploesti: The Great Ground-Air Battle of 1 August 1943*, Random, New York, 1962.

Dunn, Walter S., Jr., *Second Front New—1943*, University of Alabama Press, University, Ala., 1980.

Dyer, George D., *The Amphibians Came to Conquer: The Story of Admiral Richmond Kelly Turner*, vols. I and II, Department of the Navy, Washington, 1969.

Eccles, Marriner S., *Beckoning Frontiers*, Knopf, New York, 1951.

Edmonds, Walter D., *They Fought with What They Had: The Story of the Army Air Forces in the Southwest Pacific, 1941–1942*, Little, Brown, Boston, 1951.

Ehrman, John, *Grand Strategy*, vols. V and VI, H. M. Stationery Office, London, 1956.

Eichelberger, Robert L., with Milton MacKaye, *Our Jungle Road to Tokyo*, Viking, New York, 1950.

Eisenhower, Dwight D., *At Ease: Stories I Tell to Friends*, Doubleday, Garden City, 1967.

Eisenhower, Dwight D., *Crusade in Europe*, Doubleday, Garden City, 1948.

Eisenhower Foundation, *D-Day: The Normandy Invasion in Retrospect*, Abilene, Kans., 1971.

Eisenhower, John S. D., *Allies: Pearl Harbor to D-Day*, Doubleday, Garden City, 1982.

Eldridge, Fred, *Wrath in Burma*, Doubleday, Garden City, 1946.

Ellis, L. F., *Victory in the West, Vol. I, The Battle of Normandy*, H. M. Stationery Office, London, 1961.

Erickson, John, *The Road to Berlin*, Weidenfeld and Nicholson, London, 1983.

Esherick, Joseph W., *Lost Chance in China: The World War II Dispatches of John S. Service*, Random, New York, 1974.

Evans, Geoffrey, *Slim as Military Commander*, B. T. Batsford, London, 1969.

Evans, Geoffrey, and Anthony Brett-James, *Imphal: A Flower on Lofty Heights*, Macmillan, New York, 1962.

Feis, Herbert, *The Road to Pearl Harbor*, Princeton University Press, Princeton, 1950.

Fergusson, Bernard, *The Watery Maze*, Collins, London, 1961.

Ferrell, Robert H., ed., *The Eisenhower Diaries*, Norton, New York, 1981.

Frank, Pat, and Joseph D. Harrington, *Rendezvous at Midway: U.S.S. Yorktown and the Japanese Carrier Fleet*, Warner, New York, 1968.

Frankland, Noble and Christopher Dowling, eds., *Decisive Battles of the Twentieth Century*, McKay, New York, 1976.

Fraser, David, *Alanbrooke*, Atheneum, New York, 1982.

Freeman, Douglas S., *Lee's Lieutenants*, vol. I, Scribner, New York, 1946.

Freeman, Roger A., *Mustang at War*, Doubleday, Garden City, 1974.

Freidel, Frank, *Franklin D. Roosevelt, Vol. I, The Apprenticeship*, Little, Brown, Boston, 1952.

Freidin, Seymour, and William Richardson, eds., *The Fatal Decisions: Kreipe, Blumentritt, Bayerlein, Zeitzler, Zimmerman, and Manteuffel*, William Sloan, New York, 1956.

Fuchida, Mitsuo, and Masatake Okumiya, *Midway: The Battle That Doomed Japan*, U.S. Naval Institute Press, Annapolis, 1955.

Fuller, J. F. C., *The Conduct of War 1789–1961*, Rutgers University Press, New Brunswick, 1961.

Fuller, J. F. C., *The Second World War 1939–45: A Strategical and Tactical History*, Eyre and Spottiswoode, London, 1948.

Gabel, Christopher R., *Seek, Strike, and Destroy: U.S. Army Tank Destroyer Doctrine in World War II*, Leavenworth Papers No. 12, Combat Studies, Fort Leavenworth, 1985.

Galland, Adolf, *The First and the Last: The Rise and Fall of the German Fighter Forces*, Holt, New York, 1954.

Gavin, James M., *On to Berlin: Battles of an Airborne Commander 1943–1946*, Viking, New York, 1978.

Glines, Carroll V., and Wendell F. Moseley, *Grand Old Lady: Story of the DC-3*, Pennington Press, Cleveland, 1959.

Greenfield, Kent R., *American Strategy in World War II: A Reconsideration*, Johns Hopkins University Press, Baltimore, 1963.

Greenfield, Kent R., *Command Decisions*, Office of the Chief of Military History, Department of the Army, Washington, 1960.

Greenfield, Kent R., Robert R. Palmer, and Bell I. Wiley, *The Organization of Ground Combat Troops*, Historical Division, Department of the Army, Washington, 1947.

Grew, Joseph C., *Ten Years in Japan*, Simon & Schuster, New York, 1944.

Griffith, Samuel B. II, *The Battle for Guadalcanal,* Nautical & Aviation Publishing Company, Annapolis, 1963.

Grigg, John, *1943: The Victory That Never Was,* Hill & Wang, New York, 1980.

Groves, Leslie R., *Now It Can Be Told: The Story of the Manhattan Project,* Harper & Brothers, New York, 1962.

Gunther, John, *Eisenhower: The Man and the Symbol,* Harper & Brothers, New York, 1952.

Gunther, John, *The Riddle of Douglas MacArthur,* Harper & Brothers, New York, 1951.

Gunther, John, *Roosevelt in Retrospect,* Harper & Brothers, New York, 1950.

Gurney, Gene, *Journey of the Giants,* Coward, McCann, New York, 1961.

Hagan, Kenneth J., ed., *In Peace and War: Interpretations of American Naval History 1775–1978,* Greenwood Press, Westport, 1978.

Halsey, William F., and J. Bryan III, *Admiral Halsey's Story,* McGraw-Hill, New York, 1947.

Hamilton, Nigel, *Master of the Battlefield: Monty's War Years 1942–1944,* McGraw-Hill, New York, 1983.

Hancock, W. K., and M. M. Gowing, *British War Economy,* H. M. Stationery Office, London, 1949.

Harriman, Averell, and Elie Abel, *Special Envoy to Churchill and Stalin, 1941–46,* Random, New York, 1975.

Harris, Arthur, *Bomber Offensive,* Macmillan, New York, 1947.

Harrison, Gordon A., *Cross-Channel Attack,* Office of the Chief of Military History, Department of the Army, Washington, 1951.

Harrison, Gordon, *Mosquitoes, Malaria, and Man,* Dutton, New York, 1978.

Hassett, William D., *Off the Record with F.D.R. 1942–1945,* Rutgers University Press, New Brunswick, 1958.

Hastings, Max, *Overlord: D-Day and the Battle for Normandy,* Simon & Schuster, New York, 1984.

Haugland, Vern, *The AAF Against Japan,* Harper & Brothers, New York, 1948.

Hayes, Grace P., *The History of the Joint Chiefs of Staff in World War II: The War Against Japan,* Naval Institute Press, Annapolis, 1982.

Hersey, John, *Men on Bataan,* Knopf, New York, 1942.

Hinsley, F. H., *Hitler's Strategy,* Cambridge University Press, Cambridge, 1951.

Hinsley, F. H., with E. E. Thomas, C. F. G. Ransom, and R. C. Knight, *British Intelligence in the Second World War: Its Influence on Strategy and Operations,* vol. I, Cambridge University Press, New York, 1979; vols. II and III, part 1, H. M. Stationery Office, London, 1981, 1984.

Hinton, Harold B., *Air Victory: The Men and the Machines,* Harper & Brothers, New York, 1948.

Historical Division, Department of the Army (Ruppenthal, Roland G.), *Utah Beach to Cherbourg,* U.S. Government Printing Office, Washington, 1947.

Historical Division, War Department, *The Admiralties: Operations of the 1st Cavalry Division (29 February–18 May 1944),* U.S. Government Printing Office, Washington, 1945.

Historical Division, War Department, *Merrill's Marauders (February–May 1944),* U.S. Government Printing Office, Washington, 1945.

Historical Division, War Department (Taylor, Charles H.), *Omaha Beachhead,* U.S. Government Printing Office, Washington, 1945.

H. M. Stationery Office, *Combined Operations: The Official Story of the Commandos*, Macmillan, New York, 1943.

Hobbs, Joseph P., ed., *Dear General: Eisenhower's Wartime Letters to Marshall*, Johns Hopkins University Press, Baltimore, 1971.

Holmes, W. J., *Double-Edged Secrets: U.S. Naval Intelligence Operations in the Pacific during World War II*, Naval Institute Press, Annapolis, 1979.

Holmes, W. J., *Undersea Victory: The Influence of Submarine Operations on the War in the Pacific*, Doubleday, Garden City, 1966.

Hough, Frank O., *The Assault on Peleliu*, Historical Division, U.S. Marine Corps, Washington, 1950.

Hough, Frank O., Verle E. Ludwig, and Henry I. Shaw, Jr., *History of the U.S. Marine Corps Operations in World War II: Pearl Harbor to Guadalcanal*, Historical Branch, U.S. Marine Corps, Washington, 1958.

Howarth, David, *D-Day: The Sixth of June*, McGraw-Hill, New York, 1959.

Howe, George F., *Northwest Africa: Seizing the Initiative in the West*, Office of the Chief of Military History, Department of the Army, Washington, 1957.

Hull, Cordell, *The Memoirs of Cordell Hull*, vols. I and II, Macmillan, New York, 1948.

Hunt, Frazier, *The Untold Story of Douglas MacArthur*, Devin-Adair, New York, 1954.

Huntington, Samuel P., *The Soldier and the State: The Theory and Politics of Civil-Military Relations*, Harvard University Press: Cambridge, 1957.

Ickes, Harold L., *The Secret Diary of Harold L. Ickes, Vol. I, The First Thousand Days 1933–1936, Vol. II, The Inside Struggle 1936–1939; Vol. III, The Lowering Clouds 1939–1941*, Simon & Schuster, New York, 1954.

Ienaga, Saburo, *The Pacific War, 1931–1945*, Pantheon, New York, 1978.

Ike, Nobutaka, ed., *Japan's Decision for War: Records of the 1941 Policy Conferences*, Stanford University Press, Stanford, 1967.

Irving, David, *The Destruction of Dresden*, William Kimber, London, 1963.

Isely, Jeter A., and Philip A. Crowl, *The U.S. Marines and Amphibious War*, Princeton University Press, Princeton, 1951.

Ismay, Hastings, *The Memoirs of General the Lord Ismay*, Heineman, London, 1960.

Jablonski, Edward, *Airwar, Vol. I, Terror from the Sky; Vol. II, Tragic Victories; Vol. III, Outraged Skies; Vol. IV, Wings of Fire*, Doubleday, Garden City, 1979.

Jablonski, Edward, *Flying Fortress*, Doubleday, Garden City, 1965.

Jacobsen, H. A., and J. Rohwer, *Decisive Battles of World War II: The German View*, Putnam, New York, 1965.

James, Clayton D., *The Years of MacArthur, Vol. I, 1880–1941; Vol. II, 1941–1945*, Houghton Mifflin, Boston, 1970, 1975.

Janeway, Eliot, *The Struggle for Survival*, Weybright and Talley, New York, 1951.

Johnson, J. E., *Wing Leader*, Ballantine, New York, 1957.

Jones, Ralph E. *et al.*, *The Fighting Tanks Since 1916*, National Service, Washington, 1933.

Jones, R. J., *Most Secret War*, Hodder and Stoughton, London, 1979.

Jungk, Robert, *Brighter Than a Thousand Suns*, Victor Gollancz, London, 1958.

Kahn, David, *The Codebreakers*, Weidenfeld and Nicolson, London, 1973.

Kahn, E. J., Jr., *The China Hands*, Viking, New York, 1975.

Kahn, E. J., Jr., *McNair: Educator of an Army,* Infantry Journal, Washington, 1945.

Kase, Toshikazu, *Journey to the Missouri,* Yale University Press, New Haven, 1950.

Keegan, John, *Six Armies in Normandy: From D-Day to the Liberation of Paris,* Penguin, New York, 1983.

Kemp, P. K., *Key to Victory: The Triumph of British Sea Power in World War II,* Little, Brown, Boston, 1957.

Kennan, George, *Memoirs 1925–1950,* Atlantic Monthly Press, Boston, 1967.

Kesselring, Albert, *Kesselring: A Soldier's Record,* Morrow, New York, 1954.

King, Ernest J., and Walter Muir Whitehill, *Fleet Admiral King: A Naval Record,* Norton, New York, 1952.

Kirby, S. Woodburn, *The War Against Japan, Vol. II, India's Most Dangerous Hour;* H. M. Stationery Office, London, 1958.

Klein, Burton H., *Germany's Economic Preparation for War,* Harvard University Press, Cambridge, 1959.

Knocke, Heinz, *I Flew for the Führer,* Holt, New York, 1954.

Koch, Hansjoachim W., *The Hitler Youth: Origins and Development 1922–45,* Stein & Day, New York, 1976.

Kouwenhoven, John A., *Partners in Banking,* Doubleday, Garden City, 1968.

Krueger, Walter, *From Down Under to Nippon: The Story of Sixth Army in World War II,* Combat Forces Press, Washington, 1953.

La Farge, Oliver, *The Eagle in the Egg,* Houghton Mifflin, Boston, 1949.

Lamb, Richard, *Montgomery in Europe 1943–1945,* Franklin Watts, New York, 1984.

Langer, William L., and S. Everett Gleason, *The Undeclared War,* Harper & Brothers, New York, 1953.

Larrabee, Harold A., *Decision at the Chesapeake,* Clarkson Potter, New York, 1964.

Lash, Joseph P., *Roosevelt and Churchill: The Partnership That Saved the West,* Norton, New York, 1976.

Leahy, William D., *I Was There,* McGraw-Hill, New York, 1950.

Leckie, Robert, *Challenge for the Pacific: Guadalcanal—The Turning Point of the War,* Doubleday, Garden City, 1965.

Lee, Clark, and Richard Henschel, *Douglas MacArthur,* Holt, New York, 1952.

LeMay, Curtis E., *Mission with LeMay,* Doubleday, Garden City, 1965.

Lewin, Ronald, *The Chief: Field Marshal Lord Wavell,* Farrar, Straus, Giroux, New York, 1980.

Lewin, Ronald, *Churchill as Warlord,* Stein & Day, New York, 1973.

Lewin, Ronald, *Slim: The Standardbearer,* Pan Books, London, 1978.

Liddell Hart, B. H., *History of the Second World War,* Putnam, New York, 1970.

Liddell Hart, B. H., *The Liddell Hart Memoirs,* vols. I and II, Putnam, New York, 1965.

Liddell Hart, B. H., ed., *The Rommel Papers,* Harcourt, New York, 1953.

Liebling, A. J., *Liebling Abroad,* Wideview Books, New York, 1981.

Loewenheim, Francis L., Harold D. Langley, and Manfred Jonas, *Roosevelt and Churchill: Their Secret Wartime Correspondence,* Dutton, New York, 1975.

Lohbeck, Don, *Patrick J. Hurley,* Regnery, Chicago, 1957.

Lord, Walter, *Day of Infamy,* Holt, New York, 1957.

Lord, Walter, *Incredible Victory,* Harper & Row, New York, 1967.

Love, Robert W., Jr., *The Chiefs of Naval Operations,* Naval Institute Press, Annapolis, 1980.

Lu, David J., *From the Marco Polo Bridge to Pearl Harbor: Japan's Entry into World War II,* Public Affairs Press, Washington, 1961.

Luvaas, Jay, ed., *Dear Miss Em: General Eichelberger's War in the Pacific, 1942–1945,* Greenwood Press, Westport, 1972.

MacArthur, Douglas, *Reminiscences,* McGraw-Hill, New York, 1964.

MacDonald, Charles B., *The Last Offensive,* Office of the Chief of Military History, Department of the Army, Washington, 1973.

MacDonald, Charles B., *The Siegfried Line Campaign,* Office of the Chief of Military History, Department of the Army, Washington, 1963.

Maclean, Fitzroy, *Take Nine Spies,* Atheneum, New York, 1978.

Macmillan, Harold, *The Blast of War 1939–1945,* Carroll & Graf, New York, 1983.

Mahan, Alfred T., *The Influence of Seapower upon History 1660–1783,* Sagamore Press, New York, 1957.

Manchester, William, *American Caesar,* Dell, New York, 1978.

Mansfield, Harold, *Vision: A Saga of the Sky,* Duell, Sloan and Pearce, New York, 1956.

Marshall, Katherine T., *Together: Annals of an Army Wife,* Tupper and Love, Atlanta, 1947.

Marshall, S. L. A., *Night Drop: The American Airborne Invasion of Normandy,* Atlantic Monthly Press, Boston, 1962.

Martienssen, Anthony, *Hitler and His Admirals,* Dutton, New York, 1949.

Martin, George, *Madam Secretary: Frances Perkins,* Houghton Mifflin, Boston, 1976.

Martin, John B., *Adlai Stevenson of Illinois,* Doubleday, Garden City, 1976.

Masters, John, *The Road Past Mandalay,* Harper & Brothers, New York, 1961.

Matloff, Maurice, and Edwin M. Snell, *Strategic Planning for Coalition Warfare 1941–1942,* Office of the Chief of Military History, Department of the Army, Washington, 1953.

Matloff, Maurice, *Strategic Planning for Coalition Warfare 1943–1944,* Office of the Chief of Military History, Dept. of the Army, Washington, 1959.

May, Ernest R., ed., *The Ultimate Decision: The President as Commander in Chief,* George Braziller, New York, 1960.

McCarthy, Dudley, *Australia in the War of 1939–1945, Vol. V, South-West Pacific Area—First Year: Kokoda to Wau,* Australian War Memorial, Canberra, 1959.

McKee, Alexander, *Strike from the Sky: The Story of the Battle of Britain,* Souvenir Press, London, 1960.

McMillan, George, *The Old Breed: A History of the First Marine Division in World War II,* Infantry Journal, Washington, 1949.

Middleton, Drew, *Crossroads of Modern Warfare,* Doubleday, Garden City, 1983.

Middleton, Drew, *The Sky Suspended,* Longmans, New York, 1960.

Miles, Milton E., *A Different Kind of War,* Doubleday, Garden City, 1967.

Miller, John, Jr., *Cartwheel: The Reduction of Rabaul,* Office of the Chief of Military History, Department of the Army, Washington, 1959.

Miller, John, Jr., *Guadalcanal: The First Offensive,* Office of the Chief of Military History, Dept. of the Army, Washington, 1949.

Millis, Walter, *This Is Pearl! The United States and Japan—1941*, Morrow, New York, 1947.

Millis, Walter, ed., *The Forrestal Diaries*, Viking, New York, 1951.

Millis, Walter, ed., *The War Reports of General of the Armies George C. Marshall, General of the Armies H. H. Arnold, and Fleet Admiral Ernest J. King*, Lippincott, Philadelphia, 1947.

Milner, Samuel, *Victory in Papua*, Office of the Chief of Military History, Department of the Army, Washington, 1957.

Montgomery, Bernard L., *Normandy to the Baltic*, Houghton Mifflin, Boston, 1948.

Moore, John H., *Over-Sexed, Over-Paid, and Over Here: Americans in Australia, 1941–1945*, University of Queensland Press, Brisbane, 1981.

Moran [Charles Wilson], *Churchill Taken from the Diaries of Lord Moran*, Houghton Mifflin, Boston, 1966.

Morgan, Frederick, *Overture to Overlord*, Doubleday, Garden City, 1950.

Morison, Elting E., *Turmoil and Tradition: A Study of the Life and Times of Henry L. Stimson*, Houghton Mifflin, Boston, 1960.

Morison, Samuel E., *History of United States Naval Operations in World War II, Vol. I, The Battle for the Atlantic; Vol. II, Operations in North African Waters; Vol. III, The Rising Sun in the Pacific; Vol. IV, Coral Sea, Midway and Submarine Actions; Vol. V, The Struggle for Guadalcanal; Vol. VI, Breaking the Bismarcks Barrier; Vol. VII, Aleutians, Gilberts and Marshalls; Vol. VIII, New Guinea and the Marianas; Vol. IX, Sicily—Salerno—Anzio; Vol. X, The Atlantic Battle Won; Vol. XI, The Invasion of France and Germany; Vol. XII, Leyte; Vol. XIII, The Liberation of the Philippines; Vol. XIV, Victory in the Pacific; Vol. XV, Supplement and General Index*, Atlantic Monthly Press, Boston, 1955–1962.

Morris, Eric, Christopher Chant, Curt Johnson, and H. P. Willmott, *Weapons and Warfare of the Twentieth Century*, Derbibooks, Secaucus, 1976.

Morrison, Wilbur H., *Hellbirds: The Story of the B-29s in Combat*, Duell, Sloan and Pearce, New York, 1960.

Morton, Louis, *The Fall of the Philippines*, Office of the Chief of Military History, Department of the Army, Washington, 1953.

Morton, Louis, *Strategy and Command: The First Two Years*, Office of the Chief of Military History, Department of the Army, Washington, 1962.

Mosley, Leonard, *Gideon Goes to War*, Scribner, New York, 1955.

Mosley, Leonard, *Hirohito: Emperor of Japan*, Prentice-Hall, Englewood Cliffs, 1966.

Motley, John J., and Philip R. Kelly, *Now Hear This!*, Infantry Journal Press, Washington, 1947.

Murphy, Robert, *Diplomat Among Warriors*, Doubleday, Garden City, 1964.

Neustadt, Richard E., *Presidential Power: The Politics of Leadership*, Wiley, New York, 1960.

Newcomb, Richard F., *Savo: The Incredible Naval Debacle Off Guadalcanal*, Holt, New York, 1961.

Nicolson, Nigel, ed., *Harold Nicolson: Diaries and Letters, Vol. II, The War Years 1939–1945*, Atheneum, New York, 1967.

Nixon, Edgar B., ed., *Franklin D. Roosevelt and Foreign Affairs*, vols. I–III, Harvard University Press, Cambridge, 1969.

Ogburn, Charlton, *The Marauders,* Harper & Brothers, New York, 1956.

Okumiya, Masatake, and Jiro Horikoshi, with Martin Caidin, *Zero!,* Dutton, New York, 1956.

Palmer, Robert R., Bell I. Wiley, and William R. Keast, *The Procurement and Training of Ground Combat Troops,* Historical Division, Department of the Army, Washington, 1948.

Parton, James, *"Air Force Spoken Here": General Ira Eaker and the Command of the Air,* Adler & Adler, Bethesda, 1986.

Pendar, Kenneth, *Adventures in Diplomacy: Our French Dilemma:* Dodd, Mead, New York, 1945.

Perkins, Frances, *The Roosevelt I Knew,* Viking, New York, 1946.

Petillo, Carol M., *MacArthur: The Philippine Years,* Indiana University Press, Bloomington, 1981.

Pogue, Forrest C., *George C. Marshall, Vol. I, Education of a General 1880–1939; Vol. II, Ordeal and Hope 1939–1942; Vol. III, Organizer of Victory 1943–1945,* Viking, New York, 1963, 1966, 1973.

Pogue, Forrest C., *The Supreme Command,* Office of the Chief of Military History, Department of the Army, Washington, 1954.

Politics and Strategy in the Second World War, Papers presented under the auspices of the International Commission for the History of the Second World War, San Francisco, 1975.

Prange, Gordon W., Donald M. Goldstein, and Katherine W. Dillon, *Miracle at Midway,* McGraw-Hill, New York, 1982.

Pratt, Fletcher, *Ordeal by Fire: An Informal History of the Civil War,* William Sloane Associates, New York, 1958.

Pratt, Fletcher, *Eleven Generals: Studies in American Command,* William Sloane Associates, New York, 1949.

Pratt, Fletcher, *Empire and the Sea,* Holt, New York, 1946.

Pratt, Fletcher, *The Heroic Years: Fourteen Years of the Republic 1801–1815,* Smith and Haas, New York, 1934.

Pratt, Fletcher, *The Marines' War: An Account of the Struggle for the Pacific from Both American and Japanese Sources,* William Sloane Associates, New York, 1948.

Pratt, Fletcher, *Preble's Boys: Commodore Preble and the Birth of American Sea Power,* William Sloane Associates, New York, 1950.

Rame, David (A. D. Divine), *Road to Tunis,* Macmillan, New York, 1944.

Reichshauer, Edwin O., *The United States and Japan,* Harvard University Press, Cambridge, 1957.

Reynolds, Clark G., *The Fast Carriers: The Forging of an Air Navy,* McGraw-Hill, New York, 1968.

Reynolds, Quentin, *Only the Stars Are Neutral,* Random, New York, 1949.

Rogow, Arnold A., *James Forrestal: A Study of Personality, Politics, and Policy,* Macmillan, New York, 1963.

Romanus, Charles F., and Riley Sunderland, *Stilwell's Mission to China; Stilwell's Command Problems; Time Runs Out in the CBI,* Office of the Chief of Military History, Department of the Army, Washington, 1953, 1956, 1959.

Roosevelt, Eleanor, *This I Remember,* Harper & Brothers, New York, 1949.

Roosevelt, Elliott, *As He Saw It,* Duell, Sloan and Pearce, New York, 1946.

Roosevelt, Elliott, ed., *F.D.R.: His Personal Letters,* vols. I and II, Duell, Sloan and Pearce, New York, 1947–1948.

Roosevelt, James, with Bill Libby, *My Parents: A Differing View,* Playboy Press, Chicago, 1976.

Rosenman, Samuel I., *Working with Roosevelt,* Harper & Brothers, New York, 1952.

Rosenman, Samuel I., *The Public Papers and Addresses of Franklin D. Roosevelt,* vols. 1941–1943, Harper & Brothers, New York, 1950.

Rumpf, Hans, *The Bombing of Germany,* Holt, New York, 1963.

Ruppenthal, Roland G., *Logistical Support of the Armies,* vols. I and II, Office of the Chief of Military History, Department of the Army, Washington, 1953, 1959.

Rust, Kenn C., *Twentieth Air Force Story,* Historical Aviation Album, Temple City, 1979.

Ryan, Cornelius, *The Last Battle,* Simon & Schuster, New York, 1966.

Sanborn, Frederic R., *Design for War: A Study of Secret Power Politics 1937–1941,* Devin-Adair, New York, 1951.

Saunby, Robert, *Air Bombardment: The Story of Its Development,* Harper & Brothers, New York, 1961.

Schaller, Michael, *The U.S. Crusade in China, 1938–1945,* Columbia University Press, New York, 1979.

Schlesinger, Arthur M., Jr., *The Age of Roosevelt, Vol. I, The Crisis of the Old Order; Vol. II, The Coming of the New Deal; Vol. III, The Politics of Upheaval,* Houghton Mifflin, Boston, 1957–1960.

Schroeder, Paul W., *The Axis Alliance and Japanese-American Relations,* Cornell University Press, Ithaca, 1958.

Seagrave, Gordon, *Burma Surgeon,* Norton, New York, 1943.

Sevareid, Eric, *Not So Wild a Dream,* Knopf, New York, 1946.

Sheean, Vincent, *Between the Thunder and the Sun,* Random, New York, 1943.

Sherrod, Robert, *History of Marine Corps Aviation in World War II,* Combat Forces Press, Washington, 1952.

Sherwood, Robert E., *Roosevelt and Hopkins: An Intimate History,* Harper & Brothers, New York, 1948.

Shirer, William L., *The Rise and Fall of the Third Reich,* Simon & Schuster, New York, 1960.

Shulman, Milton, *Defeat in the West,* Dutton, New York, 1948.

Slessor, John, *The Central Blue: The Autobiography of Sir John Slessor, Marshal of the RAF,* Praeger, New York, 1957.

Slim, William, *Defeat into Victory,* Cassell, London, 1956.

Smith, Bradley F., *The Shadow Warriors: O.S.S. and the Origins of the C.I.A.,* Basic Books, New York, 1983.

Smith, Holland M., and Percy Finch, *Coral and Brass,* Scribner, New York, 1949.

Smith, Robert R., *The Approach to the Philippines,* Office of the Chief of Military History, Department of the Army, Washington, 1953.

Smith, Robert R., *Triumph in the Philippines,* Office of the Chief of Military History, Department of the Army, Washington, 1963.

Snyder, Earl, *General Leemy's Circus,* Exposition Press, New York, 1955.

Soldiers and Statesmen, Military History Symposium, U.S. Air Force Academy, Washington, 1973.
Sontag, Raymond S., and James F. Beddie, eds., *Nazi-Soviet Relations 1939–1941,* Dept. of State, Washington, 1948.
Spear, Thomas G. P., *India, A Modern History,* University of Michigan Press, Ann Arbor, 1961.
Spector, Ronald, *Eagle Against the Sun: The American War with Japan,* Free Press, New York, 1985.
Speer, Albert, *Inside the Third Reich,* Macmillan, New York, 1970.
Stafford, Edward P., *The Big E: The Story of the USS Enterprise,* Random, New York, 1962.
Stagg, J. M., *Forecast for Overlord,* Ian Allen, London, 1971.
Steele, Richard W., *The First Offensive: Roosevelt, Marshall, and the Making of American Strategy,* Indiana University Press, Bloomington, 1973.
Stiles, Bert, *Serenade to the Big Bird,* Norton, New York, 1947.
Stilwell, Joseph W., Theodore H. White, ed., *The Stilwell Papers,* William Sloane Associates, New York, 1948.
Stimson, Henry L., and MacGeorge Bundy, *On Active Service in Peace and War,* Harper & Brothers, New York, 1948.
Storry, Richard, *The Double Patriots: A Study of Japanese Nationalism,* Houghton Mifflin, Boston, 1957.
Stouffer, Samuel A. *et al., The American Soldier,* vols. I and II, Princeton University Press, Princeton, 1949.
"Strategicus" (H. C. O'Neill), *A Short History of the Second World War,* Faber, London, 1950.
Swinson, Arthur, *The Battle of Kohima,* Stein & Day, New York, 1967.
Sykes, Christopher, *Orde Wingate: A Biography,* World, Cleveland, 1959.
Taylor, A. J. P., *English History 1914–1945,* Oxford University Press, Oxford, 1965.
Taylor, Theodore, *The Magnificent Mitscher,* Norton, New York, 1954.
Terkel, Studs, *"The Good War,"* Ballantine, New York, 1985.
Thomas, Hugh, *The Spanish Civil War,* Harper & Brothers, New York, 1961.
Thompson, Kenneth W., *Winston Churchill's World View: Statesmanship and Power,* Louisiana State University Press, Baton Rouge, 1983.
Thompson, R. W., *The Battle for the Rhineland,* Hutchinson & Co., London, 1958.
Thompson, R. W., *The Eighty-Five Days: The Story of the Battle of the Scheldt,* Ballantine, New York, 1957.
Thompson, R. W., *Generalissimo Churchill,* Scribner, New York, 1973.
Thorne, Christopher, *Allies of a Kind: The United States, Britain, and the War Against Japan 1944–1945,* Oxford University Press, New York, 1978.
Toland, John, *Infamy: Pearl Harbor and Its Aftermath,* Doubleday, Garden City, 1983.
Toland, John, *The Last 100 Days,* Random, New York, 1966.
Truscott, Lucian K., *Command Missions,* Dutton, New York, 1954.
Tuchman, Barbara, *Stilwell and the American Experience in China 1911–1945,* Macmillan, New York, 1970.
Tugwell, Rexford G., *The Democratic Roosevelt,* Doubleday, Garden City, 1957.
Tuleja, Thaddeus J., *Climax at Midway,* Norton, New York, 1960.
Tully, Grace, *F.D.R.: My Boss,* Scribner, New York, 1949.

U.S. Bureau of the Budget, *The United States at War,* U.S. Government Printing Office, Washington, 1946.

Vagts, Alfred A., *A History of Militarism,* Meridian, New York, 1959.

Vandegrift, Alexander A., as told to Robert B. Asprey, *Once a Marine,* Norton, New York, 1964.

Vandenberg, Arthur H., Jr., ed., *The Private Papers of Senator Vandenberg,* Houghton Mifflin, Boston, 1952.

Van Der Rhoer, Edward, *Deadly Magic: An Account of Communications Intelligence in World War II,* Robert Hale, London, 1978.

Viorst, Milton, *Hostile Allies: FDR and Charles de Gaulle,* Macmillan, New York, 1965.

Walton, Francis, *Miracle of World War II: How American Industry Made Victory Possible,* Macmillan, New York, 1956.

War Department, *Lessons from the Tunisian Campaign,* U.S. Government Printing Office, Washington, 1943.

Ward, John W., *Red, White, and Blue,* Oxford University Press, New York, 1969.

Watson, Mark S., *Chief of Staff: Prewar Plans and Preparations,* Historical Division, Department of the Army, Washington, 1950.

Wedemeyer, Albert, *Wedemeyer Reports,* Holt, New York, 1958.

Wedgwood, C. V., *The Thirty Years War,* Anchor, Garden City, 1961.

Weigley, Russell F., *Eisenhower's Lieutenants: The Campaign of France and Germany,* Indiana University Press, Bloomington, 1981.

Weigley, Russell F., *Towards an American Army: Military Thought from Washington to Marshall,* Columbia University Press, New York, 1962.

Werth, Alexander, *Russia at War 1941–1945,* Dutton, New York, 1964.

Wescott, Lynanne, and Paula Degen, *Wind and Sand: The Story of the Wright Brothers at Kitty Hawk,* Eastern Acorn Press, Philadelphia, 1983.

Wheeler, Burton K., *Yankee from the West,* Doubleday, Garden City, 1962.

White, Dorothy S., *Seeds of Discord: De Gaulle, Free France, and the Allies,* Syracuse University Press, Syracuse, 1964.

Whitney, Courtney, *MacArthur: His Rendezvous with History,* Knopf, New York, 1956.

Williams, T. Harry, *Lincoln and His Generals,* Knopf, New York, 1952.

Willoughby, Charles A., and John Chamberlain, *MacArthur 1941–1951,* McGraw-Hill, New York, 1954.

Wilmot, Chester, *The Struggle for Europe,* Harper & Brothers, New York, 1952.

Winterbotham, F. W., *The Ultra Secret,* Harper & Brothers, New York, 1974.

Wintringham, Tom, *The Story of Weapons and Tactics,* Houghton Mifflin, Boston, 1943.

Wohlstetter, Roberta, *Pearl Harbor: Warning and Decision,* Stanford University Press, Stanford, 1962.

Wolff, Leon, *Low Level Mission,* Doubleday, Garden City, 1957.

Wood, Derek, and Derek Dempster, *The Narrow Margin: The Battle of Britain and the Rise of Air Power 1930–40,* McGraw-Hill, New York, 1961.

Wright, Gordon, *The Ordeal of Total War 1939–1945,* Harper & Row, New York, 1968.

Zimmerman, John L., *The Guadalcanal Campaign,* Historical Division, U.S. Marine Corps, Washington, 1949.

INDEX

Acheson, Dean, 64, 81, 634
Adams, Phelps H., 186
Adams, Philip, 523
Aizawa, Lieutenant Colonel Sabura, 71, 72, 73
Albion, Robert G., 24
Alexander, General Sir Harold R. L. G., 428, 430, 433, 434, 436–437, 474, 497, 501, 531, 599; on American soldiers, 436–437; and Stilwell, 526, 528, 529–530
Alison, Lieutenant Colonel John R., 551, 552
Allen, Edmond T., 608, 609
Allen, General Terry de la Mesa, 132, 144, 151
Allen, Major General A. S., 324–325
Allies of a Kind (Thorne), 632
Alsop, Joseph W., Jr., 545, 569–571, 574, 575, 631
Ambrose, Stephen, 184, 431, 433, 450, 454, 476, 506, 507
Amery, Leopold, 550
America First Committee, 227, 228
Andrews, Major General Frank, 213–214
Andrews, Vice-Admiral Adolphus, 177, 179
Appold, Major Norman, 248, 251
Araki, General, 68
Arcadia (Washington conference), 17–18, 20, 21, 35, 187, 587, 588
Armstrong, Colonel Frank, 590, 592
Army, U.S., 107–108, 113–114, 307, 336–338; Americal Division of, 292, 295, 303; compared with German Army, 137, 468–469; reform of, 109, 111–112, 113–121, 142–143; size of, 114–115, 122, 145. *See also* Marshall, General George Catlett, Jr.; *individual generals*

Army Air Forces, U.S. (USAAF), 221, 226, 240, 243, 334–335, 394, 396, 628, 638; and "Big Week," 600–601, 603; and long-range bombers, 579–583, 584, 585, 588–600, 602–611, 614, 641; and long-range fighter planes, 251, 601–604, 637; No. 1 Air Commando, 551, 552; before World War II, 208, 212–214. *See also* Arnold, General Henry H.; Bombing; Carriers, aircraft
Army-Navy Board, Joint, 16, 21, 49, 50, 81
Arnold, General Henry H. ("Hap"), 180, 185, 206–255, 386, 485, 533, 551, 623; administration of, 215, 233; on air power, 230, 254, 588, 598; and American air force, 209, 210, 212, 214, 219, 220, 223, 224, 470, 594, 596, 602, 623
Army Flyer, 587; and Atlantic Charter Meeting, 236, 237, 238, 239; background of, 208, 211–212; and bombers, 587–589, 608–610, 613, 615; character of, 11, 209–210, 253–255; and Chennault, 570–571; and FDR, 12, 14, 28, 223–224, 229, 340, 587, 623, 643; *Global Mission*, 229, 251, 580; and Guadalcanal, 284, 295; illness and death of, 253, 254; and Joint Chiefs, 20, 21, 255; and Kilner Board, 606–607; and King, 174, 254, 365, 609; and LeMay, 616, 617; and Lindbergh, 224–228, 229, 606; in London, 229, 230–231; and Lovett, 215–216, 218–219, 223; and MacArthur, 253, 310, 335, 580; and Marshall, 97, 141, 142, 150, 208, 252–254; and Nimitz, 253, 580; and North African invasion, 254, 291; and Pacific strategy, 340, 344,

707

712 INDEX

ABOUT THE AUTHOR

Born in Massachusetts in 1922, Eric Larrabee graduated *cum laude* from Harvard in 1943. For his service during World War II in Tank Destroyers and in Military Intelligence, he was awarded a Bronze Star and the Army Commendation Ribbon.

He has since been continuously active—as author, editor, professor, and member of various boards, councils, and panels of the New York State Council on the Arts, the New York Council for the Humanities, and the National Endowment for the Arts.

He has been associate editor of *Harper's Magazine* (1946–58), then managing editor of *American Heritage* (1958–61), managing editor of *Horizon* (1961–63), and editorial consultant to Doubleday & Company (1963–69). As well as being a regular contributor of articles and reviews to national magazines, he has written and edited several books on art and American society. He was Provost of the Faculty of Arts and Letters at SUNY Buffalo, has taught there and at Sarah Lawrence College and Columbia University, and is now Dean of Arts and Design at Pratt Institute.

He and his wife, an architect, live in New York City and own a Frank Lloyd Wright house in Buffalo, New York.